STAFF

Tina N. Grant, *Editor*

Miranda H. Ferrara, *Project Manager*

Laura S. Berger, Joann Cerrito, David J. Collins, Steve Cusack,
Nicolet V. Elert, Jamie C. FitzGerald, Kristin Hart, Laura S. Kryhoski,
Margaret Mazurkiewicz, Michael J. Tyrkus, *St. James Press Editorial Staff*

Peter M. Gareffa, *Managing Editor, St. James Press*

Library of Congress Catalog Number: 89-190943

British Library Cataloguing in Publication Data

International directory of company histories. Vol. 27
I. Tina N. Grant
338.7409

ISBN 1-55862-386-8

Printed in the United States of America
Published simultaneously in the United Kingdom

St. James Press is an imprint of The Gale Group

Cover photograph: Smithsonian Institution Castle, Washington, D.C.
(courtesy of Smithsonian Institution)

10 9 8 7 6 5 4 3 2 1

International Directory of
COMPANY
HISTORIES

International Directory of

COMPANY HISTORIES

VOLUME 27

Editor

Tina N. Grant

ST. JAMES PRESS

AN IMPRINT OF THE GALE GROUP

DETROIT • SAN FRANCISCO • LONDON
BOSTON • WOODBRIDGE, CT

CONTENTS

Company Histories

PREFACE

The St. James Press series *The International Directory of Company Histories (IDCH)* is intended for reference use by students, business people, librarians, historians, economists, investors, job candidates, and others who seek to learn more about the historical development of the world's most important companies. To date, *IDCH* has covered over 3,700 companies in 27 volumes.

Inclusion Criteria

Most companies chosen for inclusion in *IDCH* have achieved a minimum of US$50 million in annual sales and are leading influences in their industries or geographical locations. Companies may be publicly held, private, or nonprofit. State-owned companies that are important in their industries and that may operate much like public or private companies also are included. Wholly owned subsidiaries and divisions are profiled if they meet the requirements for inclusion. Entries on companies that have had major changes since they were last profiled may be selected for updating.

The *IDCH* series highlights 10% private and nonprofit companies, and features updated entries on approximately 40 companies per volume.

Entry Format

Each entry begins with the company's legal name, the address of its headquarters, its telephone, toll-free, and fax numbers, and its web site. A statement of public, private, state, or parent ownership follows. A company with a legal name in both English and the language of its headquarters country is listed by the English name, with the native-language name in parentheses.

The company's founding or earliest incorporation date, the number of employees, and the most recent sales figures available follow. Sales figures are given in local currencies with equivalents in U.S. dollars. For some private companies, sales figures are estimates. The entry lists the exchanges on which a company's stock is traded and its ticker symbol, as well as the company's principal Standard Industrial Classification codes.

Entries generally contain a *Company Perspectives* box which provides a short summary of the company's mission, goals, and ideals, a list of *Principal Subsidiaries, Principal Divisions, Principal Operating Units,* and articles for *Further Reading.*

American spelling is used throughout *IDCH*, and the word ''billion'' is used in its U.S. sense of one thousand million.

Sources

Entries have been compiled from publicly accessible sources both in print and on the Internet such as general and academic periodicals, books, annual reports, and material supplied by the companies themselves.

Cumulative Indexes

IDCH contains two indexes: the **Index to Companies**, which provides an alphabetical index to companies discussed in the text as well as companies profiled, and the **Index to Industries**, which allows researchers to locate companies by their principal industry. Both indexes are cumulative and specific instructions for using them are found immediately preceding each index.

Suggestions Welcome

Comments and suggestions from users of *IDCH* on any aspect of the product as well as suggestions for companies to be included or updated are cordially invited. Please write:

> The Editor
> *International Directory of Company Histories*
> St. James Press
> 27500 Drake Rd.
> Farmington Hills, Michigan 48331-3535

ABBREVIATIONS FOR FORMS OF COMPANY INCORPORATION

A.B.	Aktiebolaget (Sweden)
A.G.	Aktiengesellschaft (Germany, Switzerland)
A.S.	Atieselskab (Denmark)
A.S.	Aksjeselskap (Denmark, Norway)
A.Ş.	Anomin Şirket (Turkey)
B.V.	Besloten Vennootschap met beperkte, Aansprakelijkheid (The Netherlands)
Co.	Company (United Kingdom, United States)
Corp.	Corporation (United States)
G.I.E.	Groupement d'Intérêt Economique (France)
GmbH	Gesellschaft mit beschränkter Haftung (Germany)
H.B.	Handelsbolaget (Sweden)
Inc.	Incorporated (United States)
KGaA	Kommanditgesellschaft auf Aktien (Germany)
K.K.	Kabushiki Kaisha (Japan)
LLC	Limited Liability Company (Middle East)
Ltd.	Limited (Canada, Japan, United Kingdom, United States)
N.V.	Naamloze Vennootschap (The Netherlands)
OY	Osakeyhtiöt (Finland)
PLC	Public Limited Company (United Kingdom)
PTY.	Proprietary (Australia, Hong Kong, South Africa)
S.A.	Société Anonyme (Belgium, France, Switzerland)
SpA	Società per Azioni (Italy)

ABBREVIATIONS FOR CURRENCY

DA	Algerian dinar	M$	Malaysian ringgit
A$	Australian dollar	Dfl	Netherlands florin
Sch	Austrian schilling	Nfl	Netherlands florin
BFr	Belgian franc	NZ$	New Zealand dollar
Cr	Brazilian cruzado	N	Nigerian naira
C$	Canadian dollar	NKr	Norwegian krone
RMB	Chinese renminbi	RO	Omani rial
DKr	Danish krone	P	Philippine peso
E£	Egyptian pound	Esc	Portuguese escudo
Fmk	Finnish markka	SRls	Saudi Arabian riyal
FFr	French franc	S$	Singapore dollar
DM	German mark	R	South African rand
HK$	Hong Kong dollar	W	South Korean won
HUF	Hungarian forint	Pta	Spanish peseta
Rs	Indian rupee	SKr	Swedish krona
Rp	Indonesian rupiah	SFr	Swiss franc
IR£	Irish pound	NT$	Taiwanese dollar
L	Italian lira	B	Thai baht
¥	Japanese yen	£	United Kingdom pound
W	Korean won	$	United States dollar
KD	Kuwaiti dinar	B	Venezuelan bolivar
LuxFr	Luxembourgian franc	K	Zambian kwacha

International Directory of

COMPANY
HISTORIES

AARP

601 E Street N.W.
Washington, D.C. 20049
U.S.A.
(202) 434-2277
(800) 424-3410
Fax: (202) 434-2588
Web site: http://www.aarp.org

Nonprofit Organization
Incorporated: 1947 as National Retired Teachers
Association
Employees: 1,700
SICs: 8600 Services, Membership Organizations

AARP (The American Association of Retired Persons) is a not-for-profit association with 33 million members, a membership second only to the Catholic Church in the United States. This gives its publication *Modern Maturity* a colossal circulation. *Fortune* polls found it to be the most influential lobby on Capitol Hill; the group spent $35 million lobbying in 1995. Although it sells health insurance, among other things, the organization is considered a nonprofit group and receives many tax breaks and federal grants ($86 million in 1997). Its economic influence goes far beyond its membership revenues, administrative allowances, and commissions on product offerings, which include various types of insurance and financial products, and its pharmacy service, which controls ten percent of the mail-order market. Investigative journalist Dale Van Atta estimated "that the total revenue for AARP and its partners in 1994 was $5.6 billion."

1940s Origins

Even AARP detractors credit California educator Dr. Ethyl Percy Andrus as "one of the truly great women of recent American history," as Dale Van Atta put it. Andrus had become the first female high school principal in the state of California, and upon her retirement she became interested in the poverty of her fellow retired teachers trying to live on tiny pensions.

Andrus founded the National Retired Teachers Association (NRTA) in 1947. She started a nursing home for teachers but was unable to find health insurance for them until joining forces with Leonard Davis, who had succeeded in securing this for a group of retired New York teachers. Their first policy went into effect in 1956; within a year the number of subscribers had leapt from 5,000 to 15,000. The policies were highly profitable, pulling in $75,000 in premiums per month and laying out only $25,000 in claims. The Continental Casualty Company, which had developed an insurance plan to be sold by mail, found the NRTA members to be reliable customers.

In 1958 Andrus and Davis created the American Association of Retired Persons to share the insurance benefits the NRTA had gained with the general retired population. Davis provided the $50,000 of start-up capital. The company publication, *Modern Maturity,* consumed much of this capital but proved an effective marketing tool, touting an "invitation to security" in the organization's health insurance plans. A company publication, the *Bulletin,* described the group's lobbying efforts. Thousands of volunteers also worked to promote the offerings of AARP/ Colonial Penn.

Rocking the Drug World in the 1960s

Andrus and Davis started an early mail-order pharmacy, the "AARP Drug Buying Service," in 1959, to help older persons manage the high cost of filling prescriptions. In fact, Andrus and pioneer drug discounter Herbert Haft, who briefly ran the service, testified at congressional hearings on high pharmaceutical prices. Established pharmacists tried to ban the drug program stores and in some cases boycotted its distributors. Pharmacists' groups, who resented the fact that neither AARP nor Retired Persons' Services, Inc. (RPS) paid taxes on their sales, continued to provide opposition based on safety, community, and service issues.

John McHugh took over the drug service in 1962 and managed it for 30 years. Upon his retirement, it employed 250 pharmacists and filled eight million prescriptions per year. Besides price, privacy and convenience were key selling points. A line of generic products was added. The company's catalog expanded to include sundries, which eventually generated 40 percent of its sales. The service operated as a separate nonprofit organization, Retired Persons' Services, Inc., ''not owned or controlled by AARP.'' Van Atta reported its sales as $440 million in 1993, with a one percent commission on gross sales payable to AARP.

Media Scrutiny in the 1970s

In 1963 Davis bought 750,000 policies from Continental and set up a holding company, the Colonial Penn Group. According to Morris, Colonial Penn's revenues grew from $46 million to $445 million between 1967 and 1976, thanks to NRTA/AARP members, which provided most of its health insurance revenues. This made Colonial Penn the most profitable company in the United States, according to *Forbes* magazine. At the same time, *Consumer Reports* published a highly critical review of Colonial Penn's service to AARP members. A U.S. Postal Service investigation into the organization's use of nonprofit mailings ensued. The post office, in fact, recommended that criminal federal prosecutors bring charges against AARP and Colonial Penn for fraud. Charles Morris and Dale Van Atta reported, however, that Leonard Davis had been expunged from official AARP histories because of his questionable reputation. In fact, he lost his insurance license in 1965 in a New York bribery scandal. Andrus died in 1967, the year the Age Discrimination in Employment Act was passed.

In 1978, after being fired by Davis, Executive Director Harriet Miller (who eventually became mayor of Santa Barbara, California) filed a $4 million suit leveling many of the same charges, contending that control of the organization rested in the hands of Colonial Penn. A *60 Minutes* exposé demoralized AARP workers, members, and volunteers, and Davis left the organization in February 1979. AARP settled Miller's suit for $480,000 and began inviting competitive bids for its insurance business in 1981. Prudential Insurance Co. won the contract and devoted a staff of 4,500 to the project.

New Offerings in the 1980s

In 1983 Davis retired from Colonial Penn. A couple of years later, the company, which had lost AARP's health insurance contract, sued its former partner for not allowing competitors to advertise in *Modern Maturity*.

The NRTA and AARP had merged officially in 1982. The membership age was lowered from 55 to 50, allowing for a larger pool of potential members. South Carolina native Horace Deets, a former Catholic priest, became chief executive of AARP in 1988. The organization lobbied to standardize Medigap coverage in the late 1980s, which *Smart Money* reported had the effect of drying up competition.

AARP tried putting together a federal credit union, which was vigorously opposed by other bankers. AARP Federal failed within two years, since it decided not to open any regional branches, and senior citizens proved wary of placing transactions without speaking to tellers in person. Van Atta reported that the AARP Travel Service was another seemingly logical marketing concept that soon failed. In the mid-1990s an offering of a simplified cellular phone, the Roadphone, fell apart when the provider, ASCNet, went bankrupt. Van Atta noted that AARP initially refused to compensate members for the $200 phones but relented after an intense public outcry.

Battling for Boomers in the 1990s

AARP fought another publicity battle when Republican Senator Alan Simpson attacked the organization's tax exempt status in congressional hearings. Deets characterized these proceedings as ''an absolute witch hunt.'' At the same time, articles in *National Review, Fortune,* and others lamented an intergenerational inequity in the Social Security system. They observed that the current generation of retirees would reap many more benefits from the money-losing program than their children ever would—the funds simply were not there to support them. As Simpson put it, ''Do any of you care a crap about your grandchildren?'' Chrysler Chairman Lee Iacocca delivered much the same message at the 1992 AARP convention.

AARP still faces the challenge of capturing the Baby Boomer generation, something it must do to survive as natural attrition trims two million people a year from its rolls. It has tried marketing tactics such as sending alternate magazine covers to younger (less than 60 years old) members and even has considered changing the publication's name from *Modern Maturity* to something more appealing to the more hip and independent group demographic. In fact, at least one analyst urged the organization to change its own name to something more positive as well. One of its own ads implored: ''Forget for a moment that the word 'retired' is in our name.'' In 1998 the group began using the acronym AARP (pronounced to rhyme with ''harp'') as its official name. *Direct Marketing* writer James Rosenfield summed up the organization's image problem: ''Experiencing adolescence in the '50s was a mite different from adolescence in the '60s. Were two decades ever more in contrast?''

As politicians and providers tossed about solutions for the impending Medicare crisis, some observers criticized AARP for impeding the debate. Bill Clinton's universal health care plan, for example, foundered without AARP support. Critics accused the organization of using scare tactics on its elderly members and, generally, campaigning for liberal causes that primarily would benefit its relatively affluent population.

In 1996 AARP test-marketed a retail drug program administered through Arizona-based PCS (Pharmaceutical Card System). The organization decided to cancel its group health insurance contract with Prudential in 1997. United HealthCare, Metropolitan Life, and ITT Hartford won the right to administer the $4 billion program.

While few discount the influence of this venerable organization, AARP faces serious threats to existence in the next century. Although the U.S. elderly population was expected to double by 2040, the children of Woodstock have values different from those of the children of the Depression. Perception is reality in lobbying and marketing; the group is trying to maintain the appearance of power and prestige while at the same time staying relevant and credible with its varied membership constituency.

Principal Divisions

NRTA.

Principal Operating Units

Information and Education (AARP Andrus Foundation); Community Service; Advocacy; Member Services.

Further Reading

Besack, Mike, "AARP Gets Ready for the Boomers," *Workforce,* December 1997, pp. 27–28.

Birnbaum, Jeffrey H., "Washington's Power 25," *Fortune,* December 8, 1997, pp. 144–52.

——, "Washington's Second Most Powerful Man," *Fortune,* May 12, 1997, pp. 122–26.

Finger, Anne L., "What This Man Wants, You May Get," *Medical Economics,* February 23, 1998, pp. 177–91.

Geist, Bill, "Surviving Your AARP Attack; A Boomer Will Turn 50 Every Eight Seconds, and the Ugly Reminder Is Sure To Follow," *Washington Post,* January 26, 1999, p. Z12.

Gupta, Dipak K., et. al., "Group Utility in the Micro Motivation of Collective Action: The Case of Membership in the AARP," *Journal of Economic Behavior and Organization,* February 1997, pp. 301–20.

Machan, Tibor R., "AARP Turns Extortion into a Group Activity," *Arizona Republic,* April 10, 1998, p. B7.

McAllister, Bill, "AARP Alters Name to Reflect Reality," *Washington Post,* November 18, 1998, p. A25.

McArdle, Thomas, "Golden Oldies," *National Review,* September 11, 1995.

Moore, Wayne, and Monica Kolasa, "AARP's Legal Services Network: Expanding Legal Services," *Wake Forest Law Review,* Summer 1997, pp. 503–44.

Morris, Charles R., *The AARP: America's Most Powerful Lobby and the Clash of Generations,* New York: Times Books, 1996.

Rosenfield, James R., "AARP: Slaying the Mail-Order Insurance Dragon," *Direct Marketing,* May 1997, pp. 42–44.

——, "Boomers and Branding: The Agonies of AARP," *Direct Marketing,* August 1998, pp. 60–62.

Smith, Lee, "Rebelling Against the Tyranny of the Old," *Fortune,* March 22, 1993.

Van Atta, Dale, *Trust Betrayed: Inside the AARP,* Washington, DC: Regnery Publishing, 1998.

Waldrum, Shirley B., and H. Geral Niemira, "Age Diversity in the Workplace," *Employment Relations Today,* Winter 1997, pp. 67–73.

Walker, Sam, "Congress May Bite Hand that Feeds Members," *Christian Science Monitor,* June 28, 1995.

—Frederick C. Ingram

Academy Sports & Outdoors

1800 North Mason Road
Katy, Texas 77449
U.S.A.
(281) 579-1555
Fax: (281) 646-5204
Web site: http://www.academy.com

Private Company
Incorporated: 1973
Employees: 4,000
Sales: $435 million (1998 est.)
SICs: 5941 Sporting Goods, Retail; 5661 Shoe Stores

Privately owned by the Gochman family, Academy Sports & Outdoors operates the fourth largest chain of retail sporting goods ''megastore'' outlets in the United States. In 1999, it had 35 stores in Texas, three in Oklahoma, two in Alabama, three in Louisiana, and one in Florida. The majority of these are ''superstores,'' ranging from 35,000 to 50,000 square feet in size. In them, Academy carries an extensive line of name-brand equipment and clothing and shoes for competitive sports, physical fitness training, and outdoor recreational activities such as camping, hunting, fishing, and boating. Included among its name brands are Champion, Jantzen, Justin, K-Swiss, Nike, Reebok, Rollerblade, Spalding, and Wrangler. Academy's company headquarters are located in Katy, Texas, a suburb of Houston, where it also owns a large warehouse used for effective inventory control and distribution.

1970s: Early History and Directions

Academy Sports & Outdoors came into existence in 1970, when Arthur Gochman and his business partner purchased Southern Sales, a Houston-based army-navy surplus chain comprised of six stores that were by that year no longer making any profit. At the time, Gochman was a practicing attorney in San Antonio. He had not been formally educated as a businessman, but he had learned much about the surplus retail business from his father, Max Gochman, who had owned a surplus goods

outlet in San Antonio and in 1970 still owned and operated a small chain of stores in Austin.

Gochman bought out his partner in 1973 and changed the company's business name from Southern Sales to Academy Corp. The Academy name was borrowed from his father's stores. It came from a now-defunct San Antonio Catholic school named St. Henry's Academy. Max Gochman had opened his first store across the street from the school in the 1930s, selling pre-World War II surplus goods. Later, when he moved to Austin, he used the name for his four army-navy surplus stores. Because many University of Texas students and graduates lived in the Houston area and were familiar with the Austin stores, Max Gochman permitted his son to use the name, knowing that it would help his son's business.

For the first few years of Academy's operation, Arthur Gochman's involvement was, in large part, passive. He continued to practice law in San Antonio until 1978, when he gave up his practice and moved to Houston to assume active control of the company and complete the overhaul of its basic merchandising policies.

1980s: From Surplus to Sporting Goods

Gochman made streamlining the chain's image his first priority. He closed two of the original stores and completely discontinued the sale of military surplus goods, responding to market changes reflecting new tastes and lifestyles. Academy already had begun refurbishing its image in the late 1970s, when, prompted by the increasing popularity of athletic shoes and leisure wear, it had begun selling sporting goods and clothing. In the 1980s the company's management completed the Academy changeover into a chain of outlets offering a wide and competitively priced range of brand name, top quality sporting goods and clothing—creating the company image that it has since retained.

Under Gochman's tutelage, the company began its continuing growth cycle. At first it widened its in-state operating area, in part as the result of family loss. Max Gochman died in 1985, and Arthur Gochman took over his father's four Austin stores, refurbishing them in Academy's new image as sporting goods

Company Perspectives:

While there are retailers in the market who sell lower quality goods at discount prices, and those who sell the absolute top of the line equipment and products at premium prices, we strive to consistently offer everyday low pricing on comparable products. In conjunction with price and quality, we stress service. Our strategy is to have knowledgeable and friendly salespeople assisting customers and to make returning merchandise as pleasant as purchasing it.

megastores. The Austin market was both reliable and profitable, and it helped Academy's gradual "transition from 'giant killer' to a retail giant in its own right." It also brought the number of stores in the chain from eight in 1980 to 12 in 1985.

Smart responses to market realities also helped the company's growth. In the 1980s, through surveys of his customers, Gochman realized that the great majority of them were men. To encourage women to shop in Academy outlets, he introduced lines of women's casual clothing and aerobic wear. It was a wise policy move, for within a few years women would account for 50 percent of the chain's shoppers.

Starting in 1986, Academy also adopted an EDLP (Every-Day Low Pricing) sales philosophy, rejecting the widely used deep discounting of select items to attract customers. That policy assures Academy shoppers that they will pay low prices across the entire line of merchandise and not be penalized by the higher markups many stores put on nonsale items to offset the deep discount prices on their "specials."

Wisely, too, Academy retained much of a regional identity, offering the company's home base Texas customers several lines not carried by other sporting goods outlets. An important example is Western footwear. By 1990 the company was selling more cowboy boots than any other chain in the United States. In that year alone, its sale of women's Western-style boots increased by a full 70 percent over the previous year.

By the end of the 1980s Academy had become a very popular Texas chain. Among other things, its outlets sold more state fishing licenses than its chief competitor, Oshman's Sporting Goods, or any other group of stores in the state. But its success in Texas also raised new possibilities. In the mid 1980s the company began an impressive sales record, with yearly increases in revenue matched with stable margins and excellent cash flow. The health and stability of the company encouraged its expansion, both in Texas and, starting in the 1990s, beyond.

1990s: Expansion, Managerial Changes, and Successful Strategies

By 1990 Academy had grown to 18 stores. It also began a period of more rapid expansion, jumping to 34 stores by 1995, the year after it first moved into two adjoining states. It opened its first store outside Texas in Edmond, Oklahoma in June of 1994, then added a store in Lafayette, Louisiana the following November, thus ending the company's exclusive Texas identity.

Academy's roots will remain in Texas, though, no matter how far away it locates new outlets. The epicenter of the company's business always has been the greater Houston area. Almost half of its stores are located there, as are the company headquarters and its distribution facility. As it has expanded beyond its home base, Academy has sought "hot-market" locales, places that from careful market analysis offered the promise of high-volume sales. The result has been that it has never had to close one of its new stores, all of which have been profitable since their first day of operation.

In 1995 David Gochman, the founder's son, joined Academy on a full-time basis. By that time his father, then 65, had built Academy into a $350 million retail chain and was ready to turn control of the business over to his 30-year-old son. David Gochman initially served as vice-president of store operations and general counsel, but in the following year he succeeded his father as Academy's chairman, president, and CEO.

Like his father's, David Gochman's formal education indicated that his career plans would take him in some other direction. He completed an M.A. in East Asian Studies at Harvard before earning a law degree from the University of Texas. Yet David Gochman has found the business fascinating. He and his sister Molly, 13 years his junior, now own a controlling interest in the company. Arthur Gochman has continued to handle some of the firm's legal work and remains the chief of store operations, but he prefers to remain in the background, giving son David and his team a free hand. He deferred to David's decision to change the company's name from Academy Corp. to Academy Sports & Outdoors. It has been both an important and successful change, necessitated by the company's move outside its home territory of Houston, to locations where "Academy" alone had no name recognition and could easily be confused with a private or technical school or even a dance studio. The full Academy Sports & Outdoors name both reflects the range of goods that the company markets and identifies the basic nature of its stores.

It is, in fact, the variety and range of merchandise that makes Academy Sports & Outdoors unique. Its strategy has been to provide "one-stop shopping" for all family members, including women and children. It has proved to be a very successful strategy, especially in light of the fact that domestic sales of women's casual wear and shoes surged upward during the 1990s. By 1997 women's purchases accounted for 44 percent of Academy's annual sales, up from 30 percent two years earlier, prompting the company, for the first time, to run print and TV ads aimed specifically at women customers.

Just as important, Academy stocks its outlets with much more than the standard equipment that typical sports equipment stores sell, and it makes sure that each of its outlets maintains a full stock. As the "Outdoors" part of its name suggests, Academy meets the needs of almost any outdoor activist, offering, for example, not just bats and gloves but barbecue pits and cooking gear, not just rods and shotguns but boats and motors and duck blinds and decoys. The name change has already successfully helped identify the company's business in its new markets.

The one-stop strategy is also reflected in Academy's selection of locations and in its store design. A key concept is customer convenience. Potential sites without an easy-in and easy-out accessibility and ample parking, even if in promising neighborhoods, are dropped from consideration. The interior layout of the stores is also important, designed for efficient shoppers who, from a single visit, know where to find things. According to David Gochman, Academy stores "arrange things where people can get in and out in about five minutes if they want to."

Both its merchandising efficiency and range and quality of merchandise have helped ensure Academy's great success. It has managed to keep its prices competitive through an effective control of inventory and distribution at its 775,000-square-foot facility in Houston. Through computerized monitoring of sales and accurate and efficient inventory control, the company can restock any of its outlets' depleted items within a day or two. As soon as a store sells an item, its replacement is ordered and virtually on its way.

Beyond the Houston epicenter, some urban communities have encouraged Academy to open two or more outlets. For example, in early 1999 it opened an additional Austin store, which, added to the four stores originally owned by Max Gochman, brought the total number of Austin outlets to five. The new 52,500-square-foot facility reflected the rationale behind the company's site selection. As CEO David Gochman explained, the locale was chosen because "demographically it's a very strong area, in terms of population and income." It is a site with a cluster of retail stores and other businesses, an area that promised to draw many "drop in" shoppers. As in the case of all of Academy's new stores, its accessibility was also a major factor.

Academy's low-price, high-volume formula has resulted in a steady increase in retail sales and earnings through the 1990s, which, respectively, grew at an average rate of about 25 percent and 35 percent per annum. Its rapid expansion also is seen in its increase in the number of its employees. In 1997 alone there was a 14.3 percent boost in that number. In 1998 that sustained growth propelled Academy into the ranks of top 100 specialty stores in the nation, moving it past 19 other companies to rank 81st. In that year its total number of stores numbered 44.

Future Plans

Academy has plans for cautious but continued expansion and seems well positioned to meet its current projections of a rate of expansion equaling that of the 1990s. In addition to opening new outlets in four of the states in which it currently operates—Texas, Oklahoma, Louisiana, and Alabama—it intends to expand its market into additional states in the Southeast. One selected location outside its current four states is in Franklin, Tennessee, where the company hopes to open a new store in the summer of 1999. In all, management anticipates that five to eight new stores will be opened each year for the next several years. If the rate of growth that occurred in the 1990s is any indication, Academy's should remain an ongoing success story for a long time.

Although David Gochman has stated that going public is not impossible, the company is likely to remain private for the immediate future. It has always been able to finance its operations and growth from its profits and from loans from the Chase Bank of Texas, with which it has maintained an excellent business relationship.

Further Reading

Elder, Laura E., "From Civil Rights Champion to Sporting Goods Star," *Houston Business Journal,* December 15, 1995, p. 14.

Feitelberg, Rosemary, "At the Super Show: Women's Impact Big, But Lots More To Do," *Women's Wear Daily,* February 20, 1997, p. 1.

"High-Stepping Times," *Houston Business Journal,* October 29, 1990, p. 2.

Hudgins, Matt, "Academy Indicates Graduating Retail Area," *Austin Business Journal,* September 21, 1998.

Marchese, Amy, "Academy Sports & Outdoors Shooting for Summer 1999 Opening," *Tennessean,* August 20, 1998, n.p.

"NRF's *Stores* Magazine Released List of Top 100 Specialty Stores," *PR Newswire,* August 5, 1998, p. 21.

Simon, Dana, "Sports Retail Center Planned for Site," *Tulsa World,* Bus. Sec., June 19, 1998.

"Sports Store Opens with Special Events," *Daily Oklahoman,* Community Sec., October 2, 1998.

—John W. Fiero

Accor SA

2, rue de la Mare-Neuve
91021 Évry Cedex
France
(33) 1 69 36 80 80
(800) 207-2542 (Accor North America Group)
Fax: (33) 1 69 36 79 00
Web site: http://www.accor.com

Public Company
Incorporated: 1983
Employees: 121,000
Sales: $5.3 billion (1997)
Stock Exchanges: Paris
SICs: 7011 Hotels & Motels; 5812 Eating Places; 4724
    Travel Agencies; 7514 Passenger Car Rental

Accor SA, a Paris-based conglomerate comprising hotels, restaurants, travel agencies, car rental companies, and restaurant voucher firms, has a history of remarkably rapid expansion. By the late 1990s, Accor operated more hotels than any other hotelier in the world. The company maintained a strong presence in all sectors of the hotel market in Europe, from luxury Sofitels to budget Formule 1s, in the United States with its Motel 6 chain, and in the Asia/Pacific region, Africa, the Middle East, and Latin America. Accor was also 50 percent owner of Carlson Wagonlit Travel, the second largest travel agency in the world, and 50 percent owner of Europcar, Europe's second largest car rental business. Its service voucher business was the largest in the world.

Early History

In 1967, Gérard Pelisson and Paul Dubrule opened their first Novotel hotel on a roadside near Lille in northern France. Travel was booming in France in the 1960s, and the hotel industry had not yet expanded to meet the demand, as French hotels, in general, were either rural inns or luxury hotels in city centers. Dubrule decided to build American-style highway ho-

tels in the medium price range and collaborated with Pelisson, a former head of market research at IBM-Europe. Through Pelisson's connections, the partners were able to secure a bank loan, and their Novotel company was launched. The company's ensuing success was facilitated largely by its being first to break into the unexploited European market for highway lodging. Each Novotel provided standardized rooms, ample parking facilities, and restaurants featuring local cuisine. Soon Novotels were also established at airports as well as popular vacation sites, such as the seaside and mountain areas.

Pelisson and Dubrule developed their expanding company with a philosophy of decentralized management and a unique dual chairmanship. Although to comply with French law the partners took turns holding the official position of chairman, they made all decisions jointly and generally shared responsibilities, immersing themselves in all aspects of the business. The company's specialty became variety, providing hotel chains to fit every need. In 1973, Sphere SA was created as a holding company for a new chain of two-star, no-frills hotels, called Ibis; the first Ibis was opened the following year. During this time, the company also acquired Courte Paille, a chain of roadside steakhouses, founded in 1961, which reflected many of the same priorities as Novotel: practicality, easy parking, consistent quality, and quick service. The purchase of the Mercure hotel chain in 1975 pushed the company into metropolitan areas and the business traveler market, and again, as with Novotel, these hotels varied according to regional demands in style, character, and restaurant offerings. By the end of the 1970s, Novotel had become the premier hotel chain in Europe with 240 establishments in Europe, Africa, South America, and the Far East.

New Ventures in the Early 1980s

In 1980, Novotel invested in Jacques Borel International, which owned restaurants and luxury Sofitel hotels. Jacques Borel had begun his career with the establishment of one restaurant in 1957, and, by 1975, when he took over Belgium's Sofitel chain, he was Europe's top restaurateur. After losses in the hotel business forced Borel to sell the Sofitel chain to Pelisson and Dubrule in 1982, Novotel and its holdings were incorporated under the name Accor and became one of the top ten hotel

Company Perspectives:

L'esprit ACCOR is the art of blending skills, of combining traditions of the past with modern innovation, adding the generosity, discipline, imagination and warmth which can carry our work to a higher level of excellence. For the Company, L'esprit ACCOR is a conquering vision of success. The men and women of ACCOR have inherited a unique cultural legacy: the sense of hospitality, the unfailing ability to anticipate and meet the needs of their guests, with genuine attention to detail. ACCOR people know techniques and practices which mark the everyday with a sense of style and turn simple services into real experiences for the guest. It is a trade, it is an art, it is their particular talent. Seeking the best of everything, creating better places just to be, our one wish is to share it all with you. This is L'esprit ACCOR, the breath of France that kindles the spark of conviviality, no matter where you are in the world.

operations in the world, an elite group typically dominated by American firms. The merger doubled the partners' holdings and infused new talent into the senior management, as Bernard Westercamp became vice-president and general manager of Accor. Sofitel's luxury services, which were aimed at business and holiday travelers and located in the center of international cities, near airports, and in prestigious tourist areas, introduced Accor to the higher-priced end of the hotel industry.

Accor's initial expansion into the American market, which began in 1979 with the opening of a hotel in Minneapolis, was not as successful as its ventures in Europe, due to a saturated market in the United States and Accor's slow development. The company brought Novotel, Ibis, and Sofitel hotels to the United States, as well as a chain of eateries in California called Seafood Broiler, but all operated at a loss. Nonetheless, Pelisson and Dubrule made American-style service culture fundamental to their business in Europe. After visiting training schools at McDonald's Corporation and Disneyland, they opened Accor Academy at the company headquarters in Évry in 1985. The academy offered seminars in topics ranging from phone etiquette to team-building skills and the exploration of new technologies. Accor spent a reported two percent of its annual payroll on training.

During the mid-1980s, Accor developed investments in the restaurant and travel businesses. The company opened Pizza del Arte, a chain of Italian restaurants, in 1983, installing them in commercial and city centers, and entered into a partnership with the bakery and catering company Lenôtre two years later. Accor also entered the travel industry during this time, buying into Africatours, the largest tour operator to Africa, which became the third of its major investments, along with hotels and restaurants. The company expanded its tour operations to North and South America, Asia, and the South Pacific through the purchases of Americatours, Asietours, and Ted Cook's Islands in the Sun. In an effort to attract weekend clientele in Europe, Accor developed Épisodes, an agency specializing in short trips offering weekend rooms in hotels usually filled by business travelers.

In 1985, Hotec, a subsidiary of Accor, brought forth a completely new idea in the hotel industry with the creation of Formule 1, a one-star budget hotel chain that offered no reception staff, no restaurant, and no private bathrooms. Travelers simply inserted a credit card at the entrance to gain access to the rooms, which were plain yet practical and cost $15 a night. Formule 1 hotels appealed to vacationing young people and families of limited financial resources. Costs were kept to a minimum by the use of prefabricated construction and staffs of only two to run each 60-room hotel. Occupancy rates were high, and ten Formule 1s were in operation by early 1987, and another 30 were under construction across Europe.

Continued Expansion in the Late 1980s

From 1981 to 1986, Accor's revenues doubled to around $2 billion, with net profits of $32 million. Novotel, with hotels in 31 countries, remained the most profitable of Accor's holdings, whereas Sofitel faced stiff competition in the luxury hotel market, particularly from American firms. Nevertheless, Accor expanded at a far swifter rate than its international rivals. The company was the largest operator in Europe. It led the market in France, West Germany, and the Benelux countries and was expanding in the medium and economy range in Spain, Italy, and Britain with its $75 million investment budget. The company's European base provided three-quarters of its revenue, with more than half coming from hotels and the rest from restaurants, catering, and lunch tickets.

In 1985, Accor took control of Britain's Luncheon Voucher, the company that invented meal tickets, which companies distributed to their employees as a benefit. Accor overhauled the company's communications and management systems and restored its market presence through a new sales drive. By 1987, Accor was the world leader in restaurant vouchers for employees and was exploring similar voucher programs for child care in the United States and groceries in Latin America.

In 1987, Accor exploited another growing market: homes for the elderly. The company's Hotelia homes provided 24-hour medical and nursing care, as well as more traditional hotel services. Also that year, Accor created the successful Parthénon chain of residential hotels in Brazil. In 1988, the company invested in France Quick, ranked second in the French fast-food market, and launched the Free Time fast-food chain. With several partners, Accor then invested in Cipal-Parc Astérix, a theme park north of Paris, based on a Gallic cartoon character, and expressed interest in providing catering and lodging for the then projected EuroDisney amusement park. Accor's rapid growth was not without its setbacks, however, as it made a failed bid for the Hilton International Co. and tried unsuccessfully to merge with Club Méditerranée.

In early 1987, the company underwent a large-scale reorganization in order to help it better cope with its diversification of products and its two decades of growth. The group was restructured according to product, so that each chain would have its own general management. Accor was still committed to decentralization and expected the management of each chain to act autonomously as directors of small- or medium-sized companies. Pelisson and Dubrule maintained a flexible, dynamic structure and were committed to remaining accessible. During this reorganization, the company's business continually improved, with 1989 profits up 30 percent from 1988, on sales of $3.6 billion. Accor enjoyed yearly 12 percent earnings-per-share increases from 1983 to 1989. Steady growth allowed the company to sell equity, including a $340 million issue in January 1990.

Acquisitions in the Early 1990s

Accor made a major move into the U.S. market when it purchased the Dallas-based budget hotel chain Motel 6 in 1990 for $1.3 billion. The deal made Accor the second largest hotel company in the world in terms of rooms, 157,000, and represented an attempt by Pelisson and Dubrule to build an American hotel empire to match their extremely successful operation in Europe, where 85 percent of their hotels were located. Accor paid a hefty price to enter the crowded U.S. market and took on an additional $1 billion debt from the seller, Kohlberg Kravis Roberts & Co. However, Pelisson and Dubrule were committed to expanding in America, planning to implement the same cost-cutting measures which had worked so well for Formule 1, including credit card payment and limited maintenance staff. The company used a radio ad campaign and transatlantic marketing to lure Europeans to Motel 6. Although Accor agreed not to overhaul the management of Motel 6's parent company, Motel 6 G.P. Inc., it did sell a 60 percent stake of Motel 6 to French institutional investors. In 1991, Accor bought 53 Regal Inns and Affordable Inns from RHC Holding Corp. in order to expand Motel 6 into the preeminent budget hotel company in the world. Motel 6's success in the early 1990s was due in part to Accor's financial backing and ability to pay cash, as well as its decision to purchase company-owned properties outright rather than franchising them.

In 1990, with Société Générale de Belgique, Accor bought a 26.7 percent stake in Wagons-Lits, a Belgian company that dominated the European railroad sleeping car business and was the second largest hotel chain in continental Europe, owning about 300 hotels in Europe, Thailand, and Indonesia. In 1992, the European Community approved Accor's nearly $1 billion bid for a 69.5 percent controlling interest in Wagons-Lits. At the end of the year, Accor became the world leader in its industry with 2,100 hotels, 6,000 restaurants, and 1,000 travel agencies.

With the privatization of industry in Hungary, Accor entered into a partnership in 1993 to buy 51 percent of the hotel company Pannonia from the Hungarian government. Pannonia owned medium-priced hotels in Hungary, Germany, and Austria and gained exclusive rights to develop under Accor in Bulgaria, Albania, Romania, Slovakia, Hungary, and the former Soviet Union and Yugoslavia, as well as to develop the Mercure chain in Austria. Accor also launched the Coralia label in 1993 to distinguish holiday hotels from business hotels. Around 30 Accor hotels in the Mediterranean and Indian Ocean regions added the Coralia label by 1994 and more were planned in the Caribbean, Central America, and Venezuela.

In the early 1990s, Accor subsidiary Atria was developing economic centers in cities and towns, composed of conference centers, offices, and hotels, particularly Novotels and Mercures, in conjunction with local chambers of commerce. The company also had investments in Thalassa International spas and luxury hotels

and casinos in France. Accor began a hotel-rebranding strategy in June 1993 to eliminate the Pullman Hotels International chain, which it had acquired in 1991, while expanding its Sofitel International and Mercure brands. Through renovations, the company transformed 27 Pullman hotels into its four-star Sofitel hotels, while another 25 Pullman hotels became Mercure hotels.

Similarly, Accor continued to expand its restaurant business in the early 1990s, with L'Arche cafeterias, L'Écluse winebars, Boeuf Jardinier steakhouses, Café Route highway cafés, Actair airport restaurants, Terminal train station buffets, and Meda's Grills in Spain. The company increased its partnership in France Quick and began building independent ''villas'' for Pizza del Arte. In 1994, Lenôtre, the bakery and catering chain that Accor had developed in six countries, merged with Rosell, a chain specializing in organization, expansion, and management of catering services, for mutual advantages.

With Wagons-Lits, Accor continued its expansion in restaurants and sleeping compartments aboard trains. In the car rental business, the company shared control of Europcar Interrent International with Volkswagen in 89 countries in Europe, Africa, and the Middle East. In March 1994, Accor agreed to merge its travel agency business with Carlson Travel Network, a subsidiary of Carlson Companies, to form a network of 4,000 agencies, in 125 countries, worth $10.8 billion. The new enterprise, named Carlson Wagonlit Travel, would be 50 percent owned by Carlson Companies and 50 percent owned by Accor. The integration of the two businesses would occur gradually over the next several years.

Divesting Assets in the Mid-1990s

Accor's rapid expansion lost some momentum in the mid-1990s, as its debt accumulated and a recession hit the travel industry. One of the first signs its steamrolling expansion would not continue was the loss of Accor's 1994 bid for a 57 percent stake in the four-star hotel chain Meridien. Although Accor found funding through the Saudi hotel financier Prince Al Waleed, the company's bid still fell FFr 200 million short of the highest bidder.

In 1994 Accor sought to reduce its debt and free up funds for further expansion by selling some of its real estate and periphery businesses. Accor's principal strategy was to sell more expensive hotel real estate; however, it continued to manage the hotels. The same year, Accor sold several Dutch Wagon-Lits enterprises. In 1995 the company received $936 million for its catering operations from the British contract-catering company Compass.

In the mid-1990s Accor's nonhotel businesses were taking an increasingly prominent position in the conglomerate. The Carlson and Wagonlit Travel partnership was thriving, with sales rising from FFr 19.4 billion in 1993 to FFr 21 billion in 1995. Europcar, Accor's joint venture with Volkswagen, had become Europe's largest car rental company; in addition to its car rental fleet, by 1995 the company had 3.2 million leased vehicles. Net income for Accor as a whole had been rising since its 1993 low of FFr 423 million, to reach FFr 923 million in 1995.

Accor's hotel operations, however, remained the company's mainstay. By 1997, Accor operated 2,605 hotels with 289,200 rooms around the world. Sales from its hotel operations rose 16.6 percent in 1997, to FFr 18.6 billion. The company had placed its hotels in two groups: the business and leisure group, which comprised Mercure, with 43,000 rooms, Novotel, with more than 50,000 rooms, Coralia, with 23,500 rooms, and Hotel Sofitel, with 20,500 rooms, and the economy group, which comprised Motel 6, with 84,500 rooms, Ibis, with 45,000 rooms, Hotel Formule 1, with 22,000 rooms, and Etap Hotel, with 13,000 rooms. Accor continued to open new hotels, especially internationally. Its Asia-Pacific subsidiary, which the company had launched in 1993, controlled 144 hotels in 18 countries by 1996. With 56 more projects in the works, Accor Asia-Pacific had become that region's leading hotel group. Accor's Africa/Middle East group operated 99 hotels by 1997, and its Latin America group, 89.

In 1997 the company's founders, Dubrule and Pelisson, reorganized the management of the company to reduce their involvement in the day-to-day decision making. The two co-chaired the new supervisory board but ceded the chair of the management board to Jean-Marc Espalioux. The same year, the merger of the travel agency businesses of Accor and Carlson was completed, making Carlson Wagonlit Travel one of the largest travel agencies in the world.

Accor continued to fund expansion through sales of hotel real estate and certain businesses. In 1997 the company sold General de Restaurantes SA, its Spanish concession restaurant subsidiary, for FFr 275 million. By 1998, Accor had received $800 million from various sales of Motel 6 properties and FFr 1.1 billion from properties sold in Europe. In addition to funding its growth in Asia and the Pacific, these sales helped Accor acquire Postiljon, a Dutch hotel chain the company planned to incorporate into its Mercure hotel chain. In the late 1990s, the company's goals included the opening of 250 hotels a year.

Principal Subsidiaries

Academie Accor; Buffet Montparnasse SA; Devimco; HOTEC; Lenôtre; Pullman International Hotel; Resinter; Resteurop; S.E.A.V.T. SA; S.E.P.; SEPHI; SFPTH SA; SHSO; Sedri; Serare; Soblafhor; Société Hotelière Paris Vanues; Société Internationale des Hotels Novotel; Sphere SA WLFF SA; Accor North America (U.S.); Europcar (50%); Carlson Wagonlit Travel (50%; U.S.); Accor Asia Pte (Singapore); Accor Gastonomie AG (Germany); Accor Hong Kong Ltd.; Accor UK; Accor TRB (Belgium); Group Accor Espana (Spain); Luncheon Vouchers Ltd. (U.K.); Novotel Goteborg AB (Sweden); Novotel UK Ltd.

Further Reading

Bergsman, Steve, ''Accor Gains Ground with U.S. Acquisitions,'' *Hotel & Motel Management,* May 27, 1991, pp. 3, 60–61.

Bond, Helen, ''Motel 6 Eyes More Moves,'' *Hotel & Motel Management,* May 27, 1991, pp. 1, 76.

Bruce, Leigh, ''The Two-Headed Chairmanship That Keeps Accor Soaring,'' *International Management,* January 1987, pp. 26–28.

''Circling the Wagons,'' *Economist,* January 27, 1990.

Jones, Sandra, ''Accor Launches Rebranding, Proposes Venture with Air France,'' *Hotel & Motel Management,* July 3, 1993, p. 11.

McDowell, Edwin, ''Not Just Leaving the Light On,'' *New York Times,* October 28, 1998, p. C1.

''Meat and Drink,'' *Economist,* July 8, 1995, p. 7.

''Playing Monopoly: Luxury Hotels,'' *Economist,* May 7, 1994, pp. 77–78.

Reier, Sharon, ''Bedroom Eyes,'' *Financial World,* June 9, 1992, pp. 56–58.

''Rest Assured,'' *Economist,* January 10, 1998.

Riemer, Blanca, ''This Buy-America Bandwagon Could Hit a Few Potholes,'' *Business Week,* July 30, 1990, p. 21.

Toy, Stewart, ''Accor Goes with the Modified American Plan,'' *Business Week,* October 1, 1990, pp. 78–79.

—Jennifer Kerns
—updated by Susan Windisch Brown

Performance Companies, Inc.

Action Performance Companies, Inc.

4707 E. Baseline Road
Phoenix, Arizona 85040
U.S.A.
(602) 337-3700
Fax: (602) 337-3810
Web site: http://www.action-performance.com

Public Company
Incorporated: 1992
Employees: 418
Sales: $252 million (1998)
Stock Exchanges: NASDAQ
Ticker Symbol: ACTN
SICs: 2321 Men's & Boys' Shirts, Except Work Shirts;
  2331 Women's, Misses, & Juniors' Blouses & Shirts;
  3089 Plastics Products, Not Elsewhere Classified;
  3229 Pressed & Blown Glass, Not Elsewhere
  Classified; 3944 Games, Toys, & Children's Vehicles,
  Except Dolls & Bicycles

Action Performance Companies, Inc. is one of the United States' leading corporations manufacturing and distributing souvenirs and apparel related to motor racing. The company runs a variety of racing-related enterprises. Its main business is producing die-cast miniature race car replicas. These are sold through a collectors' club, at racing events, and through other mainstream distribution channels. Action also manufactures other racing souvenirs, such as miniature replica drivers' helmets, and sells racing-style clothing for children and adults. In addition, it handles licensing agreements for prominent stock car drivers through its Action Sports Marketing Division. Under contract with the company are many of the most popular and successful drivers in the country. The company's enormous growth in the 1990s came as interest in stock car racing soared in the United States. Few other companies were serving this niche market, and Action Performance rode the wave of racing popularity to admirable financial reward.

Early History

Action Performance was founded by Fred Wagenhals, an inventor and former race car driver. Wagenhals attended college for two years, intending to become an engineer, but his real love was car racing, and he left school in order to drive. He raced for the next five years, and then began working for himself as a designer and inventor. Wagenhals had many ideas, and he claimed in a 1997 interview with *Chain Store Age Executive* that many of them failed. Nevertheless, he held eight patents by the time he was 21, and had made a million dollars by the time he was 30. Wagenhals pioneered a two-man jet-pumped boat, which was eventually manufactured by Ski-Doo, and he created a computerized motor for a mechanical bull featured in the movie *Urban Cowboy*. Wagenhals also made gas-powered one-third scale cars used in the film *Smokey and the Bandit* and in the television show *Fantasy Island*.

In the 1980s Wagenhals was in business with two partners in Tempe, Arizona, to sell these minicars. Wagenhals and his partners Joe Hrudka and Ed Fochtman incorporated in 1986 as Action Products, Inc. This company sold the gas-powered cars as well as pedal cars, electric cars, radio-controlled cars, and something called the "Funder Wheels Go Kart." Action Products was able to sell its minicars to such substantial clients as Coca-Cola, Pennzoil, Dial Corp., and Quaker State. These customers used the cars in promotional events. Action Products also sold a significant number of miniature cars patterned after the vehicle shown in the movie *Back to the Future II*. Despite the small company's promising sales, with revenues just under $5 million in 1987 and up to $6 million in 1988, cash flow problems plagued it, and Action Products operated at a loss. The company went public in 1989, hoping to raise close to $3 million in its initial stock offering.

While he was doing business as Action Products, Wagenhals got an idea for a new venture. In 1989 he came across an article on the baseball card collectibles market, and decided it might be lucrative to sell stock car racing collectibles. Because of his familiarity with the racing world, he was in a good position to know it had not been done before. The popular miniature cars that children collected, such as Hot Wheels and Matchbox,

---

Company Perspectives:

Action Performance Companies, Inc. is the leader in the design, marketing and distribution of licensed motorsports-related apparel, souvenirs, die cast car replica collectibles and other memorabilia.

---

offered race cars, but they were not modeled on specific vehicles. Wagenhals decided to make premium collectible miniatures with a wealth of detail, and to market them directly to members of a racing club.

To get the rights to reproduce one well-known car, driver Dale Earnhardt's black number three, Wagenhals paid Earnhardt $300,000. It seemed a big investment at the time, yet Wagenhals knew that he had a corner on what could be a burgeoning market. He proceeded to produce die-cast miniatures of Earnhardt's car and sold them through a Georgia-based fan club called the Racing Collectables Club of America. Interested consumers paid a membership fee to join the club, and then were offered Wagenhals' collectibles as well as other merchandise licensed from the National Association of Stock Car Automobile Racing (NASCAR). Even though he was still president of Action Products, Wagenhals ran this new venture through another company he formed with different partners, called Racing Champions. This new company took off, while Action Products continued to flounder. With some acrimonious jostling among the partners, Action Products went out of business in 1992, Wagenhals took his share of the assets, and formed a new company, Action Performance. (His former partners in Action Products sued Wagenhals, and the breach of contract suit was settled in 1997 for $4.9 million.)

Growth of the New Company

Because of Wagenhals' extensive contacts with NASCAR drivers and team owners, he was able to wangle many prime licensing deals to duplicate cars and use drivers' images and endorsements. Action Performance began selling its products directly to racing enthusiasts, bringing a trailer to racing events across the country. The company also bought up the Racing Collectables Club of America, Inc. and Racing Collectables Inc. These were two enterprises owned by brothers Andrew and Stan Gill in Atlanta. Racing Collectables Inc. made model cars, and the club was founded in May 1991. By mid-1993, the Racing Collectables Club had some 24,000 members, and the number continued to go up. Action Performance manufactured over 50 different collectible cars by 1993, including models it bought when it took over Racing Collectables Inc. Manufacturing was done in China, and with the growing club membership and interest in stock car racing, the company was soon producing hundreds of thousands of miniatures each month. These were sold not only through the collectors club but through some 8000 retail outlets as well. The model cars were built to 1/64th size, and sold for just under $2 to around $6. But the company also produced limited edition models for the collectors club, and these were quite pricey. After paying close to $30 to join, club members then might shell out over $70 for a limited edition model race car.

Meanwhile, Action Performance continued the sell the one-third scale minicars that had been the prime product of the old Action Products. It also acquired Race Z, Inc. in May 1992, a company that specialized in staging Grand Prix-type races for minicars. Action Performance began to have an extremely integrated business. It sold minicars to companies that wanted to stage races as fundraisers, and conducted the races. Its minicar customers also often bought the collectible models, as gifts or premiums for their clients.

The popularity of stock car racing climbed in the mid-1990s, and Action Performance prospered. By 1996, more people were watching professional auto racing than any other sport in the U.S., and industries associated with racing were pulling in a combined $1 billion. Action Performance's growth rocketed, as its sales climbed and it acquired more related companies. The company also shed some businesses, getting rid of its race-staging business in 1994 and selling off its minicar manufacturing division in 1995. Then in 1996, Action Performance started a new division, Action Sports Management. The company hired Bill Seaborn, Jr., to head the new enterprise. He had worked for NASCAR, the stock car racing association, for 14 years, ultimately heading their licensing program. Action Performance hired Seaborn to market their licensed clients, hoping to turn stock car drivers into the kind of ubiquitous presences of many of the top basketball, football, and baseball stars. The new marketing division's first coup was to sign up the single biggest star of drag racing, John Force, a six-time Winston Cup champion. Merchandise with Force's image already made up over 40 percent of racing souvenir stand sales.

Action Performance also forged an alliance with giant toy-maker Hasbro in 1996. In a joint agreement, the two companies planned to develop a line of racing toys called Winner's Circle. Action Performance also bought up a marketing and distribution firm called Sports Image Inc., owned by former NASCAR champion Dale Earnhardt (whose car had been Action's first miniature collectible). Sales for 1996 were stellar, rising to just over $44 million from $26 million the previous year. This huge increase in sales was accompanied by a doubling of net income.

The company continued to buy up related businesses. In 1997 it acquired a marketing and promotions firm owned by another former NASCAR champion driver, Jeff Gordon, and his partners. Action Performance put down more than $5 million in cash for Gordon's concerns. Then in July 1997 the company spent another $4.25 million for a Georgia firm, Image Works, Inc. Image Works marketed racing-related apparel. Then in August the company bought up the collectibles business of one of its competitors, Simpson Race Products. Action Performance then quickly initiated a deal to buy the die-cast collectibles unit of another competitor, Revell-Monogram Inc. Revell-Monogram had three lines of die-cast race cars, in addition to a huge business in plastic model kits. It sold primarily to hobby shops, where it had significant brand recognition. Action Performance paid $25 million for Revell's motor die-cast unit, hoping for an in with the hobby shop consumer. The acquisition gave Action Performance an estimated 50 to 60 percent share of the total die-cast collectible race car market. And this one acquisition alone was expected to bring in over $20 million in new sales for the company.

As sales and earnings multiplied for the company, Action Performance dubbed itself "the Franklin Mint of auto racing." Between 1993 and 1997, sales grew more than eightfold, from around $15 million to over $130 million. Stock car racing was the fastest growing sport in the United States, with attendance at the Winston Cup finals rising more than 65 percent from 1990 to 1996. More than six million fans showed up for the Winston Cup in 1997, while 123 million watched the race on television. Action Performance had plenty of money to spend, and it continued to buy up smaller companies. Around the time the company announced its major purchase of Revell-Monogram's motor die-cast unit, Action also paid $8 million for the licensing and merchandising firm Rusty Wallace Merchandising Inc. The company also acquired a small Wisconsin collectibles firm called Brookfield Collectors Guild, Inc.

In 1998 the firm expanded into the European market for the first time. It bought an 80 percent interest in Minichamps, a company that designed and sold die-cast miniatures of Formula 1 racers. It also had licensing agreements with European drivers and racing teams, including Michael Schumacher, Jacques Villeneueve, Ferrari, and McClaren. Action Performance acquired a controlling interest in the firm, and also agreed to let Minichamps manage Action's European business. Then, expanding in a different direction, Action went into cyberspace, buying Tech 2000 Worldwide Inc. in November 1998. This privately held company ran racing related Internet sites. After spending $4.27 million for the company, Action Performance announced it would use Tech 2000 to develop a motor sports on-line shopping mall and information site, to be called www.goracing.com.

The Future

By 1998, Action had positioned itself as one of the major toy makers in the United States. NASCAR toys were said to be the third bestselling item in the entire toy industry, and Action Performance had some 50 to 60 percent of the NASCAR niche. Action continued to plan more acquisitions for the end of the 1990s and into the next century, and also claimed it would follow up on its European expansion. One possible brake to Action's growth though was the slowdown in new members of its collectibles club. In 1995, for example, the club grew by over 80 percent. The number of new members in 1998 however was up only 22 percent over the previous year. The company was predicated on the continuing boom in racing's popularity, and any downturn would presumably effect Action's sales. But the company itself worked assiduously to make racing interesting, sponsoring special paint jobs for its drivers, for example, coming up with Elvis cars at the Las Vegas Winston Cup Gala, and fostering a promotional tie-in with its cars in the movie *Small Soldiers*. The company seemed to have tireless marketing strength. Wagenhals himself saw stock car racing as still with its best years ahead in the late 1990s. In an interview with *Stock Car Racing* in November 1998, he declared that "NASCAR is very similar today to where baseball was in the early '60s," and he predicted more tremendous growth in the sport over the next five years. Since the company and the sport were so closely tied, that would mean more growth in Action's future, too.

Principal Subsidiaries

Race Z, Inc.; Action Products, Inc.; Racing Collectables Inc.; Mini Wheels West; Racing Collectables Club of America Inc.; Fan Fueler, Inc.

Further Reading

"Action Purchases Internet Company," *Knight-Ridder Tribune Business News,* November 25, 1998.

Berggren, Dick, "Making It in Racing: Fred Wagenhals," *Stock Car Racing,* November 1998.

"Fred J. Wagenhals," *Chain Store Age Executive,* December 1997, p. 130.

Golfen, Bob, "Lawsuit Targets Chief of Arizona's Action Performance," *Knight-Ridder/Tribune Business News,* May 9, 1996.

——, "Tempe, Ariz. Firm Shifts Gears to Rev Up Racers' Images," *Knight-Ridder/Tribune Business News,* September 7, 1996.

Jacobson, Gianna, "From Zero to Millions," *Success,* June 1996, p. 30.

Luebke, Cathy, "Maker of Miniature Cars Buys Atlanta Competitor," *Business Journal* (Phoenix), August 27, 1993, p. 6.

"Race Car Boom Fuels Profits of Arizona Marketing Firm," *Knight-Ridder/Tribune Business News,* December 4, 1996.

Rodrian, Scott, "Tempe-Based Mini-Car Builder Files with SEC for Stock Offering," *Business Journal* (Phoenix), October 23, 1989, p. 2.

Schifrin, Matthew, "Streetwalker," *Forbes,* December 14, 1998, p. 276.

Western, Ken, "Action Increases Its Share of Race Car Collectibles Market," *Knight-Ridder/Tribune Business News,* January 2, 1998.

—A. Woodward

ADVANTICA
restaurant group

Advantica Restaurant Group, Inc.

203 East Main Street
Spartanburg, South Carolina 29319-9966
U.S.A.
(864) 597-8000
Fax: (864) 597-8780

Public Company
Incorporated: 1979 as Trans World Corporation
Employees: 85,000
Sales: $2.6 billion
Stock Exchanges: NASDAQ
Ticker Symbol: DINE
SICs: 5812 Eating Places; 6794 Patent Owners &
    Lessors; 6719 Holding Companies

Advantica Restaurant Group, Inc., is one of the largest restaurant companies in the United States, operating 3,300 restaurants. In the late 1990s its moderately priced chains included Denny's, Coco's, Carrows, and El Pollo Loco. Originally part of a much larger and more diverse conglomerate, Advantica, formerly known as Flagstar, was formed through a series of corporate mergers and divestitures, which ultimately produced a company focused on restaurants. The company's legacy of corporate restructuring, however, left it with large debts, and it went through Chapter 11 bankruptcy reorganization in 1997.

Company Origins

Flagstar emerged in the early 1990s from the Trans World Corporation, which was created in 1979 as a holding company for Trans World Airlines (TWA), Hilton International hotels, and the Canteen Corporation, a contract food-services company. Later that year Trans World acquired Century 21 Real Estate and Spartan Food Systems, which owned the restaurant chain Quincy's Family Steakhouse and is the largest franchisee of Hardee's restaurants. In the mid-1980s Trans World moved to streamline its diverse operations, spinning off TWA to its shareholders and selling Century 21 to the Metropolitan Life Insurance Company.

In 1986 Trans World's profits declined sharply after its purchase of American Medical Services, a nursing home operator in poor financial shape. As a result of this acquisition, the company's stock price dropped dramatically, attracting the attention of corporate raiders, who sought to buy up the inexpensive shares of Trans World stock, take over the company, and sell off its other valuable constituent parts for a profit. To ward off such hostile takeover attempts, Trans World was forced to restructure. The company's stock was liquidated on December 31, 1986, and new stock, for a company called TW Services, Inc., was issued. This new entity included the assets of Canteen, Spartan, and American Medical Systems, along with other businesses.

The following year TW Services moved to consolidate its operations further, and it sold its hotel operations, Hilton International, to Allegis, Inc. At the same time, TW Services expanded and strengthened its restaurant operations, purchasing Denny's, a restaurant chain with 1,200 outlets, and El Pollo Loco, another chain of 70 eateries specializing in chicken. After this process of corporate restructurings, TW Services emerged as an operator of chain restaurants and other food services. The company's five principal food-oriented businesses included Denny's, Hardee's, Quincy's Family Steakhouse, El Pollo Loco, and the Canteen Corporation.

Early History of the Canteen Subsidiary

The oldest of TW Services' units was Canteen, founded in July 1929 by Nathaniel Leverone and two other partners. Just before the onset of the Great Depression, Leverone acquired the Chicago Automatic Canteen Corporation, the vending operations of an American Legion chapter in Chicago. The company oversaw the operations of 100 five-cent candy bar machines stationed throughout the Chicago area. In 1930 Leverone changed the name of his company to the Automatic Canteen Company of America, and he began to seek out franchise operators, who would be given an exclusive contract to operate Canteen machines in different areas of the country. By 1931, 15 different franchises had been established.

Wartime shortages in the early 1940s challenged the abilities of Canteen's franchise operators. At the end of the war, however, a sharp increase in the manufacture of consumer goods proved a boon to Canteen operators, since many of their machines were located in factory lunchrooms. The company thrived throughout the 1950s, and in 1960 its operations were expanded with the purchase of Nationwide Food Service, which also provided food services for people in their workplace. In the mid-1960s American Canteen shortened its name to the Canteen Corporation. Three years later the company was purchased by International Telephone and Telegraph (ITT).

Under ITT, Canteen's operations continued to expand, as it moved into the fields of hospital and college campus food services. In 1973 Canteen was sold to the Trans World Corporation, and over the next several years Canteen became involved in running food services for the National Aeronautics and Space Administration (NASA), as well as concession stands in national parks and at convention centers, sports arenas, and massive entertainment complexes.

Early History of Denny's

The second oldest of the TW Services restaurant units was Denny's, founded as a doughnut stand in Lakewood, California, in 1953. Originally called Danny's Donuts, the shop was opened by Harold Butler, who planned to offer coffee and doughnuts 24 hours a day. By the end of its first year in operation, Butler's doughnut stand had garnered profits of $120,000. In 1954 Danny's Donuts became Danny's Coffee Shops, and Butler began expanding his operations, opening additional stores. Five years later the chain of coffee shops became Denny's restaurants, and doughnuts were phased out of the menu.

In choosing locations for his restaurants, Butler concentrated on major highway and freeway exits, where travelers would be plentiful at all hours of the day and night. The expansion of a national network of interstate highways during this time prompted increasing numbers of Americans to travel by car, and Denny's restaurants became a rapid success.

In 1967 Denny's opened its first foreign restaurant, located in Acapulco, Mexico, and eventually established additional outlets in Mexico as well as Hong Kong. In 1969, in an effort to streamline and centralize its food production, Denny's bought Delly's Food, changing the name of that concern to Proficient Food Company. This subsidiary was responsible for running warehouse and distribution operations to keep the company's restaurants supplied. Four years later Denny's opened its own food processing facility, called Portion-Trol Foods, in Mansfield, Texas. In the mid-1980s Denny's was purchased for $800 million by a group of investors in a leveraged buyout. Two years later these investors sold the company to TW Services for $843 million.

Early History of Spartan Food Systems

TW Services also owned and operated the largest franchisee of Hardee's, one of the units of Spartan Food Systems. The first Hardee's franchise was opened in October of 1961 in Spartanburg, South Carolina. A second Hardee's franchise outlet was soon opened in another area of Spartanburg. This restaurant, which was a walk-up operation rather than a drive-in, was owned and run by Jerry Richardson and four other investors, who contributed a total of $20,000 and called their enterprise Spartan Investment Company.

Offering hamburgers, french fries, and beverages priced between 10 and 15 cents, the franchised Hardee's was a success, and the Spartan investors soon opened other outlets. Within five years they were running 15 different Hardee's restaurants. In 1969 the partnership changed its name to Spartan Food Systems and began to offer stock to the public. In 1976 Spartan was listed on the New York Stock Exchange for the first time.

The following year, with the money raised from this stock offering, Spartan purchased the Quincy's Family Steakhouse chain, founded in 1973 as the Western Family Steak House, a single restaurant located in Greenville, South Carolina. By 1976 nine Western Family Steak Houses were in operation, and the company's name was changed to Quincy's, in honor of co-founder Bill Brittain's grandfather. By 1978 the number of Quincy's restaurants had almost tripled, and this rate of rapid growth continued after Spartan was purchased by Trans World in 1979. Over the next five years, an additional 189 Quincy's steakhouse restaurants were opened throughout the Southeast.

TW Services also acquired El Pollo Loco, Spanish for "The Crazy Chicken," a company that got its start in Mexico in 1975. Francisco Ochoa opened a modest restaurant by the side of a road in the small town of Gusave, serving flame-broiled chicken that had been marinated with his family's recipe of fruit juices, herbs, and spices. Ochoa's operation expanded rapidly in Mexico, as 90 outlets in 20 cities were opened during the 1970s.

At the end of 1980 the company opened its first restaurant in the United States, on Alvarado Street in Los Angeles, and within three years 16 more American restaurants were established. In 1983 the Ochoa family sold its American restaurants to Denny's, retaining the El Pollo Loco Mexican operations. Under its new owner, the American El Pollo Locos were expanded to include several new outlets in California and Nevada, before being purchased by TW Services in 1987.

With a stable group of food service properties in place, TW Services announced in 1987 that it planned to invest $700 million in expanding and improving its operations in an effort to strengthen its presence in the food services industry. Toward this end the company cut back the administrative staff at Denny's headquarters and simplified the chain's menus, improving the company's profitability.

Hostile Takeover in Late 1980s

Before other efforts had begun to take effect, however, TW Services found itself in the midst of another corporate takeover battle in the fall of 1988. Coniston Partners, an investor group known for breaking up and selling off parts of other big corporations, sought to buy TW Services for $1.14 billion. In response, the company put in place a "poison pill" defense intended to make it extremely expensive for any outsider to buy more than 20 percent of its stock. Coniston challenged this move in court, while continuing to purchase increments of TW Services stock. By mid-December 1988, 85 percent of TW

Services' stock had been purchased by Coniston, and by the middle of the following year the deal had been completed. Coniston bought TW Services for $1.7 billion. The company's new owners planned to keep its food services units and sell off its less profitable nursing home unit.

In 1990 American Medical Services was divested, along with two other smaller units, The Rowe Corporation and the Milnot Corporation. In addition, the company consolidated the administration of all of its restaurant chains, moving the headquarters of TW Services from Paramus, New Jersey, to Spartanburg, South Carolina, where its Hardee's franchises were based. In the months following, the headquarters of Canteen was moved from Chicago to Spartanburg as was Denny's administrative staff, which transferred from Irvine, California. Only El Pollo Loco, whose restaurants were located exclusively in the western states, retained its headquarters outside the new central company facilities.

These moves were intended to help TW Services run more efficiently, to offset its high debt, and to stem its losses, which reached $67.8 million in 1990. The transfer of operations was completed in 1991, but the company still finished 1991 with losses of $67.6 million. Help for the beleaguered company came in 1992, when TW Services cut a deal with the venture capital firm Kohlberg Kravis Roberts & Company, which contributed $300 million in capital to TW Services, in return for a 47 percent stake in the company.

Denny's Discrimination Problem in the Early 1990s

Hope for financial improvements was offset, however, by disturbing news on another front: African-American customers at Denny's restaurants in California began to complain that they had been discriminated against and denied service. Specifically, the customers alleged that some Denny's restaurants either refused adequate service or forced them to pay in advance for their meals, while white customers in the restaurants were not asked to do the same.

As the U.S. Justice Department began an investigation into Denny's, TW Services began an effort to control the public relations damage to its reputation. The company apologized to customers, made contact with civil rights groups, fired or transferred problematic employees, and implemented a cultural relations team designed to educate employees on issues of race. Negotiations with the Justice Department continued throughout 1992. In March 1993, TW Services signed a consent decree with the Justice Department that called for an end to prejudicial practices. The company agreed to initiate improved training guidelines for employees and to allow for the spot testing of Denny's restaurants for compliance with its nondiscriminatory policy.

Nevertheless, the company's legal troubles continued, as aggrieved customers pressed lawsuits. Moreover, in May 1993, six African-American Secret Service agents sued Denny's, claiming that they had been denied service at a restaurant in Annapolis, Maryland. The charges received extensive media exposure, as critics charged that Denny's employees exhibited such consistent racist behavior that it constituted a part of the company's culture.

In the midst of these image problems, TW Services changed its name in June 1993. Shedding all vestiges of its past association with Trans World, the company took Flagstar as its new moniker. Flagstar also hired its first African-American executive, a human relations administrator who vowed to tackle the problems at Denny's.

One month later, Flagstar announced an ambitious minority advancement program developed in conjunction with the NAACP. To demonstrate its good faith in its effort to stamp out racism, Flagstar announced that it would double the number of Denny's franchises owned by minorities to 107, hire 325 African-American managers, and pledge $1 billion to be earmarked for goods purchased from minority-owned contractors over a seven-year period. Moreover, the company promised to maintain a policy of designating 12 percent of its purchasing budget, ten percent of its marketing and advertising budget, and 15 percent of its legal, accounting, and consulting budget, exclusively for minority-owned firms.

Financial Trouble in the Mid-1990s

Flagstar continued to suffer financial difficulties. Surveys showed that the customer traffic in its Denny's chain, which contributed the bulk of its revenues, was down by seven percent. In an effort to draw more people into its restaurants, Denny's inaugurated an all-you-can-eat promotion, which had to be canceled in the summer of 1993 when it became too expensive. By the end of the year the company's losses had reached $1.7 billion, which included a $1.5 billion write-off of goodwill and other intangible assets. In addition, in January 1994, Flagstar announced that it would take a $192 million restructuring charge to close or franchise 14 percent of its restaurants, primarily Denny's outlets. The company also announced that it would embark upon a modernization program for its 1,000 company restaurants, installing new facades and menus, additional lights, and contemporary logos in facilities that, in many cases, had not been updated in 20 years.

The company's poor financial performance prompted the layoff of 300 employees in March 1994. Although the company had announced in February an 18-month program for gradual downsizing, it considerably accelerated the plan. The eliminated positions were primarily in support staff, particularly clerical, payroll, and building services.

In June 1994 Flagstar announced that it had completed the sale of the Canteen food and vending operations to London-based Compass Group PLC for $450 million. At the same time Flagstar began searching for buyers for its Volume Services and TW Recreational Services divisions. These efforts reflected the company's decision to focus on its restaurants, Flagstar's core business.

By December 1995, Flagstar had agreed to pay a total of $54 million to plaintiffs in three class action lawsuits against Denny's. This sum represented the largest and broadest settlement ever made in such suits. With this move, the company hoped to settle 4,300 claims against it, contained in legal proceedings taking place in Maryland, Virginia, and California. At the same time, the company renewed its commitment to improving race relations at Denny's, setting up discrimination testing programs and monitoring employee behavior.

Flagstar CEO Jerry Richardson brokered the settlements and hired Ron Petty to take over as president of Denny's, with clear instructions to solve the chain's race relations problems. Richardson faced other problems, however, namely $2.3 billion in debt and five straight years of losses by the end of 1994. In January 1995 he was replaced as CEO by Jim Adamson. Adamson moved decisively to change the company's environment of racial discrimination. He instituted diversity training for his employees, set up management training programs to help minorities rise into executive positions, increased recruitment of minorities for both company positions and for franchise ownership, and sought out minority suppliers.

The company's financial problems proved more difficult to overcome. In 1995 Flagstar lost $55 million on revenues of $2.6 billion. Struggling with a poor image and with annual interest payments of $230 million, the company had lost Wall Street's confidence; the stock price had fallen to a low of $2.88 in 1995. The company's mainstay, Denny's, had begun to recover in 1994, with revenues up 35 percent. That growth stalled in 1995 as Flagstar sold 45 company-owned restaurants to franchisees, resulting in Denny's revenues dropping from $1.55 billion in 1994 to $1.49 billion in 1995. Hardee's was also a drain in 1995, as revenues fell almost six percent to $660 million. Hardee's same-store sales showed a depressing decline of 8.6 percent.

Adamson tackled the company's problems on several fronts. Flagstar already had begun refocusing on its restaurant businesses; Adamson completed that task by divesting all of the company's nonrestaurant businesses by mid-1996. To offset competition at Denny's from fast food restaurants, he lowered prices, introducing five morning meals under $2 to supplement the chain's popular $1.99 Grand Slam breakfast. In addition, Denny's added a "value" lunch menu, with meals from $2.99 to $4.99. To regain Hardee's customer base, Adamson ordered a cut in burger prices and an increase in burger size. In addition, he brought in a new president, Craig Bushey, to rejuvenate the 580-store chain.

In May 1996 Flagstar acquired two family dining chains, Coco's and Carrows, hoping to add more consistent performers to its stable of restaurant chains. Unable to continue under its staggering burden of debt, however, Flagstar spent 1997 reorganizing under Chapter 11 bankruptcy protection. The company finished the year with revenues of $2.61 billion, a slight increase over 1996, but reported yet another net loss, this time of $134.5 million.

In January 1998, Flagstar emerged from Chapter 11 with a new name, Advantica Restaurant Group, and a debt load $1.1 billion lighter. Adamson remained CEO, but the company had a new board of directors and newly issued common stock trading over NASDAQ. In February Advantica signed an agreement to sell its Hardee's franchise subsidiary to CKE Restaurants, Inc. The $427 million deal comprised $381 million in cash and $46 million in debt obligations. Soon after, Advantica sold its Quincy's Family Steakhouse chain as well. Advantica planned to use the cash from the two transactions to further reduce its debt and to invest in its other restaurant chains. Not only was Advantica in a more hopeful financial position in mid-1998, it was receiving recognition for its dramatic turnaround in race relations. *Fortune* magazine named Advantica the number two best company in the country for Asians, African-Americans, and Hispanics. With a rejuvenated balance sheet and image, Advantica hoped to complete a solid turnaround by the end of the decade.

Principal Divisions

Denny's; El Pollo Loco; Coco's; Carrows.

Principal Subsidiaries

FDR Acquisition Co.

Further Reading

Allen, Robin Lee, "Family Feud," *Nation's Restaurant News,* June 22, 1998, pp. 130–38.

Carlino, Bill, "Flagstar Cuts 300 Jobs, Steps Up Restructuring," *Nation's Restaurant News,* March 14, 1994, p. 3.

Deveny, Kathleen, "Do These Raiders Really Want To Start Flipping Burgers?," *Business Week,* October 10, 1988.

Fairclost, Anne, "Guess Who's Coming to Denny's," *Fortune,* August 3, 1998, pp. 108–10.

Frank, Robert, "Flagstar Loss Is $1.65 Billion on Big Charge," *Wall Street Journal,* January 25, 1994.

Holden, Benjamin A., "Parent of Denny's Restaurants, NAACP Agree on Plan To Boost Minorities' Role," *Wall Street Journal,* July 1, 1993.

Labaton, Stephen, "Denny's Restaurants To Pay $54 Million in Race Bias Suits," *New York Times,* May 25, 1994.

"On the Griddle," *Forbes,* October 7, 1996, p. 128.

Rice, Faye, "Denny's Changes Its Spots," *Fortune,* May 13, 1996, pp. 133–38.

Ringer, Richard, "Denny's Parent Has Loss After a Large Write-Off," *New York Times,* January 25, 1994.

Serwer, Andrew E., "What To Do When Race Charges Fly," *Fortune,* July 12, 1993.

—Elizabeth Rourke
—updated by Susan Windisch Brown

AHL Services, Inc.

3353 Peachtree Road N.E.
Suite 1120, North Tower
Atlanta, Georgia 30326
U.S.A.
(404) 267-2222
Fax: (404) 267-2231
Web site: http://www.ahls.com

Public Company
Incorporated: 1979
Employees: 16,282
Sales: $276 million (1997)
Stock Exchanges: NASDAQ
Ticker Symbol: AHLS
SICs: 7363 Help Supply Services; 4111 Local &
    Suburban Transit; 7389 Business Services, Not
    Elsewhere Classified

AHL Services, Inc. provides contract staffing and management of labor-intensive operational support functions such as security, baggage handling, and transportation, on an outsourced basis throughout the United States and Europe. The company, which had global sales of $276 million in 1997, focuses on recruiting, hiring, training, motivating, and managing the large numbers of personnel required for its clients' support services. A primary focus is in services for the aviation industry, which include pre-departure screening, passenger profiling, and other passenger services. AHL's non-aviation clients include Federal Express, America On-Line, Georgia Power, BellSouth, Nike, and Motorola. Through its 83 offices in the United States, along with 28 offices in six European countries, AHL is a multinational corporation with a particularly strong presence in the United Kingdom, which alone accounted for nearly one-quarter of its revenues in 1997. In the latter year, its first as a public company, AHL had some 630 service contracts, mostly with *Fortune* 1,000 companies.

A Dozen Quiet Years in the 1980s

AHL Services, Inc. began life in 1979, when founder Frank Argenbright Jr. created it as a replacement for Argenbright

Holdings Ltd. The latter ultimately became a subsidiary of AHL. Argenbright, who would remain chairman and CEO of AHL Services in the late 1990s, was already building a successful security agency under the Argenbright name; with AHL he expanded the company's offerings. The key to expansion emerged from the company's core specialty: Argenbright provided security to airlines, and it was relatively easy to make a lateral move into cargo handling and shuttle bus services for the airlines as well.

In a 1998 listing of its top clients, AHL showed two that had been with it for 17 years, almost to the time of the company's founding: Delta Airlines and Northwest Airlines. The other companies, and the lengths of their relationships with AHL, suggested the successive layers of growth by which the company had expanded over the preceding years. Next longest was Federal Express, to whom AHL had contracted its services for 12 years, or since the late 1980s; then United Airlines (nine years); BMW and *Reader's Digest,* with eight years apiece; British Airways, Ford, and Publishers' Clearing House, all with seven years; and Mattel, with which AHL had been working for just a year.

Clearly, a large portion of the company's growth had begun in the early 1990s; during its first dozen years, AHL's expansion proceeded quietly. Initially, it offered, along with security, a polygraph service; then in the early 1980s the company began providing shuttle bus services for Delta at the latter's headquarters in Atlanta. A decade later AHL was ready for a big push: thus as Tom Walker observed in the *Atlanta Constitution,* "It took 14 years for AHL Services to reach $100 million in annual revenue, but only three more to top $200 million."

Turning Point in the Early 1990s

According to Celeste Bottorff, AHL Services' vice-president of marketing and strategic planning, the firm reached a "turning point" in 1995. It was then, wrote Evelina Shmukler in the *Atlanta Business Chronicle,* that "it decided it would move from being a small company to a large one. AHL has recruited all its top executives since 1995."

To a degree, however, the turning point may have begun earlier, in 1992. That was the year when the company, its revenues having reached $80 million, began to expand internationally by purchasing the passenger shuttle service operations of British Airways at London's Heathrow Airport. To facilitate that acquisition, in March 1992 AHL had formed ADI, which it has since used as a platform for expansion in Europe. The second move toward international growth occurred in August 1993, when ADI bought Express Baggage Reclaim Services Limited, which provided lost baggage delivery and replacement services in Great Britain.

Also in 1992, AHL began providing profiling services in Europe. According to the company's own information, "Passenger profiling seeks to identify a potential threat"—e.g., of hijacking or other airborne security dangers—"before it materializes by means of interviewing, document verification, and behavioral analysis. This procedure results in the classification of the vast majority of passengers as low risk, thereby enabling more scrutiny to be focused on higher risk passengers." With some 233 employees dedicated to profiling, this has become a specialty with AHL, which maintains that it "would be well-positioned to quickly implement profiling procedures for its U.S. clients" if the Federal Aviation Administration (FAA) mandates this security procedure for flights within the United States.

The Beginnings of Explosive Growth in the Mid-1990s

Starting in 1993, the year when receipts first topped $100 million, the company began to build its top layer of management, and this was in place, in large part, by the middle of the decade. Prominent among the key management figures AHL took on during the early- to mid-1990s was Frank Mellett, co-chief executive officer (CEO) of the company and former senior vice-president of Coca-Cola, who joined in 1994. In 1993, A. Trevor Warburton, former senior vice-president of Ground Services for Ogden Aviation Services in England, became managing director of the ADI Group Limited. Likewise Bottorff, the company's leading female executive, joined in 1996 after serving with Holiday Inn Worldwide as director of strategic planning and the *Atlanta Journal Constitution* as marketing director. Tom Marano, who like Mellett came from Coca-Cola, became president and chief operating officer (COO) of Argenbright Holdings Limited, the holding company for the company's U.S. operations, in mid-1995.

In the mid-1990s AHL began to expand through acquisitions, but before it did so, it sold off one holding: in October 1995, the company divested itself of Intergram, Inc., a wholly owned subsidiary of Argenbright that provided drug testing services, for $1.3 million. AHL in 1996 entered into a joint venture with British Airways whereby it would provide a variety of services at the latter's Nice, France operation, including passenger and baggage check-in.

July of 1996 saw the third in a series of acquisitions that had begun with the purchase of British Airways' Heathrow passenger service in 1992. The company was Intersec, Inc., which AHL acquired for $2.5 million in cash and $1.155 million in notes payable. Intersec provides access control services—i.e., personnel and equipment to protect against entry by unauthorized persons—for businesses in Washington, D.C. and surrounding areas. This third corporate purchase would be followed by a rapid-fire series of acquisitions in 1997.

A Series of Acquisitions in 1997 and 1998

AHL went public in mid-1997 and quickly established itself as a powerful market force. "AHL Services, Inc. is flying high," wrote Zach Coleman in the *Atlanta Business Chronicle* that summer. "In the two-and-a-half months since the Atlanta-based airport services and security company went public, its stock has risen more than 70 percent and it has closed on almost as many acquisitions as it did in 17 years as a private company." In May, the company commenced yet another involvement with British Airways, this time in a joint venture to purchase Executive Aircraft Services (EAS), a division of British Airways. EAS performs ground handling, passenger handling, and concierge services for large private executive aircraft. The licensing rules at Heathrow Airport prevented AHL from making an outright purchase, hence the joint venture, which was combined with an agency agreement whereby AHL kept the option to purchase the entire business if and when the licensing rules changed. AHL paid British Airways $2.8 million and agreed to pay more than $500,000 per year for three years if the new division performed to certain standards.

Also in May 1997, AHL bought the access control business of USA Security Systems, Inc., a New Jersey firm, for some $2.6 million in cash. It followed this up in September by acquiring Lloyd Creative Staffing of Chicago for $5 million in cash along with contingent consideration based on future operating results. A light industrial staffing company, Lloyd provides staff for warehouse "pick and pack," along with other light industrial functions, in the Chicago area. During the following month AHL acquired Van Nuys, California-based RightSide Up, Inc., an order fulfillment firm that serves the entertainment industry, for more than $6 million. Finally, in December, the company closed out 1997 by adding Midwest Staffing Systems to its growing list of subsidiaries. Based in Chicago like Lloyd Creative Staffing, Midwest also provides staff for warehouse "pick and pack" and light industrial functions.

The acquisitions just kept coming in 1998, and growth spread to the European continent. AHL purchased SES Staffing Solutions, a light industrial and warehouse company located in Maryland, in February, and in April bought the German firm of TUJA. July saw the conclusion of a $1.1 million purchase agreement for Gage Marketing Support Services Group, and in the following month AHL added its second German industrial staffing company, EMD. The latter purchase was its largest to that point: $42 million. Also in August, AHL announced that it intended to purchase Right Associates, a British industrial staffing company.

Four Lines of Service

By any standard, AHL in the late 1990s experienced a dizzying rate of growth, but its expansion made sense in that each new area of expertise had the common factor of service. Thus the company's statement of its Core Competency: "Professionally manage large workforces that perform non-core, repetitive, operational support tasks for clients, on a 'recurring' contractual basis." AHL now offered four lines of service, including what had once been its singular focus, Aviation Services. Under the latter heading comes pre-departure screening, passenger profiling, sky caps, wheelchair service for disabled passengers, cargo handling, and into-plane fueling: hence, as Mellett said in a 1998 interview with Jan Hopkins of Cable News Network Financial News (CNNFN), "We don't fly airplanes. But we'll do almost anything else for them."

In addition to Airline Services, AHL offers Facility Support Services (access control, shuttle buses, commercial security); Operational Support Staffing Services (assembly, warehousing, shipping, electrical, and mechanical); and Marketing Execution and Fulfillment Services (consumer/trade fulfillment, e-commerce fulfillment, trade support, and customer service support). Just as it had rapidly broadened its focus from Aviation Services, so the company's projections called for a diminished emphasis on aviation and increased attention to other lines. Whereas Aviation Services had made up 58 percent of its business in 1997, AHL projected that it would constitute 29 percent in 1998. Facility Support Services would decrease slightly, from 39 percent to 30 percent. Operational Support Services, on the other hand, would expand enormously, from three percent to 25 percent. But the greatest proportional expansion would occur in Marketing Execution and Fulfillment Services, which had not even been a part of AHL's lines of service in 1997 but which the company's leadership predicted would make up 16 percent of its business in 1998.

Describing AHL's variety of services in the *Constitution,* Walker wrote: "Commerce would come to a halt without the rank-and-file workers who handle packages, load cargo, shuttle people from place to place by bus, and do a long list of other necessary chores. Theirs is the occupational stratum AHL Services has defined as its niche in the fast-growing field of outsourcing and contract staffing. And that's just the reverse of what most competitors in the highly fragmented staffing business are doing." As Mellett told Walker, most of AHL's competitors were saying, "We are going into the information technology business."

In his interview with CNNFN, the co-CEO expanded on the distinction between his company and other players in the temporary-services industry: "We are really not in the temporary kind of business. We're in contract staffing and outsourcing. And that is really one of the points of distinction between us and other staffing companies. What we do is provide workforce management for large numbers of people, relatively low-skill jobs . . . repetitive kinds of things in the non-core elements of our clients' business. But we do that on a contractual basis, a long-term basis with the average length of our contract about three years. So I guess, really, if you were looking for some help, for a receptionist for a day or a secretary for a week, you would not call us."

The Growing Ranks of AHL

For many companies, the number of employees—with the concomitant payroll and benefits commitment—is a liability rather than an asset. Hence the urge toward downsizing that began in the 1980s. With a personnel services firm such as AHL, however, employees are indeed an asset, and the company proudly proclaims its growing numbers. Likewise it draws attention to its efforts at recruitment and retention in lines of work that are not known for long terms of service. This is certainly the case with the job of security guard, for which the median salary in the Atlanta metropolitan area in 1997 was $12,480, according to the U.S. Department of Labor. Bottorff pointed out to Gene Tharpe of the *Atlanta Constitution* that more and more women are being drawn to security guard jobs. This can be attributed to the decrease in the proportion of armed security positions, which is in turn explained by increased liability and insurance concerns that have led to such a decrease.

With the need to retain more competent and reliable people in such positions, AHL has had to maintain a competitive position in the labor market, a fact of which its leadership is keenly aware. According to the company's annual report, "Historically, non-core support services workers have a high turnover rate. We work hard—and invest substantially—to recruit and keep people, and our efforts are rewarded. The Company has a relatively low turnover rate—approximately one-half that usually reported among large-volume, non-core work forces."

As it continued to grow its ranks, AHL likewise expanded its holdings. Thus in October 1998 it entered into a definitive purchase agreement to acquire Unicco Security Services, an access control and security services company based in Chicago. The latter counts among its clients BASF Corporation, Bell Atlantic, and Yale University. Meanwhile, overseas expansion continued. AHL, which provides security for Federal Express at Subic Bay in the Philippines, clearly had its eye on Asian expansion. "We like the Pacific Basin," Mellett told Walker. "If you look at the 21st century, that's where the growth in aviation is going to be." Argenbright told Walker, "I believe that in five years, 50 percent of AHL's business will come from outside the United States." He reinforced the Pacific Basin theme, saying, "We continue to explore for a partner in that area. The third priority would be Latin America."

Principal Subsidiaries

Argenbright Holdings Limited; Argenbright, Inc.; RightSide Up; Lloyd Creative Staffing; Midwest Staffing; Argenbright Security, Inc.; Intersec USA Security; The ADI Group Limited (United Kingdom); ADI U.K. Limited (United Kingdom); Aviation Defence International (United Kingdom); Argenbright Motor Coach, Inc.; Argenbright Substance Testing, Inc.; IPS Training Institute, Inc.

Further Reading

Coleman, Zach, "AHL Is Landing in More International Airports," *Atlanta Business Chronicle,* July 18, 1997, p. 10A.

Hopkins, Jan, interview with AHL Services Co-CEO Edwin Mellett, CNNFN (Cable News Network Financial News), March 31, 1998.

Luke, Robert, "AHL Services Hurt by Market Weakness," *Atlanta Journal and Constitution,* August 25, 1998, p. 4D.

Shmukler, Evelina, "Atlanta Staffing Company Extends Its Reach Overseas," *Atlanta Business Chronicle,* August 28, 1998, p. A20.

Tharpe, Gene, "Booming Market for Security Guards, But Fewer Carry Firearms, Because of Liability Issues and Insurance Restrictions," *Atlanta Constitution,* November 16, 1998, p. 6E.

Walker, Tom, "Handling Chores Works for AHL: Company Has Carved Its Niche Providing Contract Staffing in Labor-Intensive, High-Turnover Jobs," *Atlanta Constitution,* May 17, 1998, p. 8P.

—Judson Knight

Air-India Limited

Air-India Building
Nariman Point
Mumbai 400 021
India
(91) 22 202 3732
Fax: (91) 22 204 8521

State-Owned Company
Incorporated: 1946
Employees: 18,700
Sales: Rs 3.81 billion (US $1.01 billion) (1997)
SICs: 4516 Air Transportation, Scheduled

Air-India Limited operates passenger and cargo flights from Bombay to destinations in the United States, Europe, the Middle East, Africa, the United Kingdom, Russia, China, Japan, and other countries. It holds the distinction of being the world's first all-jet airline. Founded as a small, private, domestic carrier in 1932, Air-India is now government owned. Once regarded as a "little jewel" of an airline, its reputation became somewhat tarnished as service and profits slipped. Significant changes, however, have rejuvenated the airline, put it back in the black, and restored its ranking among the better airlines of the world. Three million passengers a year fly Air-India.

Origins

Air-India began operating in 1932 as Tata Airlines, named after J. R. D. Tata, its founder. The line carried mail and passengers between the Indian cities of Ahmadabad, Bombay, Bellary, and Madras, and Karachi, Pakistan. Within a few years Tata Airlines' routes included the Indian cities of Trivandrum, Delhi, Colombo (in Sri Lanka), Lahore, and other locations in between.

In 1946, at the conclusion of World War II, the airline became a public company and was renamed Air-India Limited. In just two years, with the government having a 49 percent share in the company, the airline was flying further outside of India, with regular flights to Cairo, Geneva, and London. The line's name changed again to reflect its new scope of operations, becoming Air-India International Limited.

India enjoyed more success in the airline industry than most other developing countries for a number of reasons. Whereas others had to rely on foreign pilots to fly their planes, Air-India used mostly native-born pilots. Similarly, skilled Indians were plentiful enough to maintain India's fleet as well as to train and supervise its personnel; many other countries had to go outside for this kind of expertise. Air-India benefited from these advantages along with its sister carriers.

Air-India first encountered competition for its routes in the early 1950s. Many new airlines were forming, propelled into business by the availability of inexpensive, war-surplus DC-3s. No fewer than 21 airlines had been established, with 11 of them licensed to fly the skies of India. A 1985 article in the *Economist* cited Tata's foresight of what this plethora of airlines could lead to: "The scene was well and truly set for the ultimate debacle."

To prevent that debacle from occurring, the Indian government in 1953 took control of all of the airlines within its borders. Along with the nationalization the government created two corporations. Indian Airlines Corporation, which merged Air-India Limited with six smaller lines, served the country's domestic travel needs. Air-India International Corporation flew routes overseas. By 1960 the international airline had routes to Singapore, Sydney, Moscow, and New York. By 1962, when the name was shortened to Air-India, it had become the world's first all-jet airline.

The Jet Age

Beginning in the 1970s, however, Air-India saw difficult times. It suffered a net loss in three of the years between 1976 and 1985. The downturn in the world economy had a significant effect on air travel throughout the world, and India was no exception. In addition, the government kept a number of unprofitable routes open simply for prestige purposes—a strictly commercial airline may have closed those routes. Its flights to New York, for example, resulted in losses for a number of years, even though many of those flights were full. At one point an airline official estimated that only about ten percent of Air-India's passengers to New York were business travelers who would buy the more expensive seats. Flights to Canada were even less profitable, flying at around 55 percent of capacity. Another factor in the airline's financial problems was that, to compete for American and European travelers with American and European airlines, Air-India had to discount many of its fares. In addition, the airline depended heavily on local citizens—"ethnic traffic"—which generally meant lower fares.

The routes that had proven to be most profitable for Air-India had been those to the oil-producing nations. Flights to the Persian Gulf accounted for 35 to 40 percent of Air-India's traffic in the mid-1980s. Working with Gulf Air, Air-India operated 60 flights each week between the Gulf and India. But even these routes saw profits fall, as revenue in the gulf states declined. Another problem was the shortage of tourists traveling to India. Communal violence and the assassination of Indian Prime Minister Indira Gandhi in 1984 kept tourism down. In addition, to combat the terrorism that was becoming a major problem at many of the world's airports, the government imposed heavy restrictions at airports, giving tourists another reason to stay away.

The darkest note in Air-India's history was the tragedy that took place in June 1985 when one of its 747s, on a flight from Toronto to Bombay, crashed to the sea with 329 passengers aboard. A Canadian Safety Board Report, addressing an inquiry by Indian High Court Judge Bhupinder Nath Kirpal, concluded that an explosive device was the probable cause of the crash. The board reported that an X-ray machine at Pearson International Airport in Toronto broke down before all the luggage had been checked. Nonetheless, the effect on the reputation of Air-India was severe.

Despite these problems, Air-India's productivity was high. By acquiring large-body airliners, its productivity almost doubled from the year 1974–75 to the year 1983–84. In terms of rupees, this productivity figure translated to a per-employee production of Rs 125,000 (US $16,000) in operating revenue in the 1974–75 year and Rs 439,000 in the 1983–84 year. In 1985 Air-India flew 8.1 billion passenger-kilometers (number of passengers times distance), a figure that prompted the International Air Transport Association to rank Air-India 15th out of 136 member airlines in passenger-kilometers on scheduled services.

Nevertheless, Air-India lost US $23 million in the 1987–88 fiscal year. To stem such losses, Prime Minister Rajiv Gandhi named Rajan Jetley chairman of Air-India. Jetley took command of an airline that was overstaffed, mired in sticky negotia-

tions with unions, and struggling under difficult working conditions. In addition, some bureaucratic meddling and high gasoline taxes interfered with procedures and made operating the airline expensive.

A number of these factors came together to have a significantly negative impact on the airline. Specifically, Air-India was flying many flights with intermediate stops, while competing airlines were flying the more attractive nonstop flights. One reason for these intermediate stops was the pilots' refusal to fly more than nine hours. A second reason was that, to minimize the effect of the high cost of fuel, Air-India did much of its refueling outside of India's borders. Jetley dealt with these problems by convincing the government to reduce its gasoline tax and by convincing the pilots to fly longer flights.

According to Jetley, as quoted in a 1990 *New York Times* article, the carrier was "packing the back of the bus" on many of its routes. In addition to selling coach fares, Jetley hoped to entice affluent fliers to purchase the more profitable business-class seats. Toward that end he bought new planes and changed the look of the airline, ordering a new logo and a redesign of the planes' decor and employees' uniforms and improving in-flight service and meals. He increased the number of flights to Europe, making Frankfurt, Germany, a hub and enabling passengers to connect to other European cities. In addition, he adjusted the timing of flights, making it more convenient for passengers to connect with other flights. Under Jetley's direction, Air-India turned the loss of the previous year into a profit of US $23 million. The airline rose to number 22 on the International Air Transport Association's list of the world's most profitable airlines. The revitalized Air-India saw record profits of US $41 million in the year 1989–90, then topped that the following year with profits of US $42.7 million. These accomplishments were all the more startling because they came at a time when many of Air-India's flights to the Persian Gulf had to be suspended because of the conflict between Iraq and Kuwait and the ensuing Persian Gulf War. The airline, though, did experience activity during the conflict, launching a massive airlift to help 110,000 Indians flee war-torn areas. Ravi Mani, deputy general director of cargo for Air-India, was quoted by the *Journal of Commerce* as saying that compared with this airlift, "the Berlin airlift was chicken feed."

Air-India was intent on continuing its success of the early 1990s. Although it controlled 28 percent of air passenger traffic out of India, that was a drop from 32 percent just a few years before. Subbash Gupte, acting chairman after Jetley left his post, explained, as quoted by the *New York Times:* "The reason for the drop is simple. Other airlines have expanded, bought new aircraft; we haven't." Between 1982 and 1986 the airline had kept its capacity at a standstill. While Jetley was still in command, however, plans were implemented to increase capacity by six to eight percent each year from 1990 to 1995, reducing the average age of its fleet—13 and one half years in 1990—to about four and one half years by the turn of the century.

Succeeding Jetley was Chairman and Managing Director Yogesh Deveshwar, who outlined the airline's direction for the 1990s. As reported in *Travel Weekly* in 1992, Deveshwar said: "We want to make Air-India a boutique carrier, as opposed to a department store.'' Parts of those plans called for expanding the carrier's United States routes to include Chicago, Los Angeles, and Newark. Flights to Los Angeles, it was hoped, would attract many ethnic Indians, who were using other carriers to other points in the Far East and then transferring to Air-India. New aircraft, including long-haul 747-400s, would help to bring those plans to fruition.

In addition to passengers, cargo has always been a large portion of Air-India's business. Its major cargo markets are the Persian Gulf countries, Europe, the United States, the United Kingdom, and Japan. In 1989 (the last year for which figures were available) Air-India ranked 19th among all International Air Transport Association carriers in scheduled international freight tons. The carrier handled 66,000 metric tons of cargo that year.

One of the major goals of Air-India for the 1990s was to increase its cargo operations still further. At the beginning of the decade Air-India had about 30 percent of the country's air cargo market, while more than three dozen airlines from other countries carried the balance of the country's cargo. The airline planned to lease additional jet freighters to increase its capacity to carry exports. The International Airports Authority of India improved the infrastructure and ground handling at the gateways it operates, making them more attractive to carriers and freight forwarders. With these changes under way, cargo revenue for fiscal 1990 amounted to US $195 million, 21 percent of Air-India's revenue.

The Challenging 1990s

Air-India lost $171 million in the three years beginning with 1994–95. The airline gained a reputation for poor service and poor on-time performance. The company initiated a generous incentive program to motivate employees, which proved successful. In addition, a computerized flight system and updated lounges and cabin interiors were added to update the company's image among customers. Management cut fares drastically and provided two-for-one discounts.

In the summer of 1997 the carrier negotiated code-sharing deals with Air France and Singapore Airlines. Streamlining the carrier's route network became an ongoing process. In fact, Air-India was notorious for constantly adding and dropping routes. Its network dropped Canada, Australia, and South Africa in an attempt to cut losses.

Air-India sought to offer its $150 million annual North American income streams as debt securities, pending the approval of a hesitant Indian government. The company also planned to raise cash (it already had reserves of more than $110 million) by selling its Hotel Corporation of India subsidiary, worth at least $220 million, as well as some older Boeing 747-200s, valued at $60 million.

Still, the company owed $900 million on new aircraft purchases. In spite of this impressive sum, Air-India found itself chronically short of medium-sized long haul aircraft, reported *Air Transport World*. Most of its planes were too large to be profitable on their particular routes, a liability previously covered by an especially profitable Persian Gulf market.

A recovery seemed to be in place upon the announcement of a quarterly profit of $10 million in the fall of 1997. More positive results were projected. Operating revenue was expected to reach Rs 4,189 million in 1997–98.

It was later announced that these results had been overly optimistic; the $10 million profit was in fact a $10 million loss. Managing Director Michael Mascrenhas announced the news after taking over from Brijesh Kumar, whose two-year term had just expired. Mascrenhas colored the news in the best possible light, noting in *Air Transport World* that Air-India had lost money only "six times in the last 43 years."

A planned merger between Air-India and Indian Airlines was canceled in spring 1998. Nevertheless, closer ties between the two carriers remained after the aborted deal. As Air-India cut routes, it maintained code-sharing deals with Air France, SAS, Singapore Airlines, and Austrian Airlines. Still, market share fell from 35 percent to 20 percent in 1997–98.

Reducing its annual payroll costs of $40 million was a top priority for Air-India, which had not found sufficient productivity increases to match its generous incentive programs. *Air Transport World* reported that Mascrenhas trimmed $23 million in other areas.

In spite of these savings, Mascrenhas predicted Air-India would not pull out of the red for another two years after projecting a 1997–98 loss of $44 million. To raise desperately needed cash, the airline offered its hotels and two 747 airliners for sale. As the carrier planned for its $150 US/Canada security issue, the Indian government also was considering a rescue plan.

Principal Divisions

Ground Services; Engineering and Maintenance; Engine Overhaul.

Further Reading

"Air-India's Chief Eyes Chicago, Los Angeles Routes," *Travel Weekly,* February 6, 1992.
Hazarika, Sanjoy, "Air-India's Head Quits to Join Private Sector," *New York Times,* July 18, 1990.
"India's Airlines: Keeping Aloft," *Economist,* July 27, 1985.
Janigan, Mary, "A Tragedy's Haunting Legacy," *Maclean's,* June 23, 1986.
Kaufman, Lawrence H., "Air India Turns to Jet Leasing to Ease Cargo Capacity Crunch," *Journal of Commerce,* October 15, 1990.
Lefer, Henry, "A One-Way Freight Operation," *Air Transport World,* May 1991.
Mamu, H.P., "Air-India on the Rebound," *Interavia Aerospace Review,* October 1989.
Mhatre, Kamlakar, "Air-India Battles Back," *Air Transport World,* September 1997.
——, "Mumbai Mirage," *Air Transport World,* March 1998, pp. 107–08.
"Record Profit for Air-India," *New York Times,* August 6, 1991.

—Cosmo Ferrara
—updated by Frederick C. Ingram

Airtours Plc

Wavell House
Holcombe Road
Helmshore Rossendale
Lancashire
BB4 4NB
England
(44) 1 706 240 033
Fax: (44) 1 706 232 089

Public Company
Incorporated: 1972 as Pendle Travel Services Ltd.
Employees: 14,000
Sales: £3.05 billion (US $)(1997)
Stock Exchanges: London
Ticker Symbol: Airtours
SICs: 4724 Travel Agencies; 4725 Tour Operators

Airtours Plc is one of the largest integrated tour operators and travel agents in the European and North American markets. Based in England, where the group is the second largest holiday package vendor after Thomson Travel Group, Airtours has been expanding rapidly in the late 1990s, achieving leading tour and travel positions in the Scandinavian, German, Dutch, French, and Belgian markets, while also building a strong position in the United States and Canada.

Airtours' operations are divided into three areas. The first is the company's holiday tour package sales, represented by the Airtours and other brand names, including Spies in Scandinavia; Sunquest Vacations in Canada; Suntrips in California; Sun International SA in Belgium; Direct Holidays, a direct sales package seller in the United Kingdom; and others, such as the company's 1998 additions of Frosch Touristik in Germany, Panorama Holidays in Ireland, and Vacation Express, based in Atlanta, Georgia. Added to the company's tour operations is Airtours' own network of nearly 800 travel agencies under the Going Places brand name in the United Kingdom. Since the mid-1990s Airtours has been building operations in a new area:

cruise lines. In 1998 the company counted three cruise ships in its possession, carrying more than 90,000 vacationers to more than 40 ports. A fourth cruise ship was expected to be added in 1999. Supporting Airtours' activities is a solid infrastructure that includes not only company-owned resort and other hotels, but also the company's own charter airline. The company operates a fleet of some 20 airplanes, ranging from Airbus A320s to Boeing 767s.

Airtours continues to be led by founder David Crossland. A public company listed on the London stock exchange, Airtours is partly owned by the United States' Carnival Cruise Lines, the world's leading cruise line operator, which bought up nearly 30 percent of Airtours in 1996. After rising to the top of the British tour market in the 1990s, Airtours has been actively participating in the ongoing consolidation of the international tour and travel industry, as well as expanding into new markets. Already boasting a string of acquisitions, in December 1998 the company floated a convertible bonds issue, boosting its war chest by more than £250 million.

From Travel to Tours in the 1970s

David Crossland entered the travel business by a side road in the early 1960s. After leaving a self-described ''mediocre'' school career at the age of 16, Crossland sought work in hospital management. Crossland's lack of qualifications, however, prevented him from finding work in this field. Instead, Crossland found a job stamping brochures for a local travel agent. That job turned out to be an eye-opener for Crossland. As he told the *Financial Times:* ''It was super leaving school and this was a marvelous opportunity, lots of colorful brochures and different places. It was like someone had opened the door and there was this big, shining light.''

The shining light proved to be Crossland himself. After only three months, he added salesman's duties, selling holidays for the agent. Crossland turned out to be a natural salesman, with a knack for recognizing his customers' needs—a quality that would come into play strongly in his later career. Crossland's career received its next boost in 1971, when he met a couple preparing their retirement who were looking to sell their two

Lancashire travel agencies. The couple offered to sell to Crossland, who jumped at the opportunity. "To this day, I don't know why I didn't say I had no money," Crossland told the *Financial Times*.

Buying the travel business would cost Crossland some £11,000. The agencies' owners themselves loaned Crossland £4,000, and Crossland sold a one-third share to his sister for £3,000. The remaining £4,000 came from Barclays Bank. Crossland quickly began earning back that loan—by the time he had signed the papers, he had sold a holiday package to the bank's manager. In 1972 Crossland took over Pendle Travel Services Ltd. It would take Crossland only nine months to pay off his company's debts.

Crossland proved to be not merely a good salesman, but a good manager as well. Over the next decade, Crossland sought out more travel agents who were looking to sell their agencies to retire. By the end of the 1970s he had built a chain of 12 travel agencies. Yet Crossland's ambitions would lead him into a vast expansion over the decade to come.

"Serious Business" in the 1980s

Despite Crossland's success, Pendle remained a relatively small company. A new inspiration in 1980, however, would lead the company into a new era. In that year Crossland recognized an opening in the tour packages industry. "I could see that passengers were coming in and asking for products that the tour operators weren't manufacturing," Crossland told the *Daily Telegraph*. "They weren't listening to the customers so in the 1980s we started a tour operation."

The opening Crossland spotted was in holiday packages for his working class customers. Whereas most tour packages at the time were being offered on a Wednesday-to-Wednesday basis and, therefore, were not easily adapted to customers' vacation schedules, Crossland began designing Saturday-to-Saturday tours. The shift to the weekend made all the difference. In 1980 Pendle would take some 900 customers on holidays to Malta. By the following year, that number would grow to more than 23,000, and the company began offering a choice of destinations. By 1983 Crossland's tour operation—created as a separate division dubbed Pendle Air Tours—had expanded the company to 23 agencies and more than 200,000 tour customers per year.

Until then, Crossland had led Pendle Travel Services as an entrepreneurial concern. But in the mid-1980s Crossland recognized his own limits and the limits of entrepreneurship. As he told the *Financial Times:* "I can remember thinking, 'I haven't got the capability to work any more hours, so if I want to expand the company, I'll have to find people with business disciplines I don't have.' In my own mind that was one of the turning points for the group, changing from a one-man entrepreneur into a serious business."

Crossland began recruiting a management staff, bringing in former executives from such firms as Marks & Spencers, Kellogg's, and Granada. The new team began reshaping Pendle from its former travel agent business to a full-fledged tour operator. By 1986 the company's tour business had become the primary source of revenues and growth. In that year Pendle sold off its 25 Pendle travel agency chain stores, and renamed itself Airtours, concentrating solely on its booming tour package operations.

Airtours continued to expand rapidly in the late 1980s. Fueling this expansion was the company's listing on the London stock exchange in 1987. The public company, and Crossland in particular, would be credited with bringing a new level of professionalism to the traditionally volatile travel business. Airtours also would prove adept at discovering new travel niches. In 1990, for example, Airtours launched its EuroSites brand of self-drive camping holidays. In keeping with the popular European-style camping holiday—where a "camping" often resembles a small resort more than a simple campground, complete with restaurants and recreational facilities—a EuroSites holiday offered a tent or mobile home rentals, as well as a choice of location in England, Holland, Germany, Denmark, and other European continent countries. The EuroSites concept proved to be a hit, bringing Airtours to one of the leading positions in that segment.

Vertically Integrated Travel Giant in the 1990s

The 1990s would see Airtours transform itself from tour package operator to a vertically integrated holiday provider. The company took an important step toward this transition in March 1991, when the company launched a new division, Airtours International, offering charter flights on the first of a soon-to-expand company-owned fleet of airplanes. The addition of Airtours International would help propel Airtours to the U.K. lead in the air-inclusive tour operators segment.

The following year Airtours reentered the travel agency business with the acquisition of Pickford Travel Agencies and that company's 330 travel agencies in the United Kingdom. The return to retail travel sales enabled the company to move closer toward vertical integration—a move that would be completed as the company began to acquire its own resort and hotel locations.

The troubled travel industry of the early 1990s—hit by the triple blow of overcapacity, traveler fears arising from the Persian Gulf War, and the recessionary economic climate—provided fresh opportunities for growth for Airtours, as the company began seeking out more acquisitions. In 1993 Airtours bought Aspro, Ireland's largest tour operator and the number seven ranking tour operator in the United Kingdom as a whole. The Aspro acquisition also extended Airtours' airline activities, as it included Aspro's Inter European Airways subsidiary.

At the time that the Aspro acquisition was made, Airtours also purchased the Hogg Robinson Travel Agency and its chain of 214 retail stores. At the end of 1993 Airtours combined the Hogg Robinson and Pickford travel agent chains into a single operation, renamed Going Places. Further acquisitions would build the Going Places chain to more than 700 stores before the end of the decade.

These acquisitions would prove to be only the first of many more to come, as Airtours began seeking expansion beyond its U.K. base, as well as a diversification of its product offerings. After buying up Tradewinds, the leading long-haul tour operator in the United Kingdom, in December 1993, Airtours turned to a new market opportunity. With the purchase of the *MS Seawing,* Airtours entered the growing cruise ship market. By 1995 the company had added a second liner, the *MS Carousel,* and had launched its fly-cruise holiday packages.

The company's international expansion began in earnest in 1994 with the acquisition of Sweden's Scandinavian Leisure Group AB (SLG), which included not only that company's Ving, Saga, and Always tour brands, but also SLG's 50 percent ownership of Premier airlines, the largest charter airline operator in the Scandinavian countries. In addition to giving Airtours SLG's tour and airline operations, the acquisition placed SLG's Sunwing Hotel Group under Airtours' wing, giving the company a number of resort hotels in popular holiday destinations such as Majorca, Spain. Capping 1994, Airtours acquired a new retail operation in the form of Late Escapes, a teletext-based direct sales holiday provider.

After launching its cruise line operations in 1995, Airtours turned its attention to North America, purchasing Sunquest Vacations and Silverwing Holidays, two prominent Canadian-based holiday providers. These would be followed in 1996 with a move to consolidate Airtours' position as the leading tour operator in Scandinavia with the acquisition of the tour operators Spies and Tjaereborg, the hotel group Stella Polaris, and the acquisition of full control of Premier airlines.

Airtours' strong growth and its rapidly expanding cruise ship division, which was reaching more than 75,000 passengers per year, caught the eye of others in the travel industry, in particular the United States' Royal Caribbean Cruises, the largest cruise line operator in the world. In April 1996 Royal Caribbean became Airtours' leading shareholder with the purchase of 29.54 percent of the company's stock. The purchase sparked rumors of a possible takeover bid by Royal Caribbean; a possibility that neither side could discount completely for the future. Meanwhile, the shareholding position provided the basis for a partnership between the two companies, including the sale of one of Royal Caribbean's cruise ships to Airtours, which renamed the ship *MS Sundream.*

If the mid-1990s presented a difficult market, with increasingly consolidated, global competition sparking a price war that cut deeply into the company's profits, the second half of the decade would show impressive growth in Airtours. From revenues of £1.7 billion in 1995, the company would reach more than £3 billion by 1997.

Among the company's acquisitions during the period were the joint venture purchase with Royal Caribbean of Italy's Costa Cruises, which held the lead in the Mediterranean market and the number five spot worldwide; the acquisition of Northern California's Suntrips tour operator; and the 1998 acquisition of Sun International SA, bringing the company into the Benelux and French markets, as well as strengthening Airtours' short-break holiday business in the United Kingdom.

Airtours would show no sign of slowing down its expansion through 1998. After the Sun International purchase in February of 1998, the company would add a new cruise ship to support its booming cruise division, before moving into the German market with the purchase of a 30 percent stake in Frosch Touristik. By the end of September, Airtours had further strengthened both its U.K. and U.S. presence, with the acquisitions of Panorama Holidays in Ireland and Vacation Express in Atlanta, Georgia.

Under Crossland, Airtours promised continued growth for the future. After moves in December 1998 to move into the Polish market, under the Ving brand name, and the extension of the company's U.K. travel agency division with the purchase of the 116-outlet Travelworld, Airtours showed its hand with the launch of a £250 million bond issue. As the worldwide travel market entered a new phase of consolidation, Airtours appeared likely to take its place among the upper ranks of travel's global leaders.

Further Reading

Daneshhu, Scheherazade, "David Crossland Takes an Occasional Break," *Financial Times,* October 10, 1998.

Pratley, Neil, "Airtours Man Still Has Far to Go," *Daily Telegraph,* December 13, 1997.

Yates, Andrew, "Record Season for Airtours as Bookings Take Off," *Independent,* November 12, 1997.

—M.L. Cohen

Allstate®

The Allstate Corporation

Allstate Plaza
2775 Sanders Road
Northbrook, Illinois 60062
U.S.A.
(847) 402-5000
(800) 416-8803
Fax: (847) 836-3998
Web site: http://www.allstate.com

Public Company
Incorporated: 1931 as Allstate Insurance Company
Employees: 51,400
Total Assets: $80.91 billion (1997)
Stock Exchanges: New York Chicago
Ticker Symbol: ALL
SICs: 6311 Life Insurance; 6331 Fire, Marine & Casualty
Insurance; 6351 Surety Insurance; 6371 Pension,
Health & Welfare Funds; 6719 Holding Companies,
Not Elsewhere Classified

The Allstate Corporation is the holding company for Allstate Insurance Company, the second largest property and casualty insurance company by premiums in the United States. Allstate controls about 12 percent of the U.S. home and auto insurance market, second only to State Farm Insurance Companies. In addition, Allstate Life Insurance Company offers life, annuity, and pension products, and its Business Insurance offers select coverages for small and medium-sized businesses. Allstate's 20 million customers are served by 15,200 full-time ''captive'' agents, and thousands of independent agents, in the United States and Canada. Personal property and casualty policies account for over three-fourths of Allstate's revenue, while Life Operations account for 15 percent. In June 1993, Sears, Roebuck and Co. offered nearly 20 percent of Allstate's stock to the public in the largest initial public stock offering in U.S. history, making Allstate the nation's largest publicly held personal property and casualty insurance company. The remaining 80 percent of Allstate became publicly owned in 1995, when Sears spun the rest of the company off to its shareholders.

Formed in 1931

The idea for Allstate came during a bridge game on a commuter train in 1930, when insurance broker Carl L. Odell proposed to his neighbor, Sears, Roebuck and Co. president and CEO Robert E. Wood, the idea of selling auto insurance by direct mail. Odell suggested that selling insurance by mail could sharply reduce costs by eliminating commissions paid to salesmen. The idea appealed to Wood, and he passed the proposal on to the Sears board of directors, whose members were also intrigued by the concept. Allstate Insurance Company, named after an automobile tire marketed by Sears, went into business in April 1931, offering auto insurance by direct mail and through the Sears catalog. Lessing J. Rosenwald was Allstate's first chairman of the board, and Odell was named vice-president and secretary.

The company's early success proved Odell and Wood correct with regard to cost-cutting. Selling primarily through the regular Sears catalog, Allstate took in $118,323 in premiums on 4,217 policies in 1931, with a staff of 20 employees based at Sears headquarters in Chicago. Although the company showed underwriting losses in its first two years of operation, by 1933 it earned a profit of $93,000 from 22,000 active policies. That year, the first sale made by an Allstate agent was completed from a Sears booth at the Chicago World's Fair.

In 1934, Allstate opened its first permanent sales office in a Chicago Sears store, marking the beginning of a transition from direct mail to agents as its principal avenue of sales. The use of Sears stores enabled the company to keep a lid on costs even with the added expense of agents' commissions. Allstate's growth through the remainder of the Depression was slow but steady. By 1936, the company's premium volume had reached $1.8 million. Revenue from premiums more than tripled by 1941, reaching $6.8 million from over 189,000 policies in force. In 1943, James Barker was named chairman of Allstate's board.

The United States' participation in World War II slowed Allstate's growth somewhat, since automobile production and

Company Perspectives:

Consumer surveys indicate the insurance industry has a long way to go to satisfy customers completely. Customers want insurance to be friendlier and easier; they want the claims process to be fairer and more efficient; and they want their agents to be loyal and highly familiar with their needs.

Thus we've undertaken one of the most important initiatives in Allstate's history—to generate faster, more profitable premium growth by aligning the entire company to deliver more of what customers say they want and need. We know the outcome will mean significant changes, over time, in the way we do business. But with our financial and organizational strength, we see these changes as tremendous opportunities for growth.

usage were curtailed. New legislation, however, helped pave the way for a period of explosive growth that the company would experience after the war's end. In 1941, when only about a quarter of U.S. drivers had auto liability insurance, a law was passed in New York firmly establishing the financial responsibility of drivers for damage or injuries resulting from auto mishaps. New York's law inspired a flurry of legislation in other states, and by the mid-1950s nearly every state had some sort of financial responsibility law on its books.

Postwar Boom Years

During the ten-year period after World War II, Allstate grew at a phenomenal pace, nearly doubling its size every two years. There were 327,000 Allstate policyholders paying premiums totaling over $12 million in 1945, and by 1955 Allstate's sales had risen to $252 million, with more than 3.6 million policies in force.

Growth was facilitated by a change in the company's structure that was implemented in 1947. That year, Allstate decentralized its operations, adopting a three-tiered structure. Research and policy development were conducted at Allstate's home office. Zone offices were created to interpret company directives, and in turn oversee the regional offices, where the programs were put into effect. Some regions were further organized into district service offices and local sales/service centers. The restructuring extended to the first foreign offices as well. Allstate became an international company in 1953 when its first Canadian office opened. Along with the restructuring, the 1947 introduction of the Illustrator Policy, which simplified the language of policies and added pictures to enhance customers' understanding of their coverage, facilitated growth.

During the 1950s, Allstate became more than an auto insurer. Throughout the decade, Allstate expanded its services to include the entire spectrum of insurance. Personal liability insurance was introduced in 1952. In 1954, Allstate began offering residential fire insurance. Commercial fire, personal theft, and homeowners insurance were all added in 1957. Through a subsidiary, Allstate Life Insurance Company, life insurance became part of the company's package in 1957 as well. In 1958,

personal health and commercial liability insurance were added to the Allstate line. By the end of the decade, boat owners, group life, and group health insurance were all being offered. A new entity, Allstate Enterprises, Inc., was created in 1960 as an umbrella for a whole batch of non-insurance businesses to come. Among the activities eventually conducted under the Allstate Enterprises banner were a motor club and a number of finance operations, including vehicle financing, mortgage banking, and mutual fund management.

Allstate's now well-known slogan, "You're in Good Hands With Allstate," first appeared in 1950 after its creation by the company's general sales manager, Davis W. Ellis. By the end of the decade it was used in the company's first network television advertising campaign, which featured actor Ed Reimers.

Allstate's growth throughout the 1950s paved the way for continued growth over the next few decades. Not only did the company increase its sales volume but it increased its offerings and its operating space. In 1963, the Allstate Life Insurance subsidiary passed the $1 billion mark in insurance in force, after only six years of operation. By that time, over 5,000 agents were selling Allstate life, automobile, home, and business insurance. Two new subsidiaries, Allstate Insurance Company of Canada and Allstate Life Insurance Company of Canada, were formed the following year. In 1966, the Judson B. Branch Research Center (later renamed the Allstate Research and Planning Center) was opened in Menlo Park, California. The company's home office was moved to a new 723,000-square-foot complex in the Chicago suburb of Northbrook, Illinois, a year later. Meanwhile, Allstate continued to make additional types of insurance available to its customers throughout the decade, including worker's compensation insurance in 1964, surety bonds in 1966, ocean marine coverage in 1967, and a business package policy in 1969.

The 1970s: Diversification and International Expansion

By 1970, there were 6,500 Allstate Insurance agents. That year, Allstate unveiled a mutual fund. In 1972 Allstate entered the mortgage banking business by acquiring National First Corporation. The following year, the company purchased PMI Mortgage Insurance Company, marking its initial entry into that field. Around the same time, Allstate insurance became available through independent agents in rural areas not covered by agents working directly for the company. For 1973, Allstate generated earnings of $203 million, nearly 30 percent of parent company Sears's total.

The 1970s also saw Allstate increase its presence abroad dramatically. In 1975, the company entered the Japanese market through a joint venture (Seibu Allstate Life Insurance Company, Ltd.) and purchased Lippmann & Moens, a group of Dutch insurance operations. The remainder of the decade also included the formation of Tech-Cor, Inc., an auto-body research and reclamation firm, in 1976; the establishment of a Commercial Insurance Division (later called Allstate Business Insurance) to oversee the company's commercial operations in 1978; and the formation of a new wholly owned subsidiary, Northbrook Property and Casualty Insurance Company, in 1978. Allstate Reinsurance Co. Limited, a London Subsidiary of Allstate

International, was incorporated in 1978. Two new policies, the Basic Homeowners Policy and the Healthy American Plan (life insurance), were introduced in 1978 and 1979, respectively.

Allstate was the sixth largest insurance group in the United States by 1980. At that time, the company was operating four zone offices, 31 regional offices, 219 claim-service offices, 687 automobile damage inspection stations, and 2,720 sales/service centers. For 1980, the company reported $450 million in net income on revenue of $6.2 billion, as well as assets of $10.5 billion and 40,000 employees. In 1981, two Dean Witter Reynolds insurance companies, Surety Life Insurance Company and Lincoln Benefit Life Company, became part of the Allstate Life Insurance group. Allstate, Dean Witter, and Coldwell Banker joined forces the following year to form the Sears Financial Network, first appearing in eight Sears stores and later expanding to many other locations.

Donald F. Craib, Jr., was named chairman of the board at Allstate in 1982. Under Craib, a major reorganization of Allstate's corporate structure was initiated. The "New Perspective," as it was called, entailed the elimination of zone offices, as well as other streamlining and decentralizing moves. A new, more flexible life insurance plan, the Universal Life policy, was also unveiled that year. By the end of 1983, Allstate's claim staff consisted of 12,500 employees, the largest force in the industry.

In 1985, Allstate rolled out its Neighborhood Office Agent (NOA) program. In its first year, the NOA program placed 1,582 agents in 944 locations. The following year, the company launched an extensive $30 million advertising campaign that included nine new television commercials and the creation of a new tag line: "Leave It to the Good Hands People." The campaign, which extended to print and radio as well, emphasized family protection. For 1986, the company reported income of over $750 million on revenue of $12.64 billion.

A number of business insurance developments took place at Allstate in 1987. First, the company's Commercial Insurance Division and Reinsurance operation were combined under the Business Insurance umbrella. In addition, two new programs were launched in that area. The "Topflight" program created special ties between the company's Northbrook subsidiary and certain independent agents. The STAR-PAK program offered a new business package policy that provided special services such as the delivery of price quotes within five hours. Allstate also launched the Allstate Advantage Program, a three-tiered rating system for auto insurance, in 1987. A new board chairman and chief executive officer, Wayne E. Hedien, was named in 1989.

Throughout the 1980s, the company had grown at a rate that could not be supported by its profits. It had roughly doubled its premiums during the decade, but in doing so it had burdened itself with a large number of high-risk policyholders. This growth had increased the company's costs both in terms of claims payouts and regular operating expenses. Meanwhile, the company also had to contend with customer backlash against insurance rates, including an ongoing court battle in California involving the 1988 passage of Proposition 103, which called for a rollback on premium rates. Allstate's income shrank from $946 million in 1987 to $701 million in 1990. Resolving Proposition 103 issues put some major concerns behind the company.

The 1990s: Natural Disasters and Spinoff from Sears

After a solid year in 1991, Allstate suffered losses from Hurricane Andrew in 1992 that obscured an otherwise outstanding year for the company. This natural disaster led to a net loss of $825 million for the year. Subsequently, an insurance crisis developed in Florida. The legislature was unable to enact a solution the following spring, and Allstate announced a plan to not renew some 300,000 Florida property customers living in high hurricane risk areas. A state-mandated moratorium on nonrenewals was imposed until November 15, 1993. On November 9, 1993, the Florida Legislature approved a catastrophe fund bill designed to protect insurance consumers and the insurance industry from the financial devastation caused by severe hurricanes. The bill enabled Allstate to renew about 97 percent of its Florida property customers in 1994.

In June 1993, 20 percent of Allstate was offered to the public. The offering was an extraordinary success, generating $2.4 billion in capital. That sum was the largest ever raised in an initial public offering in the United States. The separation of Allstate from Sears was part of Sears's new focus on its traditional business of merchandising. With newly found financial strength from the successful public offering, Allstate posted impressive numbers for 1993: a record net income of $1.3 billion on revenue of $20.9 billion.

A dip in profits followed in 1994, however, in the wake of another natural disaster which involved massive claims against Allstate. The Northridge, California earthquake, which struck in January, resulted in claims totaling over $1 billion. In its wake, as had happened following Hurricane Andrew, Allstate (and most other insurers) attempted to stop writing policies for homeowners' insurance in the state, and California eventually passed legislation creating a state Earthquake Authority to help pay future catastrophe claims.

Allstate became completely independent in June 1995, when Sears gave up its 80 percent stake in the company, distributing 350.5 million shares of Allstate stock to its own stockholders. Allstate also streamlined its operations, selling off the PMI Mortgage Insurance subsidiary to raise funds for corporate growth. A smaller hurricane in 1995, Opal, resulted in a more manageable amount of damage than Andrew, and the company's yearly totals were a record-setting $22.8 billion in revenues and $1.9 billion in income.

Concurrent with the positives of Allstate's independence and financial success, controversies were surfacing on a number of fronts. In Texas, the company's use of Allstate-run law firms to represent claimants in court was being examined, while in California Allstate was accused of falsifying engineering reports to minimize earthquake damage claims. In several other states, attorneys general were investigating allegations that the company was overcharging single car owners for auto insurance. Additional states were examining the practice of mailing out pamphlets to auto accident claimants which attempted to dissuade them from consulting an attorney. The company fought these and all such actions vigorously. Allstate, along with a number of other insurance carriers, was also accused of "redlining," or denying insurance to inner city and minority homeowners. In this case, the company announced it was making changes to its policy guidelines which would improve the opportunity for such customers to obtain insurance.

Strong years were again seen in 1996 and 1997, with record revenues and income posted in each. The company began trying new methods of insurance sales, using more independent agents and exploring the possibility of telephone or Internet sales. This was a delicate subject, as the 15,000 plus traditional full-time company agents were strongly opposed to such competition. Allstate also divested itself of several smaller subsidiaries and finished selling off its real estate holdings, a move which had been started in 1991. In late 1998 the company founded a bank, Allstate Federal, which it began to use to handle many of the company's own financial transactions.

In January 1999, a new CEO was installed, Edward M. Liddy. Liddy had been with Allstate only five years, following a longer stretch with Sears, but had quickly moved into the positions of president and COO, and was expected to closely follow the pattern set by his predecessor Jerry Choate. As the company approached the year 2000, it was as strong as it had ever been, and appeared likely to continue in that position for some time to come.

Principal Subsidiaries

Allstate Insurance Company; Allstate Life Insurance Company; Allstate Indemnity Company; Allstate County Mutual Insurance Company; Allstate Holdings, Inc.; Allstate International, Inc.; Allstate New Jersey Holdings, Inc.; Allstate Property and Casualty Insurance Company; Allstate Texas Lloyd's, Inc.; Deerbrook Insurance Company; Forestview Mortgage Insurance Company; Pinebrook Mortgage Insurance Company.

Principal Operating Units

Property-Liability; Life and Annuity; Investments.

Further Reading

"Allstate Insurance: Playing the Field from Now On," *Business Week,* July 11, 1959, pp. 76–88.

Berss, Marcia, " 'We Grew Too Fast' (Allstate Insurance Improves Finances)," *Forbes,* February 13, 1995, p. 103.

Boe, Archie R., *Allstate: The Story of the Good Hands Company,* New York: Newcomen Society, 1981.

Bowe, Christopher, "New Thrift Targets 'Disenfranchised' Customers," *Wall Street Journal Europe,* December 17, 1998, p. 25.

Cole, Robert J., "Allstate Chief Heads an Investment Army," *New York Times,* May 3, 1970, p. F3.

Durgin, Hillary, "Allstate IPO Scores Big," *Crain's Chicago Business,* June 7, 1993, p. 38.

——, "A New Hand Dealt to 1990s Allstate," *Crain's Chicago Business,* December 20, 1993, p. 1.

Elsner, David M., " 'Good Hands People' Play Tough, Propelling Allstate's Profits Up," *Wall Street Journal,* October 4, 1974, p. 1.

Flood, Mary, "Allstate Sued over the Use of Lawyers," *Wall Street Journal,* November 11, 1998, p. T1.

Levin, Gary, "Allstate's Ads Hand It to 'Family'," *Advertising Age,* January 20, 1986, p. 1.

Opdyke, Jeff D., "How Allstate Tried to Skirt State Laws," *Wall Street Journal,* January 4, 1995, p. T1.

Scism, Leslie, "Allstate Relaxes Standards on Selling Homeowners' Policies in Poor Areas," *Wall Street Journal,* August 14, 1996, p. A3.

——, "Auto Insurers May Be Facing Slowdown," *Wall Street Journal,* June 5, 1998, p. C1.

——, "To Avoid Disaster, Allstate Hands Off Home Policies," *Wall Street Journal,* July 11, 1995, p. B4.

"Something New in Stock for Sears Shoppers," *Business Week,* April 25, 1970, pp. 120–22.

Steinmetz, Greg, "Allstate Stock Sale Raises $2.12 Billion," *Wall Street Journal,* June 3, 1993, p. A3.

Stires, David, "SmartMoney Online: Allstate: On Shaky Ground?," *Dow Jones News Service,* May 13, 1998.

This Is Allstate, Northbrook, Ill.: Allstate Corporation.

Wahl, Melissa, "Allstate President to Be Next Chairman, CEO," *Knight Ridder/Tribune Business News,* September 22, 1998.

—Robert R. Jacobson
—updated by Frank Uhle

American Classic Voyages Company

2 North Riverside Plaza
Chicago, Illinois 60606
U.S.A.
(312) 258-1890
Fax: (312) 466-6001
Web site: http://www.amcv.com

Public Company
Incorporated: 1985 as Delta Queen Steamboat Company
Employees: 1,404
Sales: $ 177.9 (1997)
Stock Exchanges: NASDAQ
Ticker Symbol: AMCV
SICs: 4489 Water Passenger Transportation; Not
    Elsewhere Classified; 7011 Hotels, Motels; 6719
    Holding Companies, Not Elsewhere Classified

American Classic Voyages Company is parent company to two pleasure cruise companies, the Delta Queen Steamboat Company, which offers paddlewheel steamboat cruises on the inland waterways of the South and Midwest, and American Hawaii Cruises, which offers ocean liner cruises in the Hawaiian Islands. With origins reaching as far back as the 1890 establishment of Greene Line Steamers, later known as the Delta Queen Steamboat Company, American Classic Voyages is the oldest cruise line to operate under U.S. flag and adopted its current name in 1994.

History of Steamboating

Greene Line Steamers originated as a family-owned and operated business established by Captain Gordon C. Greene and his wife, Captain Mary Greene. After working his way from deck hand to captain, Gordon Greene purchased his first steamboat with his own savings in 1890. The last years of the 19th century and first years of the 20th were prosperous for steamship lines, and the Greenes purchased several "packet" steamers which carried both passengers and freight. Their riverboats traveled on the Ohio River from the port at Cincinnati to Charleston, Pittsburgh, and other ports along the way, transporting agricultural products to the west and general goods to the east.

In the 1920's the railroads came to dominate freight transport, and many packet steamer companies folded. Greene Line Steamers, however, survived by building modern steamships which could carry more freight, by capitalizing on shorter trade routes, as well as by initiating passenger pleasure cruises. Though the business of pleasure cruising stalled during the Great Depression, the Greene Line's freight business endured. Greene Line Steamers directed a fleet of 26 steamboats when Captain Tom Greene, son and successor of Gordon Greene, purchased the *Delta Queen* in 1946.

Since its inaugural voyage on June 1, 1927, the *Delta Queen* has become "legendary" as the last original overnight paddlewheel steamboat in full operation. Captain A.E. Anderson, head of the California Transportation Company (CTC), had reportedly defied conventional wisdom when he built the *Delta Queen* and its twin, the *Delta King*. They were the largest, most extravagant sternwheel riverboats of their time, built at a cost of $1 million each. A crystal chandelier, stained-glass windows, and a grand staircase with accents of Honduran mahogany and bronze filigree were just some of the adornments to grace the *Delta Queen*. Though river transportation was in decline, CTC successfully operated both boats on the Sacramento River, offering "Luxury and Comfort Afloat" on overnight passages between San Francisco and Sacramento.

After some years out of service during the Great Depression, the *Delta Queen* and *Delta King* were leased to the U.S. Navy in the late 1930's for barracks, for naval training and, later, to be used to transport men wounded at Pearl Harbor from oceangoing vessels to military hospitals in San Francisco. After extensive electrical and mechanical maintenance and a coat of navy gray paint, the steamboats provided general ferry transportation between naval bases in the San Francisco Bay area. When World War II ended, the *Delta Queen* and *Delta King* were sent to the mothball fleet. Tom Greene purchased the *Delta Queen* from the Maritime Commission with a bid of $46,250. (Another company bid higher for the *Delta King*, which eventually became a floating conference center in Sacramento.)

Tom Greene's vision to place the *Delta Queen* into operation on the Mississippi River faced many challenges. To transport the flat-bottomed boat without damage over rough ocean waters—from northern California, along the coast of Mexico, through the Panama Canal to New Orleans—the *Delta Queen* would have to be towed. Most of the mechanical parts were dismantled and wood planks were mounted on the external framework of the first two decks to protect the ship's interior. The *Delta Queen* arrived safely in New Orleans on May 19, 1947, after a month-long voyage. With the steamboat's paddlewheel reinstalled and its steam engine realigned, the *Delta Queen* powered itself to the Dravo Shipyard in Pittsburgh for a complete refurbishment and overhaul. On June 30, 1948, the *Delta Queen* made its inaugural voyage under the banner of Greene Line Steamers from its port at Cincinnati.

The 1950s–60s: *Delta Queen* on the Mississippi

A variety of problems beset Greene Line Steamers in the following years. The company had incurred a large debt from the $750,000 renovation of the *Delta Queen,* while competition from the trucking industry reduced freight rates, exacerbating the company's financial difficulties. Frequent engine problems on the *Delta Queen* were also a hindrance. The company eventually purchased internal mechanical components from the owner of the *Delta King* for use as replacement parts, including the paddlewheel shaft which was replaced in 1980.

The premature death of Tom Greene in 1950 placed his wife Letha in charge of the company. To stay in business, Greene Line Steamers eventually sold all of the boats in its fleet except for the *Delta Queen,* including family namesakes, the *Chris Greene,* the *Tom Greene,* and the *Gordon C. Greene.* In 1958, without funds to market the company for the next steamboating season, Letha Greene decided to fold the company and put the *Delta Queen* up for auction.

The fate of the *Delta Queen* and Greene Line Steamers changed unexpectedly with the involvement of Richard Simonton. Letha Greene had returned this man's check for a reservation in early 1958 with a letter explaining that the company was going out of business. Simonton had relished a steamboat trip with his family the previous season and was disappointed to learn of the company's imminent demise. Simonton rescued the company with a $25,000 loan, a $25,000 stock purchase, and the assumption of $70,000 of the company's debt. His friend E. Jay Quinby was named chairman of the board, with the primary responsibility for publicizing the company. Quinby purchased an antique calliope, a steam-pipe organ, and installed it on the *Delta Queen,* making it the centerpiece of his efforts to promote steamboating. Quinby played the calliope for passengers as well as to attract the attention of the people in the shore towns who could hear the music as the paddlewheel boat traveled along the Mississippi River. Dressed in vintage clothing, Quinby traveled in advance of the *Delta Queen* to distribute old-style handbills and to promote the riverboat to the local media. Quinby's formula successfully increased passenger bookings so that by 1962 the company's mortgage and other debts were paid in full.

However, new legislation in 1966, the Safety of Life at Sea Law (SOLAS), threatened the *Delta Queen*'s existence as an overnight passenger ship. The law was enacted to prevent the risk of fire danger on overnight vessels carrying 50 or more passengers; the wooden superstructure of the *Delta Queen* was considered unsafe under the law. Two consecutive two-year exemptions were granted, but the company did not have funds to build an all-steel replacement. Overseas National Airways (ONA) purchased Greene Line Steamers in 1969 with the intention of building a new steamboat.

At the same time, company president Bill Muster and publicist Betty Blake continued the fight to maintain the *Delta Queen*'s presence on the Mississippi River by securing it a place on the Register of Historic Places in 1970. They fought for permanent exemption from SOLAS based on the *Delta Queen*'s perfect safety record, its on-board fire safety devices and the fact that it was not on ocean-going vessel but was always in sight of land. Public officials in support of a permanent exemption from the law included members of Congress, governors and other government officials in the cities and states along the Mississippi River. Public outcry to preserve the *Delta Queen* and river steamboating heritage included thousands of signatures on petitions to "Save the Queen."

All was to no avail, however, and a final voyage was planned for October 1970. Publicity by Muster and Blake attracted large crowds to watch the *Delta Queen's* final passage on the Mississippi River. This public support won the *Delta Queen* an exemption to 1973 after a rider was placed on unrelated legislation and by-passed the House Merchant Marine and Fisheries Committee. (Exemption status continued to be renewed; in 1998 it was extended to 2008.)

1970s: *Delta Queen Steamboat Company is Formed*

The 1970's brought many changes to Greene Line Steamers. No longer a family-owned and -operated business, in 1973 the company changed its name to the Delta Queen Steamboat Company (DQSC) in honor of the *Delta Queen.* Under financial duress due to another renovation of the *Delta Queen,* new boat construction, and problems at ONA, the DQSC was sold to the Coca-Cola Bottling Company of New York in 1973, and Betty Blake became president. Blake had joined the company in 1962 and immediately made her mark when she revitalized the tradition of steamboat racing. As president she would oversee the premier voyage of the *Mississippi Queen* on July 27, 1976. The *Mississippi Queen* was the first boat of its kind to be built in the United States since the *Delta Queen* and *Delta King* in 1926. It was also the largest at 385 feet long, with seven decks, and the capacity for 416 passengers. At a cost of $27 million, modern amenities were fused with turn-of-the-century decor on the new, all-steel paddlewheel steamboat.

National attention continued to shine on the DQSC and the popularity of steamboating grew in the 1980's. In 1979 the national media followed President Jimmy Carter and the first family on a week-long Mississippi River cruise on the *Delta Queen.* The *Mississippi Queen* and its ports-of-call were filmed during an actual cruise and featured on the television show "Real People" in November 1983. DQSC promoted the show through travel agencies nationwide, resulting in a 50 percent increase in the volume of calls. Other television shows which put a national spotlight on the DQSC's Ohio and Mississippi

River steamboating cruises included segments on shows featuring known celebrities such as Phil Donahue, Glenn Campbell, and Conway Twitty. Also, during the 1984 World's Fair in New Orleans, a procession of historic vessels like that of the 1776 Bicentennial in New York Harbor was lead by the *Delta Queen.* In 1989 the steamboat became a National Historic Landmark.

Possibility and Adversity in the 1990s

Around the time of its 100-year anniversary in 1990, DQSC was prospering and expanding. The company endured the national recession by attracting an affluent, retired customer market. Between 1989 and 1992 reservations increased from 80.7 percent of passenger capacity to 95 percent of passenger capacity. Fares rose 28.3 percent, thus boosting operating income from $800,000 in fiscal year ending March 1990 to $9.8 million two years later. In 1992 DQSC went from a privately-held company with a $26.3 million debt and $9.2 million equity to a publicly traded company with $33.2 million equity and no debt. (DQSC had returned to private ownership under billionaire Sam Zell and his partner Bob Lurie when they acquired control of the company in 1981.)

Building on its success, DQSC began construction of a third paddlewheel steamboat, the *American Queen,* in 1993. The 436-passenger ship featured Victorian-era interior design with several authentic antiques, and a grand staircase and a formal dining room modeled on the famous J.M. White steamboat much admired by Mark Twain. Complementing a salvaged 1930s Nordberg steam engine with modern diesel technology, the *American Queen* cost $67 million to build. Service was initiated in June 1995.

In the midst of expansion, DQSC and, later, American Classic Voyages experienced some financial reversals. The Mississippi River flood in the summer of 1993 adversely affected revenues when a number of reservations were canceled due to changes in cruise itineraries. Acquisition of American Hawaii Cruises (AHC) in August 1993 also presented a mixture of legal and financial difficulties. Though DQSC earned $4.2 million in 1993, by 1994 American Classic Voyages, which became the parent company that year, experienced a loss of $983,000. In 1995 the company lost $9.7 million. The losses in both years were attributed to an accounting adjustment at AHC of $.20 per share, totaling $5.8 million, and cost overruns for renovation of its ocean liner, the *Independence.*

AHC was in bankruptcy when the company was acquired by DQSC in 1993. AHC was created by American Global Lines, Inc. in November 1979 to offer overnight pleasure cruises in the Hawaiian islands on the *Independence.* Service was expanded with the acquisition of the *Constitution,* which began operating in Hawaii in June 1982. Despite a monopoly on inter-island travel and some initial success in providing Hawaiian cruise vacations, the company continually lost money. Financial problems eventually led the senior management along with outside investors to acquire AHC from American Global Lines, Inc. in 1985. After being forced into bankruptcy by its lenders, AHC was acquired by the DQSC with approval by the U.S. District Court in Honolulu.

The transformation of AHC was precarious at first. American Classic Voyages paid over $100,000 in fines for garbage illegally dumped in the ocean prior to the purchase of AHC, and the poor condition of the two ocean liners proved costly. Moreover, cost overruns from the refurbishment of the *Independence* led to a legal dispute with the Newport News Shipbuilding and Dry Dock Company. The ship was put into dry dock in July 1994 with an expected return to service in October. After Newport News Shipbuilding seized the ship in November for the outstanding debt, American Classic Voyages sued the company for fraud, breach of contract and wrongful seizure. A court-ordered bond allowed the *Independence* to return to service but some voyages had been canceled by this time. The original cost estimate of $13 million was paid in July 1995 and the disputed difference of $16.8 million was settled out-of-court in February 1996. AHC also suffered a financial loss in 1996 when a $60 million estimate for renovation of the *Constitution* was determined to be too expensive for its return on investment. A write-down of $38.4 million was absorbed by American Classic Voyages.

The bright side of fleet reduction was that AHC was able to focus its attention on the cruise vacation market for the *Independence.* A successful renewal of AHC occurred under Executive Vice-President Jim Nobles, who joined the company in July 1995. Nobles created an more genuine Hawaiian vacation experience on the *Independence* by redesigning the interior decoration and providing activities which highlight native Hawaiian arts and culture. AHC won several travel industry awards for its cultural themes, including its "Aloha Festival/Hawaiian Heritage" theme cruise, which was recognized by the Hawaii Visitors and Convention Bureau in 1997. Service improvements, additional passenger capacity, upgrades to its classic ocean liner cabins, a new appeal to families and a variety of theme cruises worked positively for the company. New sales and repeat business increased, while a revision of the fare structure further increased revenues.

Fleet Expansion for the 21st Century

In October 1997 American Classic Voyages announced plans to expand its Hawaii fleet with two new, 71,000 ton, 840-foot long oceangoing vessels. A year later Ingalls Shipbuilding of New Orleans (a division of Litton Industries) was awarded the contract to build the passenger ships at an estimated $400 million each. Fleet expansion was motivated by the U.S. Flag Cruise Ship Pilot Project Statute, enacted by Congress to improve the reserve of oceangoing vessels operating under U.S flag which could be used in case of war, and to support an industrial base for the U.S. Navy. In addition to guaranteeing a 30-year monopoly on inter-island ocean travel to American Classic Voyages, the U.S. Defense Department allocated $250,000 for the design of the two ships. Jon Rusten was appointed president of the Ocean Development Company, a new subsidiary created for the construction of the ships. In February 1999 Roderick K. McLeod, a well-known cruise industry veteran, was hired to oversee construction and marketing as CEO and president of "Project America." The first ship was scheduled to begin service by late 2002 and the second ship nine to eighteen months later.

American Classic Voyages also initiated plans to provide vacation cruises in other U.S. coastal areas, featuring the regional cultures and countryside of Northern California, the Pacific Northwest, and the Eastern Seaboard from Miami to Halifax to the Great Lakes. Five new 300-foot, diesel-powered boats would be small enough to fit through the locks of the St. Lawrence Seaway. Seattle-based Guido Perla & Associates, Inc., Naval Architects, was contracted to design the ships in the style of the old packet steamboats. Delta Queen Coastal Cruises was established to oversee the project with inaugural service expected to take place in 2001.

Fleet expansion at American Classic Voyages became possible under the direction of company chairman Samuel Zell. Zell recruited Philip C. Calian who was named CEO and president of American Classic Voyages in 1995. Some of Calian's strategies for alleviating American Classic Voyages's financial difficulties included debt refinancing, with an expected annual savings of $1.8 million, the sale of the Maison-Dupry Hotel in New Orleans for $22 million, and the sale of the *Constitution* for $1.8 Million. In July 1996 Zell purchased 170,000 shares of American Classic Voyages stock, raising the its value from $6.50 per share to over $9.00. This was substantially less than the November 1993 price of $16 per share, but by March 1998, with plans for fleet expansion underway, the value of American Classic Voyages stock was $22 per share. Repurchase of up to one million shares of stock was approved by the board of directors in June 1997; as of November 1998 only 51,000 shares had been purchased.

Principal Subsidiaries

The Delta Queen Steamboat Company; DQSB II, Inc.; Cruise America Travel, Incorporated; Great River Cruise Line, L.L.C.; Great Ocean Cruise Line, L.L.C.; Great AQ Steamboat, L.L.C.; DQSC Property Co.; Delta Queen Coastal Cruises; Great Hawaiian Cruise Line, Inc.; Great Independence Ship Co.; Oceanic Ship Co.; Great Hawaiian Properties Corporation; American Hawaii Properties Corporation; CAT II, Inc.; Ocean Development Company.

Further Reading

"ACV to Order US-Built Ships; Rusten to Oversee Project," *Journal of Commerce and Commercial,* August 27, 1998, p. 2B.

Ambler, Charles Henry, *A History of Transportation in the Ohio Valley,* Glendale, Calif.: Arthur H. Clark Company, 1932.

"American Hawaii Cruises to Quadruple Passenger Capacity in the Next Eight Years," *Business Wire,* October 20, 1997, p. 10201419.

"American Hawaii Cruises Wins Hawaii's Top Tourism Award," *PR Newswire,* April 16, 1997, p. 0416CLW033.

"Black Ink From the Mississippi," *Business Week,* August 25, 1997, p. 156.

"Court OKs Delta Queen Takeover," *Travel Weekly,* June 28, 1993, p. 1.

Determan, Wendy, "American Classic Merges Management," *Tour and Travel News,* May 13, 1996, p. 4.

——, "American Hawaii to Stick With One Ship," *Tour and Travel News,* April 15, 1996, p. 2.

Fritz, Michael, "Rising Tides Lift Zell Cruise Ships," *Crain's Chicago Business,* September 16, 1996, p. 3.

Garvey, Stan, *King and Queen of the River: The Legendary Paddle-Wheel Steamboats Delta King and Delta Queen,* Menlo, Calif.: River Heritage Press, 1995.

Greene, Letha, *Long Live the Delta Queen,* Hastings House, 1973.

Huber, Lisa, "Owner of Cruise Ship Seized over Debt Countersues," *Journal of Commerce and Commercial,* November 10, 1994, p. 9B.

——, "Shipyard to Settle with American Classic Voyages," *Knight-Ridder/Tribune Business News,* February 7, 1996, p. 2070175.

Kamhis, Jacob, "Refurbished Independence Back to Work," *Pacific Business News,* June 23, 1997, p. A12.

Lynch, Janet, "Senior Executives, Investors Will Buy American Hawaii," *Travel Weekly,* December 9, 1985, p. 1.

Marino, Donna, "American Hawaii Brings Back 'Heritage Cruises'," *Tour and Travel News,* May 26, 1997, p. 30.

——, "New Legislation a Boon to American Hawaii Cruises'," *Tour and Travel News,* October 20, 1997, p. 8.

Mehlman, William, "Delta Queen Making Splash with Affluent Customer Base," *The Insider's Chronicle,* September 28, 1992, p. 1.

"New Riverboat to Echo Gilded Past," *Travel Weekly,* September 5, 1994, p. C14.

Perez, August, et al., *The Delta Queen: Last of the Paddlewheel Palaces,* Gretna, La.: Pelican Publishing Company, 1973.

Seiden, Allan, "Rebuilding AHC," *Travel Agent,* February 3, 1997, p. 105.

"Swell for Zell," *Chicago Tribune,* October 9, 1998.

—Mary Tradii

American Italian Pasta Company

1000 Italian Way
Excelsior Springs, Missouri 64024
U.S.A.
(816) 502-6000
Fax: (816) 502-6080
Web site: http://www.pastalabella.com

Public Company
Incorporated: 1986
Employees: 400
Sales: $189.3 million (1998)
Stock Exchanges: New York
Ticker Symbol: PLB
SICs: 2098 Macaroni & Spaghetti; 5149 Groceries &
    Related Products, Not Elsewhere Classified

The second largest pasta producer in North America, American Italian Pasta Company (APIC) produces more than 80 dry pasta shapes, selling its pasta to supermarket chains, food processing companies, and food service companies. APIC produces pasta for private label brands and its own brand, Pasta LaBella. The company's manufacturing facilities, located in Excelsior Springs, Missouri and Columbia, South Carolina, are vertically integrated operations using the most advanced production technology in the industry. APIC's manufacturing facilities, capable of producing more than 600 million pounds of pasta per year, are key to its success. In late 1998 the company's third production facility, located in Kenosha, Wisconsin, was under construction.

Origins

Richard C. Thompson brought an eclectic professional past with him when he founded APIC in 1986. During the 1970s he was involved in real estate surrounding the Houston Astrodome. During the early 1980s he turned his attention to the oil and gas business, forming an exploration firm, Kinson Resources Inc., to make a living wildcatting in North Dakota. The cyclical nature of the oil and gas business, which descended into one of its deepest ruts during the early 1980s, convinced Thompson to search for a

business with fewer market fluctuations and led him to explore food manufacturing as an option. Food production sprang to mind not only because "there's always a demand for food," as Thompson once remarked, but also because North Dakota was home to a prized crop: durum. Renowned for its superior pasta-making qualities, North Dakota durum was imported by Italian companies, who converted the wheat into pasta and then exported the pasta back to the United States. Thompson decided to use North Dakota durum to start his own pasta-making company, and he began enlisting the support of financial backers. From the start, he decided to focus on producing premium-grade pasta and avoid competing against low-priced, mass-produced brands manufactured by industry giants such as Hershey Foods and Borden Inc. "If we're going to survive," Thompson explained, "we cannot compete on price. If we do, we'll get stepped on, thrown away, chewed up, and walked over." Accordingly, Thompson devoted a considerable amount of time to researching pasta making. He spent four years in the United States and two years in Italy learning how to make pasta, searching for the method his company could use to produce superior pasta. "I want my pasta to be known as the finest in the world, bar none," Thompson declared, "including the Italians."

Aside from producing a premium brand that would limit direct competition with low-priced brands, Thompson's strategy also hinged on something else, something that would make his company a rarity among U.S. pasta producers. Most manufacturers purchased their pasta flour from commercial mills, rather than producing it on their own, but from the start Thompson preached vertical integration, striving to realize the financial benefits of owning his own flour-making facility and the greater control over quality such ownership would give him. He decided to build his production plant in Excelsior Springs, Missouri, selecting the location because of the presence of pure spring water and, more important, because of Excelsior Springs' proximity to rail lines accessing North Dakota durum. The $50 million, state-of-the-art facility began production in 1988, officially making Thompson's APIC a participant in the growing pasta industry. At the time, pasta consumption in the United States was on the rise, a trend that would continue into the 1990s as a national passion for pasta intensified. The average American ate 17 pounds of pasta a year in 1988, up from 13 pounds a year in 1981, which translated into a $2 billion market by the time Thompson's plant began producing its first shipments. Into this market APIC entered as a newcomer in 1988; a decade later the company would hold sway as a dominant force, ranking as the second largest pasta producer in the United States.

Business began on a high note when Thompson secured contracts to supply his pasta to the A&P grocery chain and SYSCO Corp., the largest restaurant supply firm in the country. These two customers purchased the company's initial production output, pushing APIC's first-year sales into the $20 million range, while Thompson pursued contracts with other institutional customers and began negotiations with brokers in several foreign countries. Thompson's goal was to make APIC the first U.S. company to ship pasta to Italy, a feat that would go a long way toward legitimizing his pasta as the "finest in the world." To accomplish this objective and to give APIC a product to increase sales domestically, Thompson invested his efforts in the creation of what he termed a "super-premium" brand, the pasta product that would drive the company's sales upward, distinguish APIC as a premier pasta maker, and fuel expansion into foreign markets, particularly into the much-vaunted Italian market. The company's signature brand debuted in January 1990, introduced under the name Pasta LaBella. As Thompson had planned, APIC's flagship brand stood apart from other mass-produced brands such as American Beauty and Creamette. Pasta LaBella was stocked in the deli section, away from competitors shelved on the pasta aisle, and its retail price of approximately $2.65 for a one-pound package was $1.50 more than most other American brands. Although the sales generated by Pasta LaBella only accounted for five percent of APIC's revenue volume during the brand's first year, the brand attracted a wealth of new business that promised to be the beginning of more to come. The 800-store Kroger chain began stocking LaBella, as did several other large retail chains, such as IGA, Payless, Hy-Vee, and Price Chopper. Several restaurant chains replaced their Italian pasta brands with LaBella as well, but in Thompson's mind the true measure of success was LaBella's entry into the Italian market. "Everyone remembers the first company to do something," Thompson mused, "just like everyone remembers the first person to walk on the moon. But who cares about the second or third?"

APIC's place in the annals of business history was secured in May 1990 when Thompson attended a European trade fair for food brokers. At the trade fair Thompson reached an agreement to sell LaBella through an Italian grocery store called Casa di Risparmio di Parma, making APIC the first U.S. company to sell pasta in Italy. APIC's historic achievement fanned excite-

ment at company headquarters, inducing Thompson and his management team to develop ambitious plans. As negotiations were under way to sell LaBella through a 400-store distributorship in Italy, a LaBella pasta sauce was developed, slated for introduction by the end of December 1990, while LaBella olive oil and LaBella breadsticks were in earlier stages of development. By the end of 1990 sales were up 60 percent from the previous year's total, prompting Thompson to expand production capacity. He increased production capabilities at the company's Excelsior Springs plant 200 percent, giving APIC the ability to make 150 million pounds of pasta per year.

New Management in 1991

In 1991 a host of changes swept through APIC that few outside observers could have foreseen. According to one report, the investors who had financially helped Thompson build his Excelsior Springs plant grew worried by the end of 1990 that APIC would not meet certain financial objectives and would fall short of reaching the new, expanded production capacity at the company's plant. In the midst of this reported anxiety, a $76 million buyout of APIC by Hershey Foods was announced in early 1991. Thompson welcomed the deal, but the U.S. Justice Department intervened and launched an investigation into the proposed buyout. After a three-month inquiry, the Justice Department ruled against the proposed acquisition in March, stating that the union of APIC and the second largest pasta producer in the United States would result in higher prices for consumers. In the wake of the scuttled buyout, Thompson stepped aside, vacating his posts of president and chairman of the board to make room for what industry pundits termed "professional managers." Horst Schroeder, formerly the chief operating officer for Kellogg, was named chairman of the board, and Timothy Webster, formerly APIC's chief financial officer, was promoted to president, along with a number of other promotions that gave APIC a revamped management team. The change in leadership was a smooth transition, without any finger-pointing at Thompson or much to suggest that Thompson's leadership had led to failure. "This is a step all entrepreneurial companies go through," explained Webster, "where the creator hands the baton to his managers." Thompson, who ranked as APIC's largest shareholder, retained a seat on the company's board. Under the new management, however, a new business plan emerged, one that was substantially different from the philosophy espoused by Thompson. Said Webster, "Our focus is on the high-volume segments. We need to be a manufacturing-driven company until the plant [capacity] is utilized."

From 1991 forward APIC strove to be a low-cost producer of pasta, rather than a company seeking to make the "finest pasta in the world." The new strategy sought to utilize the full strength of the company's unique manufacturing capabilities, capitalizing on the vertically integrated operations that had been established by Thompson. Although making quality pasta had not been abandoned as a company goal (APIC touted itself as the only pasta maker to use high temperature drying, reportedly the best way to process wet pasta), operating as a low-cost producer had moved to the forefront of the company's pursuits. Toward this end Webster and his staff achieved encouraging results. Using aggressive marketing and citing the advantages of the company's own mill operations, Webster convinced a number of large customers to purchase their pasta from APIC. Supplier contracts with companies such as Wal-Mart, Publix, Pillsbury, Kraft, and General Mills fostered consistent, strident financial growth, assuaging any anxiety investors might have experienced. Sales rose to $39 million in 1992 and then began increasing by at least 20 percent each year as APIC headed toward the mid-1990s. As the company's customer base of grocery chains, restaurants, and food processing companies increased in number, pushing sales upward and stretching production capacity to its limit, a different type of APIC took shape. The APIC of Thompson's era had sought to distinguish itself from the established giants in the industry by producing a higher-priced, higher-quality product, but during Webster's era the pursuit of becoming a low-cost producer had developed APIC into a giant itself. By the mid-1990s APIC was one of the major producers with which it had avoided directly competing during the late 1980s and was well on its way toward becoming the largest pasta producer in the United States. The prospect of reaching the industry's number one position was not a "goal in and of itself," Webster noted, as the company steadily increased its market share. "But we do want to continue to grow," he added. "If it were to happen, we'd certainly have grins on our faces."

Late 1990s Expansion

By 1995 any fear of not reaching full production capacity at the company's Excelsior Springs plant had been thoroughly eliminated. The company was ready, in fact, to build a second manufacturing facility. Construction of the new plant began in 1995 in Columbia, South Carolina, its completion lifting APIC's production capacity to roughly 300 million pounds of pasta per year. By the end of 1996 sales had eclipsed the $100 million mark, climbing to $121 million. APIC, by this point, was the third largest pasta producer in the United States, trailing only Hershey Foods and Borden Inc., and it was regarded widely as the most efficient producer. Its two manufacturing plants, which made more than 80 shapes of pasta, utilized the most advanced production technology in the industry, a distinction used as a persuasive marketing tool to win new customers and one that was making it increasingly difficult for other companies to compete with APIC on a low-price basis. The fruits of APIC's decade-long investment in its manufacturing facilities were realized in 1997, a year that saw the company achieve great strides while its largest competitor began to retreat.

In early 1997 CPC International, a global food company that marketed 45 varieties of pasta, announced APIC would become the exclusive producer of its Mueller's brand of pasta, the leading brand in North America. The contract represented an extraordinary boon to APIC's business, one that could not have been gained without its state-of-the-art manufacturing facilities. "By joining with APIC," a CPC International senior executive remarked, "we make a leap from the oldest production technology in the industry to the newest." The addition of the Mueller's brands led to a $45 million expansion at APIC's Columbia plant, where Mueller's was scheduled to begin production in January 1998. News of the Columbia facility expansion was followed by the announcement of a $20 million expansion at the company's Excelsior Springs plant, which had been planned for at a later date but was accelerated once APIC executives learned of their biggest rival's future plans. In mid-1997 Borden announced that it

would start to close its pasta-producing plants after deciding to stop manufacturing private-label brands and pasta for the "ingredients business," which included making noodles for products such as Hamburger Helper. APIC moved in to fill the void created by Borden's retreat, implementing an expansion program designed to increase its production capacity by 60 percent, making it the second largest pasta producer in North America.

As work was under way to increase APIC's production capacity to more than 600 million pounds of pasta per year, the company decided to convert to public ownership. In October 1997 APIC's initial public offering on the New York Stock Exchange raised $87 million in net proceeds, giving the company the financial resources to pay for expansion. Following the public offering, Thompson stepped forward to remark, "It's been wonderfully exciting and a dream come true. I'm a proud papa." There was good reason for Thompson's elation. "Everything looks to be going very, very well for them," one stock analyst remarked. "They continue to gain market share." In November 1997 the likelihood of further gains in market share appeared assured when APIC announced preliminary plans for a third pasta production plant in Kenosha, Wisconsin, to be constructed through a joint venture with Harvest States. Following this exhaustive period of expansion, the company entered its tenth year of production, by which time both expansion projects at Columbia and Excelsior Springs were completed. The results were impressive. In 1998 revenues increased from $129 million to $189 million and net income swelled from $5 million to more than $15 million, both record results. On this bright note, APIC prepared for its second decade of business, having successfully climbed the rungs of its industry to hold sway as a dominant presence in the North American pasta market.

Further Reading

Bassing, Tom, "Pasta Maker Restructures After Buyout Bid Squelched," *The Kansas City Business Journal,* June 14, 1991, p. 2.

Brockhoff, Anne, "Romance, Intrigue of IPOs Intoxicate Some Executives," *The Kansas City Business Journal,* December 12, 1997, p. 22.

Clevenger, Brenda, "That's Not Italian," *Ingram's,* November 1990, p. 59.

Collins, Martha, "Using Their Noodles," *Ingram's,* July 1992, p. 40.

Davenport, Carol, "Richard C. Thompson, 38," *Fortune,* November 6, 1989, p. 196.

Everly, Steve, "American Italian Pasta Co. To Expand Excelsior Springs, Mo. Plant," *Knight-Ridder/Tribune Business News,* July 2, 1997, p. 7.

Levine, Joshua, "Yankee Noodles Dandy," *Forbes,* November 12, 1990, p. 310.

"Missouri Pasta Maker To Sell 5.4 Million Shares of Common Stock," *Knight-Ridder/Tribune Business News,* April 30, 1998, p. 4.

Otto, Alison, "Where Are They Now?," *Prepared Foods,* October 1991, p. 47.

Reeves, Scott, "No Fireworks, Just Pasta: An IPO with Real Growth and Actual Earnings," *Barron's,* October 6, 1997, p. 39.

Roth, Stephen, "Public Offering Poises American Italian for No. 1," *The Kansas City Business Journal,* November 14, 1997, p. 3.

Welbs, John, "Pasta Giant Expands in South Carolina To Begin Production for Mueller's," *Knight-Ridder/Tribune Business News,* April 15, 1997, p. 41.

—Jeffrey L. Covell

American Media, Inc.

600 East Coast Avenue
Lantana, Florida 33464-0002
U.S.A.
(561) 540-1000
Fax: (561) 540-1018
(800) 288-4890
Web site: http://www.nationalenquirer.com

Public Company
Incorporated: 1990 as Enquirer/Star Group, Inc.
Employees: 550
Sales: $307.7 million (1998)
Stock Exchanges: New York
Ticker Symbol: ENQ
SICs: 2721 Periodicals: Publishing & Printing

American Media, Inc. is a leading U.S. publisher best known for the periodicals *National Enquirer, Star, Weekly World News, Soap Opera Magazine, Country Weekly,* and *Soap Opera News,* with a current aggregate weekly circulation of over five million copies. *National Enquirer* and *Star* have the second and third largest single copy circulation, respectively, of any weekly periodical. American Media Operations, Inc., a wholly owned subsidiary of American Media, conducts all of the company's business operations and owns substantially all of the company's assets including the capital stock of its subsidiaries. American Media derives more than 85 percent of its revenues from circulation, predominantly single copy sales in supermarkets and other retail outlets, with the remainder from advertising and other sources. Another subsidiary, Distribution Services, Inc. (DSI), markets American Media's periodicals, as well as those of its client publishers, in approximately 175,000 locations in the United States and Canada. In addition, DSI provides merchandising and information gathering services for nonpublisher third parties.

Pope Acquires the New York Evening Enquirer: 1952

In 1952 the 25-year-old Generoso Pope, Jr., acquired the *New York Evening Enquirer,* a weekly that focused on horse racing news and crime stories, for $75,000. He modified the paper to a tabloid format and altered it to include unique and unusual news items. He also gave the paper more of a national focus and in 1957 renamed the paper *National Enquirer.* By the mid-1960s weekly circulation reached one million copies. Anticipating that urban newsstands would become less numerous, he had the paper distributed through supermarket chains. To make the paper more acceptable to shoppers and the general public, he reduced coverage of crime stories and increased coverage of celebrity and human interest stories.

Pope moved the *National Enquirer* to Lantana, Florida, in 1971. Circulation of the *National Enquirer* peaked in the late 1970s at about six million copies a week. Pope began publishing *Weekly World News* in 1979. It was a black and white tabloid devoted to entertaining and unusual news and feature stories. Most of its content was derived from stories and purchased photographs from agencies and periodicals around the world.

1989 Sale of the Company

Pope died in 1988, and in June 1989 GP Group Acquisition Limited Partnership acquired the *National Enquirer* and *Weekly World News* from Pope's estate for $413 million in cash. The general partners of the GP Group Acquisition were Boston Ventures Limited Partnerships III and IIIA and Mcfadden Holdings L.P. Management of the company consisted of several key executives associated with Mcfadden and Boston Ventures. Mcfadden was known as the publisher of *True Confessions, True Stories,* and other magazines.

Following the acquisition, a program of revenue enhancements and cost reduction measures began. The cover price of the *National Enquirer* was raised from $.75 to $.85 in the United States and from C $.75 to C $.89 in Canada. The subscription price also was increased, as were mail order and classified ad rates. These actions resulted in an additional $15 million in annual revenues.

Cost reductions included renegotiating major supplier contracts and new printing contracts. An outmoded printing facility in Pompano Beach, Florida, was closed, and the page count of the *National Enquirer* was reduced. Television advertising was discontinued because it was ineffective. Editorial staff was reduced, and free-lancers were paid less for articles and photographs. These measures resulted in an estimated annual savings of more than $20 million.

Enquirer/Star Group, Inc. Forms in 1990

In June 1990 the Enquirer/Star Group, Inc. was organized as a holding company for the purpose of acquiring the *Star* from News America Publishing Inc. and one of its affiliates for $200 million in cash and $200 million in convertible preferred stock. Enquirer/Star, Inc. was a wholly owned subsidiary, originally incorporated in 1981 under a different name, of the Enquirer/Star Group that conducted substantially all of the company's operations and represented substantially all of the Group's assets.

The *Star* was launched in 1974 by Murdoch Magazines, a division of News America Publishing Inc. It was a weekly periodical focusing on celebrity news and feature stories and was distributed through the same outlets as the *National Enquirer*. The *Star*'s editorial staff worked from offices located in Tarrytown, New York, and operated independently of the editorial staffs of the *National Enquirer* and *Weekly World News*, whose offices were located in Lantana, Florida.

Cost reduction measures were introduced following the acquisition of the *Star*. Production of the *Star* was changed from heatset offset to the more cost efficient rotogravure printing. The change also improved reproduction quality and allowed for the use of lower-cost newsprint. Certain distribution, print, and pre-press operations were combined to achieve additional cost savings, as were advertising sales staffs, accounting, and other support functions. These measures resulted in annual savings of more than $20 million.

Enquirer/Star Group Goes Public: 1991

In July 1991 13.5 million shares of Class A common stock were offered to the public at $14 per share, and the stock of the Enquirer/Star Group began trading on the New York Stock Exchange. Just prior to the initial public offering (IPO), the *National Enquirer* began distribution in the United Kingdom. The tabloid was so well accepted that the company began printing a separate U.K. edition in Switzerland and was exploring the possibility of selling *Weekly World News* in the United Kingdom as well.

Soap Opera Magazine was launched in October 1991 as a weekly publication, with editorial offices in Tarrytown, New York. Within three months of its launch it was being sold at 70,000 checkout counters across the country, and after nine months it had reached the break-even point in sales. The 48-page weekly provided in-depth coverage of 11 network daytime soap opera programs, with circulation consisting primarily of single copy sales. Its content included summaries of current story lines, exclusive interviews, and extensive photo coverage of soap opera stars.

During fiscal year 1991 (ending March 31) the company began publishing special issues of the *National Enquirer* and the *Star*. Each issue was topic-specific, had 72 color pages, and stayed in circulation for six to eight weeks. They were priced at $1.95 in the United States and C $2.25 in Canada. During fiscal year 1992 six special *National Enquirer* issues and five *Star* special issues were published.

For fiscal year 1992 (ending March 30) the company reported excellent financial results, with increases in operating cash flow, operating income, and net income. It realized net income of $5.7 million on sales of $283.7 million. Newsstand circulation and advertising sales continued a downward trend, due in part to a continuing recession and competition from other media who were devoting more space to personality journalism. The company planned to launch a brief television ad campaign to boost circulation and improve ad sales. Cover prices for the *National Enquirer* and the *Star* were raised to $.99 from $.95 to cover promotion costs. The company planned to grow its business by launching new magazines, expanding distribution to Europe, and exploring the possibility of television production. DSI, the company's distribution and merchandising subsidiary, was expanding its operations by increasing its client base. During fiscal year 1992 it added *US* and *Rolling Stone* magazines.

In May 1992 the cover prices of the *National Enquirer* and the *Star* were raised to $1.25. At the same time a substantial television ad campaign was launched. For fiscal year 1993 the company reported net income of $19.4 million on sales of $275.4 million. During the year a new distribution agreement for the United Kingdom was completed. The company also formed a joint venture in Australia with Australian Consolidated Press to publish an Australian version of the *National Enquirer,* which went on sale June 9, 1992. It suspended publication in December 1993 after 29 issues, because of lower than anticipated single copy sales. With no plans to resume publication of the Australian version, the company resumed distribution of the U.K. version in Australia.

In June 1993 the GP Group Acquisition Limited Partnership was dissolved and its assets, consisting primarily of 21.5 million shares of common stock, were distributed to its general partners and two limited partners. These general partners, The Boston Group and Mcfadden Holdings L.P. submitted a proposal on April 28, 1994, to acquire all of the outstanding shares of Class A Stock not owned by them for $17.50 per share in cash. At the time the majority stockholders controlled about 76 percent of the company's voting stock. The proposal involved taking the company private, with all stock being converted into cash and no longer being traded on the NYSE.

In May 1994 the board established a committee to consider the proposal. In April and May a total of seven lawsuits were filed by the company's shareholders. These lawsuits all claimed the same thing, namely, that the proposal was "a scheme to eliminate the public shareholders of the [company] at a grossly unfair or inadequate price in violation of Delaware law and that the defendants, in either pursuing or acting on this scheme, have breached their fiduciary duties of good faith, loyalty, fair dealing, due care and candor to the minority public shareholders." The plaintiffs generally alleged that the proposal was made at a time when the company's stock price was severely depressed and that the offer price of $17.50 per share did not adequately reflect the company's prospects for earnings growth. The proposal to take the company private was rejected because of the opposition of the minority shareholders.

American Media, Inc. is Created in 1994

The company's fifth periodical, *Country Weekly,* was launched in April 1994. It was devoted to all aspects of country music, lifestyles, events, and personalities. In its first full year of publication *Country Weekly* had average weekly sales of 290,000 copies, of which 225,000 were single copy sales.

The company changed its name to American Media, Inc. on November 21, 1994, to reflect its broader publishing base of five major periodicals. The name American Media became available when the former American Media, an owner of several radio stations, was acquired and merged into another company.

For fiscal year 1995 the company reported net income of $11.8 million on sales of $315.3 million, compared with net income of $27.8 million on sales of $300 million the previous year. Sales of the *National Enquirer* were down about ten percent from 3.3 million copies per week in fiscal year 1994 to 3.0 million in fiscal year 1995. The *Star*'s average weekly copy sales fell from 2.8 million in fiscal year 1994 to 2.7 million in fiscal year 1995, and *Weekly World News* fell from 558,000 copies per week in fiscal year 1994 to 510,000 copies in fiscal year 1995. In addition to declining sales, which could be offset by higher cover prices, the company's financial results continued to be affected by higher paper costs, declining advertising revenue, and higher interest expense due to increased debt.

Sales of four of the five major periodicals declined even more during fiscal year 1996, while the recently introduced *Country Weekly* gained about 15 percent in sales. Average weekly sales of the *National Enquirer* dipped to 2.6 million copies, and sales of the *Star* dropped more than ten percent to 2.4 million copies. *Weekly World News* also declined about ten percent to 459,000 copies, and *Soap Opera Magazine* fell below the 300,000 mark to 284,000 copies for the first time since it was introduced.

Television coverage of the O.J. Simpson trial was having a big effect on sales of the company's periodicals. Not only were people buying fewer tabloids, they also were watching daytime soap operas less faithfully. As a result, American Media reported a net loss of $1 million for fiscal 1996 on declining sales of $295.1 million.

For fiscal year 1997 (ending March 31) American Media reported higher sales of $316.0 million and net income of $12.0 million. Average weekly sales of *Soap Opera Magazine* and *Country Weekly* both increased by approximately 15 percent, and the declining sales of the *National Enquirer,* the *Star,* and *Weekly World News* leveled off at less than ten percent.

Steve Coz, a Harvard University graduate, was named editor of the *National Enquirer* in 1996. Coz pledged that the tabloid would feature more stories on celebrities and contain less sensationalism. Reviewing his first year as editor, he noted that the *National Enquirer* refused to publish such sensational items as the autopsy photographs of Ron Goldman and Nicole Simpson or the murder pictures of six-year-old JonBenet Ramsey, even though its main competitor the *Globe* did. Publishing those photographs helped the *Globe* reach the one million mark in circulation.

Time magazine named Coz one of the most influential people of 1997, and under Coz's editorship the *National Enquirer* won praise for its coverage of the O.J. Simpson case, the JonBenet Ramsey murder case, and the murder of Bill Cosby's son. The *National Enquirer* also broke the story of President Clinton's advisor, Dick Morris, leaking presidential secrets to a female "acquaintance."

Nonetheless, in Coz's first year as editor, the *National Enquirer* had six lawsuits brought against it by celebrities, including Don Johnson, Dabney Coleman, Lisa Marie Presley, and Tammy Wynette. Eddie Murphy's lawsuit was dismissed, but Clint Eastwood won a $150,000 judgment when the *National Enquirer* was found guilty of misrepresenting a syndicated interview as an exclusive. Then in 1997 Martha Stewart brought a $10 million lawsuit against the *National Enquirer* for an article entitled, "Martha Stewart Is Mentally Ill."

Entering Television Entertainment in 1997

Production of a one-hour *National Enquirer* special, "25 Years of Scandals," marked American Media's entry into television entertainment. The program aired in June 1997. The company had been exploring television shows based on its tabloids since the early 1990s. In 1993 television executive Brandon Tartikoff announced he would produce a show based on stories from *Weekly World News.* In 1994 Celebrity Entertainment, Inc. produced a one-hour television pilot based on stories from the *National Enquirer.* Other television projects that never aired included an "Enquiring Minds" game show, which was considered by a major network for the 1992–93 season, and an infotainment show based on *Soap Opera Magazine.* A third project being explored was a series of one-hour specials tentatively titled, "From the Secret Files of the *National Enquirer.*"

American Media launched its sixth periodical, *Soap Opera News,* in March 1997, with editorial offices in Tarrytown, New York. Circulation for the weekly digest-sized publication was 163,000 for its first year, of which 146,000 were single copy sales. It covered all aspects of daytime television's soap opera programming, including news, features, and behind-the-scenes stories about the shows and their stars.

For fiscal year 1998 American Media reported net income of $5.5 million on sales of $307.7 million. In its annual report it noted that adverse publicity resulting from the August 1997 death of Princess Diana affected single copy circulation of the *National Enquirer* and the *Star.* Greater coverage of celebrity news in other forms of media also was having a negative impact on the company's revenues. The company continued to raise cover prices in an effort to offset declining sales. Of the company's six periodicals, only *Country Weekly* showed circulation gains, as its average weekly sales rose from 389,000 copies in fiscal year 1997 to 416,000 copies in fiscal year 1998.

Following nearly a decade of declining sales since it was incorporated in 1990 as the Enquirer/Star Group, American Media will continue to build on its strong trademarks such as the *National Enquirer,* the *Star,* and *Weekly World News.* Interest in celebrity news remains high, and the company will face significant competition as other forms of media devote more time and effort to covering celebrities and personalities in the news.

Principal Subsidiaries

American Media Operations, Inc.; National Enquirer, Inc.; Star Editorial, Inc.; SOM Publishing, Inc.; Weekly World News, Inc.; Country Weekly, Inc.; Distribution Services, Inc.

Further Reading

Altaner, David, "Trail and Error: Tabloid Firm Jumps O.J. Simpson Bandwagon, Hits Bump in Road," *Sun-Sentinel,* August 16, 1995, p. 1D.

"American Media Cleans Up by Digging Dirt," *Sun-Sentinel,* April 30, 1995, p. 3F.

"American Media Inc. Announces Acquisition of MediaOne Inc.," *Business Wire,* October 3, 1996.

Antilla, Susan, "A Tabloid Publisher's Unsensational Performance," *New York Times,* May 1, 1994, p. F11.

Cohen, Adam, "With a Tip from a Tab," *Time,* March 24, 1997, p. 54.

"Enquirer/Star May Change Name," *Palm Beach Post,* August 4, 1994, p. 6B.

"Enquirer/Star Shareholders Sue," *Palm Beach Post,* April 30, 1994, p. 5B.

"Entertainment Makes Announcement," *Business Wire,* February 22, 1994.

"Feud of the Week," *Time,* December 1, 1997, p. 105.

Gleick, Elizabeth, "Leader of the Pack," *Time,* January 9, 1995, p. 62.

Herubin, Danielle, "Media Inc.: Shareholders Don't Count," *Palm Beach Post,* August 14, 1996, p. 5B.

Peterson, Iver, "The National Enquirer Cuts Back on Sensationalism, But Is Still Haunted by Its Past," *New York Times,* September 9, 1997, p. D11.

Pogrebin, Robin, "The National Enquirer Turns to a Consultant To Improve Its Sales at Supermarkets," *New York Times,* October 20, 1997, p. D11.

Pounds, Stephen, "Owners to Buy Up Enquirer/Star Shares," *Palm Beach Post,* April 29, 1994, p. 5B.

"Tabloids' Shocker: Big Debt, Big Returns," *Palm Beach Post,* May 22, 1995, p. 48.

Vorman, Julie, "Enquirer Plans Magazine, TV Shows," *Reuter Business Report,* December 28, 1993.

"Weekly World News, Tartikoff in TV Special," *Reuter Business Report,* September 28, 1993.

—David Bianco

American National Insurance Company

One Moody Plaza
Galveston, Texas 77550
U.S.A.
(409) 763-4661
Fax: (409) 766-6663
Web site: http://www.anico.com

Public Company
Incorporated: 1905
Employees: 6,900
Sales: $1.74 billion (1997)
Stock Exchanges: NASDAQ
Ticker Symbol: ANAT
SICs: 6311 Life Insurance; 6321 Accident & Health
   Insurance; 6331 Fire, Marine & Casualty Insurance;
   6351 Surety Insurance; 6324 Hospital & Medical
   Service Plans; 6282 Investment Advice

American National Insurance Company is one of the 100 largest life insurance companies in the United States in terms of insurance in force, providing personal life insurance and related financial services to more than seven million policy owners in 49 states, the District of Columbia, Guam, Puerto Rico, and American Samoa. Directly and through its subsidiaries, American National offers a broad line of coverage, including individual life, health, and disability insurance; group life and health insurance; personal lines of property and casualty insurance; and credit insurance. The company also offers a variety of mutual funds and annuities.

Founded in Texas in 1905

American National Insurance Company traces its origins to the entrepreneurial spirit of William Lewis Moody, Jr., a Texan with diverse business interests who prospered in the cotton and banking industries during the latter part of the 19th century before turning his attention to insurance in the early 1900s. In 1904—at a time when the insurance industry was dominated by large east coast companies writing most of the life insurance policies in Texas—the 39-year-old Moody became president of American National Insurance and Trust Company of Houston and relocated that company's headquarters to Galveston, where Moody's family owned a bank.

The following year Moody organized and became president of American National Insurance Company, which then took over $800,000 worth of insurance policies covered by American National Insurance and Trust. Chartered as a life insurance company with $100,000 of capital and $20,000 surplus, American National Insurance Company began operating with ten employees in the original Moody Bank building in Galveston. Initially, American National paid no dividends because Moody, who held controlling interest in American National, believed that during a company's early years all profits should go toward financing future growth.

Moody's plans for growth paid off, and within five years American National's assets had risen to more than $1 million. Between 1905 and 1910 American National's insurance in force also rose considerably—from $2.1 million to $22 million—and in 1911 the company paid its first dividend. The following year the company's home office work force had expanded to 70 employees, and the number of American National field representatives totaled more than 700. In 1913, to accommodate its growing work force, American National moved into a new 11-story office building, initially claiming two of its floors.

American National's premium revenues increased rapidly during the 1920s, with the deadly influenza epidemic of 1918–19 fresh in the memories of potential customers. American National's growth was also fueled by a stream of acquisitions, and by 1928 the company had absorbed 27 other insurance companies and was employing 500 persons in its home office.

During the decade of the 1920s American National's assets increased more than 400 percent—compared with the national average for insurance companies at the time of 160 percent—climbing from $7.3 million to $38 million. Insurance in force rose from about $100 million to more than $600 million.

Stability During the Depression Years

In large part as a result of its carefully selected investment portfolio, American National weathered the worst of the Great Depression without laying off employees or suffering annual losses. In 1933, with the nation's banks closed, American National continued to meet its financial obligations as policyholders paid small weekly premiums in cash.

Between 1930 and 1935—the worst years of the Depression for most businesses—American National's assets grew by 37 percent, while its capital and surplus funds nearly doubled, rising from $6 million to $11.5 million. During that same period American National's insurance in force declined only about three percent, or at half the rate of the insurance industry as a whole. The company's insurance sales picked up in 1936, and by 1939 American National had assets of $82 million, with insurance in force totaling $777 million.

At the onset of World War II, the company's assets and sales grew dramatically, and in 1942 American National became the first Texas insurance company to claim $100 million in assets. Two years later the company's insurance in force passed the billion dollar mark. During the war, American National was a significant financial contributor to the military efforts of the United States, purchasing about $33 million worth of government war bonds.

In 1950 American National made its first major diversification move, entering the accident insurance field through the purchase of Commonwealth Life and Accident Insurance Company of St. Louis, Missouri. That year the company also entered the health, hospitalization, and credit insurance fields through acquisitions of other companies operating out of St. Louis and Dallas. By the end of 1950, American National had $2 billion worth of insurance in force.

In 1954, after nearly 50 years of running the company he founded, W.L. Moody died. Moody left behind a business legacy that included control of American National, as well as ownership of newspapers, hotels, and businesses operating in the fields of banking, printing, and ranching. Before his death, Moody's assets were used to establish a family trust, as well as the Moody Foundation, with the latter holding a controlling interest in American National as well as responsibility for future distribution of nonprofit grants. Moody's daughter, Mary Moody Northen, succeeded her father as president of American National. The company continued to prosper under Northen, and by 1959 American National's insurance in force had grown to $5 billion.

Moody Family Influence Decreases in the 1960s

During the late 1950s the Moody Foundation's four-member board became deadlocked on numerous issues, with Shearn and Robert Moody, great-grandsons of W.L. Moody, opposing the two other board members. Texas state officials responded to the foundation feud by increasing the board's size and adding nonfamily members, beginning a long battle between Shearn Moody and nonfamily foundation trustees.

In 1961 Mary Moody Northen retired, and American National's presidency and chair passed out of the Moody family to W.L. Volger, executive vice-president since 1944. Two years later R.A. Forbush took over the presidency of the company, whose assets had grown to more than $1 billion.

Under the leadership of Forbush and Volger, American National made several moves to expand the company's business activities. In March 1967, American National acquired Securities Management & Research, Inc. (SM&R), the investment management company of Citadel, Inc.'s mutual fund. With the acquisition of SM&R, which became American National's first major wholly owned subsidiary, the company entered the investment oriented financial services field and began offering mutual funds under the name American National Growth Fund, Inc. One month after acquiring SM&R, American National also entered the savings and loan field by acquiring a majority interest in Southern California Financial Corporation, a holding company based in Los Angeles with control over Southern California Savings & Loan Association and $200 million in assets.

In December 1967, American National—in another strategic acquisition—purchased controlling interest in Trans World Life Insurance Company of New York, the only state in which American National was not already licensed to operate. Between 1967 and 1968 American National also extended its operations beyond the United States and was licensed to operate in Western Europe.

The acquisitions and expansion moves helped boost revenues, and by 1968 American National had $10 billion worth of insurance in force. In 1969 Phil B. Noah, an executive vice-president since 1962, became president and chairperson of American National. American National continued to expand its life insurance operations that year by acquiring Equitable Insurance Company of Texas, which became American National Life Insurance Company of Texas (ANTEX), American National's second major subsidiary. During its initial years under American National's control, the operations of ANTEX were focused primarily in the areas of credit, life, accident, and health insurance.

By 1969 American National's home office work force had grown to more than 1,000 employees and field representatives included more than 7,000 agents and office workers. In response to the growth of its work force, during the late 1960s American National began construction of its 20-story American National Tower in Galveston. The new headquarters was completed in 1971.

Continued Growth in the 1970s and 1980s

In 1970 Glendon E. Johnson was named president, assuming the additional duties of chairperson in 1973. That year American National created a third principal subsidiary, American National Property and Casualty Company (ANPAC), based in Springfield, Missouri. Designed to broaden the scope of coverage available to its customers, ANPAC was licensed in 40 states and chartered to handle multiple lines of insurance, including automobile and homeowner's policies. Between 1973 and 1974 American National also expanded its activities in New York and acquired complete control of Trans World Life.

During the early 1970s Shearn Moody filed a lawsuit aimed at ousting Moody Foundation trustees accused of allowing American National to make large, low collateral loans to Las Vegas gambling casinos. Shearn Moody won the suit, and in 1973 his family regained control of the Moody Foundation. But Shearn Moody's battles with the law and the foundation board continued into the next two decades. During the late 1980s he was convicted of mail fraud and improperly taking money from the Moody Foundation and was subsequently voted off the foundation board. In 1990 the conviction was overturned.

In 1976 American National took over control of Standard Life & Accident Insurance Company, a unit of Standard Life Corporation based in Oklahoma. Standard Life & Accident Insurance, which had filed for bankruptcy and had been charged with securities fraud prior to being acquired, became American National's fourth major wholly owned subsidiary. The following year Orson C. Clay assumed the presidency of American National.

Late in 1980 American National sold Trans World Life to a Mutual of Omaha Insurance Company subsidiary. During this time American National created its fifth major subsidiary, American National General Insurance Company. American National General was chartered to handle most lines of property and casualty insurance and, like ANPAC, was based in Springfield, Missouri.

In 1981 the subsidiary ANTEX discontinued its credit insurance operations and became active in the business of reinsuring ordinary life and individual annuity policies written by other companies. That year SM&R began offering its American National Money Market Fund. The following year the leadership of American National was returned to the Moody family when Robert Moody was named as chair of American National's board of directors. American National doubled the size of its credit insurance operations in 1986 when it acquired the operations of World Service Life Insurance Company of Colorado and two of its affiliates. American National's total assets climbed above the $3 billion mark in 1986, and by 1987 the company's insurance in force had grown to more than $25 billion.

In 1987 American National acquired the universal and life insurance operations of American Health & Life Insurance Company. The following year the company purchased three Primerica Corporation insurance companies—Pennsylvania Life Insurance Company, Executive Fund Life Insurance Company, and Trans Pacific Life Insurance Company—specializing in various kinds of individual life, accident, and health insurance.

Between 1985 and 1988 ANTEX wrote no new insurance policies, turning its attention to the acquisition of business through the assumption of reinsurance agreements, including two large blocks of individual life and annuity contracts that were acquired during this time. In 1989 ANTEX resumed writing individual life insurance polices and also began marketing individual accident and health insurance.

The 1990s: Focus on Marketing

In 1989 American National's annual revenues exceeded $1 billion for the first time, and one year later the company's insurance in force topped $30 billion. Pushing sales upward during the early 1990s were acquisitions of life insurance business and a marketing diversification program. In 1990 ANTEX significantly expanded its direct policy writing activities after entering into the association group health market, with health, accident, and hospitalization coverage offered under an agreement with an outside sales agency and group polices sold through the National Business Association.

In 1990 American National also acquired American Security Life Insurance Company, a Texas life insurer licensed in 31 states. American Security Life was sold the following year after American National assumed the former company's insurance portfolio.

In 1991 Robert Moody assumed the additional duties of chief executive officer. That year the company expanded its investment fund sales channels when SM&R began a new marketing program and expanded its distribution outlets to include banks, savings and loan associations, and credit unions. In an effort to broaden its insurance sales force, in 1992 American National began recruiting noncareer insurance agents, association groups, bank affiliates, auto dealers, and other groups to sell its insurance products.

In June 1992, American National expanded its distribution channels further, paying $41.1 million to acquire Garden State Life Insurance Company, a direct-response insurance company based in New Jersey. Licensed to do business in 49 states, Garden State's activities included television and direct mail marketing of term life insurance policies with a face amount of $100,000 or more.

In large part as a result of its increasingly diversified sales and marketing efforts, in 1992 American National saw significant financial gains. In July 1992, American National sold the insurance portfolio of Commonwealth Life and Accident Insurance Company for $14.2 million. Net income for the year rose $40 million to $168 million, and revenues increased better than ten percent, climbing from $1.1 billion to $1.3 billion. Assets exceeded the $5 billion mark for the first time in 1992, and life insurance in force swelled by almost 20 percent, climbing to more than $37 billion.

American National entered 1993 having paid annual dividends for 82 consecutive years and having raised its dividend 19 straight years. In terms of industry measuring sticks, in 1993 the company received A.M. Best Company's top rating (A-double-plus) and held $156 in assets for every $100 in liabilities, which was one of the better assets-to-liability ratios in the insurance field.

The company had begun expanding its sales of annuities in the early 1990s, marketed in large part through third parties, and this area became a strong source of revenue over the next several years. In 1994 Garden State began to explore offering life insurance policies to customers of credit card companies and banks, with the first sales taking place in the fall of 1995. Initial sales were modest, however, and Garden State's overall revenues were stagnant during the mid- to late-1990s. Garden State introduced a new form of Critical Illness health insurance in late 1997, which the company expected to bring revenues back up.

Sales of health insurance for American National and its subsidiaries declined during the mid-1990s with the company's restructured home service division in fact discontinuing sales of major medical insurance policies altogether. American National's field agent force had been halved during an eight-year period beginning in the late 1980s, with only 2,200 licensed agents left by 1998. Sales of life insurance policies now were increasingly being made by the company's multiple line, rather than single line, agents.

The Standard Life and Accident subsidiary, which primarily offered medicare supplement insurance policies, also had seen a decline in sales since the early 1990s, though a number of new products were added in 1995–96. Four-fifths of Standard's net premiums still consisted of this ''medigap'' coverage, however, and this market was highly vulnerable to changes in state and national health insurance laws. Standard made moves to diversify, seeking increasing life and annuity sales.

American National's bread and butter remained life insurance, and this area continued to contribute more than 70 percent of the company's earnings. Life insurance in force totaled $43.8 billion in 1997, with the company's overall consolidated assets standing at $8.5 billion. Net income for the fiscal year 1997 was up 15 percent from 1996, to $248 million, with stockholder dividends increased yet again. A.M. Best Company's ratings were still A-double-plus, or ''Superior.''

As the year 2000 approached, the company's outlook appeared to be quite solid. Conservative by nature, with the life insurance business remaining primarily stable and predictable, there appeared to be few major obstacles to continued prosperity. As a result of its diversified sales force and marketing techniques, which had been expanded substantially in the 1990s, American National expected to reap continued growth in revenues and assets. It remained guardedly optimistic about the ramifications of potential national health care programs on health insurance premiums and the company's overall operations. The heirs of founder William Moody, through the Moody Foundation and The Libbie S. Moody Trust, continued to control more than 61 percent of the company as it neared the end of its first century in business.

Principal Subsidiaries

American National Life Insurance Company of Texas; Garden State Life Insurance Company; Standard Life and Accident Insurance Company; American National Property and Casualty Insurance Company; American National General Insurance Company; American National Lloyds Insurance Company; ANREM Corporation; Securities Management & Research, Inc.

Principal Divisions

Home Service; Multiple-Line; Independent Markets; Group Insurance; Individual Health; Credit Insurance.

Further Reading

Hackett, George, with Daniel Shapiro, ''In Galveston, Moody's Blues: a Saga of Sex, Violence and Money, Texas Style,'' *Newsweek,* February 2, 1987.
History of American National, Galveston, Texas: American National Insurance Company, 1975.
Norman, James R., ''Texas Gothic,'' *Forbes,* October 22, 1990, pp. 345–49.

—Roger W. Rouland
—updated by Frank Uhle

Armor Holdings, Inc.

13386 International Parkway
Jacksonville, Florida 32218
U.S.A.
(904) 741-5400
(800) 654-9943
Fax: (904) 741-5403
Web site: http://www.armorholdings.com

Public Company
Incorporated: 1969 as American Body Armor and
    Equipment, Inc.
Employees: 1,830
Sales: $97.2 million (1998)
Stock Exchanges: American
Ticker Symbol: ABE
SICs: 3999 Manufacturing Industries, Not Elsewhere
    Classified; 7381 Detective, Guard, & Armored Car
    Services

Prior to 1997 Armor Holdings, Inc. operated in one business segment, manufactured products, which included the development, manufacture, and distribution of ballistic protective equipment, less-than-lethal products, and narcotic identification and evidence equipment. Its customers included law enforcement agencies, local police departments, state police agencies, state correctional facilities, highway patrols, and sheriffs' departments. The company's products were sold primarily through a network of independent distributors who served law enforcement communities.

With the acquisition of DSL Group Ltd., based in the United Kingdom, Armor Holdings entered the security services market and established its Integrated Security Services Division to complement its Manufactured Products Division. With operations in more than 20 countries, the Integrated Security Services Division became the world's leading provider of specialized security services in high risk and hostile environments around the world. The core of the company's security services business is to create and implement solutions to complex security prob-

lems. It conducts detailed and targeted analyses of potential threats to security and assists in the secure design of facilities. It also provides highly qualified personnel with extensive international experience and conducts on-going training of security personnel. These experienced security personnel act as planners, trainers, managers, advisors, instructors, and liaison personnel. Other security services provided by the company include humanitarian mine clearance and ordnance disposal, maintenance of secure lines of communication, and high risk insurance services.

Armor Holdings is also a leading systems engineer for sophisticated electronic and computer-driven security and fire alarm systems. Its specialty is high-speed analog and digital transmission designs for life safety, communication, alarm, access control, television, and security systems. These systems have been installed in airports, banks, government buildings, hospitals, prisons, universities, and other locations.

1969 Origins

Armor Holdings was founded in 1969 as American Body Armor and Equipment, Inc. It was primarily a manufacturer of armored products such as ballistic resistant vests and tactical armor. In August 1985 the company was acquired by Unifast Industries, Inc., for $1.7 million. In March 1989 Unifast and American Body Armor and Equipment completed a public offering of common stock which reduced Unifast's ownership interest from 100 percent to 55.6 percent. Proceeds were used to reduce bank debt.

Bankruptcy and New Owners in the 1990s

In May 1992 the company filed for relief from its creditors under Chapter 11 of the U.S. Bankruptcy Code following a general decline in operations. The company had reported significant operating losses in 1989 and 1991. It also was unable to collect $1.5 million related to a shipment of vests to a customer in the Middle East in April 1991. In September 1993 the company emerged from Chapter 11 with a new reorganization plan. For the fourth quarter of 1993 the company reported revenue of $3 million and net income of $138,000. In 1994, its first full year of operations following bankruptcy protection, the

---

Company Perspectives:

Armor is a leading provider of effective security solutions to the increasing level of security threats encountered by domestic and foreign law enforcement personnel, governmental agencies and multi-national corporations. These solutions include a broad range of high quality branded manufactured products such as ballistic resistant vests and tactical armor, bomb disposal equipment, less-than-lethal munitions and anti-riot products and sophisticated security planning, advisory and management services, including the provision of highly trained, multi-lingual and experienced security personnel in violent and unstable areas of the world.

company reported net income of $423,000 on revenue of $11.4 million. Results for 1995 were about the same, with net income improving to $520,000 on slightly higher revenue of $11.7 million.

In January 1996 the company underwent a change in control following the purchase by Kanders Florida Holdings, Inc. and other investors of all of the company's capital stock that was owned by Clark Schwebel, Inc. and Hexcel Corporation, who were both suppliers of raw material to the company. As a result of acquiring the stock of the company's two largest shareholders, Kanders owned approximately 66 percent of the company. A new name, Armor Holdings, Inc., was adopted on August 21, 1996.

With new ownership, Armor Holdings began pursuing a strategy of growth through acquisition of other businesses in the security industry. Its goal was to become the preeminent global provider of security products and services. It made six major acquisitions between January 1996 and March 1998, and in 1997 adopted a holding company structure and completed a public offering of four million shares of common stock. Two additional acquisitions were completed in 1998, and two more were pending.

NIK Public Safety Product Line was acquired in July 1996 for $2.4 million worth of stock. NIK assembled and distributed portable narcotic identification kits, which were used by law enforcement agencies to identify narcotic substances. NIK also distributed specimen collection kits, evidence collection kits, and tamper guard evidence tape.

Defense Technology Corporation of America was acquired in September 1996 for approximately $5.5 million in cash and stock and the assumption of certain liabilities. DTC manufactured less-than-lethal and anti-riot products, including pepper sprays, tear gas, distraction devices, flameless expulsion grenades, and specialty impact munitions. As a result of these acquisitions, Armor Holdings reported significantly higher revenue of $31 million in 1996, with net income of $689,000.

In April 1997 Armor Holdings moved to a new corporate headquarters in Jacksonville, Florida. In June a holding company structure was adopted. Operating assets were transferred to a subsidiary, and the company became a holding company. It owned directly or indirectly all of the outstanding capital stock of its subsidiary corporations and no longer conducted any manufacturing operations directly. In July Armor Holdings issued four million new shares of common stock and netted $38.1 million, which was used to repay the company's outstanding debt on its credit facility.

Acquisitions in the Mid-1990s

Supercraft (Europe) Ltd. was acquired in April 1997 for an initial purchase price of $2.6 million, less some $410,000 of future consideration that Armor Holdings was not required to pay. Supercraft was a European manufacturer of military apparel, high visibility garments, and ballistic resistant vests. Its clients were law enforcement and military agencies throughout Europe, the Middle East, and Asia.

DSL Group Ltd. was acquired in April 1997. Based in the United Kingdom, DSL was a leading provider of specialized security services in high risk and volatile environments. To finance the acquisition, Armor Holdings issued common stock valued at $10.9 million to be traded for the common stock of DSL, paid $7.5 million for DSL's preferred stock, and subsequently paid $6.9 million plus interest on DSL's outstanding credit facility.

The acquisition of DSL marked the company's entry into the security services market and resulted in the establishment of the company's Integrated Security Services Division to complement its Manufactured Products Division. DSL was originally established in 1981, and by 1997 it was operating in 20 countries. In 1997 it contributed $48 million in revenue to Armor Holdings.

Part of the DSL acquisition included a 50 percent interest in Gorandel Trading Ltd. In June 1997 Armor Holdings acquired the remaining 50 percent interest in Gorandel for $2.4 million in cash and stock. Gorandel provided specialized security services throughout Russia and Central Asia. For 1997 Armor Holdings reported significantly higher net revenues of $78.3 million. Net income jumped to $3.2 million.

Low Voltage Systems Technology, Inc. was acquired in January 1998 for about $750,000 in cash and stock and $200,000 in assumed debt. It was a leading systems engineer specializing in sophisticated electronic and computer-driven security and fire alarm systems.

Asmara Ltd. of London, England, was also acquired in early 1998. The company specialized in business intelligence services, including commercial due diligence and intelligence, asset tracing, litigation support, and other investigative work.

Armor Holdings completed its acquisition of Federal Laboratories, a division of Mace Security International, Inc., in July 1998 for a purchase price of $4.6 million in cash and an additional $600,000 held in escrow. The acquisition included the law enforcement division of Mace Security International, Inc., including the Federal Laboratories Division, and the right to use the MACE trademark in the law enforcement market.

In May 1998 Armor Holdings announced that it intended to acquire Pro-tech Armored Products for $1.6 million. Pro-tech specialized in manufacturing hard armor products and added substantial engineering talent to Armor Holdings' hard armor production.

CDR International Ltd. was acquired in June 1998. CDR's specialty was intangible asset protection, including intellectual property management and protection. It had offices in London, Los Angeles, Charlotte (North Carolina), and Moscow.

Alarm Protection Services, Inc., located in Kampala, Uganda, was acquired in July 1998. Armor Holdings had managed APS through DSL Group Ltd. since 1996. APS had about 900 employees and annual revenues of approximately $2.5 million.

In December 1998 Armor Holdings signed a letter of intent to acquire The Parvus Company, a consulting firm based in Washington, D.C., that specialized in international investigations, corporate intelligence, and security services. The Parvus Company was founded in 1984 by Gerard P. Burke, who had held several senior positions in the National Security Agency and had served as President Nixon's executive director of the President's Foreign Intelligence Advisory Board.

As Armor Holdings acquired companies, they became business units in one of the company's two divisions, the Manufactured Products Division or the Integrated Security Services Division. Business units in the Manufactured Products Division included American Body Armor, NIK Public Safety, Defense Technology, Supercraft, Pro-Tech Armored Products, and Federal Laboratories.

Armor products manufactured under the brand name American Body Armor included ballistic resistant vests, sharp instrument penetration armor, and bomb protective gear. The company also marketed a broad range of other personal armor products.

Under the trademark First Defense the company manufactured pepper sprays and a wide range of specialty impact munitions that could be used against either individuals or in crowd control situations. These manufactured products were generally available for use only by authorized public safety agencies.

Armor Holdings also assembled and marketed portable narcotic identification kits under the NIK brand name as well as evidence collection kits and evidence tape. It was also the exclusive distributor of Flex-Cut and Key-Cuff disposable restraints.

The Manufactured Products Division contributed net revenues of $30 million during 1997, a 66 percent increase over 1996. Approximately three-fourths of the company's manufactured products were sold in the United States during 1997.

The company's second division, its Integrated Security Services Division, was a provider of specialized security services in high risk and hostile environments around the world. It was established in the second quarter of 1997 following the acquisition of DSL Group Ltd. The division also included Low Voltage Systems, Asmara Ltd., and the pending acquisition of CDR International.

Approximately 38 percent of Armor Holdings' security business in 1997 involved multinational petrochemical companies, and 11 percent was accounted for by mining and construction companies. The company's security clients typically had significant investments in remote and hostile areas of the world. Other significant clients included the United Nations, governmental embassies, projects funded by the World Bank and the European Commission, and a variety of other organizations and companies engaged in international trade and commerce.

Future Expectations

Armor Holdings planned to continue to identify acquisition targets in areas that complemented its existing businesses in the security market. Its strategy was to expand its product line and increase its geographical diversity. It was hoped that growth through acquisitions would result in better gross margins and more efficiencies from consolidating administrative overhead. These measures would also improve the company's access to capital in the coming years.

Principal Subsidiaries

Armor Holdings Properties, Inc.; American Body Armor and Equipment, Inc.; Armor Holdings Ltd. (U.K.); Defense Technology Corporation of America; NIK Public Safety, Inc.; Defense Technology Europe Ltd. (U.K.); Supercraft (Europe) Ltd. (U.K.); Pro-Tech Armored Products; DSL Holdings Ltd. (U.K.); Defense Systems Colombia S.A.; U.S. Defense Systems, Inc.; USDS Congo SPRL (Democratic Republic of Congo); Gorandel Trading Ltd. (Russia); Defense Systems Eurasia Ltd. (Kazakhstan); Defensetse Systems Ecuador USDSE SA; Defence Systems Eurasia Ltd. (Ukraine); Low Voltage Systems Technology, Inc.; Asmara Ltd. (U.K.); Armor Holdings Venezuela S.A.; Defence Systems (South Africa) Pty Ltd.; Defence Systems France SA; Defence Systems (Jersey) Ltd.; DSL Security (PNG) Pty Ltd. (Papua New Guinea); DSL Security (Asia) Pte Ltd. (Singapore); Jardine Securicor Gurkha Services Ltd. (Hong Kong); Maximum Security Indochina Ltd. (Hong Kong).

Principal Divisions

Integrated Security Services; Manufactured Products Division.

Further Reading

"Armor Holdings, Inc. Signs Letter of Intent to Acquire the Parvus Company," *PR Newswire*, December 2, 1998.
"Armor Increases Corporate Holdings," *Florida (Jacksonville) Times-Union*, February 25, 1999.
Barker-Benfield, Simon, "Armor Holdings Executive Has Plenty to Worry About," *Florida (Jacksonville) Times-Union*, October 20, 1997.
Snite, Eleanor, "Armor Grows with Purchase of Mace, Pro-Tech," *Jacksonville Business Journal*, April 10, 1998.
Thompson, Brian L., "Armor Holdings Acquires Two Companies for $4 Million," *Jacksonville Business Journal*, January 30, 1998.

—David Bianco

AXA Colonia Konzern AG

Colonia-Allee 10-20
D-51067 Köln
Germany
(49) (221) 148-105
Fax: (49) (221) 148-21704
Web site: http://www.axa-colonia.de

Public Company
Incorporated: 1839 as Kölnische Feuer-Versicherungs-
   Gesellschaft
Employees: 9,280
Total Assets: DM 11 billion (1997)
Stock Exchanges: Frankfurt/Main
Ticker Symbol: COL.G.
SICs: 6311 Life Insurance; 6321 Accident & Health
   Insurance; 6324 Hospital & Medical Service Plans;
   6331 Fire, Marine, & Casualty Insurance; 6351 Surety
   Insurance; 6361 Title Insurance; 6371 Pension,
   Health, & Welfare Funds

AXA Colonia Konzern AG is Germany's fourth largest primary insurer based in Cologne. Through its operative subsidiary, Colonia Versicherung Aktiengesellschaft, the group provides a broad variety of personal and property insurance services such as general and professional liability, accident, fire, auto, transportation, life, and health coverage to private and corporate clients. Major brand names are Colonia, Nordstern, Darag, and Deutsche ärzteversicherung.

AXA Colonia is part of the world's largest insurance holding company, the AXA-UAP Group, which holds about 69 percent of AXA Colonia shares. As part of AXA-UAP, AXA Colonia offers international coverage concepts for multinational companies. The AXA Colonia group also offers several financial services including asset management, construction financing, bond funds, and real estate funds. Forty-eight companies in Germany and abroad are consolidated in AXA Colonia's annual accounts. Major subsidiaries include Colonia Versiche-

rung AG, Colonia Bausparkasse AG, Colonia Krankenversicherung AG, Deutsche Ärzteversicherung AG, and Nordstern Allgemeine Versicherungs-AG.

Early Years As Fire Insurer: 1839–1902

AXA Colonia's origins go back to a law enacted in 1837, banishing most foreign—mainly French—insurers from the German state of Prussia. This was the chance for the two brothers Abraham and Simon Oppenheim, of the Cologne-based Oppenheim bank, to pursue their plans for a fire insurance business in the form of a joint stock company within the thriving heart of the Rhineland. On June 22, 1839, five founders gave birth to Colonia by signing the company agreement after they had received a concession from the Prussian emperor Kaiser Wilhelm III: the Cologne bankers Simon Oppenheim, Heinrich Ziegler, Wilhelm Ludwig Deichmann, and Carl-Eduard Schnitzler, and Cologne's Chamber of Commerce president Peter Heinrich Merkens who became chair of the board. They were joined by other Cologne businessmen to constitute the first executive board of the Kölnische Feuer-Versicherungs-Gesellschaft (Fire Insurance Company of Cologne). The company's first fire insurance plan covered buildings and furniture consumed or damaged by fire and lightning. However, documents, money, precious gemstones, and gunpowder mills, as well as fire resulting from earthquakes or acts of war, were not covered.

Johann Heinrich Daniel Kamp, an experienced banker and entrepreneur residing in Cologne, became the company's first director and took the first steps to get the business going, which meant to create a close network of representatives as soon as possible. By 1843, 59 general agencies in 57 towns including over 260 subsidiaries represented the newly licensed firm. Because the name Kölnische Feuer-Versicherungs-Gesellschaft was not easy to remember by potential customers, the name ''Colonia'' was used instead, referring to the female allegorical figure that gave the city of Cologne its name. In 1841, the company's first brand name was approved by the Ministry for the Interior as a prefix to the company name.

Colonia's initial business concession allowed the company only to do business in the German state of Prussia. However, in

Company Perspectives:

We offer a comprehensive line of coverage in all areas of personal and property insurance, focused on the needs of private, commercial and industrial clients. We promote a solid foundation for assets and the financial security of our clients by means of an extensive variety of financial services: construction financing, bond funds, real estate funds, and other financial instruments. Our strengths are the close relationship of our representatives to clients, the continuous work on new types of insurance and financial services and the development of innovative special products. Our staff is characterized by their competent counsel, their comprehensive understanding of customer service and their acknowledged reliability. We are aware of our responsibility for the life-planning, health care, and secure livelihood of our clients. We understand that our job as an insurance company is an ethical and social one as well. In our work we take into account the latest findings of science, technology and environmental studies. We observe in advance economic and social changes and do our business in harmony with environmental needs.

the years after its founding, it modestly expanded into a few small German states as well as into the Netherlands and Denmark. A devastating fire in the German harbor town of Hamburg in 1842 was Colonia's first big challenge. Because of the company's high share capital basis, all claims—amounting to more than one-third of Colonia's annual premium income—were settled through cash payments within five weeks. Resulting from this experience, the board of directors decided to establish Colonia's own reinsurance company. After the first European economic crisis had delayed this project for several years, the Rückversicherungs-Aktien-Gesellschaft Colonia was set up under Colonia's third managing director, Jakob Gilbert, who served the company in this position between 1868 and 1883. Until the end of the 19th century, Colonia offered fire insurance only. In 1853, Concordia, Cölnische Lebensversicherungs-Gesellschaft, a life insurance provider, was opened and closely linked to Colonia through Abraham Oppenheim as a member of both companies' boards of directors.

New Products, Alliances, and Crises: 1903–45

Since its founding, Colonia had been a driving force in setting up alliances to promote the mutual interests of insurance companies. In the late 19th century, it joined five other insurance companies in founding the ''Federation of German Private Fire Insurers,'' an organization that provided statistics linked with their business. While it was not a price cartel, minimum rates for fire insurance were set beginning around 1900. Between 1903 and 1917, Colonia added new insurance products to its business: a burglary and theft insurance; an insurance against loss of rent caused by fire, lightning, or explosion; a burst pipes insurance; a consequential loss insurance; a price difference insurance (i.e., for the sugar trade); and a marine insurance. By 1914, Colonia employed over 70 people.

Beginning in 1919, Colonia entered two decades of new alliances through mergers and acquisitions to compete in the consolidating insurance sector. In December 1919, the company agreed to merge with the Kölnische Unfall-Versicherungs-Aktiengesellschaft (K.U.), another Cologne-based insurer active in the industrial liability as well as in individual accident, collective, passenger, sea voyage, and glass and valuables insurance, in which Colonia had been holding a substantial share since 1880. Colonia took over all of K.U.'s assets and insurance contracts—and its full name. The new Colonia Kölnische Feuer- und Kölnische Unfall-Versicherungs-Aktiengesellschaft, however, entered troubled times.

First of all, the merger went anything but smoothly. K.U.'s workforce could not get used to the more bureaucratic Colonia culture and none of the parties was willing to give up its independence. In addition, Germany's economy went through difficult times after World War I, including dwindling markets through lost territories and a collapse of the German currency due to inflation in 1920. Colonia as a fire insurer was not allowed by law to do business in foreign currency—a fact that put Colonia's reinsurance subsidiary, which had to pay back loans in foreign currency, into deep debt. Thanks to the brisk intervention of Colonia's supervisory board in the spring of 1923, the company was able to survive the turmoil. In October, Dr. Christian Oertel, a highly respected German insurance manager, was elected as chairman of Colonia's board. He successfully reorganized and streamlined management, sales, and administration, replaced bureaucracy by a more participatory culture to motivate Colonia's and former K.U.'s employees, increased Colonia's share capital, and rearranged its holdings.

In response to rapidly increasing competitive pressure, Colonia entered an agreement with the two other main insurance companies of the Rhineland to support each other if needed in 1921, sealed by a mutual exchange of shares. However, the agreement was hit hard in 1929, when one of the partners went bankrupt. In the years after 1924, Colonia bought holdings in several companies, many of which were sold again over the next ten years, when the company retained shares in ten companies, among them a 35 percent share in the Berlin-based Nordstern Allgemeine, and a 40 percent share in the Cologne-based reinsurer Kölnische Rückversicherungsgesellschaft. In 1938, the company was renamed Colonia Könlische Versicherungs-AG. Before World War II began, Colonia was Germany's third largest private insurance company with a workforce of about 880.

Postwar Boom and Major Mergers: 1946–72

In Colonia's first balance sheet after the war, the company's assets displayed were worth less than 60 percent of the prewar value. About a third of Colonia's buildings in the western part of Germany were destroyed. In the ''Soviet Zone,'' Colonia's property was expropriated: ten branch offices and about 40 percent of the company's business volume were lost. Dr. Robert Pferdmenges, a close acquaintance of West Germany's new president, Konrad Adenauer, who had rescued the Oppenheim bank during the Nazi years and succeeded Simon Alfred von Oppenheim as a partner, led Colonia's reconstruction efforts as chair of the supervisory board. Colonia's chairman of the management board was Karl Haus, another representative of the Oppenheim bank in charge of its insurance holdings, who became the first president of the Association of German Insurers. While Colonia mainly focused on reconstruction in the early 1950s, the first signs of the postwar boom were seen when Colonia's traditional branches made profits again. Colonia's premium income increased by 15 percent from 1954 to 1955 to a total of DM 76.6 million. The company especially participated in the postwar boom of auto insurance, and new products such as livestock and textiles insurance were offered. Otto Vossen, an experienced insurance manager who had joined Colonia in 1946, took over chairmanship of the management board in 1963. An engineer with a creative mind, he pioneered Colonia's product management by introducing machinery, contract works, warranty, and building contractors' insurance for businesses, as well as an early version of renter's insurance and a new-value insurance for houses, among other offerings. A brand new office building in Cologne built in 1968 included a "drive-in-station" for the fast settlement of claims. By 1969, Colonia's workforce reached 2,160, up from about 1,000 in 1953.

In 1967, Dr. Nikolaus Graf Strasoldo, former assistant of Dr. Robert Pferdmenges and successor of Karl Haus as a personally liable partner of the Oppenheim bank, became Colonia's chairman of the supervisory board himself. Together with Otto Vossen, he created a new corporate structure in one of the biggest merger deals in the history of Germany's insurance market. In a first major step, Colonia merged with the Lübeck-based National Versicherung with which it was already closely connected through majority shareholdings of the Kölnische Verwaltungs-AG and the Oppenheim bank, as well as through a community of interests. All of National's assets and obligations were transferred to Colonia and the new company was renamed to Colonia National Versicherungs-Aktiengesellschaft. In a second step, Colonia merged with two other major insurers, the Gladbacher Feuerversicherungs-Gesellschaft and the Schlesische Feuer, after it received major holdings in those companies from its "Rhineland Group" partner Aachener and Münchener in a share exchange transaction. Colonia also integrated the Westdeutsche Schlachtvieh-Versicherungsgesellschaft, a wholly owned subsidiary since 1959. Including those major deals, a total of 12 well-established German insurers were merged with Colonia, making it one of the largest insurance companies in Germany with DM 685 million in premium income. Internally, Vossen and Strasoldo energetically pushed Colonia through a rapid restructuring program eliminating 24 of the former 30 executive board members of the merged companies after 1972. The 79 divisional offices of those companies were managed by Cologne headquarters while sales and claims settlement divisions were decentralized. At the end of the legal part of Colonia's major coup, it was given the new name Colonia Versicherungs Aktiengesellschaft in 1971.

A New Leader and a New Identity: 1973–88

While legal matters were settled and Colonia's turnover tripled through the merger to about DM 3 billion, the new giant had to be merged internally—an even more challenging task. Dieter Wendelstadt, a 45-year-old dynamic leader and outsider, not at all familiar with the insurance business, was chosen by Graf Strasoldo as representative of Colonia's major shareholder, the Oppenheim bank, to accomplish that task. Strasoldo became chairman of the supervisory board while Wendelstadt

took over as CEO. Soon after, he presented his fresh and unconventional concept for Colonia to increase service efficiency, expand internationally, and substantially improve internal communication among the different company divisions. In order to increase service quality, separate sales offices were established for corporate clients to better serve their special needs. To get closer to customers, new local offices were set up. To improve service quality, a new training center was opened in 1976. Claas Kleybold, Colonia's new marketing and sales executive, concentrated on the reorganization of the sales channels and the introduction of a comprehensive electronic data processing system. By 1979, Colonia's service network was one of the largest in Germany's insurance landscape, including 80 local offices, 1,700 full-time agents, and 13,000 part-time agents.

Colonia's decision to expand internationally was mainly driven by the ongoing internationalization of its corporate clients. In order to provide insurance services for its subsidiaries abroad, but also to further distribute Colonia's own risks, the company started working with experienced local partners through minority holdings. Colonia's first foreign subsidiary—Colonia Insurance Company (UK) Ltd.—was established in London in 1975. One year later, Colonia was the first German insurer to receive a license for conducting business in the United States, namely in New York. In the following years, Colonia gradually expanded into most of the other states as well as in Europe, Canada, Brazil, and Saudi Arabia.

After the big merger Colonia's headquarters were spread over 13 different locations in Cologne, making internal communication quite complicated. A symbol of the new concept of "live communication" (open and participatory management style) a DM 250 million office complex was erected for Colonia employees in December 1983. At the end of the 1980s, Colonia was one of Germany's leading all-round insurance groups including its main subsidiaries, Colonia Lebensversicherung AG (life insurance), Colonia Krankenversicherung AG (health insurance), the Colonia Bausparkasse (construction financing), and its majority shareholdings Nordstern Allgemeine Versicherungs-AG, Kölnische Rückversicherungsgesellschaft (reinsurance), and Rheinisch-Westfälische Boden-Credit-Bank (real estate financing). Private policies, auto and life insurance in particular, contributed about one-third of Colonia's premium income while fire insurance and industrial liability insurance were its most important products for businesses. Some 1,300 independent agents exclusively offering Colonia policies were supported by 85 local sales offices, 16 divisional and branch offices, traveling salespeople, part-time agents, and brokers.

International Expansion with New Partners: 1989–99

Between 1989 and 1991, major changes in the marketplace as well as from the side of its shareholders forced Colonia to adapt quickly. In its 150th anniversary year, Colonia's quiet financial backer, the Oppenheim bank, sold its majority share to the second biggest private French insurance firm, Compagnie Financiere du Groupe Victoire. Together with two other Victoire subsidiaries, the Danish Baltica and the Dutch Nieuw Rotterdam, Colonia belonged to the newly created Vinci B.V. headquartered in Utrecht, Netherlands, which ranked fifth in Europe's insurance market with about DM 19 billion.

After the two German countries were reunited, Colonia expanded into the new East German market. The first branch office was opened in Dresden in 1990, and expanded to a network of 19 branch offices, 180 sales managers, and 12 general agents by the mid-1990s. In 1990 Colonia acquired a 40 percent share in DARAG, the reinsurer for East German firms involved in international trade, refocusing the business towards insuring operational risks for large and middle-sized clients. New offices were also opened in Poland and Hungary.

A new group structure became effective in 1991. The Colonia Versicherung AG transferred its business to its wholly owned subsidiary Wikinger Lloyd Versicherungs-AG, Köln, which was renamed Colonia Versicherung AG and took over operations. The "old" Colonia Versicherung AG became the new Colonia Konzern AG and functioned as a management holding company for the whole group. Claas Kleybold succeeded Dieter Wendelstadt, the man who had freed the marketing and sales position on the management board for Kleybold in 1973, as CEO in 1991. A passionate art collector, Kleybold later developed a Colonia specialty—art insurance.

The first consolidated result of the new Colonia group was a gross premium income of DM 7.6 billion. In 1994, the abbreviation CKAG was added to Colonia's name. In the same year, the U.S. firm General Re, the world's fourth largest reinsurance firm, acquired a majority share in Colonia's reinsurance subsidiary Cologne Re in a $630 million deal, creating the world's third largest reinsurance company and strengthening Cologne Re's capital backup. In 1996, premium income of the Colonia group amounted to DM 10.8 billion, the third largest among Germany's insurers. After several changes of majority shareholders in the mid-1990s, the French Compagnie Union des Assurances de Paris (UAP) finally became Colonia's parent company in 1996 and then merged with the French AXA SA—with DM 100 billion in world sales and DM 770 billion of managed assets—in a $9 billion deal in 1997. The AXA group now held about 69 percent of Colonia's equity capital and, consequently, CKAG Colonia Konzern AG became AXA Colonia Konzern AG in 1997. As a part of one of the world's leading insurance groups, Colonia was enabled to offer its business clients comprehensive international coverage. In 1997, AXA's net profit was DM 260 million, a ten percent growth over 1996 profits.

In 1998, the AXA Colonia group founded AXA Colonia KAG and AXA Colonia Asset Management GmbH, two asset management subsidiaries with assets worth DM 35 billion, and launched a 24-hour-customer service center with about 100 employees. One of Colonia's major cases in that year was the tragic accident of the International City Express train near the German town of Eschede in June 1998. With total premium income slightly lower than in 1997, AXA Colonia predicted total sales of about 10.4 billion and an eight percent decrease of its workforce down to about 8,580 for 1998. In early 1999, AXA Colonia was working on new products such as private pension funds combined with life insurance, and planning to merge the Nordstern companies with AXA Colonia. It was also planning to take over the Hamburg-based competitor Albingia for DM 1.66 billion, depending on the approval of Albingia's British parent company Guardian Royal Exchange Plc. Albingia, the world market leader for insuring sports events with a mass audience, generated a premium income of approximately DM 2 billion in 1997. AXA Colonia also announced that Dieter Wendelstadt would retire after the annual meeting in 1999 while Claas Kleybold would resign as CEO and succeed retiring Dieter Wendelstadt as chairman of AXA Colonia's supervisory board.

Principal Subsidiaries

Colonia Versicherung AG; Colonia Bausparkasse AG (66.7%); Colonia Krankenversicherung AG (51%); Colonia Lebensversicherung AG (97.8%); Deutsche ärzteversicherung (97.8%); Nordstern Allgemeine Versicherungs-AG (97%); General Re-CKAG Reinsurance and Investment S.a.r.l. (Luxembourg; 49%); Sicher Direct (50%); RBS Beratungs- und Servicegesellschaft für die Vermittlung von Finanzdienstleistungen mbH.

Further Reading

"Der Außenseiter," *Capital,* October 1975.
Brennan, Eilis, "Insurance Sector Spree Reaches $9bn," *European,* October 21, 1994, p. 25.
"Claas Kleybold 60," *Börsen-Zeitung,* September 3, 1997.
"Claas Kleybold 60 Jahre," *Frankfurter Allgemeine Zeitung,* September 3, 1997.
"Company Profile," Cologne: AXA Colonia Konzern AG, 1998.
Die Colonia von 1989 bis 1992, Cologne: Colonia Konzern AG, 1992, 3 p.
"Dieter Wendelstadt 60 Jahre," *Börsen-Zeitung,* December 12, 1989.
"France's Axa SA to Take Over UAP in Stock Swap," *Minneapolis Star Tribune,* November 13, 1996, p. 3D.
"Gen Re Deal with Colonia a 'Home Run'," *National Underwriter,* July 11, 1994 p. 3.
"Der harte Graf," *Capital,* June 1976.
Looking Back to the Future—150 Years of Colonia Versicherung AG, Cologne: Colonia Versicherung AG, 1989, 78 p.
"The Insurance Industry Is in Trouble," *Economist,* January 16–22, 1999.

—Evelyn Hauser

Ballantyne of Omaha, Inc.

4350 McKinley Street
Omaha, Nebraska 68123
U.S.A.
(402) 453-4444
(800) 424-1215
Fax: (402) 453-7238
Web site: http://www.ballantyne-omaha.com

Public Company
Incorporated: 1995
Employees: 298
Sales: $75 million (1998)
Stock Exchanges: New York
Ticker Symbol: BTN
SICs: 3861 Motion Picture Equipment & Suppliers; 3589
    Service Industry Machinery; 5046 Restaurant
    Equipment & Supplies; 5099 Exporters; 7923
    Theatrical Equipment & Supplies

Ballantyne of Omaha, Inc. is a leading developer, manufacturer, and distributor of commercial motion picture equipment and long-range follow spotlights in the United States and abroad. The company's product lines are distributed on a worldwide basis through a network of more than 200 domestic and international dealers to major movie exhibitors, ride simulation operators, and sports arena and amusement park operators. The company's broad range of both standard and custom-made equipment can completely outfit and automate a motion picture projection booth and is currently being used by major motion picture exhibitors such as AMC Entertainment, Regal Cinemas, Act III Theaters, Cinemark USA, and Cineplex Odeon. The company also manufactures commercial food service equipment, which is sold to convenience store and fast food restaurant operators and to equipment suppliers for resale on a private label basis.

The Early Years

Robert Scott Ballantyne of Hartington, Nebraska, founded the Scott-Ballantyne Company in Omaha in 1932. Ballantyne, who had two decades of experience working at film corporations and managing movie theaters, devoted his motion picture theater supply house to manufacturing sound and air conditioning equipment. By 1938 the Scott-Ballantyne Company was marketing its own 35mm projector, similar to the industry standard Simplex, and shortly thereafter it joined forces with Largen Manufacturing, another Nebraska business, to market and later manufacture the Largen line of amplifiers and soundheads and two lines of light houses. That year, Ballantyne moved his operation to Omaha's "film row," a street housing many of the city's motion picture businesses.

During WWII almost all of Ballantyne's production was taken up by the armed forces, but by war's end the young company was positioned to take advantage of the new postwar rage: the drive-in theater. By 1949 Ballantyne had equipped 282 of the 846 drive-ins then operating in the United States with speakers, and by 1952 Scott-Ballantyne was selling everything needed to assemble a drive-in theater: speakers, projectors, amplifiers, pole-mounted junction boxes, and premanufactured screen towers. At the same time, the company positioned itself to keep pace with new developments in improved indoor sound by manufacturing its Royal Soundmaster systems, which utilized four- and six-channel amplifiers. In the early 1960s, in an effort to capture a portion of the concession business that accompanied drive-ins, Scott-Ballantyne expanded its scope of operations to include the manufacture of pressure fryers. These were followed by production of rotisserie and barbecue ovens.

From Drive-In to Multiplex: 1960s–80s

When Robert Ballantyne retired in 1960, he sold his company to ABC Vending Corporation of New York. ABC renamed the company Ballantyne Instruments and Electronics and sold it seven years later to Ogden Corporation. In 1970 Ogden sold Ballantyne again, this time to a group of investors headed by Ballantyne's former managers. The company, now Ballantyne of Omaha, moved back to Nebraska, and with drive-in theaters on the wane, it introduced the Pro-35 projector, the first new American-made projector in 25 years. This equipment became increasingly popular with the "special venue" market found in museums and theme parks, such as Epcot

Company Perspectives:

Ballantyne believes that its position as a fully-integrated equipment manufacturer enables it to be more responsive to its customers' specific design requirements, thereby giving it a competitive advantage over other manufacturers who rely more on outsourcing components. In addition, the company believes its expertise in engineering, manufacturing, prompt order fulfillment, delivery, after-sale technical support and emergency service have allowed the company to build and maintain strong customer relationships.

Center, Universal Studios, and the simulation rides offered by Imax and the Iwerks Group.

The company changed hands again in 1976, this time when Canrad-Hanovia of New Jersey, a diversified manufacturer, purchased the business for $1 million. A short while earlier, Canrad had acquired the Toledo-based Strong Electric, known for its movie projector lamphouses and for setting the industry standard for arenas, stadiums, large theaters, and auditoriums in the 1950s with its Super Trouper, a carbon arc spot, and, in the 1970s, with its xenon-bulb Super Trouper. Canrad appointed Ronald Echtenkamp, a native Nebraskan and longtime Ballantyne employee, to be the company's president and chief operating officer in 1981. In the mid-1980s Canrad merged Strong into Ballantyne's operations in Omaha and created Strong International.

Echtenkamp positioned the company ideally to take advantage of the boom in the moving theater industry as the multiplex theater got under way. In 1982, with Ballantyne's sales stalled at $7 million because of the decline in the drive-in industry, he bought the then-floundering Simplex Projection Company for $800,000, the cost of its inventory and accounts receivable in 1983. His vision and timing could not have been better. From 1983 to 1987, the number of screens in the United States went from 18,000 to 23,500, and sales of the sturdy Simplex doubled, while those of the original Ballantyne projectors increased as well. The trend toward multiplexing began to accelerate internationally at about the same time, prompting Ballantyne to look overseas to develop its market in the early 1990s.

Despite good prospects for continued growth, however, and with Ballantyne's sales at a little more than $10 million, in 1988 Canrad decided to unload Ballantyne. ARC International Corporation, a Toronto builder of ice-skating rinks and manufacturer of products for cable television and telecommunications—satellite dishes, coaxial cables, electronic equipment, and ultraviolet lamps—headed by chairman Arnold Tenney, stepped in and purchased Ballantyne for $12 million in a leveraged buyout, reducing its debt by selling off Canrad's other assets. Soon afterward, when Ballantyne outgrew its manufacturing plant, ARC went further into debt to buy a 140,000-square-foot factory in north Omaha that by 1989 housed Simplex, Ballantyne, and Strong.

The company now consisted of three divisions—Strong International spotlight, Flavor-Crisp restaurant division, and

Strong International cinema—which experienced steady growth during the next several years. AMC, Cineplex Odeon, Cinemark USA, and Regal Cinemas all purchased standard projectors from Ballantyne, and Disney, Universal Studios, Imax, and Iwerks purchased specialized, custom-made equipment. Sales went from $16 million in 1989 to $29 million in 1994 by which time the company employed around 200 employees. With Strong and Ballantyne companies under one roof, Ballantyne technicians began to assemble, wire, and test units in-house before shipping them to theaters, an innovation that saved new or renovating theaters the trouble of assembling projector assemblies on site.

Strategic Acquisitions in the Early to Mid-1990s

Beginning in the early 1990s, Ballantyne undertook to broaden its sales base and clinch control of the projector market, while also looking for strategic acquisitions in the restaurant and spotlight industries. Sales in the latter two markets accounted for 7.8 percent and 6.5 percent of Ballantyne's revenues, respectively. In March 1993, Tenney, chairman of the company, and Echtenkamp purchased the ailing cinema products division of Optical Radiation Corporation, manufacturer of the Century projector, a Simplex competitor. This acquisition gave Ballantyne control of about 65 percent of the movie projector market in the United States. In 1994 the company also acquired the Hong Kong firm of Litton-Westrex and renamed it Strong Westrex, to assist in the sales, service, and shipping of cinema and spotlight equipment to its customers in Hong Kong, mainland China, and Taiwan. This move enabled expansion of Ballantyne's services into Malaysia, Japan, and other parts of Asia.

In September 1995 Ballantyne went public, raising $7.8 million to pay off ARC's accumulated debt with the sale of 35 percent of the company, or 1.2 million shares of common stock. The company's initial share price was set at about $7, but by the end of 1996, shares had risen to $19.87, quadrupling in value sometime in 1997, before settling down again in July at $22.50. During this period ARC lowered its holdings in Ballantyne from 50 to 23 percent, thereby raising fresh capital to pursue its main business and broaden its investor base.

At the same time, the demand for Ballantyne's projection equipment reached an all-time high in 1997 with sales of projection booths rising from 1,500 in 1995 to 2,140 in 1996 to 2,500 in 1997. Thus surge was accompanied by an increase in the nation's screen count to 29,731 at the end of 1996, up 30 percent since 1990. Revenues for the company were $70 million in 1997—up from $51.7 million in 1996—89 percent of which came from the company's theater division. The company responded to this increase by expanding its Omaha plant, adding a $1.5 million, 21,000-square-foot addition to its manufacturing facility to help speed production and relieve the pressure of cramped working areas.

Related Markets in the Middle to Late 1990s

Echtenkamp, now vice-chairman of the board, also elected to initiate a strategy of aggressive expansion into the entertainment lighting business in 1997. This strategy had a dual rationale. Strong spotlights were already in use in numerous sports venues, including Chicago's United Center and the Toronto Skydome; they were taken on tour by the Rolling Stones and

Pink Floyd and accounted for about 85 percent of the follow spot market in the United States in 1995. Yet Ballantyne's share of light sales had reached only $5.4 million in 1997 and, although this figure represented an annual doubling of revenues since 1995, Echtenkamp reasoned that it could go much higher with a larger segment of the industry under Ballantyne's control. Then, too, the motion picture theater industry had experienced increasing competition from in-home sources of entertainment and, whereas the multiplex market showed no signs of abatement, according to the National Association of Theater Owners, some analysts believed that the domestic market for new projectors was nearly saturated. Even factoring in the as yet untapped European and Asian multiplex markets, Ballantyne recognized that growth in the production of projectors could not be limitless.

The first phase of the acquisition strategy initiated by Echtenkamp occurred with the 1997 acquisition of Xenotech, a California-based manufacturer and distributor of high-intensity searchlights and lighting systems. The rationale behind this purchase was to build Xenotech's share of the entertainment lighting market by leveraging Ballantyne's capital resources. Previously outsourced components began to be manufactured at Ballantyne's expanded plant, and the Hong Kong-based Westrex subsidiary was assigned the role of increasing Xenotech's equipment sales and rental business to a full-service, global distribution network. Later in 1997, Ballantyne opened its Seattle Xenotech office and also added Skytracker of America to its Xenotech operation. Skytracker was a manufacturer of single- and multiple-head xenon searchlights, such as those used to attract customers to business locations such as car dealerships. In 1998 the Xenotech-Strong division of Ballantyne launched a new business unit, Nocturn, focusing on ultraviolet effects for entertainment and architectural applications.

At about the same time that Ballantyne was expanding through acquisitions, it increasingly began to focus its theater supply sales on overseas markets. In the United States in the late 1990s, there was one screen for every 9,800 people, in Germany there was one screen per 17,700 people, and in Mexico there was one screen per 61,000 people. AMC opened a 13-screen theater in Japan in 1996, and Cinemark USA built 92 screens in Mexico in a period of two years in the mid-1990s. According to a U.K.-based media market research firm that year, Europe's screen count would increase by approximately 2,000 through the year 2000. Ballantyne's net sales to foreign customers had increased from $11.3 million in 1995 to $18.5 million in 1997, representing about 27 percent of Ballantyne's sales abroad, and Echtenkamp projected that by 2001, 40 percent of the company's theater revenues would come from abroad.

New Technology: Late 1990s and Beyond

The company also sought to protect its future by diversifying into new realms. Ballantyne management expected film projec-

tors to remain the film-delivery method of choice until at least the end of the first decade of the 21st century; in 1998, however, they entered into an agreement with MegaSystems of Wayne, Pennsylvania to manufacture a 3D large-format projection system to be distributed by Megasystems. In 1998 Ballantyne acquired Design and Manufacturing, an Illinois-based supplier of film platter systems with 16,000 units then in use in movie theaters throughout the world. Ballantyne had been Design and Manufacturing's largest customer and the acquisition was intended to reduce costs and increase efficiency in the projection system assembly process. Ballantyne also began to develop theater automation systems, capable of connecting to a desktop or laptop computer, that enabled remote control of a cinema megaplex. And the Simplex was updated as the Simplex Millenium with LED framing illumination and other improvements.

Although the company had a leading position in the domestic motion picture projection equipment market by the end of 1998, with a 56 percent gain in profits on a 36 percent rise in sales, both the domestic and international markets for its products were highly competitive, with competition coming chiefly from Cinemeccanica S.p.A., an Italian privately held company, and from the domestic Christie Electric. The markets for its long-range follow spotlight and other illumination and restaurant products were also highly competitive, leading Ballantyne to capitalize on its ability as an integrated manufacturer of customized products to seek to become the leading provider of state-of-the-art special venue products. Yet Ballantyne remained optimistic about its future at the close of the 1990s, as evidenced by its late-1998 decision to repurchase up to ten percent of its outstanding common stock. It competed and planned to continue to compete primarily on the basis of the quality, prompt delivery, price, and product customization of its goods and the after-sale technical support it provided.

Principal Divisions

Ballantyne Fabricators, Inc.; Flavor-Crisp of America, Inc.; Strong-Westrex, Inc.; Xenotech Rental Corp.

Further Reading

Helliker, Kevin, ''Far from Hollywood, a Film Veteran Shines,'' *The Houston Chronicle,* March 1, 1998, p. 12.
Hendee, David, ''Analyst Expects Dip in Retail Beef Price,'' *Omaha World Herald,* February 2, 1997, p. 1B.
Kelley, Matt, ''Ballantyne Finally Steps Out from Behind Its Spotlights,'' *Omaha World Herald,* October 9, 1995, p. 12.
Spiegel, Peter, ''Prairie Moguls,'' *Forbes,* May 6, 1996, p. 64.
Sterngold, James, ''For a Projector Maker, Multiplexes Are a Ticket to Growth,'' *The New York Times,* August 31, 1997, p. 3.

—Carrie Rothburd

Bernard Chaus, Inc.

1410 Broadway
New York, New York 10018
U.S.A.
(212) 354-1280
Fax: (212) 921-4619

Public Company
Incorporated: 1975
Employees: 334
Sales: $191.5 million (1998)
Stock Exchanges: New York
Ticker Symbol: CHS
SICs: 2331 Women's, Misses' & Juniors' Blouses &
   Shirts; 2337 Women's, Misses' & Juniors' Suits,
   Skirts & Coats; 2339 Women's, Misses' & Juniors'
   Outerwear, Not Elsewhere Classified; 5621 Women's
   Clothing Stores

Bernard Chaus, Inc. designs and markets an extensive range of women's career and casual sportswear at the high end of the "upper moderate" price range. This clothing is marketed as coordinated groups of jackets, skirts, pants, blouses, sweaters, and related accessories that, while sold as separates, are coordinated by styles, color schemes, and fabrics, and are designed to be merchandised and worn together. The company's products are sold by department store chains, specialty retailers, and other retail outlets.

Garment District Dynamo: 1945–85

A track star at Boys' High School in Brooklyn, Bernard Chaus dropped out in his junior year and sought a job with Henry Rosenfeld, a legendary figure in New York City's garment district. Rosenfeld wanted salesmen who were college graduates and more than six feet tall. "Since I was neither," Chaus recalled, "I had to talk myself into a job in the shipping department. Within two years I was his assistant." It was the beginning of a lucrative career for the supersalesman whom a *Bobbin* columnist later called "part Jackie Mason, part Charlie Chaplin, part Ebeneezer Scrooge and part P.T. Barnum."

Chaus became part-owner of Major Blouse Co. in 1958 at the age of 29, taking annual sales, he said, from $1 million to $5 million in three years. After the business was purchased by Genesco, Inc., in 1965, Chaus sold the Genesco stock he received and retired. A year later he became a partner of Joanna Blouse Co. According to Chaus, he took the company's sales up to $3 million within two years. After the firm was acquired by Lilly Lynn five years later, Chaus once again cashed in his profit and departed.

Josephine Ferraro was a 22-year-old buyer for a New Jersey store when she met the 44-year-old Chaus in 1973. After a year traveling together cross-country by motorcycle, they became partners of newly founded Bernard Chaus, Inc. in 1975. She became his second wife shortly after. Although she bore two children, she remained active in the firm, first as director of design and later of production as well, and she was named president in 1980. Otherwise Chaus essentially presided over his eponymous firm as a one-man band, with no secretary, marketing director, advertising agency, or showrooms outside Manhattan. To sell his company's sportswear he cultivated store buyers. "Bernie started from nothing and built relationships," a former company executive told a reporter in 1991. "Eventually the people he dealt with became heads of the store."

The fledgling firm built its collection around the concept that working women wanted colorful, moderately priced separate articles that could be easily coordinated with a fashion flair. Its founder pioneered the practice of selling moderately priced sportswear on the main floors of department stores as an impulse purchase. The Chauses, according to a 1986 *Forbes* piece, "quietly have built a loyal following among conservatively dressed working women who would rather not spend $150 on a blouse." By the end of 1982 (the year ended June 30, 1982) the firm's sales had reached $91.2 million and its net income was $6.9 million, even though it did no advertising in print or on television except for a minor amount of so-called cooperative ads in which the costs were shared with retailers. All manufacturing was being performed by suppliers in the Far East.

The Founder's Last Years: 1986–91

After net income of $12.9 million on sales of $155.3 million in 1984, Bernard Chaus fell slightly into the red the next year because one of its biggest accounts, R.H. Macy & Co., dropped Chaus's line of blouses and sportswear, largely in favor of its own private brands. But the company had record net income of $35.3 million in 1986 on record net sales of $278.8 million. That summer Bernard Chaus went public, netting $95.7 million by selling stock at $17 a share. The Chauses received $86.4 million of that total and still retained 62 percent of the firm. Now the envy of the garment district, Bernard Chaus's founder fielded a stable of thoroughbred racehorses, went on fishing trips ranging from Alaska to Argentina, and became a collector of modern art. When not in their renovated Upper East Side townhouse, the couple relaxed on a working Connecticut farm they purchased. They also were active in philanthropic pursuits.

The Chauses' good fortune would not last long, however. In 1987 sales reached a record $333.9 million, but net income slipped to $13.3 million. Then the firm lost money in 1988 and 1989—$10.9 million in 1988 alone. Bernard Chaus blamed his company's problems primarily on having raised prices higher than the market would bear, but his wife also pleaded guilty to leaving "the design direction of the company to others without giving them the focus they needed." The couple's response was to cut costs, trimming staff by 30 percent, shipping goods from the Orient primarily by sea rather than air, and closing all four of the company's retail outlets. The Chauses also delegated more day-to-day responsibilities to other executives, hired additional designers—overseen by Josephine Chaus—and conducted marketing research to better determine the needs of the company's customers.

Bernard Chaus raised its sales in 1990 and ended the year with a net profit of $1.5 million. During this period 90 percent of its merchandise was being sold to between 50 and 65 major department stores. Macy's was again a big buyer, taking about $40 million of Chaus's goods annually, but in 1990 the department store dropped the firm's goods after one of the founder's horses threw the wife of Macy's chairman during a weekend visit. In addition, other department store bankruptcies in this recessionary period limited the number of outlets for the firm's apparel.

Neither husband nor wife had allowed their fortune to lessen their motivation or work habits. When not overseeing the company's six contiguous floors of showroom and office space in Manhattan, Bernard Chaus was, according to a 1989 *Women's Wear Daily* story, often on the road, conducting seminars, visiting store managers, or traveling to the Far East, where four offices were established to monitor the firm's suppliers. This was not the full story, however, for Chaus's founder had been stricken with cancer. Shortly after he died in May 1991, the company ended its fiscal year with a $12 million loss on sharply lower sales of $232.4 million. His widow was forced to extend the firm a $10 million loan from her own resources to keep bankers from canceling its credit lines after long-term debt reached a record $24.7 million.

Drowning in Red Ink: 1992–97

One of Josephine Chaus's first decisions was to stimulate sales by lowering prices. This became feasible by consolidating manufacturing into fewer plants and shifting some of it to lower-cost factories in Central America. She added sporty weekend apparel to the career-oriented blouses, skirts, and jackets and emphasized the firm's clothing as a collection rather than separates to be mixed and matched with other lines. Bernard Chaus also began to open retail stores and regained Macy's as a customer following the departure of its chairman. In her first full year at the helm—fiscal 1992—sales rose to $254.2 million, and the company registered a net profit of $5.5 million. The number of retail stores reached a peak of 36 in 1994.

Bernard Chaus, Inc.'s resurgence did not last long. The company's sales fell to $235.8 million in 1993, and it registered an $11 million loss. Results were even worse in 1994, with sales sliding to $206.3 million and a loss of $46.8 million, which included write-offs and restructuring costs. In September 1994 Andrew Grossman left the presidency of rival Jones Apparel Group Inc.—a struggling company he had helped turn around—to become president and chief executive officer of Bernard Chaus. Josephine Chaus, who remained chairwoman, extended the firm $3 million in credit in early 1994 and another $14.4 million in September of that year, of which an unprecedented $6.2 million went to Grossman as a signing bonus.

Besides hiring Grossman, who was considered one of the garment district's brightest stars, Josephine Chaus recruited a highly regarded chief financial officer to pare expenses through consolidation and layoffs and persuaded the firm's banks to waive covenants on its $60 million credit line. "She's a champ," said a securities analyst. "Most people in the world would go bankrupt and start again. She keeps plugging." He added that she had "kept the Chaus name relatively clean" by not selling to chains and discount stores.

Grossman's strategy for Bernard Chaus was to return the company's merchandise to the upper-moderate price range with a new strategy emphasizing fashion-forward looks. "We want to be current with fashion, just like the better and designer lines," he told stockholders at the company's annual meeting in November 1994. "We don't want to chase it, as we had in the past, but be a leader." However, in 1995 sales fell again to $181.7 million, and the company, despite having cut operating costs and raised gross margin, incurred a loss of $27.9 million.

In September 1995 Bernard Chaus attempted to turn its fortunes by signing a licensing deal with Nautica Apparel, Inc. to manufacture and market apparel for women under the Nautica label, which had previously only been for menswear. David Chu, president and designer of Nautica Enterprises, the parent company, was to design the line. Under the agreement, Bernard Chaus had to raise at least $10 million in equity capital by the end of the year and devote at least $7 million to fulfill obligations, including minimum royalty and advertising payments and the construction of a separate showroom for the display of licensed Nautica products. The company raised $15 million, before underwriting costs, in November 1995 by selling five million shares of common stock at $3 a share.

Bernard Chaus's bestsellers at Macy's in-store shops during the spring of 1996 included rayon and silk blouses, two-piece dressing, linen, and viscose jackets, knit cardigans, and linen-blend pants. Grossman's plans to move the company's apparel upscale were said to have backfired, however. A *Women's Wear Daily* article said that, according to retail executives, without a suitable home in many stores the merchandise was rejected by traditional customers, who were puzzled by its dramatically updated fashions, such as plaid slip-dresses and retro Forties dresses. Bernard Chaus subsequently dropped its money-losing dress division. Company sales again fell in 1996, to $170.6 million, and it incurred a net loss of $24.4 million.

Bernard Chaus unveiled its Nautica line of apparel in August 1996. Marketed in 120 in-store shops, Nautica's sportswear included coordinating knits, blouses, wovens, sweaters, pants, skirts, jackets, outerwear, and sportswear dresses. The results were disappointing, with only $24 million in sales during 1997. Company sales declined again in the year, to $160.1 million, although its net loss narrowed to $16.5 million. In November Bernard Chaus announced that it would close all of its 22 outlet stores except the one adjacent to its warehouse in Secaucus, New Jersey.

In order to obtain new financing to replace an expiring credit line of $72 million, Josephine Chaus agreed to provide $12.5 million in cash collateral to pay off a loan extended by BNY Financial Corp. She also agreed to spend up to $12.5 million buying company stock in a new rights offering to existing stockholders enabling them to buy 10 million shares at $1.43 each. This rights offering, effective January 1997, was part of an overall debt structuring that converted $40.6 million owed by the firm to Josephine Chaus into stock, established a new $81-million bank line, and created a 1-for-10 reverse stock split. The offering, which raised $20 million in new equity capital, half from Josephine Chaus, was oversubscribed by $8.2 million. As a result of these actions, her stake in the company grew from 51.3 to 69.5 percent. Bernard Chaus's long-term debt was $13.5 million at the end of 1998.

Turnaround in 1998

In September 1998 Bernard Chaus reported its first annual profit since 1992, earning $4.3 million on sales of $191.5 million—up almost 20 percent from the previous year and 36 percent when taking into consideration the phase-out of the retail stores. Grossman said that robust gains in the Chaus line had offset continuing weakness in the licensed Nautica line. He added that soft dressing looks in general and long skirts and long jackets in particular had been key sellers for the firm.

The Nautica line was relaunched in 1997 with a narrower focus on casual but higher-priced sportswear. Sales fell to $15.3 million, however, in 1998, and Bernard Chaus announced it was in discussions to terminate the license, which was not due to expire until the end of 1999. Lynn Buechner, formerly vice-president of sales for the Liz Claiborne Collection, was hired in October 1997 to manage the Nautica line. She was the designer of the Nautica apparel presented by Bernard Chaus for the fall of 1998.

Bernard Chaus's products, at the end of 1998, were being sold under the brand names Chaus, Chaus Woman, Chaus Petite, and Nautica, with suggested retail prices ranging from $24 to $280. Career sportswear accounted for 61 percent of sales and weekend casual for the remaining 39 percent. The leading brand was Chaus, followed by Chaus Sport, Chaus Woman, Chaus Petite, and Nautica.

These goods were being sold nationwide to an estimated 1,800 individual stores operated by about 160 department store chains, specialty retailers, and other retail outlets. During the year about 82 percent of the company's net sales were made to department store customers owned by four single corporate entities. Sales to Dillard's accounted for 43 percent and sales to nine department store companies owned by The May Department Stores Company for 29 percent. Eighty percent of Bernard Chaus's products were being manufactured by 35 Far East suppliers, with the remainder manufactured in the United States and the Caribbean. The company continued to maintain corporate headquarters and a showroom in Manhattan's garment district and a warehouse and retail store in Secaucus, New Jersey. It was also leasing offices in Hong Kong and South Korea.

Principal Subsidiaries

Bernard Chaus International (Hong Kong), Inc.; Bernard Chaus International (Korea), Inc.; Bernard Chaus International (Philippines), Inc.; Bernard Chaus International (Taiwan), Inc.; Chaus Retail, Inc.; Chaus Specialists, Inc.

Further Reading

Agins, Teri, "U.S. Apparel Makers Feeling Pinched," *Wall Street Journal,* August 3, 1988, p. 22.

"Bernard Chaus, 62, Innovative in Selling Women's Sportswear," *New York Times,* June 1, 1991, p. 34.

D'Innocenzio, Anne, "Andrew Grossman Quits Jones Apparel for Chaus CEO Slot," *Women's Wear Daily,* December 7, 1994, pp. 1, 5.

——, "Chaus Seeks New Line at Upper-Moderate End," *Women's Wear Daily,* November 23, 1994, p. 3.

D'Innocenzio, Anne, and Seckler, Valerie, "New Hurdles for Chaus Revival," *WWD/Women's Wear Daily,* June 12, 1996, p. 12.

Feitelberg, Rosemary, "Chaus to Make Nautica Women's Line," *WWD/Women's Wear Daily,* September 8, 1995, pp. 2, 15.

Furman, Phyllis, "Ailing Chaus Pens New Chapter with Fresh Fashions, Leaders," *Crain's New York Business,* November 21, 1994, p. 16.

——, "Can Chaus' Widow Rally Apparel Maker,?" *Crain's New York Business,* October 28, 1991, pp. 3, 42.

Gault, Ylonda, "Can New Nautica Line Be Lifesaver for Chaus?," *Crain's New York Business,* March 4, 1996, pp. 3, 34.

Hartlein, Robert, "Bernard Chaus Deceased at 62," *Women's Wear Daily,* June 3, 1991, pp. 2, 10.

——, "Bounces Back," *Women's Wear Daily,* October 4, 1989, Sportswear Supplement, p. S16.

——, "Chaus Poised for a Better '89," *Women's Wear Daily,* May 17, 1989, pp. 10–11.

"Josephine Chaus Opens Wallet Again to Ease Firm's Losses," *Women's Wear Daily,* September 26, 1994, pp. 1, 31.

Millstein, Alan G., "The Teams at the Top," *Bobbin,* October 1989, pp. 38, 40, 42, 44.

Oppenheim, Charles, "Low-Key," *Forbes,* August 11, 1986, p. 113.

Ryan, Thomas J., "Chaus Has 1st Profit Since '92," *WWD/Women's Wear Daily,* September 3, 1998, p. 12.

——, "Chaus Shrinks Loss, Gets $81M Financing," *WWD/Women's Wear Daily,* October 20, 1997, p. 4.

Strom, Stephanie, "A Survivor for Seventh Ave.," *New York Times,* March 7, 1993, p. 12.

—Robert Halasz

Bethlehem Steel Corporation

1170 Eighth Avenue
Bethlehem, Pennsylvania 18016-7699
U.S.A.
(610) 694-2424
Fax: (610) 694-6920
Web site: http://www.bethsteel.com

Public Company
Incorporated: 1904
Employees: 15,600
Sales: $4.63 billion (1997)
Stock Exchanges: New York
Ticker Symbol: BS
SICs: 3312 Blast Furnaces & Steel Mills; 3731 Ship
Building & Repairing; 3443 Fabricated Plate Work-
Boiler Shops; 3317 Steel Pipe & Tubes

Bethlehem Steel Corporation is the second largest steel producer in the United States, with control of supply sources, production, and distribution, from raw materials to a wide variety of steel mill products. Also a long-time repairer of ships and offshore drilling platform businesses and manufacturer of forgings and castings, Bethlehem had curtailed many of these activities during the late 1990s. The company is the nation's number one supplier of steel to the domestic construction industry, as well as a major supplier for railroads and automobile companies. It manufactures almost ten million tons of steel annually, a tenth of the nation's supply.

Early Years of Rapid Growth

The company began operations in 1857 as the Saucona Iron Company in South Bethlehem, Pennsylvania. Its primary business was the rolling of iron railroad rails. In 1899, after broadening the product line to include heavy forging for electric generators, tool steels for metal cutting, and armor plate for U.S. Navy ships, the company's name was changed to the Bethlehem Steel Company.

Bethlehem Steel was incorporated in December 1904 by Charles M. Schwab, a former Andrew Carnegie disciple and first president of United States Steel Corporation (U.S. Steel). Schwab left U.S. Steel over difficulties that he felt inhibited his freedom to run that company properly. At its incorporation the company included Bethlehem Steel, a Cuban iron ore mine, and several shipbuilding concerns in California and Delaware. Schwab became president and chairman of the board.

Soon after the formation of the company, Schwab hired an electrical engineer, Eugene G. Grace, whose management skills allowed the more entrepreneurial Schwab the freedom he needed to plan the growth of the company. Together, the two men became the team that built Bethlehem from a small producer with an ingot capacity of less that one percent of the national total in 1905 to the world's second-largest producer in fewer than 35 years.

In 1908 the two men staked the company's future on a new type of mill invented by Henry Grey. It was capable of rolling a wide flange structural steel section that was stronger, lighter, and less expensive than the fabricated steel sections that were being used at the time. The gamble paid off for Bethlehem. The wide-flange section made it possible to build skyscrapers and modern cities.

In the years preceding World War I, the company acquired an interest in a Chilean iron ore mine with ore of a higher quality than available from the U.S. upper Great Lakes region. As a result of the acquisition, the company built a fleet of ore carriers and entered the ocean transportation business. With the outbreak of the war, Bethlehem became a business of international scope, building warships for Great Britain at the company's shipyards. Bethlehem also filled orders for guns and munitions, armor, and ordnance placed by the British, French, and Russian governments. In the process of contributing to the Allied cause in Europe, Bethlehem created a financial base that would help in expanding the company's steelmaking facilities.

Grace was named president of the company in 1916, with Schwab staying on as chairman of the board. In that same year, bolstered by wartime profits, Bethlehem acquired American Iron and Steel Manufacturing Company, Pennsylvania Steel

Company, and Maryland Steel Company. In the years following World War I, the company continued its growth with the acquisition of Lackawanna Steel & Ordnance Company, Midvale Steel and Ordnance Company, and Cambria Steel Company. In the years preceding the Great Depression, the company boosted its steelmaking capacity to 8.5 million tons and employed more than 60,000 people.

Bethlehem's growth was tied to an incentive program from which its upper management profited handsomely. In 1929 Grace received a bonus in excess of $1.6 million, or about 3.3 percent of earnings. The policy of paying out such large awards to its executives eventually caused problems. In early 1931 a group of stockholders filed suit against Schwab and 12 other officers of the company, charging that the bonus program constituted a misuse of company funds. The suit asked that a total of $36 million in bonuses distributed since 1911 be returned to the company's coffers. The action resulted in the formation of the Protective Committee for Stockholders of Bethlehem Steel Corporation, a watchdog group that sought the elimination of the bonus program in its existing form. Though no funds were returned to the company, the suit was settled in July 1931, about six months after it was filed. The settlement resulted in a new policy that included the publication of executive bonuses in the company's annual reports and a revised executive salary and bonus package. In subsequent years labor unions used the bonus issue in their demands for higher compensation and benefits for the rank-and-file steelworkers.

Depression Struggles and Wartime Demand

The 1920s were years of growth for Bethlehem. In the early years of the Great Depression, the company weathered the economic storm and continued to improve its production plants and introduce new products. The Depression caught up with Bethlehem in September 1931 when the company posted a quarterly loss for the first time since 1909. In the face of a stagnant economy and an eroding demand for steel products, the company had overexpanded and was forced to shut down many of its facilities, including a newly constructed, jumbo-sized open hearth at the Sparrows Point, Maryland, plant. Bethlehem, along with other major steel producers, struggled through the Depression. Help arrived with President Franklin D. Roosevelt's New Deal and the National Industrial Recovery Act of 1933. The government suspended antitrust laws, and the steel industry established codes approved by the National Recovery Administration providing for labor reform, workers rights to organize, minimum wages, and maximum work hours. In December 1933 Bethlehem reported a modest net profit in excess of $600,000 after nine quarters totaling more than $30 million in losses.

During the 1930s Bethlehem acquired steelmaking plants in Los Angeles and San Francisco, California, and Seattle, Washington. McClintic-Marshall, a large fabricator and builder of bridges, was also purchased, enabling Bethlehem to participate in the construction of San Francisco's Golden Gate Bridge. Through this subsidiary, Bethlehem was also involved in the construction of other large bridges and notable buildings, including Rockefeller Plaza and the Waldorf Astoria Hotel in New York City; the Chicago Merchandise Mart; and the U.S. Supreme Court Building in Washington, D.C.

During the mid-1930s Bethlehem went through an expensive retooling. With the largest capital expenditure since before the Depression, the company spent approximately $20 million on the construction of a continuous strip and tin-plate mill at Sparrows Point. A primary reason for the new project was beer. After six years of research and development, the American Can Company had produced a coated tin can suitable for packaging beer, and the tin-plate market exploded.

Schwab died in September 1939, leaving Bethlehem under the tight controls of Grace. With U.S. involvement in World War II imminent, Grace geared the company's entire capacity toward war production. Furnaces, shops, and mills worked around the clock producing armor plate for ships and structural steel for defense plants, munitions, and aircraft engines. Between 1941 and 1944 Grace pushed production at Bethlehem to 101 percent of usual capacity. During the war, the company's 15 shipyards produced more than 1,100 ships, including aircraft carriers, destroyers, heavy cruisers, and cargo ships. In 1943 alone the company built 380 vessels.

During World War II, from 1940 to 1945, Bethlehem produced more than 73 million tons of steel. This total represented almost one-third of the armor plate and gun forgings used by the United States in the war. Prior to the U.S. entrance into the war, the company's gross sales were $135 million. In 1945 sales topped $1.33 billion, with more than 300,000 employees. Bethlehem became a global giant in the steel industry. In December 1945, six years after the death of Schwab, Grace was elected the company's chairman. Arthur B. Homer, director of the Bethlehem's wartime ship building program, became president.

Expansion through Early 1970s

With the war's end, the global demand for steel was even greater than during the conflict. Consumer demands for new cars and household goods, along with the massive amounts of structural steel needed to rebuild war-torn economies, resulted in further expansion. Bethlehem built new furnaces and mills at many of its plants and by the late 1950s was capable of producing 23 million tons of steel annually. The nature of the company's shipbuilding business began to change as Bethlehem produced larger, longer cargo ships. Forerunners to supertankers, the new ships produced by Bethlehem cost less per unit, carried more tonnage, and were able to cruise at speeds 30 percent faster than their prewar predecessors. More iron ore was delivered in less time. In 1957, Bethlehem's peak postwar production year, the company made more than 19 million tons of steel and earned $190 million on sales of $2.6 billion. At the close of the decade, Bethlehem's full-time postwar employee roster stood at 165,000.

In 1960 the United States imported more steel than it exported for the first time in the U.S. steel industry's history. This situation was a harbinger of things to come. The deterioration of Bethlehem's enterprises, as well as those of other U.S. steel manufacturers, can be traced to several major factors. High wages, foreign competition, and the enormous costs of environmental clean-up of the lands and waters around the company's many production plants cut deeply into the company's profits and cash reserves. In addition, decades of unlimited growth, expansion, and profits had made Bethlehem's leadership complacent. Antitrust and price fixing suits against several U.S. steel giants including Bethlehem followed. Throughout the 1960s and 1970s, company leaders believed that procedures could continue as they had been for over a half century without change in processes or structure.

Bethlehem's leaders did not engage in product research, innovation, or reorganization. The company, like its competitors, relied on continual price increases to protect profits. These policies allowed opportunities for entrance into the U.S. market by Japanese and other foreign steelmakers, who rebuilt their steel industries after World War II and captured the competitive edge worldwide. This new competition, a shrinking domestic market, and the expansion of steel substitutes such as aluminum and plastics, created a still-existent threat to Bethlehem's future. Following Grace's death in 1960, Homer, the company's new chairman, committed the company to a $3 billion modernization and expansion program. The old mentality still prevailed as the company pushed to produce more tonnage. Bigger still seemed to be better.

Two important factors permitted Bethlehem to sustain its business and expansion through the early 1970s. First, pressure was put on the U.S. government to limit the amount of foreign steel allowed into the country. Early in 1969 the State Department persuaded Japanese and European steel producers voluntarily to cut their imports to the United States by 25 percent. The second factor that helped sustain Bethlehem during the 1970s was the Vietnam War, which stimulated production in all sectors of the U.S. economy. Bethlehem again pushed for more production and higher steel prices. After the price of steel rose steeply in 1969, the administration of President Richard Nixon instituted price controls on steel in August 1971.

The company faced growing competition from mini-mills. These small operations challenged the premise that the steel business had to be huge and integrated to survive. Using scrap metal melted down in electric furnaces, the small operations were capable of producing simple iron and steel products at a much lower cost than the large steelmakers. In light of increased competition, the company chose to grow with the construction of a huge blast furnace at Sparrows Point. Named Big L, it was built at a cost of $275 million. The furnace began operations three years after the end of the early-1970s boom years and one year after the company had shown a net operating loss of over $448 million. Bethlehem Steel was in trouble.

Major Reorganization in the 1980s

As the 1970s ended, drastic action was needed to save the company. In 1980 Donald Trautlein, Bethlehem's controller, was named chairman, and he began to cut away at the company's cost of doing business. The company possessed outmoded production plants, steep labor costs, rising foreign and domestic competition, and eroding profits at a time when the steel industry was experiencing the worst downturn in more than 50 years. Trautlein had other problems as well. He knew little about the business of steelmaking; he felt that most of Bethlehem's problems were due to external forces beyond the company's control. Trautlein chose first to diversify, then to remain exclusively in the steel business, and then began a diversification that was not completed.

The company's new chairman began cutting costs at the top. Salaries were cut by 20 percent over a four-year period. Lump-sum retirement packages were offered to employees over the age of 55; vacations were cut back; and by the fall of 1982, 13 upper echelon executives had taken early retirement. These measures were accompanied by mass firings and layoffs. Further cutbacks eliminated such perquisites as company limousines and drivers, security forces for executives' homes, and a fleet of jet airplanes. By 1984, the number of Bethlehem employees had shrunk by almost 50 percent. Trautlein replaced some of the executive-level positions made vacant with professional managers who had little or no experience in the steel business; many positions were left unfilled.

The company also began the liquidation of some subsidiaries. During the 1980s, 11 of the company's operations were sold. In that same period, Bethlehem began to consolidate many of its steelmaking operations by closing marginal facilities and modernizing aging plants. The company closed its West Coast steel plants and scaled back shipbuilding operations, and in 1983 steelmaking was discontinued at the Lackawanna plant.

Between 1982 and 1985 the company posted losses of $1.9 billion. Under pressure and criticism, Trautlein resigned in 1986. He was replaced by the company's president, Walter F. Williams, who had more than 30 years of experience in the business. Williams was faced with a downward momentum that would be difficult to reverse. The company's stock hovered around an all-time low of $4 per share.

Williams instituted a campaign to improve and revitalize Bethlehem's basic steel business. He began by selling off the assets that were not related to steel. He smoothed relations with both customers and suppliers and persuaded bankers to stay with the company. Slowly, Williams's program began to make a difference. For the year ending December 31, 1987, the company reported more than $174 million in profits compared to a net loss of over $150 million the previous year. In 1988 the company increased its sales volume another 18 percent over 1987 sales figures and reported record earnings of more than $400 million. Two important problems were solved in 1989. First, a 50-month labor contract that included cost-of-living increases and profit sharing was signed with the United Steelworkers. Second, the U.S. government's steel-trade-liberalization program with other countries extended voluntary restraint arrangements previously negotiated with other countries by President Ronald Reagan's administration.

1990s: Recession and Foreign Competition

In 1990 and 1991 Bethlehem worked at increasing its market share in products that produced higher profit margins. Further, the company focused on modernization and the development of high-technology production methods, and increased research and development into new products and processes. The severe economic recession of the early 1990s, however, hit Bethlehem earlier than most U.S. industries, offsetting the benefits of management's determined modernization and streamlining efforts. Steel prices and domestic demand sank to all-time lows. With the capacity to produce 16 million tons of steel annually, Bethlehem produced only eight million tons in 1991. Unfortunately, the economic recession also exacerbated longstanding problems of the company, such as high employment costs and, in particular, skyrocketing health insurance costs, which were reportedly two to three times higher than those of foreign steel competitors. By the end of 1991 Bethlehem posted a $191 million loss.

Nevertheless, under the leadership of Chairman and CEO Williams, Bethlehem forged ahead with $564 million worth of capital expenses for the modernization of Sparrows Point, improvement of flat rolled operations at the Burns Harbor plant, and completion of a new galvanizing line for the production of coated sheet products. In 1991, the worst year of the recession, such leading automotive companies as Ford, Mazda, and Nissan presented the Burns Harbor plant with outstanding quality awards.

Restructuring continued as Bethlehem sold its Freight Car Division and most of its coal properties. The company discontinued the manufacture of trackwork at its Steelton, Pennsylvania, plant as well as its coke production operations at its Sparrows Point, Maryland, plant. These capital outlays and structural changes were all part of management's comprehensive plan (which was approved by the board of directors in January 1992) to revitalize Bethlehem during the recession.

The plan also called for the elimination of the quarterly stock dividend and a reduction in the work force by 6,500 employees. The leaner, more streamlined company weathered the storm, just as it had in previous and even more severe economic downturns. By 1993, Bethlehem had recovered its 12 percent domestic market share and had become a world producer of coated sheet products for both the construction industry and domestic and U.S.-based foreign automobile companies.

Demand for steel increased steadily in the mid-1990s, especially in view of the federal government's plan to invest billions of dollars in upgrading the nation's infrastructure of bridges (40 percent of 576,000 bridges were found to be in need of serious repairs), highways (60 percent of 1.1 million miles of highway in need of repairs), and public transportation systems. With a return to profitability, Bethlehem became the biggest low-cost steel producer in the United States. The company also boasted thoroughly modern, world-class facilities for producing steel—especially high quality flat rolled sheets, a product that held great future promise and accounted for 80 percent of the company's sales.

Getting Bethlehem back on track was the major accomplishment of Chairman Williams, who retired in the mid-1990s. The challenge for incoming CEO and Chairman Curtis H. Barnette, former top counsel in Bethlehem's legal department, would be not only to maintain this record but to try to make Bethlehem the number one steelmaker on the domestic scene as the 1990s closed.

Outlook in the Late 1990s

Under the new leadership of Barnette, Bethlehem went through drastic restructuring. The company had accumulated substantial debt, as well as a huge unfunded pension liability ($1.6 billion in 1993) that had to be corrected. In 1996 the company adopted a comprehensive restructuring plan which resulted in the planned sale of several poorly performing businesses, among them the Iron Ore Company in Canada and Sparrows Point Shipyard, and the sale or discontinuation of operations at the Bethlehem Coke Division. 1997 saw a slight drop in sales but a return to profitability with $280 million in net income. By the end of that year the pension liability also had been reduced to only $440 million.

Bethlehem focused on its core businesses and entered into several agreements with other companies in an attempt to strengthen its financial footing. Its chief ongoing businesses were the Burns Harbor Division, Pennsylvania Steel Technologies, and Sparrows Point Division. Burns Harbor accounted for more than half of the company's revenues, shipping five million tons of products annually. Bethlehem planned major improvements to this division's facilities in order to keep the division profitable. It also earmarked $300 million for a new cold rolling mill complex at Sparrows Point, which brought in more than one-third of the company's revenues. Pennsylvania Steel Technologies maintained its position as the largest domestic rail producer.

Bethlehem also expanded its operations in several directions in the late 1990s, funding three new sheet coating lines and entering into several joint ventures and acquisitions. Chief among these transactions was Bethlehem's 1998 purchase of Lukens, Inc., a major manufacturer of steel plate and sheet used in industrial equipment. After acquiring Lukens, Bethlehem merged it into its own plate operations and created the new Bethlehem Lukens Plate Division, which began to concentrate on alloy steel and carbon products. In turn Bethlehem sold its existing stainless steel production facilities to Allegheny Teledyne, which would continue to operate some of these facilities and sell a portion of the completed products to Bethlehem.

Even with all of these organizational changes improving Bethlehem's infrastructure, its financial outlook in the near future remained somewhat challenged due to events in the international market. The end of the 1990s saw a major threat to the domestic steel industry; foreign markets, especially in Asia, were in crisis and foreign demand was down.

The drop in sales to foreign markets was not a significant problem for Bethlehem, since most of its products were sold within the United States, with export sales totalling only two percent in 1997 (a drop from three percent in 1996 and five percent in 1995). However, at the same time, foreign steel producers who could not sell their products in their own countries began to sell them at reduced prices within the United States. As a result, domestic producers were facing a drop in both prices and demand for their products. In 1998 a group of leading domestic steel companies, including Bethlehem, filed federal trade complaints against several countries, among them Brazil, Japan, and Russia. The companies hoped for federal protection from foreign-made steel being "dumped" in the United States, in the form of increased import duties on foreign steel products.

Principal Subsidiaries

Pennsylvania Steel Technologies, Inc.

Principal Divisions

Bethlehem Lukens Plate Division; Burns Harbor Division; Sparrows Point Diyision.

Principal Operating Units

Basic Steel Operations; Steel Related Operations.

Further Reading

"Analysts Disagree on Bethlehem Steel Stock," *Morning Call* (Allentown, Pa.), December 14, 1997.

Bethlehem Will Shut Down Coke Div.," *New Steel,* January 1998.

A Brief History of Bethlehem Steel, Bethlehem, Pa.: Bethlehem Steel Corporation, 1990.

Cotter, Wes, "Still Suffering U.S. Steel Producers Seek Relief from Product Dumping," *Pittsburgh Business Times & Journal,* July 6, 1992.

Fisher, Douglas Alan, *The Epic of Steel,* New York: Harper & Row, 1963.

Hessen, Robert, *Steel Titan: The Life of Charles M. Schwab,* Pittsburgh: University of Pittsburgh Press, 1990.

Jesdanun, Anick, "Illegal Steel Imports Cited," *Associated Press,* December 23, 1998.

Kleiner, Kurt, "Steel Companies Crying Foul," *Baltimore Business Journal,* July 10, 1992.

Kuchta, David, *Memoirs of a Steelworker,* Easton, Pa.: Canal History and Technology Press, 1995.

McQueen, Rod, "U.S. Charges Likely Against Canada's Steel," *Financial Post,* June 30, 1992.

Prizinsky, David, "Steel Firms Benefit as Bethlehem Drops Lines," *Crain's Cleveland Business,* July 20, 1992.

Reutter, Mark, *Sparrows Point: Making Steel-the Rise and Ruin of American Industrial Might,* New York: Summit Books, 1988.

Ritz, Joseph P., "Bethlehem Workers Eye Bleak Future as Bar Mill Closes in Lackawanna," *Buffalo News,* September 26, 1992.

Scolieri, Peter, "Walter F. Williams Takes Union Regret Into His Retirement," *American Metal Market,* October 27, 1992.

"Steel Makers Unite to Seek Higher Flat-Rolled Prices," *Cincinnati Enquirer,* October 9, 1992.

Strohmeyer, John, *Crisis in Bethlehem: Big Steel's Struggle to Survive,* Bethesda: Md.: Adler & Adler, 1986.

"U.S. Agency Finds Evidence of Steel Dumping," *Reuters News Service,* December 18, 1998.

Woutat, Donald, "Restructured Steel Firms Face New Problems," *Los Angeles Times,* February 9, 1992.

—William R. Grossman
—updated by Gerry Azzata

Block Drug Company, Inc.

257 Cornelison Avenue
Jersey City, New Jersey 07302-9988
U.S.A.
(201) 434-3000
(800) 365-6500
Fax: (201) 434-5739
Web site: http://www.blockdrug.com

Public Company
Incorporated: 1970
Employees: 3,380
Sales: $863.06 million (1998)
Stock Exchanges: NASDAQ
Ticker Symbol: BLOCA
SICs: 3843 Dental Equipment & Supplies; 2843 Surface
   Active Agents; 2834 Pharmaceutical Preparations;
   3991 Toothbrushes, Except Electric; 2844 Shampoos,
   Hair

Block Drug Company, Inc. develops and manufactures a variety of pharmaceutical products, including dental care, oral hygiene and professional dental care products, and other types of over-the-counter healthcare and consumer goods. Block's most popular brands include Polident denture cleanser, Poli-Grip dental adhesive, Nytol sleeping aids, Tegrin medicated shampoo, Lava hand soaps, Beano and Phazyme anti-gas products, Balmex diaper rash ointments, and Sensodyne desensitizing toothpaste. Dental products account for over two-thirds of the company's sales, with consumer goods comprising the rest. Block Drug is a family-run business, now in its third generation. Block's products are sold in over 125 countries, with 60 percent of revenues generated outside the United States.

Beginnings

Although Block Drug Company was incorporated in 1970, the history of the company can be traced back to 1907 when Alexander Block, a Russian immigrant, opened a small drug-store on Fulton Street in Brooklyn, New York. By 1915 he turned wholesaler, and by 1925 he was in the drug manufacturing business, acquiring a 50 percent interest in Wernet's Dental Manufacturing Company.

Continuing to grow through acquisitions in the 1930s, Block entered the dental care products business, which would be the company's most profitable over the years. In 1931 Block bought Antikamnia Remedy Company, a small drug and dental care products company, as well as Pycopay toothbrush and Romilar cough syrup. During this period Block also developed Polident dental powder, which eventually spawned brands including Poli-Grip denture adhesive.

Heavily advertised brand names and slightly differentiated products became Block's trademark for success. In the 1950s, Block was a pioneer in the use of network television commercials, which succeeded in making his products household names. This led to huge growth and new products; for example, he built an entire family of products around the Polident name. An ex-product manager at Block once commented that Block Drug "could hide in the bushes, then . . . push a button and TV would sell the product."

After Alexander Block died in 1953, his son Leonard took over the company. He has run the operation since, keeping earnings and sales growth at around ten percent per year. Commentators have noted that while Block Drug does not have the capital to compete directly with such large pharmaceutical companies as Warner-Lambert, its innovative advertising has meant safe niche markets alongside the bigger brand names.

The 1960s: Advertising and Marketing Drive Sales

By 1966 Block was spending $10.5 million annually to advertise its very successful Polident denture cleanser against fierce competition. Warner-Lambert had introduced Efferdent denture cleanser tablets, which reportedly gained 20 percent of the market in its West Coast debut. In response to this move, Block stepped up advertising in 1966, with the company delivering 1.5 billion messages (twice as many as in 1965) in an attempt to reach the denture wearer who watched television.

Company Perspectives:

From dental care, to treating dentinal hypersensitivity, adult periodontitis and beyond, people around the world experience better oral health as a result of the strong partnership between Block Drug Company and the dental professional.

As we look to the new millennium, Block Drug Company remains committed to this relationship. We will continue to dedicate our energies and resources to develop cutting-edge products and to create strategic alliances that will enable the Company to expand its product line to enable the dental professional to better serve the patient.

Block developed a slightly differentiated product, Polident "tablets" for the "portable denture wearer," and also developed new decorator boxes. The new tablets took 15 percent of the entire denture cleanser market by the end of 1965 and had expanded the total denture cleanser market volume by 25 percent. The ad campaign by Polident (costing twice the amount spent on the 1964 Democratic presidential campaign) also included a Block version of Efferdent, called SteraKleen.

The late 1960s were a period of growth for Block Drug. Income increased from $4.8 million in 1967 to $6.6 million for the year ending March 31, 1971. The drug products segment of the business went from nine percent to 29 percent of total business, while dental care products fell from 85 to 65 percent of the total. Foreign sales and television and radio ad expenditures were both on the rise.

In 1970 Block Drug incorporated, and the following year the company went public, placing 275,000 shares of common stock on the market. Revenues rose by seven percent in fiscal 1971 and net income jumped eight percent over the same period. International sales in 125 foreign countries had 15 percent of the business in 1971. Television was still the company's favored advertising vehicle, with Polident the most advertised Block product in 1971. Nonetheless, Polident lost ground to competitor Efferdent, holding a 36 percent market share compared to Efferdent's 40 percent. Block's other leading products, including Nytol, held their own, and Block added a medicated soap to the Tegrin shampoo line.

In the early 1970s the company was able to cut distribution costs of spot and network commercials by 35 percent by using videotape rather than film. Block turned to Advertel, a tape company in Toronto, to distribute Block commercials, whatever the original production medium, and hence reduce the costs of duplicating. For a company that relied so heavily on television advertising, this outsourcing of distribution was an important breakthrough in cost reduction.

Problems in the Early 1970s

In 1972 Block's advertising reputation was dealt a blow when the federal government and the National Association of Broadcasters asked Block to downplay its promotion of sleeping pills. The government asked that Block's Nytol (along with

J.B. Williams Company's Sominex and Whitehall Labs' Sleep-Eze) ads show sleeping pills as an aid to, rather than a direct cause of, sleep. The ads were modified to comply with the request.

Block's sales began to stagnate in the early to mid-1970s as larger competitors such as Procter & Gamble and Warner-Lambert entered its markets. Some attributed Block's problems to an apparent move away from TV advertising into other merchandising and marketing activities, in which the company could not compete effectively with the giants. It was also noted that Block needed other strategies, such as more aggressive new product development. According to Melvin Kopp, Block's controller, "Our products must constantly be replaced by newer products. We fell behind on that."

Block kept Polident and Tegrin competitive by increasing the ratio of its advertising to sales, focusing especially on television. In 1976, for example, Block spent $30 million or 23 percent of its sales on advertising, while Procter & Gamble, with the largest total advertising budget in the industry, spent $445 million, or eight percent of sales; Warner-Lambert spent 15 percent of its sales on advertising.

While sales of dental care products declined domestically, sales abroad increased from ten percent of net income in 1971 to 26 percent of net income in 1973. One concern over the denture cleanser market was that the market was becoming saturated and that there would be a reduced number of people who use dentures as dental hygiene improved during the 1960s and 1970s.

More advertising battles followed as the struggle between Polident and Efferdent continued. Block brought suit against Warner-Lambert, charging that Warner-Lambert "falsely and deceptively" disparaged Polident tablets in its ads. Block withdrew the suit when Warner-Lambert agreed to revise the contested spot.

Block ran into advertising trouble of its own in 1977. The Federal Trade Commission (FTC) ordered Block to stop what it considered false and misleading advertising, taking exception to Block's claims that users of Poli-Grip or Super Poli-Grip could eat such foods as apples or corn-on-the-cob without difficulty. The FTC also stated that Block did not have reliable scientific evidence to substantiate the claim that its new Extra Effervescent Polident denture cleanser would clean better than Warner-Lambert's Extra Strength Efferdent.

Getting Back on Track with
Headache Powders: The 1980s

In the 1980s Block aggressively pursued its niche marketing strategy, including a successful campaign to revive the popularity of powdered pain killers. Targeting the southern United States, where powdered pain killers have retained popularity, Block marketed a "better-tasting," granulated pain killer through folksy ads; soon the "fast-acting powders," as they were known, became available throughout the United States. Sales of powders more than doubled between 1980 and 1986.

The company reorganized its front office in the late 1980s. In 1988 Leonard Block, chairman, was named senior chairman of the board, a newly created post. He was succeeded by James A. Block, who had been president of the company; Thomas Block was named president.

Block's advertising made news once again in the late 1980s as the company developed a new line of commercials for its Super Poli-Grip product. The company sought to develop TV spots with the "real touch," a new trend in product endorsement. This approach involved showcasing an average "Joe" or "Jane" who used the product to speak on its behalf. To develop the Poli-Grip TV spots, Block spent two years—with the help of commercial casting consultants—to find an ideal "real" candidate to promote their new Super Poli-Grip denture adhesive: a woman between the ages of 35 and 50 who was physically active and attractive, wore dentures, and used the Poli-Grip line.

Block continued to expand into new product areas and to market other companies' products. As part of a joint venture with Chemex Pharmaceuticals, Inc., Block Drug marketed Chemex's Actinex Cream, designed to treat pre-malignant skin lesions. Relying on its expertise in dental products, Block also contracted to market Ciba-Geigy Corporation's Habitrol nicotine skin patch, a smoking cessation aid, to dental professionals. Habitrol was the leading nicotine patch, with sales of about $350 million.

Block's sales grew by 12 percent in 1992, and its profits increased by ten percent. However, a year later sales had slowed, dropping two percent, with profits declining by 22 percent. The company again pushed up its advertising budget, announcing that it would spend over $35 million in that area in 1994, an increase of ten percent. The same year the company entered into another new co-promotion agreement, with Wyeth-Ayerst Laboratories, to assist in the marketing of Lodine, a non-narcotic dental anti-inflammatory analgesic. Block also purchased Goody's Pharmaceuticals, Inc. of North Carolina, a well-known maker of headache powders.

1995: Acquisitions and a Divestiture

The year 1995 was a busy one for Block, with a number of new acquisitions and a major divestiture. In June, the company announced it was selling off its U.S. Reed and Carnrick Pharmaceuticals Division to Schwarz Pharma KermersUrban, a unit of the German Schwarz Pharma AG. The move was partly in response to the increasing likelihood of healthcare reform in the United States, as well as increased pressure from generic drug manufacturers, which had for some time been cutting into the profits of brand name pharmaceutical producers. On the acquisition front, Block added the well-known cleaning and deodorizing products of Reckitt and Coleman, Inc., which had been forced by an antitrust ruling to divest itself of its Carpet Fresh and Rug Fresh brands. Also in 1995, an agreement was signed with U.S. Biomedicals Corporation to market its Bioglass technology, which regenerated bone that had been lost due to periodontal disease.

Another major acquisition for Block was the Lava soap brand, purchased in late 1995. The hand soap, with its grains of pumice for heavy-duty cleaning, had been owned for 68 years by Procter and Gamble, having originally been introduced in 1893. In December 1995 further acquisitions were announced, including Nature's Remedy laxatives, purchased from Smith-Kline Beecham, Parodontax oral hygiene products, from Madaus AG in Germany, and the English brand Setlers antacids, also obtained from SmithKline Beecham. These purchases, and the divestiture of Reed and Carnrick, were part of a declared strategy to focus on Block's strongest areas, those of consumer, dental, and household products.

Over the next several years such strengths were further bolstered by other acquisitions, including the Baby's Own line of baby care products in June 1996 and the maker of Beano antigas tablets in October 1997. Marketing alliances with Atrix Laboratories (for periodontal disease treatment products) and Wyeth-Ayerst (for a new dental analgesic, Duract) were also added, in December 1996 and September 1997, respectively. The company had consolidated its manufacturing operations as well, announcing the planned closing of six of its 12 plants in a February 1997 restructuring. Further streamlining of Block's product mix occurred in early 1998, when the company sold its 2000 Flushes and X-14 toilet bowl cleaning lines, and the Carpet Fresh Rug and Room deodorizer business, again citing the need to focus on the company's strengths of dental and medicinal products. In mid-1998 a joint venture with Access Pharmaceuticals of Texas yielded the first-ever drug approved to treat canker sores, Aphthasol.

With its consistently profitable product mix, and its demonstrated ability to purchase existing brands and maximize their potential, Block Drug appeared robust as it approached the end of its first century. A public company, Block nevertheless remained a family affair, Block family members holding three top positions with the company and the family controlling 100 percent of the company's voting stock and 50 percent of the non-voting stock. Block was generally risk-averse, preferring to keep a good portion of its retained earnings in the form of long-term bonds, which generated increasing amounts of tax-free income. The company's taxes had been generally kept low by the location of major subsidiaries in such tax sanctuaries as Ireland and Puerto Rico.

Principal Subsidiaries

Ada Products Company; Block Drug Corporation; Dentco, Inc.; Reedco, Inc.; Stafford-Miller International, Inc.

Further Reading

Alsop, Ronald, "Folksy Ads Help in Reviving Old-Time Headache Powders," *Wall Street Journal,* June 19, 1986.

Anderson, James, "Block Coaxes Big Gains out of Smaller Brands," *SmartMoney,* September 1, 1996, p. 27.

"Block Drug Co.'s Ads for Denture Products Are Cited by FTC Aide," *Wall Street Journal,* October 28, 1977.

"Block Drug Exec Tallies Savings in Shift to Tape," *Advertising Age,* February 15, 1971.

"Block Drug Introduces Instant Mildew Stain Remover," *Spray-Technology-and-Marketing,* January 1992.

"Block Drug Unit Goes to McAdams," *Advertising Age,* August 10, 1970.

"Block Drug Will Sell Ciba-Geigy's Nicotine Skin-Patch to Dentists," *Wall Street Journal,* September 30, 1992.

"Block Gives Grey BC; SSC&B Picks Up New Products," *Advertising Age,* January 1, 1973.

"Block Struggles to Regain Winning Formula of Old," *Advertising Age,* August 19, 1974.

Gebeloff, Robert, "Airwick Maker Is Sold—Block Drug Buys R&C Subsidiary," *Record (Northern New Jersey),* June 1, 1995, p. B1.

Giges, Nancy, "Block, W-L Cold-Fighters Bow," *Advertising Age,* July 23, 1984.

Harrington, Jeff, "Procter Washes Hands of Lava Brand Being Sold to Block Drug After 68 Years," *Cincinnati Enquirer,* November 21, 1995, p. B7.

"Just Itching for Sales: Tegrin Shampoo Cuts Price, Rethinks Ad Strategy," *Advertising Age,* May 18, 1992.

"New Chip at the Old Block?," *Forbes,* May 29, 1978.

Overstreet, James, "Block Drug Plans to Open Center for Distribution," *Memphis Business Journal,* November 10, 1997, p. 1.

Phalon, Richard, "In Anonymity They Thrive," *Forbes,* December 25, 1989.

"$10,500,000 Ad Campaign Boosts Block's Polident," *Advertising Age,* May 16, 1966.

"Three Sleep Aid Makers Agree to Tone Down Ads," *Advertising Age,* June 12, 1972.

—John A. Sarich
—updated by Frank Uhle

Bridgford Foods Corporation

1308 North Patt Street
P.O. Box 3773
Anaheim, California 92803
U.S.A.
(714) 526-5533
(800) 854-3265
Fax: (714) 526-4360
Web site: http://www.bridgford.com

Public Company
Incorporated: 1952
Employees: 640
Sales: $127.9 million (1997)
Stock Exchanges: NASDAQ
Ticker Symbol: BRID
SICs: 2013 Sausages & Other Prepared Meat Products;
    2022 Natural, Processed & Imitation Cheese; 2045
    Prepared Flour Mixes & Doughs; 5141 Groceries,
    General Line

Bridgford Foods Corporation manufactures and distributes frozen, refrigerated, and snack food products for both retail and food service establishments in the United States and Canada. Bridgford products include a variety of sliced luncheon meats and cheeses, wieners, bacon, dry and semidry sausages, frozen Micro-Ready sandwiches, biscuits, and bread and roll dough items. The company also purchases for resale a variety of jerky, cheeses, salads, party dips, Mexican foods, nuts, and other delicatessen-type food products. In all, Bridgford was manufacturing or distributing a line of about 450 food products in 1997. With the majority of its stock in the hands of the founding Bridgford family, the relatively small company competes effectively with such industry giants as ConAgra, Hormel, and Sara Lee. The company's strategy, in the words of chairperson Allan Bridgford in a 1995 article in *Barron's,* is to be "a niche marketer and find unusual products that fit in between [those of its] very big competitors."

Origins During the Great Depression

The company traces its origins to 1932, when Hugh Bridgford, formerly an employee in a San Diego grocery store, started his own butcher shop with $65 he had saved from his paychecks. Success ensued at the small shop; over the years, Bridgford opened up several more such markets in the area and eventually established a wholesale meat business that sold Bridgford meats to local hotels and restaurants.

By 1944 Hugh Bridgford had also entered the frozen food distribution business, first offering frozen corned beef hash and baked beans, foods that he noticed retained their fresh taste even after they had set in his freezer for some time. Also that year, he moved the hub of his operations and management headquarters to a 50-year-old meatpacking plant he purchased in Anaheim, California. Bridgford's various operations were organized as the Bridgford Foods Corporation in 1952.

Product Innovations in the 1960s

Bridgford Foods was the first to manufacture and market frozen bread dough, which it did in 1962. This reportedly came about one evening when a company baker, tired from the day's work, opted to store some already-mixed dough in the freezer that night and to bake it the next day. The bread baked and tasted fine, and after adjusting the quantity of yeast so that the dough would still rise after being frozen for months, the company began marketing the heat-and-serve product, which would become its staple. In 1966 the company developed the Bridgford Demi-Loaf for the food service trade; it would later estimate in 1991 that two-thirds of the miniature bread loaves served in U.S. restaurants were made from Bridgford frozen dough.

Allan Bridgford later recalled that his father was "an innovative man and seemed to come up with ideas that people liked," adding that his father was "always searching for new product development." Not all of the ideas worked out: holiday hams, marketed covered with red-and-green candied cherries in the 1950s failed when the cherries fermented, causing the hams to spoil within their wrappers, and a pizza-making kit introduced in 1980 foundered on the impatience of consumers who

---

Company Perspectives:

Uniqueness, high quality and consistency of products are the main objectives of Bridgford Foods Corporation.

---

would not wait for the dough to defrost. "For every 100 product ideas, we'll try ten and maybe one will stick," Hugh's son H. William ("Bill") Bridgford commented.

Hugh Brigford's sons began working at the company part-time when they were boys; after college—both graduated from Stanford University with degrees in economics—they took full-time positions at Bridgford Foods, with Allan focusing his energies on sales and marketing and Bill overseeing production.

Beginning in 1964, Bridgford Foods' sales would increase every year for the next two decades. Moreover, after 1965, when the cost of expanding to the East Coast by establishing a breadmaking plant in Secaucus, New Jersey, resulted in a $93,000 loss, the company would also make a profit each year. In 1966, Bridgford had sales of $8.4 million and net income of $163,367; for 1970, these figures were reported at $14.1 million and $195,267, respectively. Bridgford Foods offered a small portion of its stock to the public in 1968 at $8.75 a share.

Steady Growth in the 1970s

In 1970, Hugh Bridgford remained chairman of the company he had founded, while Bill Bradford served as president and Allan Bridgford was vice-president. Besides the main Anaheim plant and the Secaucus facility, the company maintained a meat wholesaling facility in San Diego during this time and leased a plant in Dallas for breadmaking.

By this time, Bridgford Foods was manufacturing and distributing wholesale processed meats and other delicatessen foods packaged for consumer convenience, manufacturing and selling fresh, frozen, and smoked wholesale meats, and manufacturing and selling frozen bread-dough products. The company's products were being sold through about 4,000 retail outlets in California and Arizona—largely convenience stores, delicatessens, and independent markets—serviced by Bridgford's own delivery sales force, and also through about another 15,000 retail outlets in California and elsewhere, serviced by distribution through food brokers, cooperatives, chain-store warehouses, independent food distributors, and other sources.

Packaged luncheon meats, bacon, wieners, smoked pork products, cheese, and other delicatessen foods had accounted for 68 percent of Bridgford Foods' sales in the late 1960s, while bread, dough, and related products constituted 18 percent and fresh meat and other products the remaining 14 percent. In the following years, however, bread dough and related products gained steadily in importance, accounting for 42 percent of Bridgford's sales in 1974, compared to 47 percent for delicatessen-type food and 11 percent for fresh meat and other products.

Bridgford Foods grew considerably in the 1970s. In 1972 it purchased the Dallas plant it had been leasing, and in 1975 it purchased a plant in Chicago for meat processing, with heavy emphasis on dry and semidry sausage. During this decade the company also leased warehouse and/or office space in Oakland, California; Phoenix and Tucson, Arizona; and Beaumont and San Antonio, Texas. Although the Beaumont and San Antonio leases lapsed in 1979 and 1984, respectively, a warehouse in Modesto, California, was leased out in 1985, and a second Dallas breadmaking plant was opened that year.

Ups and Downs in the 1980s

Net sales continued to grow year by year through the decade, increasing from $14.1 million in fiscal 1971 to $40.7 million in fiscal 1980. In the latter year the company's products were being sold through about 7,000 convenience-store retail outlets in California, Arizona, Texas, Nevada, and New Mexico, and also throughout the country to about another 20,000 retail outlets and 12,000 restaurants and institutions.

For the first time in two decades, sales slipped slightly at Bridgford in 1985, due only to the fact that the previous year had been a 53-week fiscal year. The upward march resumed the following year, however, and Bridgford Foods was also able to eliminate its modest long-term debt at that time. The company exceeded net income of $1 million for the first time in 1987, earning $1.6 million on net sales of $56.5 million. Analysts began to take note of the small company, and in 1987 Bridgford Foods took second place in a *Forbes* list of the best stocks of the year, with an impressive 221-percent return to investors. Between 1985 and 1990 the stock price, adjusted for splits, appreciated more than tenfold.

At 78 years of age, Hugh Bridgford was still active in the company in 1987, running the Chicago production plant, while Bill and Allan Bridgford presided over headquarters, working out of a shared, modest, linoleum-floored "executive suite" in a corner of the Anaheim plant, an area permanently chilled by the meatpacking operations, prompting the brothers to don heavy work jackets over their Oxford shirts while in their office. The unpretentious Bridgfords—"low-cost operators and penny pinchers," in the words of one stock analyst—did not even keep a secretary. The family atmosphere was augmented by the fact that many of the company's work force of 450, which included more than a dozen other family members, had been working for Bridgford for decades.

Bridgford Foods' products were being sold in more than 20,000 stores and stocked by more than 15,000 restaurants and institutions by 1988. In addition, the number of convenience stores carrying Bridgford products reached 10,300 in 25 states. These products consisted mainly of traditional snack foods such as pepperoni and salami sticks that were based on recipes going back hundreds of years. Accordingly, although supermarkets carried the Bridgford line, these products seemed to be doing best in convenience stores, delicatessens, and liquor stores, where profit margins were wider and Bridgford did not face as much competition from giant companies such as Pillsbury, ConAgra, and Oscar Meyer. One California store owner commented, "They're not a company for this day and age, but maybe that's why they do so well."

But Bridgford Foods was not conceding the supermarket trade to its big rivals, either. The sales staff made things easier for their retail customers by putting price tags on Bridgford products at the plant, stocking the supermarket shelves itself, and reimbursing the stores for unsold items. "We do everything but sweep the floor," Allan Bridgford told a reporter. Although the sales force of 110 was expensive to retain, "nothing replaces the personal touch," he added. As a promotional tool, Bridgford also sent out to its distributors full-color calendars every year featuring frozen bread-dough recipes such as those for "Incredible Pizza Layer Loaf" and "Hand-Wiches." By contrast, the larger food companies generally were selling their products through food brokers whose distributors simply dropped the goods on the store loading dock.

Bridgford Foods introduced microwave-ready hamburgers, cheeseburgers, roast beef and ham-and-cheese sandwiches, and chili dogs in 1988. *Forbes,* in an informal taste test in 1990, rated "the Bridgford flame-broiled cheeseburger by far the tastiest" in the microwave sandwich market. By now the number of company products had risen to more than 100.

Forging Ahead in the 1990s

Sales volume reached $84.3 million in 1990, and net income rose to $3.9 million. Bridgford Foods had no long-term debt and, in 1991, about $4 million in cash. As a result of its enviable position, the company was rated one of "The Best 200 Small Companies in America" by *Forbes* during 1990–93. Between 1992 and 1996 the company averaged an annual 13-percent return on assets.

Bridgford Foods opened a frozen-foods plant in Statesville, North Carolina, in 1996 and modernized its Chicago and Dallas facilities. It closed its Secaucus plant in 1995. The company continued to have no long-term debt and owned valuable parcels of land in Chicago, Dallas, and Anaheim. Bridgford Foods had issued a dividend in every year since 1966 except for 1983 and 1986.

Nevertheless, in March 1997 Bridgford Foods' thinly traded stock was being quoted at only about $8 a share, compared to a high of $24 in 1992. One problem was price hikes of as much as 40 percent in 1996 for the company's main ingredients, wheat and pork. This led to a decline in profits of 15 percent in 1996 in spite of record sales of $118.3 million. The following year net income rose 19 percent, to $6.6 million on sales of $127.9 million.

Hugh Bridgford died in 1992. In 1996 Bill, who had retired from day-to-day operations but retained a seat as chairman of the executive committee, moved to Dallas to oversee the recently expanded bakery plant there, leaving Allan Bridgford, the company's chairperson, in sole possession of the Anaheim office. A third generation of Bridgfords was also moving up the corporate ladder, with William Bridgford, Jr., Allan Bridgford, Jr., and Bruce Bridgford in charge of subsidiaries and a total of eight members of the Bridgford family in management positions. Major decisions were still being made by the three-member executive committee, consisting of the two senior Bridgfords and Robert E. Schulze, the company's president.

In 1997 Bridgford Foods was selling about 450 items through some 180 salespeople to 25,200 retail food stores in 49 states and Canada. It was also selling Bridgford products, through wholesalers, cooperatives, and distributors, to about 18,000 retail outlets and 19,000 restaurants and institutions. Moreover, the company was advertising its products in Sunday newspaper food circulars and sending executives to more than 400 trade shows a year. Products manufactured or processed by the company represented 82 percent of sales, with items manufactured or processed by third parties for distribution accounting for the remaining 18 percent. Frozen-food products accounted for 44 percent of sales and refrigerated and snack-food products for 56 percent. Bridgford Foods maintained plants in Anaheim, Chicago, Dallas, and Statesville, North Carolina. About two-thirds of the company's stock was held by Bridgford family members.

Principal Subsidiaries

A.S.I. Corporation; Bridgford Distributing Company; Bridgford Foods of Illinois, Inc.; Bridgford Meat Co.

Further Reading

Brammer, Rhonda, "Recipe for Growth: Dry Sausage + Biscuits," *Barron's,* March 27, 1995, p. 19.
——, "Recipe for Recovery," *Barron's,* March 24, 1997, p. 20.
Cox, Tony, "Family-Run Bridgford Targets Food Niches," *Orange County Business Journal,* April 29, 1991, p. 8.
Fulmer, Melinda, "Roll Model," *Los Angeles Times,* August 30, 1997, pp. D1, D8.
Heise, Kenan, "Hugh Bridgford, Founder of Frozen Food Company," *Chicago Tribune,* April 16, 1992, p. B8.
Palmeri, Christopher, "Family Affair," *Forbes,* November 12, 1990, pp. 228, 232.
Tighe, John Charles, "Food Maker Forgoes Tradition with Line of Microwave Burgers," *Los Angeles Times,* April 22, 1988, pp. D1, D12.
Woodyard, Chris, "Bridgford Skips Frills to Make Bread, Profits," *Los Angeles Times,* April 30, 1991, p. D3.

—Robert Halasz

Briggs & Stratton Corporation

12301 West Wirth Street
Wauwatosa, Wisconsin 53222
U.S.A.
(414) 259-5333
(800) 274-4477
Fax: (414) 259-5773
Web Site: http://www.briggsandstratton.com

Public Company
Incorporated: 1909
Employees: 7,265
Sales: $1.33 billion (1998)
Stock Exchanges: New York
Ticker Symbol: BGG
SICs: 3519 Industrial Combustion Engines; 7699 Repair
    Services

Briggs & Stratton Corporation is the world's largest producer of air-cooled gasoline engines for outdoor power equipment. The company designs, manufactures, markets, and services its products for various manufacturers worldwide. In the 1990s, with increased competition from both domestic and Japanese engine makers, the company has sold off its non-core technology holdings and has shifted jobs from Wisconsin to southern factories in efforts to cut costs.

Early 20th-Century Beginnings

In 1909, Stephen Foster Briggs was a young college graduate and inventor when he and Harold M. Stratton, a successful grain merchant, founded Briggs & Stratton Corp. The partners incorporated their company in the state of Wisconsin and with $25,000 began to produce a six-cylinder, two-cycle engine that Briggs had made while a student at North Dakota State College. They experienced tough times at first as their six-cylinder engine proved too costly for mass production. A brief foray into the automobile assembly business also failed, nearly driving the partners into bankruptcy.

Nevertheless Briggs had a knack for inventions, and in 1910 he received a patent for a new gas engine igniter, which included a novel mechanism that could start an automobile engine with a single spark. Although it was not an overwhelming success, the company had found its niche as a producer of electrical specialties for the booming automobile industry. The business soon took off, becoming by 1920 the largest producer of specialty lights, ignitions, regulators, and starting switches in the United States. Sales also shot up, approaching $4 million. Briggs & Stratton customers included all the major automobile makers, including Chevrolet, Dodge, Ford, Hudson, Hupp, Kissell, Maxwell, Nash, Studebaker, and Willys-Overland. The market for electrical specialties proved so profitable that it accounted for two-thirds of Briggs & Stratton's total business through the mid-1930s. In 1920, the company expanded operations into the East Plant, a five story concrete and steel building at 13th and Center Streets in Milwaukee. The plant employed 1,400 workers with an annual payroll of $1.5 million.

In the early years, Briggs & Stratton ventured into various new markets, often with little success. The production of refrigerators, crystal radios, headsets, radio tuners, and a device called the battery eliminator all were short lived. The company also tried making oil filters, air cleaners, and a series of stamped metal items, including key storage cabinets, soap containers, calendar banks, candy display stands, and coin operated paper towel dispensing cabinets.

In 1924, Briggs & Stratton reincorporated in the state of Delaware. That year, with profits soaring, the company discovered another profitable market: the automotive lock business. A new die cast automobile lock cylinder outsold competing brass models, and within five years Briggs & Stratton had become the largest producer of automotive locks with more than 75 percent of the total market. Briggs & Stratton's new BASCO auto body hardware, including door handles, inside knobs and levers, compartment locks, door locks, hinges, and keys also became standard features on many of the leading models of motor cars. For the ever-expanding automobile market, the company introduced in 1938 the Cushion Action Starter Drive, a new automobile self-starting mechanism that became standard on the Ford V8, Mercury, and Lincoln Zephyr. Its automotive division also provided supplies to airline, marine, and cabinet manufacturers.

In 1919, the company acquired the A.O. Smith Motor Wheel and the Flyer, a two-passenger buckboard-like vehicle. The Motor Wheel was a gasoline-engine driven wheel, designed for attachment to the rear of a bicycle, thus converting it into a kind of motor cycle. The wheel sold for about $90 and could get approximately 100 miles per gallon. Briggs & Stratton had high hopes for sales worldwide and tried to market the Motor Wheel in Spanish-speaking countries and in Asia where it could also be used on rickshas. When sales proved disappointing, Briggs & Stratton re-engineered the Motor Wheel to produce the first American motor scooter. Despite being one of the least expensive automobiles on the road, the Flyer could not compete with the Ford Model T and other popular models. Only 2,000 Flyers sold between 1920 and 1923. In 1924, the Motor Wheel and related items were sold off.

The company soon became successful, however, in the engine manufacturing business by producing a stationary version of the Motor Wheel, which could power various kinds of equipment. In 1923, the Model PB engine was introduced, providing a popular and compact power source for washing machines, garden tractors, and lawn mowers. Production in 1925 of the overhead valve, ¾ horsepower, Model F series engine proved useful for a wide variety of industrial and agricultural equipment, including compressors, generators, and pumps. In 1931, Briggs & Stratton introduced a best-seller for washing machine producers, a small low-profile engine that could fit under washing machine tubs. This engine remained popular until 1936 when the Model WM (Washing Machine) engine rolled off the assembly line. The washing machine business was the company's major market for engines until the Second World War.

In 1928, Briggs & Stratton acquired the Evinrude Outboard Motor Company, which it sold less than a year later. Founders Stephen Briggs and Harold Stratton had differing views on the market potential for outboard motors. Stratton was against di-versifying the company's products. Briggs, on the other hand, was enthusiastic, and he formed a new company, Outboard Motors Corp., with Ole Evinrude, a maker of outboard motors since 1909. The new partners merged Evinrude's company, Evinrude Light Twin Outboard, with Lockwood-Ash Motor Co. and purchased the Evinrude Outboard Motor Co. from Briggs & Stratton. Briggs served as chairman and Evinrude as president.

Success as a producer of electrical specialties and small engines proved a boon for the company's fortunes during World War II. Briggs & Stratton quickly became one of the nation's 200 largest military suppliers, producing everything from deto-nating fuses and artillery ammunition, to ignition switches for airplanes and airplane guns. The company also profited as a supplier of engines for electric and radio generators, pumps, compressors, ventilating fans, saw rigs, mobile kitchens, repair shops, emergency hospitals, and water purification equipment. The war effort proved so lucrative that between 1938 and 1944 net income increased six-fold, from $785,000 to more than $6,000,000.

Postwar Success with Lawn Mower Engines

Following the war years, Briggs & Stratton, already the biggest producer of small gasoline engines, pursued a greater share of the market for lawn and garden equipment caused by the postwar boom. With the rapid suburbanization of America, the Briggs & Stratton name became virtually synonymous with the lawn mower. The rapidly growing market for powered home use equipment also stemmed from the appearance of inexpen-sive rotary lawn mowers, powered by relatively lightweight two-cycle engines. Briggs & Stratton's original four-cycle en-gine, weighing about 40 pounds, was too cumbersome for lawn mowers and garden equipment. As a result, the company intro-duced in 1953 aluminum die cast engines with chrome plated pistons. These were not only lighter than competing models but also could withstand greater engine pressure and temperatures. In 1954, Briggs & Stratton patented its new die cast technique for the production of four-cycle engines, which rapidly became the industry standard. The company subsequently filed a patent infringement suit against the Clinton Machine Company, one of its major competitors. Briggs & Stratton eventually lost the case, allowing the industry to freely use the newly developed die cast process. In 1955, Briggs & Stratton opened a new plant in Wauwatosa, Wisconsin, to keep pace with rising demand for the aluminum engines. The plant was expanded in 1967 and again seven years later to increase production.

In 1948, Briggs resigned to join Outboard Motors Corp., the company he helped found. Briggs had been president of Briggs & Stratton from 1909 until 1935 when he became chairperson. While with the company, Briggs had received about 60 patents for various inventions, mostly for lighting switches and locks and their mechanisms produced for the automobile industry. Later, at Outboard Motors Corp. he would receive patents for engine components, including a starting circuit, valve lifters, and a valve actuating mechanism that could be mechanically self-adjusted.

Briggs was succeeded by Charles Lyons Coughlin, a fellow electrical engineering student who had known Briggs at North Dakota State College. Coughlin had joined the company in 1910, but left in 1918 for the Ladish Drop Forge Company. In 1923, he rejoined Briggs & Stratton as vice-president and gen-eral manager. He became company president in 1935 and later chief executive officer and chairperson in 1970.

Coughlin's leadership brought Briggs & Stratton rising profitability. Net sales more than doubled from $40 to $90 million between 1953 and 1959. By 1965, sales volume had risen to a record $105.1 million. Briggs & Stratton's profitability stemmed from a conservative approach in sticking with its two principal lines of manufacturing, the production of small air-cooled gasoline engines and the production of automobile parts. The company also benefitted enormously from a market that was not big enough to attract major competition. In 1966, *Forbes* magazine estimated that 90 percent of its sales were in "small engines, used mostly in power lawn mowers but also in air compressors, pumps, generators, etc." The remaining ten percent were in auto locks and switches.

In 1970, Vincent R. Shiely was named president of Briggs & Stratton. Shiely had joined the company in 1959 as administrative vice-president, later becoming executive vice-president in 1963. Shiely stayed with Briggs & Stratton's conservative approach, which continued to pay impressive dividends. In the 1970s, net sales shot up from about $212 million to almost $591 million from 1973 to 1979. The company's purchase of a manufacturing plant in Milwaukee from the Square D Co. expanded its production capacity for various components, and brought new facilities for research and development, engineering, and sales. The Burleigh plant, built in Wauwatosa in 1955, was also expanded to keep pace with demand for Briggs & Stratton engines. In 1976, Shiely became the company's chairperson and, by the time of his death in 1976, was also chief executive officer.

Following Shiely's death, Lawrence G. Regner was elected to the chair, and Frederick P. Stratton, Jr., became president and chief operating officer. By 1980, Briggs & Stratton remained unrivaled as the world's lowest-cost producer of small engines. The company enjoyed rising profits while selling motors to power-equipment makers at prices they could never match if they tried to produce their own. Among Fortune 500 companies, Briggs & Stratton ranked 405th in sales but 94th in profit margin (8.2 percent) and 44th in stockholders' return on equity (23.5 percent).

Competition from Japan in the 1980s

For all its success, however, the company was soon on the run from Japanese competitors. "In many ways," said a reporter in *Forbes* in 1986, "Briggs & Stratton was a sitting duck." Big Japanese producers, Honda in particular, began targeting the small engine market after sales for motorcycles peaked in the early 1980s. In 1984, Honda reportedly spent $12.5 million advertising its lawn and garden equipment, fully 20 percent of the industry's total advertising budget. Honda's move into the small engine market came at a bad time for Briggs & Stratton. In the 1970s, a weak dollar had boosted the company's market share worldwide. However, a recession and a strong dollar in the early 1980s allowed such competitors as Honda, Kawasaki, Suzuki, and Mitsubishi to make inroads by supplying U.S. equipment makers with engines at lower cost.

For the most part, due to its overwhelming market dominance and low production costs, Briggs & Stratton fended off the competition. Despite a strengthening dollar, the company retained its markets in Europe but lost considerable ground in

Asia as its cost advantage disappeared. Its exports precipitously dropped from 25 percent of sales or $179 million in 1980, to 14 percent of sales or $99 million in 1985. In the United States, Briggs & Stratton relied on low manufacturing costs to beat out Japanese producers in the engine market itself. However, the Japanese were quick to provide more sophisticated engines aimed at the higher-priced segment of the market where Briggs & Stratton's cost advantage was less overwhelming. In response, the company produced a slew of new products, including an improved line of its basic 3.5 and four horsepower engines introduced in 1985, as well as a wholly redesigned line of other engines. The company also doubled spending on engineering and research and launched a $2 million consumer advertising campaign to bolster its brand name.

In addition to trying to maintain market share, Briggs & Stratton concentrated on cost reduction to ensure its position as the industry's low cost producer. Labor costs, which accounted for 50 percent of total expenses, also were 50 percent higher than those for the Japanese. Briggs & Stratton's ability to remain competitive with this considerable cost disadvantage reflected its remarkable efficiency. In 1983, the company experienced a three-month strike to win additional flexibility to remain competitive. Also during this time, Briggs & Stratton opened a highly automated nonunion engine plant in Murray, Kentucky, which required far fewer employees than at the main engine facility in Wauwatosa, Wisconsin. The new plant provided not only significant savings in labor costs, but greater flexibility with which to experiment with new manufacturing techniques.

None of these efforts, however, produced an immediate payoff. In 1985, earnings dropped 31 percent from their $49 million 1980 high, operating margins fell from 13.8 percent to 10.8 percent, and return on equity from 22.3 percent to 12.1 percent. The big difference occurred in sales volume, which declined a precipitous 30 percent since 1980.

In 1986, George A. Senn was elected as Briggs & Stratton's fifth president. Senn had joined the company the year before as an executive vice-president. When he resigned in 1988, Richard E. Marceau was elected president and chief executive officer. Marceau had risen through the company, first as human resource director and then as vice-president for administration. In 1991, Marceau retired, and Frederick Stratton Jr., grandson of co-founder Harold M. Stratton, assumed the office as president.

During this five-year transitional period, the company's fortunes continued to waver. In 1989, Briggs & Stratton suffered its first major loss in more than 50 years, incurring a $20 million net drop in income. The company continued aggressive efforts to improve its position in the industry. Capital expenditures in 1989 totaled a record $79.5 million, including spending on new equipment and tooling for its new nonunion assembly plant in Poplar Bluff, Missouri.

What looked like a decline in the 1980s was reversed in the early 1990s as Briggs & Stratton began recovering market share from such formidable competitors as Kawasaki and Suzuki. A boost in productivity stemmed partly from lower raw material costs and lower operating expenses. Moreover, Briggs & Stratton benefitted from a weakening dollar relative to the yen as well as from substantial increases in product development spending, which grew from 1.5 percent of sales in the early 1980s to 2.5 percent of sales in 1992. The company's two nonunion plants also were manufacturing engines more cheaply and efficiently.

Briggs & Stratton continued to strengthen its market position, an impressive feat given the stiff competition that now characterized the small engine industry. The company faced tough domestic competition from Tecumseh Products Company, Kohler Co., Kawasaki Heavy Industries, Ltd., and Onan Corporation. Two domestic lawnmower makers, Lawn Boy Inc. and Honda Motor Co., also produced their own engines. Eight Japanese small engine manufacturers were worldwide competitors, the largest being Honda and Kawasaki, while Italy's Tecnamotor S.p.A., owned by Tecumseh, was a major competitor in Europe.

In 1992, Briggs & Stratton reincorporated in the state of Wisconsin. At this time, engines, parts, and related products accounted for 93 percent of Briggs & Stratton's total sales, a percentage that had changed little since 1983. The company's chief market continued to be air-cooled four-cycle gasoline engines in the two- to 18-horsepower range. The lawn and garden equipment industry, holding remarkably steady since the early 1980s, accounted for 86 percent of its engine sales. Manufacturers installed Briggs & Stratton engines mostly on walk-behind mowers, riding mowers, garden tillers, and shredders. Briggs & Stratton engines also powered snow throwers, garden tractors, lawn edgers, vacuums, generating pumps, pressure washers, and various other equipment. The majority of its engines were still produced at the main engine facility in Wauwatosa, Wisconsin.

The engines were sold in the United States and Canada by Briggs & Stratton's own sales force. In overseas markets, the company relied primarily on independent representatives, assisted by a network of regional offices in Norway, Switzerland, the United Arab Emirates, Singapore, and Milwaukee. Exports accounted for 21 percent of all engines and parts sales in 1992, up from 14 percent of sales in 1984. One reason for Briggs & Stratton's success had been its emphasis on customer service, which included a worldwide service network of over 35,000 authorized service dealers through which it sold replacement engines and service parts.

1994: Jobs Shifted to Southern Plants

Despite its ability to maintain market share in the face of strong competition, the company remained focused on increasing profits and made plans for additional cost cutting measures. The corporation had adopted an Economic Value Added business philosophy in 1990, which emphasized earning a cash return that was higher than the cost of capital. In the early 1980s, Briggs & Stratton had maintained a ratio of operating capital to net income of three to one, but this ratio had slipped to nine to one by 1990. Efforts to reduce this ratio included cutting manufacturing costs, increasing productivity, boosting quality, and ensuring on-time delivery of products.

Having already built two plants in the South which had lower labor costs and a more productive work force, Briggs & Stratton made the decision in mid-1994 to move 2,000 jobs from Wisconsin to three new plants in the South within the next four years. These would be located in Statesboro, Georgia (a $75 million, 800 employee plant); Auburn, Alabama (a $30 million and 500 worker site); and Rolla, Missouri (a $38 million, 600 employee facility). The southern states offered incentives which included tax abatements and worker training programs, in addition to a wage scale, given a lower cost of living, of almost half that found in Wisconsin. The news hit the Milwaukee area hard, and the United Paperworkers International Union, which represented Briggs & Stratton's workers there, became increasingly antagonistic toward the company. Corporate officials expressed sympathy for the workers but maintained that there had been no choice but to take such a step. Fortunately, by 1996, as demand for the company's die-cast products suddenly surged, Briggs & Stratton was able to add 1,000 workers to its Wauwatosa plant, half of which had been idle since the lay-offs.

In early 1997 the company and the U.S. Environmental Protection Agency reached an agreement to comply with new, stricter emissions standards for the small engines the company manufactured, a challenge faced by all such manufacturers. These new engines were to be phased in between the years 2001 and 2005. Briggs & Stratton expected to spend a significant amount of money complying with the standards, though it already had some engines in production which were in compliance.

Divestitures in the mid- and late 1990s helped streamline Briggs & Stratton. In February 1995, the company spun off its Strattec Security Co. subsidiary, leaving the automotive lock and key business for good. In July 1997, it sold its gray iron foundry, and a year later its ductile iron foundry, both of which would continue to produce camshafts, crankshafts, and other products for the company under their new owner, JTC. In July 1998, the company also sold its Powercom-2000 subsidiary.

In late 1998 Briggs & Stratton and the United Paperworkers held talks aimed at reaching common ground, which purported to yield a new spirit of cooperation. As a result, the union gave up a piecework pay system in exchange for receiving increased retirement benefits. As the company's Wisconsin work force was aging, 500 workers had already taken an early retirement package in 1996. An immediate sign of the improved union-management relationship was the announcement that some 71 jobs would be shifted from the South back to Wauwatosa. Some analysts suggested at this time that the company's southern plants had not delivered the cost savings initially anticipated, though the company maintained that it was still in the process of getting the new plants up to capacity.

As Briggs & Stratton reached the end of the 1990s, it remained the world's largest manufacturer of small gasoline engines. Moreover, the streamlining and focusing of energies that had followed the adoption of the Economic Value Added model were showing some signs of strengthening the company's bottom line.

Principal Subsidiaries

Future Parkland Development Corporation.

Further Reading

"Briggs Axing 2,000 Jobs Here; Norquist 'Bitterly Disappointed'," *Milwaukee Sentinel,* May 18, 1994, p. 1.

Cook, James, "We Are the Target," *Forbes,* April 7, 1986, pp. 54–56.

Fauber, John, "Briggs' Primary Rivals are Nearby; Tecumseh and Kohler Post the Biggest Threat, Not the Japanese," *Milwaukee Journal,* May 29, 1994, p. 1.

The History of Briggs & Stratton Corporation, Wauwatosa: Briggs & Stratton Corporation.

Kinkead, Gwen, "An American Company Honda Can't Mow Down," *Fortune,* July 28, 1980, pp. 54–55.

"The Little Engine Company that Could," *Forbes,* February 5, 1990, p. 205.

Romell, Rick, "Deal Sets Small-Engine Emissions; Briggs, Kohler Among Firms Agreeing to Costly Pollution-Control Effort," *Milwaukee Journal Sentinel,* January 11, 1997, p. 1.

Romell, Rick, "Wauwatosa-Wis.-Based Briggs & Stratton Moves Slowly into South," *Knight-Ridder Tribune Business News (KRTBN),* November 12, 1998.

Savage, Mark, "Briggs Bringing 71 Jobs Back to Wauwatosa Plant," *Milwaukee Journal Sentinel,* November 12, 1998, p. 1.

Savage, Mark, "Mow Money for Briggs: Engine Maker's Path to Change Turns Out to be Tough Lawn to Cut," *Milwaukee Sentinel,* January 23, 1995, p. 4D.

Savage, Mark, "1,000 Workers Will Move In: New Life for Briggs' Burleigh Plant," *Milwaukee Journal Sentinel,* June 16, 1996, p. 1.

"Worthy Heir," *Forbes,* June 22, 1992, p. 12.

—Bruce P. Montgomery
—updated by Frank Uhle

BTR Siebe plc

BTR House
Carlisle Place
London SW1P 1BX
United Kingdom
(44) 171 834-3848
Fax: (44) 171 834-3879
Web site: http://www.btrsiebe.com

Public Company
Incorporated: 1819 as Siebe plc
Employees: 49,779
Sales: $6.13 billion (1998)
Stock Exchanges: OTC
Ticker Symbol: BSBE
SICs: 8711 Engineering Services

Already the worldwide leader in the design, manufacture, distribution, and installation of controls and control systems, Britain's Siebe Plc. is positioned to become a diversified manufacturing giant as it merges with the British manufacturing conglomerate BTR plc. in 1999. While analysts have questioned the wisdom of Siebe's move from a relatively "pure play" controls and controls systems group to a diversified engineering and manufacturing empire, there is no doubt that the emerging BTR Siebe will become one of the world's leading manufacturing concerns, with industry dominance in the high value added controls and automation industries. The merger, at a price of approximately £6 billion, represents only the latest in a long span of acquisitions that have enabled Siebe to grow from a company producing revenues of just £370 million in the mid-1980s to a giant with annual sales of nearly £3.7 billion in 1997. The BTR merger was expected to more than double Siebe's annual sales.

The proposed portrait of the post-merger BTR Siebe suggests more of an acquisition than a partnership, as Siebe's management, including key figures CEO Allen Yurko and Chairman Lord Colin Marshall, will retain the top positions.

Nonetheless, BTR, which has been struggling through much of the 1990s, will provide several of its own top figures, including its CEO Ian Strachan, who will serve as the merged group's deputy chairman, and Kathleen O'Donovan, who will continue her previous position as the new group's chief financial officer. After the merger, Siebe shareholders will retain 55 percent of the company's shares.

Siebe's product line numbers more than 10,000 individual products produced by more than 150 subsidiaries around the world and includes such well-known brand names as Foxboro, Robertshaw, APV, Univam, ACL-Drayton, Eberle, and many others. Siebe manufactures controls and control systems ranging from components for small appliances to sophisticated turnkey control automation systems for such projects as nuclear power stations and offshore drilling platforms. In addition to its manufacturing, Siebe also produces the software to drive its control systems under various computer platforms.

BTR, which has its own history of rapid expansion through acquisition, will add its diversified range of products, centered around four primary areas: process controls; specialized engineering systems; power drives for gear boxes and motors; and drive train and other systems for the automotive industry. At the same time, the company is expected to continue the process of shedding BTR's more diversified interests, which included subsidiary companies in the packaging, laminates, building products, sporting goods, and office furniture industries, among others.

Siebe's Change of Strategy in the 1970s

Siebe's beginnings stemmed from the arrival of former Austrian cavalry officer Augustus Siebe in London in 1819. A natural inventor, Siebe would be credited with a number of innovative products, ranging from water pump and rifle components designs to the product that would come to define Siebe for much of the 20th century—the world's first diving suit. The success of the Siebe diving suit led the company to focus on this new market, and from the 1890s the company developed into a specialized marine engineering company with an emphasis on

---

Company Perspectives:

BTR and Siebe have merged to create a world class engineering group with global leadership in the high-value-added controls and automation industry.

safety and rescue systems. As such, Siebe became a supplier to the British Royal Navy, among others, developing breathing apparatus and submarine emergency escape equipment. As the world took to the skies in the early part of the 20th century, Siebe adapted its underwater breathing apparatus to use in high-altitude conditions. By then, Siebe's designs had gone underground, as the company developed safety and rescue equipment for mining operations. Among noteworthy Siebe products were its Proto and Salvus rescue suits—the Proto name eventually would become synonymous with rescue stations in Britain's mining community.

Siebe remained a small, barely profitable manufacturing company. Until well into the 1960s the company's revenues hovered below the £1.5 million mark; the company's overhead, including an extended payroll, left little of its revenues as profits. By then, however, the company had acquired new management, in the person of Barrie Stephens, formerly with General Dynamics and later granted the royal title "Sir." Taking the managing director's position at Siebe in 1963, Stephens would spend the 1960s restructuring Siebe's operations, trimming staff by more than half, and expanding the company into new directions. At the end of the 1960s Stephens would lead Siebe into the first of what would become a long string of acquisitions. By the end of the decade, while bringing the company's revenues past the £2 million mark, these moves also had quintupled Siebe's profits. Siebe's business, which remained primarily British-based, would double to reach £4 million by 1972.

In the 1970s Stephens would start the process of transforming Siebe from a small domestic safety products company to a global group targeting the broader engineering controls category. Stephens's taste for acquisition had only just been whetted. In 1972 the company made its first significant acquisition, the purchase of leading safety product specialist James North & Sons. This company, larger than Siebe itself, was the leading European manufacturer of safety products and systems and gave Siebe its first strong foothold on the European continent. The James North acquisition also would mark another company trait: rather than place the Siebe name on North's operations, Siebe continued to market its new subsidiary's products under the North brand name. The same pattern would recur with Siebe's new acquisitions, to the extent that the Siebe name would remain relatively unknown, even though its brands led their respective markets.

The North purchase gave a new impulse to Siebe's revenue growth. By year end 1973 Siebe's sales had topped £18 million, before reaching the £20 million mark the following year. Steady and continued growth followed throughout the 1970s, despite the international recession caused by the Arab Oil Embargo. By the end of the decade Siebe had topped £50 million in sales.

Controls Specialist in the 1990s

Siebe continued to build its U.K. and European business, while eyeing entry into a new market: that of North America. The company would find a portal in 1982 with the acquisition of Tecalemit, one of the leading garage equipment and automotive tubing suppliers. This addition would help raise Siebe's sales to more than £156 million by 1984. The Tecalemit purchase also would lead the company into a new direction. Included in the Tecalemit acquisition were two subsidiaries producing electronic controls systems. These did not, however, fit together with Siebe's other businesses, and the company searched for a buyer for the two subsidiaries. The search was not successful, as a long slump in the computer and electronics industries had weakened the marketplace. Nonetheless, the controls subsidiaries remained profitable operations.

The Tecalemit controls subsidiaries also would provide essential pieces of the Siebe puzzle. With the company undergoing rapid growth and strong profits, Stephens's war chest provided opportunities for still larger acquisitions. The next Siebe acquisition came in 1985, with the purchase of compressed air systems and equipment specialist CompAir. That acquisition proved doubly interesting: in addition to providing Siebe with a complement to its North American garage equipment and safety equipment markets, CompAir brought with it three subsidiaries specialized in hydraulic controls systems. The new controls category fit neatly with the Tecalemit controls subsidiaries, and a new Siebe division was born.

By the end of the decade the child had grown larger than the parent. The new subsidiaries had given Siebe a solid footing in the North American market. But they also would encourage the company to invest more heavily in what was still a fairly young industry. The long-predicted reliance on computers and computers systems was becoming more and more of a reality in the 1980s, particularly with the widespread adoption of numeric control manufacturing systems and processes and the increasing use of automation and robotics in manufacturing.

In just five years Siebe would build a worldwide presence in the controls industry. The company's revenues would soar past £1.2 billion. Although the company continued its safety equipment and other manufacturing activities, controls would become its core focus. Three important acquisitions brought Siebe to this point. The first, made in 1986, added the United States' Robertshaw to the growing Siebe portfolio of subsidiaries. One of the leading controls manufacturers in the North American market, Robertshaw added its specialty category—appliances—to Siebe's list.

Siebe quickly reinforced its entry into appliance controls with the acquisitions of two more U.S. companies, Ranco and Barber-Colman, in 1987. These acquisitions also gave Siebe entry into industrial and commercial building control systems as well as into automotive control systems. In the appliance control segment, meanwhile, Siebe had achieved a worldwide leadership position. Ranco also added more than 75 years of experience in the heating and air conditioning temperature control segment, as well as control systems for commercial and home refrigeration. The Ranco and Barber-Colman acquisitions pushed Siebe's turnover past the £1 billion mark in 1988.

Siebe leader Stephens, who had raised the company's revenues more than 1,000 times in less than 30 years, began moving toward retirement in the 1990s. At the start of the decade, Stephens named the American Allen Yurko as the group's managing director and COO. During the years to follow Stephens would transfer the company's day-to-day leadership to Yurko, who was name CEO in 1994.

In the meantime, Siebe had gained global leadership of the controls industry. A significant acquisition came in 1990, with the purchase of the Foxboro Company, a world leading process controls automation company based in Foxboro, Massachusetts that had fallen on hard times in the 1980s. At a price of approximately US $650 million, Siebe added Foxboro's more than US $500 million in sales of its Unix-based control automation and other control systems products. Foxboro's specialty—that of implementation of large-scale control systems for oil refineries, chemical and pharmaceutical plants, nuclear and other power generation plants, and control systems adapted to the pulp and paper industries—placed Siebe firmly at the forefront of the world's control process industry. After restructuring Foxboro's operations, including trimming an oversized management and a vast private security staff, Siebe returned its new subsidiary to profitability by 1992.

Between 1992 and 1998 Siebe would conclude an impressive number of acquisitions, ranging from the 1993 purchase of Germany's Eberle, to the 1996 acquisition of Unitech plc, the company's largest acquisition to that date. Unitech brought the company its electronic power controls, while adding significant reinforcement to Siebe's Asian Pacific sales, which continued to lag behind its U.S. and Europe sales. Other acquisitions during this period include those of Eckardt AG and Schmidt Armaturen, both of Germany, Sweden's NAF Group, Triconex Corporation, Appliance Control Technology Inc., Eliwell SpA, LeROI International, Fabex Inc., and Satchwell Control Systems, the U.K. leader in the building automation segment. The 1997 purchase of APV Plc. marked Siebe's second bid for that leading food, beverage, dairy, and pharmaceutical process automation control specialist (the first takeover attempt having been fought and lost by Siebe in the mid-1980s).

Siebe's acquisition activity enabled the company to maintain its revenue and profit growth in the face of the difficult economic climate of the first half of the 1990s. By its year end 1996, the company neared £2.6 billion in revenues. The company, which, despite its worldwide dominance of the control systems market, remained in large part unknown to the public, nonetheless became known for its so-called "black belts," a staff of some 300 managers sent into newly acquired subsidiaries to assist in the restructuring and integration in the Siebe group.

Sir Barrie Stephens retired in 1998, passing on full leadership of Siebe to Allen Yurko in that year. The company's chairmanship was delegated to Lord Colin Marshall. Yurko would lead Siebe on its most aggressive acquisition year ever, one that would catch industry observers by surprise. Throughout 1998 the company made a number of acquisitions, including that of manufacturing process execution software designer Wonderware, which would be merged with the company's existing Foxboro operations. The company also added Electronic Measurement, a maker of power supply controls, and Eurotherm, which specialized in temperature controls. To accommodate these acquisitions, Siebe engaged on a restructuring drive, eliminating a number of jobs, a process that would continue through the end of the year and prepare the way for Siebe's largest-ever acquisition.

In November 1998 Siebe announced that it had agreed to merge with British manufacturing conglomerate BTR to form BTR Siebe. The deal, which was expected to be finalized in February 1999, would add BTR's £4.8 billion annual sales to Siebe's £3.9 billion and create one of the United Kingdom's largest manufacturing groups. The deal also left Siebe basically in control of the merged entity, with Yurko remaining in place at the new manufacturing giant's helm.

The addition of BTR gave Siebe not only that company's process controls divisions, specialized in valves, meters, and batteries, but also its specialized engineering activities, principally in airplane repair, filtration and railroad signaling systems, and in automotive and power drive manufacturing. Although Siebe was criticized for abandoning its "pure play" status to take on a new role as a diversified manufacturing conglomerate, the BTR acquisition nonetheless presented a number of opportunities for synergy, while adding to Siebe's own manufacturing lines. Meanwhile, Siebe's long experience in integrating and restructuring subsidiaries, while sustaining its own steady growth, made the BTR acquisition seem less of a risk.

Principal Subsidiaries

The Foxboro Company (U.S.); BTR Nylex Ltd. (Australia); Hawker-Siddeley Group Ltd.; Stowe Woodward; CompAir (U.S.); Eaton Technologies (U.S.); Mesnel (France); Metzeler Automotive Profiles (Germany); Perfiles (Spain); Weavexx (U.S.); Westinghouse Brake & Signal (U.K. and Australia).

Principal Divisions

Aerospace and Sensors; Appliance Controls; Automotovie Systems; Climate Controls; Environmental Controls; Industrial Equipment; Instrument & Valve; Intelligent Automation; Pneumatics; Power Controls; Specialist Equipment.

Further Reading

Edgecliff-Johnson, Andrew, "Time for Siebe to Weave Its Magic at BTR," *Financial Times,* November 25, 1998.
Holmes, David, "Siebe Merger Debate Hots Up," *Reuters Finance UK,* November 27, 1998.
"Siebe Company History," London: Siebe plc, 1998.
"Siebe's Driving Force Takes a Tighter Grip on the Controls," *Financial Times,* November 24, 1998.

—M.L. Cohen

Burlington Northern Santa Fe Corporation

3800 Continental Plaza
777 Main Street
Fort Worth, Texas 76102-5384
U.S.A.
(817) 333-2000
Fax: (817) 333-2377
Web site: http://www.bnsf.com

Public Company
Incorporated: 1994
Employees: 44,500
Sales: $8.41 billion (1997)
Stock Exchanges: New York
Ticker Symbol: BNI
SICs: 4011 Railroads, Line-Haul Operating; 6719
    Holding Companies, Not Elsewhere Classified

Burlington Northern Santa Fe Corporation is one of the great success stories in the history of American railroad. Merging Burlington Northern, Inc. and Santa Fe Pacific Corporation in 1995 gave rise to one of the largest railroad networks on the North American continent, with more than 34,000 route miles across 28 states and the Canadian provinces of British Columbia and Manitoba. The company's railroad networks extend over a vast distance, from the Pacific Northwest and southern California seaports to the Midwest, Southeast, and Southwest, and from the Gulf of Mexico up to the flatlands of Canada. With more than 44,000 employees, the Burlington Northern Santa Fe Railroad transports large amounts of coal, grain, chemicals, forest products, metals and minerals, consumer goods, and automobiles.

Early History

Burlington was founded in 1849 in the small town of Aurora, Illinois, and its early fortunes were linked with the burgeoning midwestern railway industry and the growing nearby city of Chicago. In the years from 1845 to 1848, swarms of settlers began to push west, lured by vast tracts of arable land and the promise of gold in California. By 1848 Illinois had already be-

come the largest grain producer in the nation, requiring links with established eastern markets as well as with developing western settlements. The state's promise was reflected most clearly in Chicago's explosive growth as a railroad center. In 1847 Chicago had not even a single mile of railroad, but by 1854 it had become the railway capital of the United States.

Astutely anticipating Chicago's ascendancy, Aurora businessmen in 1848 proposed the construction of a railroad to connect with the Galena and Chicago Union Railroad, thus linking Aurora not only to the hub of the Midwest but also to the markets of the East. The State of Illinois charter for the Aurora Branch Railroad was signed into law on February 12, 1849, by Governor Augustus French. It authorized 12 miles of track to connect with the Galena Railroad. The Aurora commissioners immediately issued stock, selling more than a quarter of the total issue in nine days, and elected five members to its board of directors with Stephen F. Gale as its president.

Construction of the Aurora Branch progressed swiftly. By August 27, 1850, six miles of rail were laid; by October 21 of the same year the fledgling railroad began regular service to Chicago. The company encountered stiff competition from the beginning. In 1850 the U.S. Congress ceded 2.5 million acres of public land in Illinois for the construction of a railroad throughout the length of the state. Eager to promote the railroad industry, the Illinois legislature in turn granted numerous charters to new rail firms during its first session of 1851. Potential routes then crisscrossed the state, some quickly materializing and threatening to cut off or supersede the Aurora Branch.

To safeguard their young firm, Aurora directors moved to consolidate with three other new lines: the Central Military Tract Railroad, Peoria and Oquawka Railroad, and Northern Cross Railroad. The move was financed by eastern interests bent on profiting from the developing Illinois railroad industry. In January 1852 Boston financiers bought enough stock to elect John W. Brooks, who represented Boston interests, to the Aurora board.

Chauncey Colton, a promoter of the Central Military Tract, met with Elisha Wadsworth, an Aurora director, and James Grimes, a Peoria and Oquawka director, proposing to consolidate their three lines into one through-route between Chicago and the Mississippi River. John Brooks in turn persuaded John Murray Forbes, the leader of the Boston group, to fund the consolidation. In 1852 the respective charters were amended to accommodate the territorial changes, and the Aurora Branch officially changed its name to Chicago and Aurora Railroad Company. Eventually, Northern Cross, which extended southwest from Galesburg, Illinois, joined the group. The original 12-mile Aurora branch now reached from Chicago through Aurora and Galesburg to Burlington, Iowa and Quincy, Illinois, two small towns on the Mississippi River, thus fulfilling the intent of Colton's original plan. In 1855 the Chicago and Aurora again changed its name, this time to The Chicago, Burlington and Quincy Railroad Company (CB&Q). By 1864 the various segments of the system had been united into a single corporate entity under the control of the Chicago, Burlington and Quincy, which became the parent company.

CB&Q received its impetus from the urgent expansion and stiff competition of the young railroad industry rather than from a single visionary leader. In the first few years presidents rapidly succeeded one another. In 1851 director Elisha Wadsworth followed Gale as president, but exactly a year later, Gale was re-elected to succeed Wadsworth. In 1853 an easterner, James F. Joy, was elected president, reflecting the enlarging interests of the Boston financial group in the future of the company. In 1857 John Van Nortwick became president, holding the post until 1865, the longest term of any president to date. For each of these men, running the railroad was only one of many responsibilities; CB&Q was not to have a full-time president until 1876.

Van Nortwick guided the firm through the financially rocky years of the late 1850s. With Boston capital supplementing local dollars, the railroad had established a solid financial footing by 1852. The panic of 1857, however, wiped out earlier successes. Wheat and corn crops were abnormally small in 1858 and 1859, providing little for railroads to haul. In the company's fiscal year 1858–1859, tonnage moved by CB&Q amounted to only three-quarters of the previous year's haul, and the number of passengers carried was 20 percent less than the preceding year. Revenues in 1858 were only 60 percent of what they had been in 1857. Bonds and a mortgage were issued to cover outstanding bills. A portion of the income from these sources, however, was earmarked to repay old bonds. One million dollars was set aside to cover the cost of a new entry into Chicago, and a sinking fund was established to liquidate the debt on or before its maturity, bespeaking a prudent approach to financial management that guaranteed CB&Q's future. By fiscal year 1860–61 total revenues were up 38 percent.

The Civil War and Late 19th Century

The Civil War closely followed the lean years of the late 1850s, and the wartime economy launched CB&Q's full eco-

nomic recovery. The company's primary wartime challenge was to manage the increased traffic in goods and people. The railroad's physical plant and facilities were enlarged and adapted to meet this demand. During the war years the company doubled its supply of freight cars and improved its roadbed, track, and terminal facilities in Chicago, Aurora, and Galesburg. Revenues and profits increased with the traffic. For the fiscal year ending April 30, 1863, CB&Q experienced a 90 percent rise in net income.

Expansion and improvement continued in the postwar years. From 1864 to 1873, CB&Q track and traffic increased fourfold. Technical improvements kept pace. In 1867 the firm laid its first steel rails, replacing iron ones. During the 1870s and 1880s the route was expanded in Iowa, Nebraska, and Illinois, and preparations were made to reach farther toward the Pacific. The push west generated intense competition among railroad companies. Although revenues increased 2.5 times in the first postwar decade, traffic climbed more quickly. After guiding CB&Q through the financial panic of the late 1850s and the Civil War, Van Nortwick resigned as president in 1865, and James Joy was re-elected. Following him, James Walker was elected president in 1871 and Robert Harris became president in 1876.

As the railroad industry expanded in the 1870s, it also experienced increased government regulation and labor unrest. In the early 1870s most of the states on the Burlington route, as CB&Q's network was called, passed stiff regulatory measures known collectively as the Granger Laws. Such laws fixed passenger fares and freight rates, providing that the latter be based on distance rather than the quantity or nature of the commodity shipped. In 1874 under Walker's leadership, CB&Q challenged the constitutionality of Iowa's Granger Laws. In 1877 the Supreme Court ruled in favor of Iowa. This suit was only one of many of the Granger cases. Together, these cases established the precedent of government intervention in and regulation of businesses that provided public services.

In 1877 in solidarity with railroad workers nationwide, CB&Q workers struck in Chicago, Galesburg, and Iowa. In Chicago, President Harris discontinued freight service but kept passenger lines open. Charles Perkins, vice-president of CB&Q, refused to do the same in Iowa; acting independently, he completely shut down the Iowa leg. His disagreement with Harris over labor relations provoked corporate struggles that eventually moved Harris to resign. John Forbes, the eastern financier who had funded the original Aurora Branch, took over as president in 1878. Remaining in Boston, he joined forces with Perkins, who became the western partner in this two-man leadership team.

Together, Forbes and Perkins developed a highly efficient corporation. In 1881 Forbes resigned and let Perkins take over as president. Under Perkins, leadership was consolidated in the president's hands, ending the power shifts between board and president that had characterized the first 30 years of CB&Q's existence. Perkins's 20-year presidency was marked by periods of financial success in the 1880s and financial downturn in the 1890s. These years were punctuated by ongoing contests both with the government and with labor.

The early and middle 1880s were years of general economic improvement with small fluctuations. Because CB&Q's freight was primarily agricultural, it was vulnerable to changing crop yields, and in 1881, for example, net income declined after a poor season. The 1883 crop was excellent, however, and net income rose to $8.7 million, the highest company income in the 19th century. In that year CB&Q was among 17 railroads serving Chicago, yet it carried 41 percent of all corn received in the city, 34 percent of all rye, 33 percent of all wheat, and 21 percent of the oats, and delivered more livestock than any other company. The year 1887 was the firm's best to that time in terms of traffic hauled and gross earnings.

Technical improvements also contributed to CB&Q's success in the 1880s. In 1886 and 1887 company engineers improved the air brake, previously devised by Westinghouse for use on heavy freight trains. The better brake allowed higher train speeds and the railroad instituted its fast mail coach in 1884. In general technical developments permitted rapid expansion. In 1882 Burlington completed a through line to Denver and, in 1886, to St. Paul-Minneapolis, Minnesota. All told, from December 31, 1880, to December 31, 1890, CB&Q track increased in length from 2,771 miles to 5,160 miles.

In the late 1880s another episode of labor unrest compromised some of the early successes of Perkins's tenure. On February 27, 1888, CB&Q engineers struck, beginning a walk-out that lasted until January 4, 1889. Labor finally capitulated to management, but not without damage to the company. After the hugely successful 1887, fiscal year 1888 was disastrous. Freight revenue dropped by more than 17 percent from the previous year, while operating expenses increased by the same percentage. By year's end there was a net loss of almost $250,000.

Perkins was concerned about increasing government regulation. In 1887 President Cleveland signed the Interstate Commerce Act, a measure that Perkins strongly opposed as a restraint to the continued viability of the railroad industry. Along with the Chicago and Northwestern and the Union Pacific railroads, CB&Q tested the constitutionality of Nebraska's Newberry Law, passed in 1893, which established maximum rates on all freight transported in the state. This time, the U.S. Supreme Court decided in favor of the railroads.

In the 1890s circumstances coincided that reversed the financial successes of the 1880s. Increasing competition and regulation, economic depression following the panic of 1893, and rising taxes combined to decrease net income for the eight years following 1888; during those years it was only 60 percent of what it had been from 1881 to 1887. Improvements in physical plant were kept to a minimum, reflecting CB&Q's usual conservative fiscal policy. From 1889 to 1896 new acquisitions fell well behind the national average. In 1898 John Forbes died, closing the founding era.

The 20th Century

By the mid-1890s CB&Q's corporate structure had become large and unwieldy. Most of the smaller railroads it had acquired were independently owned and operated, affiliated with CB&Q only through lease arrangements or stock ownership. In 1899 Perkins financed the purchase of most of the companies, greatly simplifying the corporate structure of the Burlington system. Meanwhile, E.H. Harriman, chairman of the Union Pacific Rail-

road, and James J. Hill, chairman of the Great Northern Railroad a controlling voice of the Northern Pacific, were both looking longingly at the entire Burlington network. CB&Q still controlled the Chicago traffic, the major prize that had eluded both of these men. For their part, Perkins and other CB&Q executives recognized the need for a link to the Pacific Northwest with its rich supplies of lumber. In April 1901 Hill agreed to purchase two thirds of CB&Q stock, and CB&Q became a subsidiary of the Great Northern and Northern Pacific Railroads. Although Perkins completed the negotiations for sale, he resigned from his post in January 1901. George Harris, second vice-president of CB&Q, succeeded Perkins as president.

The period preceding World War I was a time of smooth and regular expansion for CB&Q. Because Hill made few changes in management and operation, CB&Q was, for the most part, unaffected by the purchase. Harris continued as president, and the entire firm simply became one efficiently functioning unit of a larger system. In 1910 Harris resigned and was followed by Darius Miller. When Miller died suddenly in 1914, Hale Holden, general counsel for CB&Q, became president. CB&Q's primary challenge after 1901 was to fill in the gaps in its rail network. From 1901 to 1915, trackage increased by 1,373 miles, 17.2 percent, to a total of 9,366 miles. These years made up the last great period of expansion; in 1916 the firm reached its peak mileage.

Financial performance during this period reflected smooth and steady development. Both freight and passenger revenues climbed during the prewar period but more steeply in the earlier than in the later years. By 1908 total revenues were up 56.8 percent over 1901, but by 1915 were only 82.2 percent over 1901. In the same period, operating expenses also increased. Because Hill had modernized track and physical plant after the acquisition, 1908 expenses showed a 72.5 percent increase over 1901. After 1908, however, the effect of modernization was reflected in reduced operating expenses. By 1915 the increase over 1901 was only 86.4 percent.

CB&Q began to feel the effects of World War I before the United States was directly involved. In 1916 traffic, revenues, and operating expenses all increased. When the United States declared war in 1917, the U.S. government authorized the formation of the Railroads' War Board, a committee of five top railroad executives, including Hale Holden. The board monitored the flow of rail traffic and managed railroad personnel to maximize efficiency for the war effort. In late 1917, however, the government took complete control, regulating compensation rates as well as traffic flow. Each railroad was guaranteed an annual compensation equal to its average annual operating income for the three years ending June 30, 1917. For CB&Q this amounted to $33.3 million.

During these years the company's haulage of livestock and agricultural products increased substantially and it set all-time records for transporting coal. The U.S. government relinquished control of the railroads on March 1, 1920, one day after passage of the Transportation Act. The act modified what had been a policy of encouraging competition among railroads; passage of the new plan permitted any mergers or acquisitions that met Interstate Commerce Commission (ICC) standards for approval and exempted railroads from antitrust laws to the extent necessary to permit these combinations. The law gave railroads broad leeway in devising policies generally, although the ICC had the final say in how the companies carried out these policies.

During the 1920s CB&Q focused on two broad tasks: testing the new industrywide regulatory policy and reorganizing its prewar plant and traffic. In response to the new Transportation Act, Holden urged the railroad industry to follow the act's mandate and initiate policy. Hill and Holden and other officials were themselves formulating a new financial arrangement between the CB&Q, the Great Northern, and the Northern Pacific. In 1930 the ICC rejected the proposal, and the group remained in its original 1901 configuration.

Physical plant improvements and technical innovations characterized CB&Q's internal development during the 1920s. For the first time in the firm's history, there was no net growth in railroad mileage. The number of locomotives and cars actually decreased. Carrying capacity increased, however, because of technical improvements. Throughout this decade CB&Q consistently made money; although passenger revenues declined, operating expenses also declined, and income remained steady.

Hard Times During the Great Depression

Early in 1929 Holden resigned to become chairman of the Southern Pacific. Frederick E. Williamson was chosen to replace him as president. Soon afterward the stock market crashed. CB&Q felt the effects immediately. By March 1930, as the Great Depression engulfed the economy, gross revenue was less than in any comparable month since 1919. Overall in 1930, business decreased more than 12 percent compared with 1929. By June 1932 the number of employees had dropped to 23,135, a decrease of more than 7,000 since June 1931. In the first quarter of 1933 CB&Q fell short in meeting fixed expenses by $1.5 million. In the second quarter of that year, however, stimulated in part by New Deal legislation, the firm began a slow recovery. In May it not only met its expenses but also showed the first increase in gross revenue over the corresponding month in the previous four years. In 1931 Williamson resigned to become president of the New York Central, and Ralph Budd, president of the Great Northern, was chosen to replace Williamson as president of the CB&Q.

New Deal legislation that aided the railroad industry included 1933's Emergency Transportation Act, which sought to eliminate duplication of services and promote financial reorganization of railroads. New Deal legislation, however, also helped labor, and in 1934 the National Railroad Board of Adjustment was established to settle labor disputes over rates of pay, work rules, and working conditions. Two other measures passed in 1935, the Railroad Retirement Act and an accompanying pension act, cost CB&Q $1.44 million in addition to the funds already paid into the company's existing pension plan.

The railroad industry also suffered during the 1930s from the effects of stiffening competition as the number of passenger cars, trucks, and airplanes increased. CB&Q met that competition with technological advancements, especially in the area of passenger service. In 1934 it introduced the *Zephyr,* the first diesel-electric locomotive, which often cut travel times in half.

Resurgence During World War II

In 1940, even before the United States entered World War II, the government began to mobilize resources for a wartime economy. Rather than follow World War I practice and nationalize the railroads, the Roosevelt administration worked through such existing organizations as the Interstate Commerce Commission and the Association of American Railroads. The government did appoint an advisory commission to the revived Council of National Defense; Ralph Budd was appointed commissioner of transportation to this board.

By 1941 CB&Q had emerged fully from the Depression. Net income in that year was $10.4 million—in excess of $10 million for the first time since 1931. Wartime traffic and income continued to soar. Although miles of track actually were reduced during the war, CB&Q improved its traffic control and communications and modernized many of its facilities, rising to the demands of a wartime economy. From 1940 through 1945 CB&Q increased the amount of freight and passengers by 88 percent and 179 percent, respectively, over the previous six-year period. Net income for the years 1942 through 1945 was 98 percent of total net income for the years 1929 through 1941.

In the immediate postwar period the U.S. economy continued its prosperous trend. The railroad industry, however, was faced with stiffening competition from the airline and automobile industries, its wartime successes curtailed by rising operating and compensation costs. Although CB&Q's total operating revenues did not decrease in the years 1945 to 1949, total operating expenses increased nearly 14.5 percent during the same period. The company met these challenges primarily by concentrating on passenger rail improvements.

In 1949 Ralph Budd resigned as president to become chairman of the Chicago Transit Authority. Harry C. Murphy was appointed as his successor. During Murphy's tenure, which lasted until 1965, CB&Q continued to face rising wage costs and competition from other forms of transportation. To counter these challenges, the firm ceased operating 343 miles of underused track between 1950 and 1963. In addition, from 1949 through 1963, CB&Q spent more than $430 million to improve plant and equipment, resulting in higher efficiency for handling freight and passengers. During these years the firm maintained its reputation for innovations in passenger service. From 1949 to 1963, a period when the number of passengers declined on other railroads, the number of passengers on CB&Q increased 10.2 percent. Net income during these years ranged from a high of $33.8 million in 1950 to a low of $12.5 million in 1960.

In the 1960s CB&Q, the Great Northern, and the Northern Pacific proposed to merge into one corporate entity. Murphy resigned in 1965, before the ICC could rule on the proposal. L.W. Menk succeeded him as president and chairman. In 1966 Menk resigned to become president of Northern Pacific and was succeeded by William J. Quinn.

In 1968 the ICC approved the merger plan under the name Burlington Northern Inc. In March 1970 the three firms and two smaller railroads formally consolidated, and Menk became president and chief operating officer of the new company. Burlington Northern in 1970 sought to acquire the Missouri-Kansas-Texas Railroad (Katy) but subsequently dropped its bid without comment. Industry observers speculated that the Katy's debt load may have discouraged Burlington Northern or that the ICC would have been unlikely to approve the merger.

In the early 1970s Burlington Northern diversified into natural resources management, focusing especially on coal development. It also added an air freight subsidiary. Management structure changed in the 1970s; Menk became chairman and chief executive officer, with Robert Downing, Norman M. Lorentzsen, and Richard Bressler, serially, filling the dual posts of president and chief operating officer.

In 1972 Burlington Northern and Union Pacific sought joint control of Peninsula Terminal Co., a switching line in Portland, Oregon, but the U.S. Supreme Court reversed the ICC's approval of the plan. The following year brought merger negotiations between Burlington Northern and Chicago, Milwaukee, St. Paul & Pacific Railroad. The ICC rejected this merger plan. In 1980, however, Burlington Northern succeeded in acquiring the St. Louis-San Francisco Railway.

By 1978 the company had record profits, still in large part from the railroad division. In 1982 Bressler became chairman, president, and chief operating officer. He streamlined existing operations by selling the air freight unit and unsuccessful segments of the railroad and by continuing efforts to develop the company's coal, timber, and gas reserves. In 1983 Burlington Northern acquired El Paso Natural Gas Company, a diversified energy concern that specialized in producing natural gas, and in 1985 it bought Southland Royal Company, producer of oil and gas. Initially these moves profitably supplemented Burlington's development of resources on its own railroad land. In June 1988, however, the company suddenly reversed its diversification trend and announced the spinoff of the energy resources operation as Burlington Resources Inc., an independent public company. The spinoff enabled Burlington Northern to avoid pending legal claims that remained against the former El Paso Natural Gas Company, which had been sued for breach of contract, and to recover from falling energy prices. Burlington Northern also sold its trucking subsidiary, Burlington Motor Carriers Inc., in 1988. The buyer was an investor group that included the subsidiary's top management.

Bressler continued as chairman of Burlington Northern and Burlington Resources, while Gerald Grinstein, who had been vice-chairman of both companies, became Burlington Northern's president and chief executive officer in 1989. Bressler retired in 1990, and Grinstein assumed the additional post of chairman. In the early 1990s Burlington Northern was focused on its railroad business, the company's historic strength. It was seeking increased flexibility in its labor contracts in an effort to improve efficiency and was investing in track improvements and new rolling stock.

History of the Santa Fe Pacific Corporation

In the early 1990s Santa Fe Pacific Corporation (SFP) was a holding company for subsidiaries engaged in transportation, mining, and petroleum products transmission. One of its wholly owned subsidiaries was the Atchison, Topeka and Santa Fe Railway Company, one of the nation's major freight railroads, serving 12 states. Another subsidiary, Santa Fe Pacific Minerals

Corporation, had significant coal mining operations and was a large producer of precious metals. Santa Fe Pacific Pipelines, Inc., the third subsidiary, transported gasoline, diesel, and jet fuel.

The Early Period

The history of SFP began with a railroad. In 1859 Cyrus K. Holliday founded the Atchison and Topeka Railroad Company. The Kansas drought hit immediately thereafter and the company foundered. Through the early 1860s the company searched for funding and land grants. The company name became Atchison, Topeka and Santa Fe Railroad (ATSF) in 1863, but the first train movement did not take place until 1869, on a line of about 26 miles from Topeka to Burlingame, Kansas. The ATSF became the pioneering railroad of the southwest portion of the United States. The East had fairly reliable railroad service by 1860, but the West was still largely untouched. The ATSF started in eastern Kansas and ultimately reached Santa Fe, New Mexico, paving the way for the growth of towns and commerce. The company was built upon faith in the prospects of the West and Southwest.

By 1873 the company had more than 130 miles of track. In 1875 the road expanded eastward toward Kansas City. The first train entered Las Vegas, Nevada, in 1879, and Albuquerque, New Mexico was entered in 1880. ATSF acquired the Sonora Railway in 1882. Hardships in the southwestern United States were crippling the Gulf, Colorado and Santa Fe Railroad in 1885. ATSF absorbed that company, thus stretching to Houston, Texas, and the Gulf of Mexico. Other smaller additions to the ATSF were being transacted through the company's subsidiary—the Chicago, Kansas and Western Railroad Company. Many of these branches were not completed until 1887.

The company also worked to protect its presence in California. In 1886 ATSF purchased from the fading Chicago and St. Louis Railway a right of way into Chicago. After rusted tracks were replaced and bridges built, train service began in 1888. In 1890 the company purchased the St. Louis and San Francisco Railway and the Colorado Midland Railway. In 24 years the ATSF had grown from the Topeka ground-breaking to a system of 9,300 miles, linking Lake Michigan, the Gulf of Mexico, and the Pacific Ocean. It served Chicago, Dallas, Denver, St. Louis, Los Angeles, Kansas City, and San Francisco.

During this time the company's growth was characterized by quality construction. It was the creation of railroad men, not financiers, and lines often were built ahead of traffic, leading the way for trade and settlement. ATSF absorbed and repaired dozens of bankrupt lines along the way.

The company suffered some setbacks around the turn of the century. In 1889 the California boom stalled, and passenger business dropped. During the financial panic of 1893, banks and rail empires crashed. Crop failures and dropping rates due to competition between 1889 and 1895 had weakened the company. Its troubles compounded by purchases and upkeep, the ATSF was pinched financially. The company went into receivership and in 1895 the financially troubled system was sold to Edward King, representing a reorganization committee, for $60 million. The company was reincorporated as the Atchison, Topeka and Santa Fe Railway Company, and reorganization began with the sale of the two lines acquired in 1890. Other unprofitable lines were sold and business picked up. By 1898 the company's line had been trimmed to about 7,000 miles. The new president of the reorganized company was Edward P. Ripley.

Growth in the New Century

Pruning continued, but the company revitalized enough to purchase the unfinished San Francisco and San Joaquin Valley Railway in 1899. The line was operative by 1900. Numerous short lines also were acquired. In 1901 the Santa Fe, Prescott and Phoenix Railroad was purchased, giving ATSF exclusive presence in Arizona, then a promising area. By 1902 the company had added almost 1,000 miles to its reorganized line. Careful purchase and expansion continued as ATSF extended through Arizona, New Mexico, northern California, and Texas.

Between the company's inception and 1917, passenger travel rose 600 percent. The railway was operated by the U.S. government between 1917 and 1920, because of its strategic importance during World War I. Between 1920 and 1929 the ATSF concentrated on maintenance and improvement of equipment and lines. There were ups and downs in operating revenue as the postwar economy surged and faltered in the regions serviced by ATSF, but the decade overall was a good one. The company in 1928 purchased the Orient Line, a system that included about 300 miles of line in Mexico.

The Depression and World War II

During the Great Depression the company's business suffered. In 1935 the company started a track-improvement program between Chicago and California to institute a new fast schedule. At the same time the first diesel-electric locomotive was being built. By 1938 ATSF was running two of the new diesel-electric trains between Chicago and the West Coast. The trains were much faster and more economical than their predecessors, a boon to both passenger and freight services. While the number of passengers dropped, travel distances had increased. Freight traffic was hit hard by the Depression. To offset this, the company reduced operating costs by increasing efficiency, primarily by equipment replacements. ATSF also began branching into other forms of transportation. It bought bus operations and acquired a system of truck lines. In 1935 it purchased the Southern Kansas Stage bus lines. The motor-carrier companies that ATSF acquired were consolidated into the Santa Fe Trail Transportation Company in 1937. By the decade's end ATSF owned 15 diesels and 44 motor coaches. By 1940 a freight-handling system was coordinated between the company's truck operations. Just as ATSF was enjoying economic recovery, World War II broke out.

The Postwar Boom

With the war came a surge in traffic, both passenger and freight. War halted the delivery of needed new locomotives, but availability was resumed right after the war. Despite the strain, the line and equipment survived the record-breaking traffic. The result was the development of an automated system of centralized control. In 1946 the company established the Santa Fe Skyway, Inc., offering air freight service to round out its business with shippers. Complete transportation integration was prevented by the Civil Aeronautics Board and the ICC. The skyway was discontinued in 1947. Truck and bus operations continued, covering 12,000 and 9,400 miles, respectively, by 1949.

In another postwar development, the ATSF returned its attentions to improving equipment and methods. Streamlined train use was expanded. The 1950s were marked by the complete phasing out of steam locomotives; by 1954 ATSF was entirely dieselized. During the 1950s many railroads began deemphasizing passenger service as a result of the growth of air travel and the improvement of highways due to U.S. President Dwight Eisenhower's Interstate Highway Act. In contrast, ATSF, whose reputation had been built on passenger service, applied itself to upgrading passenger travel, buying passenger rail cars and developing high-quality, high-speed service.

Growth and Expansion

In the late 1950s and early 1960s the company pursued greater diversification that led to the creation of separate companies involved in pipelines, energy resources, and trucking. In 1968 Santa Fe Industries Inc. (SFI), a new parent company, was established as the holding company for these separate enterprises. Also in 1968 SFI inaugurated the fastest freight train in the world. During this time ATSF began to enter a new market segment—the intermodal truck-train-container business—which allowed freight to be shifted from ships to trucks to trains more fluidly. In the early 1990s 60 percent of its trains were intermodal and 40 percent of the railroad's revenues came from intermodal operations.

The shift in emphasis was auspicious; by the late 1960s railroads lost mail contracts to jets and thus lost the main revenue subsidizing passenger service. In 1968 ATSF's losses on passenger service necessitated the sale of trains. It was a prelude to turning passenger service over to Amtrak in 1971. This marked the end of an era for ATSF and the start of a new focus on freight service.

In 1972 SFI sought and found resources in its underused acreage in New Mexico and Arizona: tons of coal. Diversification made sense, and the company committed to mining the coal itself in 1982. The following year John Schmidt took over as chairman and CEO, and Southern Pacific Company (SPC) agreed to merge with SFI, creating an umbrella holding company—Santa Fe Southern Pacific Corporation (SFSP), with $11 billion in assets. The merger application was filed with the ICC in 1984. At the time of the merger, SPC was not performing well. The company had diversified into industrial parks and office complexes. SFI had diversified into transportation, natural resources, and real estate. The ATSF and SPC were then the two least profitable of the major U.S. railroads. Joining forces would shorten routes, create economies by cutting overlaps, and eliminate competition with each other. Other major railroads were moving to merge in the early 1980s, making the ATSF and SPC merger necessary for survival.

While awaiting ICC approval, SPC's rail business could not be operated by SFI, so SFI looked to SPC's real estate to generate income. In 1983 real estate income supplied nearly a third of SFSP's revenue. Development projects became a new source of income. Its natural resource division also contributed significantly to operating profits.

ICC hearings continued through 1985 and into 1986. SFSP suffered from being unable to run 40 percent of its business— the Southern Pacific Railroad. Placed in trust, the railroad deteriorated. Then the ICC ordered divestiture of either the Santa Fe or Southern Pacific rail operations, claiming the merger would create a monopoly on some important routes. By 1986 SFSP's major businesses—transportation and fuel—were suffering, and real estate earnings also were down. In 1985 SPC contributed one third of SFSP's real estate earnings, which accounted for nearly half of the company's operating profit that year. In 1987 the ICC refused to reconsider its rejection of the merger. SFSP reported a net loss of $138 million for 1986. Schmidt resigned as CEO, and the company underwent drastic restructuring, beginning with the sale of unprofitable businesses. Robert Krebs filled the CEO seat.

Six subsidiaries were put on the block, including three pipeline companies, a leasing company, a building contractor, and the Santa Fe Pacific Timber Company. Raiders circled the troubled company, aided by the October 1987 stock market crash. By the year's end SFSP announced the sale of SPC's rail business to Rio Grande Industries, for $1 billion. SFSP's net income was $373.5 million for 1987.

To discourage takeover, the company underwent a $4.7 billion leveraged recapitalization. Despite restructuring and the sale of subsidiaries the company remained highly diversified: in addition to being the seventh largest U.S. railroad, it held the second largest petroleum products pipeline, remained one of the largest real estate operations, and oversaw the sixth largest domestic oil and gas company. In 1988 ATSF had 12,000 miles of track. Undeveloped holdings included urban and agricultural land in 15 states and oil and mineral holdings. Income from continuing operations for 1988 was $146 million. After accounting for discontinued operations, however, the company showed a net loss of $46.5 million.

Further setbacks came in 1989. In addition to slowed shipments because of the recession, the company received a $1.04 billion verdict in a federal antitrust case brought by Energy Transportation Systems, Inc. (ETSI) in Texas. ETSI was a coal-slurry pipeline company that accused SFSP of blocking a project. The settlement was adjusted to $350 million in 1990.

The company name was changed to Santa Fe Pacific Corporation in 1989. Hard times in the industry produced greater cooperation between companies; SFP reached agreements with Burlington Northern Inc., including sharing a rail terminal.

Early in 1990 SFP sold a 20 percent stake in its real estate subsidiary. Selling assets continued to reduce the company's debt. SFP made public a portion of its Santa Fe Energy Resources, Inc. unit in 1990 and spun it off completely by year's end. SFP Realty changed its name to Catellus Development Corporation, which also was spun off as an independent company in 1990.

Survival in the 1990s

SFP continued to experience difficult times during the early 1990s. Although management had decided on a strategy of selling off assets to bolster revenues, unexpected events hastened the company's decline. Railway congestion around Houston and in places such as Phoenix and South California significantly delayed the timeliness of SFP deliveries, with the consequence of declining revenues. Soon SFP was looking for a potential candidate with which to merge its operations and, luckily, management found Burlington Northern a willing suitor.

The merger had significant benefits for both railroad companies. For SFP the advantages were obvious: capital to stabilize its worrisome financial condition; access to trackage and new shippers; an agreement to improve its carriers; and the potential for long-term growth. Burlington Northern likewise was given new opportunities, including access to trackage and new shippers throughout the SFP railway system; a vastly improved competitive position throughout the Western United States due to the merger; more access to the Gulf coast petroleum belt; a single line route from British Columbia to San Diego, California, which management had wanted for some time; and a projected net annual increase in revenues of more than $500 million.

Gerald Grinstein, the chairman of Burlington Northern, and Robert Krebs, the president of SFP, managed the details of the merger in both an amiable and efficient manner. The relationship between the two men cannot be discounted in assessing the merger, since it appeared that the congeniality that flowed between Grinstein and Krebs filtered down to the actual merger operations. Nearly everything went smoothly and according to plan, and within a few short years the new Burlington Northern Santa Fe Railway was the envy of the railroad companies.

By the end of 1997 the company counted more than 34,000 route miles and had a total of 5,000 locomotives and 90,000 freight cars in service, with a little more than 44,000 employees. Burlington Northern Santa Fe Railroad had become the largest transporter of low-sulfur coal in the entire world, the largest transporter of grain throughout the United States, the largest transporter of aircraft parts, beer, and aluminum in America, and had hauled enough coal in 1997 to generate almost ten percent of the country's entire electrical output.

Robert Krebs replaced Grinstein as the head of BNSF, but continued to lead the company into a period of stabilized prosperity. Revenues increased to $8.4 billion in 1997, and the company's rail also increased significantly. During the same year BNSF's work force increased by 1,000 employees, with more people expected to be hired during 1998 and 1999. The merger between Burlington Northern and Santa Fe Pacific has been one of the great railroad success stories of the late 20th century.

Principal Subsidiaries

Atchison, Topeka and Santa Fe Railway Co.; Burlington Northern and Santa Fe Railway Co.; Central California Traction Co.; Havelock Car Shop; SFP Pipeline Holdings Co.; Western Fruit Express Co.

Further Reading

''As BNSF Nears Start-Up, Management Team Takes Shape,'' *Railway Age,* October 1995, pp. 20–21.

Marshall, James, *Santa Fe: The Railroad That Built an Empire,* New York: Random House, 1945.

Overton, Richard C., *Burlington Route: A History of the Burlington Lines,* New York: Alfred A. Knopf, 1965.

——, *Milepost 100: The Story of the Development of the Burlington Lines, 1849–1949,* Chicago, 1949.

Waters, L.L., *Steel Trails to Santa Fe,* Lawrence: University of Kansas Press, 1950.

Welty, Gus, ''Managing the Mega-Mergers,'' *Railway Age,* November 1997, pp. 33–35.

——, ''Matchmakers Rob Krebs, Jerry Grinstein,'' *Railway Age,* January 1996, pp. 31–33.

Zeller, Wendy, and Kathleen Morris, ''A Desperate Effort to Clear the Tracks,'' *Business Week,* March 2, 1998, p. 46.

—Lynn M. Voskuil and Carol I. Keeley
—updated by Thomas Derdak

❒ Carnival®

Carnival Corporation

Carnival Place
MSEO 1000
3655 N.W. 87th Avenue
Miami, Florida 33178-2428
U.S.A.
(305) 599-2600
Fax: (305) 406-4700
Web site: http://www.carnivalcorp.com

Public Company
Incorporated: 1972
Employees: 18,000
Sales: $2.4 billion
Stock Exchanges: New York
Ticker Symbol: CCL
SICs: 4481 Deep Sea Transportation of Passengers,
    Except by Ferry; 4482 Ferries; 4489 Water Trans-
    portation of Passengers, Not Elsewhere Classified

Begun with one ship that ran aground on its maiden voyage, Carnival Corporation has since grown into the most successful and prominent American cruise line. Carnival is the largest cruise company in the world and either owns or has purchased interest in seven cruise lines, including Carnival Cruise Lines, Holland America Line, Windstar Cruises, Cunard White Star Line, Seabourn Cruise Line, Costa Crociere S.p.A., and Airtours' Sun Cruises. Carnival has combined these cruise lines into an operating fleet of 43 state-of-the-art ships that sail the seven seas. Through innovative vacation packaging and extensive advertising campaigns, the family-operated company has changed the face of the cruise industry by coaxing thousands of middle-class customers aboard its floating resorts. The firm's interest in numerous tour companies that provide air transportation, hotel accommodations, and land excursions makes Carnival the most popular cruise line in the world.

Early History

Carnival was founded in 1972 by Ted Arison, an Israeli immigrant. After serving in World War II with the British

Army and in Israel's War of Independence, in the late 1940s Arison founded a cargo line running between Israel and New York, but was put out of business by competition from the Israeli state-run shipping line. In 1954 he moved to the United States, where he took a position as cargo manager for El Al, Israel's national airline. He eventually founded his own air freight company, Trans Air System, which went public in the late 1960s.

In 1968, at the age of 42, Arison moved to Miami to operate a small Israeli-owned cruise ship running between Florida and the Caribbean. When the Israeli government impounded the boat to collect the owners' debt, Arison quickly filled a Norwegian Caribbean Line ship with the customers he had lined up. Convinced that he should own boats rather than operate them for others, in 1972 he entered into a partnership with former schoolmate Meshulam Riklis, who then owned the travel conglomerate American International Travel Service (AITS). They formed Carnival Cruise as a subsidiary of AITS, and for $6.5 million they purchased the ship *Empress of Canada,* which they renamed the *Mardi Gras.*

The ship's first voyage was less than spectacular: the *Mardi Gras* ran aground off the Florida coast with several hundred travel agents on board. Future voyages went more smoothly, however, and in 1974 Arison bought Riklis's share of Carnival for $1, also assuming the company's debt of more than $5 million. To cut costs, Arison sought to reduce fuel consumption by reducing the speed of the *Mardi Gras* and the number of stops it made. This simple economizing measure was to revolutionize the entire cruise industry. Since passengers would have to spend more time at sea between Caribbean ports of call, Arison added more on-board entertainment features, including a disco, casino, movie theater, and nightclubs. Carnival's marketing staff quickly dubbed the *Mardi Gras* the "Fun Ship," and other cruise lines soon followed Arison's lead.

Growth and Expansion in the 1970s

In the 1970s the hit television series "The Love Boat" helped revitalize the cruise industry, bringing people on board ships in larger numbers than ever before: between 1970 and 1986 the number of people taking cruises soared from 500,000

Company Perspectives:

Our goal is to use our brands to reach every tier of the cruise market. Regardless of customer budget, itinerary, geography, demographics or psychographics, our brands really do cover the waterfront. That makes us unique in the North American cruise market, if not in the world . . . More than anything else, these vacationers want to have fun, and they recognize that Carnival offers them the ultimate fun experience. We also meet the needs of vacationers seeking luxury, elegance, shorter vacations, exotic destinations or land/sea packages. Within our other brands—Holland America, Windstar, Seabourn, Costa and Airtour's Sun Cruises—we have vacations that appeal to virtually every potential cruise customer, a strategy that has made us a leader in every market and the most popular choice among consumers considering a cruise vacation.

—Interview with the Chairman, Micky Arison, 1997 Annual Report

to 2.1 million. By 1978 Arison had three ships running seven-day cruises from Florida to the Caribbean and in the Caribbean itself: the *Mardi Gras*; the *Carnivale*, which he bought in 1975; and the *Festivale*, which he bought in 1977. Despite a bad economy and high fuel prices, in 1978 Arison also contracted for a fourth ship, the *Tropicale*, which was completed in 1982. In 1979 Arison's 30-year-old son, Micky Arison, was named president and chief executive of the company.

The 1980s brought the cruise industry massive expansion: between 1981 and 1991 the number of berths on North American cruise ships grew from 41,000 to 84,000. Carnival was the chief exponent and beneficiary of the boom. In 1982 Carnival's four boats carried some 200,000 passengers, with the firm earning $40 million on revenues of about $200 million. During the next decade the number of passengers carried per year nearly quintupled. Beginning in 1980, Carnival's revenues grew 30 percent annually, three times faster than the average for the cruise business as a whole.

During the recession of the early 1980s, Carnival ordered three more ships, the first from the Danish Aalborg shipyard at a cost of $180 million and two additional ships from the Swedish state shipbuilding company, Svenska Varv, for a total of $262 million. With the completion of these three "superliners"—*Holiday, Jubilee,* and *Celebration*—Carnival had the world's largest cruise line fleet, with seven ships.

The 1980s and an Innovative Marketing Campaign

To help fill these ships, Carnival adopted aggressive marketing and advertising strategies. In 1984 Carnival initiated the memorable "Fun Ship" advertising campaign, which featured talk show host Kathie Lee Gifford partaking of shipboard amenities and singing "We've Got the Fun." In 1984, for what was then the largest network television advertising campaign in the cruise industry, Carnival spent $10 million to advertise during "The Love Boat" and network news shows.

To gain support from travel agents, Carnival routinely sent representatives to travel agencies to inquire about vacation options. If the agent recommended a cruise as a first option, the representative would give the agent $10. If the agent's first recommendation was a Carnival cruise, he or she would get $1,000. By the end of 1989 Carnival had given away more than $500,000 with this program.

In an attempt to attract younger, more middle-class customers to cruises, which had traditionally been the preserve of older, upper-class travelers, Carnival offered cheaper, shorter trips—in 1988 the company's low-priced air and sea packages were approximately 20 percent below industry averages. Advertising efforts targeted toward the younger market included a 1988 Fourth of July party on a Carnival ship that was broadcast on MTV. These strategies paid off: in 1989 the annual household income of passengers was between $25,000 and $50,000, while 30 percent of the passengers in the early 1990s were between the ages of 25 and 39. In addition, Carnival's ships were consistently running at full capacity.

Strategic Acquisitions

In 1987 Ted Arison sold 18 percent of the shares of his private empire, raising nearly $400 million for the company, and Carnival went on a spending spree. The company entered into a contract for the *Ecstasy,* sister ship to the *Fantasy,* which had been ordered earlier in the year. In addition Carnival attempted to buy the cruise ship business of Gotaas-Larsen Shipping Corp., which owned part of Royal Caribbean and a majority of Admiral Cruise Lines, but the sale did not go through.

In 1988 Carnival purchased the Holland America Line for $625 million. A long-standing company with four cruise ships and about 4,500 berths, Holland America sailed to the Alaska coast in the summer and the Eastern Caribbean in the winter. Holland's trips were aimed at higher-income travelers—its Caribbean cruises cost 27 percent more than a Carnival cruise of the same length. In addition, as part of the package, Carnival acquired two other companies that Holland America owned: Windstar Sail Cruises and Holland America Westours, which included Westmark Hotels.

The acquisition greatly expanded the company's operations. Windstar Sail Cruises, whose three large passenger sailing ships operated in the South Pacific, Mediterranean, and Caribbean, served the luxury market. Westours operated Westmark's 18 hotels in addition to five dayboats, 240 motor coaches, and eight glass-domed railcars in Alaska and the Canadian Northwest. Already the world's largest cruise operator based on passengers carried, with this single purchase Carnival boosted its number of berths by more than 50 percent. During the year following the acquisition, Carnival carried 579,000 passengers, generating $600 million in revenues and earning profits of $196 million.

In 1989 Carnival completed the Crystal Palace Resort & Casino, a lavish 150-acre resort in the Bahamas, which cost Carnival $250 million to develop. The 1,550 room hotel had many extravagant features, including a $25,000 per night suite that included a robot that brought bath towels and an aquarium with a stingray. With its 13 restaurants, golf course, tennis courts, and other recreational facilities, the Crystal Palace was the biggest resort in the region. Carnival's 1989 revenues surpassed $1 billion, and the firm earned profits of $193 million while carrying 783,485 passengers.

Change and Growth in the 1990s

The following year Ted Arison, at the age of 66, stepped down as chairperson of Carnival and was succeeded by his son Micky. Shortly thereafter, the industry's boom of the previous decade began to taper off. The war in the Persian Gulf brought higher fuel and airline costs and deterred tourists. The effects were reflected in Carnival's stock price, which slid from 25 points in June of 1990 to 13 points late in the year. At the same time, it became apparent that the Crystal Palace would be an unprofitable venture. At the end of fiscal year 1990, Carnival incurred a $25.5 million loss from the resort and casino operation and not long after began attempting to sell the Crystal Palace. In 1991, with no prospective buyers, Carnival agreed to turn over a large portion of the resort to the Bahamian government, in exchange for cancellation of some of the debt incurred during construction. Carnival took a $135 million write-down on the Crystal Palace for that year.

Still, in 1991 Carnival enjoyed a 26 percent share of the passengers in the $5 billion cruise-ship market, with revenues of $1.4 billion. Its average occupancy level stood at 103 percent, well above the industry's average of 90 percent. In April of 1991 Carnival signed a $300 million contract for a ship, the *Sensation,* to be delivered in 1993. In September of the same year the *Fascination,* to be ready in late 1994, was ordered at a cost of $315 million. In an effort to gain more working capital, Carnival offered 7.85 million Class A common shares for sale in 1991.

The company also entered into an agreement in 1991 to acquire Premier Cruise Lines for $372 million. Though smaller than Carnival, Premier had a lucrative contract with Walt Disney Co. to be the official cruise line for Walt Disney World in Orlando, Florida. The deal fell through, however, when a final agreement could not be reached on the price.

In 1992 Carnival agreed to acquire a percentage of Seabourn Cruise Lines. Seabourn, operated in partnership with Atle Byrnestad, served the ultra-luxury market, running tours to such locations as South America, the Baltics, the Mediterranean, and Southeast Asia. The company also signed a contract for a $330 million ship, the *Imagination,* to be delivered in the fall of 1995. Perhaps the most impressive ship introduced in the modern era was the *Carnival Destiny,* the largest passenger ship afloat at 101,000 tons and room for 2,640 people. Its maiden voyage was in 1996.

In 1997 Carnival purchased a 50 percent interest in Costa Cruise Lines, in partnership with Airtours, a travel company. These acquisitions strengthened the company's presence around the world, but especially in the Caribbean. Yet the company's most important acquisition came in 1998 when it purchased a controlling interest in Cunard White Star Line. Cunard's five ships, including the *QE2,* the *Vistafjord,* the *Royal Viking Sun,* and *Sea Goddess I* and *II* catapulted Carnival into the super-luxury cruise line business.

By 1998 the company had changed its legal name to Carnival Corporation, to emphasize the growing diversity within its cruise lines. Yet when every indicator seemed to point the way toward uninterrupted and uneventful prosperity for the company, disaster struck. In July of 1998, the cruise ship *Ecstasy* caught fire after leaving the port in Miami, Florida bound for Newport News with 2,575 passengers on board. Although no one was injured during the fire and evacuation, the ship suffered extensive damage to more than 100 cabins, while heat and smoke damaged adjacent sections of the ship. The precise cause of the fire remains unknown, but the *Ecstasy* was examined meticulously and refitted in drydock; it re-entered cruising service not long afterward.

Carnival did not suffer financially or from a public relations standpoint because of the fire on the *Ecstasy,* and it continues to look forward to further growth, building on its name recognition, which is presently the highest in the industry. Since studies show that only five percent of the 70 million Americans who can afford cruises choose that type of vacation, Carnival seemed to have plenty of room for expansion.

Principal Subsidiaries

Carnival Cruise Lines; Holland America Line; Windstar Cruises; Holland America Westours; Cunard White Star Line (68%); Seabourn Cruise Line (68%); Costa Crociere S.p.A. (63%); Airtours' Sun Cruises (26%).

Further Reading

Blum, Ernest, ''Carnival Is Expected to Postpone Re-Entry of Ecstasy Beyond July 31,'' *Travel Weekly,* July 27, 1998, pp. 1, 45.

Brown, Jerry, ''Carnival Corporation Set to Buy Cunard,'' *Travel Weekly,* April 9, 1998, pp. 1, 4.

Fins, Antonio N., ''Batten Down the Hatches and Rev Up the Jacuzzis,'' *Business Week,* August 19, 1991.

——, ''Carnival Tries Sailing Upstream,'' *Business Week,* September 25, 1989.

Golden, Fran, ''New Deals,'' *Travel Weekly,* June 4, 1998.

——, ''Ted Arison Turns Hardship into 'Fun Ship','' *Travel Weekly,* March 30, 1998, p. 44.

''Pacesetter for Cruise Industry,'' *New York Times,* July 25, 1987.

Rice, Faye, ''How Carnival Stacks the Decks,'' *Fortune,* January 16, 1989.

20 Years of Fun: A History of Carnival Cruise Lines, Miami: Carnival Cruise Lines, 1992.

Wayne, Leslie, ''Carnival Cruise's Spending Spree,'' *New York Times,* August 28, 1988.

—Daniel Gross
—updated by Thomas Derdak

Carrefour ⟨C⟩

Carrefour SA

6, avenue Raymond Poincare
75116 Paris
France
1 53 70 19 00
Fax: 1 53-7086-16
Web site: http://www.carrefour.fr

Public Company
Incorporated: 1959
Employees: 113,289
Sales: US $28.3 billion (1997)
Stock Exchanges: Paris New York
SICs: 5411 Grocery Stores; 5331 Variety Stores; 5251
   Hardware Stores; 5399 Miscellaneous General
   Merchandise Stores; 6512 Nonresidential Building
   Operators

One of Europe's leading retailers in supermarkets and hypermarkets, Carrefour SA operates almost 700 stores in France and abroad under the Carrefour, Ed l'Epicier, and Ed le Marche Discount names and has a controlling interest in the frozen food store chain Picard Surgeles. The company's founders created the concept of the hypermarket, an expanded supermarket offering a wide variety of merchandise—including groceries, electronics, clothing, and automotive supplies—that allowed consumers to accomplish most of their shopping at one store. Hypermarkets became a rapid success, revolutionizing the retail industry in France and worldwide.

Company Origins

Carrefour emerged in 1959 as a collaboration between two entrepreneurs, Marcel Fournier and Louis Defforey, in Annecy, a city in eastern France that had become increasingly industrialized since World War II. Both men came from successful, enterprising families, and each was anxious to expand his own business by building large supermarkets. Fournier already had established the department store Grand Magasin de Nouveautés

Fournier d'Annecy and had connections in the Casino supermarket company, and Defforey was president of Badin-Defforey in Lagnieu.

In the 1950s the French grocery industry consisted primarily of family operations. Traditional grocery stores, committed to providing a variety of high-quality products, accounted for 83 percent of food sales. As fewer young people entered into family businesses, however, and grocers' unions, independent wholesalers, and food cooperatives increased in number, a need for alternatives to the smaller markets developed. At the same time, big department stores, generally located in the center of cities, often proved inconvenient, and the high prices they charged for luxury items and value-added services were prompting consumers to look elsewhere for nonfood items.

Moreover, the concept of free service was becoming increasingly popular. Free service, prevalent in retail by the 1990s, was invented in 1916. Prior to its institution, consumers relied heavily on assistance from sales clerks in selecting and obtaining merchandise. Under the free service system, however, customers used bags, carts, or baskets to collect their needs—placed within easy reach and individually priced—while sales clerks served primarily as cashiers.

The supermarket, which first appeared in France in 1954, used the concept of free service. With larger facilities located outside the center of cities, supermarkets could provide fresher produce, a greater variety of products, and lower prices than the traditional grocery store. By the end of the decade, however, only 33 free service supermarkets were in operation in France, and none of them was modeled after the large discount supermarkets in the United States.

Thus, in May 1959, Fournier and Defforey decided to incorporate these virtually unexploited concepts for their store in Annecy. An offering of 7,000 shares of stock was made to ten stockholders, and a facility already under construction in Annecy was purchased. The ground floor of the building was to be used as the supermarket, while the upper floors, containing apartments, were to be sold to help finance the business. Marcel Fournier was elected president, and Denis Defforey, Louis's son, was chosen as general director. Fournier named the business Carrefour, the French transliteration of the Greek word agora, or marketplace.

During this time, a businessman named Edouard Leclerc, who was establishing supermarkets in the Rhine-Alps region, announced plans to open a store in Annecy. Fournier and Defforey knew that, to be able to compete, they had to open their store before Leclerc opened his. Thus, Fournier offered the basement of his department store, Grand Magasin de Nouveautés Fournier, for Carrefour's use. This annex was opened on January 7, 1960, six months before the opening of the larger store, and was an immediate success. In fact, four days after it opened, the annex was already out of goods and had to close for one day to restock. The threat of competition from Leclerc prompted Fournier and Defforey to offer the lowest prices they could, and, as it turned out, Leclerc never built the competitive supermarket in Annecy.

To familiarize the public with supermarkets, Carrefour embarked on an advertising campaign before opening its main store. The publicity was effective. The store opened on June 3, 1960, achieving sales that far surpassed expectations and drawing 15,000 customers in the first two days. In a little more than three weeks, Carrefour had sales of FFr 290,000, a figure most independent grocers reported for an entire year. To prevent traffic jams, the store expanded its parking lot, but the company's management soon was convinced that supermarkets in urban areas were impractical.

Expansion in the 1960s

Between 1961 and 1962, business at Carrefour increased 45 percent and salaries increased as well. The following year, another supermarket was opened in Cran-Gevrier, in the Annecy region, this time with a vast parking lot. Moreover, Carrefour installed its own discount service station in the parking lot of its first store, selling gasoline without a name brand for five centimes less per liter than the average price; making neither a profit nor a loss, the company's gas station was intended as a protest against the French government's high gasoline taxes. Carrefour's discounts angered smaller business owners, a reaction that would prove typical throughout much of Carrefour's history.

During this time, the company decided to expand into the Paris region, purchasing a tract of land 30 kilometers south of the capital in Sainte-Geneviève-des-Bois, where costs were lower and more space was available. Before construction began at the new site, Louis Defforey and his brother Jacques went to the United States to observe the American commercial structure. Seminars given by Bernardo Trujillo on such modern sales practices as free service, discount prices, and large facilities convinced the Defforeys to completely modify Carrefour's initial plans for the store outside Paris. Although Carrefour did not adopt the huge dimensions of American stores with many cashiers and large aisles, they did construct a relatively large facility and integrated the idea of low prices on every product by purchasing merchandise from wholesalers and producers. They also followed Trujillo's advice about investing less in luxury construction. The store opened in June 1963 and was referred to by the press as a hypermarket, reflecting its 2,500 square meters of space, 400 parking places, and abundance of both food and nonfood merchandise. The store was an immediate success, with each customer purchasing, on average, three times more than in a regular supermarket.

Carrefour's success was based on its discount prices, decentralization of power, reduced emphasis on aesthetics and equipment costs, and accelerated rotation of stocks. The hypermarket appealed to younger people and new suburban dwellers, as well as the budget-conscious consumer affected by the high inflation rates in the 1960s. Carrefour's innovations in weighing, pricing, wrapping, cashing, and refrigerating made its hypermarket integral to the ensuing revolution in French retail. Not everyone, however, was pleased with these developments. The company had an adverse affect on small businesses, and an independent butchers' union blocked Carrefour's trucks at an abattoir in 1964 to protest the store's discounts. Moreover, some complained that shopping at the hypermarket was an impersonal experience, lacking in the traditional rapport between shopowner and loyal customer.

In January 1965, to avoid government restrictions on expansion, Carrefour formed two divisions: Carrefour Supermarché was led by Marcel Fournier and Denis Defforey, and Grands Magasins Carrefour, a subsidiary, was led by Jacques Defforey and Bernard Fournier. A hypermarket of 10,000 square meters was opened near Lyon in 1966 as well as another of 20,000 square meters in Vitrolles. The following year, an office was opened in Paris to collect, compare, and distribute results from all the stores, and in 1968 Marcel Fournier moved his office from Annecy to Paris.

International Growth in the 1970s and 1980s

Carrefour also actively sought involvement with other companies in Europe, including Delhaize Frères-Le-Lion in Belgium, Mercure in Switzerland, Wheatsheaf Investment in Great Britain, and Italware in Italy, and made major efforts to expand into Mediterranean regions in Europe. During its international expansion, Carrefour was careful to appeal to new clientele by marketing local products, rather than exporting French products. Initially developing new stores through joint subsidiary companies in partnership with local retailers, Carrefour eventually acquired full interest in these stores. Competitors such as Auchan, Casino, and Euromarché followed Carrefour's lead over the next ten years, greatly increasing the number of hypermarkets in France.

In June 1970 Carrefour stocks went on sale at the Bourse in Paris. With high inflation in the mid-1970s, competition for food prices was fierce, and when the 1973 Royer law put restrictions on the development of large stores in France, Carrefour began to focus increasingly on expansion abroad. Between 1978 and 1982, the greatest number of new Carrefour stores was established outside of France, particularly in Latin countries. Profits proved high at its stores in Brazil, Argentina, and Spain.

By 1982 the hypermarket industry had matured, resulting in active competition for prices, standardization of product lines, and the closing of some parts of the market. The food market stagnated, and Carrefour reduced the size of some of its stores. During this time, the company entered into more partnerships with other companies, including one with Castrorama, through which it sought to satisfy increased demand for leisure and hardware products. Although Carrefour reported sales nearly double those of its immediate competitors—Casino, Viniprix, and Nouvelles Galeries—the company's primary goal was to preserve existing markets and its commercial, financial, and developmental advantages.

Marcel Fournier, who had been awarded the Legion of Honor, died in 1985, and the institute of management founded by Carrefour was named after him. By that year, Carrefour had expanded to ten countries across three continents and had a net profit of FFr 520 million. As emphasis on brand image intensified on a national scale, Carrefour introduced its own private brands as a low cost alternative, while still emphasizing quality. In 1988 Carrefour was France's leading hypermarket merchant and the top retail company in Europe, with 65 hypermarkets in France and approximately 115 in Europe and South America. In February of that year, the company opened a 330,000-square-foot hypermarket outside Philadelphia, Pennsylvania. Initial financial problems due to low customer volume were overcome, and Carrefour opened a second hypermarket in the Philadelphia area in 1991. Carrefour continued to provide autonomy to each department head through its successful policy of decentralization and continued to focus on long-term results rather than immediate successes.

Continued Growth in the 1990s

In the early 1990s all members of the founding families of Carrefour left the company's active direction and formed an advisory council. Carrefour sold its stores in Annecy and Cran-Gevrier to Casino, and, in return, Casino sold its hypermarket in Nantes to Carrefour, so that Carrefour only managed stores of more than 2,500 square meters. In 1991 Carrefour acquired competitor Euromarché for $850 million and Montlaur, a bankrupt grocery chain, for $175 million. Although France had reached the saturation point with 798 hypermarkets and governmental regulations restricted the opening of new hypermarkets, Carrefour continued to expand in foreign markets, with its own stores or partnerships in Austria, Great Britain, The Netherlands, Switzerland, Germany, Belgium, Italy, Spain, Africa, Argentina, Brazil, and the United States.

In 1992 Carrefour planned to open two new stores in Great Britain in a joint venture with Costco, a warehouse club company. In addition, the company's discount food chain, known as Ed, was established in Great Britain and Italy, providing a limited range of products at extremely low prices. Carrefour also opened new stores in Spain, Brazil, and Argentina and began plans for stores in Taiwan, Turkey, and Malaysia.

In 1993 Carrefour faced further challenges to its expansion in France in the form of a government-enforced freeze on new hypermarkets in rural parts of the country. Nevertheless, accustomed to such legislative, noncompetitive restrictions, the company continued its pattern of growth, particularly in foreign markets. In an exception to that international expansion, the company closed its two stores in the United States in 1993 and had no plans for opening others there. It continued to pull out of the U.S. market by selling its 11 percent interest in Costco, a warehouse retailer in the United States. It retained its 20 percent

stake in Costco UK, however, and as of 1998 it owned six percent of Office Depot, a U.S. office supply discounter, and eight percent of PETsMART, a U.S. discount pet supply retailer.

Expansion in Central and South America was especially strong in the 1990s. Carrefour moved into Mexico in 1993, opening the first of a chain of hypermarkets. Of the 30 stores the company opened in 1996, 15 were in Mexico, Brazil, and Argentina. By 1997 Carrefour operated approximately 60 stores in South America and was generating $7 billion in sales in Brazil and Argentina alone. Hoping to build on its successful growth in the area, Carrefour planned to open ten hypermarkets in Chile over the next decade.

By 1995 Carrefour operated more stores internationally than it did in France. Asia provided another fertile ground for Carrefour's international expansion. The company opened its first store in Seoul, South Korea, in 1996, after the South Korean government lifted some of its restrictions on foreign retailers. When the financial crisis in Asia hit in the late 1990s, Carrefour was already operating 26 hypermarkets in the region. Because of its discount strategy and the steady demand for food and other basics sold by the company, Carrefour was weathering the recession. In fact, Carrefour opened 20 more stores in Asia in 1997 and 1998.

Restrictions on the company's growth in France increased in 1996. In an effort to protect small shopkeepers, the French government placed a six-month ban on the opening of any store measuring more than 300 square meters (3,230 square feet). Unable to open new stores, Carrefour continued to expand in France by acquiring its competitors. In 1996 it bought a 41 percent interest in the owner of the Cora supermarket chain, GMB.

Carrefour's performance in France was hurt by an economic slowdown in 1996 and 1997. Carrefour store sales rose in the first half of 1998, however, by 4.1 percent. The company was in the process of refurbishing its stores in 1998; it hoped to complete 19 that year and then extend the program in the following year.

Internationally, Carrefour bought eight Eldorado stores in Brazil in 1997 and converted them in 1998 to the Carrefour name. The company planned to open 34 new stores by the end of 1998, including its first stores in Colombia, Chile, Indonesia, and the Czech Republic. Carrefour thus remained committed to growth in France through increases in same-store sales and the acquisition of rival stores and to expansion internationally through both acquisitions and the opening of new stores.

Principal Subsidiaries

Carrefour France; Erteco; Carrefour Argentine S.A.; Carrefour China; Carrefour Commercio e Industria (Brazil; 80%); Carrefour Italy; Carrefour Korea Ltd.; Carrefour Malasia; Carrefour Mexico; Carrefour Nederland B.V.; Carrefour Portugal; Carrefour Taiwan; Carrefour Ticaret Merkezi A.S. (Turkey); Cencar Limited (Thailand); Picard Surgeles; Brepa (Brazil; 80); Centros Commerciales Pryca (Spain; 77%).

Principal Divisions

Carrefour; Ed l'Epicier; Ed le Marche Discount.

Further Reading

"Asian Retailing: Going Cheap," *Economist,* August 15, 1998.

Bidlake, Suzanne, "Ed's Cut Price Bonanza," *Marketing,* February 11, 1993, p. 19.

Johnson, Jay L., "Carrefour Revisited," *Discount Merchandiser,* August 1990, pp. 24–30.

Mao, Philippe, "France: Defforey Family, Halley Family," *Forbes,* July 18, 1994, p. 202.

"Not at Any Price," *Economist,* April 6, 1996.

"Retailing in South America," *Economist,* July 12, 1997.

Sasseen, Jane, "France: Balladur Halts March of the Hypermarché," *International Management,* June 1993, p. 24.

Toussaint, Jean-Claude, *La politique générale de l'enterprise, un cas concret: Carrefour,* Paris: Chotard & Associés, 1984.

Villermet, Jean-Marc, *Naissance de l'hypermarché,* Paris: Armand Colin, 1991.

—Jennifer Kerns
—updated by Susan Windisch Brown

Cessna Aircraft Company

One Cessna Boulevard
Wichita, Kansas 67215
U.S.A.
(316) 517-6000
(800) 423-7762
Web site: http://www.cessna.textron.com

Wholly Owned Subsidiary of Textron Inc.
Incorporated: 1927 as Cessna-Roos Company
Employees: 10,779
Sales: $1 billion (1998 est.)
SICs: 3721 Aircraft; 3728 Aircraft Equipment

Based in Wichita, Kansas, the aviation capitol of the United States, Cessna Aircraft Company is the world's largest manufacturer of private aircraft. Cessna began its operations building small propeller-driven aircraft for the private pilot market, eventually expanding into the manufacture of corporate jets. The company has since become the leading private jet manufacturer in the industry. Following the 1994 signing of the General Aviation Revitalization Act, the company resumed production of single-engine piston aircraft, which it had given up in 1986.

Origins

In 1911 the company's founder, Clyde V. Cessna, a farmer who was also employed as a mechanic and auto salesman for Overland Automobiles, attended an air show in nearby Oklahoma City at the Moisant International Aviation Air Circus. Cessna was immediately taken with the urge to fly. Aware of the large sums paid to exhibition barnstormers, Cessna sensed an opportunity and traveled to New York, where he purchased a French Bleriot aircraft from the Queens Airplane Company in the Bronx. He assembled the plane from a kit, using one of his own water-cooled engines. Having never before flown, Cessna wheeled the craft out onto a salt plain near Jet, Oklahoma, to begin practice runs. As his brother Roy watched, Cessna bounced his craft on a takeoff run, eventually ending up ditching its nose into the ground.

The pilot emerged without serious injury but, determined to fly, he repaired the Bleriot for another try. Cessna smashed the airplane 11 more times before he got the hang of it. On the thirteenth try he managed to get enough altitude to avoid crashing. But because he had not yet learned to turn, he was forced to set the craft down immediately. And because he had never landed, the flight ended with yet another crash. In June of 1911, after several modifications, Cessna made his first completely successful flight, and with practice he became a fairly good pilot. He was paid $300 to perform at an air show in Jet, and before the end of the season he flew three more exhibitions.

Through the spring and summer of 1912, and for several years after, Cessna made small changes to his airplane, customizing it by incorporating new controls and changing the balance and surfaces of the craft. Each year he gave flying demonstrations throughout Kansas and Oklahoma. In the fall of 1916 Cessna was offered a rent-free space at the Jones Motor Car factory in Wichita, Kansas, to manufacture a new model. In return he was asked to paint the words "Jones-Six," the name of a car model, on the bottom of the wings of his new airplane. This craft, built over the winter of 1916–17, was the first airplane manufactured in Wichita.

Cessna's next model, the Comet, emerged in 1917. With a partially enclosed cockpit, the Comet became the manufacturer's most successful model. Cessna planned to promote the design at one of the 60 air shows in which he was booked to perform during 1917, but American involvement in World War I forced him to abandon his sales efforts. Engines, propellers, and other important supplies were earmarked for larger manufacturers. Cessna, effectively, was put out of business. He returned to his home near Rago, Kansas, and resumed farming.

In 1925 Cessna was lured back to Wichita by two business partners, Walter Beech and Lloyd Stearman, who persuaded him to begin making airplanes again. The three men established the Travel Air Manufacturing Company, with Cessna as president. While the company built a line of biplanes, a conflict began to emerge between Beech and Cessna. Beech favored the two-wing designs and Cessna wanted to build a monoplane. In 1926 Cessna rented his own shop, where he designed and built his single-wing aircraft. He later flew this plane in a demonstra-

Company Perspectives:

The Mission of the Cessna Aircraft Company is: to be the worldwide leader in the industry segments we serve by developing and producing safe, reliable, high quality aircraft that represent the best value in general aviation; to provide the most comprehensive and responsive support to every Cessna customer; to produce the financial results that create value for Textron shareholders.

tion for Beech, who was forced to concede that Cessna's design was an excellent one, resulting in the manufacture of monoplanes by Travel Air. Two later models, the City of Oakland and the Woolaroc, were the first civilian planes to be flown to Hawaii.

Cessna-Roos Company Origins in 1927

Further differences with Beech and Stearman, however, led Cessna to leave the partnership in 1927. He established his own shop in Wichita and began work on a radical design that eliminated the need for wing struts, the bars that supported the plane's wings. After successfully building his strutless "A" series monoplane, Cessna organized another firm and sold shares in his new company. Victor Roos, a major shareholder, was made a partner, and the company was incorporated as the Cessna-Roos Company on September 8, 1927. Roos helped Cessna to acquire an 11-acre site at First Street and Glenn Avenue, where they established a 5,000-square-foot factory and an adjacent paint shop. Roos, however, received a lucrative offer to become general manager of the Swallow Airplane Company and left the business in December.

Cessna reorganized his enterprise as the Cessna Aircraft Company and began offering five variations on the "A" series, each with a different type of engine. These were called AWs—the "W" stood for Wright, the engine manufacturer. Cessna then began work on a heavier BW series. The Commerce Department, however, which then certified aircraft designs, would not approve the use of a more powerful Wright engine without a lengthy stress analysis. To maintain sales, Cessna was forced to substitute a smaller engine in the BW. But he soon began work on an even more powerful third series, the CW-6, which featured a 225-horsepower engine.

In 1929, on the success of these models, Cessna financed development of an improved "D" series. Members of this series, the Chief and the Scout, were to be built at another new facility, an 80-acre site southeast of Wichita. Here, Cessna was building a 55,000-square-foot plant, although it was during construction that the stock market crashed, plunging the country into the Great Depression.

By 1930 the demand for private aircraft all but disappeared. In an attempt to bolster sales Cessna designed a glider, the CG-2, which he sold for only $398. He attempted several other experimental designs, but by 1931 was forced to close down his plant and rent out his buildings. Although the Cessna Aircraft

Company did not go bankrupt, no airplanes were built for three years. In fact, Clyde Cessna and his son Eldon were prevented by the company's board of directors from even attempting to restart operations at the plant. Instead, the pair opened another small shop and founded the C.V. Cessna Aircraft Company. At this site Cessna and his son built the CR-1, CR-2, and CR-3 racing models and the C-3 cabin cruiser.

Meanwhile, in June of 1933, Cessna's nephew Dwane L. Wallace graduated from Wichita University with a degree in aeronautical engineering. He went to work for the Beech Aircraft Company, which occupied a section of the closed Cessna factory. When Beech later moved to another plant, Dwane and his brother Dwight persuaded Cessna's board to allow their uncle to reopen the plant. Production was resumed on January 10, 1934, and the Wallace brothers joined the company as officers. The new team designed another cantilevered—sans wing struts—craft, the C-34 Airmaster, which test pilots George Hart and Dwane Wallace flew on nationwide demonstrations. The new model put the company back on its feet, particularly after it garnered numerous prestigious awards.

In 1935 Clyde Cessna, now age 55, sold his shares in the company to the Wallace brothers. He remained president of Cessna Aircraft until October 8, 1936, when he retired. He returned to his 640-acre farm in Rago and invented new farm implements until his death in 1954. Under the Wallaces, the Cessna Aircraft Company built its first twin-engine aircraft in 1938. The T-50 Bobcat was designed and built in nine months—production had barely started in March 1939 when priority military orders for the new plane began to come in. The U.S. Army used the T-50 as a trainer, designated AT-8. Meanwhile, the Royal Canadian Air Force weighed in with similar orders, calling theirs the Crane I.

Expansion During World War II

With a growing backlog of military orders, Cessna was forced to expand. The company, which employed 200 people in July 1940, had more than 1,500 workers just seven months later. As hostilities in Europe began, with Germany's invasion of France, the army increased its orders from Cessna. The company delivered several new variations on the T-50, including AT-17 trainers and UC-78 utility cargo aircraft. The basic T-50 design, however, was the mainstay at that time. In April 1942, during the darkest days of the war, the army ordered Cessna to manufacture 1,500 C-4A troop/cargo gliders. These craft, which were designed by the Waco Aircraft Company, were intended for use in an allied invasion of Europe.

Cessna built a new plant for the gliders at Hutchinson, Kansas, 60 miles northwest of Wichita. Although half the order was later canceled, Cessna and other builders were kept busy subcontracting for other manufacturers. In addition, Cessna designed a large twin-engine cargo airplane, called the C-106, that was made from freely available nonstrategic materials. The company received an order for 500 of these planes, but this was later canceled when the army decided to use planes from Douglas and Curtiss. Had Cessna been able to build its C-106s for the army, the company may have graduated into another class, with such manufacturers as North American, Boeing, Consolidated Vultee, Douglas, and Lockheed.

In 1944 Cessna occupied 468,000 feet of factory space—nearly ten times the amount it had in 1939—and employed 6,074 workers. With the end of the war imminent, however, the company was forced to turn its attention to the inevitable evaporation of military orders. Futurists had long predicted the emergence of family flight, describing sedan aircraft suitable for jaunts to grandma's house, a picnic spot, and even the grocery store. These planes were to be simple, light designs that were affordable and rugged. Before the end of the war, Cessna began work on a fabric-skin model, the 190/195 series P-780. But pilots of these air sedans would first need to learn how to fly, so the company briefly shelved the P-780 to rush two small trainers, the 120 and 140, into production.

The revolution in flight materialized shortly after the war, and although it never reached the proportions—an airplane in every garage—that futurists had envisioned, it seemed everyone was learning to fly. Cessna built nearly 8,000 trainers by the early 1950s, but the boom was short-lived. Output of 120/140s fell from 30 per day to only five. Demand for the 190/195—now with metal skins—and a new model, the 170, remained strong, however.

After the war, Cessna had established a fluid power division that manufactured hydraulic components. With limited applications in aircraft, the hydraulic products were sold mainly to manufacturers of farm equipment, though the fluid power group later became one of Cessna's most profitable divisions. In 1952 Cessna purchased the Seibel Helicopter Company. This small concern flew its first helicopter in 1954, celebrating the event a year later with a demonstration landing on the summit of Pike's Peak. The company built a YH-41 helicopter for the U.S. Army in 1957, and by 1961 was building CH-1 Skyhook models. With declining sales, however, the business of Cessna Helicopters was wound up in 1963.

Entering the Business Aircraft Market in 1954

Meanwhile, the company had begun to cultivate a new market for its winged aircraft: corporations. As executives found a greater need to travel long distances in less time, a market for business aircraft emerged. Cessna was one of the first to exploit this opening by producing the 310, an airplane designed specifically for executives in 1954. That same year Cessna entered the jet age when it began production of T-37s. These small jets were used as trainers by the Air Force, which purchased more than 1,000 T-37s. In 1959 Cessna brought out an all-metal, 100-horsepower plane, the Model 150. This aircraft was extremely popular with flight schools and flying clubs and was singularly responsible for Cessna's strong growth during the 1960s.

Output reached 3,000 per year by 1966. The following year, production of the popular 150 was relocated to a facility at Strother Field in Winfield, Kansas. The 150s were again manufactured in Wichita for a brief time during 1969 when a recession dried up the market, but production resumed at Winfield in 1973. With strong growth from the 150 program, Cessna began acquiring numerous companies in related fields. The company purchased the Aircraft Radio Corporation in 1959, and the following year took over the McCauley Company, which manufactured propellers and other aircraft components.

In 1960 Cessna became affiliated with SNA Max Holste, a French manufacturer located in Reims. Cessna later purchased 49 percent of the company, which changed its name to Reims Aviation. As Cessna's agent in the European market, Reims Aviation assembled a variety of Cessna designs, principally the Model 150. Cessna upgraded its position in the business market in 1965, when it introduced the 411, a cabin class airplane. The company also turned out its first general purpose agricultural airplane, the Ag Wagon. In 1968 Cessna began production of the A-37B twin-jet attack aircraft for the U.S. Air Force.

Lear, also located in Wichita, entered the business market in the mid-1960s with a line of business jets. As a result, Lear nearly cornered the corporate market, forcing such companies as Cessna—with the broadest product line in the industry—to respond in kind. Cessna began work on its first business jet, the Citation 500, in 1969, although the first of this series was not delivered until 1972. Nevertheless, the Citation became an important source of strength for Cessna, whose private plane business had begun to fall flat. Amid financial reverses, Cessna launched a productivity campaign and its executives—including chairman Dwane Wallace—took salary cuts. In addition, the number of employees, which was 16,200 in 1974, was cut to 13,000 by 1976.

The outlook for Cessna began to improve as it delivered its 100,000th single-engine airplane in 1975 and introduced the large Titan cargo plane a year later. In 1978 the company redesigned the successful 150, redesignating it the 152. Questions had begun to arise, however, about the integrity of Cessna's construction. Several highly publicized plane crashes seemed to indicate some propwash (the force stemming from the propellers' wake) problems with Cessna tail sections. According to a *Wall Street Journal* article, the Federal Aviation Administration (FAA) grounded one model—the Conquest—in 1977 after the National Transportation Safety Board concluded that a particular crash was the result of "poor-inadequate design." The FAA allowed the planes to return to the sky, however, after Cessna made some significant changes to the tail section.

Eager to make up for lost profits on the redesign, Cessna's chairman, Russell Meyer, who had succeeded Wallace in 1975, stepped up production of Conquests and Citations, which were in demand as business planes after the energy crisis caused airline prices to skyrocket. Before long, inventories of crucial parts became so low that Cessna was forced to store $40 million worth of half-completed jets. In addition, the company found itself competing for an appropriate number of skilled workers with such formidable rivals as Boeing, Lear, Beech, and Piper, all located in the same area. As these problems began to take their toll, the short-term debt needed to cover Cessna's faltering operations began to mount, and before long the company also was facing a $92 million debt crisis.

Meyer's response was to close the jet production line for several weeks while parts inventories were replenished. Stocked aircraft were completed and sold, and production was resumed at lower levels. By 1979 Cessna was outselling Lear, and in 1980, the year Cessna's sales topped the billion dollar mark, Cessna achieved a record high market share of 54 percent. In an attempt to get more airplanes out of the factory,

Cessna inaugurated a clever marketing scheme in 1982. Rather than try to sell its planes in a recessionary economy, Cessna offered leases with maintenance contracts. Companies now could finance the new Citation I, II, and III business jets with money from their operating budgets, rather than purchasing them with capital funds. Although customers could cancel the leases on short notice, Cessna was allowed to depreciate the aircraft, an important tax shelter.

The 1980s: New Aircraft and Ownership

In 1983 Cessna sold its ARC Avionics division to the Sperry Corporation, predecessor to Unisys. In the meantime Cessna identified an important new market: fleet sales. That year Federal Express placed the first of several bulk orders for Cessna's new Caravan turboprop utility aircraft, suitable for serving smaller metropolitan markets. With Cessna's business increasingly dominated by corporate and fleet jet sales, the private plane business became an ever smaller part of the company's operations. Still, the flight schools Cessna had established in 1970 continued to train private pilots in great numbers.

As the company's product liability insurance costs began to mount—annual premiums were in excess of $35 million—Cessna solicited bids from companies that were interested in acquiring the aircraft manufacturer. In October of 1985 General Dynamics, a large defense contractor, purchased Cessna for $663.7 million. Both companies stood to benefit from the transaction. Cessna would be able to take advantage of General Dynamics's stable cash position, technology, and experience in contracting, while providing its parent company with expertise in lightweight structures that could prove useful in cruise missile projects.

That same year, in response to increasingly stronger competition from the used aircraft market, Cessna began a campaign to refit and upgrade older Citation jets. In 1988 Cessna sold its fluid power division to the Eaton Corporation, and the following year the company's 40 percent interest in Reims Aviation, which had been manufacturing the Caravan, was purchased by Paris-based Compagnie Française Chaufour Investissement. Cessna continued its production of the successful Caravan, however. Although a part of General Dynamics, Cessna was allowed to maintain managerial autonomy. Self-insured against lawsuits, it was now also self-funded and producing a profit for its parent company, but by 1991 General Dynamics, seeking to concentrate on its core defense businesses, announced its intention to sell Cessna. Textron, parent of Bell Helicopter, offered $600 million for Cessna. The deal was completed in January 1992 with Cessna's autonomy intact, while Meyer continued as chairman.

The Early 1990s: Success as Part of Textron

Following the company's purchase by Textron, Cessna continued to expand its line of Citation business jets. The year 1992 saw FAA certification of the Citation VII and the entry level CitationJet models. The following year the prototype of the Citation X, touted as the world's fastest business jet, was unveiled. The Citation Ultra model, the successor to the Citation V, also was announced in 1993. That year the company

celebrated delivery of the 2,000th Citation. Cessna also sold its McCauley Accessory Division during 1993.

Production of single-engine piston aircraft had ceased for Cessna in 1986 due to the prohibitive cost of liability insurance. In 1994, as a result of lobbying by the aircraft industry, the U.S. Congress passed the General Aviation Revitalization Act, which established a limit of 18 years from date of manufacture on lawsuits against plane manufacturers. Cessna CEO Russ Meyer flew to Washington for the signing by President Clinton, and the company quickly announced plans to resume building piston aircraft. A site for a new manufacturing facility was selected in Independence, Kansas, some 120 miles from Wichita, and in late 1996 the first plane rolled off the assembly line. The company revived, with minor modifications and updates, its popular models 172 and 182 from the 1980s, rather than designing entirely new aircraft.

Cessna continued to do well in 1996, receiving large orders for Citation Ultras from the U.S. Army and for Citation VIIs and Xs from Executive Jet of New Jersey. The latter deal, for 45 jets, was worth a record-setting $600 million. The company delivered a total of 229 airplanes during the year. The year 1997 was even better, with the company registering a 35 percent jump in sales. A total of 180 Citation series jets, 78 Caravan turboprop aircraft, and 360 new piston planes were sold, and Cessna celebrated delivery of the 2,500th Citation in September.

The company's good fortunes continued unabated in 1998 as the Citation Excel received certification and entered production, and orders for all of Cessna's aircraft remained strong. A total of $40 million in construction projects in Wichita were planned, comprising painting, interior installation, and warehousing facilities. In October, four new Citation models were announced. Three were variations on existing planes, with the Citation Sovereign to be an all-new design. By the beginning of 1999, the company's backlog of orders topped $4 billion.

As it prepared to enter the 21st century, Cessna remained the largest private aircraft manufacturer in the United States. With its line of cargo craft and advanced private jets, including the new Citation X, Cessna still offered the broadest product range in the industry. With the company's relationship to owner Textron on solid ground, Cessna looked certain to remain America's leading small aircraft manufacturer.

Principal Subsidiaries

Cessna Finance Corporation.

Further Reading

Aarons, Richard N., "Cessna Fills Out the Citation Line," *Business & Commercial Aviation,* November 1, 1998, p. 56.

Banks, Howard, "Cleared for Takeoff," *Forbes,* September 12, 1994, p. 116.

Campanella, Frank W., "Single-Engine Aircraft Hiking Cessna's Profits," *Barron's,* January 26, 1976, pp. 60–65.

Carton, Barbara, "Cessna Says It Will Make More Small Airplanes," *Wall Street Journal,* March 14, 1995, p. B1.

"Cessna: 50 Years and 139,000 Aircraft," *Interavia,* September 1977, pp. 860–61.

"Cessna: Relying on Its Big Planes, New Sales Tactics and Austerity," *Business Week,* October 11, 1982, pp. 95–96.

"Cessna Sells Reims Interest," *Flight International,* March 4, 1989, p. 8.

Dinell, David, "Cessna Aircraft to Undertake $40 Million Worth of Projects," *Wichita Business Journal,* March 6, 1998, p. 1.

——, "Cessna Cycling Up for 1999," *Wichita Business Journal,* October 2, 1998, p. 1.

Frasier, Steve, "Cessna Aircraft Company Struggles to Overcome Design, Factory Woes," *Wall Street Journal,* December 26, 1980, pp. 1–5.

"A History of the Cessna Aircraft Company," *Cessna Guidebook,* Dallas: Flying Enterprise Publications, 1973.

McMillin, Molly, "Cessna Aircraft Prepares to Grow After Lean Years," *Wichita Business Journal,* August 11, 1995, p. 1.

"New Parent to Benefit Cessna," *Flight International,* October 12, 1985, p. 27.

Phillips, Edward H., "Cessna Aircraft Reports Record Sales, Deliveries," *Aviation Week & Space Technology,* February 16, 1998, p. 49.

Phillips, Edward H., and Anthony L. Velocci, Jr., "Cessna Officials Expect No Changes After Acquisition by Textron Corp.," *Aviation Week & Space Technology,* January 27, 1992, p. 36.

"Sales Zoom for the Light-Plane Makers," *Business Week,* March 10, 1973, pp. 157–60.

"Snafu Unsnarled," *Fortune,* June 1, 1982, p. 11.

Warwick, Graham, "General Dynamics to Sell Off Cessna," *Flight International,* October 23, 1991, p. 5.

—John Simley
—updated by Frank Uhle

LINDT & SPRÜNGLI

Chocoladefabriken Lindt & Sprüngli AG

Seestrasse 204
CH-8802 Kilchberg
Switzerland
(41)(1) 716 22 33
Fax: (49)(1) 715 39 85
Web site: http://www.lindt.com

Public Company
Incorporated: 1845 as David Sprüngli et fils Societät
Employees: 4,599 (1997)
Sales: CHF 1,344 million (1997)
Stock Exchanges: Zürich
Ticker Symbol: LISP
SICs: 2066 Chocolate & Cocoa Products

Chocoladefabriken Lindt & Sprüngli AG is one of the world's leading manufacturers of premium chocolate and chocolate-related products sold in more than 80 countries, with almost $1 billion in worldwide sales. The predominantly Swiss-owned corporation manufactures various products of its renowned Lindt brand in Switzerland, Germany, France, Italy, and Austria, as well as in the United States. The international group includes major sales and distribution firms in England, Poland, Spain, Canada, and Australia, as well as sales offices in Buenos Aires, Hong Kong, and Dubai. Lindt & Sprüngli products are distributed by a network of distributors that spans the globe.

The Origins of a Chocolate Empire

Lindt & Sprüngli's origins go back to a small confectionery shop in the Old Town of Zurich. In 1820, David Sprüngli, a poor orphan who had assisted a few Zurich confectioners, started an apprenticeship at the reputable shop. When both the master confectioner and his son died in 1836, the widow sold the house and confectionery shop to David Sprüngli. Within eight years Sprüngli paid off half of his debt. In March 1845 he and his 29-year-old son Rudolf, who had gathered experience as an apprentice in confectionery businesses abroad, announced the opening of a new chocolate factory named David Sprüngli et fils Societät.

At first, they manufactured chocolate in solid form in a small workshop they set up in the old store building, equipped with two hand-driven machines: a small roasting unit and a grinding machine. But soon the old bakery became too small to meet the demand for the new delicacy they were making from a fashionable new Italian recipe. As a result, the chocolate production was moved to a small facility in Horgen at the northern end of Lake Zurich in 1847. Sprüngli invested in machinery for processing cocoa beans and the new factory soon employed ten people. One of their tasks was to sort stones and nails out of the raw cocoa beans that traveled by boat and rail from Dutch ports to Zurich. In 1859 a second, more spacious confectionery and refreshment room was opened. At the elegant establishment, members of Zurich's high society sat at marble tables and enjoyed coffee or hot chocolate while they waited for the Sprüngli delicacies they had purchased to be packed. Between about 1860 and 1880, the Sprüngli company's diverse product range included an assortment of 20 chocolate bars of different quality, from "Economique" to "Chocolat du Cremier."

Second Sprüngli Generation Manages Expansion

In 1862 David Sprüngli died at age 86 and Rudolf Sprüngli, formerly the junior boss, took over management of the entire business. After a new boulevard was built on Zurich's Paradeplatz where the second Sprüngli store was located, the business found itself in the center of a new thriving area, surrounded by a luxury hotel, a bank, and the Stock Exchange. The chocolate production was moved again in 1870 to the Werdmühle in Zurich, a much bigger facility in a central location that included workshop buildings, warehouses, a canal that supplied water to the complex, and a residence for the Sprüngli family. A decade later, the Sprüngli factory employed about 80 people—confectioners, mechanics, carriers, salesmen, and teenage girls 15 and older, who wrapped the expensive delicacies in rich "glazed" paper. By 1882 Sprüngli chocolate bars, pastilles, croquettes, and pralines were exported to Germany, Austria, Hungary, Belgium, Italy, Rumania, Denmark, Sweden, Norway, Turkey, and even eastern India.

When Rudolf Sprüngli retired from the business in 1892, his younger son, David Robert Sprüngli, received the two confec-

Company Perspectives:

We are an international company and are recognized as the leader in the market for premium quality chocolate and chocolate related products of superior quality and value. Our working environment attracts and retains the best people. Our partnership with our consumers, customers and suppliers is mutually rewarding and prosperous. We want to be recognized as a company which cares for the environment and the communities we live and work in. The successful pursuit of our commitments guarantees our shareholders an attractive long term investment and the independence of our company.

tionery stores, while the elder son, Johann Rudolf Sprüngli-Schifferli, was given the chocolate factory. Johann Rudolf first expanded the production facility and invested in state-of-the-art machinery that sorted, roasted, and crushed the cocoa beans better and cheaper than before. Around 1890 the Sprüngli company launched ''Alpina, Chocolat au lait.'' This milk chocolate was manufactured according to a process that Daniel Peter, another Swiss chocolatier, had invented in 1875. The new technology replaced half of the cocoa used before in chocolate by condensed milk. Consequently, Swiss chocolate makers' dependence on cocoa imports shrunk, since milk was a traditional product of Switzerland. Sprüngli's marketing and new product manager at that time, Carl Georg Bernhard, launched and professionally marketed other early innovations. One was saccharin cocoa for diabetics, which was first test-marketed to doctors and pharmacists in a single Swiss town. Another was acorn cocoa, a mixture of cocoa and ground acorns with less oil marketed as health food.

After his father died in 1897, Johann Rudolf Sprüngli-Schiffeli realized that the Werdermühle facility was still too small for his ambitious plans. To be able to raise money for a new plant, the sole proprietorship was transformed into a joint stock company in 1899 under the new name Chocolat Sprüngli AG. In the years 1898 and 1899 a new factory was built under his leadership in Kilchberg at Lake Zurich. During the following decade, sales rose by 250 percent. But more than expanded production power contributed to this growth.

Entering the 20th Century with New Partners

In 1899 Chocolat Sprüngli acquired a small but famous Berne chocolate maker, Rod. Lindt fils. Entrepreneur Rodolphe Lindt, the 24-year-old founder of the company, had invented a new technology while experimenting with old machines he had bought from a bankrupt spice mill. By rolling the cocoa in the trough for a very long time and adding cocoa butter to the right mix of cocoa beans, he developed a new kind of chocolate superior to the other chocolate available at the time, which was a somewhat bitter paste with a coarse, sandy consistency. In the 1880s Lindt developed a shell-shaped trough and a fitting roller. Running back and forth in the partly covered trough for as long as 72 hours, the roller homogenized the sugar and cocoa particles through the internal warming it created, covered them

thinly with cocoa butter, and mixed the resulting mass with little air bubbles that released unfavorable bitter flavors into the air. This machine was later called a ''conche'' and became the basic equipment for chocolate production. Although demand for the new ''melting chocolate'' rose rapidly and waiting periods for customers became longer and longer, Lindt was not interested in expanding production at his own risk. For 1.5 million Swiss francs—an enormous sum at that time—and a seat at the board of directors Lindt sold his business to the Chocolat Sprüngli AG. Sprüngli acquired rights to the Lindt brand name, which had a reputation throughout Europe, together with the secret to manufacturing so-called ''melting chocolate.'' The Sprüngli company's name was changed to Aktiengesellschaft Vereinigte Berner und Züricher Chocoladefabriken Lindt & Sprüngli.

The two component companies actually were run like separate businesses, however, and serious differences arose between the managing members of the Lindt and the Sprüngli families. In the business year 1902–03, the Lindt factory in Berne produced about 40 percent of the total Lindt chocolate output, and 60 percent was made in the Sprüngli plant. But Lindt chocolate was more expensive than Sprüngli's. The Lindt facility's output represented 13 percent of total production, but 26 percent of total sales. When Rodolphe and his brother August Lindt built another factory in Berne as their private facility and rented it to Lindt & Sprüngli, the board of directors approved this arrangement. However, in July 1905 Rodolphe Lindt canceled the rental agreement and resigned from all duties at the Lindt & Sprüngli company in September. In April 1906, August and Walter Lindt, a cousin of Rodolphe Lindt, founded their own firm in Berne, thereby breaching their contracts with the Lindt & Sprüngli company.

Robert Stünzi-Sprüngli, a hardheaded cotton broker from Basle who had taken over the management of Lindt & Sprüngli in 1906 after Rudolf Sprüngli's retirement, led the firm through the following legal battle. It lasted more than two decades. While the court machinery moved slowly, Lindt & Sprüngli launched costly advertising campaigns to defend their markets from the competitor who used the famous ''Lindt'' brand name illegally. In the summer of 1927 the Berne Appeals Court sentenced the A. & W. Lindt company to a high fine and ordered them to print ''This chocolate is not the original Lindt chocolate'' on all of its packages, ads, and correspondence. One year later the firm A. & W. Lindt was liquidated after a settlement was agreed on by the heirs of the two founders, who had died in the meantime. Rodolphe Lindt, who had died in 1909, lived on in the Lindt & Sprüngli company, however. His secret recipes have never been revealed.

Surviving Economic Depression and World Wars

While the legal battle was being fought, the Swiss chocolate industry enjoyed two decades of growing sales, especially in foreign countries. The boom continued through the First World War; Lindt & Sprüngli, which was only a medium-sized company compared with other Swiss chocolate makers, participated in it wholeheartedly. Lindt & Sprüngli exported 72 percent of its products to 20 countries in 1915–16. In all, sales doubled between 1914–15 and 1919–20. Low trade activity and protectionism resulting from the global depression in the 1920s and 1930s, however, caused a steady erosion of foreign markets. In

1922–23 sales plummeted to half of what they had been in 1919–20. In 1927 Lindt & Sprüngli's general agent in Germany, the company's largest export market before the war, went bankrupt. One year later, the Schokoladenfabrik Lindt & Sprüngli AG Berlin was founded as a joint venture with the British Rowntree and Co. in York, Lindt & Sprüngli's first foreign partner. In 1930 the firm's name was changed again to the simpler Chocoladefabriken Lindt & Sprüngli AG. Exports of Swiss chocolate makers dropped by 87 percent in 1932. In the following years the Lindt & Sprüngli factory in Berne was closed down, and the Lindt subsidiaries in Great Britain and Germany were changed into licensees. Costs for all raw materials shot up, the Swiss currency was devalued significantly due to inflation, and consumer prices were frozen by the Swiss authorities. By 1937 Lindt & Sprüngli's export share had sunk to only nine percent of total sales.

When the Second World War began, the company had only its domestic market. Although prices remained high for cocoa and sugar, limited supplies were secured through imports monopolized by the government. In newly developed products, almonds and nuts replaced a good portion of cocoa, and the Lindt brand name more and more replaced the Sprüngli brand name. In 1940 Lindt & Sprüngli started paying their work force cost-of-living allowances, which rose from 4.5 percent of total pay in 1940 to 26 percent in 1944. In addition, so-called autumn allowances enabled Lindt & Sprüngli employees to buy food and fuel for the winter. From 1943 until 1946, chocolate was rationed in Switzerland to 100 grams per person per month. Despite dwindling sales figures, Lindt & Sprüngli survived—primarily because of the management's total commitment to premium quality. Arthur Weber, Lindt & Sprüngli's first sales manager, launched an advertising campaign in 1944 to keep the Lindt brand name in customer's minds while supply and demand was rationed. Every ad in various magazines began "When peace comes again."

An International Group After World War II

When peace did come again, the explosion of domestic and foreign markets once more challenged Lindt & Sprüngli's production and personnel capacity. Except for the subsidiary in England, the company was not successful in its attempt to establish facilities outside of Switzerland prior to the two world wars. Now, with worldwide demand rapidly growing, new attempts to expand internationally bore fruit. In 1947 a new licensing agreement was concluded with S.A.A. Bulgheroni & Figli, an Italian company. Other licenses were issued to companies in Germany, France, Holland, Sweden, and Denmark in the following years. Supported by a period of worldwide economic boom, Lindt & Sprüngli entered an unprecedented period of growth under the new leadership of Rudolph R. Sprüngli, son of Robert Sprüngli-Baldassari, the previous chairman from 1958 until 1962. Annual chocolate consumption increased steadily as the world economy recovered—in Switzerland alone from 3.0 kg in 1930 to 6.9 kg in 1960. Between 1961 and 1971, Lindt & Sprüngli acquired three Swiss companies. The Chocolat Grison AG in Chur, another chocolate maker, was integrated and modernized as a new production facility for Lindt & Sprüngli. Nago Nährmittel AG of Olten first agreed to produce cocoa butter and cocoa powder for Lindt & Sprüngli. The partners invested in a fully automated production facility and a 56-meter-high storage tower for cocoa beans and sugar, with a capacity of 3,000 tons. In 1971 Lindt & Sprüngli took over the Nago Nährmittel AG. The facility in Olten later became the exclusive provider of cocoa mass in fluid form for all Lindt & Sprüngli production facilities in Switzerland, Germany, and Italy. Also in 1971, Lindt & Sprüngli bought the Gubor Schokoladefabrik G. Uebersax in Langenthal, where the Central Switzerland distribution center was set up. To finance the takeovers, share capital was increased from eight to ten million Swiss Francs.

In 1972 Lindt & Sprüngli pioneered chocolate production technology in different ways. First, the so-called "Lindt & Sprüngli Chocolate Process" (LSCP) developed by the company's R&D engineers reduced processing time by more than 90 percent, down to eight hours, by pretreating the broken cocoa kernels with a water-based solution before they were mixed together with the other ingredients and refined in modernized conches. Extensive testing showed no difference in product quality. The new technology also used less energy and space. The technology was adopted later by other large chocolate makers. In the same year, a fully mechanized packaging line capable of correctly placing various pralines into 50 single layer boxes per minute was installed. In addition, innovative technologies for cooling and reheating the liquid chocolate mass and for making liqueur pralines were introduced. As a result, production capacity was quickly increased by 50 percent and Lindt & Sprüngli's sales hit 100 million Swiss Francs for the first time in 1972.

From the Second World War until 1980, about 80 percent of Lindt & Sprüngli's production was sold in Switzerland. The next step toward building an international group was taken when Lindt & Sprüngli bought 65 percent of the share capital of the French licensee CFC Consortium Francais de Confiserie in 1977 from the Perrier mineral water group. In 1983 a newly built central storage and distribution center was opened in Altendorf on Lake Zurich. Shelves measuring 15 meters high provided room for 11,000 double palettes, and direct rail connections from Altendorf to Kilchberg and Olten were opened in 1986. In the same year, the German Lindt operation became a wholly owned subsidiary. Two years later, the associated factory site also became part of the new German Chocoladefabriken Lindt & Sprüngli GmbH in Aachen. In 1986 share capital was increased to CHF 14 million when Lindt & Sprüngli shares were first quoted on the Stock Exchange in Zurich. Also in 1986, Lindt & Sprüngli's subsidiary in the United States, Lindt & Sprüngli Inc., which had existed in New York since 1925, was reactivated; one year later it was made responsible for the American market as Lindt & Sprüngli (USA) Inc. In 1989 Lindt & Sprüngli (USA) Inc. started production in a newly built facility with storage and office spaces in Stratham, New Hampshire, a $10.5 million investment. Three years later, Lindt & Sprüngli S.A. in France became a fully owned Lindt & Sprüngli subsidiary.

Geographical Expansion in the 1990s

In 1992 the German Lindt & Sprüngli subsidiary already employed more personnel and was responsible for more sales than the Swiss parent company. Consolidated group sales amounted to CHF 1,065 million, with both Germany and France accounting for about 30 percent and Switzerland accounting for another 15 percent of the group's total. In 1993 the long-term licensee, Bulgheroni SpA of Induno Olona, Italy, was acquired by Lindt & Sprüngli and given the new name Lindt & Sprüngli SpA. Thereby, all former licensees were integrated in the Lindt & Sprüngli group as fully owned subsidiaries. One year later, Lindt & Sprüngli expanded further into Austria by acquiring the famous Confiserie-Group Hofbauer in Vienna. It was integrated into the newly founded Lindt & Sprüngli (Austria) Ges.m.b.H., which was moved from Salzburg to Vienna, where both sales forces were merged.

Also in 1994, under the leadership of former Johnson & Johnson manager Ernst Tanner, who came to Lindt & Sprüngli in 1993 and was elected to the board of directors in the same year, the Lindt & Sprüngli group was restructured to encourage further international growth. As a management holding company, Chocoladefabriken Lindt & Sprüngli AG (International) in Kilchberg owned 100 percent of all subsidiaries and manufacturing sites in Switzerland, Germany, France, Italy, Austria, the United States, and selling firms in many other countries. The former parent and manufacturing plant was now responsible for production and sales in Switzerland and export markets, and its name was changed to Chocoladefabriken Lindt & Sprüngli (Schweiz) AG. A new International Sales department was created to market Lindt brand products to international corporate customers. By the end of 1994, more than 80 percent of Lindt chocolates were sold abroad. In 1997 the Lindt & Sprüngli group acquired Caffarel of Turin, an Italian chocolate manufacturer with a long tradition. In January 1998 the acquisition of the Ghirardelli Chocolate Company, founded in 1852 and based in San Leandro, California, became effective. With that move, the Lindt & Sprüngli group significantly improved its position in the world's largest chocolate market, since Ghirardelli Chocolate traditionally dominated the western part of the United States, while the Lindt brand was well established in the eastern part. In 1998 sales in Italy and the United States contributed one quarter of the group's sales, which reached CHF 1.344 billion in that year.

Finally, distribution of Lindt products was expanded and diversified. A new distribution company was founded in Australia in 1997. Joint ventures were set up with the Swiss and German Post Office to launch a new gift service that enabled customers to send Lindt chocolates to addresses worldwide between September and May. The service takes a summer break because of concerns about quality. In 1998 Lindt & Sprüngli added online shopping to their web site. Over 60 "Lindt Shops" had been opened by late 1998 in the eastern parts of the United States. Future efforts pointed toward direct sales to corporate customers in existing markets and opening up new ones, especially in Eastern Europe.

Principal Subsidiaries

Chocoladefabriken Lindt & Sprüngli (Schweiz) AG; Chocoladefabriken Lindt & Sprüngli GmbH (Germany); Lindt & Sprüngli SA (France); Lindt & Sprüngli SpA (Italy); Caffarel SpA (Italy); Lindt & Sprüngli (Austria) Ges.m.b.H.; Lindt & Sprüngli (USA) Inc.; Ghirardelli Chocolate Company (U.S.; 98%); Lindt & Sprüngli (UK) Ltd.; Lindt & Sprüngli (Canada) Inc.; Lindt & Sprüngli (Espana) SA; Lindt & Sprüngli (Poland) Sp.z o.o.; Lindt & Sprüngli (Asia-Pacific) Ltd. (Hong Kong); Lindt & Sprüngli (Australia) Pty. Ltd.

Further Reading

"Lindt Acquires Ghirardelli," *The Gourmet Retailer,* March 1998.

Mäder, Markus, and Verena Eggmann, "Der bittersüsse Duft nach Schokolade und die kleine grosse Welt darum herum," *Neue Züricher Zeitung,* December 6, 1986.

150 Years of Delight, Kilchberg, Switzerland: Chocoladefabriken Lindt & Sprüngli (Schweiz) AG, 1995.

Rüedi, Werner, "Auf Einkaufstour," *Handelszeitung,* January 13, 1998.

Schmidt, Hans Rudolf, "Die Pioniere Sprüngli und Lindt," in *Schweizer Pioniere der Wirtschaft und Technik 22,* Zurich, Switzerland: Verein für wirtschaftshistorische Studien, 1970.

—Evelyn Hauser

CompuServe Interactive Services, Inc.

5000 Arlington Center Boulevard
Columbus, Ohio 43220-2913
U.S.A.
(614) 457-8600
(800) 848-8990
Fax: (614) 457-0348
Web site: http://www.compuserve.com

Wholly Owned Subsidiary of America Online, Inc.
Incorporated: 1980 as Compuserve Corp.
Employees: 3,050
Sales: $842 million (1997 est.)
SICs: 7375 Information Retrieval Services; 7372
   Prepackaged Software; 7374 Data Processing &
   Preparation

One of the world's leading online information services, CompuServe Interactive Services, Inc. provides personal computer users in the home or office with a wide variety of online information services, communications opportunities, and software products. With approximately two million subscribers in 1998, CompuServe specializes in online services for small businesses and professionals, maintaining a separate niche from parent company America Online, recognized for its more mass-market approach. An important portion of CompuServe's business comes from Europe, where in 1998 it boasted some 850,000 subscribers.

Early History

CompuServe was established in 1969 by Jeffrey Wilkins to computerize his father-in-law's insurance company. In 1977, he expanded into computer time-sharing services. Through its pioneering efforts in videotex technology, CompuServe introduced an online service, the CompuServe Information Service, two years later. This network initially represented an extension of its core business; starting the information service was simply a matter of offering existing hardware to about 1,200 nighttime

users in its first year. The following year, CompuServe became a wholly owned subsidiary of H&R Block, Inc., which provided the financial support to foster CompuServe's rapid growth through expansion as well as research and development.

Through videotex, CompuServe enabled users to perform banking and shopping transactions and access a wide variety of information from their homes. Using CompuServe, individuals could make travel reservations and order tickets for cultural or sporting events in the convenience of their homes, or access databases offering current news, weather forecasts, sports scores, and stock prices. The usage rate for many of these services initially fell below the company's expectations, however, as it proved difficult to change consumer behavior; many simply preferred to use the telephone or other conventional channels for acquiring their goods and services. Nevertheless, as personal computing and home office environments became more common in the United States, Americans became more willing to explore videotex transactions. CompuServe reported that sales made through its home shopping service, the Electronic Mall, rose 76 percent in 1990.

Other, more popular videotex applications involved communication networks facilitated by e-mail, electronic bulletin boards, and forums. These services, which allowed users across the country to communicate through their computers, quickly became the most popular of CompuServe's offerings. CompuServe played a particularly important role in developing online forums—its most heavily used service—that offered users the opportunity to share information on areas of common interest. The company's earliest forums consisted largely of shared information on personal computing technology and thus appealed primarily to specialists and technology buffs. As the concept gained popularity, however, forums for a wide variety of subjects and hobbies emerged, allowing users to electronically discuss music, gaming, auto racing, and science fiction, or more serious topics, such as law and medicine. By the early 1990s, CompuServe had become famous for its more than 450 technical support forums; every major software developer and computer manufacturer, including Borland, IBM, Microsoft, and 3Com Corporation, began hosting its own bulletin board to share information and entertain questions from their users. Forums also began serving as a point of access to the thousands of valuable public domain software programs in circulation.

Steady Expansion in the Late 1980s

In 1986, the market research organization LINK Resources published a report in which it characterized CompuServe's growth as "slow but steady." This reflected the company's marketing strategy of focusing on the enhancement of its popular services, while avoiding "quantum leaps" into new and untried areas. This strategy proved successful, as CompuServe was one of just a few profitable videotex companies by the early 1990s.

In 1987, CompuServe entered into a joint venture with Nissho Iwai Corporation and Fujitsu Limited to offer Nifty-Serve, a version of the CompuServe Information Service, in Japan. Licensing and distribution agreements were also made during this time to bring the CompuServe Information Service to Argentina, Australia, Chile, Hungary, Hong Kong, Israel, New Zealand, South Africa, South Korea, Taiwan, and Venezuela. After establishing access and support centers in the European population centers of Bristol, Munich, and Paris, CompuServe doubled its membership on the continent between 1992 and 1993, while Nifty-Serve claimed over 350,000 members.

In March 1989, CompuServe Information Service became the first general videotex service to garner a half million U.S. subscribers. Later that year, CompuServe completed the acquisition of Source Telecomputing Corporation, thereby expanding its membership by as many as 40,000 subscribers and eliminating a competitor. The following year, CompuServe acquired MicroSolutions Inc., a Dallas-based reseller of local area network and connectivity products. By 1991, CompuServe boasted over 620,000 subscribers and annual revenues of over $200 million. That year, CompuServe introduced new software providing colorful windows and icons to help users recognize and quickly select the service of their choice.

During this time, CompuServe was a litigant in a precedent-setting case involving censorship, liability, and libel in the electronic information age. The case involved Don Fitzpatrick, the coordinator of CompuServe's Rumorville forum for journalists, who was accused of posting defamatory remarks about Skuttlebutt, a rival forum. CompuServe was named as a co-defendant, but in November 1991, Judge Peter K. Leisure of the U.S. District Court likened CompuServe's responsibility to that of the owner of a bookstore, noting that the bookseller could not possibly be responsible for the editorial content of every book sold. Two years later, CompuServe was again involved in a lawsuit and was ordered by a federal judge to pay $4 million in compensatory and punitive damages to two Massachusetts businesses for breaching an agreement in connection with the purchase of a database system by CompuServe.

Competition Increases in the Early 1990s

In the early 1990s, lower costs for computing and telecommunications technology made online services less expensive to operate. The savings were passed along to users, who were offered limited groupings of services for a single flat rate per month, regardless of the time spent using them. Spearheading flat-rate pricing, the Prodigy online service soon surpassed CompuServe as the leading videotex service in terms of active members. Moreover, the Internet, a nonprofit, global network of more than 34,000 public and private computer networks, was becoming a potential threat to CompuServe's share of the market. Subsidized by the government and managed by volunteers, the Internet derived operating revenues from its members, who paid connection fees.

Although for-profit information services did not yet consider the Internet a direct competitor—and relied on a wider variety of services and appealing color graphics to maintain their market share—the issue of cost remained a factor in subscription rates. Dave Bezair, a senior product manager at CompuServe, Inc., told the *Wall Street Journal* in September 1993 that although "everyone wants to jump on this price issue . . . the reality is accessibility, ease of use, customer service and worldwide access." In fact, the company made major strides towards accessibility and ease of use by becoming the first in the industry to offer user interface software compatible with the popular Microsoft Windows operating system. Nevertheless, CompuServe did announce a subscriber fee reduction of as much as 40 percent, effective early in 1994. Hourly connect fees, which had ranged from $12.80 to $22.80 were dropped to between $8 and $16.

During this time, CompuServe also developed new products and services to meet competition. The Executive Service Option (ESO) was introduced, featuring business data enhanced by financial, demographic, and editorial information. Communications services designed especially for business users included online brokerage firms and electronic conferencing via computer. ESO also offered stock quotes and commodity information; historical market information; major market and industry indices; and national and international business news wires. In other fields, CompuServe created a public, online forum to help find missing children, which it made freely available to both customers and competing online services. Early in 1994, Vice-President Albert Gore, Jr., an avid promoter of the "information superhighway," gave CompuServe one of the first online, interactive interviews by a major political figure.

CompuServe's revenues stood at $315.4 million in fiscal 1993, rising 12.3 percent above the previous year, while its membership increased 40 percent during the year, reaching 1.5 million. The CompuServe Information Service won the *PC Magazine* Editor's Choice Award in 1993 and was selected as the leading provider of public data network services in *Network World*'s reader survey that year. Billed in advertisements as "The Information Service You Won't Outgrow," CompuServe focused on developing and implementing new technologies to stay competitive in a rapidly changing marketplace.

In 1994 CompuServe made two Internet-related acquisitions. The first was Network Publishing, which specialized in creating Internet sites for corporations. The second, SPRY, developed Internet software, including Internet in a Box. By mid-1996 CompuServe had fully embraced the Internet, providing its subscribers access to the World Wide Web using Netscape Navigator software and committing itself to creating all new content with Internet technology.

The Late 1990s: Troubled Finances

In April 1996 H&R Block sold 20 percent of CompuServe in an initial public offering. The IPO generated less cash than H&R Block had hoped: only $454 million. In 1996 revenues rose 36 percent to $793 million and net income more than quintupled, from $9 million in 1995 to $49 million in 1996. With more intense competition from industry leader America Online and the increasing popularity of direct Internet providers, however, the growth of the company's subscriber base had ground to a halt by the end of the year. In addition, CompuServe's introduction of its WOW! online package generated such a poor response it was pulled before the year was out. Repeated delays in introducing its CompuServe 3.0 software also hurt the company, though the company managed to release it by the end of 1996.

Early in 1997 president and CEO Robert J. Massey resigned, after only two years at those posts. Soon after, CompuServe agreed to provide its content to the subscribers of germany.net, an Internet access provider in Germany.

CompuServe's financial performance plummeted in 1997, with the company reporting a loss of $120 million. By late 1997, however, H&R Block had sold its controlling interest in CompuServe to the telecommunications company WorldCom. WorldCom split the company, keeping CompuServe's networking infrastructure and using its online content and subscriber base in a deal with America Online. AOL agreed to exchange its own network infrastructure for the CompuServe online service, $175 million in cash, and networking discounts from WorldCom.

Rather than swallow its nearest competitor wholesale, AOL chose to maintain CompuServe Interactive Services as an independent subsidiary. America Online's service was known as user-friendly and extremely easy for even novice computer users to navigate. AOL planned to keep CompuServe's identity as a more sophisticated service that catered to small businesses and professionals.

In 1998 CompuServe's subscriber base remained fairly steady at approximately two million. Although it still operated at a loss that year, it came close to breaking even. It introduced a service upgrade in 1998, CompuServe 4.0, and a revamped shopping service. The new Shopping Channel featured more than 100 retailers, including Eddie Bauer, FTD, and Barnes and Noble. Late in 1998 CompuServe announced a partnership with Time Inc. News Media that would provide CompuServe's subscribers with content and information from the online editions of the Time Inc. publications *Money* and *Fortune*.

Further Reading

Brink, Susan, Margaret Mannix, and Corinna Wu, "CompuServe Embraces the Web," *U.S. News & World Report,* June 3, 1996, p. 65.

"CompuServe Posts Loss," *Computerworld,* February 24, 1997, p. 8.

Coursey, David, "The Cost of Information," *InfoWorld,* August 5, 1991, pp. 40–44.

"Gore Mistypes His Way Through On-line Forum," *Wall Street Journal,* January 14, 1994, p. B8.

Hawkins, Donald T., "Videotex Markets, Applications, and Systems," *Online,* March 1991, pp. 97–100.

Heid, Jim, "AOL and WorldCom Swallow CompuServe: Good for Online Consumers?," *PC World,* November 1997, p. 68.

Manning, Anita, "Shopping Comes Online with Computerized Ease," *USA Today,* October 25, 1990, p. D4.

Martin, Michael H., "Online Services, Now on Their Own," *Fortune,* March 18, 1996, p. 24.

O'Leary, Mick, "Product-Support Forums Fill Niche," *Link-Up,* May/June 1992, pp. 3, 16.

Picarille, Lisa, "BBS Not Liable for Libel, Court Says," *InfoWorld,* November 11, 1991, p. 130.

Schwartz, Evan, "Adventures in the On-Line Universe," *Business Week,* June 17, pp. 112–13.

Sparks, Debra, "H&R Block: Forget CompuServe," *Financial World,* May 23, 1995, p. 16.

Stecklow, Steve, "Internet Becomes Road More Traveled as E-Mail Users Discover No Usage Fees," *Wall Street Journal,* September 2, 1993, p. B1.

Webb, Joseph A., "CompuServe Purchases the Source," *Information Today,* July/August 1989, pp. 1–2.

—April Dougal Gasbarre
—updated by Susan Windisch Brown

Cost Plus, Inc.

201 Clay Street
Oakland, California 94607
U.S.A.
(510) 893-7300
Fax: (510) 893-3681

Public Company
Incorporated: 1958
Employees: 2,114
Sales: $260.5 million (1998)
Stock Exchanges: NASDAQ
Ticker Symbol: CPWM
SICs: 5331 Variety Stores

One of the leading direct-import retailers in the United States, Cost Plus, Inc. operates approximately 70 Cost Plus World Market stores, which specialize in home furnishings imported from more than 50 countries in Europe, Asia, and Africa. With the inventory of a specialty retailer and the prices of a mass merchandiser, Cost Plus built its reputation in San Francisco before expanding into Southern California and finally eastward, where the bulk of the company's stores were opening in the late 1990s. The chain more than doubled in size during the 1990s after languishing during the late 1980s, when poor financial performance after a leveraged buyout prompted sweeping alterations to the Cost Plus concept. Cost Plus's flagship store, a 40,000-square-foot store located on San Francisco's Fisherman's Wharf, was supported by the chain's smaller stores, which measured between 16,000 square feet and 18,000 square feet.

Origins in the 1950s

Cost Plus's founder, William Amthor, did not intend to create a discount direct-import retail chain—or even to open a single store—but he discovered San Franciscans had a penchant for just that sort of merchandise. His discovery occurred by chance in 1958 when he sold some extra rattan furniture he had stored in a warehouse. At the time, Amthor operated a small family-owned furniture store in San Francisco, but instead of displaying the rattan furniture in his store, he rented 4,000 square feet of warehouse space in the Fisherman's Wharf area of San Francisco. The rattan furniture sold quickly, convincing Amthor to start importing merchandise as a new business. He opened his first store devoted exclusively to imported merchandise later in 1958 and began importing wicker by the shipload. Amthor took the name for his new store from his pricing strategy. The imported goods were sold at cost, plus ten percent, the inspiration for a chain of stores that would become known as Cost Plus.

Amthor took frequent trips to foreign countries looking for merchandise, hunting down the best bargains for an eclectic array of goods. During these trips he established business relationships with vendors that Cost Plus would use 30 years later. The frequency of Amthor's trips established the company's founder as a "world traveler," words invariably used to describe the peripatetic retailer, and established Cost Plus as a unique, exotic store, filled with an ever-changing selection of merchandise. Customers never knew what they might find at Cost Plus, and this mystery had a decided appeal, making a trip to Amthor's store similar to a treasure hunt. The store's bazaar-style merchandising proved to be highly popular, its success spawning the establishment of additional stores. For years, the location of these new stores was restricted to the greater Bay area, but the stores expanded, eventually, into Southern California. During this gradual expansion, which occurred during the 1960s and 1970s, the Cost Plus chain thrived, selling tiki torches, gauze dresses, wicker furniture, and a grab-bag of other imported goods, all at discount prices.

By the 1980s, two and one half decades of expansion had created a flourishing regional chain. Midway through the decade, there were 24 Cost Plus stores in California and one in Arizona. The anchor of the chain was the company's flagship store in Fisherman's Wharf, a 40,000-square-foot unit that, despite being ten times larger than Amthor's original store, still exuded the atmosphere created by the chain's founder. Inside, amid housewares, clothing, and furniture, customers picked their way through a broad collection of merchandise, everything from an inexpensive wire whisk to a $1,000 brass buddha from India. The merchandising mix was unique, representing the efforts of the company's seven buyers who, like Amthor before them, traveled the globe looking for items in Indonesia, China, Thailand, Portugal, France, and a host of other countries. The company's other stores were considerably smaller, averaging between 18,000 square feet and 20,000 square feet, but each contained as diverse a range of merchandise as the flagship store. The smaller stores, which averaged sales of $200 per square foot, were primarily located in shopping centers, next to other retail tenants whose customer-drawing power proved to be a boon to Cost Plus's business. The expansion strategy had worked well, providing a welcomed support system of sorts that eased Cost Plus's entry into new markets. By the end of 1986 the company was ready to open two more stores, one in San Dimas, California and the other in Bakersfield, but troubles had begun to surface. As Cost Plus exited the mid-1980s, its consistent record of success began to unravel, prompting changes that ultimately led to the creation of the modern version of Cost Plus, the nearly 100-unit chain that existed during the late 1990s.

Late 1980s Decline and Resurgence in the 1990s

The turning point in Cost Plus's financial performance occurred after a 1987 leveraged buyout engineered by Bechtel Investments (later renamed Fremont Group). In the wake of the ownership change, Cost Plus's formula for success was lost, and financial losses began to mount. The quality of the merchandise declined as the stores developed a reputation for being cluttered, rather than being rich in diversity. As time passed, the problems became more severe, leading to further, escalating losses. One industry pundit remarked that Cost Plus offered ''too much hunt and too little treasure,'' characterizing the rapid deterioration of the chain's former strength. By the beginning of the 1990s the company had recorded five years of consecutive year-end deficits, an alarming record exacerbated by the $5.9 million loss posted for 1991. Clearly, changes needed to be made.

Help had arrived by the time the depressing financial figures for 1991 were released. Ralph D. Dillon, the former president and chief operating officer of Family Dollar Stores, had joined Cost Plus in 1990. It was Dillon's responsibility to muster a turnaround and revive the chain's former vitality. He began making changes in the way Cost Plus operated shortly after his arrival. The scope and the severity of the changes increased after control of the company was gained by Goldman Sachs and International Nederland Capital Corp. in 1994, but throughout the first half of the 1990s, the process of transforming Cost Plus into a healthy enterprise was under way. By the time the company entered the mid-1990s, it emerged as a different sort of retailer offering a subtly but significantly altered merchandise mix.

One of the first problems Dillon recognized was that Cost Plus had lost its focus on the proper merchandise for the stores to display. Accordingly, he launched a campaign to determine what product mix was most attractive to the chain's customers. Experiments with focus groups revealed that the typical Cost Plus customer, identified as a college-educated female between the ages of 25 and 55, desired a combination of home décor merchandise and gourmet food. Dillon reacted to the research by increasing the presence of home décor items, eliminating toys, and limiting the space devoted to jewelry and beverages. Along with these changes, the average square footage of the

stores was decreased, reduced from 20,000 square feet to somewhere between the 16,000-square-foot and 18,000-square-foot range. Despite the smaller size, Cost Plus stores continued to display roughly the same amount of merchandise, using vertical merchandising to compensate for less retail space.

Once the proper merchandise mix was identified, Dillon refined the layout of the new, prototype Cost Plus, which was christened Cost Plus World Market. The objective was to eliminate the cluttered look that had developed during the late 1980s and create a more defined design, but the layout still had to retain the open-air market atmosphere that had characterized the chain since its birth. Cost Plus relied heavily on impulse purchases, so a balance had to be struck between an orderly design and one that was conducive to browsing. To orient the customer, Dillon and his staff designed three featured areas. At the back of the store, an assortment of gourmet food and beverages composed Cost Plus's Marketplace section. One side of the store, identified by a rug wall, displayed decorative home furnishings, including textiles, pillows, and baskets. On the other side of the store, beneath a chair hung on the wall, functional home furnishings were displayed, such as furniture, glassware, and tabletops. These areas provided an easily recognizable structure to Cost Plus, serving as landmarks amid the sea of imported merchandise, but not at the expense of reducing the number of impulse purchases. The average Cost Plus customer spent 45 minutes in the store, nearly twice the time spent in a typical home store.

The changes were important, but equally important were the characteristics that were left unchanged. Although the company greatly increased its reliance on home furnishings, until they accounted for nearly 70 percent of a store's total inventory, the emphasis continued to be on stocking imported items, one of the company's original strengths. Cost Plus imported 90 percent of the home furnishings it sold, buying the merchandise in more than 40 countries in Europe, Asia, and Africa. Placemats, napkins, and rugs were shipped from India and Turkey. Wood and rattan furniture arrived from Italy, Thailand, and the Czech Republic. Cost Plus buyers procured glassware and dinnerware from England and France, baskets from China, the Philippines, and Indonesia, and collectible home artifacts from Bali, Ghana, and Namibia. The diversity of the imported merchandise had not changed and neither had the grab-bag appeal of an ever-changing inventory—an integral part of the formula that created Cost Plus's ''treasure hunt'' attraction. Roughly 60 percent of the items on display were changed every 12-month period, while certain product types were changed more frequently, usually at a monthly rate. The interior of the store harkened back to Amthor's first years as well, retaining the warehouse ''feel'' of the earliest Cost Plus units. The floors were cement, ceilings were high, beams were exposed, and fixtures were plain, creating a Spartan environment for what the company described as an ''upscale, organized version of the Third World central market-place.''

Expansion Accelerates During the Late 1990s

After the Cost Plus concept was refined and profitability was restored, Dillon was ready to usher in an era of expansion—the most prolific in the company's history—and add to the 38 stores in operation when he joined the company. The company expanded beyond its home territory in California and began opening stores in neighboring states, with the pace of expansion increasing after Goldman Sachs and International Nederland Capital Corp. assumed majority control over the company in 1994. By the end of 1995 there were 50 stores composing the Cost Plus chain, including 13 in the Bay area, more than 30 stores in California, and more than a dozen scattered in a ten-state territory.

In early 1996, after maintaining profitability for a three-year period and expanding at a modest pace, Dillon was ready to take the company to new heights. His confidence in the Cost Plus World Market concept was resolute, prompting him to develop ambitious plans for the company. First, he completed the company's initial public offering of stock in April 1996, raising $29.8 million to pay for past and future expansion. Several weeks later, Dillon announced that Cost Plus would open eight additional Cost Plus World Markets by the end of 1996 and 12 units the following year, hoping to reach nearly 90 units by the end of the decade. His long-term plan was much grander, a 300-unit chain collecting $1.5 billion in sales, exponentially higher than the $182 million Cost Plus generated in sales in 1995. "We have worked the last five years developing a prototype Cost Plus World Market store," Dillon explained, "and we are constantly testing new things. With the markets we have already ID'd nationwide, we could be 300 stores."

By the time Cost Plus converted to public ownership, expansion was under way in a number of new markets. New stores were being developed in Texas, Illinois, Missouri, and Wisconsin, established, as they had been for decades, in shopping centers where the presence of other retail tenants assured a steady stream of customers. As the company expanded eastward, its progress was made easier not only by situating its stores in established shopping centers, but also by its decades of experience in the business. Other import retailers of Cost Plus's ilk—companies such as Bombay Company, Euromarket Designs, and Pier 1 Imports—had to contend with the often troublesome process of foreign-sourcing their merchandise, that is, coordinating supply and delivery of goods from distant markets. Delays and miscommunications were frequent, but Cost Plus avoided the problems with which less experienced retailers had to contend because of the company's long-established ties with overseas vendors, many of which stretched back two generations. This was one of Cost Plus's major strengths,

enabling the company to expand eastward with relative ease. In October 1996 Dillon banked on this advantage when he announced plans for major expansion, projecting the opening of 35 stores by the end of the decade.

As Cost Plus entered the late 1990s, work was under way to reach Dillon's goal. Expansion pushed the company eastward into the Midwest, where Cost Plus World Market stores opened in Chicago, Detroit, and Cincinnati. By November 1997, when the company announced plans to open its first store in Indiana, the chain comprised 68 stores in a 12-state territory, including four stores in Chicago and three in Detroit. The company planned to open 15 stores in 1998, projecting an annual growth rate of between 15 percent and 20 percent as the end of the century approached. As the company prepared for the future, its record of success in the 1990s provided strong evidence that further expansion would yield substantial growth. Between 1992 and 1997, revenues more than doubled, jumping from $121 million to $260 million. Net income increased more dramatically, swelling from $151,000 to reach $10 million. With these figures demonstrating the strength of the Cost Plus World Market concept, the company's future expansion suggested equally robust gains in the years ahead.

Further Reading

Blackwood, Francy, "Cost Plus Treks Across America: Eclectic Retailer Opening 35 Units as It Spreads East," *HFN The Weekly Newspaper for the Home Furnishing Network,* October 21, 1996, p. 1.

Carlsen, Clifford, "Importer Maps Out Uncharted Territory," *San Francisco Business Times,* July 26, 1996, p. 4A.

"Cost Plus: Buddhas to Bakeware," *Chain Store Age Executive with Shopping Center,* September 1986, p. 36.

Huesmann, Chris, "Cost Plus Inc. Shares Begin Trading with a Rise," *Knight-Ridder/Tribune Business News,* April 5, 1996, p. 4.

Key, Peter, "Cost Plus of Oakland, Calif., to Open Carmel, Ind., Store," *Knight-Ridder/Tribune Business News,* November 4, 1997, p. 11.

Konstam, Patricia, "California's Cost Plus World Market to Open San Antonio Store," *Knight-Ridder/Tribune Business News,* August 30, 1996, p. 8.

Vincenti, Lisa, "Cost Plus Markets Intrigue," *HFN The Weekly Newspaper for the Home Furnishing Network,* May 11, 1998, p. 1.

—Jeffrey L. Covell

Cutter & Buck Inc.

2701 1st Avenue, Suite 500
Seattle, Washington 98121
U.S.A.
(206) 622-4191
(800) 929-9299
Fax: (206) 448-0589
Web site: http://www.cutterbuck.com

Public Company
Incorporated: 1990 as Jones-Rodolfo Corporation
Employees: 265
Sales: $70.1 million (1998)
Stock Exchanges: NASDAQ
Ticker Symbol: CBUK
SICs: 2329 Men/Boys' Clothing, Not Elsewhere
   Classified

A fast-growing apparel company, Cutter & Buck Inc. is known for its casual golf attire, which consists of woven and knit fabrics featuring embroidered designs. In 1998 the company derived more than half of its revenue from sales at 3,000 golf course pro shops, where the typical Cutter & Buck customer—an affluent 30- to 50-year-old male—visited frequently. The company's clothing was manufactured under contract in Hong Kong, China, and Thailand. In late 1998 Cutter & Buck opened its first retail store, a 3,400-square-foot clubhouse replica located in Seattle.

Origins

Cutter & Buck's co-founder, Harvey Jones, grew up in the apparel industry. His family owned a retail apparel business in Spokane, Washington, where Jones divided his time between school and stocking the shelves and sweeping the floor at his family's store. As an adult, Jones followed his family's example. He moved to California in 1974 and started making his own apparel, beginning with an initial investment of $7,000. With his modest start-up money, Jones began manufacturing and

marketing an apparel label called Sticky Finger Jeans. His next venture involved a second label called San Francisco Riding Gear. By the mid-1980s Jones had departed from the entrepreneurial ranks and joined an apparel design company called UnionBay Sportswear Co., where Jones first met another UnionBay employee, Joey Rodolfo. Jones and Rodolfo forged a partnership, and in early 1987 they began collaborating on starting their own apparel company. After securing financial backing from Taiwanese investors, Jones and Rodolfo were in business, ready to begin manufacturing and marketing a line of men's and women's sportswear through their new company, Bench Co. Ltd. Their plan was to manufacture the clothing overseas and ship it back to the United States, where the sportswear would be distributed to department stores and specialty shops. The plan did not fulfill expectations. Jones and Rodolfo were pleased by the results they were achieving, but their investors were not, particularly one Taiwanese investor who owned the majority of Bench. Together, Jones and Rodolfo owned one third of Bench, not enough to exert ultimate control over the company. Said Jones, "Bench's distribution had expanded to more of a specialty store clientele and had done well, but our Taiwanese partner had some real questions about where the company was going." By mid-1989, just as Bench was beginning to generate a profit, the relationship between the founders and their foreign investors had become irrevocably divisive. The philosophical disagreement that erupted led to Jones's and Rodolfo's departure from the company in July 1989, their bitterness evident. "We were really disillusioned with the fact we were leaving behind a company just kicking into high gear," Jones lamented.

After leaving Bench, Jones and Rodolfo searched for two months for a new job, exploring several opportunities to work for apparel design companies, but both felt a need to finish what they had started at Bench. In September, the pair decided to start another company together, each adamant that the second venture would be substantially different from the first. Jones and Rodolfo decided that their next company would be smaller than Bench and would target a narrower market base. Instead of marketing men's and women's sportswear, the new company would focus on male customers only, specifically 20- to 50-year-old males looking for clothes to wear on the weekend. Of

Company Perspectives:

Growing from the tradition and heritage of golf, Cutter & Buck is emerging as the premier sportswear line in America today. Our customer is the man or woman who believes that clothing is a reflection of personal style. Our design philosophy combines the inspiration of the golf lifestyle with our Pacific Northwest roots. We feature updated traditional clothing with an outdoor attitude. We are known for our strong clear colors, natural fiber fabrications, attention to detail, innovative trims, and specialized printing and embroidery; these form the Cutter & Buck identity.

primary importance, however, was avoiding any foreign involvement, both in terms of production and financing. Jones and Rodolfo wanted to keep their manufacturing in the United States and thereby shorten the time between design and production, enabling their company to offer greater flexibility to retailers. They hoped to avoid distributing to major department stores, which preferred to stock discounted merchandise, and instead concentrate on a network of between 250 and 300 specialty shops. With a rough idea of their new venture, Jones and Rodolfo were ready to go forward with their plans, but not until they found a suitable financial backer. The issue of financial support was of paramount importance. After the debacle at Bench, neither of the entrepreneurs wanted any financial help from overseas investors. "We weren't going to go ahead with the business," Jones explained, "if we couldn't get a financial partnership with someone we felt comfortable with."

Jones and Rodolfo hired a Seattle-based business consultant to help develop the financial model of their new company, which they named Jones-Rodolfo Corp., and began showing their plan to venture capital firms. They found a number of small, local investors willing to support their efforts and had a small amount of their own capital to invest, but the biggest and the most crucial investor was a Seattle-based venture capital firm named Roanoke Capital Ltd. Roanoke, which never disclosed an exact dollar amount of its investment, but reportedly offered between $1 million and $4 million, suited Jones and Rodolfo perfectly as a financial partner. "It's really nice," Jones remarked, still bristling from his experience with Taiwanese investors, "that we didn't have to sell our souls to a foreigner."

As Jones and Rodolfo searched for the capital to start their company in the fall of 1989, they also devoted time to searching for domestic fabric sources and production facilities to make their inaugural apparel line. Once an agreement was reached with Roanoke, Rodolfo, who held the title of design director, hurried to assemble the company's first line of clothes. With the help of a corporate design and administrative staff comprising eight individuals, Rodolfo began designing and making a collection of jackets and heavy-knit sportswear for the company's new label, Cutter & Buck. By early 1990 the company was ready for the Preline fashion show in Seattle, which immediately preceded more prestigious menswear shows in Los Angeles and New York. Using the Preline show as a jumping-off point, Jones-Rodolfo Corp. unveiled the first Cutter & Buck line, showcasing sweatshirts, jackets, and other garments priced between $45 and $150.

After the Preline show, the Cutter & Buck concept underwent a period of refinement, as the label's "look" took shape. By 1991 the line was predominated by richly colored, knit sweatshirts that evoked an outdoor image or, as fashion observers defined it, a "Pacific Northwest lifestyle" image. Rodolfo claimed that he drew his inspiration from "the early Eddie Bauer look," citing the name of a Seattle-based clothing manufacturer founded by outdoor enthusiast, Eddie Bauer. In fact, Cutter & Buck sweatshirts were made at a former Eddie Bauer manufacturing site, where they were embellished with embroidery and designs of fishing and hunting themes, intended to be reflective of the Pacific Northwest. The label achieved its widest acceptance away from the mountains and streams of the Pacific Northwest, however. Cutter & Buck found its most receptive audience in the southeastern United States, where the sweatshirts and other garments were most commonly found in small shops. Roughly 75 percent of Jones-Rodolfo Corp.'s merchandise was distributed to small, independent, specialty shops, with the balance retailing in department stores.

Strategic Changes in 1993

By the end of 1991 Jones-Rodolfo Corp. essentially had become the type of company envisioned by Jones and Rodolfo in late 1989. The company's products were made in the United States, they were sold in the United States, and the company itself was supported by U.S.-based investors. Further, the two founders, to a large extent, had avoided relying on department store sales, generating the bulk of their sales by distributing Cutter & Buck apparel to small specialty shops. All was as it should have been, at least according to the business plan developed in late 1989, except for one crucial aspect—the company's financial performance. Annual sales, which reached $2.6 million in 1991, were growing slowly. Profits were nonexistent. During the company's first three years of business, more than $2.3 million in losses were racked up, prompting Jones and Rodolfo to rethink their strategy and make a number of changes. The result was a type of company different from the Jones-Rodolfo Corp. of the early 1990s, as the two founders strayed from their 1989 ideals to make their company a financial success in the 1990s.

The turning point arrived in 1993, the third year of consecutive annual losses for the company. In 1993 Jones and Rodolfo narrowed their distribution of Cutter & Buck apparel to golf course pro shops, which had proved to be highly popular destinations for the company's target customer. In addition, the founders contravened their earlier resolution to keep production in the United States and began contracting nearly all of their production to Asian manufacturers. The two changes worked wonders, increasing the pace of sales growth and, more encouraging, transforming Jones-Rodolfo Corp. into a profitable enterprise. In 1994 the company reported its first year-end profit, generating $101,000 on sales of $9.9 million. Gradually, as the number of golf pro shops carrying Cutter & Buck apparel increased, the apparel itself—a collection of knit and woven sport shirts, pants, shorts, sweaters, and sweatshirts—began to take on a slightly different look, becoming a label more and more associated with the sport of golfing. By 1995 more than half of the company's garments sold in golf pro shops were embroidered with the name or the logo of the particular golf course adjoining the pro shop. Overall sales reflected the shift in focus away from specialty stores and toward golf pro shops. In 1995 sales to upscale men's specialty shops, formerly the company's mainstay distribution point, remained flat, stagnating at 1994's level, while sales to department stores plunged, falling from $1 million to $116,000. Total sales, however, were up significantly, increasing from $9.9 million to $13.5 million, which was entirely attributable to the increase in sales coming from golf pro shops.

1995 Public Offering Fuels Expansion

As evidenced by the invigorated financial growth, the company's Cutter & Buck line, which had been divided into a trendy "Fashion" line and a more traditional "Classic" line, had found its market niche by the mid-1990s. Golf pro shops offered the greatest opportunity for growth, and they were abundant, providing Jones-Rodolfo Corp. with a vast market into which to expand. In 1995, 42 percent of the company's revenue was derived from sales at 1,200 pro shops, only a fraction of the approximately 13,000 pro shops in the United States. Expanding into these shops was the direction the company was headed, but expansion required capital, so in July 1995, after changing its name to Cutter & Buck Inc., the company filed with the Securities and Exchange Commission for an initial public offering (IPO). In the August 1995 IPO approximately 44 percent of the company's stock was sold to the public. Roanoke retained 32 percent of Cutter & Buck's stock and Jones and Rodolfo held on to a combined 11 percent. The IPO raised $9.4 million, providing the financial resources to fuel expansion. Of the proceeds, nearly $1 million was set aside to finance expansion into more pro shops, $2 million was earmarked to increase inventories of the Classic line, another $1 million was designated to expand the Fashion line, and an additional $2 million went to pay off debt. The balance was invested for future use.

Following the IPO, Cutter & Buck was geared for expansion on all fronts. As the company prepared for an extraordinarily active 1996 and 1997, it did so without the day-to-day presence of the creative force who had guided Cutter & Buck during its first five years of business. Rodolfo resigned from the company at the end of April 1995, served the next two years as a consultant, and then left the company entirely in 1997 to start his own women's golf apparel company. Rodolfo's departure, however, caused little disruption to Cutter & Buck's progress, as the company began to record strident financial and physical growth in the wake of the 1995 IPO. In 1996 the company opened an in-house embroidery and warehouse facility, increased its presence in pro shops throughout the country, and strengthened its international business. The company had already established distributorships in Japan, Singapore, and Australia, but 1996 saw Cutter & Buck turn its attention in the other direction, toward Europe, where the company's apparel began appearing in the United Kingdom. The push into the United Kingdom was followed by the formation of a wholly owned subsidiary, Cutter & Buck (Europe) B.V., in Holland to govern the company's operations on the continent.

By the end of the company's fiscal year in 1996, sales had swelled to $21.6 million, ten times the total recorded five years earlier, and net income, once a sore spot for the company, had climbed to $1 million. The company was growing robustly after years of modest growth, but in the years ahead the pace of growth would become significantly more prolific. By 1997 selected collections of the company's apparel were available in approximately 2,300 pro shops scattered throughout the country. By 1998, when sales increased more than 50 percent from the previous year's total, reaching $70.1 million, 3,000 pro shops carried Cutter & Buck menswear, outerwear, and accessories, leaving 10,000 additional pro shops into which the company potentially could expand. The existence of these untapped markets suggested greater growth for years to come, but as Cutter & Buck neared its tenth anniversary, another avenue of expansion was explored. In October 1998 the company opened its first store, a 3,400-square-foot outlet in Seattle that was designed to replicate a golf clubhouse. Inside, for the first time, the entire Cutter & Buck merchandise line was available to consumers instead of the selected collections available in pro shops. Although no specific plans were announced for additional stores at the time of the Seattle store's grand opening, the possibility of retail expansion combined with the continued penetration of pro shops throughout the country pointed to a promising future for the company. As Cutter & Buck prepared to move forward with its plans, a 44 percent increase in sales and a 67 percent increase in profits for the first quarter of 1999 provided convincing evidence that the company was destined to become one the industry's most potent competitors.

Principal Subsidiaries

Cutter & Buck (Europe) B.V. (Holland).

Further Reading

"Cutter & Buck Back in Black in 3d Period," *Daily News Record,* March 26, 1996, p. 10.
"Cutter & Buck Earnings Skyrocket in 2nd Quarter," *Daily News Record,* December 19, 1995, p. 10.
"Cutter & Buck Net Jumps 34.1%," *Daily News Record,* December 5, 1997, p. 6.
"Cutter & Buck Plans IPO to Raise $9M–$11M," *Daily News Record,* August 1, 1995, p. 10.
Epes, James, "Cutter & Buck Slates an IPO to Raise Upwards of $8 Million," *Puget Sound Business Journal,* July 28, 1995, p. 4.
"Jones Adds Post at Cutter & Buck," *Daily News Record,* July 9, 1997, p. 8.
Liebman, Larry, "Lighting Up the Links," *Puget Sound Business Journal,* June 27, 1997, p. 29.
Prinzing, Debra, " 'Deep Backgrounds' Behind New Menswear Entity," *Puget Sound Business Journal,* February 26, 1990, p. 5.
Spector, Robert, "Rough Edges: Northwest Style," *Daily News Record,* April 9, 1991, p. 3.
Walsh, Peter, "Cutter & Buck Inc.," *Daily News Record,* September 6, 1995, p. 5.

—Jeffrey L. Covell

Cytec Industries Inc.

Five Garret Mountain Plaza
West Paterson, New Jersey 07424
U.S.A.
(973) 357-3100
Fax: (973) 357-3060
Web site: http://www.cytec.com

Public Company
Incorporated: 1991
Employees: 5,200
Sales: $1.29 billion (1997)
Stock Exchanges: New York
Ticker Symbol: CYT
SICs: 2899 Chemical Preparations, Not Elsewhere
   Classified

A leading chemicals company, Cytec Industries Inc. develops, manufactures, and markets specialty chemicals, specialty materials, and building block chemicals. Cytec's products were sold to end users involved in a variety of industries, including water treatment, paper, mining, coatings, plastics, aerospace, textile, and automotive. The company's distinctive quality was its vertically integrated operations, which manufactured the raw materials—the building block chemicals—used in Cytec's finished chemical products. During the mid-1990s Cytec divested a number of businesses, notably its acrylic fibers business, and concentrated on specialty chemicals and specialty materials. By the late 1990s the company's global operations included sales, laboratory, and manufacturing facilities in 36 countries.

Origins

New Jersey-based American Cyanamid formed Cytec Industries as a separate business unit in 1991, grouping its chemicals business within the new company. When Cytec was created, it joined a number of other separately run companies operating under American Cyanamid's vast, life sciences corporate umbrella. These other companies included Lederle Phar-

maceuticals; Davis & Geck, a medical device company; Storz, an ophthalmic and pharmaceutical company; and Praxis, a medical supply firm. Along with these companies and other concerns involved in agricultural products businesses, Cytec had to compete for American Cyanamid's resources. It was a struggle for the parent company's attention, a struggle that Cytec's new leader, Darryl D. Fry, had little hope of winning. Among pharmaceuticals, agricultural products, and chemicals, chemicals "ranked a low third," according to Fry, in the minds of American Cyanamid's senior executives, putting the new company and its new manager in an unenviable position. Further, it soon became apparent to Fry that American Cyanamid had Cytec slated for divestiture, reinforcing his opinion that Cytec's chemicals business occupied the lowest rung of its parent company's priorities. By the following year—one year after Cytec's formation—the business press realized American Cyanamid's intentions for its recently formed company. Cytec was to be spun off as an independent company, but the process of separation could not be completed overnight. Cytec, by itself, represented a nearly $1 billion a year business; its separation from American Cyanamid would require a substantial amount of time to complete. During this interim period spanning Cytec's formation and its spin-off from American Cyanamid, Fry devoted his energies to shaping the company into an enterprise that could stand on its own.

Early on, Fry began to make fundamental changes in the way Cytec operated. His goal was to implement as many of the changes as possible before Cytec's spin-off, or, in his words, to take "all the psychological and morale hits before the spin." Toward this end, there was much to be done. Cytec physically separated itself from American Cyanamid before the spin-off, moving its headquarters to West Paterson, New Jersey, away from its parent company's campus in Wayne, New Jersey. Before and after the move, Cytec had to be restructured, layers of management needed to be stripped, and costs had to be cut drastically. Further, and perhaps most difficult, a new mentality among all employees had to be instilled, one that replaced the ingrained habits and practices existing under the American Cyanamid regime. Fry intentionally established what he described as a period of "discontinuity," a period of purposeful, noticeable disruption that let everyone know nothing would be

---

Company Perspectives:

Cytec's diverse portfolio of products and technologies is supported by vertical integration, which distinguishes us from most other specialty chemical companies. We produce the major building block chemicals used as intermediates in manufacturing many of our specialty chemicals and specialty materials. This provides us with a better balance through economic cycles.

---

as it once had been. Austerity measures were implemented to create what Fry envisioned as a "classless" corporate culture, a company without executive dining rooms, without corporate jets, and without executive parking lots. Part of the reason for the sweeping changes was the burdensome inheritance Cytec was slated to receive as part of the spin-off. Upon gaining its independence, the company was to assume roughly $400 million in employee retirement, health, and insurance liabilities, as well as approximately $225 million in environmental clean-up liabilities. "Things couldn't get any worse," Fry remarked, recalling the ominous future the company faced during the early 1990s. Cytec, an industry analyst noted, echoing Fry's assessment, "has to dig its way out of a deep ditch."

1993 Spin-Off

The various businesses Fry was struggling to shape into an efficient, cohesive whole comprised American Cyanamid's global chemicals business, which in 1992 generated $951 million in revenue. The scope of the business included American Cyanamid's process chemicals, commodities chemicals, coating resins, water treating and mining chemicals, and paper chemicals assets. In December 1992 Cytec received another business from American Cyanamid, the company's acrylic fibers segment, which manufactured fibers for apparel and industrial uses. With the addition of the acrylic fibers segment, which was organized as the Fibers division, the major components of Cytec's business were in place and the company was ready for the much-awaited spin-off date. The spin-off occurred on December 17, 1993, but its arrival did not evoke any sense of a new beginning. According to Fry, Cytec's employees felt "kicked out by Cyanamid." Investors, who were presented with the opportunity to invest in Cytec for the first time, were generally apathetic. Fry conceded "expectations were very low," but he remained positive, declaring "we've exceeded expectations since day one." Despite Fry's optimism, there was not much hope that Cytec could be fashioned into a vibrant, financial success. There were, however, several factors working in the company's favor. Cut free from American Cyanamid, Cytec no longer had to clamor for resources from a parent company with priorities that did not always mesh with its own needs. Second, Cytec's operations were unique, giving the company an advantage that not all of its competitors enjoyed. The company manufactured a handful of its own raw materials, including ammonia, methanol, acrylonitrile, acrylamide, and melamine, positioning the company as a "back integrated" specialty chemicals producer, a rarity among the industry's participants. The addition of the acrylic fibers business made

Cytec one of only two acrylic fibers producers in the United States, which gave the company a solid position in a market expected to grow during the mid-1990s.

As Cytec headed out on its own, its businesses were divided into three categories: building block chemicals, specialty materials, and specialty chemicals. The building block chemicals segment comprised the manufacturing operations that distinguished Cytec as a vertically integrated chemicals producer. The specialty materials group was led by the company's acrylic fibers business, but also included the production of aerospace film adhesives and advanced composites, as well as specialized sealants, molding compounds, and metal-coated fibers. Cytec's third business segment—its specialty chemicals operations—consisted of water treating, mining, and paper chemicals, as well as coating resins and polymer additives. In the years following the spin-off, much of the company's growth occurred in the specialty materials segment.

As expected, Cytec's first few months as an independent company proved difficult. The company recorded an operating loss of $89 million in 1993, yet Fry remained positive, realizing that the early 1990s were years of preparation. "In the next three years," Fry declared, projecting Cytec's course between 1994 and 1997, "we're going after top-line growth and developing a passion for the customer." The budget for capital expenditures was increased to $120 million for 1994, as the company realized its first opportunity to develop momentum, while Fry turned his attention to strengthening customer relations. "If you track my time," Fry remarked, recalling American Cyanamid's tenure of control, "the proportion that I have spent with customers has been deplorable. I plan to pick that up heavily." Fry planned to diversify the geographic composition of the company's customer base as well, hoping to increase Cytec's business outside the United States and Canada. During the mid-1990s Cytec derived 75 percent of its sales from the United States and Canada, but Fry envisioned an even split between business outside North America and business within North America. Accordingly, the company began exploring business opportunities in Western Europe, Latin America, and the Far East, with a particular emphasis on China and Southeast Asia as high-growth regions.

To the outside observer, Cytec's most noticeable activity took place on the acquisition and divestiture fronts, away from the behind-the-scenes efforts to improve customer relations and expand geographically. First, the company began to shed businesses and properties, discarding assets that no longer matched its priorities. The first hint of the divestitures to follow arrived in early May 1996, when the company announced its decision "to explore all strategic options available to enhance the value of its acrylic fibers business including the possible sale of the business." Although the Cytec was one of only two acrylic fibers manufacturers in North America, the business no longer fit the company's strategic plans. Cytec's vice-president of corporate development explained: "We feel that fibers are not our key strength. Chemicals are our key strength as a company. Fibers require a different priority." A week later, Cytec announced similar plans for its aluminum sulfate business, a producer of chemicals used by paper mills to improve paper quality and used by municipalities to purify drinking and waste water. The aluminum sulfate business was the first to go, sold to GEO Specialty

Chemicals, Inc. in mid-December 1996. The divestiture stripped Cytec of seven manufacturing plants in the southeastern United States and an additional plant in Georgia. One week later Cytec reached an agreement with Sterling Chemicals, Inc. for the sale of the company's acrylic fibers business, a $140-million-revenue producer in 1996. The transaction, which included a plant in Pensacola, Florida, was completed at the end of January 1997 for approximately $100 million. Fry explained, "The divestiture is consistent with Cytec's strategy to concentrate on value-added, technology-intensive specialty chemicals."

Late 1990s Acquisitions

At the same time of the sale of the acrylic fibers business, Cytec underwent a change in management. As had been announced in the early 1990s, Fry intended to retire in January 1999 at age 60, but the leadership transition began at the beginning of 1997, when David Lilley took over as president and assumed control of operations. Fry stayed on as chief executive officer and chairman, but it was Lilley who oversaw Cytec's first major acquisition, the purchase of Fiberite, Inc. In September 1997 Cytec purchased Fiberite from Stamford FHI Acquisition Corp. for an estimated $344 million, completing a move aimed toward strengthening its aerospace business. Fiberite, which was expected to generate $250 million in revenues in 1997, manufactured epoxy and resin systems for the interiors and exteriors of commercial and military aircraft at factories in Texas, California, Minnesota, Pennsylvania, and Delaware. Internationally, the company operated facilities in France and in Germany. Fiberite's operations were merged subsequently with a Cytec subsidiary named Cytec Engineered Materials Inc., which was renamed Cytec Fiberite Inc.

With the acquisition of Fiberite, Cytec's specialty materials segment accounted for approximately 40 percent of total operating profits for 1997. Of this total, 80 percent was derived from sales to the commercial and military aerospace industry, which was becoming the central focus of the company's plans as the late 1990s progressed. In this business area, Cytec stood well positioned, despite the reverberating effects of the Asian economic crises. The collapse of Asian economies was important to Cytec because the financial catastrophe touched off a rash of aerospace order cancellations, impacting the customers who were becoming increasingly important to Cytec's financial well being. At first blush, Cytec appeared dangerously exposed to the market downturn, but the company's focus on advanced composites provided substantial protection from the crises. The majority of the aerospace cancellations were for Boeing 747s, which used less than 2.5 percent of their structural weight in advanced composites. Boeing 777s, by comparison, used a greater percentage of the type of advanced composites made by Cytec, roughly eight percent more than the Boeing 747s. To

Cytec's fortune, Asian cancellations of Boeing 777s were replaced by orders from non-Asian airlines.

Evidence of the confidence in the future of aerospace business was found in Cytec's next big move on the acquisition front. In October 1998 the company acquired The American Materials & Technologies Corporation (AMT) for roughly $30 million. Lilley, who had been named chief executive officer in May 1998, announced, "AMT provides us the opportunity to enhance our existing aerospace product portfolio as well as realize significant cost synergies." Wall Street, which initially had been indifferent to Cytec's existence, applauded the company's increasing penetration of the aerospace market. Said one specialty chemicals analyst, "I would be hard pressed to find any negatives for Cytec right now." Fry, in his last weeks as chairman of the company following the AMT acquisition, could rightly claim to have completed a remarkable turnaround, but further adjustments to Cytec's structure and operations were in the offing as the late 1990s drew to a close. The specialty chemicals market was rapidly consolidating, and Cytec was expected to take advantage of the acquisition candidates created by the consolidation. In a potential prelude to a future acquisition, Cytec sold its bulk molding compounds business in November 1998, which included a manufacturing, sales, and laboratory facility in Ohio. Looking ahead, the company was expected to increase its international business, as the era of Lilley's management succeeded Cytec's formative years under the guidance of Fry.

Principal Subsidiaries

Cytec Fiberite Inc.

Further Reading

"All Cyanamid Chemicals in Cytec Unit," *WWD,* December 22, 1992, p. 6.
"AmCy To Spin Off Cytec to Public," *Daily News Record,* September 17, 1993, p. 9.
Chang, Joseph, "Cytec Industries Is Attractive as Potential Takeover Candidate," *Chemical Market Reporter,* March 9, 1998, p. 1.
Hunter, David, "Lessons Learned," *Chemical Week,* February 1, 1995, p. 4.
Kiesche, Elizabeth S., "Cytec Industries Gets Down to Business," *Chemical Week,* March 30, 1994, p. 26.
McCurry, John, "Cytec Sells Acrylic Fiber Biz," *Textile World,* February 1997, p. 23.
Simon, Ellen, "Cytec Industries of West Paterson, N.J., To Buy Aerospace Materials Firm," *Knight-Ridder/Tribune Business News,* August 26, 1997, p. 82.
Wood, Andrew, "Cytec Builds Confidence; Pleasing Investors—and Employees," *Chemical Week,* January 15, 1997, p. 24.

—Jeffrey L. Covell

Darty S.A.

BP 103
14, route d'Aulnay
93141 Bondy Cedex
France
(33) 1 48 02 36 19
Fax: 01 48 02 35 55
Web site: http://www.darty.fr

Wholly Owned Subsidiary of Kingfisher Plc
Incorporated: 1957
Employees: 8,196
Sales: FFr 9.93 billion (US $1.8 billion) (1997)
SICs: 5722 Household Appliance Stores

With its "contract of confidence," Darty S.A. has gained the confidence of the French consumer, raising this national chain of retail appliance stores to France's sector leader. Darty also has gained the confidence of British retailing group Kingfisher Plc, parent of Darty since 1993, which has placed Darty at the center of its European expansion. As such, Darty joins the store groups Comet and BCC in The Netherlands, New Vanden Borre in Belgium, and Kingfisher's U.K. holdings, including Woolworth's and B & Q. In the late 1990s Darty also has acquired a majority holding in another leading French appliance and furniture retailer, But.

The Darty chain continues to enjoy steady expansion in its native France, at six stores in 1998 to top 160 stores. The average size of a Darty store is 12,500 square feet. Darty stores feature a wide-ranging selection of household and electrical appliances, including computers and peripherals and stereo systems. The company also operates a number of after-sales service centers, including emergency repair services.

With nearly FFr 10 billion in annual sales, and consistent net profits, Darty has proved to be the motor of Kingfisher's 1990s growth and has helped the British group weather the extended European economic crisis during the decade. Darty is led by managing director Jean-Noël Labroue.

Electric Beginnings in the 1950s

The Darty family ran a small fabric shop in Montreuil, near Paris, in the 1950s. When brothers Natan, Marcel, and Bernard Darty joined their father at the store, the family decided to expand by purchasing the neighboring store. According to that store's lease, however, the Darty family was required to maintain the store's former occupation: that of a retail center for radio and television. Bernard and Marcel Darty took over the new store's operation. As a means for attracting customers, the brothers began exhibiting their new stock on the sidewalk.

This simple beginning would prove just the start of a long history of successes. Within days after taking over the new store, the Darty brothers had sold off its entire inventory. Joined by brother Natan, the Darty brothers decided to build their fortune through radio and television, quickly adding other electrical appliances. Their company, Darty, was established formally in 1957. Over the next several years, the brothers continued building a clientele, while also gaining experience in both customer relations and in their products.

Customer satisfaction quickly became a house rule. Not content simply with sales of their merchandise, the Darty brothers soon added delivery and post-sales services, as well as an emergency repair service. The Darty dedication to customer service was a novelty for much of France. Before long, the company's service department would become as well known as its retail operations and would begin offering repairs independent of sales. By the mid-1960s the Darty brothers had added a warehouse to distribute inventory to its Montreuil store, but also to supply the company's next step in its growth: the opening of a second small store in the Parisian region. Darty's later growth would follow a similar model of retail stores grouped around a regional distribution center and service facility. Post-sales service had grown to be an important component of the Darty brothers' business, aiding not only in building client fidelity, but also in providing continuous revenues.

In 1967 Darty moved its warehouse to a new building in Bondy. The Darty brothers, however, had purchased a building and lot far larger than they actually needed. This provided them with the opportunity to test out a new idea for the French consumer market. On a trip to the United States, the Darty brothers had marveled at an American innovation, that of large-surface specialty stores, later known as "category killers." The Darty brothers felt that this formula could be adapted to the French market. In 1968, they opened France's first large-surface home appliance store. With its 800 square meters, the store enabled Darty to offer a larger selection at lower prices. Extending the range of products in its store had another objective as well: to continue to build the company's after-sales service component.

The new store was a hit with the French consumer. Darty began plans for greater development, based around its "Choice, Price, and Service" concept. Although the company had continued to operate as a family business through the 1960s, at the start of the 1970s the Darty brothers instituted a tighter management structure, with Bernard Darty taking the company's lead. In 1970 the company opened its second large-format store, in Pierrefitte. Darty also began supplying its competitors, forming a wholesale component, Caprofem, providing cash-and-carry services to other professionals. The large assortment and higher volume also enabled Darty to achieve higher margins on its own retail sales.

Confidence in the 1970s

By 1973 Darty had expanded to nine retail stores while adding a new distribution depot at Tremblay-les-Gonesse (former name of Tremblay-en-France). As the company's chain of retail stores expanded—and began to include franchised stores—Darty took steps to maintain centralized control of the Darty image. Communications and advertising soon were recognized as an important component of the growing company. Whereas previous publicity had been conducted on the local scale, Darty now brought this activity under the responsibility of its headquarters. In 1973 the company contracted with Havas-Conseil, then the country's largest advertising agency, to create Darty's first nationwide campaign, placing advertising spots on the radio (television programming, controlled by the French government, remained as yet commercial-free).

This campaign would take place under the company's famed "Contract of Confidence." Instituted in 1973, this "contract" offered something new to the French consumer: a guarantee of price, choice, and service. The contract certainly proved to be a confidence builder with the customers, as the company's sales continued to grow. In that same year the Darty family opened the company to outsiders, bringing in investment capital from Paribas, Compagnie Bancaire, and UAP. This capital was needed for Darty's next step: developing its chain beyond the Paris region. For this, the company brought in Philippe Francès, who was named Director of Development before being named the company's president in the 1980s.

In 1975 the company consolidated its warehousing to a new site in Mitry-Mory. The company's future development would be built around the centralized warehousing model, breaking with its competitors' model of grouping retail and warehousing activities in the same location. Centralizing its warehouses enabled Darty to open new retail stores at a relatively low cost, as inventory needs could be handled away from the new store sites. While inventory was centralized, however, the company's

national expansion would take a different route, focusing on regions, rather than the entire country. Each region would be grouped under a separate subsidiary, operating more or less independently. The first Darty to open beyond the Paris region was established in Lyon in 1975. By the end of the decade the company had created four regional subsidiaries: Darty Nord-Pas-de-Calais; Darty Provence Méditérranée; Darty Alsace-Lorraine; and Darty Normandie.

The company's growth was aided by Darty's introduction on the Paris stock exchange in 1976. Although the Darty family maintained majority control, the family would begin making plans to transfer control of the company, in part to protect the company against any attempts at a hostile takeover—the rage in the business world of the 1980s. In the mid-1980s Darty began transferring shares in the company to its employees as part of their salary and benefit plans. At the start of the decade, however, Darty had begun looking at diversification.

Transferring Control in the 1980s and 1990s

Despite the company's continued success—by the mid-1980s Darty would take the leadership in French retail sales, with more than ten percent of the market—its efforts to diversify were more trouble-prone. At the start of the 1980s Darty attempted to export its retail concept to Spain. Difficult market conditions in that country, however, doomed the effort, which was abandoned less than two years later. Darty's next move to diversify kept the company in France, but looked at a new and growing product category: sports retailing. In 1982 the company launched its Sparty concept, building a chain of 11 sport-specialty retail stores by mid-decade. This development proved to be not enough to counter the rapid growth of competitors Intersport and Décathlon; in 1987 Darty transferred control of its sports stores to rival Go Sport, taking a 20 percent share of that company in exchange.

If the company had been forced to place a cap on its diversification moves, its appliance retail core continued its vigorous growth. For much of the decade the company would book revenue advances of as much as 15 percent per year and profit growth as high as 25 percent per year. By 1987 the company's sales had topped FFr 6.5 billion, posting net income of more than FFr 400 million. While expanding its chain through its headquarters and through its regional subsidiaries, Darty also adopted an "integrated management" concept for the less populated areas of the country. The new addition to Darty brought a franchised concept to the chain, breaking from the centralized logistics model in favor of independent operation under the Darty brand name. In 1984, Darty also created a new distribution subsidiary, Dacem, which provided warehousing and distribution of spare parts and appliance accessories to the Darty chain stores and service centers.

At mid-decade the Darty family began facing succession issues. Eager to preserve the independence of its appliance empire, which would near 90 stores by 1986, the Darty family began looking for ways of transferring its shareholdings, without sacrificing the company to foreign ownership. In 1986 Darty opened its capital internally, giving its employees the opportunity to buy stock in the company. Some 99 percent of the company's employees would participate in the private transaction. By the beginning of 1988 Darty's employees held some six percent of the company in stock and options. The stock market crash of October 1987, which saw Darty's stock price tumble dramatically, paradoxically opened the way to a new opportunity.

In April 1988 the Darty family announced their decision to sell the company to its employees. The idea of a management buyout, which had become quite popular in the United States during the 1980s, was still relatively novel for France. The Darty proposal would be the largest employee buyout ever attempted in the country, valuing the company at some FFr 6.5 billion. Moreover, where the buyout option typically had been reserved for businesses in failing health, Darty's revenue growth and profitability remained robust. By the summer of 1988 the company had been placed under employee control: the company's employees had gathered some 56 percent of the company. Their holdings were grouped with the Darty family's 25 percent and the 16.5 percent held by a collection of the company's institutional investors to form the Financière Darty shareholding group, with 95.2 percent control of the company. The new shareholders engaged, meanwhile, to maintain their shares until 1993.

As the Darty family retired from active control of the company—with Philippe Francès named as president and CEO—the buyout would raise complaints from several of the company's minority shareholders, who, excluded from the buyout, would institute an investigation by the French COB (Commision des Opérations de Bourse, equivalent to the United States' SEC). The Darty example—which was supposed to lead the way to a whole wave of employee buyouts in France—had become the Darty scandal. Meanwhile, however, Darty continued its steady growth. With an objective of a minimum of six new store openings per year (the company would, in fact, often top ten and more new stores per year), the number of Darty stores would top 120 by the early 1990s. At the same time the company purchased a minority holding in Belgium's New Vanden Borre, a 13-store chain of retail appliance stores.

Darty's success continued even in the face of a withering economic climate that would grip France in a recessionary crisis into the later half of the decade. Yet, even as its market was shrinking, Darty still could boast profits margins of more than six percent. Nonetheless, the company, which faced the end of the freeze on employee stock sales in 1993, also had began to look for ways to reinforce its growth opportunities in the soon to open European market. Reluctant to repeat its internal expansion, after its negative experience in Spain in the early 1980s, Darty instead began looking for partnerships beyond France.

In March 1993 Financière Darty agreed to transfer its holdings to the British retailing group, Kingfisher Plc. In exchange for 11 percent of Kingfisher—making the Darty shareholding group one of Kingfisher's principal shareholders—Darty became a Kingfisher subsidiary, alongside its U.K.-based Woolworth's, B & Q, and Superdrug chains. In this way, both Darty and Kingfisher could further their European ambitions, uniting Darty with Kingfisher's Comet—the largest chain of appliance stores in the United Kingdom—and BCC, based in The Netherlands.

After taking 100 percent control of New Vanden Borre, Darty would move to reinforce its French presence. In 1996 the company reached an agreement to purchase 20 percent of the appliance-furniture retail chain But, which, with 37 company-owned stores and 195 franchised stores, counted among France's leading furniture and household appliance retailers. Darty's holding would later be augmented, according to the agreement with But's founders, the Venturini family, reaching 26 percent in 1998.

Under Kingfisher's ownership, and now led by managing director Jean-Noël Labroue, responsible for Kingfisher's appliance retailing expansion on the continent, Darty continued to register strong growth, nearing 160 French stores in 1998 and the FFr 10 billion mark in 1997. With the backing of Kingfisher's more than US $5 billion per year in annual sales, Darty was certain to maintain its leadership position in France, while extending, with its partners, a contract of confidence throughout the European market.

Principal Subsidiaries

But (France); New Vanden Borre (Belgium).

Further Reading

Nouzille, Vincent, ''Darty: la mort du RES à la française,'' *L'Expansion,* September 21, 1989, p. 175.

Pierre-Angel, Guy, ''Darty s'offre 20% du capital de But,'' *Les Echoes,* November 1, 1996, p. 13.

Roche, Marc, ''Le géant anglais Kingfisher absorbe Darty,'' *Le Monde,* February 20, 1993, p. 18.

—M.L. Cohen

Death Row Records

10900 Wilshire Boulevard
Suite 1240
Los Angeles, California 90024
U.S.A.
(213) 852-5000
Fax: (213) 852-5027

Private Company
Incorporated: 1992
Employees: 10
Sales: $325 million (1997 est.)
SICs: 6794 Patent Owners and Lessors

Death Row Records, a private company established in 1992, is one of the most lucrative rap labels in the music industry. Since its inception the company has produced several multiplatinum records, grossed hundreds of millions of dollars, and has become the driving force behind the popularization and commercial success of gangsta' rap music. In an industry known for its distinct personalities and eccentricities, Death Row Records stands out not only for its phenomenal financial success but for the label's well publicized confrontations and legal battles.

1990s Origins

Death Row was conceived and founded by Marion Knight, a former professional football player known to all in the music industry as "Suge." Raised in the Los Angeles neighborhood of Compton by parents who were both musically and athletically inclined, Knight parlayed his early talent as a football player into a full scholarship at the University of Nevada at Las Vegas and, later, a brief career with the Los Angeles Rams. After retiring from football, Knight became a bodyguard, working security for Los Angeles rap concerts as well as for R & B singer Bobby Brown, and thus developed business connections throughout the rap music industry. In 1990 Knight met the producer and rapper Andre "Dr. Dre" Young, at that time under contract to Ruthless Records, and together the two formed a partnership (initially funded in part by Sony and Solar Records), which eventually became Death Row.

Soon after the creation of Death Row, the company struck a distribution deal with Interscope, a relatively new record company which had made a name for itself through its willingness to support and distribute obscure or controversial bands. Interscope, headed up by James Iovine and the financial magnate Ted Field, was partly owned and financed by Warner Music Group, a division of Time Warner, and thus gave Death Row the financial clout necessary for a successful debut.

The Commercial Success of Gangsta Rap

In 1992 Death Row released its first effort, an album entitled "The Chronic," which was written and produced by Dr. Dre. Dre was regarded as one of the most gifted producers in the business; his involvement with Death Row's first project therefore gave the label an unusually high level of marketability. "The Chronic" proved to be an immediate commercial and critical success, remaining on Billboard's Top Ten for over eight months, and established Death Row as a leading and innovative force in the rap music industry.

In the early 1990's the commercial viability of gangsta' rap was still unknown. Though the mid-1980s had seen the popularization of rap, with such groups as Public Enemy, Run D.M.C., and LL Cool J selling millions of albums, the genre thus far had been essentially viewed as a new form of dance music, with antecedents in the soul and funk sounds of the 1970s. Gangsta' rap, however, with its explicit lyrics and overtly subversive edge, was a subgenre of rap, the willfully controversial nature of which promised to be an inherent risk to large music labels. At the time of Death Row's creation, the only successful gangsta' rap album had been N.W.A.'s "Straight Outta Compton," the lyrics of which had ignited a flurry of political controversy and public outrage. However marketable gangsta' rap appeared to executives in the industry, it could also be seen that with sales came scandal for which publicly held companies had to answer. Death Row, after its release of "The Chronic," proved not only its willingness to take a risk where other companies refused, but also that the notoriety of gangsta' rap's lyrics translated into huge profits.

In November 1993 Death Row released "DoggyStyle," an album by the rapper Snoop Doggy Dogg, which debuted at number one on Billboard's Top Ten and which eventually sold over four million copies. During this period as well Death Row's music videos began to receive regular rotation on television's MTV, an occurrence previously unheard of for rap videos, and which greatly increased gangsta' rap's exposure to a large audience. Pop radio stations as well began to play Death Row singles from Snoop Doggy Dogg and Dr. Dre, thereby boosting the label's sales and making gangsta' rap's stars recognizable to a broader consumer base.

Legal Battles

For all its sudden success, however, the label was also besieged by legal troubles. The same year in which "Doggy-Style" was produced, Snoop Doggy Dogg was arrested and charged with the murder of a man in Compton. The previous year Death Row's CEO, Marion Knight, was put on probation for a widely publicized assault on two singers. Moreover, in 1994, Knight received federal probation for an illegal weapons charge. When the daughter of the Los Angeles District Attorney who had brokered the federal probation deal with Knight was signed to a recording contract with Death Row, becoming the company's only white artist, further controversy surrounded the label.

By 1995 Death Row was the largest rap label in the industry, eclipsing in sales both its East Coast competitor Def Jam Recordings and other, longer-established West Coast labels. Gangsta' rap had become the most popular and marketable form of contemporary music for both black and white audiences, with its albums consistently achieving multiplatinum status and selling millions of copies. However, as gangsta' rap's popularity grew, so did the public protest against what was perceived as that music's blatant encouragement of drug use and violence. Gangsta' rap, and the industry executives and artists who produced it, became the subject of a very public political debate.

In the fall of 1995 Death Row was engaged in preparing an album called "Dogg Food" by the group Tha Dogg Pound which was being marketed as containing particularly prurient and violent lyrics. During the time in which "Dogg Food" was set to be released, a Washington-based political group called the National Political Congress of Black Women (NPCBW) launched a public protest against gangsta' rap and the genre's artists and producers. C. Delores Tucker, the leader of NPCBW, attempted to block the release of "Dogg Food" by publicly revealing that Time Warner, a company which previously had attempted to distance itself from controversial music, was through its financial involvement with Interscope indirectly supporting the production of gangsta' rap. Tucker appeared at a press conference in August of that year to condemn the pernicious effects of gangsta' rap, and she specifically singled out Death Row and Time Warner as exerting a negative influence over young people.

Though "Dogg Food" was eventually released, and grossed over $100 million in sales, Tucker's efforts were not without effect: the undesired publicity brought on by her campaign caused Time Warner to jettison its 50 percent ownership of Interscope, thus leaving Death Row's distributor without necessary financial backing. Several months later, however, Interscope sold Time Warner's former shares to Seagram's Universal Records at a profit of $150 million.

Only three years after its creation, Death Row's roster included both Dr. Dre and Snoop Doggy Dogg, two of the most successful rap artists in the industry. Added to that list in the fall of 1995 was a gifted singer/songwriter named Tupac Shakur. Despite the commercial success of his albums, Shakur had made himself unpopular with industry executives, given his extensive criminal record, which included the shooting of two police officers and charges of assault. When Death Row signed Shakur to the label, the singer was serving out a jail sentence for sexual assault, and part of Shakur's contract included the payment of over $1,000,000 for his bail. The label's investment paid off: early in 1996 Shakur recorded the album "All Eyez on Me," which within one week of its release sold 500,000 copies and would eventually sell over seven million copies.

Shakur's success with Death Row, however, was short-lived. On September 7, 1996 Shakur and Knight were attending a boxing match between Mike Tyson and Bruce Seldon in Las Vegas. After the match the two men got into a fist fight with reputed gang members in the lobby of the MGM Grand. Later that evening, Shakur was fatally shot while riding in Knight's car.

Important Players Leave the Label

The events of that evening created more problems for Death Row than the loss of its top-selling artist. Knight, who had been on probation for assault, was arrested for his role in the fight at the MGM Grand. In February 1997, after a short but highly publicized trial, Knight's probation was revoked, and he was sentenced to nine years of prison in the California state penitentiary.

From the beginning of the company's creation, Death Row had been dominated and shaped by Knight. According to Lynn Hirschberg, writing in *The New York Times,* Knight "was on top of everything at Death Row—from choosing artwork, promotional materials, singles and the track for the B side, to hiring the video director." As California law forbids an inmate from running a business from prison, upon Knight's incarceration, Death Row was left without one of its most vital players.

More losses ensued as in March 1996 Dr. Dre had creative differences with Knight and left Death Row to establish his own label. Nevertheless, even while the company experienced internal conflict and legal turmoil, it grossed $75 million in profit by year's end.

In 1997 Death Row's legal problems mounted. With Knight in prison and Death Row's long time general manager Norris Anderson acting as CEO in his stead, federal authorities launched a RICO (Racketeer Influenced and Corrupt Organizations) investigation into Death Row's history and business practices. At issue were questions of the label's reputed connection to street gangs and Knight's alleged relationship with a convicted drug dealer. Subpoenas were issued to 15 companies that had ties to the label.

Among the subpoenaed was Solar Records, the company which had helped in the initial funding of Death Row, and which several months earlier had filed suit against the label, claiming they had never received compensation for their involvement in the production of "The Chronic." Also during this time, the Shakur estate filed a $150 million suit against

Death Row, demanding back payment in royalties and the return of Shakur's master recordings, of which Death Row claimed ownership. The case was later settled out of court, with Shakur's masters being returned to his estate.

The first album Death Row released after Knight's imprisonment was by female rap singer Lady of Rage. The album, called "Necessary Roughness," did not sell well and created some question as to the viability of Death Row operating successfully without Knight at the helm. With the death of Shakur and the departure of Dr. Dre, there was tremendous pressure on the label to produce marketable artists. Though a posthumous release from Shakur, as well as Snoop Doggy Dogg's "Tha Doggfather," each premiered at No. 1 on Billboard's chart, Death Row's roster was less promising in 1997 than it had been the previous year. To add to the label's trouble, its last highly successful crossover singer, Snoop Doggy Dogg, left Death Row in January 1998, leaving the company with only a handful of bankable acts.

New Directions for the Future

Ultimately, Death Row's controversies proved to present too much of a risk to Seagram's Universal Records, which owned 50 percent of Interscope. Several months after Knight went to jail, Interscope, bending to pressure from Universal, ended its distribution deal with Death Row, marking the first time in the company's history in which the latter's records had no permanent distributor. Death Row began developing distribution deals with other companies on a record by record basis; Shakur's posthumously released soundtrack to the film "Gang Related," for instance, was distributed by Priority Records, a company known for its readiness to distribute and promote material deemed undesirable or too risky by other labels.

Though Death Row was embroiled in conflicts both legal and political, the label's sales continued to climb. In 1997 alone, Death Row saw sales of $325 million, an increase of 225 percent. Moreover, the company has made efforts to branch out into more traditional, and less conspicuous, forms of pop music, such as R & B and soul, evidenced by the label's contract with the soul and jazz singer Danny Boy.

In August 1998 the California Court of Appeals approved a new hearing for Knight, giving rise to hopes that the CEO would be released from prison before serving out his full term. Still, the controversy surrounding the company's relatively brief history has prompted speculation about Death Row's future. Neil Strauss, writing in the *New York Times,* suggested that "Since a record label has few assets beyond its executives, its acts, and its distribution arrangements, the losses suffered by Death Row have raised serious questions about its future." Much would depend on its leadership.

Further Reading

Hirschberg, Lynn, "Does a Sugar Bear Bite?," *New York Times Sunday Magazine,* January 14, 1996, pp. 26–57.

Morris, Chris, "Grand Jury Looking into Death Row," *Billboard,* March 8, 1997, pp. 6–8.

——, "Knight Sentenced to Nine Years; Impact on Death Row Uncertain," *Billboard,* March 15, 1997, pp. 12–14.

——, "New Questions over Funding of Death Row," *Billboard.* September 13, 1997. pp. 5–7.

Nelson, Havelock, "Upbeat Year for Rap, Despite Legal Matters," *Billboard,* December 28, 1996, pp. 31–34.

Ro, Ronin, *Have Gun Will Travel: The Spectacular Rise and Violent Fall of Death Row Records,* New York: Doubleday, 1998.

Strauss, Neil, "Rap Empire Unraveling as Stars Flee," *New York Times,* January 26, 1998, pp. 2–7.

—Rachel Martin

DIMON Inc.

512 Bridge Street
Danville, Virginia 24543-0681
U.S.A.
(804) 792-7511
Fax: (804) 791-0377
Web site: http://www.dimon-inc.com

Public Company
Incorporated: 1904 as Dibrell Brothers, Inc.; 1920 as
    A.C. Monk & Co.
Employees: 4,000
Sales: $2.17 billion (1998)
Stock Exchanges: New York
Ticker Symbol: DMN
SICs: 5194 Tobacco & Tobacco Products

DIMON Inc. is the second-largest independent leaf-tobacco merchant in the world and is engaged in virtually all areas of the industry, including purchasing, processing, storing, and selling leaf tobacco. The company owns tobacco leaf growing companies in the United States and more than 30 other countries, as well as 15 factories for processing the product, which is then sold to manufacturers of American-blend cigarettes throughout the world. The company was formed from a 1995 merger of Dibrell Brothers, Inc. and Monk-Austin Inc.

The History of Dibrell Brothers

The origins of DIMON go back to the 1850s, when Richard H. Dibrell became a tobacco merchant in Richmond, Virginia. When Union troops set fire to the capital of the Confederacy shortly before the close of the Civil War, the contents of his warehouse went up in smoke, but not in the form he had anticipated. This resulted in Dibrell's decision to relocate a portion of his operations in Danville, Virginia. In 1873 he sent his two sons to Danville, where they became leaf-tobacco brokers and formed Dibrell Brothers, a partnership incorporated in 1904 with Richard L. Dibrell as president.

Dibrell Brothers purchased raw tobacco from individual growers or at auction, cured and stored the product, and then sold and transported the processed tobacco to manufacturers. The high cost of transportation, however, made its practice of purchasing tobacco in one state, shipping it to another for processing, and then reshipping it to manufacturers inefficient. Accordingly, the company began acquiring branches, subsidiaries, and affiliates soon after 1900. It also found new buyers abroad. Sales grew from over 65 million pounds of tobacco in 1919 to nearly 93 million pounds in 1931, and the company's net equity tripled over this period to $3 million. It began, in 1925, a tradition of paying a dividend to its stockholders each year.

The Great Depression of the 1930s failed to halt the growth of Dibrell Brothers, and in this decade the larger U.S. cigarette manufacturers began, for the first time, to do substantial business with the firm. During the 1960s the company installed advanced tipping and threshing equipment to accommodate the requests of its customers for tobacco shipped in strip rather than leaf form. In 1967 Dibrell Brothers built a modern processing facility in Ringgold, Virginia. It also diversified that year for the first time by acquiring Richmond Cedar Works Manufacturing Co., a producer of home ice-cream freezers and decorative woodenware. In 1968, Dibrell Brothers had net income of $1.2 million on net sales of $106.6 million.

The following decade was a period of explosive growth for Dibrell Brothers. Its tobacco operations expanded into Central and South America, the Far East, India, and Italy, with more than 60 percent of its 1980 sales to foreign customers for use in their manufactured tobacco products. At home, the parent firm and its subsidiaries were buying leaf tobacco at auction markets in eight states and processing it at plants in Kentucky, North Carolina, and Virginia. Dibrell Brothers now was believed to be the second-largest independent processor of leaf tobacco in the United States. In addition to Richmond Cedar Works, the company was operating Kentucky Rib-Eye, a chain of eight steak restaurants in three states. Net income in 1980 came to $3.65 million on net sales of $325.3 million.

By acquiring a Dutch company in 1981, Dibrell Brothers gained access to tobacco growers in Brazil, the Dominican

Republic, and Zimbabwe. It sold the steakhouse chain in 1983. After rising to $381 million in fiscal 1985, however, company sales dropped as low as $308 million two years later, when Dibrell Brothers lost $1 million—the only year it lost money—and closed three of its five U.S. facilities. Also in 1987, however, the firm acquired a majority stake in Florimex, a German-based worldwide distributor of fresh-cut flowers that led the way to a resumption of healthy profits. In 1990 net sales reached $765.4 million, and net income was $12 million. The company sold Richmond Cedar Works that year and also completed the purchase of Florimex by buying out the minority interests. Florimex doubled its annual revenues between 1989 and 1993.

During the late 1980s consumers throughout the world, but especially in the United States, were turning to low-priced, generic cigarettes. This trend, which intensified during the early 1990s, was beneficial to Dibrell Brothers, which had been importing a sizable amount of inexpensive tobacco for years.

In addition, the company responded early to another tobacco industry trend—the popularity of lighter, ''American-blend'' cigarettes, especially among Eastern Europeans, who previously had smoked very strong, dark-tobacco cigarettes. By 1993 Dibrell held a dominant position in the Brazilian leaf-tobacco market, which trailed only the United States as a source of export. Thirty-seven percent of its fiscal 1992 tobacco revenues came from Brazilian operations.

The History of Monk-Austin

Born on a small tobacco farm outside Durham, North Carolina, in 1876, Albert C. Monk left the farm at age 20 to take a job in a Durham tobacco warehouse. He became a speculator and commission buyer of the product, moving to Farmville, North Carolina, in 1907, where he was instrumental in the formation of the town's tobacco market. During his first years in Farmville, Monk and his brother J.Y. Monk packed the green tobacco he purchased into hogsheads and shipped it to processors from the local railway station. As the business grew, he built a small factory to house a redrying machine. The firm was incorporated as A.C. Monk & Co. in 1920.

Over the next three decades, A.C. Monk & Co. expanded through part ownership or full interest in tobacco plants in six North Carolina communities: Greenville, Kinston, New Bern, Robersonville, Wendell, and Wilson. It was one of the first U.S. companies to move into the German market after World War II, and by the time the founder died in 1948, had established a worldwide reputation in the tobacco industry. Under the direction of his eldest son, Albert C. Monk, Jr., who became president, and his two other sons, the company continued to prosper. Beginning in 1956, the company moved its New Bern stemming

operation to a newly purchased plant in Farmville. In 1972 a ten-acre processing plant, equipped with the most advanced machinery, was opened there. By 1979, all of Monk's U.S. processing was located at this complex.

A.C. Monk also was expanding abroad. Its efforts during the 1970s resulted in operations in Brazil, Canada, Guatemala, Italy, and South Korea. By 1977, some 80 percent of the firm's tobacco was being exported to foreign countries. Monk was the nation's third-largest tobacco supplier and the largest privately held one. A third generation had entered the business, and Albert C. Monk III assumed the presidency in 1984.

A.C. Monk had net income of $7.1 million on net revenues of $296.1 million in 1990. Despite its prosperity, however, the company was doing only one-fifth the business volume of Universal in an era when small, family-owned companies were rapidly becoming obsolete. Accordingly, in 1990, A.C. Monk acquired, for $32.7 million, The Austin Co., a smaller, privately held firm based in Greeneville, Tennessee. It quickly shut Austin's Greeneville processing plant while retaining a more modern Austin processing facility in Kinston, North Carolina.

Monk-Austin became a giant overnight, with 1991 revenues of $630 million. While sales fell slightly the next year, net income almost tripled, to $27.7 million. That year the company had five operating properties in the United States and one in Brazil and in Zimbabwe, plus part-ownership in properties in Brazil, Malawi, and Mexico. In order to raise more capital to compete with its rivals, Monk-Austin went public in November 1992, selling 3.6 million shares of common stock (about 20 percent of the outstanding shares) at $16.50 each. Monk family members realized about $26.4 million and continued to hold about 70 percent of the stock. The remaining $28.9 million in net proceeds was earmarked to finance expansion and reduce the company's long-term debt of $66.7 million.

U.S.-grown tobacco accounted for 71 percent of Monk-Austin's net revenues in fiscal 1990 but only 56 percent in fiscal 1992. In terms of tonnage, 1992 was the first year that Monk-Austin bought less than half of its tobacco in the United States. China was selling tobacco to Monk-Austin for about $2 a kilo, while South American leaf was $4 to $5 a kilo compared to $7 for U.S.-grown tobacco. In Brazil and elsewhere, Monk-Austin was supplying a farmer's seed, fertilizer, training, and equipment to harvest tobacco in return for a guaranteed price. ''This is our home and we are U.S. citizens, and we want to see the tobacco business grow and prosper here in the United States,'' Monk-Austin's chief financial officer told a reporter. ''At the same time, we see what is happening in the industry, and you have to follow where the business is growing,'' he added.

In 1993 Monk-Austin bought out its joint-venture partner in Malawi and acquired T.S. Ragsdale Leaf Co., of Lake City, South Carolina, a small, privately owned tobacco dealer. The company also began building a tobacco processing plant in China, where it had formed a joint venture. That year the company earned record net income of $28.7 million. In 1994 R.J. Reynolds Tobacco Co. hired Monk-Austin to buy most of the tobacco it needed for its U.S.-made cigarettes; R.J. Reynolds had been the last major U.S. cigarette manufacturer to buy all of its own tobacco supplies.

1995: DIMON is Formed

Dibrell Brothers had a disastrous fiscal 1994, chiefly because of a worldwide oversupply of tobacco. The company lost $9.1 million on revenues of $919 million—down from $1.07 billion the previous fiscal year, when it registered record net income of $39.3 million. Monk-Austin was barely profitable. At the same time, both companies were pursuing a merger with Standard Commercial Corp., a tobacco-processing company roughly the same size as Dibrell. When negotiations came to naught because of disagreements over price, Dibrell and Monk-Austin began to talk to each other. In late 1994 they agreed to merge into a new company named DIMON, with Dibrell shareholders receiving 1.5 shares in the firm for each one share given to Monk-Austin shareholders.

By agreeing to the merger, the Monk family gave up control of their firm even though several family members would assume board seats and executive positions. "We didn't see how we could be effective in this business without growing," Albert C. Monk III told a reporter. He explained, "We came to the conclusion that we might be better off long term to take a littler share of something that we thought would really be a good thing. . . . This merger will enable us to do things that neither one of us could do independently or do well." Dibrell Chairman and Chief Executive Officer Claude Owen became chairman and CEO of DIMON. Monk, chairman and chief executive officer of Monk-Austin, became president of the company and chief executive officer of the international division, located in Farmville.

By the spring of 1995 tobacco sales volume and prices were improving again, partly because manufacturers had agreed to buy part of the surplus tobacco. Another reason was the elimination of a 1994 domestic-content law that had limited the use of foreign tobacco in U.S.-made cigarettes and thus aggravated the worldwide oversupply. One of DIMON's first acts was to acquire Austrian-held tobacco operations in Greece, Turkey, and Bulgaria with combined annual revenues of about $60 million. The company also acquired two operations in Macedonia in 1998. This so-called Oriental tobacco was an important component of the American-blend cigarette tobacco increasingly popular in world markets.

DIMON lost $30.2 million on revenues of $1.94 billion in 1995. This figure reflected a pretax charge of $40.9 million on tobacco inventories and advances and $25.9 million in restructuring and merger-related charges. The following year, the company reported earnings of $41.3 million on revenues of $2.17 billion, and in 1997 had net income of $77.2 million on revenues of $2.51 billion. The totals were $43.6 million and $2.17 billion, respectively, for 1998.

In early 1997 DIMON purchased Intabex Holdings Worldwide, S.A., the world's fourth-largest leaf-tobacco dealer, for an estimated $245.6 million in cash, stock, and convertible debentures. Intabex, a privately owned Luxembourg holding company, had annual revenues of about $700 million. The acquisition increased DIMON's presence in such tobacco-sourcing

areas as Argentina, Brazil, and Zimbabwe, as well as the United States, and put the company into Thailand, Sri Lanka, and certain emerging areas within Africa for the first time. The deal also included Compania General de Tabacos de Filipinas, one of the oldest leaf-tobacco dealers in the world and the world's largest dealer of dark air-cured leaf tobacco, used primarily as cigar wrappers and filler for cigars and cigarettes. However, in 1998 DIMON filed a lawsuit charging that the former chairman and major stockholders of Intabex had misrepresented the value of the company's assets. DIMON was seeking to reduce the purchase price by $110 million.

DIMON scored a coup in December 1997, when it announced it had reached an agreement with R.J. Reynolds to process all of the cigarette manufacturer's tobacco in 1998. The agreement was a natural extension of the earlier one that had put Monk-Austin in charge of Reynolds' leaf-tobacco procuring. DIMON said it would process the leaf at the former Monk-Austin plant in Kinston. The company already was processing leaf tobacco for Philip Morris Cos., Lorillard Tobacco Co., and other cigarette manufacturers.

DIMON's Florimex subsidiary was the world's largest importer and exporter of fresh-cut flowers, with annual revenues of nearly $400 million, when the parent company agreed in August 1998 to sell it to USA Floral Products Inc. for about $90 million, plus assumed debt. This was a transaction that had been sought by Monk-Austin before its merger with Dibrell. However, DIMON had initially been unable to sell off the flower business because, according to the rules on pooling-of-interest mergers, a tax penalty would have been imposed on shareholders.

At the end of 1997 DIMON was processing about 3.3 billion of the 12 billion pounds of tobacco produced worldwide each year to produce 5.5 trillion cigarettes a year. Its share of the global leaf-tobacco market was 37 percent. During 1998 DIMON purchased tobacco in about 32 countries and sold to manufacturers in about 60 countries. Approximately 42 percent of the dollar value purchased by the company was bought in the United States. Brazil (14 percent) and Zimbabwe (nine percent) followed. In addition to its factories in Danville, Farmville, and Kinston, DIMON was maintaining three in Brazil, two in Germany and Turkey, and one each in Greece, Italy, Malawi, Thailand, and Zimbabwe. Work on a factory in Tanzania was to be completed in late 1998.

Principal Subsidiaries

Contentnea, Inc.; Kin-Farm, Inc.; DIMON International Tabak B.V. (Netherlands); DIMON International A.G. (Switzerland); Olima Holdings AG (Switzerland); DIMON International Tabak AG (S.A. Ltd.) (Switzerland); Intabex Netherlands B.V.; DIMON Do Brasil Tabacos Ltda. (Brazil); Intabex Holdings Worldwide S.A. (Luxembourg); Compania de Filipinas, S.A. (Spain); DIMON Exportadora de Fumos Ltda. (Brazil).

Further Reading

Basconi, Mary Alice, "Tobacco Road's Big Pothole," *Business Journal of Upper East Tennessee & Southwest*, March 1993, p. 1+.

Campbell, Doug, "Tobacco Middleman," *Greensboro News & Record,* January 25, 1998, pp. E1, E4.

Croghan, Lore, "The Tobacco Barons," *Financial World,* May 23, 1994, pp. 34, 36–37.

Hwang, Suein L., "Dimon Expects Profit for Fiscal 1996 Despite End of Tobacco Content Rules," *Wall Street Journal,* September 18, 1995, p. A9G.

Jones, Chip, "Dimon to Work RJR Leaf," *Richmond Times-Dispatch,* December 17, 1997, p. C1.

Mildenberg, David, "Turning Over a New Leaf," *Business-North Carolina,* August 1993, p. 40+.

Ryan, Christopher, "Tobacco Tradition Ends: R.J. Reynolds Tobacco Hires Company to Buy Tobacco Supplies," *Winston-Salem Journal,* March 19, 1994, p. B28.

Swoboda, Frank, and Martha M. Hamilton, "Two on Top of the World," *Washington Post,* July 7, 1997, bus. sec., pp. 10–11.

"USA Floral Is Acquiring Florimex from Dimon Inc.," *New York Times,* August 14, 1998, p. D4.

—Robert Halasz

Duke Energy Corporation

422 South Church Street
Charlotte, North Carolina 28242
U.S.A.
(704) 594-6200
Fax: (704) 382-3814
Web site: http://www.duke-energy.com

Public Company
Incorporated: 1905 as The Southern Power Company
Employees: 23,000
Sales: $16.30 billion (1997)
Stock Exchanges: New York
Ticker Symbol: DUK
SICs: 4911 Electric Services; 4922 Natural Gas
Transmission; 1311 Crude Petroleum & Natural Gas;
1321 Natural Gas Liquids

The largest publicly owned gas and electric utility in the United States, Duke Energy Corporation serves roughly two million electric customers in North and South Carolina and gathers, processes, and distributes natural gas in the Midwest, Northeast, and Gulf Coast. Duke Energy was the result of the 1997 merger of Duke Power Company and PanEnergy Corporation, a $7.7 billion deal that married Duke Power's electric business to PanEnergy's natural gas business. The merger, which was initiated by Duke Power, tripled revenues and transformed Duke Power from a regional electric utility into the international energy services giant that Duke Energy represented in the late 1990s. On the electric side of the business, Duke Energy served its customers in the Carolinas through coal, gas, and nuclear power-generation plants. The company's natural gas assets included more than 37,000 miles of pipeline. Duke Energy also was involved in a number of joint ventures, which spread the company's interests into a diverse range of businesses, including wireless telecommunications, residential and commercial real estate services, and international energy development projects.

Founder and Company Origins

Duke Power owes its name and origin to James Buchanan (Buck) Duke, the hugely successful founder of The American Tobacco Company. In the tradition of Rockefeller and Carnegie, Duke turned his family's modest business into a vast cartel wielding monopolistic control over the entire tobacco industry, until, like Rockefeller's, his organization was formally dissolved through antitrust action in 1911.

Duke was born in 1856 to a farming family outside Durham, North Carolina. His father's small farm and livestock holdings were ruined during the Civil War, leaving the family no choice but to peddle a barn of tobacco unnoticed by the looting soldiers. The tobacco was of the variety now known as bright leaf, a then-recently developed, mild, golden leaf grown in the Durham area and soon to become widely popular under the Bull Durham label. Young James Duke began selling tobacco with his father at age nine and never stopped; the family's bright leaf sold well, and the Duke business grew rapidly. Along with his father, Washington Duke, brother Benjamin, and half-brother Brodie, Buck Duke worked day and night to make the family's Pro Bono Publico brand of tobacco competitive with the Bull Durham leader, but as late as 1880 the Dukes remained a profitable also-ran in the booming bright leaf business.

James Duke was an ambitious young man, and in 1881 he shifted to the manufacture of cigarettes, a new and not yet fashionable form of tobacco use. Armed with a number of efficient automatic rolling machines and the excellent tobacco of his native area, Duke became a national power in the cigarette business within a few years. Relocating to New York City, Duke gained some 38 percent of the nation's cigarette sales by 1889 and in the following year engineered the formation of The American Tobacco Company, merging W. Duke Sons & Company with the four leading cigarette makers in the country. During the following two decades Duke made American Tobacco the core of what came to be known as the tobacco trust, a network of interlocking corporations controlling about three-fourths of the U.S. tobacco business. Duke became an extremely wealthy, powerful, and well-known figure in U.S. business.

Among his myriad other ventures, Duke became interested in the 1890s in the future of North Carolina hydroelectric power. Electrification was slow in coming to the rural Piedmont, an area of central North Carolina and western South Carolina, but several early investors, including W. Gill Wylie of South Carolina, had begun harnessing the power generated by the many Appalachian mountain rivers coursing through the area. Duke saw the potential value of electricity to the local textile industry, in which he and his brother Ben already had extensive interests, and in 1898 the brothers began buying Piedmont river properties for later development. Duke also met Wylie and agreed to back his existing electric projects, but it was not until 1904 that the tobacco tycoon took a serious interest in the business of power.

In that year Duke, Wylie, and Wylie's chief engineer, William States Lee, met in New York to discuss the future of electric power in the Piedmont. Impressed by Lee's detailed plans for a series of hydroelectric plants along the Catawba and Yadkin Rivers, Duke matched a $50,000 investment of Wylie's, and the two men formed The Southern Power Company in June of 1905. Southern Power, incorporated in New Jersey and capitalized at $7.5 million, would be the holding company for Duke and Wylie's power assets, which at that time included extensive tracts of land, several power stations, and manufacturing facilities. By 1907 Southern Power was operating two full-fledged electric plants, one at India Hook Shoals and the other at Great Falls, both in South Carolina. Three years later the company created a subsidiary, Mill Power Supply Company, to purchase, manufacture, and sell various types of electrical equipment.

Duke's investment in Piedmont power was not limited to the millions he poured into Southern Power, however. As he had in the tobacco business, Duke went into power expecting to change the face of the industry. Not only would he bring electricity to the Piedmont, he and his brother Ben also would bring the textile factories that would buy the electricity, in that way beginning an industrial revolution in the area with Duke power as its indispensable base. He and Ben made countless investments in new and existing textile mills, offering the financial backing of the mighty American Tobacco Company to any mill owner who would buy power from the Dukes. Many of them did, their mills prospering with the efficiencies made possible by electrified spindles. The Dukes would then sell their stock to buy into another mill and thus keep the expansionary cycle rolling. By this method the Dukes were responsible, in large part, for a surge in Piedmont textiles, where, by the early 1920s, fully one-sixth of all U.S. spindles were powered by Duke generators. Duke Power Company, as the firm was known after the mid-1920s, supplied electricity to about 300 cotton mills, in many of which it held large shares of stock, and the Carolinas' textile industry rivaled that of Massachusetts for national leadership.

In 1911 Duke's tobacco trust was broken up by the U.S. Supreme Court (coincidentally, also the year in which Rockefeller's Standard Oil was dissolved), but the change had little impact on either Duke's fortune or the growing success of his power company. Along with its many textile industry customers, Duke Power began supplying electricity to private residences in the area, a source of revenue soon to be considerably expanded by the increasing number of electric appliances in the home. Mill-Power Supply Company, Duke's equipment subsidiary, took a leading role in the appliance revolution in the Piedmont, introducing electric irons, water heaters, and other inventions to the largely rural, conservative homeowners. Together with the universal shift to electric lighting, the growth in appliance use eventually would make residential service one of Duke's three main sources of revenue, the others being industrial and commercial. Once the electrical household was firmly established and most of the modern conveniences introduced, residential sales remained at the level of about 25 percent of total company revenue.

In 1923 W. Gill Wylie died, followed two years later by James Duke, leaving W.S. Lee as the company's leader. At about the same time, Duke Power began adding to its hydroelectric generating stations a series of larger and more powerful steam plants. The company previously had used steam generators only as auxiliaries, but with the increasing demand for electricity in the Piedmont, W.S. Lee decided to embark on a comprehensive program of steam construction. The Buck Steam Station, named after the company's late founder, went on line in 1927, the first of many steam plants that were later to dwarf the original hydroelectric network. In 1989 the latter consisted of 26 units that together generated only two percent of Duke's 13-million-kilowatt capacity.

The Great Depression years were difficult for many utilities, especially those that depended heavily on industrial users for their revenue. W.S. Lee's career as one of the country's top power plant engineers came to an abrupt halt in October of 1929, the crash and ensuing lean years ending all plans for future construction in the Piedmont. With industrial usage down, Duke Power sought to increase its residential sales by once more pushing the acceptance of household appliances and several times cutting its rates. In the midst of these hard times, Lee died in 1934 at the age of 63, bringing to an end the first generation of leaders at Duke Power. Lee's grandson, also called William S. Lee, later became chairman and president of the company. It was not until 1938 that Duke built another power plant, and not until after World War II that it regained its earlier rapid pace of expansion.

Post-World War II Expansion and Nuclear Development

The postwar years brought a resurgence of business and consumer activity in the Piedmont, as it did elsewhere in the United States. Duke immediately began revamping and repairing its system of plants and soon was to spend $200 million developing a number of new and highly efficient steam facilities. The two largest of these, Dan River and Plant Lee, were in service by 1952 and together added 320,000 kilowatts to the Duke Power grid; both plants were praised as being unusually well engineered. Duke Power always excelled at the construction of power stations, doing all of its own design, building, and maintenance. The company attributed to the experience thus gained the consistently high marks its plants have earned from industry analysts. In 1982, for example, six of the eight most efficient generating plants in the United States were owned by Duke Power; as of 1989, Duke Power's team of coal-fired stations had been ranked number one nationally for 15 straight years.

It was no doubt this tradition of engineering excellence that encouraged Duke to join with three other utilities in a 1956 venture called Carolinas-Virginia Nuclear Power Association. Even as they continued adding ever-larger steam plants, more than doubling the company's capacity during the 1950s, Duke Power engineers had become much interested in the long-term potential of nuclear energy as an alternative source of electricity. Carolinas-Virginia was formed to build a small, experimental nuclear generator as a first step toward the eventual construction of complete nuclear stations. Its Parr Shoals, South Carolina plant opened in 1962, the first nuclear facility in the southeastern United States and a generally successful conclusion to the years of planning required. Duke Power officials decided that, despite the evident environmental dangers inherent in the use of nuclear energy, its engineering abilities would allow it to shift its entire power grid over a number of years, from coal and water to nuclear without an unacceptable diminution of safety. Duke Power, like all other nuclear power utilities, often was faced with formidable opposition to its nuclear program. Scientists and the general public were alarmed by the possibility of radiation leaks and the more remote chance of explosion.

Steam construction continued apace, including the world's largest such plant located at Lake Norman, North Carolina, but in 1967 Duke Power received a permit from the Atomic Energy Commission to build the first of its full-scale nuclear units, the Oconee Nuclear Station. The proportion of electricity generated by nuclear energy at Duke rose rapidly, reaching 31 percent as early as 1975, and Duke Power's overall capacity approximately doubled during the same short span. To feed its massive coal system, in 1970 Duke Power bought four coal mines in Harlan County, Kentucky, creating a new subsidiary called Eastover Mining to operate the mines. Eastover soon became embroiled in a prolonged and bitter dispute with the United Mine Workers (UMW) union, which claimed that the Duke Power subsidiary was preventing its workers from joining their ranks. The union took out full-page ads in leading national financial newspapers urging investors to boycott Duke stock for the company's anti-union stance and an assortment of other alleged corporate misdeeds, including pollution and poor worker housing. To make matters worse, the economy was rocked by the OPEC oil embargo of 1973, inducing a recession

just as Duke began the most intensive campaign of capital expenditures in its history, a ten-year, $6.6 billion program to run until 1982. In 1974 a belated rate hike approval from the North Carolina Utilities Commission buoyed the company, with sales in that year hitting $823 million and net income $103 million. The dispute with the UMW was settled eventually, and Duke Power later divested itself of the mines.

By 1977 sales again had jumped, to $1.3 billion, but Duke Power already had begun scaling back its plans for a wholesale shift to nuclear power. The 1979 accident at Three Mile Island further darkened the nuclear horizon; although Duke Power continued to bring on line the nuclear plants it had under construction, by 1985 it had canceled or postponed a total of six new units. The rising tide of opposition to nuclear power was especially painful for Duke Power, which had already gained a reputation for outstanding work in the nuclear field and whose chairman, William S. Lee, had been called the leading expert on nuclear power in the utility industry. The company did not initiate new construction on any nuclear units after the early 1980s, confining development to a massive hydroelectric pumped-storage station in South Carolina. Duke Power nevertheless remained an ardent supporter of nuclear power, which in 1989 supplied 63 percent of its total kilowatts. That year Lee was elected president of the new World Association of Nuclear Operators (WANO), an organization he was instrumental in creating. WANO provides a forum in which owner-operators of the world's more than 400 commercial nuclear reactors can meet to discuss safety and related technical issues.

Further evidence of Duke Power's continued commitment to nuclear power was its 1989 formation, with four other companies, of Louisiana Energy Services, a joint venture to build the nation's first privately owned uranium enrichment facility, capable of supplying 15 percent of the U.S. nuclear industry's uranium needs. Also that year, Hurricane Hugo swept through the Carolinas, interrupting service to 700,000 of Duke Power's customers and causing extensive damage to transmission lines and other company equipment. Repairs took up to two weeks of nonstop work by a crew of 9,000, but Duke Power's response to the crisis seemed to have been generally well received and the effect on its financial performance was negligible. In 1990 construction proceeded—ahead of schedule—on Duke's $1.1 billion Bad Creek Hydroelectric Station. Also that year, Duke Power split its common stock two-for-one, to make the shares more accessible to individual investors, and sold Mill-Power Supply, whose business was too small to have a significant impact on corporate earnings.

1990s: Deregulation and PanEnergy Merger

Ranked in 1990 as the country's seventh largest public utility, Duke Power appeared to be situated to prosper in any future energy environment, which was a decided advantage given the fundamental changes that would sweep through its industry during the decade. The electric utility industry, like the airline, trucking, and telecommunications industries before it, was slated for deregulation. The common fear was that it would be a fitful transition, aping the trend established by other industries as they struggled to move from regulation to deregulation. The trucking industry, for example, provided justifiable cause for the concern among electric utilities facing deregulation. Of the 100 largest trucking companies in the country at the time of deregulation in 1978, only 38 were still in existence by the beginning of the 1990s, a precedent large utility companies such as Duke Power feared would be repeated. With history serving as a nagging reminder, the question of how a company responded to the forces ignited by deregulation loomed as a crucible for the future, and at Duke Power the responsibility for formulating an answer to that question fell to a new leader. The era of Lee's leadership was over.

Lee was succeeded in 1994 by William H. Grigg, a Duke employee since 1963 and the company's chief financial officer for the previous two decades. In several important respects, Grigg was the opposite of Lee. Lee was charismatic, possessing the type of personality that shined at social functions. Grigg was described as detail-oriented, known for spending 14 to 16 hours a day in his office, devoting his time to pouring over the practical details of business and pondering pragmatic solutions. Grigg was only four years away from Duke's mandatory retirement age of 65 when he was named chief executive officer, leading observers to speculate that the replacement of the visionary Lee with the more myopic Grigg merely gave the company time to groom a younger, more dynamic leader from within its executive ranks. Grigg surprised outside observers, however, by dispelling the perception that he was a caretaker appointed to maintain the status quo. Under Grigg's leadership, Duke Power made the boldest move in its history, completing an acquisition that ranked as the largest of its kind in the history of business. Grigg, few could disclaim, had inherited the scepter of a visionary and wielded it like no other before him.

The inexorable approach of deregulation prompted Grigg's uncharacteristic response. "I really believe," he stated, "that any electric utility that keeps doing what it's been doing is in a slow, downward spiral." From his vantage point, Grigg saw a need to consolidate to avoid the fate the majority of large trucking companies suffered in their postderegulation era. He declared to *Forbes* magazine in early 1995: "We plan to expand our business through acquisitions." He then attempted to follow through on that statement by examining a series of other electric utilities as acquisition candidates before considering a more profound move. In July 1996 he approached executives of Houston-based PanEnergy Corp. about working together, without specifically stating his intentions. PanEnergy officials surmised Duke Power was interested in a possible joint venture, but Grigg was envisioning a deal on a much grander scale. PanEnergy was the third largest natural gas company in North America, operating in 33 states through more than 37,000 miles of pipeline stretching as far west as Montana and north to Massachusetts. Grigg wanted all of PanEnergy, and he began working toward his goal of uniting the two companies to create an energy giant.

When it became apparent to PanEnergy officials that Grigg's "appetite was a little bigger than just a discussion of a potential joint venture," as one PanEnergy official termed it, a series of meetings ensued. As representatives from the two companies labored over the details of a merger, the negotiations were kept a close secret at Duke Power, referred to only as "Project Venus" or "Wayne." The last detail to be negotiated was the most staggering—the price—agreed to by both parties in late November 1996. The deal was valued at $7.7 billion according to a stock-swap to be completed once the merger was announced. With this last stumbling block cleared, Duke Power and PanEnergy executives checked into New York City hotels under assumed names, and then the secret became public knowledge. It was the largest merger of an electric utility and a gas company ever. The announcement stirred investor interest, with one analyst's comments characterizing the reaction: "Duke saw the future and realized it couldn't remain one of the world's best utilities by staying in the Carolinas. To grow earnings, they had to go out and become a big factor in the North American market. To succeed you have to be a complete player."

The merged companies became Duke Energy Corporation, a company with three times the revenue volume of Duke Power. Overnight, the old Duke Power was transformed from an electric utility with 1.8 million customers along the Interstate 85 corridor in North and South Carolina into a national energy services company—the "complete player" to which the analyst had referred. Grigg stepped down as chief executive officer once the merger was completed, paving the way for Duke Energy's first chief executive officer, Richard B. Priory. During the first six months of Priory's leadership, Duke Energy continued to move forward on the acquisition front, though on a far less ambitious scale. The company acquired three West Coast power plants from San Francisco's PG&E Corp. for $500 million. Although Priory was not planning on another multibillion deal before the end of the 1990s, he did intend to acquire parts of other companies, both domestically and abroad. As Duke Energy prepared for the 21st century, therefore, future acquisitions seemed highly likely.

Principal Subsidiaries

Duke Energy Group Inc.; Duke Energy Power SVC; DukeSolutions, Inc.; Duke Energy International; Duke Energy Trading and Marketing L.L.C.; Duke Energy Marketing Limited Partnership (Canada); Duke/Louis/Dreyfus L.L.C.; Algonquin Gas Transmission Co.; Nantahala Power and Light Company; Crescent Resources, Inc.; Duke Energy Corp.; Duke Engineering & Services, Inc.; Duke/Fluor Daniel, Inc.

Further Reading

Baldwin, William, "They Got the Power," *Forbes,* February 9, 1998, p. 14.
"BHP Sells Stake in Eastern Gas Pipeline to US Giant," *AsiaPulse News,* December 23, 1998, p. 10.
"CMS Energy to Buy Gas Pipeline Assets from Duke for $2.2 Billion," *The Oil Daily,* November 3, 1998, p. 3.
Gray, Tim, "Energy to Burn: Though Never Considered a Visionary, Bill Grigg Pulls Off a Megadeal that Puts Duke Power in Whole New Light," *Business North Carolina,* July 1997, p. 32.
Johnson, Leslie Williams, "Expansion into New England Gives Duke Energy a Competitive Edge," *Knight-Ridder/Tribune Business News,* October 17, 1997, p. 10.
Maynor, Joe, *Duke Power: The First 75 Years,* Charlotte, N.C.: Duke Power Company, 1979.
Shook, Barbara, "Duke Power; PanEnergy Plan Merger in $7.7 Billion Stock-Swap Agreement," *Oil Daily,* November 26, 1996, p. 1.
Winkler, John K., *Tobacco Tycoon,* New York: Random House, 1942.

—Jonathan Martin
—updated by Jeffrey L. Covell

EgyptAir

Cairo International Airport
Heliopolis, Cairo
Egypt
(20) 2290-8518
Fax: (20) 2245-9316

State-Owned Company
Incorporated: 1932 as Misr Airwork
Employees: 13,000
Sales: $1.05 billion (1996)
SICs: 4516 Air Transportation, Scheduled; 4522 Air
    Transportation, Nonscheduled

EgyptAir is the second largest airline on the African continent (exceeded only by South African Airways) and is the second largest Arab airline (exceeded only by Saudi Arabian Airlines). However, in a historical sense the Egyptian national carrier has no rivals; with origins going back to 1932 it can claim to be the oldest airline servicing both Africa and the Arab world. Although several other airlines sprang up in Africa during the 1930s, no other airlines were developed in the Arab world until the mid-1940s. In addition, until the meteoric growth of Saudia as a result of the oil boom of the mid-1970s, the only Arab airline to even approach EgyptAir in size was Lebanon's Middle East Airline. This background has given EgyptAir a unique leadership role among its Arab neighbors, despite the many serious setbacks it has suffered during its existence. The company's network extends throughout Europe, the Middle East, the Far East, Africa, Australia, India, and North America.

Imperial Origins

EgyptAir's early start can be traced back to the pivotal position played by Egypt in the development of Britain's imperial air routes. Within a few months of the armistice that brought World War I to an end, the Royal Air Force (RAF) was dispatching ground surveys parties to establish both the routes and the basic route facilities for future air services southward from Cairo to Capetown and eastward from Cairo to Baghdad. By the mid-1920s the RAF was operating regular services on both these routes. In 1925 the British government agreed with newly formed Imperial Airways that the airline would gradually take over from the military. This resulted in Imperial Airways starting regular service from Egypt to Iraq in 1927, extending to India via Iran in 1929. Service from Egypt to British East Africa started in 1931. Both services connected in Egypt with Imperial Airways service between the United Kingdom and Egypt.

By 1931 Egypt had developed into a vital hub on Britain's Imperial network. At this time a prominent Egyptian economist, Talaat Harb, realized that the importance of Egypt as a hub was soon to be significantly increased by two new developments: in 1932 Imperial Airways was due to extend its African service the entire length of the continent from Cairo to Capetown; and the airline expected to transform its Indian service by shifting the route from the politically difficult Persian shore of the Arabian Gulf to the friendlier Trucial Coast on the Gulf's southern shore.

Both these developments did indeed take place in 1932, by which time Talaat Harb had discovered a suitable British partner in the form of Airwork, a well-established company with wide interests in aviation and with ambitions to develop regular air services alongside Imperial Airways. This led to the formation in May 1932 of Misr Airwork, with the Misr Bank of Cairo putting up 85 percent of the initial E£20,000 capital, Airwork contributing ten percent, and Talaat Harb and his Egyptian colleagues furnishing five percent.

The first step by the new company was to set up a flight school at the rapidly developing Almaza airport on the outskirts of Cairo at Heliopolis. Airwork was by this time heavily involved in pioneering the development of flight training programs in Britain and Talaat Harb was enthusiastic to encourage airmindedness in Egypt. A small fleet of De Havilland Gypsy Moth aircraft were imported and these provided the foundation on which Egypt's airline industry was to develop. In the summer of 1933 Airwork arranged the import of a Spartan Cruiser on temporary lease from the fleet of the parent company.

In July 1933 this aircraft ran a daily service from Cairo to the western port of Mersa Matruh via Alexandria. Strong traffic demand resulted within one month in an extra daily flight being added between Cairo and Alexandria. With the start of the winter tourist season a new route up the Nile Valley from Cairo to Aswan via Assiut and Luxor was opened in December 1933 on a twice-weekly basis.

The following year Misr Airwork launched its first international service to Lydda and Haifa in Palestine. Further expansion took place in 1936 with a new service to Cyprus and Baghdad. By this time the airline was operating with its own all-De Havilland fleet, its flagship being the 14-seat DH86 Express, of which it had four. This was a period when tourism rapidly developed in Egypt and Palestine, due in part to promotion by the pioneering travel agency Thomas Cook of the newly opened services of Imperial Airways.

World War II and Nationalization

With the outbreak of World War II, control and ownership of the airline was taken over by the Egyptian government, which continued to operate over the same network but at a much increased frequency under the new name Misr Airlines. Immediately after the war the Egyptian airline, still under government control, reverted to civil operations, its first priority being to re-establish the flight training program using a fleet of ten newly acquired U.S.-built Beechcraft. By early 1948 the prewar network had been re-established but it soon became evident that larger aircraft would be needed, if only to compete with the DC-3s rapidly coming into widespread operation in the region.

Regularly scheduled service was resumed in 1949 when the airline took delivery of a fleet of ten Vickers Viking aircraft. These twin-engine 28-seat aircraft allowed rapid expansion, with the route network doubling between 1949 and 1952 and the number of staff climbing to 1,000. It was at this time that the airline adopted the name Misrair. During this period Misrair continued to work closely with its old partner Airwork (from which it had acquired the Viking fleet and with which it maintained close technical relations). Airwork continued to be additionally active in the region, forming Sudan Airways in 1946. Shortly afterwards Airwork launched its own ''colonial coach'' scheduled services to East and Central Africa, using its own fleet of Vikings, with stops at Cairo and Khartoum.

July 1952 was a turning point for the airline—and for Egypt—for it marked the successful military coup that ended the rule of King Farouk and which led in 1953 to the country becoming a republic, at first under Major General Mohammed Naguib and from 1956 under Gamal Abdel Nasser. Under Naguib the airline stagnated. New routes were introduced and then suspended. New aircraft types were introduced but then withdrawn. But with the assumption of power by Nasser a renewed priority was given to the development of the national airline.

The first step was the placing in service in 1956 of a fleet of British-built Vickers Viscounts. The next step was the purchase in 1958 of a fleet of DC-3s to allow modernization of the domestic network within Egypt. The final step was the purchase in 1960 of a fleet of De Havilland Comet 4 jets for long-haul services. Arrival of the Viscounts allowed Misrair to fulfill a longstanding ambition to open service to London. This soon developed into the airline's single most important destination.

Similarly, arrival of the Comet jets allowed another ambition to be realized with the opening of service in 1961 to Bombay and in 1962 to Tokyo.

The Turbulent 1960s

The year 1962 was to prove another turning point in the airline's history. Until then Misrair had a consistent record of profitability, even in the lean mid-1950s, the only exception being the revolution in 1952. However, in 1962 the company experienced a massive loss of revenues. There were several reasons for this change in fortune, including very low yield traffic on the Bombay route, a highly competitive Tokyo service, and difficulty pitting the Comet against the Boeing 707s and Douglas DC-8s then coming into general service on long-haul routes.

But a more fundamental problem was the marketing situation that resulted from the political decision in 1958 to merge the airlines of Egypt, Syria, and Iraq into a single new enterprise to be called United Arab Airlines, this being the joint airline of the newly formed United Arab Republic (UAR). Syria joined Egypt to form the UAR in 1958 but withdrew in 1961; Iraq never joined.

Although the Egyptian government formally restructured and renamed Misrair as United Arab Airlines early in 1960, it was only later that year that the Syrian government finally agreed to the merger of Syrian Airways, the main problem having been the reluctance of privately owned Syrian Airways' shareholders to accept the merger terms. Nevertheless, during the previous two-year negotiation period several useful developments had taken place as a result of the planned merger, including the opening of a much-needed direct service between Cairo and Aleppo and the introduction of promotional fares to generate travel between Egypt and Syria. From early 1961 the operations of the Egyptian and Syrian partners were indeed merged under the banner of UAA. But this arrangement failed to survive to the end of the year, for by October Syria had pulled out of the union and had created a new government-owned Syrian Arab Airline, which quickly restored the network operated by its private-enterprise predecessor.

Whereas Syrian Arab then embarked on a program of modest expansion and modernization—its first trunk route to Europe was opened in 1963—UAA (as Misrair was then called) was plunged into financial crisis. The name change and the erratic political circumstances with which it was associated created a major marketing problem. Another problem was the airline's dubious safety record following no fewer than four fatal accidents—involving the loss of two Comet 4s and two DC-3s—in a 14-month period in 1961–62.

An underlying problem was Egypt's shift towards socialism and its alliance with the USSR, which had a negative effect on tourism—a striking example being the poor quality of service that spread through Egypt's newly nationalized hotels—but it also presented the airline with particular problems. Difficulty in raising Western loan funds resulted in an order for Boeing 707s, originally placed in 1961, never being completed. There were chronic foreign-exchange difficulties in maintaining adequate spares for the Comet and Viscount fleets. Yet another issue was the uncontrolled escalation in staff numbers which soon developed into a major managerial problem.

Matters were brought to a head by the national disaster of the Six-Day War in 1967. Although this was a humiliating experience in military terms, which inflicted a period of extreme austerity on the country as a whole, the actual defeat precipitated changes that gradually worked to the advantage of Egypt and its national airline. In the immediate aftermath of the war there was a surge of Arab sympathy for Egypt. Several Arab governments even proclaimed that their citizens should relieve Egypt's plight by going there on holiday. As a result the number of Arab visitors to Egypt by 1970 had recovered to the prewar record level of 1966. Arab funds were also forthcoming to allow the belated purchase in 1968 of the airline's first 707s, thus allowing the return of service to Tokyo and an overdue upgrading of the quality of service.

Unfortunately for the airline a new political problem now developed with the launch of plans to merge—or to at least integrate—Egypt and its two African neighbors, Libya and Sudan. This soon led to the idea of a new United Arab Airlines which would combine the Egyptian national airline with Libyan Arab Airline and Sudan Airways. Were it not for the political difficulties that finally wrecked the scheme, on economic grounds alone this incarnation of the UAA made much more sense than its ill-fated predecessor. The three member airlines were all outfitting their fleets with 707s and would benefit from commonality of equipment. The route networks of the three substantially overlapped and could benefit from rationalization both of services and of ground facilities. By comparison with most European carriers, each of the three were disadvantaged by the low frequency of flights, typically only two or three flights a week on any one route. In addition, by merging it would be possible to obtain better terms when negotiating traffic rights with foreign governments. This development would also have advanced Egyptian hopes of making Cairo the center for technical servicing of Boeing 707s throughout the Middle East.

Progressing Under Sadat

By 1970 the project had already advanced to the point where plans were being prepared for joint overseas sales offices to replace the existing separate offices and for a joint overseas sales force. Looking forward, a joint operational program was being prepared whereby all European and Asian services would be based in Cairo, all North African services would be based in Tripoli, and all other African services on Khartoum. However, another event took place in 1970 that was to lead Egypt and its airline in a different direction: the coming to power of Egyptian President Anwar Sadat. This almost immediately led to the final collapse of the political concept of the UAR and to the consequent adoption by the national airline in 1971 of the name it bears to this day, EgyptAir. Even more significantly, Sadat's appointment led to Egypt's success against Israel during the October War in 1973, the severance in 1974 of Egypt's special relationship with the USSR, and to the re-establishment of close relations between Egypt and the United States.

Despite these fundamental changes, continuing fears of war in the Middle East together with rising fears in the Middle East that Egypt had betrayed the Palestinian cause, imposed a severe brake on the development of trade and travel between Egypt and the outside world. In its most extreme form—after the Camp David accord between Egypt and Israel—Egypt had to endure a virtual boycott by the wealthy oil-producing states of the Gulf, which had a drastic impact on the airline. With a relatively slow-growing traffic base, the airline continued to maintain its services with a mixed fleet of Boeing 707s and early model 737s. Meanwhile it suffered the indignity of seeing itself being overtaken by Saudia and IranAir and being threatened by better-equipped rivals such as Gulf Air.

Transformation in the 1980s

Once again it was an external event which was to transform the situation facing EgyptAir. Following the assassination of Sadat in 1981, Hosni Mubarrak rose to lead the nation. Although Sadat had supported an open-door policy, seeking to promote foreign investment, he had failed to steer Egypt away from the socialist path favored by his predecessor. In contrast, Mubarrak realized that Western economic aid and investment would only flow into Egypt once it started moving towards a market economy.

Mubarrak was also interested in aviation and was concerned over the unimpressive performance of the national airline. At this time, sounds of public criticism of EgyptAir were starting to be heard and Mubarrak decided that strong leadership was needed. He invited a senior air force officer, Air Vice-Marshal Muhammed Rayan, with a solid knowledge of the technicalities of aviation and with a reputation for getting things done, to take over as chairman of EgyptAir.

Since his appointment, Rayan brought about a remarkable transformation in the airline. His first priority was to ensure that the airline was properly equipped. Starting with an order in 1981 for eight Airbus 300s, the airline emerged with a fleet of over 30 low-mileage, front-line aircraft. Rayan resisted the temptation to embark on high-risk new routes, preferring instead to consolidate EgyptAir's regional base. He developed the airline's own terminal at Cairo, introduced computerized reservations, and imposed an ambitious training program for the airline's staff.

A move into a modern, efficient headquarters complex at the airport allowed staff to vacate much of the obsolete and inefficient accommodations to which they had been tied. EgyptAir also enacted a $30 million, multi-stage plan to create a regional maintenance facility.

Another appointment by President Mubarrak which proved of fundamental importance in the modernization of EgyptAir was the selection of Fouad Sultan as minister of Aviation and Tourism. With a distinguished background in merchant banking, and a firm belief in the market economy, Sultan masterminded the restructuring of Egypt's air transport industry to prepare for a more competitive international environment while at the same time weaning EgyptAir off the government protection it enjoyed in the past. Although EgyptAir was not subsidized and by law had to finance its own aircraft purchases, the government nevertheless fielded some criticism for protecting its flag carrier market at the expense of its privately owned domestic competition. Further, its workforce of 15,000 also seemed bloated to outside observers.

EgyptAir suffered one of the deadliest hijackings in history in November 1985, when terrorists took over a flight from Athens to Cairo. Sixty passengers were killed. After serving part of a jail term in Malta and living on the lam for several years in Africa, the surviving terrorist was finally captured and tried in the United States in the mid-1990s.

New Horizons in the 1990s

EgyptAir reported a loss of $33 million in the 1990–91 fiscal year, a year disrupted by the Persian Gulf War, which increased the cost of fuel and insurance and frightened travelers away from the Middle East (although EgyptAir spirited many Egyptians out of Kuwait and Iraq during the crisis). However, the carrier soon recovered, posting an equivalent gain for the first six months of 1992–93 as tourism in the area boomed. EgyptAir found extra capacity at the same time due to a postponed aircraft sale and the delivery of $2.4 billion worth of new aircraft. The arrival of the new planes necessitated massive retraining among more than 300 pilots.

EgyptAir teamed with Kuwait Airways to create the non-scheduled carrier Sharouk (''Sunrise'') Air in the spring of 1992. Its significance to religious groups made the region's market especially partial to charter flights, which accounted for a quarter of EgyptAir revenues, although the company had only a 20 percent market share of charters into Egypt. EgyptAir controlled 51 percent of the Sharouk venture, which arose out of a leasing agreement with Kuwait Airways.

Rayan told *Aviation Week* EgyptAir planned to be a major airline in Africa and the Middle East, and the company contin-ued to upgrade its fleet. EgyptAir received a Boeing 777-200 in 1997, the same plane that Boeing used to set speed and distance records for its class. The aircraft was configured to seat 319 passengers. (Oddly, a worker's mallet was later found inside the tail of this plane during an inspection.) EgyptAir also operated several Airbus types. In 1997, it became the first to order the extended version of the Airbus ultra-long range A340, a direct challenger to the venerable Boeing 747. The aircraft could carry 400 passengers and was expected to be delivered in 2003. It was designed to fly up to 7,500 nautical miles.

As with many other national airlines, the prospect of privatization was discussed. The government resisted such plans, including one to offer bonds worth 20 percent of the company's value.

Principal Subsidiaries

Sharouk Air (51%).

Further Reading

''EgyptAir Convertible Bond Issue Unlikely,'' *Airfinance Journal,* April 1997, p. 23.

Lane, Polly, ''Worker's Tool Found in Another Boeing Jet,'' *Seattle Times,* November 11, 1998.

Vandyk, Anthony, ''EgyptAir: Back in the Black,'' *Air Transport World,* August 1992, p. 84.

Lenorovitz, Jeffrey M., ''EgyptAir, Kuwait Form Join Carrier for Charter Passenger, Cargo Flights,'' *Aviation Week and Space Technology,* April 20, 1992, pp. 40–41.

—John Seekings
—updated by Frederick C. Ingram

EIFFAGE

Eiffage

2, rue de Laborde
75418 Paris Cédex 08
France
(33) 1.01.44.90.44.44
Fax: (33) 1.01.44.90.44.90

Public Company
Incorporated: 1844 as Fougerolle
Employees: 42,501
Sales: FFr 31.89 billion (US $6.87 billion) (1997)
Stock Exchanges: Paris
Ticker Symbol: Eiffage
SICs: 8711 Engineering Services

Eiffage is one of France's leading construction and civil engineering groups, posting nearly FFr 32 billion in total sales. Conceived as a federation of companies—with more than 500 subsidiaries in France alone—Eiffage is the result of the 1993 acquisition by Fougerolle of Société Auxiliaires des Entreprises (SAE). Eiffage member companies are specialized in private sector and public construction and civil engineering projects, including building construction, highway and road construction, electrical installation, and civil engineering (bridges, stadiums, and other public structures). Other leading names in the Eiffage group are Quillery, Eiffel, Gerland, SCR-Beugnet, Forclum, and Norelec.

Each of Eiffage's member companies operate independently of the others, with their own equipment, resources, networks, employees, and corporate cultures, while providing opportunities for synergy and cooperation among member companies. Member companies reflect a similar federation structure, operating more or less as holding vehicles for their own subsidiaries. In this way, Fougerolle, for example, counts more than 40 subsidiary companies, ranging from 80 to 200 employees each, providing the flexibility of localized and specialized services, while offering the backing of a national operation. This localized approach enables Eiffage to respond to a wide range of construction needs, from small renovation projects to large-scale engineering intensive works such as the construction of a new Parisian Metro line completed in 1998.

Although the 1990s have been a difficult period for the French construction industry, Eiffage has been able to contain the damage somewhat. Despite the recessionary French economic climate during much of the decade, Eiffage has managed to limit to some extent its slip in revenues, balancing domestic losses with increased international activity. After posting losses of more than FFr 900 million in 1996, the group recovered to achieve more than 400 million in profits for the 1997 fiscal year. France's return to healthy economic growth in the late 1990s has stimulated new construction and public engineering needs. Nonetheless, Eiffage has been criticized for its focus on France—more than 80 percent of its revenues are achieved domestically—and has begun to step up its foreign presence, including acquiring subsidiaries Soficom in Belgium and Walter Bau in Germany, as well as construction contracts in Africa, Asia, and other European countries. Eiffage also has begun to expand into the services industry, particularly through the group's 17.1 percent shareholding position in Cofiroute, one of the country's leading exploiters of the public autoroute network, but also through the development of building and site maintenance activities, through subsidiary Avenir Entretien.

The formation of the Eiffage group has occurred under longtime Fougerolle leader Jean-François Roverato, who serves as company president and CEO. A publicly held company traded on the Paris stock exchange, Eiffage also is majority-owned by Eiffage employees, the result of the 1980s employee buyout of founding company Fougerolle. That company, which celebrated its 150th anniversary in the 1990s, is also France's oldest continuously operating construction and engineering firm.

19th Century Foundation

The Fougerolle name would enter French history with the completion of the Nivernaise canal, a structure totaling 174 kilometers and joining the Loire and Yonne Rivers in the Burgundy region in the 1840s. Philippe Fougerolle, a mason from the central Creuse River region of France, later joined by Jacques Fougerolle, founded what would become France's oldest construction firm in the 1844. The company would participate in many of France's greatest public works projects.

Jacques Fougerolle would lose his life in the construction of the Saint Gothard tunnel in the Swiss Alps on the Swiss-Italian border, which, at 15 kilometers in length and carved through the 3,200-meter tall Saint Gothard mountain, remains one of the region's most important railroad and highway structures. Jacques Fougerolle's death did not, however, spell the end of the family's company, which would complete the Saint Gothard tunnel in 1882.

Before the end of the century Fougerolle's activity would spread through much of France and include for the first time projects in Paris, later to become a principal site of Fougerolle projects. An early Parisian project was the digging of the Metro line connecting the Porte de Clichy with the Place de la Trinité. While Fougerolle expanded its operations in France, it also was participating in international projects, including the construction of the Namur fortifications in Belgium by 1890. In 1903 the company put into place the Adolphe bridge for Luxembourg.

By the turn of the century Fougerolle was receiving projects from farther abroad. In 1908 Fougerolle received the contract for the construction of the Rio Grando del Sul port in Brazil. At the same time, the company was completing some 2,500 kilometers of roads for the soon-to-disappear Ottoman Empire. The outbreak of the First World War, while restricting the company to its French operations, nevertheless called Fougerolle into service; for one project, carried out in 1915, Fougerolle was contracted to add a second passage to the railroad between Paris and Amiens to ensure the supply chain to the French army in its effort to halt the advancing German army.

Building the 20th Century

After the First World War, Fougerolle, now organized under the company name Le Soliditit Français, returned to both its domestic and international activities. A chief French project of the period was achieved in 1921, when Fougerolle constructed a series of large-scale dirigible hangars at Orly, later the site of the country's domestic airport. In the 1920s, in addition, Fougerolle was contracted to build the refitting supports in the shipbuilding port of Toulon; the resulting structure set scale records for the time. The 1920s saw the company extend its business into the French-controlled colonial regions, with the construction of the port of Dakar in 1927 and the building of the Deir Ez Zor bridge over the Euphrates on the border between Iraq and Syria. In the next decade Fougerolle would receive the contract to build a road from Mogaidscio to the Ethopian border.

In the climate of approaching war in the 1930s, Fougerolle participated in the building of the Maginot line, a series of fortifications designed to protect France against German invasion. Just prior to the outbreak of hostilities, the company finished constructing an arm of the Parisian Metro, leading to the Porte de Montreuil.

In the postwar period Fougerolle would play a central role in the French reconstruction, while also fulfilling major projects in the soon-to-be-former French colonies of Africa. Fougerolle had continued to expand its operations, chiefly through adding subsidiaries, while remaining largely decentralized. Its subsidiaries, which tended to range in size from 80 to 200 employees, kept their own names and continued their operations on an essentially local scale. Fougerolle itself remained a relatively small operation, clinging to its independence as the construction industry in France gravitated to a small circle of large, government-influenced or publicly held conglomerates.

Among the company's major projects of the postwar period are the digging of a hydroelectric tunnel in Tanzania; a role in the construction of the 1,420-meter suspension bridge at Tancarville, near the city of Le Havre; the construction of the Bin el Ouidane dam in Morocco in 1954, followed by the Serre-Ponçon dam in the French Alps in 1960 and the dam and tidal power plant at Rance on the English Channel; and construction of the Terminal One structure of the new Roissy international airport outside Paris. In 1970 the company reorganized under the name Société des Entreprises Fougerolle Limousin.

Becoming a Major in the 1990s

Fougerolle remained primarily a family-led company into the 1970s. The company, buoyed after nearly two decades of French economic growth, prepared to expand its activities, buying out the Société Nouvelle de Constructions et de Travaux, a building construction specialist, in 1973, and taking over the company Gifor, specialized in laying foundations, in 1974. The Arab Oil Embargo of 1973, and the resulting economic crisis, would cut deeply into Fougerolle's growth plans. A friendly attempt was made by the French banking leader Paribas to merge Fougerolle into the larger Sopie-Batignolles in 1980. Fougerolle's insistence on independence, however, would block that move. Then the company ran into trouble on a number of its international construction sites, most notably in Iraq and Nigeria, at the start of the 1980s; taking losses on these projects, Fougerolle was lashed by a new recession and a collapse of the French construction market. By 1982 Fougerolle had been brought near the edge of bankruptcy.

Fougerolle would be rescued by several important shareholders and financial backers, including Paribas, the French oil giant Total, and the French conglomerate Générale des Eaux, the last of which, taking some 30 percent of Fougerolle, began making plans to merge Fougerolle into its own construction and civil engineering subsidiaries. Placed in charge of rebuilding Fougerolle was Jean-François Roverato, heir-apparent to then CEO Louis Lesne. Roverato, who had entered the company in 1975 at the age of 30, already had served as the company's head of French development and later served as head of its international division. Roverato would quickly succeed in restoring Fougerolle to health—enabling Resne to refuse Générale des Eaux efforts to take control of the smaller company.

Roverato was named the company's CEO in 1987. By then, he had initiated the company on an expansion drive, leading Fougerolle into a number of acquisitions of smaller construction, road-building, and engineering firms. As noted, these firms were allowed to continue their independent, locally oriented operations. By the mid-1990s the company would count more than 50 subsidiary companies, operating throughout France and on the international front as well.

Assuming command of Fougerolle, Roverato had asked for—and received—from the company's major investors the right to open the company to new capital at will. This would come to serve Fougerolle well in its struggle to maintain its independence. By the late 1980s Générale des Eaux was pushing harder for a merger of the now mid-sized Fougerolle with CGE's construction division. Paribas, ally and owner of 40 percent of Fougerolle, refused to sell its shares to CGE, thwarting the conglomerate's aims.

In 1989 Roverato performed a coup that would prevent CGE from proceeding with a hostile takeover. With the participation of Paribas, Roverator announced an employee buyout of Fougerolle's operations. More than 10,000 Fougerolle employees participated in the operation, which created the employee shareholding group Financière Fougerolle and gave Fougerolle majority control of 56 percent of its operations. CGE, which had seen its dream of taking over Fougerolle thwarted, increased its own position in the company to 34 percent, giving it a minority position and the ability to block further moves by the company, particularly should Fougerolle seek a fresh expansion of capital. But this block would become effective only after June 1992.

In April 1992 Fougerolle announced that it was taking over the Société Auxiliaire d'Entreprise, or SAE, France's second largest building construction firm. With nearly FFr 30 billion in annual revenues, SAE was close to three times Fougerolle's size. Yet SAE had been facing difficulties, with the collapse of the worldwide construction market in the late 1980s, followed by the Persian Gulf War and economic recession of the early 1990s. At the start of the 1990s, with its share price weakened, SAE was facing the threat of a hostile takeover. In 1990 the company weathered a raid on its stock by the Belgian promoter Michel Pelège. SAE was rescued at the time by Fougerolle and Paribas, each of which took some ten percent of SAE's shares. Two years later, Roverato—eager to shed CGE's influence on Fougerolle before the June 1992 deadline—approached SAE with a proposition: in exchange for shares in Financière Fougerolle, the smaller Fougerolle would take over SAE's operations.

The operation, worth some FFr 5 billion, was a success, bringing SAE and Fougerolle together, while following the company's long-held federation concept. The united companies, which would adopt the name Eiffage in 1993, became France's fourth largest construction and engineering firm, with nearly FFr 38 billion in annual sales. Following the takeover, CGE's part in the group was reduced to less than 33 percent, depriving the conglomerate of its minority block. By 1997 CGE would begin looking to sell off its Eiffage holdings.

Despite the economic crisis of the 1990s, which would wreak havoc on the French and international construction industries, Eiffage continued the expansion course that had been begun by Fougerolle at the start of the decade. The SAE takeover had followed on Fougerolle's acquisitions of IGB, Fontaine, Gallego, and Clément in 1990, and of Batiment et Génie Civil Thélu, Rosina, GCI, Cattirolo Lepage, as well as 40 percent of Germany's Walter Bau, and a share in Paris-based maintenance services firm Avenir Entretien in 1991. Following

the SAE merger, the company hardly rested, adding more than ten new subsidiaries in 1992 alone, including the Dutch Fraanje and the Belgian Delens. Now known as Eiffage, the company would absorb a number of existing SAE subsidiaries, including Quillery, Eiffel, and Norelec. Several Fougerolle subsidiaries specializing in building construction would be regrouped under Eiffage as well.

After taking control of Walter Bau, with 74 percent of the German company's shares, in 1994, Eiffage enhanced its French road construction capacity with the 1995 acquisition of Beugnet. In response to the depressed construction and public works market, Eiffage began extending its services capacity, including augmenting its share of Avenir Entretien and acquiring 100 percent of SIES, Paris-based specialist in cleaning services worth some FFr 400 million in annual sales.

Eiffage had managed to resist the collapsing construction market into the mid-1990s. But in 1996, with its revenues slipping back to FFr 32.7 billion, the company posted a loss of nearly FFr 890 million. The company would be forced to make cuts, notably in its real estate and services subsidiaries, without renouncing, however, its interest in building a stronger position in these sectors. At the same time, Eiffage continued to insist on its federation model of construction and public works subsidiaries—despite the inevitable competition that existed among some of its subsidiaries.

France's return to economic growth would come none too soon for Eiffage. By the end of 1997 the firm's losses would prove short-lived, as the company once again reported profits for the year—of FFr 605 million, despite the continued decline of its revenues. Although Eiffage would be criticized as too heavily reliant on the French market, which continued to account for more than 80 percent of the company's sales in 1998, Eiffage's continued extension into the real estate and services market, including a strong share of the highly profitable Autoroute services company, Cofiroute, looked likely to balance the company's construction and civil engineering projects in the future.

Principal Subsidiaries

Fougerolle; Quillery; SAE; Eiffel Construction Metallique; Gerland; SCR-Beugnet; Forclum; Norelec; Soficom; Avenir Entretien; Walter Bau (Germany); SCR; Cofiroute (17.1%).

Further Reading

Barjonet, Claude, "Eiffage entend consolider son redressement en 98," *Les Echoes,* March 19, 1998, p. 10.
——, "La reprise du bâtiment donne du tonus à Eiffage," *Les Echoes,* September 15, 1998, p. 14.
Bauer, Anne, "Fétant ses cent cinquante ans Fougerolle affirme son rôle de fédérateur," *Les Echoes,* October 4, 1994, p. 11.
Chevlolot, Pascal, "Bonne surprise sur Eiffage," *Option Finance,* March 23, 1998, p. 25.
Nouzille, Vincent, "Et Roverato, le patron de Fougerolle, poursuite son rêve: égaler Bouyges," *L'Expansion,* February 20, 1992, p. 52.

—M.L. Cohen

800-JR Cigar, Inc.

151 E. Broad Street
Statesville, North Carolina 28677
U.S.A.
(704) 872-9555
(800) JRCIGAR; (800) 572-4427
Fax: (973) 884-9556

Public Company
Incorporated: 1997
Employees: 1,150
Sales: $240.34 million (1997)
Stock Exchanges: NASDAQ
Ticker Symbol: JRJR
SICs: 5191 Tobacco & Tobacco Products; 5961
  Catalogue & Mail Order House; 5399 Miscellaneous
  Merchandise Stores; 5993 Tobacco Stores & Stands;
  6719 Holding Companies

800-JR Cigar, Inc. is one of the largest distributors and retailers of tobacco and tobacco-related products in North America. Management believes that the company ranks as the leading retailer of brand name cigars in the United States. In addition, the company is the largest customer of many of the world's top cigar manufacturers, including Consolidated Cigar Holdings, Inc., General Cigar Holdings, Inc., Swisher International Group, Inc., and Villazon & Co. The company markets its products via direct mail and through its six specialty cigar stores and three large discount outlet stores.

Steady Growth: 1970s–90s

Industry commentators have noted that for the past 100 years, the popularity of stogies has mirrored the peaks and troughs of the stock market in the United States. Cigar sales declined markedly following the stock market crash of 1929, and again in 1973 as the country met with a bear market. Surprisingly, however, while cigar sales declined steadily from 1973 to 1993, 800-JR Cigar's business was growing. Lew and LaVonda Rothman opened their small, corner candy and tobacco store in 1970, just three years before cigar sales surged to an all-time high, and then began their steady 20-year decline. The business, originally named JR Tobacco after Lew's father, Jack Rothman, quickly outgrew its original location at 6th Avenue and 45th Street in Manhattan, New York, and went from being a "mom and pop" shop to a bustling wholesale and direct mail retail operation.

According to *Barron's,* the early 1990s marked a social backlash against the fit, careerist, Yuppie lifestyle that had been promoted and caricatured in the 1980s, and JR Cigar benefited from the shift. Helped by good times on Wall Street, the cigar industry indirectly encouraged many recently arrived professionals to explore new avenues of decadence. Cigars became associated with the sort of "refined rebellion" championed by the Baby Boomers, then 30- or 40-something and enjoying a time of life that lent itself to reveling in success. These individuals, male and female alike, helped build an industry that enjoyed a compounded annual growth rate of 20 percent, reaching $2 billion a year in total volume by 1997. Between 1991 and 1997, as the Dow climbed threefold, sales of premium cigar brands rose more than fourfold. An estimated 500 million cigars were imported into the United States in 1997.

All of this spelled good news for 800-JR Cigar, which by then ranked as one of the largest distributors and retailers of premium and mass market cigars in the United States and the largest customer of each of the world's largest cigar manufacturers. Premium cigar imports increased an average of 37.6 percent a year between the years 1993 and 1996. Yet according to Rothman, major manufacturers, who increased their production by 50 percent or more, still could not meet the distribution demands of a swelling market. About six million Cuban cigars began to be smuggled into the United States yearly, but even these could not match the needs of this country's estimated one million premium cigar smokers, whose demand created a situation in which there were 80 million cigars on back order. 800-JR Cigar's net sales increased approximately 25 percent each year from 1995 to 1997, from $152.7 million to $192 million to $240.3 million—all without benefit of advertising.

Company Perspectives:

800-JR Cigar's objective is to enhance its position as the leading retailer and distributor of an unmatched selection of tobacco products, including over two hundred brands of premium and mass market cigars. The company's buying acumen and selling power enables it to earn a significant savings on purchases, and to pass those savings on to customers in the form of discounted prices. The company also markets an extensive selection of value-priced, private label, premium cigars which it believes compare favorably to nationally branded cigars selling at substantially higher prices. 800-JR Cigar believes that its success is due in part to its ability to purchase in large quantities from a broad range of suppliers.

Changes in Cigar Demographics: Mid-1990s

By 1994, the scarcity of premium, brand name products caused a horde of start-up companies, some foreign. As many as 150 small manufacturers of inferior cigars sprang up to meet the new need to provide smokers with the perishable product they desired, inundating the American market with lower-quality cigars. These ''Don Nobodies'' sold for as much as the better quality, better known brands due to a supply and demand imbalance. The established premium companies, whose products accounted for 40 percent of sales in dollar terms (ten percent of product sold), faced further competition from another set of foreign companies, mostly Caribbean, that used the shortage to establish a bigger foothold in the United States for their handmade cigar brands.

In addition, the renaissance in cigar smoking drove up prices—by as much as 20 percent per year on premium products. This increase largely accounted for the wholesale price of quality tobacco leaf which went into premium cigar wrappers and which took at least three years to develop from seed to rolling desk. Prices for the most expensive kind of shade tobacco surged to $40 a pound in the mid-1990s, up from $17 only a few years earlier. Also in short supply was skilled labor, especially cigar rollers, who saw their wages increase fivefold in as many years, up to as much as $300 per week by 1997.

A Glut in the Market Spells Opportunity: Late 1990s

Then, in the late 1990s, the situation reversed. By 1997 the major manufacturers had caught up with production demands, and there developed an industry surplus consisting mainly of cigars with no brand equity. This situation caused sudden widespread discounting of the foreign no-names, which could no longer compete with the better quality and better known premiums. Of the approximately 500 million cigars imported into the United States in 1997, only 325 million or so were purchased. This turn of affairs spelled disaster for recognized name-brand manufacturers, such as Consolidated Cigar, General Cigar, Swisher, and Matasa, but opportunity for 800-JR Cigar. ''What's good news for the major manufacturers is normally good for us.

And what's bad for the major manufacturers is normally good for us as well . . . ,'' announced Rothman in a *Wall Street Transcript* interview. The mark-up on an inferior cigar is essentially the same as that on a high-end item, so as the upstart companies attempted to liquidate their inventories at vastly lower prices, 800-JR Cigar bought up the excess and sold it to its customers at reduced prices. With no competitors of its scope or scale, 800-JR Cigar experienced greater than the combined growth of its closest four or five competitors in 1997.

While analysts began voicing some concern that the peak in the cigar industry was over early in 1998, pointing to a sell-off of common stock by Consolidated Cigar, General Cigar, and 800-JR Cigar stock in 1997, business for 800-JR Cigar continued to boom. During the last quarter of 1997, it moved its Bergen County, New Jersey store to a new location in Paramus, New Jersey, and in that same quarter made its first sales to a distributor in Germany and another in Canada. Shortly afterward, it began looking into the possibility of opening duty-free areas in airports. Its stock, which sold for $17 at its initial public offering in June 1997, increased in value to $38 and then dropped back down to $27.

In 1998 the company formed a subsidiary, JR Tobacco of Burlington, Inc., which opened a new 128,000-square-foot JR Outlet Center in North Carolina in October of that year to serve as a distribution point and shipping facility for the company's wholesale accounts. The outlet, which provided a significant improvement in 800-JR Cigar's ability to efficiently process and ship orders, also allowed for additional product lines to be added to its retail, wholesale, and mail-order operations and provided the venue to test out these new items. Some of this merchandise constituted what Lew Rothman called ''oral'' products— cashews, coffee, pistachios. Others were ''male-oriented''— shirts, jeans, fishing rods, designer fragrances—quality items that took into account the tastes and pocketbook of 800-JR's established, typically male and well-to-do customer.

In March 1998 the company opened a 10,000-square-foot, upscale cigar humidor and bar in the heart of New York's financial district in the New York Cocoa Exchange, a building steeped in history and known for its outstanding architecture and decor. Later that same year, another wholly owned subsidiary of 800-JR Cigar, Santa Clara, N.A. Ltd., became the exclusive U.S. distributor of Romeo y Julieta Cigars. The company also became the exclusive importer of all cigars produced in Nicaragua when it purchased a controlling interest in a factory producing 80,000 or more handmade cigars daily, Nicaraguan American Tobacco Inc. The price gap between these cigars— selling at 800-JR Cigar prices, which were 20 to 30 percent less than that of other companies in 1998—and other brand equity names was enormous.

Slowdown in the Industry

By March 1998, many stocks of cigar companies were nearing 52-week lows, and shares of the four largest public enterprises—Swisher International, General Cigar Holdings, Consolidated Cigar Holdings, and 800-JR Cigar—had dropped 20 to 46 percent since October 1997. There was a proposed multibillion-dollar tobacco settlement before Congress; in addition, a lengthy monograph at the National Cancer Institute, drawn from all salient research on medical implications of cigar smoking, was due out soon. As a result, industry watchers were predicting a slowdown in the sales of cigars and related products. These specialists were saying that, after years of annual growth in the nine percent range, cigar sales likely would taper off to around half that in 1998. The slowdown was expected to be especially marked in the premium cigar segment.

Still 800-JR Cigar remained optimistic. In the third quarter of 1998, it continued its unbroken string of record sales and earnings with its largest-to-date earnings of $73.2 million. After the opening of the new Burlington outlet, the company leased approximately 45 billboards on the interstate highway and moved warehousing and shipping into the world's largest, 2.2-million-cubic-foot humidor. While sales were soft at the company's specialty retail stores, wholesale and mail-order shipments of proprietary JR brands took over shelf space from the newer, overpriced entries of the recent cigar boom. 800-JR Cigar launched its new Bolivar premium cigar brand, and the company sought to dispel fear about recent hurricanes that had struck in several cigar-producing countries. Its literature assured stock owners and customers that the impact on the supply of raw materials and finished goods would be minimal, while at the same time urging shipments of clothing, tools, housewares, and food to the Dominican Republic and Nicaragua. 800-JR even organized a few such shipments and matched monetary donations sent in by its customers.

Whether cigar smoking would, in fact, prove a fad remained to be seen. Big cigars, long a symbol of success, confidence, and power, have always been bought by brand, and thus remained somewhat immune to price competition. Despite strong sales, the industry was still nowhere near its all-time peak of 11.3 billion cigars sold in 1973. Yet optimists assumed that the industry would continue to grow, albeit more slowly than it had in recent years. 800-JR Cigar sought to capitalize on the fact that cigar smokers are repeat customers by investing in advertising and software that would enable it to serve its current and future clients more quickly. Stressing the fact that it is not a matter of whether the customer will return, but where, Lew Rothman articulated his company's philosophy: Fast, fresh and cheap. "Just keep all our old customers happy and make new customers at a conservative pace and our business will grow," said Rothman. "All you have to do is treat people nicely and they're going to come back. . . . From the bottom up, it's a feeling of trust between ourselves and our vendors . . . [and] customers."

Principal Subsidiaries

JR Tobacco Company of Michigan, Inc.; Cigars by Santa Clara NA Inc.; JR Tobacco Discount Outlet; JR Tobacco NC Inc.; J&R Tobacco New Jersey Inc.; JR Tobacco Outlet Inc.; JR-46th Street Inc.; JNR Grocery Corp.

Further Reading

"CEO Interview: 800-JR Cigar, Inc.," *Wall Street Transcript,* March 16, 1998, pp. 86–91.
Flanagan, William G., "Cigar Madness," *Forbes,* April 21, 1997, pp. 134–36.
Santoli, Michael, "Snuffed Out," *Barron's,* November 24, 1997, pp. 31–35.
Siwolop, Sana, "Investing It: It's Brand Over Bargain in the World of Cigars," *New York Times,* March 1, 1998, Sec. 3, p. 4.

—Carrie Rothburd

Fab Industries, Inc.

200 Madison Avenue
New York, New York 10016
U.S.A.
(212) 592-2700
Fax: (212) 689-6929
Web site: http://www.fab-industries.com

Public Company
Incorporated: 1955 as Fab-Lace, Inc.
Employees: 1,600
Sales: $160.9 million (1997)
Stock Exchanges: American
Ticker Symbol: FIT
SICs: 2257 Weft Knit Fabric Mills; 2258 Lace & Warp
Knit Fabric Mills; 2295 Coated Fabrics, Not
Rubberized; 2392 Housefurnishings, Except Curtains
& Draperies

Fab Industries, Inc. is a major manufacturer of textile fabrics sold to a wide variety of manufacturers of ready-to-wear and intimate apparel for men, women, and children. Other uses of Fab products are found in the home furnishing, industrial, and specialty markets. The company also manufacturers comforters, sheets, blankets, and other bedding products, selling them to retail stores, catalogue and mail-order companies, airlines, and health-care institutions.

Mid-Century Origins of Fab Industries

Fab Industries was incorporated in 1966, bringing together all of the outstanding stock of Adirondack Knitting Mills, Inc., Lamatronics Industries, Inc., and Fab-Lace, Inc., which had been established in 1955, in addition to an 81-percent interest in Mohican Corp. held by Bankers Life & Casualty Co. One of the company's founders, Samson Bitensky, would continue to oversee operations into the 1990s as CEO and a major shareholder.

As one of the nation's largest manufacturers of warp knit fabrics produced on tricot and raschel machines, the company was engaged in the knitting, dyeing, finishing, converting, laminating, and bonding of tricot and raschel fabrics, circular and novelty knits, laces, and settings. Its knit tricot fabrics were sold primarily to manufacturers of lingerie, blouses, dresses, and menswear, and to the shoe trade.

The company's chief plant became Mohican's facility in Lincolnton, North Carolina. This factory handled Fab's dyeing and finishing operations, raschel lace, and certain tricot knitting operations. The major portion of the company's tricot and laminating operations was being conducted at a plant in Amsterdam, New York. Fab also leased a warehouse in Carlstadt, New York, and headquarters, including a showroom, in New York City's garment district.

Fab Industries lost $382,279 on sales of $17 million in 1965. This deficit was attributable to the acquisition of money-losing Mohican, which was merged into Fab in 1968, following the purchase of additional shares. At this time the company also bought out the minority interest in Fab-Craft Inc., a subsidiary of Fab-Lace. Late in 1968 Fab Industries became a public company by selling a minority of its shares of common stock at $13.50 per share. Sales and net income grew annually during 1966–70, reaching $32.2 million and $2.3 million, respectively, in fiscal 1970.

Fab Industries, in 1968, was engaged in the knitting of synthetic yarns (largely nylon, acetate, and polyester), provided by its suppliers, on both raschel and tricot machines. It dyed and finished all its fabrics on its own equipment. Fab was also laminating polyurethane foam to fabrics and laminating fabrics through adhesive bonding. More than half of its fiscal 1968 volume came from the sale of knitted tricot fabrics to manufacturers of lingerie, blouses, dresses, and ski and wind jackets. Sales also came from circular double- and single-knit fabrics to manufacturers, chiefly for use in women's and children's dresses and sportswear and men's shirts and sportswear, as well as from raschel laces, primarily sold to manufacturers of women's apparel in the dress, blouse, sleepwear, and lingerie fields.

New Fabrics and Facilities in the 1970s

Fab Industries doubled the capacity of its Lincolnton plant during 1968–69 and also, in 1969, introduced cling-free "Swing-a-Way" tricot material, using Celanese Corp.'s Fortrel polyester yarn. During this time, Fab also introduced a similar line of cling-free nylon tricot, chiefly for use in lingerie and blouses. The company's shipments of warp fabrics reached 273.9 million pounds in 1970, of which tricot accounted for 87 percent and raschel and lace for the remainder. A decline in Fab's raschel fabrics was observed during this time, related principally to a drop in girdle sales as women's preferences turned to pantyhose.

Up to this point, warp knits had been used almost entirely in lightweight garments, but with the application of polyester these fabrics became suitable for almost all types of outerwear, closely resembling the solid color and striped fabrics produced on double-knit machinery. Accordingly, in 1969 Fab Industries took steps to introduce knitted polyester fabrics for men's slacks, suits, and sports coats. A sales and merchandising division was established specifically for the sale of uniform fabrics designed by Fab from its own line of these fabrics.

Fab Industries purchased a new plant in 1971 in Maiden, North Carolina, for both warp knits and circular double and single knits. It also leased a new facility in Amsterdam for laminating and bonding operations, enabling the previous Amsterdam plant to be entirely devoted to warp knitting. The Carlstadt warehouse was vacated in 1973. That year Fab Industries formed a subsidiary to make leather-substitute products at the new Amsterdam plant. This subsidiary, Frontier Urethane Corp., manufactured outer material, insert backers, and foam tricot linings for the shoe industry. The handbag, upholstery, and apparel industries also became clients for the urethane-coated products of this subsidiary, which was subsequently renamed Gem Urethane Corp. Also in 1973, Fab added machinery in Lincolnton for heat-transfer printing on knit fabrics.

In 1974 Fab Industries introduced Supersuede, a suede-like knitted fabric made with a special blend of triacetate and nylon developed by Celanese. Panavelle, introduced in 1976, was made from the same fabric. In 1978 the company introduced Bouclette, a loop knit fabric simulating the look of fine cotton terry and particularly suited for softer dresses and blouses. Fab later added Wispa Suede and Crepe Candide to its array of artificial fabrics.

With the exception of fiscal 1972, Fab Industries enjoyed steadily increasing revenues in the 1970s. Net income generally rose too, increasing every year between 1975 and 1979, when it peaked at $8.7 million on net sales of $112.7 million. The company first began issuing dividends in 1977, and thereupon did so on an annual basis. In 1979 Fab Industries acquired two bankrupt knit companies, Travis Mills Inc. and Travis Knits Inc., and assets of an affiliated fiber-texturing concern, for about $8 million. This acquisition included a mill in Lititz, Pennsylvania, for warp knitting and dyeing, and a plant in Cherryville, North Carolina, for circular knitting, dyeing and finishing, and printing.

Financial Strength in the 1980s

Fab Industries' net sales reached a peak of $119.7 million in fiscal 1980, of which textile products accounted for 89 percent and urethane fabrics for the remaining 11 percent. With the advent of the steep 1981–82 recession, sales fell as low as $94

million in fiscal 1982. Net income remained at a comfortable level, however, and reached a record $10.7 million in fiscal 1986.

Fab Industries entered the bedding field in 1983, using Dacron filament on warp knit equipment installed in a new plant in Salisbury, North Carolina, for blankets, Fortel for flannel sheets, and Ceylon for satin sheets. A showroom in New York City was displaying Fab blankets and sheets and also coordinated comforters made of Fab fabrics by Carolina Creations. Fab's heat-transfer printing capability was being used on sheets and comforters.

Fab Industries had record net income of $10.9 million on net sales of $167.9 million in fiscal 1990. Both sales and profits advanced in the next three years, with record sales of $189.6 million and net income of $17 million in fiscal 1993. Investment analysts considered the company's stock, at less than twice book value, seriously undervalued. In early 1994 Fab had cash in investments of about $62 million and virtually no long-term debt. Bitensky said at this time that management's goal was to add $100 million in sales over the next four or five years, partly by finding and acquiring a mid-sized specialty weaving company.

After reaching net sales of $189.8 million in 1994, however, Fab Industries began to slump in sales volume, which was only $156.1 in 1996 and $160.9 million in 1997. Net income was lower, too: $8.8 million in 1996 and $9.4 million in 1997. Nevertheless, the company's rock-solid finances and low stock price continued to make it a favorite of investment analysts. Writing in *Barron's* in 1996, Mike Price called Fab "one of the cleanest, best-run companies" in what this publication termed a "notoriously treacherous industry." That year the company spent $5 million to buy back its own stock. In 1997 Peter Schlieman of Babson Enterprise Fund noted that because of its cash reserves Fab could "go out and purchase fabric at the right time. They can hedge against prices. And they have very good manufacturing facilities."

The 1990s and Beyond

In 1997 Fab Industries augmented its position in the lace business by purchasing the copyrights, trade name, and certain other assets of Wiener Laces Inc., a manufacturer of raschel and leavers lace goods. The company, in the same year, also acquired the copyrights, trademarks, and certain assets of JBJ Fabrics Co., offering an upscale line of wet and pigment prints of knits and wovens. Also in 1997, Gem Urethane formed Sandel International, Inc. for the purpose of creating fire and flame retardant industrial fabrics made from glass filament yarns.

Fab's Raval Lace Division was named "Lace Supplier of the Year" for 1997 by Sara Lee Intimates, Sara Lee subsidiaries representing about ten percent of Fab's business at the time. Fab Industries also won a Technical Achievements Award in 1998 from Cotton Inc. Fab was the largest blanket supplier to the U.S. airline industry at this time.

During this time, Fab Industries acquired bankrupt Lida Stretch Fabrics, Inc. in order to expand its better-price offerings in the stretch circular-knit business. Lida was operating a mill and corporate office in Charlotte, North Carolina, and a dyeing and finishing plant in Gastonia, North Carolina. This acquisition came shortly after Fab's purchase of SMS Textile Mills, a manufacturer of wide elastic fabrics. SMS's production facility in Allentown, Pennsylvania, was retained, while the finishing operation was moved from Norwich, Connecticut, to Fab's finishing plant in Lincolnton.

In 1997 Fab Industries' Raval Lace division was producing raschel laces for sale to manufacturers and jobbers of sportswear, dress, blouses, and other related outerwear industry. The new Wiener Lace division made laces for manufacturers of intimate apparel and bridal wear. The JBJ Fabric division offered an upscale line of wet and pigment prints of knits and wovens used in sportswear, dresses, children's wear, evening wear, and other apparel. Gem Urethane was producing a line of polyurethane-coated fabrics and a variety of flame, adhesive, and ultrasonically bonded items for apparel, accessories, healthcare, environmental, and industrial products. It was also manufacturing Sandel, a silica-based material coated with high-performance polymeric fire-fighting compounds and was marketing this material through Sandel International, Inc., which had become its subsidiary. Fab also was offering a comprehensive line of heat-transfer prints for sleepwear, robewear, outerwear, and activewear.

Fab Industries' knitting, dyeing, finishing, and printing operations, including warp and raschel knitting, were being conducted at the Lincolnton facility. Dyeing and finishing were also being performed at the Cherryville facility. The Maiden plant was performing a variety of operations, including warping for the tricot and lace machines and single and double knitting of fabrics. The Salisbury plant was the site of Fab's consumer and institutional products manufacturing, retail, and over-the-counter operations. The Amsterdam facilities were devoted to tricot warping and knitting and warehousing, but also for the production of a line of polyurethane-coated fabrics and a variety of flame, adhesive, and ultrasonically bonded items.

Some of Fab Industries' fabrics were registered trademarks. For example, circular-knit Fabiella was being used in many national brands of intimate apparel, sleepwear, and children's wear. Stratofleece was the company's proprietary outerwear line.

Supersuede and Microflex were other outerwear fabrics, as was Ultracoat MVT, a registered trademark of Gem Urethane Corp.

Samson Bitensky, at age 78, was still at the helm of Fab Industries in 1998, continuing to hold the positions of chairman and chief executive officer. He owned 26.6 percent of the stock at this time.

Principal Subsidiaries

Adirondack Knitting Mills, Inc.; Fab International Ltd.; Fab-Lace, Inc.; Gem Urethane Corp.; Lamatronics Industries, Inc.; Mohican Mills, Inc.; Salisbury Manufacturing Corp.; Sandel International, Inc.; Travis Knits, Inc.

Principal Divisions

Circular Knit; Consumer Products; Fab Print; Fab Warp Knit; Gemsonic; JBJ Fabric; Lace Designer; Raval Lace; Singer Retail; Wiener Lace.

Further Reading

Brammer, Rhonda, ''Price and Value,'' *Barron's,* February 19, 1996, p. 15.
——, ''Value of Enterprise,'' *Barron's,* May 5, 1997, p. 27.
Cedrone, Lisa, ''Back to School,'' *Bobbin,* September 1992, pp. 36. 39.
Chiris, Stuart, ''Fab Agrees to Acquire Lida Stretch,'' *WWD—Women's Wear Daily,* April 29, 1998, p. 17.
''Fab Industries Set to Fashion Smart Advances in Sales, Profits,'' *Barron's,* April 28, 1969, pp. 36–37.
''Fab Says Profit Was Better Than Expected in Its Fourth Quarter,'' *Wall Street Journal,* January 31, 1994, p. B5A.
Levine, Al, ''Unique Constructions Play a Big Hand at Fab,'' *HFD—Home Furnishings Daily,* August 27, 1984, p. 61.
Needham, Tara C., ''Fab Industries,'' *Wall Street Transcript,* November 15, 1971, pp. 26,111–112.
''Plastics Corner,'' *Journal of Commerce,* June 5, 1973, p. 5.

—Robert Halasz

Real Italian. Real *Fast.*®

Fazoli's Systems, Inc.

2470 Palumbo Drive
Lexington, Kentucky 40509
U.S.A.
(606) 268-1668
Fax: (606) 268-2263
Web site: http://www.fazolis.com

Wholly Owned Subsidiary of Seed Restaurant Group Inc.
Incorporated: 1990
Employees: 6,000
Sales: $204.2 million (1996)
SICs: 5812 Eating Places

Fazoli's Systems, Inc. is the operator and franchiser of an Italian fast-food restaurant chain in the United States under the name Fazoli's. One of the most popular and fastest growing restaurant concepts in the country by the late 1990s, Fazoli's came to fruition at a time when people in the United States were searching for an alternative to the traditional fast-food menu of burgers and fries. The company either operates or franchises over 320 restaurants throughout 27 states.

The Early Years

Although the Fazoli's restaurant concept was created in 1989, Fazoli's Systems, Inc. was actually formed in 1990, when the chain consisted of just five restaurant locations in Lexington, Kentucky. At that time, the restaurants were owned and operated by Jerrico Inc., which was also the parent company of the Long John Silver's seafood restaurant chain. Jerrico decided to focus solely on developing Long John Silver's, however, and Fazoli's was put up for sale. Entrepreneur Kuni Toyoda—Jerrico's Asian franchise vice-president—joined forces with Japan-based Duskin Co. Ltd. and purchased the tiny restaurant chain. They formed Seed Restaurant Group Inc. to own and manage the enterprise, and Fazoli's Systems, Inc. became its subsidiary.

When Toyoda acquired the Fazoli's chain, the restaurants were selling a pretty equal mix of pizza and pasta items. Toyoda decided that it would be almost pointless to compete in the well-established pizza industry, especially because Fazoli's did not offer home delivery. Therefore, Fazoli's began phasing out pizza and instead focused mainly on its pasta selections. Toyoda upgraded the ingredients that Fazoli's used, while also making changes such as the creation of larger portions and a shift toward cooking the pasta more firmly (known as "al dente").

The early 1990s marked a trend toward health consciousness in the United States. Grocery store shelves were lined with "fat free," "low fat," and "reduced fat" alternatives to most popular items, and Toyoda realized that he could capitalize on this trend with the Fazoli's concept. In the August 1995 issue of *The Lane Report,* he noted, "Pasta is here to stay, simply because the Italian segment is the most popular ethnic segment. Pizza used to dominate, but now people are so used to eating pasta. They know what good pasta is." He began marketing Fazoli's as a more healthful alternative to the traditional fast-food menu of burgers and fried foods.

Toyoda also promoted Fazoli's as an affordable alternative to most full-service casual restaurants. Each Fazoli's restaurant featured an ample, comfortably decorated dining room where the manager was likely to be seen serving patrons hot bread-sticks as they ate. Dine-in customers were treated to an unlimited supply of the breadsticks, as well as free drink refills. A typical individual check at Fazoli's was under $4, while a family of four could usually eat there for less than $15. For those prices, each customer was buying six to eight ounces of food, whereas most hamburgers were only two ounces.

Fazoli's soon began opening more restaurant locations, focusing at first on gaining a presence in small- and medium-sized towns. For one thing, real estate prices were usually lower in such areas, and the healthful, low-cost Fazoli's concept appealed to their residents. Fazoli's also benefited from the fact that its restaurant set-up was flexible enough to allow the company to purchase other failed restaurant buildings and convert them, rather than having to actually build all of its new structures.

Company Perspectives:

Fazoli's management believes its greatest assets are its food and service along with exceptional value. Most items are priced under $4 and all are made fresh, never frozen and reheated.

From the start, the new company placed a great emphasis on customer service. New employees were required to complete a one-week training seminar, while store managers underwent a five-week program. Rather than focus most of its attention and resources on adding restaurants and increasing in size, Fazoli's focused instead on making sure each of its locations was able to properly represent the company's principles. According to Toyoda in a 1998 issue of *Kentucky Business Viewpoint*: "We could grow faster, but we don't want to grow fast. . . . It takes time to develop competent general managers that really understand Fazoli's system. We tend to focus more on service."

Rapid Expansion in the Mid-1990s

Within a couple years, however, the chain was, in fact, expanding rapidly. By 1992, the company had grown to include over 35 Fazoli's restaurants. It almost doubled that figure in 1993 by adding 25 additional locations, giving Fazoli's a total count of 62 restaurants throughout the states of Kentucky, Florida, and Indiana. Of those, 53 were company-owned and nne were franchised.

Not only did the company expand quickly in terms of the number of restaurant locations, it also exponentially increased the amount of sales that each location achieved each year. When Toyoda took over the operations of Fazoli's in 1990, the average unit volume for each of the five restaurants had been about $500,000 per year. Within five years, that figure had increased to around $1 million per year. This made expansion quite easy financially, because start-up costs ranged from $150,000 for conversions to $500,000 for newly constructed buildings. At those costs, most locations could turn a profit in the first year of operation.

Fazoli's expanded its prototype unit as well, from 2,800 square feet and 100 seats, to over 3,000 square feet and 140 seats. This helped each unit handle higher volumes of dine-in business. In 1994, the company's takeout orders represented only 30 percent of its total sales. Most of the restaurant's business was done in its dining room, with about 60 percent of it taking place during the dinner hours.

In early 1994, the company brought aboard Toyoda's former boss at Jerrico—Ernest Renaud—as a marketing vice-president and special consultant. Renaud, who was already a board member of Fazoli's parent, Seed Restaurant Group, had actually done a lot of the start-up work on the Fazoli's chain in its early years. Along with Toyoda, he set out to help the young enterprise compete with the other players in the fast-food Italian niche, including market-leader Sbarro and Pizza Hut's Fas-

tino's concept. A goal was set to open at least 120 Fazoli's units by 1996.

In late 1994, Fazoli's began testing the potential for food court and strip mall versions of its restaurants to achieve success. This move may have come about as a means of competing with Sbarro, which operated most of its units within shopping malls. Fazoli's knew, however, that its strength was in its freestanding restaurants, and it therefore continued to expand mainly in that area. The company posted 1994 sales of $59 million.

By mid-1995, the company had grown to include 112 units in 120 states. Of those, only 30 were franchised. In the June 19, 1995 issue of *Business First—Louisville*, however, Ernest Renaud stated that the vast majority of new units in the coming years would be operated by franchisees. This would help the company offset the cost of start-ups, as each franchisee would pay a one-time $25,000 fee for Fazoli's rights, in addition to all start-up costs and five percent of the restaurant's gross annual sales each year.

In August 1995, Fazoli's made headlines when *Nation's Restaurant News* published its "Second 100 Chains" rankings, based on growth in three different areas. Fazoli's was ranked third in the area of systemwide sales growth, second in the growth of company-owned units, and first in the growth of franchised units. At year's end, the chain was composed of 164 Fazoli's restaurants, each of which generated an average of $964,000 in annual revenue.

The Turn of the Century and Beyond

Within a year, Fazoli's units numbered 214 in 23 different states throughout the country. Meanwhile, in a surprising move, Seed Restaurant Group introduced a new Italian restaurant concept called Bella Notte in 1996. According to Toyoda in a 1998 issue of *Kentucky Business Viewpoint,* "We try to duplicate Trattoria, the neighborhood, casual restaurant in Italy where people go to have fun over great quality food." While some may have felt that the company was potentially diluting its market base and creating competition for Fazoli's, Seed did not see it that way. Bella Notte would be pricier than Fazoli's, with an average individual check double that of its older sibling. In reality, the new entry would more appropriately serve as competition for such established Italian restaurants as the Olive Garden chain.

Entering 1997, the company was altering its market strategy slightly as it moved into bigger cities. Its most recent entries into larger markets dictated that the company needed to change its advertising strategy in order to maintain the sales volume it had achieved in smaller locales. Regional television advertisements surfaced. The company knew that it was important for things such as the Fazoli's tagline—"Real Italian. Real Fast."—to be in the public eye and permeate the potential consumer's awareness.

Toyoda invested himself mainly in his employees, however. In a January 21, 1997 article about him in *Nation's Restaurant News,* he contended, "To be a success in a people-driven industry like ours, you definitely have to take care of your people.'' Not only did he ensure that the company operated on its founding principles of open communication, idea sharing, teamwork, and excellence, but he also actually invested in his employees. Toyoda offered half of his 50 percent ownership of the company to his management team. (The other 50 percent was owned by Duskin Co. Ltd.)

Corporate management also began offering each of its restaurant units incentives for maintaining a high level of customer service. Each month, a ''mystery shopper''—that is, a customer who actually reports back to the company about the level of service received—visited Fazoli's restaurants on multiple occasions. Any unit that received scores of 90 or higher three times within a month received bonuses for all of its employees.

In late 1997, and early 1998, Fazoli's received more accolades within the industry. *Restaurant Business* released its list of top 50 growth chains in July 1997, and Fazoli's was ranked seventh overall. The company also received a number seven ranking in terms of sales increases, and a number 13 ranking with regard to increases in number of units. The following March, *Restaurants and Institutions* ranked quick-service restaurant chains on multiple attributes; Fazoli's came out on top in overall rankings, as well as in the areas of value and service. Fazoli's also ranked second to Starbucks in the atmosphere rating, and third in cleanliness—just barely behind Starbucks and Bruegger's Bagel Bakery.

In December 1997, Fazoli's opened its 300th restaurant. As the company entered 1998, Toyoda began announcing that some time in the near future, the company would be going public in order to fund a true nationwide expansion campaign. The company hoped to double its unit count by the year 2002.

Further Reading

Baldwin, Amy, ''Fazoli's Opens 300th Restaurant, Plans National Expansion,'' *Lexington Herald-Leader,* December 10, 1997.

''Blast off,'' *Restaurant Business,* July 1, 1997, p. 43.

Clancy, Carole, ''Fazoli's Cooks Up Bay Area Expansion,'' *Tampa Bay Business Journal,* July 12, 1996, p. 1.

Coeyman, Marjorie, ''Making it Simple,'' *Restaurant Business,* January 15, 1997, p. 40.

Cooper, Ron, ''Fazoli's Adding Two Restaurants, Sees More Growth,'' *Business First—Louisville,* June 19, 1995, p. 9.

''Fazoli's Parent to Open New Italian Dinner House,'' *Nation's Restaurant News,* July 22, 1996, p. 2.

''Fazoli's,'' *Restaurant Business,* July 1, 1996, p. 78.

''Fazoli's Tests Food Court, Strip Malls,'' *Nation's Restaurant News,* November 28, 1994, p. 2.

''Full-Service Winners vs. Quick-Service Winners,'' *Restaurants and Institutions,* March 1, 1998, p. 68.

Hayes, Jack, ''Kuni Toyoda,'' *Nation's Restaurant News,* January 21, 1997, p. 214.

——, ''Pronto! Fast-Serve Italian Niche Swells,'' *Nation's Restaurant News,* March 14, 1994, p. 1.

Howard, Theresa, ''Fazoli's: Like Going Home to Mom's,'' *Nation's Restaurant News,* May 16, 1994, p. 62.

Kass, Mark, ''On the Menu: Drive-Through Pasta, Pizza?'' *Business Journal Serving Greater Milwaukee,* May 13, 1995, p. 3.

''Second 100 Chains Ranked by U.S. Systemwide Sales Growth,'' *Nation's Restaurant News,* August 21, 1995, p. 62.

Walter, Grady, ''Area Restaurateurs Replicate Success through Franchising,'' *The Lane Report,* August 1995, p. 20.

Wood, Campbell, ''The Seed Restaurant Group—Flourishing Italian Style,'' *Kentucky Business Viewpoint,* Second Issue 1998, p. 15.

—Laura E. Whiteley

Fédération Internationale de Football Association

FIFA House
Hitzigweg 11, PO Box 85
Zurich
Switzerland
(41) 1-384-9595
Fax: (41) 1-384-9696
Web site: http://www.fifa.com

Non-Profit Association
Incorporated: 1904 as Fédération Internationals de
  Football Association
Employees: 65
Sales: $310 million (1997)
SICs: 7941 Sports Clubs, Managers & Promoters

The world's governing body for football, the Fédération Internationale de Football Association (FIFA) is the not-for-profit association responsible for regulating the rules of play, superintending international transfers of players, establishing uniform standards of refereeing, and organizing international competitions. FIFA-sponsored competitions included the World Cup, the Olympic Football Tournament, the World Youth (under-20) Championship for the FIFA/Coca-Cola Cup, the under-17 World Championship for the FIFA/JVC Cup, the FIFA World Championship for Women's Football, the FIFA Futsal (Indoor Football) World Championship, and the FIFA/Confederations Cup. In the late 1990s FIFA had 203 member associations—the national football associations that competed internationally under FIFA auspices. The legislative body of FIFA, the Congress, wielded the greatest power within the association, convening every two years to determine and implement FIFA statutes and to elect a president every four years. The majority of the profits realized by FIFA from ticket sales, television rights, corporate sponsorship, and merchandising were awarded to the finalist teams in each competition, with the balance retained by FIFA to finance its administrative costs and its efforts to promote and develop the sport of football.

Origins

The impetus for FIFA's formation arose from the spontaneous act of a 19th century football player in central England. In the town of Rugby in 1823 a player for the home team scored a goal by picking up the ball and running with it. The loosely organized, largely uncodified, sport of football was changed forever. The player's inspired use of his hands divided the sport of football into two groups: "association football," which forbade the use of hands and was distinguished by the use of a round ball, and "Union football," whose derivatives included rugby and American football, which used an oval-shaped ball. FIFA was formed to distinguish unequivocally association football from Union football and to serve as a governing organization that could provide international standards and unity to the numerous national association football organizations. The driving force behind FIFA's formation was a journalist named Robert Guérin, the president of France's national association football organization, who reportedly began spearheading an effort to create a governing body for international association football after a match between Belgium and France. On May 21, 1904, Guérin achieved his goal when delegates from Belgium, Denmark, France, The Netherlands, Spain, and Sweden gathered in Paris to found FIFA and formally adopt the term "association football" as their own.

At the organization's inaugural meeting, Guérin was elected president of FIFA, a post he would hold for two years. The possibility of a tournament among FIFA members—a "World Cup"—was first discussed at the meeting in Paris, but it would be years before the organization's signature event was staged. At FIFA's Annual Congress in 1920, however, momentum began to build toward staging a tournament. The Antwerp meeting resulted in the election of France's M. Jules Rimet as president and the unanimous agreement that a FIFA championship should be staged. It was debatable which decision was more important to the long-term success of FIFA. Rimet was the organization's first genuinely influential leader and its longest serving president in the 20th century, occupying the post of president until 1954. Under Rimet's direction, FIFA moved laboriously toward organizing the first World Cup, its progress slowed by the numerous political difficulties inherent in reaching accord

Company Perspectives:

FIFA is committed by its statutes not only to the positive promotion of football through development programmes, but also to supervising international competition and to safeguarding the sport and its good image against abuse of its rules and regulations. And FIFA sees to it that the game is played to one unified set of rules, the Laws of the Game, all over the world. Football's ever growing popularity, its enormous appeal especially to young people, its expanding economic, social and even political significance and, not least, its importance for the media have all combined to make the sport a vital common denominator for varied interest groups. This trend also means that FIFA is obliged to deal also with matters outside its immediate sporting sphere of activity.

among disparate nations. It was not until the Annual Congress of 1928, held in Amsterdam during the Ninth Olympic Games, that Rimet prevailed and the final decision was made to "organize a competition open to representative teams of all affiliated national associations." The divisive issue as to where the tournament was to be held was not resolved until the Annual Congress in Barcelona in 1929, when FIFA officials agreed to stage the event in Uruguay, the reigning football champion for the previous two Olympic Games. For FIFA, with its European roots, the decision to hold the first World Cup in South America nearly led to an embarrassing failure.

Following the 1929 Annual Congress, construction began on a 100,000-seat stadium in Montevideo, where the tournament was scheduled to take place in the summer of 1930. As preparations continued and the date of the first match neared, organizers grew anxious when it became apparent that no European teams were interested in participating. To travel to Uruguay by sea and compete required three months, a sacrifice European teams were unwilling to make. Disaster loomed; as late as two months before the I FIFA Championship was scheduled to begin, organizers still had not received a formal entry from a European country, but then Rimet exerted his formidable influence. Using his persuasive powers, Rimet convinced four European nations to make the southward voyage, bringing France, Belgium, Yugoslavia, and Romania to Montevideo to compete against Argentina, Mexico, the United States, Chile, Brazil, Bolivia, Peru, Paraguay, and the host country, Uruguay. By the time the FIFA World Cup trophy was awarded to victorious Uruguay, the 13 nations had played 18 matches witnessed by more than a half million spectators. FIFA, with 46 member associations at the time, had successfully staged its first international event, the popularity of which supported the organization's mission to promote and govern what would become known as the "beautiful game."

Preparations for the second World Cup began soon after closing ceremonies in Montevideo. For the next World Cup, FIFA's Congress decided Europe should be the stage, but it required eight lengthy conferences to select Italy as the host nation. Interest in the tournament had grown measurably, prompting FIFA officials to implement two changes for the 1934 World Cup that became hallmarks of the unique competition in the decades to come. Instead of playing all the matches in one city, the 17 matches scheduled to be played were spread throughout the country, divided among eight cities, with Rome as the site for the final match. In addition, greater interest in the tournament—29 nations entered the 1934 World Cup—required qualification games to be played throughout the world to reach the 16 finalists scheduled to compete in Italy.

Italy won the 1934 World Cup and repeated the feat at the 1938 World Cup, which was held in France. The selection of France as the host country aggravated the tensions between Europe and South America, exacerbating the jealousies that had been building since the 1930 World Cup. In 1934, the reigning champion Uruguay had refused to travel to Italy as retribution for the lack of interest by European teams in the 1930 World Cup. Argentina, believing that location of the World Cup would alternate between Europe and South America, had lobbied vigorously for the rights to the 1938 World Cup, but its efforts were in vain. The selection of a European nation for a second consecutive tournament led Argentina to boycott the event entirely, a decision aped by Uruguay, still miffed by the lack of European support. Other South American teams bowed out as well, leaving Brazil as the lone South American representative to enter the 1938 tournament. The tensions between Europe and South America, and later between Europe and the rest of the world, would dominate FIFA's activities as the popularity of the FIFA World Championships increased, making the president's job in large part a political exercise in diplomacy. After the conclusion of the 1938 World Cup, however, political events of a far more nefarious nature called a halt to the quadrennial celebration of football. The outbreak of the Second World War canceled the tournaments scheduled for 1942 and 1946, invoking a 16-year respite from the heated battle for football supremacy.

Post-World War II Maturation

During the interim war years FIFA's membership increased from the 57 associations composing the organization in 1938 to 70 members by the time the 1950 World Cup was under way. Rimet, whose influence on FIFA and the sport of football was acknowledged by renaming the World Cup trophy the "Jules Rimet Cup" in 1950, ushered FIFA and the sport into the postwar era, the last years of his presidency. Perhaps mindful of the gulf separating European and South American nations at the III FIFA Championship, Rimet issued a mission statement in 1948, stating that it was FIFA's goal to establish "world unity of football, unity both moral and material." It was a sweeping statement, broad and overarching, befitting the expansive reach of FIFA during the second half of the 20th century, but at the time Rimet penned the words, FIFA and the football nations it governed were struggling to recover from the devastation wrought by the war. Of the 31 countries that originally entered the 1950 World Cup to compete for the 16 final positions, only 13 made the trip to Brazil, to whom FIFA, in an effort to achieve Rimet's "unity," had awarded the rights to the IV FIFA Championship.

Following the 1950 World Cup, won by Uruguay after a 20-year absence from the tournament, Rimet implemented an organizational change that created FIFA's structure for the remainder of the century. From its outset FIFA had worked with regional federations, but beginning in 1953 FIFA authorized the formation of continental confederations. South America had been represented by its confederation, Confederacion Sudamericana de Futbol (CONMEBOL), the oldest unit affiliated with FIFA, since 1916, and was joined by other continental confederations in the wake of the 1953 ruling. The Union of European Football Association (UEFA) and the Asian Football Confederation (AFC) were formed in 1954, followed by the Confederation Africaine de Football (CAF) in 1956. North American, Central American, and Caribbean nations joined together in 1961 to form the Confederacion Norte-Centromericana y del Caribe de Futbol (CONCACAF) and five years later Australia, New Zealand, and South Pacific island-nations organized the Oceania Football Confederation (OFC).

By the 1954 World Cup, Rimet's last as president, footballing nations had recovered fully from the Second World War and their level of participation reflected a rejuvenated passion for competing internationally. Held in Switzerland, where FIFA had moved its headquarters in 1932, the 1954 World Cup marked the 50th anniversary of FIFA and attracted formal applications from 38 countries who played 57 qualifying matches and 26 final matches. Rimet's 24-year term as president was followed by two comparatively brief stints by Belgian Rodolphe William Seeldrayers (1954–55) and Englishman Arthur Drewry (1955–61), who oversaw the first worldwide television transmission of a World Cup at the 1958 tournament held in Sweden. Drewry was succeeded by fellow countryman Sir Stanley Rous, whose 13-year reign marked the last time a European would control FIFA for nearly a quarter of a century. Rous's ouster marked a turning point in FIFA's existence, not only because of the historic shift away from the European power base but also because the organization was suffering from years of institutional neglect and needed a new, dynamic leader. At the last two World Cups during Rous's presidency (1966 in England and 1970 in Mexico), attendance had eclipsed 1.6 million, each a record high. Further, the 1970 tournament reached worldwide television audiences greater than any other event in history, which, coupled with the legions of spectators flocking to the event, suggested the existence of a commensurately strong FIFA. FIFA, however, was nearly bankrupt, struggling lethargically to stay afloat financially while the sport it governed and the worldwide tournament it sponsored stood ready for commercial exploitation.

1974 Election of Havelange

The individual who tapped into the marketability of football was Rous's successor, Joao Havelange, FIFA's president from 1974 until 1998. He was, in the words of one of his FIFA colleagues, "the right man at the right time in the right place." Havelange was Brazilian, the first non-European to preside over FIFA, and keenly aware that FIFA's survival depended on securing lucrative deals with the corporate sector. One year after his election, which he won in large part through African votes, Havelange completed a sponsorship deal brokered by Horst Dassler, the head of sporting goods manufacturer Adidas, with The Coca-Cola Company. With the money received from the sponsorship agreement with Coca-Cola, FIFA's coffers were replenished, giving Havelange the resources to focus on developing football in the Third World, where his constituency was based and where he sought to usher in, as one pundit described it, "football's economic golden age." The general sponsorship agreement with Coca-Cola proved to be instrumental to FIFA's growth during the 1970s, leading to the creation of the FIFA World Youth Tournament for the FIFA/Coca-Cola Cup in 1977, an international competition for players younger than 20 years old. Renamed the World Youth Championship in 1981, the tournament served as Havelange's "ambassador" in developing countries and was just one of several new FIFA-sponsored tournaments created during Havelange's tenure. For the 1982 World Cup, hosted by Spain, Havelange made good on the promise implicit in his election to help non-European countries play a larger role in international football. He expanded the tournament from the traditional 16 finalists to 24 finalists, thereby creating more room for African and Asian teams. For the first time at a World Cup, attendance eclipsed two million in Spain, and television viewership soared into the hundreds of millions. Havelange's recipe of combining big business with multimillion-dollar television agreements and incorporating a greater geographic diversity into FIFA-sponsored events had revolutionized the world of football.

Along with the praise for Havelange's success in increasing the might and scope of FIFA came an equal amount of criticism, with the harshest critics claiming that Havelange's efforts had sullied the sport. His style of management was described as autocratic, his behavior striking some as more in accordance with a head of state than with the president of a nonprofit organization. Havelange, referred to as "Have-a-Lunch" by his detractors because of a growing FIFA expense account, created a vast bureaucracy of FIFA committees, over which he presided with resolute control, prompting one executive committee member, Michel D'Hooge, to remark, "He [Havelange] is everywhere . . . heaven and hell . . . like the Pope." For nearly a quarter century Havelange held onto the reins of power like no other FIFA president before him and, criticism aside, the financial and political power of FIFA increased exponentially. In 1985 the FIFA Under-16 World Tournament (renamed the Under-17 World Championship in 1991) was added to FIFA's ever-growing calendar of events, and in 1989 Havelange directed the development of the first indoor football international competition, the Futsal World Championship. In 1991 the FIFA World Championship for Women's Football—the Women's World Cup—debuted in China, further broadening the scope of FIFA's involvement in football. With the addition of these international tournaments and a flourishing World Cup that included the participation of 112 countries in preliminary rounds for the 1990 finals, FIFA boasted a global reach unrivaled by any other sports organization. Havelange, for better or worse, had built an organization whose lucrative sponsorship deals had transformed the sport of football into big business.

The 1994 World Cup, hosted by the United States, was an unqualified success, drawing a record 3.5 million spectators and reaching a cumulative television audience of a staggering 37 billion viewers. Havelange's tight control over FIFA, however, was already beginning to slip. Prior to the 1994 World Cup,

Pele, a Brazilian player widely regarded as the greatest footballer of all time, had alleged that Havelange's son-in-law was involved in corruption within Brazilian domestic football, an accusation to which Havelange responded by banning Pele from the ceremonies of the 1994 World Cup draw. Havelange's reaction was regarded as a political mistake, one from which he never fully recovered, but before he made his exit Havelange completed one more FIFA deal of epic proportions. In 1996 FIFA sold the worldwide television rights for the 2002 and 2006 World Cups to a partnership comprising Bavarian media mogul Leo Kirch and a Swiss company named Sporis for $2.2 billion, exponentially more than the $92 million paid for the television rights to the 1990, 1994, and 1998 World Cups.

Havelange announced his retirement in early 1998, touching off a power struggle between FIFA's general secretary, Joseph S. (Sepp) Blatter, to whom Havelange referred as his "foreign minister," and Lennart Johansson, the head of Europe's football confederation, UEFA. Havelange, who supported Blatter's candidacy, accused Johansson of conspiring to create a new European football empire and exhorted "Latin countries to rebel." Johansson countered by explaining that Europe was the historical power base of football, where UEFA countries generated "80 to 90 percent of football's income." A bitter, two-month-long campaign for FIFA's presidency ensued, ending two days before the opening ceremonies of the 1998 World Cup in France. Blatter emerged as the winner, with his victory promising the continued development of football as a worldwide sport. The selection of Japan and Korea as co-hosts of the 2002 World Cup underscored FIFA's commitment to expanding the geographic horizons of football. As FIFA's second century of operation was under way, it was Blatter's duty to ensure that expansion into every corner of the globe was achieved.

Further Reading

Boehm, Eric, "Jocks Itchy Over Costly Cup," *Variety,* June 8, 1998, p. 1.

Coman, Julian, "Fight To Control the Game That Turned to Gold," *The European,* June 8, 1998, p. 8.

Hogan, Kevin, "World Cup Wired," *Forbes,* April 11, 1994, p. SI124.

Islam, Shada, "Playing by New Rules," *Far Eastern Economic Review,* September 19, 1996, p. 64.

"Old Man's Game: Soccer," *The Economist,* January 6, 1996, p. 35.

"Why Switzerland Won After All," *The Economist,* July 9, 1994, p. 66.

—Jeffrey L. Covell

Ferolito, Vultaggio & Sons

5 Dakota Drive, Suite 205
Lake Success, New York 11042
U.S.A.
(516) 812-0300
(800) 832-3775
Fax: (516) 326-4988

Private Company
Founded: 1972
Employees: 250
Sales: $300 million (1997 est.)
SICs: 2082 Malt Beverages; 2086 Bottled & Canned Soft
    Drinks & Carbonated Waters

The seemingly overnight success of AriZona Iced Tea in the early 1990s made its owner, Ferolito, Vultaggio & Sons, a major player in the multibillion-dollar "New Age" beverage market, which offers alternatives to traditional colas and other carbonated drinks. Since its early 1970s founding in Brooklyn, New York, as a beer distributorship, Ferolito, Vultaggio & Sons (FV&S) was intent on proving that, in co-founder John Ferolito's words, "We're high class enough to be No. 1, and low class enough to know how to get there." Inspired by the success of the Snapple brand of beverages, FV&S strove to provide a popular ready-to-drink tea beverage that soon distinguished itself primarily by its unique packaging: oversized, brightly-colored cans bearing southwestern-style graphics. In the late 1990s, the privately owned company, having moved its headquarters to Lake Success, New York, followed up its iced tea success with a line of fruit drinks and another line of carbonated drinks, as well as a beer called Mississippi Mud.

From Distributorship to Malt Liquor Maker

John Ferolito and Don Vultaggio went into business together in the early 1970s, soon after graduating high school. While they held delivery jobs at a brewery and beer distributorship, they decided to team up, part-time, to form their own business on the side. Together, the Brooklyn natives purchased a used Volks-

wagen bus for a couple of hundred dollars, ripped the seats out of the back, and proceeded to work delivering reduced-price beer and soda to Brooklyn homes and grocery stores.

This venture soon became full-time work, and the men purchased a used truck to make wholesale deliveries. Their territory centered on such neighborhoods as Crown Heights and Bedford-Stuyvesant, known as tough, high-crime areas that other union drivers tended to avoid. Vultaggio and Ferolito were eventually successful enough to acquire a small fleet of trucks, though they were still second-tier distributors flogging beer at cut-rate prices.

Not satisfied with their role as distributor, the pair soon decided they'd rather make their mark with their own product. They established the Hornell Brewing Co. in the mid-1980s to oversee this new venture, and Ferolito, Vultaggio & Sons eventually became a division of Hornell. The first product FV&S tried, and ultimately failed, to market was Spence & Wesley, a flavored seltzer water named for Vultaggio's sons.

The partners achieved a higher profile with their next product, a malt liquor, with a high alcohol content, named Midnight Dragon. Ferolito and Vultaggio made the product available at a cheap price and promoted it vigorously, reportedly targeting the streets of Manhattan's and Brooklyn's black and Hispanic neighborhoods in particular, every night for a year, shaking hands with passersby and thanking owners of small stores for their orders. Citing Ferolito's and Vultaggio's approach as an example, one *Wall Street Journal* reporter noted disapprovingly that companies employing such tactics "play a part in the cycle of poor nutrition that is approaching crisis levels in the inner city."

Ferolito, Vultaggio & Sons also publicized the brew with suggestive point-of-sale posters, notably one displaying a woman clad in red lingerie, sipping the brew through a straw, with the accompanying tagline, "I could suck on this all night." This ad was withdrawn following protests by the National Organization for Women, although Ferolito was said to have told the *Wall Street Journal* in 1989: "Real men like sex and sex sells beer. I'm not interested in wimps and achievers who want to suck on a lime and drink Corona." Although available only in the New York City metropolitan area at the time, Midnight Dragon had estimated sales of one million cases in 1988. The following year FV&S formed a joint venture with a Cincinnati brewer to introduce Midnight Dragon to other major U.S. markets and to handle additional marketing and production.

Ferolito, Vultaggio & Sons next launched a new brand of malt liquor it called Crazy Horse, named after the Sioux leader, with a label that bore a drawing of an Indian in a feathered headdress. Produced by G. Heileman Brewing Co. and sold in 40-ounce bottles, the beer was marketed in New York City and five states.

The brand soon drew negative attention. In 1992 the U.S. Surgeon General called the brandname "an insensitive and malicious marketing ploy" aimed at Native Americans, who had long been experiencing a high rate of alcoholism and alcohol-related illness. The U.S. Bureau of Alcohol, Tobacco and Firearms, which had approved the product only two months earlier, then reversed itself, citing technical violations that it said, along with the clear-glass, 40-ounce bottle and dark color of the beverage, "all combine to create the misleading impression that the product is a bottle of whisky." Congress passed a 1992 law essentially banning the product, but in 1993 a federal judge overturned the act on First Amendment grounds. In 1997 FV&S would still be fighting legislation that banned Crazy Horse in some states, as well as contending with an organized boycott. Annual sales of the brew had dropped by that time from a peak of three million to some 240,000 cases, according to Vultaggio.

Entering the Iced Tea Market: 1992–95

Ferolito, Vultaggio & Sons' Hornell Brewing Co. was earning annual revenues of about $10 million, when, in 1992, FV&S launched the less controversial product—AriZona Iced Tea—that was to make its fortune. Some 200 ready-to-drink teas had been introduced in the previous two years, produced by such industry giants as Lipton and Snapple, but AriZona stood out for its pastel-colored packaging, vaguely reminiscent of Native American artwork, and its jumbo 24-ounce can. "You know how much time you have at the cooler when the consumer's thirsty?" Vultaggio asked a reporter rhetorically. He answered, "A split second. Make it easy and they'll buy it." The six-foot-eight co-founder credited the can's creation to "my partner, myself, my wife, and a gal in South Jersey who does our mechanicals."

The brand name, Vultaggio said, came to him when he was standing in front of a map in his office and asking himself "Where is hot?" and "What sounds good?" The idea for the product, he confessed, was inspired by rival Snapple Beverage Corp., which was also founded in Brooklyn. "We had been beer guys all our lives and we only knew beer," Vultaggio told a *Beverage World* reporter, noting "Iced tea was foreign to us." Nevertheless, he and Ferolito thought they could do whatever the three founders of Snapple had done. Vultaggio relayed that his company paid more for extra tea flavoring and higher-grade sweeteners but marketed 24-ounce AriZona for the same 99 cents as the 16-ounce bottle of Snapple's iced tea. Production was handled by the same Cincinnati company that made Midnight Dragon, Hudepohl-Schoenling Brewing Co.

The product's success was also reportedly inspired by the partners' experience selling in urban neighborhoods. "We learned a lot working up and down the street," Ferolito told a *Brandweek* reporter. "Party King was a popular soft drink that taught us pretty colors worked in the inner city. Sweetness worked too; that's why Nehi was a success." Twenty-four-ounce beer cans were already available in these markets.

Ferolito and Vultaggio knew all about the beverage wholesaling game after more than 20 years in the business. They ordered wholesalers—mostly large beer distributors of Budweiser and Miller—to repack their products into "rainbow cases" that would provide small retailers with an assortment of the four AriZona Iced Tea flavors—lemon, diet lemon, raspberry, and tropical—even if the retailer only ordered one case. The multiethnic FV&S sales team was told to get the product placed in all its existing beer accounts. The company resisted paying "slotting allowances" to supermarkets. "I don't like retail chains," Ferolito said in 1994. "They're a pool of sharks that you can't sell your products to like a human being." (By late 1997, however, FV&S would give in, routinely paying slotting fees to chain stores.)

By mid-1993 the four AriZona teas each were available in 7.7- and 16-ounce sizes as well as in the big can, in more than 30 states. FV&S sold more than ten million cases of AriZona in 1993, even though 80 percent of the sales were in only four markets—New York, New Jersey, Miami, and Detroit. AriZona had come from nowhere to take fourth place among ready-to-drink teas in the United States.

The point man for the expansion of Ferolito, Vultaggio & Sons products was Michael Schott, who was minority owner and vice-president of Hudepohl-Schoenling when that company had contracted to produce and distribute Midnight Dragon. Schott was running a Detroit beer-wholesaling operation when FV&S introduced AriZona Iced Tea. He brought it to Detroit and took it to the top there in its first year, moving 900,000 cases of the beverage in 1993. FV&S then hired Schott as its chief operating officer and charged him with making the drink national. Before the end of 1994 AriZona Iced Tea was being sold in all 50 states, with estimated sales of $300 million a year, compared to an estimated $10 to $20 million in 1992 and an estimated $130 million in 1993. Ferolito and Vultaggio each pocketed $30 million in aftertax profits in 1994.

By the end of 1993, FV&S had also begun making AriZona Iced Tea available in a proprietary 20-ounce long-neck, widemouth bottle (produced by Anchor Glass) that proved even more popular than the big can. Packaging innovations continued, as they began offering the beverage in milk-style wax cartons, large aseptic packs, and even in powdered form. The AriZona design was licensed for lollipops and freeze pops, beach towels, shirts, and other goods. In early 1994 FV&S widened the beverage line by introducing AriZona Cowboy Cocktails, a juice-based drink in such flavors as Mucho Mango and Strawberry Punch, with Kiwi Strawberry and Pina Colada added later. Soon the company was also putting out lemonade and a nonfat, chocolate-flavored drink. During this time Canadian distribution was also achieved through an agreement with Molson Breweries.

By this time Ferolito, Vultaggio & Sons was seeking to move from its overcrowded 6,000-square-foot Brooklyn warehouse, where, Vultaggio said, ''we have been burglarized about 20 times and the roof is impossible to repair.'' In the fall of 1994 the company began moving to a corporate office park in Lake Success on Long Island, although the sales staff would remain at the Brooklyn site. During this period the partners decided against taking FV&S public and also reportedly turned down an offer of about $400 million for the company from Heileman.

FV&S began 1995 by introducing its iced tea in a fifth flavor—ginseng—in 20-ounce, cobalt-blue bottles. Later in the year the company introduced the first of what became its Soda Shop line of carbonated soft drinks—Chocolate Cola, Diet Chocolate Cola, Vanilla Cola, Chocolate Covered Cherry Cola, and Root Beer Float—under the AriZona name. The root beer drink included milk and cream, which, according to Vultaggio, was unprecedented in a carbonated beverage. These drinks were marketed in a thicker 19-ounce bottle to accommodate the carbonation, and with labels featuring the distinctive AriZona package graphics. FV&S's estimated sales of $285 million in 1995 included 20.3 million cases of Arizona Iced Tea. Earnings were said to be $45 million before taxes. (A later estimate put 1995 sales at $355 million.)

The Going Gets Tougher: 1996–98

In 1996 FV&S introduced Mississippi Mud, a black-and-tan beer that was a blend of English porter and continental pilsner. The first alcoholic beverage since Crazy Horse to be marketed by the company, the brew came in a 32-ounce glass jug inspired by the rustic clay whiskey-drinking vessel John Wayne hoisted in the film *The Alamo*. Despite the broadened scope of its product line, or perhaps because of it, AriZona's sales slipped to an estimated $337.3 million in 1996. Moreover, its share of the iced-tea market fell to 9.6 percent, compared to 10.7 percent in 1994. FV&S's totals would have looked worse, according to a *Newsday* article, if the company had not raised prices sharply and introduced new superpremium-priced flavors.

By the spring of 1997 Schott and several FV&S sales and marketing executives had departed, forcing Vultaggio to assume the position of sales manager himself. One job that demanded action was to smooth the ruffled feathers of some of the company's 500 distributors, angered by what they considered broken promises and strong-arm tactics. At least five distributors had filed lawsuits against FV&S, charging that the company had breached contracts for distribution rights. In early 1997 the company shifted its business in many markets from beer wholesalers to soft-drink bottlers, thereby, according to one account, throwing its distribution system into chaos.

FV&S next began shipping its goods directly to major national retail chains, paying local distributors a per-case fee of about $1.50 for circumventing the wholesale end of the business. The company also switched from 24-unit to 12-unit cases for some of its higher-priced packages, thereby enabling retailers to invest less money in AriZona inventory while continuing to stock a variety of flavors. (Some warehouse-club stores had been reluctant to spend $300 to $400 to stock the brand, and

some suspected that the 24-unit cases were so heavy that clerks might avoid restocking shelves.)

By this time the partners were reportedly reconsidering their determination to hold the annual advertising budget to $1 million—trivial compared to Snapple's $33 million and Lipton's $17 million in 1996. The company had sponsored the Schwinn Cycling & Fitness racing series and other bicycling events in major metropolitan areas in 1996 but dropped this promotional effort, which included AriZona uniforms, posters, and banners, after a single year.

Despite earlier urgings from Schott, and even at one point from Ferolito, Vultaggio had in 1995 vetoed a plan to hire an advertising agency from more than a half-dozen interviewed. Beverage-industry consultants considered the rejection a mistake. ''AriZona had a great burst in the beginning because of the packaging, but the consumer is tired of that,'' said one, adding ''If you don't spend money to promote your brand, you will fall to the earth and crash.''

By this time Strawberry Punch, tropical-flavored tea, and the carbonated line of beverages all had failed—the latter, according to a distributor, because FV&S failed to get the message out that AriZona now had such drinks, while marketing them in bottles similar in size and appearance to that of the teas and juices. ''I saw people shaking it up in the store, thinking it was tea,'' he said.

Still, the company continued to innovate and achieved some success. By the spring of 1997 AriZona's new Green Tea with Ginseng and Honey had become one of FV&S' biggest hits. It also introduced an egg cream called Lite Chocolate Fudge Float and added to its line a Herbal Tea the ingredients of which included chamomile, ginseng, bee pollen, and honey. While some AriZona products maintained the original southwestern motif in their packaging, others seemed to take reflect designs of the Far East or recapitulated American artwork of the 19th century. Still others had a ceramic appearance ''like they were handpainted in Tuscany,'' according to Vultaggio. FV&S also added a line of diet teas, a proprietary 16-ounce bottle, and a squeezable plastic sports bottle made to look like a metal can. The product line extended to nearly 50 stock keeping units (SKUs) in late 1997.

In the fall of 1998 FV&S test-marketed Blue Luna iced coffee, its first nonalcoholic beverage line not under the AriZona brand name. Introduced in Cafe Latte and Lite Cafe Mocha forms and sweetened with the newly approved product Splenda, Blue Luna came in elaborate 12.5-ounce bottles shaped like double-handled Roman jugs. Earlier in the year, FV&S had commissioned pop artist Peter Max to create a limited-edition series of 16-ounce bottles for its core Lemon Tea line.

While industry observers agreed that FV&S's unique, award-winning packaging designs have contributed in large part to the company's sales and success, some have expressed concern over the company's meager advertising budget and strains on relations with its distributor network. Ferolito and Vultaggio, however, considered such reports overstated, and, with their reputation for product and packaging innovation, planned to enter the next century as popular as ever.

Further Reading

Berkowitz, Harry, "Half Empty or Half Full?," *Newsday,* April 7, 1997, pp. C7, C9–C10.

Bird, Laura, "U.S. Moves Against Label of a New Brew," *Wall Street Journal,* April 24, 1992, p. B4.

Christy, Nick, "The Call from Ferolito, Vultaggio & Sons: Here Comes the Jug, Here Comes the Mud," *Beverage World,* October 31, 1996, p. 17.

Collins, Glenn, "A Feisty Brand's Newest Frontier: Premium Colas," *New York Times,* October 28, 1995, p. 35.

Freedman, Alix M., "Poor Selection: An Inner City Shopper Seeking Healthy Food Finds Offerings Scant," *Wall Street Journal,* December 20, 1990, p. A1.

Jochum, Glenn, "Tea for Two on LI?," *LI Business News,* April 25, 1994, p. 1.

Khermouch, Gerry, "Between Coke and a Hard Place," *Brandweek,* June 22, 1998, pp. 36, 38.

——, "Grand Can Yen," *Brandweek,* November 7, 1994, pp. 23–24, 26–29.

——, "Still Winging It," *Brandweek,* October 27, 1997, pp. 38, 40.

Prince, Greg W., "Tall Order," *Beverage World,* June 1994, pp. 22–24, 26, 28, 32.

Roth, Daniel, "Just Call Us Cockroaches," *Forbes,* August 26, 1996, p. 58.

"Vultaggio, AriZona Never Take a Holiday from Package Design," *Beverage World,* August 15, 1997, p. 24. ·

—Robert Halasz

Firearms Training Systems, Inc.

7340 McGinnis Ferry Road
Suwanee, Georgia 30024
U.S.A.
(770) 813-0180
Fax: (770) 622-3505
Web site: http://www.fatsinc.com

Public Company
Incorporated: 1984 as Firearms Simulations Technology,
   Inc.
Employees: 464
Sales: $73.5 million (1998)
Stock Exchanges: NASDAQ
Ticker Symbol: FATS
SICs: 7999 Gun Safety and Marksmanship Instruction;
   3484 Firearms Manufacturers; 7373 Computer
   Integrated Systems Design

Firearms Training Systems, Inc., better known by the acronym FATS, provides weapons training for law enforcement agencies, military forces, and individuals. Its headquarters are in Suwanee, Georgia, which at the time of the company's founding in 1984 was still a sleepy town some 45 minutes north of downtown Atlanta. By the late 1990s, however, Suwanee was another bustling suburb to one of the nation's fastest-growing metropolises, and FATS had become what one analyst called "the 'Kleenex' of firearms training." International from its origins as the brainchild of South African race-car driver Jody Scheckter, the company has facilities not only in the United States, but in Canada, Barbados, Great Britain, The Netherlands, and Singapore. Among its clients are the U.S. Army, Air Force, and Marine Corps, along with the Bureau of Alcohol, Tobacco, and Firearms (BATF), the Federal Bureau of Investigation (FBI), and the Los Angeles Police Department. Its international clients include the armies of Great Britain, Italy, The Netherlands, Singapore, and many other countries. With the attractiveness of simulation over live-fire exercises—both in terms of safety and of cost—it is likely that the client list of FATS will continue to grow.

From Auto Racing to Weapons Simulation

In 1979, South African race-car driver Jody Scheckter won the Formula One championship for Ferrari. He then decided to quit while he was ahead and chose to settle in Atlanta and start his own company. Many other sports figures had similarly retired in a blaze of glory and started a business—only to fail abysmally in the world of commerce, or to make an abortive comeback to the arena that had given them so much satisfaction in the past, or both. Scheckter did neither. He did spend a lot of time in the mid-1980s "playing around with laser disc technology," in the words of the *Atlanta Constitution*'s John McCosh. "There was a lot more tinkering than profiting in the early days," according to McCosh.

This was the—by Scheckter's reckoning at least—inauspicious beginning of Firearms Simulation Technologies, Inc. "I always felt I was really stupid," Scheckter told McCosh, "when I'd run into a guy who imported plastic wheelbarrows and he was doing $2 million a year doing trade shows and I had all this technology and was doing $1 million a year." Geoff Lonsdale, head of European operations during the Scheckter era at FATS, gave Philip Swinden of *Corporate Location* quite a different appraisal of his boss: "He runs this company like he drives cars—flat out."

The idea behind FATS was to use computer technology to provide interactive live-fire simulations for police forces, the military, and hunters. Thus the company could not have existed prior to the explosion in computer technology that occurred in the mid-1980s; as it was, the world was certainly waiting for its product. "We think we have chosen the best system we could find on the market," J.H.J. Rosenboom of the Netherlands Ministry of Defence told McCosh, adding "There is savings on ammunition and savings on trainers. With the FATS system there is one trainer for 10 soldiers, rather than one trainer for almost every soldier on the shooting range."

That one of FATS' most significant contracts should come from The Netherlands was no accident, given the fact that its founder was a descendant of the Dutch colonists who founded South Africa. FATS itself was at that time a subsidiary of THIN International N.V., formerly known as Firearms Training Sys-

Company Perspectives:

FATS' simulation systems enable users to train in highly realistic situations through the integration of video and digitized projected imagery and modified, laser-emitting firearms that retain the fit, function, and feel of the original weapon.

tems International N.V., a Netherlands Antilles corporation. By 1992, the company had facilities in The Netherlands to supply its Dutch army contract. Discussing the decision to expand from England to Holland, Lonsdale told Swinden that the British location ''wasn't really good enough'' to manage the company's Dutch accounts. ''We also needed the capability to speak in Dutch. Although people in Holland speak English very well, they don't always know all the technical words, and if any of the military people had a problem with the equipment they really didn't want to be ringing England,'' Lonsdale related.

But that was in 1992; in its earliest years of operation, during the mid-1980s, FATS built is client base much closer to home. In 1985, it produced its first simulation training system for the U.S. Post Office, thus beginning a tradition of involvement between the company and agencies of the federal government. It also began developing relationships with the police forces of major urban centers, and by 1988 its systems were in use by the police departments of Los Angeles, New York, Philadelphia, and San Francisco. By then FATS had begun to establish a presence overseas as well.

FATS Goes to War in the Persian Gulf

FATS technology makes use of film, which creates a realistic backdrop for simulations. Thus although participants are actually conducting their fire exercise inside a darkened studio, projected images of various scenarios—an urban landscape, a battlefield, farmhouses and open fields—create a sense of a particular environment. The company made training films in California's Mojave Desert, which the U.S. military put to use in 1990 for training personnel in Operation Desert Storm. Though the Iraqi desert in which the forces operated in the Persian Gulf War was on the other side of the planet from the Mojave, to some extent a desert is a desert, and the company's simulation technology proved a great asset during the Gulf War.

Moreover, the war gave FATS great exposure as well. With the Cold War over, military forces around the world were scaling back. Not only were they cutting costs, they were no longer preparing for a nuclear armageddon or some other superpower confrontation, but for a clash with smaller forces—whether religious fundamentalists, nationalist splinter organizations, or other groups. In such an environment, characterized by the redirection of funds from the military to other uses, a reallocation nicknamed ''the peace dividend,'' FATS proved one of the beneficiaries. ''We were in the right place at the right time with the peace dividend and with everyone having less money,'' Scheckter told McCosh, explaining ''They save money by training for less.''

Scheckter Sells the Company

By the mid-1990s, FATS' growth had begun in earnest. As McCosh reported, it was rapidly becoming too big for its facilities, then located at Peachtree Corners on Atlanta's north side. Not only had it secured the Dutch contract in 1992, it had added the British military to its client list, and in just a few weeks' time it had taken in $80 million work of contracts. Given estimates by the U.S. Air Force that it had saved several million dollars by using the FATS system, it was clear that the contracts would continue to mount up—with no end in sight. ''We can double our business again next year,'' Juan de Lebedur, head of the international department, told McCosh. ''This is just the tip of the iceberg.''

Lebedur, who had previously worked in military information systems and spoke six languages, was an example of the highly skilled personnel that had been recruited by Scheckter. Ed Schumacher, director of marksmanship training, had in his earlier army career trained with the AT4 antitank weapon he now wielded in demonstrations at FATS—only the army's version fired live ammunition, whereas the FATS version fired harmless lasers akin to those used in a laser-tag arcade. Schumacher was one of 45 FATS employees, nearly one-third of its work force at that time, with an extensive military background.

With a lock on the police and military market, in 1995 FATS expanded its offerings when it introduced a simulator, complete with woodland scenarios involving wildlife, specifically for hunters. By the end of that year, the company had become a $30 million enterprise with 250 employees, a far cry from the shoestring operation it had been when Scheckter founded it more than a decade before. Its revenues doubled in 1996, to $65 million, and in July 1996 Scheckter sold FATS to a New York-based private equity investment firm called Centre Partners. ''He built the company through sheer entrepreneurial energy,'' said the new chief executive officer (CEO), Peter Marino, ''but he wanted to raise his children back in England.''

Going Public in 1996

With the end of Scheckter's 12 years of leadership, the company began to move in new directions. On the recommendation of Craig Fields, chairman of the Defense Science Board—which acts in an advisory capacity for the U.S. Secretary of Defense—FATS brought in Marino, who had spent 17 years with the Central Intelligence Agency (CIA) before going on to a second career as a defense contractor. Marino took the CEO position in the fall, just before the company's initial public offering (IPO) in November.

The company had a number of factors on its side as it went public. Certainly not the least of these was the sheer romantic appeal of its enterprise, training the warrior for combat, and no doubt many corporate warriors saw themselves in a similar position. Thus Bethany McLean of *Fortune,* which listed FATS among ''Companies to Watch'' in March 1997, noted that ''during the company's November IPO road show, banker types, crouched behind M-16s, gleefully took out targets.'' But entertainment value alone did not explain what McLean called the ''whopping paper profit'' of more than $120 million which Centre Partners made on the stock offering. There was also the fact that FATS enjoyed the trust of the U.S. government—and the fact of its outstanding bottom line. In 1995, it had made $2.8 million profit on $30 million in revenues; and in 1996, as sales figures more than doubled, profits increased by almost five times, to $12.7 million.

Coupled with these selling points was the fact that FATS had established itself as a leading player in a new and exciting—not to mention profitable—field. McLean, while observing that "interactive simulation is in infancy," went on to quote analysts regarding a $4 billion potential market, much of which would come from expanded offerings to the existing customer base among the military and police. Hence the comment by John Hancock Funds portfolio manager Kevin Baker that FATS was the "Kleenex" of firearms training: just as Kleenex had long been such a leader among tissue manufacturers that its brand name had become a generic term for tissue, so FATS' name had become more or less synonymous with the entire interactive simulation market—of which it controlled 80 percent.

Still, such exposure carried liabilities. FATS' outstanding performance could not help but attract the attention of investors—and potential competitors. "One of the pitfalls of going public is that it broadens the awareness of a potential market," Chief Financial Officer David Apseloff told Jason Kelly of the *Atlanta Business Chronicle,* noting "Before, we could labor in relative obscurity." And life in such a growth company was no place for someone who wanted a restful job: "Working here is like being on a treadmill running full speed at the highest incline," Marino told Kelly.

New Products and Acquisitions in the Late 1990s

FATS maintained its edge with continual research and development (R & D). According to a company publication, "A rigorous qualification process has produced a highly capable, dedicated engineering staff, with Ph.D. and Masters degrees, each devoted to the development of advanced simulation products. Capabilities include Booch Method software development, 3-D audio, interactive 3-D graphics, Distributed Interactive Simulation (DIS), video special effects, lasers, extremely accurate ballistics, optics, image processing, Newtonian-based target modelling, and motion platforms."

Out of its R & D department in 1997 came two important new products. The first of these was its Vessel Weapons Engagement Training System (VWETS), for training military or law-enforcement personnel—including river police, the Navy, and the Coast Guard—for operations in a marine environment. Also, FATS developed what it called an Indirect Fire Trainer (IFT), an artillery application complete with a full authoring suite and interactive targets. In October 1997, the Canadian Department of National Defence became the first customer for this product.

In 1998, FATS made two important acquisitions. In March, it purchased all the outstanding stock of Simtran Technologies, Inc., a simulation training company based in Canada. Working extensively with the Canadian Department of National Defence, Simtran produced an air defense missile trainer, an appended armored vehicle crew trainer, and a stand-alone armored vehicle crew trainer. In April of that year, FATS acquired Dart International, a hunter/sports simulation company based in Colorado, which thenceforth took over all of FATS' hunter and sports business.

Also in 1998 the company experienced one of the only setbacks in its history when it lost its bid to provide the U.S. Army Engagement Skill Trainer. "As many of you are aware," Marino announced in the shareholders' letter that accompanied the 1998 annual report, "all of us at FATS were quite surprised at this announcement as FATS has consistently been the overwhelming first choice of military and law enforcement professionals around the world for interactive small arts training systems. To date, the U.S. Army has not awarded a contract for small arms simulators. We are exercising every approach available to correct this situation as we are confident that FATS offers the best simulator solution." It was a rare negative experience for a company whose history had been almost unremittingly positive, and the resolve with which the leadership at FATS proposed to redress the problem was characteristic.

The military made up 70 percent of the company's revenues in 1998, compared with 29 percent from law enforcement and just one percent from the hunter and sportsman market—a category expected to grow in coming years. The split between domestic and international business was almost even, with 54 percent for the former and 46 percent for the latter. FATS continued to improve its product lines, which included some 1,000 scenarios involving more than 180 varieties of weapon ranging from small arms to artillery. Using real firearms as their model, FATS technicians created non-lethal versions which in all other respects (including recoil) duplicated the qualities of their more dangerous counterparts. As Marino noted at the conclusion of his shareholders' letter, FATS remained the leader in its field by a long shot: "Few companies in the world can offer the combined expertise in weapons, simulation, training, and international sales that FATS represents."

Principal Subsidiaries

FATS, Inc.; FSS, Inc.; DART International, Inc.; Firearms Training Systems Limited (U.K.); F.A.T.S. Singapore PTE Ltd.; F.A.T.S. Foreign Sales Corporation (Barbados); Firearms Training Systems Netherlands, B.V. (Netherlands); FATS Canada, Inc.; Simtran Technologies, Inc. (Canada); FATS Canada Holdings, Inc.

Further Reading

Kelly, Jason, "Arms Are Fake, But Profits Real," *Atlanta Business Chronicle,* February 28, 1997, p. 3A.

McCosh, John, "Weapons Training Scores a Big Hit," *Atlanta Constitution,* January 14, 1993, p. F1.

McLean, Bethany, "Companies to Watch," *Fortune,* March 3, 1997, p. 198.

Swindlen, Philip, "Camouflaged Cost-Saver," *Corporate Location,* November/December 1995, pp. 26–29.

—Judson Knight

Frymaster Corporation

8700 Line Avenue
Shreveport, Louisiana 71106
U.S.A.
(318) 865-1711
Fax: (318) 862-2418
Web site: http://www.frymaster.com

Wholly Owned Subsidiary of Welbilt Corporation
Founded: 1935
Employees: 650
Sales: $105 million (1997 est.)
SICs: 3556 Food Products Machinery; 3589 Service
Industry Machinery, Not Elsewhere Classified; 3634
Electric Housewares & Fans; 3822 Environmental
Controls; 5046 Commercial Equipment, Not
Elsewhere Classified; 5099 Durable Goods, Not
Elsewhere Classified

Frymaster Corporation, a subsidiary of Welbilt, is the leading manufacturer of commercial, open-pot fryers in the United States. It also manufactures pasta cookers and three different gas-fired fryers not utilizing the open-pot design. Its primary units, its deep-well, high volume open-pot fryers, are used for preparing a wide-range of fried foods in restaurants and fast-food chains both in the United States and abroad, particularly in Europe's Common Market countries. According to the company's president, David E. Mosteller, "nine out of the top 10 hamburger chains in the U.S. use Frymaster either predominantly or exclusively." The same equipment is used by these chains operating overseas. Frymaster's ultimate parent is London-based Berisford International PLC, an international conglomerate with investments in food, property, and commodity trading as well as kitchen equipment and building materials. Berisford has customers in over 65 countries.

Depression-Era Origins

Frymaster was founded in Shreveport, Louisiana, in 1935 by P.F. Ratcliff, who was then struggling to keep his family business, Ratcliff Barbecue and Market, viable, a tough job during the Great Depression. Although he never progressed beyond a grade-school education, Ratcliff was a gifted amateur inventor who constantly tinkered in his two-car garage in Shreveport. It was there that he fabricated the first Frymaster deep fryer using the new idea of the open frypot and master jet burner, a design eliminating the need for visible heat exchangers that made pot cleaning difficult.

His business was slow in developing, partly because Ratcliff was forced to pinch pennies. His first fryers looked crude, but he was able to sell them to area restaurants because they worked better than established-brand fryers. Although it was tough going, he gradually began selling fryers to a widening circle of customers, transporting his wares in the trunk of an old Ford coupe that he continued to use until the end of World War II.

In 1939, Ratcliff was able to move his operation from his home garage into a storefront located on Marshall Street. He also hired two men, neither of whom had any previous shop experience. In 1940, just before the war, he added a third employee. The fryers then cost about $50, a price that represented only a small markup above the cost of materials and labor. With the economy in the doldrums throughout the 1930s, there was a relentless need to find sufficient operating funds.

World War II to Ratcliff's Retirement: 1941–55

Ratcliff's inventive genius helped his company survive the hard times, both in the Depression and World War II. He worked with a Shreveport doughnut bakery to develop glazing machines and doughnut-proofing boxes, eventually getting patents for the processes. By 1953, the doughnut-making equipment would account for about 20 percent of Frymaster's sales. However, deciding to specialize in fryers, in the late 1960s the company stopped making the doughnut equipment and sold its patents to another manufacturer.

World War II brought special problems in the form of material shortages and government regulations. In 1942, Frymaster had to get a ruling from the War Production Board stipulating that its fryers did not constitute heating appliances, devices placed under a wartime manufacturing moratorium.

Company Perspectives:

It is our goal to continually meet and exceed the expectations of those we serve by performing our work in a quality manner. We not only intend to be error free, but we always work to improve previous performance. Quality has a special meaning with regard to Frymaster's customers. We will design, build and service our products in a manner which makes us the best fryer manufacturer anywhere in the world. The emphasis in quality extends from the smallest detail to the issues of greatest importance. Frymaster's success rests solely on the degree to which each of us makes the quality of our performance our most important objective.

Planned expansion was also slowed. Although a slab for a new manufacturing site was poured in 1942, the building was not completed until war's end. In addition, both raw material and labor were scarce, which slowed down operations considerably.

Growth remained very slow through the late 1940s and into the 1950s. In 1953, there were 29 fryer manufacturers nationwide, and Frymaster ranked dead last in size and sales. But important changes were underway. In that same year, Ratcliff hired the company's first engineer, L. Frank Moore. Until that time, he had used contract draftsmen for design specifications necessary for patent applications and client literature. Then, in 1955, Ratcliff decided to retire and sold the company to three men: Moore; Hershel H. Herring, the company's CPA; and Robert L. Dunkelman, who came to Frymaster from General Electric. Herring served as Frymaster's president from 1956 to 1966, when he retired and sold most of his stock to Travis E. Schermerhorn, Jr., who served as the company's CFO. Upon Herring's retirement, Moore became Frymaster's president and CEO, serving in that capacity until 1982.

Technological Development and Growth: 1956–84

In 1955, Frymaster had gross sales of about $400,000. It was still housed in its 28,000-square-foot plant on Fortson St. built at the end of the war. Growth remained slow for another two years, until the company began fabricating more accurate temperature controls and earned design certification on its standard models from the American Gas Association. Its high-efficiency gas fryers gave Frymaster a needed growth nudge, for it was these fryers, equipped with built-in filtration and later computer control, that would eventually attract such customers as McDonald's and Burger King and turn Frymaster into the world's leading manufacturer of commercial gas and electric fryers.

The company's determination to adapt to new technologies accounted for much of its success. In addition to using the open-pot design, early on Frymaster developed and patented fryer jet burners and its doughnut making equipment. In 1954, it built its precision 1° F action thermostat to replace the much less accurate units then in use. Over the next several years it would add cooking computers for precise cooking control, automatic basket lifters, built-in fat filtration systems, integrated pasta cook-

ers, and high-efficiency gas fryers. In combination with the accurate temperature and computer controls and built-in filtration, the high-efficiency fryers provided Frymaster with a fast-growing worldwide market.

Although the company's customers still include independent restaurants and cafeterias, starting in the 1960s, most of the company's growth came from rapidly increasing sales to fast-food chains. Besides the fryers' efficiency, other features appealed to quick-service drive-ins, especially the automatic basket lifters. Frymaster's first large chain account was Kentucky Fried Chicken. It was followed by Marriott's, Bob's Big Boy, and Dairy Queen. McDonald's joined the ranks of customers after extensive testing of a new, high-performance fryer. For that large and demanding chain, Frymaster incorporated special features, including an automatic melt cycle for frying with shortening and extra safety devices.

In 1965, the company moved to a new site on Hollywood Avenue, made necessary by the spiraling demand for its fryers. The new plant nearly doubled the size of the Fortson St. facility, and over the next few years was enlarged twice, to reach 96,000 square feet, finally to be replaced when Frymaster moved to its current 22-acre site in the 1980s.

By 1975, when Dunkelman retired, Frymaster's gross sales went over $5 million for the first time. Five years later, in 1980, sales had tripled to over $15 million, with 25 percent coming from foreign orders. The company bought the new site in that year, but signs of market softening put building plans on hold for a couple of years, even though between 1980 and 1984 Frymaster's sales doubled again.

In 1982, Moore and the Welbilt Corporation formed Welmoore Industries, a joint venture created to purchase four companies in the Sunbeam (Allegheny International) group of equipment manufacturers, including Frymaster. Moore, as Welmoore's president and CEO, appointed Schermerhorn president of Frymaster. Two years later, Moore sold his interest in Frymaster to Welbilt.

Welbilt, founded in 1929 by Henry and Alexander Hirsch, started out making ovens and survived the Depression; but after an ambitious expansion in the 1950s and 1960s, the company almost failed in the economic downturn of the 1970s. Forced to retrench, it restricted its line to commercial cooking equipment and, under the control of Henry Hirsch's son, Richard, began purchasing companies that manufactured such equipment, a policy that continued after Jerome Kohlberg bought the company in 1987 and Richard Hirsch left the company in 1991. Despite ongoing financial problems, the company survived and by the middle 1990s had became a solid market performer, with Frymaster recognized as being "a strong pillar of Welbilt's success." In January 1995, through a stock buyout, Welbilt and its subsidiaries were acquired by London-based Berisford International PLC, Frymaster's ultimate parent.

It was in 1987 that David E. Mosteller became president of Frymaster, coming to the company from Toastmaster Corporation, where he had served as president from 1985 to 1987. Before that he had served as vice-president of operations for ITT-Blackburn and also in managerial positions with L.P. Nelson Corporation and GE Food Service Equipment Division. In

1990, he also became Welbilt's vice-president of international operations. Since Mosteller directed two other Welbilt subsidiaries—Varmixer and Dean—Frymaster enjoyed a close working relationship to two other manufacturers of commercial cooking equipment. Dean fabricated fryers at its facility in Gardena, California, while Varimixer, also located in Shreveport, manufactured commercial mixers, featuring more sizes than any other line. Dean fryers appealed to a different market segment than Frymaster's and used an entirely different Thermo-Tube heat-transfer rather than an open-pot design.

Throughout the 1980s, Frymaster continued to lead the industry in adapting to changes in technology. It refined its highly efficient infrared burners and fully-controlled programmable cooking, utilizing fryers that automatically adjusted the cooking time and temperature, filtered out the waste, and shut themselves down. These features justified their cost, which in 1987, for example, ranged from $1,600 to $5,500, depending on size and features. Importantly, the automated and computerized controls guaranteed uniformity in taste, an extremely important factor in sales to giant food chains.

1990s: Physical Expansion and Automation

In 1991, Frymaster began transforming its 170,000-square-foot manufacturing plant in Shreveport into a state-of-the-art facility. The company planned a system that could employ computer-assisted automation, utilizing bar codes and radio frequency data communications (RF/DC) to streamline its operation and track and validate business orders and inventories. It also began using CAD/CAM automation, cutting unit parts from sheet metal with laser precision and moving them to assembly or inventory storage locations on fully-automated vehicles. Bar code scanners and RF/DC terminals were introduced to keep track of both inventories and work-in-progress, speeding both the handling and shipping of buyers' orders.

In 1992, when it employed about 430 workers, Frymaster won the coveted "E Star" award given by the U.S. Department of Commerce for excellence in exporting. At that time, about one-third of the company's annual sales of over $50 million were made in foreign markets. It also registered with the International Standards Organization by meeting the five ISO 9000 standards for quality assurance accepted around the world, a virtual must for companies doing business in Europe.

Since 1992, the company has made additional modifications to improve its operation. For a brief time, company executives considered expanding into surrounding states or even Mexico, but giving a vote of confidence to the workers in the Shreveport area, decided to stay and grow in Louisiana. By the mid-1990s, Frymaster had enlarged it plant to 250,000 square feet and further refurbished its operation. In 1997, new tooling was also introduced. Until that year, Frymaster had used Mate Precision Tooling's standard 112 tools for its stamping operations, but its new, high-speed turret machines needed a better system. The company found that the old 112 tools were wearing too quickly, either getting dull too soon or failing altogether. For example, the 0.109″ round punch, used for nibbling corners in steel panels, had to be replaced after each run. The solution was to move to Mate Precision Marathon Tooling, which provided much more durable service and improved the quality of the machined parts. The new tools lasted an average of 15 times longer before requiring resharpening and greatly curtailed the need for the manual intervention of tool operators. In 1998 Frymaster again expanded, adding 150,000 square feet to its plant. It also began recruiting additional employees, boosting its workforce to about 650, with plans to eventually bring that figure to around 720.

Company Problems and Prospects

Throughout its history, Frymaster has led the field in many important innovations. It introduced the first high-efficiency fryer, the first fryer with a built-in, automated filtration system, and the first system to use computer-controlled frying. It experimented with a system that virtually eliminated the chance of human error or contamination, automatically taking food from a freezer, depositing it in a fully-automated fryer, removing it when done, and conveying it to the appropriate dumping stations. The company continued to pride itself on the high quality, energy-efficient, and space-saving design of its cookers. Its compact, small-footprint fryers were built to reduce labor and waste. However, responding to consumer trends towards healthier, low-fat foods, Frymaster was also experimenting with oven preparation alternatives to deep-frying. One possibility was oven baking, though there were serious limitations to the method. It both changed the taste of food and made thorough cooking very difficult for fast-food operations.

"We are working on solving these problems, as are many others," said Mosteller, in a February 1996 article in *Appliance Manufacturer*. He continued, "If fryers are going to become obsolete someday, then we want to be the ones who make it happen with our own products." Still, he remained confident that fryers would never be passé. They provided too many foods with a special flavor that no other method of preparation can duplicate. The ubiquitous french fry was a special case in point.

The company continued to push towards the completely automatic fried-food preparation system described above. A prototype of this automated system was introduced in 1994 at the National Restaurant Association Show, but the finished product still remained on the drawing board. However, the company recently introduced SinBaD, a single basket hopper that kept fries frozen and automatically dispensed them into the open-pot fryer one basket at a time. The dispenser saved time, eliminated waste, and reduced food handling and labor, making it particularly well suited to preparing fries during high-volume rush periods. This sort of improvement kept and promised to keep Frymaster on the leading edge of its industry.

Further Reading

Babyak, Richard J., "Frymaster Sizzles As Market Leader, *Appliance Manufacturer,* February 1966, pp. W20–W24.
"Frymaster Corp.," *Journal of Commerce and Commercial,* March 5, 1993, p. 4A.
"Frymaster Receives ISO 9000 Registration," *Nation's Restaurant News,* January 4, 1993, p. 46.
Remich, Norman C., Jr., "Tool Has 15 Lives," *Appliance Manufacturer,* July 1997, pp. 41–44.

Ringer, Richard, "Welbilt Sets Merger Agreement," *New York Times,* December 21, 1994, p. D4.

"Stamping Out a French-Fry Maker," *Manufacturing Engineering,* February 1997, pp. 78–81.

"Strahan to Rep Frymaster, Dean and Bevies," *Nation's Restaurant News,* October 19, 1998, p. 80.

Welsh, Jonathan, "Welbilt to Be Acquired by Berisford in Transaction Valued at $312.7 Million," *Wall Street Journal* (Eastern Edition), December 21, 1994, p. A6.

"When It's Hot, It Sizzles," *Automatic I.D. News,* September 1996, pp. 18, 41.

—John W. Fiero

Garden Ridge Corporation

19411 Atrium Place, Suite 170
Houston, Texas 77084
U.S.A.
(281) 579-7901
Fax: (281) 578-0999

Public Company
Incorporated: 1979 as Garden Ridge Pottery
Employees: 3,125
Sales: $304.7 million (1998)
Stock Exchanges: NASDAQ
Ticker Symbol: GRDG
SICs: 5331 Variety Stores

Fast becoming a national retailer, Garden Ridge Corporation operates a chain of more than 25 stores scattered throughout the southern and southeastern United States. Strictly a Texas-based retailer until 1995, Garden Ridge accelerated its expansion after a May 1995 conversion to public ownership. Management during the late 1990s projected that the company would operate on a national basis and generate sales in excess of $1 billion by the early 21st century. The impetus for the chain's rapid expansion during the latter half of the 1990s stemmed from a successful overhaul of the company's strategy and retail concept during the early 1990s. Spearheaded by the company's chairman and chief executive officer, Armand Shapiro, the changes focused on revamping and organizing the stores' floor plan and design. Merchandise, 70 percent of which was private label, was categorized into ten departments: home accents; silk and dried flowers; pottery; crafts; housewares; candles and scents; baskets; party supplies; pictures and frames; and holiday decorations. Roughly 25 percent of the company's total revenues were derived from silk and dried flower sales. The typical Garden Ridge store measured 125,000 square feet.

Origins

Garden Ridge was founded by a Texas businessman named Eric White, who opened his first store in San Antonio in 1979.

Over the course of the next decade, White opened two more of his "Garden Ridge Pottery" stores, establishing each in his home state of Texas. By 1988 White was ready to retire, and he sold his company to a group of investors, marking the end of a relatively serene first decade of business for the three-store chain. Under new ownership, however, Garden Ridge experienced the disruptive and damaging problems commonly endured by start-up companies, as the White era of control proved to be the calm before the storm. Garden Ridge's new managers were woefully inept, quickly steering the modestly sized business toward financial ruin. The investors were shackled by heavy debt incurred from purchasing the company from White, they implemented ill-conceived changes in the chain's merchandising strategy, and they failed miserably in an effort to expand. In a matter of months, Garden Ridge was headed toward bankruptcy, prompting the group of investors to put the company up for sale. In 1990 Garden Ridge was sold to a new management team that included two individuals who would be responsible for mounting the company's comeback; their names were Armand Shapiro and Jack Lewis.

Shapiro arrived at Garden Ridge in February 1990, just after the company reported its latest annual financial totals. The three stores had generated $44 million in sales and lost $2.9 million, providing tangible evidence that sweeping changes needed to be made. Shapiro graduated with a degree in architecture and engineering from New York's Rensselaer Polytechnic Institute, gaining an academic footing that, in his words, "was great training on how to think, analyze, and solve problems . . . a great background for retail." In the early 1980s he joined a computer retail chain based in Houston named Computer-Craft, which he successfully developed into a viable concept before engineering its expansion into a six-state chain as the company's president. Faced with the challenge of transforming Garden Ridge into a viable concept, Shapiro enlisted the help of another ComputerCraft executive, Jack Lewis. Lewis had spent 25 years working for Sears, Roebuck & Co., dividing his efforts between home fashion buying and marketing and national advertising. In 1989 he was appointed vice-president of ComputerCraft, one year after Shapiro had left ComputerCraft to join a company called Modern Furniture Rentals Inc. as chief operating officer. In 1990 the pair joined forces and began transforming Garden Ridge into a profitable retail chain.

What Shapiro and Lewis had to work with and correct were massive, cluttered stores that confused customers and consequently lost money. The Garden Ridge units were 250,000-square-foot giants stocked with merchandise with diversity that went one step beyond what could be described as eclectic. To most, Garden Ridge's merchandise was an unfathomable heap. Inside, customers were confronted with disparate merchandise categories that included automotive parts, jewelry, pet supplies, lawn equipment, and toys, all confusingly organized in small, drab rooms. The store layout and merchandising strategy was perplexing, yet surprisingly the Garden Ridge name had cultivated considerable customer loyalty. Customers demonstrated an expectant patience that the store's concept could somehow be clarified. Said Shapiro: "Jack [Lewis] and I looked at the store and realized customers had a love affair with Garden Ridge. But they were desperately trying to hang on as customers, and they were begging that we listen to them." The typical Garden Ridge customer was a female between 18 and 54 years old who spent an average of three hours in the stores on a single visit. She was enthusiastic about the merchandise, receptive to the concept—however murky it was—but in the end frustrated and confused.

Strategic Changes in the Early 1990s

Shapiro and Lewis began to implement changes, and as they did so, their individual talents came to the fore. Lewis gained the reputation as the "creative" half of the duo, and Shapiro earned the moniker "Numbers Guy," although both Lewis and Shapiro disapproved of the characterizations. First, to reduce operating costs, the pair significantly reduced the size of the prototype Garden Ridge, cutting the space down to between 125,000 square feet and 140,000 square feet. Merchandise was focused on home décor items, while pet supplies, toys, jewelry, lawn equipment, and much of the chain's former diversity disappeared. Advertising spending was increased, as was the buying staff, who traveled overseas to purchase some of the chain's more exotic, seasonal merchandise. Meanwhile, Lewis, who was responsible for the design of the stores, made some of the most profound changes distinguishing the Garden Ridge of the late 1980s and the Garden Ridge of the 1990s. The goal was to make shopping simpler, to make the warehouse-style stores shopper friendly for the company's core customer. "Eighty-five percent of our shoppers are women," Lewis explained, "and

we try to appeal to them with everything from colors to fragrances and bright lights." Toward this end, Lewis redesigned the stores' interiors, using boldly designed graphics, color accents, and a color-coded system for specialty areas, which were identified further by seven-and-a-half-foot, sculpted foam and masonite signs. Navigation throughout the stores was made far easier as a result, particularly if the customer followed the 26-foot-wide, red "racetrack" on the floor, which directed the customer past seasonal and promotional products. The emphasis on seasonal merchandise, rotated every three to four weeks, was a change as well, intended to keep customers interested and lure them back for return visits. Another change—one of great importance to Lewis and Shapiro—was an emphasis on customer service. The company conducted monthly focus groups, asking shoppers what they wanted, and employees underwent training to help customers with decorating ideas.

After the changes were made, the first prototype Garden Ridge opened in Houston in 1992. Inside, under exposed ceiling structures and bright lights, the store's merchandise was arranged according to Lewis's color-coded scheme. Merchandise was organized into ten departments, the most prominent of which was the collection of Garden Ridge silk and florals. Artificial flowers and silk florals occupied roughly 25,000 square feet of the new Garden Ridge store, accounting for a quarter of the revenue generated by the company. The other merchandise categories were as follows: home accents; pottery; crafts; housewares; candles and scents; baskets; party supplies; pictures and frames; and holiday decorations. Of all the merchandise, which comprised more than 80,000 separate items, 20 percent was private label, a percentage that would increase during the middle and late 1990s. As the new store concept was undergoing its first test, Lewis and Shapiro began developing their own Garden Ridge label, a move designed to increase the name recognition of the stores. Lewis explained: "Most of our vendors are importers or small vendors that don't have high brand recognition. That's why we're trying to build up an identity with the Garden Ridge label. I've never seen a customer yet that asks for a branded flower or basket or pot."

1995 Public Offering Spurs Expansion

After the Houston prototype store, Shapiro and Lewis opened two more Garden Ridge units during the next two years, establishing both in Texas. The performance of these new units served as a test of the new concept's viability, determining whether or not customers would embrace the changes made by Shapiro and Lewis. The financial totals recorded at the end of Garden Ridge's experimental expansion answered in the affirmative. At the end of 1994 the six-store chain collected $64 million in sales and had transformed from a money-loser into a profit-maker, posting $4.6 million in net income. With a proven formula for success, Shapiro and Lewis were confident that the Garden Ridge concept they created was ready for expansion. To finance the chain's expansion, they converted to public ownership in a May 1995 initial public offering (IPO), raising $39.6 million in proceeds. With the cash obtained from the IPO, all long-term debt was paid off, with $11 million left over to fund expansion. Although Shapiro and Lewis continued to fine-tune Garden Ridge's retail strategy, the essence of the blueprint for expansion was established by the 1995 IPO. In the years ahead the company extended its geographic presence beyond the borders of its home state of Texas and began to assume the stature of a national retailer.

Garden Ridge took its first step outside Texas before the end of 1995, when a store was opened in Louisville, Kentucky. The company opened four Garden Ridge units in 1995, lifting sales for the year above the $100 million mark, the first of several prodigious leaps in the company's revenue total. *Chain Store Executive* magazine, an industry publication, took notice of the startling success, selecting Garden Ridge as "Home Center Retail Store of the Year" for 1995. A year later, after new store openings extended Garden Ridge's presence into Oklahoma, Tennessee, North Carolina, and Florida, Ernst & Young selected Shapiro as "Entrepreneur of the Year." Amid the accolades, Garden Ridge swelled in size, with new store openings lifting sales to $148.1 million at the end of 1996. In 1997, seven new stores were opened, which combined with a ten percent increase in sales at existing stores, increased revenues 52.1 percent above 1996's total, to $225.3 million. By this point, after a half-decade of unbridled growth and unchecked success, Shapiro and Lewis envisioned the development of a chain five times larger than the company's size in 1997. They foresaw Garden Ridge as a 100-unit chain capable of generating sales in excess of $1 billion. With growth occurring at an approximate annual rate of 30 percent, few outside observers disputed the feasibility of the pair's ambitious plans. "We see no limitation in terms of merchandise assortment to create a national chain," Lewis said. "Most of our merchandise is drop-shipped, so we're not dependent on a central distribution point, so it gives us flexibility in locating stores in various geographic areas."

To drive their bid toward their lofty goal, Lewis and Shapiro had a slightly altered prototype as their vehicle for expansion. One of the new stores opened in 1997 was a unit in Lewisville, Texas, a store that was the model for the future. As the chain expanded beyond its ten-state operating territory, future units were expected to be smaller, closer to the 100,000-square-foot range. Inside the stores, new features had proven to be successful in the late 1990s and were expected to be included in future units. Plants and snack bars had made their debut, and the emphasis on customer service had produced in-store arts and crafts classes and cooking lessons. Further, great strides had been achieved in the company's private label program. By the end of 1997 between 60 percent and 70 percent of the company's merchandise was private label, bearing what was regarded by a substantial number of customers as the trusted Garden Ridge label.

In 1998 Garden Ridge began working toward its goal of opening six stores during the year, but the year's most dramatic news came from company headquarters, not from the advancing front line of the chain's expansion. In October 1998, Lewis resigned from his posts as president and chief operating officer, explaining that he was departing to "pursue other interests." Garden Ridge's chief financial officer shed more light on the reasons behind Lewis's departure, revealing more than Lewis's terse farewell. "We expect to generate nearly $400 million in sales this year," she said, "and in the next few years we project a billion in sales. Lewis's resignation was mutual agreement

between Lewis, Shapiro, and the board of directors. Different leadership skills are needed to run a larger entity, and we're looking for a seasoned retail veteran to come in as president." Shapiro's comment on the matter corroborated the chief financial officer's statement. "Jack and I," he said, "reached the agreement that this was a good time for him to strike out and do new things."

In the wake of Lewis's departure, Shapiro assumed the responsibilities of president in addition to his duties as chairman and chief executive officer. As the end of 1998 approached, an executive search firm was looking for a permanent replacement for Lewis's presidential post. Meanwhile, the company pushed forward with its plans to develop into a national retailer. Shapiro planned to open seven or eight stores in 1999 and ten or 11 stores in 2000, aiming to grow by 25 percent to 30 percent annually until the company reached the hotly pursued goal of $1 billion in sales. Considering that the company had yet to reach the halfway mark by the end of the 1990s, the 21st century promised to see a proliferation of new Garden Ridge stores opening across the country.

Principal Subsidiaries

Garden Ridge Management, Inc.; Garden Ridge Investment, Inc.; Garden Ridge Finance Corporation; Garden Ridge, L.P.

Further Reading

"Armand Shapiro," *Chain Stores Age Executive with Shopping Center Age,* December 1996, p. 89.

Duff, Mike, "Garden Ridge: The Serious Business of Casual," *Discount Store News,* March 23, 1998, p. H40.

Elder, Laura, "Flower Power," *Houston Business Journal,* May 8, 1998, p. 16A.

Erlick, June Carolyn, "Mega Minded," *HFN: The Weekly Newspaper for the Home Furnishing Network,* August 14, 1995, p. 1.

"Garden Ridge Announces Third Quarter Results," *PR Newswire,* November 19, 1998, p. 6458.

"Garden Ridge President Exits," *HFN: The Weekly Newspaper for the Home Furnishing Network,* October 5, 1998, p. 8.

"Goin' South," *HFN: The Weekly Newspaper for the Home Furnishing Network,* March 25, 1996, p. 8.

Hassell, Greg, "President of Houston-Based Garden Ridge Steps Down," *Knight-Ridder/Tribune Business News,* September 25, 1998, p. 3.

Mathis, Karen Brune, "Garden Ridge To Open First Florida Store Next March," *Knight-Ridder/Tribune Business News,* September 5, 1995, p. 91.

Meyer, Nancy, "Garden Ridge: Trend-Right Home Décor at Sharp Prices," *HFN: The Weekly Newspaper for the Home Furnishing Network,* June 1, 1998, p. 29.

Rutherford, Dan, "Garden Ridge To Open Housewares Store in Tulsa," *Knight-Ridder/Tribune Business News,* November 22, 1995, p. 11.

Silberg, Lurie, "Garden Ridge Blooms by Knowing Its Customer," *HFN: The Weekly Newspaper for the Home Furnishing Network,* June 1, 1998, p. 8.

Wilensky, Dawn, "Garden Ridge Offers 'Home' Style Feast for Senses," *Discount Store News,* July 17, 1995, p. 27.

—Jeffrey L. Covell

Gateway, Inc.

610 Gateway Drive
North Sioux City, South Dakota 57049
U.S.A.
(605) 232-2000
(800) 846-2000
Fax: (605) 232-2023
Web Site: http://www.gateway.com

Public Company
Incorporated: 1985 as TIPC Network
Employees: 13,300
Sales: $6.29 billion (1997)
Stock Exchanges: New York
Ticker Symbol: GTW
SICs: 3571 Electronic Computers; 5961 Catalogue and
Mail Order Houses

Gateway, Inc., is the leading American seller of personal computers by mail. Started in the mid-1980s in a small Iowa town, the company grew by keeping its own costs at a rock-bottom level and undercutting its competitors on price. As its sales skyrocketed in the early 1990s, Gateway began to experience growing pains, as some customers complained about low quality and poor service. The company moved to address these concerns while attempting to expand its market to include corporate buyers and European customers. Other efforts at diversification included introduction of a combination widescreen TV and PC, and creating an Internet access service exclusively for Gateway owners.

Mid-1980s Beginnings

Gateway was founded in 1985 by Ted Waitt, who had attended two different colleges before returning to his family's cattle farm in Sioux City, Iowa. After spending nine months working at a computer store in Des Moines, Waitt felt that he had learned enough about the business of selling computers to allow him to carve out his own market niche.

Waitt noticed that at the time computers tended to be either inexpensive models with extremely limited capabilities or top-of-the-line models with capabilities that few people would ever need. He decided that a middle path made more sense and devised a "value equation," which stipulated that extra technology should not be added to a computer unless it provided extra value to a customer.

In addition, Waitt observed in his retail job that computers could be sold over the phone by an educated salesperson. This led to the idea that overhead could be virtually eliminated. Because he had no money to invest in his new business, Waitt took over some empty space in a farmhouse that his father's shrinking cattle brokerage business had left empty, and moved in upstairs. Joining him in the business was Mike Hammond, the salesman who had trained him at his computer store job.

In September 1985, the two started up a mail order business that they called the TIPC Network. Waitt was 22 years old. Placing advertisements in computer magazines, TIPC sold peripheral hardware and software to people who owned Texas Instrument computers. Because these computers did not conform to the IBM-compatible standard, some considered them obsolete, and many computer stores did not offer additional features for the machines once they had been sold.

Waitt charged each of his customers a $20 membership fee, which gave him start-up capital. Because his costs were so low, he and Hammond could undercut competitors' prices, and within four months, the fledgling business had racked up $100,000 in sales. Six months after they started, Waitt's brother, Norman Waitt, Jr., bought half of the company and began to offer financial advice.

Waitt's goal in starting the company had not been to sell computer accessories, but to sell computers themselves. In 1986 TIPC Network experimented with assembling its own computers, and even sold them to local customers. Nevertheless, these made only a small contribution to the company's first-year revenues of nearly $1 million.

In mid-1987, however, TIPC was given an opportunity to break into the computer field when Texas Instruments inaugu-

Company Perspectives:

Vision: *To be the leading marketer of personal computer products in the world.* Values: *Respect, caring, teamwork, common sense, aggressiveness, honesty, efficiency and fun.* Mission: *To profitably grow our business faster than the competition by better understanding and serving the desires of our customers and aggressively marketing the highest value directly to our chosen markets.*

rated a program to let its buyers trade in their old machines for new, IBM-compatible units at a price of $3,500. Waitt and his partners decided that they could offer a similar IBM-compatible machine, put together from parts offered by other mail order dealers, for less than half as much. Employing Waitt's value equation, and his sense of what customers would be willing to pay for, the company created a machine with two floppy disk drives of different sizes, a color monitor, a large memory, and a keyboard with function keys, and a cursor keypad for $1,995. TIPC's competitors offered far fewer features for a similar price.

With the introduction of this computer, TIPC's sales took off. In 1987 the company had revenues of $1.5 million. In the following year, TIPC changed its named to Gateway 2000, and the company's sales exploded, hitting $12 million.

In expanding its product line beyond its initial Texas Instrument computer trade-in offer, Gateway eschewed research and development and a staff of designers. Instead, the company relied on Waitt's own sense of what customers would want. "We didn't do a whole lot of market research on it," Waitt told *Inc.* magazine. "A lot of it was instinctive." Hammond elaborated further: "The first question would always be, 'would I buy it'," he told *Inc.* "Everyone wants smaller, faster, cheaper, so it's a fairly educated guess."

Gateway's clientele of sophisticated users did not make high demands for service or back-up support and shopped on the basis of price. Accordingly, despite its rapidly increasing sales, Gateway was not forced to increase its overhead, and the company was able to keep its prices low. With its growth in sales, the company moved from the Waitt family farmhouse to a 5,000-square-foot space in Sioux City's 100-year-old Livestock Exchange building, paying $350 a month in rent. The cow manure was cleaned from the building and Gateway's new offices were furnished with used furniture. Because of Gateway's rural Midwestern location, Waitt discovered that he could pay his employees $5.50 an hour and experience virtually no turnover. In 1988 the company began to supplement these wages with monthly cash bonuses based on profits.

Gateway's advertising, too, was cut-rate, although effective. Eschewing the services of a professional advertising agency, the company's founders devised their own promotions. Gateway strove to present an image of reliability and trustworthiness to counteract customer fears that their low-priced products were being supplied by a fly-by-night outfit. In the company's first full-page ad, run in computer magazines in 1988, Gateway displayed a picture of Waitt's father's cattle herd, with the Sioux City water tower looming in the background. Playing on the novelty of the company's midwestern location, the ad asked, "computers from Iowa?" In this way, Gateway was able to remind customers that their products were manufactured in the United States. In addition, the ad stood out in a magazine filled with pictures of computers.

1990: Gateway Moves to South Dakota

Spurred by these promotional efforts, which consumed only 2.5 percent of company revenues, Gateway sales continued their meteoric rise, reaching $70.6 million in 1989. By that time, Gateway had expanded beyond the confines of its second office, and the company moved to South Dakota in January 1990. This location was selected in part because South Dakota collected no income taxes.

In 1990 Waitt also hired an advertising manager, a local photographer, and a designer, and produced a series of eye-catching and humorous new Gateway ads that began appearing in computer magazines every few months to keep up momentum in the fast-changing industry. Rather than hiring models, the ads frequently featured company employees, particularly Waitt and his brother. An ad released in July 1990 showed Waitt dressed as an 1890s card shark, flashing a royal flush. Subsequent ads featured other company employees. One showed Gateway staffers standing in a pasture under the slogan, "we're out standing in our field." In a nod to its history, and in an effort to further play up its rural roots, Gateway adopted a cow as its mascot. The company began to ship all its products in white boxes with black spots that looked like the markings on a Holstein. This black-and-white design also kept printing costs low.

By the end of 1990, Gateway's revenues had nearly quadrupled from the previous year, to $275 million. In just five years, the company had grown an impressive 26,469 percent. This extremely rapid expansion brought problems of its own, and Gateway was forced to confront some of the consequences of its new size. "The biggest challenge for us right now," Waitt told *Inc.* in 1991, "is figuring out how to add the necessary bureaucracy without becoming slow moving." To expand the company's executive pool, Gateway recruited six vice-presidents from large computer makers and a public accounting firm to help mastermind the company's future growth. In addition, Gateway set up a number of new administrative branches. The company established a 20-member group to investigate new technology, and set up a "Road Map Group" to evaluate choices. Waitt began meeting with ten top assistants, known as the Action Group, every two weeks. Gateway hired a media buyer to systematize its advertising and established a five-member marketing department, which evaluated customer satisfaction by conducting telephone interviews.

To increase productivity in its manufacturing operations, Gateway built a new 44,000-square-foot building down the road from its headquarters in the summer of 1991. In constructing this facility, Gateway stuck to its low-cost, no frills philosophy, to create "the largest metal building I've ever seen," as Waitt told *Marketing Computers.* "It's a big ugly building, but it's very functional," he added. Inside this structure, Gateway reorganized its computer-assembly workers into separate teams. This change was expected to increase output by 30 percent.

Gateway also began an effort in 1991 to expand into lucrative corporate accounts. In the fall of 1991, the company began to run ads that showed a group of conservative executives huddled around a Gateway computer, with the slogan, "because we've stood the test of time."

To further shore up its image as a legitimate computer dealer, Gateway began to divulge some quarterly financial results, in the form of press releases. The company also began to offer the more extensive customer service that corporate clients required, including training programs and troubleshooting procedures. By the end of 1991, Gateway's sales had reached $626 million, and the company was named the fastest-growing private company in America by *Inc.* magazine.

Gateway doubled the pace of its advertising schedule in the following year, releasing new promotions every month. Created by a nine-member in-house team, the ads ran in nine different computer industry magazines, two of which were published weekly. The faster pace was designed to keep up with the company's release of new products and changes in price for old ones.

With the vast increase in the volume of products it sold, Gateway had fallen somewhat behind in technological innovation. "We've been playing catch-up for the last two years," Waitt told *Marketing Computers* in 1992. "We're still not anywhere near where we want to be or need to be, but we're improving our processes continuously and we're learning from our mistakes." As part of its program to regain the lead in technology, Gateway released a notebook computer, called the HandBook, which weighed 2.7 pounds, in 1992. Rather than trying to manufacture this new technology itself, Gateway had the HandBook made by another company.

Gateway also moved to diversify its marketing strategy. Rather than assuming that all customers had the same needs— good value for a good price—the company set out to target the special needs of different segments of the market. "You won't see us introducing separate product lines, but you will see us doing separate sales and marketing efforts and a different level of customization," Waitt told *Marketing Computers.*

By the end of 1992, Gateway's sales had reached $1.1 billion, an increase of 76 percent over the previous year. At a time when other computer makers were reporting losses, Gateway's earnings reached $1.1 million, as the company took the lead in the mail order computer business.

Gateway's 1,500 employees were supplemented by 200 new hires at the end of 1992. These new workers were assigned to bolster Gateway's sales and support staff in hopes of alleviating some of the company's growing pains. The push to augment Gateway's staff came as the company discovered that finding and training a large number of technical support and computer assembly workers in the middle of South Dakota was not an easy task.

Growing Pains in the Early 1990s

Starting in late 1992, Gateway found itself deluged by a wide variety of customer complaints, alleging problems ranging from delays in delivery to improperly constructed computers. Gateway buyers complained that the company's quality control had fallen apart, and that its efforts to address complaints were inadequate. The company blamed the shortcomings on extremely high demand for its products in the final quarter of 1992, which made it impossible for all orders to be filled.

Although Gateway's revenues for the first three months of 1993 remained strong, as the company moved to clear its back orders, during the second quarter the company reported its first drop in revenues. The slowdown was attributed to the company's quality control problems, and also to its aging merchandise, which needed to be updated with new products. Gateway responded with a color notebook computer and a sub-notebook based on a new computer chip, which had previously been in limited distribution.

In the fall of 1993, Gateway's competitors began an effort to capitalize on its problems: the Dell Computer Corporation started an ad campaign boasting "performance that blows the gates off Gateway." In addition, the company faced growing competition in the mail order field from industry giants such as IBM. To protect Gateway's market share, and to insure future growth, the company made plans to move more aggressively into the corporate market, and to enter foreign markets.

To increase the company's corporate sales beyond their 1992 level of 40 percent, Gateway formed a major accounts team, headed by a former IBM employee. The company's technical support staff was doubled to more than 400, and its on-line technicians were doubled to 14, in order to better service corporate clients. Late in 1993, Gateway inaugurated a separate phone line to provide support services to companies, in which each company was assigned its own personal service representative.

During this time, Gateway also opened its campaign to move into the European market. Previously, foreign sales had accounted for just three percent of the company's revenues. In early October, Gateway opened a headquarters in Dublin, Ireland, with sales, marketing, support, and manufacturing facilities. From this base, the company began to sell mail-order computers in Britain. In the future, the company intended to branch out into France and Germany. However, this plan was complicated by well-established competitors and by the need to customize both machines and marketing programs for each country.

Both Gateway's corporate sales initiative and its expansion into Europe brought with them higher costs than the company had experienced in its South Dakota sales and marketing operations. In an effort to offset the impact of those expenses, Gateway surprised Wall Street by unexpectedly announcing its intention to sell stock to the public in October 1993.

In December 1993, Gateway went public, raising $150 million through the sale of 10.9 million shares, which accounted for 15 percent of the company. Waitt and his brother retained the other 85 percent of Gateway. With this infusion of capital, the company planned to finance current operations, as well as its European push, and also to expand its range of products to include printers, networking products, fax modems, and software. In addition, Gateway announced that it would consider the acquisition of other companies in its field.

In the spring of 1994 Gateway moved to further enhance its corporate marketing effort. The company announced a multifaceted overhaul of its support operations to placate disgruntled customers and win new ones. This program involved a two-year extension of Gateway's one-year warranty, 24-hour-a-day phone lines for technical support, and one-day delivery for replacement parts. In May 1994, the company announced that it would continue to provide technical support free of charge, despite the fact that several of its competitors had begun to charge for this service.

In 1995, Gateway continued to grow, announcing plans to build an $18 million manufacturing plant in Hampton, Virginia, and acquiring 80 percent of an Australian computer maker, Osborne Computer Corp. Revenues for the year were up again, to $3.7 billion, an increase of $1 billion over 1994. 1995 also saw a manufacturing plant opened in Malaysia to serve Far Eastern markets and establishment of the company's Web Site at http://www.gateway.com.

New Marketing Initiatives in the Late 1990s

Early in 1996 the company tried its hand at a new product, the Destination 2000, a combination PC and wide-screen TV. It was designed to be used as a home entertainment center that could also be linked to the Internet. Initial sales were slow, but the company had purposely invested a minimal amount in research and development. After a few months of barely perceptible sales, Gateway announced plans to offer Destinations through such retail outlets as Nobody Beats the Wiz and CompUSA. The price was also dropped by over 20 percent. During this year a small number of Gateway Country Stores were also opened in suburban locations. These stocked no merchandise, but were intended mainly to offer first-hand contact with the company's products. Computers were still ordered over the telephone and shipped directly to the customer. Within the next two years over 140 Country Stores were opened.

With Gateway's success came increased interest from other companies bent on acquisition. In early 1997 a $7 billion purchase offer from Compaq was nearly finalized before being rejected by CEO Waitt. In May, the company switched its stock listing from the NASDAQ to the New York Stock Exchange. A month later Gateway purchased Advanced Logic Research, Inc., a producer of server computers for business applications. This move was part of a newly intensified effort by the company to seek a larger share of the business computer market, as penetration of home PCs reached near-saturation levels. Later in the year, the company announced further measures to increase corporate sales, including removing the ubiquitous cows from its advertising in an attempt to refine its image. Gateway also formed a new subsidiary, Gateway Major Accounts, which focused on sales to business. 1997 was another record year, with revenues of $6.29 billion and profits of over $1 billion.

In early 1998, the company announced that it was dropping the "2000" from its name and would be moving some offices to San Diego. The latter move was partly to be closer to the mainstream of the business world, as well as because CEO Waitt wanted to live in California. Gateway was also attempting to get a piece of the Internet pie, launching a new Internet connectivity service, http://www.gateway.net, which was made exclusively available to its customers, at prices comparable to America Online and other major services. In June 1998 the company also began to install Netscape Navigator software on its machines along with Microsoft Internet Explorer, which was being bundled with Microsoft's Windows 98. Gateway's Internet service was slow getting off the ground, with only 200,000 subscribers by the beginning of 1999. After a number of problems with the Internet service provider it had chosen, Gateway switched to MCI Worldcom.

As it neared the end of the 1990s, Gateway had come a long way from its humble beginnings. Despite the relatively indifferent responses to its Destination and http://www.gateway.net initiatives, the company's direct sales of PCs were still strong, and it was increasingly targeting the business market, with hopes that it would finally succeed in pulling significant sales away from rival Dell.

Principal Subsidiaries

Gateway Europe; Gateway Country Stores, Inc.; Gateway Major Accounts, Inc.; Advanced Logic Research, Inc.; Osborne Gateway 2000 Pty. (Australia; 80%).

Further Reading

Beatty, Sally, and Evan Ramstead, "Gateway 2000 Plans Shorter Name, Longer Client Talks and No Cows," *The Wall Street Journal,* April 28, 1998, p. B6.

Britt, Russ, "Computers & Technology Going Corporate: Gateway Changes Spots," *Investor's Business Daily,* October 30, 1997, p. A1.

Hyatt, Joshua, "Betting the Farm," *Inc.,* December, 1991.

Impoco, Jim, "Why Gateway Isn't Cowed by the Computer Price Wars," *U.S. News and World Report,* July 26, 1993.

Kasler, Dale, "Will TV-Like Computer Propel Gateway into the Big League?," *Gannett News Service,* June 13, 1996.

Krause, Reinhardt, "The New America: Gateway 2000 Adding 'Nuances' to Direct-Selling Strategy," *Investor's Business Daily,* May 29, 1996, p. A4.

McWilliams, Gary, "Gateway Inc. Sues to End Contract With Web America," *Wall Street Journal,* January 20, 1999, p. B6.

Ridgeway, Michael, "Gateway Executives Going Big City," *Gannett News Service,* August 28, 1998.

Smith, Dawn, "Home on the Range," *Marketing Computers,* December 1992.

Therrien, Lois, "Why Gateway Is Racing to Answer on the First Ring," *Business Week,* September 13, 1993.

Turner, Nick, "Gateway's Unusual Move: When Direct Meets Retail," *Investor's Business Daily,* September 29, 1998, p. A10.

Zimmerman, Michael R., "Gateway Plots New Corporate Program," *PC Week,* April 25, 1994.

——, "Gateway Seizes Moment," *PC Week,* November 1, 1993.

—Elizabeth Rourke
—updated by Frank Uhle

**Leading Technologies.
Individual Solutions.**

GEA AG

Dorstener Strasse 484
D-44809 Bochum
Germany
(49) (234) 980-0
Fax: (49) (234) 980-1087
Web site: http://www.gea-ag.com

Public Company
Incorporated: 1920 as Gesellschaft für Entstaubungs-
   Anlagen mbH
Employees: 16,747
Sales: DM 4.71 billion (1997)
Stock Exchanges: Frankfurt
SICs: 3443 Fabricated Plate Work (Boiler Shops); 3564
   Industrial and Commercial Fans and Blowers and Air
   Purification Equipment; 3565 Packaging Machinery;
   3567 Industrial Process Furnaces and Ovens; 3569
   General Industrial Machinery and Equipment, Not
   Elsewhere Classified; 3585 Air-Conditioning and
   Warm Air Heating Equipment and Commercial; 3594
   Fluid Power Pumps and Motors; 3629 Electrical
   Industrial Apparatus, Not Elsewhere Classified; 3823
   Industrial Instruments for Measurement, Display, and
   Control; 8711 Engineering Services

GEA AG is one of the world's leading suppliers for food and process engineering, and thermal engineering technology. The global group, headquartered in Germany, is active in more than 50 countries. GEA supplies proprietary engineered products and systems in the fields of process technology, thermal and energy technology, air treatment, and dairy farm systems. The GEA group's 150 operating companies generated DM 4.7 billion in sales in 1997: about one-fifth of it in Germany, two-fifths in other European countries, one-fifth in both Asia and the Americas, and about three percent in Africa. More than half of the group's 16,700 employees work outside of Germany. The group serves primarily companies in the food and beverage, chemical, pharmaceutical, cosmetics, petrochemical, and utility industries. The main subsidiaries of the GEA group are Grasso's Koninklijke Machinefabriken (Netherlands), Tuchenhagen GmbH (Germany), Niro Holding A/S (Denmark), and Westfalia Separator AG (Germany).

GEA's Thermal Technology Division develops and produces systems for heat rejection and exchange such as wet and wet/dry cooling towers; heat recovery and energy conservation systems; heat exchangers; waste heat boilers; and equipment for nuclear power stations. The Energy Technology Division offers air-cooled condensers for power stations and waste-to-energy facilities; air-cooled process heat exchangers and re-cooling systems; dry cooling towers; and oil tank farms. Main products of the Air Treatment Division are central and decentralized air-conditioning equipment; air-unit heaters; clean-room systems; and air filters. The Refrigeration Division offers reciprocating and screw-type compressors and compressor units; refrigeration engineering services; evaporators and condensers; chillers for air-conditioning systems; ice machines and freezers; and valves and other fittings for refrigeration engineering. The Liquid Processing Division's product range includes complete process lines for liquid and food processing; automated process control systems; heaters; degassing, carbonation, and nitrogenation plants; mixing and dosing systems; plate-type and tube-bundle heat exchangers; ultra-high temperature plants; cleaning-in-place (CIP) and sterilization-in-place (SIP) systems; valves, in-line instrumentation and pipework components; aseptic process systems; and form, fill, and seal machines. The Powder Technology Division's main products are industrial dryers; agglomerators, granulators, coaters, and pelletizers for powder processing; and powder bagging and packaging systems. Specialty Products include evaporators and heat exchangers; jet pumps and vacuum systems; keg cleaning and filling systems; crystallizers, homogenizers and other equipment. The Mechanical Separation Division sells separators and decanters (centrifuges), process lines for centrifugal separation, and butter churns. The product range of the Dairy Farm Systems Division includes vacuum equipment for milking systems, milking parlors and other milking equipment; milk cooling and heat recovery systems; cleaning equipment; herd management and disinfecting systems; and animal care products.

Company Perspectives:

All group companies focus on their customers and their specific needs. GEA staff are capable of listening to their customers and are their partners at the regional, international and global levels. Our employees are a key to our success. Their knowledge, their abilities and their commitment give us our competitive strength. They chart out our course to future success.

The 1920s: From Air Cleaning to Air Cooling

GEA traces its history to the formation of The Gesellschaft für Entstaubungs-Anlagen mbH, a limited liability corporation for dust removal equipment. This company was founded on February 2, 1920 in Bochum in the heart of the Ruhr, at the time one of Germany's most important industrial centers, where coal mining and steel production were the dominant industries.

The company's founder was Otto Happel, an entrepreneur gifted with both technical and commercial insight. The first company he worked for after he completed his commercial training was Balcke, a family-owned mechanical engineering firm in Bochum, another town in the Ruhrgebiet. One of his jobs was to design filters to clean the cooling air used in electricity generators and motors. The bag filters common at that time didn't function very well nor did they generate good profits. However, Otto Happel believed that there was a market for such filters and that he would be able to design better and more profitable ones. In 1919, Balcke agreed to help him establish his own business, which Happel started one year later in a small workshop in Bochum.

During the next two years, the company's first new product—a closed-circuit air cooling system that used air circulating in a metal tube built around the electrical engine—was developed for large electrical machinery. While this technology was already used widely in the United States, England, and France, it was unknown at that time in Germany. Happel pioneered this technology in collaboration with Professor Ludwig Prandtl, director of the Aerodynamic Research Institute in Göttingen, and together they invented a new air-cooling device: the elliptical finned tube.

In 1925, Otto Happel acquired the Metallwerk Westfalia GmbH in Bochum, a company that had made equipment for him earlier. All production was moved to the site of the new acquisition, and the company's name was changed to GEA Luftkühlergesellschaft, Bochum. The company rapidly built a reputation, and in the following years different kinds of air coolers were developed based on the elliptical finned tube: for transformers, rectifiers, compressors, diesel and steam locomotives. Other new products included air heaters for heating systems and air coolers for air conditioning systems. In 1928, a new large factory and a laboratory for thermodynamic and aerodynamic tests were built on a property in Wanne-Eickel near Bochum that was large enough for further growth.

In 1929, the successful, medium-sized enterprise was hit hard by the Great Depression. During the next three years, sales dropped by more than two-thirds, and many workers either lost their jobs or were cut back to part-time work.

Not all news was bad, however. In 1934, the German Patent Office granted a patent for the elliptical finned tube with turbulators. That same year, GEA engineers entered new spheres of business which were designed to reduce customers' energy costs. Economizers and boilers for central heating systems and greenhouses were developed which re-used the waste-heat from power plants.

In 1935, Otto Happel together with the German engineer Dr. Kurt Lang, started working on air-cooled condensers for stationary steam turbines used for electricity generation. In 1939, GEA commissioned the first pilot project using an air-cooled condenser for stationary steam turbines at the Waltrop Colliery in the Ruhr. Although met with skepticism, Happel's team decided to pursue the technology further, which turned out to be successful for GEA in the following decades.

The War Era

When the Second World War began, about 200 people were on GEA's payroll, enjoying over-average benefits such as the company's own indoor swimming pool and a sports ground, and free fruit and vegetables grown in the experimental greenhouses. The company tried to maintain is business activities despite several bombardments, an endeavor which became impossible towards the end of the war.

Production started up again with about 70 employees in a small, undamaged building a few weeks after the war ended. At that time, many business transactions—including salaries—were barter deals. While reconstruction work progressed in the following years, the company was hit hard once again. The day after Christmas in 1948, GEA's founder Otto Happel died. His widow, Elisabeth Happel, who had given birth to her son Otto—named after his father—just eleven months earlier, took over the company's management. In the late 1940s and early 1950s, funds from the Marshall Plan provided for the reconstruction of power plants helped GEA get back on track.

Successful Start in the 1950s

The year 1950 saw two GEA firsts. The company produced and sold its first convectors—multiple stage radial blowers which controlled temperature electronically, used for heating, ventilation, and cooling—and it entered the field of systems engineering when the first complete air-cooled condenser was delivered to a small coal-run power plant in Hausham, Bavaria. Extensive series of tests carried out by the Process Engineering Institute of the Technical University in Karlsruhe provided a valuable database for GEA engineers, who developed larger units afterwards. Based on the principle of replacing water as the cooling element with by air, and thereby cutting operation costs and lowering negative environmental impacts, GEA engineers developed closed circuit coolers for large generators, and new cooler models for large diesel engines, chemical and steel producing facilities, and other cooling and condensation processes. In 1952, GEA was awarded a major contract which guaranteed work for the entire year. This contract included the delivery of air-cooled condensers for 90 locomotives to the German company Henschel.

In 1953, two new subsidiaries were founded: the GEA Wärmeaustauscher Berlin GmbH in Berlin for heat exchanger production, and the GEA Konvektorenbau Happel KG in Wanne-Eickel. The latter was the beginning if a profitable business segment for convectors and air heaters. The first marketable GEA K 54 Convector was developed in only one year's time, and the first big shipment of 1,200 convectors went to a Hilton hotel in Ankara, Turkey. Under the leadership of managing director Helmut Schmiegel, GEA Konvektorenbau soon became German market leader in the field of air heaters. Schmiegel would manage this subsidiary for 30 years.

In 1958, the GEA Gesellschaft für Luftkondensation mbH was founded in Bochum to develop air-cooled condensers for steam and gas turbines—a growing market at that time. GEA Luftkühlergesellschaft, the parent company, developed new air cooling solutions for various applications in process engineering. As one result, large orders were placed by companies from the petrochemical industry for oil refineries starting in 1959.

Expansion in Germany and Abroad in the 1960s

In the 1960s, GEA had to catch up with growing demand for its products in Germany as well as abroad. In 1962, GEA established a joint venture in Glasgow, Ireland—James Howden-GEA Ltd.—which included a production facility in Northern Ireland. It served the British Commonwealth and was later renamed to GEA Airexchangers Ltd. London. In 1963 and 1964, other new subsidiaries were founded in Austria, the United States, Italy, the Netherlands, and Spain, and licenses were granted to a Japanese and a Swiss company.

The GEA Konvektorenbau branch enjoyed a period of healthy growth. After founding its first foreign subsidiary in Austria in 1963, a new German factory was opened one year later in Obershausen in Hessen, thereby doubling its production capacity. In the following years, new products were developed such as the oil and gas-fired air heater in 1965, roof-mounted ventilation systems in 1966–67, and the first central air handling units in 1968.

When natural draught wet cooling towers were introduced to German power plants in 1965, GEA decided to market this new technology which fit well into its product line, especially for the utility industry. In the year of GEA's 50th anniversary, the company proudly presented the results of half a century of engineering work; 135 of GEA's air-cooled condensers for steam turbines, 8,000 air-cooling systems in various processing facilities, and 500,000 air heaters in all kinds of buildings had been installed all over the world.

New Markets and a New Leader in the 1970s

In the 1970s, GEA Gesellschaft für Luftkondensation intensified efforts to break into the utility market with air-cooled condensers for big power plants. This technology, which made water obsolete as a cooling agent for power generation, was successfully installed and tested in a 72 megawatt (MW) power plant in Italy; a 160 MW power station opened in 1971 in Utrillas, Spain; and a 365 MW power station in Wyodak, Wyoming, opened in 1977. Based on these successful operations, air-cooled condensers became feasible for power plants of any size. Prompted by the 1973 energy crisis, GEA Luftkühlergesellschaft developed heat exchangers that recovered process energy in large processing facilities in the chemical, steel producing, and other industries. GEA Konvektorenbau developed water-to-water heat pumps in 1974, and before long it dominated the European market for heat pumps for almost a decade.

In 1975, Otto Happel, Jr., who had just received his Ph.D. in engineering science, took over the management of the 3,000-employee company. In the same year, GEA won its largest contract to date, as Aramco, a Saudi Arabian company, ordered air coolers for a petrochemical plant worth DM 120 million.

Right from the beginning, Happel favored a more commercial orientation of the company, which had been run by engineers for half a century. Following the path his mother had set out on, he also worked on the further internationalization of the group. Between 1975 and 1978, GEA founded or acquired companies in South Africa, Brazil, France, and again in the United States. The latter included the engineering company GEA Power Cooling Systems, Inc. in San Diego, California, and the manufacturing firm GEA Rainey Corp. in Tulsa, Oklahoma.

In 1979, GEA diversified into the food and process engineering market by taking over the Eduard Ahlborn GmbH in Hildesheim, northern Germany, a firm specialized in plate heat exchangers used for thermal treatment of milk, fruit juices, and beer. As a result of continuous innovation and expansion, sales for the GEA Luftkühlergesellschaft grew 20-fold between 1954 and 1979.

New Applications in the 1980s

GEA entered the new decade reorganized by divisions, departments, and regions headed by a central management company. In 1982, the company made the biggest single deal in its history when it received a contract worth DM 360 million for air-cooled condensers for a 4,000 MW power station in Matimba, South Africa. For this gigantic facility, GEA engineers developed new finned tubes using fans of ten meters in diameter.

However, the market for heat pumps collapsed completely between 1981 and 1983 for GEA Konvektorenbau, due to the second energy crisis in the early 1980s. With R&D shifting towards energy and environmental engineering after the two oil crises, GEA's Environmental Engineering Division began developing heat transfer systems for the removal of sulfur and nitrogen from the emissions released by coal-based power stations in 1983.

Between 1984 and 1988, new subsidiaries were established or acquired for the new GEA Food and Process Engineering Division established in 1985, including four German manufacturers of products such as evaporators, equipment for breweries, and cooling equipment, as well as two companies in France and Belgium.

A new management holding company—GEA AG & Co.—replaced GEA GmbH in 1988. Three new divisions—Thermal and Energy Technology, Air Treatment and Refrigeration, and Food and Process Engineering, coordinated by a three-person executive board—replaced the old structure. By then, the GEA group included about 30 firms, employed about 4,900 people, and generated about DM 946 million in annual sales.

1989 was not only a historical milestone for the German people, but also for the GEA group. In order to finance further expansion, the company went public in December 1989, and raised DM 775 million. The Happel family preserved 37.5 percent of the total share capital in ordinary shares. However, preference shares had nonvoting status, so that the Happels actually held 75 percent of the voting rights. At the end of the decade, the sum of sales and received orders went beyond the DM 1 billion mark for the first time.

Expanding Internationally in the 1990s

In 1990, another DM 280 million was raised for the new GEA AG through a capital increase. The financially strengthened group was now able to enter a new stage of expansion which began by moving into its newly built futuristic headquarters in Bochum. At the end of 1991, GEA took over Grasso's Koninklijke Machinefabrieken N.V., a DM 300 million Dutch refrigeration specialist with an international reputation. Consequently, GEA's Air Treatment and Refrigeration Division was able push sales over DM 800 million.

In 1992, activities were extended into eastern Europe when GEA purchased a Hungarian engineering firm specialized in dry cooling for power stations and a Czech company active in the fields of heating, ventilation, and air conditioning. One year later, the GEA group took its biggest step towards becoming a global player when it acquired the DM 700 million Danish group NIRO A/S, located in Soborg near Copenhagen. The firm (which specialized in equipment for industrial drying, homogenization, concentration, membrane filtration, and other processes for treating liquids and solid materials used in the food, pharmaceutical, and environmental industries) not only brought 50 years of know-how to the GEA group, it also lent its strong presence in North and South America, Asia, Australia, and New Zealand. As a result of the NIRO group's integration into GEA's Food and Process Engineering Division, the division's share in the whole group's sales doubled from 21 percent to 42 percent in 1993, and NIRO's president Ole Anderson became its head and joined the executive board of the GEA AG.

In 1994, the group continued expanding in the field of food and process engineering with the acquisition of Westfalia Separator AG, the world's second largest supplier of centrifuges for the food, pharmaceutical, chemical, and petroleum industries with 4,000 employees and DM 810 million in sales.

With the acquisition of the Otto Tuchenhagen GmbH & Co. KG, a DM 330 million German firm with headquarters in Büchen near Hamburg specializing in process integration and automation systems for the brewery, dairy, beverage, and other industries, GEA became the world's second largest supplier for food and process engineering technology after Alfa Laval. In 1995, when GEA celebrated the group's 75th anniversary, sales had surpassed DM 4 billion, generated by more than 17,000 employees. The group was now able to offer fully integrated processing equipment instead of only system components.

The latter half of the 1990s began with another organizational restructuring effort, the results of which were introduced in February 1997. The GEA AG management holding company was headed by an executive board of three managers jointly responsible for the group's business affairs. Nine divisions (including Thermal Technology, Energy Technology, Air Treatment, Refrigeration, Liquid Processing, Powder Technology, Specialty Products, Mechanical Separation, and Dairy Farm Systems) each managed by a division president, constituted the next management level.

Between 1990 and the end of 1997, group sales tripled and net income almost doubled in the same period. The number of employees peaked in 1995 at 17,740, and decreased slightly in the following years, reaching 16,747 in 1997. 32 percent of GEA's DM 4.7 billion total sales in 1997 came from the food processing industry; 24 percent from the chemical, petroleum, and other basic industries; 12 percent from refrigeration products; nine percent from heating, ventilation, and air conditioning products; eight percent from both the energy and waste management as well as mechanical engineering industries, and seven percent from agriculture.

In November 1998, GEA announced only slightly increased sales, but net profits growth "well in the double-digit range," showing that the decline of Asian markets was more than compensated by cost reduction measures. In 1998 GEA also took over the French Hugonnet Group, a producer of milk cooling systems, and announced the takeover of the U.S. firm Zajac, Inc., expected to be complete by January 1, 1999. Zajac, an engineering contractor for the pharmaceutical, cosmetics, and beverage industries, was expected to strengthen GEA's presence in the North American market and to complement the Liquid Processing Division's product line.

In early February 1999, GEA and the German raw materials conglomerate Metallgesellschaft AG, Frankfurt am Main, announced they were planning to merge and that the Metallgesellschaft would take over the GEA AG by acquiring a majority share of 74.85 percent of the common stock from institutional and private GEA shareholders, including the Happel family which held 50.1 percent. The European Commission was reviewing the transaction for antitrust violations. It was expected that the GEA name as well as its other trade names would be maintained.

Principal Divisions

GEA Happel Klimatechnik (Germany); Grasso's Koninklijke Machinefabrieken N.V. (Netherlands); Niro A/S (Denmark); Westfalia Separator AG (Germany); Tuchenhagen GmbH (Germany); GEA Erge-Spirale et Soramat (France); GEA Integrated Cooling Technologies; GEA Spiro-Gills (U.K.); GEA Rainey; GEA do Brasil Intercambiadores (Brazil); Polacel (Netherlands); GEA Engine Cooling Systems; GEA Klimator (Poland); GEA Aircooled Systems (South Africa); EGI-Contracting/Engineering (Hungary); GEA Iberica (Spain); GEA Scambiatory di Calore (Italy); LVZ (Czech Republic).

Further Reading

Barber, Tony, "Metallgesellschaft Aims To Buy GEA," *Financial Times,* February 9, 1999, p.20.

Bauer, Ina, "Metallgesellschaft Shares Soar on Plans to Buy GEA," *Wall Street Journal Europe,* February 9, 1999.

GEA 1920–1995, company document, Bochum, Germany: GEA AG, 1995.

"GEA Sells Sugar/Sweetener Unit To Danish Group," *European Report,* September 5, 1998.

Hagos, Ghion, "German-Invested GEA Technology Equipment (Shanghai) Co. Ltd. Opens," *Asia Info Services,* November 13, 1996.

Lindemann, Michael, "GEA Posts Sharp Advance in Sales to 4.2 Billion Deutschmarks," *Financial Times,* March 2, 1995, p. 26.

——, "Sales at GEA Fall Short of Forecasts," *Financial Times,* May 7, 1996, p. 21.

Marsh, Peter, "GEA Hails Profits Recovery," *Financial Times,* March 10, 1998, p. 33.

——, "GEA to Spend DM2bn on Expansion," *Financial Times,* May 11, 1998, p. 26.

"Tuchenhagen Shifting Location," *Minneapolis Star Tribune,* September 12, 1995, p. D4.

—Evelyn Hauser

GEHE AG

Neckartalstrasse 155
D-70376 Stuttgart
Germany
(49) (711) 5001-00
Fax: (49) (711) 5001-500
Web site: http://www.gehe.de

Public Subsidiary of Franz Haniel & Cie. GmbH (50.1%)
Incorporated: 1835 as Gehe & Companie
Employees: 23,755
Sales: DM 25.03 billion (1997)
Stock Exchanges: Frankfurt/Main
Ticker Symbol: GEHG.F
SICs: 5047 Medical, Dental, & Hospital Equipment &
    Supplies; 5122 Drugs, Drug Proprietaries, &
    Druggists' Sundries; 5912 Drug Stores & Proprietary
    Stores; 5961 Catalog & Mail-Order Houses; 7352
    Medical Equipment Rental & Leasing

GEHE AG is the largest drug wholesaler in Europe. Through main wholesale subsidiaries in Germany, France, and the United Kingdom, GEHE generated 85 percent of its DM 25 billion sales in eight European countries in 1997. In Germany where GEHE is headquartered, the company held the second largest market share in drug wholesales of about 19 percent in 1997. Eighty percent of the group's turnover was generated outside Germany. GEHE's OCP Group is the French market leader, with a 40 percent share. The OCP Group is also active in Belgium, Italy, and Portugal. In the United Kingdom, GEHE is represented through its AAH Group division, leading British drug wholesalers with a 37 percent market share. Through the Lloyd's Pharmacy subsidiary, AAH also accounts for over ten percent of pharmacy retail sales in Great Britain and owns 1,290 pharmacies. The GEHE Healthcare Services Division provides supplies and services for rehabilitation, elderly care, and other home healthcare needs through the Pro Reha group in Germany and through Orkyn' in France. GEHE's special mail-order company—Kaiser + Kraft GmbH (K + K)—supplies over one million businesses worldwide with more than 20,000 products for offices, warehouses, and transportation, ranging from designer furniture to forklifts, through catalogues, CD-ROMs and the Internet. GEHE is majority-owned (50.1%) by the German trade and services group Haniel & Cie. GmbH.

Gehe's Founder Pioneers Drug Wholesaling: 1835–1903

On May 1, 1835, 25-year-old merchant Franz Ludwig Gehe founded Gehe & Co. OHG, the first German drug wholesale business, in Dresden. After working as an assistant servant at a wholesale business for six years, he stated a clear vision about his new enterprise: "... to satisfy completely the requirements of the pharmacy in all its dealings." At that time, pharmacy-made medicines were a luxury only rich people could afford. In its first year, the Gehe company employed three people full-time. Ten years later, Franz Ludwig Gehe moved his enterprise to Dresden's Koenigstrasse, where he opened a drug wholesale house. Gehe & Co. sold unprocessed raw materials for drug manufacturing such as minerals and substances from plants and animals. Right from the beginning, Franz Ludwig Gehe worked on developing a far-reaching trading network through offices in two European "trade capitals," Hamburg and London, and served customers all over the world. He traveled to the United States in 1876 and visited the world exhibition in Philadelphia, one of America's most important pharmaceutical manufacturing centers at that time. Gehe's wholesale business was based on traveling salespeople using company-owned coaches and delivery carried out by Dresden-based carriers. Deliveries to remote places were transported by rail or boat to GEHE subsidiaries or to railroad stations where customers picked them up.

When Gehe's nephew, pharmacist and chemist Dr. Rudolph August Luboldt, joined the company in 1859, GEHE's workforce was up to 29. He engaged in adding manufacturing of medicines to the wholesale business. In 1865, the first production facility for pre-produced drugs and drug finishing was built in Dresden's Leipziger Strasse and started operation one year later as Gehe & Co., Drogen-und Appreturanstalt. The new branch enabled GEHE to deliver raw materials of higher quality, purified and tested at the new facility. The property was also

Company Perspectives:

As the market leader in Europe, we wish to understand the public health systems and the differing, oftentimes complex, conditions in each of the principal European countries. It is our desire to actively influence the changes in order to share the experience of our companies with our customers. Our philosophy of quickly adapting to ever-changing market conditions helps us to position ourselves as leaders in the industries and countries where we have established a presence.

an excellent basis for transportation, including direct rail and boat connections. In the second half of the 19th century, more and more finished medicines were brought to market by newly founded pharmaceutical manufacturers. On the other hand, international delivery by mail became more and more accepted after the Bern Convention of 1875 simplified international mail delivery in 21 mainly European countries. Consequently, the frequency of orders per customer went up steadily. In addition, demand for pharmaceuticals increased after a law became effective in Germany in 1883, making public health insurance obligatory for industrial workers, with benefits such as free medication. Price and product information of the GEHE company were provided to its growing international pharmacist clientele in five languages, and GEHE employees were sent out to explore new trade possibilities literally everywhere in the world, from northern Europe to Africa, from North America to the Orient.

In 1882, company founder Franz Ludwig Gehe died. According to his will, a foundation named after him was opened in 1885 in Dresden, offering various educational opportunities for merchants, civil servants, tradespeople, and workers. Gehe's death made Rudolph August Luboldt the sole proprietor of the GEHE enterprise, which by then already had 80 employees— 12 of them certified pharmacists and chemists—and 150 factory workers on its payroll. When Rudolph August Luboldt died in 1894, his son, chemist Dr. Walter Luboldt, took over the GEHE business as sole proprietor and managed the firm until 1903. GEHE also published, in 1894, the first specialty catalogue for industrially produced drugs. The so-called ''Verzeichnis neuerer Heilmittel'' consisted of 14 pages containing information on about 400 drugs, including their place of origin, consistency, and effects.

Expansion After Going Public in 1903

In 1903 GEHE was transformed into a public stock company with the new name Gehe & Co. AG, starting out with a capital of DM 2 million, a work force of 400 people, and Dr. Walter Luboldt as its first CEO. In 1908 GEHE extended production capacity by taking over the Chemische Fabrik Schoenprissen in Aussig, a Czech chemicals factory, which was merged into Gehe & Co., Aussig, in 1924. In 1909 GEHE's first drug wholesale house in Koenigstrasse was closed after the construction of a new house at the Leipziger Strasse location. In the 1920s, GEHE expanded its wholesale business in Stuttgart by purchasing two local drug wholesalers, and founded a publish-

ing branch in Dresden for the ''GEHE Codex.'' In the 1930s, GEHE set up new subsidiaries in Germany, Spain, and Poland through new acquisitions. In 1935 GEHE employed 560 people, among them 39 sales representatives in Germany and 95 abroad. By 1943 GEHE had established five sales offices in Germany, one in Spain, and two in Poland.

In 1910 GEHE's first ''Codex'' was published, a 390-page reference book for pharmacists and doctors including information on all industrially manufactured drugs and their composition, usage, and dosage, as well as information about cosmetics and important technical products. The compendium was aimed to give a comprehensive and objective overview of the fast-growing market of pre-manufactured pharmaceuticals. Only four years later, the second edition came out with almost double the pages. In the fourth edition of 1926 the number of pages had almost doubled again; the book included information on drug manufacturers for the first time. In 1929 German explanations of pharmaceutical terms in foreign languages were added. After several customers complained about the ever growing size of the book, GEHE decided to restrict the ''Codex'' to all drugs for which authentic data were available from manufacturers. However, the ''Codex'' was extended again in 1935, including more foreign preparations and new homeopathic medicines. In addition, a separate publication, the ''Rote Liste'' (red list) with listings of prices for German pharmaceuticals, was launched in the same year. By 1937 information on chemicals for cleaning, disinfecting, and pesticides was added.

An Unexpected New Beginning in 1948

After World War II, GEHE lost its headquarters in Dresden, which was located in the Russian sector. In 1947 Gehe's main office in Dresden was renamed and transformed into a publicly owned entity. Three years later, the former Gehe & Co. AG was merged with two Dresden-based pharmaceutical companies into Volkseigener Betrieb Arzneimittelwerk Dresden, owned by the East German government. The West German remains of GEHE started from scratch with 17 people—including CEO Dr. Max W. Ecker—in the West German sales offices in Sulzbach-Rosenberg and Kassel, and C.H. Burk GmbH in Stuttgart which GEHE had owned since 1921. In 1948, GEHE's headquarters were moved from Dresden to Munich. At the end of that year, sales for GEHE's first balance sheet after the war and after the introduction of a new currency in the West German sectors were DM 1.9 million. By the end of the following decade, they tripled, reaching DM 6.6 million in 1958. In that year, GEHE's West German branches were reorganized. New branches were opened in Bavaria, the Sulzbach-Rosenberg office was closed, and the C.H. Burk GmbH in Stuttgart was integrated as a branch.

GEHE entered the 1960s with a significant boost in sales. The figure of DM 36.7 million in that year was almost five times higher than a year before. Total sales rose at an increasing rate during the decade, between 9 and 13 percent until 1964, mainly caused by generally rising demand. In the second half of the 1960s, GEHE's sales increased at a rate of 25 percent and up annually, mainly due to a row of mergers and acquisitions, including the takeover of three German drug wholesalers in 1966 and 1967. In the record year of 1968, sales grew by 28 percent compared with 1967, reaching DM 147 million. In

1969, GEHE acquired the German drug wholesaler Heitzer & Co. KG in Hamburg, strengthening the company's position in northern Germany. In the same year, GEHE ceased publication of the "Codex" which was one year later replaced by the "Gelbe Liste" (yellow list), a pharmaceuticals index published by Drotax in Frankfurt/Main.

New Partners, Technologies, and Markets: The 1970s and 1980s

GEHE's future was affected significantly when Franz Haniel & Cie. GmbH, based in Duisburg, Germany, became a majority shareholder in 1973. With Haniel as a new partner, the GEHE group entered a new period of expansion. In 1976, four German drug wholesale subsidiaries of the Haniel group were merged with GEHE. In 1979, Dr. Dieter Schadt became GEHE's new CEO. To significantly improve GEHE's domestic market position, existing branches were reorganized in 1981, including two acquisitions and two closures. After moving headquarters from Munich to Stuttgart and changing its name to GEHE AG in 1981, GEHE acquired Ruwa GmbH, one of its main competitors, in 1982.

Another crucial step on GEHE's path to become a market leader was heavy investment in state-of-the-art technology. Beginning in the 1970s, the way the pharmaceutical wholesale business functioned changed completely, driven by emerging electronic data processing and computer technology. Telephone orders from pharmacists were entered into computer terminals and processed electronically in GEHE's branches. Later on, orders were directly transmitted through electronic data transfer from the pharmacies to GEHE's warehouses. A second wave of rationalization affected the way orders were handled, and manual commissioning was gradually replaced by machinery, significantly lowering the order error rate. Another result was that GEHE's workforce dropped by 25 percent in only five years, from 1,608 in 1976 to 1,217 in 1981. In 1985, the firm's 150th anniversary year, GEHE was the first German drug wholesaler to introduce fully automated commissioning in its newly built Darmstadt/Weiterstadt branch. GEHE also pioneered robot utilization in its warehouses in 1988, where approximately 45,000 orders had to be filled daily, 80 percent within a window of about four hours, selected from an inventory of some 75,000 different products. Automated commissioning was used to fill orders for approximately 2,000 articles most in demand, accounting for about 35 percent of GEHE's sales. The automates, controlled by a central computer, were able to fill about 1,500 orders totaling 15,000 articles per hour. In comparison, commissioning robots were slower, but more flexible. Equipped with an optical recognition system able to recognize different products, the robots were able to grab an article out of a shelf in four seconds, assemble eight orders at a time, and fill about 500 orders per hour.

In the second half of the 1980s, GEHE diversified into the mail-order business by purchasing the German Kaiser + Kraft Group, which supplied corporate clients with office, warehouse, and transportation equipment. GEHE's international trading network was extended, covering 14 European countries and the United States. In 1987 and 1988, the takeover of the German GAERNER GmbH & Co. KG and Milwaukee-based C & H Distributors, Inc., strengthened GEHE's new mail-order divi-

sion. In 1989, GEHE again added pharmaceutical manufacturing to its portfolio when the group acquired a 26 percent share in Azuchemie GmbH, Gerlingen, Germany's second largest generic drug maker. In 1989, sales of the GEHE group reached almost DM 3.3 billion, and the number of employees was up to 4,170.

Becoming a European Market Leader in the 1990s

With the reunification of Germany, GEHE launched its largest investment plan to date in 1990, aimed at the extension of the drug wholesale activities to eastern Germany. Immediately after the fall of the Berlin Wall, GEHE started contacting pharmacies in the former GDR and started supplying them from branches in western Germany as well as provisional warehouses in eastern Germany. In 1991, six newly established branches were opened in the east German states. In 1991 and 1992, the east German Jenapharm GmbH, Jena, was acquired and a new production facility—mainly for hormone preparations—was opened in Weimar. After a record growth of 13 percent in drug wholesales in 1990 mainly caused by the growing domestic market, the same market collapsed in 1993, due to new regulations introduced by the German government in order to restrict the explosion of public healthcare costs, which immediately resulted in drug sales dropping by 15 to 20 percent. In the same year, GEHE went through a restructuring program. GEHE AG was organized as a holding company. The new pharmaceutical wholesale division, GEHE Pharma Handel GmbH, managed 17 branches in Germany. Pharmaceutical production and mail-order became separately managed business divisions. In 1993, Dieter Schadt resigned as GEHE's CEO and became chairman of its supervisory board.

After reorganizing business in Germany, GEHE entered a period of unprecedented international expansion. It began with the establishment of new drug wholesale enterprises in Poland, Czechoslovakia, and Russia between 1991 and 1993. With taking over the French Office Commerciale Pharmaceutique S.A. (OCP), GEHE became Europe's number one drug wholesaler. Two other deals secured GEHE's top position in the wholesale business: the "hostile takeover" of AAH plc in 1995, which controlled 30 percent of the British and 40 percent of the Irish wholesale markets and owned 250 retail pharmacies. This transaction was closely followed by the purchase of Lloyds Chemists plc in 1997 after a year-long bidding battle with British rival Unichem Plc. Thus, GEHE also entered the business it had served devotedly since the company's founding: the pharmaceutical retail business of which it controlled some 1,300 stores in the United Kingdom in the late 1990s.

While entering the drug retail market was considered a strategic step towards concentration on GEHE's core business after excessive wholesale expansion, other ventures were given up. Initiated in 1996, almost all pharma production subsidiaries were sold for DM 1.2 billion. GEHE's subsidiaries in Poland and Russia had been sold in 1996. In order to further concentrate on its core business—trading pharmaceuticals—GEHE was planning to spin off its mail-order division Kaiser + Kraft to its shareholders in September 1999.

However, as a result of massive international expansion in the 1990s, GEHE's workforce exploded almost fivefold, from

5,032 in 1990 to 23,755 in 1997. Within the same period of time, sales jumped from DM 3.78 billion to DM 25 billion, while net income rose from DM 58.6 million to 285.1 million—a nearly 500 percent increase. For 1998, GEHE's new CEO, Dr. Fritz Oesterle, who replaced Dieter Kaemmerer at the beginning of 1999, reported that he expected the GEHE group's net profit (before taxes) to reach DM 500 million for the first time in its history.

Principal Subsidiaries

GEHE Pharma Handel GmbH; Office Commercial Pharmaceutique-OCP S.A. (France; 97.05%); AAH plc (U.K.); Lloyds Retail Chemists Ltd. (U.K.); AAH Retail Pharmacy Ltd. (U.K.); Pro Reha Handelsgesellschaft fuer Krankenpflegeartikel und Rehabilitationshilfen mbH & Co. KG; Pharma Dom S.A. (France; 99.44%); Kaiser + Kraft GmbH; Gaerner GmbH & Co. KG; Topdeq International GmbH; C & H Distributors Inc.

Principal Divisions

Pharmaceutical Wholesale (Gehe Group; OCP Group; AAH Group); Pharmacy/Retail; Healthcare Services; Mail Order.

Further Reading

"AAH Fights Gehe's 'Cheap' Bid," *Chemist & Druggist,* March 25, 1995, p. 515.

"AAH Pledges Saving of 14 million Pounds Sterling As Gehe Ups Bid to 445p per Share," *Chemist & Druggist,* April 15, 1995, p. 611.

Birt, Jonathan, "German Firm Wins British Drugstore Chain," *Reuters Business Report,* January 13, 1997.

Blackwell, David, "Business As Usual After Gehe's Big Win," *Financial Times,* May 8, 1995, p. 15.

"Financial World Top CEOs 1994," *Financial World,* July 19, 1994, p. 46.

"Gehe Goes for Top Spot," *Mergers & Acquisitions International,* March 13, 1995, p. 6.

"Gehe kauft Apotheken zu," *Handelsblatt,* February 8, 1999.

"GEHE Short Chronicle," Stuttgart: GEHE AG, 1997.

"Gehe's 1993 Group Net Rose Only 3% Despite an Increase of 87% in Its sales," *Wall Street Journal (Europe)*, March 30, 1994, p. 5.

"Gehe vollzieht den Kurswechsel sanft," *Frankfurter Allgemeine Zeitung,* February 8, 1999.

Jones, Liz, "Survival of the Fittest: AAH Confident of New Euro Role," *Chemist & Druggist,* May 27, 1995, p. 858.

Kempf, Andreas, "Pharmagroßhändler Gehe kauft englische Apothekenkette," *Stuttgarter Zeitung,* February 8, 1999.

"Konzept: Globalisierung," *Wirtschaftswoche,* November 20, 1997, p. 181.

L'Aimable, Guy, "Digesting an Empire," *Chemist & Druggist,* June 6, 1998 p. 32.

"Schering AG to Boost Share of Hormone Market with Jenapharm," *Pharmaceutical Business News,* June 8, 1996, p. 6.

"Seit 150 Jahren: Gehe AG," *Deutsche Apotheker Zeitung,* May 16, 1985.

Shields, Michael, "Sandoz to Buy German Drug Maker for $416 Million," *Reuters Business Report,* October 15, 1996.

"Tough Battle for AAH: German Wholesaler Gehe's Move on AAH Could Be Hard for the Group to Resist," *Investor's Chronicle,* March 10, 1995, p. 70.

—Evelyn Hauser

Genesee & Wyoming Inc.

71 Lewis Street
Greenwich, Connecticut 06830
U.S.A.
(203) 629-3722
Fax: (203) 661-4106

Public Company
Incorporated: 1899 as Genesee and Wyoming Railroad
    Co.
Employees: 771
Sales: $103.6 million (1997)
Stock Exchanges: NASDAQ
Ticker Symbol: GNWR
SICs: 4011 Railroads, Line-Haul Operating; 4731
    Arrangement of Transportation of Freight & Cargo;
    4741 Rental of Railroad Cars; 6719 Offices of
    Holding Companies, Not Elsewhere Classified

Through its subsidiaries, Genesee & Wyoming Inc. (GWI) oversees the operations of short-line and regional freight railroads and provides related railroad services, such as switching and rail-car leasing and repair. Celebrating its 100th anniversary in 1999, GWI had come a long way from its role as a regional hauler of rock salt, and in 1997 comprised 15 U.S. railroads—in New York, Pennsylvania, Illinois, Louisiana, and Texas—hauling bulk cargos such as coal, petroleum products, pulp and paper, lumber, and metals over about 1,500 miles of track. Nevertheless, the company maintained a link to its past in that Mortimer B. Fuller III, great-grandson of GWI's patriarch, retained an interest in the company. In the late 1990s, GWI made some acquisitions intended to enhance its size and scope within the niche market of short-line railroading. Interest in a Canadian company that owned and operated two short-line Canadian railroads was purchased in 1997, and the company also began operating freight service along about 900 miles of track in Australia. In addition, GWI acquired Rail Link, Inc., a leading provider of railroad switching and related services.

Late 19th Century Origins

The company traces its history to the 1899 founding of the Genesee & Wyoming Railroad Co., itself a successor of the Genesee & Wyoming Valley Railway in Livingston County, Pennsylvania. At the time, the company operated about 16 miles of railroad, which was used to transport rock salt from a mine in Retsof, in western New York. Its main line ran from Retsof to Pittsburgh and Lehigh Junction, with shorter branches running from Retsof to Greigsville and Retsof Junction. In 1899, this small railway was purchased by E.L. Fuller, who reorganized the company as the Genesee & Wyoming Railroad.

The cargo aboard trains on the Genesee & Wyoming during this time was supplied by the Retsof Salt Mining Co., which controlled the road in that area. Expansion activities during this time were limited to leases of short stretches of track, and for years the Genesee & Wyoming continued to be dependent on a single industry, salt mining. Fuller's son Mortimer B. Fuller served as the company's president at this time, and the company's main office was located in Scranton, Pennsylvania. By 1913, the company's gross income had reached $113,855 with net income of $71,250.

By 1920 the Genesee & Wyoming, still running on a little over 17 miles of track, had purchased two passenger coaches as well as six locomotives and two cabooses. Gross revenues that year had risen to almost $500,000, and net income was reported at $270,065. The Genesee & Wyoming railroad experienced its own Depression early, with operating revenues falling every year from 1922 to 1932, when they came to less than half what they had been at the peak. Net income dropped as low as $30,000, but the company never lost money and continued its tradition, established in 1900, of paying quarterly dividends.

The Genesee & Wyoming continued to prosper in subsequent decades. It passed $1 million in annual operating revenues in 1955 and $2 million in 1970, when net income came to $512,622. The company's main office had by then moved to Clarks Summit, Pennsylvania. While its "line of road" comprised only about 13 miles, the railroad's equipment, or "rolling stock," had increased significantly and now included seven

---

Company Perspectives:

The core purpose of Genesee & Wyoming is to be a leader in rail related services, anticipating and responding rapidly to customers' requirements and the dynamics of a competitive market place.

---

diesel locomotives, 97 50-ton boxcars, 47 60-ton hopper cars, and two cabooses. Operating revenues were $3.3 million and net income $662,000 in 1978.

Expansion in Mid-20th Century

Mortimer B. Fuller III, great-grandson of the founder, purchased a controlling interest in the firm in 1977 and began seeking contracts from industries that would make the railroad its sole supplier. Under his leadership the company, which was renamed Genesee & Wyoming Industries, Inc. and moved its main office to Greenwich, Connecticut, first entered the rail-car leasing business and then began making rail-line acquisitions, seeking contracts from industries that would make the railroad its sole supplier. Within a decade GWI became a leading provider of short-line and regional rail transportation and related services.

The U.S. railroad industry underwent significant change after the passage of a 1980 Federal act that deregulated the pricing and types of services provided by railroads. The larger railroads focused their management and capital resources on their long-haul core systems, and certain of them sold branch lines to smaller and more cost-efficient rail operators willing to commit the resources necessary to meet the needs of shippers located on these lines. GWI was one of these smaller, more cost-efficient operators and began acquiring such lines in 1985, when it purchased The Dansville & Mt. Morris Railroad, a line with headquarters in Leicester, New York, and eight miles of track running a little south of G&W's own line.

The company acquired the Ashford Junction-Rochester line in 1986 from railroading giant CSX Corp. This railroad, which GWI renamed the Rochester & Southern Railroad (R&S), was losing money and in very poor condition at the time of purchase because of deferred maintenance; the threat of derailment kept train speeds below normal, limiting the amount of traffic the railroad could carry. Under the parentage of Genesee & Wyoming, however, improvements were made; revenue carloads increased 36 percent between 1986 and 1988, and the company had 39 customers in 1989, including Eastman Kodak Co. In 1991 the R&S reached Buffalo via a connection at Silver Springs, New York, with a Canadian Pacific Railway line and by 1997 operated 66 miles of track in the Rochester, New York, area.

During this time, Genesee & Wyoming also acquired the Buffalo & Pittsburgh Railroad (B&P) from the Pennsylvania division of CSX. Like R&S, this railroad had its origins late 1880s, when it was founded as the Rochester & Pittsburgh Railroad, hauling coal as the chief source of income and carrying passengers until 1955. After acquiring this line, which would become GWI's biggest, GWI implemented cost savings

by cutting crew sizes and requiring that rail workers be able to function in roles as varied as engineer and track repairer. In 1997 the B&P had 279 miles of track, some of it leased, and was carrying scrap steel for Armco Butler, oil from refineries in northwestern Pennsylvania, paper from a Willamette mill, coal glass, forest products, and automobiles moving down the line from Canada. Coal composed 40 percent of its business in 1996, with chemicals from 15 to 25 percent and mixed freight accounting for the rest.

When GWI acquired 149-mile-long Allegheny & Eastern Railroad in 1992, the B&P, R&S, and A&E became virtually one railroad, with shared customer service, dispatching tasks, and pooled power. The A&E operated an extension west from the B&P at Johnsonburg, Pennsylvania, and an extension east at Ridgeway, Pennsylvania.

In 1993 GWI also acquired four-mile-long Bradford Industrial Rail. This line had its headquarters in the same place as the A&E—Punxsutawney, Pennsylvania.

GWI had also expanded its geographic scope, having in 1987 purchased a part of the Southern Pacific Railroad that it named the Louisiana & Delta Railroad. This enterprise had its headquarters in New Iberia, Louisiana, and a main line running between Lafayette and Avondale, Louisiana. Some of its 87 miles of track were leased rather than owned by GWI.

Other geographic expansion occurred in 1993 when the company purchased the Willamette & Pacific Railroad from Southern Pacific Rail Corp. This Far West railroad, with 185 miles of track in 1997—some of it leased—included a main line between Portland and Monroe, Oregon, and a branch line from Corvallis east to Albany—the railroad's headquarters— and west to Toledo. Another branch ran south from Albany to Eugene. In 1995 GWI opened the Portland & Western Railroad (P&W) on tracks leased from the Southern Pacific. The new line ran around Portland, Hillsboro, Beaverton, Tigard, Sherwood, and Newberg, via Milwaukie and Lake Oswego. It connected at Newberg with the Willamette & Pacific, which pooled locomotive servicing, track maintenance, accounting, administration, and customer service with the P&W. P&W had 198 miles of track in 1997, including a 92-mile line linking Astoria and other Columbia River ports to Portland and continuing south to Quinby, acquired from Burlington Northern Inc. that year.

Genesee & Wyoming Railroad itself was moving about two million tons of salt a year for Azko Nobel Salt Inc. when this Retlof, New York, mine met with disaster, collapsing and flooding in 1994. Only nine other businesses were using the 26-mile railroad, and they were accounting for only about ten percent of its revenue before the disaster, but the Genesee & Wyoming continued operations, including serving a salt distribution center at the site of the collapsed mine. An investment group was planning to build a new salt mine in the same area in the late 1990s.

Going Public and Further Acquisitions

In June 1996, the company went public, offering about 2.5 million shares at $17 apiece. The offering reportedly raised about $46 million, which the company planned to use to pay down the debt it was incurring during its recent period of acquisitions.

Another acquisition, in 1996, added the Chicago & Illinois Midland Railroad (C&IM) to Genesee & Wyoming's corporate umbrella. This line began in 1889 as the Pawnee Railroad. The Chicago & Illinois Midland Railway Co. extended the line west to Auburn and east to Taylorville in 1906, thereby providing rail services through the rich coal fields of Sangamon and Christian counties. Eventually a new main line ran north from Taylorville through Springfield to Peoria. At its peak in 1940, C&IM employed 750 people and operated around the clock, providing fuel for Chicago's Commonwealth Edison utility company. After GWI purchased the railroad, it was renamed Illinois & Midland.

Also in 1996, Genesee & Wyoming purchased the 224-mile-long Pittsburg & Shawmut Railroad for $11.7 million. This western Pennsylvania line—also based in Punxsutawney—connected to the Buffalo & Pittsburgh Railroad at Brockway. Along with the Pittsburg & Shawmut, GWI acquired two other coal-country lines—the Red Bank Railroad and the Mountain Laurel.

In a diversification move in 1996 Genesee & Wyoming purchased an industrial switching subsidiary, Rail Link, Inc. Based in Virginia, Rail Link had three Virginia-based subsidiaries of its own: Carolina Coastal Railway (17 miles of track), Commonwealth Railway (17 miles), and Talleyrand Terminal Railroad (ten miles).

Genesee & Wyoming's rail system expanded beyond domestic operations in 1997, when it took on a 47.5 percent interest in a Canadian company that owned and operated two short-line railroads in Canada. One of these lines, Huron Central Railway, won a lease that year to operate Canadian Pacific's 180 mile line between Sudbury and Sault Ste. Marie, Ontario. Huron Central's customers included Algoma Steel and E.B. Eddy Forest Products.

International operations were bolstered by the 1997 purchase of certain freight-railroad assets of Australian National, a railroad company owned by the federal Australian government. The subsequently renamed Australia Southern Railroad (ASR), was an operation with 900 miles of track, and the land under the tracks was leased from the state of South Australia for 50 years. ASR was hauling six types of commodities, including grain, coal, and gypsum, for six major customers and also acquired contracts to operate "hook and pull" trains for three customers over the 2,100-mile-long corridor between Melbourne and Perth.

Genesee & Wyoming Industries, Inc. was renamed Genesee & Wyoming Inc. in 1995. The company's domestic railroads and switching operations served more than 300 customers in 1997, the largest being Commonwealth Edison, which accounted for about 15 percent of company revenue that year. Coal, coke, and ores represented by far the largest commodity

group hauled in 1997, accounting for 37.4 percent of GWI's 219,706 carloads. Also among the commodities it hauled were metals, pulp and paper, lumber and forest products, petroleum products, farm and food products, minerals and stone, chemicals, and autos and auto parts.

Genesee & Wyoming's operating revenues increased from $53.4 million in 1995 to $103.6 million in 1997. Of the 1997 total, freight accounted for 71 percent, switching and storage for 18 percent, and rail-car hire and rental for six percent. Net income rose from $1.7 million in 1995 to $8 million in 1997. In March 1998 Mort Fuller, the founder's great grandson, held 5.4 percent of Genesee & Wyoming's Class A shares of common stock and 77.9 percent of the Class B shares, giving him 52.8 percent of the voting power.

Principal Subsidiaries

Allegheny & Eastern Railroad, Inc.; Australian Southern Railroad Pty Limited (Australia); Bradford Industrial Rail, Inc.; Buffalo & Pittsburgh Railroad, Inc.; Corpus Christi Terminal Railroad, Inc.; The Dansville & Mt. Morris Railroad Company; Genesee & Wyoming Investors, Inc.; Genesee and Wyoming Railroad Company; Genesee & Wyoming Railroad Services, Inc.; GWT Canada, Inc.; GWT Dayton, Inc.; GWT Leasing Corporation; GWT Rail Management Corporation; Illinois & Midland Railroad, Inc.; Louisiana & Delta Railroad, Inc.; Pittsburg & Shawmut Railroad, Inc.; Portland & Western Railroad, Inc.; Rail Link, Inc. (and its subsidiaries, Carolina Coastal Railway, Inc., Commonwealth Railway, Inc., and Talleyrand Terminal Railroad Company, Inc.); Rochester & Southern Railroad, Inc.; Willamette & Pacific Railroad, Inc.

Further Reading

Astor, Will, "Railroad Rolling Toward Offering," *Rochester Business Journal,* July 5, 1996, p. 5.

Bird, Wendy, "Soo to Sudbury Line Finally Leased," *Northern Ontario Business,* February 1998, p. 6.

Craig, Gary, "Blow to Railway Might Be Fatal, Says Its Top Official," *Rochester Democrat and Chronicle,* April 23, 1996, p. 1A.

Fischer, Ryan R., "Big Kid in the Alleghenies," *Trains,* January 1997, pp. 46–53.

"Genesee and Wyoming Railroad Absorbs C&IM," *St. Louis Post Dispatch,* April 29, 1996, p. 8I.

"Genesee & Wyoming Trades Higher," *Traffic World,* July 22, 1996, p. 15.

Grund, John M., "The Second Train Rolls In," *Oregon Business,* September 1997, p. 26.

Johnston, Phil, "Young Railroad's Fate Rides on U.S. Support Plan," *Rochester Business Journal,* April 17, 1989, p. 22.

MacKenzie, Bill, "Suburban Short-Line Railroad Starts Up," *Oregonian,* August 22, 1995, p. B14.

McKay, Jim, "Off the Beaten Track: Short Lines are in It for the Long Haul," *Pittsburgh Post-Gazette,* June 16, 1996, p. C1+.

—Robert Halasz

GPU, Inc.

100 Interpace Parkway
Parsippany, New Jersey 07054
U.S.A.
(201) 263-6500
(800) 452-9155
Fax: (201) 263-6822
Web site: http://www.gpu.com

Public Company
Incorporated: 1906 as Associated Gas & Electric
    Company
Employees: 9,387
Sales: $12 billion
Stock Exchanges: New York
Stock Symbol: GPU
SICs: 4911 Electric Utilities; 6719 Holding Companies,
    Not Elsewhere Classified

GPU, Inc., a public utility holding company, is an international firm that holds all the stock of three electric operating subsidiaries that provide over two million customers with 39 billion kilowatt-hours of electricity in a service territory covering about half the land area of New Jersey and Pennsylvania. Jersey Central Power & Light Company accounts for about half of the GPU system's revenue and supplies about 43 percent of New Jersey with power. Pennsylvania Electric Company serves a largely rural 17,000-square-mile area that includes many mining, manufacturing, and agribusiness customers. Metropolitan Edison Company's 3,274-square-mile service area in Pennsylvania contains a wide range of manufacturing, agricultural, recreational, and tourist facilities. In addition, through the GPU International Group, the company develops, manages, owns, and operates numerous transmission and distribution facilities that serve another 2.3 million people overseas. GPU Advanced Resources, Inc. sells retail energy and services throughout the mid-Atlantic States, GPU Generation, Inc. and GPU Nuclear, Inc. operate the company's domestic generating facilities, while GPU Services, Inc. provides an extensive network of corporate support to all the operations within GPU.

Early History

GPU was originally incorporated as Associated Gas & Electric Company (Ageco) in 1906. A group of small-town promoters around Ithaca, New York, created Ageco as a holding company for 12 small gas and electric properties: ten in south central New York and one each in Pennsylvania and Ohio. The total value of the properties was $1.2 million. In spite of some minor acquisitions over the next several years, Ageco remained a group of small, rural New York companies as late as 1921, with assets under $7 million. In 1922, however, Ageco entered a period of almost two decades of dramatic growth tied in with incredibly convoluted and often illicit financial manipulations.

In 1908 at the age of 26, Howard C. Hopson had been hired by the New York State Public Service Commission as chief of its division of capitalization. In this position, Hopson was a central figure in New York state public utility regulation from 1908 to 1915. Here he met John I. Mange, general manager of Ageco and president of several of its operating subsidiaries. Hopson and Mange became close friends. In 1915 Hopson left the commission to become an independent consultant. In 1922, through an amazing series of transactions involving dummy companies, Hopson and Mange bought all the stock in Ageco. With the pair now firmly in power, Mange became president of Ageco, and Hopson became treasurer and vice president. The expansion that followed turned Ageco into a utilities giant, including about 180 intricately connected subsidiaries and service companies, possessing properties in 26 states and in the Philippines.

By 1924 Ageco's assets were up to $65 million, and more than tripled to $217 million in 1925. The most significant acquisitions of this period were the Pennsylvania Electric Corporation and the Manila Electric Company. Hopson funded these purchases by issuing the first of several unusual types of convertible securities that were to become his standard operating method. Hopson's method involved complex juggling of assets between holding companies and subholding companies. The process was so complicated that accountants, lawyers, and shareholders could not follow it, enabling Hopson to derive huge sums from the system by way of his personally held service companies, which performed various tasks for the operating companies and charged them outrageous rates. In the three years preceding the stock

182

market crash of 1929, Hopson sold nearly $500 million worth of Ageco debentures convertible to stock. Because stock prices were rising so fast during this time, people were anxious to exercise these conversion rights and bought up the bonds quickly. Ageco ended 1929 as one of the five largest holding-companies in the nation. With the collapse of the stock market, however, Hopson was no longer able to support Ageco's pyramid-like structure through the sale of new securities.

The Great Depression and World War II

By 1932 Ageco was in a desperate situation. The Depression had slowed revenue growth of the operating companies, and Ageco had difficulty raising money to pay off maturing bonds. In an effort to save his empire, Hopson announced in early 1932 that over the last few years all of Ageco's income-producing assets had been shifted into a subsidiary, Associated Gas & Electric Corporation (Agecorp), formerly called Associated Utilities Investment Corporation. Ageco security holders suddenly discovered that their stock was subordinate to any debt that Agecorp might create.

Then, in a further attempt to avoid bankruptcy, Hopson unveiled his plan for recapitalization, in 1933. Under the plan, investors were given the option of exchanging their Ageco debentures for Agecorp securities. The catch was that they would have to take either a 50 percent reduction in their principal amount, or retain their principal and accept a significant cut in interest rate.

Although the recapitalization plan was somewhat successful as a stalling tactic, a group of security holders attempted to force Ageco into receivership. This litigation and similar legal attacks lasted until 1937, when a compromise was struck. The compromise required Hopson to appoint three independent directors to his board to help work out a more equitable reorganization plan and to protect the shareholders' interests. At the same time as this battle raged, the Treasury Department was trying to collect $54 million in back taxes from Ageco. Throughout these attacks Hopson personally continued to fare very well financially. He and his family collected at least $3.6 million between 1934 and 1938 from the service companies alone.

Meanwhile, Congress had begun its work on the Public Utility Holding Company Act, passed in 1935. Hopson's furious lobbying against the act helped to make him a target for investigation by the Securities and Exchange Commission

(SEC) and other federal agencies. In the course of its investigation, the SEC put a halt to certain illegal accounting practices used by Ageco and Agecorp, and both companies filed for bankruptcy in January 1940. Hopson himself eventually was convicted of mail fraud and sentenced to five years in prison.

The reorganization that followed bankruptcy was a success. The reorganization staff included Albert F. Tegen, who had served on the SEC investigation team and then became president of Ageco, and Willard Thorp, a leading economist, who became chairman of the board. During this period of trusteeship, creditors received Ageco stock, claims were settled, reduced power rates improved customer relations, the tangle of securities and holdings was simplified, and $14 million a year in interest savings was filtered back into previously delayed maintenance and new construction projects. By 1945 Ageco stock was six times as high as it had been in 1942, and the new streamlined Ageco was the pride of the SEC. The company's name was changed in 1946 to General Public Utilities Corporation.

Growth During the Postwar Era

The end of World War II led to increased growth for utility companies throughout the country. Although GPU's growth in territory was about average, its gains in earnings were considerably higher than the industry average during these postwar years. In the decade after the war, GPU's operating revenues more than doubled, surpassing $174 million in 1955. A major reason for this exceptional growth in earnings was tremendous progress in operating efficiency. In 1948 1.35 pounds of coal was required to generate one kilowatt-hour of electricity. By 1955, 36 percent less coal was needed. The new Shawville station of the Pennsylvania Electric subsidiary was highly efficient, requiring less than 0.75 of a pound of coal to produce one kilowatt-hour. By 1955, even after divesting several properties by order of earlier SEC rulings, the GPU system was making electricity for 1.2 million customers in New Jersey, Pennsylvania, and the Philippines. Of these customers 43 percent were residential, 29 percent industrial, 21 percent commercial, and seven percent in other categories. The variety of industries that comprised the industrial sector was extremely wide, with the metals industry making up ten percent of this segment.

In the 1960s GPU began turning to nuclear power. In 1963 the Jersey Central Power & Light subsidiary signed a $68 million contract with General Electric for construction of a nuclear facility at Oyster Creek, New Jersey, making it the first U.S. company to lay out money for a nonexperimental nuclear generator. The Oyster Creek station was scheduled to begin producing in mid-1967, but did not actually go into service until December 1969—the kind of delay that would come to be expected in the construction of nuclear facilities. Because of this delay, GPU was forced to spend $79 million in these two years on power from other sources in order to meet its expanding electricity demands. Despite the fact that the Oyster Creek generator cost $60 million more than expected, and GPU's capital outlays had tripled in the latter half of the 1960s—largely due to nuclear projects—GPU President William Kuhns remained committed to a growing emphasis on nuclear energy, including construction of two generators at the now-notorious Three Mile Island site in Pennsylvania. Throughout the decade, operating revenues rose slowly but steadily, from $205 million in 1960 to $384 million in 1970. By 1970 the combined service area of GPU's three utility subsidiaries was approaching its early 1990 size.

The 1970s and 1980s

Nuclear power remained GPU's great hope for the future into the mid-1970s. With oil prices skyrocketing, nuclear generation was increasingly seen as the method of choice. The cost of nuclear fuel to generate one kilowatt-hour in 1974 was less than one-third that of coal and about one-eleventh that of oil. That year, the fuel used by GPU for generating was 58 percent coal, 22 percent nuclear, and 20 percent oil. This was also the year that the first Three Mile Island unit went into commercial operation.

GPU entered 1979 as the 17th-largest utility in the United States, with assets of $4.6 billion. In the previous year, GPU had earned $139 million on $1.3 billion of operating revenues. On March 28, 1979, an accident occurred at the new, second nuclear generator at Three Mile Island, which had been producing electricity for only a few months. A valve at the unit failed to close, allowing cooling water to escape from the reactor. The plant, run by a Metropolitan Edison subsidiary, was operating at 97% of capacity at the time, and the absence of the cooling water caused the plant's core to overheat, damaging fuel rods and releasing radioactive particles, thereby contaminating the building.

The costs of the accident were enormous. GPU estimated the cost of cleaning up Three Mile Island at $1 billion. In addition, it would cost GPU $2.3 billion to maintain electrical service to all of its customers, including $24 million per month to purchase power to replace that which was no longer being produced at Three Mile Island. At this time, $400 million came due on maturing securities. With net earnings drastically reduced, investors wary, and the Pennsylvania Public Utility Commission threatening to cancel Metropolitan Edison's franchise, it appeared that GPU could become the first public utility to go bankrupt since the Depression.

GPU's recovery from the devastation of the Three Mile Island accident was slow. Profits were much lower through the first half of the 1980s. A major obstacle to GPU's return to stability was the length of time it took for the Nuclear Regulatory Commission (NRC) to determine whether the undamaged Three Mile Island unit could be returned to operation, and if so, whether it could be operated by GPU. The company's competency to run a nuclear facility was questioned, by the NRC and by many other critics. Members of Congress urged that GPU Chairman and Chief Executive Kuhns and President Herman Dieckamp be replaced. Criminal charges were filed against Metropolitan Edison alleging that records regarding the leakage of coolant had been falsified.

The turning point finally came in November 1985, when the NRC ruled that GPU could return Three Mile Island to operation, ending more than six years of inactivity. The ruling almost instantly added $1 per share to company earnings and allowed rates to be lowered in both New Jersey and Pennsylvania, since the need to purchase power from outside sources was dramatically reduced. In May 1987, GPU reinstated dividends to shareholders for the first time since 1980. In 1988 earnings rose to

$284 million, from $259 million the previous year, and dividends were increased twice. These results were achieved partly due to record-setting operation by the company's generating units, particularly those fueled by coal. GPU-owned generators produced 31 million megawatt-hours in 1988.

In 1989 Kuhns retired as president, chairman, and CEO, and was replaced by Standley H. Hoch. Kuhns, who had been chief executive for 20 years, had first retired two years earlier, but that initial retirement had proved temporary, as he had returned to active duty upon the death of his successor, John O'Leary. Hoch, who had been executive vice-president and chief financial officer of General Dynamics Corporation, continued to reshape GPU into a more streamlined and cohesive system, focusing on improved communication networks among the parent company and operating subsidiaries; on eliminating unnecessary work and positions; and on maximizing production efficiency. GPU increased its dividends twice in 1989 and once each in 1990 and 1991.

The 1990s and Prospects for A New Millennium

The year 1990 brought the completion of the Three Mile Island cleanup, a project that drained GPU financially and made consideration of further construction projects much more difficult. Also in 1990, a 6.1 percent rate increase was approved for Jersey Central, the first such hike since 1986, meaning an additional $95.5 million in revenue. The company's operating and maintenance expenses were lower than in 1989, and when 24 officers retired in a 15-month period, only eight were replaced, reflecting the stated commitment to streamlining. In addition, an agreement was reached with DQE, a western Pennsylvania utility, which agreed to produce and transmit electricity from western Pennsylvania, where demand was lower, to the eastern part of the state over 240 miles of transmission line.

GPU's status as a regulated public utility had helped to prevent its demise, in spite of regulations that sometimes hinder profits and require spending on safety and environmental control. By the mid-1990s, however, management at the company acknowledged that revenues were flat due to increasing competition within the electric utility industry, and a reassessment of GPU's entire operation was required. The result of this internal evaluation was far-reaching and dramatic. GPU made the announcement that it was beginning a process to sell all of the fossil fuel and hydroelectric generating facilities owned by the company. Comprised of over 26 operating stations, the book value of the sale was estimated at over $1 billion. In addition, both the Oyster Creek Nuclear Generating Station and Three Mile Island Unit 1 were put up for sale. At the same time, the company reached an agreement with The Williams Company to jointly market electricity, natural gas, oil, and energy-related services to an expanded market from New York to Virginia. Management thought it beneficial to combine Williams' background as America's largest volume transporter of natural gas with its own expertise within the electric industry.

This was only the beginning of a comprehensive restructuring process. GPU also made a strategic decision to expand overseas, especially within Australia. In 1997, the company purchased PowerNet Victoria, from the state of Victoria, Australia for $1.9 billion. PowerNet Victoria owns and operates the electricity transmission system throughout Victoria, an area that covered over 87,000 square miles and had a population of approximately 4.5 million. A new management team had decided to focus on aggressively expanding the company's international operations to offset fluctuations in the domestic market.

GPU's continued success was expected to be greatly influenced by regulations imposed on the industry, as well as its ability to expand into related energy markets and services. Yet the company's strategic vision of diversifying overseas would no doubt lessen the impact of any unforeseen developments within the domestic market.

Principal Subsidiaries

Jersey Central Power & Light Company; Metropolitan Edison Company; Pennsylvania Electric Company; GPU Service Corporation; GPU International, Inc.

Further Reading

"Agreement Reached to Sell Stake in Australian Concern," *Wall Street Journal,* December 1997.

"An End to Hopson's Labyrinth," *Business Week,* December 8, 1945.

"GPU Closes PowerNet Purchase," *Wall Street Journal,* November 1997.

"New York Utility, GPU Aim to Sell Stakes in Generating Station," *Wall Street Journal,* February 1998.

Stranahan, Susan Q, "Wanna Buy a Reactor? Three Mile Island Becomes a Hot Property," *Fortune,* November 10, 1997, p. 40

"Through the Wringer with A.G.&E.," *Fortune,* December 1945.

"Williams Cos. and GPU Venture," *Wall Street Journal,* December 1997.

—Robert R. Jacobson
—updated by Thomas Derdak

Groupe DMC (Dollfus Mieg & Cie)

10, avenue Ledru-Rollin
75012 Paris
France
(33) 1.49.28.10.00
Fax: (33) 1.43.42.51.91
Web site: http://www.dmc-cw.com

Public Company
Incorporated: 1746 as Koechlin, Schmalzer & Co.
Employees: 7,600
Sales: FFr 5.95 billion (US$ 1.1 billion) (1997)
Stock Exchanges: Paris Frankfurt
Ticker Symbol: Dollfus Mieg & Cie
SICs: 2211 Broadwoven Fabric Mills—Cotton; 2221
   Broadwoven Fabric Mills—Manmade; 2299 Textile
   Goods, Not Elsewhere Classified; 2399 Fabricated
   Textile Products, Not Elsewhere Classified; 5949
   Sewing, Needlework & Piece Goods; 2284 Thread
   Mills

A household name among the world's needlepointers, France's Groupe DMC (Dollfus Mieg & Cie) is also the world's leading designer and producer of printed fabrics for the apparel and other industries, as well as a leading designer and manufacturer of household and protective textiles and trimmings for the clothing industry. Since the mid-1990s DMC has also expanded upon its needlepoint and other hand crafts expertise to open a chain of retail hand crafts specialty stores.

An extensive reorganization of DMC and its subsidiary companies in the late 1990s has grouped the company's operations under four major divisions: Apparel Fabrics; Crafts; Trimmings; and Household Textiles. The company's Apparel division, which groups subsidiaries such as KBC (Germany), Velcorex of France (U.S.A.), DMC Tissus (France) and others, markets to the casualwear, sportswear, and other categories under brand names including SAIC, KBC, Herose, Inoseta, DMC Prints, Maya, CDW, and Texunion. Apparel, at some 49 percent, contributes the largest share of DMC's revenues.

Reducing its reliance on its apparel sales—and on the European market, which accounts for 70 percent of the company's sales and, until recently, the major portion of its manufacturing—has become a company priority in the 1990s. As such, the company is using its longstanding dominance of the world needlepointing market as a platform on which to penetrate deeper into the growing crafts market. While DMC subsidiaries, including founding house Dollfus Mieg & Cie in France, DMC Creative World in the United Kingdom, and DMC Inc. in the United States, produce needlepoint thread and accessories, DMC has branched out into retailing with its chain of *Loisirs et Creation* stores. This retail concept, specializing in hand crafts, is a first for France and Europe. Introduced with two stores in 1995, the Loisirs et Creation concept has expanded to ten stores in 1998, with plans to build a chain of more than 30 stores in France and Europe by the year 2000. In addition to the retail stores, DMC has also launched a network of Hobbyland in-store boutiques. With the worldwide crafts market estimated to be worth some US$20 billion, DMC expects its crafts division to contribute a growing part of its annual sales. In 1997, this division represented 17 percent of the company's total sales.

DMC is also a leading producer of industrial sewing threads, linings and interlinings, and other trimmings products for the worldwide garment industry. These activities represent 14 percent of the company's sales. DMC's Household Textiles division not only encompasses the company's upholstery and bed linens subsidiaries, but also serves as the company's springboard into the wider household fashions market. Household Textiles added nine percent of the company's 1997 sales of FFr 5.9 billion.

18th-Century Origins

DMC was founded in 1746 by Jean-Henri Dollfus, Jean-Jacques Schmalzer, and Samuel Koechlin in order to produce so-called Indian print fabrics in Mulhouse, in what was then the Alsace region of Switzerland (Mulhouse was annexed by France in 1798). The firm, originally known as Koechlin, Schmalzer & Co., linked Dollfus's artistic talents with Koechlin's financial backing and Schmalzer's wholesale experience. The company's development took off especially under the leadership of Dollfus's son, Daniel, who, upon his marriage to Anne-Marie Mieg in 1800, added his wife's name to his own.

The company adopted the Dollfus-Mieg name in recognition of Daniel Dollfus-Mieg's contribution to its growth.

By the beginning of the 19th century, Dollfus-Mieg et Compagnie had already begun to achieve national recognition for the quality of its fabrics, winning a prestigious silver medal at the 1806 French Industrial Exhibition. The following year, Dollfus Mieg joined the nascent Industrial Revolution, becoming the first textiles company to operate a machine capable of printing in 12 colors. At this time, also, Dollfus Mieg began expanding beyond Mulhouse, although that city would remain its principal manufacturing site through the late 1990s. After opening a sales office in Paris, the company spread throughout France and then began establishing offices throughout Europe as well. Throughout the 19th century, Dollfus Mieg & Cie established more than 100 sales offices, not only in Europe, but throughout the world.

Dollfus Mieg continued to build its production capacity, introducing power weaving machinery and reaching production levels of more than two million yards of fabric annually by the 1830s. The company's sales expanded beyond Europe during this period, bringing Dollfus Mieg products to the United States for the first time. The company continued to improve on its manufacturing techniques, improving the quality of its fabrics, a process crowned, in 1864, by the gold medal award at the French Industrial Exhibition. At the same time, the company had also developed a reputation for its social policies, opening schools and daycare centers, and even building a community of homes for its workers. Many of these housing "settlements" were still in use by DMC employees into the 20 century. In 1842, the company founded the Société Industrielle de Mulhouse as part of its research and development activities.

After nearly a century concentrated on printed textiles, Dollfus Mieg began eyeing expansion into other markets. In 1841 the company began production of sewing thread. Dollfus Mieg's threads gained in importance especially after the company bought the patent rights to a process called mercerization.

Developed by the English calico printer John Mercer, the process involved dipping cotton yarn into a caustic alkali solution. The mercerized threads were stronger, more lustrous, and also more easily dyed. Where cotton threads before had found difficulty competing against silk yarns, the mercerized threads presented rivaled silk yarns in appearance, while remaining much less expensive.

Dollfus Mieg's thread and yarn production took off, and before the end of the century the company had established itself as one of the world's premier producers of sewing threads and decorative yarns. Aiding the company's reputation—and sales—was the 1886 publication of the *Encyclopedia des Ouvrages des Dames*, written by Austria's Theresa von Dillmont and published by Dollfus Mieg. The *Encyclopedia*, later retitled the *Encyclopedia of Needlework*, contained some 800 pages, and was eventually translated into 17 languages, with sales of more than two million copies. The *Encyclopedia*, after a number of revisions and updates, remained a bestseller among needle crafts practitioners into the late 1990s.

Industry Dominance in the 20th Century

Thread production had overtaken printed fabrics as the company's chief revenue generator by the end of the 19th century, a process aided by the introduction of embroidery floss in 1898. By the early years of the 20th century Dollfus Mieg had achieved worldwide dominance of the thread market and had become a leader in printed fabrics as well. While much of its production remained centered in its Mulhouse base, the company's products were available in more than 100 countries worldwide—and particularly its sewing threads enjoyed near-monopoly positions in many of the company's markets.

These positions were interrupted by the outbreak of World War I, and further disrupted by the World War II years, as the company found itself cut off from much of its export markets. Nevertheless, in the 20th century Dollfus Mieg began a policy of expansion that greatly increased its industrial base. While part of the company's growth came internally, including increasing its implantation in the United States with the formation of the DMC Corporation in New York City in 1934, Dollfus Mieg began a series of acquisitions that not only greatly increased its existing printed fabrics and sewing threads portfolio, but extended the company into a range of complementary fabrics and textiles production.

Shares of Dollfus Mieg were first offered to the public on the Paris stock exchange in 1922. The company's expansion took it into such fabrics categories as protective and fireproof textiles, home decor textiles, denim and corduroy fabrics, as well as fabrics specially developed for the sportswear market. The company also invested heavily in research and development of new thread-making methods in the 1950s and 1960s, helping the company rebuild its position lost during World War II. In 1961, the company changed its name to DMC, upon the merger of Dollfus Mieg & Cie with the operations of Ets. Thiriez & Cartier Bresson, a relationship that did not, however, survive into the 1980s.

By the start of the 1970s, the DMC group represented an extensive array of diverse subsidiaries. In keeping, the company was formally transformed into a holding company. The following decade, however, proved nearly disastrous for the company. By the start of the 1980s, DMC was losing money and facing bankruptcy. The arrival of Julien Charlier in 1982 as the company's chief turned DMC's fortunes around. Instituting a drastic reorganization—including cutting the company's workforce by more than 35 percent, resuming direct control of its thread production activities, and restructuring its subsidiaries around their various textile specialties—Charlier succeeded in bringing the company back to profitability by 1983.

Beyond stabilizing DMC's profits, however, Charlier took the company on an aggressive expansion program during the second half of the decade. Expansion took the form of acquisition, particularly as the company sought to enter new market areas. In 1986, the company acquired Hervillier (resold in 1990), as well as a part of SAIC Velcorex (later increased to 100 percent). Two years later, DMC stepped up the pace, acquiring 50 percent of Bozkurt, the textile subsidary of the Turkish Koç conglomerate; the company also purchased a textile printing facility in Orangeburg, South Carolina, and a second facility in Lyon, France. While establishing a new company in Egypt, Thread Makers Cy, DMC acquired three fabric makers, Polilinha in Portugal; Donisthorpe in the United Kingdom; and Boule de Neige in Switzerland.

The following year DMC continued its expansion, with the acquisition of the Netherlands' Watermelon, and a 50 percent share (in partnership with the Dutch Ten Cate) of Irish denim makers Atlantic Mills. That same year the company established new operations in the United States, under the names Promotex and Fashion Fabrics of America, and formed a joint venture, Maya Fashion Print, that brought the company into Hungary. The company also began development of a retail distribution network, Descamps, with operations focused on the United States.

Sliding in the 1990s

By 1990, DMC's revenues had topped FFr 10.35 billion with net profits of nearly FFr 300 million. By the end of the decade, however, the company saw its sales drop by nearly half—and at one point its net losses approached FFr 600 million. A number of factors had come together to bring the company to a new crisis by mid-decade. The company's ambitious expansion program had taken it into too many directions, and especially beyond its core products of printed textiles and sewing threads. The company's sales were also hit by DMC's long reliance on the European marketplace—while the majority of the company's sales came from exports, fully 70 percent of the company's revenues were generated within the European community. Yet, through most of the 1990s, Europe weathered an extended economic crisis, particularly severe in France and in the reunified Germany. The company's printed fabrics catalog was also considered as having fallen out of fashion. DMC, plagued by management in-fighting and competition among subsidiaries, watched as its fabric sales eroded. Equally critical to the company's difficulties was its overemphasis on European locations for its manufacturing park at a time when the market had clearly shifted to the lower-cost production centers in Asia and other developing regions.

By 1994, the company's sales had slipped back to FFr 7.9 billion, with a net loss of FFr 148 million. The company's reorganization appeared to redress its position: after selling off a number of subsidiaries, exiting several markets, including zipper production, and regrouping its other operations, in 1995 the company, despite a continued slump in sales to FFr 7.1 billion, eked out a profit of just FFr 3 million. The company's difficulties led to the exit of CEO David Suddens, brought in by Julien Charlier just nine months earlier. Charlier, who continued to oversee the company from a position as president of the board of directors, appointed Jacques Boubal to lead the company. Meanwhile, DMC's fortunes continued to fade, with revenues slumping to FFr 6.2 billion in 1996 for a net loss of FFr 592 million—nearly ten percent of the company's revenues.

DMC, led by Boubal, once again restructured its activities, focusing its activities on four primary markets, including its clothing fabrics and sewing threads, but also trimmings and fabrics for home decoration. The company also took steps to move the bulk of its production to the Asian, African, and eastern European markets to take advantage of lower wage costs, while maintaining only high valued-added operations in western Europe. Particularly promising for the company was its newly created chain of Loisirs et Creation stores. Launched in 1995, the retail chain featured a crafts specialty focus, a concept that, while long a success in the United States, was new for Europe. Initial success of the chain was encouraging enough for the company to open ten French stores by 1998, with plans to reach 30 throughout France, before expanding throughout Europe. In addition to the Loisirs et Creation concept, DMC also introduced a network of Hobbyland in-store boutiques, featuring a more limited selection of crafts supplies and kits. By 1998, Hobbyland boutiques had been opened in more than 85 Carrefour hypermarkets, with agreements to introduce the concept into the Continent and Cora hypermarket chains as well. The company expected its retail crafts activities to represent as much as FFr 500 million by the end of the century.

The results of DMC's restructuring remained to be seen; however, the company's initial expectation to restore profits and revenue growth by 1999 were considered too optimistic. Nevertheless, the company hoped to have solved its latest difficulties by the year 2000, while maintaining its position as a world leader in the textile industry.

Principal Subsidiaries

DMC Tissus; Gebruder Bochmann (Germany); Buntweberei Ahornberg (Germany); Veclorex of France (U.S.); Inoseta (49%); KBC (Germany); Herose Textil (Germany); Maya Fashion Print (Hungary); DMC Prints (U.S.); CDP Textiles Ltd. (China; 51%); China Dyeing Holdings (49%); Dollfus Mieg & Cie; DMC Creative World (U.K.); DMC Espagne (Spain); DMC Italie (Italy); The DMC Inc. (U.S.); DMC Needlecraft Asia (Singapore) DMC Accessoires; Donisthorpe (U.K.); DMC Industria (Spain); Polilinha (Portugal); DMC Czeckia (Czech Republic); DMC Polska (Poland); Fileteries du Mahgreb (Morocco); DMC Mediterranee (Tunisia); Satexco (Colombia); Toga Linings (South Africa; 50%); Tejidos DMC (Spain); KBC Textile Wohnen (Germany).

Principal Divisions

Apparel Fabrics Divison; Crafts; Trimmings; Household Textiles.

Further Reading

Chirot, Françoise, "DMC accélere son développement international," *Le Monde*, December 22, 1988, p. 27.
Epinay, Bénédicte, "Le groupe DMC diffère une nouvelle fois son retour à l'équilibre," *Les Echoes*, September 23, 1998, p. 9.
Lagoutte, Christine, "DMC sous l'oeil des investisseurs," *Le Figaro Economique*, February 2, 1998, p. 16.
Leboucq, Valérie, "DMC tisse sa toile sur les travaux manuels," *Les Echoes*, June 9, 1998, p. 49.
Payne, Mark, "Profiles of DMC and Chargeurs," *Textile Outlook International*, July 1997, p. 70.
Tissier, Corinne, "La tempete que DMC pouvait eviter," *Le Nouvel Economiste*, March 14, 1997, p. 48.

—M. L. Cohen

GRUNDIG

Grundig AG

Kurgartenstraße 37
D-90762 Fürth
Germany
(49) (911) 703-0
Fax: (49) (911) 70 53 76
Web site: http://www.grundig.de

Private Company
Incorporated: 1945 as Radio Vertrieb Fürth
Employees: 6,114
Sales: DM 2,833 million (1997)
SICs: 3579 Office Machines, Not Elsewhere Classified;
3651 Household Audio & Video Equipment; 3661
Telephone & Telegraph Apparatus; 3663 Radio &
Television Broadcasting & Communications
Equipment; 3823 Industrial Instruments for
Measurement, Display, & Control of Process
Variables, & Related Products

Grundig AG is a German consumer electronics manufacturer with significant shares in the market for television sets, video recorders, satellite reception equipment, and digital audio and television reception equipment in major European countries. Almost half of the company's DM 2.83 billion in sales in 1997 was generated from television sets; 12.6 percent of sales came from car audio equipment, ten percent from audio/hi-fi and video equipment, 7.5 percent from satellite reception equipment, 3.4 percent from professional electronics, and two percent from telecommunication equipment such as mobile phones. Only three percent of Grundig's sales revenues came from non-European countries, whereas of the lion's share—about 88 percent—half was generated in Germany and half in other countries of the European Union. Headquartered in Nuremberg, Germany, Grundig runs production facilities in Germany, Portugal, Great Britain, and Austria and development centers in Denmark, Great Britain, Austria, and the United States. Of Grundig's share capital, 95 percent is held by a group of Bavarian investors.

Dynamic Beginnings After World War II

In 1945 Max Grundig, a 37-year-old German entrepreneur who had stored the equipment of his electrical workshop in a small Bavarian village, set up shop in Fürth near Nuremberg. He rented space for his new business, Radio Vertrieb Fürth, and began producing transformers for radio receivers. Soon after, Grundig ran out of space and—after long negotiations with the city government—moved to premises near the city limit on a long-term lease. While the first buildings were going up at the new location, Max Grundig hired the best engineers and business administrators he could find in Germany. With 45 employees, Grundig produced the do-it-yourself radio kit "Heinzelmann." This single-circuit receiver was freely available in the otherwise highly rationed consumer goods market of postwar Germany and it became an instant success. Grundig heavily expanded his business to meet the huge demand for radio receivers. In 1948 Max Grundig founded Grundig Werke GmbH. The company soon employed 650 people and new production facilities and research labs were built.

In the 1950s the Grundig company's growth was breathtaking. Grundig's output of pioneering innovations included the world's first miniature television cameras for the inspection of pipelines and boreholes, Europe's first mass-produced VHF receivers, Germany's first television camera for monitoring systems, auto radios, music cabinets with 3-D sound, portable radio sets, tape recorders, dictating machines, and measuring instruments. Grundig became Europe's largest radio manufacturer in 1952, the world's largest producer of tape recorders in 1955, and the world's largest manufacturer of radiograms in 1956. Grundig entered the office equipment market in 1957 by acquiring a majority share in two important German companies: the Triumph Werke in Nuremberg and the Adler-Werke in Frankfurt/Main. In the same year the world's largest production facility for tape recorders was set up in Bayreuth in upper Franken. Within only a decade Grundig's work force climbed to 12,000 in 1956, and it more than doubled again within only three years, reaching 26,000 in 1959. By that year seven million machines had left Grundig's assembly lines.

More Innovations and Growth Outside Germany in the 1960s

Grundig entered the 1960s with 30,000 employees, 8,000 of them working in the main facilities at the company's headquarters in Fürth. More Grundig innovations, such as TV sets with wireless remote controls, the smallest German pocket AM radio receiver weighing just 250 grams, and the first portable TV sets made in Germany were put on the market in 1960 and 1961. Later in the 1960s Grundig pioneered developments in the hi-fi consumer market and technologies for storing and transmitting images for professional applications. In the hi-fi field, a series of modular units was introduced that allowed consumers to design their own configuration. A fully transistorized hi-fi amplifier was introduced in 1963, followed by the first Grundig hi-fi receiver in 1967. In the consumer television market, Grundig introduced the first German high-definition TV set with 875 lines in 1962 and demonstrated for the first time the transmission of broad-band television waves via a twin-core telephone line. In 1968 Grundig designed the first video transmission for professional applications. The new technology, developed by Grundig engineers, enabled television images to be transmitted over a telephone line; within a minute they were then available as a photographic record. A year later Grundig publicized its so-called "leakage cable technology," which allowed cordless picture transmission between fixed and moving parts of professional television systems.

Responding to the ever-growing demand for measuring instruments, Grundig entered the planning stage for a new electronics production facility in 1960. In addition, in response to the shortage of skilled personnel, Grundig's facilities for professional education were enlarged one year later. In a first attempt to expand abroad, a tape recorder factory was set up in Northern Ireland in 1960. Five years later the second foreign facility was built in Braga, Portugal. In 1968 Grundig sold its office equipment subsidiaries Triumph and Adler to the American firm Litton and concentrated on strengthening its consumer electronics business. In 1969 a newly built production facility for TV sets was opened in Rovereto, Italy. Another Grundig factory was opened in Creutzwald, France, in 1971.

Expanding at Home in the 1970s

In the 1970s Grundig expanded its facilities in Nuremberg. First, a factory for the production of color TV sets and a production plant for plastics were opened in 1970. Then in 1973 the central customer service department as well as the Nuremberg sales office were opened in "Grundig-City" in the Langwasser district of Nuremberg. In 1978 a new video recorder factory started production. On April 1, 1972, the Grundig-Werke GmbH was transformed into a public company—the Grundig Aktiengesellschaft (Grundig AG).

In the following years Grundig received two large orders from corporate customers. As an official supplier for the Olympic Games in Munich in 1972, Grundig delivered 9,000 monochrome and color television sets for informational displays. In 1974 Grundig equipped 140 operating centers of the Deutsche Lufthansa with a television information system. In the consumer electronics market, new product introductions included the first cassette deck for hi-fi systems, "Super Color" television sets with fully transistorized chassis, the first German portable color television (which was among Grundig's most successful products ever), the world's first dictating cassette recorder with a built-in minute display, the first Grundig car radios with cassette players, and the first German color television projector.

Sales passed the DM 2 billion mark for the first time in the financial year of 1974–75, and in 1978–79 Grundig products generated sales of more than DM 2.9 billion. In 1979 "an equity link with the Dutch Philips group was established," according to Grundig.

Changing Owners and Mastering Difficulties in the 1980s

By 1982 Max Grundig's empire consisted of 23 manufacturing plants and employed about 31,500 people. One year later, it generated more than DM 3 billion in sales for the first time in its history. The company was struggling, however, with profitability. When the company's founder retired from company management in 1984 and sold his firm to the Netherlands-based Philips Electronics N.V., Europe's largest consumer electronics company, more than 170 million Grundig radios and television sets had been sold worldwide. Philips took over leadership of the Grundig E.M.V. Elektro-Mechanische Versuchsanstalt Max Grundig GmbH & Co. KG, Fürth, which had been the parent company of Grundig AG since 1972, and agreed to pay a dividend of about DM 45 million annually to the Max-Grundig-Stiftung, the founder's family foundation, whether or not Grundig AG turned a profit.

Led by Hermanus Koning, the new head of the executive board, Grundig managed to get out of the red within only two years. The price paid for this, however, was a cutback of the work force by almost 40 percent—down to about 19,200. On the other hand, Grundig intensified marketing efforts and had a good hand with some new product introductions. After investing DM 80 million into the reconstruction of a production facility for a new flow production line, the first video recorders went into production there in 1986. In the same year Grundig made some of its most successful market introductions: the world's first mass-produced 100 Hz color TV set, a technology that solved the problem of large-area flickering in conventional TV screens, and two "Jumbo" TV sets with screens of 82 cm and 95 cm in diameter. Demand for those innovations were so high that orders were placed on waiting lists. A new marketing strategy was pursued when Grundig introduced a new hi-fi product line of extraordinary quality. As the name, "Fine Arts by Grundig," suggests, the line was aimed at the professional hi-fi equipment market dominated by specialized firms. Another group of high-priced products was marketed under the "Design by F.A. Porsche" label, which was aimed to take advantage of the renowned auto maker's reputation, including color TV sets and car radios with alphanumeric station display and automatic frequency selection. When Chief Executive Hermanus Koning retired in 1987, Grundig reported a net profit of DM 100 million for the first time after many years of losses, and sales reached DM 3 billion again.

After the new chief executive, Johan van Tilburg, took over, Grundig's strategy was redirected to better compete in a Japanese-dominated electronic consumer goods market. A facility in Malaysia was purchased for the production of audio equipment. Beginning in 1988, Grundig supplied the two Japanese electronics giants Matsushita and Hitachi with video heads. In 1989 Grundig entered the market of environmental monitoring technology. At the end of the 1980s Grundig's sales reached DM 3.43 billion, net profits amounted to DM 140 million, and about 18,800 people were on the group's payroll. In December 1989 the company's founder Max Grundig died at the age of 81.

Surviving Turmoil in the 1990s

In 1990 Grundig's largest facility for the production of color TV sets and plastic cabinets in Nuremberg was modernized and interconnected. After the German reunification, Grundig started distributing its product range to the new East German market and enjoyed two extraordinary years of growth in sales. In the financial year 1989–90 sales rose by 10.7 percent, which was much higher than the industry average, and in the record year 1990–91 sales jumped again by 20 percent, to DM 4.55 billion. In the same year, Grundig reported a net profit of DM 190 million and employed 21,170 people. Aside from the run on Grundig products by East German consumers and cost reductions through rationalization, other factors—such as new system solutions in industrial and office electronics offered by Grundig's newly formed "Systems Technology" division, Grundig's introduction of a cordless telephone, a new hotel communication system, and in particular a new television set with the new 16:9 picture ratio—contributed to this success. When CEO Johan van Tilburg resigned of his own accord at the end of 1991, however, Grundig entered a decade of instability and restructuring in a stagnating consumer electronics market.

Due to worldwide overcapacities and increasing competition, a Spanish TV production company that belonged to the Grundig group, Fabricantes Europeos de Televisores, S.A., closed in 1992. In 1994 Grundig underwent a restructuring program. All Grundig divisions were transformed into legally independent companies that became subsidiaries of Grundig AG, which functioned as a management holding. The TV production facility in France was sold. At the same time, sales fell by nine percent because of decreasing prices for consumer electronics, an area that generated about 85 percent of Grundig's total sales. Consequently, Grundig reported a loss of DM 348 million in the financial year 1993–94. Hopes to get out of the red in 1995—Grundig's 50th anniversary year—were thwarted. Due to further declines in prices for consumer electronics in a stagnating market, together with the growing strength of the Deutsche Mark against the dollar and several other European currencies, Grundig reported a net loss of DM 598 million. About 50 percent of it was caused by extraordinary expenses for restructuring and by financial support to an Argentine licensee.

At a press conference in 1996 Grundig's supervisory board announced that it and Philips had mutually agreed to end Philips's domination of Grundig by the end of 1996. Thereafter, Grundig aimed to concentrate on its core competencies in consumer electronics. It sold or closed down facilities connected with other markets such as professional electronics. It closed down the production facility in Malaysia and cut down a quarter of its work force. Grundig's sales in markets outside of Europe contributed about six percent to total sales in 1996. Through its own sales offices in Poland, Russia, and the Middle East, and through cooperation with other firms, sales rose by 30 percent in Central European, Middle Eastern, and Asian markets. On the other hand, the decision of two other German electronics giants—Siemens and Blaupunkt—to cease production of entertainment electronics cost Grundig DM 227 million in lost components sales to those companies.

Grundig announced losses of DM 631 million at the end of the financial year 1996. After spending about DM 1.5 million in the previous years—about $950 million at that time—to keep Grundig out of debt, Philips announced on January 8, 1997 that it would give up control over Grundig and restrict its responsibility for any further losses to its duties as a passive minority shareholder. Philips also withdrew DM 250 million from Grundig's capital. In the middle of January the Grundig supervisory board replaced Grundig CEO Pieter van der Wal, who officially resigned on February 3. According to Reuters, van der Wal cited an overconcentration in the European and German markets and an overly broad product array as the two primary reasons for Grundig's serious problems. When Grundig reported net losses of DM 631 million for 1996 in June 1997, Philips fought Grundig's demand that it be compensated by Philips for the whole sum. In March, Grundig had announced a DM 553 million loss, which now also included restructuring costs resulting from Philips's decision to end its participation in Grundig. On July 18, 1997, Philips announced that it would cut its share in Grundig from 31.6 percent to five percent, and it sold 26.6 percent to Botts & Company Ltd. in London. The British investment bank acquired another 16.4 percent, which the Hohenstaufen Vierundvierzigste Vermögensverwaltung GmbH in Cologne had purchased from the Grundig family through Philips. Philips also was planning to sell 52 percent of Grundig shares held by the Max-Grundig-Stiftung to the Botts & Company immediately, which would have made them the owner of 95 percent of Grundig's shares. Philips could not reach an agreement with the Max-Grundig-Stiftung, however, which was obliged to sell its Grundig shares to Philips by 2004. The new speaker of Grundig's executive board, Pieter de Jong, criticized Philips sharply since he and Bavaria's minister for economy had already offered Philips a takeover by a Bavarian group of investors.

After Grundig's former head of its supervisory board, Christian Schwarz-Schilling, resigned his position in mid-1997, the former chief executive of Krauss Maffei AG, Burkhard Wollschläger, became the new chair of Grundig's supervisory board on August 1. With the support of the Bavarian Minister of Economics, Otto Wiesheu, Wollschläger worked out an agreement that resolved the dispute with Philips. Among other things, Philips agreed to pay another DM 400 million to compensate Grundig's 1996 losses. Pieter de Jong, speaker of Grundig's executive board, resigned after the first session of the new Grundig supervisory board on September 24, 1997. He was succeeded by Herbert Bruch, who formerly headed Grundig's Personnel and Industrial Relations divisions. Four other top executives left the company in the same year. On December 18, the contract between Philips and the new owner group Bayerische Wagnisbeteiligung GmbH led by Bavarian Banks was officially signed in Fürth. It included the cancellation of Philips leadership over Grundig AG.

At the end of 1997 Grundig reported a net loss of DM 118 million and sales of DM 2.8 million. In February 1999, Philips's share in Grundig was down to 0.5 percent, and Grundig's work force amounted to 5,700. It was planned that the remaining production facilities in Portugal, Great Britain, and Austria, as well as the two German factories in Bayreuth and Nuremberg, would continue operations, while Grundig headquarters would be moved to Nuremberg by spring 1999.

For the first time since 1972, the Grundig AG was independent again. In the 1998 annual meeting, Grundig shareholders decided to boost capital by DM 134 million and to concentrate on Grundig's strengths: high quality products and technological leadership. In a press release the company announced a slightly positive result for the first half of 1998 and aimed to concentrate on its core business—consumer electronics—and promising niche markets such as office electronics and measuring instruments. In November 1998, Grundig launched a new advertising campaign that emphasized Grundig's technological and innovative strength featuring four of the company's star products: the brilliant 100 Hz TV sets, an Internet Box, an audio compact set with space-fidelity technology, and the first serial digital audio broadcast component for use in cars. While looking for new strategic partners, Grundig's R&D efforts were directed in particular toward the market introduction of equipment for new digital services delivered by satellite, terrestrial, and cable. In February 1999, Grundig announced the founding of the new subsidiary, Grundig Digital Systems, headquartered in San Jose, California, and the takeover of R&D capacities for digital television broadcasting from TV/COM International, another California firm located in San Diego, where it was planning to work on new generations of set-top boxes and integrated digital modules for TV sets. In January 1999, Grundig had acquired a license from the American firm Macrovision Corp. for its pay-per-view copy protection technology to be included in its set-top decoders, which restricts unauthorized recording of pay-TV programs by consumers.

Principal Subsidiaries

Grundig Fernseh-Video Produkte und Systeme GmbH (Germany); Grundig Marketing und Vertrieb Europa GmbH (Germany); Grundig CAR Audio-Produkte GmbH (Germany); Grundig Austria Gesellschaft m.b.H. (Austria); Grundig Audio Internacional Lda. (Portugal); Grundig UK Ltd. (Great Britain); Grundig International Marketing & Sales GmbH (Germany); Grundig Gulf FZE (United Arab Emirates); Grundig Digital Systems.

Further Reading

''Competition: Commission Set To Clear TV/VCR Makers' Power-Saving Deal,'' *European Report,* January 5, 1996.

Die Geschichte des Hauses Grundig, company document, Fürth, Germany: Grundig AG, 1998.

''Germany's Grundig Still in the Red,'' *Tech Europe,* January 9, 1996.

''Grundig-Chef tritt zurück,'' *Die Welt,* September 25, 1997.

''Grundig-Konsortium noch nicht unter Dach und Fach,'' *Die Welt,* September 30, 1997.

''Grundig rechnet mit Philips ab,'' *Die Welt,* January 22, 1997.

''Grundig Sales Down, Narrows Loss,'' *Reuters Business Report,* August 29, 1997.

''Grundig To Stop Making TV Sets in Germany,'' *Reuters Business Report,* December 20, 1996.

Grundig Umweltbericht 1997 (environmental report), company document, Fürth, Germany: Grundig AG, 1998.

''Grundig will nächstes Jahr die Nullinie durchbrechen,'' *Die Welt,* September 20, 1997.

''HAVi Backers to Promote Compatibility with Sun's Jini,'' *Newsbytes News Network,* January 21, 1999.

''Heftiger Streit um den Grundig-Verlust,'' *Die Welt,* June 5, 1997.

''Philips beendet sein Engagement bei Grundig,'' *Die Welt,* January 9, 1997.

''Philips Disputes Grundig 1996 Loss,'' *European Report,* January 5, 1996.

''Philips, Grundig & Olympus Define Digital Dictation Standard,'' *Newsbytes News Network,* February 28, 1996.

''Philips to Become Passive Minority Shareholder in Grundig,'' *Xinhua News Agency,* January 8, 1997.

''Philips trägt schwer an Grundig,'' *Die Welt,* April 25, 1996.

''Philips Unloads Its Grundig Shares,'' *Xinhua News Agency,* July 19, 1997.

''Technology Report: Philips Bows Out of Grundig Pact,'' *The Dallas Morning News,* January 9, 1997, p. 11D.

''Viel Bewegung bei Grundig,'' *Die Welt,* July 19, 1997.

Wildhagen, Andreas, ''Treueschwüre für Grundig,'' *Die Welt,* January 24, 1997.

—Evelyn Hauser

Ha-Lo Industries, Inc.

5980 Touhy Avenue
Niles, Illinois 60714
U.S.A.
(847) 647-2300
Fax: (847) 647-5999
Web site: http://www.ha-lo.com

Public Company
Incorporated: 1972
Employees: 4,000
Sales: $589.6 million (1998)
Stock Exchanges: New York
Ticker Symbol: HMK
SICs: 7389 Business Services, Not Elsewhere Classified

The largest marketer and distributor of promotional products in the United States, Ha-Lo Industries, Inc. offers more than 300,000 promotional giveaway products to a lengthy list of customers—more than 30,000 in total—that includes many of the elite *Fortune* 500 corporations. One of the fastest-growing companies in the country, Ha-Lo recorded prodigious growth during the 1990s by acquiring dozens of competitors in domestic and international markets. By the end of the 1990s, the company's marketing and promotional capabilities included promotion marketing through UPSHOT, brand identity and packaging through LAGA, telemarketing through Market USA, and sports-related promotions through Ha-Lo Sports. In addition to the services provided through its subsidiaries, Ha-Lo provided corporate event planning and communication and design services. Logo-emblazoned coffee mugs, apparel, watches, and scores of other items represented Ha-Lo's mainstay business. Clients included Ford Motor Company, General Electric, General Mills, IBM, and Siemens.

Origins

Lou Weisbach was 23 years old when he struck out on his own as an entrepreneur. A former high school basketball coach in Chicago, Weisbach made his start by borrowing $3,500 from

his mother for the capital to launch his own business, Ha-Lo Industries, named after himself and his brother Hal. With the money he received from his mother, Weisbach began selling calendars to butcher shops and beauty shops—the type of promotional calendars imprinted with the name of the particular shop. His choice of business was far from glamorous, and not an occupation expected to produce a multimillionaire. The $3,500 he started with in 1972 blossomed into a $500 million business during the ensuing three decades.

Weisbach's arena of achievement—known variously as the promotional products or corporate premium business—had roots stretching back to the late 19th century, when corporate giveaways first appeared. The first to use such promotional items were small-town newspapers and print shops, whose business owners, in an effort to generate new business, printed the name of their enterprise on virtually anything that would accept ink. Customers received horse blankets, buggy whips, playing cards, flyswatters, and a host of other inexpensive goods that were the predecessors to the logo-emblazoned pens, coffee mugs, and baseball caps prevalent a century later. In the decades following their inception, promotional giveaway items appeared in various shapes, sizes, and types, each bearing the name of the business they were intended to promote. Initially, the promotional gifts were made by the shop owners and business operators themselves, but gradually companies began to emerge whose sole occupation was to produce such items for other businesses. One of the first great successes registered by this new breed of business competitor was a St. Paul, Minnesota, company named Brown & Bigelow. During the 1940s and 1950s, Brown & Bigelow created calendar giveaway promotions for John Deere, Ford, and Pillsbury, whose corporate banners were imprinted alongside the artistic work of Norman Rockwell and Maxfield Parrish. In their day, the calendars were as well known as the most frequently aired television commercials of the late 20th century.

Although Brown & Bigelow's calendars enjoyed national distribution, the corporate premium industry contained few companies that operated on a national basis. Instead, the industry was a collection of small companies with a local or regional focus. This characteristic of the industry—as highly frag-

---

Company Perspectives:

The arena for any company's product or service is extremely competitive. A favorable position in the mind of your customer or prospect is a never ending challenge. At Ha-Lo, we understand the communications clutter in today's market place. We also believe that promotional products can play an important role in making a lasting impression with your customers and prospects as well as your employees.

---

mented, without an upper tier of national leaders—endured as the corporate premium business grew during the latter half of the 20th century.

1992 Conversion to Public Ownership

The industry did not begin to consolidate or produce a dominant national leader until Weisbach took aim at becoming the biggest and best competitor in the corporate giveaway sector. Before Weisbach began earnestly pursuing this objective, Ha-Lo was similar to the thousands of other distributors of promotional products in the nation: relatively small and operating within a limited territory. Weisbach began devoting resources toward national expansion 20 years after he started the company, making a late but propitiously timed bid toward dominance. The U.S. promotional products industry was a $4.9 billion-a-year business in 1989, according to Promotional Products Association International. During the ensuing seven years, distributors' sales shot upward, more than doubling to $9.5 billion. Midway through this prolific growth spurt, Weisbach launched his expansion campaign, touched off by a 1992 initial public offering (IPO) of stock. The IPO raised $7.9 million, giving Weisbach the resources to fund an acquisition campaign and achieve geographic expansion by swallowing up other firms.

Aside from aggressively acquiring companies, Ha-Lo's progress during the 1990s was aided by another aspect of Weisbach's strategy: an emphasis on innovation. Ha-Lo distinguished itself by developing new types of giveaway items. Instead of relying on ubiquitous coffee mugs and pens, the company piqued its customers' interest by imprinting corporate banners on a vast and ever-changing selection of items. Ha-Lo distributed logo-engraved wine bottles, disposable cameras that printed a company's name on each photo, and, in one special case, the company sold 250 logo-bearing condoms to the Cook County Public Defenders Office. Ha-Lo also catered to the particular needs of individual clients, developing promotional items designed for specific corporate events and giveaways unique to an industry. For the movie theater chain Cineplex Odeon, Ha-Lo created ceramic vases shaped like popcorn bags. When the food conglomerate Kraft Foods wanted to call attention to its new packaging for Parmesan cheese, Ha-Lo developed heat-sensitive coffee mugs whose designs changed from the old label to the new label after the introduction of hot coffee. With these innovative products and the more traditional items such as paperweights, luggage tags, and apparel, Ha-Lo was a comprehensive supplier to businesses both large and small. Once Weisbach began expanding his operations and extending his geographic reach through acquisitions, the company's sales began to mushroom.

Following the 1992 IPO, Weisbach wasted little time in his acquisitive pursuits. There were 12,000 distributors in the corporate premium business at the time of Ha-Lo's stock market debut, providing a wealth of acquisition candidates from which to choose. Between 1992 and 1996, Weisbach acquired 11 competitors, as well as advertising agency Duncan & Hill, and had diversified in two important directions. In 1995, the company broadened its promotional capabilities by forming Ha-Lo Sports. The subsidiary was created to provide promotional items for sports teams, including endorsements and vendor programs. The following year, Weisbach acquired Market USA, which moved Ha-Lo into telemarketing, giving the company operations that served the United States and Canada. This initial acquisition spree had a significant effect on Ha-Lo's stature, executed at a time when the corporate premium industry ranked as the fastest-growing segment in the advertising business. By the end of 1996, Ha-Lo's annual sales had swelled to $255 million, but Weisbach was just beginning his assault on competitors. During the late 1990s, Weisbach moved steadfastly forward, causing an industrywide trend toward consolidation that would distance Ha-Lo from all rivals.

Late 1990s Acquisitions

As a medium, corporate giveaways generated more revenue annually than outdoor billboard advertising and not much less than magazine advertising generated. It was big business, but still highly fragmented, with approximately 15,000 distributors in existence during the late 1990s. Weisbach, pursuing a greater share of the nearly $10 billion worth of business available, was intent on reducing the number of distributors in the industry through his own acquisitive efforts. He embarked on his second round of acquisitions in 1997, quickly outpacing his record of expansion between 1992 and 1996.

In January 1997, Ha-Lo completed the acquisition of Creative Concepts in Advertising, a Beverly Hills, Michigan, specialty advertising products company with annual sales of $100 million. Creative Concepts ranked as the third largest distributor in the industry, with large corporate clients in the United States, Canada, and, importantly, Europe. One month later, Weisbach signed an exclusive agreement with Champion Products Inc., a leading brand in sports apparel, that gave Ha-Lo the exclusive rights to sell branded Champion apparel to the corporate promotional market, marking the first time an apparel brand with mass appeal became available for corporate promotional purposes. In April, Weisbach picked up a corporate premium distributor in Detroit, Bradley Marketing Group, with $9.7 million in annual sales and large corporate clients such as the United Auto Workers, Audi, and Ford. Next, Weisbach strengthened Ha-Lo's presence in New York, acquiring a 45-year-old promotional products distributor named Lees/Keystone, Inc. With annual revenues of $10 million, Lees/Keystone added clients such as IBM, Weight Watchers International, and MasterCard International to Ha-Lo's growing roster of more than 15,000 customers. After entering an exclusive agreement with Roots Canada—the largest Canadian manufacturer and retailer of apparel and fabric goods—that was similar to the deal struck with Champion, Weisbach acquired a nine-year-old company named

The Corporate Choice/Red Sail Merchandising, Inc. in July 1997. The acquisition added offices in San Francisco, Chicago, and northern New Jersey, bolstering Ha-Lo's presence in the New York market and adding an estimated $14 million in annual sales.

A brief respite followed the acquisition of The Corporate Choice/Red Sail Merchandising, offering an opportunity to reflect on the company's prodigious growth. During this lull in acquisitive activity, *Fortune Magazine* selected Ha-Lo as one of the country's 100 fastest-growing companies, crediting the company's "hard charging sales culture," and concluding that Ha-Lo "rules what is now the second-biggest part of the ad industry." Weisbach remarked that the recognition provided "an additional incentive to pursue our successful strategies for growth," and quickly made good on his words, acquiring $15-million-in-sales Joking, Spa. in September 1997. Joking, one of Italy's largest promotional products companies, added large European clients such as American Express Europe, Fiat, and Motorola; offices in Florence, Buenos Aires, and Mexico City; and furthered the international expansion inaugurated by the acquisition of Creative Concepts earlier in the year. By the end of the year, the frenetic activity had led to record financial results. Net income in 1997 increased 68 percent to $13.9 million and sales rose 20 percent, reaching $413.8 million.

In 1998, Weisbach continued to push forward on the acquisition front, as he spearheaded a drive to push Ha-Lo past the half-billion sales mark. In February, the company purchased R&T Specialty, Inc., a promotional products company based in Peoria, Illinois. Ha-Lo's next purchase was an Illinois-based company as well, the country's third highest-rated promotion marketing agency, Chicago-based UPSHOT. With annual revenues of $35 million, UPSHOT offered a diverse range of marketing services, including strategic and creative planning, promotion, merchandising, promotional advertising, retail planning, and event marketing. The company, described as a creative boutique agency, boasted an enviable list of clients such as The Coca-Cola Company, Sony Electronics, Anheuser-Busch, and Proctor & Gamble Cosmetics—the *Fortune* 500 corporations that Ha-Lo thrived on. The acquisition of UPSHOT was followed by the August 1998 purchase of Lipson Alport Glass & Associates (LAGA), the largest independent brand identity and package design firm in the United States. The acquisition, which added $21 million in revenues, broadened the scope of Ha-Lo's marketing services, increasing its ability to meet the diverse marketing and promotion needs of its clientele. In December 1998, Weisbach completed his next acquisition, purchasing New York City-based Siebel Marketing Group. A privately owned promotion marketing agency with $25 million in annual sales, Siebel was organized as part of UPSHOT following its acquisition by Ha-Lo and renamed UPSHOT, NY.

Early 1999 saw Ha-Lo continue the trend it had established during the previous six years. The company acquired Parsons International Trading Business, one of Europe's largest corporate premium companies. Based in Paris, Parsons maintained sales offices in Holland and Italy and generated revenues in excess of $40 million. In February 1999, the company completed its acquisition of Idea Man, Inc., one of California's leading promotional products companies and one of three acquisitions announced by the company in late 1998. Ha-Lo also had agreed to acquire Premier Promotions and Marketing, Inc., which developed and implemented specific consumer-oriented promotions for major global corporations, and Smith Advertising Specialties, Inc., a promotional products company based near Harrisburg, Pennsylvania. As Ha-Lo prepared for the 21st century, the company was expected to continue acquiring competitors both domestically and internationally. With annual sales reaching $589 million in 1998, it was evident that Weisbach's strategy of purchasing small competitors by the handful was reaping lucrative financial rewards.

Principal Subsidiaries

Creadis Group, Inc. (Canada); Creative Concepts in Advertising, Inc.; Fletcher, Barnhardt & White; Flow Plastics, Inc.; HMK International Holdings, Inc. (Netherlands); HA-LO Sports, Inc.; Joking, Spa. (Italy); Lees Keystone, Inc.; Market USA, Inc.; Marusa Marketing, Ltd. (Canada); Wolff Marketing Group, Inc.

Further Reading

"Champion Goes Corporate," *WWD,* February 6, 1997, p. 10.
"The Charlotte Observer, N.C. Business Briefs Column," *Knight-Ridder/Tribune Business News,* December 22, 1995, p. 12220221.
"Ha-Lo Acquires Siebel Marketing Group," *PR Newswire,* December 21, 1998, p. 7441.
"Ha-Lo Announces Acquisition of Three Promotional Products Companies," *PR Newswire,* December 2, 1998, p. 2887.
Hayes, John R., "As Long As It's Free. . . .," *Forbes,* January 30, 1995, p. 72.
"Idea Man Is Acquired by Ha-Lo Industries in Premium Deal," *PR Newswire,* December 16, 1998, p. 0739.

—Jeffrey L. Covell

Hain Food Group, Inc.

50 Charles Lindbergh Boulevard
Uniondale, New York 11553
U.S.A.
(516) 237-6200
Fax: (516) 237-6240

Public Company
Incorporated: 1926 as Hain Pure Food Co.
Employees: 110
Sales: $104.3 million (1998)
Stock Exchanges: NASDAQ
Ticker Symbol: NOSH
SICs: 2099 Food Preparations, Not Elsewhere Classified;
    5142 Packaged Frozen Foods; 5149 Groceries &
    Related Products, Not Elsewhere Classified

Hain Food Group, Inc. markets and distributes about 550 branded natural food products and is a leader in many of the top 15 natural food products, a category consisting of foods that are minimally processed, mostly or completely free of artificial ingredients, preservatives, and other nonnaturally-occurring chemicals, and are as near to their whole natural state as possible. It also markets and distributes a full line of sugar-free and low-sodium products, kosher frozen foods, and snack foods, and manufactures, markets, and sells under license about 60 Weight Watchers dry and refrigerated products.

Hain Pure Food Co.: 1926–94

Hain Pure Food Co. was founded in 1926 in Stockton, California, by Harold Hain, who began by marketing carrot juice. A Hollywood line, chiefly of vegetable cooking oils, was added in 1955. With the introduction of Hain Yogurt Chips in the early 1970s, Hain began developing diet and health snacks. By 1983 the company, which was acquired by Ogden Corp. in 1981, was offering more than 300 natural and health food items. Most of these were manufactured in its own Los Angeles facility, where it also maintained its headquarters, and the majority of the products carried the Hain name.

Hain's product development was based on good taste, as determined by consumer panels, without adding sugar or any artificial ingredients. Many of the nearly 40 snack items were low in sodium or contained no salt. A line of kosher foods was produced as well. The company's products were found in supermarkets, health food stores, and specialty shops throughout the United States and abroad in countries such as Austria, England, Germany, and Japan.

Ogden sold its food products subsidiary, which included Hain Pure Food Co., in 1986. The purchaser was IC Industries Inc., which assigned the acquired companies to its Pet, Inc. specialty foods subsidiary. But in 1991 the former IC Industries, which had become Whitman Corp., spun off Pet, which became an independent company. Hain was one of the marginal food operations that Pet shed in 1993 to focus on its core businesses. The buyer, in April 1994, was Kineret Acquisition Corp., a specialty foods company based in Jericho, New York, that paid $22 million in cash and stock for the operation. At this time Hain was marketing more than 160 natural food products, including the Hollywood line of specialty cooking oils, carrot juice, mayonnaise, and margarine, and had sales of about $50 million a year.

Simon's Food Acquisitions: 1992–93

Kineret was a kosher food company recently acquired by Irwin Simon. The son of a Canadian grocer, Simon became a product manager for a Toronto food conglomerate before moving to New York City in the mid-1980s at the age of 25 to work for Pillsbury Co. on projects such as developing Haagen-Dazs ice cream outlets. In 1991 he moved to Slim-Fast Foods Co. as vice-president of sales and marketing. When his contract expired a year and a half later, Simon decided he "couldn't take the idea of working at another corporation."

Instead, Simon went into business for himself with a grubstake of $500,000, in part derived from his savings and a second mortgage on his apartment. His objective was to buy specialty food companies that were mismanaged or not realizing their potential, including those selling natural, low-fat, or ethnic foods. "The traditional food business is flat," he told an interviewer in 1995, "but specialty foods are growing in double digits. And the categories are still too small for the big guys like ConAgra, Kraft, and Pillsbury, so we don't have to compete against them. . . . I didn't want to invest in brick and mortar, so we get contract manufacturing and focus on management and marketing.'' His company originally was named 21st Century Food Products.

Simon used his savings in March 1993 to buy California Slim, a struggling diet drink and diet-powder competitor of Slim-Fast, for $50,000 and a seven-year royalty agreement. His next step, two months later, was to purchase Kineret, a $4 million-a-year manufacturer of kosher frozen foods, for $2 million. Simon then incorporated under the name Kineret Acquisition Corp. In August 1993 Kineret acquired from Tree Tavern, Inc., for $300,000 and stock, a frozen soy-based pizza product line marketed under the Pizsoy name. Three months later Simon's company purchased Barricini Foods Inc., a firm producing nondairy frozen Ice Bean desserts and frozen organic products combining pita bread with grains and vegetables under the Pita Classics name. These products also were marketed under the Farm Foods name. Kineret paid $195,000 plus stock for the acquisition.

To pay for these acquisitions, Simon took Kineret public, raising $4 million in November 1993 by selling 48 percent of the company's common stock at $3.25 a share, plus warrants. To underwrite the offering, however, he had to turn to Lew Liberbaum & Co., a firm with a history of securities regulations violations that took 30 cents on the dollar as its commission. Simon recalled, ''After I paid lawyers, underwriters and everyone else [including the sellers of Kineret], I probably had enough money to pay for a taxi home.''

Adding Hain and Other Companies: 1994–97

The Hain acquisition, purchased with debt financing from Argosy Group LP, ''made us a major player in the natural-food industry,'' Simon said. ''It allowed me to hire a different level of people, and from a company standpoint, it allowed me to be able to participate in certain advertising and promotions and upgrade systems.'' A Super Bowl promotion of merchandising kits, supported by radio spots and full-page trade ads, was designed to increase male patronage for Hain products, for which three quarters of the customer base consisted of college-educated women between the ages of 25 and 49.

About 40 percent of Hain's sales was coming from all-natural rice cakes. Simon repackaged the line in brightly colored, resealable cardboard cartons, introduced rice cake snack bars, and marketed Mini Munchies, a new line of bite-size rice cakes in several flavors, including ''strawberry cheesecake.'' Although Quaker Oats dominated this market, Simon did not let the food giant faze him. ''People always ask me, 'Doesn't Quaker frighten you?' '' he told a *Forbes* reporter in 1996. ''But every time I see Quaker ads on TV I just shout, 'Yeah!' They're growing the category.''

Simon moved his company to Uniondale in August 1994 and changed its name to Hain Food Group four months later. In fiscal 1994 (the year ended June 30, 1994), the company reported a loss of $502,000 on sales of $15 million. But it also came up with 24 new products to market. With the completion of the Hain acquisition, revenues rose to $58.1 million in fiscal 1995. The company moved into the black that year, with $2.4

million in net income. Hain raised $7.6 million in 1994 from the conversion of warrants to common stock in connection with the company's initial public offering. The funds were used to retire a $7.9 million loan.

In late 1995 Hain Food Group purchased Estee Corp., a deficit-ridden producer of sugar-free and low-sodium products for persons on medically directed diets, including diabetics, and other health-conscious consumers, for $11.3 million. Simon immediately closed the company's New Jersey plant, dismissing 180 employees and contracting production to a Canadian firm. Hain's acquisitions continued in 1996, when Simon purchased Growing Healthy Inc., a fledgling baby food company, and Harry's Premium Snacks, a potato chip and pretzel maker.

During fiscal 1996 the company had revenues of $68.6 million and earnings of $2.1 million, and it upped the number of its food products to 250. Simon was running a very lean operation, with only 43 employees, by farming out manufacturing and distribution. Nevertheless, when sales declined to $65.4 million in fiscal 1997, a drop that was attributed in large part to a $10.5 million sales fall-off for Hain's rice cakes, net income fell to $1.1 million. That year the company marketed 71 new products.

In March 1997 Hain reached an agreement to manufacture, market, and sell soups, snacks, and other food products of Weight Watchers Gourmet Food Co., a subsidiary of H.J. Heinz Co., with the products to continue to be sold under the Weight Watchers name. These 60-odd products were the dry and refrigerated goods that had generated only $17 million in sales for Weight Watchers in 1996 but at one time had done $100 million a year in business before becoming ''lost within the Heinz infrastructure,'' according to Simon. Under the five-year agreement, Weight Watchers would receive royalties and a share of the profits. This transaction made Hain, according to one of its executives, the nation's leading marketer of foods sold to dieters and other consumers with special medical needs. Hain repackaged the line to connect it more closely to Weight Watchers ''1-2-3 Success'' theme and added 30 new products.

Hain Food Group's next major acquisition, in October 1997, was that of Westbrae Natural, Inc., a California-based company with sales of nearly $38 million the previous year, for $23.5 million in cash. Westbrae's leading product was soy milk. The purchase allowed Hain to strengthen its presence in natural food stores, where Westbrae averaged 250 to 300 stockkeeping units (SKUs). Following the transaction, Hain's product line reached 1,000 SKUs spanning 13 brand lines. Other 1997 acquisitions included Alba Foods, a Heinz line of dry milk products, and Boston Popcorn Co., a snack food firm. Having sold the manufacturing facilities of its acquisitions, Hain now was dealing with a network of 95 co-packers. Simon was named 1997 Entrepreneur of the Year by Ernst & Young and one of *Business Week*'s Best Entrepreneurs of the Year.

Hain Food Group in 1998

In April 1998 Hain Food Group announced that it had agreed to acquire four closely held natural foods businesses for $60 million, plus the assumption of about $20 million in debt, from Shansby Group, a San Francisco investment company, and other owners. These firms were Arrowhead Mills Inc., DeBoles Nutritional Foods Inc., Dana Alexander Inc., and Garden of

Eatin' Inc. The acquisition was completed in July. In June of that year Hain contracted to handle sales and distribution of Heinz's Earth Best organic baby foods to natural food stores and to develop new products under the Earth's Best label.

By this time Simon, who had a five-year plan to increase company sales to $500 million by 2002, was paying more attention to promoting Hain Food Group products among consumers rather than merely distributors and retailers. The company had become involved in a number of promotional campaigns, including ones involving Weight Watchers, the American Diabetic Association, schools, and several cancer groups. "As we move into the 21st century," he told a reporter, "there is more awareness about nutrition and healthy foods. . . . We see the market (for better-for-you foods) growing drastically." Accordingly, Hain, in the latter half of 1998, introduced Chicken Broth and Noodles with Echinacea, Country Vegetable with Echinacea, Creamy Split Pea with St. John's Wort, and Chunky Tomato with St. John's Wort. These products were described on their labels as "herbal supplements," rather than soup, probably because dietary supplements were subject to less government regulation than were foods.

Hain Food Group made a new public offering of 2.5 million shares of common stock at $9 a share in December 1997. The proceeds of about $21 million were used to pay down debt, which was $16.6 million in mid-1998. In large part because of the Westbrae acquisition, net sales rose to $104.3 million in fiscal 1998. Net income increased to a record $3.3 million, inspiring the price of the stock to rise as high as $28.625 a share in the summer of 1998.

One of the company's supporters was billionaire George Soros, whose Soros Fund Management bought a 16 percent stake in early 1997 and still owned nearly ten percent in October 1998. White Rock, a Texas corporation and limited partnership, owned 20.1 percent. Simon held 10.7 percent of the shares.

In addition to its Hain and Westbrae lines of natural food products, Hain Food Group's products, in mid-1998, consisted of the Hollywood Foods line, the Estee and Featherweight lines of sugar-free and low-sodium products, kosher frozen foods under the Kineret and Kosherific labels, the licensed Weight Watchers products, and about 40 snack food items under the Boston Popcorn and Harry's Original names. The additions from the July 1998 acquisitions consisted of 360 ready-to-eat grains, nut butters, and nutritional oils produced by Arrowhead Mills and DeBoles, about 48 natural food vegetable chip items by Terra Chips, and a variety of tortilla chip products from Garden of Eatin'. Nondairy drinks accounted for about 19 percent of Hain's fiscal 1998 net sales.

All of Hain Food Group's products was being manufactured by nonaffiliated co-packers in mid-1998. With the July 1998 acquisitions, the company inherited a Brooklyn facility for making Terra Chips as well as plants in Hereford, Texas and Shreveport, Louisiana, for Arrowhead Mills and DeBoles products. The long-term future for these facilities was uncertain. In addition to leasing corporate headquarters in Uniondale, Hain was leasing warehouse and office space for its West Coast distribution in Compton, California, a smaller warehouse and distribution center in East Hills, New York, for its kosher products, and a small Boston Popcorn warehouse and distribution center in Foxboro, Massachusetts. The majority of Hain's products was being marketed and sold through independent distributors.

Principal Subsidiaries

Arrowhead Mills, Inc. and subsidiaries; Hain Pure Food Co., Inc.; Kineret Foods Corp.; Westbrae Natural, Inc. and subsidiaries.

Principal Divisions

Grocery/Mass Market; Natural Foods; Snack Foods.

Further Reading

Ain, Stewart, "A Dynamo in the Food Marketing Arena," *New York Times,* April 12, 1998, Sec. 14 (Long Island Weekly), p. 2.

Anderson, Duncan Maxwell, "Free At Last," *Success,* July/August 1995, p. 14.

Davids, Meryl, "Healthy Harvest," *Chief Executive,* May 1998, p. 25.

Dwyer, Steve, "Hain's 'Natural' High," *Prepared Foods,* April 1998, pp. 12–13, 15–16.

"Hain Food Seals 4-Store Acquisition," *Newsday,* July 2, 1998, p. A60.

"Quality and Taste Spur Hain Snack Line Growth," *Snack Food,* March 1983, pp. 20–22.

Siklos, Richard, "Real Men Do Eat Niche," *Financial Post,* October 16, 1997, p. 12.

Studnick, Alison, "Ricequake," *Food & Beverage Marketing,* January 1995, pp. 26–27.

Sugarman, Carole, "Magic Bullets," *Washington Post,* October 21, 1998, p. E1 and continuation.

Tascarella, Patty, "Heinz Puts on a New Baby Face," *Pittsburgh Business Times,* June 5, 1998, p. 1.

Waters, Jennifer, "Growing Healthy Leftovers for Sale," *Minneapolis-St. Paul CityBusiness,* May 3, 1996, p. 1.

Woods, Bob, "Healthy Appetite," *Food & Beverage Marketing,* May 1998, p. 8.

Wooley, Scott, "The Slipstream Strategy," *Forbes,* October 7, 1996, pp. 78, 80.

—Robert Halasz

Harveys Casino Resorts

P.O. Box 128
Lake Tahoe, Nevada 89449
U.S.A.
(702) 588-2411
(800) 553-1022
Fax: (702) 588-2411
Web site: http://www.harveys.com

Public Company
Incorporated: 1955
Employees: 4,010
Sales: $283.6 million (1997)
Stock Exchanges: New York
Ticker Symbol: HVY
SICs: 7999 Amusement & Recreational Services, Not
　　Elsewhere Classified; 5812 Eating Places

Founded in 1944, Harveys Casino Resorts is an established owner, operator, and developer of high quality hotel/casinos in Nevada and new gaming jurisdictions. Through its subsidiaries, the company owns and operates Harveys Resort/Casino, the largest hotel/casino in Lake Tahoe, Nevada; Harveys Wagon Wheel/Casino in Central City, Colorado, the first major hotel/casino in the Denver area; and Harveys Casino Hotel, a riverboat casino and hotel/convention center in Council Bluffs, Iowa. In 1999 the company merged with an affiliate of Colony Capital, Inc., a real estate investment firm.

A Family-Run Business in the 1940s

When Harvey Gross, a successful meat retailer from Sacramento, and his wife, Llewellyn Gross, moved to South Lake Tahoe, there were no phones, water, sewer, or power lines in the area. There was no highway maintenance and as soon as a significant amount of snow fell on Echo Summit, the road closed. Gross worked delivering meat and running a summer market for a few years before he and Llewellyn opened Harvey's Wagon Wheel Saloon & Gambling Hall in 1944 on seven acres of land near Stateline on Highway 50. The one-room, log cabin resort housed a six-stool lunch counter, three slot machines, two blackjack tables, and the only gas pump open 24 hours a day between Placerville, California and Carson City, Nevada. Harvey and Llewellyn worked 16-hour days preparing food, pumping gas, and dealing cards.

The Grosses were a devoted couple—partners from the start. It was Llewellyn's idea to give the club a western theme with its trademark wagon wheel and longhorn skull. William Ledbetter, who married the couple's only daughter, became Harveys' vice-chairman in 1983 and has described the two as "complementing each other." She was a "woman of action"; he had a "plodding business nature." In their gaming escapades, she was acknowledged as the driving force. The Wagon Wheel was very much a family affair; in the early years, when business slowed, family, friends, and employees sat around Harveys' fireplace in the casino eating popcorn and telling stories.

In the 1950s Tahoe boomed as a tourist playground, and Harveys boasted "more slot machines under one roof than any other casino in the world." By then the Wagon Wheel encompassed an entire city block, and a maintenance station topped Echo Summit to keep Highway 50 open during the winter. Giant billboards advertising Harveys dotted nearby highways, and Harveys offered shuttle service to customers between the casino and their hotel, along with a free keno game and a meal. Business was so good that Harvey Gross put off plans to retire and, instead, built an 11-story, 197-room hotel, changing Harveys Wagon Wheel to Harveys Resort Hotel & Casino. In the early 1960s Harveys' flagship casino expanded, adding on gaming tables and more hotel space, and by the time Gross died in 1983, at the age of 79, his operation was earning $4.1 million on revenues of $70 million and had virtually no debt. Even so, Harvey Gross refused to expand beyond Lake Tahoe. When asked why, he always gave the same answer: "I have a nice little business. . . . How many steaks can I eat?"

Gross had made a commitment to Lake Tahoe, and he was not about to back out of it. He was committed to "spending money where he made it," sponsoring scholarships for local students, and providing job opportunities for disabled citizens. He and Llewellyn were instrumental in opening Highway 50 to year-round traffic. He also played a key role in establishing the South Lake Tahoe airport, a medical center at Al Tahoe, and Barton Memorial Hospital at South Shore.

The Early Yturbide Years

William Ledbetter, Gross's son-in-law, who assumed control of the business shortly before Harvey's death, had different ideas. On a borrowed budget of $70 million, he moved to double the size of the casino and triple the number of rooms by 1985. Three years after Gross's death, in 1986, the project was slightly less than about three-quarters complete and the money gone. Ledbetter then called upon Thomas Yturbide to run the business. Yturbide, an experienced casino hand who had worked for nearly three decades for the competition, Harrah's, cut the staff back by ten percent, refinanced the construction loan, and finished a revamped expansion for an additional $30 million.

Yturbide also revamped Harveys' marketing program. Gross had relied upon nearby Harrah's to lure people to Lake Tahoe, in turn luring them from Harrah's with his billboards and his well-known $2.99 steaks and cheap drinks. In 1988 Yturbide approved a $10 million marketing budget, five times more than Harveys had ever spent. He bought radio and television spots and plastered Highway 50, the main artery between Sacramento and Lake Tahoe, with dayglo signs which read, "The Party's at Harveys." His plan brought results. Between 1987 and 1994, Harveys market share rose from 21 percent to 28 percent, the second highest among Tahoe hotels.

Beyond Lake Tahoe: Two New Casinos in the 1980s

Then, in 1988, Yturbide began to pursue expansion beyond Lake Tahoe. His first plan to partner with the Council Bluffs, Iowa Sioux in building a casino fell through after four years of discussion and planning when the land they had hoped to develop upon proved unavailable. Yturbide then tried to acquire the bankrupt Bally's hotel in Reno, but Hilton outbid him in his effort to buy. Harveys' luck turned around when Peter Morton, founder of the Hard Rock Cafes, approached Harveys to jointly launch a Hard Rock hotel and casino in the mid-1990s. The idea was that Morton would provide seven and one half acres in Las Vegas and Harveys would supply $66 million of the $88 million the two businesses needed to finance the project. Together they planned to buy another eight and one half acres and split another $24 million capital contribution.

The first deal was not yet even closed when Yturbide signed on to another. Partnered with Mountain City Casino Partners, Harveys would build a 118-room hotel and casino in Central City, Colorado, 35 miles east of Denver. Yturbide committed his business to putting up $9.4 million and guaranteed $28 million of debt and $7.5 million worth of gambling equipment. He then took the company public in 1993, selling 2.25 million shares of common stock (and another 1.2 million that belonged to the heirs of Harvey Gross) to raise capital for the planned ventures. At $14 a share, the sale raised $48 million.

The Wagon Wheel opened in Central City in 1995. It was designed from the outside to resemble ten separate, vintage storefronts and businesses, in keeping with the Western theme, and contained a 400,000-square-foot casino with 938 slot machines and 24 gaming tables, two restaurants, and a two-level underground parking garage. In subsequent years the complex also included a 118-room hotel, restaurants, and entertainment lounges. Before the year was out, however, it had defaulted on a $4 million principal payment to one of its minority investors. Earnings had not met expectations, and Harveys was exploring ways of restructuring its $11.9 million debt. It did so by buying out its minority partner and making Harveys Wagon Wheel a wholly owned subsidiary of Harveys Casino Resorts.

The Hard Rock Hotel also opened in 1995, tiny by Vegas standards with only 340 rooms. In keeping with the rock theme, slot machines had arms shaped to resemble guitar necks and roulette tables were shaped like pianos. The $25 chips were purple and featured Jimi Hendrix's profile and the title of his hit, "Purple Haze." Morton, whose entrepreneurial genius had dreamed up the first Hard Rock Cafe in London more than 20 years earlier, was in agreement with the Harveys philosophy of treating the guest well. The rooms in the Hard Rock Hotel had windows and supplied room service, to make the guests feel at home, rather than to chase them out into the casino.

More expansion was afloat back in Council Bluffs, Iowa. There, in exchange for $1.5 million and another $1.5 million to be spent on the construction of an athletic field complex on public land, the city council voted to sell Harveys a docking site on the Missouri River for its *Kanesville Queen*. The project cost Harveys $70 million and, in addition to the 2,352-passenger riverboat casino, which housed 1,100 slot machines, 48 table games, and seven poker tables, included a futuristic-looking, 251-room hotel, 20,000 plus-square-foot convention center, and docking site. In December of 1995, the *Kanesville Queen* received a ceremonial christening.

A Focus on Established Markets in the 1990s

Things quieted down for the next year or so. After the Wagon Wheel in Colorado failed to make expected earnings and missed its principal payment on $11.9 million in bonds that had been sold to help finance its building, Harveys proposed buying out the venture's minority partner, Mountain City Casino Partners. When New York State appeared about to open its doors to big-time gaming in 1996, Harveys took out an option on 27 acres of land in upstate Greene County. When the pending gambling bill stalled, however, no new ground was broken; Harveys decided not to seek approval for casino gaming in new markets, but instead to focus strategically on open markets where gaming was already legal—Nevada, Mississippi, and Atlantic City.

Also in 1996, Harveys hired Bill Cosby to serve as casino spokesperson. Cosby's role included promoting the firm's properties via television, radio, and billboard, and raising money for charities through benefit concerts. In keeping with the tradition of Harveys Project Care, an in-house corporate contributions program that in 1992 gave $416,000 to education, health, youth, and service organizations regionally, Cosby's six concerts raised more than $100,000 for charitable, educational, and youth groups across the country.

By 1997 Harveys had captured 28 percent of Tahoe gaming revenues, a conspicuous achievement in a market that included two other leading national casino companies. In Council Bluffs, net revenue increased approximately 44 percent over the previous year and market share increased to 33 percent. In Central City, revenue reached $320 million and market share was at 15 percent, while the Wagon Wheel Casino added a self-parking garage and 160 additional slot machines, bringing the total number of machines to 1,000. The company as a whole posted 1997 net revenues of $283,563,000 and net income of $30,775,000. It sold its stake in the Las Vegas Hard Rock Hotel and Casino to its joint venture partner, Hard Rock Hotel, Inc. for $45 million cash when it became clear that Harveys and Peter Morton had different ideas on how to best expand the property.

In 1998 Harveys also reached a second agreement with Hard Rock Cafe International to bring the Hard Rock Cafe brand to Harveys Resort Hotel and Casino in Lake Tahoe. According to this plan, a Hard Rock Cafe was built on the main casino floor of Harveys, outfitted with rock and roll memorabilia. The new cafe and retail outlet, completed by the busy summer season, encompassed approximately 6,500 square feet, with seating for about 200.

Harveys was going strong, posting earnings per share at the end of the first fiscal quarter of 1998 slightly less than double analysts' estimates. Chuck Scharer, chairman, president, and chief executive officer, attributed these results to strong performances assisted by mild weather at all properties. "In Colorado, our property continues to experience the benefits of the new 530 parking structure. In Iowa, the Council Bluffs market has continued to show its strength and support as we continue to lead as the state's top performing riverboat. And at Lake Tahoe, favorable weather patterns and road conditions . . . lead to increased volume at the property."

Scharer also stressed that the company had remained true to its initial focus on people as well as products. "As we aggres-

sively seek to take the company to the next level, our goal is to translate the essence of Harveys—the best possible service, quality and customer experiences—to new properties in new markets. The positive feedback from our customers tells us we are doing just that, and we intend to continue raising the bar in service and quality." Management at Harveys believes that it is the personal involvement of Harveys personnel that drives the company's success, and they insist that their front-line employees respond quickly to guests' needs, empowering workers to do "whatever it takes" to make the customer happy.

But times were changing at Harveys. Acquisitions and consolidations were becoming common in the casino industry and growth was slowing after the mid-1990s boom. In 1998 the company was sold to the real estate investment firm of Colony Capital and some Harveys executives for $420 million, including assumed debt, putting an end to the era of family control. Chuck Scharer continued to run the company, and Harveys' 4,000 employees retained their jobs, while three members of Harvey Gross's family continued to sit on the Harveys board. But the Ledbetters, who retained 40 percent of the company's shares through a family trust, were no longer central to Harveys' day-to-day operations. The sale to Colony Capital, completed in early 1999, was designed to provide a big financial boost to the company, affording it the resources necessary to explore new opportunities, such as building a luxury hotel next to Harveys in Lake Tahoe, returning to Las Vegas, and building a $300 million casino in Salisbury Beach, Massachusetts. At the time of the sale in February 1998, Harveys' stock soared to $27, showing investors' continued faith in Harveys' future.

Principal Subsidiaries

Harveys Tahoe Management Company, Inc.; Harveys C.C. Management Company, Inc.; Harveys L.V. Management Company, Inc.; Harveys Iowa Management Company, Inc.

Further Reading

Gubernick, Lisa, "Moving on Vegas," *Forbes,* October 10, 1994, p. 16.
Chan, Gilbert, "L.A. Real Estate Firm Agrees to Buy Harveys," *Sacramento Bee,* February 3, 1998, p. G1.
"Colony Capital to Acquire Harveys Casino Resorts," *New York Times,* p. D2.
"Harveys Casino Resorts Announces Hard Rock Cafe to Be Built at the Company's Lake Tahoe Property," *PR Newswire,* February 4, 1998.
Louis, Arthur M., "Colony Capital Puts Its Chips on Harveys Casino Purchase," *San Francisco Chronicle,* February 3, 1998.
Newman, Gary, "Harveys Casino Proposal May Reach Council First," *Omaha World Herald,* p. 20.
——, "Harveys Opens Colorado Casino," *Omaha World Herald,* p. 13SF.
Shanahan, Deborah, "Harveys Bond Default Won't Affect Bluffs," *Omaha World Herald,* December 12, 1995, p. 1.

—Carrie Rothburd

Hayes Lemmerz International, Inc.

38481 Huron River Drive
Romulus, Michigan 48174
U.S.A.
(734) 941-2000
Fax: (734) 942-8772
Web site: http://www.hayes-lemmerz.com

Public Company
Incorporated: 1927 as Kelsey-Hayes Wheel Corporation
Employees: 11,000
Sales: $1.26 billion (1998)
Stock Exchanges: New York
Ticker Symbol: HAZ
SICs: 3714 Motor Vehicle Parts & Accessories; 3465
   Automotive Stampings; 3711 Motor Vehicles & Car
   Bodies

The largest manufacturer of automobile wheels in the world, Hayes Lemmerz International, Inc. makes steel and aluminum wheels, brake parts, tractor trailer wheels, and other automotive components. Hayes Lemmerz supplied nearly every major automobile manufacturer in the world through 36 production facilities in North America, Europe, and Asia and through joint venture operations in South Africa, Turkey, Venezuela, India, Brazil, Thailand, Mexico, and Canada. During the 1990s the company's growth was derived from an expanding market for aluminum wheels, which were supplanting steel wheels as the preferred choice of automobile manufacturers, and from several major acquisitions. In 1996, when the company operated as Hayes Wheels International Inc., it purchased Motor Wheel Corp. The following year it acquired Lemmerz Holding GmbH, a German wheel producer, and was renamed Hayes Lemmerz. In late 1998 the company purchased CMI International Inc., which produced components that worked in conjunction with wheels and brakes.

Origins

Hayes Lemmerz's earliest predecessor originated from the Hayes side of the business, a company called Hayes Wheel,

founded by Clarence Hayes in 1908. The following year John Kelsey and John Herbert started their own automobile wheel manufacturing company, the K.H. Wheel Company, which produced wooden-spoked wheels for Henry Ford's Model T and other early automobile models. In 1927 the two companies merged to form the Kelsey-Hayes Wheel Corporation, which was reorganized in 1933 and renamed the Kelsey-Hayes Wheel Company. Meanwhile, the Lemmerz side of the business had been in business for more than a decade. Founded in 1919, when the Lemmerz family began producing their first automotive wheels in Konigswinter, Germany, the enterprise remained at its original location until merging with the direct descendant of Kelsey-Hayes Wheel Company, Hayes Wheels International Inc., in 1997.

While Lemmerz carved a place for itself as one of the leading manufacturers of wheels for the European market, the Kelsey-Hayes Wheel Company developed into one of the United States' largest suppliers of wheels, eventually controlling a substantial percentage of the domestic market. The company also did pioneering work in other areas of the automotive components industry, particularly in the development of brakes. During the early 1960s Kelsey-Hayes completed developmental work on rear-wheel anti-skid systems and in 1968 began supplying such systems to Ford Motor Co. This aspect of the company's business often was overlooked because of Kelsey-Hayes's dominance as a wheel producer and also because for many years the company operated under the auspices of a larger parent company. For Kelsey-Hayes, however, operating as a subsidiary company had more profound drawbacks than limiting its exposure to the business press. The company suffered considerably during its time as a subsidiary, incurring damage not necessarily from its own mistakes but primarily from the problems of an embattled parent company. The effect of these ''secondhand'' problems that trickled down to Kelsey-Hayes eventually led to the company's independence and the merger with the German Lemmerz operations. The backdrop for these two signal events—independence and the Lemmerz merger—occurred during the 1980s.

Business in the 1980s and 1992 Spin-Off

During the mid-1980s Kelsey-Hayes operated as a subsidiary of Fruehauf Corp., with other businesses that included a trailer manufacturing company and shipbuilding operations. At the time Kelsey-Hayes's annual sales hovered in the $1 billion range, supported by manufacturing facilities throughout North America. The company's product lines included wheels, disc brakes, drum brakes, brake valves, front hub assemblies, electromechanical sensors, automotive engine components, iron castings, and precision aluminum die castings. Aside from its prominence as a wheel producer (the company had manufactured more than one billion wheels by this point in its history), Kelsey-Hayes also ranked as the world's leading manufacturer of rear-wheel antilock braking systems (ABS), producing 1.3 million systems a year for all of the full-sized pickup trucks manufactured by Ford and General Motors Corp. The company had begun serving the aerospace industry, developing a business comprising five separate divisions, and it operated a Heavy Duty Systems business group, which included two companies, Gunnite and Fabco, that produced brake systems for heavy trucks, trailers, and off-road vehicles. Owing to the diversity and the magnitude of Kelsey-Hayes's operations, the company stood as Fruehauf's primary subsidiary when a corporate raider named Asher Edelman launched a hostile takeover of Fruehauf in the late 1980s. Fruehauf's management entrenched itself and fought a bitter, five-month-long battle against Edelman, eventually staving off the takeover specialist, but at considerable expense. In the aftermath of the hostile takeover, Fruehauf was forced to sell many of its profitable subsidiary operations, including a considerable portion of Kelsey-Hayes's diversified strength. Kelsey-Hayes was forced to sacrifice its aerospace-related business and its Heavy Duty Systems business segment, causing its work force to be trimmed from 9,000 to 6,000. The divestitures stripped the company of 30 percent of its annual sales.

Despite the blow the divestitures represented, Kelsey-Hayes's management remained positive about the company's future, confident that the undiminished strength of their automotive business could fuel a return to the company's former size. Robert G. Siefert, president and chief operating officer of Kelsey-Hayes, talked of expanding the company's automotive business, particularly in the growing market for ABS and cast aluminum wheels. Although the company found itself operating under a parent company strapped for cash, plans were developed for a new plant to be constructed in 1989 in Michigan that would nearly triple Kelsey-Hayes's ABS production capacity. "We've had assurances at our latest meeting with the banks that we can get more capital money," Siefert explained. "We haven't diverted any efforts or retracted anything in engineering or research and development . . . we're going to open that new antilock plant," he vowed.

It was not long, however, until Kelsey-Hayes's future course underwent a significant change in direction. Fruehauf Corp. sold Kelsey-Hayes in 1989 to a Canadian company named Massey-Ferguson Ltd. for $161 million in cash and $436 million worth of notes. Massey-Ferguson was reincorporated in the United States in July 1991, moved to Buffalo, and renamed Varity Corp. Within Varity's corporate structure, Kelsey Hayes operated alongside U.K.-based Perkins Engines, a leading maker of diesel engines and the Massey-Ferguson line of agricultural equipment. Of all of Varity's businesses, however, Kelsey-Hayes was the jewel, accounting for half of its parent company's sales and two-thirds of total profits. Despite Kelsey-Hayes's strength, reflected in the $1.35 billion in sales the company collected in 1991, Varity was in grave trouble shortly after acquiring the wheel and brake producer from Fruehauf.

Financial losses quickly mounted, leading to a staggering $178 million loss reported in early 1992. Amid Varity's financial woes, rumors surfaced that Varity was looking to sell Kelsey-Hayes to ease its financial worries, but Varity officials declined to comment on the matter. In October 1992 Varity's chairman attempted to end the speculation by unequivocally denying the possibility of a sale. "Kelsey-Hayes is an outstanding business with long-term potential that we intend to hold onto for the long-term," he remarked.

Despite assurances to the contrary, the ties connecting Varity and Kelsey-Hayes began to unravel one month after the chairman's statement. In November 1992 Varity sold 50.2 percent of the subsidiary to the public in an initial public offering (IPO). The IPO constituted Kelsey-Hayes's Hayes Wheels International Inc. business, which accounted for roughly 40 percent of the U.S. wheel market. Varity retained 46 percent of Hayes Wheels' shares and used the proceeds to pare down more than $860 million in debt, leaving a whittled down version of the former Kelsey-Hayes to compete in the automotive wheel market. Buffeted again by the troubles of its parent company, the new, publicly traded company moved forward without much of the diversity of operations that had characterized it previously. Hayes Wheels' business, in the wake of the 1992 spin-off, was focused tightly on wheel production instead, the company's mainstay line since the early 20th century. Expansion of this business occupied the company's energies during the early 1990s, including the construction of a $20 million aluminum wheel casting plant in Gainesville, Georgia in 1993. Construction of the new plant began shortly after Hayes Wheels began exporting cast aluminum wheels to Nissan, the first shipments of a $12-million-a-year contract announced in 1990. In addition to providing greater capacity for North American customers, the Gainesville facility also strengthened Hayes Wheels' access to overseas markets, which became increasingly important as the company secured foreign business similar to the Nissan deal. At roughly the same time Hayes Wheels began exporting wheels to Nissan, it signed another $12-million-a-year contract to supply fabricated aluminum wheels to German manufacturer BMW AG.

By the mid-1990s Hayes Wheels had greatly increased on its long-held domestic capabilities by expanding its presence globally. Despite the adverse environment in which the company had been operating for the previous decade, Hayes Wheels ranked as one of the world's preeminent wheel producers, with its most promising growth coming from the expanding global market for aluminum wheels. Increasingly during the 1990s, automobile manufacturers were choosing more expensive aluminum wheels over steel wheels, and in this growing market Hayes Wheels stood strongly positioned, having achieved meaningful strides in the highly fragmented European market. Varity noted as much, and in mid-1995 the company attempted to obtain complete ownership in Hayes Wheels. The bid, however, was rebuffed by Hayes Wheels management, who believed the price was too low. Following the scotched Varity deal, Hayes Wheels began looking for its own acquisition targets, touching off a series of acquisitions that lifted the company to the top of its industry by the end of the 1990s.

Late 1990s Acquisitions

In March 1996 Hayes Wheels agreed to merge with another southeast Michigan-based auto supplier, Motor Wheel Corp., in a transaction valued at $1.1 billion. Under the terms of the agreement, the Hayes name was retained, with the Motor Wheel name used for a new subsidiary. Headquarters for the combined companies were established at Hayes Wheels' central offices in Romulus, Michigan. The merger created one of the largest wheel and brake producers in the world, an employer of 4,800 workers in eight U.S. plants with foreign operations in Italy, Spain, Japan, Mexico, Venezuela, Brazil, Thailand, and the Czech Republic. For Hayes Wheels, ranked as the largest supplier of aluminum wheels in Europe before the deal, the merger gave the company the opportunity to supply complete wheel-and-brake systems to car manufacturers worldwide thanks to Motor Wheel's production facilities for light-vehicle brakes and medium- and heavy-duty wheels. Shortly after the merger was completed, a consortium of investors led by New York-based Joseph Littlejohn & Levy acquired 43 percent of the new company.

Before the end of 1996 news of another major acquisition surfaced, a transaction that gave Hayes Wheels a new name for the 21st century and solidified its presence in Europe. Hayes Wheel agreed to acquire 77 percent of Lemmerz Holding GmbH, the privately owned Lemmerz family operation in Konigswinter, Germany that ranked as Europe's leading wheel manufacturer. The merger of the two companies created the largest wheel manufacturer in the world, with combined annual sales of $1.5 billion and operations that served virtually every major automobile manufacturer on the globe. For Hayes Wheels, the acquisition of Lemmerz solved the problem of European expansion in a relatively inexpensive manner. Without the addition of Lemmerz's European production facilities, Hayes Wheels would have had to incur the cost of building its own plants, but by acquiring the German wheel producer Hayes Wheels was able to expand existing facilities at a far lesser expense. After the deal was completed, the Lemmerz family, headed by Horst Kukwa-Lemmerz, controlled 16 percent of the new company, which was renamed Hayes Lemmerz International, Inc. on November 12, 1997. Hayes Wheels' chairman, Ranko Cucuz, was selected as chairman and chief executive officer of the new Hayes Lemmerz and Kukwa-Lemmerz was named vice-chairman. The two companies were not united for long before another major acquisition was announced. In November 1998 Hayes Lemmerz signed a definitive agreement to acquire CMI International, Inc., a full-service supplier of wheel-end, suspension, structural, and powertrain automotive components. With the addition of Southfield, Michigan-based CMI, Hayes Lemmerz gained the ability to provide entire ''corner'' modules of vehicles, which comprised wheels, suspension, knuckles, calipers, rotors, and other parts.

After the CMI deal was completed in late November 1998, Hayes Lemmerz was roughly three times larger than it had been three years earlier. The acquisitions of Motor Wheel, Lemmerz, and CMI lifted annual sales over the $2.5 billion mark, extended and entrenched its presence overseas, and enabled the company to supply a greater percentage of an individual vehicle's content to automobile manufacturers. By the end of the 1990s Hayes Lemmerz supplied $800 in content for each vehicle manufactured by its long list of customers. As Hayes Lemmerz prepared for the future, swelled in stature after the late 1990s acquisitions, there was strong evidence that the company's bold moves would pay dividends in the years to come. Net income increased 81 percent during the company's third quarter of fiscal 1998,

reaching a record high of $19.7 million, while sales increased 20 percent. Holding sway as the undisputed leader in its industry, Hayes Lemmerz appeared to be strongly positioned for robust financial growth in the future.

Principal Subsidiaries

Hayes Lemmerz International–California, Inc.; Hayes Lemmerz International–Michigan, Inc.; Hayes Lemmerz International–Indiana, Inc.; Hayes Lemmerz International–Georgia, Inc.; Hayes Lemmerz International–Texas, Inc.; Hayes Lemmerz International–Ohio, Inc.; Hayes Lemmerz International–Mexico, Inc.; Hayes Lemmerz, S.p.A. (Italy); HLI (Europe), Ltd.; Hayes Lemmerz de Espana, S.A. (Spain); Hayes Lemmerz Japan Limited; HL Ohio Sub, Inc.; Motor Wheel de Mexico, S.A. de C.V. (75%); Hayes Lemmerz Autokola, a.s. (Czech Republic) Aluminum Wheel Technology, Inc. (98%); HL Holdings BV (Netherlands); HL Holding Germany GmbH; Hayes Lemmerz Hungary Consulting Limited Liability Company (Hungary); Newco Nr. 17 Vermogensverwaltungs GmbH (Germany); Newco Nr. 18 Vermogensverwaltungs GmbH (Germany); Hayes Lemmerz Holding GmbH (Germany; 99.9%); Hayes Lemmerz Werke GmbH (Germany); Hayes Lemmerz Werke Wohnungsbaugesellschaft mbH (Germany); Metaalgieterij Giesen B.V. (Netherlands; 91%); Hayes Lemmerz Manresa SPRL (Spain); Hayes Lemmerz System Services N.V. (Belgium; 99.7%); Hayes Lemmerz Belgie N.V. (Belgium; 99.9%); Hayes Lemmerz Comercio e Participacoes SRL (Brazil; 99.9%); Lemmerz Canada, Inc.; Hayes Lemmerz-Inci Jant Sanayi A.S. (Turkey).

Principal Divisions

Automotive Brakes; Commercial Highway & Aftermarket; North American Fabricated Wheels; European Aluminum Wheels; European Fabricated Wheels; MGG (Metaalgieterij Giesen).

Further Reading

''Betting on a '90s Status Symbol,'' *Money,* June 1994, p. 67.

Evanoff, Ted, ''Lack of Demand Forces Hayes Wheels To Close Plant, Lay Off Workers,'' *Knight-Ridder/Tribune Business News,* January 11, 1997, p. 11.

''Hayes Lemmerz Buys Brazil Wheel Venture,'' *Automotive News,* May 11, 1998, p. 26F.

''Hayes Lemmerz International Signs Definitive Agreement To Acquire CMI International,'' *PR Newswire,* November 20, 1998, p. 7153.

''Hayes Making Hay,'' *Ward's Auto World,* December 1993, p. 81.

Phelan, Mark, ''Hayes Eyes New Markets After Motor Wheel Merger,'' *Automotive Industries,* May 1996, p. 90.

Regan, Bob, ''Hayes To Build $20M Wheel Plant,'' *American Metal Market,* March 4, 1993, p. 1.

Sedgwick, David, ''Deal Boosts Hayes' Bid To Dominate Market for Steel, Aluminum Wheels,'' *Automotive News,* December 16, 1996, p. 24.

Sherefkin, Robert, ''Hayes Lemmerz Acquires CMI,'' *Automotive News,* November 23, 1998, p. 1.

Wrigley, Al, ''Hayes Consolidating Wheel Output,'' *American Metal Market,* May 7, 1998, p. 6.

—Jeffrey L. Covell

Hays Plc

Hays House, Millmead
Guildford, Surrey GU2 5HJ
United Kingdom
(44) 1483-302-203
Fax: (44) 1483-300-388
Web site: http://www.hays-plc.com

Public Company
Incorporated: 1965 as Farmhouse Securities
Employees: 17,499
Sales: £1.55 billion (US $2.53 billion) (1998)
Stock Exchanges: London
Ticker Symbol: Hays
SICs: 4225 General Warehousing & Storage; 4515
    Courier Services; 7361 Employment Agencies

Fast-growing Hays Plc is one of the United Kingdom's leading business services groups with more than 60 business units and 17,000 employees providing logistics and other services in three primary areas: distribution; commercial, including postal and other delivery services; and personnel placement. Although more than 60 percent of the company's sales continue to be placed in Great Britain, Hays has made active forays onto the European continent during the 1990s. The company has gained particularly strong entry into the French logistics and distribution markets, through subsidiaries Fril and FDS. These two companies have given Hays the number two position in specialized next-day delivery services in France. Hays also has been making inroads into the German, Italian, and Benelux markets, and plans an extension into Spain.

A series of acquisitions in the 1990s has helped the company in its revenue growth; however, the majority of the company's growth has come internally. In its 1998 fiscal year, the company recorded sales of some £1.55 billion, a jump of more than 38 percent over the previous year. In just four years the company has been able to nearly triple turnover. Hays also has been a profit leader, with steadily rising pretax profits reaching nearly £200 million in 1998. The company's solid growth performance has won it a place on Britain's prestigious FT-100 listing and a position as one of the London Stock Exchange's leading growth stocks.

Leading Hays's charge is Ronnie Frost, company chairman, who previously served the company as its chief executive. While encouraging the company's internal growth, Frost has taken Hays on an acquisition campaign both to strengthen its core areas in its United Kingdom base and to insert the company into the European market. Hays expects to continue to strengthen its network of distribution and logistics services throughout the European continent, especially with the emergence of a single-currency market in the turn-of-the-century period. Already by the late 1990s, Hays counts as one of Europe's leading business services firms.

Hays has carved out its position by focusing on innovative niche areas. The company provides distribution services, including dairy, meat, and other food product and retail product distribution for manufacturers and retailers; chemicals transport is another important focus area for Hays. Included under its group of distribution subsidiaries are warehousing and other logistics services. The company's Commercial division competes in the busy Mail and Express Services market by focusing on same-day and early morning delivery (as opposed to overnight or next-day delivery) and by targeting specific markets of expertise, such as the banking sector, medical clinic sector, and the accountancy market. Hays's third area of focus is its Personnel services division, providing temporary personnel and personnel recruitment services especially to the banking and finance industries, but also to other specialist sectors, including the information technology and computer industries.

Hays's three-prong approach has enabled the company to maintain steadily rising revenues—and profits—despite the difficult economic climate during much of the 1990s. After focusing on internal growth in the early 1990s, Frost has taken the company on an extended drive of so-called "bolt-on" acquisitions, bringing a large number of relatively small companies under the Hays Ltd banner.

Joining Distributors in the 1980s

Although Frost would become the chief architect of Hays Plc's growth, the company had been in the distribution business for nearly 125 years before coming under Frost's sway. The Hays business had begun in 1867, operating wharf facilities on the Thames in London, where it received dairy products shipped from New Zealand and other British colonies. Hays would gradually grow into a prominent cold storage provider, especially for dairy products. The company also would extend its services to distribution, while extending its London properties to include many prime Thames-side locations, including the eponymous Hays Wharf. By the late 1970s, Hays would come under control of the Kuwaiti Investment Office, acting as a holding company. In the late 1980s, however, Hays would be taken over by Ronnie Frost, who then took Hays public in 1989.

Ronnie Frost had had his own history with the Kuwaiti Investment Office. Frost started his own company, called Farmhouse Securities, in 1965. The company's original area of business was as a poultry wholesaler. Speaking of the period with the *Financial Times,* Frost would say: "Wonderful training. You'd approach someone, and in those days it could have been John Sainsbury himself or just a market trader. You'd have to adjust immediately." Frost's ability to "adjust" would become one of the principal assets of Farmhouse Securities, as was his dedication: it was not uncommon for Frost to put in 18-hour workdays. In the late 1960s and early 1970s the ambitious Frost extended the company into the distribution sphere, with an emphasis on cold storage facilities for its poultry and other products.

In the 1970s Frost would take Farmhouse Securities on a massive expansion program, opening or acquiring cold storage and other facilities throughout the United Kingdom. By the late 1970s Farmhouse Securities had built up a network of facilities capable of providing products to more than two-thirds of the United Kingdom. The company also built a fleet of trucks—one of the country's largest—to serve its storage facilities and its customers.

Farmhouse Securities' expansion would leave the company vulnerable to changes in the economic climate. After nearly three decades of strong growth since the Second World War, the British economy, along with much of the West, collapsed in the 1970s. Spurred by the Arab Oil Embargo and the oil-producing countries' sudden decision to raise world oil prices, the recession would strike particularly hard in the United Kingdom. Farmhouse Securities' finances, given its huge fleet of trucks, came under attack both from the rising oil prices and the drop in distribution activity. Despite its efforts to surmount its fragility in the new economic climate, Farmhouse Securities quickly found itself struggling to survive.

By the end of the 1970s Farmhouse Securities was on the verge of declaring bankruptcy. Frost, however, was not about giving up, telling the *Financial Times:* "There was too much blood and time invested in this business to let it go, but it was scary. We'd got to the stage of banks stopping cheques." Frost hung on into the new decade. But by 1981 it was too late. In that year Frost sold Farmhouse Securities to the Kuwaiti Investment Office. Frost would remain in charge of the company he had founded, however.

Expansion for the 1990s

Giving up control of Farmhouse Securities had enabled the company to survive its financial problems as the British econ-omy began to recover in the 1980s. Frost had had no intention of relinquishing permanent control of Farmhouse Securities: even as he sold the company, Frost made plans to buy back not only Farmhouse Securities, but the Hays wharf and distribution business as well.

Regaining control of the company proved more difficult than expected. It was not until 1987—the day after the October stock market crash—that the Kuwaiti Investment Office finally agreed to sell Frost back his business. For pounds 257 million, Frost regained control not only of the Farmhouse Securities businesses, but the Hays Distribution companies as well, which provided the name for the new company, Hays Plc. Joining the company's ranks was also a personnel and recruitment arm, which had been founded in 1969 and added to the Hays group in 1986. Another Hays business was its Document Exchange Service, later known as Hays DX, which had started up in 1975, offering business-to-business, overnight, and other specialty mail and delivery services. Hays DX would later build a strong focus on such sectors as the banking and accounting industries.

Frost set about imposing Hays as one of the United Kingdom's premier logistics and business services groups. To fund the company's proposed expansion, Frost led Hays to a public listing in 1989. The public offering would get off to a rocky start, however. Coming on the same day as the resignation of Britain's chancellor of the exchequer, Nigel Lawson, the Hays stock float would be forced to cut its initial price by some 15 percent. This proved to be only a temporary setback. In the 1990s Hays would become the darling of the London Stock Exchange, posting some of the decade's strongest performances.

Hays's growth would come primarily from the company's own internal expansion, as the company captured a stronger share of its market and expanded into new markets. Unwilling to compete with larger firms, the company shrewdly sought out niche opportunities in which to focus its energy, capturing leading shares of such segments as the chemicals transportation and logistics segment. The company also avoided direct exposure in the retail distribution market, which was undergoing a cutthroat shakeout in the 1990s, leading to more and more meager margins as the United Kingdom slipped into the extended recession of the first part of the decade.

While parts of Hays's business inevitably suffered from the recession and the resulting drop in demand for its distribution services, the company's three-prong approach enabled it to achieve some stability. The difficult economic climate, for example, would prove a boon to Hays's personnel services division, as companies looked more and more for temporary personnel, rather than hiring permanent employees. At the same time, Hays began to look for new markets, extending the company's delivery services into more general postal services, such as sorting and other services for the British post office. Another niche of interest to the company was computer-based records management and data storage, a segment the company would come to dominate after the acquisition of Rockall Scotia Resources in 1994.

Increasing competition in other sectors would bring opportunity to Hays. When British supermarkets began installing gasoline pumps, the country's traditional service stations, including Shell and British Petroleum, found their business under extreme pressure. In response, these companies began developing onsite grocery and convenience services. Hays seized the opportunity to propose its logistics services—coordinating an extremely complex provisions operation combining goods from various segments, from foods to clothing to other products, into one service. The initiative paid off: Hays was awarded contracts from Shell, followed by British Petroleum, in 1996.

Hays had already become adept at such complex logistics operations through its association with Carrefour, the French hypermarket giant. Where the company had remained focused on the United Kingdom markets, in the 1990s the company recognized the need to expand its services onto the European continent. France would provide the company's initial entry, as Hays began making small acquisitions of companies in its three primary sectors. Germany and the Benelux countries would soon follow.

Hays continued to target internal growth, while preparing an extensive series of so-called "bolt-on" acquisitions to boost its presence in specific markets, and especially in building its continental presence. Most of these acquisitions were on a relatively modest scale. In January 1999, for example, the company announced the purchase of France Partner, one of that country's top express parcel delivery services, for £19.5 million. This acquisition, however, followed on that of Colirail, in December 1998 for £40 million, and Delta Medical Express Group, acquired for £2.2 million in 1998, boosting the company to a 20 percent market share in the next-day parcel sector in France.

These acquisitions also complemented the strong moves that the company had made in building out its logistics network, with acquisitions including FDS in 1997 and Fril in 1994, strengthening the company's presence in France and the Benelux countries, as well as the takeover of Mordhorst, in 1993, which provided Hays with its German market foothold. The acquisition of Sodibelco in April 1998 brought the company's logistics operations into Italy. In the late 1990s Hays also began spreading its personnel and recruitment wings, with acquisitions including France's Sitinfo in October 1998, itself following on the June 1998 purchases of Alpha TT, Quasar, and Arec, three French specialist recruitment agencies.

By 1999 Hays had established a firm position in each of its three specialty areas across much of Western Europe, with near-future plans to expand into Spain, as well as to build a presence in the Eastern European market as well. While Ronnie Frost remained the guiding force of the company's growth, Hays would receive credit for building a strong management team, including retaining most of the executive staff of its acquisitions. This team was expected to continue to build on Hays' status as a world-leading business services group.

Principal Subsidiaries

Hays Logistics International (UK); Hays Logistics UK; Hays Logistique France; Hays Logistics Italy; Hays Logistics Germany; Hays Logistics Benelux; Hays Logistics USA; Hays Chemicals; Hays Chemical Distribution; Hays Process Chemicals; Hays Sulfur; Hays Distillation Services; Hays DX; Hays Customer Solutions; Hays Information Management; Hays Rentacrate; Hays Clinical Support Services; Hays Paperstream; Hays DEI; Hays Accountancy Personnel; Hays Banking Personnel; Hays Recruitment; Hays Montrose; Hays Richard Owen; Hays IT; Hays Read Carroll; Hays Alpha (France); Hays Executive; Hays International.

Further Reading

Ahmad, Sameena, "Acquisitive Hays Set for Next Pounds 100m Buy," *Independent,* August 21, 1997, p. 18.
Cope, Nigel, "Hays Delivering the Goods in France," *Independent,* January 6, 1999, p. 17.
Gresser, Charis, "The Thrill of Making Money for Others," *Financial Times,* September 24, 1997.
Grimond, Magnus, "The Three Facets of Hays," *Independent,* September 17, 1997, p. 26.
"Hays Shrugs Off the Threat of Recession," *Independent,* September 15, 1998, p. 23.
Potter, Ben, "New Ideas Help Frost Chill the Opposition," *Daily Telegraph,* September 15, 1998.
Richard, Phillips, "Hays Delivers the Goods," *Independent,* December 15, 1996, p. B6.
"Return of the Milk Train," *Dairy Industries International,* November 1, 1997, p. 33.
Stevenson, Tom, "A Bargain To Be Made in Hays While It's Marked Down," *Independent,* March 4, 1997, p. 16.
Tringham, Melanie, "Hays's Sights on Euro Expansion," *Daily Telegraph,* March 5, 1998.

—M.L. Cohen

⹃HIGHMARK℠

Highmark Inc.

120 Fifth Avenue
Pittsburgh, Pennsylvania 15222-3099
U.S.A.
(412) 544-7000
Fax: (412) 544-8368
Web site: http://www.highmark.com

Private Company
Incorporated: 1996
Employees: 12,000
Sales: $7.4 billion (1997)
SICs: 6411 Insurance Agents, Brokers, and Service

Highmark Inc. is the eighth largest health insurer in the nation, with annual revenues of over $7.4 billion. The company provides health care coverage in Pennsylvania and offers dental, medical, vision, life, casualty, and other health insurance to over 18 million people. The company operates under the trade name Highmark Blue Cross Blue Shield in the 20 counties of western Pennsylvania and under the name Pennsylvania Blue Shield in the rest of the state. With operating centers located in Camp Hill, near Harrisburg, as well as in Pittsburgh, Highmark was created in December 1996, with the merger of Blue Cross of Western Pennsylvania and Pennsylvania Blue Shield. Prior to the merger, Blue Cross covered only hospital stays, while Blue Shield covered physicians' fees. While the company maintains that the Blues operate more efficiently as one health care provider, some critics have expressed concern that a company with so a great a market share may be focused on revenues more than on quality health care.

Blue Cross of Western Pennsylvania: 1937–96

While Pittsburgh was slowly recovering from the Great Depression in 1937, its hospitals were in trouble. Most were about half empty, and many of the patients couldn't afford to pay the minimum $6 per day charge for hospital service. At that time, Blue Cross of Western Pennsylvania unveiled a prepaid hospital plan that would benefit both the hospitals and the people of Pittsburgh. The plan promised individuals 21 days of hospital

service for a monthly premium of 75 cents. A spouse could be added to the plan for an additional 65 cents, and children could be added for 35 cents. Therefore, a worker could insure a large family for a total of $1.75 a month. The plan was originally called the Hospital Service Association of Pittsburgh and was chartered by the Alleghany County Court of Common Pleas on September 15, 1937. Coverage for the first subscribers became effective on January 1, 1938. Over 75,000 members were enrolled within the first year, and by 1941 enrollment had increased to 500,000.

In the 1940s, Blue Cross expanded the benefits offered in its original 21-day hospital contract to cover 50 percent of an additional 90 days of care. It also introduced "direct-pay" coverage for individuals who were self-employed or otherwise ineligible for participation in a group plan. Blue Cross also encouraged the development of the Medical Services Association of Pennsylvania to provide prepaid coverage for physician fees.

Blue Cross negotiated the first national Master Agreement with the United States Steel and the United Steelworkers of America in 1951. This agreement provided uniform Blue Cross and Blue Shield benefits to companies and unions whose operations extended across state lines.

Blue Cross' goal was to provide quality health care to all Pennsylvanians. Unlike many other insurers, Blue Cross continued coverage to its subscribers after they retired. In the 1960s, Blue Cross made available a Senior Citizen Agreement to people over 65 who were not previously insured by Blue Cross.

By the 1970s, Blue Cross had introduced the first prepaid group practice in Western Pennsylvania, called the Centerville Health Plan, and was part of the Central Medical Health Services, the first health maintenance organization (HMO) in Pittsburgh. Over the years, Blue Cross began acquiring noninsurance businesses in addition to providing insurance coverage, and in 1991, the organization changed its name to Veritus Inc. to reflect the growing importance of its for-profit operations.

Pennsylvania Blue Shield: 1964–96

Pennsylvania Blue Shield was created in 1964 when the Medical Service Association of Pennsylvania (MSAP) adopted

Company Perspectives:

Highmark's mission is to provide Pennsylvanians with access to affordable health care insurance regardless of age, health, or occupation.

the Blue Shield name. The Pennsylvania Medical Society, in conjunction with the state of Pennsylvania, formed MSAP to provide medical insurance to the poor and indigent. MSAP borrowed $25,000 from the Pennsylvania Medical Society to help set up its operations and named Chauncey Palmer as its new president. Individuals paid 35 cents a month and families paid $1.75 a month to join MSAP, which initially covered mainly obstetrical and surgical procedures.

Enrollment declined in World War II as many members left the state to support the war. Arthur Daugherty replaced Palmer as president in 1945 and recruited new, larger accounts, including the United Mine Workers and the Congress of Industrial Organizations. In 1946, MSAP became a chapter of the national Blue Shield association, which was started that year by the medical societies.

MSAP recruited the 150,000 employees of United States Steel in 1951, which brought its total enrollment to more than 1.6 million. Despite the organization's large client base, it had trouble keeping up with its payments to doctors and was forced to raise premiums. The state insurance commission disapproved of the high premiums and reminded MSAP of its social mission—to provide quality insurance to low-income households. The commission suggested that MSAP control costs rather than continue to raise premiums. In response, MSAP formed a utilization control unit the following year to help keep track of expenses.

In 1964, MSAP changed its name to Pennsylvania Blue Shield. Two years later, the organization began managing the federal government's Medicare insurance plan for the state's elderly and also started the 65-Special plan to supplement Medicare coverage. In the 1970s, the organization again fell behind in its payments to doctors. Rates were once again increased and expenses were scrutinized.

Pennsylvania Blue Shield faced serious competition in the 1980s from newly formed health maintenance organizations (HMOs) within the state. Blue Shield retaliated by creating its own HMO plans, some of which it owned jointly with Veritus.

Despite physicians' protests and state regulators' concerns, Pennsylvania Blue Shield merged with Veritus in 1996. The new company chose the name Highmark Inc. to emphasize its standards for high quality.

The 1996 Merger

The merger of Pennsylvania Blue Shield with Veritus, formerly Blue Cross of Western Pennsylvania, was highly controversial, giving Highmark a staggering 60 to 65 percent of the total market share in Western Pennsylvania. The approval of the merger by the state insurance commission on November 27, 1996 shocked those who opposed it. The approval was not without contingencies, however. Pennsylvania Insurance Commissioner Linda Kaiser required the companies to devote $65 million or 1.25 percent of their premium revenue to community service programs. Kaiser also stipulated that Highmark stay nonprofit for at least two years after its creation.

Although he approved the merger, State Attorney General Thomas Corbett, Jr., issued written comments expressing concerns that the merged company's size might impede competition. His approval was also contingent upon Highmark providing continued coverage to the poor. In addition, Highmark also could not demand exclusivity from any hospital it contracted.

The newly merged Blues had a total enrollment of roughly 2.5 million people and dominated the market in Pittsburgh. Pittsburgh's next largest insurer, HealthAmerica, had only 294,000 members. While Highmark brandished a great deal of power, its first year was not an easy one. The organization posted sizable losses in 1996 for its most popular product, the Select Blue health plan. To offset the losses, Highmark launched a plan to entice employers to offer Select Blue as the only point-of-service (POS) plan for employees. As an incentive, Highmark cut the premiums—too much.

Major Change and Competition in 1997

To compensate for the underperforming Select Blue, Highmark cut costs and expanded its dental and vision health care programs. Highmark maintained both of the former Blues' headquarters—in Pittsburgh and Camp Hill—but it downsized its staff by 4.6 percent through early retirements. At Veritus 260 out of 3,600 employees accepted; at Blue Shield 300 out of 8,500 employees accepted.

Highmark also scaled back its Medicare claims processing business. The government divides the administration of the federally funded Medicare among many different insurance carriers, and prior to the merger, Pennsylvania Blue Shield was the nation's largest Medicare carrier. However, Highmark found it necessary to cut back on its Medicare claims processing, since the federal government reduced its payment to administer these claims.

The Blues had begun expanding their dental and vision programs before the merger. In 1996, Pennsylvania Blue Shield had purchased MIDA Dental Plans, Inc., based in Southfield, Michigan, while Pennsylvania Blue Shield had purchased Davis Vision, Inc. of Plainfield, New York, which insured approximately three million people, manufactured lenses, and owned an estimated 45 retail outlets. Highmark's Clarity Vision Inc. was formed in 1997 to provide group customers with a complete package of vision products. Moreover, Highmark significantly increased its dental business when it contracted the families of active military personnel throughout the United States with one of its subsidiaries, United Concordia Companies, Inc. The military contract covered 1.8 million people and was valued at $1.7 billion over five years. The network created to service the contract included 45,000 dentists. United Concordia became the nation's sixth-largest dental insurer.

Nineteen ninety-seven brought increased competition for Highmark. Specifically, the University of Pittsburgh Medical Center (UPMC) was rapidly acquiring hospitals in the Pittsburgh area mainly through full-asset mergers. By 1997, its scope included 16 hospitals, including three prestigious tertiary care hospitals, affiliations with 12 additional hospitals, and fiscal 1997 revenues of $2.4 billion. Highmark and UPMC had originally considered designing a product that would combine their vast resources, with Highmark as an insurer and UPMC as a provider. UPMC claimed that it couldn't meet Highmark's discount demands, however, so it became an insurance provider and a serious competitor.

To compete with UPMC's programs, Highmark launched its Community Blue plan, a niche product for small employers. Community Blue offered subscribers a narrower choice of hospitals and doctors in exchange for lower premiums. The plan excluded all UPMC hospitals, except its Children's Hospital. Highmark's other managed care plans continued to offer a broad network of UPMC hospitals, however.

Physicians had mixed feelings about the competition between Highmark and UPMC. Some expressed concern that neither Highmark nor UPMC would raise rates for fear of losing market share, which meant that physicians would have to cut their own costs in order to participate in their programs. An even bigger concern, however, was that in the race to become the market leader the focus was shifting away from quality care and onto cost. "We have a totally cost-centered health care model," explained surgeon Jon Lloyd, M.D. in an article in *American Medical News.* "Purchasers select plans based on cost, and plans select providers based on cost. The consumer is at the end of the food chain in Pittsburgh," he asserted.

Legal Troubles and Damage Control in 1998

In 1998 Highmark agreed to pay the government $38.5 million to settle allegations that it had defrauded Medicare by overbilling the program between 1989 and 1996. United States Attorney David M. Barasch also announced that the government had accepted a plea agreement from Judith Krafsig-Kearney, a former corporate vice-president accused of helping to carry out the alleged scam.

Barasch maintained that Krafsig-Kearney and others at the company had manipulated what were to be random samples of processed claims to mislead auditors from the Health Care Financing Administration (HCFA) performing annual reviews. According to Barasch, Krafsig-Kearney and others had singled out claims they knew complied with HCFA standards and presented them as "random" samples. The settlement also covered accusations of fraud in Blue Shield's failure to pursue payments from other companies insuring Medicare recipients, manually overriding computer payment safeguards, not conducting reviews of kidney disease treatments required by Medicare to determine if they were medically necessary, and failing to recover overpayments resulting from computer errors. Barasch remarked that Highmark had cooperated fully and admitted some of the violations on its own.

Legal problems continue to plague the company in the late 1990s. In July 1998, the Pennsylvania Society of Internal Medi-cine (PSIM) filed a complaint with the state insurance department stating that Highmark had violated the Unfair Insurance Practicing Act by exercising unfair influence on hospitals and participating doctors. Dr. Robert B. Sklaroff, president of the PSIM in 1998, asked both the Insurance Department and the State Attorney General's office to investigate the situation. Highmark contended that the PSIM was opposing the merger in order to gain higher reimbursements for its members.

Nineteen-ninety-eight marked the third consecutive year that Highmark had to pay out more in claims than it collected in premiums. The shortfall, known as an underwriting loss, was $300 million in 1996, $154 million in 1997, and was estimated between $75 and $100 million in 1998. The narrowing loss reflected premium increases that Highmark implemented for many of its insurance products in 1998. Highmark's 1997 underwriting losses were negated by interest income from investments and by the sale of its Keystone Easy HMO to Independence Blue Cross.

To deal with the negative publicity generated from premium increases and the Medicare suit, Highmark brought in John Brouse to serve as CEO. In an article in the *Pittsburgh Business Times,* Brouse expressed his hopes that people would view Highmark as a company that anticipates change and that is "compassionate," and "exact and sharp" in its internal operations. He also wanted customers to feel that they received good value for the premiums they paid. "We're not here to be the cheapest. We want people to feel they're getting their money's worth. We want customer loyalty and we have to earn that," Brouse explained.

Brouse noted that Highmark was taking steps to ensure a positive bottom line in the future. He planned to save about $100 million in 1998 from cutting payments to hospitals and doctors and from better managing subscribers' care. Using what the company referred to as disease-management techniques, Highmark identified subscribers with such diseases as diabetes and implemented programs to help them better manage their ailments. Brouse expected to gain an additional $98 million from cutting costs in Highmark's core health care business.

Positive Reports in 1998 and 1999

As the company neared the end of the century, Brouse's management seemed to be relieving some of what ailed Highmark. Standard and Poor's awarded Highmark A+ credit ratings for its superior capitalization, excellent market position, and good liquidity. In addition, the National Committee on Quality Assurance (NCQA) awarded Highmark's Keystone Health Plan West full, three-year accreditation, which it granted to health plans with excellent programs that demonstrated continuous quality improvement and met NCQA's rigorous accreditation standards.

Highmark remained a dominant player in its traditional Pennsylvania markets. While its operating performance was still poor, it showed steady improvement as it moved toward the year 2000.

Principal Subsidiaries

Highmark Blue Cross Blue Shield; Pennsylvania Blue Shield; Keystone Health Plan West, Inc.; United Concordia Companies, Inc.; HVHC, Inc.; Clarity Vision; HealthGuard of Lancaster; Trans-General Life and Casualty Group Inc.; Alliance Ventures Inc.; Insurer Physician Services Organization; Standard Property Corporation; Keystone Health Plan Central, Inc. (50%); Inter-County Hospitalization and Health Plans (50%); Health Benefits Management, Inc. (50%)

Further Reading

Bell, Allison, "Pennsylvania Blues Consolidation Plans Approved," *National Underwriter Life and Health—Financial Services Edition,* December 9, 1996, p. 30.

Jacob, Julie A., "Pennsylvania OKs Blues Merger: Medical Groups Sue to Block It," *American Medical News,* January 6, 1997. p. 16.

"Keystone Health Plan West Awarded Full Accreditation by NCQA," *PR Newswire,* January 4, 1999, p. 1737.

McGaw, Jeff, "Pennsylvania's Largest Insurer Charged with Violating Unfair Practices Act," *Knight-Ridder/Tribune Business News,* July 28, 1998.

Robinet, Jane-Ellen, "Accreditation Fight May Hurt Blue Cross Plans," *Pittsburgh Business Times,* November 11, 1996.

——, "Blue Blood," *Pittsburgh Business Times,* September 5, 1997, p. 23.

——, "Highmark and UPMC Turned Into a Bitter Industry Rivalry," *Pittsburgh Business Times,* September 18, 1998, p. 1.

——, "Highmark Blue Cross Cuts Medicare Claims Business," *Pittsburgh Business Times,* March 17, 1997, p. 3.

——, "Insuring a Future for Highmark; New CEO John Brouse Is Grappling with the Insurer's Serious Problems," *Pittsburgh Business Times,* March 13, 1998, p. 14.

——, "It's a Blue Union of Cross, Shield," *Pittsburgh Business Times,* December 4, 1995, p. 17.

Shellem, Pete, and Jeff McGaw, "Highmark, Inc., Formerly Pennsylvania Blue Shield to Repay Millions in Fraud," *Knight-Ridder/Tribune Business News,* September 4, 1998.

"Standard and Poor's Affirms Highmark's A+ Financial Strength Rating," *PR Newswire,* November 2, 1998.

Stark, Karl, "Head of a Philadelphia Doctors' Group Asks for Hearings on Health-Care Merger," *Knight-Ridder/Tribune Business News,* August 26, 1997.

Tokarski, Cathy, "Antitrust, Social Mission Issues Cloud Blues Merger Deal," *American Medical News,* July 1, 1996. p. 6.

——, "High Noon for the Old Guard," *American Medical News,* August 17, 1998, p. 13.

—Tracey Vasil Biscontini

Hill's Pet Nutrition, Inc.

400 S.W. 8th Street
Topeka, Kansas 66601-0148
U.S.A.
(785) 354-8523
(800) 445-5777
Fax: (785) 368-5915
Web site: http://www.hillspet.com

Wholly Owned Subsidiary of Colgate-Palmolive Company
Incorporated: 1935 as Hill's Packing Co.
Employees: 2,500
Sales: $965.3 million (1997)
SICs: 2047 Dog and Cat Food; 5047 Medical and
Hospital Equipment

Hill's Pet Nutrition, Inc. pioneered and developed the concept of clinical nutrition—the idea that pets with diseases could be treated nutritionally. A subsidiary of conglomerate Colgate-Palmolive, Hill's is the leader in the premium pet food industry. Although Hill's does make food for such zoo animals as lions and orangutans, as well as special diets for police and military canines, the company focuses on products for companion dogs and cats. Hill's flagship product is Science Diet, which is available in many different varieties designed to meet an individual dog or cat's needs based on its size, age, and lifestyle. Sold in veterinary offices and pet stores, Science Diet costs about 50 percent more than pet food sold in supermarkets. Hill's also produces Prescription Diet, a line of dog and cat food that helps manage allergies and such medical conditions as heart and kidney disease. Prescription Diet is available only through veterinarians, and customers pay a premium of 200 to 300 percent for its benefits. More recent additions to Hill's lineup include HealthBlend, a food for large-breed puppies, Science Diet Savory Recipes, which contain real meat, and Science Diet Canine Maintenance Treats. In the research and development of its products, Hill's employs over 100 veterinarians. Hill's products are sold in the United States, Europe, Japan, Australia, and South America.

A Slow Start

Hill's Packing Company began producing canned dog and cat food in 1935. However, Hill's Pet Nutrition, Inc. actually began in 1943 when veterinarian Mark Morris put Buddy, one of the first guide dogs for the blind, on a special diet to treat her kidney problems. By reducing the levels of protein and minerals in Buddy's diet, Dr. Morris improved her health considerably. "For years, animals have been used for medical research into human ills, and now it's time that something was done for animals themselves," Dr. Morris later recalled. Soon thereafter, Hill's Pet Nutrition, Inc. was founded.

Hill's began slowly, selling the premium dog and cat food in specialty pet stores. While the company eventually branched out into other pet-care products, such as flea bath products and aquarium supplies, it remained a small, relatively unknown company. In the 1960s, Hill's was acquired by a string of larger concerns, all of whom failed to capitalize on the pet food brand.

The 1970s—Acquisition

As part of a diversification strategy that included food products, Colgate-Palmolive, the toothpaste and personal care product conglomerate, purchased Hill's in 1976. A few years later, as Colgate-Palmolive again restructured, management considered selling off Hill's. In fact, if it weren't for Reuben Mark, an executive vice-president in charge of Hill's who would later become CEO of Colgate-Palmolive, the company would have been sold. Mark persuaded Colgate executives that Hill's had great potential and could find a profitable "niche" in premium pet foods and clinical nutrition. Mark's pleas were heard, and Colgate executives gave him a chance to turn the company around.

Mark promptly recruited Robert Wheeler from another Colgate subsidiary, and together they refocused Hill's business away from sidelines in which the company had little expertise and into the therapeutic qualities of the Science Diet line of pet food. Mark and Wheeler agreed that the secret to making Hill's reputation was to distinguish it from the lower-priced commercial dog and cat foods sold in supermarkets. Thus they began building up a network of relationships with veterinarians, whom they encouraged to sell their products exclusively. Packaging of the Science Diet and Prescription Diet products was designed to appeal to the veterinary community; the food was marketed in plain bags and cans with plain labels to emphasis its role as a prescriptive diet. Hill's sales rose dramatically, and Wheeler was eventually made CEO of Hill's.

By 1984, Hill's Pet Nutrition, Inc. had risen to prominence in domestic markets, with sales reaching $110 million. During this time, to reach its retailers, Hill's relied on independent distributors, who furnished medical supplies and drugs in addition to food to more than 21,000 small-animal veterinarians in the United States. While this system worked well, Hill's worried that a competitor would purchase some of these independent distribution centers and it would lose access to some of its key markets. To keep this from happening, in 1987 Hill's purchased the Veterinary Companies of America (VCA), a group of seven wholesalers in the western United States.

Logistics expert Jim Keebler was hired in 1989 to run VCA as a distributor of Hill's pet food. In order to integrate VCA with Hill's remaining independent distributors, Keebler reconfigured the channels of distribution to minimize overlap, which ultimately resulted in three geographical sales territories across the United States.

Keebler also installed an information system using a network of IBM computers, which he linked to other wholesale and retail computers. With this new computer system, Hill's could more efficiently manage the 6,000 order transactions it received each day from veterinarians and wholesalers. The computer system also allowed Hill's to attune its production and distribution to customer demand in different geographical locations.

At this time, Hill's operated under a two-stage system for filling orders and distributing them. Four factories manufactured Hill's products for warehouse orders. Then, the warehouses took orders from wholesalers and shipped the product to wholesale-level service centers. Production then had to replenish depleted inventory. Keebler replaced this system with a continuous-flow production system that eliminated the warehouses at each plant location, so that the product could be shipped directly from the plants to the wholesale-level service centers. Production was thereby changed from a push system, in which the product was manufactured first and then "pushed" on wholesalers and retailers, to a pull system, in which the product was manufactured according to customer orders.

With this new continuous-flow production system, Keebler cut the time between order and shipment from two months to about two weeks, which reportedly saved the company over $7 million. By 1990, Hill's commanded 95 percent of the prescription diet pet food market in the United States.

International Expansion in the Early 1990s

While Hill's domestic sales were healthy, its international sales were low. Although the company had established a presence in Europe in the 1970s, its market share there was very small, and parent company Colgate-Palmolive, which made two-thirds of its profits abroad, encouraged Hill's to adopt a much more aggressive global marketing strategy.

Hill's management realized that in order to succeed in overseas markets, it first had to educate veterinarians and pet owners abroad about the benefits of a better diet for dogs and cats, as people had to be convinced of the benefits of Hill's before they would pay the high premium for Hill's products. The company also had to be sensitive to consumer needs in different geographical locations. The typical 40-pound bag of Hill's pet food, for example, was not suited to every international market. A November 1996 article in *Pet Product News* explained, "Petite Japanese women shoppers, who generally shop on foot, have trouble carrying such a heavy package any distance. So, for the Japanese market, Hill's developed small glossy pouches of puppy food and other products."

Richard Hawkins, vice-president of operations, was promoted to president of Hill's International and charged with building the brands' reputation abroad. He was enormously successful, even though he had no prior global sales experience. Hawkins used the domestic formula of selling the product through veterinarians to sell $50 million worth of pet food in 16 countries. In just two years, international sales rose to $215 million in 50 countries, with a staff of just 265. Hill's established its European headquarters in Hatfield, Hertfordshire, England.

Hill's rapid global success attracted the attention of such pet-food industry giants as Carnation and Ralston, the latter of whom unveiled its own line of specialty pet foods, Purina O.N.E., in 1990. However, that company spent millions to capture only a few points of market share. A more serious competitive threat came from Iams, a manufacturer of premium dog and cat food whose products were also only available in pet stores and veterinary offices.

A Changing Marketplace in the Late 1990s

The emergence of large pet superstores in the late 1990s forced Hill's to alter its marketing strategies. These pet superstores purchased large quantities of Science Diet and sold it for less than veterinarians had to pay for it. Some of these superstores also offered their own veterinary services, so they were in direct competition with the veterinarians who originally marketed Hill's. Hill's welcomed the pet superstores' business, much to the chagrin of the veterinarians who had been reaping profits from selling Hill's. To placate the veterinarians, Hill's gave them the exclusive right to sell its Prescription Diet and HealthBlend lines.

To improve its service to veterinarians and other customers, Hill's stepped up its efforts in telemarketing. In 1996, Hill's hired an outside agency, FDS, to contact its 1,400 customers on a regular basis. FDS hired only telemarketers with previous veterinary experience to offer veterinarians information about special offers and to field technical questions. The operators then took orders, which they transferred to the vet's chosen wholesaler. Hill's contacted vets every six weeks to identify opportunities for sales and training requirements.

In the late 1990s, Hill's unveiled several new products to increase sales and maintain its position as market leader. For example, Hill's introduced HealthBlend, a premium dog food for large-breed puppies—puppies that will rapidly grow to be 55 or more pounds—which are prone to common skeletal problems such as hip dysplasia and osteochondrosis. As researchers found that overfeeding puppies the wrong kinds of food increased the risk of such skeletal problems, HealthBlend was aimed at controlling levels of fat, calories, and calcium, promoting a slow and steady growth, which in turn reduced the risk of skeletal problems.

The company also unveiled its Prescription Diet Canine n/d. Developed by veterinarian David Ogilby of the Colorado State University Comparative Oncology Unit, Prescription Diet Canine n/d provided the nutritional requirements needed for dogs suffering from cancer. The high fat and low carbohydrate dog food formula was meant to "starve" cancer cells, and early results were encouraging, as the survival rates of dogs given the food and a program of chemotherapy increased to 354 days, as compared to 130 for dogs given the chemotherapy and regular dog food.

Hill's also ventured into the "treat market," introducing its first line of upscale dog treats, Science Diet Canine Maintenance Treats, available in four varieties and designed to prevent weight gain. "Our goal was to establish this product as the first premium pet treat that provides the right nutrients for every life stage and tastes better than the leading dog biscuit," explained Jim Humphrey, vice-president for marketing, in *Packaging* magazine. Hill's put a great deal of thought into what kind of container it would use for its Treats. Instead of using traditional boxes, which were not reclosable and tended to crush easily, Hill's selected an environmentally safe canister that proved more sturdy and easier for customers to handle.

As it moved closer to a new century, Hill's believed that research and goodwill were paramount to its continued success.

The company spent millions of dollars each year on research at its high-tech 179-acre facility in Topeka and donated over $250,000 a year for university research, books on small animal nutrition, and world lecture tours by prestigious veterinarians. In fact, Hill's scientists authored the most widely used textbook about small animal nutrition, *Small Animal Clinical Nutrition,* the fourth edition of which was published in 1998. Hill's also held an annual pet diet contest—the Hill's Nutrition Pet Slimmer of the Year—in the United Kingdom.

Moreover, when contacted by the World Society for the Protection of Animals (WSPA) to aid starving dogs left homeless after Hurricane Mitch devastated Honduras in 1998, Hill's stepped forward and donated five tons of dog food, which fed more than 20,000 dogs. "At Hill's, we are deeply committed to the health and well-being of companion animals," said Dr. Albert Ahn, Director of Professional Affairs for Hill's in an interview for *PR Newswire* in December 1998. "When we received the call from WSPA asking for help, we jumped into action immediately," he added.

Hill's commitment to new product development and the continued improvement of the health and care of companion dogs and cats has paid off greatly. According to *Fortune* magazine, Hill's was the top-ranked premium pet food and third in overall customer satisfaction in 1998 among 190 companies rated by the National Quality Center at the University of Michigan Business School.

Further Reading

Buttita, Bob, "Hill's Unveils Food for Canine Cancer Patients," *Pet Product News,* September 1998, p. 4.

Cooke, James Aaron, "How Hill's 'Re-Engineered' Its Logistics Network," *Traffic Management,* November 1992, p. 32.

Hoggan, Karen, "Diet Dog Food Firm to Bite Into Europe," *Marketing,* February 15, 1990, p. 2.

"Large Breed Puppies Need Special Care," *PR Newswire,* March 27, 1997.

"Roll Over for Hill's," *Food and Beverage Marketing,* February 1995, p. 26.

Thorton, Kim Campbell, "Sutton on the Premium Pet Food Market," *Pet Product News,* November 1996, p. 8.

Vogel, Jason, "Top Dog: How Hill's Pet Nutrition Became One of the All-Time Starts in the Colgate Stable," *Financial World,* June 20, 1995, p. 58.

—Tracey Vasil-Biscontini

Hunt Consolidated, Inc.

Fountain Place
1445 Ross at Field
Dallas, Texas 74202
U.S.A.
(214) 978-8000
Fax: (214) 978-8888

Private Company
Incorporated: 1934 as Hunt Production Company
Employees: 1,900
Sales: $1 billion (1997 est.)
SICs: 1311 Crude Petroleum & Natural Gas; 2911
   Petroleum Refining

Hunt Consolidated, Inc. is the holding company for Hunt Oil Company, and is run by Ray Hunt, the son of H. L. Hunt, renowned as one of the wealthiest men in the United States in the 1940s. A private company with extensive oil and gas exploration and production facilities throughout North America, Hunt Oil has made a reputation for itself by engaging in high-risk overseas ventures in Yemen, China, and Ghana that have brought the company wealth and prestige. No other company in the industry is as likely to take the chances that Hunt Oil does when exploring for oil and natural gas in remote and exotic regions around the world.

Early History

H. L. (Haroldson Lafayette) Hunt was already one of the most successful independent oilmen before founding Hunt Oil. Originally a real estate speculator, he first became involved in the oil business in Arkansas and then Louisiana in the 1920s. His strategy was to drill in already known areas, jumping into lease-buying action immediately after a discovery was made. Hunt achieved historic success in November 1930 at age 41 when, together with a partner, Pete Lake, he bought 5,000 acres in East Texas belonging to wildcatter Columbus "Dad" Joiner, shortly after a single-well discovery of which big oil companies were skeptical. Hunt secretly employed an oil scout to monitor test results at a nearby well and, before Joiner realized

the full extent of the discovery, persuaded the wildcatter to sell all his leases for $1.34 million. Hunt paid Joiner $30,000 in cash with the rest to be paid out of future production. Subsequent wells proved that Hunt had purchased rights to not only some of the richest ground in the new East Texas oil field, but to the largest single oil deposit in the continental United States (and, at that time, in the whole world), totaling 140,000 productive acres. This business deal made Hunt the largest independent in East Texas and became the financial cornerstone of Hunt Production Company, which would soon become Hunt Oil, based in nearby Tyler, Texas.

With the newly acquired valuable property, Hunt was able to secure a bank loan to expand and upgrade his equipment to make the land productive. Within a month after the Joiner deal, he founded Panola Pipeline Company and was already supplying crude petroleum from his new oil wells. By 1934, Hunt Production Company, which already had 229 wells and was still drilling on its 5,000 acres, had produced 7.5 million barrels. In 1935, the company was grossing $3 million a year. At this time, Hunt's lead over the smaller independents widened, as his company was large enough to reap the benefits of the Connolly Hot Oil Act of 1935, which regulated pumping output in order to conserve oil reservoirs and ground pressure. Hunt Production, like the major companies, had sufficient acreage leased so that it could pump oil from wells spread apart.

In 1936, Hunt split with Lake, who had held 20 percent from the Joiner deal, and incorporated his holdings under the new name of Hunt Oil Company. With assets at the time worth about $20 million, Hunt Oil was henceforth solely owned by H. L. Hunt and other members of his family. Hunt soon started a subsidiary, Penrod Drilling, composed of a fleet of 11 steam-powered land rigs to both provide his own drilling needs and to be contracted out to others. He also diversified into the refining business by buying 50 percent of the nearby Excelsior Refinery for $150,000 and renaming it the Parade Gasoline Company.

At the end of 1937, Hunt Oil moved its headquarters to downtown Dallas. With the East Texas oil field no longer the company's only center of activity, Hunt Oil managed operations in Louisiana and Arkansas in addition to other parts of Texas. During this time, the company also became involved in interna-

215

tional marketing, making a barter deal with Germany of oil for steel drill pipe and exporting oil to Japan through a California trading company. Closer to home, H. L. Hunt purchased 7,000 acres of farmland, launching Hunt Oil's continual sideline of agricultural enterprises, which have included a cattle ranch.

World War II and the Postwar Period

During World War II, the increased demand for oil led to the opening of new offices for Hunt Oil, which produced a total of over 100 million barrels during the period from 1941 to 1945, averaging 60,000 barrels a day. Following the war, Hunt Oil was able to maintain high output through expanded operations. It opened a refinery in Tuscaloosa, Alabama, and started a chain of gasoline stations in Alabama and Louisiana under the name Parade. Hunt Oil explored for oil under the names Hunt Oil and its subsidiary Placid Oil Company, drilled for oil under the name Penrod, and transported oil under the name of the Panola Pipeline. The company also acted as an umbrella corporation that provided accounting and other services for the rest of the Hunt family enterprises, which encompassed scores of separate entities, companies, partnerships, and trusts in several states, and which were spread out among the members of H. L. Hunt's families. "A maze of interlocking and interdependent relationships, the Hunt corporate structure was confusing even to employees hired to help operate it," wrote Hunt biographer Harry Hurt.

Beginning in the 1950s, H. L. Hunt began to entrust more responsibility to top associates and to his sons from his first marriage. Ownership of Penrod Drilling, which possessed about 25 drilling rigs and was worth over $25 million by the 1960s, had been transferred to three of his sons in 1948. Placid Oil also came to be managed by the children of Hunt's first marriage and, in the early 1960s, had production double that of Hunt Oil. As H. L. Hunt became less involved with the oil business, he began devoting more energy to a food and drug subsidiary of Hunt Oil, HLH Products, which he started in 1960—partly as a means to integrate his vast farmland holdings. This food division continuously lost money, however, due to being overextended with too many product lines (up to 1,340), but also because of problems with salesmanship, management, sponsorship ties to conservative political media, and even embezzlement.

In the early 1960s, Hunt Oil's production began to level off. Although by the early 1960s production was estimated at 65,000 barrels a day—the same it had been in the late 1940s—the increase in the price of oil meant that revenues were still climbing. Wells 20 to 30 years old were declining in production, while additional production from new wells was barely offsetting the depletion of the old fields. Moreover, these new wells were being drilled by subsidiary companies and not Hunt Oil itself. For the first time since Hunt Oil's inception in 1936, the company's income was based solely on wells that had been found in past years. One reason for decreased drilling by Hunt Oil was its financial obligation to cover the losses of HLH Products, which by 1969 had totaled more than $30 million—averaging $4 million per year.

Transition and Change During the 1970s and 1980s

In early 1971, H. L. Hunt auctioned off nearly all of the property of HLH Products for $9 million, leaving only the drug and cosmetics plant in Dallas, which continued to do business under the name H.L. Hunt Sales. As a result of the sale, Hunt Oil could afford to resume drilling and made a recovery. Another revenue boost at the beginning of the 1970s was the company's participation in the five-member consortium headed by Getty Oil, which in 1969 won a lease on Alaska's North Slope. Hunt Oil invested $50 million for a one-fifth share, thus becoming partial owner of one of the last great oil fields in North America. Its original investment was returned many times over. These successes, however, were no longer under H. L. Hunt's leadership. For some time already his sons Herbert and Bunker, as vice-presidents, and his nephew Tom Hunt, production manager, had become the real operators of Hunt Oil.

Upon H. L. Hunt's death in November 1974, his share of Hunt Oil—80 percent—passed to his second wife, while its management went to their son Ray, leaving the children from his first marriage with 18 percent. Two of the latter, Herbert and Bunker, who were still vice-presidents of Hunt Oil, were already becoming increasingly involved in their own business operations, while Ray, who had been employed by Hunt Oil since graduating from college in 1965, had become the one most involved with the management of Hunt Oil. Herbert and Bunker decided to form their own independent oil company, Hunt Energy, from the subsidiaries of Hunt Oil they owned, leaving Ray to become president of Hunt Oil in February 1975. Two years later, Ray obtained the remaining shares of Hunt Oil owned by his half-brothers in exchange for a specified cluster of Hunt Oil properties, including oil leases, a pipeline in North Dakota, and Florida timberlands.

After his half-brothers split off from Hunt Oil, Ray Hunt modernized the company, hiring new managers and consolidating the diverse enterprises that remained with his branch of the family: oil and gas, timber and farm properties, H. L. Hunt Sales, and his own real estate companies of Hunt Investment and Woodbine Development Company. He introduced new methods of management and operating efficiency, instituted new medical benefits and pension plans for employees, and elevated salary scales.

Concentrating once again on the oil business, Ray Hunt hired new geologists and gave Hunt Oil a bigger exploration budget. The headquarter's staff increased from 50 to 200 by the end of the 1970s, and within a few years of taking control, Hunt had increased the area of offshore drilling leases from 100,000 to one million acres. The value of domestic oil reserves under Hunt's control increased from $100 million to $300 million in five years, also due in part to the sudden increase in oil prices caused by the Arab oil embargo of 1973. He also became involved in other facets of the energy business by making a deal with Dallas-based Energy Resources to provide drilling technology for uranium mining. Under Ray Hunt, Hunt Oil increased its annual revenue by 300 percent to $750 million by 1990.

The main contributor to this phenomenal regrowth of Hunt Oil from the late 1970s onward was its good luck with new overseas drilling ventures. Up to this point, all of Hunt Oil's production, unlike that of its former subsidiary Placid Oil, had been only in the United States. Although previous attempts at foreign ventures had been made, it was not until 1976 that Hunt Oil got involved in foreign exploration. A representative of the

Sabine Corporation, a small Dallas-based oil company, was seeking a buyer for its 15 percent stake in a British North Sea exploration led by Mesa Petroleum for a price of $50,000. The representative first tried to approach Bunker Hunt at Hunt Energy but, not finding him in, went instead to the neighboring office of Ray Hunt, who decided to buy the stake. The Beatrice Field in the North Sea turned out to contain a total of 150 million barrels, more than doubling the reserves belonging to Hunt Oil. With oil prices rising in the late 1970s the value of this holding grew to more than $500 million. "We were in the club now. It allowed us the vehicle to quickly establish ourselves in the international arena," Ray Hunt told the *New York Times Magazine.*

By 1980, Hunt Oil's leases overseas had reached 21.9 million acres, including interests in Australia, Portugal, and South Korea. The company was even trying to gain an offshore lease from China, although talks broke off without an agreement. Hunt Oil's strategy with foreign exploration was to look for oil in less-developed regions of the world, even if politically unstable, focusing on high-risk, high-return investments. Then, after a discovery was made, the company formed joint-venture partnerships to absorb the cost of drilling development wells. Hunt Oil was one of the few companies to do well in out-of-the-way foreign sites, due to several factors. First, it was large enough to finance its own exploration operations without help from the larger oil corporations. Second, its private ownership structure allowed it to pursue higher risk, longer-term investments which shareholders of a publicly traded company might not tolerate. In yet another advantage over major corporations, foreign governments in some cases were reluctant to work with large corporations perceived to represent the "Western monopoly."

Hunt Oil's most profitable success of the 1980s was in Yemen, where it was responsible for the country's first oil discovery. In 1981 Hunt Oil received a production-sharing contract from the government of North Yemen to drill for oil within a 5,000-square-mile concession. According to the contract's terms, the Yemeni government would initially keep half of the oil, its share increasing as production increased. With its first well, Hunt Oil in January 1984 discovered the Alif Field, an oil basin measuring more than four million acres in a vast desert containing estimated reserves of 400 million barrels of recoverable oil. "North Yemen will mean as much to Hunt in the 1980s and beyond as the purchase of Dad Joiner's oil rights in East Texas meant to H. L. Hunt in the 1930s," Jim Oberwetter, Hunt Oil government affairs director, told the *Dallas Business Courier* in 1986.

While Hunt Oil acted alone in the exploration and drilling of the Yemeni find, it signed on partners to help with the production. Sales of shares allowed Hunt to recover almost all of its investment costs by early 1988. In 1985, Exxon bought a 49 percent share in a venture to build a refinery and a pipeline, while a consortium of South Korean companies purchased another 24.5 percent share. The following year, Hunt Oil began construction on a $300 million, 263-mile pipeline from the Alif Field refinery to the port of Hodeida on the Red Sea, across three mountain ranges and through territory controlled by sometimes unruly tribes. The line, with a 200,000-barrel-per-day capacity, was completed in December 1987, whereupon Hunt Oil made the first oil shipments out of the country after an

investment of more than $600 million. By the following year, Hunt Oil was delivering an estimated 150,000 barrels a day to tankers. By December 1990, Hunt produced more than 100 million barrels of oil from Yemen, and in 1991 had a staff of 220 that produced $100 million for the year. Although the refinery and pipeline operated by Hunt and financed by Exxon would eventually revert to the Yemeni government, Hunt Oil drilled subsequent successful wells in Yemen beyond the Alif Field and offshore in the Red Sea.

The 1990s and Beyond

Hunt Oil hoped to duplicate its success in North Yemen with two new oil and gas exploration programs in Jordan and Chile in 1988, signing production sharing agreements with authorities in each country. Although no oil was found in either country by 1992, Hunt Oil continued to drill in new places near the border of Bolivia and Peru into 1993. Elsewhere in South America, Hunt Oil obtained exploration rights to property in Guyana in 1991 after a Canadian competitor actually found oil but withdrew, believing the jungle site lacked commercial potential. In another distant country and after several years of negotiations, Hunt Oil received exploration rights with a production sharing agreement to more than seven million acres in southern Laos.

In response to Hunt Oil's rapidly expanding oil exploration activities, a reorganization of the company was announced in July 1986. The restructuring included the formation of a new holding company, Hunt Consolidated, under which all the firm's profit centers, including Hunt Oil, became subsidiaries. A new president was named for Hunt Oil—the first nonmember of the Hunt family—while Ray Hunt, owner of Hunt Consolidated, remained as chairman. In a press release, Ray Hunt stated that the growth of the company "necessitated a streamlining of our corporate holdings" in order "to operate efficiently." In 1991, as part of a strategy to shed businesses not related to its core real estate and energy exploration and production units, Hunt Consolidated sold off its health and beauty products subsidiary, Hunt Products, Co., which had been purchased by the Hunts in 1962.

In the early 1990s, Hunt Oil increased emphasis on exploration in the United States as well as overseas. Previous drillers, the company believed, have overlooked major fields that modern technology could uncover, particularly in natural gas. The new Oryx Gulf of Mexico offshore platform, of which Hunt Oil owned one-third, started producing 26 million cubic feet of gas and 720 barrels of condensate per day in January 1991. A year later, the company drilled a deep wildcat well to 25,000 feet in western Texas. Gas prices and the potential to drill deeper than before were the key to developing such gas fields.

During the mid- and late 1990s, Hunt Oil Company aggressively pursued its past successful strategy of seeking oil and natural gas reserves in out-of-the-way and exotic locations. Hunt Oil and PanCanadian Petroleum Ltd. formed a partnership in 1994 to explore for natural gas on the Port au Port Peninsula in western Newfoundland. By 1997, both Hunt Oil and PanCanadian Petroleum had not yet commented on the commercial viability of the discovery, but indications from the Canadian government seemed to imply that there was less natural gas there than originally anticipated. The partnership continued to explore the region during 1998 and early 1999. In 1996, Hunt Oil signed an exploration and production agreement with the government of Ghana in West Africa, and conducted a seismic shoot in the Western Cape Three Points Basin. With financing from the U.S. Export-Import Bank, the company received $253 million for the drilling and completion of wells, pipelines, and platforms. At the end of 1998, Ghana's first offshore gas project was progressing according to plan.

In December 1998, Yemeni men from the Jahm tribe sabotaged one of the major pipelines operated by Hunt Oil in Yemen. The purpose of blowing up the pipeline was to force the government to fund development projects in their region. Although there were no reports of casualties, millions of barrels of oil were leaking from the broken pipeline, which carried oil from the Safer field in Marie province to a nearby port located on the Red Sea. In spite of the attack, Hunt Oil remained unwavering in its commitment to explore for oil in the more remote regions around the globe.

Thus Hunt Oil continued to grow, both domestically and overseas. In 1992, the company was ranked 35th out of the 469 U.S. companies (public, private, or subsidiaries) engaged in crude petroleum and gas production, and was the fourth largest private petroleum company. By 1998 Hunt Oil had moved to 25th in the rankings, and still remained the fourth largest private petroleum firm. As long as the company continued to engage in exploration and development in remote and exotic areas around the world, there could be little doubt as to its viability and financial success.

Principal Subsidiaries

Hunt Refining Company.

Further Reading

Akani, Fred, "Ghana Expanding Its Exploration and Development," *Offshore,* July 1996, p. 22.

Bancroft, Bill, "Hunting Elephants Around the World," *New York Times Magazine,* March 24, 1992.

Blanton, Kimberly, "Hunt Oil Selling Health, Beauty Unit," *Dallas Times Herald,* May 23, 1991.

Cook, James, "Yemen: Felix Redux?," *Forbes,* February 22, 1988.

Fagan, Alphonsus, "Hunt Pipeline Bombed in Yemen," *Oil Daily,* December 11, 1998, p. 8.

——, "More Operators Set Sights on Western Newfoundland," *Oil and Gas Journal,* October 27, 1997, pp. 78–80.

Hurt, Harry III, *Texas Rich: The Hunt Dynasty from the Early Oil Days Through the Silver Crash,* New York: W.W. Norton, 1981.

Lampman, Dean, "Hunt Oil Hopes for Big Overseas Strikes," *Dallas Business Journal,* May 30, 1988.

——, "Hunt Oil's Bonanza in North Yemen," *Dallas Business Courier,* July 21, 1986.

——, "Newfoundland Frontier Draws Hefty Tract Bids," *Oil and Gas Journal,* April 1, 1996, pp. 28–30.

——, "Newfoundland's Much Ballyhooed Port-au-Port Prospect Is to Be Drilled," *Offshore,* April 1996, p. 14.

Petzet, Alan G., "Delaware-Val Verde Gas Drilling Busy," *Oil & Gas Journal,* January 13, 1992.

—Heather Behn Hedden
—updated by Thomas Derdak

Hypercom Corporation

2851 W. Kathleen Road
Phoenix, Arizona 85023
U.S.A.
(602) 504-5000
Fax: (602) 866-5380
Web site: http://www.hypercom.com

Public Company
Incorporated: 1978
Employees: 1,166
Sales: $257.2 million (1998)
Stock Exchanges: New York
Ticker Symbol: HYC
SICs: 3575 Computer Terminals; 3571 Electronic
   Computers

A leader in its field, Hypercom Corporation develops, manufactures, and markets electronic payment hardware and software for major corporations, retailers, and financial institutions. An early competitor in the electronic payments industry, Hypercom originated as an Australian company, supplying customers with point-of sales terminals that authorized credit card and debit card transactions. In 1992, after moving its headquarters to the United States four years earlier, the company began providing networking products for electronic payment systems through its Hypercom Network Systems division. Growth for the company came quickly during the 1990s, as Hypercom chased its only rival, industry leader VeriFone, Inc., seeking to win the global race for domination in the electronic payments industry. Hypercom chipped away at VeriFone's lead during the early and mid-1990s, strengthening its domestic presence while it expanded on the international front. In 1997, the company made its debut on the New York Stock Exchange and introduced a line of Internet electronic commerce products. Majority-owned by its founder, George Wallner, Hypercom distributed its products in more than 50 countries, occupying a commanding position in Latin America and the Asia/Pacific region.

Australian Origins

Hypercom's founder, George Wallner, was born in Hungary, where he studied electrical and communications engineering. Wallner put his educational training to work when he moved to Australia in 1973. For five years, Wallner strove to develop large telephone systems and data collection networks; then in 1978 he hatched an entrepreneurial plan in the kitchen of the Sydney apartment he shared with his brother Paul. The Wallner brothers were, according to George, "just engineers playing with technology," but the pair soon created a viable business by developing systems to deliver credit card authorizations to merchant terminals at high speed. Hypercom was the result of their efforts, a pioneer company in the nascent and soon to burgeon electronic payments industry.

Point-of-sale (POS) systems that enabled card-based, electronic payments were introduced in the early 1980s to accommodate consumer preferences for using credit and debit cards instead of cash or checks. Prior to the development of automated POS systems, card-based transactions generally were processed manually, using paper-based systems to obtain authorization from card-issuing banks. As the volume of credit and debit card transactions increased, however, a more sophisticated method of authorization was needed. Banks, with the backing of VISA and MasterCard, offered financial incentives to promote the development and use of POS-related technologies, which spawned the creation of electronic payment systems that improved accuracy, reduced costs, increased efficiency, and reduced credit card abuse and fraud. In the United States, one company in particular achieved prominence in the fast-growing industry, Redwood City, California-based VeriFone, Inc. Wallner, meanwhile, achieved his initial technical advances in Australia. As the electronic payment industry grew rapidly during the 1980s, maturing into an indispensable facet of modern commerce, the two companies eventually confronted one another on VeriFone's home turf in the United States.

Before Hypercom and VeriFone began their head-to-head battle, the two companies were distant competitors, operating in entirely different regions. Wallner used Hypercom's business in Australia as a springboard for the company's expansion throughout the Asia/Pacific region, providing hardware and software for banks, retailers, credit-card companies, and other businesses with transaction-processing needs. As Hypercom grew, it did so with a technology obdurately embraced by Wallner. Based on synchronous data-link control protocols rather than character-by-character asynchronous communication, Hypercom's technology was relatively common outside the United States, but in the United States the technology was unique. According to the company's claims, synchronous technology enabled POS systems to transmit data more quickly and more reliably than asynchronous technology, and at a lower cost, but the advantages did not necessarily translate into great demand. Although there was widespread agreement that the synchronous approach was superior in several important respects, many users were satisfied with existing systems and could not be persuaded to adopt a different technology. "There's something to what they have," one of Hypercom's competitors conceded, "but none of our customers have asked for it." Wallner, however, refused to bow to what the market demanded, becoming, as one colleague remarked, "the keeper of the dream," convinced that the benefits of synchronous technology would eventually win the business of enlightened customers. It was only a matter of time, he believed, until the volume of the electronic payment transactions necessitated the widespread adoption of faster, cheaper POS technology.

By the mid-1980s, Wallner had entrenched his position in markets scattered throughout the Asia/Pacific region. Hypercom, by this point, ranked as the largest supplier of POS equipment in the region, operating in 18 countries. Despite the company's preeminent market position, annual sales were a modest $5 million, held in check by the equally modest size of the electronic payments industry. Rampant growth had not yet arrived, but the industry would begin to expand beyond its initial card-acceptance base during the late 1980s and finally record explosive growth during the early 1990s. As this monumental upswing in growth was beginning, Wallner made his first move into the United States, positioning his company in VeriFone's domain just as the electronic payments industry reached a turning point in its brief history. Hypercom signed on American Express Company as a customer in 1986, entered the U.S. market the following year, and relocated its worldwide headquarters in Phoenix, Arizona, in 1988 to be closer to American Express. By this point Hypercom's systems were delivering six-second transactions, far faster than the 12- to 17-second transactions averaged by other POS systems, but it was at this juncture that Hypercom's synchronous technology met with tepid response from POS customers. Although the faster transmission rates sounded good, they were not yet a necessity and, accordingly, did not make Hypercom's penetration of the U.S. market any easier. Nevertheless, the company secured substantial, important business during the late 1980s, winning customers such as Citibank, Texaco, Smitty's, and Valley National Bank.

Rapid Industry Growth Touched Off in the 1990s

By the beginning of the 1990s, conditions were prime for the explosive growth of the electronic payments industry. Credit- and debit-card usage began to greatly increase at new locations, such as supermarkets, as the variety of electronic payment methods and programs proliferated. Consumers became in-

creasingly dependent on the magnetic stripe on their cards for everyday purchases, and the systems that handled electronic authorization, data capture, and transaction transmission and settlement consequently needed to become more sophisticated to cope with the heavy traffic. As this decade of vibrant growth began, Hypercom, according to the industry publication *POS News,* ranked third in U.S. shipments of POS equipment, controlling a 9.7 percent share of the market in the 1990s. VeriFone, by contrast, was well in the lead, controlling 62 percent of the U.S. market and collecting annual sales of $155 million, compared to the $40 million generated by Hypercom.

The gap separating Hypercom and VeriFone narrowed during the first half of the 1990s, while the rest of the competitors in the field receded into the distance, essentially leaving Wallner and VeriFone's chief executive, Hatim Tyabji, to battle for industry supremacy. As Hypercom's annual sales began to grow robustly, the company diversified the services it offered to customers. In 1992, Hypercom Network Systems, headed by Paul Wallner, was formed to develop networking products for electronic payment systems and to develop such products for other networking markets. It served as the company's telecommunications unit, a lower-profile segment of the company's business that provided cost-efficient voice and data telecommunications for Wells Fargo Bank's branch system, the 1,500 store network of Home Depot, and other customers, expanding beyond Hypercom's original business of supplying POS equipment and related services. In the same year Hypercom Network Systems made its debut, Wallner hired Albert Irato as Hypercom's president and chief executive officer, gaining the talents of an individual described as "a pioneer in the development of U.S. credit card authorization systems." Previously a senior vice-president at American Express, Irato had been responsible for merchant and automated teller machine networks for the giant credit card company.

Annual sales eclipsed the $100 million mark in 1993, the same year Hypercom tripled the manufacturing, marketing, research and development, and administrative space at its headquarters in Phoenix. The expansion, coupled with an increase in manufacturing capacity in Australia, helped fuel a 36 percent increase in shipments in 1994. With the gains achieved that year, Hypercom increased its market share to 17 percent, still well below the 59 percent commanded by VeriFone, but substantial progress nonetheless. Said Irato, "We are shipping 30 percent to 35 percent of new devices in the U.S. market. That tells me we have to be taking share away from VeriFone." Although the U.S. market accounted for the majority of Hypercom's sales by the mid-1990s, contributing mightily to the 20-fold increase in the company's revenue volume since it had first entered the U.S. market, international business was undeniably important, representing roughly 40 percent of the Phoenix-based firm's total sales. With Irato installed as president and chief executive officer, Wallner, as chairman, presided over this aspect of Hypercom's operations, overseeing the company's international activities.

Overseas Growth in the Mid-1990s

As annual sales eclipsed $200 million in 1995—twice the total recorded two years earlier—Wallner intensified Hypercom's foreign expansion. In January 1995, the company established a presence in Santiago, Chile, with the formation of Hypercom de Chile. The organization of the subsidiary followed an agreement with Transbank, Chile's largest credit card transaction processor, to provide POS terminals and an electronic payment network for 19 cities. Six months later, the company established a subsidiary office in Budapest to serve emerging markets in eastern Europe and opened a second office in London to bolster its business with European Union markets. In April 1996, the company formed Hypercom International as a subsidiary to coordinate global strategic planning and to help tailor POS equipment and networking products and the marketing of such products to different economies, political systems, and cultures. Several months later, a subsidiary in Buenos Aires was opened. By the end of 1996, the emphasis on international expansion had created substantial leads for Hypercom over VeriFone in two, fast-growing regions. In the Asia/Pacific region, Hypercom controlled 29 percent of the market, compared to 16 percent for VeriFone, and in Latin America it controlled 54 percent of the market, compared to 37 percent for VeriFone.

The attention awarded the race between Hypercom and VeriFone stemmed, in part, from the fact that there were no other competitors close on their heels. The two companies had the global market largely to themselves, and, accordingly, all eyes were drawn to the heated battle between number one and number two. There were, however, important distinctions between the two companies, distinctions that Hypercom officials were quick to expose. Aside from collecting nearly twice the revenues of Hypercom and having an employee base four times larger than Hypercom, VeriFone had diversified into a number of different business areas, including expanding its operational scope to include Internet commerce. Wallner professed no interest in following suit, declaring in late 1996, "This is not the time to be going off into cyberspace." Further, VeriFone was publicly held, while Hypercom prided itself on remaining a privately owned concern. Said Irato, "We can move more quickly and make significant investments in our future without worrying all the time about what the shareholders would say." In 1997, however, the distinctions became subtler and the battle between the companies became more difficult to follow.

In mid-1997, Hewlett-Packard Company acquired VeriFone in a $1.2 billion transaction. Following VeriFone's absorption into the vast structure of its new parent company, financial figures and other yardstick results were consolidated into Hewlett-Packard, making the head-on competition with Hypercom more difficult to follow. Also in 1997, Hypercom converted to public ownership, filing for an initial public offering (IPO) after VeriFone had been acquired by Hewlett-Packard. In November 1997, Hypercom's IPO raised $180 million. The company planned to use the proceeds to repay $21 million of debt and to fund $20 million of facility expansion, with the balance set aside for research and development and the possibility of future acquisitions. The same year that Hypercom debuted on the New York Stock Exchange, it also entered the Internet commerce business, only several months after Wallner had disparaged such a move. Hypercom's line of Internet commerce products was based on Secure Electronics Transaction (SET) technology, a standard supported by VISA, MasterCard, IBM, GTE, Microsoft, and Netscape.

Although the Asian economic crisis delivered a palpable blow to Hypercom in 1998, particularly affecting its Hypercom Network Systems business group, the company's first year as a publicly traded concern was positive. With the proceeds ob-

tained from its IPO, Hypercom completed two small acquisitions during the year, purchasing companies that distributed Hypercom equipment in both transactions. In April, the company reached an agreement to acquire the Australian operations of its distributor, Advantage Group Ltd., for $1.5 million. In November, Hypercom acquired Horizon Group Inc., a U.S. distributor of POS equipment with $24 million in annual sales. Looking ahead, Hypercom was intent on remaining focused on POS equipment, as VeriFone pushed deeper into Internet commerce. In late 1998, VeriFone controlled 45 percent of the market for POS terminals, compared to the 15 percent controlled by Hypercom, but continued growth by Hypercom promised to narrow the gap. To fuel this expected growth, the company had a new generation of POS payment systems—its Interactive Customer Equipment line—that employed new modem technology called FastPOS. Capable of providing faster transactions and reading personal signatures, the new technology instilled confidence that the company's 20th anniversary would be a springboard for future growth.

Principal Subsidiaries

Hypercom (Arizona), Inc.; Hypercom U.S.A., Inc.; Hypercom Latino America, Inc.; Hypercom Manufacturing Resources, Inc.; Hypercom do Brasil Industria e Comercio Limitada (Brazil); Hypercom Asia Ltd. (Hong Kong); Hypercom Australia Pty., Ltd.; Hypercom Europe, Inc.; Hypercom FSC, Inc. (Barbados); Hypercom Financial, Inc.; Hypercom Net Transactions, Pty., Ltd. (Australia); Hypercom Hungary KFT; Hypercom Network Systems Ltd. (Hong Kong); Hypercom Far East, Ltd. (Hong Kong); Hypercom Asia (Singapore) Pte Ltd.; Hypercom Canada Ltd.; Hypercom de Mexico; Hypercom de Argentina; Hypercom de Chile, S.A.; Hypercom de Venezuela.

Principal Operating Units

Hypercom USA/Canada; Hypercom International; Hypercom Network Systems; Hypercom Manufacturing Resources.

Further Reading

Gilbertson, Dawn, "Phoenix Firm Hypercom Goes Public," *Knight-Ridder/Tribune Business News,* November 17, 1997, p. 11.
Kutler, Jeffrey, "Hypercom Calmly Chipping Away at No. 1," *American Banker,* February 16, 1995, p. 16.
——, "Hypercom Hires High Execs from Rival VeriFone," *American Banker,* July 23, 1998, p. 4.
——, "Hypercom Strengthens Marketing in Europe," *American Banker,* June 8, 1995, p. 15.
——, "Transaction Automation's 'Other Visionary,'" *American Banker,* December 19, 1996, p. 14.
Luebke, Cathy, "Pact Could Launch Valley's Firm's Business into Hyperspace," *Business Journal* (Phoenix), October 21, 1991, p. 12.
Marjanovic, Steven, "Hypercom Files for $11M-Share IPO," *American Banker,* September 15. 1997, p. 20.
Piskora, Beth, "Hypercom Establishes a Unit in Budapest," *American Banker,* September 11, 1995, p. 31.
Quittner, Jeremy, "Hypercom Forms Global Unit with Sights on Asia, E. Europe," *American Banker,* April 4, 1996, p. 16.
Rolwing, Rebecca, "Chairman of Arizona-Based Hypercom Said to Have Vision and High Energy," *Knight-Ridder/Tribune Business News,* December 8, 1998, p. 83.

—Jeffrey L. Covell

IDG Books Worldwide, Inc.

919 E. Hillsdale Boulevard
Suite 400
Foster City, California 94404
U.S.A.
(650) 655-3000
(800) 434-3422
Fax: (650) 655-3299
Web site: http://www.idgbooks.com

Public Company
Incorporated: 1990
Employees: 450
Sales: $141.5 million (1998)
Stock Exchanges: NASDAQ
Ticker Symbol: IDGB
SICs: 2731 Books, Publishing

The fastest growing computer book publisher of the 1990s, IDG Books Worldwide, Inc. made publishing history when it introduced *DOS for Dummies* in 1991. The book quickly sold out its initial print run and in the first 14 months sold 1.5 million copies. It was the beginning of the immensely popular "for Dummies" series of black and yellow books on topics ranging from sex to golf. By the end of 1998 IDG Books had published approximately 350 titles in the series, which annually accounted for some two-thirds of the company's revenues.

1990 Origins as a Subsidiary

IDG Books Worldwide was founded in April 1990 as a subsidiary of the privately held International Data Group (IDG), one of the world's leading information technology publishers (*Computerworld, Macworld, PC World*). Its mission was to publish quality computer books. Based in Foster City, California, IDG Books was co-founded by John Kilcullen and IDG founder Patrick J. McGovern.

After a string of unsuccessful titles, IDG Books published *DOS for Dummies,* written by Dan Gookin, in November 1991.

The idea of the "for Dummies" series originated in 1987. John Kilcullen, then an employee of Bantam Doubleday Dell Publishing Group in New York, had overheard a software customer request a simple, basic book on the DOS operating system. Not knowing anything about computers, the customer suggested, "Something like DOS for dummies."

The remark stuck with Kilcullen. In 1991 he was attending a publishing conference as the co-founder and publisher of IDG Books Worldwide. One of the speakers at the conference was author Dan Gookin. Impressed with Gookin's take on the publishing industry, Kilcullen signed him up to author *DOS for Dummies.*

The first print run of *DOS for Dummies* was 7,500 copies. The book appeared six months after the release of MS-DOS version 5.0. It initially was met with skepticism. Most bookstore chains did not want to stock it. Critics said the book should have been released when MS-DOS 5.0 was released, not six months later. They also were afraid the "for Dummies" title would offend readers.

Kilcullen countered that the "for Dummies" branding strategy would endear the book to customers as something they could immediately relate to and identify with. As it turned out, Kilcullen was right. *DOS for Dummies* sold out its initial print run in about a week, and in its first 14 months the book sold more than 1.5 million copies.

Marketed as "A Reference for the Rest of Us," the "for Dummies" series with its bright yellow and black covers stood out as different. Helping achieve a strong brand identity was the Dummy character. The "for Dummies" series of books was designed to be informative yet entertaining. The text contained some humor, and illustrations and icons were used to guide readers to key points. Each book's chapters were ordered logically to make it easy for readers to find the information that was needed.

The success of *DOS for Dummies* caused rival computer book publisher, Macmillan Publishing USA, to launch its own "Complete Idiot's Guide" series, including *The Complete Idiot's Guide to Personal Computers.* Macmillan later launched a successful "Teach Yourself" series of computer books. Although IDG Books was headquartered in Foster City, California, it edited and produced its computer books from its Indianapolis office. Macmillan's editorial offices for computer books also were located in Indianapolis. IDG Books CEO John Kilcullen had worked at Que Corporation in Indianapolis in the early 1980s, and he felt there was an editorial talent pool in the city because of Macmillan's presence there.

By early 1993 the company had seven "Dummies" titles in print, and all of them were on bestseller lists. Two new series were planned to launch later in 1993. When Microsoft Corporation launched its MS-DOS 6.2 upgrade in November 1993, it made a groundbreaking agreement with IDG Books. IDG Books would publish a special edition of its *DOS for Dummies* book called *MS-DOS 6.2 Upgrade for Dummies* with three Microsoft disks holding the actual DOS software. Both companies would distribute the book-and-software package. It was the first time a major software product was marketed with an independent publisher's book. The first printing of *MS-DOS 6.2 Upgrade for Dummies* was 250,000 copies.

"for Dummies" Expanded to Non-computer Topics: 1994

The "for Dummies" books were intended to help the average consumer overcome the frustration they felt about technology and other confusing subjects. At first, the series covered computer and technology-related subjects. Then, in April 1994, IDG Books expanded the scope of the "for Dummies" series beyond technology with the publication of *Personal Finance for Dummies,* by Eric Tyson. The book was an immediate success, selling out in bookstores within three weeks. Later that year Dr. Ruth Westheimer penned *Sex for Dummies* for IDG Books.

Expanding the scope of the "for Dummies" series led to dividing the Dummies Press into two groups: Dummies Technology Press, which published computer and technology titles, and Dummies Trade Press, which published general interest titles. Among the areas covered by the Dummies Trade Press were sports and leisure (*Golf for Dummies*), education and test preparation (*The SAT I for Dummies*), food and beverage (*Red Wine for Dummies*), the arts (*Shakespeare for Dummies*), health and fitness (*Pregnancy for Dummies*), home and garden (*Painting and Wallpapering for Dummies*), business and personal finance (*Mortgages for Dummies*), and more.

By mid-1995 IDG Books had about 150 "for Dummies" titles in print, and more than 15 million "for Dummies" books had been sold. The company launched a number of new formats to complement its "for Dummies" line, including a "Quick

Reference" line, a "Dummies 101" tutorial series, a "For Teachers" line, and calendars. The company also experimented with the CD format, producing its first CD-book package in a licensing agreement with Angel Records called *Classical Music for Dummies.*

As IDG Books celebrated its fifth anniversary in 1996, it had 213 titles in print, translations into 30 languages, and previous year's sales of $50 million. It was virtually the only computer book publisher that had achieved success in the trade market, selling to consumers through bookstores rather than through computer stores.

At the end of the year, Steven Berkowitz was promoted from chief financial officer (CFO) to president and publisher. Former president and co-founder John Kilcullen remained the company's chief executive officer (CEO). Berkowitz had joined IDG Books in 1994 as CFO and formerly was the publisher at MIS:Press and M&T Books in New York City.

Acquisition of MIS:Press and M&T Books: 1997

In 1997 IDG Books acquired two computer book publishers, MIS:Press and M&T Books, from Henry Holt and Company for $5.4 million. In 1997 MIS:Press and M&T Books published about 80 titles.

By the end of the year IDG Books had published 300 technology titles and more than 55 non-computer trade books in its "for Dummies" series. Of those 355 titles, 29 had achieved sales of more than 250,000 copies, including *The Internet for Dummies* and *PC's for Dummies*. With estimated annual revenues of $150 million, IDG Books was regarded as the number two computer book publisher behind Macmillan Computer Books.

Going Public: 1998

When IDG Books published *DOS for Dummies* in 1991, there was already a book for dummies on auto repair in print by another publisher. In February 1998 IDG Books acquired three "Dummies" books from Ten Speed Press: *Auto Repair for Dummies, Auto Repair for Dummies Glove Compartment Guide,* and *Wheeling and Dealing for Dummies.* IDG Books would revise and repackage the books to fit into its own "for Dummies" series for fall 1998. *Auto Repair for Dummies* was first published in 1976 by Ten Speed Press and had sold about 750,000 copies.

In a move to further merchandise the "for Dummies" strong brand identity, IDG Books signed an agreement with game and toy manufacturer Pressman Toy Corporation of New York to produce three board games based on the series: *Trivia for Dummies, Crosswords for Dummies,* and *Charades for Dummies.*

After filing registration statements with the Securities and Exchange Commission (SEC) in May, IDG Books had its initial public offering (IPO) in July 1998. The company planned to raise $50 million from the sale, of which $38.4 million would go to parent company International Data Group (IDG) as a debt repayment. After the IPO, IDG would continue to hold a majority interest in IDG Books.

The SEC filing revealed that revenues at IDG Books had increased some 357 percent from fiscal 1993 (ending September 31) through fiscal 1997, reaching $120.7 million. Net income for the period rose 84.2 percent to $7 million in fiscal 1997. The ''for Dummies'' series accounted for approximately two-thirds of the company's revenues, reaching $82 million in fiscal 1997. Technology titles accounted for the remaining $38 million of revenues in fiscal 1997. At the time of the IPO, IDG Books had about 700 active titles, about half of which were ''for Dummies'' books.

Revenues for fiscal 1998 (ending September 31) were $141.5 million, a 17 percent increase from the previous year, and net income rose 45 percent to $10.2 million. Sales of the company's technology titles increased 33.8 percent, while those of the ''for Dummies'' series rose 9.3 percent.

In December 1998 IDG Books acquired Cliffs Notes, based in Lincoln, Nebraska, for $14.2 million. Founded by Cliff Hillegass, the company had about 300 backlist titles consisting of literary study guides, test preparation guides, and advanced placement guides. Commenting on the acquisition, IDG Books President Steven Berkowitz told *Publishers Weekly,* ''Our strategy in building the company is to build brands, and Cliffs Notes is well-known among its core audience of students 12 to 20 [years old]. We intend to invest heavily in the brand and feel we can extend the Cliffs Notes name beyond its current audience.'' It was not yet decided whether the Cliffs Notes editorial staff of about 55 people would remain in Lincoln.

Outlook

At the end of 1998 IDG Books launched a new ''for Dummies'' series on health, beginning with *Alternative Health for Dummies* and *Herbal Remedies for Dummies.* For 1999, the company planned to release 400 titles, including new and revised editions, of which more than 200 would be in the ''Dummies'' series.

IDG Books implemented a strategy of achieving wider distribution by taking a 49 percent stake in a new Canadian publishing company for about $1.7 million. The new company was to be formed jointly with Macmillan Canada, a division of Canada Publishing Corporation, and would be called CDG Books Canada Inc.

For spring 1999 IDG Books and Netscape Communications Corporation planned to jointly produce a line of books and book-and-CD-ROM packages under a new Netscape Press imprint. It was not clear how America Online's announced acquisition of Netscape would affect the agreement.

The growing use of personal computers and people's frustration with using new technologies—two factors that contributed to the success of *DOS for Dummies*—promised a strong market for IDG Books' ''for Dummies'' series well into the 21st century. Although the company had many competitors, it had built a strong brand identity for the ''for Dummies'' series that would enable it to increase readership, reach new markets, and grow its market share in computer and trade publishing.

Further Reading

Barlyn, Suzanne, ''The Dummying of America,'' *Fortune,* May 1, 1995, p. 28.

Dobie, Maureen, ''Dummies vs. Complete Idiots: How Indiana Became the World's Computer-Publishing Capital,'' *Indiana Business Magazine,* December 1997, p. 6.

Farmanfarmaian, Roxane, '' 'Dummies' Titles Change Hands,'' *Publishers Weekly,* February 16, 1998, p. 110.

——, ''No Dummies They: IDG's Five-Year, $50-Million Success Story,'' *Publishers Weekly,* November 4, 1996, p. 15.

——, ''Sales, Earnings Up at IDG Books,'' *Publishers Weekly,* November 9, 1998, p. 14.

Foege, Alec, ''Nobody's Fool: Ignorant and Proud—and Prescient—Publisher John Kilcullen Gets Rich Hawking How-To Books,'' *People Weekly,* February 2, 1998, p. 63.

Hilts, Paul, ''Microsoft in Revolutionary Release of New DOS—with Book,'' *Publishers Weekly,* October 4, 1993, p. 9.

——, ''1.5 Million Dummies Can't Be Wrong,'' *Publishers Weekly,* February 22, 1993, p. 49.

''IDG Buying Holt's Computer Imprints,'' *Publishers Weekly,* November 17, 1997, p. 11.

Jordan, Steve, '' 'Dummies' Publisher to Buy Lincoln, Neb.-Based Cliffs Notes,'' *Knight-Ridder/Tribune Business News,* December 8, 1998.

Milliot, Jim, ''IDG Books Plans $50-Million Public Offering,'' *Publishers Weekly,* June 1, 1998, p. 19.

——, ''IDG Books to Acquire Cliffs Notes,'' *Publishers Weekly,* December 14, 1998, p. 10.

''Netscape and IDG Books Worldwide Announce Book Publishing Partnership; New 'Netscape Press' Imprint Created,'' *Business Wire,* January 7, 1999.

''Netscape, IDG Form Joint Book, CD-ROM Publishing,'' *Reuters,* January 7, 1999.

''Steven Berkowitz to Head IDG Books,'' *Publishers Weekly,* December 2, 1996, p. 14.

—David Bianco

Il Fornaio (America) Corporation

770 Tamalpais Drive, Suite 400
Corte Madera, California 94925
U.S.A.
(415) 945-0500
Fax: (415) 925-0906
Web site: http//www.ilfornaio.com

Public Company
Incorporated: 1980
Employees: 2,000
Sales: $83.14 million (1998)
Stock Exchanges: NASDAQ
Ticker Symbol: ILFO
SICs: 5812 Eating Places; 2051 Bakery Products

Il Fornaio (America) Corporation owns and operates 17 full-service, upscale Italian restaurants and five wholesale bakeries. The company's name, *Il Fornaio,* is Italian for "the baker." The restaurants are located mostly in California, but an Il Fornaio restaurant and bakery can also be found in each of the following cities: Portland, Oregon; Denver, Colorado; Las Vegas, Nevada; and Seattle, Washington. These white-tablecloth *Il Fornaio Cucina Italiana* (restaurants with bakeries) serve premium-quality Italian cuisine based on authentic regional Italian recipes. Each restaurant houses a retail market (known as a *panetteria*) offering the company's unique baked goods, prepared foods, and a variety of Il Fornaio-brand products. The company's five California-based *Il Fornaio Panificio* production bakeries offer more than 50 varieties of handmade breads and rolls as well as pastries and other baked goods for sale in the company's own locations and to quality grocery stores, specialty retailers, hotels, and other upscale restaurants. Since 1997, the Burlingame, California, bakery also functions as the Accademia del Fornaio, a training facility or "School for Bakers." In 1998 Il Fornaio (America) Chairman Laurence B. "Larry" Mindel was among select restaurant industry leaders to receive the International Foodservice Manufacturers Association's 1998 Foodservice Operator of the Year and Gold Plate award, the top distinction among Silver Plate Awards, and one of the restaurant industry's highest honors. Mindel, a self-described Italophile, also was the first American and the first person of non-Italian descent to receive the Italian government's Caterina de Medici Medal for excellence in preservation of Italian heritage and culture outside of Italy.

A New Italian Bakery Concept: 1970–86

In 1972 in Barlissina—a small village outside of Milan, Italy—a family of furniture and fixture makers, committed to the goal of preserving the disappearing craft of Italian artisan baking, created the Il Fornaio Baking School. Carlo Veggetti and his family gathered centuries-old recipes from every region in Italy. In this school bakers learned the methods needed to prepare these traditional recipes; furthermore, the school provided the baker-students with the materials necessary for opening their own bakeries under the Il Fornaio name. From this modest beginning, Carlo Veggetti developed his concept of the "neighborhood baker" into what eventually became the largest bakery chain in Italy.

The Il Fornaio bakery concept was introduced to the United States in 1980 when the company acquired exclusive rights in the United States to the Il Fornaio trademark and to certain recipes that remained central to the company's bakery concept. Howard Lester, chairman of Williams-Sonoma Co., discovered the Il Fornaio bakeries during a 1981 business trip to Florence and fell in love with the Old World bakeries. He tracked down Carlo Veggetti, chairman of this largest chain of Italian bakeries, and negotiated an agreement for the rights to Il Fornaio (America) in North America. According to Steve Kaufman's article titled "Innovation Is House Specialty," published in the October 12, 1998 issue of the *San Jose Mercury News,* Lester opened eight bakery outlets by year-end 1984. The enterprise was not successful, however; Williams-Sonoma sold the company to a group of private investors who hoped to build a wholesale business by having a central bakery supply many additional outlets. When that venture also failed, reporter Kaufman noted that the investors asked Larry Mindel "if he would try his hand at turning the company around." Previously, Mindel had served as president of the restaurant division of

Company Perspectives:

Il Fornaio's mission is to provide our customers with the most authentic Italian experience outside of Italy. We realize our mission by being students and teachers of Italian culinary traditions, preparations and presentations, infusing our heritage into everything we do. We realize our mission by putting our employees first so that our customers can come first. We realize our mission by executing a profitable business strategy that rewards our shareholders without compromising the quality of our products. We realize our mission by developing an atmosphere of camaraderie and fun in all our endeavors, of celebrating every day the Italian in all of us.

Saga Corp. and had created eight successful Italian restaurants. He agreed on the condition that he be allowed to phase out the bakeries gradually and replace them with Italian restaurants having in-store bakeries, thereby introducing a new approach to the restaurant business. Mindel later served as president, chairman of the board, and chief executive officer at Il Fornaio (America) Corporation.

A New Restaurant Concept: 1987–95

The competitive distinction that Mindel had in mind was a new business strategy that, in addition to Il Fornaio's freestanding retail bakeries, focused on the development of full-service restaurants. He envisioned these restaurants and bakeries as showcasing baked goods produced by the company's bakeries and offering a varied menu of premium-quality Italian foods and beverages. This strategy was predicated on the development of an Il Fornaio brand based on the company's authentic Italian heritage. To this end, the company incorporated a retail market into the design of each location so that guests could purchase and bring home Il Fornaio-baked goods, prepared foods, and other branded products. In October 1987 the company opened its first full-service restaurant and bakery. By year-end 1995 the company had opened 11 full-service *Il Fornaio Cucina Italiana* (restaurants with bakeries) in California and operated five wholesale bakeries.

Il Fornaio's strategy focused on differentiating its restaurants from other restaurants in the Italian food segment by offering creatively prepared, premium-quality Italian cuisine based on authentic regional recipes. The core menu, served at both lunch and dinner, featured a variety of dishes: house-made and imported pasta, poultry and game roasted over a wood-fired rotisserie, meat and fresh fish from a charcoal grill, pizza from a wood-burning oven, soups, salads, and desserts. Native-born Italian chefs developed all of the core menu items. Each month, as part of the company's *Festa Regionale* 1995 marketing program, these chefs developed special menus based on the local cuisine and culinary style of one of Italy's 20 geographic regions.

Il Fornaio believed that its restaurants, wholesale bakeries, and retail markets worked together to reinforce its image as a provider of authentic Italian food. The wholesale bakeries supplied the same fresh, award-winning breads and other baked goods served at its restaurants to quality grocery stores, specialty retailers, hotels, and other fine restaurants. The retail markets also offered an Il Fornaio-brand Chianti Classico from a Tuscan vineyard originally planted in the 11th century and designated for Il Fornaio's exclusive use. To create a distinctive authentic Italian atmosphere in its restaurants, the company chose designs unique to each location. Design elements—such as terra-cotta or European slate floors, marble bars, mahogany trim, outdoor piazzas, hand-painted ceilings, and fine art—were selected to evoke the charm and elegance of a memorable dining experience in Italy. Il Fornaio's Sacramento restaurant received the grand prize for best new restaurant design worldwide, one of the five grand prizes in hospitality design awarded in 1995 by the national magazine known as *Hospitality Design.*

To foster a strong corporate culture, Il Fornaio provided extensive training, attractive compensation, and significant opportunities for employee feedback and advancement. In 1995 the company instituted a Partnership Program, which provided equity participation to chefs and restaurant managers. Furthermore, Il Fornaio provided medical, dental, and other benefits to hourly employees; these benefits contributed in part to an employee turnover rate that was below the industry average. At year-end 1995, Il Fornaio posted total revenues of $54.14 million, compared with revenues of $38.51 million at the end of 1992 and with annual revenues of close to $6 million in 1987.

Growth in California and Elsewhere: 1995–97

In 1995 Michael J. Hislop, who had served four years as chairman and chief executive officer of Chevy's Mexican Restaurants and guided that company's expansion from 17 to 63 restaurants, joined Il Fornaio as president and chief operating officer. Mindel, Hislop, and seven other members of senior management continued to develop Il Fornaio restaurants in both existing and new markets and to locate these restaurants at sites in affluent urban and suburban areas. The flexibility of the Il Fornaio concept enabled the company to establish successful hospitality restaurants in a variety of locations, including residential neighborhoods, shopping centers, office buildings, and hotels.

Il Fornaio opened its first out-of-state restaurant and bakery in Portland, Oregon, in 1996 and in January 1997 opened another full-service restaurant and bakery in Las Vegas, Nevada, in the New York, New York Hotel & Casino. In November still another *Cucina Italiana e Panetteria* was opened in Santa Monica, California, overlooking the Pacific Ocean. The company's fifteenth restaurant and bakery opened in December in the lower downtown (''LoDo'') district of Denver, Colorado, three blocks from Coors Field.

Demand for the company's traditional Italian bread and pastries soon exceeded Il Fornaio's capacity for production. In March 1997 the company opened a free-standing 12,000-square-foot wholesale bakery in Burlingame, California. This facility allowed the company to use improved processes that enhanced the quality and consistency of its products while maintaining the Il Fornaio commitment to preservative-free, handmade, authentic Italian breads. This bakery, which replaced two small bakeries and brought about a substantial increase of profits, provided freshly baked goods to all of the company's restaurants and wholesale customers throughout the San Francisco Bay area. Furthermore, to assure the continuing visibility and longevity of its heritage, in May Il Fornaio (America) opened its own Accademia del Fornaio—that is, "School for Bakers"—in this bakery.

Another 1997 highlight was Il Fornaio's successful completion of an initial public offering; in September the company was traded on the Nasdaq National Market under the ticker symbol ILFO. Revenues grew 18.6 percent to $72.12 million in fiscal 1997 from $60.75 million in fiscal 1996. Net income grew to $2.58 million ($0.48 per share diluted) from $1.45 million ($0.32 per share diluted) in 1996: an increase of 77.8 percent. The company shared its success by creating an employee stock-purchase program. In his 1997 Annual Report, Chairman Mindel commented that "a new niche is evolving in the restaurant business, somewhere between 'casual dining,' with an average guest check of $15 and 'fine dining,' where a guest routinely pays in excess of $50. We call this niche 'sophisticated dining.' Our definition of sophisticated dining applies to the handful of restaurant groups that offer great food, professional service, beautiful and worldly wise environments, but with a check average of *under* $25. After all, fundamentals are the reasons that people dine so often at Il Fornaio." As a matter of fact, "two separate company-sponsored research studies indicate that our customers dine at Il Fornaio an average of sixteen times per year, a visitation frequency normally associated with quick-service restaurants," Mindel emphasized.

Further Expansion: 1998 and Beyond

In the *San Jose Mercury News* story mentioned above, newswriter Kaufman attributed much of Il Fornaio's success to its management structure, creativity, and attention to details. For instance, chefs and general managers were offered generous stock options and had to buy into the company's vision that profits would follow if quality was "the top priority." One of the ways that Mindel strove to implement the company's mission of providing customers "with the most authentic Italian experience outside of Italy" was to take about ten chefs and managers on an annual two-week trip to Italy to immerse them in that country's food, wine, culture, and lifestyle. Furthermore, once back home the chefs enjoyed much leeway for the preparation of food; every month they alternated the preparation "of supplementary menus customized to the cuisine of one of Italy's 20 regions," Kaufman pointed out. "Executive Chef Maurizio Mazzon reviewed the recipes, photographed the dishes and jotted down the details of the recipes—including instructions for proper pronunciation—for dissemination to the rest of Il Fornaio's chefs," wrote Kaufman.

Il Fornaio opened its sixteenth unit in Seattle, Washington, in October 1998. Located in that city's Pacific Place retail/entertainment complex, the restaurant and bakery shared space with the introduction of a new concept: a fast-serve restaurant called a Risotteria. According to the *Il Fornaio Online Magazine,* the menu featured six to eight risotto preparations, five to seven pastas, and three to four gnocchi—rotated seasonally along with salads, soups, antipasti, and desserts. Entered from the street level or from the Il Fornaio flagship restaurant situated above, the Risotteria had an open kitchen, no tablecloths, a prominent win-

dow for to-go orders, 92 seats for the customers who chose to stay—and everything was priced under $10. In an interview with Robert Klara, who gave news about this complex in the July 1, 1998 issue of *Restaurant News,* Il Fornaio Vice-President Michael Mindel said that the company had "long believed that there's an opportunity to do something more casual with a lower-price point without going down to fast food."

The Pacific Place's location at the crossroads of business and tourist traffic was the impetus for the idea. "A typical lunch break," Mindel noted, "is 29 minutes. We've long been looking for a way to accommodate people like that." He was quick to make the point that the Risotteria-type eating place would "never be a dominant business for us. We're still a full-service restaurant," he emphasized. But even the Seattle Risotteria had a unique Il Fornaio touch; for instance, Mantovana Risotto—a typical lunch item—consisted of radiochio, sausage, balsamic vinegar, and goat cheese! Il Fornaio opened its seventeenth *Cucina Italiana e Panetteria,* a 12,000-square-foot unit, in downtown Walnut Creek, California in November 1998. This restaurant and bakery could seat approximately 160 guests. The retail bakery, offering Il Fornaio's signature baked goods, coffees, fresh fruit, and juices, opened at 7:00 a.m. weekdays and at 8:00 a.m. on weekends.

By year-end 1998 Michael J. Hislop had been appointed president and chief executive officer; Larry Mindel continued to be chairman of the board. Sales and profits reached all-time highs, driven by an increase of five percent in same-store sales. In addition, sales at the restaurants increased by 3.3 percent for the fourth quarter of 1998, a percentage that represented the twelfth consecutive quarter of increases in same-store sales. Expansion into new markets also helped drive earnings per share to new heights. Total revenues peaked at $83.12 million for fiscal 1998, compared with $72.12 million for fiscal 1997. Net income for fiscal 1998 increased by 21 percent to $3.1 million versus $2.6 million for the prior year.

Although Il Fornaio became one of the more prominent chains in the upscale dining category, Chairman Mindel and President/CEO Hislop maintained strict standards to keep the company from becoming "chain-like." All but one of the Il Fornaio executive chefs were first-generation Italian and personally created half of the menus. All chefs and general managers were partners in the company. In his October 1998 interview with newswriter Kaufman, Hislop pointed out that the word *chain* connoted a prototype and implied that the same food was served in each of the company's restaurants. "That's not the case," said Hislop. "Becoming the best Italian restaurant means not only making the best Italian food but also being creative and innovative in each market where we are located."

According to Clifford Carlsen's report in the December 21, 1998 issue of *American City Business Journals Inc.,* during 1999 Il Fornaio planned to open five full-scale restaurants and bakeries, thereby propelling sales to more than $100 million. Chairman Mindel told Carlsen that with expansion set at five or six new restaurant units a year, Il Fornaio could reach $200 million in annual revenues within five years. "We have enough money to finance expansion internally for at least the next 18 to 24 months. And since the [1997] initial public offering we have put in infrastructure and management that can take us to $200 million a year,'' said Mindel.

Indeed, as the 21st century drew near, Il Fornaio's expansion continued at a rapid pace. All was on track for a May 1999 opening of *Il Fornaio Canaletto,* the company's 18th restaurant unit—its second in Las Vegas—as well as for a number of other restaurants under construction. Furthermore, with a lease in hand for a new 8,000-square-foot restaurant and bakery in Ashwood Restaurant Park, in the upscale ''Perimeter'' section of Atlanta, Georgia, Il Fornaio would soon have its first *Il Fornaio Cucina e Panetteria* east of the Rockies. According to newswriter Carlsen's story mentioned above, Chairman Mindel predicted that over the next five years about one-fourth of Il Fornaio's locations would be in West Coast markets, with the remainder farther afield. ''We think there are 100 markets for Il Fornaio,'' said the enterprising restaurateur. ''There are just a handful of restaurant companies that are on the radar screen of developers today, and we are one of them.''

Further Reading

Carlsen, Clifford, ''Il Fornaio Sets Table for New Round of Growth,'' *American City Business Journals Inc.,* December 21, 1998.

Galli, Franco, *The Il Fornaio Baking Book: Sweet and Savory Recipes from the Italian Kitchen,* San Francisco: Chronicle Books, 1993.

Il Fornaio Online Catalog, http://www.infornaio.com/catalog.html.

Kaufman, Steve, ''Innovation Is House Specialty,'' *San Jose Mercury News,* October 12, 1998.

Klara, Robert, ''Gnocchi at Noon,'' *Restaurant Business,* July 1, 1998, p. 1.

''NationsBanc Montgomery Analyst Forecasts Favorable Outlook for Restaurant Industry,'' *PR Newswire,* January 29, 1999.

—Gloria A. Lemieux

Imo Industries Inc.

Imo Industries Inc.

1009 Lenox Drive
Building 4 West
Lawrenceville, New Jersey 08648
U.S.A.
(609) 896-7600
Fax: (609) 896-7688

Public Subsidiary of II Acquisition Corporation
Incorporated: 1901 as De Laval Steam Turbine Company
Employees: 2,100
Sales: $316 million (1997)
Stock Exchanges: New York
Stock Symbol: IMD
SICs: 3829 Measuring & Controlling Devices Not Elsewhere Classified; 3511 Turbines & Turbine Generator Sets; 3566 Speed Changers, Drives & Gears; 3826 Analytical Instruments; 3714 Motor Vehicle Parts & Accessories

Imo Industries Inc. is a multinational industrial manufacturer. The company manufactures a wide array of products through three core divisions: the Power Transmission business segment which designs and manufactures electronic speed motor drives, speed reducers, and various gears; the Pumps business segment which designs and manufactures rotary pumps; and the Morse Controls business segment which designs and manufactures remote control systems and push-pull cables. During the late 1990s, Imo Industries experienced a comprehensive financial and operational restructuring, largely due to legal suits from people who alleged injury caused to them by exposure to asbestos, widely regarded as a cancer-causing substance. In August 1997, the company was acquired by II Acquisition Corporation, whose management immediately implemented a cost-reduction program.

Imo Delaval, Inc., renamed Imo Industries, Inc. in 1989, was created as a public company in December 1986, when Transamerica Corporation, which had acquired the De Laval Steam

Turbine Company in 1962, distributed Imo stock to its shareholders on a one-for-ten basis. In 1986 Imo Delaval, with 21 plants in North America and Europe and close to 3,500 employees, had revenues of $358 million. The newly independent company launched an aggressive strategy on several fronts. Through the late 1980s and early 1990s, Imo actively sought to acquire companies involved in related business areas to strengthen and enhance existing product and service lines. Continuing the company tradition, resources were dedicated to development of engineering applications and solutions in a number of areas, including efforts to respond to worldwide environmental concerns.

Imo's long-established reputation and stability had been grounded in the success of its turbines, compressors, pumps, and motion control equipment, which are still produced by Imo companies, including Delaval Turbine, Imo Pump, Warren Pumps, Boston Gear, and Delroyd Worm Gear. The energetic acquisitions campaign of the late 1980s had effected a greater diversity in current activities. Revolutionary night vision and laser systems produced by new subsidiaries Baird (acquired in 1987) and Varo (acquired in 1988) made Imo a major force in electro-optical systems. A one-piece door lock developed by Roltra, a major supplier to Fiat and 100 percent Imo-owned since 1991, attracted attention in European and other automobile markets. Other products such as sensors and pressure switches from Gems Sensors (acquired in 1969) and Barksdale (acquired in 1964), respectively, had been redesigned for detecting leaks in underground storage tanks and piping systems. Likewise, a Gems electronic liquid level switch has been instrumental in revolutionizing Freon gas recycling and recovery systems.

Late 19th Century Origins

The history of Imo Industries begins in Stockholm, Sweden, in March 1890, when Dr. Carl Gustaf Patrik de Laval—known as the "Thomas Edison of Sweden"—founded Gustaf de Laval Angturbin Fabrik to produce his single stage geared turbine. The motivation behind his steam-turbine invention was to find a way to power large versions of the automated cream separators that he had introduced a number of years before and which were being produced in Sweden and, since 1883, in the United States by the De Laval Separator Company in Poughkeepsie, New York.

Dr. de Laval's geared steam turbine generator was the first of its kind in the United States when it was exhibited at the 1893 World's Fair in Chicago. The finished design incorporated an expanding nozzle, flexible shaft, and double helical gears, and initially could be produced in different-sized units ranging from five to 200 horsepower. (This unit and a Baird spectrometer are two Imo Industries products on permanent display at the Smithsonian Institution in Washington, D.C.) Realizing the potential of his invention to increase industrial efficiency while reducing power-generation costs, Dr. de Laval wanted to introduce his turbine to industries in the United States as well as in his home country. His continuing experiments quickly led to new industrial applications for the turbine, including powering outdoor lighting and shipping.

In 1896, in what was possibly the first commercial application of a steam turbine for electric power generation in the United States, the New York Edison Company imported and installed two 300 horsepower De Laval turbines, establishing the first electric generating stations in New York City. While financial setbacks delayed Dr. de Laval's plans to manufacture the steam turbine engines in the United States, other companies such as Westinghouse and General Electric acquired patents and gained a valuable head start.

On December 9, 1900, an article in the *Trenton Sunday Advertiser* announced that the De Laval Steam Turbine Company would be opening a new plant in New Jersey the following May and was expecting to employ "a large number of skilled mechanics" in the manufacture of steam turbine engines. A group of U.S. investors (who were 30 percent owners) was led by Francis J. Arend, director of the De Laval Separator Company. By the end of 1902, the Trenton plant was producing gears, centrifugal pumps and compressors, and allied high-speed equipment in addition to the steam turbines. The company originated and became a major supplier of city waterworks pumping equipment.

In application after application, high-speed centrifugal turbines were replacing steam driven equipment, and De Laval was an industry pacesetter. Year after year the De Laval engineers made notable advances in engineering achievements in response to the needs of U.S. industry. During World War I, the company was a key supplier of power generating equipment to the U.S. Navy. And during the postwar building program the company supplied precision reduction gearing for 60 destroyers and 11 cruisers. At this time, requirements of the U.S. defense industry led to the lessening of ties between the U.S. manufacturing company and its Swedish parent. Arend was made the company's first U.S. president in 1916; he served until his death in 1942.

In the 1920s, instead of retooling to provide large turbines to drive the central power station generators that were needed to supply power to communities across the United States, De Laval chose to concentrate on marine sales and industrial power generation. By the end of the decade and during the next few years, as the company weathered the Depression, sales decreased and operations were pared down.

In 1932 the company acquired a license to sell three-screw positive displacement pumps manufactured by the Swedish firm AB Imo-Industri. Some of De Laval's most important achievements in the coming years came from efforts to design, produce, and expand applications of these pumps and the design and production of precision gears for marine propulsion. Pump orders took off following the events in Europe in 1939, and when the U.S. Navy began building its Mahan class destroyers, the De Laval double-reduction geared turbines were on board. Those not manufactured in the Trenton plant were produced elsewhere using De Laval designs. One of the few U.S. manufacturers with the experience, staff, and machinery to build the large, complex propulsion equipment needed to power warships and freight carriers, De Laval was awarded the Navy's "E" award for excellence for these vital contributions to the war effort.

The Post-World War II Period

Continuing research and development after the war and through the 1950s concentrated on products for peacetime markets, such as the centrifugal compressor for high-pressure gas pipeline transmission needed to pump natural gas from well-heads to consumers. Domestic and worldwide marketing efforts were expanded to increase sales and to offer licenses to manufacture selected products in remote locations. The Imo pump was still strong, and worm gear products, whose sales had declined, were strengthened through a partnership with the John Holroyd & Co. of Great Britain, known for its worm gearing made to involute helicoid thread form. In the 1960s, Delroyd (a combination of the names De Laval and Holroyd), with some of the most advanced worm gear manufacturing equipment in the world, began operations in a new addition to the greatly expanded Trenton plant.

Two World Wars, the Depression, the Korean conflict, and other world events and trends, such as a worldwide shipbuilding boom in the mid-1950s, had caused De Laval's operations to rise and fall and had influenced product decisions. Swedish control of the De Laval Steam Turbine Company by AB Separator had been diminished although the financial tie remained. By the late 1950s the Swedish firm needed additional funding to grow with Europe's dynamic peacetime economy and began looking for a buyer for its 70 percent of De Laval. It was not until several years later, in April 1962, that an investment group headed by Lehman Brothers became full owners of the newly named De Laval Turbine Company. The following year Lehman Brothers found a buyer for the company: Transamerica Corporation, a large insurance and financial services firm based in San Francisco. Transamerica was looking for a business to complement General Metals, a manufacturing subsidiary that was one of its many industrial holdings.

Although Transamerica's acquisition of De Laval was not unanimously approved, once accomplished the advantages were capitalized upon and turned into assets. Realizing that De Laval's sales and professional personnel (experienced in targeting the marine and utility markets) could benefit General Metals's Enterprise diesel engines (to date a mediocre performer) and Barksdale valve and switch lines as well as De Laval products, Transamerica decided in 1964 to merge General Metals and all of its industrial holdings into one manufacturing operation: De Laval. Fortunately, the new management also recognized that product development was fundamental to the De Laval enterprise and kept it a priority. In fact, within the next few years, as De Laval concentrated on marine, electric utility, gas transmission, municipal, process, and general industrial markets—in other words, not only military—Transamerica saw earnings increase over 90 percent to account for 7.3 percent of the parent company's reported earnings. Under W. J. Holcombe, who became De Laval president in 1965 after having managed Transamerica's western manufacturing companies, sales continued to increase each year and by 1970 had more than doubled, with net income increasing nearly 12-fold. As the company entered 1971 with a $113 million backlog, the future looked bright.

Growth and Expansion during the 1970s and 1980s

In 1971, to accommodate some of its manufacturing divisions' growth, the De Laval corporate offices were moved from Trenton to nearby Princeton. At this time, the company comprised three product divisions (aero components, industrial components, and heavy equipment) and more than a dozen companies. Growth continued through the 1970s, particularly in the area of aero components, with the acquisition of E.B. Wiggins (1975) and Red-Lee Metal Finishing (later Airfoil) (1978) and expansion of production capability. Diverse new products included Imo's geared twin screw pump and, from Wiggins Connectors, a fuel service system that permitted rapid refueling of racing cars and off-road vehicles without contamination-causing leakage. By 1976 De Laval's $22 million net income accounted for almost 20 percent of Transamerica's consolidated income.

Beginning in the 1970s, and extending into the next decade, continuing company growth was accompanied by global outreach. Early milestones included: the opening of a compressor plant in Toronto, Canada; joint ventures in Mexico (EPN-Delaval, SA) and the Netherlands (Delaval-Stork); and the procurement of orders for utility and petrochemical applications from Poland and Yugoslavia. Sales offices were established around the world, from London and Paris and the Hague to Athens and Saudi Arabia to Singapore and Hong Kong. The 1986 acquisition of Imo AB, in Stockholm, the original Swedish patent holder, brought the company full circle as well as supporting its leadership in the worldwide screw pump market.

The growth period of the 1970s and 1980s was also marked by changes in company leadership. W. J. Holcombe moved to an executive position in Transamerica and assumed De Laval chairmanship in 1972 before leaving the company in 1975. Ivan Monk, who had joined De Laval in 1961, presided over the company for two years, followed by Donald T. Bixby, who served as president from 1974 to 1983 and chairman of the board until his retirement in 1985. It was Bixby who broke ground in Lawrenceville, New Jersey, for the new company headquarters in 1979. In 1983 Truman W. Netherton moved from Westinghouse to become De Laval's president. Three years later, in 1986, W. J. Holcombe returned to the newly independent company as chief executive officer and was named president the following year.

Independence from Transamerica in 1986 brought with it many fundamental changes. A loss of $21.8 million—the first in 25 years—occasioned the divestment of several divisions (Enterprise, Texas Forge, and Pumptron) whose business depended on depressed markets like oil, gas, agricultural, and nuclear utilities. At the same time, focusing on companies involved in the manufacture and sale of complementary profit-making product lines, the company began a strategic acquisition campaign. As a means of delimiting the company's course, Imo was reorganized to form its two current primary businesses: Instruments and Controls, and Power Systems. Management was restructured to better coordinate sales and operations and to accommodate future business opportunities. More attention was directed to serving the extensive aftermarket needs of the energy marketplace.

Beginning in 1987, the newspapers were filled with accounts of Imo acquisitions, large and small. Among the largest were Baird (in 1987 for $55.8 million), manufacturer of spectrometers and optical systems; Incom International Inc. (in 1987 for $145.8 million), a group of manufacturers of electronic controls and power transmission devices; and Varo (in 1988 for $117 million), a major supplier of night vision equipment to the military. Less costly but important acquisitions included Warren Pumps and Roltra (1989), Quabbin Industries (1990), an aftermarket service company and producer of retractable seals to increase turbine efficiency, and Opto-Electronic Corp., which was merged with Varo.

The 1990s and Beyond

Earnings at Imo in the early 1990s were depressed. Gross profit margins slipped from 29.1 percent in 1989 to 25.8 percent in 1991. Paying down accumulated long-term debt from its acquisition program and lessened potential recovery momentum. However, the company expected to have some long-term protection from up-and-down behavior in various markets with its carefully developed multiple-niche strategy.

During the early 1990s, company-wide efforts were directed toward increasing the competitive advantage through marketing initiatives and manufacturing efficiencies and diminishing the effects of market fluctuations. The year 1991 saw a nine percent work force reduction as manufacturing processes designed to increase productivity and reduce lead times were implemented. Streamlining strategies also resulted in the integration of like operations such as the combining of Varo and OEC (Electro-Optical Systems) and the consolidation of a new Turbo-Care group. Multi-division marketing such as the recent Pacific-area program based in Singapore exemplified the company's efforts to reach expanded global markets.

Still, the company had difficulties maintaining its financial health and operational viability. Thus, in 1992, Imo Industries implemented a strategy to reduce its outstanding debt through the sale and divestiture of certain businesses. To this end, the company completed the sale of its Delevel Turbine and Turbo-Care divisions in 1995, sold its Varo Electronic Systems and Baird Analytical Instruments division, and the rest of its Electro-Optical Systems division around the same time. In 1998, the company completed the sale of its Instrumentation business, and Roltra-Morse businesses. The sale of company assets contributed toward paying off a substantial portion of its debt, but the revitalization of Imo Industries and its operations were significantly hindered by lawsuits brought forth by both individuals and the U.S. government.

Specifically, Imo Industries had been identified by the U.S. Environmental Protection Agency as the potentially responsible party for hazardous waste at a number of its facilities throughout the United States, especially in the state of Washington. In addition, legal suits against the company alleging injury caused by asbestos were also filed by nearly 7,000 individuals. Although the company and its subsidiaries had never produced asbestos, the suits alleged that numerous industrial and marine products sold by the company contained asbestos.

Unable to climb out of its increasing financial difficulties, Imo Industries was purchased by II Acquisition Corporation in 1997, whose management immediately implemented a cost reduction program that included the closing of certain company manufacturing facilities, the consolidation of others, reduction of the firm's work force, and a reorganization plan designed to breathe new life into company operations. New management was also brought into the company, including a new CEO, Philip W. Knisely, in 1997.

As it approached the end of the century, the company's focus on products for transportation, industrial, utility and cogeneration, and oil, gas, and process markets that stress efficiency and environmental initiatives underscored management's concern about financial stability and could well contribute to long-term profitability and recovery. Yet Imo Industries had a long road to travel before finding the shelter it sought.

Principal Divisions

Imo Industries Ltd. (UK); Imo Industries Gmbh; Morse Controls SARL; Morse Controls S.L.; Imo Industries PTE, Ltd.; NHK Morse Co., Ltd.; Imo AB; Imo-Pumpen GmbH; Imo Industries, Inc. (Canada); Delsalesco, Inc.; Imovest, Inc.; Baird Corporation; Incom Transportation, Inc.; Boston Gear Industries of Canada, Inc.; VHC Inc.; Warren Pumps, Inc.; Deltex Service, Inc.; Shanghai Dong Feng Morse Control Cable Co., Ltd.; Bombas Imo De Venezuela C.V.

Further Reading

"Constellation Capital Partners Affiliate Launches Tender Offer for Imo Industries," *PR Newswire,* July 1997.
IMO 1890–1990: An Industrial Evolution, Lawrenceville, N.J.: Imo Industries, 1991.
"Imo Industries Announces Sale to II Acquisition Corp.," *PR Newswire,* June 25, 1997.
"Imo Losses Widen," *United Press International,* October 11, 1996.
"Imo Reports Earnings of 14 Cents Per Share," *PR Newswire,* June 17, 1997.

—Margaret Barlow
—updated by Thomas Derdak

Indiana Energy, Inc.

1630 North Meridian Street
Indianapolis, Indiana 46202-1496
U.S.A.
(317) 926-3351
Fax: (317) 321-0498
Web site: http://www.indiana-energy.com

Public Company
Incorporated: 1945 as Indiana Gas and Water Company, Inc.
Employees: 984
Sales: $465 million (1998)
Stock Exchanges: New York
Ticker Symbol: IEI
SICs: 4924 Natural Gas Distribution

Indiana Energy, Inc. (IEI) is a holding company with subsidiaries in natural gas distribution and related services. The company's primary subsidiary, Indiana Gas, is a public utility that provides natural gas to approximately 489,000 residential, commercial, and industrial customers in Indiana. A second subsidiary, IEI Investments, operates as a holding company for the parent company's interests in non-regulated industries. The subsidiary companies of IEI Investments are Energy Realty, a limited partner in three affordable housing complexes in the Indiana Gas service area, and IGC Energy. IGC Energy is a joint owner of ProLiance Energy L.L.C., a strategic partnership formed to supply natural gas and related services to Indiana and surrounding states. The co-owner of ProLiance is Citizens Gas and Coke Utility, a natural gas distribution company serving Indianapolis, Indiana.

The Early Years: Reorganization, Incorporation, and Trouble-Shooting

Indiana Energy, Inc. began its existence as Indiana Gas & Water Company, a utility under the corporate umbrella of the large multi-utility Public Service Indiana. PSI, which included gas, water, electric, and transportation divisions, was formed at the beginning of the 20th century as part of Middle West Utilities, a gigantic Chicago-based holding company. Through the 1910s and 1920s, PSI evolved by acquiring and operating a number of small individual utility companies in communities throughout central and southern Indiana. In the early 1930s, however, undercapitalized and hit hard by the Depression, PSI's parent company Middle West Utilities, filed for reorganization and the company was ordered into receivership. In 1941, as part of its reorganization plan to emerge from bankruptcy, PSI proposed divesting of its gas and water divisions. The plan was approved by the Securities and Exchange Commission, and four years later, the Indiana Gas & Water Company was incorporated.

Most of the total cost of the new company was financed by issuing 277,500 shares of stock worth $8.5 million to PSI. The balance of the purchase price came from $6 million worth of bonds. At the time of its incorporation, the Indianapolis-based Indiana Gas & Water provided gas to approximately 61,000 customers in 42 southern, central, and central-northern Indiana communities. Water service was provided to just over 29,000 customers in 19 communities.

The spin-off company faced an immediate and formidable problem: its gas distribution system was outdated and not well maintained. Through the Depression and the early years of World War II, PSI had lacked both the funding and materials necessary to adequately maintain and expand the system. For the most part, therefore, no improvements had been made since the early 1930s. The newly organized Indiana Gas & Water set about improving the situation in early 1946, with an ambitious three-year, $3 million construction program. The project involved building 60 miles of new gas line and adding more than 4,500 new customers.

A second major problem was the inadequate supplies of pipeline gas available from the company's suppliers. In the years immediately following Indiana Gas & Water's incorporation, the use of natural gas grew at an unprecedented rate, and the suppliers were often unable to keep up with the demand. To alleviate part of the shortage, in 1947 the company built a transmission line southward to connect with a major pipeline operated by the Texas Eastern Gas Transmission Corporation.

As the gas squeeze grew tighter in the late 1940s, Indiana Gas & Water installed a number of small liquefied-petroleum air gas plants to provide standby gas during peak demand days. Even so, gas remained in short supply throughout the 1940s and into the early 1950s, and the company was forced to move slowly in its expansion efforts.

Strengthening and Expanding the System

The second half of the 1950s was a time of rapid growth for the gas industry throughout the United States. New natural gas fields were discovered in Mexico, Canada, Louisiana, and North Dakota, and the first offshore gas pipeline was built in the Gulf of Mexico. It appeared that the shortage was at an end, and the gas industry boomed. Indiana Gas & Water used the decade to further strengthen and broaden its gas distribution and storage system. By the early 1950s, the company had sold several of its small-town water properties to the Hoosier Water Company and used the proceeds to purchase additional natural gas facilities. Near the end of the 1950s, storage became the company's focus. Following the industry trend toward underground storage, Indiana Gas & Water developed three underground fields capable of storing more than three billion cubic feet of gas. The newfound gas supplies also allowed the company to take more gas from its suppliers, upping its daily take from 52.5 million to 140 million cubic feet of gas between 1959 and 1961.

With the upgraded distribution system, the addition of new storage fields, and the greatly increased gas supply, Indiana Gas & Water was poised for expansion. The company entered the 1960s with a growth strategy that quickly played out. Projecting that population growth in central Indiana would be concentrated in the suburban areas around Indianapolis, the company started the decade by installing distribution lines to three new communities in the Indianapolis region. (This decision proved to be both foresighted and pivotal. As predicted, the size of these new communities did increase dramatically: in the years between 1960 and 1990, their population would more than double.) Indiana Gas & Water followed this expansion with further growth as the decade progressed—to include more than 20 new communities in its service area. The strategy paid off almost immediately. By 1965, the company was one of the state's fastest-growing utilities, with a service area of 76 communities throughout southern, central, and north-central sections of Indiana.

The second half of the 1960s was marked by a series of acquisitions and one major divestiture. Between 1965 and 1968,

Indiana Gas & Water purchased four existing gas utility companies, expanding its service territory to include more than 20 new communities. The company also made the decision to sell off its remaining water utilities to three Chicago investors for the price of $13.4 million. With the divestiture of the water companies, a name change was necessary—and Indiana Gas & Water became Indiana Gas Company. In 1970, the company was listed on the New York Stock Exchange under the ticker symbol IGC.

The Gas Shortage Years

Leaving the boom years of the late 1950s and 1960s behind, the gas industry fell on hard times again in the 1970s with the onset of the fuel shortage. The gas that had been so abundant in the previous decade was suddenly in short supply. A main factor behind the shortage was the Federal regulation of natural gas prices. Under this regulation, gas producers were unable to command high enough prices to make feasible the costly exploration and drilling for new gas sources. As a result, domestic exploration and drilling had declined, and the U.S. gas industry had become increasingly dependent upon foreign sources.

In 1970, Texas Eastern, one of Indiana Gas's suppliers, announced that it would begin curtailing gas shipments to some of its customers. Indiana Gas responded by dividing its customers into "firm" and "interruptible" categories, informing its industrial customers to be prepared to switch to other fuels in case of curtailment. A few months later, the company was notified by its suppliers that they could provide no further volume increases under contract. Gas supplies got even tighter in 1973, with the OPEC Oil Embargo, instituted by the Arab nations to protest U.S. support of Israel. To partially ameliorate the crunch, Indiana Gas built a propane storage installation, and purchased 840,000 gallons of liquid propane from Texas Eastern. By mixing the propane with 48 percent air, the company was able to produce a gas similar in quality to natural gas.

Despite the continued gas shortage, Indiana Gas broadened its base in the mid-1970s by purchasing the Muncie-based Central Indiana Gas Company. Central Indiana Gas Company was a company of substantial size, with 538 employees and more than 100,000 customers in 62 east central Indiana communities. The purchase, when completed in 1976, made Indiana Gas Company the state's second largest gas-distribution utility, with more than 292,000 customers.

The shortage that plagued Indiana Gas throughout the first part of the 1970s was aggravated near the end of the decade by some of the worst winter weather of the century. Contending with increased customer demand for gas for heating purposes, Indiana Gas announced curtailments for 234 large-volume customers in December 1975. Along with the shortages and curtailments came price hikes. By 1977, the company was paying its suppliers more than 150 percent more for gas than it had been paying only four years earlier. At the same time, the cost of virtually everything else was increasing. Inflation, which had been held at bay during the early postwar years, was climbing steadily. In 1977, to offset its increased expenses, Indiana Gas asked the Public Service Commission to approve a rate adjustment. The approved 9.8 percent increase allowed the company to recover approximately $15.25 million per year.

Deregulation, High Prices, and the Gas Bubble

The last years of the 1970s marked the beginning of a new and turbulent era for Indiana Gas. In 1977, President Jimmy Carter proposed a sweeping package of energy legislation that was to completely alter the way gas companies did business. When Congress passed the bill in 1978, the piece of legislation that had the greatest impact on the gas industry was the Natural Gas Policy Act. This act provided for a steady increase in gas prices for producers at the wellhead between the years of 1978 and 1985. On January 1, 1985, under the same legislation, the natural gas industry would be completely deregulated. There were to be further price regulations on gas discovered after 1977. In addition, the new policy enabled gas companies, and even large industrial and commercial customers to purchase gas directly from the producers. Until this time, the *pipelines* had purchased gas from the producers, and in turn sold it to the distributors. The Natural Gas Policy Act was designed to encourage domestic exploration for new gas sources by creating a more competitive marketplace and allowing producers to command higher prices—and it worked. Gas producers all across North America stepped up exploratory drilling, and new gas sources were made available. The gas shortage began to ease late in 1978.

The reversal came at a high price, however. In 1978, the CEO of Indiana Gas, John Kavanagh, cautioned gas customers of what was likely to come. "All of the activities to provide additional gas require very large capital outlays, and it appears that high inflation will affect costs in the 1980s," he noted in an essay for the *Indianapolis News*. "Therefore, efforts to obtain gas supplies for present and future consumers will be reflected in higher delivered prices," he cautioned. Kavanagh was correct in his prediction. With the loosening of price controls, natural gas pipeline suppliers increased their rates rapidly and recklessly. In 1982, Indiana Gas' major supplier raised its gas price by 40 percent in just one adjustment.

The sudden jump in gas prices at the supplier level sent Indiana Gas to the Public Service Commission to petition for a series of rate increases. A 7.8 percent increase in 1980 was followed by an 11.1 increase in 1982 and a 5.2 percent hike in 1983. The company was finally able to access enough gas to service all of its customers—but both the customers and the company were paying exorbitant amounts for it. The high prices led to two natural reactions from gas customers: dissatisfaction and conservation. Faced with prices that were going through the roof, both residential and commercial customers began conserving gas. Many commercial customers switched to alternative fuels, such as electricity, coal, and propane. Indiana Gas was faced with a problem that was the polar opposite of the gas crunch: it had more supply than demand.

The gas surplus, called "the gas bubble" by industry economists, was by no means limited to Indiana Gas or to the state of Indiana. Eventually, this so-called bubble affected the price of gas at the supplier level, and in 1983, the pendulum swung back the other way. Indiana Gas received a reduction in purchase costs from pipeline suppliers, and was able to lower its rates for the first time since 1978. Gas prices continued dropping throughout the 1980s.

Meeting the Challenges of the New Marketplace

In the wake of the turbulent gas shortage and facing the challenges of deregulation, Indiana Gas moved into a period of change and reorganization. The first major change came in 1985, when Indiana Energy, Inc. (IEI) was created as a holding company for Indiana Gas. Then CEO Duane Amundson said the purpose of the reorganization was "to establish a more flexible corporate structure that will position us to diversify our income sources and to expand our energy-related operations."

The second half of the 1980s was taken up with revamping, both major and minor. The company's materials distribution and dispatching functions were centralized in a former Indianapolis warehouse. The company's 27 commercial officers were consolidated into six regional offices, and meter-reading routes were reorganized to improve efficiency and save time. The marketing department kicked off a major new campaign to both win new and retain existing customers. Along with these restructuring projects, the corporate culture changed to become more in keeping with the tenets of the 1985 mission statement. The company became more customer-focused, and the management style slowly evolved from a top-down to an employee-participation approach.

With the task of restructuring largely behind it, Indiana Energy began the processes it was created for: expansion and diversification. In 1990, the company acquired Richmond Gas Corporation and Terre Haute Gas, adding about 47,000 customers. With the two new additions, Indiana Gas had a customer base of 391,000 customers and annual revenues of about $390 million. To begin diversification, IEI formed the subsidiary IEI Investments, Inc., which served as a holding company for all non-regulated businesses. This structure in place, IEI began to invest in businesses that were outside the gas distribution industry—such as flexible gas piping and real estate.

IEI took a major step in 1996, with the formation of ProLiance Energy L.L.C., a strategic alliance of IEI Investments subsidiary IGC Energy, Inc. and a subsidiary of Citizens Gas and Coke Utility. The alliance was formed to supply gas, power, and marketing services to both Indiana Gas and Citizens Gas, as well as other companies. As the sole supplier for these companies, ProLiance had the ability to negotiate favorable prices for gas supplies. It was this fact, however, that led 18 Indiana businesses to protest the ProLiance-Indiana Gas gas-purchasing agreement, claiming that it gave ProLiance a monopoly over gas supplies and prices. Although the Indiana Utility Regulatory Commission upheld the agreement, the Indiana Court of Appeals reversed the decision in 1998. IEI petitioned for the case to be transferred to the Indiana Supreme Court.

Two similar alliances were formed in 1997, again between IEI and a subsidiary of Citizens Gas and Coke. CIGMA L.L.C., was designed to combine the purchasing power of the companies to obtain better pricing, reduce combined inventory, and allow for quick inventory turnover. Energy Systems Group L.L.C. evaluated institutional and industrial customers' use of energy, and designs, finances, and installed upgrades to maximize energy efficiency and operational performance. A fourth alliance, Reliant Services L.L.C., was formed in 1998 with

Indiana electric company, Cinergy Corp. Reliant Services offered locating and trenching services to gas, electric, water, and cable companies.

The year 1998 also brought changes to IEI's corporate structure. The company divided into separate and distinct business units: Indiana Gas, IEI Investments, and a new, third division, IEI Services. IEI Services served as the company's administrative arm, providing human relations, information technology, accounting, tax, and building and fleet management services to the IEI companies.

Moving into the 21st Century

In 1997, Indiana Energy's Board of Directors approved a growth strategy to support the company's transition into the more competitive deregulated market between the years of 1998 and 2003. The twin goals of the plan were for IEI to become a "leading regional provider of energy products and services" and to increase its consolidated earnings per share by an average of ten percent annually through 2003. Achievement of this goal would likely mean earnings of $2.40 per share by the end of the five-year period. IEI's strategy relies largely upon growing the earnings from its non-regulated businesses to more than 25 percent of total annual earnings. Increased earnings and customer base for Indiana Gas was another key tenet of the strategy. Indiana Gas earnings were projected to increase five percent yearly for the foreseeable future. IEI also pledged to reduce costs during the five-year plan period. In June 1997, the company announced its intent to reduce the number of full-time employees from 1,025 to approximately 800 by the end of the year 2002. It also committed to selling, abandoning, or otherwise disposing of certain assets, including buildings and gas storage fields.

Principal Subsidiaries

Indiana Gas Company, Inc.; IEI Services L.L.C.; IEI Investments, Inc.; IGC Energy, Inc.; Energy Realty, Inc.; Indiana Energy Services, Inc.; Energy Financial Group, Inc.; IEI Financial Services L.L.C.; ProLiance Energy L.L.C. (50%); Reliant Services L.L.C. (50%).

Further Reading

Andrews, Greg, "Indiana Energy Stock Spikes," *Indiana Business Journal,* October 13, 1997, p. 1.

Beck, Bill, *Natural Gas for the Hoosier State: An Illustrated History of Indiana Gas Company, Inc. 1945–1995,* Indianapolis: Indiana Gas Company, Inc., 1995.

Eckert, Toby, "Indiana Energy Sets New Growth Goals," *Indiana Business Journal,* August 11, 1997, p. 4.

Tussing, Arlon, and Bill Tippee, eds., *The Natural Gas Industry: Evolution, Structure, and Economics,* Cambridge, Mass.: Ballinger Publishing Company, 1984.

—Shawna Brynildssen

Intermountain Health Care, Inc.

36 South State Street
Salt Lake City, Utah 84111
U.S.A.
(801) 442-2000
Fax: (801) 442-3565
Web site: http://www.ihc.com

Private Company
Incorporated: 1975
Employees: 22,000
Sales: 2,008.7 million (1997)
SICs: 8062 General Medical & Surgical Hospitals; 8063
    Psychiatric Hospitals; 8069 Specialty Hospitals Except
    Psychiatric; 8011 Offices & Clinics of Medical
    Doctors

Intermountain Health Care, Inc. (IHC) is the largest hospital chain and health care organization in the Intermountain West. With 23 hospitals, it serves more than 425,000 individuals in Utah (its main market), Idaho, and Wyoming. It is a vertically integrated company with not only hospitals, but also 75 clinics plus health insurance plans for individuals, families, companies, and institutions. More than 2,500 medical doctors are affiliated with IHC, including 400 directly employed by the firm. It has pioneered innovative management methods for the nonprofit health care industry, resulting in cost-effective quality care, and its executives have served in numerous leadership roles in that field. IHC also has faced major legal and public relations problems concerning taxation and antitrust, issues that have received considerable attention by the media and public policy experts.

1970s Origins: The LDS Church Hospital System

IHC grew out of the hospital system of The Church of Jesus Christ of Latter-day Saints (the ''Mormons''). Although the Episcopalians built St. Mark's Hospital, Utah's first permanent hospital, in 1872, the LDS church by the early 1900s had built its two main facilities: the LDS Hospital and the Primary Children's Hospital, both in Salt Lake City.

After World War II, the church acquired other facilities, including some, like Provo's Utah Valley Hospital, which had originated as community hospitals. In 1970 the church integrated its health care system by forming the LDS Health Services Corporation. In the early 1970s that nonprofit corporation operated 15 hospitals with more than 2,000 beds, one of the nation's largest hospital chains.

In 1974, however, the church surprised many by announcing that it would quit the hospital business, ''because the operation of hospitals is not central to the mission of the Church.'' Reasons for that change included 1) a booming worldwide missionary effort that required more church resources, 2) old hospitals that needed about $100 million to upgrade, and 3) concern over more federal laws and regulations on medicine, including the 1973 U.S. Supreme Court decision (*Roe v. Wade*) that legalized abortion.

So in 1975 the church gave its hospitals to a new nonprofit entity called Intermountain Health Care. Its founding chairman, William N. Jones, a prominent businessman, headed an interdenominational board of trustees. IHC chose Scott Parker as its first president, a Salt Lake City native who had graduated with his master's degree in hospital administration from the University of Minnesota and then gained much experience as a hospital administrator in Minnesota, Arizona, and California.

IHC started with the following 15 hospitals: LDS Hospital, Salt Lake City (largest in the chain); Primary Children's Hospital, Salt Lake City; Utah Valley Hospital, Provo, Utah; Bear River Valley Hospital, Tremonton, Utah (managed); Cassia Memorial Hospital, Burley, Idaho (managed); Cottonwood Hospital, Murray, Utah; Fillmore Hospital, Fillmore, Utah; Fremont General Hospital, St. Anthony, Idaho (managed); Garfield Memorial Hospital, Panguitch, Utah; Logan Hospital, Logan, Utah; Idaho Falls Hospital, Idaho Falls, Idaho; McKay-Dee Hospital, Ogden, Utah; Sanpete Valley Hospital, Mt. Pleasant, Utah; Sevier Valley Hospital, Richfield, Utah; and Star Valley Hospital, Afton, Wyoming. IHC thus followed the trend started in the 1960s for hospitals to cooperate to save money and compete more effectively. In 1968 Hospital Corporation of America became the first for-profit chain. By 1986 about one-

Company Perspectives:

The mission of Intermountain Health Care's nonprofit hospitals and clinics is to provide quality care to those with a medical need, regardless of ability to pay. Excellent service to our patients, health plan members, customers, and physicians is our most important consideration. We will provide our services with integrity. Our actions will enhance our reputation and reflect the trust placed in us by those we serve. Our employees are our most important resource. We will attract exceptional individuals at all levels of the organization and provide fair compensation and opportunities for personal and professional growth. We will recognize and reward employees who achieve excellence in their work. We are committed to serving diverse needs of the young and old, the rich and poor, and those living in urban and rural communities. We will reflect the caring and noble nature of our mission in all that we do. Our services must be high quality, cost-effective, and accessible, achieving a balance between community needs and available resources. It is our intent to be a model health care system. We will strive to be a national leader in nonprofit health care delivery. We will maintain the financial strength necessary to fulfill our mission.

third of the United States' acute-care hospitals were affiliated with a multihospital organization.

Early Expansion and Improvements

In its first few years IHC emphasized refurbishing its original hospitals, adding some new facilities, and generally improving hospital operations. It purchased three hospitals in Utah (St. George, Cedar City, and Orem), two in Evanston, Wyoming, and one in Pocatello, Idaho.

IHC also expanded centralized services to its growing chain of facilities. In cooperation with other nonprofit hospitals, IHC formed the Associated Hospital System (AHS) in 1978 to save money on joint purchases. AHS merged with the United Hospital System in 1984 to form the American Hospital Systems, again to take advantage of economy-of-scale purchasing power.

Scott Parker and his management team took advantage of the centralized budgeting started by the LDS hospital system. In IHC's 1995 corporate history, Parker said, "Other hospital systems hadn't done it [consolidated their finances]. [The LDS Church] bit the bullet and said, 'The money is going to come centrally and we're going to bank it, invest it and control it centrally.' That's a big, big problem to get over. Some systems that have prominence and reputations across the country still haven't done it." IHC began a cost-saving program to save on insurance and risk management. In 1976 it teamed up with hospitals in other states to create Multihospital Mutual Insurance, Ltd. to provide liability coverage.

In these early years, IHC saved some small rural hospitals, such as Valley View, which in 1977 regained it accreditation. IHC's total revenues grew from $92 million in 1975 to $223

million in 1980, a ten percent real growth rate after adjusting for inflation. Its "ambitious program of building, renovating, and managing was being accomplished without significantly raising the cost of care," according to its corporate history.

Diversification and Restructuring in the 1980s

While continuing to add more hospitals and horizontally integrate its chain under centralized leadership, IHC in the early 1980s constructed or purchased several facilities for ambulatory patients who did not need hospitalization. Included were surgical centers for elective surgery, InstaCare Centers or clinics near residential areas, and occupational health centers, like the one built to serve the workers of Intermountain Power Plant near Delta, Utah. In 1986 more than 100,000 patient visits were recorded at these various smaller IHC facilities.

In 1983 IHC created its Home Health Agency to provide nursing care, physical therapy, medical social work, intravenous therapy, and other services to patients at home. Such new and diverse programs led IHC in 1983 to reorganize as a parent company with five subsidiaries. IHC Hospitals, Inc. managed the firm's hospitals in Utah, Wyoming, and Idaho. IHC Professional Services, Inc. ran surgical centers and WORKMED occupational clinics, and IHC Foundation, Inc. raised funds and administered grants to help rural hospitals. The fourth subsidiary, IHC Health Plans, Inc., included a preferred provider organization called Health Choice and three health maintenance organizations: IHC Care, IHC Care-Group, and the Utah Small Employer Health Plan. IHC Affiliated Services, the fifth subsidiary, was a for-profit operation with group purchasing programs and computer software sold to other hospitals.

Sociologist Dr. Paul Starr called such a corporate restructuring a form of vertical integration, defined as a "shift from single-level-of-care organizations, such as acute-care hospitals, to organizations that embrace the various phases and levels of care, such as HMOs." IHC owned primary care facilities, such as clinics and small hospitals, secondary care hospitals with the ability to handle routine operations and diagnostic tests, and tertiary care hospitals with quite advanced capabilities.

Integration and Consolidation in the 1980s and 1990s

IHC eventually realized that it had overexpanded geographically by comanaging some clinics far from Salt Lake City. To save travel costs and focus on its core markets in the Intermountain West, IHC finally abandoned surgical centers in New Jersey and California and an Ohio occupational health center. Although IHC computer software had been sold to more than 200 hospitals nationwide, the company sold that business in 1988 to focus on its main goals.

In the late 1980s, as most hospital bed occupancy rates had fallen to about 50 percent, IHC was forced to find other ways to become more efficient and consolidate its operations. Thus in 1989 the company eliminated 20 management positions, a fairly typical move in the Information Age when middle management was becoming increasingly irrelevant.

Meanwhile, IHC faced other major problems in the 1980s. Its doctors faced higher malpractice insurance premiums, a nationwide trend. In the 1982 case *Hunter v. IHC,* the jury decided that the Hunter family should be awarded $4.7 million because of malpractice at IHC's Utah Valley Hospital. The largest malpractice lawsuit in Utah at the time, that one case probably helped raise liability rates for all Utah doctors.

IHC's toughest long-term legal and public relations challenge arose when some county governments decided that IHC hospitals should pay property tax because of the increasing business orientation of all health care operations, whether for-profit or nonprofit. IHC argued that its hospitals were charitable institutions and thus should be tax-exempt, based on the Utah Constitution that stated tax exemption could be granted to only charitable, religious, or educational organizations. In 1985 the Utah Supreme Court ruled in *Utah County v. Intermountain Health Care, Inc.* that two IHC hospitals were not automatically considered charitable and thus might be subject to taxation. In the fall 1986 election, Utah voters defeated Proposition One, which would have amended the state constitution to "allow property owned by a nonprofit entity that is used exclusively for hospital or nursing home purposes to be exempt from property tax."

In spite of the court ruling and the defeat of Proposition One, IHC hospitals have not paid taxes because they were able to prove on an individual basis that they qualified under state rules as charitable institutions. Some people complained because IHC input was used to write new rules concerning what exactly qualified as a charitable unit.

The bottom line was that IHC survived this challenge and continued into the 1990s as a legally charitable organization, based on its numerous gifts to the community. Those included free care to those who could not pay for aid, plus numerous grants from IHC foundations to support a wide variety of community-based organizations. In 1997, for example, IHC helped fund 114 programs, such as those for the American Cancer Society, the Salvation Army, the Utah Hispanic-American Festival, and the Salt Lake County Aging Services. After 20 years of operations, IHC by 1995 had provided more than $130 million in charitable care for patients. The company's total benefit in the form of community education, free health screening, and medical training came to $1 billion.

IHC worked hard to integrate its physicians into the corporate structure and culture, a difficult task considering that doctors traditionally valued autonomy and professionalism under their own direction. IHC created the Great Basin Physician Corporation. Three officers of that corporation also sat on the IHC Board of Trustees as a way of giving MDs more say on overall IHC policy.

IHC used advanced technologies to help integrate its services. For example, its laboratory leaders in the late 1980s began a coordinated program that eventually networked IHC hospital labs together. Automated inventory and medical records programs followed suit. In 1986 the company installed its satellite network, which was used mainly for continuous medical education programs, seminars, and teleconferences.

In the late 1980s IHC also began implementing the ideas of W. Edwards Deming to promote continuous quality improvement (CQI) in all phases of its work. Using statistics, empowering employees, reducing waste, and improving communication were a few of the basic concepts used here. National and international recognition of these innovative programs soon came. For example, in 1991 IHC received the Healthcare Forum/Witt Award for Commitment to Quality, similar to the Malcolm Baldrige National Quality Award.

In the 1990s IHC extended its integration strategy by pushing for systems and clinical integration. For example, it emphasized a wide range of health care operations, from short-term acute emergencies and surgery to long-care strategies based on prevention. In 1997 it began serving healthy children by creating the state's first Family Health Center at Salt Lake City's Lincoln Elementary School, a pilot program in a medically underserved neighborhood where many Hispanics and other minorities lived. In cooperation with other organizations, IHC supported health fairs, health education classes, and various other support groups as part of the national Healthy Communities program. For businesses, it provided through its IHC Health Plans free onsite screenings for employees with risk factors such as high blood pressure. IHC also backed programs for at-risk women to prevent premature births and to help individuals quit smoking. In addition to its hospital-based surgeries and advanced diagnostics, IHC provided home-based health care for temporary or long-term patients. IHC called this holistic approach clinical integration, which included families, neighborhoods, communities, businesses, and other providers in a long-range plan to help individuals in their quest for optimal physical and mental health.

Facing reform efforts by the Clinton administration and state government, IHC in the 1990s stressed the cooperation and synergy created when hospitals, health plans, and doctors worked together. Its subsidiary IHC Health Plans offered several kinds of health insurance, from managed care HMOs to plans that gave patients more freedom to choose their doctors.

By the 1990s IHC faced three major competitors in its main Utah market, the urban Wasatch Front from Provo in the south to Brigham City north of Salt Lake City. First, Columbia/HCA Healthcare Corporation, a for-profit chain based in Nashville, owned St. Mark's Hospital, other Wasatch Front hospitals, and several clinics. The University of Utah HealthNetwork included the University of Utah Medical Center and several clinics. Third, Paracelsus Healthcare Corporation ran the Salt Lake Regional Medical Center, formerly known as Holy Cross Hospital, along with three smaller hospitals and some clinics.

Because of IHC's dominance in its main market, it sometimes was accused of creating a health care monopoly and violating federal antitrust laws. For example, when it built the new Primary Children's Medical Center next to the University of Utah Medical Center, the federal government investigated antitrust charges that ultimately were dropped.

Developments in 1997 and 1998

After many years as Utah's main blood bank, in 1997 IHC ended that activity after having difficulty meeting the increasingly demanding requirements of the Food and Drug Administration. The American Red Cross took over the region's blood banking after IHC's departure.

Also in 1997, IHC received the following awards or honors. A National Research Corporation survey found that IHC was the top-rated HMO in the Salt Lake City area. After examining 500 U.S. firms, the magazine *PC Week* rated IHC as Utah's number one company in the use of computers and information technology. In addition, IHC received the Smithsonian Computerworld Award for its use of the Internet in quality care tracking systems. The American Hospital Association's *Hospitals and Health Networks* magazine, after studying more than 630 systems, named IHC one of the nation's top eight integrated health care systems.

At the end of 1998 Scott Parker retired after 23 years as IHC's first and only president/CEO. He had served as the chairman of the American Hospital Association, president of the International Hospital Federation, chairman of the Hospital Research and Development Institute, and as a director of several major corporations.

Parker's replacement, William H. Nelson, took over the nation's seventh largest nonprofit hospital chain. Nelson had earned an MBA in 1971 from the University of Southern California and worked as a healthcare consultant for the accounting firm later known as Ernst and Young before joining IHC in 1976. As part of IHC's senior management team for many years, Nelson was well positioned to take over the reins of the growing firm.

In 1998 IHC's chairman was David Salisbury, an attorney who had joined the Salt Lake City law firm of Van Cott, Bagley, Cornwall and McCarthy in 1952 after graduating from the Stanford Law School. His law career included work in taxation and estate planning and clients such as Mountain States Telephone and Telegraph Company.

Like all health care organizations, IHC confronted recent trends such as increased consumer awareness, questioning of professional roles, and the rise of holistic or alternative medicine. In reality, IHC and other hospitals generally arose during the Industrial Revolution, along with other centralized entities like factories and libraries. But with the advent of computers and advanced telecommunications, decentralization became the dominant trend. Almost all hospitals since the 1980s had about a 50 percent occupancy rate. That basic fact propelled IHC to search for new ways to serve the community.

In 1998 IHC seemed to be doing a good job of adapting to what many have called a health care revolution, in part by balancing what author John Naisbett in *Megatrends* called high-tech and high-touch approaches. Significantly, IHC's costs ranged about 30 percent lower than the national average, a rather remarkable achievement.

Two 1998 developments seemed typical of IHC's history. On a positive note, officials from IHC, the University of Utah,

and the Huntsman Cancer Institute announced a joint program to develop standardized cancer therapies. According to the December 19, 1998 *Salt Lake Tribune,* this cooperative effort was "the first time in the United States such a venture has been initiated in a population within a single geographical area. Similar programs involve medical institutions and patient populations located far from each other." Such clinical innovation was part of IHC's legacy.

The company, however, faced yet another in a series of public relations/legal difficulties. Shortly after receiving the bid to become the health care provider for the Salt Lake Winter Olympics in 2002 A.D., the public learned that IHC had provided nearly $28,000 worth of free care for three Africans associated with the International Olympic Committee before the IOC awarded the games to Salt Lake City. An IHC spokesman said the company had responded as part of a community effort to win the games and that IHC had been told the three individuals lacked adequate funds or that the requested services were unavailable in their home nations. These developments were part of an ongoing bribery and ethics investigation concerning not only IHC and Salt Lake City Olympics leaders, but the Olympic Games in general. As the new millennium approached, IHC President Nelson and Chairman Salisbury faced such controversies along with their main task of keeping costs down while providing quality care.

Principal Subsidiaries

IHC Affiliated Services; IHC Foundation, Inc.; IHC Health Plans, Inc.; IHC Hospitals, Inc.; IHC Professional Services, Inc.

Further Reading

Divett, Robert T., *Medicine and the Mormons: An Introduction to the History of Latter-day Saint Health Care,* Bountiful, Utah: Horizon Publishers, 1981.

Knudson, Max B., "What Is the Secret of IHC's Success?," *Deseret News,* November 5, 1995, p. M1.

Rammell, Phelon S., and Robert J. Parsons, "Utah County v. Intermountain Health Care: Utah's Unique Method for Determining Charitable Property Tax Exemptions—A Review of Its Mandate and Impact," *Journal of Health and Hospital Law,* March 1989, pp. 74–75.

Starr, Paul, *The Social Transformation of American Medicine,* New York: Basic Books, 1982.

Vitelli, Tom, *The Story of Intermountain Health Care,* Salt Lake City: Intermountain Health Care, 1995.

Wagner, Norma, "After 23 Years at Helm, IHC Boss to Sail Off into Retirement," *Salt Lake Tribune,* April 7, 1998, p. D1.

——, "Cancer Effort Aspires to Better Care," *Salt Lake Tribune,* December 19, 1998, p. E1.

——, "Free Care, IHC Lists Specifics of Games-Related Donations," *Salt Lake Tribune,* December 15, 1998, p. A1, A5.

Walden, David M., "Intermountain Health Care, Inc.," in *Utah's Health Care Revolution: Pluralism and Professionalization Since World War II* (M.A. thesis), Provo, Utah: Brigham Young University, 1989.

—David M. Walden

INTERNATIONAL SHIPHOLDING CORPORATION

International Shipholding Corporation, Inc.

650 Poydras Street, Suite 1700
New Orleans, Louisiana 70130
U.S.A.
(504) 529-5461
Fax: (504) 529-5745

Public Company
Incorporated: 1947 as Central Gulf Steamship
  Corporation
Employees: 960
Sales: $391.1 million (1997)
Stock Exchanges: New York
Ticker Symbol: ISH
SICs: 4449 Shipping Agents; 4412 Deep Sea Foreign
  Transport of Freight; 4489 Steamship Companies

Tracing its history to the formation of the Central Gulf Steamship Corp in 1947, International Shipholding Corporation, Inc. (ISC) is Louisiana's oldest existing steamship company. Through its subsidiaries, ISC operates a diversified fleet of U.S.- and international-flag vessels that provides international and domestic maritime transportation services to commercial customers and agencies of the U.S. government under medium- to long-term charters or contracts. ISC is the only significant operator of the LASH transportation system, which it pioneered in 1969; the company owns 13 such LASH vessels, in addition to four LASH feeder vessels and 1,865 LASH barges.

The Originator of the LASH Shipping System

The company was founded as Central Gulf Steamship Corporation by Niels F. Johnsen and his sons, Niels W. and Erik F. Johnsen. Incorporated in 1947, the new company was backed by a group of New Orleans businessmen and professional leaders. It immediately purchased and began operations with one World War II Liberty ship, renamed the *Green Wave* in honor of Tulane University, alma mater of the two younger Johnsens.

Central Gulf undertook to consolidate its management and expand its fleet during the 1950s. The company opened offices in New Orleans and New York and formed a network of marketing and operating agents in major cities worldwide. During the 1960s, ISC increased its fleet to 36 vessels and became the number one U.S.-flag carrier between the United States and the Middle East. ISC also inaugurated its practice of becoming a niche operator during this period—identifying and meeting customers' special shipping needs—and pioneered the LASH (Lighter Aboard SHip) system in 1969. That year and the next, the company began to operate the world's first two LASH vessels, designed by naval architect Jerome Goldman.

The LASH transportation system used specially designed barges of uniform size which were loaded with cargo, towed to a centralized fleeting area, loaded aboard a large oceangoing LASH vessel by the vessel's 500-ton capacity shipboard crane, and then transported overseas, where the process was reversed. In its transoceanic liner services, ISC used the LASH system to gather cargo in ocean ports as well as on rivers and island chains and in harbors too shallow for traditional vessels. ISC's 400-ton capacity LASH barges were ideally suited to transport larger unit size items such as project cargo, forest products, natural rubber and steel that could not be transported efficiently to and from such areas in container ships.

Trans Union Corporation, a Fortune 500 company, was quick to perceive the advantages of the LASH system. In early 1971, Trans Union merged with Central Gulf, allowing it to launch three new U.S.-flag LASH vessels, which operated from the Gulf to the Middle East and Southeast Asia, and to commission and commence operating a new series of float-on/float-off heavy-lift vessels. In 1978, International Shipholding Corporation was spun off from Trans Union and formed to act as a holding company, its only significant assets the capital stock of its subsidiaries, which at the time consisted of Central Gulf and certain other affiliated companies. By 1981, ISC had paid off its remaining debt to Trans Union, after securing a $41 million, six-year loan, $9 million of which went to its LASH Carriers subsidiary. The company then, through its subsidiaries, began to operate a diversified fleet of U.S.- and international-flag vessels that provided international and domestic as well as

---

Company Perspectives:

The company's strategy is to (i) identify customers with high credit and marine transportation needs requiring specialized vessels or operating techniques, (ii) seek medium- to long-term charters or contracts with those customers and, if necessary, modify, acquire or construct vessels to meet the requirements of those charters or contracts and (iii) provide its customers with reliable, high quality service at a reasonable cost.

---

government maritime transportation services. As part of the spinoff, common stock in ISC was issued to Trans Union stockholders in 1979.

Diversification in the 1980s

During the 1980s, ISC steadily expanded operations. It reflagged to the U.S. registry and began operating two ice-strengthened multipurpose vessels under charter to the U.S. Navy's Military Sealift Command. In 1984, ISC moved to new headquarters in the Poydras Center Building in New Orleans. In 1986, Central Gulf purchased Forest Lines from International Navigation Ltd., a subsidiary of International Paper Company. International Paper had had contracts with ISC units since 1969, and this acquisition included ongoing, guaranteed transportation contracts with the paper manufacturer. Forest Lines began to operate three additional LASH vessels between New Orleans, Savannah—later Charleston—and the United Kingdom and North Europe. It also signed a 22-year contract with a Florida-based utility to transport coal from Mt. Vernon, Indiana, to Florida and began operating two of the first four pure car carriers to fly the American flag, transporting vehicles for Honda and Toyota beginning in 1987.

ISC had begun repurchasing shares of its common stock from time to time throughout the 1980s, and, in 1986, it announced its intentions to continue this practice. With net income of $11 million in 1988 and revenues of $170.4 million, the company's business was booming. That year its stock hit an all-time high at $44.25 per share, and the company began offering its shareholders a dividend. After ISC's 1989 purchase of Waterman Marine Corporation, Wall Street analysts were calling it "one of the premier U.S. shipping companies," notably one of the few to add to its fleet during a period of industry decline. ISC offered 920,000 shares of common stock for sale in 1989, raising about $15.2 million, to help offset the $34 million cost of buying Waterman Marine Corporation, which operated the Waterman Steamship Corporation.

Acquiring Waterman Marine Corporation

Prior to the Waterman acquisition, ISC was operating eight U.S.-flag ships and ten international-flag vessels between ports in the U.S. Gulf and the Atlantic and those in the Red Sea, Indian Ocean, South Asia, and Southeast Asia. The purchase of Waterman involved the transfer of its six U.S.-flag vessels to a new International Shipholding subsidiary, Waterman Steamship Corporation, bringing ISC's total number of vessels to 24. Three of the Waterman ships were chartered LASH vessels which ISC continued to use in a liner service between the U.S. Atlantic and the Gulf and ports in the Middle East and South and Southeast Asia, while the remaining three roll-on roll-off vessels were operated under existing charter arrangements with the Military Sealift Command. Also included in the Waterman deal were subsidy contracts worth about $13.1 million which Waterman held with the Transportation Department's Maritime Administration (Marad). These subsidies were provided as part of the 1936 Merchant Marine Act enacted by Congress to help owners of U.S.-flag vessels, who were required to hire U.S. unionized labor, offset the cheaper operating costs of international-flag competitors. Waterman had suffered financial losses in the early 1980s so severe that it was forced to let these government contracts lie dormant. However, once ISC bought Waterman, Central Gulf's ships could be used by Waterman to fulfill its government charters, and its financial losses conferred tax benefits on ISC.

ISC's purchase of Waterman was subject to the approval of Marad, since U.S. shipping law barred the operation of foreign vessels by subsidized carriers or their affiliates without prior Marad permission. The Administration consented to the Waterman purchase over the objections of the Seafarers International Union and another shipping company, Afram, both of whom contended that the merger was in violation of the 1936 act. The grounds for their objection was the fact that ISC owned two unsubsidized companies, Central Gulf and the Liberian-flag LCI, while Waterman received about $12 million in operating differential subsidies from Marad in 1988. Afram, which operated liners along the same trade route as Waterman, insisted that Waterman's merger with ISC "could confer an unconscionable windfall on Waterman and ISC," forcing Afram to compete with a subsidized line that also received a premium rate to transport government preference cargoes. The Maritime Administration's Subsidy Board, however, ruled in favor of ISC's acquisition once the company pledged to keep its other subsidiaries separate from Waterman. In fact, Transportation Secretary Samuel K. Skinner later decided in 1990 to revise and lengthen Waterman's vessel subsidy contract on condition that the company use no more than four subsidized vessels on its newly consolidated trade route.

Waterman, in fact, proved a boon to ISC's financial strength and resources, making expansion possible for the company as it headed into the 1990s. ISC's 1990 income totaled $15.1 million, up 20 percent from 1989 with most of this increase attributable to Waterman's earnings. Meanwhile, ISC's other subsidiaries continued to do business as usual. In 1989, Central Gulf was awarded a $6.4 million contract to provide transportation and safe storage for Department of Defense watercraft. In 1990, the company acquired a total of two new ships—one US-flag LASH vessel and a 148,000 dead weight ton Cape-Size bulk carrier, the largest ship in its fleet. Also in 1990, ISC purchased 159 additional LASH barges from Marad for $1.2 million and instituted a $30 million program to refurbish 1,000 barges, continuing an effort begun in 1989 when the company's service arm, LASH Marine Services, awarded contracts worth $12 million to two shipyards to refurbish a total of 250 barges.

Uneven Growth in the 1990s

The Persian Gulf War of 1991 created ample opportunity for ISC to meet its goal of adding stable, military business to its more cyclical, commercial operations. The company's 1991 earnings of $15.2 million on revenues of $328.4 million were bolstered in part by government contracts to charter vessels to carry equipment to Middle East ports, and once again led analysts, who praised ISC's diversification, to rate ISC as a good buy. The company became listed on the New York Stock Exchange, which enabled it to broaden investor base.

By contrast, 1992 was a poor year financially for ISC. Profits and revenues were both down, to $3.28 million and $324.6, respectively, in part due to the drop in income after Desert Storm, and also partly due to the fact that cargo markets for products such as liquefied petroleum gas and iron ore were weak following recession at home and economic woes in Europe and Japan. The slump was clearly not part of a trend, however, and did not prevent ISC from expanding operations yet further that year.

One such expansion, by far ISC's most unusual venture of the early 1990s, was the LASH Intermodal Terminal Company (LITCO), a 1992 partnership between Cooper/T. Smith Stevedoring Company and ISC, which resulted in a hub terminal, the largest fully enclosed barge warehouse in the nation's midcontinent. This 237,000-square-foot facility (later expanded to 287,000 square feet) was used to transfer many types of non-containerized cargo, known as breakbulk, between barges and surface carriers in Memphis, and allowed LASH vessels to dispatch barges up the Mississippi to transfer cargo to motor and rail carriers at the new terminal. Another 1992 collaboration took place between ISC and a major mineral resource company, which agreed to build an oceangoing carrier to transport molten sulphur to begin operation in 1994 by ISC.

The next three years saw a steady rise in revenues on a relatively steady base for ISC. In 1993, revenues rose to $341.7 million, exceeding 1991 levels, while income increased 80 percent to $5.9 million. In 1994, the company reached $342.3 million, with profits of $13 million, and in 1996, the company set a new record of $378.9 million, despite the costs of buying out its partner in a Singapore shipping agency and expanding operations in Southeast Asia. The company took title in September 1995 of the *S.S. Energy Independence*, a self-unloading, conveyor-belt equipped U.S.-flag coal carrier eligible for domestic trade. The 38,000 dead weight ton vessel, renamed the Energy Enterprise, completed shipyard work and commenced service in February 1996 under a long-term charter to a New England electric utility company carrying coal in the coastwise and near-sea trade. In the mid-1990s, ISC bought out Cooper's share of the LITCO terminal.

The 1993 Maritime Security and Competitiveness Act, part of the longer term legacy of the Gulf War, also created opportunities for ISC. As the United States withdrew from its bases overseas, it had come to rely increasingly upon prepositioned supply ships. During the Persian Gulf War, for example, the United States had had to turn to international-flag supply vessels for more than half the 365 commercial vessels it hired. However, the 1993 Act created a program designed to subsidize the U.S. merchant marine fleet and ensure that the nation had ample commercial vessels during a military emergency. This Act, which revamped the 1936 law, created the Maritime Security Fleet Program, stipulating payment to companies of about $2 million per vessel over the next ten years to keep 47 ships in U.S. registry and to replace old vessels with new, more efficient ships. In exchange for the subsidy, the company had to agree to make the vessel available to the government during wartime. The program later became the Maritime Security Act of 1996, which went into effect in 1997. ISC had a total of seven U.S.-flag vessels operating under provision of that Act when it began.

By 1997, ISC operated a diversified fleet of 31 ocean-going vessels, 18 towboats, 128 river barges, and 26 special purpose barges, in addition to its LASH barges and related shoreside handling facilities. The company placed one LASH vessel in reserve that year, acquired two others, and entered into an agreement to have two special purpose barges built. It replaced its international frame-relay network with an Internet connection between Singapore and its New Orleans headquarters, becoming the first in its industry to rely upon the internet as a wide-area network for financial and billing transactions. The company enjoyed revenues of $391.6 million, once again its highest yet, and raised its dividend paid to shareholders. However, operating profits were lower than in 1996 due to the cost of outfitting and refurbishing the newly acquired vessels, lower subsidy payments from the government for the Waterman liner service, and the fact that 1997 was a soft market period for the shipping industry.

As it entered 1998, ISC had to contend with a decrease in subsidies for four of its Central Gulf LASH vessels as specified by the Maritime Security Program and a loss from start-up costs for a planned service between the Gulf of Mexico and Brazil, which was later canceled. All told, however, the company was confident that this leveling off of ISC's growth trend would be temporary. The company enjoyed by then a fairly balanced operation between its commercial and military shipping and had the resources necessary to weather leaner times.

Principal Subsidiaries

Central Gulf Lines, Inc.; Forest Lines Inc.; Waterman Steamship Corporation.

Further Reading

Beller, Margo, "Shipowner Urges Release of Loss Data, 'Maverick' Hits P&I Secrecy," *Journal of Commerce,* September 14, 1994, p. 11A.

DiBenedetto, William, "International Shipholding Seeks OK on Purchase of Waterman and Units," *Journal of Commerce,* November 18, 1988, p. 1B.

——, "ISC Completes Waterman Deal," *Journal of Commerce,* March 31, 1989, p. 1B.

——, "Waterman Bidder Claims Hearings Aren't Needed," *Journal of Commerce,* December 16, 1988, p. 3B.

Dunlap, Craig, "New Breakbulk Hub Operation to Service Barges in Memphis," *Journal of Commerce,* February 11, 1992, p. 8B.

Klose, Roland, "Cargo; Port Warehouse Opens, Boosts City's Trade Role," *The Commercial Appeal,* June 24, 1992, p. B4.

"Maritime Subsidies Sail through House," *The Times-Picayune,* November 5, 1993, p. C1.

Mongelluzzo, Bill, "Second Central Gulf Car Carrier Makes Initial Voyage to U.S.," *Journal of Commerce,* November 19, 1987, p. 3B.

Prat, Marie, "Waterman Deal Set to Close; Protest Filed," *Journal of Commerce,* March 13, 1989, p. 12B.

Roberts, Allen S., "International Shipholding Expected to Win the Military Supply Race," *Journal of Commerce,* August 14, 1992, p. 1B.

Sansbury, Tim, "CP-Lykes Deal Hits More Choppy Waters," *Journal of Commerce,* May 8, 1997, p. 8B.

Toll, Eric, "International Shipholding, Inc. Seen Entering a Period of Slower Growth," *Journal of Commerce,* January 30, 1991, p. 3B.

Vail, Bruce, "Financial Analysts Bullish on International Shipholding," *Journal of Commerce,* May 30, 1989, p. 1A.

Wallace, Bob, "Shipper Saves Money by Using the Net as it WAN," *Computerworld,* July 14, 1997, p.8.

—Carrie Rothburd

Jitney-Jungle Stores of America, Inc.

1770 Ellis Avenue, Suite 200
P.O. Box 3409
Jackson, Mississippi 39207-3409
U.S.A.
(601) 965-8600
Fax: (601) 346-2187
Web site: http://www.jitney.com; http://www.jjsa.com

Private Company
Incorporated: 1946
Employees: 17,500
Sales: $2.2 billion (1998)
SICs: 5411, Grocery Stores; 5141, Groceries, General
   Line; 5113, Industrial & Personal Service

Jitney-Jungle Stores of America, Inc., one of the largest, privately owned grocery chains in the nation, operates in six southern states: Alabama, Arkansas, Florida, Louisiana, Mississippi, and Tennessee. It is the largest retailer in Mississippi, its home base, where it enjoys a 25 percent share of the grocery market. Its 198 stores include Jitney-Jungles and Delchamps, traditional supermarkets, as well as Sack & Saves and Megamarkets, discount stores, and Jitney and Delchamps Premiers, more gourmet-conscious, upscale grocery outlets. Also included are 54 Pump & Save service stations and ten liquor stores. Although a private company throughout its long history, it has given serious thought to going public to facilitate its plans for greater expansion. As of early 1999, however, no definitive steps to effect the changeover had been taken by the company's owners.

The Early Years: 1919 to the Great Depression

Three cousins of the Holman and McCarty families from rural Carroll County, Mississippi, founded Jitney-Jungle in 1919 as a private company. William Bonner McCarty served as the company's first president, Judson McCarty Holman served as president of McCarty-Holman, the company's wholesale operation, and William Henry Holman, Sr. served as president of the retail operation. Throughout most of the history of Jitney-Jungle, these men and their descendants kept the ownership and control of the company within the two families.

Jitney-Jungle actually emerged from an earlier grocery business, the Jackson Mercantile Co., owned by William McCarty's father, William Henry McCarty. Before he died in 1910, the senior McCarty had hired Jud Holman as his bookkeeper. Jud and his brother William bought the business from the McCarty estate, enabling Will McCarty to go to law school. They operated branch stores in Jackson, which, by the end of World War I, they began converting to self-service, cash-and-carry operations after one of their charge-and-delivery stores ran into financial problems because of a railway workers' strike.

On April 19, 1919, under the new partnership arrangements, and guided by the principle that they would save their customers "a nickel on a quarter," the cousins opened their first Jitney-Jungle store as a cash-and-carry grocery. It was located in downtown Jackson, on East Capitol Street. The name came from a slang term for a nickel and a play on the word "jingling" in the popular catch phrase "jingling your jitneys in your pockets." Within a year the new store had made more money than all the other McCarty-Holman stores combined, which were soon either converted to Jitney-Jungles or phased out.

Near the first store was a Piggly-Wiggly, another cash-and-carry store. In 1920 Piggly-Wiggly brought suit against Jitney for patent infringement, claiming that it had exclusive rights to the cash-and-carry system. Finally, after Will McCarty proved that such a system pre-existed the founding of Piggly-Wiggly, the U.S. Supreme Court ruled in favor of Jitney-Jungle. The legal victory helped remove a significant barrier to expansion.

There were, however, significant risks involved in the changeover to the self-serve, cash-and-carry merchandising system adopted by Jitney. People who had always relied on credit purchasing did not always have money readily available, and the possibility of resentment toward stores denying credit to customers was very real. There was also the problem of "shrinkage," especially the losses incurred through shoplifting made easier by the self-service system. But folks adapted to the changes quickly, particularly women, who turned shopping at

Jitney-Jungles into social outings. As a result, Jitney was able to begin its rapid growth, honoring McCarty's motto "expand or expire." In the early 1920s the company opened its first stores outside Jackson—in Greenwood, Yazoo City, and Canton, Mississippi.

New Triumphs in Difficult Years: 1929–50

Jitney fared comparatively well in the Depression, in part because the cash-and-carry system did not strap it with credit charges its customers simply could not pay. Still, to help its financially pressed shoppers, the stores did accept checks and managed an enviable record of receiving payment from customers who sometimes were not able to meet their obligations for several years.

Jitney also took an important step in 1934, when it opened its first real supermarket in Jackson. It involved a change of shopping styles, depending on parking lots and prototypes of the modern bag boy who would deliver packages of groceries to customers' cars. Jitney's first supermarket was the second such store to be air conditioned, and it included the first women's restroom in any of its stores, as well as other amenities, like chairs for children who had to wait while their mothers shopped. That first store served as a model for the company's other supermarket buildings.

During World War II, despite such problems as food rationing, Jitney continued to expand. The supermarket had caught on, and by 1946, when the company's gross sales mounted to $7.5 million, Jitney finally incorporated. The move, which named the three presidents' wives to vice-presidencies, was in large part a strategic response to mounting tax liabilities, but because Jitney's customers were 90 percent women, it was also a good public relations move.

At about the same time, a new generation of McCarty and Holman family members began their association with the business. William Bonner McCarty, Jr. went on board after completing his Army service in World War II. A few years later William Henry Holman, Jr. followed, after completing his Army service in the Korean War.

Decades of Adaptation and Change: 1950–70

After Jud Holman's death in 1950, William Holman, Sr. took on the additional responsibility of managing the wholesale operations. Under his control, McCarty-Holman Co. would be transformed into a distribution and service warehouse for Jitney-Jungle stores. By the end of the decade, the company was sending its own refrigerator trucks throughout the United States to bring back fresh, top-quality produce for its Mississippi customers. As its own wholesaler, Jitney was able to keep costs down by eliminating wholesale jobbers. The result was that it could keep its retail prices lower and highly competitive.

Jitney responded to changes wisely, though sometimes reluctantly. A new fad of the 1950s was the shopping center, many of which had as their centerpiece a large supermarket whose customers might be attracted to the merchandise in other stores. Jitney-Jungle, in its home market, Jackson, opened the first such shopping center supermarket in Morgan Center, the city's first of its kind. Jitney also solved problems that plagued its operations. For example, in 1954, after years of being unable to make satisfactory arrangements with independent bakeries, Jitney bought a nearly insolvent bakery in Columbia, Tennessee and began making its own bread and other baked goods. It soon proved to be a very successful operation. But the company was less enthusiastic about another craze of the 1950s—the ubiquitous trading stamps. For a time the company held out, even in the face of pressure from customers who demanded them. Finally, in 1958, despite objections from the senior family members, Jitney relented, but with a solution typifying its independence: it created Associated Merchandisers, Inc., its own trading stamp company.

In 1962, after William Henry Holman, Sr.'s death, his son William, then executive vice-president of McCarty-Holman Co., began a five-year term as the presiding officer of the board. In 1967 he was elected president and served as CEO until 1998. In that period, Jitney continued its ambitious expansion, growing from a chain of 32 stores, all located in Mississippi, to a chain of almost 200 stores operating in Mississippi and five other southeastern states.

In the 1960s the most important step Jitney took was to join Topco, a national, cooperatively owned purchasing association that wielded as much purchasing power as the largest supermarket chains. The move made it possible for Jitney to purchase grade-A foodstuffs and related merchandise at competitive prices. The company also started expanding through the purchase of other franchises, starting with five stores located on the Gulf Coast. Over the next several years it would grow through strategic acquisition of other chains, some of which were operating outside Mississippi.

Another important move was first undertaken in 1965, when Jitney created a discount division that sold goods at the lowest possible prices while suspending the use of trading stamps. For a time, its discount stores operated in the same neighborhoods as the older Jitney-Jungles, which still gave the stamps, but the company eventually phased them out completely. It proved to be a good move, for in its first year of operations completely without the stamps, Jitney's sales rose a full 25 percent over the previous year.

By 1973, Jitney, with a payroll for 1,700 employees, was operating 38 food stores, five drug stores, and six gasoline stations. One of the stores, located in Jackson, just off Interstate 55 North, was a prototype for the future Jitney megastore, a giant food discount store that also included a pharmacy and gasoline service. With annual sales quickly passing $10 million, it proved to be the most worthwhile investment in Jitney's history to that point and encouraged the company to expand its operations in the super discount store market.

Expansion and New Ownership: 1980s and 1990s

Jitney continued a relatively slow expansion through the late 1970s and the next decade. It had by then purchased small grocery chains in other states, starting in the late 1960s with a purchase of five stores in northwest Florida. There was some slowing in the 1980s, when the Gulf Coast economy cooled down with the drop in oil prices. The financial backing necessary for a more vigorous expansion did not materialize until 1996, when the New York-based investment firm, Bruckmann, Rosser, Sherill & Co. acquired a controlling interest for about $400 million. Until that time, members of the Holman and McCarty families owned a controlling interest in Jitney and served as the company's chief officers. With the sale to Bruckmann, Rosser, Sherill & Co., Michael E. Julian, Jitney's president, succeed William Henry Holman, Jr. as chairman of the board. Holman, still the CEO of McCarty-Holman, was named chairman emeritus.

The financial backing that resulted from the buyout enabled Jitney to begin a major expansion and refurbishing program, including moves into new market areas. Changes rapidly ensued. The most significant occurred in July of 1997, when Jitney acquired the Mobile-based Delchamps, Inc. in a merger scheme. Delchamps agreed to be purchased at $30 per share, for a total cost of $213 million. The buyout had an immediate impact on Jitney-Jungle's rankings in *Forbes* Private 500, moving it up from the 143rd spot it held the previous year to 59th in 1997. It was also the only Mississippi company to be featured on *Forbes*' annual list. Its total annual sales for the fiscal year ending in April 1998, which included receipts from the Delchamps stores, climbed to more than $2.2 billion. In a 12-week period ending June 20, 1998, the company reported an increase in sales of 58.7 percent over the sales of the same period in the previous year. This increase, according to CEO Michael E. Julian, matched the company's expected increase in revenue from the purchase of the Delchamps chain.

That purchase increased Jitney-Jungle's operation in Florida by 14 stores, in Alabama by 45, in Louisiana by 41, and in Mississippi by 17. Jitney divested ten of the Delchamps stores, however, selling eight in Mississippi and two in Florida to Supervalue. Additional selective Delchamps stores were closed after a careful analysis of their market share in their host communities and their financial histories. The Delchamps stores in Mississippi were converted to operate under the Jitney-Jungle name. The remaining stores operating under the Delchamps name were reorganized and restocked in accordance with the Jitney system. Jitney also closed Delchamps administrative offices in Mobile and its 635,000-square-foot distribution warehouse located in Hammond, Louisiana, a facility that Jitney planned to sell. Its operations moved to Jackson, Jitney's headquarters.

Changes also involved extensive building and remodeling. To handle the increased volume of produce, the company built a $7 million produce warehouse, expanding its 900,000-square-foot distribution warehouse by an additional 175,000 square feet. It also added full-service pharmacies to its Megamarkets

and new food lines to its stores, with drastic reductions in the price of most of its merchandise.

Because it has expanded further into geographical areas beyond its Mississippi base, Jitney has created four separate regions with managerial teams sensitive to the distinct needs of their stores' customers. Jackson is the hub of the company's operations, where purchasing and planning is done, but each region has its own vice-president of human resources and loss prevention and a vice-president of sales and merchandising. The central region, headquartered in Jackson, includes the northern parts of Mississippi and Alabama down to Jackson and Birmingham. The southwest region, headquartered in Mandeville, consists of Louisiana, and the southeast region, headquartered in Mobile, covers the coastal areas in Mississippi, Alabama, and northwest Florida. The northern group, headquartered in Memphis, covers Memphis and Little Rock. According to Jitney's CEO Michael Julian, the company does not want ''to lose the local flavor of these areas,'' while, at the same time, it endeavors to achieve maximum purchasing power through its centralized control in Jackson.

Current Strategies and Future Prospects

Jitney strives to be efficient so that it can remain highly competitive in a tough market. Many of its recent policies reflect that aim. For example, in October 1998 the company signed a contract with Illinova Energy Partners to streamline its utility accounting, an important improvement because utility costs are a major part of store overhead costs. But Jitney also strives very hard to make a positive impression on its sites' communities. It stresses the freshness of its foodstuffs and the friendliness of its personnel. It also offers its customers its popular Gold Card, which both simplifies checkouts and guarantees savings on select items. In addition, Jitney has given much back to its customers in the form of charitable donations to such agencies as the United Way. Through its Gold Card Community Gift Program, it has donated food, gift certificates, and direct financial aid to customer-designated schools, churches, and other charitable organizations.

The company also endeavors to stay abreast of national trends in supermarket services. In 1996 Jitney's in-store banking facilities were limited to ten of its 106 stores in Mississippi, but the service will be included in future expansion and remodeling of existing stores. In one of its Mississippi Jitney Premiere stores it has started experimenting with drive-through banking.

Jitney's current plans are to open at least five new stores per year and continue its remodeling program, an ambitious aim in the face of competition that is growing stiffer, even in Mississippi, its home base. Albertson's, the rapidly expanding Idaho-based supermarket chain, recently opened two stores in Jackson and announced plans for additional expansion in the state. That competition may force Jitney to go public, but plans to make that move considered in the fall of 1998 were deferred until a later, undisclosed date.

Principal Subsidiaries

Delchamps; Sack and Save (McCarty-Holman Company, Inc.); Foodway, Inc.; Megamarkets.

Further Reading

Bennett, Stephen, "The Power of Produce," *Progressive Grocer,* December 1994, pp. 97–98.

Donegan, Priscilla, "Leap of Faith," *Progressive Grocer,* September 1993, pp. 48–52.

Holman, William Henry, Jr., *"Save a Nickel on a Quarter": The Story of Jitney-Jungle Stores of America,* New York: Newcomen Society in North America, 1974.

"Jitney Jungle Opens CFC-Free Supermarket," *Chain Store Age Executive with Shopping Center Age,* May 1993, p. 174.

"Lower Humidity = Lower Costs at Jitney Jungle," *Progressive Grocer,* January 1991, p. 26.

"A Pleasant Surprise," *Progressive Grocer,* June 1996, p. 48.

Snyder, Glenn, "In Promotion, a Little Can Go a Long Way," *Progressive-Grocer,* May 1988, pp. 247–48.

Tanner, Ronald, "A New Look in the Deep South," *Progressive Grocer,* May 1984, pp. 39–40.

Weinstein, Steve, "Diversity in Action," *Progressive Grocer,* June 1996, p. 44.

—John W. Fiero

Kelsey-Hayes Group of Companies

**LucasVarity plc Light Vehicle Braking Systems
    Division (LVBS)**
12025 Tech Center Drive
Livonia, Michigan 48150
U.S.A.
(734) 266-2600
Fax: (734) 255-4594

Incorporated: 1927 as Kelsey-Hayes Wheel Company
Absorbed: 1998 into LucasVarity's Light Vehicle
    Braking Systems
SICs: 3714 Motor Vehicle Parts & Accessories

The Kelsey-Hayes Group of Companies, once a major supplier of wheels, brakes, and other components to the worldwide automobile industry, ceased to exist as a separate entity after being acquired and absorbed by London-based LucasVarity plc in 1996. Formed by the merger of Lucas Industries and Kelsey-Hayes' former parent Varity Corporation, LucasVarity reorganized its holdings, and Kelsey-Hayes became part of the LucasVarity Light Vehicle Braking Systems (LVBS) Division. Originally a supplier of wooden wheels to the fledgling automobile industry in the early 20th century, Kelsey-Hayes had evolved into a major international corporation and had been the leading producer of electronically controlled antilock brake systems before the acquisition.

Beginnings as Wooden Wheel Manufacturer

Kelsey-Hayes was originally formed in 1927 as the result of a merger of the Kelsey Wheel Company and the Hayes Wheel Company. The parallel wheel-making history of founders John Kelsey and Clarence B. Hayes began much earlier.

John Kelsey formed the K. H. Wheel Company (with partner H. J. Herbert) in 1909 with the hopes of developing a spring wheel. Advised by Henry Ford to focus instead on the production of traditional wheels made of hickory wood, Kelsey took his advice and by 1919 his company was producing wooden wheels at a rate of two million per year and in 1915 the Kelsey Wheel Company was reincorporated for $13 million. Ford gave Kelsey his flying start, buying more than three quarters of the company's wheel production in 1909. Afraid of becoming too dependent on Ford, Kelsey diversified, giving Ford less than one-third of his business in 1910 and, following a disagreement with Ford, less than ten percent in 1912. While still selling to Ford, by 1915 the company's business had grown to $3.5 million in total revenues and had 15-20 percent of the wheel market, supplying not only Ford but also Hudson, Paige, Chalmers, and Studebaker. Government demand for artillery type wheels provided a further boost to profitability—in 1918, 80 percent of production was devoted to defense type wheels—and by the end of World War I the company was solidly profitable.

A major cost cutting innovation was a wheel with a metal felloe band that cut the amount of wood needed in the production of wheels. This enabled Kelsey to capture a larger market share and, coupled with the boom in car and truck sales, Kelsey's wheels were on 70 percent of Ford's cars by early 1920. Kelsey Wheel was on its way and growing.

While John Kelsey was achieving great success, Clarence B. Hayes was building a company of his own. Beginning with a one year stint at the Kalamazoo Wheel Company, which built wooden buggy wheels, Hayes quickly moved on to become the vice-president, then president and general manager of the Imperial Wheel Company where he worked with W. C. Durant, who later founded General Motors.

In 1909 Hayes formed the Hayes Wheel Company. After buying out the National Wheel Company plant in Jackson, Michigan, he began to phase out the production of buggy wheels and switched exclusively to the production of wooden car wheels. Hayes would expand his operations to five more plants during the decade and by 1920 he had 60 percent of the U.S. automobile wheel business.

While both the Kelsey Wheel Company and the Hayes Wheel companies got their start with the production of wood wheels, by the 1920s both were expanding into the production of wire wheels. Wire wheels were cheaper to produce and they were replaceable and transferrable from one axle to another (while wood wheels came as part of the entire axle assembly). Wire wheels were on one-quarter of all new vehicles by 1927 and clearly represented the wave of the future. This competitive pressure, a threat to the very existence of wooden wheel makers, was certainly a major motivating force behind the 1927 Kelsey-Hayes merger. The Kelsey-Hayes Wheel Company was born.

John Kelsey's wheel company had been producing wire wheels throughout the 1920s but had been accused of violating a patent for wire wheels that had been issued to Edward Cole of the Wire Wheel Corporation of Buffalo, New York. This company was primarily involved with patent licensing. The nature of the patent dealt with the critical issue of mountability of the wheel and Wire Wheel refused a license to Kelsey and threatened to sue for patent infringement. John Kelsey died early in 1927 and George Kennedy became the company's president. Kennedy's solution to this legal imbroglio was to purchase the Wire Wheel Company to get control of the patent but this wasn't the end of the problem: the patent was actually owned by the Packard Co., which had been receiving royalties from Wire Wheel. Kennedy paid $500,000 to Packard and production of wire wheels was now fair game. By 1929, the new Kelsey-Hayes Corporation was producing 10,000 wire wheels a day. The company also entered the brake field, supplying brakes for Ford's Model A.

Depression and Labor Problems

During the lean years of the Great Depression the company solidified its hold on its General Motors market by purchasing the General Motors subsidiary Jaxon Steel Products Company of Jackson, Michigan. Kelsey-Hayes also provided the wheels for Henry Ford's invasion of the European market. By 1931, with the depression in full swing, the company lost $667,000 and in 1932 it lost $1.1 million. George Kennedy's Kelsey-Hayes corporation had accumulated massive amounts of short-term debt, mostly owed to banks and to General Motors. After the losses in the early to mid-1930s, Kelsey-Hayes went through a financial restructuring and cost-cutting campaign which resulted in small but growing profits in 1938 and 1939. Ever conscious of the need for new product development, Kelsey-Hayes began supplying standard-equipment hydraulic brakes to Ford and developed a new brake drum. Kelsey-Hayes had weathered the storm and would be prepared for the coming war production effort.

In 1940, Kelsey-Hayes began producing machine guns for the mounting war effort, first for the United Kingdom and then for the United States. It made tank components, wheels and accessories for ordnance vehicles, aircraft wheels, brakes and other parts. In anticipation of the transition to a post-war economy, Kelsey-Hayes acquired French & Hecht, Inc., a leader in the agricultural and construction industry wheel business.

Although the period following the war was a time of massive innovation, the road out of the government regulated war economy was not completely peaceful. With unemployment on the rise and real wages of workers falling, the United States experienced a wave of strikes that shut down much of the U.S. industry for at least some part of 1946. Kelsey-Hayes was not immune. A wildcat strike by 4500 members of the United Auto Workers in 1946 closed the company down for 46 days.

Developing New Products in the Late 1940s

With the strike settled, Kelsey-Hayes looked to cost-cutting measures and product diversification. In 1946 the company also began supplying power brakes to Buick and Chrysler and in 1947 Kelsey-Hayes acquired Lather Company, which also made brake components. The innovation and product diversification continued through the early 1950s as the company reached the highest profit margins in its history. During the Korean War the company made inroads into the aircraft industry.

In recognition of the diversification and expansion, the company changed its name, becoming simply the Kelsey-Hayes Corporation. Kelsey-Hayes was now at the front of new product innovation, introducing chrome-plated wheels, the first aluminum wheels, and power brakes, and was the leading producer of auto wheels, brakes, and other components. The strategy was to diversify in order to grow, both through research and development and through acquisition of other promising companies. To move into research and development for the burgeoning aircraft industry, Kelsey-Hayes acquired Control Specialists, Inc. The company also moved into the production of wheels and brakes for truck trailers, buses, and agricultural equipment.

In 1958 the company began explorations into the development of antilock brake systems for automobiles. Though the technology had been developed much earlier, antilock brake systems had only been employed as a safety measure on commercial aircraft. This basic technology eventually resulted in the development of electronic sensors that could read wheel speeds and send the information to a computer to prevent wheel lock on large automobiles. This evolving technology would be a mainstay of Kelsey-Hayes's business for years to come.

The product innovations continued into the boom years of the 1960s when Kelsey-Hayes was a pioneer in the development of disc brake systems. Kelsey-Hayes disc brake systems beat out the competition and became standard equipment on Lincoln Continentals and Thunderbirds, and by the time the 1970s rolled around, 85 percent of U.S. cars came with Kelsey-Hayes disc brakes. Kelsey-Hayes replaced Bendix as the number one brake supplier to Ford. Not only had Kelsey-Hayes become a leading brake producer, but there were also Kelsey-Hayes parts in virtually every jet engine.

Organizational Turmoil in 1970s and 1980s

While the 1960s were years of expansion and diversification, the 1970s were extremely volatile. As was often the case for Kelsey-Hayes, as goes the automobile business, so goes the business of automobile suppliers. The challenge for Kelsey-Hayes following the oil crunch of the early 1970s was to develop products tailored to the new lighter, more fuel efficient, cars of the future. Towards this end, Kelsey-Hayes opened a research and development center in Ann Arbor, Michigan, designed to accelerate new product development, intensify the application of new manufacturing processes and search for new material applications for new and existing products. At the same time that the company was implementing this longer term strategy its sales continued to expand, topping the half billion dollar mark in 1973.

By 1973, however, in the face of a severe economic downturn, Kelsey-Hayes found itself over-extended in credit markets and, with its stock value plummeting, takeover loomed. In 1973 Kelsey-Hayes Corporation became a wholly owned subsidiary of Fruehauf Corporation, a leading producer of truck trailers. The takeover was only a small bump in the road for Kelsey-Hayes, however. The new financial support provided from Fruehauf enabled Kelsey-Hayes to continue its growth and by 1975 Kelsey was supplying disk brakes for all new subcompact cars including Volkswagen in Germany. Fruehauf commented in its 1975 annual report: "Kelsey-Hayes recognized the trend toward smaller cars several years ago. All of its automotive manufacturing plants have the flexibility to manufacture the required smaller components." Kelsey-Hayes was also maintaining its market share in wheels, brake components, and axles, as well as in helicopter transmissions, parts for jet engines, and hydraulic brake systems for the military. Kelsey-Hayes had become Fruehauf's shining star, accounting for 60 percent of Fruehauf's corporation revenues and becoming the company's only profitable business.

By 1978 Kelsey-Hayes was in full development of aluminum wheels as a cost cutting improvement over the traditional steel wheels. In addition, with the auto market in a severe slump beginning in 1978, Kelsey began to increase its share of the automobile replacement parts market. Since the auto makers were selling less new cars, older cars were staying on the road longer and hence the demand for replacement parts was rising. Thus, the replacement parts market buffered the negative effects of declines in automobile production.

In the late 1970s Kelsey-Hayes also began looking toward new production processes and, through its purchase of Compositek Engineering Corporation, the company had a new expertise in fiber-reinforced plastics that allowed substantial weight savings in wheel production. By 1979 the company could manufacture every type of wheel, from the traditional steel wheel to a light weight, low-alloy steel wheel. This technological breakthrough, of course, allowed Kelsey-Hayes to make lighter weight die castings and other lighter, stronger, parts.

The success of Kelsey-Hayes following its merger with Fruehauf was not without controversy. Fruehauf's acquisition of Kelsey-Hayes was ruled by the Federal Trade Commission, in 1978, to violate anti-trust laws in three Kelsey-Hayes product lines: heavy-duty wheels, anti-skid braking devices, and truck trailers. The argument was that these markets were serviced by few suppliers and the buyout would reduce effective competition through the possibility that Fruehauf would deny other suppliers the opportunity to sell to Fruehauf. Since Fruehauf had, in the past, attempted to make some of the same products as Kelsey-Hayes, a merger of the two companies was ruled to be a restraint on trade. Fruehauf was ordered to divest itself of some of its Kelsey-Hayes assets in order to enforce competitive behavior. The legal battle dragged on into the 1980s.

Further complicating the matter was the flurry of leveraged buyouts that affected many businesses in the United States in the 1980s. Following a protracted unfriendly takeover bid, Fruehauf was divested and Kelsey-Hayes became the remaining operation. This new successor to Fruehauf became the K-H Corporation, selling its trailer division and the Fruehauf name to the Terrex Corporation. K-H became the holding company for the Kelsey-Hayes Corporation. For the first time in a long time, K-H became a publicly traded, independent corporation. Thanks to booming sales of its antilock brake systems, aluminum wheels, and electronic sensors its profits grew by more than ten percent in fiscal year 1987.

But the independent K-H Corporation did not last long. At the time, some experts believed that K-H could make a go of it as an independent company. However, saddled with interest payments on a debt load of over $600 million, which drained its growth potential, the K-H Corporation went looking for a suitor. In 1989 the Varity Corporation, a Toronto-based farm equipment and auto parts manufacturer, purchased K-H Corporation for $577 million in cash and securities.

Yet Another Owner in the 1990s

After the buyout by Varity in 1989, Kelsey-Hayes evolved into the Kelsey Hayes Group of Companies, a wholly owned subsidiary of Varity. It was reorganized into business units in order to focus on individual product lines: anti-lock brake systems, brakes, aluminum wheels, steel wheels, and others. The Group remained solidly profitable and an integral component of Varity's operations for several years. Kelsey-Hayes's revenues of $1 billion in fiscal year 1990 were nearly one-third of Varity's total revenues. Despite relatively weak markets, Kelsey-Hayes continued to compete aggressively in a global market. The company introduced a four-wheel anti-lock brake system line (that became standard on many cars by the end of the decade) that was compatible with virtually every car and light truck made anywhere in the world.

Hand-in-hand with the development of the antilock brake systems was the development of electromechanical products. Aluminum wheels, originally developed by Kelsey-Hayes in the 1950s, became one of the company's fastest growing markets. These innovations and continued refinement of new products and processes accompanied expansion of overseas production in the Asian-Pacific region, including a joint manufacturing venture with Japan's Topy Industries Ltd.

The Kelsey-Hayes Group of Companies thrived under the parentage of Varity until 1996, when business dealings originating in London would change its future forever. That year, Varity was purchased by a larger corporation, London-based Lucas Industries, which manufactured automotive and aerospace equipment. Lucas had been looking to expand its presence in the United States, following a late 1980s downturn in the U.K. automotive market.

In 1996, Lucas acquired Varity and its subsidiaries, and Kelsey-Hayes became a subsidiary of newly formed LucasVarity plc, which, in turn, became the second largest brake manufacturer and one of the ten largest automotive component manufacturers in the world. The widespread use of the Kelsey-Hayes antilock braking system (ABS) in automobiles established LucasVarity as a major player in the United States, and also allowed it to expand into Asia, Eastern Europe, and Latin America. The company's worldwide annual ABS sales grew to more than five million units.

However, the merger also resulted in massive restructuring expenses, and LucasVarity began to reorganize its operations. In 1998 the former Kelsey-Hayes brake manufacturing business was rolled into LucasVarity's new Light Vehicle Braking Systems (LVBS) division. Kelsey-Hayes ceased to exist as a separate company. LVBS became the largest division of LucasVarity; headquartered in Michigan where Kelsey-Hayes had operated for so many years, LVBS manufactured products at 23 plants, located in North America (where it was the leading two-wheel and four-wheel ABS manufacturer), Latin America, and Europe. Some of the division's major customers included Chrysler, Ford, General Motors, Volkswagen, and Renault.

Further Reading

A Billion Wheels Later, Romulus, Mich.: Kelsey-Hayes Company, 1984.

Callahan, J. M., "Life After Buyout," *Automotive Industry,* August 1987.

"Canada's Varity Agrees to Buy K-H For Reduced Price," *Wall Street Journal,* October 5, 1989.

Jewett, Dale, "GM Denies Corrosion Causes Poor Performance in Antilock Brakes," *Detroit News,* January 15, 1998.

May, George S., *A Most Unique Machine: The Michigan Origins of the American Automobile Industry,* Grand Rapids, Mich.: Eerdmans, 1975.

—John A. Sarich
—updated by Gerry Azzata

Kennecott Corporation

Rio Tinto plc
Six St. James Square
London
England
44-171-930-2399
Fax: 44-171-930-3249

Incorporated: 1915 as Kennecott Copper Corporation
Absorbed: 1997 into Rio Tinto plc
SICs: 1021 Copper Ores; 1041 Gold Ores

Kennecott Corporation, the world's leader in copper output throughout most of the 20th century, had by 1997 ceased to exist as a separate entity. That year it was divided into a group of wholly owned subsidiaries of the British metals and mining company Rio Tinto plc. Rio Tinto, formed by the 1995 merger of Kennecott's owner RTZ Corporation and CRA Limited, continued to operate Kennecott's chief U.S. businesses: Kennecott Utah Copper, Kennecott Minerals, and Kennecott Energy. However, these operations were absorbed into Rio Tinto's copper and energy units. The RTZ-CRA merger, pulling in all of Kennecott's holdings, made Rio Tinto an international giant in the mining and minerals industry.

Origins in the Alaskan Wilderness

The chain of events that would lead to Kennecott's founding began in 1901. With financial backing from the Havemeyer family, a young mining engineer named Stephen Birch acquired mining rights on a sizeable chunk of promising copper property near the Kennicott Glacier in Alaska (the difference in spelling between the glacier and the company was the result of a clerical mistake). Birch returned East to seek additional investors in the venture, and was introduced by the Havemeyers to J. P. Morgan and to members of the Guggenheim family the following year.

At that time, the Guggenheims were the most powerful force in the industry, controlling the vast majority of copper reserves and nearly all of the smelting capacity in the western United States. These two financial giants formed the Kennecott Mines Company to develop mining operations on the claims purchased from Birch, and Birch was named general manager of the organization. In 1907, Morgan and the Guggenheims, calling themselves the Alaska Syndicate, purchased the Alaska Steamship Co., a large fishing fleet, the Beatson Copper Co. of LaTouch Island, Alaska, and, most importantly, 200 miles of right-of-way on which they completed a $25 million railroad that led to the copper mine. The Alaskan ore proved to be very rich in copper, and with the railroad and shipping line in place to transport the ore to civilization, the operation was quite profitable for the syndicate.

The mine at Kennicott, however, appeared to contain only about 20 years' worth of copper ore. In addition, the high cost of building the Copper River and Northwestern Railroad had required the sale of millions of dollars in stocks and bonds. In 1915, in order to both dilute the railroad's cost and find new ventures for the capital produced by the Alaskan mine, Kennecott Copper Corporation was incorporated out of the various financial interests involved, with Stephen Birch as President.

The Guggenheims were by this time already actively working copper mines in Chile and Utah. Upon Kennecott's creation, they decided to merge their Braden Copper Co. property in Chile, as well as 25 percent of the Utah Copper Co., into Kennecott, concentrating on the smelting end of the industry as the family's primary business interest. These moves gave Kennecott possession of Braden's El Teniente, the world's largest underground mine, in the Chilean Andes. In 1936 Kennecott acquired the remainder of Utah Copper Co. and its huge Bingham copper pit, which would become the heart of Kennecott's operations for decades to come.

The Bingham pit was developed by Daniel Cowan Jackling, the metallurgical engineer who pioneered the mass mining of low-grade ores from open pit mines. Jackling also used his revolutionary methods at mine locations in Nevada, Arizona, and New Mexico, all of which were eventually bought by Kennecott.

253

Struggles and Expansion During 1930s and 1940s

Unlike many new companies, Kennecott made money every year in its early history. The company did not suffer its first operating loss until 1932, at the bottom of the Great Depression. World War I had created high demand for all metals, and when it ended, the copper industry found itself stuck in high gear, overproducing in the face of slowed demand. Kennecott was able to remain profitable mainly because production at the Alaskan site was among the cheapest in the industry, including extremely low labor costs.

The trend among copper companies in the 1920s was toward vertical integration. Companies such as Anaconda and Phelps Dodge created their own fabricating operations in order to guarantee outlets for the products of their copper mines. Kennecott participated in this trend, but to a far lesser extent than did its main competitors. The company's only significant non-mining acquisitions during this period were the Chase Companies Inc. (which became Chase Brass and Copper Co.) in 1929, and American Electrical Works (changed to Kennecott Wire and Cable Co.) in 1935.

In 1933, following Kennecott's first unprofitable year, Birch was succeeded as president and chairperson by E. T. Stannard, a director of J. P. Morgan and Company. Around that time, the market was beginning to show the effects of a new flood of copper from Rhodesia. Since Kennecott was set up as a high-production outfit, and also had to keep Chase Brass operating full tilt, cutting back production was not a practical strategy. Stannard instead sought out new markets. Although this policy made no significant gains, Kennecott was bailed out in the late 1930s, as was the copper industry in general, by greatly increased demand for copper in preparation for entry into World War II.

Stephen Birch died in 1940, leaving management of the company firmly in Stannard's hands. Through the first half of the 1940s, the war kept production moving at a healthy pace, and Kennecott's operating revenues reached a peak of $265 million in 1943. When the war ended, however, Stannard saw that Kennecott's continued growth would depend upon its willingness to diversify and explore new geographical and geological arenas. In 1945, Stannard allotted half a million dollars for exploration, a figure comparable to that spent by its main competitors Phelps Dodge and Anaconda.

Oil, gold, and titanium were the principal commodities on which Kennecott began to focus. In 1945, the company teamed up with Continental Oil for a joint prospecting and drilling venture. By this time, Kennecott was already a major U.S. gold producer, since that metal is often a natural byproduct of copper mining. But not until 1947 did the company go looking for gold directly. That year, Kennecott's exploration chief, Anton Gray, was sent gold-hunting in South Africa. This action resulted in the creation of the Kennecott-Anglovaal Exploration Co., Ltd., a joint gold-exploration firm.

More important was the company's entry into the titanium business. Titanium is found in ilemite, one of the most abundant minerals in the earth's surface. Ilemite had been discovered in parts of Quebec in the early 1940s, and Kennecott began its search in the region in 1944. Two years later, Kennecott's explorers, led by Gray, discovered the largest ilemite deposit in the world, over 100 million tons, at Lake Tio in eastern Quebec. Kennecott spent a half million dollars finding, claiming, and measuring the mine. In 1948, Quebec Iron and Titanium Corp. (Q.I.T.) was formed, with Kennecott controlling two-thirds interest and New Jersey Zinc Co., which had been exploring the area as well, owning the remaining share.

An airplane crash in September 1949 claimed the lives of three important company officers: the retiring president; his designated successor, Arthur D. Storke; and R. J. Parker, a vice-president. The executive vacuum created by the disaster was quickly filled by Charles Cox, formerly head of Carnegie-Illinois Steel.

Mid-Century Giant in the U.S. Mining Industry

By 1952, Kennecott was easily the biggest copper producer in the United States; 46 percent of the nation's primary copper output was produced by Kennecott that year. With addition of the Braden mine in Chile, the company accounted for about 25 percent of the entire copper production of the free world. Kennecott was still far less integrated than Anaconda or Phelps Dodge, with only 25 percent of the company's copper production used by its fabricating subsidiaries, Chase Brass and Kennecott Wire & Cable. The Bingham mine in Utah alone provided about two-thirds of Kennecott's domestic copper output in 1952, and 29 percent of the entire nation's production. Braden represented about 30 percent of the company's copper volume. Kennecott's operating revenue reached $470 million that year.

Expansion into other metals and oil continued into the 1950s under Cox. In 1952, three test wells were drilled in western Texas as part of the joint program with Continental Oil. About $42 million was invested in the two South African gold mining ventures by 1956. Kennecott purchased the Kaiser Aluminum and Chemical Corp. in 1953, as well as 76 percent interest in a Nigerian firm, Tin and Associated Minerals Ltd. In 1957, the company joined forces with Allied Chemical and Dye Corp. to launch Allied-Kennecott Titanium Corp., formed to build a North Carolina plant to produce and sell titanium. This venture proved to be short-lived, and the company dissolved seven years later. An attempt was made in 1958 to vertically integrate further into the wire and cable fabricating field, with the purchase of Okonite Co. This idea was also thwarted, however, when in 1966 Kennecott was forced to sell Okonite at a loss due to perceived antitrust violations, just as modernization investments were beginning to pay off in increased earnings.

During Cox's tenure as Kennecott's president from 1950 to 1960, difficulties were encountered finding areas in which to expand. In that timespan, the company's copper production actually decreased. Kennecott's domestic copper output dropped from about 418,000 tons to 339,000 tons in the first half of the decade alone. Only $12 million was invested in the Chilean operations between 1946 and 1956, compared to over $200 million invested by Anaconda in that country. Furthermore, Q.I.T. had problems processing the titanium that was mined in Canada, and the South African gold mines turned out to be busts, losing about $36 million. Nevertheless, Kennecott's earnings remained solid throughout the decade, thanks largely to a steady flow of cheaply produced copper from the seemingly bottomless Bingham mine. In 1956, it cost only 12 cents to mine a pound of copper at Bingham, which was the lowest cost per pound in the United States. About half of the company's copper was used to make some type of wire. Thirty percent of the output was used by electric companies, 12 percent by the military, and about 13 percent by automotive companies.

Cox retired in 1961. Frank Milliken, an engineer and metallurgist, was promoted from executive vice-president to take his place. The following year Milliken launched a $110 million program to expand domestic copper production capacity by 28 percent over five years. A new corporate division was organized in 1964, the purpose of which was to develop new mining properties. These new operations included a lead, zinc, and silver mine in Utah, a lead mine in Missouri, and a Canadian molybdenum mine. In 1967, Kennecott sold 51 percent of the El Teniente mine to the government of Chile for $80 million. The company then lent $93 million to Chile as part of an expansion program at the mine.

In 1968, Kennecott undertook its most aggressive diversification project yet, the acquisition of Peabody Coal Co., the largest producer of coal in the United States. The purchase price for Peabody was $622 million, about 70 percent greater than Peabody's market value. Three years later, however, the Federal Trade Commission (FTC) ordered Kennecott to divest itself of Peabody, on the grounds that the company should have diversified by either starting up its own coal operation or by acquiring a smaller one. The FTC argued that purchasing Peabody eliminated a potential competitor from the field. Kennecott fought the ruling for several years, investing over $500,000 in Peabody. However, Peabody did not prove to be especially profitable for Kennecott. Between 1968 and 1976, Peabody's profits were less than one-sixth as high as the $431 million earned by Continental Oil's Consolidation Coal Co., Peabody's nearest competitor in steam coal production. After a number of failed legal challenges, Kennecott finally complied with the FTC in 1977, selling Peabody to a group headed by Newmont Mining for around $1 billion.

1970s: Losses and Corporate Battles

In 1971, Chilean President Salvador Allende nationalized that country's copper mines, stripping Kennecott of its partial ownership of El Teniente, the largest underground copper mine in the world. Aware of growing nationalistic sentiment in the 1960s, company leadership had foreseen the possibility of Chile's appropriation of the mines, and the sale a few years earlier of 51 percent interest in El Teniente to the government of Chile turned out to be a very wise move. By the time of the takeover, the share of Kennecott's income that came from Chile had been reduced to 11 percent from 25 percent in the 1960s, and though the event was certainly unsettling, Kennecott suffered far less than Anaconda, which had continued to invest heavily in that country. In 1972 an agreement was reached with the Overseas Private Investment Corp. (OPIC), the U.S. government agency that had insured Kennecott's 1967 loan to Chile. Under the terms of the settlement, Kennecott received $66.9

million from OPIC, taking a $9.8 million loss on the loans, on which Chile had made only two payments.

The 1970s were sluggish for Kennecott. The copper market was at its most depressed state since the 1930s, with prices down due to an abundant supply from new mines in Africa and elsewhere. New competition arose in the United States from growing companies such as Magma Copper Co. and Cyprus Mines Corp. These developments contributed to a $10.9 million loss for Kennecott in 1976, excluding Peabody, on $956 million in sales. Kennecott's annual capital investments were just over half those of Anaconda or Phelps Dodge during the mid-1970s, even though the production capacities of those two companies was smaller. While Kennecott was losing money in 1976 and 1977, both of those main competitors recorded profits.

Late in 1977, Kennecott acquired the Carborundum Co., a manufacturer of industrial products such as abrasives and pollution control equipment. Although Carborundum was a profitable company, with sales growing at a pace of about 15 percent a year, some stockholders felt that the $568 million Kennecott paid, about half the money from the sale of Peabody and twice Carborundum's market value, was too high. A group of Kennecott stockholders filed a suit to block the acquisition. Though no action came about as a result of the suit, criticism of Kennecott's management began to simmer, focusing on Milliken in particular.

With dissatisfaction growing, a proxy fight was launched in 1978, led by T. Roland Berner, chief executive of Curtiss-Wright Corp., a maker of aircraft engines. Berner promised that, if successful in taking over control of Kennecott, he would immediately sell off Carborundum and use the proceeds to pay out $20 a share to stockholders. By March 1978, Curtiss-Wright owned 9.9 percent of Kennecott's stock. After much complex legal wrangling, Milliken managed to fight off the challenge. One result was the integration of several Carborundum executives into top Kennecott management positions. Another result of the struggle was the occupation by Berner and two associates of seats on the Kennecott board of directors.

Following the proxy battle, Milliken retired. Thomas D. Barrow, a senior vice-president at Exxon, was named Kennecott's new chief executive. Barrow, upon accepting the position, immediately bought over three-quarters of a million dollars of Kennecott stock, making him the company's largest single stockholder. In 1981, Barrow negotiated the sale of Kennecott to Standard Oil Company of Ohio (Sohio) for $1.8 billion. Although Kennecott was still the nation's largest copper producer, it had been severely weakened by the industry-wide problems of the 1970s. With copper shortages expected in the 1980s, Kennecott needed to find hundreds of millions of dollars with which to modernize its facilities in order to take advantage of the elevated copper prices created by the new cycle of short supply. Sohio, flush with cash from its huge oil field at Prudhoe Bay in Alaska, came forward to supply the necessary funds. The purchase in turn gave Sohio an insurance policy against the depletion of its oil reserves.

In 1985 the Bingham Canyon mine was temporarily shut down because of depressed copper prices. During that time, the company invested $400 million to modernize the Utah Copper operations, including construction of an in-pit crushing and conveying system. A few months later, Kennecott purchased part of Anaconda's copper mine at Carr Fork, Utah. Kennecott had been trying to acquire the property, which bordered Bingham Canyon, for several years, and the mine had been closed since 1981. The following year, Sohio decided to focus all of its copper efforts on Bingham Canyon. With that decision, Sohio sold all of its other copper mines, dealing its Ray Mines division in Arizona to Asarco, and selling New Mexico's Chino Mines division to Phelps Dodge.

Buyouts Lead to Absorption into Rio Tinto

Kennecott became a subsidiary of BP Minerals in 1987, when BP purchased an outstanding minority interest in Standard Oil in June 1989. BP Minerals was then acquired by RTZ Corporation plc, Britain's largest mining company. In July of that year, construction began on Kennecott's Denton-Rawhide gold mine in Nevada's Mineral County. A joint venture was launched in 1990 with U.S. Energy Corp. to mine uranium in southern Wyoming.

In December 1991, the Environmental Protection Agency (EPA) issued a complaint charging Kennecott with 217 counts of mishandling hazardous wastes and chemical byproducts. In April 1992 the company reached an agreement in principle with federal and state environmental agencies on establishing a pilot program to clean up the wastes in the area of its Utah copper operations over a ten-year period. President G. Frank Joklik stated that the agreement's framework was "the product of a Kennecott concept brought to the U.S. EPA and the Utah DEQ over a year ago."

The Fourth Mill Line at Bingham Canyon began operating in January of 1992, adding an additional 32,000 tons of copper and 84,000 ounces of gold to the company's production capacity annually. Plans were also made in 1992 for the construction of a new $880 million smelter west of Salt Lake City. It was hoped that the new smelter would enable Kennecott to process all of its own concentrate, rather than send 40 percent elsewhere to be refined.

Restructuring and Shaky Market in Late 1990s

In 1995, Kennecott's parent RTZ merged with Australia's CRA Limited, forming the RTZ-CRA Group, the largest mining company in the world. In mid-1997, that company's name was changed to Rio Tinto plc and headquarters were established in London. The merger, while creating a multinational mining giant, also created the need for a management restructuring, which ultimately shook up the Kennecott operations. In 1997, Rio Tinto announced the closing of the Salt Lake City corporate headquarters, as well as the division of Kennecott Corporation into three separate operations: Kennecott Utah Copper Corporation, Kennecott Minerals Company, and Kennecott Energy Company. Kennecott Exploration Company (responsible for seeking new mineral resources) would be connected to and assist all three of these subsidiaries.

Kennecott Utah Copper, as part of Rio Tinto's massive copper unit, had 1997 net earnings of $139 million from production of copper, gold, silver, and molybdenum. It was the third largest U.S. copper producer in the late 1990s, producing 15 percent of the domestic copper supply. The revamped Bingham Canyon open pit mine near Salt Lake City (2.5 miles wide at the rim and half a mile deep) remained the cornerstone of this operation, moving 320,000 tons of ore daily. However, environmental concerns continued to plague Kennecott Utah operations. In 1995, Kennecott, the EPA, and the state of Utah had entered into an agreement under which Kennecott would have to clean up its Bingham Canyon operation, which was largely responsible for widespread contamination of ground waters in the area. A 1998 report by the EPA ranked Utah as the seventh worst state for toxic chemical releases, with Kennecott Utah Copper being the largest releaser in the state of bioaccumulative toxic chemicals. Kennecott Utah Copper hoped that its new plant would drastically cut the amount of future toxins released.

The other Kennecott operations were operating on a much smaller scale than Kennecott Utah Copper. Kennecott Minerals, which also operated from within Rio Tinto's copper unit, was created to develop and operate mineral properties throughout North America. Its headquarters remained in Salt Lake City after the reorganization. Kennecott Minerals accounted for $15 million of Rio Tinto's net earnings in 1997. Kennecott Energy (with $70 million in net earnings in 1997) was a major producer of coal in the United States, via surface mines in Colorado, Montana, and Wyoming. Its chief customers were electric utilities in the western United States.

In the late 1990s, the U.S.-based Rio Tinto operations suffered from an economic crunch, as did many other mineral and metal producers. The United States accounted for almost one quarter of the world's copper production, and consumption had grown steadily through the early and mid-1990s. The U.S. copper mining industry had begun to rely strongly on the expanding markets in Asia, particularly in China, Indonesia, Japan, Malaysia, South Korea, and Thailand. However, it became clear that the Asian economic crisis of the late 1990s would have serious repercussions for the copper mining industry. Copper prices hit a four-year low in December 1997, although there was some recovery in early 1998; the drop in the price of gold was even more serious, reaching an 18-year low. As a result, Kennecott Utah Copper was forced to lay off 150 workers in early 1998. Many experts predicted that the copper market could expect continuing problems.

Further Reading

Abrahamson, Peggy, "Kennecott Agrees on Cleanup," *American Metal Market*, April 8, 1992.
Argall, George, "Takeovers Shake USA Mining Companies," *World Mining*, May 1981.
"The Battle of the Lightweights," *Forbes*, May 1, 1978.
"Big Plan in Copper Country," *ENR*, April 20, 1992.
Clark, C.A. Jr., "Kennecott Copper," *Barron's*, March 16, 1953.
Cook, James, "A Man Who Knows Where He's Going," *Forbes*, April 30, 1979.
Davidson, Lee, "Pollution Report Slams Kennecott Over Groundwater," *Deseret News*, September 16, 1997.
Ehbar, A.F., "Kennecott After the Battle," *Fortune*, June 5, 1978.
"Excellence and Style," *Engineering and Mining Journal*, August 1989.
Jordan, Carol, "Anaconda Sells Part of Mine to Kennecott," *American Metal Market*, October 3, 1985.

"Kennecott Collects on Its Insurance," *Business Week,* December 23, 1972.

"Kennecott Copper," *Forbes,* April 15, 1972.

"Kennecott Renews Itself with Sohio's Oil Money," *Business Week,* April 26, 1982.

Knudson, Max. B., "Kennecott to Lay Off 150 As U.S. Copper Prices Rise," *Deseret News,* March 3, 1998.

——, "Kennecott's Parent Firm May Take a New Name," *Deseret News,* April 17, 1997.

Loving, Rush Jr., "How Kennecott Got Hooked With Catch-22," *Fortune,* September 1971.

McDonald, John, "The World of Kennecott," *Fortune,* November 1951.

Thurlow, Bradbury, "Kennecott Copper," *Barron's,* February 20, 1956.

"Utah Is 5th in Toxic Releases," *Deseret News,* November 25, 1998.

Voynick, Steve, "The Secret To Staying Young," *Mining Voice,* January/February 1998.

Welles, Chris, "The Kennecott Blunders," *Financial World,* March 1, 1978.

"Where Copper is Not Quite King," *Business Week,* December 7, 1968.

Zipf, Peter, "Kennecott Output Capacity Sale Seen Having Little Effect on Copper Mart," *American Metal Market,* September 16, 1986.

—Robert R. Jacobson
—updated by Gerry Azzata

Kerry Group plc

Princes' Street
Tralee
County Kerry
Ireland
(353) 66 22433
Fax: (353) 66 22353

Public Company
Incorporated: 1974 as Kerry Co-Operative Creameries
Limited
Employees: 9,800
Sales: IR£ 1.34 billion (US $1.92 billion) (1997)
Stock Exchanges: Dublin London
Ticker Symbol: Kerry
SICs: 2051 Bread, Cake & Related Products; 2099 Food
Preparations, Not Elsewhere Classified; 2034
Dehydrated Fruits, Vegetables & Soups; 2045
Prepared Flour Mixes & Doughs; 2011 Meat Packing
Plants; 2013 Sausages & Other Prepared Meats; 2015
Poultry Slaughtering & Processing; 2021 Creamery
Butter; 2022 Cheese—Natural & Processed; 2026
Fluid Milk

Kerry Group plc is fast becoming one of the world's leading food ingredients suppliers. Based in Ireland, the Kerry Group has expanded its operations worldwide, with a strong presence throughout Europe and the United States, and a growing presence in the Pacific Rim region. Kerry operates manufacturing plants in 14 countries, with sales of its more than 7,000 products reaching more than 70 countries. Kerry continues to expand rapidly, primarily through a strong program of acquisitions. After acquiring the U.S.' DCA Food Industries in 1994—giving Kerry a prominent position in the North American ingredients market—the company went after bigger fish in 1998, acquiring the ingredients operations of fellow U.K. producer Dalgety PLC. That acquisition is expected to boost Kerry's 1998 revenues past IR£ 2 billion.

Kerry's operations are separated along three primary market targets. The first and most important for the company's annual sales is its Food Ingredients division, which accounts for more than half of Kerry's sales and nearly three-quarters of its annual operating profits. Supplying primarily multinational and other food processors, Kerry Ingredients produces more than 6,000 individual products for categories including seasonings and coatings; dehydrates; dairy; fruit preparation; bakery goods, including a leading share of the U.S. donut mix market; and specialty ingredients. The company's ingredients include flavoring agents, functional ingredients—such as those required for processing yogurt or ice cream, and the many consistency and flavor enhancers and additives found in processed foods. A primary market for this division is the seasonings and coatings market segment, including crumb and batter systems for meat, poultry, fish, and convenience foods.

Through subsidiaries Lucas Ingredients, Produits Jaeger, PAC, Morton Foods, and ABC, Kerry has captured the European leadership for these products. Kerry's Ingredients division also produces pre-packed flour and baked goods mixes for the private label market and for the company's own Homepride and Greens labels, themselves leaders in many European and other global markets. Other Kerry ingredients brands include Kerry PSF, Aptunion, and Ravifruit, which have captured leading positions in the fruit processing market; and the company's Trumato line of enhanced powdered tomato products, developed in the company's "greenseed" Irapuato, Mexico facility.

In the United States, Kerry's DCA and other subsidiaries have enabled the company to take a leading share of the processed cheese and dairy products categories. Kerry has also targeted the South American market for growth, with a production facility in Brazil serving that country and the Argentinean and Chilean food production markets. Kerry is also making moves to expand its presence in the Asia-Pacific region. In addition to a manufacturing facility in Sydney, Australia, Kerry has purchased a second production plant in Johor Bahru, Malaysia, from which to serve the booming population of the region.

Representing approximately one-third of the Kerry Group's annual revenues, the Kerry Foods division is one of the United

Company Perspectives:

Kerry is committed to being a leader in its selected markets through technological creativity, total quality and superior customer service. The Group is focused on contintuing to expand its presence in global food ingredients markets and on the further development of its consumer foods businesses in Europe.

Kingdom's leading manufacturers of refrigerated food products for the company's own Richmond, Wall's, Denny, Ballyfree, and Mattessons brands, as well as for private label and other third-party brands. Kerry Foods specializes in five product categories, with an emphasis on pork and other meat products, cold cuts, poultry, dairy, and convenience foods products. Kerry Foods focuses primarily on the Irish and U.K. markets, in which the company has built up an extensive distribution network, while continuing a steady expansion in the European Community markets. All of the division's manufacturing facilities are located in the United Kingdom and Ireland, including the company's Shillelagh, Ireland pork processing facility, commissioned in 1994, which remains one of Europe's most technologically advanced food processing plants.

In addition to meat products, which account for approximately 80 percent of Kerry Foods production, this division also manufactures and distributes dairy products, yellow fat products, including the company's popular ''Move Over Butter'' and Kerrymaid brands, and fruit juices and bottled waters.

The last of the three Kerry divisions is Kerry Agribusiness, which represents the company's founding focus. Kerry Agribusiness is responsible for the coordination of the company's 4,000-strong contingent of raw milk and other dairy suppliers. Kerry Agribusiness provides services to its network of dairy farm suppliers to assist them in maintaining the nutritional quality of their milk products while maximizing their production and cost efficiency. Kerry Agribusiness provides technical services, including breeding technology, services, and research, as well as a fleet of milk delivery vehicles and feed products to complement traditional grazing methods.

These three divisions enable Kerry to provide a vertically integrated food production, processing, and distribution system that has grown to take a leading role in the United Kingdom and European markets. The chief architect of the company's growth has been Denis Brosnan, managing director, who has overseen the company since its public listing in the mid-1980s.

Dairy Co-Op in the 1970s

The Kerry Group was formally established as Kerry Cooperative Creameries Limited in 1974, in Kerry County, Ireland. The Cooperative combined the dairy and dairy processing interests of a number of the region's dairy farms, including a dairy and dairy ingredients processing plant opened in Listowel, Ireland, in 1972. In less than 30 years, the company would grow from this small provincial creamery to one of the world's leading specialist food ingredients producers and distributors. The introduction of the company on the Dublin and London stock exchanges in the mid-1980s made millionaires out of many of the co-op's founding members.

A primary component in Kerry growth was its steady expansion through acquisition, as well as a willingness to invest in new production and other facilities. Through the 1970s, Kerry grew to include a large number of dairy farms and processing plants in the counties of Cork, Killarney, Galway, and Limerick, supplying to the company's Dairy Disposal Company, established in 1974 as the originator of the later Kerry Foods division. By the mid-1980s, the Kerry Co-op counted several thousand members.

In the early 1980s, Kerry began branching out from its dairy core into other food product categories. An early addition was the pork products category, which the company entered with the acquisitions of two prominent Irish pork products producers, Duffy Meats and Henry Denny & Sons, both acquired in 1982. The move into food processing raised Kerry to a prominent position in Ireland's food industry. By the middle of the decade, Kerry's annual sales topped IR£200 million.

By then the little dairy co-op had expanded to include a number of manufacturing and other food processing facilities, located throughout Ireland and Northern Ireland. In 1986, the co-op made the decision to transform into a full-fledged corporation, listing its shares on the Irish stock exchange. Leading this transformation was Denis Brosnan, who also served as the chief executive of the founding Kerry Co-Op. The newly public company reported strong growth after its first full year of operations, with revenues nearing IR£ 300 million, and net profits of nearly IR£ 6.3 million.

Brosnan led Kerry on an accelerated drive to build the business into a vertically integrated food production conglomerate, doubling the company's revenues before the end of the decade. The company continued its expansion in Ireland with the 1986 acquisition of Snowcream Dairies Moate, and the formation of a Convenience Foods division, bringing the company into this increasingly prominent market—particularly with the steady adoption of this food trend among European consumers. Parallel to this move was the stepping up of Kerry's specialty ingredients business. At the same time, Kerry also established a presence in the United States, opening a dairy processing facility in Jackson, Wisconsin in 1987. Kerry continued to build its U.S. presence, adding additional facilities in Wisconsin and Illinois especially. Part of the company's U.S. growth came from the acquisition of existing businesses, including the 1988 acquisition of Beatreme Food Ingredients.

Rounding out the 1980s, Kerry's acquisitions included Grove and Ballytree, adding turkey products to the company's food production division. These companies were added in 1988, as was S.W.M. Chard, which gave Kerry a presence in the English market. At the end of 1989, Kerry, which had reached revenues of IR£ 584 million, began looking to expand onto the European continent. This was achieved the following year when the company purchased Milac, of Germany.

Leading the Ingredients Market in the 1990s

At the end of 1991, Kerry's annual sales surged to IR£ 755 million. The company had continued to invest in its British expansion, acquiring Eastleigh Flavors for its ingredients business in 1990, as well as food processors A.E. Button and Sons and Miller-Robirch. The company added several more U.K.-based businesses in the early 1990s, including the foods division acquisitions of Buxted Duckling, and Kantoher Food Products, and the food ingredients producer Tingles Ltd. At the same time, Kerry increased its market focus with the formation of Kerry Spring Water in Ireland. Between 1990 and 1993, Kerry also added Dairyland Products and Northlands to its ingredients division, both in the United States. These were joined by the company's move into Canada, with the 1993 acquisitions of Malcolm Foods and Research Foods, in Ontario and Vancouver. In 1994, Kerry added to its North American presence with the commissioning of a state-of-the-art dairy processing facility in Irapuato. In Ireland, the company began construction on one of the pork processing industry's most advanced plants, in Shillelagh.

Kerry's acquisition drive continued into the late 1990s, bringing the company into France and Italy, with the purchases of Ciprial S.A. and its Aptunion, Ravifruit, Gasparini, and Gial subsidiaries in 1996; into Poland, with the acquisition of U.K.-based Margetts in 1994; to Malaysia, in 1997, with the purchase of SDF Foods; and Brazil, with the acquisition of Star & Arty in 1998. In the United Kingdom, Kerry added both Mattessons and Walls to its list of brands.

Two important acquisitions highlighted Kerry's expansion. The first came in 1994, when the company acquired the food processing business of DCA, elevating the company to a major position among North America's specialty ingredients producers, especially among the coatings and bakery market segments. The DCA purchase, which cost the company some IR£ 250 million, also introduced it to the Australian and New Zealand markets. After digesting this purchase, including restructuring its U.S. holdings into the new subsidiary, Kerry Inc., the Kerry Group once again began eyeing a new large-scale acquisition.

The opportunity for renewed expansion came in February 1998, when the Kerry Group announced its agreement to purchase the food ingredients businesses of the U.K.'s Dalgety PLC. For a price of IR£ 384 million, Kerry acquired Dalgety Food Ingredients' plants in the United Kingdom and in Hungary and the Netherlands—new markets for Kerry—as well as plants in France, Italy, and Germany. The Dalgety acquisition firmly established Kerry as the top specialty ingredients producer in Europe, and one of the world's leaders in its specific categories.

With the Dalgety acquisition expected to boost Kerry's revenues beyond IR£ 2 billion for its 1998 fiscal year, Kerry was already turning its attention to two new markets: the Far East and South America. Both of these markets represented a huge pool of potential customers, both for the company's own food products and brands, and for its ingredients products. The company's initial forays into these markets included plant acquisitions in Malaysia and Brazil, while the company forecasted that these markets would reach some 25 percent of the company's revenues early in the next century.

Principal Subsidiaries

Castleisland Cattle Breeding Society Ltd.; Dawn Dairies Ltd.; Duffy Meats Ltd.; Glenealy Farms (Turkeys) Ltd.; Grove Turkeys Ltd.; Henry Denny & Sons Ltd.; Kerry Holdings Ltd.; Kerry Ingredients Ltd.; Kerry Agribusiness Holdings Ltd.; Kerry Creameries Ltd.; Kerry Farm Supplies Ltd.; Kerrykreem Ltd.; Snowcream (Midlands) Ltd.; A.E. Button & Sons Ltd. (U.K.); G.R. Spinks & Co. Ltd. (U.K.); Kerry Foods Ltd. (U.K.); South West Meat Ltd. (U.K.); Henry Denny & Sons (NI) Ltd. (Northern Ireland); Kerry Group BV (Netherlands); Pegromar Sp.z. O.O. (Poland); Ciprial S.A. (France); Kerry Ingredients France S.A.; G.I.A.L. S.r.l (Italy); Gasparini S.r.l (Italy); Kerry Ingredients GmbH (Germany); Kerry Ingredients Australia Pty. Ltd.; Kerry Ingredients (New Zealand) Ltd.; Kerry Inc. (U.S.A.); Kerry (Canada) Inc.; Kerry Ingredients S.A. de C.V. (Mexico); Kerry Ingredients (S) Pte. Ltd. (Singapore).

Further Reading

Canniffe, Mary, "Kerry Group Annual Profit Surges 18.6% to £51.2m," *Irish Times*, March 5, 1997.
——, "Kerry Group Well Positioned to Raise Profits," *Irish Times*, March 5, 1997.
Harding, Ted, "Kerry Group Set to Exceed the Revised Profit Forecasts," *Sunday Business Post (Ireland)*, March 9, 1998.
"Kerry Buys Malaysian Food Company," *European Report*, May 1, 1996.
McGrath, Brendan, "Co-op to Cut Stake in Kerry Group to 39%," *Irish Times*, May 16, 1996.
——, "Kerry Group Looks to Far East Market," *Irish Times*, May 27, 1997.
——, "Mega Deals Create £600m Debt," *Irish Times*, January 27, 1998.
O'Sullivan, Jane, "Kerry Group Pays £394m for Dalgety," *Irish Times*, January 27, 1998.

—M. L. Cohen

KESKO

Kesko Ltd. (Kesko Oy)

Satamakatu 3, Helsinki
P.O.B. 135, FIN-00016 Kesko
Finland
358 10 5311
Fax: 358 1053 23481
Web Site: http://www.kesko.fi

Public Company
Incorporated: 1940
Employees: 10,672
Sales: FIM $34.82 billion (US $6.39 billion) (1997)
Stock Exchanges: Helsinki
SICs: 2095 Roasted Coffee; 5064 Electrical Appliances,
TV & Radios; 5083 Farm & Garden Machinery; 5091
Sporting & Recreational Goods; 5099 Durable Goods,
Not Elsewhere Classified; 5112 Stationery & Office
Supplies; 5136 Men's and Boys' Clothing; 5137
Women's and Children's Clothing; 5139 Footwear;
5141 Groceries; 5142 Packaged Frozen Goods; 5143
Dairy Products; 5148 Fresh Fruits & Vegetables; 5191
Farm Supplies; 5199 Nondurable Goods, Not
Elsewhere Classified; 5411 Grocery Stores; 5311
Variety Stores; 5511 New & Used Car Dealers; 5551
Boat Dealers; 5561 Recreational Vehicle Dealers

The largest trading company in Finland, Kesko Ltd. is the parent corporation of the K-Group, comprising some 2,400 independent retailer-shareholders who operate nearly 2,700 stores specializing in groceries, leisure goods, and consumer durables. Kesko's largest division by far is Foodstuffs, which represents 71 percent of the K-Group outlets and 59 percent of corporate sales. Other corporate Divisions include Builders' and Agricultural Supplies, and Home and Specialty Goods, each of which includes both wholesale and retail operations. Kesko also serves as one of Finland's major importing firms, handling such international brands as Audi, Brooks, Browning, Daewoo, Fuji, Volkswagen, and Yamaha.

Early 20th Century Origins

Kesko was formed following mergers and dissolutions of nearly a dozen retailer-owned wholesale companies active in Finland prior to World War I. By the beginning of World War II, only four such companies, called the group of rural retailer companies, were left to vie for market share against other competitors in the rural foodstuffs industry. These four were Maakauppiaitten Oy, founded in 1906 and headquartered in Helsinki; Kauppiaitten Oy, founded in 1907 and located in Vaasa; Oy Savo-Karjalan Tukkuliike, founded in 1915 and centered in Vyborg; and Keski-Suomen Tukkukauppa Oy, founded in 1917 and located in Jyväkylä. The early association of these four main companies represented a transition in Finland's goods distribution system from traditional wholesale trade to owner-operated wholesale companies, a transition upon which Finland's entire cooperative movement was ultimately modeled. Two large central companies already in existence, the Finnish Co-operative Wholesale Society SOK and the Central Cooperative Society OTK, would eventually be surpassed by this group that joined to form Kesko. Even during their infancy, three of the core four—Maakauppiaitten, Kauppiaitten, and Savo-Kaijalan Tukkuliike—represented sizeable businesses with extensive office networks and net sales second only to the two central co-ops.

According to the corporate publication *50 Years of Kesko*: "Attempts were made to merge the retailer-owned wholesale companies almost from the very beginning, as the first negotiations on the matter took place as early as in 1908." Although prior to the formation of Savo-Karjalan Tukkuliike or Keski-Suomen Tukkukauppa, these original negotiations led to a series of meetings throughout the 1910s and 1920s, during which time several small mergers took place. A large merger of the core four almost succeeded in 1928, prevented only by "the 'strong men' of the two biggest companies," who had "firm opinions about the principles of the new company, and the other companies could not accept them." The firm opinions, of course, pertained to how the new company would be managed and what degree of administrative clout each of the original managers would retain following the merger.

One positive outcome of the 1928 negotiations was the foundation of two organizational bodies, Vähittäiskauppiaiden

261

Tukkuliikkeiden Yhdistys (VTY) and Kauppiaitten Keskuskunta. The purpose of the former was to serve as a consortium for more uniform purchasing by the four; the latter was to serve as a joint-service cooperative for the importation of wholesale goods as well as domestic industrial production, as the Kauppiaitten company already operated a Lahti shirt factory and a Helsinki coffee roastery. According to *50 Years of Kesko*, "Kauppiaitten Keskuskunta did not become a very significant company during the 1930s but, in the end, it became the seed of Kesko" because of its registration of the K-emblem and the Kesko logo. In late March 1940, following another decade of ongoing but disappointing negotiations as well as the conclusion of the Winter War with Russia, new talks among the four companies resumed. Despite one potentially considerable stumbling block—Savo-Karjalan Tukkuliike's loss of most of its eastern Finland operations to Russian control during peace negotiations—Kesko Oy became a reality by October. Combined sales at the time totaled FIM $1.25 billion; retailer-shareholders for the group numbered some 5,800.

Fittingly, the chair of the largest merged company, Maakauppiatten's Oskari Heikkilä, was elected Kesko's first chairperson. The company's original supervisory board consisted of 21 other members, with seats apportioned according to the net sales of the predecessor companies. The name Kesko, which had no historical ties to any of the founding companies, was adopted. Interestingly, the formation of Kesko did not legally constitute a merger because all four companies dissolved themselves and distributed their net assets to shareholders, who in turn subscribed to new shares of capital in Kesko, a wholly new limited liability company.

Postwar Growth

From the end of World War II to 1950, Kesko's district network grew from 19 to 22 regional offices while K-emblems spread to the stores of some 3,700 shareholders. Through the formation of consultative Committees, introduction of purchase discounts, and implementation of support services, Kesko began to transform itself from a strictly wholesale concern to a central company devoted to its members. Beginning in 1950, the emphasis on district expansion and internal restructuring was exchanged for diversification beyond foodstuffs, into the related areas of animal feed, fertilizer, and agricultural machinery, as well as the construction industry.

During the late 1950s, as Finland altered from a primarily agrarian and rural to a primarily industrial and urban economy, Kesko adapted itself as well. Large numbers of K-stores located in outlying regions had to be closed, while nearly as many new K-stores had to be erected closer to urban centers. Coincident with this dramatic upheaval for Kesko retailers, the central company faced shortages in capital, spiraling growth in personnel, and mounting transportation and distribution expenses.

The most significant action taken by the company during this period of growth and transformation was the decision to take Kesko public, through a division of the company's stock into exclusive and ordinary shares. Thus, in 1960, Kesko was listed on the Helsinki Stock Exchange, and new capital was available to solve its problems while governance of the company remained in the hands of the exclusive shareholders, the retailers themselves. Enormous advancements during the 1960s, including the completion of a central warehouse in 1965 and the implementation of long-term retail development programs, paved the way for significant growth during the 1970s. During this decade, Kesko came into its own and saw its combined market share rise from 23 percent to almost 30 percent. Confident, after weathering the rationing policies and manufacturing shortages of the 1950s and 1960s, that foodstuffs could steadily generate at least half of corporate sales, Kesko poised itself for more rapid growth in its Agricultural and Builders' Supplies division.

Changes in the 1980s and 1990s

During the 1980s, Kesko fulfilled its longtime plan of divesting itself of most of its manufacturing operations, which over the years had come to include a margarine factory, flour mill and bakery, match factory, rye crisp company, meat processing company, bicycle factory, clothing factory, and coffee roasting plant. The process had been a slow one, for at the beginning of the decade the last three still remained within the company's holdings. Management decided to retain only the roastery, the strongest performer in net sales of all Kesko's manufacturing units. "The necessity of having a coffee roastery of our own has been generally approved," according to *50 Years of Kesko,* "because coffee has been the most important campaign product ever since the Second World War." Kesko's establishment in 1991 of Viking Coffee Ltd., a roastery jointly owned with a Swedish central company, affirms the company's continuing commitment to this important "micro-market."

Having become the largest central trading company in Finland, Kesko entered the 1990s streamlined (its district offices progressively pared down to just nine) and prepared for strong continuing growth. However, due to a depressed national and global economy, the company saw net sales decline by 6.5 percent from 1991 to 1992. Chair and Chief Executive Eero Utter nonetheless found cause for optimism in the increased market share for most of Kesko's product groups: "Although the Kesko Corporation's profit for 1991 decreased from the previous year, the Corporation and the whole K-Group has coped and will continue to cope with the recession very well in comparison with other companies.''

The company was back on track soon, with profits for 1994 of FIM $462 million, up from FIM $285 million the year before, on a sales increase of 4.8 percent. The following year was even better, with a total profit of FIM $689 million on sales of FIM $26.4 billion. Expanding outside Finland, Kesko had begun opening several different types of stores in Sweden, and later in Russia. The K-stores chain had restructured in 1994, with stores now classed into four different size categories, ranging from "One-K," the smallest, to "Four-K," with a store's sign now showing from one to four letter "K"'s on it as appropriate. Each size had a different emphasis, with the smallest ones, for example, posting a list of "10 principles" on the wall near the entrance which stated such ideals as, "You can always have a few words with the shopkeeper," or "You'll always feel cozier in our store than in big supermarkets." Despite the variations in size, the stores were organized identically, enabling shoppers to find things easily in any store in the chain.

The year 1996 saw Kesko acquire a large commercial trading house, Kaukomarkkinat Oy, while it sold Keskometalli Oy, a steel and metal service center and distributor. An attempted acquisition of the Tuko chain of supermarkets, however, was thwarted by the Commission of the European Union after the Finnish government requested that it examine the case. The country could not intercede itself, as it had no laws governing large corporate mergers. Control of Tuko, the second largest supermarket chain in Finland after K-stores, would have given Kesko nearly 60 percent of this market, and the EU ruled against Kesko because it believed that this would significantly impede competition. Having already begun the acquisition process, Kesko was forced to sell off most of the portions of Tuko that had already been purchased.

This setback was not a total debacle, however, as Kesko reported that it was selling off its Tuko stake at cost, and by 1998 the company was posting yet another record year for profits and sales. The company installed a new CEO, Matti Honkala, and announced plans to add wine sales to its food retail outlets and expand further into the Baltic States. Another acquisition had come in late 1997, that of Academica Oy, an information technology company, which boosted Kesko's presence in the computer marketplace. Kesko also reorganized its Foodstuffs and Home and Specialty Goods Divisions around this time.

Despite relative anonymity in the United States, Kesko is a singularly important Finnish company, controlling some 40 percent of the country's over-all grocery market, and looming large in other areas including department stores, wholesaling, importing, and coffee roasting. It appears to have become a permanent fixture in the Finnish landscape.

Principal Subsidiaries

Kaukomarkkinat Oy; VV-Auto Oy; Antilla Oy; K-maatalousyhtiöt Oy; Rautia Oy; Viking Coffee Oy (50%).

Principal Divisions

Foodstuffs; Builders' and Agricultural Supplies; Home and Specialty Goods.

Further Reading

A Capital K Is the Key to the Finnish Market, Helsinki: Kesko Corporation, 1991.
Fifty Years of Kesko, Helsinki: Kesko Oy, 1990.
"Finland: Kesko-Tuko Case—The Finnish Experience of the Use of the 'Dutch Clause'—Castren & Snellman," *Mondaq Business Briefing,* February 6, 1997.
McCabe, Jane, "Commanding Respect (Finland's Coffee Industry)," *Tea & Coffee Trade Journal,* February 2, 1995, p. 16.
Raphael, Murray and Neil Raphael, "The One-Idea Trip—Innovative Ideas For Grocery and Convenience Stores," *Progressive Grocer,* March 1, 1996, p. 23.

—Jay P. Pederson
—updated by Frank Uhle

KeySpan Energy Co.

175 East Old Country Road
Hicksville, New York 11801
U.S.A.
(516) 755-6650
Fax: (718) 643-2277
Web site: http://www.keyspanenergy.com

Public Company
Incorporated: 1998 as MarketSpan Corp.
Employees: 8,000
Sales: $3.12 billion
Stock Exchanges: New York
Ticker Symbol: KSE
SICs: 4931 Electric & Other Services Combined; 4932
    Gas & Other Services Combined; 6719 Offices of
    Holding Companies, Not Elsewhere Classified

KeySpan Energy Co. is a holding company formed by the 1998 merger of Brooklyn Union Gas, the nation's fourth largest natural gas utility, and the nonnuclear electric-generating assets of Long Island Lighting Co. (LILCO). In addition to providing gas and electricity service to millions of New Yorkers, KeySpan was, in 1998, involved in developing energy projects and markets both in the United States and abroad. It also held investments in other energy companies and facilities.

The Predecessor Companies to 1991

Brooklyn Union Gas Co. was providing service in 1991 to nearly 1.1 million customers in New York City's boroughs of Brooklyn, Queens, and Staten Island, and Long Island's Nassau and Suffolk counties. Incorporated in 1895 from the merger of seven competing Brooklyn gas-lighting companies, Brooklyn Union Gas traced its roots back to 1824. Originally it lit Brooklyn's streets with methane obtained from heating coal. By 1952, however, the utility had completely switched over to natural gas. This fuel was so cheap and readily available that Brooklyn Union Gas reduced rates 27 times between 1952 and 1969. Supply problems developed in the 1970s, but the company built

liquefied gas storage tanks and constructed a synthetic natural gas plant. It became part-owner in a pipeline, opened in 1992, that transported natural gas from Canada to the northeastern United States.

Long Island Lighting Co. (LILCO) was, in 1991, supplying electric and gas service to about 2.8 million people in Nassau and Suffolk counties and the Rockaway Peninsula in New York City's borough of Queens. The company was incorporated in 1910 by the merger of four small Suffolk County utilities. As this essentially rural area was drawn into New York City's orbit, LILCO's revenues and generating facilities grew greatly. It converted most of its plants from coal to oil in the 1960s and, following the run-up of oil prices in the 1970s, raised its rates 13 times in 12 years to offset its rising costs.

To reduce its dependence on expensive oil, LILCO began construction of a nuclear power plant at Shoreham, Long Island, in 1973. It was completed in 1984 but never began operations because of safety concerns. LILCO sold it to a state-created power authority in 1989 for $1 and the company's right to raise rates for ten years to pay down $4 billion of its debt of about $5.3 billion for building the facility. The huge debt that LILCO incurred required its electricity rates to rise higher than those of any other utility in the United States outside of Hawaii.

Long Island Lighting: 1991–97

By early 1995, when LILCO requested and received a one-year rate freeze, the utility was in much better shape. In 1994, for the first time in more than 20 years, it registered a positive cash flow, and it ended 1995 with $800 million in cash. These results were achieved in part by reducing its work force and converting some of its power plants to burn gas rather than oil. By the summer of 1996 LILCO had reduced its debt by $1.1 billion since 1994. Even so, the company's ratio of long-term debt to capital remained a high 62 percent in September 1995, and the utility's customers continued to chafe at its high rates. LILCO's autocratic chairman and chief executive officer, William J. Catacosinos, was a frequent public target.

In March 1997 Governor George Pataki announced a long-awaited agreement to cut electric rates on Long Island. It called for a new holding company to absorb both LILCO and Brooklyn Union Gas. The state-owned Long Island Power Authority (LIPA) would buy LILCO's power lines, its customer services, and its share of an upstate nuclear plant, issuing $7.3 billion in tax-free bonds to purchase about $2.5 billion of the new holding company's stock and to retire $3.6 billion of its remaining $4.5 billion debt for the abandoned Shoreham plant. Rates would drop by 23 percent over five years in Nassau County and 20 percent in Suffolk County. In addition, Long Island homeowners would receive rebate checks of $100 to $232.

LIPA also won the right to buy LILCO's power-generating plants after three years. Although the new holding company would run the transmission and distribution system under a contract, after the eighth year the power authority would have the right to reassign the contract to a qualified lower bidder. The authority would set electricity rates. It would, in theory, be free to buy cheaper power elsewhere, but a 15-year contract obligated it to purchase almost all of its power from existing power plants on Long Island. The new holding company would continue to own gas lines and sell gas to customers.

Brooklyn Union Gas: 1991–97

A merger with LILCO made sense to Brooklyn Union Gas because it long had sought LILCO's gas business in a possible breakup and sale of the company by the state. Some 160,000 LILCO customers were using gas for cooking but not for heating, and two-thirds of Long Island homes did not have gas heat. In addition, as the gas industry in New York became increasingly deregulated, Brooklyn Union Gas had been moving into energy fields other than natural gas, including the sale of electricity. Unregulated subsidiaries of the company— mainly gas exploration, marketing, and cogeneration operations—had been responsible for profits of $12.8 million in fiscal 1995, about 14 percent of the parent company's total and a tenfold increase over the previous five years. In 1995 the utility formed a joint venture with Houston-based Pennzoil Corp. to sell more than 1.5 billion cubic feet of natural gas per day.

In September 1997, following the adoption of the plan to merge LILCO and Brooklyn Union Gas, the latter company revamped its structure, establishing KeySpan Energy Corp. as a holding company, with Brooklyn Union Gas as its subsidiary. The change was intended to enable KeySpan to propose acquisitions of other companies in a more timely manner than Brooklyn Union Gas, whose dealings were subject to review by the state's Public Service Commission. KeySpan, in December 1997, sold Gas Energy Inc. and Gas Energy Cogeneration Inc., which had participated in the development, operation, and ownership of cogeneration projects, for $100 million.

One of the parent company's most dynamic subsidiaries was KeySpan Energy Management Inc., formed in 1996 with the mission of building, maintaining, upgrading, and operating the fuel-powered mechanical systems of large energy users, initially in the tristate New York City metropolitan area but ultimately in 19 eastern states. This unregulated subsidiary, poised to take on the fuel-oil suppliers that had long dominated the Long Island market, had a five-year revenue goal of more than $150 million. Another unregulated KeySpan subsidiary was KeySpan Energy Services Inc., also created in 1996. Its mission was to save commercial clients money in meeting their fuel needs.

Brooklyn Union Gas, in February 1998, announced it would turn over the management of its $500-million-a-year business of buying, transporting, and storing natural gas to a subsidiary of Houston-based Enron Corp. Enron guaranteed Brooklyn Union Gas a higher rate of return because, according to the subsidiary's chief executive, his company could do a better job than the utility of negotiating gas supply, sale, transport, and storage contracts since it had a staff of 200 on trading floors in Houston.

MarketSpan and KeySpan in 1998

The parts of LILCO not taken over by the state power authority merged with KeySpan, the parent of Brooklyn Union Gas, on May 28, 1998, to form MarketSpan Corp. LILCO shareholders received slightly more shares of stock in the new company for each share of LILCO stock they owned than KeySpan shareholders received for each share of their stock. (LILCO had fiscal 1997 revenue of $3.12 billion compared with KeySpan's $1.48 billion, but the latter was considered to be in much better financial shape.)

A controversy developed a week later, when the governor and power authority disclosed that LILCO had made $67 million in secret payments to 26 of its executives who automatically succeeded to jobs at MarketSpan. Catacosinos, who became chairman and chief executive officer of the new company, received $42 million. Pataki said the payments were violations of LILCO's 1997 agreement with the state, which included a no-layoff guarantee and a ban on severance pay, and he called for Catacosinos' resignation. Public documents indicated, however, that the payments were collectible accrued compensation or benefit payments.

Catacosinos, who was slated to bow out as chief executive anyway in a year, kept his payment and resigned his post on July 31. He was succeeded by Robert Catell, the former president of Brooklyn Union Gas and KeySpan and the president of MarketSpan. Seventeen of the other 25 executives also chose to leave the company rather than relinquish their payments. Twenty-two lawsuits challenging the payments were filed: 21 by stockholders and one by Suffolk County.

Meanwhile, Catell was addressing the complaints of shareholders unhappy because MarketSpan's stock price had fallen from $37.625 a share on the day of its inception to as low as $26.50 in July. Calling the company's stock price "greatly undervalued," he announced August 3 that the company would buy back as much as a tenth of its 158 million shares, using some of the approximately $2 billion it had collected from LIPA from selling part of the former LILCO. The company had spent about $450 million for this purpose when it announced, in October, that it would spend up to $500 million more in a second stock buyback of about 12 percent of its shares.

The same institutional investors who had been demanding a company buyback of stock to raise the price also were calling for MarketSpan to be sold to another company. Their chief concern was that, in the rapidly consolidating energy business, MarketSpan would only have two choices: to sell out or to construct its own energy empire by acquisition, an alternative that might depress its stock price further. One securities analyst ventured the opinion that eventually MarketSpan probably would be sold, even if it made acquisitions beforehand, but that short-term, the company had not yet determined its strategy.

MarketSpan announced in August 1998 that its KeySpan Energy Development Corp. unit would join Duke Energy Corp. and the Williams Cos. in developing the Cross Bay Pipeline project, which would transport gas from interstate pipelines in New Jersey to New York City and Long Island. This decision was in keeping with Catell's intention to expand MarketSpan's natural gas business, which he said had long been neglected by LILCO. Fewer than 30 percent of all Long Island homes were being heated with gas, compared with 80 percent in Brooklyn Union Gas's territory. Two months later the company agreed to acquire, for $189 million, a half-interest in Gulf Canada Resource Ltd.'s gas processing, storage, and transport business in western Canada.

MarketSpan Corp. changed its name to KeySpan Energy Co. in September 1998. One month later it announced a third-quarter loss of $26.4 million. A company spokesman said the loss was due to cuts in rates before "synergy" savings were achieved from the merger of LILCO and Brooklyn Union Gas. In the second quarter of 1998 the company had net income of $37.25 million on total revenues of $582.6 million.

In late 1998 KeySpan Energy was operating five steam power plants and 42 smaller facilities with an aggregate-rated generating capacity of 3,978 megawatts to generate electricity to its customers under a contract with LIPA and was managing the transmission and distribution of this energy under the same contract to more than one million customers. Brooklyn Union Gas was providing natural gas service to 1.57 million customers.

KeySpan Energy Management was designing and operating energy systems and providing a broad range of energy-related services to large commercial and industrial businesses in the New York City metropolitan area, including design, construction, and engineering. KeySpan Energy Services was marketing natural gas and electricity services to customers throughout the Northeast. KeySpan Energy was providing service and maintenance for heating equipment, water heaters, central air conditioners, and gas appliances.

KeySpan International Ltd. was involved in gas distribution and cogeneration activities in selected developing gas markets in Europe and Latin America. KeySpan Energy Development Corp. was identifying and developing investment opportunities and strategic partnerships and alliances in unregulated energy areas, both domestically and internationally.

In addition to its joint venture with Enron, KeySpan had a 64 percent interest in Houston Exploration Co., which held offshore oil and gas properties in the Gulf of Mexico and onshore properties in Texas and West Virginia. KeySpan also held a 52 percent interest in Honeoye Storage Corp., which owned an underground gas storage facility in Ontario County, New York, and a gas storage facility in Steuben, Mew York. KeySpan owned the North East Transmission Co., the second largest equity holder in the 375-mile-long Iroquois pipeline, which was transporting natural gas from Canada to the northeastern United States.

Principal Subsidiaries

The Brooklyn Union Gas Company; Honeoye Storage Corp. (52%); Houston Exploration Co. (64%); KeySpan Energy Development Corp.; KeySpan Energy Management Inc.; KeySpan Energy Services Inc.; KeySpan International Ltd.; North East Transmission Co., Inc.

Further Reading

"At Deadline," *Crain's New York Business,* November 16, 1998.

Benkelman, Susan, "Lilco Still Unsettled," *Newsday,* September 24, 1995, pp. A4, A54.

Bunis, Dean, "Plans in the Pipeline," *New York Newsday,* February 25, 1991, pp. 33, 36–37.

Fagin, Dan, "An Artful Deal," *Newsday,* March 20, 1997, pp. A5, A44.

Gross, Jane, "A Utility Chief Who Remembers His Roots," *New York Times,* August 27, 1998, p. B2.

Halbfinger, David M., "In Deal, LIPA and Utility End Clash Over Pay to Ex-Officers," *New York Times,* December 22, 1998, pp. B1, B8.

Holden, Benjamin A., "Long Island Lighting, Still Detested, Nears a Takeover by State," *Wall Street Journal,* April 26, 1996, pp. A1, A5.

Lambert, Bruce, "New Marketspan Chairman Announces Share Buyback," *New York Times,* August 4, 1998, p. B2.

——, "Power Authority Imposes Penalties and Asks Dismissals in Pay Deals," *New York Times,* June 17, 1998, pp. B1, B8.

——, "Utility Chief Resigns Post Over Lilco Pay," *New York Times,* August 1, 1998, pp. B1–B2.

Lentz, Philip, "Brooklyn Union Sets Aggressive Expansion Effort," *Crain's New York Business,* March 25, 1996, pp. 3, 64.

Malone, James T., and Caryn Eve Murray, "Cooking with Gas," *Newsday,* January 6, 1997, p. C7.

Murray, Caryn Eve, "Power Struggle," *Newsday,* May 12, 1997, pp. C12–C13.

Ravo, Nick, "Marketspan Pursues More Big Changes," *New York Times,* August 9, 1998, Sec. 14 (Long Island Weekly), pp. 1, 8.

Salpukas, Agis, "Brooklyn Gas to Turn Over Some Business to Enron," *New York Times,* February 13, 1998, p. B6.

Smith, Andrew, "Gas Market," *Newsday,* January 1, 1997, pp. A7, A49.

—Robert Halasz

Kone Corporation

PO Box 8, Kartanontie 1
FIN-00331 Helsinki
Finland
(358) 204 751
Fax: (358)-204-75-4375
Web site: http://www.kone.com

Public Company
Incorporated: 1910
Employees: 22,499
Sales: Fmk 122.55 billion (US $2.25 billion) (1997)
Stock Exchanges: Helsinki
Ticker Symbol: Kone
SICs: 3534 Elevators & Moving Stairways

Kone Corporation is a world-leading designer and manufacturer of elevators, escalators, and ''autowalks.'' Based in Helsinki, Finland, Kone has developed an international organization of 150 subsidiaries and nearly 22,500 employees, who produce and install 12,000 units per year. The late 1990s introduction of the company's Monospace elevator concept, which reduces space and energy requirements, has helped invigorate Kone's business in a difficult economic climate. Yet sales of new elevators, escalators, and autowalks represent only 41 percent of the company's sales. Since the late 1980s Kone has built a strong business in elevator maintenance and modernization. In 1997 the company held maintenance and modernization contracts on more than 400,000 elevators worldwide.

Whereas Europe traditionally has been the company's primary sales base, representing 55 percent of company revenues in 1997, the company has made strong inroads into the U.S. market, which provides 29 percent of company sales. In the 1990s Kone has stepped up its position in the Asia-Pacific region, including opening a new elevator and escalator factory in Kunshan, China in 1998. At 11 percent of annual sales, this region represents a still limited share of Kone's revenues, sparing the company the brunt of the late 1990s economic crisis there. Nonetheless, the company remains committed to devel-

oping this market. Kone also delivers elevators and escalators to the African and South American markets, which together represent only five percent of annual sales.

Kone had been a diversified materials handling equipment company until the 1990s, when the conjunction of a worldwide recession and a too-rapid expansion forced the company to streamline its operations, returning to its long-time core elevator and escalator components. The company retains the number three spot among leading elevator producers, behind Otis Elevator, of the United States, and Schindler, of Switzerland. Kone Corporation is led by President Anssi Soila; the founding Herlin family is represented by Chairman Pekka Herlin and his son, Deputy Chairman and CEO, Antti Herlin.

Rising in Prewar Finland

Kone Corporation originated almost as an afterthought of the Finnish electric motor manufacturer, Strömberg. Although Strömberg's primary business was the manufacture and sale of new motors, it also had developed an active business of refurbishing its used motors. Rather than develop sales of the rebuilt units under its own name, however, Strömberg sought a new brand name for its refurbished motors. In 1910 Strömberg incorporated its electric motor refurbishing arm as a separate company, dubbing the company simply ''Kone'' (Finnish for ''machine''). The Kone company began business as little more than a machine shop in a converted stable on the lot of Strömberg's Helsinki factory.

Another offshoot of Strömberg's electric motor business had been elevator sales and installation. The company did not produce the elevators itself, but instead acted as the Finnish licensee for Sweden's Graham Brothers, then the leading elevator manufacturer in Scandinavia. In 1912, Lorenz Petrell, head of Strömberg's elevator activities, was named managing director of its Kone subsidiary. Petrell did not abandon the elevator line, however; instead, he transferred all of Strömberg's elevator business, with its engineering, installation, and other personnel, to Kone. For the time, Kone continued to represent the Graham elevator line.

Company Perspectives:

Kone's innovative products and comprehensive services are designed to enhance the value and usefulness of our customers' property. Customer include planners, developers, builders and owners of public and private facilities. Kone's commitment to long-term customer support ensures reliability in its products and services and quality in its employees' performance. Commitment to R&D keeps Kone in the forefront of innovation in the elevator and escalator industry.

For more than a century Finland had been dominated by its Russian neighbor, which had made the tiny country a Grand Duchy at the start of the 19th century. In the years leading to the First World War, Finnish manufacturers, including Kone, were called on to supply the Russian military effort. To meet production demands, Kone moved to larger Helsinki quarters. The Russian Revolution that followed on the heels of World War I gave Finland the long sought for opportunity to declare its independence.

Kone, too, had decided that the time was ripe for independence. In 1918 the company ended its long-held licensing agreement with Graham Brothers, and began producing its own elevators, installing its first four elevators that same year. By then, the company had grown to 50 employees. The company's initial elevator experience was positive, prompting the company to turn its focus to elevators in the early 1920s. By then, the company, still a subsidiary of Strömberg, was producing more than 100 elevators per year. The company's sales focus was wholly on the Finnish market, which only had begun to develop multistory building structures necessitating elevator technology.

By 1924 Kone's parent company began to struggle financially; a member of its advisory board, Harold Herlin, recommended that Strömberg sell off its noncore businesses, including its Kone elevator division. Herlin, who held an engineering background, himself offered to buy Kone from Strömberg, an offer which was accepted. Herlin took the position as Kone's chairman, while assuming the chairman and president position of Strömberg as well. Lorenz Petrell, meanwhile, was named as Kone's president. The pair set to work building the newly independent Kone into the country's leading elevator manufacturer, hiring many of the failing Strömberg's engineering and commercial staff to boost Kone's development.

Helsinki was undergoing rapid expansion in the 1920s, and Herlin's variety of business interests, which extended into ship-building, utilities, and other construction, placed Kone in a strong position to furnish the growing market for elevators. In 1927 Kone moved into new, far larger production facilities, after buying a former margarine factory. By the end of 1928 the company had produced more than 1,000 elevators. In that same year the next generation of Herlins joined the company. With an engineering degree from Helsinki University of Technology, Heikki Herlin had spent four years working for Otis Elevator in the United States and for Brown Boveri in Germany, before joining what would become the Herlin family company. As

Kone faced the Great Depression, Lorenz Petrell retired and was replaced by Heikki Herlin.

The younger Herlin proved to be an impassioned leader, whose engineering background enabled him to become involved in all aspects of the company. Kone, which had been struggling to compete against the higher technology of its foreign rivals, now began producing elevators again to meet international standards. The drop in elevator orders caused by the Depression economy paradoxically aided Kone in its technological advancement effort. Forced to look elsewhere for sales in the early 1930s, Kone saw an opportunity to move into the crane market, where it could easily adapt its elevator technology. At the same time Kone also began producing its own electric motors. This gave the company full control of its elevator manufacturing, enabling Kone to satisfy higher quality standards. During the 1930s the company's production continued to expand, into electric hoists, and then into conveyor belt systems.

Elevator production once again picked up at the end of the decade, enabling the company to top more than 3,000 elevators sold. The Second World War—and Finland's uncomfortable position—would interrupt Kone's elevator growth, as production was turned to supplying the country's effort against the Soviet army. Heikki Herlin took over the chairmanship of the company upon his father's death in 1941. Two years later Kone stepped up its production of industrial cranes, opening a new production plant in Hyvinkää, outside of Helsinki. Supplying the war effort replaced much of Kone's production, however, while the company would maintain its prewar production levels to a large extent. On the losing side at the end of the war, Finland was forced to pay a heavy reparations bill. Kone's production was turned as well to this end, producing—at government cost—its elevators and other industrial equipment for the Soviet victors.

Postwar Diversity and Internationalization

Kone would find a positive note in its production for the Soviets. Despite receiving no profit from its production—which included 100 elevators and close to 200 cranes, paid for by the Finnish government—Kone found other benefits. For one, many of the elevators and cranes demanded by the Soviets were of a larger design, featuring more advanced technology than Kone had been using. As the company adapted to these requirements, it also was able to expand its production capacity, increasing not only the number of production units, but also their tonnage capacities as well. By the end of the 1940s, as reparations wound down, Kone had developed the technology to enter a new market, that of harbor cranes.

During the 1950s Kone continued to introduce new technology into its elevators, including automatic doors, hydraulic lifts, and advanced control features. The company also was growing into an important producer of cranes and hoists, as well as conveyor belts and other materials handling equipment technologies. A prime source of sales was Finland's dominant forestry and paper industries; in the 1960s Kone would increase its position in these industries with various lumber handling machinery. Yet elevators remained the company's core product; by the 1960s, Kone, which had become the leading elevator supplier for Finland, was finding little room for further domestic growth.

The arrival of the next generation of Herlins to the company's leadership would introduce a new era to Kone's history. When Heikki Herlin retired in 1964, he was replaced by son Pekka, who had joined the company in 1958. Unlike his engineering-oriented father and grandfather, Pekka Herlin held a degree in economics. The younger Herlin would chart a new course for the company: that of international growth. As such, Kone would become one of the first Finnish companies to eye international expansion, leaving the company with no predecessors upon which to model its expansion.

In 1966 the company opened a new, state-of-the-art elevator production facility in Hyvinkää. Then the company began looking for new markets, in particular, across the borders of its Scandinavian neighbors. In 1968 Kone made its first acquisition, buying the elevator and escalator business of Sweden's Asea. The purchase of the larger, yet money-losing Asea-Graham unit (which, incidentally, gave the company control of its former supplier, Graham Brothers) catapulted Kone to the position of Scandinavian market leader. It would take six years for Kone to reverse its new subsidiary's losses. By then, however, the company had continued to fuel its overseas expansion, acquiring elevator subsidiaries throughout Europe. In 1974 the company bought out the entire European elevator and escalator production of Westinghouse, doubling Kone's revenues.

By the mid-1970s Kone was producing elevators, escalators, and the new "autowalks" under such brand names as Graham, Hävemeier & Sander, Marryat & Scott, Armor, Sabiem, and Westinghouse, and the company featured production facilities in France, Germany, the United Kingdom, Austria, Sweden, Norway, Denmark, Spain, and elsewhere in Europe. Pekka Herlin also would continue the company's product diversification, adding electronic hospital and laboratory equipment, and expanding Kone's crane, harbor crane, and other materials handling businesses. Developing these activities led Kone into a new area, with the 1982 acquisition of Navire Cargo Gear and the 1983 acquisition of International MacGregor. These acquisitions did more than bring Kone into the cargo access market, including ship hatches and ramps and other materials for loading, unloading, and RoRo (rollin rollout) processing—adding Navire and MacGregor established Kone as the world leader in this category.

By the mid-1980s Kone had joined the ranks of the world's leading materials handling companies. Despite its diversification, Kone still relied on its elevator and escalator businesses for more than 63 percent of its sales, which continued to be heavily centered on Europe. The collapse of the worldwide building market, and the extensive economic recession that would grip Europe through much of the 1990s, would force Kone to rethink its global strategy.

Streamlining in the 1990s

By 1995 Kone had either sold off or spun off its non-elevator and non-escalator operations. First to go was the company's conveyor and bulk handling businesses, which were sold off in 1986. Kone would jettison its wood handling arm in 1994, selling its Kone Wood division to Austria's Andritz AG in 1994. Next, the company's cargo access wing, MacGregor-Navire, was sold to Incentive Group, based in Sweden, in 1993.

The company's crane production subsidiaries were incorporated as a separate company, sold to Sweden's Industri Kapital, and then introduced as a public company on the Helsinki stock market as KCI Konecranes International. Finally, the division grouping the company's high-tech analyzers, monitors, and other hospital and laboratory equipment businesses was spun off through a management buyout and reformed as Kone Instruments in 1995. In turn, Kone moved to reinforce its escalator arm, acquiring Montgomery Elevator Company, then the United States' fourth largest elevator and escalator company, which also gave Kone a major boost into the North American market. With the addition of 100 percent control of Germany's O&K Rolltreppen in 1996, Kone emerged firmly as the world's leading escalator and autowalk supplier.

The newly streamlined Kone had not finished its restructuring. Throughout its 20-year acquisition and development drive, Kone had maintained a hands-off policy on its new subsidiaries. The result was a collection of independently operating subsidiaries, each with its own culture, products, brand names, and production methods. In the 1990s Kone at last took steps to create a single corporate culture, enforcing the Kone brand name on a new generation of modular products. The company's push to restructure and homogenize its operations would be capped by the 1996 introduction of its Monospace elevator design. Hailed as revolutionary by the industry, the Monospace eliminated the need for a dedicated wheelhouse for the elevator's machinery, cutting its cost and reducing its energy requirements.

While building its new corporate culture, Kone also had been developing a new market area designed to complement its elevator and escalator core operations, as well as bridge that business's inherently seasonal, cyclical nature. In a program started during the 1980s Kone built a new maintenance services group, which during the 1990s would grow to become the company's strongest revenues provider. More than simply offering maintenance and repair services, Kone proposed a modernization program, enabling customers to upgrade, rather than entirely replace, their elevator parks.

As the company developed its maintenance and modernization arm, reaching more than 400,000 elevators under contract by 1998, the company's newly introduced Monospace design would help boost Kone's sales after years of a withering economic climate. Kone's strong push into the North American market promised to give the company greater balance during such economic cycles. Similarly, in the late 1990s Kone stepped up its efforts to expand into the developing Asian markets. Despite the faltering economy of much of the region, beginning in 1997 Kone continued to invest in production capacity, opening a new state-of-the-art production facility in Kunshan, China in October 1998.

Principal Subsidiaries

Kone Asensores S.A. (Argentina); Kone Elevators Pty. Ltd. (Australia); Kone Sowitsch AG (Austria); Kone Belgium S.A.; Kone International S.A. (Belgium); Kone Elevadores Ltda. (Brazil); Montgomery Kone Elevator Co. Ltd. (Canada); Kone Elevator Ltd. (Hong Kong); Kone Elevators International Ltd. (China); Kone Aufzug Gmbh & Co KG (Germany); O&K Escalators S.A. (France); O&K Rolltreppen Gmbh & CO KG

(Germany); Kone Elevator India Ltd.; Kone Italia S.p.A; Sabiem S.p.A.(Italy); Kone Japan Co., Ltd.; Kone Starlift B.V. (Netherlands); Kone Aksjeselskap (Norway); Arabian Elevator & Escalator Co. Ltd. (Saudi Arabia); Thai Lift Industries Public Co. Ltd. (Thailand); Montgomery Kone Inc. (USA); Kone Lifts Ltd. (UK); Ellis & McDougall Lifts Ltd. (UK); ZAO Kone Lifts St. Petersburg (Russia).

Further Reading

Simon, John B. (ed.), ''Special History Issue,'' *New and Views In-house Magazine,* Helsinki: Kone Corporation, 1998.

—M.L. Cohen

KOREAN AIR

Korean Air Lines Co., Ltd.

7F, Korean Air Operations Center
1370 Gonghang-Dong, Kangso-Ku
Seoul
Korea
(82-2) 656-7114
Web site: http://www.koreanair.com

Public Subsidiary of The Hanjin Group
Incorporated: 1962 as Korean Air Lines
Employees: 14,100
Sales: W 4.29 trillion (US $3.03 billion) (1997)
Stock Exchanges: Korea
SICs: 4512 Air Transportation, Scheduled; 4522 Air
    Transportation, Nonscheduled; 3721 Aircraft; 3728
    Aircraft Part & Auxiliary Equipment, Not Elsewhere
    Classified

Korean Air Lines Co., Ltd. (KAL) is South Korea's leading airline and part of the giant Hanjin Group, which deals in land, sea, and air transport, construction, heavy industry, finance, and information services. KAL has embarked upon a huge fleet expansion to handle the increase in overseas travel in and out of Korea; the average age of its airliners is less than eight years. In 1997, 25.5 million passengers flew KAL, which boasts the largest cargo operations of any passenger airline.

Origins

The Hanjin Group has its origins in the Hanjin Transportation Co., founded by Choong-Hoon Cho, who is still the chairman of the group today. Cho started the company in 1945, at a time when the Korean economy was in a state of chaos following World War II. Korea was occupied by the Imperial Japanese Army and was effectively under Japanese control. Upon liberation by U.S. forces in 1945, the country was poverty stricken. Cho saw a market for trucking services, and his first major customer was the United States Armed Forces, who were busy establishing bases in Seoul, Pusan, and other Korean cities.

The hostilities between North and South Korea from 1951 to 1954, which involved combined United Nations Forces against North Korean and Chinese forces, proved beneficial to business in South Korea. The huge U.S. military investment in South Korea required various local services, transport being one of the most important. Hanjin expanded rapidly and in 1956 was the prime transporter of U.S. military cargo in Korea. In 1960 the company was granted an air transportation license, which proved important in its later expansion in this sector. The company founded Air Korea, which initially dealt with cargo. In 1961 and 1964, respectively, Hanjin Sightseeing Bus Company and Korea Vehicle Transportation were established, with the Daejin Shipping Company joining the group in 1967. Cho's company had become a leading private transportation firm in South Korea. In 1969 the South Korean government recognized Hanjin for its performance as an earner of foreign exchange and presented it with the Presidential Flag Citation. This same year the Korean government would transfer operations and ownership of the bankrupt national airline KAL to the Hanjin Group, under Cho's control.

In 1962 Korean National Air Lines, the forerunner of KAL, folded because of a combination of low demand, inability to compete with foreign carriers, and inexperienced management dealing with poor technology. The state-owned enterprise had been started by the government shortly after World War II and consisted of nine small aircraft; the Korean government could not afford to keep the airline afloat, however, and began the search for suitable private-sector investors. The task of rehabilitating the airline was at first taken on by Choong Hoon Cho's Hanjin Group, in part out of a sense of patriotic duty and in part as a business challenge. At the time the prospect of a mismanaged, ill-equipped airline competing with the world's largest carriers seemed daunting. Cho realized that the domestic market for air travel within South Korea was limited by the country's small size, and international travel originating out of country was severely restricted by a government ban on its citizens traveling abroad. Despite these limitations Cho

Company Perspectives:

Before privatization, the company was a small regional airline, lacking in resources like aircraft, network and managerial efficiency. Just seven months after Choong Hoon Cho, Chairman of The Hanjin Group took over, new flights were launched to Japan and Southeast Asia. Korean Air has gone a long way—via devotion and achievement—and now boasts extensive routes spreading to 74 cities in 27 nations with a youthful fleet of 112 aircraft.

set about putting his acute business sense to work on the airline, which he officially named KAL when he acquired it in March 1969.

Building the National Carrier in the 1970s

The first step Cho took was to build up an Asian network based on cargo rather than passenger business. The freight business remained a mainstay of KAL, accounting for 40 percent of revenues. But although a freight network could be built up to service the explosion of manufacturing that was taking place at the time, finding a passenger market proved to be a different matter. The growing volume of business travel and visits to South Korea by tourists was not enough to maintain a civil carrier, and Cho's strategy, therefore, was to use Seoul as a transit route in the busy Asian region. Japan proved to be the strongest market in this category, with cost-conscious tour groups prepared to travel an indirect route to the United States or Europe via Seoul.

The first activities of the new airline consisted of the opening of branches in Taipei, Hong Kong, Saigon, and Bangkok, plus the commencement of service to Osaka in Japan from Pusan, followed by flights to Taipei, Hong Kong, and Bangkok from Seoul. In 1970 KAL moved into a new 26-story building built by the Hanil Development Company, a member of the Hanjin Group. New hangars also were constructed in 1970 to accommodate KAL's new fleet of planes. The operation of a Seoul-to-Los Angeles cargo route was followed closely by the 1973 acquisition of KAL's first Boeing 747, which was put into immediate service on the route. Although KAL began its first regular flight to Europe with a cargo service to Paris in 1973, the airline remained at a severe disadvantage in flying to Europe. Whereas other Asian airlines took advantage of the direct route to Europe over the USSR, South Korean aircraft were not granted such privileges by a Soviet government that still refused to recognize South Korea as an independent state. KAL, therefore, concentrated on trans-Pacific service to the United States and became the first airline to offer an all-cargo 747 service across the Pacific. Cho saw the need to keep pace with his international competitors' technological advances. KAL opened a modern engine shop at Seoul's Kimpo International Airport and introduced an IBM mainframe computer in its push toward full computerization. In 1975 KAL became one of Airbus's first customers with the purchase of three A300s, which were put into immediate service in the Asian routes.

In 1976 KAL established an aerospace division to contribute to South Korea's aviation and defense industry. Borrowing engineers from its maintenance department and using the resources of the Hanjin Group, KAL formed the Korean Institute of Aeronautical Technology as a subsidiary in 1978. The company was involved initially in the assembly of helicopters for McDonnell Douglas of the United States; in 1981, with the help of Northrop, it built South Korea's first domestically produced fighter aircraft, the F-5EF. The aerospace division planned to develop a short-range commuter aircraft eventually. On the civil passenger side of operations KAL continued its expansion with services to Paris, Manila, Bahrain, Zurich, Nagoya, Kuwait, Colombo, and Abu Dhabi by 1979. To accommodate these routes KAL placed an order with Boeing that represented the second largest single order in commercial aviation history—18 Boeing 747 jets. Nonstop KAL service to New York and Los Angeles began shortly thereafter. The lack of access to trans-Siberia passage to Europe continued to be problematic for KAL, which was forced to fly to destinations in Europe via Anchorage.

Weathering the Challenges of the 1980s

In 1983 disaster struck on a flight that strayed off course into Soviet airspace. The KAL jet was intercepted and destroyed by a squadron of Soviet fighter aircraft; 269 passengers and crew members were killed. The incident resulted in international condemnation of the USSR and counter accusations by the Soviet government that the KAL flight was being used to gather intelligence—a claim hotly contested by KAL and the South Korean government. The incident was a severe setback for the airline and strained relations between South Korea and the USSR for several years afterward. KAL's strategy for the next three years was to increase its freight network, and the airline invested heavily in freight terminals in Tokyo, Los Angeles, and New York.

KAL acquired a state-of-the-art control system for its freight network and in 1983 computerized its passenger reservation system with the introduction of a ticketing system called TOPAS. KAL scored a first in 1986 when it became one of the first airlines to supply Boeing with parts for its aircraft, in the form of a contract to deliver wing-tip extensions for the Boeing 747-400. KAL continued to be one of Boeing's prized customers with an order for ten of the aircraft in 1988. In that year KAL began services to London, Vancouver, Toronto, Jakarta, and Frankfurt. The Olympic Games held in Seoul in 1988, although marred by a boycott from the USSR and other Communist nations, was a financial success for the country. KAL was named official carrier for the games and took advantage of the influx of visitors to the country to display the full range of comforts it offered passengers. Cho had long stressed the need to offer quality service on par with the world's best airlines. As a result, KAL's first-class service is noted worldwide for its comfort and convenience.

Governmental restrictions on overseas travel by South Korean citizens were lifted in 1989, resulting in a 100 percent annual increase in passenger volume out of the country in each of the last two years, with more growth predicted in the near future. KAL's first scheduled flight to Moscow from Seoul occurred in 1991, and the break-up of the USSR eased relations between South Korea and the former Soviet states. The airline aimed at continued aggressive expansion and sought strategic partners to achieve this. Leading contenders in this included the Philippines' national airline, PAL.

The company also began serving Chinese destinations. Negotiation for "beyond" rights, however, the right to carry passengers from Beijing to another international destination, remained a point of contention. Still, KAL's long-term ambitions included establishing Seoul as a gateway to China (contingent upon development of the Korea's new airport at Inchon). In addition, scheduled cargo flights were not included in the Sino-Korean agreement.

Up and Down in the 1990s

In the 1990s, buoyed by generally excellent financial results, KAL maintained its ambition of being the "world's best airline with a route network extending round the globe," as *Air Transport World* reported. New routes were continually added. KAL became the first Asian airline to fly directly to Africa. A vigorous acquisition policy kept the company supplied with new planes. Operating revenues passed $3 billion in 1993 as Korean travelers took to the skies in unprecedented numbers, thanks to the relaxation of travel restrictions in 1988 and a booming domestic economy. The cargo market was even more robust. As the world's third largest freight carrier, the company grew 20 percent a year in the mid-1990s. Operating revenue reached $4.4 billion in 1995. At the same time, increasing competition from international carriers and potential industry overcapacity gave KAL managers cause for concern.

In 1996, thanks to these worries and rising jet fuel prices, KAL lost money on revenues that remained steady from 1995. It was the first of three years of losses, compounded by unfavorable exchange rates. The 1996 deficit was $235.5 million and in 1997 it was $281.9 million.

A second catastrophic accident befell the company in August 1997 when Flight 801 crashed in Guam, killing 226 people. U.S. investigators implicated pilot error as the precipitating factor. KAL officials, however, blamed inadequate airport landing instruments.

In the late 1990s the devalued won had made Korea an attractive destination to Korean expatriates in the United States, and domestic travelers flew less. While its smaller rival Asiana lost a deposit on a large Airbus order, KAL coped with lessened demand by selling aircraft as new shipments of Boeings continued. The company also laid off a tenth of its upper level managers.

Aircraft production projects in the 1990s included the UH-60 Black Hawk helicopter for the Korean air force, as well as military fighter and trainer programs. The aerospace division had grown to 2,400 employees. The company also operated an extensive maintenance division, providing support for more than 30 airlines. Its catering operation served an equivalent number of carriers and garnered the International Flight Catering Association's top in-flight meal award in 1998.

Such advantages allowed KAL to again announce a profit, of 250 billion won, for 1998. The results seemed to justify the company's aircraft purchases, which let it boast one of the youngest fleets in the world, as well as sales of about 18 older aircraft in 1997. Asian and Pacific traffic was expected to account for half of all air travel by 2010, according to the International Air Transport Association. Still, a $5 billion debt guaranteed navigating the company would remain a challenge for Cho Yang Ho, who succeeded his father as president in 1992. KAL would also have to figure possible Korean unification into its plans.

Principal Subsidiaries

Air Korea Co. Ltd. (68%); Hanjin Construction Co., Ltd. (20%); Hanjin Heavy Industry Co., Ltd. (11.08%); Hanjin Information Systems and Telecommunication Co., Ltd. (99.35%); Hanjin International Corporation; Hanjin International Japan (55%); Hanjin Shipping Co., Ltd. (13.02%); Korea Air Terminal Service Co. Ltd. (11.2%); Pyunghae Mining Development Co., Ltd. (50.31%); T.O.M.I (25%); G.L.S. (27.01%); Korean French Banking Corp. (1.56%).

Principal Divisions

Aerospace; Maintenance; Air Cargo; Passenger.

Further Reading

"Aircraft Deals Lift Korean Air Profit," *South China Morning Post,* February 23, 1999.
"Korean Air," *Airline World,* March 27, 1989.
"Korean Air Seeing Red," *Business Korea,* September 1997, p. 63.
Korean Air Service Guide, Seoul, South Korea: Korean Air, 1990.
Mackey, Michael, "Pall Over Asia," *Air Transport World,* September 1998, pp. 30–38.
——, "The 'Reluctant Dragon'," *Air Transport World,* April 1996, pp. 43–47.
——, "Unification Watch," *Air Transport World,* August 1994, pp. 87–88.
Mecham, Michael, " 'Instant Success' Fuels Korean Air Expansion," *Aviation Week and Space Technology,* November 27, 1995, pp. 28–30.
Nelms, Douglas W., "Make, Manage and Maintain," *Air Transport World,* August 1997, pp. 97–98.
"On a Won and a Prayer," *Economist,* November 15, 1997, p. 69.
Ortiz, Elizabeth, "Next Destination: Seoul," *Business Korea,* September 1996, p. 59.
Proctor, Paul, "KAL Growth to Soar with New Seoul Airport," *Aviation Week and Space Technology,* June 9, 1997, pp. 36–38.
"The Skies in 1992," *Airline Business,* 1992.
Vandyk, Anthony, "Korean: Still Riding the Tiger," *Air Transport World,* June 1993, p. 204.
Weinberg, Neil, "The Benefits of Having a Rich Neighbor," *Forbes,* December 30, 1996, pp. 43–44.
The World of Korean Air, Seoul, South Korea: Korean Air, 1990.

—Dylan Tanner
—updated by Frederick C. Ingram

Krause's Furniture, Inc.

200 North Berry Street
Brea, California 92821-3903
U.S.A.
(714) 990-3100
Fax: (714) 990-3561
Web site: http://www.krauses-castro.com

Public Company
Incorporated: 1973 as The Sofa Factory
Employees: 1,006
Sales: $115.2 million (1997)
Stock Exchanges: American
Ticker Symbol: KFI
SICs: 2512 Wood Household Furniture, Upholstered;
    2519 Household Furniture, Not Elsewhere Classified;
    5712 Furniture Stores

Krause's Furniture, Inc. is a vertically integrated manufacturer and retailer of custom-crafted upholstered furniture, including sofas, sofa beds, chairs, sectionals, incliners, and recliners, and accessories purchased from other suppliers, including occasional tables and chairs, area rugs, lamps, and fashion accessories. In January 1998 it was operating 83 showrooms in 12 states under the names Krause's and Castro Convertibles. It was the nation's largest manufacturer/retailer of made-to-order furniture.

Custom Sofas: 1973–90

Krause's Sofa Factory (originally incorporated as The Sofa Factory) was founded in San Diego or La Mesa, California, a suburb, in 1973 by Kalman and Bernelle Krause. At first they built, sold, and delivered each of their sofas themselves. As the business grew they established a factory in Brea, California. The Krauses believed that prospective customers should be able to walk into a company showroom and pick out a sofa style and fabric tailor-made for them. By 1986, when they sold the company (renamed Krause's Sofa Factory in 1984) for $30 million, there were 56 Krause's showrooms. The buyers were Ayse Kenmore and her husband, Robert, who took a 54 percent stake, and Michael Gibbons.

Krause's Sofa Factory had sales of $103 million in 1989, making it the largest factory-direct sofa manufacturer in the United States and the 17th largest furniture maker in the nation. It also believed itself to be the largest combined retailer and manufacturer of custom upholstered furniture in the United States. Its retail showrooms in 1990 averaged between 17,000 and 20,000 square feet in size to accommodate a representative sampling of 100 different sofa styles, each of which was available in 50 sizes and 1,000 fabrics or leathers. In all, the company was offering eight million combinations of custom-made sofas, love seats, and chairs.

These were not the same offerings as in the past, for Ayse Kenmore, a former *Vogue* and *Mademoiselle* staffer, had eliminated the industrial woven fabrics and box-sofa styles of Krause's early years in favor of broad stripes, delicate floral patterns, and even goose down and leather pillows for sofas ranging in price from $500 to more than $1,000. "She has a very clear idea of where she wants to take Krause's, which is toward upscale affordability," said a supervisor at Basso & Associates, which handled Krause's advertising, in a 1990 article in the *Orange County Business Journal.*

Krause's Sofa Factory expanded out of California for the first time in 1990, when it opened two showrooms and a distribution center in Houston. By May 1991 there were 67 showrooms, of which 46 were in California and 21 in six other western states. About 75 percent of its products were being manufactured at its leased 250,000-square-foot plant in Brea. The company, however, was not doing well, incurring a net loss of $2.6 million in fiscal 1990 (the year ended September 30, 1990), on sales volume that had slipped to about $86.6 million.

Mired in Red Ink: 1991–96

In April 1991 a subsidiary of Worth Corp., Keegan Management Co. (a subsidiary of KMC Enterprises, Inc.), purchased 62 percent of the outstanding common stock of Krause's Sofa Factory for $6.14 million. (Worth was one-third owned by Worms & Co., the U.S. unit of a French investment firm.) Other investors also purchased common stock that resulted in total net new equity of about $5 million for Krause's. Gibbons, now the largest individual shareholder, remained president and chief executive officer of the firm.

With this cash in hand, Krause's Sofa Factory began picking up other furniture stores struggling to survive in recession-struck California. By the end of 1991 the company had taken over two former RB Furniture stores, in Seattle and near Mesa, Arizona. Earlier, it had occupied three former Furnishings 2000 locations in southern California. Krause's also expanded its product line, adding more leather at the high end of the market ($1,400 to $1,999) while also introducing $399 promotional made-to-order sofas for the first time since the 1970s. The company lost money again in fiscal 1991, but Gibbons said the figure was only about $1 million, less than the deficit in the previous fiscal year. Later, however, the 1991 loss was put at $6.7 million on revenues of $89 million. Still heavily exposed to the struggling California economy, Krause's lost $3.4 million in calendar 1992 on revenues of $87 million.

Krause's Sofa Factory had long been planning an entry into the Midwest, and in December 1992 Gibbons said the company would enter the Chicago metropolitan area during the following year. After that, he vowed, it would fix its sights on the East Coast. The company's five-year goal, Gibbons added, was 250 units nationwide. Krause's California factory/warehouse complex had been expanded in 1990 to support up to 115 showrooms. After the Chicago stores were in place, Gibbons said, the company would assess its production needs and likely would expand or add facilities to support growth.

Krause's Sofa Factory's move to the East Coast came sooner than expected. In May 1993 the company acquired Castro Convertible Corp., a privately held firm with 18 showrooms in the tristate metropolitan New York City area and Florida and annual sales of about $20 million. The business was founded by Bernard Castro, a Sicilian immigrant who began reupholstering sofas in New York City in 1931. He was an early pioneer in developing the trifold mechanism for sliding a bed frame and mattress out of a sofa that found a ready market among apartment dwellers with limited space.

Like Krause's, Castro Convertibles offered a variety of frames and covers that customers could mix and match. At one point the company had two factories producing 100 designs and selling sofas out of 48 showrooms in 12 states, but business shifted to lower-priced makers. Although Castro's showrooms and retail employees were retained, the remaining factory, at New Hyde Park, Long Island, was closed, with production assumed at Krause's Brea plant. The acquisition raised the number of company showrooms to 87.

Worth Corp., later in 1993, purchased the remaining stock of Krause's Sofa Factory, exchanging it for its own stock in a transaction valued at $7 million to $7.5 million. Stephen Anderson then replaced Gibbons as president of the firm. At the end of the year Worth announced it had raised $12.2 million from the

sale of shares of convertible preferred stock and would use the money to finance Krause's growth and prepay some high-cost debt. When Worth sold its 18 percent share in Mr. Coffee, Inc. in 1994 for $23.2 million, more capital became available for Krause's, which was now Worth's only business. Worth renamed itself Krause's Furniture Inc. in December 1994.

Anderson concentrated his efforts on improving factory production. Like many companies, Krause's Furniture was registering a high proportion of its sales from a relatively small percentage of product. Yet production was based alphabetically by style, without considering that 20 to 30 percent of the styles were responsible for 70 percent of the volume. Anderson changed this so that high-volume items would move through the plant first. This enabled the company to trim delivery time from five weeks to four. He was also planning, in mid-1995, to cut the number of frames, or chassis, used in production from the current eight to ten to only three or four, without reducing the number of styles or fabrics used.

After incurring a record loss of $10 million on revenues of $97 million in 1993, Krause's emerged in the black the following year, earning net income of $5.8 million on record revenue of $116.5 million. This, however, was only due to $12.1 million from the Mr. Coffee sale, which was applied toward virtually eliminating the company's long-term debt of $17.7 million at the end of 1993.

Anderson's attention turned in 1996 from improving production to upgrading Krause's Furniture's stores, which in April of that year consisted of 83 company-owned showrooms and four franchised outlets. These currently averaged about 13,500 square feet, with some in the 15,000- to 20,000-square-foot range, but Anderson said the optimum size would be 7,000 to 8,000 square feet, claiming that the existing stores were displaying too wide a variety of upholstery. "We really need to show 30 or 50 [of the 100 or more] styles at the most," he said. The number of fabric offerings had been halved to about 500 by this time. Accordingly, the company had begun subleasing space in some of its large stores to complementary home furnishings retailers.

Krause's also was paying more attention to selling occasional tables, lamps, rugs, and other merchandise needed to create appealing living room vignettes. "We used to just line up sofas and accent them with some tables," Herb Friedman, senior vice-president of marketing and strategic planning, told a *Furniture Today* reporter. "What we're really trying to do now is create room environments that best show our mass customization capabilities." These accessories, obtained from outside sources, were accounting for about 10 percent of Krause's sales, but the company wanted to double the ratio to 20 percent.

Under Hawley's Management: 1996–98

Although Krause's Furniture's revenues rose to $122.3 million in fiscal 1995 (the year ended January 29, 1996), the company lost $8.7 million, and its stock sold for as little as 50 cents a share. In August 1996 Philip M. Hawley was appointed the company's new chief executive officer. He had formerly run Carter Hawley Hale Stores, a retailing giant that—renamed

Broadway Stores—was purchased by Federated Department Stores in 1995 after emerging from bankruptcy. Hawley hoped to turn the company around with a $10 million investment from GE Capital Services—half in stock and half in debt—and $4 million raised by selling new stock at $1 a share to other private investors, including Hawley himself. Another $3 million of existing debt was converted to common stock at $1 a share. GE Capital Services was a unit of GE Capital Corp., which was in turn part of General Electric Co.

One of Hawley's first moves was to replace the Krause's Furniture executives who he claimed "never walked away from the factory-outlet business." He continued the previous policy of upgrading the company's stores, announcing in August 1997 that Krause's would remodel 50 of its 80 showrooms over the next 30 months and also would open 36 new outlets. "We have always had an excellent product," Hawley declared, "but in recent years, sales have unquestionably been hurt by the dated and austere look of our stores—many of which have changed little since our company was founded." The new showrooms, based on three already completed, were to feature brighter colors and better lighting as well as displaying the sofas in living room groupings instead of arranged in rows as in a warehouse. The company was also quietly changing the name of its main retail chain from Krause's Sofa Factory to merely "Krause's," with the subtitle, "Custom Crafted Furniture."

Paying for this program presented a problem, since Krause's Furniture in early 1997 ended another fiscal year in the red—a record $13.4 million on falling revenues of $112.7 million. However, the company had lined up $7.5 million in new financing, underwritten by GE Capital Services and the Permal Group—two of the largest stockholders—plus Congress Financial Corp. This came in the form of a $3.5 million standby credit facility, a $1 million addition to an existing revolving credit line, and $3 million in long-term debt, which would be used to pay down existing revolving loans.

During fiscal 1997 (the year ended February 1, 1998), Krause's Furniture endured its seventh consecutive year of operating deficits, recording a net loss of $7.5 million on net sales of $115.2 million. Hawley pressed on, however, with the plan to remodel the stores—even accelerating it with the vow to remodel 65 by the year 2000, with the remaining 15 to close their doors and reopen in better locations. Twenty-two existing showrooms had been remodeled by the end of January 1998. In addition, Krause's intended to open 20 new stores in both 1998 and 1999 and 25 stores a year thereafter. A Castro Convertibles gallery was to be placed in all Krause's remodeled and new showrooms.

The new outlets, Hawley said, although costing about $285,000 each to open, would pay for themselves in 9 to 12 months and then contribute to positive cash flow. Many were to be in underrepresented markets such as New Mexico and Florida. By clustering stores in a few markets the company could save on advertising expenses. Hawley intended to try to put new and relocated stores right next to Krause's competitors. He explained, "We like to think if people have a choice, we'll win." The company was also trying to improve its bottom line by raising prices, cutting promotional discounts, changing the sales commission structure, and refocusing advertising efforts. In addition, it introduced 12 new sofa styles in fiscal 1997.

Some 4.4 million shares of Krause's Furniture stock (2.3 million new shares plus 2.1 million offered by Worms et Cie, the French investment firm) were sold to the public in March 1998 at $3 per share. GE Capital continued to be the main stockholder, with 30 percent of the shares at the end of April 1998. Worms still held 14 percent.

At the end of fiscal 1997 Krause's Furniture was operating 83 furniture showrooms in 12 states, 69 under the Krause's name and 14 under the Castro Convertibles name. Forty-one were in California and 13 in the New York City metropolitan area, including New York, New Jersey, and Connecticut. The other states with company showrooms were Arizona, Colorado, Florida, Illinois, Nevada, New Mexico, Texas, and Washington. Selling space in retail showrooms varied in size from 1,400 to 23,400 square feet, with an average size of 12,100 square feet.

Customers were able to choose from more than 60 styles and 40 sizes of sofas, incliners, recliners, sectionals, sofa beds, and chairs, which they could customize with 800 fabrics and 50 leathers. During the fiscal year accessories, custom-made chairs, and recliners accounted for five, eight, and seven percent, respectively, of company sales. Except for a few styles of occasional and reclining chairs that Krause's purchased from outside vendors, the company was manufacturing all of the upholstered furniture offered in its showrooms in its Brea facility. An assortment of tables, area rugs, lamps and wall decor, and nonupholstered custom-made chairs and recliners were being supplied by outside vendors. Merchandise purchased from other suppliers was accounting for about nine percent of net sales.

Principal Subsidiaries

KMC Enterprises, Inc.; Krause's Custom Crafted Furniture Corp.

Further Reading

Barron, Kelly, "Sofa So Good: Krause's Couches Move Upscale with Vogue Touch," *Orange County Business Journal*, December 10, 1990, p. 1+.

Calkins, Laurel Brubaker, "California Sofa Maker Decides to Set Up Shop in Houston," *Houston Business Journal*, October 1, 1990, p. 20.

Cutler, Ivan S., "Investment Firm Buys Krause," *Furniture Today*, May 6, 1991, pp. 1, 12.

Edmonds, Tom, "Krause's Pushes East with Castro Acquisition," *Furniture Today*, May 17, 1993, pp. 1, 32.

Engel, Clint, "Krause's Gets $17M in Cash," *Furniture Today*, September 2, 1996, pp. 1, 26.

——, "Krause's Planning First Phase of Major Store Expansion Plan," *Furniture Today*, August 25, 1997, pp. 1, 29.

——, "Krause's Realigns to Improve Efficiency," *Furniture Today*, July 3, 1995, pp. 4, 25.

——, "Krause's Seeks Partner to Speed Upgrading," *Furniture Today*, April 8, 1996, pp. 2, 94.

Fiscus, Chris, "A Game of Retail Musical Chairs," *Arizona Business Gazette*, February 14, 1992, p. 9.

Greene, Jay, "Business Legend Philip Hawley Comes out of Retirement to Update Krause's Furniture and Immediately Turn It Around," *Orange County Register*, December 7, 1997, p. K1.

Hevesi, Dennis, "Bernard Castro, an Inventor, 87; Founder of Convertible Sofa Chain," *New York Times,* August 26, 1991, p. B7.

James, Gary E., "Krause's Will Enter Metro Chicago in '93," *Furniture Today,* December 14, 1992, pp. 1, 21.

McIntosh, Jay, "Krause's Expansion Plans Include RB Furniture Units," *Furniture Today,* December 9, 1991, pp. 1, 19.

——, "Mr. Coffee Sale to Perk Up Krause's Finances by $18M," *Furniture Today,* May 30, 1994, p. 39.

——, "Worth to Gain 100% of Krause's Stock," *Furniture Today,* August 16, 1993, p. 2.

Marks, Peter, "Folding an Era: Imagine Castro-Less Convertibles," *New York Times,* June 11, 1993, p. B5.

Marsh, Barbara, "Philip Hawley: He's Back and Not Forgotten," *Los Angeles Times,* September 3, 1996, pp. D1–D2.

Veverka, Mark, "Krause's Furniture Store Revamp May Bolster Its Bid for a Comeback," *Wall Street Journal* (western edition), April 15, 1998, p. CA2.

—Robert Halasz

Lamar Advertising Company

5551 Corporate Boulevard
Baton Rouge, Louisiana 70808
U.S.A.
(225) 926-1000
Fax: (225) 923-0658
Web site: http://www.lamar.com

Public Company
Founded: 1902
Employees: 1,200
Sales: $200.5 million (1997)
Stock Exchanges: NASDAQ
Ticker Symbol: LAMR
SICs: 7312 Outdoor Advertising Services; 7311
     Advertising Agencies; 7319 Advertising, Not
     Elsewhere Classified

Lamar Advertising Company is the third largest outdoor advertising company in the United States, ranking behind Outdoor Systems, Inc. and Clear Channel Communications, Inc., both of which have more assets and larger networks than Lamar. Lamar has closed the gap with its recent acquisitions, however, and is now the nation's second largest "pure-play" outdoor advertising company. Through two of its subsidiaries—Lamar Outdoor Advertising and Lamar Transit Advertising—it manages approximately 71,000 billboards and displays on buses, bus shelters, and benches in 101 primary markets, with operations in 36 states. Through a third subsidiary, Interstate Logos, Inc., it provides 22,700 logo displays for limited access highways, including federal Interstates. These are signs that post information about food, gas, and lodging services at or near highway exits. Lamar also has secured contracts in Ontario Province, Canada, and in 18 of the 22 states that allow private contractors to fabricate the signs. It is the primary provider of such services in the United States. The company also offers graphic design and production services for its customers. In total, Lamar operates 94 outdoor advertising companies through its subsidiary network. Although its central management offices are housed in its 53,500-square-foot headquarters in downtown Baton Rouge, Louisiana, much local autonomy is allowed the managers of each of these companies, and they remain in charge of day-to-day company operations. Even though it is a public company, Lamar remains a family business under the control of third and fourth generation family members of the Lamar and Reilly families.

Early Development: 1902–58

Lamar's history goes back to 1902, when its founder, Charles Wilbur Lamar, Sr., began operating a poster-advertising concern in his spare time in Baton Rouge, Louisiana. It was a relatively new industry. Just a decade earlier, in 1891, poster makers had created the Associated Bill Posters' Association, generally credited with being the nation's first association of advertisers. At the time, posters were used to advertise on what were called billboards but were nothing like the large, steel-frame structures used today. Then they were nothing more than town and city wall spaces used to advertise businesses or, just as often, upcoming public events. They were more like modern bulletin boards, with posters stripped away or covered up after the events occurred.

It proved to be a timely venture, however, for although Lamar's business was the design and fabricating of wall displays, it placed Lamar in a position to finance expansion into a new realm of advertising just as modern technology created a need for it. Before the company's first decade of business ended, it became clear that the auto would soon replace the horse and buggy and that roads would be needed to accommodate it. By 1912, when Henry Ford introduced the Model-T, the nation had begun its durable love affair with the car. Important, too, Ford's assembly-line method of manufacturing had begun putting the automobile within reach of middle-class Americans. Lamar's response was to move into the new area of outdoor, roadside advertising.

Despite the Great Depression and the fact that its markets were in states with few paved roads, Lamar soon turned roadside advertising into its primary business. Like others in the industry, Lamar was aided by Outdoor Advertising Incorporated, an organization formed in 1931 to promote billboard sales nationwide. Charles Lamar and his two sons, Charles Jr. and L.V., slowly expanded the business, purchasing five outdoor advertising companies in Louisiana and Florida, areas where a paved road infrastructure was, like the company, rather slow to develop.

Although it was a growth industry, the billboard advertising business was a tough one. In the industry's early years, many billboards had to be hand-painted on the actual display surfaces, a tedious process. Eventually that process gave way to printing the billboard displays on sheets and assembling them at the ''plant'' (the site of the billboard). Today, most billboard advertisements are prefabricated as computer-designed and precision cut vinyl pieces with an efficiency far beyond the technology of Charles Lamar's day.

There were soon other problems, especially state and local zoning regulations that did everything from imposing permit requirements to specifying the allowed locations and size and shape of the displays. Nevertheless, the industry steadily grew, especially after World War II, when the average American family again could afford to buy an automobile. Between 1940 and 1960, the industry increased its yearly revenue from $44.7 million to more than $200 million.

New Expansion and New Directions: 1958–89

A new period of expansion for Lamar began in 1958, under the leadership of president and CEO Kevin Reilly, Sr. Over the next 15 years, Lamar purchased an additional eight companies in Florida, Alabama, and Louisiana. Growth was abetted by the fact that Florida had become a tourist and retirement mecca, and its roads were improving quickly.

Reilly also faced serious problems, however, some of which were industrywide, including growing public resistance to billboard advertising. Critics felt that the industry was cluttering the highways with eyesores, blocking out the natural beauty of the landscape. They even offered proof that billboards were dangerous distractions for drivers and caused unnecessary accidents. By the late 1950s the federal government began paying attention to the critics, adding the strong possibility of additional regulation. The rumbling prompted some important efforts by the industry to govern itself, particularly through the agency of the Outdoor Advertising Association of America and the Institute of Outdoor Advertising. But the critics prevailed. Enlisting the aid of Lady Bird Johnson, the industry's gadflies

prompted a milestone piece of legislation: the Highway Beautification Act of 1965, a law designed to limit and govern outdoor advertising along 300,000 plus miles of federal highways. The act, strongly opposed in southern oil-producing states, ended the indiscriminate erection of billboards on the right-of-ways along all federally funded roads. It was a heavy blow to the outdoor advertising industry.

Lamar only reeled with the punch, however, and, in the long haul, may have benefitted from the setback. Although the act brought unit growth of billboard displays to a virtual standstill, it forced Lamar to develop adequate contingency planning and to diversify.

In 1973 the original company and its acquired companies, totaling 13, were organized into the Lamar Corporation, a network of affiliates created to provide a central and more efficient system of accounting and management. Ten years later, Lamar gained total ownership of all of its 15 affiliated partnerships. It also acquired Creative Displays, Inc., which added another ten billboard markets to the company's total.

Additional Expansion and New Looks: 1989–99

In February of 1989 Kevin Reilly, Jr. became Lamar's president and CEO. He had first joined the company in 1978, the year after earning a B.A. from Harvard University. Until assuming the presidency, he had served as president of Lamar's Outdoor Division, starting in 1984. Under his tutelage, Lamar has greatly expanded its operations.

In 1988, just before Reilly took over the company's reins, it entered the business of fabricating interstate logo signs, winning a contract from the State of Nebraska in Reilly's initial year and eventually expanding to become the principal provider of logo signs in the United States. Thanks to the burgeoning superhighway infrastructure, the need for signs on public rights-of-way for approved franchises continued to grow, and Lamar's logo sign business, through competitive bids, won contracts from 18 states.

Through the 1990s Lamar expanded its operations into other important areas, including transit advertising and wireless communications. It began creating and maintaining advertising displays on buses, bus shelters, and commuter benches in 14 of its primary markets as well as three other states: South Carolina, Utah, and Georgia. It also has begun contractual negotiations with electronic communications providers to allow them to attach receiving and transmitting devices to its billboards on properties it owns. To date, it has made agreements with four of the principal providers of such services in the United States.

The company also went public, making an initial stock offering in August of 1996. Although Lamar is a public company, to a large degree it is still a family-owned and operated business. In fact, despite its rapid expansion, Lamar prides itself on its friendliness and the experience and loyalty of its managerial personnel. On the average, its regional managers have been with the company for 25 years. A controlling interest is owned by two families. CEO Kevin Reilly Jr. owns approximately 40 percent of the business, and Charles Lamar III and his sister, Mary Lee Lamar Dixon, great-grandchildren of the company's founder, own about 27 percent.

Lamar undertook a vigorous acquisitions program in the 1990s, despite the fact that it faced some problems. A major, industrywide setback was the steady decline in the billboard advertising of tobacco products, which had begun in 1992. Leading tobacco companies, yielding to both governmental mandates and societal pressures, began a drastic reduction in their outdoor advertising, a policy that continued over the next several years. It cut fairly deep into the billboard advertising business and left many billboards blank. Recovery was slow. It was not until 1996 that the industry, with 396,000 operating displays, came close to the 400,000 of the peak year, 1985. In 1992 tobacco advertising accounted for 12 percent of Lamar's net revenue, and although it had only dropped by three percent by 1997, Lamar was faced with the prospect that settlements in suits against the tobacco industry would lead to a total ban of outdoor advertising of tobacco products. It responded by planning the total elimination of tobacco advertising, to be completed by April 1999.

Lamar will easily weather the end of its tobacco accounts, however. Many non-tobacco advertisers have been waiting for billboard locations to free up. In any case, most of Lamar's real growth in outdoor advertising has come from its transit and logo displays, areas in which Lamar has put major efforts in the last few years. It has proved to be a fruitful strategy. In 1996 Lamar purchased FKM Advertising. In the next year its revenue increased by 61 percent over the previous year and its earnings rose by 74 percent, reaching $92.3 million.

During 1997 Lamar also continued to expand through important acquisitions. In fact, it was a year of tremendous growth, accounting for 24 of the 106 acquisitions the company made between 1983 and 1997. It increased its total number of outdoor displays by a hefty 47 percent. In April it purchased Penn Advertising, gaining close to 7,000 displays in New York and Pennsylvania, and in June it bought Headrick Outdoor, adding close to 3,200 bulletin displays and providing entry into four new states—Arkansas, Illinois, Kansas, and Missouri. It also bought McWhorter Advertising and some markets from National Advertising Company (3M), owned by Outdoor Systems, Inc., and several smaller acquisitions. These resulted in expanded markets plus a significant increase in the total number of outdoor bulletin displays operated by Lamar.

The ''accretive acquisitions'' continued in 1998. By July it had completed the purchase of an additional 24 concerns; by October it had five more. Early in the year, after purchasing Ragan Outdoor in Iowa and Illinois, Derby Outdoor in South Dakota, and Pioneer Outdoor in Missouri and Arkansas, Lamar also signed an agreement to buy Northwest Outdoor, which, in addition to adding about 4,000 displays, allowed the company entry into markets in Washington, Montana, Oregon, Idaho, Wyoming, Nebraska, Nevada, and Utah. In May it acquired two more companies: Sun Media and Odegard Outdoor Advertising, L.L.C. A major acquisition followed in October, when, for $385 million and a debt assumption of about $105 million, Lamar purchased Outdoor Communications, Inc., adding 14,700 displays in 12 southeastern states. Lamar also has plans for other acquisitions, including the assets of Imperial Outdoor of Lincoln and Omaha, Nebraska, scheduled to close in February 1999. To help finance its purchases and offset its indebtedness, Lamar has used equity sales, the last of which was completed at the end of 1998. The sale, netting $219.8 million, added 6.9 million shares, bringing Lamar's total to 61.5 million.

Lamar's future continues to look bright. Among it strategies for growth, the company plans to firm up its position as the largest logo sign operator by adding new state franchises and, possibly, new acquisitions. In an industry that is highly fragmented at best, Lamar continues to work toward consolidation of its various operations without sacrificing its local identity in the various communities served by its individual companies. It will remain a major player among the 600 companies in the outdoor advertising business, successfully competing with both rival display concerns as well as media advertisers vying for the same market share.

Principal Subsidiaries

Lamar Outdoor Advertising; Interstate Logos, Inc.; Lamar Transit Advertising; Interstate Graphics.

Further Reading

Atlas, Riva, ''Billboard Mania,'' *Forbes,* November 4, 1996, p. 371.

Beatty, Sally Goll, ''Billboard Firms Ease into Smokeless Era,'' *Wall Street Journal* (Eastern Edition), October 30, 1997, p. B6.

Brownlee, Lisa, ''Sign of the Times: Billboards IPOs Catch Eye with Oversize Gains,'' *Wall Street Journal* (Eastern Edition), September 12, 1996, p. B6.

Harrison, Joan, ''A Face Lift for a Drab Industry,'' *Mergers and Acquisitions,* May/June, 1997, pp. 46–47.

Sparks, Debra, ''Musical Billboards Are the Hottest Advertising Medium. Then Why Is the Smart Money Bailing Out?,'' *Financial World,* February 18, 1997, pp. 48–51.

—John W. Fiero

Learjet Inc.

One Learjet Way
Wichita, Kansas 67277-7707
U.S.A.
(316) 946-2000
(800) 289-5327
Fax: (316) 946-2220
Web site: http://www.learjet.com

Wholly Owned Subsidiary of Bombardier, Inc.
Incorporated: 1964 as Lear Jet Corporation
Employees: 4,975
Sales: $551 million (1998 est.)
SICs: 3721 Aircraft; 3769 Guided Missile & Space
    Vehicle Parts & Auxiliary Equipment

An innovator in aircraft technology, Learjet Inc. is one of many legacies of the 20th-century inventor and industrialist William Powell Lear. Best known for his bold effort to build the world's first private jet, Lear had a distinguished history of other inventions that are seldom acknowledged; it was the fortune from these earlier ventures that provided Lear with the capital to establish the Learjet company. Currently part of Bombardier Inc., a Canadian conglomerate which also owns several other aviation manufacturers, the company has been forced to change its independent ways and adapt to a new horizontally-integrated structure. Nevertheless, Learjet continues be a market leader in several categories of small and mid-size corporate jets.

William Powell Lear: Inventor

William Powell Lear was born in 1902 into a poor family in Hannibal, Missouri. When he was six, after his parents divorced, Lear moved to a Chicago tenement with his mother. Completing his education through the eighth grade, Lear befriended a young junk dealer and began spending much of his time tinkering with discarded electronic devices. At age 16, Lear began work as a mechanic at Chicago's Grant Park Airport. There he gained technical knowledge and skills relating to aircraft, while he acquired exposure to the business world and proper social comportment during his brief tenure as an assistant in the office of a prominent businessman.

By the age of 20, Lear was an experienced self-taught radio technician. He established a small shop in Quincy, Illinois, and set out to improve home radio sets. He succeeded in miniaturizing radio coils, eliminated the need for storage batteries, and made other modifications that are still in use today. His business became profitable, and his work soon brought him to the attention of such major manufacturers as Majestic and Motorola.

Still fascinated with flying, Lear bought a small airplane, learned to fly, and began work on an aircraft navigation radio. In 1931 he began a sales tour, demonstrating his Lear Radioaire. However, few pilots had the money to purchase such a radio during the economic hardships of the Great Depression, and fewer still saw the need for such a communication device since it was common at that time for pilots to navigate simply by following railroad lines between cities.

By 1934, Lear had exhausted his small radio fortune and was bankrupt. Depressed, but determined, he returned to his workshop and began mapping out yet another invention. This next product was the "Magic Brain," a common electronic chassis that could be used in a variety of radio set models. Lear assembled, demonstrated, and sold the idea in only two weeks, receiving a contract for $250,000 from RCA.

Next Lear returned his attention to aircraft navigation, using his second fortune to develop the Learscope Direction Finder, a radio triangulation device. These advances earned Lear an honored place in the development of aviation and won him the friendship of such prominent aviation pioneers as Amelia Earhart. More importantly, with access to the nation's leading manufacturers, Lear was able to easily market other advances, including an improved omnidirectional navigation device that could home in on any ground station, regardless of frequency.

During World War II, Lear concentrated the efforts of his company on electromechanical devices for military aircraft, including cowl controllers and auto pilot devices. After the war, Lear Incorporated pioneered all-weather flying instruments that won Lear a commendation from President Truman and an honorary degree from the University of Michigan.

1950s Venture into Business Aviation

By 1959 several airplane manufacturers began to exploit the new market for business aircraft. During this time, however, these predominantly piston-powered business airplanes were relatively slow, and Lear began to envision a smaller, quicker jet-powered craft with superior flying characteristics. He was especially impressed with a jet-powered Swiss fighter-bomber called the P-16 and began laying plans to model a passenger jet after the Swiss airplane. But with no outright demand for such a craft, Lear encountered adamant opposition from his own board of directors. If a market existed, they reasoned, some other major manufacturer would be working on it.

Determined to build the jet, Lear sold his controlling interest in his $100 million company to the Siegler Corporation (which later became Lear-Siegler). He then moved to St. Gallen, Switzerland, where he began to design a factory using Swiss machine tools, which he considered the finest in the world. During this time, Lear also worked with the French aircraft manufacturer Sud-Aviation (now Aerospatiale), AirFrance, and Lear-Siegler to develop a ''blind landing'' device for the French Caravelle jetliner.

Returning to the United States, Lear decided to locate his new company in Wichita, Kansas, home of competitors Cessna, Beech, and a major Boeing facility. There, he reasoned, he could draw upon an experienced work force and deal with banks that were familiar with aircraft manufacturing. With $10 million of his own money, plus an additional $8 million borrowed from Wichita banks, he set up a factory at Wichita Municipal Airport in January, 1963, employing a work force of 75 people.

In a bold move, Lear decided to skip the normal step of hand-building a prototype for flight testing, instead moving directly into production. Without a prototype, he risked the possibility that his designs might fail, forcing him into a costly redesign and retooling process that would surely sink his company. However, Lear reasoned that in the two years it might take to perfect a prototype, competitors would have ample time to develop similar models, and he was unwilling to invite competition. As a result, Lear had to be absolutely sure of every aspect of the Learjet's design. He considered the aircraft's P-16 heritage to be a good basis for refining the design and handling characteristics.

Exactly nine months later, on October 7, 1963, the first Learjet Model 23 rolled out of the 96,000-square foot facility for its maiden flight. Despite a later nonfatal crash of the first

model, others flew exactly as Lear envisioned they would, and sailed through FAA certification in a near record nine months. When the first Learjet was delivered on October 14, 1964, Lear had collected 72 firm orders for the new jet. This sent other companies scrambling into the market. However, it was five years before Cessna produced a jet, and even longer before companies such as Dassault could make a dent in the market. Thus, Lear's bold gamble paid off. He had, for the time being, a monopoly on the business jet market. ''In a situation like this,'' he remarked, ''you're either very right or very wrong.''

Because of its jet-fighter progenitor and a good marriage of air frame and General Electric engines, the rugged Learjet exhibited astonishing climb performance and high cruise speeds. It could transport up to six passengers in spacious comfort at up to 540 miles per hour and climb to 40,000 feet in only seven minutes. The Learjet-23 also was highly economical to operate, costing an average of only 50 cents per mile to fly.

Despite an impressive backlog of orders for the jet, the Lear Jet Corporation lacked the capital necessary to proceed with production. Having exhausted his investment—and that of the banks—Lear decided to take his company public. On November 30, 1964, Lear sold a 38 percent interest in his company to the public for $5 million. During the following year Learjet shares fluctuated between a low of $8 and a high of $89.

Other Lear Ventures of the Mid-1960s

Meanwhile, Lear continued work on several other projects, including the briefly popular 8-track audio tape system, which offered listeners the convenience of being able to play an entire tape of music without interruptions for rewinding or turning the tape over. With this invention he founded a stereo division of Learjet, based in Detroit, in 1965. Later that year he established an avionics division at Grand Rapids, where Learjet engineers designed and built aircraft electronics systems. In September 1966, to reflect its diversification, the company changed its name to Lear Jet Industries.

In the meantime, Bill Lear grew bored with his administrative duties. He pursued a variety of personal projects, including the development of a costly steam-powered bus and several profitable real estate transactions. He could, at any time, be found on the production line, in the drafting rooms, out flying or, by one account, cooking himself a hamburger in the company cafeteria.

Lear's diversity of interests and disinclination to be tied down to a desk sometimes caused him to make hasty or ill-conceived decisions. He purchased a small helicopter manufacturer that produced little more than losses, and his stereo division continued to lose millions of dollars as the 8-track tape declined in popularity.

However, the greatest weakness in Learjet Industries was the sales network. Eager to get orders for the jets, Lear hastily assembled a list of dealerships throughout the country. Many of these dealers ignored their sales boundaries and few had ever sold an airplane in the Learjet's price range. As a result, the front line sales force was fragmented, disorganized, and unprofessional. Without an effective marketing program, even the profitable Learjet could no longer stem the wider losses. That year, the company lost $12 million on sales of only $27.5 million.

1967: Lear Partners with Gates

Once again starved for capital, Lear sought an able, deep-pocketed partner. Early in 1967 he began negotiations with Charles C. Gates, president of the Denver-based Gates Rubber Company. At the time, Gates was attempting to diversify into aircraft properties. He had just acquired two large retail aircraft service companies, Combs Aircraft in Denver and the Roscoe Turner Aeronautical Corporation in Indianapolis, renaming them the Gates Aviation Corporation.

Meanwhile, Lear had upgraded the Model 23 to include a stronger windshield and engine fire suppression and a new pressurization system. The Model 24, as it was called, also allowed 500 additional pounds of take off weight. However, the cost of developing and certifying these improvements were costly, and Learjet continued to experience financial difficulties. Fortunately, Gates agreed to purchase Lear's 62 percent share of the company on April 10, 1967, only a few weeks before a potentially disastrous annual meeting.

Lear remained as chairperson of the newly formed Gates Learjet company until April 2, 1969. During that time, Gates Rubber pumped $16 million into the failing subsidiary, helping to launch a new eight-passenger Model 25. Gates Learjet lost $4.6 million on $34.6 million in sales in 1968, but a year later turned a $2 million profit on $58 million in sales. Gates's vision of a synergistic manufacturing and service organization began to take shape. In 1969 Gates merged his Gates Aviation Corporation services companies with Learjet to form a single operation that included manufacturing, sales, and maintenance. With the addition of another service facility in Palm Springs, California, and four more sales offices, Gates established an effective sales organization to replace the earlier hodgepodge dealer network.

The 1970s: Streamlining The Company

In October 1970, unable to properly manage both Gates Rubber and Learjet, Gates asked G.H.B. Gould, head of Learjet's marketing department, to lead the aircraft company. Gould was killed in a car crash only six months later and was succeeded by Harry Combs, who had joined Gates Rubber after his own company, Combs Aircraft, was acquired by Gates.

In May 1971, Combs oversaw the reorganization earlier proposed by Gould of the Learjet properties. The troubled stereo division was absorbed by Gates Rubber, leaving three aircraft properties: Learjet manufacturing, Combs-Gates sales and service, and the Jet Electronics and Technology (JET) avionics operation. In addition, the Lear helicopter business was closed, and a training agreement was established with Flight Safety International—the pioneer simulator-training firm—to help pilots avoid errors that had resulted in a number of crashes in early-model Learjets.

Under Combs's leadership, Gates Learjet became even more viable, marking a $6.9 million profit on $115.4 million in sales in 1975. Profit nearly doubled the following year, but fell to $9.3 million in 1977. This dip was mainly attributable to devel-

opment costs for a new "Longhorn" series of Learjets featuring a new wing design and construction of a $3 million, 75,000-square foot manufacturing facility at Tucson, Arizona.

Like Wichita, Tucson had become an aircraft Mecca during World War II, when manufacturing operations were expanded to meet the demand of local air force bases. The location offered its own pool of experienced aerospace workers, and provided Gates Learjet with a specialized facility. The Wichita factory produced a number of unpainted Learjets that were flown to Tucson where they were painted and their interiors were finished. This eliminated a troublesome bottleneck in Wichita that slowed output.

During those years, Gates Learjet developed several new aircraft, including the fanjet-powered Models 35 and 36, and Century III series, which featured improved "Softflite" wing leading edges. In April, 1977 the Models 24 and 25 were certified to fly at 51,000 feet, well above weather and all but military air traffic. The Longhorn Models 28 and 29 featured longer wings and vertical wingtip fences known as winglets that improved lift and maneuverability. These new models were the first Learjets without wing tanks.

Bill Lear, who founded two large companies, received 150 patents, and was instrumental in the development of modern avionics and business jets, died of leukemia in a Reno, Nevada, hospital on May 14, 1978. Although no longer associated with Lear-Siegler or Gates Learjet, his name remained with both companies, and his innovations continued to be in wide use in the aviation industry. Bill Lear's last business aircraft venture continued after his death. The all-composite Lear Fan, which he had conceived several years earlier, flew in 1980.

After Harry Combs was promoted into Learjet's parent company, Gates appointed Bermar "Bib" Stillwell to head the aircraft company. In the months that followed, Gates Learjet added five new service facilities overseas and purchased the Connecticut-based Air-Kaman service company.

Stillwell retired in 1985 and was succeeded by James B. Taylor, who took the helm of Gates Learjet at a time when "bizjet" sales had fallen so much that Learjet had to temporarily halt production. To reduce costs, Taylor laid off employees, and to raise cash, he sold the company's Jet Electronics & Technology division to BF Goodrich.

1987: Purchase by Integrated Acquisition

In August 1987 Gates received an offer for its 64.8 percent share of Learjet from Integrated Acquisition, a New York-based financial group. Eager to cut its losses, Gates agreed to part with its Learjet shares for nearly $57 million.

Integrated Acquisition initially retained Taylor as head of the company. However, in January 1988, after buying up all outstanding shares in Learjet, the partners fired Taylor in favor of Beverly (Bev) Lancaster, head of the company's growing aerospace division. The company subsequently dropped Gates from its name and sold its Combs Gates service operations to AMR, the parent of American Airlines.

During the 1980s, Learjet had been named as a major subcontractor to numerous defense, aerospace, and commercial aviation projects headed by Boeing, Martin Marietta, LTV, Textron, General Dynamics, and McDonnell Douglas. These projects included work on F-5, F-111, F-15 and F-16 fighter jets, B-1B bombers, KC-135 tankers, and later the Space Shuttle. All of this work was conducted in Wichita, which was a significant factor in much of the Learjet production being transferred to Tucson.

The company also discovered an important new market in military sales. Special versions of the Learjet 35 and 36 were built for the Brazilian, Thai, Japanese, Finnish, and Mexican military forces. The largest military order for Learjets came from the United States Air Force, which ordered more than 80 Model 35s, designated C-21As. Learjet also won a contract to service this fleet and created the Gates Learjet Aircraft Services Corporation (Glasco) for that purpose.

Despite a recovery in jet sales, Integrated Resources was saddled with repayment obligations on $2 billion in debt that it could no longer meet. Learjet was profitable but unable to secure loans because of its parent company's poor condition. Nevertheless, in 1989 Learjet succeeded in acquiring the thrust reverser business of the Aeronea company, which it transferred from Middletown, Ohio, to Wichita. The addition of these devices to Learjet aircraft substantially reduced landing distances, enabling it the use of shorter runways.

1990: Bombardier Steps In

By 1990 Integrated had fallen under Chapter 11 bankruptcy protection. Several new acquisitors expressed interest in purchasing Learjet, including Chrysler's Gulfstream Aerospace unit, British Aerospace, and Toyota Motor Sales. During this crisis, Brian Barents, a former marketing vice-president at Cessna and Toyota, was appointed president of Learjet. Within months he had negotiated Learjet's rescue by the Canadian manufacturing conglomerate Bombardier.

Bombardier gained fame during the 1960s as the manufacturer of Ski-Doo snowmobiles. With the passing of the snowmobile fad, the company expanded into the mass-transit railcar industry, buying out troubled manufacturers such as Pullman-Peabody, Budd, and UTDC. In 1986 Bombardier took over the loss-ridden aircraft company Canadair (at the time owned by the Canadian government) and expanded its presence in the aerospace market in 1989 by acquiring Belfast-based Short Brothers Aviation. The company bid for Learjet only one year later and in early 1992 purchased DeHavilland Canada from Boeing.

Bombardier took control of Learjet on April 9, 1990, paying $75 million and assuming $38 million of debt. The acquisition was favorably received. Learjet, with great manufacturing capacity and a strong customer base, could benefit from the stability provided by a financially strong parent company and manufacturing and marketing synergies with other Bombardier aerospace companies. Bombardier had assembled a product line ranging from light business jets to large commuter aircraft.

Like other Bombardier subsidiaries, Learjet remained an autonomous, independently managed unit. It occupied an important position in the company's product line, manufacturing jets for markets independent of those of its sister companies. Learjet's smaller models of aircraft provided a strong complement to the larger Canadair Challenger—which Bill Lear had also helped to develop. Within the first three years of its purchase by Bombardier, Learjet experienced dramatic growth, doubling its number of employees and expanding its manufacturing capacity. Bombardier also moved the testing of all its subsidiaries' jets to Wichita. In late 1992 the Model 60, an eight to ten passenger mid-size jet with a range of nearly 2,500 miles, was introduced. Sales were good, and 1993 was the company's best year ever, with delivery of over 40 airplanes.

However, Learjet's corporate culture was undergoing changes during this time, which caused problems. The company had been so vertically integrated that, as a former executive told *Business and Commercial Aviation* magazine, "Learjet [was] used to pushing in aluminum at one end [of the plant] and pulling airplanes out the other." As competition heated up, and the cost of development and manufacturing increased, plane building became a cooperative venture involving different subsidiaries of Bombardier. Within several years Learjet fuselages were being manufactured by Short Brothers in Ireland, wings were assembled by DeHavilland in Canada, and only final assembly occurred in Wichita. Morale among both workers and top management began to slip as these changes took place.

In September 1992 the company announced plans for its first plane in 30 years to be a "clean sheet" design—one which was not a variation on an existing aircraft. The new plane was expected to offer mid-size comfort and features in a lighter jet, one that carried six to eight passengers. The new Model 45, like the original Model 23, was slated to make it to market in an astoundingly short period of time, in this case about three-and-a-half years from the inception of the design process. However, a number of technical problems and a much-delayed FAA flight certification (partially caused by new, more rigorous standards adopted by that agency) resulted in a delay of over two years. During this time Learjet was still selling its other models of aircraft and doing relatively well, but the delay in launching the Model 45 further damaged morale, creating a "pressure cooker" environment for designers and executives at the company. Between 1996 and 1999 the company was overseen by four different presidents.

When the Model 45 was finally ready, its price had risen to nearly $8 million from the announced ceiling of $6 million. Delivery of initial orders was delayed by problems with early production aircraft, which required modifications to several systems, including the de-icing equipment. Despite the long, frustrating development process, the end result received rave reviews for its design and performance, and orders for nearly 150 aircraft came in. As Learjet struggled to adapt to its new identity as a part of Bombardier, it appeared that it would be a significantly different kind of company from that which William Powell Lear had founded in 1964, but one which could still create jet airplanes that stood out from the pack.

Further Reading

"Brian Barents Departing Learjet, Jim Robinson Named President in Unexpected Management Changes at Bombardier Unit," *Weekly of Business Aviation,* January 29, 1996, p. 41.

Christy, Joe, *The Learjet,* Tab Books, 1979.

"Development of the Learjet Model 23," *American Aviation Historical Society,* Fall 1989.

Dinell, David, "Bombardier Execs Predict More Learjet Growth Ahead," *Wichita Business Journal,* June 19, 1998, p. 3.

Dinell, David, "New President at Learjet Inc. Seeks Stability," *Wichita Business Journal,* August 9, 1996.

"Gates Agrees to Sell its Learjet Stake For a Third Time," *Wall Street Journal,* March 11, 1987, p. 30.

"Gates Learjet Halts Civilian Production Line," *Aviation Week Space Technology,* September 24, 1984, p. 26.

"Gates Learjet Postpones Consolidation," *American New Market,* December 31, 1984, p. 32.

George, Fred, "Learjet 45 Home Stretch: The Final Spring Toward Certification," *Business and Commercial Aviation,* September 1, 1997, p. 67.

——, "Learjet 45: Learjet is Making Good on its Promises for this Clean-Sheet Design," *Business and Commercial Aviation,* November 1, 1996, p. 66.

"Lear Jet Again Seeking Potential Suitors," *New York Times,* December 2, 1989, p. 35.

"Learjet Launch to Bridge the Gap," *Flight International,* September 18, 1990, p. 20.

Learjet Milestones, Wichita, Kan.: Learjet, Inc., 1997.

"Lear 60 Deliveries to Begin in January," *Flight International,* May 19, 1992, p. 16.

"Let's Make a Deal," *Forbes,* April 27, 1992, pp. 62–64.

"New Life for Learjet," *Business and Commercial Aviation,* July 1990, pp. 41–44.

Serling, Robert J., *One Grand Story,* company document, Wichita, Kan.: Learjet Inc.

William Powell Lear, Sr., company document, Wichita, Kan.: Learjet Inc.

—John Simley
—updated by Frank Uhle

Lifetime Hoan Corporation

One Merrick Avenue
Westbury, New York 11590
U.S.A.
(516) 683-6000
Fax: (516) 683-6116
Web site: http://www.lifetime.hoan.com

Public Company
Incorporated: 1945 as Lifetime Cutlery Corporation
Employees: 527
Sales: $100.02 million (1997)
Stock Exchanges: NASDAQ
Ticker Symbol: LCUT
SICs: 3421 Cutlery; 3429 Hardware, Not Elsewhere
Classified; 3914 Silverware, Plated Ware & Stainless
Steel Ware

Lifetime Hoan Corporation designs, markets, and distributes household cutlery, kitchenware, cutting boards, and bakeware under both owned and licensed brands. Among the trademarks the company owns are Hoffritz, Tristar, Old Homestead, Hoan, Roshco, Baker's Advantage, and Smart Choice; licensed brands include Farberware, Revere, and various brands under license from The Pillsbury Company (for example, the Pillsbury Doughboy, Green Giant) and Walt Disney Company, Inc. (for example, Mickey Unlimited and Mickey Stuff for Kids). Each year, Lifetime's 12-person design department creates in excess of 300 new products, ranging from entry-level items through the mid-priced sector and to the upscale. The company farms out production to about 45 contract manufacturers located primarily in east Asia, with final assembly and packaging completed in a company-owned factory in New Jersey. Marketing is handled through both the company's own sales force as well as a network of independent sales representatives. Lifetime includes among its customers about 1,800 national retailers, department store chains, mass merchant retail and discount stores, supermarket chains, warehouse clubs, direct marketing companies, specialty chains, and other channels. Its largest customer is the Wal-Mart Stores, Inc. chain, which accounts for about 17 percent of net sales. Through its Outlet Retail Stores, Inc. subsidiary, Lifetime Hoan also owns and operates about 50 Farberware outlet stores located in 25 states.

Cutlery Beginnings

The founder of Lifetime Hoan—and the chairman, CEO, and president of the company into the late 1990s—was Milton Cohen, born in 1929, the son of a garment worker. Following high school, Cohen began working as a scissors and shears salesman. He eventually gained a position, at age 26, managing sales on the east coast for a large cutlery firm.

Wanting to be his own boss, Cohen joined in 1957 with partner Sam Siegel to start a knife factory in Brooklyn under the name Reo Products. In 1960 Reo Products acquired 1945-founded Lifetime Cutlery Corporation, a larger distributor of knives than Reo. Cohen adopted Lifetime's name for his company.

Cohen, in a 1995 interview with the *New York Times*, estimated that there were about 100 cutlery manufacturers in the United States in the late 1950s, but that their numbers dwindled over the decades to three. Most of the companies failed because of increasing imports of cheap goods from Asia. A key to his company's survival, Cohen had concluded, was the 1961 decision to shift manufacturing overseas. That year the company began contracting with manufacturers in Japan for the production of parts. The parts were then shipped to the Brooklyn factory for assembly and packing. Freed from the production of basic parts, Cohen and Siegel could concentrate on design, packaging, and marketing. Over the years, Lifetime Cutlery shifted its production from one east Asian country to the next, progressing to Korea, Taiwan, the Philippines, Malaysia, Indonesia, Thailand, and China.

Between 1965 and 1967 Lifetime sold 50 million steak knives to Shell Oil for ten cents each. Shell gave one of the ivory-plastic-handled knives out to each customer coming in for a fill-up. Cohen told *Business Week* in 1994, "It was a lot of business and just a lot of hard work and no profit."

By staying away from such risky gimmicks and especially through relentless marketing, Cohen, Siegel, and a third partner increased sales by 1980 to $13 million. Within a year, however, both of Cohen's partners died. Needing cash for himself and to provide for his partners' families, Cohen—in collaboration with his former partners' sons, Jeffrey Siegel and Craig Phillips—executed a $16 million leveraged buyout (LBO) of the company in April 1984. Siegel and Phillips became executives at Lifetime, remaining in executive positions and on the board of directors into the late 1990s.

Acquired Hoan Products in the Mid-1980s

Cohen and his new partners acquired a controlling interest in Hoan Products Ltd. in 1986; they soon owned the company outright, through a total investment of $4 million. Hoan Products was an unprofitable supplier of kitchen tools and gadgets generating annual sales of $14 million. Lifetime Cutlery became Lifetime Hoan Corporation following the takeover.

Still headquartered in low-cost Brooklyn, Lifetime Hoan moved the Hoan operation there, selling its New Jersey headquarters for $5 million. Other changes included redesigning the Hoan line, cutting the costs of manufacturing Hoan products, and selling them through Lifetime's established channels. The last of these maneuvers was particularly strategic as both Lifetime cutlery and Hoan kitchenware were positioned in the entry-level and middle-market sectors, selling well in supermarkets, mass merchandisers, and specialty shops. By the early 1990s half of the company's sales came from the Hoan line.

In 1987 Lifetime Hoan moved its manufacturing operation to Dayton, New Jersey, maintaining its headquarters in Brooklyn. That same year the company entered into its first licensing agreement. In a deal with Walt Disney Company, Lifetime obtained the right to develop and market a line of Disney flatware and a line of kitchen gadgets under the Chef Mickey name. After some ups and downs, the two companies settled on profitable lines of children's housewares featuring Mickey and Minnie Mouse on such items as bag clips, party goods, bottle stoppers, and flatware.

Farberware and Pillsbury Licenses Marked Early 1990s

Revenues reached $38.5 million by 1989, while net income stood at $800,000. At this time Lifetime Hoan's cutlery lines, which included the Tristar and Old Homestead brands, remained on the lower end of the market. The company made its first move up the scale in early 1990 when it entered into a license agreement with Farberware, Inc. to market cutlery, kitchen gadgets, and barbecue accessories under the well-known and respected Farberware name. Founded in 1900, Farberware made its reputation with the stainless steel cookware it introduced soon after the end of World War II and the beginnings of the postwar boom years. In 1966 Farberware was acquired by Walter Kidde & Co., which sold the company to British conglomerate Hanson PLC in 1987. Under Hanson, Farberware began broadening the range of products bearing the famous brand, with the agreement with Lifetime Hoan a notable part of that trend. The Lifetime-created Farberware products were mid-priced and aimed at department stores and specialty shops, a retail sector already well acquainted with the Farberware name. This strategy enhanced both the probability that stores would stock the items and that consumers would buy them.

A similar licensing deal involving the leveraging of a familiar brand was reached in April 1991, this time with Pillsbury for a line of moderately priced bakeware and kitchen accessories. Launched in mid-1992, the line eventually included items such as nonstick cookie sheets and pie pans, spatulas, whisks, and cookie cutters featuring the Pillsbury Doughboy logo, as well as accessories such as peelers, can openers, kitchen hooks, and steamers incorporating the Green Giant character. These products were aimed at the supermarket channel, where the Pillsbury brands were long established.

In June 1991 Lifetime Hoan sold 40 percent of the company to the public in an initial public offering (IPO) that raised $19.4 million. Portions of the proceeds were used to virtually eliminate Lifetime's outstanding debt (some stemming from the 1984 LBO) and to redeem all outstanding preferred stock, leaving about $7.7 million in working capital. The offering not only strengthened the company's balance sheet, it also positioned Lifetime to grow through continued aggressive new product development and through acquisition. In addition, the offering provided some liquidity for Cohen and the second generation Siegel and Phillips shareholders, a lesson Cohen learned from the surprise deaths of his original partners. As of 1993, Cohen and his family held a 24 percent stake in Lifetime Hoan, while the Siegel and Phillips families held another 27 percent.

The company launched a new brand, Smart Choice, in 1993. This was a line of gadgets, packaged as impulse purchases and geared strictly for supermarkets, drug store chains, and mass merchandisers. Smart Choice helped fuel a new product blitz whereby Lifetime introduced 500 new items in 1994, compared with 150 the previous year. By 1994 the company offered about 3,000 different products.

Sales reached $77.4 million in 1994, nearly double the figure of 1989. Profits stood at $8.6 million, which translated into a profit margin of 11.1 percent, quite impressive for a maker of mainly low-priced housewares. The Farberware license was responsible for much of the increase in both sales and profits, as the Farberware line accounted for more than a quarter of overall sales and an even larger portion of profits. The decision to sell more higher priced products (a Farberware set of knives might be priced three times higher than a similar set under one of Lifetime's other brands) was clearly beginning to pay dividends. The company's shareholders benefited thereby from a 3-for-2 stock split in late 1993.

Lifetime Hoan moved its headquarters to Westbury, New York (on Long Island), in October 1994. The company had outgrown its space in Brooklyn, but also found difficulty in attracting employees there. Of particular importance was hiring new computer-literate designers since the design department was being expanded and computerized during this period. The move to Long Island enabled Lifetime to bring in the highly skilled people it needed and to improve its productivity. The company paid $5 million for a 40,000-square-foot building, used as headquarters and for a showroom for visiting buyers. Previously, because many buyers were reluctant to venture into Brooklyn, Lifetime had had to maintain a showroom in expensive Manhattan, where high rents limited its size. At this new building, the company had a huge showroom, with the added benefit of being able to show buyers both the showroom and Lifetime's high-tech design shop at the same time. Meantime, Lifetime continued to contract out its manufacturing to its Asian partners, with final assembly and packaging handled at its New Jersey factory.

Made Hoffritz and Farberware Deals in the Mid-1990s

The middle to late 1990s saw an ever more aggressive Lifetime Hoan complete a series of acquisitions and enter into new licensing and partnership deals. Having established itself as a leader in the entry-level and mid-priced segments of the housewares market, Hoan sought to enter the high-end market. To do so, it decided to acquire an instantly recognizable brand, rather than license one. After a two-year search, Lifetime settled upon the upscale 60-year-old Hoffritz brand, acquiring it in September 1995 from Alco Capital Group, Inc., an investment firm that had purchased Hoffritz in late 1992 from the bankrupt C.W. Acquisitions. At one time, there had been 197 Hoffritz stores selling upscale cutlery and kitchenware, but by the time Lifetime acquired the brand there were only six (and these were closed shortly thereafter).

Lifetime launched a new line of Hoffritz products in the spring of 1996, a line that within a few years exceeded 300 items. It featured knives, scissors, and shears; kitchenware, including spatulas, ladles, peelers, ice cream scoops, lemon zesters, serving spoons, graters, thermometers, and colanders; barbecue accessories; cutting boards; pepper grinders; bar accessories; and personal care implements, such as nail files and clippers, tweezers, manicure sets, and pocket knives. Lifetime marketed Hoffritz products in department and specialty stores through a ''shop within a store'' concept.

In 1995 Hanson spun off Farberware and 33 of its other smaller U.S. subsidiaries, forming U.S. Industries Inc. The new company soon began shopping Farberware around, having designated it a noncore asset. In April 1996 Lifetime Hoan joined with Syratech Corporation, an East Boston-based maker of tabletop and giftware products, to acquire most of the assets of Farberware for a total of about $52 million, $12.7 million of which was paid by Lifetime in cash. Syratech gained Farberware's cookware and small electrical appliances business. Lifetime and Syratech simultaneously entered into a 50-50 joint venture that gained outright ownership of the rights to the Farberware trademarks. Through this joint venture, Lifetime acquired a 200-year, royalty-free, exclusive right to the Farberware name in connection with the cutlery, kitchen gadgets, and barbecue accessories covered by the 1990 licensing agreement; in essence Lifetime thereby owned the trademark for these product categories. The company also acquired 50 Farberware outlet stores. In July 1997 Lifetime struck a deal with Meyer Corporation, the licensed manufacturer of Farberware cookware, in connection with these stores. Lifetime would continue to own and operate the stores, while Meyer and Lifetime would be jointly responsible for merchandising and stocking them, with Meyer handling the cookware and Lifetime the rest of the stock. Meyer would receive all revenue from sale of the cookware and reimburse Lifetime for 62.5 percent of the stores' operating expenses. Through this arrangement, the stores returned to profitability.

In April 1997 the company entered into a long-term agreement with the Microban Products Company to incorporate Microban antibacterial protection into cutting boards, kitchenware, and cutlery. The Microban technology acted to inhibit the growth of common kitchen bacteria, as well as molds, fungus, and mildew. In September 1997 Farberware cutting boards and such kitchen items as pastry and sink brushes, all with Microban protection, made their debut. The following month Lifetime Hoan announced that it had initiated payment of cash dividends on its stock, starting with the third quarter of 1997, a move reflecting a company confident of its long-term prospects.

Not resting on its laurels, Lifetime in August 1998 acquired Roshco, Inc., a Chicago-based, privately held distributor of better-quality bakeware under the Roshco and Baker's Advantage brands. The addition of Roshco, which had revenues of $10 million in 1997, not only extended the company further into the bakeware sector, it also added to the already strong array of higher-end products Lifetime could aim at department and specialty stores. In late 1998 Lifetime achieved similar aims through the signing of a license agreement with Corning Consumer Products Company for the design and marketing of cutlery and cutting boards under the well-known Revere brand. The first products from this line were introduced in early 1999.

Over the course of the 1990s Lifetime Hoan made a dramatic transition from a marketer of lower-end, lesser-known trademarks to that of higher-end, better-known brands. Farberware and Hoffritz quickly became Lifetime's most important brands, with these lines accounting for about 60 percent of overall sales in 1996, 70 percent in 1997, and 75 percent in 1998. The addition of the Roshco and Revere brands to the company stable were logical extensions of the same strategy. In the early 21st century Lifetime Hoan was likely to continue to seek out complementary acquisitions to fuel growth; its balance sheet was solid enough to fund such purchases easily. The company also seemed certain to leverage the highly desirable brands it now owned outright (or through the partnership with Syratech) by serving increasingly as a licenser.

Principal Subsidiaries

Outlet Retail Stores, Inc.

Further Reading

Bernstein, James, ''Lifetime Hoan Pays $41M in Farberware Acquisition,'' *Newsday,* February 6, 1996, p. A33.

Byrne, Harlan S., ''Cutting Edge,'' *Barron's,* February 6, 1995, p. 16.

Gault, Ylonda, ''Purchase of Hoffritz a Deal of a Lifetime,'' *Crain's New York Business,* October 2, 1995, p. 27.

Hill, Dawn, ''Hoan Adds Hoffritz,'' *HFD—The Weekly Home Furnishings Newspaper,* September 25, 1995, pp. 47+.

——, "The Next Frontier: Lifetime Hoan Heads for the High End," *HFD—The Weekly Home Furnishings Newspaper,* July 31, 1995, pp. 27+.

Konig, Susan, "Why One Business Planted Its Headquarters in Westbury," *New York Times,* January 8, 1995, Sec. 13, Long Island Weekly, p. 2.

Meeks, Fleming, " 'I Work Too Damn Hard To Do It for Nothing'," *Forbes,* April 11, 1994, pp. 124–25.

Sinisi, John, "Doughboy's $10M License To Bake," *Brandweek,* September 28, 1992, p. 7.

Weiss, Lisa Carey, "Chance of a Lifetime: Lifetime Hoan Corp. Targets New Opportunities in Cutlery, Gadgets in Expansion Plans," *HFD—The Weekly Home Furnishings Newspaper,* December 23, 1991, pp. 43+.

—David E. Salamie

Lucky

Lucky Stores, Inc.

Northern California Division
1701 Marina Boulevard
San Leandro, California 94577-4202
U.S.A.
(510) 678-4200
Web site: http://www.luckystores.com

Southern California Division
6565 Knott Avenue
Buena Park, California 90620
U.S.A.
(714) 739-2200
Web site: http://www.luckystores.com

Wholly Owned Subsidiary of American Stores Company
Incorporated: 1931 as Peninsula Stores, Ltd.
Employees: 121,000 (American Stores Co.)
Sales: $19.13 million (American Stores Co. 1998)
SICs: 5411 Grocery Stores

Lucky Stores, Inc. is a wholly owned subsidiary of American Stores Company, one of the largest food and drug retailers in the United States. American Stores is now a division of Albertson's, the number two ranked company among all U.S. food and drug retail companies. Lucky Stores, which continues to operate as Lucky (grocery stores) and Lucky/Sav-on (grocery/drug store combinations), is composed of two separate divisions: one in northern California, and one in southern California. Each division has its own management team.

The Early Years

The beginnings of Lucky Stores, Inc. can be traced to 1931, at which time a man by the name of Charles Crouch joined forces with four other investors to purchase a small chain of grocery stores in San Francisco, California. Located on the peninsula of San Francisco, the six stores had been named Peninsula Stores, Ltd. upon their inception. After the purchase, Crouch and his investment team operated the Peninsula store chain successfully for a couple of years before making the decision to expand.

When the company began making moves to open additional stores in the East Bay area of San Francisco, the new store locations were even more successful than were their predecessors. Crouch soon began referring to these new stores as his "lucky stores," and thus the company eventually underwent a name change. In 1935 the identification "Lucky" first appeared on the outside of the company's store at Shattuck and Bancroft Streets in Berkeley, California. The name stuck, and the store chain has been known as Lucky Stores, Inc. ever since.

The small grocery chain saw success for approximately the next ten years or so. In 1947 Lucky decided to expand its scope. At that time, the company decided to open a larger version of itself—a true "supermarket"—the first of its kind west of the Mississippi River. The new store carried expanded offerings and easily beat out its competitors in terms of its size and the range of its product selection. Almost immediately, the store began receiving accolades. The *Wall Street Journal* named it the "store of the year," citing its innovations as being years ahead of their time.

Diversification and Expansion in the 1950s and 1960s

By the early 1950s the Lucky chain was made up of more than 40 store locations. After having achieved great success in the San Francisco Bay area and its surrounding communities throughout the 1930s and 1940s, Lucky decided to expand to other markets throughout California in the early 1950s. By 1956 the company had purchased and converted 48 stores from other companies throughout the state. The Lucky purchases included ten Jim Dandy stores in the Los Angeles metro market, six Food Basket stores in the San Diego area, and a whopping 32 Cardinal stores in the Sacramento area. Not only did the acquisitions double Lucky's store count, but they also gave the company firmer footing in the California grocery store market. That year, Lucky achieved more than $100 million in annual sales for the first time in the company's history.

By 1959 Lucky operated 117 stores in the states of California and Washington. That year, the company began building "discount centers"—larger versions of its supermarkets offering everything from food and household grocery items to pharmacy services, liquor, and apparel. The year 1960 marked the beginning of Lucky's foray into the areas of general merchandise retailing, membership department stores, automotive retailing, and fabric retailing units. The company expanded its scope through the purchase of a membership department store in southern California. Soon, Lucky's Gemco and Memco membership department stores began appearing throughout the western states of California, Arizona, and Texas, as well as in the eastern and midwestern states of Maryland, Virginia, and Illinois.

Within the next decade, Lucky had advanced to the point that it could expand its supermarket chain on a national level. In 1968 the company negotiated a deal with the Eagle store chain and the May's drug store chain in Illinois, Iowa, and Wisconsin. Also purchased in 1968 was Tanne-Arden, Inc., which operated multiple retail apparel stores. Within four years, however, the retail apparel stores were divested.

Another area in which Lucky diversified its holdings was in the development of manufacturing facilities. Such activity led to Lucky's involvement in the L & G sporting goods chain in southern California, Harvest Day bakeries, Lady Lee milk processing plants, and various meat processing plants.

The 1970s and 1980s

Lucky continued to diversify in the early 1970s, through the 1972 purchases of Hancock Textile Co., Inc., Dorman's, Inc., Kragen Auto Supply Co., and Thurmond Chemicals, Inc. Hancock was involved in the manufacture of fabric goods, and Dorman's and Kragen Auto Supply both were involved in the retail sale of auto accessories and parts. Thurmond, on the other hand, manufactured and distributed household cleaning products. All four entities, in addition to Lucky's previous holdings, helped the parent company post sales of almost $2 billion in 1972. At that time, the company announced that it was ranked sixth in size in the United States among food chains, seventh among department store chains, and eleventh among all U.S. retail companies.

Lucky further increased its grocery store count when it entered the Florida market in 1979 through the purchase of 48 Kash 'n' Karry supermarkets in Tampa, Florida. The company continued to expand throughout the early 1980s and by 1985 was posting annual sales of almost $6.23 billion.

Unfortunately, Lucky had diversified so much by the mid-1980s that its holdings seemed not to fit under the corporate umbrella quite as well as they once had. The company had gotten to a point where it was dabbling in so many different areas that it could not realistically address the needs of each of its holdings. Thus in 1986 the company initiated a massive multimillion dollar restructuring program.

At the foundation of the restructuring effort was the goal of returning Lucky to its roots as a food retailer. Therefore, the company began selling off its peripheral businesses—a process that was concluded by mid-1987. At the close of its restructuring process, Lucky operated 481 grocery stores in California,

Nevada, Arizona, and Florida under the names Lucky, Food Basket, and Kash 'n' Karry.

Emerging with a rejuvenated focus on food retailing, Lucky made efforts to improve its customers' experiences in its store locations. For example, the company introduced its "Three's a Crowd" service policy, which stated that every time there were three people waiting in a checkout line, the store would open another checkout counter until all counters were in use. Also introduced was EZ-Checkout, which allowed customers to use their bank ATM cards to purchase groceries by deducting directly from their own bank accounts. Lucky also arranged its stores with short aisles, bold and legible signage, and a logical order in the placement of its merchandise, so customers would find shopping at its stores easy and convenient.

These efforts proved successful, and in 1987—Lucky's first full year after the restructuring—the company posted sales of $6.92 billion. According to company chairman and CEO John M. Lillie in Lucky's 1987 annual report, "Lucky Stores has emerged from its 1986 restructuring in excellent condition." Lillie also noted that industry giant American Stores Company had approached Lucky with a takeover proposal.

American Stores had gotten its start in Philadelphia, Pennsylvania in 1891 as Acme Market. After merging with several other Philadelphia area grocery store chains in 1917, the company changed its name to American Stores Company. Throughout the decades that followed, the company grew rapidly until being purchased by Skaggs Drug Centers, Inc. in 1979. The new company stuck with the American Stores name and went on to acquire numerous other grocery chains in the United States, including Jewel Companies, Inc., in 1984. Jewel consisted of Jewel Food Stores, Star Market, Osco Drug Stores, and Sav-on Drug Stores.

In 1988 American Stores completed its negotiations with Lucky Stores and purchased the growing supermarket chain. At the time, Lucky was California's leading grocery retailer—due in part to the fact that it was the only chain with a significant presence in both northern and southern California. The acquisition catapulted American Stores into the number two position among food and drug retailers in the United States.

In the years that followed the acquisition, American Stores made efforts to improve the overall financial strength of its Lucky holdings. Unprofitable store locations were disposed of, while the company focused instead on increasing the growth and profitability of the stores that it kept within its control. The company split itself into two divisions—a Northern California Division and a Southern California Division—to better address the differing needs of each of its two main regions. Although Lucky continued to exist as one entity under the American Stores umbrella, each of the two divisions gained their own separate management teams and operated from different locations.

Obstacles To Overcome in the 1990s

As Lucky headed into the 1990s, it became the subject of multiple headlines involving labor and human relations disputes. In early 1993 the company endured an impasse during contract negotiations with the International Brotherhood of Teamsters, involving approximately 1,300 truck drivers and warehouse workers in northern California. The issue became so heated at one point that the Teamsters' union boycotted 188 Lucky stores in the Northern California Bay area and filed a charge of unfair labor practices against Lucky. The problem was settled eventually in March 1993.

Soon thereafter, it was announced that Lucky had agreed to settle a massive class action lawsuit that had been filed against the Northern Division by some of its current and former female employees. The suit alleged that Lucky had forced many of its female employees and prospective new hires into low-paying, nonmanagerial, ''dead-end'' jobs where they were denied promotion opportunities. After the two sides spent more than a year negotiating the terms of the settlement, Lucky agreed to pay $74.25 million—an average of approximately $5,000 to $14,000 per employee in question. The November 23, 1993 edition of the *San Francisco Examiner* called it ''the second-largest sex discrimination settlement in U.S. history, behind the $240 million agreed to by State Farm Insurance in April 1992.''

Then in late 1994 the Teamsters dispute reared its ugly head again, as more contract negotiation difficulties threatened to force 235 Lucky stores in southern California to close. This time, the problem involved Lucky's Southern California Division and approximately 1,700 truck drivers and warehouse workers. With the help of a federal mediator, the two sides came to an agreement in December 1994.

Almost six months later Lucky faced another strike situation, this time involving the United Food and Commercial Workers union. During the difficulty, the union led a nine-day strike against one of Lucky's competitors—Safeway—which then led to a lockout by the Lucky and Save Mart chains. The strike was based on the union's disapproval of the grocery companies' new policy changes regarding such things as medical leave and health insurance. In mid-April 1995, however, the store chains and the union were able to reach an agreement.

Meanwhile, Lucky began putting into action plans to create a chain of warehouse-style grocery stores in northern California. The plan, initiated in 1994, was an effort to help Lucky compete with the many discount grocery chains springing up in its home market. The new foray into discounting actually marked parent company American Stores' entry into the warehouse grocery market as well. The new Lucky discount stores, named Super Saver Food, carried more bulk goods and offered lower prices. Lucky also announced that all of its own new stores would be larger in size and offer more in-store services such as bakeries, deli shops, florists, photo departments, and full-service banks. Up to that point, Lucky's typical store size was around 25,000 square feet; the new superstores would be approximately 60,000 square feet.

In early 1996 Lucky once again made headlines; this time, however, the topic was a bit more upbeat—the story of a grocery chain doing good deeds and beating the IRS at its own game. Back in 1983, Lucky had begun the practice of donating its unsold four-day-old bread to food banks and other charitable organizations. At the same time, the company kept track of the retail price of all donated bread, and then filed for charitable deductions at tax time. The IRS disallowed the deductions, stating that the bread's value should have been discounted at the

time of the donations. After a battle, in 1996 the U.S. Tax Court sided with Lucky's interpretations and the years of deductions stood.

The Turn of the Century and Beyond

Near the end of the decade, Lucky continued its efforts at customer satisfaction. In January 1997 a partnership between Lucky and Wells Fargo & Co. was announced, whereby Wells Fargo would open 24 full-service banks within selected Lucky store locations. The arrangement benefited both parties. Wells Fargo gained access to a larger potential customer base, whereas Lucky was able to offer its customers the opportunity to take care of more of their errands in one stop.

Soon thereafter, Lucky once again appealed to its customers with the introduction of the ''Rewards Card'' frequent shopper program. In basic terms, customers at 540 Lucky and Sav-on stores in California and Nevada could sign up for the cards, which when scanned at checkout would track purchases and lead to rewards. Not only would the cards entitle members to advertised discounts on selected items each week, but they also would help the store chain capture data about individual purchasing habits and trends. It was thought that the chain could better address the needs of its customers through the use of such data. To go along with the introduction of the reward program, Lucky launched a television advertising campaign featuring the slogan ''Savings Made Simple.''

In late 1998 Lucky's parent company, American Stores Company, was purchased by Albertson's Inc. The $11.7 billion purchase was the biggest in Albertson's history and helped it at the lead of the pack of U.S. grocery and drug store chains, with more than 2,470 stores in 37 states. Albertson's stated its intent to retain the store names of most of its new subsidiaries, including Lucky. Company spokespeople predicted that the main differences that customers would notice would be lower prices and a better selection.

Further Reading

''California Supermarkets Pay Millions for Discrimination Settlement,'' *Women's International Network News,* Winter 1994, p. 73.

Cimini, Michael H., and Behrmann, Susan L., ''Unions Settle at Two Grocery Chains,'' *Monthly Labor Review,* March 1993, p. 52.

Cimini, Michael H., and Muhl, Charles J., ''Grocery Settlements,'' *Monthly Labor Review,* July 1995, p. 73.

——, ''Lucky Stores, Teamsters Settle,'' *Monthly Labor Review,* December 1994, p. 58.

Cuicchi, David L., ''Corporate Donor Turns Old Bread into New Dough,'' *Memphis Business Journal,* March 4, 1996, p. 5.

Dawson, Angela, ''Frequent Buyers Get a Bonus; Grey Launches Lucky Stores Plan,'' *Adweek—Western Edition,* February 17, 1997, p. 5.

Duan, Mary, ''Lucky Falls Behind in Low-Cost Survey,'' *Business Journal Serving San Jose & Silicon Valley,* March 4, 1996, p. 6.

Fontana, Dominick, ''Wells To Open 24 Offices in Lucky Stores,'' *American Banker,* January 13, 1997, p. 5.

''Food Strike Ends,'' *Chain Store Age Executive with Shopping Center Age,* May 1995, p. 26.

Ginsberg, Steve, ''Lucky Rolls Dice in San Francisco with Two New Stores,'' *San Francisco Business Times,* October 23, 1998, p. 17.

Guynn, Jessica, and Pascual, Psyche, ''Supermarket Chain Buys Lucky Stores,'' *Contra Costa Times,* 1998.

Lewis, Len, "Lucky Strike," *Progressive Grocer,* January 1997, p. 5.

"A Lucky break and Oat Bran Mania, Part II," *Snack Food,* February 1996, p. 44.

Marsh, Gary, "Superstores Fitting Bill for Safeway and Lucky," *Business Journal Serving San Jose & Silicon Valley,* April 24, 1995, p. 3.

"Supermarkets," *Chain Store Age Executive with Shopping Center Age,* February 1994, p. 10.

Symons, Allene, "Lucky, Sav-on Debut Rewards Card," *Drug Store News,* February 17, 1997, p. 3.

Taylor, Dennis, "Safeway and Lucky Stores in a Food Fight," *Business Journal Serving San Jose & Silicon Valley,* September 23, 1996, p. 1A.

Wright, J. Nils, "Lucky Denies Retreat from Super Saver, But Plans To Switch Store," *Sacramento Business Journal,* July 15, 1996, p. 9.

——, "Lucky Eyes Warehouse Stores," *Sacramento Business Journal,* April 4, 1994, p. 1.

——, "Unions Vow To Hit Discount Grocers," *Sacramento Business Journal,* April 17, 1995, p. 1.

—Laura E. Whiteley

GROUPE MANITOU

Manitou BF S.A.

B.P. 249
44158 Ancenis Cedex
430, rue de l'Aubinière
44150 Ancenis
France
(33) 2.40.09.10.11
Fax: (33) 2.40.09.10.96
Web site: http://www.manitou.fr

Public Company
Incorporated: 1945 as Etablissements Braud
Employees: 1,800
Sales: FFr. 2.76 billion (US $502 million) (1997)
Stock Exchanges: Paris
Ticker Symbol: Manitou
SICs: 3531 Construction Machinery

Manitou BF S.A. of Ancenis, France, is the inventor and world's leading producer of all-terrain forklifts, as well as lift-trucks, pallet movers, and related vehicles for the construction, forestry, agricultural, environmental, and other industries. Manitou also produces a wide range of crane and derrick vehicles and bulldozer/loaders. In addition to the company's own line of Manitou brand vehicles and equipment, Manitou BF produces a range of similar vehicles through Toyota Industrial Equipment (TIE), a manufacturing partnership with Toyota, in which Manitou holds 34 percent. In 1998 the company reached a similar agreement to produce lifting vehicles for Fiat's New Holland subsidiary.

Manitou offers an extensive line of lifter/loaders and other vehicles for nearly every industrial, warehousing, construction, agricultural, and other light- to medium-weight lifting and loading purpose. The company's products are separated in four primary lines: flagship forklifts; Maniscopic telescoping lifts; the Maniloader line of bulldozers and articulated loaders; and a line of platform and basket lifts. Manitou produces lifting systems for a wide range of applications, from hand-operated pallet trucks for warehousing operations to platform cranes capable of raising as much as 9,000 pounds to heights of more than 50 feet. In addition to the Manitou lines, the company produces a related line of bulldozer vehicles for the construction industry through its Germany-based Ahlmann Baumaschinen subsidiary, acquired in 1994; a line of warehouse-specific pallet transporters produced by subsidiary Loc Manutention, based in France; the TIE line of electric-powered forklifts and loaders; and the company's small-quantity, professional-grade cement mixers, produced under the Braud et Faucheux name.

While the company's main production facility is located at its headquarters site in Ancenis, near Nantes in northwestern France, Manitou operates 17 subsidiaries, including an additional six production facilities, in France, Germany, the United Kingdom, Italy, Israel, the United States, Belgium, Turkey, Portugal, and Singapore. In France, the company's sales are conducted through a network of some 50 authorized dealers, backed by more than 100 service centers throughout the country. International sales are conducted by a network of some 400 distributors, bringing Manitou vehicles to more than 90 countries. Foreign sales account for approximately 55 percent of the company's sales. Despite a long economic crisis in Europe, Manitou has been able to maintain its growth, with annual sales topping FFr 2.75 billion for net earnings of FFr 138 million in 1997. Manitou is led by president Marcel Braud and his son, and vice-president, Marcel Claude Braud.

Inventing a Market in the 1950s

The Braud family's involvement in machinery for the construction and other industries began before the Second World War, when the family's patriarch drafted plans to build a manufacturing plant producing cement mixers, derrick cranes, and motorized winches. These Braud products were to feature their founder-inventor's designs, for which Braud already had been granted a number of patents. World War II interrupted the family's plans, and Braud himself would not live to see the start of his company's operations: in 1944, during the liberation of the family's home town of Ancenis in the Loire region, Braud was killed.

Braud's widow determined to carry on her husband's plans. In 1945 the company was incorporated as Etablissements Braud under Madame Braud's leadership. Joined by son Marcel Braud, the company would begin production on the late Braud's designs. By 1946 the company was able to present its first line of products, chiefly cement mixers as well as a derrick winch, and other products dedicated to the construction industry. The devastation of much of northern France's infrastructure during the war years and the ensuing reconstruction effort would bring a strong demand for the company's products from both the public works and building construction sectors. The company continued to enlarge its product offerings, expanding sales beyond its Ancenis base.

In 1953 Braud formed a partnership with another local construction materials producer, renaming the company Braud & Faucheux. The company's product line now extended to include its first cranes, and the company's production facilities expanded to meet the demand brought on by France's steady economic recovery. By then, Marcel Braud, who had inherited his father's talent for invention, had begun work on what would become the company's flagship product.

In 1957 Marcel Braud presented the first all-terrain forklift design. Using a three-wheeled dump truck as a base, Braud had invented a motorized forklift attachment that would prove far more versatile for the construction industry. By 1958 Braud had refined his design, manufacturing an all-terrain forklift with a four-wheeled MacCormick tractor as its base. The model, the MC 5, with a reach of up to 2.8 meters, was capable of lifting up to 1,000 kilos. The MC 5 would became the first Braud & Facheux machine to adopt the brand name Manitou, proposed during a family picnic (and suggesting a contraction of the French words for "handle" and "all"). Although the MC 5 was directed primarily as a warehousing aid for construction materials wholesalers, Braud quickly saw the means to extend his invention into new areas.

Before the end of the decade the MC 5 was joined by the larger MC 6, capable of vertical lifts of up to 2,000 kilos. The MC 6 also increased the MC 5's lifting range, with a vertical height of three meters. The MC 6 found ready acceptance in the construction industry, but also brought the company into the lumber industry, where the Manitou series would become a fixture.

By 1961 Braud & Faucheux had sold more than 500 forklifts. Less than a decade later the company would record the sale of its 10,000th forklift. The Manitou line expanded continuously through the decade, including the addition of the MC 7, which brought a weight range up to 3,000 kilos and would lead to the MB 20, with a vertical lifting range of nearly four meters. The Manitou line also exhibited a quality that would remain a company feature through the 1990s: subcontractors' components, both from the company's subsidiaries and from third party manufacturers, such as the MacCormick and, later, International Harvester engines of the early Manitous, to complement the company's own production. In this way, Braud & Faucheux built up a high level of expertise in specific areas of competence, including design and development, welding and assembling, and painting. This openness to third party products would prove important to the company's growth in the 1970s.

International in the 1970s

By the end of the 1960s Braud & Faucheux boasted not only the sales of more than 10,000 forklifts, but it also had developed an expanded line of derrick cranes, with production of these equaling those of its forklifts. The company's cement mixers, too, had been selling successfully more than 30,000 by the start of the 1970s. The Manitou forklifts, however, would take special prominence in the company's growth over the following decades, allowing the company to claim international leadership in this product category, while also leading the way to the expanded range of Manitou equipment.

Manitou sales had gone international in the early years of the 1960s, with the company's exports reaching Germany, Belgium, Greece, and Portugal by 1963. By the early 1970s the company, which had grown to nearly 400 employees, had outgrown its original Ancenis quarters. In 1972 the company began construction on an expanded Ancenis location, which eventually would reach more than 60,000 square meters of production space. Meanwhile, upon Faucheux's retirement in 1971, the company came under the leadership of Marcel Braud.

Marcel Braud would orient the company more firmly to the international markets. In 1973 the company opened its first foreign distribution subsidiary, Manitou Site Lift Ltd. in the United Kingdom. This subsidiary would come to represent one of the company's primary exporters, while also aiding the company to expand and adapt its product line beyond the construction industry to the agricultural market as well. In France, meanwhile, the company had built up a distribution network of some 60 Manitou dealers.

This distribution network would gain the attention of Toyota, which was preparing to introduce its own line of electric-powered forklifts to France. Toyota proposed that Manitou become its distribution partner for the Japanese giant's complementary line of forklifts—which were oriented primarily to lighter weight warehousing use. Manitou agreed, setting up a separate partnership company, Compagnie Française de Manutention (CFM), for the distribution agreement. Although CFM later would come under 98.9 percent control of Manitou, the partnership agreement marked only the first step in a long relationship with Toyota.

World Leader for the 1990s

By the beginning of the 1980s Braud & Faucheux could celebrate its 50,000th Manitou. By 1981 the importance of that brand name finally was featured in the company's name, which was changed to Manitou BF. That same year saw the expansion of the company's product lines with the introduction of the first of its Maniscopic telescoping lifts. Manitou also was building its international presence, launching its U.S. subsidiary, KD Manitou, Inc., in Waco, Texas, bringing its production capacity beyond Europe for the first time.

After introducing automated production techniques in its Ancenis plant and expanding its forklift fleet with its own line of warehouse-ready electric forklifts, Manitou joined the Paris stock exchange in 1984. The newly public company quickly made its first acquisition, that of Sociéte Materials Termit, followed by the purchase of a controlling share of Italy's Fargh, which would be renamed as the company's Manitou Costru-zioni Industriali SRL (MCI) manufacturing subsidiary.

Toward the end of the 1980s Manitou deepened its relationship with Toyota, reaching a licensing agreement to manufacture Toyota forklifts for the European community. By the mid-1990s more than 25,000 Toyota lifts would leave the Manitou production lines. Rounding out the decade, Manitou strengthened its warehousing equipment capacity with the formation of Compagnie Industrielle de Matérials de Manutention (CIMM). At the same time, as the Manitou reached weight limits of 5,000 kilos, the company introduced the latest development in its Maniscopic line, the MLT series of lifter/loaders.

Manitou would continue to expand its product range in the 1990s. In 1991 the company joined with Treco to create its Belgian subsidiary Mantrec S.A., responsible for the production of a new line of electric-powered pallet loaders under the Manitrec brand name; this range would be expanded two years later with the addition of the complementary line and with the acquisition of controlling shares in Paris-based LOC Manutention. After celebrating the production of the 100,000th Manitou in 1992, the company moved to reinforce its position in the growing Asian market, establishing its Manitou Asia subsidiary in Singapore.

By 1992 Manitou had reached sales of more than FFr 1.35 billion. The company's sales would be hurt in the 1990s, because of an extended economic recession, forcing the company to lay off workers and take steps to lower its production costs. Manitou nonetheless began to see relief as early as 1993, as sales once again picked up, enabling the company to near FFr 1.8 billion in 1994. Aiding this growth was the company's purchase of the rival forklift line from Germany's Ahlmann, creating Manitou's Ahlmann Baumaschinen subsidiary. At the same time Manitou increased its share of Mantrec to 96 percent, while acquiring Empilhadores de Portugal—in time for the vast construction program related to Lisbon's hosting of the 1998 Universal Expo. The company also established a Turkish subsidiary, Manitou HMK.

These moves helped Manitou top FFr 2.5 billion in annual sales in 1995. In that year Manitou's long-standing relationship with Toyota reached a new level, as the companies agreed to establish the Toyota Industrial Equipment (TIE) subsidiary (held 34 percent by Manitou) for the assembly of Toyota's forklifts for the European market. The agreement called for Manitou to transfer its existing Toyota assembly activities to the new joint venture, which launched its activities in 1996; nonetheless, Manitou still was able to produce a light growth in its revenues for the 1996 year.

The following year Manitou entered a partnership with another competitor, New Holland, the Fiat subsidiary and European leader in agricultural vehicles. As the agricultural market began abandoning traditional loaders for the Maniscopic-type telescoping forklift, New Holland approached Manitou with the proposition of participating in the creation of a French-based plant for the manufacture of a line of New Holland-branded telescoping lifts. While cannibalizing to some extent the market for Manitou's own line of telescoping lifts, the 1997 agreement, which called for Manitou to produce some 2,000 New Holland vehicles per year, would represent a strong boost in Manitou's revenues, as well as reinforcing Manitou's position as the world's leading manufacturer of all-terrain forklift equipment. In the year following the New Holland agreement Manitou saw its revenues top FFr 2.75 billion.

Principal Subsidiaries

Compagnie Française de Manutention; Compagnie Industrielle des Matériels de Manutention; Manitou Tous Terrains & Industriels; Savim (98.95%); Loc Manutention (66.5%); Manitou Site Lift (UK); KD Manitou (USA); Manitou Construzioni Industriali (Italy; 61%); Ahlmann Baumaschinen (Germany); Manitou HMK (Turkey; 48%); Epmilhadores de Portugal; Toyota Industrial Equipment (34%); Mantrec (96%).

Further Reading

Du Guerny, Stanislas, "Des chariots Manitou pour la concurrence," *L'Usine Nouvelle,* September 3, 1998, p. 59.

Jadoul, Arnaud, "Une cooperation et un nouveau concurrent," *L'Usine Nouvelle,* May 15, 1997, p. 44.

"Le Manitou a 40 ans," Manitou BF S.A., 1998.

"Manitou a reussi son rapprochement avec Toyota," *Les Echoes,* February 12, 1998, p. 21.

"Manitou connait une forte reprise de son activité," *Les Echoes,* October 17, 1994, p. 20.

"Manitou digère son alliance avec Toyota," *Les Echoes,* April 14, 1997, p. 12.

—M.L. Cohen

McCORMICK & COMPANY, INC.

McCormick & Company, Incorporated

18 Loveton Circle
P.O. Box 6000
Sparks, Maryland 21152-6000
U.S.A.
(410) 771-7301
Fax: (410) 771-7462
Web site: http://www.mccormick.com

Public Company
Incorporated: 1903
Employees: 7,600
Sales: $1.88 billion (1998)
Stock Exchanges: NASDAQ
Ticker Symbol: MCCRK
SICs: 2099 Food Preparations, Not Elsewhere Classified;
    2087 Flavoring Extracts & Syrups, Not Elsewhere
    Classified

McCormick & Company, Incorporated has been the largest U.S. seller of spices, seasonings, and flavorings for nearly the entirety of the 20th century, and now has grown to become the largest firm within the spice industry throughout the world. Its estimated market share is more than double that of its closest competitor, Durkee Foods. McCormick now operates seven divisions, including: McCormick Consumer Products, which provides a wide variety of spices, seasonings, and extracts under well-known brand names; McCormick Food Service, which offers spices and various other food products to foodservice distributors and membership warehouse clubs; McCormick Flavors, which supplies natural and artificial flavors for industrial needs; McCormick Foods Australia, which produces 400 items and markets them throughout the Asia and Pacific regions; Schwartz Herbs and Spices, the number one brand of herbs, spices, and seasonings in the United Kingdom; SupHerb Farms, which produces frozen and freeze dried culinary herbs; and Tubed Products, the leading producer of plastic squeeze tubes within the United States.

Early History

A 25-year-old Baltimore man named Willoughby M. McCormick founded the company in 1889 when he began making fruit syrups, juices, flavoring extracts, and root beer in his home. McCormick enlisted three young assistants to help with production and with door-to-door sales. Early marketing techniques included the use of the Bee Brand and Silver Medal labels and the adoption of the motto: "Make the Best—Someone Will Buy It." The company earned a reputation not only for its condiments and other consumables but also for such household and medicinal products as Iron Glue ("Sticks Everything But the Buyer") and Uncle Sam's Nerve and Bone Liniment ("For Man or Beast").

Within a year, the company was profitable enough to move to larger quarters. At this time, McCormick added a number of new products, including food colorings, cream of tartar, liver pills, castor oil, talcum powder, witch hazel, blood purifier, cold cream, bay rum, tooth powder, and toilet water. Three years later, after McCormick's brother, Roberdeau A. McCormick, had joined the business, the company again moved. Soon even more everyday products—bluing compound, ammonia, roach traps, flypaper, and bird seed—were added to the line. By 1894, the company had begun to export overseas. The following year the corporation was dissolved so that a partnership could be formed between Willoughby and Roberdeau (the two ultimately incorporated in 1903). This year the Clover Brand made its debut. In 1896 the company took a crucial step forward by acquiring Philadelphia-based F.G. Emmett Spice Company and firmly committing itself to the spice industry. Promotions that coincided with this event included the sale of the first McCormick cookbook and a novelty premium offer.

At the turn of the century the company opened an export office in New York City and began shipping its products to and from the East and West Indies, South Africa, Europe, and Central and South America. In 1902 the company acquired a four-story plant and unveiled the Banquet Brand for its line of spices and mustards. Promotions continued apace. With such slogans as "McCormick Means Merit" and the title of "Manufacturing Chemists, Drug & Spice Millers, Importers and Exporters," McCormick was fast becoming the East Coast leader

297

Company Perspectives:

When people hear the name McCormick, they think of the spices they use every day. Indeed, we are the world's largest spice company. Yet, the Company is also the leader in the manufacture, marketing and distribution of not only spices, but seasonings, flavors and other food products to the entire food industry—to foodservice and food processing businesses as well as to retail outlets. In addition, our packaging group manufactures and markets specialty plastic bottles and tubes for food, personal care and other industries. McCormick products are sold in more than 100 countries. How do we manage this complex business from the growing fields to the consumer purchase? It all starts with Multiple Management, an enlightened corporate philosophy and system of participative management begun in 1932. Multiple Management fosters the importance and power of people by encouraging participation at all levels of employment and sharing the rewards of success. This interaction of people is instrumental in shaping our Corporate culture and enhancing strengths throughout McCormick.

---

in its selected fields. Although in 1904 a great fire in Baltimore destroyed the majority of the company's assets and records, temporary quarters were quickly established, and the company eventually regained its foothold through new product introductions. These included Clover Blossom spices and Banquet teas. The company gained welcome publicity in 1907 at the Virginia Exposition in Jamestown, when it received gold medals for a number of its branded products.

Growth, Expansion, and the Challenge to Succeed

The next two decades were characterized by more rapid growth and the company's rise to national prominence. In 1910 the company was among the first in the country to introduce gauze-pouch tea bags. This same year Willoughby was chosen to preside over the newly formed Flavoring Extracts Manufacturing Association, the purpose of which was to ensure uniformity in materials and packaging while elevating the status of regional spice companies. Willoughby's nephew, Charles P. McCormick, joined the company as a part-time shipping clerk in 1912; years later, Charles would prove instrumental in resuscitating the business following Willoughby's death. At the onset of the Roaring Twenties, the company was manufacturing over 800 products, embracing the national mood of prosperity and optimism. In 1921 it started construction of a new corporate headquarters: a nine-story building, replete with printing plant, analytical lab, machine shop, cafeteria, and railroad siding, overlooking the inner harbor of Baltimore. Five years later, McCormick stock was offered to wholesale grocers for the first time. Although the company would not achieve coast-to-coast distribution until after World War II, it hired Scotch bagpipers (the symbol for the company's Bee Brand) to advertise its products on the streets of large cities across the United States.

Sales reached $5 million in 1928, prompting the company to schedule office openings in Houston and San Francisco within

the next few years. However, the stock market crash and the Great Depression placed the company in serious peril by 1930. Willoughby McCormick's initial response to plummeting sales was to drastically reduce wages. Within two years, he was forced to seek outside capital from New York investors to sustain the company's operations. McCormick died of a heart attack before accomplishing his mission, and it was left to his nephew, 36-year-old Charles P. McCormick, to turn the business around.

As the new president and chair of a floundering company, the potential for expansion of which was still enormous, Charles instituted a new business philosophy, which he termed "Multiple Management." McCormick's guiding belief was that a company, whatever its products or services, was nothing without its workforce, and an empowered workforce made for an empowered, efficient, and successful company. He established junior boards of directors to implement this philosophy and to provide regular forums for the exchange of ideas which might ultimately lead the company to become more productive and to seek new directions for growth. A radical departure from established business practices at the time, McCormick's plan also included a ten percent increase in general wages and a reduction in weekly hours from 56 to 45, all steps which would seem to preclude the company's downfall.

McCormick's leadership and his emphasis on employee productivity enabled the company to return to profitability within a year. Pioneering programs in profit sharing and medical benefits were among the company's rewards to its dedicated employees. The Multiple Management system became ingrained in the McCormick corporate culture and soon found hundreds of adherents in businesses across the United States, Canada, and Great Britain. McCormick's unique views and experiences were published in book form in 1938 as *Multiple Management* (reprinted as *The Power of People*) and *The McCormick System of Management*. A corporate pamphlet commemorating 50 years of the McCormick system declared that: "C. P. McCormick understood human nature and respected people. That was one of the reasons he got good results. Those who knew him and worked with him testify that he valued the opinions of others, didn't feel threatened by contrary ideas and was willing to change when a better idea came along."

Within the first five years under the new McCormick system, some 2,000 separate ideas were generated and implemented by the junior boards. Among the company's most visible innovations were a spoon-sift top and new metal containers for its spice line. In 1938 a McCormick research team developed a spice fumigation process called "McCorization" that produced the highest grade spices available without any detectable flavor loss. The early 1940s were distinguished by McCormick's undisputed rebirth as the East Coast's largest seller of spices. It was at this time that the company also began consolidating its product line under the McCormick name and the big "Mc" trademark.

The Postwar Era

In 1947, McCormick gained coast-to-coast distribution with the acquisition of A. Schilling & Company of San Francisco. A spice, coffee, and extract concern with a history older than that of McCormick, Schilling's house brand was so popular that it was retained for domestic spice sales west of the Mississippi. "United to Serve the Nation's Good Taste" became the new corporate slogan, and sales surpassed $25 million during the first full year of consolidation. Because of McCormick's growing presence overseas, with exports to 44 countries, the company opened the 1950s with yet another slogan: "From All the World—Known the World Over." Acquisitions, joint ventures, and the formation of new subsidiaries have since become an area of concentration for McCormick. Highlights of the company's early acquisitions included the 1959 purchase of Canada's largest spice company, Gorman Eckert & Co. (whose name was later changed to Club House Foods); the 1961 purchase of California-based Gilroy Foods, a producer of dehydrated onions, garlic, and other vegetables; the 1962 purchase of Baker Extract Co., a venerable New England competitor; and the 1968 purchase of Tubed Chemicals Corporation, a packer and manufacturer of plastic tubes.

Diversification Within a Changing Marketplace

McCormick remained busy on other fronts as well. In 1959 it introduced its Gourmet line of spices. Four years later, it modified its spice tins with a plastic duo-flip top and also established the industrial products division to provide custom service for food processors. However, McCormick's most dynamic move occurred outside the food and spice industry. In 1962, while searching for a 50-acre plot near Baltimore to satisfy its needs for expansion, the company learned of a much larger piece of commercial property whose developers were in financial trouble. Guided by then President John Curlett and Chairperson C. P. McCormick, the company decided to form a real estate company, Maryland Properties, Inc. (later renamed McCormick Properties), to purchase and bring the Greater Baltimore Industrial Park project to completion. Through various leasing arrangements, the subsidiary made money during its first year, and soon it began acquiring and developing other properties in the Washington, D.C., and Baltimore areas. From 1973 until 1988, McCormick's real estate arm operated as an unconsolidated subsidiary. In one of its best years, 1983, it reported a strong profit of $13 million on revenues of $86 million. Three years later, a *Financial World* article recorded chairperson Harry Wells's plans to build the subsidiary, with operating assets of close to $300 million, into a $1 billion operation by 1991. Shortly after that, new leadership determined that the company's long-term health would be best served by a concentrated refocus on its food-and-spice businesses.

Despite the regular introduction of new products, new slogans, new subsidiaries, and new distribution arrangements, McCormick's core industry had suffered from slowing growth almost since the time of C. P. McCormick's death in 1970. Depressed stock values during the late 1970s enhanced the possibility of a takeover, and one company, Sandoz Ltd., appeared as though it might become the majority shareholder in McCormick. An immense Swiss chemical and pharmaceutical firm, Sandoz succeeded in acquiring almost five percent of McCormick's nonvoting stock in 1979 at $19 a share; it then offered to buy the remainder of the company for $37 a share. Nearly a year later, McCormick succeeded in buying its shares back, at $28 apiece, amidst wild rumors on Wall Street and rollercoaster speculative trading. Sandoz had made a profit, but McCormick, more importantly, had recovered its equilibrium, at least for a time.

Reorganization and Revitalization in the 1980s

In 1982 trouble reappeared within the company's grocery division. It was found that for a four-year period, from 1977 to 1980, expense accounting had been delayed in order to satisfy corporate profit goals. Stockholder suits quickly followed. Because of this dereliction, the heretofore exclusive board of directors now decided to open its doors to outside executives.

This change alone was not enough to deflect further setbacks related to profits. During the first half of the 1980s, domestic spice consumption dropped an alarming 20 percent. The company unveiled a new gourmet line of spices in 1985, supported by a massive consumer education campaign and the slogan: "McCormick/Schilling Gourmet. Quite simply, the best spices on earth." Two years later, the company planned another major rollout with the biggest marketing budget in its history. Saturation of this sort had been atypical of the venerable company, and, according to Janet Novack in an article in *Forbes*, "McCormick had always figured that in the spice business it was enough to woo retailers, and consumers would follow. After all, its full line of 103 gourmet and 107 regular spices takes so much space . . . that once established, it leaves little room for competitors' products." By Wells's admission, the company was slow to react to changing consumer trends—so slow that, "for a while there," wrote Novack, "an alert and strong competitor, had there been one, could have knocked it right off its lofty perch." Despite its increased attention to marketing, however, McCormick's profits and market share were still crumbling at the end of 1986.

The spice company's modern rebirth came with the ascension of Charles P. McCormick, Jr., grandnephew of the founder, to the positions of president and CEO in 1987. Assisted by then COO Bailey A. Thomas (elected chairperson and CEO in 1993), McCormick sold off the real estate and underperforming food divisions and sunk some $200 million into consumer marketing and product development. The revitalization campaign, known as Project One, involved shelving the traditional red-and-white spice tins in favor of elegantly labeled clear plastic bottles, produced by a corporate subsidiary. Other product rollouts included a line of dehydrated sauce mixes. The company also began fortifying its relations with the industrial and foodservice businesses and by the early 1990s counted at least 80 of the 100 largest U.S. food processors as its clients.

The 1990s and Beyond

McCormick's strategy for future growth included increasing its domestic market share to around 50 percent. The most important step toward meeting this goal involved the implementation of a comprehensive and aggressive acquisitions strategy, including the 1991 purchase of Mojave Foods Corporation and the 1993 acquisition of the Golden Dipt Division of DCA Food Industries. More importantly, however, the company's other primary strategy was to increase its international presence, which it hoped to do through a series of joint ventures and through expansion of its foreign subsidiaries. Without wasting any time, management formed a joint venture with KG of Heidelberg, Germany, in 1990; and acquired Glentham International Ltd. of Northhampton, United Kingdom, in 1992; Grupo Pesa, a Mexican seasoning company; Tuko Oy, a spice company in Finland; Butty of Switzerland, an affiliate of Unilever; and Minipack, a packaging company in Southampton, United Kingdom, all in 1994. In 1995, the company continued its acquisition strategy in Europe, Asia, and India, but also announced a restructuring of the entire company, including staff reductions, plant and departmental consolidations, and a streamlined yet more aggressive marketing campaign. Unfortunately, Bailey Thomas was not able to see the fruits of his labor—he died unexpectedly of a heart attack in 1994 and was replaced by H. Eugene Blattman as CEO.

As the spice supplier for such expanding global chains as McDonald's and Burger King, McCormick was also growing in this area. During the late 1990s, the company's U.S. Consumer Business and Food Service Group reported record revenues, and the formation of a Global Industrial Group signalled management's commitment to expand its packaging operations around the world.

After a long and complex history, the new McCormick remained much the same as the McCormick of early Multiple Management days in its commitment to employees, innovations, and product excellence worldwide. Yet the company had even developed a whimsical sense of its place within the industry. In 1998, as part of a special printing process, management contracted a printing press company to include the scent of vanilla on its annual report.

Principal Subsidiaries

Festin Foods Corp. (50%); Gilroy Foods, Inc.; Glentham International, Ltd. (U.K.); Golden Dipt Co.; Grupo Pesa, S.A. (Mexico); Kancor Flavours and Extracts Limited (40%); Lukcor, S.A. (50%); McCormick & Wild, Inc. (50%); McCormick Canada, Inc.; McCormick de Centro America, S.A.; McCormick de Mexico, S.A. de C.V. (50%); McCormick de Venezuela, C.A.; McCormick Foods Australia Pty. Ltd.; McCormick Ingredients Southeast Asia Pte Ltd.; McCormick GmbH; McCormick-Lion Limited (49%); McCormick S.A. (France); McCormick U.K. plc; Mojave Foods Corporation; Sesaco Corporation (22.5%); Setco, Inc.; Shanghai McCormick Seasoning & Foodstuffs Co., Ltd. (35%); Stange (Japan) K.K. (50%); Tubed Products, Inc.; Tuko Oy (Finland).

Principal Divisions

Food Service Group; McCormick Flavor Division; McCormick Ingredients; McCormick Schilling Division.

Further Reading

Abelson, Reed, "Spicy Days at McCormick," *Fortune,* January 15, 1990.

Bangsberg, P.T., "Pepsi and McCormick Launch China Spice, Seasoning Venture," *Journal of Commerce and Commercial,* April 11, 1990.

Brown, Paul B., "Unlikely Landlord," *Forbes,* February 27, 1984.

Clark, Kim, "McCormick Turns 100 with Zest," *Sun,* September 27, 1989.

Cochran, Thomas N., "McCormick & Co.: Cogeneration Project Adds Spice to Profit Prospects," *Barron's,* July 4, 1988.

Dodds, Lynn Strongin, "Well Seasoned: Spices and Real Estate Do Mix," *Financial World,* September 2, 1986.

Levering, Robert, Milton Moskowitz, and Michael Katz, "McCormick & Company, Inc.," *The 100 Best Companies to Work for in America,* Reading, Mass,: Addison-Wesley Publishing Company, 1984.

Levering, Robert, and Milton Moskowitz, "McCormick," *The 100 Best Companies to Work for in America,* New York: Doubleday, 1993.

Linden, Dana Wechsler, "Hot Stuff," *Forbes,* November 26, 1990.

Litwak, David, "Second Chance Sales," *Supermarket Business,* November 1998, p. 108.

Madden, Kelly Hays, "Spicing Things Up," *Distribution,* January 1997, pp. 46–48.

"McCormick & Co. Elects Bailey A. Thomas and H. Eugene Blattman to Executive Positions," *Milling & Baking News,* January 19, 1993.

"McCormick & Co. Posts Record Results in Fiscal 1992," *Milling & Baking News,* January 19, 1993.

"McCormick Buys Consumer Product Line of Golden Dipt from DCA," *Milling & Baking News,* January 19, 1993.

Miles, Christine, "Spice and Sugar," *Forbes,* September 29, 1980.

Novack, Janet, "A Close Call," *Forbes,* January 26, 1987.

Oliver, Joyce Anne, "Spice in His Life Comes from Motivating His Workers," *Marketing News,* February 17, 1992.

100 Best Recipes for 100 Years from McCormick, Hunt Valley, Md. and Elmsford, N.Y.: McCormick & Company and The Benjamin Company, 1988.

Step Back into the Future: Fifty Years of Multiple Management, 1932–1982, Hunt Valley: Md.: McCormick & Company, 1982.

Sullivan, C.C., "Compressing Energy Needs," *Energy User News,* September 1998, pp. 12–13.

This Is McCormick, Hunt Valley, Md.: McCormick & Company, 1984.

—Jay P. Pederson
—updated by Thomas Derdak

MCI WorldCom, Inc.

515 East Amite Street
Jackson, Mississippi 39201-2702
U.S.A.
(601) 360-8600
(800) 844-8350
Fax: (601) 974-8350
Web site: http://www.mciworldcom.com

Public Company
Incorporated: 1998
Employees: 75,000
Sales: $30 billion (1998 est.)
Stock Exchanges: NASDAQ
Ticker Symbol: WCOM
SICs: 4813 Telephone Communications, Except Radio;
4822 Telegraph & Other Message Communications;
4899 Communication Services, Not Elsewhere
Classified; 7379 Computer Related Services, Not
Elsewhere Classified

MCI WorldCom, Inc. is one of the largest telecommunications companies in the world. Formed on September 15, 1998, from the $37 billion merger of MCI Communications Corporation and WorldCom, Inc., the company's operations are organized around three divisions: MCI WorldCom, U.S. telecommunications; UUNET WorldCom, Internet and technology services; and WorldCom International. The MCI WorldCom division is the second largest long distance company in the United States (after AT&T), with a 45,000-mile nationwide fiber optic network, that provides local phone service in more than 100 markets and offers data, Internet, and other communications services. UUNET WorldCom maintains a highly reliable backbone network that provides local access to the Internet from more than 1,000 locations in the United States, Canada, Europe, and the Asia-Pacific region, in addition to a wide range of other Internet services. WorldCom International is a local, facilities-based competitor in 15 countries outside the United States, connecting to the company's overall global network

more than 5,000 buildings in Australia, Belgium, Brazil, France, Ireland, Germany, Hong Kong, Italy, Japan, Mexico, The Netherlands, Singapore, Switzerland, Sweden, and the United Kingdom.

Before the 1998 merger MCI Communications, founded in 1968, was well known as the company that led the charge in introducing competition in the telecommunications industry and precipitated the breakup of AT&T's Bell System. Following the breakup, MCI quickly became a multibillion-dollar global enterprise. WorldCom began as a reseller of long distance services in 1983 before emerging as the fourth largest long distance provider and a full-service telecommunications powerhouse in the mid-1990s. WorldCom's growth was aided by a series of major acquisitions, including Resurgens Communications Group, Inc. and Metromedia Communications Corporation (1993); IDB Communications Group, Inc. (1994); WilTel Network Services (1995); MFS Communications Company, Inc. and UUNET Technologies, Inc. (1996); and Brooks Fiber Properties, Inc., CompuServe Corporation's data network, and America Online Inc.'s network services subsidiary (all in 1998).

MCI's History Began with 1963 FCC Application

Founded in 1968 as Microwave Communications, Inc. (MCI) by John Goeken, owner of a mobile radio business, MCI's regulatory history began in 1963, when Goeken filed an application with the Federal Communications Commission (FCC) for permission to construct a private line microwave radio system between Chicago and St. Louis, Missouri. Goeken proposed to erect a series of microwave towers between the two cities that would carry calls on a microwave beam. AT&T actually had developed the technology and used microwaves on many of its long distance routes. Unlike the Bell System, which had to expend enormous sums to maintain and operate the basic wire-and-cable network, however, Goeken proposed to offer a much cheaper alternative by employing microwave technology exclusively. As *Fortune*, April 1970, noted, Goeken contended that he would provide a service not offered by any of the existing telephone companies: "... wider choice of bandwidths, greater speed, greater flexibility ... and prices as much as 94 percent cheaper than A.T.&T.'s." In addition to carrying voice transmissions, the company stated that its greatest appeal would be to those who wanted to send data or a combination of data and voice messages.

Goeken's application set the stage for one of the great corporate battles in U.S. history by challenging the prevailing public service principle that had been developed and applied to telephony during the 19th and 20th centuries. The public service principle derived from the philosophy that universal availability of telephone service could be achieved only through one independent and interconnecting network. It was believed by those who built the system and those who came to regulate it that the communications industry was a natural monopoly, in which quality and service were best achieved through one integrated system rather than through the play of competing interests. At the time when Goeken filed his application, AT&T saw him as a small but important threat to its position as the nation's basic provider of phone services.

In 1964 several corporations, including AT&T, its Illinois Bell subsidiary, Western Union, and GTE's Illinois-based subsidiary, petitioned the FCC to deny Goeken's application. The corporations argued that Goeken's proposed service would be redundant. More important, AT&T charged that Goeken's service would skim the most profitable segment of the communications market at the expense of universal service provided by Bell. AT&T depended on charging high rates for some of its intercity services—such as private line, WATS, and regular long distance—to subsidize the vast expense of constructing and maintaining the nation's communications network. AT&T also used the revenue derived from these services to subsidize the price of local service, making the cost of basic phone service affordable to the average customer. If Goeken and others were allowed to compete openly in the market, this delicate system of rate averaging would be disrupted. Although it was in the interest of AT&T and the others to stall proceedings as long as possible in the hope that Goeken would not pursue his plan, most of the delays stemmed from Goeken himself. Filing deficiencies caused endless delays.

The seeds of change in the regulatory climate were sown in the revolution of new technologies that arose during and after World War II. Rapid technological advances in the fields of microwave relay, satellites, computers, and coaxial cable, in addition to other technologies such as mobile radio, recording devices, and answering machines, gave rise to a number of small, aggressive firms seeking to enter the telecommunications field. As these firms, armed with the new technologies, demanded increasingly more access to the telecommunications

market, the FCC was compelled to respond. In a string of rulings, the FCC first in 1956 decided that under certain conditions non-Bell terminal equipment could be attached to the Bell System network. In 1959 the FCC permitted firms to operate private microwave communications systems for internal use.

With these two decisions, the FCC paved the way for entry of competitive firms into certain markets. The FCC completely opened the terminal equipment market in 1968. Almost immediately dozens of small firms entered the market seeking to sell equipment in competition with Bell products.

In this changing regulatory climate of the early 1960s, Goeken arrived on the scene proposing a supplemental service that he claimed was not being provided by any company. Goeken claimed that he was seeking only a peripheral submarket much too small to disrupt AT&T's system of rate averaging. AT&T, however, opposed the entry, claiming that the ostensibly new and innovative service was merely a variation of a service already offered.

McGowan Arrived at MCI in 1968

In 1968, as the FCC was considering the newly incorporated MCI's application, the fortunes of the small company took a dramatic turn when William McGowan joined the company as chairman and chief executive officer. McGowan saw promise in the company, put his money behind it, and soon devised a strategy that would lead MCI to phenomenal success. When McGowan joined the firm, MCI's major asset was a five-year-old application to provide point-to-point private-line service by microwave between Chicago and St. Louis.

Almost immediately, McGowan set up a new company, Microwave Communications of America, to attract private investors to finance MCI-affiliated companies around the country. At the same time the company announced plans for an 11,000-mile system that would run through 40 states and be operated by 16 affiliates. Most important, McGowan began to orchestrate a legal-political strategy that would serve MCI extraordinarily well in later years when the company lobbied the FCC and Congress to grant its license.

On August 13, 1969, in a four-to-three decision, the FCC authorized MCI's Chicago-St. Louis application. The decision also assured MCI that it could interconnect with the Bell System network to enable MCI to provide its proposed services. Instead of settling the AT&T-MCI dispute, however, the FCC's MCI decision set the stage for a major battle over telecommunications policy as a result of the commission's failure to delineate clearly the boundaries of competition. The market threatened by MCI's entry was considerably larger than the market opened by the FCC's 1959 decision, which had allowed individual firms to set up their own in-house microwave communications systems. AT&T repeatedly charged that MCI would not be providing any new technologies or services but only would be skimming the most profitable routes, which AT&T needed to support unprofitable rural routes and basic local phone service.

It was clear to McGowan that to build MCI into a major national telecommunications network, AT&T's monopoly would have to be dismantled. McGowan launched a three-pronged offensive, lobbying Congress, the FCC, and the courts.

The company hired Kenneth Cox in 1971 as a senior vice-president who was assigned to lobby the FCC. Cox was a former FCC commissioner who had voted for approval of MCI's application in 1969.

AT&T responded aggressively to the FCC's MCI decision and was joined by Western Union and GTE in petitioning the FCC to reconsider MCI's application. Since other firms were then seeking entry to provide similar microwave private-line services, the companies argued that MCI could no longer be considered an isolated experiment and that increased competition would lead to higher prices, interfere with universal service, and undermine the basic system of rate averaging. MCI countered that these concerns were unfounded. The FCC denied the petitions, and in 1971 MCI received final approval to build its Chicago-St. Louis route.

Ultimately the 1971 FCC decision led to open entry into the private-line market. The FCC's 1971 deregulatory move, however, was narrow in scope and intent, designed to open only a specialized segment of the market. It was not the initial intention of the FCC to encourage full-scale competition with AT&T. The goal was to allow other firms to provide services not available from AT&T.

Verged on Collapse in Early 1970s

On June 22, 1972, MCI issued public stock, raising more than $100 million, and, assisted by a $72 million line of bank credit, it began construction of the Chicago-St. Louis route. The company also laid plans for its national microwave network that would run from coast to coast. MCI soon ran into trouble with AT&T, however, over the issue of interconnection with Bell's basic phone network. The FCC ruling had assured MCI that it could use Bell's local phone network to provide its service, but it did not stipulate at what cost or how quickly AT&T should install MCI's lines. At the same time AT&T announced that it was instituting a new pricing system called HI/LOW to compete directly with MCI and others on private line routes. By 1973 MCI was in financial trouble. Just months away from opening its nationwide microwave network, the company defaulted on its line of bank credit and was on the verge of collapse. Also in 1973 Microwave Communications, Inc. reorganized as MCI Communications Corporation.

Because the FCC's rulings—especially the decision on MCI—had spawned such competition, the commission had a political stake in MCI's success. McGowan understood the FCC's commitment to the survival of competition. To ensure MCI's preservation he worked quickly to enter the more profitable markets, capitalizing on the FCC's support. In the fall of 1973, McGowan, badly in need of cash, urged the FCC to authorize MCI to enlarge its services to include FX lines. Such lines connect a single customer in one city to another city, in which any number can be reached. The service, however, required the use of Bell's switched network, which AT&T saw as a violation of the intent of previous FCC rulings. In the protracted legal battle that ensued, MCI won a major victory that served as a prelude to the company becoming a full-scale long distance competitor of AT&T.

In 1973 MCI also began lobbying the antitrust division of the Justice Department to file a suit against AT&T to break apart the Bell System. On March 6, 1974, MCI filed a civil antitrust suit of its own, seeking damages from AT&T. Shortly thereafter, the Justice Department filed an antitrust case against AT&T to break up the Bell System.

Execunet Saved MCI, Led to Long Distance Competition in the Late 1970s

Even though MCI had succeeded in enlarging its markets by winning approval to provide FX services, the company had yet to make a profit. Between March 1973 and March 1975, the company lost working capital at the rate of $1 million a month. It needed new markets and, in a risky gamble, began to offer Execunet, a service nearly identical to AT&T's regular, very profitable long distance service. If the company was successful it could become a wealthy corporation, but if it failed, MCI faced the possibility of bankruptcy.

In 1975 V. Orville Wright joined MCI. Wright soon became president. Also in 1975, AT&T protested to the FCC that by providing Execunet, MCI had flagrantly exceeded its mandate. The FCC concurred, and MCI was directed to cease providing Execunet service. MCI won an appeal, and in 1978 the Supreme Court refused to review the appeal court's ruling that overturned the FCC ban on Execunet and ordered Bell to offer interconnection service to MCI. The breakthrough Execunet victory saved MCI from possible financial collapse. The company, in opposition to both AT&T and the FCC, had won the right to provide long distance service. In effect, MCI had cracked the Bell System monopoly. MCI soon began offering its long distance service to residential as well as business customers; in March 1980 MCI became the first AT&T competitor in the residential market when it launched residential service in Denver. As a full-scale competitor in the lucrative long distance market, MCI saw its revenues increase sharply. By 1981 MCI's annual revenues approached $1 billion. The Execunet victory also opened the long distance market to other small firms. Few, however, could afford to expend the enormous sums needed to build and maintain their own network facilities.

1984 Bell System Breakup Led to Difficulties

By the early 1980s it was clear that the government was winning its antitrust suit against AT&T. On January 8, 1982, the Justice Department and AT&T announced agreement in the seven-year-old case, providing for the divestiture of the 22 wholly owned local Bell operating companies. MCI's successful crusade for deregulation and divestiture, however, placed the company under financial strain in the immediate aftermath of the Bell System's breakup in 1984. AT&T, responding to the competitive inroads made by MCI and others, began reducing its rates drastically. MCI's profit margins collapsed as it was compelled to reduce rates. Higher access charges also squeezed the company. In 1985 MCI's stock plunged from more than $20 per share to under $7 per share, and in 1986 the company, despite having the second largest share of the long distance market, posted a loss of $448.4 million. From the beginning, MCI's profits derived not from superior technology or innovative processes, but from its cost advantage over AT&T, which it passed on to customers. Once the local Bell operating companies were divested, MCI's artificial cost advantage disappeared.

In 1985 MCI was awarded a disappointing $113.3 million in its civil antitrust suit against AT&T. Also in 1985, in need of capital to expand MCI's national network and to finance an aggressive marketing campaign to win new long distance customers, McGowan struck a deal with IBM, which bought 18 percent of MCI for cash with the option to expand its holdings later up to 30 percent.

McGowan continued to argue the need to regulate AT&T for several years before open competition could be considered viable. Whereas McGowan had led the charge for deregulation throughout the 1970s, he now argued that only vigorous regulation could guarantee that MCI and other competitors would be able to compete effectively with AT&T. The following year, MCI called for the removal of all remaining regulatory restraints. The odd alliance was created by the companies' shared perception that deregulation would enable both to improve their financial outlook by increasing rates. The two companies also had a shared interest in opposing proposals advanced by the FCC and the Justice Department to relax regulation of the former Bell operating companies, which had become competitors of MCI and AT&T.

MCI was involved early on in what would later be dubbed the Internet. In September 1983 the company launched MCI Mail, a new nationwide e-mail system. Five years later the National Science Foundation Network (NSFNet) was launched; constructed by MCI, this ultra-high-speed digital network linked a number of academic computer centers and became the "backbone" of the Internet. Meantime, in 1985 V. Orville Wright retired as president of MCI, but continued to serve as vice-chairman until 1990. He was replaced as president by Bert C. Roberts Jr.

By the early 1990s MCI had weathered the wake of AT&T's divestiture and had expanded rapidly into providing a wide range of domestic and international voice and data communications services. The company's communications services included domestic and international long distance telephone service, international record communications services between the United States and more than 200 countries, and a domestic and international time-sensitive electronic mail service. Long distance telephone service accounted for 90 percent of MCI's total revenues in 1989. The company had bolstered its position in domestic and international markets through a series of investments, including acquisition of Satellite Business Systems, RCA Global Communications, Inc., and certain assets and contracts of Western Union's Advanced Transmission Systems division. In 1990 MCI also purchased a 25 percent interest in INFONET Services Corporation, a provider of international data services, and acquired for $1.25 billion Telecom*USA, then the nation's fourth largest long distance company. With the acquisitions, MCI had approximately a 16 percent share of the domestic long distance market.

MCI's Friends & Family Program Launched in 1991

In March 1991 the company announced that it had acquired Overseas Telecommunications, Inc., provider of international

digital satellite services to 27 countries worldwide. That same month, one of the key events in later company history occurred—the launching of the Friends & Family marketing program, which offered 20 percent discounts to groups of MCI customers with members who phone each other. AT&T had been finding success winning back MCI customers through follow-up calls and an aggressive advertising blitz. Consequently, in the second half of 1990 MCI market share dropped to 13 percent. Friends & Family helped MCI attract seven million new customers, pushing its market share to 20 percent by the end of 1993.

In December 1991, the same month that MCI completed the conversion of its entire nationwide network from analog to digital transmission, president and COO Roberts was named to the additional post of CEO, with McGowan remaining chairman. McGowan, a heart transplant recipient in 1987, died of a heart attack the following June, at the age of 64. Roberts was named to succeed him as chairman, retaining the CEO post as well.

MCI Diversified Under Roberts in the Mid-1990s

While the company focused almost exclusively on the long distance market when McGowan was in charge, MCI under Roberts's leadership began diversifying in anticipation of both the further deregulation of the U.S. telecommunications market and the predicted convergence of telecommunications, computers, and entertainment. In September 1992 MCI entered into an alliance with Canadian long distance firm Stentor to create the first fully integrated digital network linking the United States and Canada. MCI introduced 1-800-COLLECT in May 1993, the first collect calling service of its kind.

In June 1993 MCI and British Telecommunications plc (BT) announced that they would form a worldwide alliance to provide advanced global network services. Following regulatory approval in mid-1994, BT purchased a 20 percent stake in MCI for $4.3 billion. MCI and BT set up a joint venture called Concert Communications Company, which was 75 percent owned by BT and 25 percent owned by MCI. Concert offered worldwide voice and data services to multinational corporations.

In January 1994 MCI formed MCImetro, entered the long distance market in Mexico, and unveiled networkMCI. Through MCImetro MCI planned to build a $2 billion fiber optic phone network, bypassing local phone companies and offering alternative local service. By 1995 the company had received regulatory approval as a competitive local carrier in 15 states. The Telecommunications Act of 1996 (signed into law in February 1996) opened up competition even more, allowing local phone and long distance companies to compete in each other's markets and providing additional opportunities for MCImetro. In Mexico, MCI formed an alliance with banking group Grupo Financiero Banamex-Accival (Banacci) to form Avantel, a joint venture to provide competitive long distance service in Mexico. In September 1995 Avantel began construction of Mexico's first all-digital fiber optic network. After completion of the 3,400-mile network, Avantel in August 1996 became the first company to provide alternative long distance service in Mexico. By July 1997 the new venture had captured about ten percent of the $4 billion long distance market in that country. NetworkMCI, meantime, was a software package aimed at small and medium-sized businesses that bundled e-mail, fax, paging, document sharing, Internet access, and videoconferencing.

MCI invested $1 billion for a ten percent stake in The News Corporation Limited in August 1995. The two companies subsequently announced that they would develop a direct broadcast satellite (DBS) system in the United States, purchasing one of only three DBS licenses in 1996. News Corporation and MCI then set up American Sky Broadcasting (ASkyB), a joint venture aiming to provide digital satellite services to homes and businesses by late 1997.

In September 1995 MCI entered the cellular phone market by paying about $210 million for Nationwide Cellular Service, Inc., the largest independent reseller of cellular services. Over the next few months MCI expanded Nationwide through additional contracts to resell service, so that the company was able to offer service to 75 percent of the U.S. population by early 1996. MCI thereby had quickly gained a significant presence in this fast-growing telecom sector without having to invest billions of dollars developing a wireless infrastructure. In November 1995 MCI paid $1.13 billion to acquire Canadian firm SHL Systemhouse Inc., a leading systems integration and outsourcing company, providing information technology services to commercial and governmental enterprises. The following April MCI introduced MCI One, a service providing consumers and small business owners a single source for a full range of communications needs, including long distance, cellular, paging, Internet access and e-mail, calling card, and a personal "One Number" with intelligent routing.

During 1996 Gerald H. Taylor was named CEO, with Roberts retaining the chairmanship. That November MCI and BT entered into a $24 million merger agreement to create a global communications power called Concert plc. As the merger moved through the process of clearing regulatory hurdles on both sides of the Atlantic, MCI announced in July 1997 that its start-up local telephone operation would lose nearly $800 million in 1997, about twice what BT had expected. BT, concluding that MCI was worth less than it originally thought, forced MCI to renegotiate the merger agreement. The companies announced in August that BT would pay $19 million to acquire the 80 percent of MCI it did not already own, a 22 percent reduction from the previous deal. This opened the door, however, to other, unsolicited bidders. WorldCom came forward on October 1 with a $30 billion stock swap bid for MCI, a company more than three times its size. Two weeks later, GTE Corporation stepped into the fray with an all-cash offer of $28 billion. On November 10 MCI accepted a sweetened takeover offer from WorldCom, amounting to a $37 billion stock swap.

WorldCom Began as LDDS in 1983

WorldCom's history began with that of Long Distance Discount Services, Inc. (LDDS), which was formed in 1983 in Hattiesburg, Mississippi, when the breakup of AT&T enabled thousands of competitors to start reselling long distance telephone service to individual and business customers. Bill Fields convinced several investors to lease a local Bell System Wide-Area Telecommunications Service (WATS) line and resell time on the line to businesses. Long distance resellers like LDDS bought time from regional Bell companies in volume and sold

it, often at a discount, to business customers. LDDS owned the switches, or nodes, of its network and leased the lines from local providers. The sophisticated long distance technology was designed to handle a high volume of calls. Some observers compared the long distance telephone industry with the airline industry: there was a fixed cost for getting calls or seats from one place to another, and the more customers a telecommunications company or airline had, the lower its costs would be. Price competition among these companies was ruthless. Assuming that the "Baby Bells" would continue to lease the lines at a fixed rate, Fields signed up 200 customers. But when Bell started raising the charges for the use of the lines, LDDS began to lose money.

By the early months of 1985 the fledgling business was losing $25,000 each month. It became clear to Fields that he was failing at the day-to-day management of LDDS, and he first tried to sell the company. Later in 1985 several owners signed LDDS over to Bernard Ebbers, one of the initial investors. By the time Ebbers became president and chief executive officer, LDDS was $1.5 million in debt.

Ebbers was a Canadian who came to the United States on a basketball scholarship to Mississippi College. After graduation he became a high school baseball coach. He later worked in the garment trade as a distributor, but lost interest in the low-margin industry. Ebbers seized the chance to buy a 40-room motel in Columbia, Mississippi, in the 1970s, borrowing the necessary money to establish himself in the business. In the real estate market of the late 1970s, the value of prime properties could double over the course of five years. Ebbers parlayed his one hotel into 12 by the early 1980s, garnering healthy operating and asset gains.

As head of LDDS, Ebbers worked to control costs. He kept overhead low with lean operations and unpretentious offices. The streamlined LDDS brought on new clients with a claim of customer service that larger long distance companies could not offer. LDDS did not use telemarketing to solicit new business, but mobilized a direct sales force to make personal contacts. After the initial face-to-face solicitation, LDDS made monthly, and sometimes weekly, office calls to ensure that the customers' service was satisfactory. The company provided an alternative to the major long distance carriers' across-the-board packages by tailoring service to each customer's calling patterns, which simultaneously maximized routing efficiency and cut costs. The major long distance carriers at this time also were exerting a great deal of effort to secure big-ticket clients; LDDS was able to take advantage of this by concentrating on small business customers who were falling through the cracks.

LDDS Grew Rapidly Through Acquisition in the Late 1980s and Early 1990s

Within six months of Ebbers's move into the driver's seat, the company had moved into the black. In 1986 revenue rose to $8.6 million, and a year later sales had grown to $18 million. By 1988 annual revenues had skyrocketed to $95 million. Consolidation and acquisitions were the principal factors that enabled LDDS to accomplish this rapid growth during the last five years of the 1980s. The company leveraged its order to buy other third-tier long distance companies, including: Telesphere Network, Inc. (1987); Com-Link 21, Inc. of Tennessee (1988); Telephone Management Corporation (1988); Inter-Comm Telephone, Inc. (1989); ClayDesta Communications of Texas (1989); Microtel, Inc. (1989); and Galesi Telecommunications of Florida (1989). The acquisitions cost the company a total of about $35 million, but expanded LDDS's geographic network to include Missouri, Tennessee, Arkansas, Indiana, Kansas, Kentucky, Texas, Alabama, and Florida.

Each company over which LDDS assumed control performed better after acquisition. Part of the success was attributed to the LDDS standards of customer service, but the economies of scale gained when more companies came on line also brought higher profitability. LDDS applied its customer service ideals to new acquisitions through a decentralized system wherein each state office set its own sales goals. Companies in the system formulated their own marketing strategies in response to local market conditions.

LDDS's annual earnings grew from $641,000 in 1986 to more than $4.5 million in 1989. That same year the company merged with 17-year-old, Nashville-based, Advantage Company, a public company that was losing money when the two consolidated. The merger benefited both companies—it enabled LDDS to reduce its debt and finance future purchases through stock offers, and it brought Advantage into profitability. LDDS was now a public company, incorporated under the name LDDS Communications, Inc. By the end of 1989, LDDS's revenue-per-employee stood at $360,000, more than double the industry average, and triple that of some of LDDS's higher-priced competitors. LDDS also pursued other avenues to spur growth. Its 14 percent annual internal growth rate was fueled by thorough infiltration of its growing markets.

Despite the economic downturn of the early 1990s, LDDS continued its upward climb. The long distance telephone business was not adversely affected by the economic climate, as the telephone had long since established itself as an indispensable part of the business world. In fact, LDDS made two acquisitions that year, purchasing Mercury, Inc. for $10.3 million and Tele-Marketing Corporation of Louisiana for $15.5 million. Despite the recession, LDDS's 1990 profit was $9.8 million, ten times its 1986 total. Sales had grown sixteenfold in that same time span.

LDDS made three acquisitions in 1991, using cash, stock, and bank debt to finance purchases that totaled $90 million. National Telecommunications of Austin was purchased with a combination of $27 million in cash and stock. The acquisition of Phone America of Carolina established an LDDS presence in North and South Carolina and eastern Tennessee. These two companies had combined annual revenues of $51 million. LDDS also made its largest acquisition up to that time with the purchase of Mid-American Communications Corporation. Mid-American provided long distance service to Nebraska, Missouri, Kansas, Illinois, Wisconsin, North Dakota, Minnesota, Colorado, New Mexico, and Arizona. The acquisitions enabled LDDS to increase its sales by 71 percent over 1990 to $263.41 million.

Between 1983 and 1991, LDDS spent more than $200 million to purchase about 24 smaller companies. The additions brought the LDDS network to 27 states, a system that excluded only the Northeast and Northwest. The downside of all of this

growth was that it left the company with $165 million in long-term debt, as well as a negative net worth.

At about the same time, AT&T started trying aggressively to win back customers of all sizes. Despite its dramatic success, LDDS and other third-tier long distance companies had captured about one percent only of the total long distance market at this point. In the 1990s the big three telecommunications companies aimed for the small- and medium-sized businesses they had previously neglected.

LDDS Became Fourth Largest Long Distance Company in 1992

LDDS did not stand idly by, however. In 1992 LDDS acquired Shared Use Network Systems, Inc.; Automated Communications, Inc.; Prime Telecommunications Corporation; TFN Group Communications, Inc.; and Telemarketing Investments, Ltd. These companies, combined, expanded LDDS service in Arizona, Florida, Iowa, Nebraska, Nevada, New Mexico, New York, Ohio, Utah, Virginia, and West Virginia. The new affiliates filled in LDDS's service network and brought a total of $66 million in annual revenues.

But a much more important development for the company in 1992 was its merger with Advanced Telecommunications Corporation (ATC). The Atlanta-based company had $350 million in annual sales spread over a network of 26 southern states. The merger increased LDDS's annual revenues by 30 percent to $801 million in 1992. Although merger-related expenses caused LDDS to take a loss of $8 million for the year, the company expected to realize significant cost savings, increased opportunities for acquisitions, and a wider variety of products with the consolidation. Cost savings were achieved through LDDS's ever-enlarging networks, which produced a situation in which a larger percentage of the company's calls originated and terminated within its service area. Therefore, more calls stayed on the network of low-cost transmission facilities that were owned or leased by LDDS. Of course, increased volume lowered the per-minute costs. LDDS's acquisition of ATC also made the consolidated company the fourth largest long distance provider in the United States (behind AT&T, MCI, and Sprint).

In March 1993 LDDS acquired Dial-Net Inc., which had operations spread throughout half of the United States. Two months later, the company moved into a new headquarters in Jackson, Mississippi. LDDS had dodged rumors and predictions of imminent takeover almost since its inception; in an effort to put to rest such speculation, in September 1993 the company merged with Metromedia Communications Corporation (MCC) of East Rutherford, New Jersey, and Resurgens Communications Group, Inc. of Atlanta. Through the three-way transaction, valued at $1.2 billion, LDDS shareholders collected about 68.5 percent of the fully diluted equity of the combined company, while MCC and Resurgens shareholders secured the remainder. LDDS issued 19 million new common shares in conjunction with the merger and made a private placement of $50 million in convertible preferred stock. The merger extended LDDS's network to include all 48 mainland states, with MCC's strength in the northeast and Resurgens's strength in California of particular importance. The new entity was renamed LDDS Communications, Inc.; John Kluge, who had been chairman of MCC, became chairman of LDDS Communications, and Ebbers was named CEO.

Diversified LDDS Emerged as WorldCom in 1995

LDDS Communications dramatically broadened its telecommunications offerings in the mid-1990s through a series of significant acquisitions. In December 1994 the company acquired Culver City, California-based IDB Communications Group, Inc. in a $900 million stock deal that greatly expanded its international capabilities. Gained through the purchase were gateways to 65 countries, voice and data networks, undersea cables, and international earth stations and satellites. The next month LDDS completed the acquisition of WilTel Network Services for $2.5 billion in cash from The Williams Companies, a pipeline company. Williams had created an 11,000-mile fiber optic cable network, much of it snaked through unused oil and gas pipelines. It was one of only four national networks in the United States. LDDS had quickly moved from being a leaser of a larger rival's phone lines to having one of the most sophisticated U.S. networks, as well as international gateways and networks. With its eye on becoming a global leader in telecommunications, the company changed its name to WorldCom, Inc. in May 1995. Basketball superstar Michael Jordan started a stint as a corporate spokesperson for the company in December of that year. For the year, WorldCom recorded revenues of $3.70 billion, a 65 percent increase over the prior year.

Having added international capabilities and a nationwide network to its core long distance business, WorldCom next aimed for a piece of the local communication service market. It was helped in this effort by the February 1996 signing into law of the Telecommunications Act of 1996, which permitted local and long distance companies to enter each other's markets. Following the passage of this landmark legislation, WorldCom signed agreements to become the primary provider of long distance service for GTE, Ameritech, and SBC Mobile Systems. The company received permission from state regulators in Connecticut, Florida, Illinois, California, and Texas to provide local telephone service. In December 1996 WorldCom acquired MFS Communications Company, Inc. for $14.4 billion in stock. MFS was a leading provider of alternative local network access facilities—bypassing the Bell networks—through digital fiber optic cable networks it had built in and around more than 50 U.S. cities as well as several in Europe. The addition of MFS made WorldCom the first company to offer both local and long distance services over its own network in the United States since the AT&T breakup. MFS also owned a trans-Atlantic fiber optic link and had just acquired—in August 1996—UUNET Technologies, Inc., the world's largest Internet service provider (and also the first). MFS Chairman James Q. Crowe was named chairman of WorldCom following the merger, UUNET CEO John W. Sidgmore was named vice-chairman, and Ebbers remained president and CEO. WorldCom revenues reached $4.49 billion in 1996, although the company recorded a net loss of $2.21 billion, reflecting a $2.14 billion charge related to the acquisition of MFS.

WorldCom could now offer an impressive array of individual services—local, long distance, Internet, and international—as well as "bundled" services that were particularly attractive to businesses. One area in which it was clearly lacking was

cellular, although in 1996 it had purchased Phoenix, Arizona-based Choice Cellular, one of the leading cellular resellers in the United States. But WorldCom was not done dealing. From September through November 1997 the company announced acquisitions of CompuServe Corporation, Brooks Fiber Properties, Inc., and MCI. CompuServe was acquired from H&R Block Inc. in January 1998 for $1.2 billion in stock. WorldCom retained CompuServe's data network but swapped its consumer online service division for America Online's ANS network services subsidiary. These network additions significantly bolstered UUNET's capacity. January 1998 also saw WorldCom complete its $2.9 billion purchase of Brooks Fiber, like MFS a provider of alternative local access networks in the United States. Brooks Fiber added an additional 34 cities to the 52 markets where WorldCom already offered alternative local phone services.

MCI WorldCom Created in 1998

For 1997 WorldCom posted revenues of $7.35 billion, a 64 percent increase over 1996. The combination of WorldCom and MCI, however, was expected to add up to a company with revenues exceeding $30 billion. The $37 billion merger (including $7 billion in cash paid by WorldCom to acquire BT's 20 percent stake in MCI), which was consummated on September 15, 1998, was at the time of its announcement in November 1997 the largest merger ever, although it soon was eclipsed by other deals in the merger frenzy of the late 1990s. The resultant MCI WorldCom, Inc. boasted of 22 million customers, 25 percent of the long distance market in the United States, some 933,000 miles of fiber for long distance service, local network facilities in 100 U.S. markets, 508,000 fiber miles for local service, and an international presence in more than 200 countries. European regulators, fearful that MCI WorldCom would have too much control of the Internet backbone, forced MCI to divest all of its Internet assets, and MCI agreed in July 1998 to sell them to Cable & Wireless PLC for about $1.6 billion in cash. MCI WorldCom, however, was able to keep WorldCom's prized UUNET Internet operation. As with other WorldCom takeovers, Ebbers took the posts of president and CEO of the new entity, and MCI's Roberts was named chairman.

In March 1998, meanwhile, Telefonica de España S.A. joined with WorldCom and MCI in business ventures that aimed at expanding MCI WorldCom's reach in Europe and Latin America. WorldCom in August 1998 sold $6.1 billion in bonds, the largest corporate bond deal in history, raising funds to help pay for its purchase of MCI. In December 1998 EchoStar Communications Corp. agreed to buy the satellite television business of News Corporation and MCI WorldCom (including ASkyB) in a stock transaction valued at more than $1 billion, with MCI WorldCom slated to be left with a stake of about seven percent in EchoStar. In August 1998 BT agreed to buy MCI's 24.9 percent stake in the Concert joint venture for $1 billion, effectively bringing to a close the two companies' partnership. It was not the end of Concert, however, as BT had in the meantime formed a new global joint venture with AT&T to provide multinational clients a host of telecommunications and data services; Concert was melded into this joint venture. In late September 1998 the newly charged competitive environment was clearly evident when MCI WorldCom launched its own bundled service for multinationals, called On-Net. Certainly the telecommunications wars—which MCI had helped precipitate—were only just beginning, and MCI WorldCom was certain to be on the front line of nearly every battle.

Principal Divisions

MCI WorldCom; UUNET WorldCom; WorldCom International.

Further Reading

Barrett, Amy, and Elstrom, Peter, ''Making WorldCom Live Up to Its Name,'' *Business Week,* July 14, 1997, pp. 65–66.

''Bernie Ebbers Saved the Company,'' *Mississippi Business Journal,* November 1989, p. 316.

Cantelon, Philip L., *The History of MCI: 1968–1988, the Early Years,* Dallas: Heritage Press, 1993.

Coll, Steve, *The Deal of the Century: The Breakup of AT&T,* New York: Atheneum, 1986.

Donlon, J.P., ''Convergence Calling,'' *Chief Executive,* May 1996, pp. 32–36.

Elstrom, Peter, ''The Axman Cometh?: WorldCom's Pattern: Shopping, Then Chopping,'' *Business Week,* October 20, 1997, pp. 36–37.

Elstrom, Peter, and others, ''The New World Order,'' *Business Week,* October 13, 1997, pp. 26–30, 32–33.

Epstein, Joseph, ''Private-Label Long Distance,'' *Financial World,* April 22, 1996, pp. 52–54, 56.

Faulhaber, Gerald R., *Telecommunications in Turmoil: Technology and Public Policy,* Cambridge: Ballinger Publishing, 1987.

Frank, Robert, and Holden, Benjamin A., ''LDDS Agrees To Acquire IDB in Stock Swap,'' *Wall Street Journal,* August 2, 1994, p. A3.

Gianturco, Michael, ''Telephone Numbers,'' *Forbes,* June 22, 1992, p. 108.

Jones, Kevin D., ''LDDS: From Zero to $150 Million in Six Years, But Analysts Say It's a Takeover Target,'' *Mississippi Business Journal,* November 1989, pp. 26–30.

Kahaner, Larry, *On the Line: The Men of MCI—Who Took On AT&T, Risked Everything and Won,* New York: Warner Books, 1986.

Keller, John J., and Lipin, Steven, ''The Battle for MCI Takes Another Twist: Now, It's GTE's Turn,'' *Wall Street Journal,* October 16, 1997, pp. A1, A10.

——, ''WorldCom, MCI Deal Could Rewrite Script for a New Phone Era,'' *Wall Street Journal,* November 11, 1997, pp. A1, A6.

Keller, John J., and Naik, Gautum, ''Merger Poses a Bold Challenge to Bells: WorldCom, MFS Confirm $12.4 Billion Accord,'' *Wall Street Journal,* August 27, 1996, p. A3.

Kupfer, Andrew, ''MCI WorldCom: It's the Biggest Merger Ever. Can It Rule Telecom?,'' *Fortune,* April 27, 1998, pp. 118+.

Lewyn, Mark, ''MCI: Attacking on All Fronts,'' *Business Week,* June 13, 1994, pp. 76–79.

——, ''MCI Is Coming Through Loud and Clear,'' *Business Week,* January 25, 1993, pp. 84–85.

Lipin, Steven, and Keller, John J., ''WorldCom's MCI Bid Alters Playing Field for Telecom Industry,'' *Wall Street Journal,* October 2, 1997, pp. A1, A8.

Mehta, Stephanie N., ''WorldCom Quietly Completes MCI Communications Purchase,'' *Wall Street Journal,* September 15, 1998, p. B6.

Naik, Gautam, and Keller, John J., ''BT Cuts Purchase Price for MCI by $5 Billion,'' *Wall Street Journal,* August 25, 1997, p. A4.

Schiesel, Seth, ''The Re-engineering of Bernie Ebbers,'' *New York Times,* April 27, 1998, pp. D1, D5.

Selz, Michael, ''LDDS Communications Wins Big by Thinking Small,'' *Wall Street Journal,* July 26, 1991.

Simon, Samuel A., *After Divestiture: What the AT&T Settlement Means for Business and Residential Telephone Service,* White Plains, New York: Knowledge Industry Publications, 1985.

Sprout, Alison L., ''MCI: Can It Become the Communications Company of the Next Century?,'' *Fortune,* October 2, 1995, pp. 107+.

Spurge, Lorraine, *Failure Is Not an Option: How MCI Invented Competition in Telecommunications,* Encino, Calif.: Spurge Ink!, 1998.

Stone, Alan, *Wrong Number: The Breakup of AT&T,* New York: Basic Books, 1989.

Thomas, Emory, Jr., ''LDDS Prospers Through Aggressive Acquisitions,'' *Wall Street Journal,* May 9, 1994, p. B4.

Thomas, Emory, Jr., and Caleb Solomon, ''LDDS to Buy WilTel Unit from Williams,'' *Wall Street Journal,* August 23, 1994, p. A3.

Tunstall, Brooke W., *Disconnecting Parties, Managing the Bell System Breakup: An Inside View,* New York: McGraw-Hill, 1985.

Ward, Judy, ''Critic's Choice: As It Steps Out from AT&T's Shadow, MCI Finds Itself More Scrutinized Than Ever,'' *Financial World,* July 18, 1995, pp. 32–34.

—Bruce P. Montgomery and April S. Dougal
—updated by David E. Salamie

McKee Foods Corporation

P.O. Box 750
Collegedale, Tennessee 37315-0750
U.S.A.
(615) 238-7111
(800) 522-4499
Fax: (615) 238-7127
Web site: http://www.mckeefoods.com

Private Company
Incorporated: 1957 as McKee Baking Company
Employees: 5,345
Sales: $831 million (1998)
SICs: 2051 Bread, Cake & Related Products; 2052
Cookies & Crackers; 2043 Cereal Breakfast Foods

Family-owned and operated, McKee Foods Corporation is the David to such Goliaths as Nabisco Brands, Lance, and Interstate Bakeries. McKee Foods' threat to these and other food giants is the niche of snack cakes, the driving force behind the company's persistent growth in sales in the 1980s and 1990s. This growth was all the more remarkable in view of the company's comparatively low profile, lack of a full-scale national sales force, and cautious approach to expansion. The secret to McKee's success was its Little Debbie snack cake line, which dominated the market for snack cakes in the United States in the second half of the century, frequently with a greater than 50 percent market share. By comparison, McKee's closest competitor, Ralston-Purina's Continental Baking, generally posted less than a 20 percent market share. Nutty Bars, Figaroos, Oatmeal Creme Pies, Caravellas, Golden Cremes, Devil Cremes, Swiss Rolls—some 66 varieties in all graced the Little Debbie snack cake line in 1999. McKee Foods also marketed granola bars, granola cereals, and other bakery products under the Sunbelt label.

Company Origins

The company was born during the heart of the 1930s depression. A young North Carolina couple, O.D. and Ruth McKee, lost their savings after a bank failure and moved from their home in Hendersonville to Chattanooga, Tennessee, in 1933. O.D. found work as a bakery salesman, selling Virginia Dare Cakes from Becker's Bakery, a local establishment, for five cents each. By 1934 O.D. had purchased his own delivery truck. He then found out that Jack's Cookie Company, another Chattanooga bakery, was up for sale. O.D. cashed in his truck and he and Ruth became owners and operators of their first business. According to the company publication *The Story Behind Little Debbie Snack Cakes,* the two ''were ideal business partners because her cautious, conservative nature was the perfect complement to his risk-taking, adventuresome spirit.''

In 1935 the couple moved the business to a new location and began making soft cookies and cakes. A year later they handed the business to Ruth's father, Symon D. King, and returned to North Carolina to launch a new bakery. Located in Charlotte and named Jack's Cookie Company like its predecessor, the business was highly successful. In 1946, O.D., who ''always had a gift for innovation and automation,'' built a new, state-of-the-art plant. During this period he also invented a soft oatmeal creme pie, ''the company's oldest continuous product,'' according to *Milling and Baking News.*

The McKees sold their Charlotte business in the early 1950s and considered retiring. They decided instead to return to Chattanooga to manage the original Jack's, now called King's Bakery and owned by Ruth's brother, Cecil King. In 1954 O.D. and Ruth purchased the company stock, and the foundation for the McKee Baking Company was born. As he had previously, O.D. served as salesman, inventor, and production manager while Ruth operated as purchaser, personnel manager, and office manager. In 1957, when they outgrew the Chattanooga bakery, the operation moved to nearby Collegedale. It was at this location that the company established its headquarters and grew into a major private corporation. The original Collegedale plant was expanded more than a dozen times before a sister plant was added. In 1982 the McKee family launched a third plant in Gentry, Arkansas; a fourth followed eight years later in Stuarts Draft, Virginia. By this time Ruth had passed away and O.D. had transferred management to his sons, Ellsworth and Jack, while retaining his chairmanship.

Company Perspectives:

We take pride in working together to provide great-tasting snack foods of outstanding value to delight customers throughout all of North America.

Introduction of Little Debbies in 1960

In 1960 the company made history in two ways. First, after leading the industry in mass production of small snack cakes, it conceived the "family" pack of 12 individually wrapped cakes sold as one multipack unit. Second, it began affixing the Little Debbie brand, named after Ellsworth's daughter Debra, to its products. Both Little Debbie and the family pack remain the company's most significant generators of sales. A proliferation of snack cake varieties since that time—including the introduction of the Sunbelt line in 1981—has been fueled by the momentum of these two landmark events.

By 1982 McKee Baking, with $130 million in sales, ranked 22nd in the industry, behind such billion-dollar giants as Continental and Interstate. Sales at the time were concentrated principally in the Midwest, Southwest, and West. By 1987 the company was able to boast annual sales growth of ten to 15 percent since the advent of Little Debbie, a product line that had now expanded to 32 varieties available in 41 states. McKee succeeded in conquering Continental's Hostess, Interstate's Dolly Madison, and other major national brands through its low pricing. According to *Forbes* writer William Stern, the feisty competitor sells its products through supermarkets for 50 percent to 70 percent less than other comparable items. More surprisingly, the company's net margins after such heavy undercutting are approximately six percent, while the average for the industry is 5.5 percent. "What's to stop McKee's giant competitors from matching its low prices?" queries Stern. "Common sense. . . . They are giant corporations with giant overhead, while McKee is a family business. And, even with lower prices, it would take them years to get the economies of scale McKee gets from its overwhelming market share." McKee maintains its low overhead by employing an independent distribution system and by expanding production only to keep pace with demand. Another advantage it has over the competition is the long shelf life of its naturally preserved products—some three to four times as long as that of Hostess Twinkies.

After 1980 McKee enhanced its market share by selling to convenience stores as well as supermarkets and by periodically rolling out national television campaigns, the most memorable of which was launched in 1985 featuring impersonator Rich Little. New products, including Little Debbie Fancy Cakes and the Little Debbie Snack Favorite line, also served as powerful inducements to buyers, at least half of which were age 15 and under. The company changed its name in 1991 to McKee Foods Corporation. Under chief executive officer Ellsworth McKee, the Tennessee bakery preserved its highly private identity and strong family management (many third-generation McKees hold high positions within the company). Although investment houses and bakery competitors, especially Continental, have

hoped for the family to sell, Ellsworth has responded: "There's no way we can be forced to." With its highly profitable status as the largest independently owned company of its kind in the country, and with consumer demand and snack cake share still rising, there would be little sense in doing so.

Continued Market Leader in the 1990s

The recession in the early 1990s provided fuel for the company's growth. With their lower prices, Little Debbie and Sunbelt brands attracted new consumers looking to shave expenses. To keep up with the company's steady growth, McKee Foods opened two new bakeries, one in Gentry, Arkansas, and the other in Stuarts Draft, Virginia. In keeping with the company's conservative approach to expansion, the new plants provided just enough capacity to keep up with existing demand. McKee produced baked goods only to fill orders. By 1999 the bakery in Gentry was employing 1,265 people, and the one in Stuarts Draft employed 925 people.

In the mid-1990s Ellsworth McKee handed the reins to his brother Jack, who took over as president and chief executive officer. Ellsworth continued to provide input into running the business from his position as chair of the board.

McKee Foods continued to rely on brand recognition and customer loyalty to generate sales, rather than national advertising campaigns and a national sales force dedicated to drumming up orders and garnering shelf space in grocery and convenience stores. Sales rose from $525 million in 1991 to approximately $825 million in 1997. Although sales were up only a modest 0.7 percent in 1998, to $831 million, the company still dominated the snack cake market segment.

The company's Sunbelt brand benefited from the tremendous growth in the granola bar market in the 1990s. By 1998 the Sunbelt Granola Bar line accounted for $33.5 million in annual revenues. Americans were spending nearly a billion dollars a year on granola bars, however, and Sunbelt held only a fraction of that market, behind Kellogg's Nutri-Grain brand, the clear leader; Quaker Oats' Chewy granola bar line; and Kellogg's Rice Krispies Treats. McKee was used to battling the big-name brands, and the company moved to capture a greater piece of the granola bar category in the late 1990s. McKee began a national marketing campaign in 1998 to promote its granola bar line in general and its new S'mores variety in particular. With print advertising in *People* magazine and television ads on game shows, talk shows, and home shows, the company hoped to reach its target audience of 25- to 49-year-old female heads of households with children aged six to 17. Employing a strategy that worked well with its Little Debbie brand, the company also challenged its competitors with lower prices, suggesting retail prices ranging from $1.49 to $2.49 per carton.

Despite competition from baking giants Nabisco and Interstate Bakeries, McKee maintained its lead in its chosen snack cake niche and pursued modest expansion in the granola segment. Still family-owned and family-operated as of the late 1990s, McKee had reached number 247 on *Forbes'* Private 500 list, and family members showed no sign of letting the company slip from their hands.

Principal Subsidiaries

Sovex Natural Foods.

Further Reading

"Family Clout Backs Philosophy of Independence in Era of Mergers," *Milling & Baking News,* November 11, 1988.

"McKee Baking Sets July Start for Production at New Virginia Plant," *Milling & Baking News,* May 8, 1990.

"McKee Plans 'Little Debbie' Plant in Virginia," *Bakery Production,* May 1987.

"McKee's New Snack Plant Begins Production," *Bakery Production,* August 1990.

Stern, William, "Mom and Dad Knew Every Name," *Forbes,* December 7, 1992.

The Story Behind Little Debbie Snack Cakes, Collegedale, Tenn.: McKee Foods Corporation.

Thompson, Stephanie, "McKee Eyes S'More Media for Sunbelt," *Brandweek,* October 19, 1998, p. 10.

—Jay P. Pederson
—updated by Susan Windisch Brown

Meijer Incorporated

2929 Walker Avenue N.W.
Grand Rapids, Michigan 49504-9428
U.S.A.
(616) 453-6711
Fax: (616) 791-2572
Web site: http://www.meijer.com

Private Company
Incorporated: 1934
Employees: 60,000
Sales: $6 billion (1997)
SICs: 5411 Grocery Stores; 5141 Groceries—General
Line

Meijer Incorporated, according to *Forbes* magazine,''is one of the 15 largest growing private companies'' in the United States; it is the country's fifth largest discount retailer, according to *Discount Store News.* The company operates 117 supercenters in Michigan, Ohio, Illinois, Indiana, and Kentucky. The company also owns and operates four office centers, two divisions of property services, and more than ten distribution centers. What makes Meijer such an overwhelming success is simple: its stores are open 364 days a year, 24 hours a day; each store has 40 departments, which sell more than 120,000 products; and one can buy almost anything at a Meijer store—from applesauce to flour to pants to lawn furniture to zinc oxide. Customers also can get prescriptions filled or shoes repaired.

Meijer entered the wholesale shopping segment in 1992 with the development of SourceClub, warehouse-shopping designed for the individual shopper, as well as the more traditional targeted customers from small businesses and affiliated groups. In business since 1934, Meijer has created up to 10,000 private-label brands.

Early History

Hendrik Meijer emigrated from The Netherlands to the United States in 1907, settling in Michigan. In 1914 he opened a barbershop, expanding it to a double storefront by 1923. When the Depression hit, Meijer had trouble finding a tenant to rent the new space in his Greenville, Michigan location. He decided to open a grocery store, hoping to cover the building rent and operating costs from store profits. With $338.76 of goods bought on credit, Hendrik Meijer opened his food store in 1934, competing with a grocer across the street as well as more than 20 competitors in town.

With his son Frederick, born in 1919, Hendrik Meijer traveled as far as necessary to find the best goods for his grocery at the lowest prices available. In keeping with the needs of the 1930s United States, Meijer's goal was to help customers of his Thrift Market store save money. To speed shoppers' progress through the store, Fred built a space designed to display 12 hand-held baskets. Above the baskets was a handwritten sign inviting customers to take one and help themselves. This ''self-service'' innovation of 1935 increased the number of customers Meijer could serve, thus aiding the growth of the business. By 1937 Hendrik Meijer had doubled the size of his original store.

Growth and Expansion: 1940s to Mid-1960s

As the grocer across the street from the original Meijer store mowed his neatly kept lawn, Hendrik noticed the more trampled path to the front door of his shop with pride. In 1942 Meijer opened a second store. With the help of wife Gezina, daughter Johanna, and son Fred, Hendrik Meijer's business succeeded through the 1940s. In the 1950s the family built four new stores and opened a supermarket chain in western Michigan. After a fire leveled Meijer's first Greenville store, the company relocated to its present Grand Rapids, Michigan headquarters.

Meijer had more than ten stores in operation in Grand Rapids, Muskegon, and Holland, Michigan by the late 1950s. Trading stamps became popular in supermarkets across the country through the next two decades. Meijer, though offered a stamp program from some of the major vendors, declined. Then the company, with some trepidation, initiated its own Goodwill stamp campaign in 1956 at a cost of $10,000 a week. Although gross sales increased, overhead costs increased as well, keeping Meijer's profits steady.

In 1961, with 14 supermarkets in operation, Meijer decided to drop the stamp program. According to the owner, there was neither profit nor reputation to be gained from doing what nearly all other retailers were doing at the time. With a thorough campaign planned, Meijer began a series of advertisements designed to promote its singular position as a supermarket that maintained a strong customer base simply by offering below-average prices. Beginning with a week-long newspaper series, Meijer ran ads with no identification to spark the interest of readers. A picture of a baby and the statement, "It's about time somebody wakes up!" was followed with another infant photo and the words, "Nobody, but nobody gets nothin' for nothin'." In the following Sunday paper, Meijer identified itself and announced that it was closing stores the following Monday to lower hundreds of prices. Banners urged buyers to "Save U.S. Green Currency—Redeemable Anywhere for Almost Anything!" Finally, Meijer revealed its plan to drop stamps. When shoppers arrived at Meijer on Tuesday, they found shelves lined with a profusion of tags listing "Typical Stamp Store Price" as compared with "Meijer No-Stamp Price." The company continued its barrage, with circulars detailing price lists, comparing as many as 540 items with competitors' prices. While the competition offered double- and triple-coupon savers, Meijer nonetheless increased its market share as a result of the campaign it waged to keep its image as a different kind of supermarket.

By 1961 Meijer had 14 supermarkets in the Grand Rapids area, with more on the way. In 1962 the company opened its first Thrifty Acres Discount Department Store, a combination food/retail item store similar to a hypermarket that had opened in Belgium the previous year. Within two years Meijer had three Thrifty Acres built, with two more in the planning stages. These large capacity discount markets vastly increased Meijer's lead in the retail segment. The growth of Meijer was overshadowed, however, by the death of founder Hendrick at age 57 in 1964. Fred continued expansion after his father's death, building Meijer's reputation as a low-cost retailer.

From State to State: 1960s–80s

Extending further into Michigan through the late 1960s, Meijer entered the Ohio market as well. The Meijer one-stop shopping theme, which the company claims to have pioneered, gave the customer a chance to buy these items in addition to food, checking all of the following merchandise out at one counter: garden and pet supplies, small appliances, jewelry, sporting goods, clothing, and home fashions. Growth remained steady through the 1970s. Meijer had more than 20 stores open, some set up with gasoline pumps as well. Though Meijer planned to build more retail/gas station combination stores, its plans were stalled by a 1978 law prohibiting a business from selling both gasoline and alcohol unless it was in a village, town, or municipality with a population less than 3,000.

By the 1980s the hypermarket was a concept destined to remain. On the national scene, retail giants like Kmart and Wal-Mart dominated; locally, competitors increased advertising and low-price wars. As more and more stores increased their square footage and challenged Meijer in the discount retail segment, the company had to carve out its niche more aggressively. There was no way around it; Meijer increased advertising dramatically. In 1984 the business bought 880 inches of page space in the *Grand Rapids Press*; by December 1985 Meijer had increased space to 2,800 inches.

The company introduced in-store delis, bakeries, and fresh meat and fish departments in the mid-1980s, promoting the changes under the slogan "Rediscover Meijer's." An example of the low-price wars was the December 1985 scuffle over banana sales. Meijer advertised them at 14 cents a pound. When an independent offered bananas for 11 cents, Meijer countered with a ten cents a pound offer. Another competitor planned on selling the fruit for five cents a pound. The goal was to get more and more customers in the door, the price of bananas being simply a sideshow. As Grand Rapids market owner David Daane, quoted in the January 20, 1986 trade journal *Supermarket News,* commented: "You know what they say in the grocery business: One guy jumps off the cliff and the others follow." Important to note is how Meijer resembled its competitors in strategy, and when, and if, it differed from them.

In February of 1987 Meijer marched into the Columbus, Ohio market, claiming more than 20 percent of the shopping public with only one store open in the area. The company planned at least one more unit in Columbus, which was gaining other wholesale club stores as well at the time.

A major change in Meijer's practices occurred a year later when the company announced it would keep most of its Michigan and Ohio stores open 24 hours after March 7, 1988. A total of 43 of 46 stores were designated to be open round the clock, departing from the previous policy of closing Meijer stores for Thanksgiving, Easter, Christmas Day, and a half-day on Christmas Eve. Employees sent a letter to Fred Meijer, requesting that he reconsider the change and allow them the chance to spend holidays with families and friends. Meijer chose not to reverse the new policy, however.

In an effort to sell alcohol in its Michigan stores, in March 1988 Meijer pushed passage of a state bill to change the ten-year-old law prohibiting the sale of alcohol and gasoline from the same location. The bill would allow gas pumps on a site where liquor was sold provided the shopping center had 50,000 square feet of space or an inventory of at least $250,000. Opponents included the Associated Food Dealers of Michigan and the Package Liquor Dealers Association. The latter group stated that the bill was discriminatory and served the interests of the big chains only.

Meijer had reason enough to compete at any level possible; by 1988 the company, still unknown outside its Michigan/Ohio retail segment, ranked number 42 in the Fortune 400 private companies. Fred Meijer, son of the founder, had an estimated wealth of more than $400 million. After 50 years in business, company sales were estimated at $2 billion. Meijer proved a serious challenge to any small retailers in its market and could even go up against the mega-retailers Kmart and Wal-Mart. In addition to its Meijer stores, the company owned 36 Sagebrush casual clothing stores, 16 Tansy women's clothing stores, and either owned or leased various in-store services such as postal stations and dry-cleaning units.

By year-end 1988 Meijer phased out its Sagebrush and Tansy facilities as leases expired. Meijer stores increased to 53, and the company put $20 million into the construction of its tenth distribution center, its largest to date, near Detroit. Since construction was delayed at the distribution center, a halt was called on the progress of four new stores slated for the Dayton, Ohio region, and one in Columbus. Four other store constructions, at the prototypical size of 225,000–250,000 square feet, were on target schedules. Two were in Detroit suburbs, one near Ann Arbor, and one in Springfield, Ohio, which could replace the Meijer store already there (49,000 square feet, one of the smallest the company operated).

A Meijer innovation in early 1989 was an electronic checking system. The Meijer 1 Card allowed customers to withdraw from their checking accounts automatically, with no paperwork or identification verification necessary. Patrick Gavin, vice-president of pharmacy, service, and retail technology, stated in the *Grand Rapid Press* that Meijer would be "the first in the world to set up a paperless software system through its cash registers." The company and banking institutions could save money, up to a total of $1.75 per check, on processing fees.

By mid-1989 sales for the entire Meijer chain were estimated at $65 million per week, bringing the annual sales figure to approximately $3 billion. Store sales were not the only indicator of Meijer's success, however; each new Meijer store cost $18 million to put up, and Meijer was opening up to five per year during the 1980s. The company researched expansion possibilities in new markets such as Toledo, Ohio, and both South Bend and Indianapolis, Indiana.

In keeping with its growth, Meijer decided to make a historical advertising shift, moving from Grand Rapids' Johnson & Dean to Southfield, Michigan-based W.B. Doner & Company. Near Detroit, Doner had national marketing expertise, something Meijer looked for in a changing marketplace. Johnson & Dean had had the Meijer account for 33 years, a record time period in advertising, producing 200 radio and 150 television ads per year. In *Advertising Age,* Patricia Strnad commented that, historically, "Meijer appear to have relied on copying other advertising ideas rather than creating new ones."

Two months after Wal-Mart advertised its environmentally friendly stance, and at the same time as two unrelated supermarket chains in San Diego and Pittsburgh promoted similar concepts, Meijer initiated its environmental awareness program in late 1989. In-store posters, grocery bags, and shopping cart signs stated, "We Care About the Earth We Share." Videos, pamphlets, and other educational publications were slated for distribution as well. Grand Rapids-based D&W Food Center, a long-time Meijer competitor, had established an environmental program years before; the chain considered making its efforts more public in response to consumer interest in the issue.

Meijer awarded an advertising package to the Nappies biodegradable diaper manufacturer, Ontario-based Dafoe & Dafoe, in response to that company's efforts. While experts questioned whether the plastics used in the product were indeed biodegradable, Meijer countered by stating that the emphasis of its program was on consumer education. As quoted in *Supermarket News,* Meijer stated, "We're not interested in debating the specific merits of each manufacturer's claim. We're just trying to make it easier for customers to research these issues." The trade journal went on to observe that environmental issues would move to the forefront of retailers' agendas through the 1990s and into the next century.

The 1990s and Beyond

Early in 1990—as it had done 30 years earlier—Meijer once again led its peers in abandoning double-coupon promotions. Beginning in its metropolitan Detroit stores, Meijer dropped the promotion in February. Ryan Mathews, Detroit-based editor of the journal *Grocery Marketing,* was quoted in the *Detroit Free Press,* describing such campaigns as "the most senseless act of marketing that stores can engage in." Luckily for Meijer, the retailer was known for its excellent customer service. The company could then use advertising to emphasize that aspect of its image, rather than concentrate on prices only, as most competitors did. Drawing from founder Hendrik Meijer's steady, practical approach to retailing, Meijer's ad agency W.B. Doner & Company planned television spots based on that theme, with the slogan: "Meijer. The store built on common sense."

Meijer store openings planned included three in Michigan in 1990 and seven in 1991, with three planned for the Dayton, Ohio market and four slated for Toledo. Wal-Mart confronted Meijer in its own backyard, moving into the Ohio market with the construction of a new distribution center there. Industry analysts noted Meijer's traditionally loyal customer base as a hedge against the Wal-Mart presence. Digging its heels in, Meijer took advantage of the exit of retailers Ames and Hills from the Cincinnati area to reenter a market it had pulled out of in 1987. (After six years of operating eight stores offering general merchandise only, Meijer had sold its stores to Zayre, which Ames acquired in 1988. Both Ames and Hills filed Chapter 11 bankruptcy in 1991.)

Management changes in April 1990 paved the way for Fred Meijer's eventual retirement. His sons Doug and Hank Meijer were named co-chairmen, and Fred became chairman of the executive committee, with plans to work with senior management on the company's day-to-day operations. Other key executives included Mark Meijer, a member of the "Office of the Chairman," and Earl Holton, president and chief operating officer. Vice-Chairman Harvey Lemmen retired during the changeover.

The company continued growing through the early 1990s as a premier discount retailer in the Midwest, maintaining a low profile and high profit margins. With sales at $3 billion, Meijer led in the field of hypermarket supercenters. But Fred Meijer's vision of an expanding network of supercenters throughout the Midwestern United States was not yet achieved. During the mid-1990s the company established a supercenter on the north side of South Bend, Indiana, a state-of-the-art retail store with 40 departments and more than 100 products sold within it. Within a few years Meijer opened a second store just east of the city, designed with the same format and convenience for customers.

In March of 1998 Meijer opened its first store in Louisville, Kentucky, with four more planned to open during the next two years. The family's most risky expansion site, however, would be Chicago, where the company planned to open ten new supercenters beginning in 1999. Competing with such giants as Wal-Mart and Target, Meijer was preparing a sophisticated strategy to enter and capture this new market. One of its most innovative moves, an express self-checkout lane for customers with just a few items, was designed to attract people to shop at Meijer supercenters in Chicago.

Meijer is one of the fastest growing supercenter stores in the nation, and there seems to be no end in sight for continued expansion. Having reported revenues amounting to $6 billion in 1997, Meijer is clearly meeting the shopping needs of people throughout the Midwest.

Further Reading

Cipriano Pepperl, Jo-Ann, "Meijer: Serving Customers an Array of Choices," *Greater Lansing Business Monthly,* February 1, 1992.

Couretas, John, "Most Meijer Stores To Open 24 Hours," *Grand Rapids Press,* February 6, 1988.

DeNitto, Emily, "Meijer Breaks Store-Wide 'Earth Friendly' Program," *Supermarket News,* November 6, 1989.

"Don't Just Drop Stamps—Give Customers Something Better," *Progressive Grocer,* February, 1963.

Duff, Mike, "Meijer Enters Louisville Market," *Discount Store News,* May 11, 1998, pp. 3, 130.

Halverson, Richard C., "Meijer to Enter New Markets," *Discount Store News,* March 9, 1998, pp. 1, 83.

——, "Meijer to Re-Enter Cincy After Hills, Ames Exit," *Discount Store News,* June 17, 1991.

Kaplan, Rachel, "Meijer Ads Heat Up Grand Rapids Market," *Supermarket News,* January 20, 1986.

Kelly, Mary Ellen, "Traditional Columbus Chains Brace for Superstore Assault," *Discount Store News,* February 16, 1987.

"Longtime Super Store Meijer Poised for Growth After Completion of DC," *Discount Store News,* December 19, 1988.

"Meijer Faces Challenge from Wal-Mart Thrust," *Discount Store News,* July 16, 1990.

"Meijer Finds Right Combination for Midwest," *Discount Store News,* July 17, 1989.

"Meijer Leads Field as Hyper/Supercenter Challengers Take Aim," *Discount Store News,* July 22, 1991.

"Meijer to Adopt Self-Checkout," *Discount Store News,* September 21, 1998, p. 5.

Moukheiber, Zina, "Squeezing the Tomatoes," *Forbes,* February 13, 1995, p. 55.

Muller, Joann, "Meijer First Store To Cut Double Coupons," *Detroit Free Press,* February 20, 1990.

Power, Denise, "Meijer's, A Hypermarket Chain, Ramps Up Self Checkout," *Daily News Record,* September 9, 1998, p. 8.

Radigan Lohr, Mary, "Meijer Inc. Switching to Detroit-Area Ad Agency," *Grand Rapids Press,* August 8, 1989.

——, "Meijer Stores to Use Electronic Checking System," *Grand Rapids Press,* March 12, 1989.

Strnad, Patricia, "Hypermarket Pioneer Changes Tack," *Advertising Age,* September 25, 1989.

——, "Meijer Hyper in Midwest Markets," *Advertising Age,* February 15, 1988.

——, "Meijer Shapes Ads on Common Sense," *Advertising Age,* April 16, 1990.

—Frances E. Norton
—updated by Thomas Derdak

Melamine Chemicals, Inc.

Highway 18 West
Donaldsonville, Louisiana 70346
U.S.A.
(225) 473-3121
Fax: (225)473-0550
Web site: http://www.melamine.com

Wholly Owned Subsidiary of Borden Chemical, Inc.
Incorporated: 1968
Employees: 153
Sales: $60 million (1997)
SICs: 2819 Industrial Inorganic Chemicals; 2821 Plastic
    Materials and Resins; 2873 Fertilizers—
    Manufacturers

Melamine Chemicals, Inc. (MCI), is a wholly owned subsidiary of Borden Chemical, Inc., which has its corporate headquarters in Columbus, Ohio. Its ultimate parent is Borden, Inc. MCI's combined M-I and M-II plant, in Donaldsonville, Louisiana, is one of the world's major producers of melamine crystal and one of only two such plants in the Western Hemisphere. Its only U.S. competitor is DSM Melamine America, which has its plant in Fortier, Louisiana. Melamine is a specialized chemical crystal made from urea (ammonia and carbon dioxide) and is used in industrial and commercial products and applications. Four-fifths of it produced by MCI is used to make melamine-formaldehyde resins, which are widely used in adhesives, paper and other surface coatings and laminates, plastic moldings, and in foams and textiles. Worldwide, about 95 percent of all produced melamine is used in melamine-formaldehyde resins, but it is also used in fluorescent dyes and as a flame retardant in fabrics. Melamine's uses differ widely from one area of the world to another. In the United States, about three-fourths of it is used for surface coatings (37 percent), laminates (32 percent), and molding compounds (seven percent), whereas in Japan, for example, almost 60 percent is used in adhesives. Melamine, albeit invisibly, is present in almost all modern houses and garages—in, for example, kitchen counter surfaces, plastic ta-bleware, laminated furniture, plywood sheathing, and automotive paint.

Beginnings and Growing Markets: 1968–88

MCI was incorporated in 1968, but it did not start producing melamine until 1971, when First Mississippi Corporation and Ashland, Inc. constructed MCI's first plant, the M-I, named after the process used to produce the chemical from urea. It was located on an eight-acre site near Donaldsonville, Louisiana, next to the Mississippi River, a site that MCI has continued to lease from Triad Nitrogen, Inc. since MCI first started operations. Triad, a wholly owned subsidiary of Mississippi Chemical Corp., also has been MCI's principal supplier of urea and ammonia, the necessary raw materials needed for making melamine crystals.

The largest investors in MCI were First Mississippi (reorganized as ChemFirst, Inc. in 1996) and Ashland, both of which owned 22.7 percent of MCI's outstanding common stock when the company was sold in 1997. These companies anticipated an increasing melamine market, both at home and abroad. New uses for the chemical as an additive in coatings, laminates, and adhesives were being found at a time when, in general, plastics and other synthetics were replacing more costly woods and metals in almost all phases of construction. Since there was only one competitor in North America, the investment seemed both prudent and prescient. Available supplies of natural construction materials were dwindling and spiraling upward in cost, creating an ever-increasing and irreversible need for synthetics. From the outset, an important part of MCI's mission was the development of both new and more efficient processes for making melamine and an applications technology to help spread melamine's industrial uses.

Through the 1970s and 1980s, MCI grew at a slow but steady rate. Melamine production worldwide reached a five percent per year average increase by 1986. By that time MCI was stable enough to cut some of its strings to its financial backers. In June 1987 it bought its M-I plant from First Mississippi and Ashland, but it continued to lease its 5,500 square feet of office space from Triad, which is still included in its plantsite lease. On its site, MCI owns and maintains a 17,600-square-foot warehouse and four silos, with a combined capability of storing 5.5 million pounds of melamine.

In the late 1980s MCI also built its second plant, based on the patented M-II technology invented by chief engineer Dave Best and former MCI president Roger Thomas. The new $20 million plant, adjacent to the old plant, utilizes a high-pressure high-temperature, noncatalytic process of converting urea into melamine crystals. Unlike the older plant, the M-II remains in constant operation, not requiring the mandatory shutdown for maintenance that takes M-I production off-line for up to three weeks each year. By the late 1990s the M-II plant was producing about 25 million pounds of melamine per year, slightly less than 25 percent of MCI total output.

The Lean Years and the Recovery: 1989–96

MCI faced a succession of "plague years" starting in 1989. Up until that time, the annual worldwide demand for melamine had been increasing at a fairly steady rate, but then a recession hit the economies of both Europe and the United States. MCI sales started into a tailspin, which, over a five-year period, amounted to about a $40 million drop and annual net losses. These peaked at $3.5 million in 1993, when market prices fell and fluctuated as low as $0.40 a pound, down from a high of $0.62 at the end of 1989.

Melamine had become a glut on the market, in part because of the economic doldrums, but also because cheaper imports were beginning to flood into the United States, forcing prices down. In 1993, 8.3 million pounds of melamine were imported. DSM Melamine America alone brought in 3.3 million pounds from its struggling Dutch parent company just to fill one specific order. The market was best in the Far East, a fact that finally prompted DSM to dismantle its 110-million-pound melamine plant at Geleen in The Netherlands and ship it to Indonesia, there to be reconstructed. It had been built at Geleen in 1992 and had only been in operation a few months when key markets in the former Soviet Union collapsed, forcing the plant to shut down. The relocating move cost DSM upwards of $115 million and kept the plant out of operation for two years.

By 1994 MCI and other melamine producers began benefitting from reversing market trends. By that year, although world production of melamine had reached almost 900 million pounds, 27 percent of which was produced in the United States, the global demand also reached its highest level in several

years, suddenly revealing a shortage made worse by the fact that DSM's relocating plant was not yet on line. Economic recovery both in the United States and abroad played a major role in the market turnaround. Spurred by the upswing in new construction, demand for melamine resins sharply increased, and so did prices. In the beginning of 1994 melamine was selling at $0.43 per pound in the United States, but by July had risen to $0.48 per pound, a much more profitable figure for the nation's two melamine producers but still far short of the $0.60 per pound being paid in Europe. As a result, U.S.-produced melamine became very competitive worldwide, and its exports shot up to almost 50 percent.

The increasing demand led MCI to undertake some necessary changes. It overhauled both its M-I plant and M-I process, which first launched the company and still accounted for more than 75 percent of the 106 million pounds of melamine annually produced by MCI. It also instituted a preventative maintenance regimen that effectively reduced plant repair costs from $6.5 million to $3.9 million per annum.

In 1994, the year it which it received ISO 9002 certification, MCI enjoyed increased sales of almost 50 percent. At the time, it had a producing capacity of about 105 millions pounds per year. Its only U.S. competitor was American Melamine, which had a capacity of 140 million pounds. With the melamine market tightening sharply, MCI's projections for sales in 1995 were $46 million, increasing in 1996 to $57 million. Yet, despite the upsurge in the global demand for melamine, in 1996 MCI had to abort two projects and write off costs of about $1.9 million. One was a joint venture urea plant in Norway, with Norsk Hydro, which Norsk broke off when it reconsidered its priorities; the second was a joint construction venture of a melamine plant with Arcadian of Memphis, Tennessee. The plant was to have had an annual production capacity of 66 million pounds of melamine. The project was aborted, however, because MCI and Arcadian could not reach final agreement on the contract terms before Arcadian was sold to another corporation. At the time, MCI CEO and president, Fred Huber, expressed regret that the planned ventures failed to materialize but noted that MCI could turn the setback into an "opportunity to debottleneck and expand" MCI's two Donaldsonville plants.

Sale of Process Patents and Acquisition by Borden Chemical: 1997

In 1997 MCI took two very important steps. First, in February, it sold its patented high-pressure (M-II and M-IV) production technologies to DSM Melamine B.V., a business group of DSM Melamine, N.V., headquartered in The Netherlands. The companies then began a joint research and development program at MCI's Donaldsonville plant to test and improve the high-pressure M-II and M-IV technologies. Under the terms of the agreement, DSM got global rights to MCI's M-II and M-IV patents and related technologies, but MCI retained the right to use these technologies and to build two additional plants in the Western Hemisphere. DSM agreed to pay MCI $25 million, with payments completed in 2005, and also agreed to assist MCI in modifying its low-pressure M-I facility to implement process improvements developed by DSM. Second, after engaging Goldman, Sachs & Co. as financial advisors, MCI's directors sold the company. The sale was completed months after MCI rejected a buyout bid by Ashland, Inc. made on June 30. Ashland had made an offer to buy all shares of MCI that it did not already own, first at $12.50 per share and then later at $14.75 per share. In November, after a final rejection of Ashland's bid, MCI's board sold the company to Borden Chemical, Inc., a subsidiary of Borden, Inc. headquartered in Columbus, Ohio. Borden paid a far more lucrative $20.50 per share for the outstanding shares, with a total cost to Borden of about $112.8 million.

MCI's biggest jump in sales came in 1996, with an increase of about $10 million over the previous year. Still, the $55.62 million figure was less than the company's own projections made in 1994. In addition, the gross profits were only up about $1.35 million over profits in fiscal 1995. If from June 1994 to June 1995 MCI had charged out the red, by 1997 it was clear that although growth would continue it would probably do so at a more moderate rate. In that same year, as well, MCI had to reduce its production of melamine for almost two months while Triad overhauled its own plant equipment. The repairs cut back MCI's melamine output by seven million pounds, causing a substantial drop in the expected first-quarter earnings. Still, annual sales for 1997 were up about $3.3 million over the previous year, though profits increased by only $200,000.

Future Expansion and Promise

MCI's prospects look very good. The worldwide demand for melamine has now risen well above one billion pounds per year. Like most companies dependent on GDP-type growth, however, MCI relies on an expanding economy and corresponding growth of a variety of other enterprises. In fact, given its export potential, MCI's fate is tightly linked to both the U.S. and global economies. Of particular import for MCI are the fortunes of the building construction industry. When it does well, so does MCI. In general, if the U.S. economy continues growing, future demand for melamine also should increase. Projections are that the United States' needs should reach about 325 million pounds in the year 2000, up from 255 million pounds in 1995, for an average annual increase of about 4.5 percent.

That prospect encouraged MCI's parent company, Borden Chemical, to permit MCI to build the additional 66-million-pound-per-year melamine plant it had planned but had to abort in 1966, the year before it merged with Borden. It will be built on the original site near Memphis, Tennessee, and is scheduled to be completed in January 2001. In tandem with its Louisiana facility, the new plant will make MCI a close second to DSM as the world's largest producer of melamine. The plant will be located on land purchased from the Potash Corp. of Saskatchewan Inc. (PCS), a Canadian company that had previously acquired Arcadian, MCI's former partner in the aborted project. PCS produces urea in a nearby facility and will provide the MCI plant with its raw materials.

Analysis has suggested that the increased need for melamine is there, thanks in part to a growing use of it in industrial synthetics. Currently, MCI produces four size grades of melamine crystals: unground, ground, Superfine, and G. P. Crystal. Each is used for different applications, most of which incorporate the crystals in a melamine-formaldehyde amino resin. MCI's product is used primarily in laminates (e.g., on kitchen countertops), molding compounds (e.g., in plastic dinnerware), adhesives (e.g., in plywood veneers), coatings (e.g., on auto parts and panels), fire-retardant foam (e.g., in pillows), and concrete superplasticizers. Its use in laminates, principally tied to new home construction and renovation, should continue to expand as natural materials continue to grow scarcer and more expensive. For example, in furniture manufacturing, there will be an increasing use of pressed wood or particle board and laminates, even in high-quality furniture. In Europe, almost 90 percent of furniture uses laminates over particle board, a figure that may be reached in the United States in the early 21st century. Melamine's flame retardant applications also may gain wider use as fire codes become stricter and more rigorously enforced. If, for example, fire-retardant foams were required in home furniture, it would have a positive impact on the chemical's production. Only melamine's application in textiles and paper coatings is expected to decline, the result of health concerns over formaldehyde emissions. That should be offset both by its wider use in its existing applications and the discovery of new ones.

Principal Subsidiaries

Foreign Sales Corp. (U.S. Virgin Islands).

Further Reading

"Borden's Completes Acquisition," *The Wall Street Journal,* November 17, 1997, pp. C13, B11.

Bongiorni, Sara, "Future Bright at Melamine Chemicals," *Business Report,* April 1, 1997, pp. 48–50.

Brand, Tony, "Melamine and DSM Link in Technology Agreement," *Chemical Market Reporter,* March 3, 1997, pp. 3, 13.

Freedman, William, "Melamine Takes Write-off for Two Aborted Projects," *Chemical Week,* July 17, 1996, p. 15.

Jennings, Robert, "Melamine Upturn Puts Pressure on US Supplies," *Chemical Marketing Reporter,* October 31, 1994, p. 5.

Loffredo, Douglas, "Melamine Prices Depressed While Exports Show Promise," *Chemical Marketing Reporter,* February 10, 1992, p. 12.

McConville, J., "Melamine Chemicals Plots a Cautious Growth Plan: New Technology Lifts Sales and Profits," *Chemical Week,* January 18, 1995, p. 23.

"Melamine," *Chemical Marketing Reporter,* October 14, 1996, p. 37.

"Melamine Chemicals Cancels US and European Expansions," *Chemical Marketing Reporter,* July 8, 1996, p. 3.

Urey, Craig, "Borden To Build Melamine Plant," *Plastic News,* January 4, 1999, p. 9.

Westervelt, Robert, "Melamine Chemical Cuts Production," *Chemical Week,* September 17, 1997, p. 19.

—John W. Fiero

Microsoft Corporation

One Microsoft Way
Redmond, Washington 98052-6399
U.S.A.
(425) 882-8080
Fax: (425) 936-7329
Web Site: http://www.microsoft.com

Public Company
Incorporated: 1981
Employees: 29,159
Sales: $14.5 billion (1998)
Stock Exchanges: NASDAQ
Ticker Symbol: MSFT
SICs: 7372 Prepackaged Software; 3577 Computer
    Peripheral Equipment Not Elsewhere Classified

With annual revenues of more than $14 billion, Microsoft Corporation is more than the largest software company in the world: it is a cultural phenomenon. The company's core business is based on developing, manufacturing, and licensing software products, including operating systems, server applications, business and consumer applications, and software development tools, as well as Internet software, technologies, and services. Led by Bill Gates, the world's wealthiest individual and most famous businessman, Microsoft has succeeded in placing at least one of its products on virtually every personal computer in the world, setting industry standards and defining markets in the process. The company is known as a ferocious competitor whose tactics have engendered the scrutiny of the Antitrust Division of the U.S. Department of Justice. It has been vilified by the press, its competitors, and many computer-savvy users who view its dominant position in the industry as a stranglehold that forestalls competition, stifles innovation, and leads to inferior products; at the same time, millions of users testify to the success of the company's products, and respondents to survey after survey name Microsoft the most admired company in the United States.

Origins of an Empire

Bill Gates was born in Seattle in 1955, the second of three children in a well-to-do family. His father, William H. Gates II, was a lawyer, while his mother, Mary Gates, was a teacher, a regent of the University of Washington, and member of several corporate boards. Gates was first exposed to computers at school in the late 1960s with his friend Paul Allen, the son of two Seattle librarians. By the time Gates was 14, the two friends were writing and testing computer programs for fun and profit.

In 1972 they established their first company, Traf-O-Data, which sold a rudimentary computer that recorded and analyzed traffic data. Allen went on to study computer science at the University of Washington and then dropped out to work at Honeywell, while Gates enrolled at Harvard. Inspired in 1975 by an issue of *Popular Electronics* that showed the new Altair microcomputer kit just released by MITS Computer, Gates and Allen wrote a version of BASIC for the machine. Later that year Gates left college to work full time developing programming languages for the Altair, and he and Allen relocated to Albuquerque, New Mexico, to be near MITS Computer, where Allen took a position as Director of Software Development. Gates and Allen named their partnership Micro-soft. Their revenues for 1975 totaled $16,000.

A year later, Gates published "An Open Letter to Hobbyists" in the Altair newsletter, in which he enjoined users to avoid illegally copied software. Arguing that software piracy prevented "good software from being written," Gates wrote prophetically, "Nothing would please me more than being able to hire ten programmers and deluge the hobby market with good software." In November 1976 Allen left MITS to devote his full attention to Microsoft, and the company's tradename was registered. In 1977 Apple and Radio Shack licensed Microsoft BASIC for their Apple II and Tandy computers, with the Apple license going for a flat fee of $21,000. As Apple sold a million machines complete with BASIC, Microsoft's unit revenues dropped to two cents a copy.

That same year Microsoft released its second programming language, Microsoft FORTRAN, which was followed in 1978 by a version of COBOL. Both were written for the CP/M operating system, one of many available in the rapidly expanding but still unstandardized microcomputer market, and as CP/M was adopted by computer manufacturers including Sirius, Zenith, and Sharp, Microsoft became the leading distributor for microcomputer languages. By the end of 1978 Microsoft had 13 employees, a sales subsidiary in Japan, and $1 million in revenues. The following year Gates and Allen moved the company to Bellevue, Washington.

The Early 1980s: Associations with IBM and Apple

Microsoft's big break came in 1980 as IBM began developing its Personal Computer, or PC. While IBM contracted Microsoft to develop languages for the PC, IBM's first choice to provide an operating system was the leader in the field, Digital Research; however, IBM and Digital Research were unable to agree on terms, so the contract for the operating system was awarded to Microsoft. As Microsoft was under a tight deadline and did not have an operating system of its own, the company purchased the rights to one from Seattle Computer Products for $75,000. Originally dubbed Q-DOS (for ''Quick and Dirty Operating System''), the product was renamed MS-DOS (for ''Microsoft Disk Operating System'') and modified for IBM's purposes. Under the terms of the agreement, Microsoft retained the right to sell the operating system to other companies and to consumers, while IBM could not. Neither company could have foreseen the value of this arrangement: as other manufacturers developed hardware compatible with the IBM PC, and as personal computing became a multibillion dollar business, the fast and powerful MS-DOS became the industry's leading operating system, and Microsoft's revenues skyrocketed.

1980 also saw the arrival of Steve Ballmer, a close friend of Gates's from Harvard, who was hired to organize the non-technical side of the business. Ballmer later recalled the company's stormy beginnings under Gates's leadership: ''Our first major row came when I insisted it was time to hire 17 people. He claimed I was trying to bankrupt him.'' Conservative in his spending, Gates dictated that the company must always have enough money in the bank to operate for a year with no revenues. Nearly 20 years later that policy still stood—in 1999 Microsoft had cash reserves of more than $13 billion and no long-term debt—while Ballmer, who had by then become Microsoft president, remained Gates's closest friend and advisor.

In 1981 the company was incorporated as Microsoft, Inc., with Gates as president and chairman and Allen as executive vice-president. The company closed the year with 128 employees and revenues of $16 million. Two years later Allen left Microsoft after being diagnosed with Hodgkin's disease. He remained on the board of directors and continued to hold more than ten percent of the company's stock. Also in 1983 Microsoft launched a word processing program, Word 1.0, in an effort to supplant the category leader, WordStar. Simpler to use and less expensive than WordStar, Word used a mouse to move the cursor and was able to display bold and italic type on the screen. Nevertheless, some users felt that the product was too complex—designed for software engineers rather than business users—and it was quickly surpassed in the market by WordPerfect, released by the WordPefect Corporation. Word did not become a success until its greatly improved version 3.0 was released in 1986, whereupon the application became Microsoft's best-selling product.

Throughout its history, Microsoft has been known for releasing products that were initially unsuccessful but eventually grew to dominate their categories. Many reviewers have been harsh in their criticism: David Kirkpatrick, writing in *Fortune,* described the first release of one product as a ''typically unreliable, bug-ridden Microsoft mess,'' while Brent Schlender noted in the same magazine that ''from its beginnings, Microsoft has been notorious for producing inelegant products that are frequently inferior and bringing them to the market way behind schedule.'' These critics note that the success of Microsoft has been based not only—or even principally—on the company's technological prowess, but also on Bill Gates's business acumen, which combined dogged perseverance, strategic marketing, powerful alliances, and, increasingly as the years went on, highly aggressive competitive tactics.

Microsoft worked closely with Apple during the development of Apple's Macintosh computer, which was introduced in 1984. Revolutionary in its design, the Mac featured a graphical user interface based on icons rather than the typed commands used by the IBM PC, making its programs simple to use and easy to learn, even by computer novices. Microsoft introduced Mac versions of BASIC, Word, and the spreadsheet program Multiplan, and quickly became the leading supplier of applications for the Mac. Revenues jumped from $50 million in 1983 to nearly $100 million in 1984.

Convinced that the Mac's graphical user interface represented the future of end-user applications, Gates sought to develop an interface manager to work on top of MS-DOS that would convert the operating system to a graphical model that would be user-friendly and provide a single method for interacting with the many non-standardized programs designed to run on the system. Because other companies, including IBM, were working to develop similar interface managers for MS-DOS, Gates solicited support from hardware manufacturers and software publishers who were concerned about IBM's continued dominance of the PC market. Compaq, Hewlett-Packard, Texas Instruments, Digital Equipment Corporation, and others announced their support for the project, called Microsoft Windows, while IBM, in the face of this opposition, threw its weight behind VisiOn, a similar product already being marketed by VisiCalc, while working to develop its own program, called TopView. Plagued by delays in development, the release of Windows was repeatedly rescheduled throughout 1984 and 1985, causing tensions at Microsoft and with other software publishers who were forced to delay releases of the applications they were designing for the system. Finally released in November 1985, after some 110,000 hours of frantic work by programmers, Windows faced a disappointing reception. The system was slow, few applications were available to run on it, and customers delayed purchase decisions while waiting for the introduction of TopView.

In 1985 Microsoft also introduced Excel 1.0, a Mac spreadsheet product. Based on the earlier and less successful Multiplan, Excel gradually took hold against its principal competitor, Lotus 1-2-3, and eventually came to account for more than $1 billion of Microsoft's annual revenues. That same year Microsoft began collaborating with IBM on a next-generation operating system, called OS/2.

The Late 1980s: A Corporate Culture Emerges

In early 1986 Microsoft moved to a new 40-acre corporate campus in Redmond, Washington, near Seattle. Designed to provide a refuge free of distractions for those whose job was, in Gates's words, to "sit and think," the campus was nestled in a quiet woodland setting and reflected huge expenditures for tools, space, and comfort. Buildings were designed in the shape of an X to maximize light, with each programmer given a private office rather than a cubicle. The buildings featured many small, subsidized cafeterias, as well as refrigerators stocked with juice and caffeinated beverages. The self-contained, collegiate surroundings were carefully designed to promote the company's distinctive culture, which one commentator described as a close approximation of "math camp." Like most software companies, Microsoft had no dress code (although company lore recounts that in 1988 senior management did express a preference that employees not go barefoot indoors). Employees were hired on the basis of sheer intelligence, with the company selecting only a small fraction of applicants from the more than 100,000 resumes it received each year, and were expected to work brutal schedules to bring products to market as quickly as possible. Microsoft paid salaries that were distinctly lower than elsewhere in the industry, even to their senior executives, but compensated with generous stock options that have made thousands of Microsoft employees millionaires. At the same time, the company tried to maintain a small company mentality, in which executives traveled coach class, the necessity of additional staff positions was closely scrutinized, and other unnecessary expenditures were vigilantly avoided.

In March 1986 Microsoft went public with an initial public offering (IPO) of 2.5 million shares that raised $61 million. Within a year the stock had risen from $25 to $85, making Bill Gates a billionaire at the age of 31. The following year Microsoft released its first CD-ROM product, *Microsoft Bookshelf,* a collection of ten reference works, as well as Excel for Windows, its first application for the new operating system. Microsoft also purchased Forethought, Inc., for $12 million, thereby acquiring that company's PowerPoint presentation graphics program, and

released OS/2 in collaboration with IBM. In November 1987 Microsoft introduced Windows 2.0, a greatly improved version of the operating system, and by the end of the year Windows had sold more than one million copies. As Windows began to take hold, more software companies were convinced to develop applications for the operating system, which brought it increased usefulness and further sales momentum. In 1988 Microsoft surpassed Lotus Development Corporation as the leading software vendor, with more than $500 million in sales. The company was accused of copyright infringement by Apple, which alleged that Microsoft had copied the "look and feel" of the Macintosh, in a lawsuit that was finally dismissed after five years of litigation. In 1989 the company introduced Microsoft Office, a "suite" of programs that eventually came to dominate the market and become Microsoft's best-selling application product. While the initial release of Office was a discount package, later versions incorporated standard, shared features and included Word, Excel, PowerPoint, and the e-mail program Mail, with the Access database management program included in the Office Professional version.

Before 1990 Microsoft was primarily a supplier to hardware manufacturers, but after 1990 the bulk of the company's revenues came from sales to consumers. That year Microsoft became the first software company to reach $1 billion in revenues, closing the year with 5,600 employees.

Product Development in the 1990s

In 1993 Microsoft introduced *Encarta,* the first multimedia encyclopedia on CD-ROM, as well as the first version of Windows NT, an operating system for users on corporate networks. While the initial acceptance of Windows NT was disappointing, an upgrade shipped in September of the following year as NT 3.5 was a dramatic success: winning the *PC Magazine* award for technical excellence in system software and named the best operating system product of 1994, the upgrade boosted sales of NT to more than one million copies by the end of the year. Microsoft announced an agreement to purchase Intuit, the producer of the leading package of personal financial software, called Quicken; however, after the U.S. Department of Justice filed suit to prevent the takeover on the basis of antitrust concerns, Microsoft withdrew its offer. Revenues for 1994 exceeded $4 billion.

In August 1995 Microsoft launched its next version of Windows, called Windows 95, which sold more than one million copies in the first four days after its release. For the rest of the decade Microsoft expanded aggressively into new businesses associated with its core franchise. Its projects included two joint ventures with the National Broadcasting Company under the name MSNBC: an interactive online news service and a cable channel broadcasting news and information 24 hours a day. The company's Web-based services included the Microsoft Network online service, a travel agency, local events listings, car buying information, a personal financial management site, and a joint venture with First Data that allows consumers to pay their bills online. Microsoft purchased 11 percent of the cable television company Comcast for $1 billion and cut a licensing deal with the largest U.S. cable operator, TCI Communications, to put Windows into at least five million set-top boxes. The company also purchased WebTV, whose core technology allows users to surf the Internet without a PC. Microsoft's latest generation of Windows, Windows CE, was designed to expand the franchise into computer-like devices including mobile phones, point-of-sale terminals, pocket organizers, digital televisions, digital cameras, hand-held computers, automobile multimedia systems, and pagers. By early 1999 the company had secured more than 100 licensing agreements with manufacturers of these "intelligent appliances."

Legal Challenges and Competition in the Future

Microsoft's many critics believed that the company's goal in this widespread expansion was to control every delivery channel of information, thereby providing the means to control the content. According to Scott McNealy of rival company Sun Microsystems, "By owning the entry points to the Internet and electronic marketplace, Microsoft has the power to exercise predatory and exclusionary control over the very means for people to access the Internet and all it represents."

The U.S. government apparently agreed. After an intensive investigation of Microsoft's competitive practices that had gone on for much of the decade, in 1998 the U.S. Department of Justice and a group of 20 state Attorney Generals filed two antitrust cases against Microsoft alleging violations of the Sherman Act. The government sought to prove a broad pattern of anticompetitive behavior on Microsoft's part by demonstrating an array of claims, including the following: that Microsoft had a monopoly on the market for operating systems; that the company used that monopoly as a means of preventing other companies from selling its competitors' products (most notably Netscape's Internet browser); that it was illegal for Microsoft to bundle its own browser into the operating system Windows 98 as a means of precluding customers from purchasing Netscape's product; that the company sought to divide markets with competitors; that Microsoft sought to subvert the Java programming language, developed by Sun Microsystems, which it viewed as a threat to Windows; and, finally, that Microsoft's business practices were detrimental to consumers. The case was conducted under a flurry of media attention, with all parties agreeing that the stakes were extremely high: should Microsoft win, its brand of extremely aggressive capitalism would secure a legal blessing; should the company lose, the company could be forced to license the source code for Windows to competitors, thus destroying its monopoly, or could be broken up into smaller components, crippling its hold over the marketplace. A decision was expected in the summer of 1999.

The fear and resentment that Microsoft and its founder Gates have engendered are testament to the company's mythic status and Gates's role as the embodiment of the digital era. Gates's extreme wealth (in early 1999 he was worth $50 billion) makes him the subject of constant scrutiny, while the Internet is rife with Bill Gates "hate pages," named, for example, "The Society for the Prevention of Bill Gates Getting Everything." Resentment and legal action notwithstanding, with more than $14 billion in sales in 1998 and $3 billion planned for R&D expenditures in 1999, Microsoft shows no signs of slowing down. The company remains a force whose products have come to seem indispensable to millions of users worldwide, and David Kirkpatrick's 1998 *Fortune* article, "Microsoft: Is Your Company

Its Next Meal?" is just the smallest indicator that competitors still have no room to relax.

Principal Subsidiaries

Microsoft FSC Corp.; Microsoft Investments, Inc.; Microsoft Ireland Operations Limited (Ireland); Microsoft Licensing, Inc.; Microsoft Puerto Rico, Inc.; The Microsoft Network L.L.C.; GraceMac Corporation; Microsoft de Argentina S.A.; Microsoft Pty. Limited (Australia); Microsoft Gesellschaft m.b.H. (Austria); Microsoft N.V. (Belgium); Microsoft Informatica Limitada (Brazil); Microsoft Canada Co.; SOFTIMAGE, Inc. (Canada); Microsoft Chile S.A.; Microsoft Colombia Inc.; Microsoft de Centroamerica S.A. (Costa Rica); Microsoft Hrvatska d.o.o. (Croatia); Microsoft s.r.o. (Czech Republic); Microsoft Danmark ApS; Microsoft Dominicana, S.A. (Dominican Republic); Microsoft Del Ecuador S.A.; Microsoft El Salvador S.A. de C.V.; Microsoft Corporation Representative Office (Egypt); Microsoft Oy (Finland); Microsoft France S.A.R.L.; Microsoft G.m.b.H. (Germany); Microsoft Hellas S.A. (Greece); Microsoft de Guatemala, S.A.; Microsoft Hong Kong Limited; Microsoft Hungary Kft.; Microsoft Corporation Private Limited (India); Microsoft India Private Limited (R&D); PT. Microsoft Indonesia; Microsoft Israel Ltd.; Microsoft S.p.A. (Italy); Microsoft Cote d'Ivoire (Ivory Coast); Microsoft Company, Limited (Japan); East Africa Software Limited (Kenya); Microsoft CH (Korea); Microsoft (Malaysia) Sdn. Bhd.; Microsoft Mexico, S.A. de C.V.; Microsoft Indian Ocean Islands Limited (Mauritius); Microsoft Maroc S.A.R.L. (Morocco); Microsoft B.V. (The Netherlands); Microsoft International B.V. (The Netherlands); Microsoft New Zealand Limited; Microsoft Norge AS (Norway); Microsoft de Panama, S.A.; Microsoft (China) Company Limited (The People's Republic of China); Microsoft Peru, S.A.; Microsoft Philippines, Inc.; Microsoft sp. z.o.o. (Poland); MSFT-Software Para; Microcomputadores, LDA; (Portugal); Microsoft Caribbean, Inc. (Puerto Rico); Microsoft Romania SRL; Microsoft ZAO (Russia); Microsoft Manufacturing B.V. Representative Office (Russia); Microsoft Singapore Pte Ltd.; Microsoft Slovakia s.r.o.; Microsoft d.o.o., Ljubljana (Slovenia); Microsoft (S.A.); (Proprietary) Limited (South Africa); Microsoft Iberica S.R.L. (Spain); Microsoft Aktiebolag (Sweden); Microsoft AG (Switzerland); Microsoft Taiwan Corporation; Microsoft (Thailand) Limited; Microsoft Bilgisayar Yazilim Hizmetleri Limited Sirketi (Turkey); Microsoft Corporation (United Arab Emirates); Microsoft Limited (United Kingdom); Microsoft Research Limited (United Kingdom); Microsoft Uruguay, S.A.; Microsoft Venezuela, S.A.; The Resident Representative Office of MICROSOFT Corporation in Hanoi (Vietnam); Microsoft Corporation Representative Office (Zimbabwe); WebTV Networks, Inc.; DreamWorks Interactive L.L.C. (50%); MSBET L.L.C. (50%); MSFDC L.L.C. (50%); MSNBC Cable, L.L.C. (50%); MSNBC Interactive News, L.L.C. (50%); Ninemsn Pty. Limited (Australia); WebTV Networks K.K. (Japan).

Further Reading

Cusumano, Michael A., *Microsoft Secrets: How the World's Most Powerful Software Company Creates Technology, Shapes Markets, and Manages People,* New York: Free Press, 1995, 512 p.
Desmond, Edward W., "Microsoft's Big Bet on Small Machines," *Fortune,* July 20, 1998, pp. 86–90.

France, Mike, "Microsoft: The View at Halftime," *Business Week,* January 25, 1999, p. 78.

Hamm, Steve, "No Letup—And No Apologies: Antitrust Scrutiny Hasn't Eased Microsoft's Competitiveness," *Business Week,* October 26, 1998, p. 58.

Higgins, David, "The Man Who Owns the Future," *Sydney Morning Herald,"* March 14, 1998, p. 1.

Ichbiah, Daniel, and Susan L. Knepper, *The Making of Microsoft: How Bill Gates and His Team Created the World's Most Successful Software Company,* Rocklin, Calif.: Prima Publishing, 1991, 304 p.

Isaacson, Walter, "In Search of the Real Bill Gates," *Time Magazine,* January 13, 1997, p. 44+.

Kirkpatrick, David, "Microsoft: Is Your Company Its Next Meal?" *Fortune,* April 27, 1998, pp. 92–102.

——, "He Wants All Your Business—And He's Starting to Get It," *Fortune,* May 26, 1997, p. 58+.

Krantz, Michael, "If You Can't Beat 'Em. . . . Will Bill Gates' Bailout Save Apple—Or Just Strengthen Microsoft's Hand in the Web Wars?," *Time Magazine,* August 18, 1997, p. 35+.

Manes, Stephen, and Paul Andrews, *Gates: How Microsoft's Mogul Reinvented an Industry—And Made Himself the Richest Man in America,* New York: Doubleday, 1993, 534 p.

Mardesich, Jodi, "What's Weighing Down Microsoft?" *Fortune,* January 11, 1999, pp. 147–48.

Moody, Fred, *I Sing the Body Electronic: A Year with Microsoft on the Multimedia Frontier,* New York: Viking, 1995, 311 p.

Nocera, Joseph, "High Noon," *Fortune,* November 23, 1998, p. 162+.

Schlender, Brent, "What Bill Gates Really Wants," *Fortune,* January 16, 1995, p. 34+.

Stross, Randall E., *The Microsoft Way: The Real Story of How the Company Outsmarts Its Competition,* Reading, Mass.: Addison-Wesley Publishing, 1996, 318 p.

Wallace, James, and Jim Erickson, *Hard Drive: Bill Gates and the Making of the Microsoft Empire,* New York: Wiley, 1992, 426 p.

—Paula Kepos

Milbank, Tweed, Hadley & McCloy

One Chase Manhattan Plaza
New York, New York 10005
U.S.A.
(212) 530-5219
Fax: (212) 530-5219

Private Company
Founded: 1866 as Anderson, Adams & Young
Employees: 910
Sales: $204.5 million (1997)
SICs: 8111 Legal Services

With offices in New York City, London, Tokyo, Hong Kong, Singapore, Moscow, and Washington, D.C., Milbank, Tweed, Hadley & McCloy is one of the world's oldest and most distinguished international law firms. Well-known for its historic representation of the Rockefeller family and its businesses, especially the Chase Manhattan Bank, the law firm also claims several other prestigious clients, including the New York Stock Exchange. Considered one of the nation's top "white-shoe" law firms, Milbank, Tweed started the first U.S. law office in Tokyo and in 1999 continues to have a notable practice in Asia and other parts of the world.

Origins and Early History

In 1866 the law firm of Anderson, Adams & Young, the predecessor of Milbank, Tweed, Hadley & McCloy, opened for business on Wall Street in New York City. Originally located on Nassau Street, the firm moved 16 years later to an office across the street from the New York Stock Exchange.

Partner Henry Anderson, a prominent minister's son, handled affairs of the Vanderbilt family. That close affiliation with families and their business dealings was typical of law firms in the late 1800s and early 1900s.

After George Murray joined the firm in 1888, he met John D. Rockefeller, Sr. ("Senior"), through Protestant church activi-

ties, and soon the oil tycoon retained him for personal and business legal advice. That began the decades of association among the firm's attorneys, the Rockefeller family, and Rockefeller businesses.

In 1901 Ezra Parmalee Prentice joined the firm after marrying Alta Rockefeller, Senior's daughter, so the firm changed its name to Murray, Prentice & Howland.

Another marriage brought the law firm and the Rockefellers even closer. John D. Rockefeller, Jr. ("Junior"), married Abby Aldrich, which led to Abby's brother Winthrop W. Aldrich joining the firm in 1907. Aldrich provided Junior with legal counsel, just as Murray had Senior. In 1921 the firm's name became Murray, Prentice & Aldrich.

The 1920s and 1930s

In 1921 Harrison Tweed joined the law firm, in part because his father was a close friend of Murray's father. Such family connections helped the firm maintain its representation of such clients as the Manhattan Gas Light Company and Consolidated Gas Company. In 1929 the law firm represented John D. Rockefeller, Sr., when he signed a lease with Columbia University to take over 199 separate lots. Young lawyers with the firm formed Metropolitan Square Corporation to manage these properties. In 1932 the corporation became known as Rockefeller Center, Inc.

In May 1929 the two law firms of Murray & Aldrich and Webb, Patterson & Hadley merged to create Murray, Aldrich & Webb. Vanderbilt Webb specialized in real estate. His main contribution while with the law firm involved developing Virginia's Colonial Williamsburg and working with Junior to acquire properties that became the Grand Tetons National Park. Webb left the firm in 1938. Robert P. Patterson departed to work on his own and to serve as a district and circuit court judge and eventually secretary of war under President Roosevelt.

Morris Hadley brought notable clients, including Aluminum Limited, to the law firm and served on its management committee. His outstanding memory and math abilities made "it quite unnecessary for the firm to rent IBM equipment" for several years, according to Pfeiffer's history.

By 1929 the firm's main client was the Equitable Trust Company, of which John D. Rockefeller, Sr., had purchased a controlling interest in 1911. Aldrich became Equitable's president in 1929, after being pressured by Junior to do so. The following year, Chase National Bank acquired Equitable Trust, making Chase the world's largest bank. That led to a 1931 merger of the law firms that had represented the two banks. Equitable was represented by the firm of Masten & Nichols, formed in 1886 by Arthur H. Masten and George L. Nichols, both graduates of the Columbia Law School. Masten & Nichols with its senior partner Albert Milbank merged with Murray, Aldrich & Webb to create the new firm of Milbank, Tweed, Hope & Webb, with 20 partners and 28 associates. At that point, Masten, Nichols, and Murray all retired and became "of counsel" to the newly merged firm.

For decades Milbank, Tweed served mainly the Rockefellers and their businesses, including working on the estate of John D. Rockefeller, Sr., valued at $26 million in personal wealth when he died in 1937 at age 97. Other major clients were the Horn & Hardart Company and also the Borden Company, not surprising since Albert G. Milbank in 1917 had become Borden's first board chairman.

During the Great Depression the law firm received considerable work because of the many bankruptcies and conflicts at that time. For example, it represented Title Guarantee and Trust Company in many of the 800 lawsuits involving foreclosed mortgages and broken contracts filed in just three years during the Depression. Although most of those foreclosure cases were routine, Milbank represented New York State's Senator Robert F. Wagner in the foreclosure lawsuit concerning New York City's 55-story Lincoln Building.

In 1931 the law firm started representing several chain stores that claimed bankruptcies. Their major client in that area was Liggett, a national chain of 500 drugstores. In 1938 Milbank gained the New York Stock Exchange, one of its major long-term clients.

Post-World War II Expansion

In 1946 John McCloy joined the firm, the only lateral hire between 1931 and 1980. Before 1946 he spent five years as the assistant secretary of the War Department, where he met Nelson Rockefeller, who eventually persuaded McCloy to join Milbank, Tweed. Later he became president of the World Bank, high commissioner of Germany, chairman of both the Ford Foundation and the Chase Manhattan Bank, and President John F. Kennedy's special assistant on disarmament. From 1962 until his death in 1989, he remained a general partner of the law firm.

In 1955 Milbank, Tweed survived a crisis when its main client Chase National Bank merged with the Bank of Manhattan to create Chase Manhattan Bank. For years Milbank shared the bank's outside legal counsel duties with the firm later known as Dewey, Ballantine, Bushby, Palmer & Wood that had served the Bank of Manhattan for some time. Close ties with David Rockefeller, a grandson of John D. Rockefeller, Sr., who became Chase Manhattan Bank's chair in 1967, helped Milbank retain its historic ties to the family and bank.

Milbank, Tweed greatly expanded its operations in the postwar period. For example, it began assisting in setting up or revising pension plans established by Ford Motor Company, General Motors, Western Union, Credit Suisse, Swiss American Corporation, and Rockefeller Brothers, among others.

In 1977, ten years before any other U.S. law firm, Milbank, Tweed opened its Tokyo office. Other offices were started in Hong Kong in 1977, London in 1979, and Washington, D.C., in 1980. One Milbank, Tweed partner played a key role in the Iranian hostage crisis begun in November 1979 when Moslem fundamentalists captured 52 Americans and held them in the U.S. embassy in Tehran. President Carter a few days later froze all Iranian assets in U.S. banks. Chase Manhattan Bank, represented by Milbank, Tweed's Frank Logan, and other U.S. banks had huge loans to the Iranians. Logan was asked by Citibank's attorney John Hoffman of the law firm Shearman and Sterling to help negotiate financial settlements and draw up the contractual papers. Hoffman, aided by Logan and attorneys representing ten other banks, worked closely with U.S. diplomats to solve this crisis. Finally, on January 20, 1981, the situation was resolved. According to the author of *The Partners*, "The $3.7 billion in assets were electronically credited to the accounts of the twelve American banks whose lawyers, in a sense, had just bought the hostages' release."

Growth in the 1980s

In the early 1980s many law firms expanded rapidly and became more business-oriented. This trend was fueled by the U.S. Supreme Court's decision that most restrictions on advertising by professional societies violated antitrust laws and also that such promotional activities were protected as free speech under the First Amendment. Furthermore, law firms increasingly competed for prominent attorneys after Steve Brill in 1979 began publishing the *American Lawyer,* which covered the inner workings and finances of law firms.

Such firms as Skadden, Arps, Slate, Meagher & Flom and also Cravath, Swaine & Moore boomed by providing legal services to the many corporations involved in mergers and acquisitions in the early 1980s. Milbank, Tweed, however, relied on its historic Rockefeller clients and thus ignored these new opportunities. By 1984 some Milbank partners expressed concern that the firm had dropped to number 27 in national rankings with just 229 attorneys. Its $74 million in revenues and $24.5 million in profits were far less than some other firms.

That led to Milbank's executive committee in 1984 choosing partner Alexander D. Forger as its new chairman. Forger had served as the New York State Bar Association president in 1981 and 1982 and as board chair of the Legal Aid Society in 1983. Meanwhile, in the early 1980s he represented clients such as Jacqueline Onassis and Joan Kennedy, which helped the firm's Trusts and Estates Department after work for Rockefeller family wills and estates had declined.

"The practice was changing, client loyalty was changing, we were into the era of competition," said Forger in the *American Lawyer* in October 1996. He began his chairmanship by promoting several new ideas to the conservative law firm. He placed bankruptcy rainmaker John Jerome in charge of encouraging one department's clients to use other Milbank departments for their other legal needs. He also pushed "marketing . . . a totally new thing for us," according to Pollock's book on the firm.

The firm expanded its presence in Tokyo and Hong Kong and in the mid-1980s opened an office in Singapore. That Asian growth, along with a booming California economy, led Milbank to open its Los Angeles office in January 1987. Guido R. Henry, Jr., with 22 years experience as a corporate attorney at the Los Angeles firm of O'Melveny & Myers, was hired to start and manage the new Los Angeles branch. Soon bankruptcy partner David Frauman and five other attorneys moved from New York to the Los Angeles office.

One of the lateral hires who really helped Milbank in Asia was Alice Young, a Chinese-American who had graduated from Harvard Law School in 1974. She worked six years with the San Francisco firm of Graham & James before joining Milbank in the late 1980s. Almost 40 major clients followed Young when she joined Milbank.

Milbank in the late 1980s also brought in new bank clients such as Citibank, added new practice areas, and changed its partner compensation from a strict lockstep method based on seniority to having several levels of profits and bonuses depending on how much business each partner generated. The firm grew from 282 lawyers and $370,000 profit per partner in 1985 to 398 lawyers and $665,000 profit per partner in 1989, according to the *American Lawyer*'s "The Am Law 100."

Bad Times and Then Good Times in the 1990s

Milbank at the start of the decade continued its growth. For example, in early 1991 the firm moved its Los Angeles office from the 50,000-square-foot location at 515 Figueroa Street into a new 80,000-square-foot office space in the high-rise Sanwa Bank Building. At that time Milbank ran the second largest Los Angeles branch of a New York-based law firm.

In 1991 Milbank also opened a branch office in Moscow. Milbank and other U.S. law firms had gained opportunities after the Soviet Union in 1987 under Premier Mikhail Gorbachev passed its first foreign joint venture law allowing foreign firms to own part of Soviet companies. That led some business leaders to ask U.S. law firms for help in transactions in the U.S.S.R. Milbank had counseled the Soviet government about setting up a stock exchange and writing new securities laws before deciding to start its own office in cooperation with a private Russian law firm called Moscow Lawyers, opened in June 1990 by two lawyers who had been Milbank interns.

Like other law firms, Milbank's profits declined and the firm reduced its size in the early 1990s when the nation's economy declined. Milbank's profits per partner reached a low of $480,000 in 1992, when it had 450 attorneys in the firm. By that time Milbank asked senior associates, those who had not made partner after eight years, to leave the firm, unlike the 1980s when such senior attorneys were allowed to remain. About 32 Milbank partners and 70 associates lost their jobs by 1993.

Meanwhile, Milbank personnel endured a "very unpleasant and difficult environment in which to work," according to a former partner in the *American Lawyer* in October 1996.

"The focus was exclusively on billings and collections and nothing else."

Milbank slowly improved under the leadership of Francis D. Logan, elected executive committee chairman after Forger in May 1992 resigned his position to attend to his terminally ill wife. Logan replaced the firm's aging 286 personal computers with 486 models, an initially expensive change that in the long run saved the firm millions each year. Under his leadership, Milbank also cut costs by subleasing two floors in the Los Angeles office and one floor in the New York office and moving its Washington, D.C. office with 35 lawyers to less expensive office space.

In June 1993 Logan announced that Milbank was not only reducing the number of its partners by 15 percent, it also was decreasing its practice in litigation, real estate, and trusts and estates, while focusing on banking, project finance, aircraft leasing, and corporate securities and mergers and acquisitions. By 1995 such strategies helped firm profits per partner reach $590,000. In May 1996 the firm's partners elected a new and relatively young executive committee made up of Chairman Mel M. Immergut, age 49; banking and corporate finance expert Frank Puleo, age 50; and structured finance partner Trayton Davis, age 41.

Milbank's London office in October 1996 lost four partners and six associates to its New York-based competitor Shearman & Sterling. This "frenzy of lateral partner movement . . . in London . . . shows how the market is forcing both English and American firms to bridge the Atlantic," according to the *American Lawyer* in December 1996.

Such law firms competed in Europe not only against each other but also against large accounting firms with their affiliated law firms. By December 1996 Arthur Anderson claimed that through its affiliated firms it was continental Europe's largest provider of legal services. Its London-based affiliate Garrett & Company had grown to 155 lawyers in just three years. Meanwhile, Price Waterhouse legal affiliates included 350 lawyers in 17 European nations.

In November 1998, Milbank, Tweed for the third year in a row ranked as the number one law firm advising clients in global project financing, good evidence of its international status and influence. According to the survey in *Euromoney's Project Finance* magazine, the firm in 1998 completed 45 transactions with capital costs of $32.7 billion. Milbank ranked number one in the Global, North American, Eastern European, Latin American, Asia Pacific, and Central Asian areas, plus it was the third ranked law firm in South Asia and the Middle East. It also ranked first in mining, petrochemicals, and the rail, roads, bridges, and tunnels sectors, with additional top ratings in oil and gas (second), power (third), telecommunications (fifth), pulp and paper (sixth), and airport and port (seventh) industries.

Milbank, Tweed received these high rankings in 1998 by helping the following clients: the main lenders in the $4.5 billion Sincor Heavy Oil Project in Venezuela, the largest Latin American project financing on record; the senior lenders in the $1.5 billion expansion of Mexico's Cadereyta Oil Refinery; JEXIM and other Japanese lenders who financed the $937 million construction of the Philippine's San Roque Hydro-

Power Plant; and Fujian Pacific Electric Company in its development of the $755 million Meizhou Wan Power Plant, the "largest wholly-foreign-owned power project in China successfully financed to date," according to a Milbank press release.

Such Milbank success in Asia occurred in spite of major devaluation of currencies in the Philippines and other nations. For example, Milbank, Tweed had done well in Indonesian project finance projects, but in September 1997 the Indonesian government suspended about 30 projects worth $13.2 billion due to its much publicized financial problems. However, Milbank's Eric Silverman, the head of the firm's project finance practice, remained optimistic that in the long term the projects would continue.

Milbank, Tweed in 1998 continued to represent Nippon Telegraph and Telephone Corporation (NTT), Japan's largest telecommunications provider, a relationship over 20 years old. Specifically, Milbank helped NTT sell part of its ownership of NTT DoCoMo in an $18.4 billion transaction that was "the largest IPO ever," according to a Milbank press release.

In December 1998 Glasgow, Scotland-based electrical producer ScottishPower plc announced it was acquiring Portland-based PacifiCorp. Milbank, Tweed attorneys represented ScottishPower in this deal, and earlier helped it gain a listing on the New York Stock Exchange. Pending approval by federal and state agencies, this was the first time a foreign company purchased an entire U.S. utility.

The troubled Russian economy caused most U.S. law firms to make little if any money in the late 1990s. Rents were expensive—four times what it cost in downtown Manhattan, though rents started decreasing in the late 1990s. Other high overhead costs and too little work caused some U.S. law firms to shut down their Moscow offices, but Milbank kept its office open and hoped for the best.

Milbank, Tweed's growth in the late 1990s included a major expansion of its litigation practice. In a January 1998 press release, Chairman Mel Immergut said, "Milbank's litigation practice has tripled in the last two years." The firm also announced that it had hired Christopher E. Chalsen from Morgan & Finnegan as a litigation partner to lead its intellectual property litigation practice. Chalsen since 1983 had specialized in electrical and computer issues.

Elliott L. Richardson, a Milbank litigation partner from 1980 to 1992, was honored in 1998 with the Presidential Medal of Freedom, the nation's highest honor for a civilian. Richardson's career included several cabinet posts in the 1970s. During the Watergate scandal, he resigned his position as the nation's attorney general.

In 1998 two Milbank, Tweed attorneys played a key role in saving Long-Term Capital Management from collapsing. Partners Lawrence Lederman and Michael Goroff advised the hedge fund's principals. They and over 100 other attorneys from Skadden, Arps, Slate, Meagher & Flom; Sullivan & Cromwell; Simpson Thacher & Bartlett; and other New York City law firms met to negotiate a last-minute deal in which 14 financial institutions agreed to lend $3.6 billion to keep Long-Term Capital alive.

Milbank, Tweed's participation in that transaction was just one example of the law firm's influence over the years, and statistics confirmed it. The *American Lawyer* in its July/August 1998 issue ranked Milbank as the nation's 37th largest law firm, based on 1997 gross revenue of $204.5 million. The nation's top firm was Skadden, Arps with $826 million in gross revenue. Milbank's profits per partner were $860,000, though ten other firms recorded over $1 million in profits per partner. In any case, Milbank, Tweed remained one of the nation's premier and most newsworthy law firms.

Further Reading

Anderson, A. Donald, et. al., "Milbank, Tweed, Hadley & McCloy," in *Los Angeles: Realm of Possibility,* Chatsworth, Calif.: Windsor Publications, 1991, pp. 310–11.

Barker, Emily, "Making Milbank Over," *American Lawyer,* October 1996, pp. 49–56.

Beck, Susan, and Karen Donovan, "Saving Long-Term Capital on a Short Deadline," *American Lawyer,* November 1998, p. 28.

Hansen, Susan, "Lost in the Ruble," *American Lawyer,* November 1998, pp. 80–85.

"Matchmaker," *Forbes,* March 27, 1995, p. 138.

"Milbank Partner to Lehman," *Wall Street Journal,* April 27, 1993, p. B7.

"Milbank Slims Down," *Wall Street Journal,* June 18, 1993, p. B4.

Morris, John E., "Joyride Is Over in Indonesia," *American Lawyer,* November 1997, p. 13.

——, "London Braces for the Big Six Invasion," *American Lawyer,* December 1996, pp. 5–6.

Pfeiffer, Timothy, *Law Practice in a Turbulent World,* New York: Milbank, Tweed, Hadley & McCloy, 1965.

Pollock, Ellen Joan, "Milbank to Dismiss 'Senior Attorneys'," *Wall Street Journal,* February 13, 1992, p. B8.

——, *Turks and Brahmins: Upheaval at Milbank, Tweed; Wall Street's Gentlemen Take Off Their Gloves,* New York: Simon & Schuster, 1990.

Smith, Lee, "Ex-Boss of FBI, CIA Now Has More Fun," *Fortune,* December 14, 1992, p. 177.

Stevens, Amy, "Law Firm Plans for Soviet Offices Are Shelved As a Result of Coup," *Wall Street Journal,* August 21, 1991, p. B4.

Stewart, James B., *The Partners: Inside America's Most Powerful Law Firms,* New York: Simon & Schuster, 1983, pp. 19–52, 283–326, 366.

—David M. Walden

Mossimo, Inc.

9 Pasteur
Irvine, California 92618
U.S.A.
(949) 789-0200
Fax: (949) 453-0101
Web site: http://www.mossimo.com

Public Company
Incorporated: 1987
Employees: 250
Sales: $70.9 million (1997)
Stock Exchanges: New York
Ticker Symbol: MGX
SICs: 2329 Men/Boys' Clothing, Not Elsewhere
   Classified; 2323 Men/Boys' Neckwear; 2387 Apparel
   Belts; 3851 Ophthalmic Goods

A dynamic force in the apparel industry during the 1990s, Mossimo, Inc. sells men's and women's sportswear and activewear, retailing its apparel through 100 in-store shops located in department stores and specialty retailers. The Mossimo label, created by Mossimo Giannulli, gained notoriety during the late 1980s, becoming a highly popular brand of beachwear. During the 1990s the company expanded into sportswear and registered great success. Further expansion during the mid-1990s into upscale menswear yielded disappointing results, leading to numbing financial losses. The losses led to a 25 percent reduction in employment and pervasive cost-cutting measures. Giannulli, who presided as chairman and maintained creative control over Mossimo, Inc., owned 73.3 percent of the company, which also included two stand-alone retail stores. The company's headquarters and production facilities were located in Irvine, California.

Early Success Spawns Expansion

Mossimo Giannulli was born Massimo Giannulli—a slight variation on the name he used to create a half-billion-dollar apparel company. As a child, Giannulli was given the nickname "Moss," which had evolved into Mossimo by the time he enrolled at the University of Southern California and, shortly thereafter, decided to try his luck as an entrepreneur. Giannulli dropped out of the University of Southern California in 1987, borrowed $100,000 from his father (a landscape architect in Los Angeles), and retreated to his apartment on Balboa Island. There, he developed an entrepreneurial strategy based wholly on marketing, not on product innovation or on product quality. With the money he received from his father, Giannulli began making three-paneled, neon-colored beach volleyball shorts and T-shirts. On each garment, he emblazoned his signature and what would become his trademark "M." He then peddled his beachwear—referred to as "activewear" in the apparel industry—to local surf shops, loading the garments in the trunk of his car. Almost overnight, Mossimo shorts and shirts became the newest trend on Southern California beaches. The reason for their popularity, as near as anyone could determine, was the Mossimo name, which had transcended from absolute obscurity to a symbol of chic cachet in a matter of months. Though his quick success might have surprised Giannulli, the emergence of his Mossimo garments as a new fashion trend did not. From the start in his Balboa Island apartment, Giannulli was convinced of the wonders marketing could produce in the apparel industry. "From day one," Giannulli explained, "I have positioned this thing as a lifestyle company."

Drawing its marketing strength from the power of the Mossimo name, Giannulli's company recorded blistering sales growth during its first year of existence. By the end of his first year Giannulli had grossed $1 million and generated enough of a profit to pay back his father. By the end of 1989 sales had swelled fourfold to $4 million, infusing Giannulli with confidence and prompting him to test how far the popularity of the Mossimo name could carry him. He decided to expand his product line and thereby market the Mossimo name to a broader customer base, realizing that exponentially higher sales and his legitimacy as a clothing designer could only be achieved by diversifying beyond beachwear. Giannulli hired an experienced designer in 1991 and began manufacturing casual sportswear and accessories, adorning each item with the highly popular Mossimo name. The debut of Mossimo woven sweaters, knit shirts, and fleece sweatshirts marked a pivotal turning point in the company's development, moving Mossimo, Inc. from the activewear niche of the apparel industry to the decidedly larger sportswear segment. Concurrent with this shift in emphasis toward sportswear, Giannulli gradually began to move away from distributing his apparel to small surf and beachwear shops and focused instead on department stores and large specialty chains, his preferred retail locales. His diversification was a gamble, but the risk paid off. Consumers, mostly teenage customers, clamored for the new Mossimo line of sportswear and accessories, eager to purchase anything with the Mossimo label. In response, Giannulli increased prices and leveraged his success to obtain better deals from his suppliers. The result was an astounding level of profitability that by far eclipsed the net profit margins averaged by his rivals and made Mossimo, Inc. one of the most closely watched competitors in the apparel industry. "I was given a pretty wonderful name," Giannulli remarked during an interview with *Daily News Record,* attempting to explain his success. "If I was Tom, I don't know if we'd be sitting here having this conversation—that was my brother's name and he's not here."

Annual sales by 1993 pushed past $20 million, providing Giannulli with the resources to hatch increasingly more ambitious plans. By this point the company had established its headquarters in Irvine, California, where a 4,600-square-foot factory produced Mossimo activewear, sportswear, and a growing collection of Mossimo accessories, such as eyewear, wallets, belts, bags, shoes, and hats. All of these items, plus the company's men's and women's sportswear, were showcased in Giannulli's newest creation—his own 2,600-square-foot retail store. Called Mossimo Supply, the store opened in December 1993 in a mall near Costa Mesa, which reportedly attracted 18 million visitors a year. There, amid other retail stores operated by Calvin Klein, Saks Fifth Avenue, Cartier, Tiffany & Co., and Gucci, Giannulli's store stood, sharing space with some of the apparel industry's elite designers. Mossimo Supply's proximity to such company was by design. "It's a good chance," Giannulli said, "that somebody will walk out of Armani Exchange or Ralph Lauren and into our store." Giannulli then offered a telling statement that revealed his professional desires and the future direction Mossimo, Inc. would take. "I want to compete with those people in a big way," he said. In the coming years Mossimo, Inc. would be shaped by Giannulli's goal to become one of the industry's elite fashion designers.

Mid-1990s Growth and Public Offering

Any uncertainty regarding Giannulli's professional aspirations was eliminated after a 1994 interview with *Action Sports Retailer.* Giannulli said: "When I look at Calvin [Klein] or Armani or Ralph Lauren, those are the companies I want to be associated with, and I'm not settling for anything less. I will do everything in my power to get there." To ascend the fashion world's hierarchy, Giannulli sought to legitimize himself as a designer through Mossimo, Inc., which appeared more than capable of supporting its founder's climb. On the retail front, another store was opened in New York City as part of Giannulli's plan to establish a retail presence in a handful of major metropolitan areas, including Dallas, San Francisco, and Chicago, but by 1995 neither of the company's stores had shown a profit, curbing plans for further expansion. Success in the retail field had been achieved, however, through another venture. Giannulli began opening shops within department stores, establishing his in-store shops in stores such as Macy's, the Bon Marché, and Dayton Hudson. By the beginning of 1995 there were more than 30 Mossimo in-store shops, selling an apparel line that reflected the "new" Mossimo, Inc. taking shape. By the mid-1990s, activewear—the T-shirts, shorts, and sweatshirts that once represented the entirety of Giannulli's business—accounted for 60 percent of sales, its contribution to the company's revenue volume decreasing with each passing year. The balance was derived from the sale of accessories and the company's sportswear line of knit and woven shirts and denim, which accounted for 34 percent of sales in 1995, up from 20 percent two years earlier. During this transition Mossimo, Inc.'s sales shot upward, increasing at an annual compound rate of 46.6 percent during the first half of the 1990s to reach $110 million by 1995. Profits kept pace as well, primarily because consumers had demonstrated a willingness to pay increasingly higher prices for garments with the Mossimo name. In 1995 the company's net profit margin rested at 16 percent, far above the six percent averaged by rival Quicksilver and higher than the 13 percent recorded by Tommy Hilfiger, the fashion industry's phenom. It was against this backdrop of resounding success that Giannulli began, in earnest, to pursue his goal of becoming an upscale fashion designer.

In the first nine months of 1995, Mossimo, Inc. opened 11 in-store shops in nine department stores and specialty chains, giving the company a total of 46 in-store retail locations. Giannulli wanted to establish more stores and he wanted to introduce a more sophisticated apparel line that would improve his standing in the fashion world. Both pursuits required money, so in December 1995 Giannulli announced his plans to sell shares in Mossimo, Inc. to the public, intending to use the proceeds from the initial public offering (IPO) to finance the establishment of new in-store shops, reduce debt, and pay for a new headquarters and distribution facility. The IPO was completed in February 1996, making 32-year-old Giannulli the youngest chief executive officer of a company listed on the New York Stock Exchange. More important, the IPO raised $36 million, more than twice the total expected when the public offering was announced two months earlier. Mossimo, Inc.'s stock debuted at $18 a share and skyrocketed to $50 a share by June 1996, enriching investors exponentially in a four-month span. Giannulli and everyone associated with the company were ecstatic. One Wall Street analyst described Giannulli as the "next Calvin Klein," precisely the recognition Giannulli had been seeking. To spark further enthusiasm, the company's prospects pointed to an even greater growth. The entire Mossimo collection was being distributed in Japan, Canada, and Australia, with an aggressive European expansion plan slated to begin in 1998. Before the push into Europe, Giannulli planned for a high-profile fashion show in New York City in 1997 and hired approximately a dozen designers and executives from competitors such as Calvin Klein and Guess. It was difficult to imagine Mossimo, Inc. occupying a more enviable position than it did as the fall 1996 fashion season approached, but by the time the fall season did arrive, Giannulli found himself in desperate straits. Mossimo, Inc.'s stock value began to plummet, stripping Giannulli of hundreds of millions of dollars.

Late 1990s Fall from Grace

When Mossimo, Inc. reported at the end of September 1996 that its profits were down nearly 50 percent for the third quarter, the company's stock plunged to $15 a share within a month. Giannulli, who owned 73.3 of Mossimo, Inc.'s stock, saw his net worth reduced by $380 million. To blame were high production and development costs, which reduced earnings and caused the value of the company's stock to cascade downward. Giannulli conceded that "we overdeveloped," but remained optimistic despite his huge financial loss, saying, "ultimately we will hit the numbers." Traded as a publicly owned company, Mossimo, Inc. needed to demonstrate consistent, quarterly profits to maintain its value, but after years of profitability as a privately held firm, the company failed to generate profits when profits were needed most. Critics cited the company's rapid expansion as the cause, explaining that operationally Mossimo, Inc. was ill-equipped to embark on the ambitious plans developed by Giannulli. Amid this criticism, Mossimo, Inc.'s profits slid quarter by quarter, prompting one shareholder to file a lawsuit against the company, charging that Giannulli had "completely lost control of the company's operations." By February 1997—one year after the company's IPO—Mossimo, Inc.'s stock had dipped below $9 a share, causing further anxiety. The company lost $498,000 during the first quarter of 1997, compared with a $5.8 million profit for the same period one year earlier. To combat chronically deteriorating profitability, Giannulli reverted to a page from his own history, rekindling memories of his days as an upstart operating out of a Balboa Island apartment.

In May 1997, after closing his watch division, Giannulli announced plans for a new line of Mossimo activewear, the cotton T-shirts and swimwear that had given him his start. It was hoped that the introduction of this new, lower-priced line of activewear, combined with continuing efforts to reduce costs wherever possible, would arrest the company's perilous financial slide, but the losses continued to mount. By the fall of 1997, after posting a $4.8 million loss and a 46 percent decrease in sales for the company's third quarter, Giannulli had decided to seek help. "I am looking for a really good operational head who will be in partnership with me," he announced. "I want someone who will help us grow a long time, and stay for a while, not someone who will just come in and out of this joint." Giannulli dropped the titles of president and chief executive officer in favor of the more ephemeral title of "visionary," yet remained chairman as the search for a savior went forward. In January 1998 John P. Brincko, a turnaround specialist credited with reviving Barney's Inc. and Knudsen Foods, was hired as a consultant, arriving at a desperate juncture in Mossimo, Inc.'s history. For the fourth quarter of 1997 the company expected to lose roughly $14 million, nearly identical to the sum it hoped to generate in sales. In March 1998 Brincko took over as president and chief executive officer, inheriting a company that lost $18.7

million in 1997 on $70.9 million in revenues, which represented a 34 percent decline from 1996's sales volume.

By the time Brincko assumed operational control over the company, Giannulli's wealth had shriveled from $550 million in the summer of 1996 to $60 million. As Brincko scrutinized every aspect of Mossimo, Inc.'s business, including distribution, marketing, production, sales, inventory, and financial management, Giannulli's Laguna Beach estate was up for sale, making his fall from the top more precipitous than the startling pace of his ascension. Looking ahead, Brincko was hoping for the turnaround he had been hired to execute, but the company's profitability problems continued to hobble progress as the end of 1998 approached. Mossimo, Inc. reported a $6.1 million loss for 1998's second quarter, and by the fall its stock had fallen to less than $3 a share, reducing the value of Giannulli's stake to $30 million. Brincko was optimistic, however, saying that the company's 1999 line of denim and knit tops would show that Mossimo, Inc. was "headed in the right direction." The validity of such hope was to be determined in the years ahead, as Brincko sought to rebuild what had been created by Giannulli and ensure that Mossimo, Inc. could look forward to a future.

Principal Divisions

Mossimo Supply; Mossimo Swim.

Further Reading

Barron, Kelly, "Converting Clothing Line from Casual to High Fashion a Slow Process," *Knight-Ridder/Tribune Business News,* April 21, 1997, p. 42.

Ellis, Kristi, "Mossimo's Wild Ride: A Rocket to the Stars, a Plunge Back to Earth," *WWD,* November 13, 1996, p. 1.

Hardesty, Greg, "Turnaround Specialist Takes Reins at Struggling Clothing Designer," *Knight-Ridder/Tribune Business News,* March 6, 1998, p. 3.

La Franco, Robert, "A Cool Dude with Vision," *Forbes,* May 20, 1996, p. 264.

——, "Minimo Mossimo," *Forbes,* April 20, 1998, p. 16.

Marlow, Michael, "Mossimo Giannulli Trying To Catch a New Wave," *Daily News Record,* October 22, 1997, p. 12.

——, "The Moss Market: After Years of Searching, California Finally May Have Found Its Designer," *Daily News Record,* July 22, 1996, p. 32.

"Mossimo COO Resigns as Sales Plummet," *Daily News Record,* November 12, 1997, p. 4.

Mouchard, Andre, "San Francisco-Based Company To Make T-Shirts for Clothing Designer Mossimo," *Knight-Ridder/Tribune Business News,* October 5, 1998, p. 8.

Ryan, Thomas J., "Mossimo's Hot-Air Balloon Popped," *Footwear News,* February 3, 1997, p. 96.

Young, Vicki M., "Mossimo Loses $6.1 Million, But CEO Cites Cause To Hope," *WWD,* August 17, 1998, p. 24.

—Jeffrey L. Covell

Mrs. Fields' Original Cookies, Inc.

2855 East Cottonwood Parkway, Suite 400
Salt Lake City, Utah 84121
U.S.A.
(801) 736-5600
Fax: (801) 736-5970
Web site: http://www.mrsfields.com

Private Company
Founded: 1977
Employees: 4,007
Sales: $133.6 million (1998)
SICs: 2052 Cookies & Crackers; 2051 Bread, Cake &
Related Products; 5461 Retail Bakeries

Mrs. Fields' Original Cookies, Inc. bakes and sells specialty cookies, brownies, pretzels, and other baked goods. From one store started by Debbi and Randy Fields in 1977, the firm has expanded to over 1,500 stores named Mrs. Fields' Original Cookies, the Great American Cookie Company, the Original Cookie Company, Pretzel Time, Hot Sam, and Pretzelmaker. This is a true success story of an American homemaker and her husband who overcame numerous obstacles to create an international business. However, like many companies that began as family businesses, it reorganized under outside leadership and ownership. The firm's chocolate chip cookies were so popular that they became the subject of a modern urban legend in the late 1980s and early 1990s.

Everybody Said She Would Fail

Debbi Fields grew up in a Catholic working class family in Oakland, California. Her father was a welder and her mother raised Debbi and her sisters to become good wives and mothers. Growing up, Debbi held a burning desire to be special. Although she was a mediocre student, she learned to work hard and sought a way to fulfill her dreams. Debbi graduated from high school, then worked at various jobs before marrying Randy Fields, a Stanford University-trained economist, in 1976.

For about a year as a new wife, Mrs. Fields tried to fit into her husband's world as a dutiful spouse by hosting visitors and making polite conversation. However, a painful incident in which she tried to pretend she was a sophisticated person made her decide to do something else with her life. In the book *One Smart Cookie,* she said, "at last I understood that I had to do something that was mine. . . . I gave up, in that moment, the desire to succeed in other people's eyes and realized that first I had to succeed for *myself.*" She elaborated, "I couldn't be Randy's shadow any more, his tagalong. . . . Somehow I would have to change, to become an independent, self-respecting individual able to stand on my two feet."

Debbi Fields decided to start a business based on a skill she had acquired as a girl. From age 13 she had baked delicious chocolate chip cookies for her family and friends. She gradually improved the basic recipe pioneered in the 1930s by Toll House.

Her husband's business acquaintances loved her cookies, so she asked them what they thought about starting a cookie business. "Bad idea," they said with their mouths stuffed full of cookies. "Never work," they said, "Forget it." Debbi's mother, her in-laws, and her friends and fellow students at Los Altos Junior College also said she would fail.

Her husband went along with the idea, but deep down he did not really believe his wife could succeed in the business world. For one thing, market studies showed that consumers strongly preferred crispy cookies. Debbi's cookies were soft and larger than normal and would have to be sold at much higher prices than regular bakery cookies.

She went ahead anyway but needed financial backing from a bank. She and Randy approached the Bank of America, their home mortgage lender. Their banker Ed Sullivan trusted the young couple to pay back a business loan, even though he expected the cookie business would fail. Debbi said in her book that the bank "trusted *us*, not cookies. . . . As things turned out, Ed Sullivan and his bank built Mrs. Fields' Cookies."

So at age 20 Debbi Fields started her first cookie store at Liddicoat's Market in Palo Alto. She signed the lease under the name Mrs. Fields' Chocolate Chippery. On August 18, 1977, she opened her store at 9 a.m., but by noon nobody had bought even one cookie. Frustrated and afraid to fail, she took samples to people on the streets. They liked the samples so returned to actually buy cookies. Providing free samples to potential customers remained a cornerstone of her business in the years to come.

Early Expansion

Debbi Fields initially was content with her one store. Then Warren Simmons, the builder of the Pier 39 shopping area in San Francisco, told her he loved the cookies and invited her to open a store in Pier 39. She at first turned him down, then a year later changed her mind. Pier 39 had reserved a prime space for Mrs. Fields' Cookies. Employees at her first store kept asking for opportunities to grow. Since her employees were like family, Debbi Fields felt a responsibility to them. With additional loans, the second store was opened in 1979. The Pier 39 store was so successful with its long customer lines that it caused problems for nearby businesses. The pressure was on to open more outlets.

An early crisis illustrated how the young company operated. Mrs. Fields refused to replace higher cost raisins with less costly but also less tasty dates. Debbi Fields explained that, ''The point wasn't to make money, the point was to bake great cookies, and we sacrificed for that principle. From the very first, I set up a policy that we still follow today. Our cookies had to be warm and fresh and when they were two hours out of the oven, what hadn't been sold was donated to the Red Cross to be given to blood donors, or to other deserving charities, and we baked a new batch. We guaranteed everything we sold.''

By 1979 the company had three stores but had reached a turning point. Working 16 hours a day to oversee everything, Debbi Fields said, ''The cookie business had become a monster, demanding and demanding.'' She was so busy she had to schedule times to see her husband. She and Randy offered the rights to the company outside of California to Foremost McKesson, a large ice-cream maker, for $150,000, but the firm turned them down. They were crushed, but just kept on, wearily trying to handle the burdens of expansion. With the help of some key employees, they managed to survive. Eventually they received but turned down better offers for their firm, for they were learning how to handle a growing business.

Not all Mrs. Fields' stores however succeeded so easily. In 1980 the company opened its new store in the Ala Moana Shopping Center in Honolulu, but initially it failed miserably. Debbi Fields then had a kahuna or priest of the native Hawaiian culture bless her store. ''The day after the ceremony, crowds of cookie buyers appeared; since that day, the Ala Moana location has been one of our most successful and profitable stores.''

A few months later the firm reached a major milestone when it opened its first Utah store—in the Crossroads Mall in Salt Lake City. Debbi previously had been to Utah to ski, but the store was the idea of Michael Murphy, one of her company officers.

By the spring of 1981 the company operated 14 stores. At a training session, Debbi Fields was impressed with the fact that each store manager knew which cookies he had baked even when they were mixed up with those baked by the other managers. That experience assured her that the company training was successful.

In 1982 Mrs. Fields' Cookies recorded sales of about $30 million. By early 1983 the company had moved to Park City, Utah, and operated 70 stores from Honolulu to Chicago, and then it decided to open its first store in New York City.

When the firm began in the late 1970s, about 100 independent stores sold gourmet or specialty cookies. By 1983, according to *Forbes,* competition in this niche industry had resulted in just a few main companies. Mrs. Fields' Cookies competed against the Famous Amos Chocolate Chip Cookie Corporation, started in 1975 by Wally (Famous) Amos. By 1983 Famous Amos began a program to franchise 100 stores within two years. David Liederman began David's Cookies with a store in Manhattan and soon dominated the New York City market for specialty cookies. Other key firms included The Famous Chocolate Chip Cookie Company headed by President Frank Bonanno, the Original Cookie Company owned by Cole National Corporation, and Original Great American led by President Arthur Karp.

Although combined revenues from these firms were just $150 million in 1983, profit margins ran higher than in other industries, partly because of inexpensive materials. For example, batter for five pounds of cookies cost only $1.50, and cookies were relatively easy to produce. Frank Bonanno in the *Forbes* article estimated that ''Pretax profits run anywhere between 10% and 20%.''

For several years Debbi Fields rejected the idea of franchising her stores. She realized the cookies and other products could be duplicated but not the atmosphere of ''love and caring'' that was so important to the business. She also said in her book that she did not ''want anyone else to get his hands on it.'' Although in 1987 she intended to retain ''complete control and complete responsibility,'' economic necessity changed that approach in just a few years.

By 1987 Debbi Fields had created 14 different kinds of cookies: Pecan Whites; Milk Chocolate with and without walnuts; Semisweet Chocolate with and without walnuts; Semisweet Chocolate with and without macadamia nuts; Coco-Mac with coconut and macadamia nuts; Oatmeal Raisin Nut, called Debra's Special; Peanut Butter Dreams; Triple Chocolate that combined white and dark chocolate; Raisin Spice; White Chunk with macadamia nuts; and Royal Pecan. Her stores also sold five kinds of brownies, her own ice cream, candy, and muffins.

In 1987 Mrs. Fields' Cookies did well financially. It earned a profit of 18.5 percent on sales of $87 million, up from $72.6 million in 1986. The company in 1987 purchased La Petite Boulangerie, a chain of 119 French bakery/sandwich stores, from PepsiCo for $15 million. In just four weeks Randy Fields used specially developed software to help him and his wife reduce La Petite Boulangerie's administrative staff from 53 to just three individuals.

Several articles in business and computer magazines in the late 1980s praised Mrs. Fields' Cookies' innovative use of computer software to run its expanding cookie operations. The firm equipped each of its stores with inexpensive IBM-compatible computers that were linked by modems to the company's larger system in Park City. Computerization allowed the firm's retail stores to plan daily production schedules, monitor stocks and order materials automatically, communicate with headquarters using electronic mail, improve employee training, and handle payroll and other accounting tasks. Store managers spent about five minutes an hour and 20 minutes before and after work using their computers to help run their outlets. Headquarters staff in 1988 remained low at about 130 persons.

Although Mrs. Fields' Cookies management structure on paper included levels of middle management, Tom Richman in an October 1987 *Inc.* article wrote: "Randy Fields has created something entirely new—a shape if not the shape, of business organizations to come. It gives top management a dimension of personal control over dispersed operations that small companies otherwise find impossible to achieve. It projects a founder's vision into parts of a company that have long ago outgrown his or her ability to reach in person." Richman continued: "In the structure that Fields is building, computers don't just speed up old administrative management processes. They alter the process. Management . . . becomes less administration and more inspiration. The management hierarchy of the company feels almost flat."

After Randy Fields computerized Mrs. Fields' Cookies, he began selling his artificial intelligence/store management software through a subsidiary, Fields Software Group. Burger King Corporation in 1990 became one of the software customers.

In the meantime, Debbi and Randy Fields received numerous honors. In 1988 the Utah Chapter of the National Conference of Christians and Jews honored the couple with its Brotherhood/Sisterhood Award for their many community contributions in business and philanthropy. Debbi Fields served on the boards of the Cystic Fibrosis Research Foundation, the Park City Educational Foundation, and Salt Lake City's LDS Hospital. She and her husband founded Mrs. Fields' Children's Health Foundation and donated millions to study children's diseases. Randy Fields was president of Riverview Financial Corporation, the Fields Investment Group, and the Fields Consulting Group. As the president of a firm with over 700 outlets worldwide, Mrs. Fields told the National Conference attendees that, "We are very proud to receive this award, but you must remember that each time you've enjoyed Mrs. Fields' Cookies, you're the one who's allowing us to give."

Her company, however, had a bad year in 1988 when it lost $19 million and closed 85 of its 500 stores, mostly in the eastern and southeastern United States. Some argued that these problems began in 1986 with Mrs. Fields' Cookies' initial public offering on London's Unlisted Securities Market. British investors purchased only 16 percent of the 30 million shares offered at $2.46 per share. After the company said it had set up a $15 million reserve to pay for store closings, its stock price decreased to just 44 cents per share.

The company also closed its Park City candy factory in order to concentrate on building its La Petite Boulangerie bakery business in Carson, California. To integrate the new subsidiary,

Mrs. Fields' Cookies changed from having just cookie stores to full-service bakeries. Randy Fields admitted this was a difficult transition. In the February 13, 1989 issue of *Fortune,* he said, "We've been very ineffective at telling the British what we're trying to do." Some British food industry analysts said investors felt deceived after they were told it was a cookie company and then it changed directions.

In spite of these challenges, Randy and Debbi Fields continued to play a major role in developing the rapidly growing community of Park City, where more celebrities and about 300 *Fortune* 500 executives decided to move or build condominiums in the 1980s. For example, the couple developed the Summit County Industrial Park, anchored by tenant Lucas Western's $40 million aerospace manufacturing plant.

They also owned Park City's Main Street Mall, home of their corporate headquarters, the Egyptian Theatre, and other properties. In 1988 they closed their ice cream parlor so they could use the former Dudler Building for Mrs. Fields' Cookie College.

Gregg Goodwin, head of Park City Area Chamber of Commerce economic development, cited Randy and Debbi Fields as an example of corporate leaders who had moved their family and company to Park City to enjoy the area's high education levels, strong work ethic, low rates of alcohol use, and other lifestyle advantages.

In 1989 the company rebounded from a poor performance the year before. Revenues for the parent company, Mrs. Fields' Inc., increased eight percent from $120.4 million in 1988 to $129.7 million in 1989, while the firm recorded a 1989 net income of $1.5 million, a major improvement from 1988's loss of $19 million.

Also in 1989, Mrs. Fields' Cookies began making frozen cookie dough at its Carson, California plant and then shipping it to selected stores in Utah. Previously it had been the only major cookie maker that did not use frozen dough. In December 1989 the company began the process of selling its Carson plant to Van den Bergh Foods, a Unilever Group subsidiary. However, Mrs. Fields' Cookies kept the part of the plant that made its cookies.

Mrs. Fields' Inc. in 1989 reorganized by delegating certain management roles. A new executive committee included Chairman Randy Fields, President Debbi Fields, Larry Holman, Paul Baird, and Tim Pierce. Holman, an attorney, had joined the company as a senior vice-president in October 1989 to manage corporate development and real estate. Director of Operations Baird took over much of the responsibility of managing the firm's cookie stores, thus allowing Debbi Fields to emphasize development and marketing. Pierce was a CPA and company vice-president of finance. Even more significant changes would occur in the years to come, but in the meantime the company had to deal with damaging rumors or stories going around the nation.

The Urban Legend

Professor Jan Brunvand at the University of Utah and other scholars have shown that tales or stories about modern companies are sometimes told so often they become urban legends.

Often not historically true, they were told by a friend of a friend in a chain of communication.

For example, beginning in the 1950s, a story called "Red Velvet Cake" was told about a customer who paid New York City's Waldorf-Astoria Hotel a large sum of money for a red cake recipe. Starting in 1983, the story had mutated so that Mrs. Fields' Cookies was the culprit. In this version, "someone had called the Mrs. Fields' company and asked for their recipe. When told that it was available for 'two-fifty,' the caller supposedly told the phone representative to send the recipe and charge it to her credit card, learning later that the price was $250 rather than the expected $2.50."

Then, according to this tale disseminated by photocopies, the corporation's victim became upset and thus sent many bitter letters with the supposed secret recipe, and encouraged others to send out even more copies.

By 1987 Debbi Fields said in her book that, "The rumor has really hurt the company." She responded to this persistent account by placing notices in all her stores denying that the company had sold its recipe. Since average people (the folk) started and spread such legends and other forms of folklore, denunciations from the top usually had little impact. That happened with this story, which continued into the early 1990s and was also told about other firms such as Chicago's Marshall Fields, New York City's Macy's, St. Louis' Union Station, and Neiman Marcus stores in various cities.

One recipient of the photocopied urban legend tried the supposed secret recipe only to realize the resulting cookies tasted nothing like the real thing. But then Todd Wilbur spent five years trying to replicate Mrs. Fields' chocolate chip cookies and other fast-food products. He even published two cookbooks in the late 1980s and early 1990s with recipes that the *Deseret News* food editor called "clones," an unusual consequence of a modern whopper. Why would anyone believe such stories of a corporation selling its vital secret recipes?

Dr. Brunvand, the nation's leading expert on urban legends, wrote about this story in his fourth book, *Curses! Broiled Again.* He said in his 1991 newspaper column that this story about Mrs. Fields' Cookies and other companies was a "classic recipe-scam story that refuses to die, no matter how often I debunk it or how vigorously companies deny it. . . . [It] illustrates two things: that many people love stories about corporate ripoffs, and that few can resist chocolate chip cookies."

The popularity of Mrs. Fields' Cookies, the basis for the urban legend, was also seen in Congress in the late 1980s and early 1990s. Utah's congressmen about twice a year distributed free cookies, baked at local Mrs. Fields' stores in the Washington, D.C., area, to the hundreds of other representatives.

The 1990s

In 1990 Mrs. Fields' Cookies announced an agreement with the Marriott Corporation which allowed Marriott to own at least 60 stores to bake and sell the popular bakery products. Marriott gained the exclusive right to build Mrs. Fields' Cookies stores in airports, hotels, and highway travel plazas and pay the cookie company approximately five percent of its gross sales.

Mrs. Fields' in 1990 operated 45 international stores in Canada, Australia, Japan, Hong Kong, and the United Kingdom, and it planned to expand worldwide using various joint ventures or licensing contracts which promised profits without significant investment. By 1992 the firm had added stores in Thailand, and its seventh overseas market started in Mexico City with a licensing agreement with Pasteleria El Molino S.A.

In 1990 the company began remodeling some stores to allow more display space for new packaging products, cookie jars, and tins. To stimulate gift buying as well as cookie purchases, teddy bear maker Gund was commissioned to make little bears like those on the cookie tins. With new designs and decor, Debbi Fields intended to create boutiques or European-style cafés that were more colorful and exciting.

In 1993 Mrs. Fields' Cookies' stock was removed from the London Stock Exchange, and new owners reorganized the company. Four lenders, mainly the Prudential group, acquired almost 80 percent of the firm in exchange for writing off $94 million in company debt, while Debbi Fields retained a minority interest, remained board chairman, and accepted a salary cut of $150,000 to $450,000. Thomas Fey, formerly with Godiva and Pepperidge Farm, replaced Debbi Fields as president and CEO. The refinancing allowed the company to plan a major expansion of 100 new company-owned and franchised stores within the next year. Started in August 1991, the company's franchise option was praised by at least three publications: *Success, Entrepreneur,* and *Self Magazine.*

Although the company survived and retained the name of its founder, many wondered why Debbi and Randy Fields lost control. As Max Knudson, the business editor of Salt Lake City's *Deseret News* said in 1998, the couple "seemed to have it all: beauty, brains, ambition, family values, a business growing exponentially—people couldn't get enough of them."

Three reasons accounted for the huge debt and loss of control to outsiders. First, the company expanded too fast, and many stores could not afford their expensive rents. In many cases, the company had purchased property for its mall stores. Second, the nation's economic downturn in the early 1990s hurt Mrs. Fields' Cookies. Many customers no longer could afford her expensive cookies (about $1 per cookie) and the value of her real estate declined.

Last but not least, Debbi Fields's insistence on hands-on personal management and reluctance to franchise did not work. Francorp's Don Boroian, a Chicago franchising consultant, in the July 1993 *Working Woman* said he told Mrs. Fields' Cookies to franchise when it was still a young firm. "When you're trying to expand as they did, with units in malls, you can't provide close enough supervision. By the time they decided to franchise, the concept wasn't strong enough because of increased competition, fewer customers, higher rents and a downturn in the economy. They needed to add more products, and they're finally doing that now." By 1993 the company had added yogurt, coffee, and diversified with other products. It also had closed most of its mall stores by 1993.

Chairwoman Debbi Fields in early 1995 announced that the company planned to add 100 new stores overseas. At that time, five percent of the firm's 617 stores were located outside the

United States. Fields said the company had franchise agreements in Indonesia, Australia, the Philippines, Canada, and the Middle East and also was targeting European and South American markets. Fields said the firm's long-term goal was to franchise all overseas operations.

Like many other firms, Mrs. Fields' Cookies in the 1990s used the Internet to stimulate sales. The company was one of over 100 businesses included on the Utah-based virtual mall called iShopper started in July 1996.

In the 1990s the company moved its headquarters from Park City to offices on Bearcat Drive in Salt Lake City. In the summer of 1998 it moved again, this time to a new 30,000-square-foot complex in Salt Lake City's Cottonwood Corporate Center. However, it kept its facilities on Bearcat Drive and Lawndale Drive for about 40 employees. Its mail-order operation remained on Bearcat Drive.

Meanwhile, the family that started the business ended in divorce. Debbi Fields married Michael Rose, the retired chairman of Harrah's Entertainment, on November 29, 1997, and moved from Park City to live with her husband in Memphis, Tennessee. Debbi Fields Rose served as a consultant to the firm she founded and also participated in a public television show called Great American Desserts. Randy Fields continued to live in Park City and work in the software industry. Thus the firm persisted even as what *Deseret News* business writer Max B. Knudson called the "media darlings" broke up, after years of conflict and tension.

The company continued to expand in 1998 under the ownership of Capricorn Investors and the leadership of Chairman Herbert S. Winokur, Jr., and President/CEO Larry A. Hodges. Effective November 23, 1998, Mrs. Fields' Original Cookies purchased Denver-based Pretzelmaker for an undisclosed amount. This acquisition added 229 pretzel stores to the firm's already existing 1,324 cookie and pretzel stores.

Further Reading

Brunvand, Jan Harold, "Fresh Batch of Kooky Cookie Stories Is Served," *Deseret News,* October 25, 1991.

"Chips and Chocolate," *Economist,* July 23, 1988, p. 56.

Fields, Debbi, and Alan Furst, *One Smart Cookie: How a Housewife's Chocolate Chip Recipe Turned into a Multimillion Dollar Business: The Story of Mrs. Fields' Cookies,* New York: Simon and Schuster, 1987.

Funk, Marianne, "Mrs. Fields' Is Transforming Some Stores into Boutiques," *Deseret News,* July 16, 1990.

Knudson, Max B., "Fields Cookie Without the Mrs. or Mr.?" *Deseret News,* May 20, 1998.

——, "Marketing Plan for Park City Is Imaginative," *Deseret News,* December 17, 1989.

——, "Mrs. Fields' Cookies Says It Has Accord to Fuel Growth," *Deseret News,* February 17, 1993.

Madden, Stephen, "Tough Cookies?" *Fortune,* February 13, 1989, p. 112.

McKanus, Kevin, "The Cookie Wars," *Forbes,* November 7, 1983, p. 150.

Moulton, Tina, "Fieldses Honored for Compassion and Service to the Community," *Deseret News,* May 8, 1988.

"Mrs. Fields' Cookies Goes East," *Fortune,* February 7, 1983, p. 9.

"Mrs. Fields Inc. Back on Track with '89 Income of $1.5 Million," *Deseret News,* April 11, 1990.

Newquist, Harvey P., III, "Experts at Retail," *Datamation,* April 1, 1990, p. 53.

Pogrebin, Robin, "What Went Wrong with Mrs. Fields?" *Working Woman,* July 1993, p. 9.

Richman, Tom, "Mrs. Fields' Secret Ingredient: The Real Recipe Behind the Phenomenal Growth of Mrs. Fields' Cookies Cannot Be Found in the Dough," *Inc.,* October 1987, p. 65.

Williams, Jean, "Send in the Clones: Top Secret Recipes," *Deseret News,* June 18, 1996.

—David M. Walden

National Media Corporation

15821 Ventura Boulevard
Encino, California 91436
U.S.A.
(818) 461-6400
Fax: (818) 461-6525
Web site: http://www.quantumtv.com

Public Company
Incorporated: 1986 as National Paragon Corporation
Employees: 370
Sales: $278.5 million (1998)
Stock Exchanges: New York
Ticker Symbol: NM
SICs: 7319 Advertising, Not Elsewhere Classified; 7812
    Motion Picture & Video Tape Production

National Media Corporation is the world's largest publicly held direct response (infomercial) television company and a leader in the growing world of electronic commerce. The company broadcasts more than 3,000 half hours of programming each week throughout the world, bringing its programming to more than 370 million television households in more than 70 countries worldwide. As it approached the end of the century, National Media hoped to begin providing live, taped, and on-demand video programming over the Internet.

Company Origins

The television infomercial was born in 1984. Prior to 1984, the Federal Communications Commission (FCC) limited the amount of advertising to 16 minutes of commercial messages per hour. In 1984 the FCC eliminated its limitations and permitted the sale of blocks of advertising. Recognizing the advertising opportunity, infomercial producers began buying chunks of broadcast time from cable operators. Their half-hour and one-hour shows combined direct response marketing and retailing principles in a television talk show format.

Media Arts International, based in Phoenix, Arizona, was one of the first companies to produce infomercials in 1984. In No-

vember 1986 Media Arts International was acquired by National Media Corporation, then known as National Paragon Corporation, for $4 million, as part of National Paragon's approved reorganization plan. Prior to entering the infomercial business, National Paragon Corporation was engaged in the needlecraft business for more than 60 years. In 1984 it formed National Syndication, Inc., a subsidiary that managed a variety of specialty catalogs and mail-order businesses. In October 1985 National Paragon filed for bankruptcy protection under Chapter 11 of the Bankruptcy Reform Act. A year later it emerged from Chapter 11 and in November 1986 acquired Media Arts International as part of its approved reorganization plan.

On July 24, 1987, National Paragon Corporation adopted its present name, National Media Corporation. Fiscal 1988 (ending March 31, 1988) was the company's first profitable year following its emergence from bankruptcy protection, when it reported net income of $4.2 million on revenues of $31.9 million. For fiscal 1989 it had net income of $2.5 million on sales of $31.8 million. Then, in fiscal 1990, revenues increased dramatically to $92.7 million, with net income rising to $11.5 million. In September 1990, the company's stock, which had been trading on the NASDAQ, was approved for listing on the New York Stock Exchange.

Focus on Infomercials: 1991

In 1991 National Media took two steps that would enable it to focus on producing infomercials and expand into the European market. In May 1991 it sold its wholly owned subsidiary National Syndication, Inc. (NSI), to NSI's management for $5 million in cash and additional consideration based on NSI's pretax income for the next seven years. Following the sale of NSI, National Media's continuing business in the United States was conducted primarily through Media Arts International, Inc., which marketed products directly to consumers principally through television and its "Amazing Discoveries" infomercial series. The products were mainly in the areas of housewares, beauty, kitchen, automotive, and self-improvement.

Proceeds from the sale of NSI enabled National Media to acquire a leading European infomercial producer, Quantum Marketing International, Inc. Through Quantum, National Media began to expand its presence quickly in Europe. In July 1991 it signed an exclusive three-year agreement with the Super Channel, the largest pan-European entertainment satellite network. The contract allowed National Media to air 30-minute infomercials for three years beginning August 15, 1991, reaching nearly 40 million homes in more than 23 countries.

Also in 1991 the company hired several key administrative and marketing executives. These included Mark P. Hershhorn, who was appointed president and Chief Operating Officer. He joined National Media from Nutri/System, where he was senior vice-president with worldwide responsibilities. David J. Carman was appointed president and CEO of Quantum Television Marketing Ltd., National Media's international subsidiary, which would be headquartered in London, England.

Pivotal Year for National Media: 1991–92

Fiscal 1992 was a pivotal year for National Media, the first in which the company embarked on a new global vision. Its strategy was to position itself as the world's premier marketer of consumer products via direct response television. Central to the company's marketing strategy was the use of infomercials to create and heighten brand awareness. Outside factors contributing to National Media's success were the growth of satellite-driven cable television and the potential of international consumerism. The emerging economies of Europe were creating new purchasing power where none had existed before.

The company achieved a vertically integrated structure by supervising the manufacture of the products it sold as well as producing the majority of its programming. It added staff to increase the number of new product introductions. The company also owned its own fulfillment operation, giving it greater control over customer service. Product quality and customer service initiatives required higher levels of inventory and, as a result, more working capital. Consequently, the company did not declare a dividend this year and suspended future dividends indefinitely. As a result of special charges, it reported a loss of $4.9 million on revenues of $102.2 million for fiscal 1992.

Revenue Increases in Fiscal 1993

National Media reported net income of $6.3 million on revenue of $142 million for fiscal 1993. During the year the company began to implement a multichannel marketing approach. It was airing almost 600 hours of programming a week through satellite and cable television as well as local television. In addition to infomercials, National Media was using print ads, catalogs, direct mail, and point-of-purchase advertising to expose its products to a larger audience. The company was also forming strategic alliances with major direct marketers and retailers.

To fuel its multichannel marketing strategy, National Media expanded its product categories to include higher-priced items. It was also forming strategic ventures with established manufacturers and marketers to achieve more product diversification.

Internationally, National Media operated through strategic alliances with local partners in 20 different countries in Europe, the Middle East, Australia, and New Zealand. Technological developments allowed National Media to simultaneously broadcast its infomercials in four different languages: English, French, German, and Dutch. The company controlled over 200 hours a week of airtime on major European networks.

In December 1993 National Media settled a lawsuit filed earlier in the year by Positive Response Television, Inc., its business partner in the "Amazing Discoveries" infomercial series. The series spokesperson, Mark Levey, was chairman and CEO of the privately held Positive Response Television. The two companies would continue their partnership, with National Media owning the trademark "Amazing Discoveries" and Positive Response acting as exclusive producer of the infomercial series. According to the *Wall Street Journal,* the "Amazing Discoveries" infomercials, which aired late at night and offered "amazing" car waxes, hair-styling kits, and exercise videos, were responsible for approximately half of National Media's revenues.

For fiscal 1994, National Media enjoyed higher revenues of $167.9 million, but it reported a net loss of $8.7 million. The company recorded unusual charges of $9 million, mostly related to litigation costs. Based on the volume of outstanding litigation and other perceived weaknesses in the business, the company's independent auditors issued an opinion questioning whether the company could continue as a going concern.

Hostile Takeover Bid in 1994

Minneapolis, Minnesota-based ValueVision International Inc., the country's third largest home shopping network, began an unsolicited $10 per share stock and cash takeover bid for National Media in January 1994 valued at $117.5 million. When National Media's board of directors rejected the bid as "financially inadequate," ValueVision announced it would launch a $134 million two-step tender offer for National Media at $10.50 per share. This second offer was also rejected. In March 1994 the *Wall Street Journal* carried reports that National Media had accepted a $150 million offer from ValueVision to purchase its stock at $11.50 a share. However, ValueVision terminated the offer, causing National Media to file a lawsuit against ValueVision seeking $20 million in damages. National Media and ValueVision subsequently reached a settlement in April 1995, whereby the two companies would enter into a three-year agreement.

Meanwhile, National Media continued to expand internationally. In February 1994 the company entered into an agreement with Japanese trading firm Mitsui & Co. to launch a televised home shopping business in Japan. Under the agreement, National Media would supply infomercial programming, and Mitsui would handle the broadcasting and marketing. The deal was updated in early 1995 and provided for infomercial programming to 33 million Japanese households on more than 21 television stations. According to *Fortune* magazine, Mitsui was the world's largest diversified service company. In May 1994 National Media expanded its programming into Brazil and Taiwan through its subsidiary Quantum International.

Financial Challenges in the Mid-1990s

In June 1994 the company announced it needed a capital infusion to remain stable. During the year it benefited from capital investments made by its management team and outside investors. In October 1994 selected officers, board members, and other private investors made an equity investment of $1.3 million. The same month a $5 million loan was closed with an affiliate of Safeguard Scientific. In December, Safeguard Scientific, along with certain affiliates and other individual investors, purchased $5.4 million of convertible preferred stock.

National Media controlled or owned more than $65 million in media time worldwide, or more than 1,600 half-hours of media time per week, reaching over 190 million homes in North America and 49 countries around the world. Internationally, revenues from Quantum International were $80.4 million for fiscal 1995, an increase of 75 percent over the previous year. The company could take products that had matured out of the American infomercial market into international markets. Also helping international revenues was the fact that media costs were lower than in the United States. National Media estimated it accounted for an 18 percent market share of the $1 billion international infomercial business.

On April 15, 1995, management was restructured to facilitate global expansion. Brian McAdams was re-elected chairman of the board and chairman of the executive committee. Mark P. Hershhorn, who had rejoined the company a month earlier, became president and CEO of National Media as well as chairman of the board of Quantum International Ltd. David J. Carman became president and CEO of Quantum International Ltd. In order to be able to empower and trust key managers throughout the world, an office of the chairman was created to provide authority for National Media's management team. The office of the chairman, which consisted of four key executives, provided for ''efficient strategic flow between the board of directors and National Media's management team.''

For fiscal 1995 National Media reported a net loss of $672,000 on revenues of $168.7 million. Unusual charges for the year were down to $5.5 million, again related to litigation costs to resolve a variety of disputes.

Fiscal 1996, ended March 31, was the best year in the company's history, with net income of $16.6 million on revenues of $292.6 million. International revenues were $151 million, up from $80 million in fiscal 1995. During the year National Media added 70 million international television households, 10 million of them in Japan alone.

Through a tax-free exchange of common stock, National Media acquired West Coast infomercial producer DirectAmerica Corporation, which became a wholly owned subsidiary, on October 24, 1995. The stock represented about 2.6 percent of National Media's outstanding common stock.

In November 1995 National Media announced it would become partners in a joint venture with Graff Pay-Per-View Inc. to be called the Dragnet, an infomercial network that would broadcast half-hour infomercials 24 hours a day. Dragnet was set to launch December 1, 1995, with National Media supplying the infomercial programming.

Acquisitions Leave Company Financially Drained, 1996–97

In late 1995 National Media announced it had agreed to acquire Positive Response Television, Inc. The acquisition was completed in May 1996 for 1.8 million shares of common stock valued at $25.9 million. It was part of a series of acquisitions that left the company in financial straits in 1997.

For the first six months of fiscal 1997, the company's net income rose 66 percent to $9.5 million, up from $5.7 million the previous year, due in part to strong growth in emerging markets. About half of the company's sales came from foreign consumers. National Media announced it would begin airing infomercials in South Africa and other nearby African countries through an arrangement with Johannesburg-based retailer Verimark Holdings Pty. National Media would provide the infomercial programming, while Verimark would manage the venture and secure air time on broadcast networks.

National Media, which had recently entered the Indonesia market, was able to enter emerging markets with a limited amount of risk. The company simply aired its library of shows, so it did not have to make a significant new investment in programming. In March 1997 National Media announced further international expansion, extending its infomercial programming to 67 million households in Russia, Belarus, and the Ukraine.

During 1996 National Media's stock price plummeted from $20 in January to $5 in December. In 1995 the company's stock had hit a high near $21, up from around $3 in the fall of 1994. As National Media was about to announce operating losses for its fourth quarter and fiscal year 1997 ending March 31, the company appointed a new CEO, Robert N. Verratti, who was also named president and a director. He replaced Mark P. Hershhorn, who resigned. Verratti was viewed as a ''turnaround specialist''; he had previously been special advisor for acquisitions to the chairman and CEO of Safeguard Scientific, Inc., which owned about 15 percent of National Media.

Most of National Media's 1997 losses were from its U.S. operations, where media costs were relatively high and there was more pressure to produce new infomercials. For fiscal 1997, National Media reported a net loss of $45.7 million on revenues of $358.2 million. Its fourth-quarter loss was $49.3 million, compared with a year-earlier profit of $5.9 million for the quarter. As a result, National Media was in technical violation of certain loan agreements which could affect its ability to remain solvent.

National Media was in financial straits after its recent acquisitions resulted in extensive losses. The company was reported to be in talks with at least two possible acquirers or merger partners, and it laid off 85 employees—most of them at Positive Response Television—representing 19 percent of its workforce. It appeared that National Media had committed too much money to air time, but did not have any new sensational products to compare with the highly successful Ab Roller Plus, which generated $100 million a year at its peak in 1996. Because of patent infringement litigation, National Media had stopped selling the abdominal exerciser. The company hired the investment firm Lehman Brothers in April to explore a variety of strategic alternatives.

In September 1997 National Media completed the sale of $20 million worth of preferred stock and common stock warrants to two institutional investors. Under an exemption granted by the New York Stock Exchange, National Media was able to sell the stock and warrants without shareholder approval, which is normally required when a transaction may increase outstanding shares by 20 percent or more. The infusion of money from the institutional investors helped relieve the company's financial distress. By August 1997, the company's stock was trading in the $5 range, well below its 52-week high of $17.125 a share.

In January 1998 National Media and ValueVision International disclosed a merger plan that called for the formation of a new company. However, dissident shareholders at ValueVision's annual meeting in April 1998 threatened to exercise "dissenter's rights," which would require them to be paid in cash rather than in stock under Minnesota law, where ValueVision was based. As the two companies tried to renegotiate their agreement, a June 1 expiration date passed, and the merger plan was mutually terminated. In June 1998 National Media's stock was selling for around $1.25 a share. For fiscal 1998 National Media reported net revenues of $278.5 million and a net loss of $56.8 million.

New Investor Group Takes Control: 1998

With National Media shares trading at around $1 or $2 a share, Stephen Lehman and his investor group saw the opportunity to gain control of the company, improve its core business, and expand into the world of electronic commerce. Lehman was formerly president and CEO of Premiere Radio Networks. The investor group included Jacor Communications, the parent company of Premiere Radio Networks and owner, operator, or representative of more than 200 radio stations. It also included several executives from media companies such as Broadcast.com, Capstar Broadcasting Corporation, Group W Productions, Westwood One Radio Networks, and Warner Brothers Records. Radio and television personality Casey Kasem was also part of the investment group.

In July 1998 it was announced that Lehman's investor group planned to invest $30 million in National Media. At the time of the announcement Lehman's group took over control of National Media's board of directors and Lehman became acting CEO. He brought in a new management team to leverage National Media's infomercial business to establish a presence on the World Wide Web and become a major player in the world of electronic commerce.

The transaction was approved at National Media's annual shareholder meeting in October 1998. Following the meeting, Lehman was installed as National Media's CEO and chairman of the board. He articulated the company's new direction in his address to the stockholders. "This company is uniquely well-positioned to become a leader in the fast-growing E-Commerce/ Internet marketplace," he said. "We have an incredible opportunity through our $100 million in annual television media; our millions of customer contacts; our international infrastructure; and our ability to deliver live, taped, and on-demand programming over the Internet. We are a leader in electronic direct-marketing, and we will use this creativity and expertise to drive consumers to our sites and make their visits rewarding."

In November 1998 National Media expanded into electronic commerce by launching three full-time video programming channels over the Internet at www.broadcast.com/shopping.

The company's alliance with Broadcast.com created the first 24-hour-per-day live and on-demand streaming video shopping channels on the Internet as well as a link from Broadcast.com's web site. As part of its electronic commerce initiative, National Media expanded its strategic relationship with Mitsui to jointly pursue electronic commerce opportunities in Japan as well as throughout Asia and Australia.

National Media relocated its corporate headquarters from Philadelphia, Pennsylvania, to the Los Angeles metropolitan area in November 1998. The move consolidated the company's offices in Philadelphia and Encino, California. Lehman said that the move was "clearly symbolic of the change in the company's direction as we expand into the world of electronic commerce." The move was also cited as a cost-cutting measure. The new headquarters was located at the site of Quantum Television, National Media's creative and marketing center, in Encino.

National Media debuted its new web site, Everything4Less.com (or www.E4L.com), the weekend before Thanksgiving in time for the biggest shopping season of the year. Over Thanksgiving weekend a national television advertising campaign featuring "TV moms" Shirley Jones ("The Partridge Family"), Florence Henderson ("The Brady Bunch"), and Marion Ross ("Happy Days") was launched. By January 1, 1999, National Media expected to insert Everything4Less commercials in all of the infomercials that it broadcast each week.

Everything4Less was an electronic commerce web site and catalog-based shopping service. Online shoppers could choose from more than 800,000 products at guaranteed low prices, including hundreds of major brands. National Media's revenues from Everything4Less were based on membership fees rather than on the products that were sold. According to company statements, more than 25,000 people signed up for Everything4Less memberships before December 1, 1998.

Future Outlook

As the company looked to the new millennium, it was focusing its efforts on four areas. One was to improve and expand its core infomercial business. This was the company's main source of revenue. Second, cost-cutting efforts were made a top priority to reduce expenses. Third, it was seeking to reduce the cyclical nature of its infomercial business by strengthening its continuity programs, whereby customers would order products on a continuing basis throughout the year. The fourth and perhaps most promising area was the Internet and electronic commerce. As Lehman told the stockholders in October 1998, "I believe this [electronic commerce] is such a crucial and potentially rewarding area that I have made this my personal number one goal."

Principal Subsidiaries

Quantum North America, Inc.; National Media Marketing Corporation; Quantum International Japan Co., Ltd.; DirectAmerica Corporation; Positive Response Television, Inc.; Quantum Productions AG (Germany); Suzanne Paul Holdings Pty Ltd.; Quantum Far East Ltd.; Quantum Polska Sp.Z.o.o.; Quantum Asia.

Further Reading

Bird, Laura, "Infomercial Settlement," *Wall Street Journal,* December 15, 1993, p. B6.

"Board Rejects Takeover Bid from Home-Shopping Firm," *Wall Street Journal,* January 31, 1994, p. B8.

Brownlee, Lisa, "Infomercial Firms Face off in Court: Flyer vs. Strider," *Wall Street Journal,* March 7, 1997, p. B9B.

——, "Leading Player in Infomercials Talks to Suitors," *Wall Street Journal,* July 16, 1997, p. B1.

——, "National Media Taps New CEO, to Post Operating Losses in Fiscal Quarter, Year," *Wall Street Journal,* April 29, 1997, p. B14.

——, "National Media to Get Infusion from Investors," *Wall Street Journal,* August 29, 1997, p. A7B.

——, "Out of Step: Infomercial Makers Spar over Fitness Flyer," *Wall Street Journal,* March 20, 1997, p. B1.

"Common Shares to Be Issued to Settle a Holder Lawsuit," *Wall Street Journal,* March 21, 1995, p. B7.

"Everything4Less Takes America's Favorite TV Moms on Major Media Tour," *PR Newswire,* December 7, 1998.

"Everything4Less Up and Running," *PR Newswire,* November 25, 1998.

"Fiscal 2nd-Period Net Rose 59% on 73% Revenue Jump," *Wall Street Journal,* October 31, 1996, p. B16.

"Flyer/Strider Suits Settled with Guthy-Renker Corp.," *Wall Street Journal,* April 1, 1997, p. B11.

Henderson, Ted, and Stacy Forbes, *Company Research: National Media Corporation,* Janco Partners, Inc., 1998.

"Holiday Shopping Made Easy with E-Commerce Virtual Superstore: Everything4Less," *PR Newswire,* November 17, 1998.

"National Media and Mitsui to Pursue E-Commerce Opportunities; Powerful Alliance Between Japanese Trading Giant and American E-Comm Company," *PR Newswire,* November 24, 1998.

"National Media Consolidates and Moves Corporate Headquarters to Los Angeles," *PR Newswire,* November 12, 1998.

"National Media Corp. Agrees to Purchase for $150 Million," *Wall Street Journal,* March 8, 1994, p. A5.

"National Media Corporation President Resigns; Turchi Assumes Title," *Wall Street Journal,* May 4, 1994, p. B7.

"National Media Corporation (Who's News)," *Wall Street Journal,* April 22, 1993, p. B5.

"National Media Corp. Spurns Second Offer from ValueVision," *Wall Street Journal,* February 22, 1994, p. B6.

"National Media Corp. Will Take Infomercials to Southern Africa," *Wall Street Journal,* February 22, 1994, p. B6.

"National Media Names McAdams to Position of Chairman, Chief," *Wall Street Journal,* September 14, 1994, p. B6.

"National Media's Everything4Less Launches Successfully During Thanksgiving Holiday," *PR Newswire,* December 1, 1998.

"National Media Shareholders Approve Transaction with Investor Group Led by Stephen C. Lehman," company press release, October 23, 1998.

"National Media Suit Is Filed in U.S. Court Against ValueVision," *Wall Street Journal,* April 25, 1994, p. B2.

"National Media Unit's TV Pacts," *Wall Street Journal,* December 13, 1994, p. C7.

Power, William, "National Media, Famed for TV Sales Pitches Late at Night, Keeps Holders in Dark over Suit," *Wall Street Journal,* May 28, 1993, p. C2.

"Proxy Fight May Follow National Media Takeover Bid," *Wall Street Journal,* February 25, 1994, p. B10.

Sandler, Linda, "Share Price of National Media Drops in Quarter As Media Costs for Infomercial Producer Rise," *Wall Street Journal,* January 6, 1997, p. C2.

"Televised Home Shopping Planned with Japan's Mitsui," *Wall Street Journal,* February 15, 1994, p. B9.

"ValueVision International Inc.," *Wall Street Journal,* February 4, 1994, p. B4.

"ValueVision International Inc.," *Wall Street Journal,* April 22, 1994, p. B4.

"ValueVision Makes Cash-and-Stock Bid for National Media," *Wall Street Journal,* January 14, 1994, p. C6.

"ValueVision Merger with National Media Is Ended by the Firms," *Wall Street Journal,* June 3, 1998, p. C17.

"ValueVision, National Media to Drop Suit, Enter Joint Venture," *Wall Street Journal,* April 17, 1995, p. B4.

—David Bianco

Nextel Communications, Inc.

1505 Farm Credit Drive
McLean, New Jersey 22102
U.S.A.
(703) 394-3000
Fax: (703) 394-3001
Web site: http://www.nextel.com

Public Company
Incorporated: 1987 as Fleet Call, Inc.
Employees: 6,400
Sales: $738.9 million (1997)
Stock Exchanges: NASDAQ
Ticker Symbol: NXTL
SICs: 4812 Radiotelephone Communications; 5999
    Miscellaneous Retail Stores, Not Elsewhere Classified

Founded originally to develop mobile telephone service on existing radio bands, Nextel Communications, Inc. has evolved to provide specialized mobile radio services (for truck drivers, taxi cab drivers, and the like) as well as wireless telephone services. The company is one of the largest all-digital wireless communications providers in the United States, providing competition not only for wireline telephone networks, but also for conventional cellular systems. In the late 1990s, the company rapidly expanded its digital cellular network, eventually providing a coverage area for approximately 85 percent of the U.S. population by the end of the decade. Motorola holds an approximately 24 percent share of Nextel, while wireless communications pioneer Craig McCaw holds another 13 percent.

Early Beginnings As Fleet Call, Inc.

In the beginning, Nextel managed to skirt regulations that restricted the allotment of increasingly sparse radio bands by making better use of others that already existed. The company developed an all-digital system to operate within underutilized radio bands that were previously used only to dispatch taxicabs. Rather than lobbying a regulatory commission for rights to new frequencies, Nextel merely purchased those that were already there. In doing so, the company established a mobile telephone system that worked like cellular, but was not subject to the regulatory morass that precluded new start-up companies from entering the market.

Mobile radio systems had been in use since the 1930s, enabling police, firefighters, and taxi and delivery drivers to stay in touch with dispatch operators. The Federal Communications Commission (FCC) allotted special frequencies for these systems, but their limited bandwidth made them practical only for mobile fleets and not for the average motorist. During the 1970s, AT&T developed a system using a network of local transceivers that could switch a mobile telephone from one antenna, or "cell," to another as it moved from one area to the next. Technological developments greatly expanded the capacity of this service, making widespread commercial use possible. Accordingly, the FCC designated new frequencies for these "cellular" phone systems.

With the break-up of AT&T as a nationwide local service provider in 1984, local telephone companies inherited the rights to develop cellular telephone networks. To ensure speedy development, the FCC limited each market area to only two cellular companies. In such places as San Francisco, Denver, Chicago, and New York, customers were allowed a choice, but only between two cellular companies.

The companies best suited to develop cellular systems often were those with the most resources, such as established telephone companies BellSouth, Southwestern Bell, Ameritech, and GTE. Many smaller companies in the industry, unable to compete or raise financing, were steamrollered into mergers with these companies. What resulted was a regime in which pairs of competitors locked up virtually every market in the country. The entry of third tier competitors was precluded by FCC rules aimed at nurturing the market and conserving capacity on the airwaves.

Thousands of other radio wavelengths had been reserved for some future use. Others had been set aside decades before for mobile radio, using an old and highly inefficient analog signaling system—an accident of history and technology that

Company Perspectives:

The mission we set for our company was very simple: Nextel is to be a worldwide leader in wireless communications. This cannot be achieved without first taking care of business here at home. And we are. Nextel, today, is the quality service provider and the innovative product and pricing differentiation leader in the digital wireless communications industry. No competitor can provide all the features and functionality of Nextel's service—digital cellular, voice mail, text/numeric paging, and Nextel Direct Connect two-way digital radio service—all in a single handset manufactured by Motorola. Our business customers tell us that our communications solution offers the greatest productivity enhancement in the industry.

provided the seed for a new form of mobile telephony that could operate in competition with cellular systems. These specialized mobile radio networks could be converted to use digital signals, which require only a fraction of the bandwidth of conventional capacity-hogging analog signals. By going digital, previously limited radio bands could be opened up to handle thousands of calls.

Around this time, the FCC recognized that its policies had successfully allowed the cellular industry to mature to a point where greater competition could be allowed. Rather than further crowd existing cellular frequencies by allowing more competitors into each market, the commission chose instead to back the development of specialized mobile radio (SMR).

Hundreds of radio frequencies were put into play as entrepreneurs began a mad scramble for SMR frequencies. One of the key players in this trade was Morgan O'Brien, a telecommunications lawyer who represented major SMR operators in proceedings with the FCC. In 1987, O'Brien decided to get into the industry himself. He established a partnership with Brian D. McAuley, an accountant and former executive with Millicom and Norton Simon. In April of that year, O'Brien and McAuley founded a company called Fleet Call, Inc. to acquire SMR properties.

Within the next 12 months, Fleet Call had financed the acquisition of ten mobile radio companies and began laying plans for the construction of communications networks in large markets. At this early stage, Fleet Call concentrated only on acquiring SMR licenses. The task of turning SMR frequencies into a new type of cellular system was still years away.

The SMR business had long been dominated by Motorola, which not only manufactured the radio systems, but also operated dozens of networks. O'Brien and McAuley feared that Motorola would oppose their plan to build a new communication network within the SMR frequencies and, with its substantial resources, persuade the FCC to stop them. Thus, O'Brien and McAuley arranged a meeting with Motorola chairman George Fisher in order to reveal their plans. They expected Fisher to tell them that he would not allow Fleet Call to so

radically upset Motorola's SMR business, one of its oldest enterprises. But to their astonishment, Fisher not only supported the idea, he asked if Motorola could become a partner in the venture. The two companies worked out an equity stake in Fleet Call for Motorola, and developed plans for the electronics giant to build parts of the new system.

A month after the meeting with Fisher, Fleet Call had acquired 74 mobile radio businesses in such metropolitan areas as Los Angeles, San Francisco, New York, Chicago, Dallas, and Houston. Throughout the remainder of the decade, it continued to operate them as radio dispatch systems using old analog transmission technology, and provided service to more than 120,000 subscribers.

A New Focus in the Early 1990s

In April 1991, Fleet Call formally requested permission from the FCC to design and build digital communications systems that would operate on the SMR bands. The systems would continue to accommodate existing fleet dispatchers but, by going digital, would allow thousands more calls to be placed. The FCC unanimously voted to allow Fleet Call to proceed with its plans in February 1991. In its opinion, the Fleet Call system would provide a healthy form of competition for entrenched and technologically limited cellular companies, while providing customers with new options only available with digital technology.

Fleet Call decided to use a digital technology called time division multiple access (TDMA). Simply described, this system made use of periods in which no data was being transmitted (such as during pauses in conversation) by temporarily lending communication capacity to other calls. Statistically, all calls would have such pauses more or less evenly distributed. TDMA ensured that every available "channel" was not squandered by transmitting silence.

With the radio bands in its possession, and having decided on a technology for the system, Fleet Call brought in other partners to build the network with Motorola. One of them was Northern Telecom, a Canadian manufacturer of telecommunications network equipment. In December 1991 the Japanese consumer electronics giant Matsushita joined the project. Matsushita was the manufacturer of the Panasonic and Technics brands, as well as the company that had bought the Quasar line from Motorola some years earlier. Matsushita agreed to supply subscriber units (basically handsets) for Fleet Call's digital mobile networks.

In January 1992, O'Brien and McAuley took Fleet Call public. The initial offering of 7.5 million shares raised $112.5 million, which was used to fund construction of the company's first network cell site in Los Angeles. Fleet Call also received $345 million in equipment financing from Motorola, Northern Telecom, and Matsushita. In addition, the company secured a $230 million investment commitment from Comcast, a large cable television provider with significant cellular operations, in exchange for a 30 percent interest in the company.

Investor interest in Fleet Call increased dramatically when details of the company's plans—and information about its partners—got out. Share prices nearly doubled as investors clamored to get in on the business.

The company completed work on its Los Angeles cell site in May 1992, using a system that operated in the 800-megahertz band. This frequency could accommodate mobile phone service, two-way radio dispatching, alphanumeric paging and messaging, and dozens of other future applications—all clearly beyond the capability of conventional cellular systems. In addition, the combined functionality of the Fleet Call system would allow customers to receive a single bill for paging, cellular, and mobile data services, rather than the three they would receive under the previously existing systems.

The only downside to Fleet Call's system was that it was incompatible with other cellular networks, precluding "handoffs" to and from other cellular operators outside Fleet Call's service territory. Recognizing that Californians were married to their cars and spent hours on freeways, Fleet Call broadened the Los Angeles site to cover Santa Barbara, Palm Springs, and San Diego County. Plans were expanded to provide seamless service throughout California by mid-1994. The company also turned its system incompatibility into a marketing advantage by touting its superior privacy and anti-billing fraud characteristics.

Much of Fleet Call's expansion was made possible by its December 1992 merger with Dispatch Communications, another mobile radio company with the same plans as Fleet Call. The combined operation gave Fleet Call coverage in nine of the country's ten largest markets, representing a potential user population of 95.5 million people.

Further Expansion in the Mid-1990s

In January 1993, the company scored something of a coup when it hired John Caner, director of wireless data development at PacTel Cellular. In Fleet Call, Caner saw an opportunity to build an entirely new communications system without the burden of aging legacy systems and Bell-related regulatory problems.

Two months later, in March 1993, the company changed its name to Nextel Communications. The Fleet Call name was deemed inappropriate because it referred to the old radio dispatch technologies. By contrast, "Nextel" cleverly suggested to consumers that, with wave after wave of new technologies, this was the next new thing in communications.

The company established numerous service trials in California during 1993, offering service to 500 customers. This enabled the company to conduct live testing of the system, establish traffic engineering patterns, and perfect billing mechanisms. A great deal had been written about Nextel up to this point, but the company did not actually begin to offer service until August 1993, when the system was formally "turned on." Nextel remained on the hunt for radio bands in new territories, but many of these had already been snapped up by other companies. However, few of these companies had developed as far as Nextel, which made them prime future merger targets for the company.

Within the next year, Nextel concluded merger agreements with Questar Telecom and a subsidiary of Advanced Mobil-Comm. These agreements brought the company operating rights in the strategically important San Diego region, as well as in Utah, Nevada, and other mountain states. Through another merger agreement, Nextel exchanged some of its Rocky Moun-

tain and Midwestern SMR properties for an equity stake in CenCall Communications. The agreement gave CenCall access to Nextel's digital communications technology, and Nextel gained a 37 percent stake in CenCall. CenCall later changed its name to OneComm. A third merger agreement led Nextel to absorb the operations of PowerFone Holdings, a company with SMR properties in Cleveland, Cincinnati, Pittsburgh, and other Midwestern markets. These developments greatly increased Nextel's service area and potential customer base.

Perhaps the most important acquisition made by Nextel, however, came in August 1994, when the company acquired the SMR licenses of Motorola in exchange for an additional interest in the company. These properties encompassed 21 states, covering 180 million "pops," or potential customers. This transaction positioned Nextel to seriously challenge cellular communications duopolies across the country. This flurry of mergers and partnerships significantly diluted Nextel's investor base, but succeeded in establishing a platform on which the company could offer nearly seamless digital mobile radio services nationwide.

The company's largest potential competitor came not from within the digital mobile radio market but, understandably, from the conventional cellular market. Numerous cellular companies formed joint marketing agreements in an effort to build nationwide brand identities. The competitive landscape came into clearer focus when AT&T announced its intention to acquire McCaw, the nation's largest cellular communications company. In addition to providing AT&T a position in the rapidly growing mobile communications market, McCaw would give AT&T direct access to millions of local telephone customers. As a long distance company only, AT&T was now dependent on local telephone companies for access to these customers. Additionally, by merging with AT&T, McCaw would have access to AT&T's substantial financial and technological resources.

By contrast, although Nextel had substantial backing from leading equipment manufacturers, it had no link-up with a long distance provider. In order to ensure nationwide coverage to rival the AT&T/McCaw combination, Nextel began negotiations with MCI, the nation's second largest long distance carrier and AT&T's fiercest rival. A formal alliance between Nextel and MCI was announced on February 28, 1994. MCI purchased a 17 percent stake in Nextel for the right to market wireless phone, data, and dispatching services under the MCI brand name, using the Nextel network.

Although Nextel lost $10 million on only $34 million in revenue during 1993, its market value was quoted at a staggering $9.5 billion. This indication of investor confidence was based on the formidability of Nextel's emerging alliances, as well as on the future potential of its services.

Perhaps the greatest asset to Nextel's network was its involvement with Motorola, which provided the advanced digital cellular technology under which the system operated. By using the Motorola Integrated Radio System, or MIRS, Nextel entered the communications market with a state-of-the-art platform that provided far greater capabilities than any other existing system. In fact, cellular companies remained divided over which digital system to use in their own upgrade from analog to digital technology, delaying implementation of systems that could compete effectively with MIRS.

The Nextel consortium contained every element necessary to ensure successful entry into the wireless market. Nextel possessed the frequency licenses and network equipment; Motorola, the engineering and manufacturing expertise; Comcast, the experience with cellular networks; and MCI, the long distance capability, billing systems and, most importantly, a nationally recognized and highly valued brand name.

The alliance was particularly important to MCI, which early in 1994 unveiled a new business strategy called networkMCI. As part of this strategy, the long distance carrier announced its intention to establish partnerships with other communications and information industry companies to provide seamless voice and data communication to customers anywhere. With about 95 percent of the nation's population covered by the Nextel system, MCI possessed the ability to market communication services directly to nearly 250 million people. By contrast, companies such as Sprint and AT&T were relatively restricted to the limited coverage of their cellular systems or obliged to deal with local telephone companies and competing cellular operators for access to customers.

Late 1994 and early 1995 saw Nextel ink two more agreements with other companies to expand its own scope. In October 1994, the company made an agreement with Clearnet Communications, Inc. of Ontario, Canada, which gave Nextel expanded coverage in 24 of the top 33 markets in Canada. In February 1995, Nextel signed a merger agreement with Dial Page, Inc., which was the leading SMR provider in the southeastern United States.

Soon thereafter, three ironic and somewhat strange things occurred. In April 1995, wireless communications pioneer Craig McCaw (of the AT&T/McCaw combination), along with his family, decided to invest over $1 billion in Nextel. Then in January 1996, Nextel brought aboard Timothy Donahue—the former Northeast regional president of AT&T Wireless Services—as the new president of Nextel. Three months later, Daniel F. Akerson—the former president of MCI—arrived at Nextel to assume the roles of chairman and CEO.

The Late 1990s: New Services and Acquisitions

In late 1996, Nextel introduced Motorola's new iDEN technology, which combined enhanced digital cellular service, alphanumeric paging service, and two-way radio service into one telephone. Nextel had ordered approximately $100 million worth of the service from Motorola earlier in the year, and thus began a national rollout of the new service in September 1996, after a very successful Summer Olympics 1996 pilot program.

In January 1997, Nextel made news by introducing the Nextel National Network. The network was linked throughout the country, and allowed Nextel to offer its customers nationwide service without charging roaming fees. This offering was a first in the wireless communications industry, and gave Nextel a considerable edge when trying to land business people with heavy travel schedules. Soon thereafter, the company also announced a new pricing policy, in which its customers' calls would be rounded to the nearest second—not the nearest minute—for billing purposes. The announcements made clear Nextel's commitment to customer satisfaction, and made its new tagline—"Get Smart, Get Nextel"—even more effective.

Throughout the rest of 1997, as Nextel continued to launch its all-in-one iDEN service throughout the country, it also increased its presence in Canada. In May 1997, the company announced a roaming agreement with Clearnet in Canada, which allowed Nextel's U.S. customers roaming access in much of Canada. By September, Nextel had even announced that customers could roam in Canada with their home rates, and that long distance calls made while roaming in Canada would be billed at a flat rate of just 30 cents per minute.

In September 1997, McCaw—which had become a wholly owned subsidiary of Nextel earlier in the decade—changed its name to Nextel International, Inc. The newly named entity retained its standing as a leading international wireless communications service company, while drawing from the newfound advantages of the Nextel brand name. The company went about business as usual, with operations and investments in countries such as Argentina, Brazil, Canada, Indonesia, Japan, Mexico, Peru, the Philippines, and Shanghai.

The following month, in October 1997, Nextel recorded its millionth subscriber—interestingly, almost exactly ten years after Fleet Call had been formed. Nextel entered 1998 poised for continued success. In January, the company introduced its newest offering—the Nextel i600 phone. Smaller and lighter than normal, the phone actually possessed a longer battery life as well as expanded services and options. For example, the new phone included a vibration alert so customers could be notified of calls without an audible ring; the option of a second line; caller-ID; three-way calling; and different ringer styles. Nextel also announced that nationwide caller-ID would soon be available in 75 percent of its markets.

By March 1998, the Nextel National Network covered almost 80 percent of the top U.S. markets. While the service continued to expand throughout the United States, the company also made additional moves to increase its presence internationally. In May 1998, service was launched in Sao Paulo, Brazil, under the name Nextel Brazil, and a month later service was added in Buenos Aires, Argentina, under the name Nextel Argentina S.R.L. In July, Nextel began offering iDEN service in Tokyo, Japan, through J-COM, a company in which Nextel owned a 21 percent stake. Also that month, service was established in Manila, the Philippines, and in Rio de Janeiro, Brazil.

Meanwhile, domestic subscriptions were skyrocketing. By June 1998 (less than one year after the company signed its millionth customer) Nextel had signed up its two millionth subscriber. The company also entered the Hawaiian market, spending more than $30 million to offer service comprehensive enough to handle conference calls of up to 100 people. Around that same time, a national distribution agreement between Nextel and Let's Talk Cellular & Wireless was created; Nextel joined a joint venture with Nextlink Communications, Inc. and Eagle River Investments, LLC to build Level 3 Communications' national fiber optic network; and Nextel also announced a retail partnership with Office Depot.

As Nextel approached the 21st century, it was well-positioned within the still-blossoming wireless communications industry. Although there were numerous companies vying for market share within the industry, and although Nextel was competing against such giants as AT&T, GTE, and AirTouch, the company was nonetheless doing quite well. It was continuing to introduce new products and technologies (evidenced by the arrival of the i1000 in September 1998), and was achieving positive cash flow near the end of the decade. Furthermore, as wireless communications became more and more affordable for the average person, companies such as Nextel were not only targeting their services toward people for business purposes, but instead seemed to have access to a vast market of customers who could use wireless communications to enhance their everyday lives.

Principal Subsidiaries

Nextel International, Inc.

Further Reading

Drury, Tracey, "Nextel Joins Competition for Cellular Market Share," *Business First* (Buffalo), August 17, 1998.

"Fleet Call Changes Name," *Wall Street Journal,* March 24, 1993, p. A5.

"Fleet Joins Communications Consortium," *Journal of Commerce and Commercial,* March 2, 1992, p. 3B.

Kamhis, Jacob, "Conference Calls Part of Nextel package," *Pacific Business News,* August 3, 1998.

"A Leap into the Digital Future," *Management Review,* October 23, 1993, p. 24.

"Motorola to Sell 42% of Licenses in Mobile Radio," *Wall Street Journal,* October 25, 1993, p. A2.

"Nextel Communications, Inc.," *Los Angeles Times,* November 19, 1993, p. D2.

"Nextel Goes Digital, Mounts Threat to Cellular Providers," *Telephony,* September 6, 1993, p. 8.

"Nextel Keeps Making the Right Connections," *Business Week,* March 14, 1994, p. 31.

"Nextel, Motorola Deal Throws Open Wireless Market," *Business Marketing,* December 1993, p. 4.

"Nextel's Deal with Motorola Advances Wireless Vision," *Wall Street Journal,* November 19, 1993, p. B4.

"The Taxicab As Phone Company," *Forbes,* January 6, 1992, p. 41.

"A Wireless Communications Wonder," *Forbes,* April 12, 1993, p. 55.

—John Simley
—updated by Laura E. Whiteley

Norton McNaughton, Inc.

463 Seventh Avenue
New York, New York 10018
U.S.A.
(212) 947-2960
Fax: (212) 643-9316

Public Company
Incorporated: 1993
Employees: 340 (1997)
Sales: $218.78 million (1997)
Stock Exchanges: NASDAQ
Ticker Symbol: NRTY
SICs: 5137 Women's/Children's Clothing, Wholesale;
   5099 Durable Goods, Not Elsewhere Classified; 2339
   Women's/Misses' Outerwear, Not Elsewhere
   Classified

Norton McNaughton, Inc. (Norton) designs and contracts for the manufacture of a broad line of brand-name, moderately priced women's career and casual clothing. The company also markets its products—which include jackets, skirts, blouses, and sweaters—as separates coordinated for styles, colors, and fabrics. All Norton products are fabricated from natural and synthetic fibers and blends; many are manufactured in petite and large sizes, in addition to the regular junior and miss sizes. The company sells its products nationwide in an estimated 7,000 individual stores operated by more than 350 department stores, national chains, mass merchants, specialty retailers, and discount stores. Norton's product labels include Norton McNaughton and Norton Studio, marketed by subsidiary Norton McNaughton of Squire, Inc.; Erika labels, marketed through subsidiary Miss Erika, Inc.; and Energie, Currants, and Jamie labels, marketed through subsidiary Jeri-Jo Knitwear, Inc. Approximately 57 percent of Norton's net sales come from its principal customers: The May Department Stores Company (Hechts, Foley's, Robinsons-May, Kaufmann's, Filene's, Famous Barr, and Meier & Frank); Federated Department Stores, Inc. (Rich's, Burdines, Bon Marché, Stern's, and Macy's); and J.C. Penney Company, Inc. By using domestic and foreign

designers and contractors, Norton avoids significant capital expenditures and the fixed cost of managing a large production work force. The company's products generally retail for $20 to $80, averaging about $30 to $50.

The Early Years: 1981–93

Sanford Greenberg, who later served as Norton's president and chairman, worked for Squire Fashions Inc., a New York apparel firm, from 1960 to 1981. Then he joined forces with Jay Greenberg and Norton Sperling to buy out Squire; the company was renamed Norton McNaughton of Squire, Inc. The Norton McNaughton product line—Norton McNaughton, Norton McNaughton Petite, Maggie McNaughton, and Maggie McNaughton Petite—was introduced in 1981; it was marketed in miss, petite, and large sizes to department stores and national chains.

In July 1991 officers of the company formed NM Acquisition Corp. to acquire Norton McNaughton of Squire, Inc. in a leveraged buyout that led to the formation of Norton McNaughton, Inc., a holding company incorporated in January 1993. The company's net sales increased from $82.29 million in fiscal 1991 to $133.33 million in fiscal 1993, for a compound annual growth of 27.3 percent. During this period net income increased from $1.6 million to $3.33 million, for a compound annual growth rate of 44 percent.

The company's profitability in fiscal 1992 and 1993 was affected by the start-up and subsequent discontinuation of a dress division. Norton entered the dress market in early 1992 but soon realized that there were insufficient synergies in operating the dress and separates businesses. Norton discontinued the dress division's operations during the second quarter of fiscal 1993 and introduced two new products, the Pant-her and Modiano product lines. The Pant-her line—designed for women ranging in age from 40 to 70—featured traditional related separates in miss, petite, and large sizes. Norton McNaughton of Squire, Inc., now a Norton subsidiary, contracted to sell Pant-her products exclusively to May Company stores; Norton and May Company agreed to terminate their agreement effective March 1, 1998 but, at that time, May Company continued to buy Norton's other product lines.

Company Perspectives:

Norton's strategy is to increase sales to its existing customers, expand its distribution channels to include additional retailers and mass merchants, selectively expand existing product lines, and introduce new product lines in the women's segment. The company attempts to capitalize on what it believes to be a trend among its major retail accounts and to increase consumer demand for moderately priced women's clothing.

In fiscal 1993 Norton's reproductions of popular designer fashions were produced by domestic and foreign contractors, thereby allowing the company to avoid significant capital expenditures and the fixed cost of managing a large production work force. A substantial majority of Norton's products were made in the United States. Domestic contracts for manufacturing minimized excess inventory by giving the company maximum flexibility: Norton could defer production until reception of initial orders and then make a closer adjustment to buying trends. In fiscal 1993 the company engaged the services of approximately 30 sewing and knitting contractors in the United States and two overseas master contractors in the Dominican Republic and the Far East; Norton did not have any long-term supply agreements with any of its sewing or knitting contractors. The company, however, did have long-term agreements for the exclusive services of its domestic cutting contractor (Roni-Linda Productions, Inc.) and its domestic distribution contractor (Railroad Enterprises, Inc.) for initial terms ending June 30, 2000 (distribution) and June 30, 2001 (cutting), respectively.

The Middle Years: 1994–96

Norton went public in 1994 and was traded on Nasdaq under the symbol NRTY. In January 1994 the company broadened its Modiano product to a full line of related separates targeted to national and regional retail chains. The Modiano line had silhouettes similar to those of the Norton McNaughton line but sold at slightly lower prices in retail chains, such as Sears, Roebuck and Co. The company also established its own retail outlets, called Norty's, in which it sold end-of-stock, out-of-season, and other miscellaneous merchandise. Norton used these retail outlets to minimize sales to off-price retailers and as a means of liquidating excess inventory.

During 1995 and 1996 Norton presented four other product lines. The Lauren Alexandra line (June 1995), sold exclusively to Federated Department Stores, offered moderately priced career sportswear collections in miss and large sizes for women of ages 25–60. The denim-driven casual Danielle Paige line and D.P.S. product lines (August 1996) consisted of moderately priced weekend wear: jumpers, sport dresses, pants, shirts, skirts, shorts, jackets, and leggings. These lines were sold to department stores, chains, and mass merchants. The Norton Studio product line (January 1996), also sold in department stores, consisted of women's career and casual knitwear collections and—as of Spring 1997—included a large-sized product division.

As always, Norton's design philosophy was to reproduce popular designer fashions at moderate prices. The company's design team was responsible for the creation, development, and coordination of product lines that interpreted and mirrored existing fashion trends in women's better apparel. The team also sought to enhance consumer appeal by combining functional fabrics in creative looks and color schemes to encourage the coordination of outfits—and the purchase of more than one garment. Rather than buying all of its printed fabrics, Norton's design staff started with "art work" purchased from more than 25 art studios worldwide. Then, working with the art departments at mills and fabric suppliers, the company redesigned the art work by altering colors, backgrounds, graphics, and shapes to have the printed fabrics appeal to the fashion tastes of its target retail consumers.

During fiscal 1996 and fiscal 1995, approximately 57 percent and 71 percent, respectively, of Norton's products were manufactured in the United States, mostly in the New York City metropolitan area. In fiscal 1996 the company engaged the services of nearly 60 sewing and knitting contractors in the United States and nine overseas master contractors in the Dominican Republic, Central America, the Far East, the Middle East and Europe.

In fiscal 1995 net sales of $227.53 million reflected an increase of 34.9 percent from the net sales of $168.62 million in fiscal 1994. Norton's growth strategy, however, brought trouble. Foreign sourcing of products—as compared with domestic production—required a significant lead time ranging from four to eight months in the case of Dominican Republic and Central American sourced manufacturing and six to ten months in the case of Far Eastern, Middle Eastern, and European sourced manufacturing. Belated design changes forced postponements; shipments from abroad arrived late; competition increased for moderately priced women's apparel; and products entering the market too late in the fashion cycle were left on the shelves.

During fiscal 1996 approximately 43 percent of Norton's products were manufactured outside the United States. According to Yolanda Gault's story in the October 21, 1996 issue of *Crain's New York Business,* at this time there was an "industry-wide malaise in moderate wear. Norton expanded too quickly in a weak market, introducing six divisions in under three years. ... Norton—known for its nimble entrepreneurial culture—lost its fashion sense. Consumers stayed away, leading to scads of markdowns, stinging losses and Wall Street's wrath." Compared with the net sales of fiscal 1995, net sales for fiscal 1996 decreased by $6.7 million, or 2.9 percent, to $220.82 million. Over and above the aforementioned problems, this drop also was attributable to a planned decrease in sales volume as Norton began to minimize the production of merchandise that it did not anticipate could be sold at a profit and, in response to competitive pressures from other moderately priced apparel wholesalers, granted customers a higher level of sales allowances.

Adjustment to a Changing Market: 1997

In an effort to improve the profitability and position the company for future growth, in fiscal 1997 Norton implemented several strategic initiatives. These strategies included narrowing management's focus to the company's key divisions—Norton McNaughton and Norton Studio, making changes in pricing and product assortment, improving product sourcing, and significantly reducing overhead. Furthermore, to diversify its distribution channels, broaden its product offerings, increase its global product sourcing capability, and gain access to additional merchandising and managerial talent, the company adopted a special strategy for relevant acquisitions.

By early and timely attention to production planning, Norton aimed to offset the long lead time necessary for foreign sourced fabrics and manufacturing. For instance, the woven components of the Norton McNaughton and D.P.S. product lines were sourced primarily through import programs in China; a lead time of two to four months was needed to develop the required fabric. The time elapsed from the factory's fabric purchase commitment to the finished goods was generally an additional four to six months, thereby creating a total cycle time of six to ten months in the case of Far Eastern, Middle Eastern, African, and European sourced manufacturing. Norton also sourced a large portion of its woven products in countries of the Caribbean basin or in Mexico, making the most of favorable "807" customs regulations. In general, these regulations exempted from U.S. duties the products assembled abroad from U.S. components.

On May 6, 1997, Norton appointed Peter Boneparth, an investment banker whose previous firm had taken Norton public in 1994, as president and chief operating officer and director to succeed Norton Sterling, one of the company's co-founders. In a telephone interview reported by Anne D'Innocenzio in the May 7, 1997 issue of *Women's Wear Daily,* Boneparth noted that he would use his expertise in acquisitions "to play a hand in expanding Norton McNaughton's sales." Future acquisitions, he predicted, would catapult sales, which had been hovering at around $220 million, to $500 million within three to five years. "We have $50 million in shareholders' equity. The whole industry is consolidating. We want to be the consolidator," he said.

Boneparth began his tenure by following through on many of the moves the company had already begun making to get back on track. During the second quarter of fiscal 1997, Norton closed its 12 retail outlets because this division did not meet the company's profitability targets. A new merchandising strategy began to reduce excess inventory; excess merchandise could more cost-effectively be disposed of through discounters and other retailers. During the third quarter, Norton sold merchandise under its existing product lines to Sears and discontinued the Modiano product line, which had been produced exclusively for that company. A new pricing strategy, to be effective in August, was planned for the company's private-label line, which was "priced 15 percent above the traditional labels and 25 percent below such upper-moderates as Halston and Emma James," Anne D'Innocenzio wrote in the May 14, 1997 issue of *Women's Wear Daily.* For instance, jackets were to retail from $68 to $72, compared with $80 to $90 in 1996.

On September 30, 1997, Norton acquired New York-based Miss Erika, Inc., a privately held firm established in 1968. Miss Erika manufactured moderately priced knit and woven separates, including knit tops and bottoms, sweaters, dresses and jackets, and more casual apparel, such as shorts, skirts, tank tops, and jumpers. The target customer was a middle-income, budgeted-minded but fashionable woman ranging in age from 15 to 50

years old. Miss Erika's merchandise was sold primarily under the Erika label and was distributed through regional chains, department stores, and specialty chains. Miss Erika contracted for the production of its garments through a network of purchasing agents located overseas. In addition to products sold under its brand names, Miss Erika worked with retail chains to develop product lines sold under the retailers' private labels.

Upon completion of the Erika acquisition, Norton President Boneparth commented, "This transaction highlights our strategy of acquiring companies that are accretive to earnings, have strong management teams in place, and broaden our existing channels of distribution," D'Innocenzio reported in "Norton McNaughton's New Mode" in the May 14, 1997 issue of *Women's Wear Daily.* This acquisition reduced sales seasonality, since Miss Erika's revenues were weighted toward the first half of the year and Norton's sales were typically higher in the second half of the year. Norton also implemented other new distribution channels (for example, QVC and SAM's Warehouse Club) and began to sell to catalogue firms, such as Chadwick's.

In addition, in the fourth quarter, Norton discontinued the Lauren Alexandra private-label line produced for Federated Department Stores and the Pant-her private-label product line sold to The May Department Stores Company. To further streamline operations, Norton reduced its work force by close to 33 percent. Other cost-savings measures that were implemented included merchandising changes that enabled the company to produce fewer samples and reductions in executive compensation and ancillary expenses.

By October 30, the end of fiscal 1997, Norton's implementation of new strategies, discontinuation of unprofitable products and divisions, and acquisition of well-established, profitable Miss Erika boded well for the future but did not immediately show a profit. Net sales for the year decreased by one percent to $218.78 million, compared with net sales of $220.82 million in fiscal 1996. These decreases were offset in part by savings resulting from a significant downsizing of the company's work force through further centralization, by an increase in net sales of $10.2 million in the Norton Studio product line, an increase in net sales of $2.8 million in the D.P.S. product line and, following the September acquisition of Miss Erika, net sales of $10.4 million for Erika products.

Toward the 21st Century: 1998 and Beyond

A more disciplined mode of operation in the fiercely competitive women's apparel business was reenergizing Norton's niche in its industry. President and Chief Operating Officer Peter Boneparth commented, ". . . results for the first quarter of fiscal 1998 were in line with management's expectations. The company posted a 28.6 percent increase in net sales and a 26.7 percent increase in operating income over the same period" in 1997. Two significant acquisitions were completed during the third quarter of fiscal 1998: Jeri-Jo Knitwear, Inc. and Jamie Scott, Inc. Founded in 1975, New York-based Jeri-Jo/Jamie Scott designed, imported and marketed juniors' and misses' apparel. The companies retained their current management and operated together as Jeri-Jo Knitwear, Inc., a Norton subsidiary.

For the first nine months of fiscal 1998, Norton's net sales increased 59.5 percent to $227.59 million, compared with $142.7 million for the same period of the previous year. It is noteworthy that sales for the first nine months of fiscal 1998 were considerably higher than the $218.78 million net sales for all of fiscal 1997. When Peter Boneparth became Norton's president in 1997 he commented that within the next three to five years the company could reach annual sales of $500 million. As the 21st century drew near, it seemed that his expectations were within the realm of possibility.

Principal Subsidiaries

Jeri-Jo Knitwear, Inc.; Miss Erika, Inc.; Norton McNaughton of Squire, Inc.

Further Reading

D'Innocenzio, Anne, ''Boneparth Appointed McNaughton President,'' *Women's Wear Daily,* May 7, 1997, pp. 1, 18.

——, ''Norton McNaughton's New Mode,'' *Women's Wear Daily,* May 14, 1997.

Gault, Ylonda, ''A Familiar Thread at Finity: McNaughton Vet Shelves Retirement To Foster Neglected Sportswear Firm,'' *Crain's New York Business,* April 27, 1998, Profiles Sec.

——, ''Fashioning a Comeback: New Executive Peter Boneparth,'' *Crain's New York Business,* June 2, 1997, Profiles Sec.

——, ''No Casual Fling at Norton: New Executive San Sommers,'' *Crain's New York Business,* October 21, 1996, Profiles Sec.

—Gloria A. Lemieux

☾ NU SKIN®

Nu Skin Enterprises, Inc.

75 West Center Street
Provo, Utah 84601
U.S.A.
(801) 345-6100
Fax: (801) 345-3099
Web site: http://www.nuskin.net

Public Company
Incorporated: 1984 as Nu Skin International Inc.
Employees: 2,000
Sales: $890.5 million (1997)
Stock Exchanges: New York
Ticker Symbol: NUS
SICs: 2833 Medicinals & Botanicals

Nu Skin Enterprises, Inc. is one of the world's largest network marketing or multilevel marketing (MLM) firms. In 27 nations, individuals buy Nu Skin products for their own use, sell them at retail prices, and recruit others to also become distributors. The company offers over 150 skin, hair, cosmetic, oral care, general nutritional, sports nutritional, weight management, and botanical products. Partly because of the firm's rapid growth since its origins in 1984, several government agencies in the United States and overseas investigated Nu Skin, which has survived those challenges and continues to expand by promoting its message of better health and financial opportunities.

Origins and Early Expansion

The year was 1984, Ronald Reagan was in the White House, and Blake Roney graduated from Brigham Young University (BYU) with a business finance degree and great hopes for the future. He and his sister Nedra Roney and their friend Sandie Tillotson decided to start their own business. Blake Roney invested $5,000 of his own money in a business idea—to make personal care products that contained "All of the Good, None of the Bad," the core principle when Nu Skin International (NSI) was founded in June 1984. On October 15, 1984, the company was incorporated.

Since the new firm had limited funds for advertising, it decided to rely on the growing method of network or multilevel marketing (MLM), where independent self-employed Nu Skin distributors would sell products one-on-one and recruit others to do the same.

Initially the company met in the apartment of Nedra Roney. After several rejections, it finally found an Arizona company to make its first skin and hair products, which were sent to Nedra's place. Then the founders spooned their products from ten-gallon containers into jars or whatever receptacles their customers brought. By word of mouth the new business spread to family and friends and was off and running out of its home in Provo, Utah.

By 1989 sales were exploding at double-digit rates every month. That year Nu Skin hired Brent Ririe as director of management information systems, the firm's first technical employee. He helped the company choose new computer systems so that commission checks could be mailed on time and other company functions could operate efficiently. However, other serious problems waited around the corner.

Legal Challenges

In March 1991 the Michigan attorney general told Nu Skin to prove it was not an illegal pyramid scheme or face a lawsuit. At least four other states (Ohio, Pennsylvania, Illinois, and Florida) also investigated the rapidly growing firm that by 1991 claimed over 100,000 distributors in the United States, Hong Kong, Canada, and Taiwan.

Nu Skin in late December 1991 issued a press release indicating that it had negotiated an agreement with Michigan in which it would strengthen its buy-back policy by offering its distributors a 90 percent refund on any unused products and sales aids, without any limit since the time of purchase. The Direct Selling Association, which Nu Skin joined, recommended a 90 percent buy-back policy to prevent building up too much inventory. Georgia, Maryland, Louisiana, Wyoming, and Massachusetts required that 90 percent refund policy.

Without admitting any illegal activity in its Michigan settlement, Nu Skin also agreed to reemphasize its retail sales and pay Michigan $25,000 for its investigative expenses. Nu Skin spokesman Jason Chaffetz said in the December 28, 1991 *Provo Daily Herald* that his company was encouraged by the settlement after what he said was "the longest, hardest look at us."

Meanwhile, the Food and Drug Administration (FDA) investigated Nu Skin to make sure its products were safe and clearly labeled without making any illegal healing claims. It should be noted that no federal laws had been passed covering multilevel marketing. Rules and regulations of the FDA and Federal Trade Commission (FTC) applied, but most government oversight came from state laws. The FTC's senior attorney said in the November 1991 issue of *Kiplinger's* that most states considered MLM as an illegal pyramid "when the money is coming in from the recruitment of people, not the sale of products."

Such governmental checks, national media exposure, and its expanding operations brought Nu Skin more attention in 1991. In May 1991, for example, it opened its new $8 million warehouse/distribution center in Provo's East Bay. Without going into debt, Nu Skin built a 200,000-square-foot center to consolidate its nine previous Utah County warehouses. The company also built a recreation facility, basketball and volleyball courts, and picnic areas for its Provo employees.

In 1992 Nu Skin completed its new corporate headquarters. After using four other Provo offices, the firm finally had its permanent home in the ten-story Nu Skin Tower, Provo's tallest downtown building. It included fiber optics and computers to administer a growing international network of distributors and a visitors' center and theater.

In the early 1990s Nu Skin faced allegations of sex discrimination from 28 former and current female employees. In one lawsuit filed December 29, 1992, in U.S. District Court in Salt Lake City, six former employees charged that Nu Skin denied them advancement opportunities and equal benefits and paid men more for comparable work. Judge David Winder on August 6, 1993 denied the women's effort to make this a class action and dismissed the case with prejudice, so that it could not be refiled. This lawsuit was settled out of court under undisclosed terms, but both sides said they were pleased with the results. Since about half of Nu Skin's workforce were women, this was a very significant case.

The FTC in January 1994 confirmed that it had reached a settlement with Nu Skin, which agreed to pay $1.2 million without admitting any wrongdoing. The FTC had alleged that the Provo firm had made false statements about three of its products and also had exaggerated earnings claims without

telling prospective distributors that very few actually made large incomes.

Meanwhile, Nu Skin in 1992 introduced a new line of products called Interior Design Nutritionals or just IDN. Eventually the firm offered over 50 IDN products of four types: general nutrition, sports nutrition, botanicals, and weight management.

Success and Frustrations in Asia

Nu Skin commenced its Asian operations in Hong Kong in September 1991. Operating from this base through the subsidiary Nu Skin Hong Kong, several leading distributors through their downlines eventually entered other Asian markets. In February 1995 Nu Skin Hong Kong began operating in Macau.

January 1992 marked Nu Skin Taiwan's opening date. About two million individuals or ten percent of the total population of Taiwan were estimated to be involved in some form of direct marketing, mostly of nutritional products. Because of so much participation, the government strictly regulated this new form of business. Nu Skin Taiwan believed that in 1997 it was the largest direct marketing firm in that nation. Revenue growth there increased an average of 41 percent annually through 1997.

Nu Skin Japan commenced operations in April 1993 and quickly became the major success story for Nu Skin in Asia. In 1992 some $30 billion worth of goods and services were sold by direct sales in Japan, making it the world's largest direct sales market with about twice the amount sold in the United States.

Not surprisingly, in the early 1990s several other MLM firms also entered the Japanese market. For example, over one million Amway distributors in Japan recorded $1 billion sales in 1992, and the local company Pola Cosmetics sold twice that amount in 1992. Avon and Mary Kay Cosmetics also operated in Japan.

Because of the success of other MLM companies in Japan, *Business Week* on May 31, 1993 wisely included an article on Nu Skin's entry into that market. "Japan will be Nu Skin's biggest market," predicted retired baseball player Leron Lee, a major Nu Skin distributor in Tokyo. Statistics from the Nu Skin 1997 annual report (i.e., 297,000 active distributors generating revenue of nearly $600 million) proved Lee right.

What accounted for the success of MLM in Japan? Part of the answer involved close social networks already in place. "Organizations from college clubs to tea ceremony schools provide ready-made distribution frameworks," said the author of the *Business Week* article. Another likely reason was that many Japanese consumers preferred high-priced, high-quality products, unlike many Americans who always seemed to be shopping for a bargain.

Products

Nu Skin in 1998 offered a wide diversity of products for consumer use. Its facial care items included cleansing bars and various lotions, muds, moisturizers, face lift formulas, and Ideal-Eyes creme to reduce dark circles and wrinkles around the eyes. For body care, Nu Skin sold bar and liquid soaps, deodorants, moisturizers and lotions, and Sunright sunscreens, lip balm, and sunless skin tanning lotion. The HairFitness line covered shampoos, styling gel, mousse, and hair conditioners. The company's AP-24 oral care products featured floss, breath spray, mouthwash, a toothbrush, and two kinds of toothpaste. Nu Skin also sold Nutriol products, described in a product brochure as "Advanced Care from Europe": nail liquid, mascara, eyelash formula, shampoo, and hair conditioner. The firm's Nu Colour Cosmetics included mascaras, blushes, lipsticks, eye liners, and finishing powder. For the exercise crowd, Nu Skin offered five trademarked ProSync products: hair and body shampoo, antibacterial deodorant bar, antiperspirant and antideodorant, muscle rub, and a face and body lotion. Nu Skin also sold the Believe line of fragrances inspired by model Christie Brinkley, the company's spokesperson. For children, it distributed specially designed gentle skin and hair products, sunscreen, toothpaste, and floss under the Jungamals brand name.

Nu Skin developed its trademarked Epoch line with plant ingredients acquired from native cultures. From the Polynesians, Nu Skin gained an extract of the ava puhi plant used for its Epoch shampoo/hair conditioner. Generations of Polynesians also used two other indigenous plants (*Cordyline terminalis* and *Orbignya phalenata*) for moisturizing and soothing skin; Nu Skin incorporated them in its Firewalker Moisturizing Foot Cream. Other Epoch products featured botanical ingredients originally from several American Indian and Mayan cultures.

From native Haiti plant experts, Nu Skin acquired knowledge of the botanical *Citrus aurantium* that it included as a key ingredient in its Epoch deodorant. As part of its Force for Good Campaign, Nu Skin donated 25 cents from the purchase of every Epoch product to help indigenous peoples protect their habitats and traditional cultures.

Developments in the Late 1990s

Nu Skin Asia Pacific, Inc. (NSAP) was incorporated under Delaware laws on September 4, 1996 as the exclusive distribution unit for Nu Skin International products sold in Asia. On November 20, 1996 a corporate reorganization resulted in Nu Skin Japan, Nu Skin Taiwan, Nu Skin Hong Kong, Nu Skin Korea, and Nu Skin Personal Care (Thailand) becoming wholly owned subsidiaries of Nu Skin Asia Pacific. NSAP's initial public offering (IPO) of 4.75 million shares of Class A common stock was completed on November 27, 1996, resulting in net proceeds of $98.8 million. Nu Skin Asia Pacific, renamed Nu Skin Enterprises, Inc., on March 27, 1998 completed its acquisition of Nu Skin International and its affiliated companies in Europe, South America, New Zealand, and Australia.

In the late 1990s, Nu Skin began operations in the Philippines and started a new compensation plan and the new Scion product line, both designed for use in low per capita income nations. In 1998 the firm also started in Poland and Brazil.

In October 1998 Nu Skin Enterprises completed its acquisition of Generation Health Holdings, Inc., the private parent company of Pharmanex, Inc. Founded in 1994, Pharmanex researched and produced a line of 38 natural health supplements, including five proprietary formulas. From its base in Simi Valley, California, Pharmanex ran several research and production facilities, primarily in the People's Republic of China but also in Chile. The company employed about 40 scientists and collaborated with UCLA, Scripps Institute, Columbia University, and Beijing University on various projects.

Just one month after the Nu Skin acquisition, Pharmanex announced on November 18, 1998 it was removing all its products from some 30,000 mass retail stores so that it could rely completely on Nu Skin's network marketing methods. "Pharmanex's move is calculated to take advantage of the growth in direct sales in the United States," said Pharmanex President Bill McGlashan in a press release. "We have confidence in Nu Skin's distributor force .... As successful as we have been in securing coveted retail shelf space, direct selling represents a more attractive way to differentiate the benefits and unique attributes of Pharmanex products—an education that cannot be communicated adequately in the mass retail setting." Pharmanex products continued to be available from the firm's catalog, a toll-free telephone line, its Internet store, health food stores, and independent pharmacies across the nation.

Nu Skin in 1999 continued under the leadership of Blake Roney and at least two others who helped start the company in 1984. Roney was president and CEO of Nu Skin International (NSI) until May 1998 and board chairman of Nu Skin Asia Pacific from November 1996 to May 1998, when he became Nu Skin Enterprises' board chairman.

Steven J. Lund, a graduate of BYU Law School, practiced law before helping Roney found Nu Skin. He served as NSI vice-president from 1984 to 1996, when he became president/ CEO of Nu Skin Asia Pacific. In May 1998 he was chosen as the president/CEO of Nu Skin Enterprises.

Sandie N. Tillotson, a third founder, also graduated from BYU, as did almost all Nu Skin officers and directors. She helped develop the original products and create the multilevel marketing system. In 1993 *Working Woman* magazine named Tillotson one of the nation's top ten female business owners. She served as NSI vice-president from 1984 to May 1998, when she became a senior vice-president of Nu Skin Enterprises.

Nu Skin's finances continued to improve in the late 1990s. Its revenues grew from $358.6 million in 1995 to $678.6 million in 1996 and $890.5 million in 1997. Net income also rose steadily, from $40.2 million in 1995 to $81.7 million in 1996 and $93.6 million in 1997.

Nu Skin's expansion illustrated the growing popularity of direct sales among more and more consumers. In 1997 direct sales, which were largely one-on-one transactions, totaled $22 billion in the United States and over $80 billion worldwide, a doubling of sales in a decade.

It was also part of a major trend of more individuals working from their home. A 1997 Telecommute America survey estimated that about 11 million Americans used their computers and telecommunications devices to telecommute to work, instead of driving to work. In addition, the 1990 U.S. Census found that 54 percent of home workers were self-employed, compared to just 5.5 percent of workers outside the home who were self-employed. Network marketers like those in Nu Skin thus played a significant part in this dramatic economic shift from the factory and office to the home.

Nu Skin also demonstrated the important role that the state of Utah has played in the expanding network marketing field and the natural products industry. Several other herbal or natural products companies that used MLM started in or moved to Utah, including Nature's Sunshine Products, USANA, and the Sunrider Corporation. Many of these firms supported the Utah Natural Products Alliance, a Salt Lake City-based trade industry association.

Nu Skin's future looked bright in 1999. With an increasing number of high-quality products and good leadership, it continued to attract more distributors, many with high levels of education and successful careers in other fields. However, it faced plenty of tough competitors, including Amway and several other corporations involved in multilevel marketing of personal care and nutritional products.

Principal Subsidiaries

Nu Skin International; Nu Skin International Management Group; Nu Skin Canada; Nu Skin Puerto Rico; Nu Skin Guatemala; Nu Skin Mexico; Nu Skin USA; Nu Skin Hong Kong; Nu Skin Japan; Nu Skin Taiwan; Nu Skin Korea; Nu Skin Thailand; Nu Skin Philippines; Nu Skin Personal Care Australia; Nu Skin New Zealand; Nu Skin Europe; Cedar Meadows; Nu Skin U.K.; Nu Skin Belgium; Nu Skin Germany; Nu Skin France; Nu Skin Italy; Nu Skin Netherlands; Nu Skin Spain; Nu Skin Brazil; Nu Skin Argentina; Nu Skin Chile; Nu Skin Poland.

Further Reading

Anderson, Duncan, "The New Elite," *Success,* December 1995.

Bullinger, Cara M., "NuSkin Tells Its Story," *Utah Business,* October 1991, pp. 49–50.

Cilwick, Ted, "Women at Nu Skin Pile Up Claims of Sex Discrimination," *Salt Lake Tribune,* September 19, 1993, pp. F1, F3.

Conover, Christi, "Nu Skin, Michigan May Soon Have Agreement," *Provo Daily Herald,* December 28, 1991, p. A1.

Free, Valerie, "Magic Marketing," *Success,* March 1992.

Godfrey-June, Jean, "Can a Skin Cream Save the Rain Forest?," *Elle,* July 1996.

Gross, Neil, "They've Got Their Feet in the Door," *Business Week,* May 31, 1993.

May, Dennis, "Nu Skin Addresses FDA Concerns," *Utah County Journal,* October 22, 1991, p. A3.

Omelia, Johanna, "Direct Sellers Expand in Asia/Pacific Rim," *Drug & Cosmetic Industry,* September 1996.

Roha, Ronaleen R., "The Ups and Downs of 'Downlines,'" *Kiplinger's Personal Finance Magazine,* November 1991, pp. 63–64, 66, 68–70.

Romboy, Dennis, "High-Level Expansion Has Nu Skin Shedding Low-Key Image," *Deseret News,* June 12, 1991, p. B4.

Von Daehne, Niklas, "Techno-Boom," *Success,* December 1994.

—David M. Walden

OEC Medical Systems, Inc.

384 Wright Brothers Drive
Salt Lake City, Utah 84116
U.S.A.
(801) 328-9300
Fax: (801) 328-4300
Web site: http://www.oecmed.com

Public Company
Incorporated: 1942 as Orthopedic Equipment Company
Employees: 715
Sales: $188.7 million (1998)
Stock Exchanges: New York
Ticker Symbol: OXE
SICs: 3844 X-Ray Apparatus & Tubes; 3845
      Electromedical Equipment

OEC Medical Systems, Inc. is a leading manufacturer and marketer of medical imaging systems and accessories for fluoroscopic intraoperative and interventional applications—a segment of the X-ray industry. The company's digital X-ray imaging C-arms and fixed-room products are used most frequently in minimally invasive surgical settings for general, orthopedic, vascular, neurovascular, urological, and cardiac procedures. As OEC Medical Chief Executive Officer (CEO) Joseph Pepper told Christine Bushey of television network MSNBC, "It's the same technology as the big X-ray machine in the basement of most hospitals, with two exceptions. Ours is mobile . . . and also, instead of using the word 'radiographic,' which typically [refers to] X-ray film, the description of our equipment is 'fluoroscopic,' which means it's real-time imaging." Hence a surgeon, for instance, can use OEC equipment to guide his or her procedure, observing the actions as they occur. This is particularly useful in minimally invasive surgery, a technique which involves small incisions and the insertion of small equipment, rather than the more drastic measures associated with traditional surgery. OEC's surgical imaging equipment—often referred to as "C-arm" systems—is mobile, and the company has remained focused on this segment of the market.

The Early Years

Founded in Warsaw, Indiana in 1942, OEC originally marketed to orthopedic surgeons—hence, its name at that time: "Orthopedic Equipment Company." OEC's equipment for orthopedic surgeons originally included pins, plates, and other orthopedic devices necessary for correcting skeletal deformities in patients. In the process of marketing these orthopedic devices, it became apparent that providing real-time imaging to the surgeon would be an invaluable tool; thus, in the early 1970s, OEC moved in the direction of mobile X-ray imaging. In 1983, OEC was purchased by Diasonics, Inc. and became OEC-Diasonics, a subsidiary of that company.

Milipitas, California-based Diasonics had come into existence in 1978, growing quickly. In February 1983, it went public with the sale of 5.6 million shares of stock—the second-largest high-technology initial public offering (IPO) in the early 1980s. The stock had the blessing of Wall Street guru Arthur Rock, who had influenced the success of Intel Corporation and Apple Computer, and the company's price per share shot up rapidly from $22 to $29. But a year later, in February 1984, *Forbes* reported that the price per share had dropped to $6.50, and the company expected a $60 to $65 million pre-tax loss. The company, according to *Forbes,* was losing money in a number of areas. The X-ray imaging business represented by OEC-Diasonics, however, remained profitable throughout this period.

After another twenty months, the prognosis was even more negative, as *Barron's* proclaimed with a dirge-like headline in November 1985: "Burnt Offering: Why Diasonics Failed to Set the World on Fire." Much of the failure, William Alpert of *Barron's* asserted, could be blamed on "lackluster demand for the company's digital X-ray systems." With the addition of Steward Carrell to the CEO position in 1984, however, things were looking up for Diasonics. Among other changes, Carrell trimmed the company's holdings down to its three most promising lines: magnetic resonance imaging (MRI) technology, ultrasound technology, and mobile X-ray technology.

The Early 1990s: OEC Spins Off

As it turned out, Diasonics' ownership of OEC was to be only a ten-year affair. In May 1993, the *Wall Street Journal*

Company Perspectives:

We believe that healthcare economics, patient demands and new technology will continue to drive minimally invasive procedures. Most minimally invasive procedures will require improved visualization for a wide array of applications . . . and across many physical locations in the healthcare delivery network. As you will see in our annual report, OEC is already participating in many of these applications and locations. Our plan for growth is based on solidifying and extending our reach into minimally invasive healthcare.

announced that the parent company had lost $2 million in the first quarter of that year, and had opted to split into three separate corporations: Diasonics Ultrasound, Inc., Focal Surgery, Inc., and OEC Medical Systems, Inc. According to the *Wall Street Journal,* drastic health-care reform proposals then under consideration by President Bill Clinton—including a plan to have the federal government take over a large portion of the nation's health care—had helped to create the situation: "medical supply companies like Diasonics are hurting as hospitals delay capital expenditures amid uncertainties over the Clinton administration's proposed health-care reform."

Under the breakup plan, Diasonics would cease to exist—which it did in September 1993—and OEC Medical Systems would merge with the former parent and become the legal entity traded on the New York Stock Exchange under the trading symbol OXE. The company would focus on its specialty mobile X-ray imaging and urology equipment. According to a Diasonics executive quoted in the San Jose, California *Business Journal,* "Investors like simple things, things they can understand. This is inherently simpler." Hence, Jim Nash of the *Business Journal* reported, "Executives at each of Diasonics' new offspring said the move will enable each company to more fully concentrate on what it does." The parent company had become overgrown in the first place, Nash observed, because it "bought into the conventional wisdom that bigger firms were better prepared to compete than small ones." According to OEC's newly-appointed CEO, David Rose, Diasonics was "on a spending spree" when it purchased OEC. Thus, Nash wrote, "in an attempt to compete with larger players, Diasonics expanded as well. The aim was to offer a full line of medical-imaging devices."

As for OEC, which had ceased to be a Diasonics subsidiary only a week before, Nash reported that it already begun "performing better than its parent." In the second quarter of 1993, the company reported profits of $200,000 on revenues of $22.5 million. During the same period a year earlier, it had suffered losses of $400,000 on revenues of $23.5 million—due to the fact that its parent company was spending faster than OEC could earn. As it struck out on its own with 300 employees, however, the future was looking bright for OEC Medical Systems. "As an independent company," Rose told Nash, "we can focus our entire team 100 percent on what we are doing."

An Undervalued Company in the Mid-1990s?

In December 1994, OEC Medical Systems announced that it would buy back some 750,000 shares of its common stock.

"We believe OEC is significantly undervalued," Rose stated in a press release, "and believe that a buy-back of our stock is a sound investment of a portion of our cash reserves. We are the market leader in our segment . . . and we are optimistic about our potential for growth."

But when OEC announced its results for fiscal 1994 a month later, in January 1995, the news was not good. It had made $8.7 million on revenues of $98.2 million, compared with a 1993 profit of $9.8 million on $100 million in sales. Rose explained in another press release: "While much of the medical industry has suffered, we were pleased to have closed the year with anticipated earnings and healthy cash flow. However, we were disappointed that delays in shipments of the Series 9600 [one of the company's principal imaging products] in the second quarter, and weaker-than-desired gross margins throughout the year, took their toll on annual performance." Yet "On a positive note," he stated, "we are seeing a broadening acceptance of our new 9600 product." For 1995, Rose announced, the company planned to introduce new products, develop its distribution alliances, and grow its international business.

But more change was looming on the horizon, and it would affect Rose directly. A month after the year-end report was issued, in February 1995, the company announced that Rose was out. He would be resigning as CEO and president, a press release stated, to be replaced by board chairman Ruediger Naumann-Etienne. The latter, according to the press release, was a former Texas Instruments executive who had been involved with OEC Medical Systems since 1984. "While the company achieved a number of significant accomplishments during 1994," Naumann-Etienne stated, "we did not achieve our financial objectives, and are committed to improvements ahead. I remain confident of OEC's prospects, and expect a number of positive developments to be reported during the next several months."

Two months later, the situation was already looking better. For the first quarter of 1995, which ended March 31, the company had made $2.5 million on $22.8 million in revenues, as compared to $2.3 million on $23.3 million a year earlier. "The first quarter of 1995," Naumann-Etienne told *Equities* magazine, "was one of OEC's strongest first quarters for C-Arm bookings, and overall revenues were within expectations despite the softness of the urology fixed-room market." During that quarter, OEC Medical Systems had introduced the Uroview 2600 urological table and digital imaging system. "According to Naumann," *Equities* reported, "the state-of-the-art system is designed with digital advancements and enhanced product features for both the patient and clinical professional, all with no increase in cost. This value-oriented product introduction is designed to bolster the company's sales opportunities in a resource-limited market."

OEC Medical Systems's balance sheet looked so good by March 1996 that rumors of a buyout began to develop. Gene Marcial of *Business Week* reported the possibility of a buyout bid by a large medical-supply company. Marcial, who did not report the name of the company that had made the offer, wrote that the would-be buyer had made a similar proposal in 1995, "But OEC and the suitor couldn't agree on a price." He quoted an unnamed investment advisor as saying that OEC was more attractive in 1996 as an acquisition target, especially because it had "practically no debt and . . . lots of cash on hand." But the buyout rumors proved to be just that, and OEC continued to operate successfully on its own.

At that point, OEC's product line had expanded to include a new urological X-ray system that brought together both radiographic and fluoroscopic capabilities with digital image-processing. The company had signed a two-year contract, worth $10 million, with Columbia/HCA Healthcare to supply mobile C-arms and urological imaging tables. It had also developed distribution subsidiaries in France, Germany, Italy, and Switzerland.

OEC finished 1996 with a stronger balance sheet than ever. Sales were up from $102 million in 1995 to $128 million, and profits had risen from $11.8 million to $12.9 million. International sales had not grown according to the company's projections, but international bookings—leasing of equipment—had experienced a substantial upsurge. OEC had added several products, including the small and large field-of-view Mini 6600, for use in minimally invasive surgery involving extremities. Thus, by March 1997, people were again saying that OEC Medical Systems' stock was undervalued—only this time the claim was not originating from just the company's management, but from the shareholders themselves, as Marcial reported in *Business Week.*

A New Century: Growth in a Specialized Market

Joseph Pepper replaced Naumann-Etienne as CEO in 1997. Soon thereafter, during his interview on MSNBC, he described what the company's innovations in fluoroscopic technology meant for patients and doctors: "[B]efore fluoroscopic imaging," he said, "X-rays were . . . used in the operating room, but it was a portable X-ray machine that made film, and if a surgeon needed to know for some reason what he had just done, the machine was wheeled into the operating room, and then they had to wait while the film was taken some place and developed." Then, in the early 1970s, "OEC introduced the first real-time fluoroscopic imaging equipment in the United States, and . . . that allowed [the surgeon] to do . . . whatever he needed to be done, right there on the spot." As for minimally invasive surgery, this was an advancement that could not have been possible without improvements such as OEC's in imaging technology, which assisted surgeons in seeing what they were doing. "They can use our equipment to guide some catheters into the right place," Pepper said, or "to map out the veinous structure, or the arterial structure." Minimally invasive surgery involved less trauma to a patient's body, fewer negative side-effects, and shorter recovery times. OEC's advancements were making procedures such as minimally-invasive surgery easier and more feasible, and thus it was clear that the company's work in this specialized field would carry it far into the future.

As for the business end of OEC Medical, Pepper reported that the company had three distribution channels, including direct sales representatives employed by OEC; independent distributors who sell OEC's product along with other products; and "exclusive independent distributors." The latter, Pepper said, constituted a two-thirds majority, "and the relationship that OEC has built with these people over five, ten, fifteen years is a key to our success." On the international scene, in addition to its direct distribution channels in France, Germany, Italy, and Switzerland, OEC had relationships with distributors in some forty countries around the globe.

Near the end of the 1990s, OEC Medical Systems enjoyed a 55 percent share of the domestic market and a 15 percent share of the international market for its products. According to CEO Pepper, the company's "competition in the United States, in the world, for full-size C-arms are GE, Philips and Siemens. Having said that, that's the good news and the bad news. The bad news is we compete against high-quality, very powerful companies in the medical field. The good news is that we've maintained and grown this 50 percent share, a point or two a year over the past three or four years. So, we're small. Those companies have good product lines, but they do everything in X-ray. We only do one thing. We live or die by how well we design, how fast we come out with new product innovations, how well we listen to the customer . . . how responsive our sales force is."

At the end of 1997, OEC Medical Systems reported another strong year, with sales up 21 percent to $155 million. Net income had increased by an even greater percentage—up 28 percent to $12.2 million, and international sales had increased significantly. The company also completed the construction of a new 40,000 square foot expansion to its Salt Lake City headquarters. Looking into the future, Pepper set a top and bottom line growth goal for the company of 20 percent. If past performance was truly an indicator of future success, then OEC seemed to be poised to meet Pepper's goal.

Principal Subsidiaries

Barwig Medizinische Systeme (Germany).

Further Reading

Alpert, William M., "Burnt Offering: Why Diasonics Failed to Set the World on Fire," *Barron's,* November 18, 1995, p. 13.

Bushey, Christine, "Interview with OEC Medical CEO Joseph Pepper," MSNBC Business Video, September 5, 1997.

Marcial, Gene G., "A Familiar Image on This X-Ray?," *Business Week,* March 18, 1996, p. 109.

——, "In a Buyer's X-Ray Vision?," *Business Week,* March 31, 1997, p. 91.

Nash, Jim, "Diasonics Believes the Sum of Parts Is Greater Than the Whole," *Business Journal* (San Jose, Calif.), September 27, 1993, p. 5.

"OEC Medical Systems, Inc.," *Equities Reporter,* April 1995, p. 41.

Stern, Richard L., "Solid As a Rock?," *Forbes,* February 27, 1984, p. 89.

"Technology: Diasonics Posts Loss, Plans to Split Concern into Three Entities," *Wall Street Journal,* May 3, 1993.

—Judson Knight

Paul, Hastings, Janofsky & Walker LLP

Paul, Hastings, Janofsky & Walker LLP

---

555 South Flower Street
Los Angeles, California 90071-2371
U.S.A.
(213) 683-6000
Fax: (213) 627-0705
Web site: http://www.phjw.com

Private Company
Founded: 1951
Employees: 1,260
Sales: $219 million (1998)
SICs: 8111 Legal Services

With over 630 attorneys in early 1999, Paul, Hastings, Janofsky & Walker LLP is a major international law firm representing individuals and organizations of all kinds, from nonprofit associations and Fortune 500 corporations to government agencies both in the United States and abroad. From its home office in Los Angeles, the firm expanded first in California, then nationwide, and finally overseas. From its nine offices, seven in the United States and others in Tokyo and London, Paul, Hastings' attorneys practice in five major areas: business law, employment and labor law, litigation, real estate, and tax law.

1950s Origins

Lee G. Paul, Robert P. Hastings, and Leonard S. Janofsky founded the law firm of Paul, Hastings & Janofsky in Los Angeles on November 1, 1951. Janofsky, who had graduated from Harvard Law School in 1934, focused on employment law, while partners Paul focused on litigation and Hastings on business law.

The practice was one of many established in the area during this time, and business remained steady. Charles M. Walker, who had received his A.B. in 1937 and his LL.B. in 1939 from the University of Missouri, joined the firm in 1962 as a partner and founded the firm's Tax Department. Although Walker would resign from the firm in 1975 to serve as President Gerald Ford's appointment as the U.S. Treasury Department's assistant secretary for tax policy, he returned three years later to practice again at the law firm's tax department.

Two events in the 1970s influenced law firms like Paul, Hastings to become more business-oriented and expand their practices in competition against other law firms. First, in 1975 the U.S. Supreme Court decided in the case Goldfarb v. Virginia Bar Association that most attempts by professional societies to restrict advertising violated antitrust laws. Thus lawyers, doctors, and other professionals began or increased their advertising, just like other businesses.

Second, in 1979 Steve Brill started *The American Lawyer* to look at the inner workings, including finances, of law firms. Before that time, most lawyers lacked knowledge of what lawyers at other firms earned. However, with such data available, competition for top attorneys increased, and a new practice sometimes called lawyer lateral hires or raiding rival firms developed. Thus some large law firms used this method to expand. Instead of approaching potential clients directly, they simply hired top lawyers who in turn brought their clients with them to the new law firm.

The 1980s

After retiring in 1981, Charles M. Walker continued to serve his chosen profession on a *pro bono* basis. He was a director and trustee of the American Bar Retirement Association for six years and served as its 1986–87 president. Beginning in 1988, he was named a regent of the American College of Tax Counsel that included about 500 of the nation's top tax lawyers, academics, and judges. In that capacity, he helped found in 1989 the nonprofit American Tax Policy Institute. For six years he served as this think tank's president.

When Alan Barton joined Paul, Hastings in 1980, he became the firm's first attorney to specialize in venture capital transactions. A graduate of Boalt Hall law school, Barton was by the summer of 1987 heading up a team of venture capital attorneys, including seven at the downtown Los Angeles office, seven in Costa Mesa, and another seven in Santa Monica. The firm represented International Furniture and Accessories Mart Inc. in a $12.5 million private equity placement. Barton's group, including fellow attorneys Mike O'Connell, Richard Roeder, and

James Hamilton, provided counsel not only to firms needing funding, but also venture capital companies like Brentwood Associates, U.S. Venture Partners, and Interven Partners. Paul, Hastings also represented investment bankers like Morgan Stanley and Merrill Lynch in private placements, public underwritings, and mergers and acquisitions. Moreover, the law firm was special counsel to the Bank of America's Trust Department that oversaw the investment of corporate pension funds in venture capital projects.

In 1986 Barton's team at Paul, Hastings was involved in venture capital funding with capital commitments of $500 million, and Barton noted in the June 15, 1987 *Los Angeles Business Journal* that, ''I am not aware of any other law firm as active as we in this area (venture capital) or that has devoted as much resources to it.''

The firm started its Tokyo office in 1988. It was founded by Kaoruhiko Suzuki, a Japanese citizen who came to the United States as a high school exchange student and later received an A.B. from Harvard College. After receiving a J.D. from Harvard Law School, Suzuki joined Paul, Hastings as an associate and then in 1984 became a partner. The firm's Toyko office was one of 20 in Japan in 1989 and was one of the first to hire a Japanese national.

By January 1989, the end of Paul, Hastings' fiscal year, the firm had grown to almost 350 lawyers and had for the first time reached the milestones of 100 partners and $100 million in annual revenues. It was Los Angeles' fourth largest law firm, exceeded only by Gibson, Dunn & Crutcher, O'Melveny & Myers, and Latham & Watkins.

Many other law firms expanded about the same time as Paul, Hastings. In 1975, before the boom time, less than 48 American law firms had at least 100 lawyers, but by 1993 over 250 firms had that minimum number.

Although most partners at Paul, Hastings continued to rise through the ranks on an eight-year associate track requiring about 50 hours per week, managing partner Robert G. Lane in the January 2, 1989 *Los Angeles Business Journal* said that hiring ''key lateral partners'' from outside the firm had also been an effective management tool.

A 1960 graduate of the University of Southern California Law School, Lane commented on other reasons for the firm's growth: ''We have been very fortunate in that we have not lost partners to other law firms . . . and have had steady growth. Nationwide, we are probably best known for our practice in employment law, but . . . we cover a wide range of legal issues.''

By 1989 Paul, Hastings maintained eight offices, including the original in Los Angeles and others in Costa Mesa, Orange County, established in 1974; Atlanta (1980), Washington, D.C. (1980); Santa Monica, California (1983), Stamford, Connecticut (1983), New York City (1986), and the newly opened Tokyo office.

The 1990s: The Firm's Five Departments and More

Paul, Hastings continued its expansion as the new decade began. By 1991 it included over 400 lawyers from over 12 nations representing about 60 law schools. The firm grew without a single merger or acquisition of another law firm. No more than three attorneys from another firm joined Paul, Hastings, and most lateral hires came as individuals. The firm's partners were relatively young; only three of the more than 100 partners were over 60 years old. All partners shared equally in making decisions about the firm.

In 1990 the firm met with a legal challenge of its own, when the U.S. Equal Employment Opportunity Commission filed a civil lawsuit in the Manhattan federal court alleging that some Paul, Hastings personnel had sexually harassed three female employees in its New York office. According to the November 9, 1990 *New York Times,* this case apparently represented the EEOC's ''first charge of harassment by a major law firm.'' Partner Dennis H. Vaughn noted that the law firm had defended several clients accused of sexual harassment, which obviously made this case's outcome even more important. The case involved accusations of sexist language as well as the firm's having allegedly ignored and then dismissed women who complained; no demands for sexual favors were alleged. By the end of the year the firm had settled the case without admitting any guilt, agreeing to completely comply with federal sex discrimination laws and to offer training to all its attorneys in regards to the sexual discrimination problem, which was being faced by other law firms, including Chicago's Baker & McKenzie, one of the world's largest law firms.

Also during this time, the firm stepped up its efforts to use the latest in computer technology. To give clients better access to information, Paul, Hastings' Michael Stanko, director of information services in the Los Angeles office, designed proprietary software called ValuMaker, which all Paul, Hastings offices began using. This electronic system provided detailed billing records and project management data online.

In the 1990s Paul, Hastings closed its Santa Monica office and opened two new offices. In February 1997 it started its San Francisco office by attracting key attorneys from other firms. The new office emphasized commercial litigation, especially in securities and high-tech issues. Later that year, the firm opened another international office—in London's International Financial Center on Old Broad Street. This office focused on international business concerns, such as those involved when American firms start up European subsidiaries and vise versa.

In the 1990s the firm organized its practice around five specialties, all represented by attorneys in each of the firm's geographic locations: business law, employment law, litigation, real estate law, and tax law. The company was perhaps best known for its expertise in the areas of labor and employment law.

Paul, Hastings' Employment Law Department included over 155 attorneys who dealt with labor and employment issues, such as discrimination, wages and benefits, downsizing, and hiring and firing topics. Name partner Leonard S. Janofsky had established the firm's national reputation in this specialty and in 1979, when the American Bar Association elected Janofsky president, he became the first employment lawyer to serve in that position. Other key employment attorneys included Christopher A. Barreca, the chair of the firm's Stamford office who in the late 1990s chaired the ABA's Labor and Employment Law

Section, and R. Lawrence Ashe, the firm's East Coast employment law chair. Paul Grossman, a 1964 Yale Law School graduate, served as chair of the Employment Law Department. His clients included major California employers, including manufacturers, oil firms, defense contractors, and financial institutions. Named in *The Best Lawyers in America,* Grossman in a 1992 survey in the *National Law Journal* was "widely acclaimed as the top employment lawyer representing management [in the United States],"

Paul, Hastings' attorneys helped the National Association of Manufacturers (NAM) win a *pro bono* lawsuit in the U.S. District Court for the District of Columbia against the U.S. Department of Labor. The department had tried to tighten rules concerning temporary employment of foreign skilled workers, a nationwide controversy in which many high-tech firms argued they needed more skilled immigrants because they could not find enough American programmers and engineers.

The firm's employment attorneys often contributed their expert knowledge to state legislatures, Congress, courts, the National Chamber of Commerce, and others. And Paul, Hastings' literature pointed out that, "Perhaps as a testament to our particular expertise, we are frequently called upon by many of the nation's leading law firms to represent them in connection with their employment law matters."

Paul, Hastings' Business Law Department dealt with a wide range of corporate legal issues, from mergers, acquisitions, antitrust, government regulations, and bankruptcy to technology licensing, capital formation, franchising, and entertainment industry transactions.

Five business law attorneys joined the firm's New York office in 1992, including Charles B. Ortner, chair of the American Bar Association's Computer Law Division, and 20 colleagues who left the New York-based firm of Milgrim, Thomajan & Lee. The five attorneys specialized in entertainment, intellectual property, and software litigation issues. This expansion increased the size of Paul, Hastings' New York office to more than 100 attorneys and added such famous clients as Madonna and Sting to its previous stable of entertainment clients, including Walt Disney, MCA, and Warner/Chappell Music. Ortner represented many other entertainers and companies as well, including Whitney Houston, Michael Jackson, Motown Records, and A & M Records. Another well-known business law partner was Ralph B. Everett, the former chief counsel and staff director of the U.S. Senate Committee on Commerce, Science and Transportation, who would head the firm's Federal Legislative Practice. Everett served as the managing partner of Paul, Hastings' office in Washington, D.C. with 62 attorneys. Business law partner Kaoruhiko Suzuki, founder of the Tokyo office, worked out of the Los Angeles office but often traveled to Japan. In addition to his law practice, Suzuki cofounded The Century of the Pacific Conference to help build relationships among young professionals in Tokyo and Los Angeles and edited *Japan Transaction Guide,* "the most comprehensive publication on Japanese law in the United States," according to the firm. Partner Daniel G. Bergstein, in the New York office, chaired the firm's Business Law Department, which boasted about 200 attorneys in 1999.

The firm's Litigation Department included about 160 attorneys and 28 paralegals in early 1999, using their considerable experience in trials, appeals, and administrative hearings to help clients from many industries and backgrounds.

Some 85 attorneys worked in Paul, Hastings' Real Estate Department for clients involved in commercial development, land use regulation, zoning, real estate investing, and environment issues.

The Paul, Hastings Tax Department, its smallest with about 25 attorneys in 1991, advised clients on complex taxation issues involving international operations, off-shore incorporation, mergers and acquisitions, estate planning, and state and federal taxes.

In 1999 Donald A. Daucher served as the firm's managing partner, a member of its Policy Committee, and chair of its Partner Compensation Committee. A 1971 graduate of Duke University Law School, Daucher was a litigation partner in the Los Angeles office and also served as the former chair of the Watts Summer Games and as a director of many community and educational organizations.

As the century drew to a close, the attorneys of Paul, Hastings faced many challenges, in the forms of increased competition and a well-informed public. Specifically, consumers asked more questions of professionals than in the past, gained information easily from the Internet, and could use software for simple legal forms, thus reducing the need for some professional legal services.

Nevertheless, the need for legal services remained a pervasive part of modern life, especially due to rapid socioeconomic and technological change, the increasing use of lawsuits to solve conflicts, and the maze of government laws and regulations. The bottom line was that Paul, Hasting, Janofsky and Walker had plenty of work to do and thus continued to grow as the new millennium approached.

Further Reading

Anderson, A. Donald, et. al., "Paul, Hastings, Janofsky & Walker," in *Los Angeles: Realm of Possibility,* Chatsworth, Calif.: Windsor Publications, 1991, pp. 338–39.

Buckley, Bruce, "Paul, Hastings Law Firm Expands," *Billboard,* August 29, 1992, p. 89.

"Cheap Computer Services Compete with Lawyers," *Omaha World-Herald,* December 26, 1994, p. 5.

Cole, Benjamin M., "Capital Idea: Alan Barton Reaps the Fruits of a Strong Local Venture Capital Market," *Los Angeles Business Journal,* June 15, 1987, p. 4.

——, "Paul, Hastings Partner Reflects on 2 Milestones," *Los Angeles Business Journal,* January 2, 1989, p. 14.

Margolick, David, "Curbing Sexual Harassment in the Legal World," *New York Times,* November 9, 1990, p. B5.

Olson, Walter K., *The Litigation Explosion,* New York: Truman Talley Books, 1991.

Podgers, James, "Legal Profession Faces Rising Tide of Nonlawyer Practice," *ABA Journal,* December 1993, pp. 51–57.

"President Appoints Paul, Hastings Partner to Lead International Telecomm Delegation," *PR Newswire,* October 13, 1998, p. 0219.

Schmitt, Richard B., "From Cash to Travel, New Lures for Burned-Out Lawyers," *The Wall Street Journal,* February 2, 1999, p. B1, B8.

—David M. Walden

Penton Media, Inc.

1100 Superior Avenue
Cleveland, Ohio 44114-2543
U.S.A.
(216) 696-7000
Fax: (216) 696-0836
Web site: http://www.penton.com

Public Company
Incorporated: 1910 as Penton Publishing Inc.
Employees: 1,400+
Sales: $200 million (1997)
Stock Exchanges: New York
Ticker Symbol: PME
SICs: 2721 Periodicals: Publishing & Printing; 7389
   Business Services, Not Elsewhere Classified

Considered a primary business resource by marketing leaders around the world, Penton Media, Inc. provides marketing and media solutions in an important cross section of industries: design/engineering, electronics, food/hospitality, government/compliance, information technology, leisure, management, manufacturing, mechanical systems and construction, and supply chain/aviation.

Overview

Although Penton Media, Inc. became an independent public company in 1998, it has published trade periodicals for a variety of industries for more than 100 years. As Penton Publishing the company began by publishing magazines for the iron and steel industry. It gradually expanded its scope and published magazines covering a wider range of industry, equipment, and machinery. In the late 1990s the company expanded its trade show activity and began offering a wider range of media services to the industries it served. In December 1998 it acquired Mecklermedia Corporation, making Penton Media the largest publicly owned, diversified business-to-business information and media company headquartered in the United States.

John Augustus Penton Published the First Issue of Foundry, *1892*

Around 1887 John Augustus Penton began developing a trade publication to serve the casting industry. An iron molder by trade, he was a native of Canada, born in Paris, Ontario, in 1862. When he was 21 he moved to Detroit, Michigan, and served as president of the Brotherhood of Machinery Molders from 1887 to 1892 and editor of its journal, *Machinery Molders Journal.* In 1892 he published the first issue of *Foundry* in Detroit.

In 1901 John Penton moved to Cleveland, Ohio, to head the Iron and Steel Press Company. It published *Foundry* magazine and another magazine then called the *Iron Trade Review,* which eventually became *Industry Week.* In 1910 Penton moved from rented quarters to a four-story brick building that became known as the Penton Building. The company's printer, Whitworth Brothers Company, also moved into the building. In 1912 Penton Publishing purchased the Whitworth Brothers Company, giving it the ability to print its own magazines and take on contract printing work.

In 1925 Penton won printing contracts for two magazines, *Time* and the *Saturday Review of Literature.* Over time the company took on more outside printing contracts. As the circulation of *Time* grew, it became clear that Penton would have to decide whether to purchase more printing equipment. When it came time to renew the contract with *Time,* the board of directors of Penton Publishing decided not to renew the contract, thus ensuring that publishing business magazines would be the company's main business.

Machine Design *First Published, 1929*

Penton published the first issue of *Machine Design* in 1929. The idea for the magazine, which was written for design engineers, came from a salesman for *American Machinist* named Frank "Spats" Johnson. When McGraw-Hill, which published *American Machinist,* turned down Johnson's idea for *Machine Design,* Johnson quit his job and approached Penton with the idea. Penton was interested and formed a subsidiary, Johnson

Publishing Company, to publish the new monthly named *Machine Design.*

In 1930 the name of *Iron Trade Review* was changed to *Steel.* The new title reflected changes in editorial policy, advertising sales, promotion, and distribution. In 1938 Penton acquired *New Equipment Digest,* which was in bankruptcy, for $30,000. The magazine's printing forms were shipped from Chicago to Cleveland, and Penton printed the April 1938 issue only a few days behind schedule. Also in 1938 Penton began helping the U.S. Census Department develop the Standard Industrial Classification (SIC) system, which was completed in 1945.

During World War II Penton was publishing *Steel, Foundry, Daily Metal Trade, Machine Design,* and *New Equipment Digest.* Because of government restrictions, though, Penton was forced to cease publication of *Daily Metal Trade* with the March 11, 1943 issue. The editors of *Steel* and *Foundry* both were called to serve as presidential advisors during the war.

Penton Press Established, 1968

By the early 1960s the rapid growth of Penton's publications was straining its printing capabilities. In 1964 the company began looking for a site that could be converted to a printing facility. Construction of a new printing plant began in 1967 in Berea, Ohio, and on April 16, 1968 the plant that housed Penton Press opened. It featured a five-unit web offset press. The cost of building the plant exceeded $3 million.

In 1970 *Steel* magazine was renamed *Industry Week.* The name change reflected the changing scope of the magazine to include broader areas of industrial management.

Acquired by Pittway Corporation, 1976

As America celebrated its bicentennial in 1976, Penton was acquired by Pittway Corporation and merged with Industrial Publishing Company (IPC), also based in Cleveland, to form Penton/IPC Publishing. The company would be known as Penton/IPC from 1976 to 1986, when the ''IPC'' was dropped. Pittway was a Chicago-based company that produced security systems. It had acquired IPC in 1964. IPC published a large number of small trade magazines that concentrated on highly specialized, narrow market segments, such as the air conditioning and refrigeration business, fluid power, welding design, and more. IPC's publications complemented those of Penton, which had much larger circulations.

At the time of the merger, the new company's revenues were about $50 million. Three years after the merger Penton/IPC's revenues had almost doubled and pretax profits had tripled.

Began Making Acquisitions, 1985

The year 1985 marked the beginning of a period of growth through acquisitions and new product launches. The company acquired *Millimeter* in 1985, and in 1987 *Foodservice Distributor* was launched. In 1987 Penton acquired *American Machinist* and *33Metal Producing.*

A $12 million expansion of Penton Press that was begun in 1988 for its 20th anniversary was completed in 1989. It included a 28,000-square-foot addition, a massive nine-stand web press, and a $1 million binder. The expansion doubled the press's capacity.

In 1989 Penton entered the growing electronics market by acquiring the VNU Magazine Group, which included *Electronic Design, Electronics,* and *Microwaves and RF.*

New Programs and Services, 1991

Penton began a formal quality improvement program in 1991. Information obtained from employees led to the creation of the Penton Quality College, which conducted ongoing training classes for Penton employees. The company also initiated a Quality Recommendation program, which encouraged employees to submit suggestions for process improvements and new business. Input also was sought from readers and advertisers through surveys and focus groups.

These programs led Penton to expand its services into other areas of business communication. In 1992 the Custom Publishing Group was launched. It used the company's resources in writing, printing, and graphics to produce magazines, newsletters, and brochures for other companies.

In 1992 Penton acquired *Food Management* magazine from Advantar Communications. Penton launched its first CD-ROM product in September 1993. Titled *Concurrent Engineering Solutions,* it contained editorial material from the first six months of 1993 from *Machine Design,* the *MD Materials Selector, Power Transmission Design,* and *Hydraulics and Pneumatics,* as well as all directory listings from those publications. *Concurrent Engineering Solutions* was followed in 1994 and 1995 by *nowmedia* and *nowmedia II.* These were CD-ROMs produced by *Millimeter* that were designed to help others produce their own CD-ROMs.

The Penton Institute was created in 1993. It produced seminars, conferences, and trade shows on topics selected by Penton editors. They covered emerging issues and trends in the industries served by Penton periodicals.

Metal Heat Treating was acquired from Chilton Company in 1993. The company also launched *Government Procurement* and *Building Renovation.* In 1994 *Wireless Systems Design* was launched. During the early 1990s Penton also launched several foreign publications. Also in 1994 Penton's direct mail subsidiary, Curtin & Pease/Peneco, acquired a direct mail operation called Feather Fine. Both were located in Florida. In 1996 the company added *EE Product News* magazine to its list of publications.

Expanded Media Services, 1997

In September 1996 Thomas L. Kemp was named chairman and CEO of Penton. He came to Penton from San Francisco-based Miller Freeman, Inc. Under Kemp, Penton would diversify its revenue sources to rely less on advertising revenue and expand its trade show business. For 1996 Penton reported $188 million in revenues.

In January 1997 Penton made the first of three trade show acquisitions for the year when it acquired A/E/C/ Systems International. A/E/C/ Systems International was a trade show company that produced technology-based exhibitions for the architectural, engineering, and construction markets. Penton's strategy was to acquire shows and conferences in markets where it published magazines. It also wanted to make acquisitions of trade shows that would support its international growth, primarily in Europe, Latin America, and the Far East.

Later in 1997 Penton acquired the United Kingdom-based Independent Exhibitions Ltd. At the end of 1997 Penton further expanded its trade show business by acquiring Baltimore-based Industrial Shows of America and its international affiliate. The three trade show firms acquired during 1997 added 34 shows to Penton's trade show portfolio. During 1996, by contrast, Penton sponsored just seven trade shows accounting for little more than two percent of its revenues for the year. In 1997 it sponsored 15 events representing five percent of its annual revenue. At the beginning of 1998 Penton had 55 events scheduled that were expected to account for nearly 15 percent of its 1998 revenues.

Became an Independent Public Company, 1998

As early as December 1997 Pittway Corporation announced plans to spin off Penton. For the year, Penton contributed $205 million to Pittway's revenues, or 15 percent. Penton's operating income and revenues had reached an all-time high. In April 1998 Penton Publishing changed its named to Penton Media Inc. to reflect the company's broadened business scope and direction. It planned to continue to provide business customers with a complete array of media for information and marketing solutions.

Penton Media Inc. was spun off from its parent company, Pittway Corporation, in August 1998, and Penton stock began trading on the New York Stock Exchange on August 10, 1998. At the time of the spin-off, Penton published 18 directories and 42 national business and trade publications.

Penton's first acquisition as an independent company was that of Donohue Meehan Publishing Co., which served the baking and convenience store markets. Chicago-based Donohue Meehan published one directory and eight magazines and had 1997 revenues of $9.4 million.

Acquired Mecklermedia Corporation, 1998

Penton completed its $274 million cash tender offer for all of the outstanding shares of Mecklermedia Corporation toward the end of November 1998. The acquisition added several Internet-related trade magazines, the Internet World and ISPCON trade shows, and the Internet.com address. It accelerated Penton's strategic growth plans for more diversified revenue sources and added greatly to its revenue from trade shows.

In November 1998 Penton announced plans to launch *EE Product News China* and *Wireless Systems Design China* magazines in 1999. Earlier in 1998 Penton had successfully relaunched *Electronic Design China*. Penton's Electronics Group publications in China were published jointly by Penton and CCI Asia-Pacific Ltd. of Hong Kong with support from China's Ministry of Electronics Industry Technology Information Research Institute.

Outlook at the End of the 20th Century

As Penton approached the end of the century, it published approximately 90 titles and employed more than 1,250 publishing professionals in offices throughout the United States and abroad. It owned a state-of-the-art printing facility and was expanding rapidly into other areas of business-to-business communication.

Goals for the year 2001 included reducing its reliance on advertising revenues and increasing revenues from trade shows and conferences. Plans called for advertising to account for 55 percent of revenue, down from 78 percent in 1996. Revenue from trade shows and conferences was expected to account for 25 percent of revenue, up from three percent in 1996. Other areas accounting for the company's revenues included subscriptions and list rentals (steady at four percent), information and databases (increase to five percent from −1 percent), electronic products (three percent), and direct mail and printing (eight percent, down from 15 percent in 1996).

Principal Subsidiaries

Donohue/Meehan Publishing Co.; Independent Exhibitions Ltd. (United Kingdom).

Principal Divisions

A/E/C Systems International; ISOA International.

Further Reading

The History of Penton Publishing, Cleveland, Ohio: Penton Publishing, 1994.
Jensen, David, "People to Watch: Thomas L. Kemp," *MIN Magazine,* Vol. 2, No. 1, 1998.
Mather, Joan, "Penton Makes Major Move into Tradeshows in 1997 with Launches, Acquisitions," *Tradeshow Week,* March 2, 1998, p. 10.
"Penton Completes Tender Offer for Mecklermedia, Closes Acquisition," *Business Wire,* November 24, 1998.
"Penton Media Announces Launch of *EE Product News China* and *Wireless Systems Design China,*" *Business Wire,* November 23, 1998.
"Penton Media Completes Mecklermedia Buy," *Reuters,* November 24, 1998.
"Penton Media Is Successfully Spun Off from Parent Pittway Corp.," *The Simba Report on Directory Publishing,* September 1998, p. 5.

—David Bianco

PICTURETEL

PictureTel Corp.

100 Minuteman Road
Andover, Massachusetts 01810
U.S.A.
(978) 292-5000
(800) 716-6000
Fax: (978) 292-3300
Web site: http://www.picturetel.com

Public Company
Incorporated: 1984 as PicTel Corp.
Employees: 1,544
Sales: $466.4 million
Stock Exchanges: NASDAQ
Ticker Symbol: PCTL
SICs: 3669 Communications Equipment, Not Elsewhere
  Classified; 7372 Prepackaged Software

PictureTel Corp. is the world's leading manufacturer of video communications systems for use over conventional or high-speed telephone lines. The company offers several systems, including relatively inexpensive models that provide audio/visual surveillance, more complex models that enable personal computer (PC) users to view each other on their computer screens, and complex multipoint systems that allow people in several locations to communicate at once.

Origins

The concept of video communications emerged during the 1960s, when American Telephone and Telegraph Company (AT&T) developed a telephone capable of sending a series of snapshots simulating motion over its lines, which were then displayed on an accompanying video screen. The device originally was intended for use in residential markets, but when market research indicated that users were uncomfortable with the idea of being seen during telephone conversations, plans to continue with the development of the "picture telephone" were stalled.

Video communications would later have more practical applications in the business community, which welcomed less costly and time-consuming alternatives to the travel involved in corporate meetings. In the 1970s AT&T again tried to exploit its video network by establishing studios in major cities, where video communications were made available to businesses for a rental fee. The costs involved in operating the system, reflected in the rental fees, proved exorbitant, however, discouraging demand for the service. Opportunities for companies other than AT&T to develop and manufacture video communications systems were limited during this time, as the Federal Communications Commission (FCC) imposed regulations and specifications for equipment that interconnected with the public telephone network. In 1984, however, with the divestiture of AT&T, barriers to entry in the telephone equipment market came down.

Improvements in video communications were also contingent on modifications to the country's telephone network system. Designed only for voice communication, conventional telephone lines had an extremely limited bandwidth that provided only a narrow frequency range; for proper transmission, video images required enormous bandwidths. The development of digital electronics technology helped overcome this problem. Digital electronics created more data transmission space by using algorithms to replace repetitive or superfluous signals with simpler, shorter codes, a process known as data compression.

Two experts in this technology were Brian L. Hinman and Jeffrey G. Bernstein, long-time friends and colleagues in the electrical engineering graduate studies program at the Massachusetts Institute of Technology during the 1970s. At MIT, Hinman and Bernstein focused on the science of image processing through visual data compression, gaining valuable technological guidance from their faculty advisor, Dr. David Staelin. The three conceived of a plan to develop and market a line of video communication devices based on a 56-kilobit per second translating interface, or "codec," they had assembled. This system would allow images to be sent over telephone wires.

Hinman, Bernstein, and Staelin gained financial backing from Robert Sterling, an entrepreneur specializing in high-technology ventures, and the PicTel Corporation was formed on August 13, 1984. PicTel established a corporate office and laboratory in Peabody, Massachusetts, where work commenced on software and hardware for the 56-kilobit per second codec.

The company drew its management team from some of the country's most prominent corporations. Robert Bernardi and Dr. Norman Gaut were recruited from companies in Massachusetts' high-tech industrial corridor. Dr. Ronald Posner, former head of the Harris Corporation's satellite division, became president and CEO, and Thomas Spaulding, formerly of Multilink, Inc., became chief financial officer.

Before it had even developed a product, the company went public on November 8, 1984, selling 2.2 million shares at $2 per share. On December 4, the company's underwriter, S.D. Cohn & Company, purchased 330,000 shares, reflecting growing confidence in PicTel's project. Product development continued through 1985 without a single sale. Early in 1986, however, PicTel developed its MCT algorithm, which reduced the bandwidth necessary for transmission of an acceptable video image from 768 kilobits per second to just 224.

Further Technological Developments in the Late 1980s

In July the company introduced its first product based on the MCT algorithm, a software-based codec called C-2000. Although the device's applications were limited, few other companies were as far along with this technology as PicTel, and work continued on improvements in the product through 1987. During this time, the company changed its name to PictureTel to better reflect its focus on picture transmission and to distinguish its name from the technical term ''pixel,'' which referred to the picture elements in a video image.

In 1988 PictureTel developed a new image coding system, called hierarchical vector quantizing, which required a bandwidth of only 112 kilobits per second, a rapid rate made possible by the system's ability to weed out redundant image transmissions, or those that reflected little or no movement. The company also introduced two new products that year: the C-3000 video codec and the V-2100 videoconferencing system. The C-3000 was compatible with the C-2000 and performed as well as any competing system on the market, at half the price and half the size. The V-2100 system was enclosed in a wheeled cabinet that enabled users to set up a video conference from any room that was properly wired.

In January 1989, AT&T chose PictureTel as the equipment vendor for an international video conference it held. The demonstration provided two-way, full-motion voice and video connection between PictureTel headquarters and an AT&T office in Paris. Other PictureTel demonstrations followed, including one for its remote-control V-3100 videoconferencing system and another that featured the Px64, which allowed PictureTel systems to be connected to those developed by other manufacturers. By the close of 1989, PictureTel had shipped more than 70 percent of the videoconference systems in use throughout the world. While the company's revenues tripled between 1987 and 1988, to $18.6 million, PictureTel had yet to turn a profit.

Several other product extensions were introduced in 1990, incorporating larger monitors and more rugged construction. PictureTel developed a one-way transmission system for surveillance use, enabling security groups to monitor remote locations through inexpensive, simple telephone connections. The company's Software Generation 3 system provided better picture quality and seven kilohertz of audio bandwidth at the same 112-kilobit per second switched data rate. By marketing entire video systems, rather than just the codec devices, PictureTel reaped a larger margin on each system sale. Shipments of videoconferencing systems increased by 40 percent over 1989, to 770 units. Revenues increased a further 99 percent over the previous year, to $37 million.

In January 1991, PictureTel introduced a new family of videoconferencing systems under the System 4000 name. The line included four models, ranging from small consoles to large conference room devices. System 4000 included a proprietary audio technology called Integrated Dynamic Echo Cancellation (IDEC), which helped prevent feedback that could produce annoying echoes. The System 4000 became PictureTel's flagship product line. At two-thirds the cost of competing systems, it also had considerable demand.

PictureTel's primary customer base consisted of large corporations with offices in multiple locations. These customers laid out in excess of $20,000 for each system and also paid for the special switched data links necessary to form a network. Although a substantial investment, the PictureTel videoconferencing system could pay for itself in as little as a year. Executives who formerly convened in person, incurring substantial airline and hotel costs, could now meet in the comfort and convenience of their own offices.

1991: Partnership with North Supply

By 1991, however, PictureTel had nearly exhausted its market among the large Fortune 500 companies that could afford such a system, and the company began making efforts to boost sales of videoconferencing equipment to smaller companies. Key to this effort was a marketing partnership with North Supply. Under the terms of the agreement, PictureTel products were sold through North Supply dealerships. The company soon introduced a new low-cost product line, which could be used by companies of modest means or added to enhance existing networks.

In April 1991, with investor enthusiasm in the company running high, PictureTel issued another 2.3 million shares, raising more than $40 million in equity capital. In September,

PictureTel introduced its M-8000 multipoint bridge, a device that enabled users to conduct as many as eight simultaneous videoconferences among 16 users.

Although PictureTel led the industry in videoconferencing technologies, it remained a small company with limited marketing resources. To increase its capital, PictureTel established a joint marketing agreement with IBM, which welcomed the opportunity to leverage PictureTel's products into its own flagging line of computer products. As an IBM "multimedia business partner," PictureTel provided full-motion color video technologies that enhanced IBM's personal computers, allowing videoconferences to be conducted from individual work stations. PictureTel ended the year with record earnings, due primarily to the success of the System 4000 product line. Reporting a profit for each quarter, the company's revenues grew to $78 million and net income reached $6 million.

PictureTel sealed another series of important joint marketing agreements in January 1992. In one agreement, AT&T agreed to handle sales and service of an AT&T videoconferencing product based on PictureTel technology. A separate arrangement was established under which Bell Atlantic's seven telephone companies would directly handle sales and service of PictureTel products. The company also established a Japanese subsidiary to handle sales of videoconferencing products in Japan. A month later, the company finalized similar agreements with Mercury Communications in the United Kingdom, as well as with the U.S. telecommunications corporation Sprint. PictureTel videoconferencing technologies also were marketed as part of the Lotus Notes software application.

Total revenue for 1992 exceeded $141 million, net income grew to $10.7 million, and shipments numbered more than 2,850 units, marking a second year of profitable operation for PictureTel. With such success in the marketplace, however, PictureTel showed signs of vulnerability to price competition from such rivals as Vtel Corporation and Compression Labs. To prevent losses, PictureTel reduced prices on its System 4000 family by 20 percent and introduced an entry level product called the Model 150E. Priced at $18,500, the system could be leased for only $500 per month, making videoconferencing affordable for even the smallest and lowest margin businesses. Other low-cost videoconferencing products included the new PictureTel LIVE, PCS 100 desktop, and System 1000 lines, all of which were compatible with international standards and, therefore, operable with any standard-based system.

In an effort to enhance its existing product line, PictureTel acquired KA Teletech, a Baltimore-based developer of scheduling, reservation, accounting, and network management software for the videoconferencing industry. The enterprise was relocated subsequently to PictureTel headquarters in Danvers, Massachusetts.

During this time, PictureTel launched its first national advertising campaign, featuring such taglines as: "Over 70 percent of dial-up videoconferences are PictureTel. Get the Picture?"; "This isn't an ad for videoconferencing. It's a wake-up call"; and "We don't move people, we move ideas. And ideas are what move companies."

1993: PC-Based Videoconferencing

At the close of 1993, PictureTel unveiled a new product that converted PCs into videophones. Regarded as substantially higher in quality than a competing system from AT&T, the PictureTel product sold for $6,000, or $1,000 more than the AT&T model. The year 1993 also saw the company ship its 10,000th group videoconferencing system. PictureTel was ranked the 11th fastest growing company in the United States by *Fortune* magazine, up from 14th on the list the year before.

In 1994 the company continued to add new products and cut prices. It slashed the price of its PC-based desktop videoconferencing system almost in half to compete with Intel's ProShare line. PictureTel expected to come out on top in sales, as its system offered noticeably better picture quality. The company also announced new strategic alliances with a number of major corporations, including Compaq. Sales for the year were $255 million.

PictureTel reached several milestones in 1995, including conducting, in April, the world's largest multipoint, global dial-up videoconference. Conducted from New York's Hudson Theater, more than 50 sites dialed in for the hour-long demonstration. The company used the opportunity to unveil two new group videoconferencing systems and a new network server. The cost of renting phone lines for the event was $4,400, as compared with $160,000 for satellite linkup costs that other types of systems would have required. PictureTel's stock price was fluctuating wildly during this time, reaching $45 in April and $73 in November, with several ups and downs along the way. The company announced plans to move its headquarters from Danvers to Andover, Massachusetts, consolidating most of its operations under one roof.

Sales Slump in the Late 1990s

Competition from a number of different companies, particularly Intel, were eroding PictureTel's profits, however, as the company was forced to continually lower prices to compete. With 15 to 20 percent of the company's revenues now coming from its desktop systems, PictureTel's stock began to slip, even as the company posted record revenues and profits for 1996, as investors became wary of "Intel overhang." In 1997 the company began to see sales and earnings drop, and it went through a restructuring to eliminate unprofitable operations. The company reported earnings of $466 million with a net loss of $39 million. To compound this bad news, figures for 1996 had required downward revision, as significant errors in the accounting of sales and lease payments were discovered. A number of shareholder lawsuits resulted.

Despite these problems, PictureTel announced the acquisition of Andover-based audioconferencing pioneer MultiLink, Inc., as well as an expansion of the company's Japanese partnership with Nippon Telegraph and Telephone Corp. The company still held a majority of the global market in both the large "boardroom size" and smaller desktop videoconferencing systems.

Sales were still down in early 1998, and PictureTel announced layoffs in January. The company's stock was now trading at less than $10 a share. PictureTel had seen a number of top executives depart in the previous year, and in March CEO Norman Gaut left, to be replaced by Bruce Bond. Bond began immediately to take measures to right the ship. In July the company announced the acquisition of Starlight Networks, Inc., a streaming media technology company. Streaming media systems were used to send audio and video feeds over the Internet to multiple recipients. PictureTel was moving toward more Internet-based products, including ''on-demand'' services, which offered recorded programs that could be accessed from a central server when needed.

In January of 1999, PictureTel announced a major deal with Intel, in which the company would collaborate with its rival to jointly develop and distribute products. The chip maker invested $30.5 million in PictureTel, making it a ten percent owner of the company. In making this deal PictureTel was finally getting a leg up to the stability and growth that it had been seeking. It was still likely to remain a bumpy road because of the rapidly changing technology and competitive marketplace, but the combination of PictureTel's inherent strengths and the clout of industry giant Intel was a potent one. As the new century dawned, PictureTel appeared to be in its strongest position to date.

Principal Subsidiaries

Multilink, Inc.; Picturetel Securities Corp.; PictureTel AG (Switzerland); PictureTel Japan K.K. (Japan); PictureTel GmbH (Germany); PictureTel UK Ltd. (United Kingdom).

Further Reading

Ackerman, Jerry, ''President Is Leaving PictureTel,'' *Boston Globe,* October 1, 1997, p. D1.

Bulkeley, William M., ''PictureTel To Introduce $6,000 System to Make PCs Work as Video Telephones,'' *Wall Street Journal,* July 16, 1993, p. B8.

Clark, Tim, ''PictureTel Sharpens Brand Image,'' *Business Marketing,* June 1993, p. 33.

Higgins, Steve, ''Leaders & Success: PictureTel's Norman Gaut—Trying To Minimize Whatever Is Extraneous to Success,'' *Investor's Business Daily,* May 16, 1995, p. A1.

McCloy, Andrew P., ''PictureTel, Intel Fight for Home Video Market,'' *Boston Business Journal*, June 28, 1996, p. 3.

Nutile, Tom, ''On State Street: PictureTel's Stock Rockets to $72.50 a Share,'' *Boston Herald,* November 9, 1995, p. 49.

''PictureTel, AT&T Vie for Videoconferencing Growth,'' *Electronic News,* May 17, 1993, p. 15.

''PictureTel Shrinks Size and Price of Video-Conferencing Suite,'' *PC Week,* July 20, 1993.

Purdy, Janet, ''The New America: PictureTel Corp.—Videoconferencing Firm Back to Full Color,'' *Investor's Business Daily,* July 14, 1995, p. A4.

''Videoconferencing: Going Prime Time?,'' *PC Week,* May 25, 1998, p. 124.

—John Simley
—updated by Frank Uhle

Piedmont Natural Gas Company, Inc.

1915 Rexford Road
Charlotte, North Carolina 28211
U.S.A.
(704) 364-3120
Fax: (704) 365-8515
Web site: http://www.piedmontng.com

Public Company
Incorporated: 1950
Employees: 1,904
Sales: $775 million (1997)
Stock Exchanges: New York
Ticker Symbol: PNY
SICs: 4924 Natural Gas Distribution

Since its formation in 1950, Piedmont Natural Gas Company, Inc., has provided natural gas and propane to customers first in the Piedmont region of the Carolinas and, later, to those in Tennessee. In 1996, its service area encompassed a large portion of western North and South Carolina along Interstate 85 and the area in and around metropolitan Nashville, Tennessee. As is typical for utilities in the southern United States, many of its customers have been in the industrial sector, though it has served larger numbers of residential and commercial customers as well. Piedmont has also engaged in non-utility endeavors, such as the selling of propane. By the late 1990s, Piedmont had grown to become the second largest gas utility in the southeastern United States.

A Difficult Beginning

The years after World War II witnessed a natural gas pipeline "boom" in the United States, and in 1950, Henry Blackford, Sr., Priestly Conyers, Jr., and Donald S. Russell, Sr., sought to construct a pipeline from Texas to the as-yet unserved Piedmont region of the Carolinas. When the Federal Power Commission instead granted Transcontinental Pipeline Company (Transco) permission to construct a pipeline to the area, rather than giving up on the gas business entirely, the three

South Carolinians purchased from Duke Power Company the right to distribute manufactured gas to a number of North Carolina cities. The sale was finalized on May 1, 1951.

Piedmont's first year was a difficult one. The company inherited 34,000 customers and 300 former Duke employees, but reportedly had no offices, minimal and aging cast iron pipe, and a collection of rusty automobiles. Eventually, an old Studebaker dealership was pressed into service as Piedmont's first corporate office, but the conditions inside were far from comfortable. Crates served as chairs and desks, the roof leaked—sometimes flooding the office—and employees labored without benefit of air-conditioning. Moreover, plans to convert the business to natural gas by tapping into Transco's pipeline were impeded by the lack of steel pipe, a shortage caused by the Korean War. Losses during the first year totaled $1 million.

A Series of Firsts

The end of 1952 brought with it good fortune to the company in the form of two events: steel pipe became available from Great Britain, and Buell Duncan was hired as president. Duncan came to Piedmont with experience in the gas business, having served as director of Florida's Southern Atlantic Gas Company. He also possessed a background as a civic leader and the desire to increase the company's community exposure. His efforts helped initiate what John Maxheim, a later Piedmont executive, would call the company's corporate culture.

In subsequent years, Piedmont experienced significant growth and an important sequence of firsts. The company made its first profit of $373,000 in 1953, more than doubling this figure the next year by earning $760,000. A dividend—the first—of 20 cents per share was issued in 1956, and the first annual report to stockholders appeared in 1957. In the same year, revenue surpassed $10 million and net income soared to $1 million. The first shareholders' meeting took place in Charlotte, North Carolina, in 1958.

Throughout the 1950s and 1960s, Piedmont continued to expand its customer base and develop its internal resources. Between 1951 and 1957, 16,000 new customers signed on with the company, bringing the total number served to 50,000. By

1960, that number was 75,000, and in 1964, the company reached the 100,000 mark. An engineering staff was organized in 1953, and the company moved into new headquarters, complete with a gas-powered clock, in 1962. Piedmont acquired Carolina Natural Gas Company in 1968, thereby gaining 9,000 new natural gas customers and 1,000 new propane customers in Hickory and the surrounding areas.

The Gas Crisis

However, beginning with the 1970s, increasingly severe gas shortages gripped the United States, and Piedmont's period of untroubled growth was stalled. Gas suppliers nationwide, but predominantly in Texas, curtailed deliveries when regulation of the wellhead price of natural gas by the Federal Power Commission set prices at levels which did not enable them to make a profit for some wells. In response, regulatory agencies like the Federal Power Commission (FPC), the North Carolina Utilities Commission (NCUC) and the South Carolina Public Services Commission (SCPSC) set in place gas rationing plans in 1971.

Since industrial customers received lower rationing priority than residential and small commercial customers, curtailments had a noticeable impact on Piedmont's earnings. Piedmont faced gas volume curtailments of 4.3 percent in 1971, 11 percent in 1972, and 24 percent in 1973. By 1974, Piedmont's curtailments had reached 40 percent, and then edged up to 56 percent the next year. In 1974, the state regulatory commission in both Carolinas ordered Piedmont to refrain from adding customers until the shortage had abated. A mild winter in 1975 helped avert a gas crisis in North Carolina, but 1976 ushered in bitterly cold weather during which interstate pipelines could fulfill only a quarter of demand.

Nevertheless, while the situation was a difficult one for the company, it still managed to turn a profit. In the mid-1970s, the company was able to secure both NCUC and SCPSC approval for a curtailment tracking adjustment (CTA) formula that was intended to stabilize earnings by adjusting customers' rates in response to curtailments. Piedmont also sought rate increases in 1974 and 1977. By 1978, with stock prices plummeting, Piedmont still claimed a net income of $5 million and 185,000 customers.

By the mid-1970s, gas shortages nationwide had become "politically intolerable," according to some, and in 1978, Congress passed the Natural Gas Policy Act (NGPA), which took the first steps toward deregulating the gas industry and created a new agency, the Federal Energy Regulatory Commission, to replace the Federal Power Commission. John Maxheim, head of Piedmont Natural Gas, was critical of portions of the act that he feared would increase gas prices. Signs of deregulation, however, were welcome, and the company routinely began to voice its pro-deregulation stance. Curtailments essentially ended in 1979. In 1982, Piedmont joined with three other utilities to call for a nationwide conference to discuss the challenges emerging in the new marketplace.

A Deregulated Market in the 1980s

Piedmont experienced strong growth during the next several years. In 1979 alone, the company provided fuel to 6,500 new customers, an increase greater than any throughout the previous six years. A total of 9,000 customers joined Piedmont's rolls in 1980. The company recorded $9.3 million in net income during the same year, a 60 percent increase over 1979, and embarked on a $16.3 million program of system expansion. By 1981, when demand for natural gas was at an all-time high, the company gained 11,000 customers and finished a new corporate headquarters building in Charlotte. Although the following recession year witnessed a 16 percent decline in earnings, cold temperatures in 1983 reversed the downward trend as Piedmont benefitted from record-breaking consumption.

Still there were rough times ahead. Inflation was an ongoing problem, and gas prices rose as predicted in the wake of the NGPA, with consumers paying 80 percent more for natural gas in 1983 than in 1978. As a result, much new residential construction had turned to electricity to meet home heating needs during the early 1980s. Piedmont and other gas utilities thus had to build non-revenue producing pipeline through the electrical "doughnuts" these subdivisions had created. The state of the wholesale natural gas market was somewhat unpredictable, and Piedmont had to contend with widely fluctuating gas prices from its suppliers. In 1981 and again in 1982, Piedmont sought rate increases, citing fluctuating oil prices and low consumption of natural gas as damaging to its competitiveness. It dropped its request in 1981, instead offering a decrease, when Transco dropped the wholesale price of natural gas.

To shield itself from this uncertain situation, the company and its subsidiaries moved to diversify. Piedmont had sold propane fuel and marketed natural gas- and propane-powered appliances since the 1950s; in the 1980s, it moved into a number of new areas as well. In 1981, PNG Energy Company purchased Gilley and Tolley Fuel Company and began to operate its coal business under the name of PNG Coal and Oil Company. Also during that year, PNG Communications Company entered the cable television market, and PNG Conservation Company began selling solar water heaters, branching out into electricity-producing solar voltaic cells in 1983. All told, by 1984, non-utility endeavors represented 4.4 percent of business.

Explosive Growth in the Late 1980s

By the late 1980s, the gas market was functioning more predictably, and Piedmont was providing fuel to a total of 300,000 customers, a number which represented a rate of increase that was three times the national average. The company acquired Tennessee Natural Resources, the parent of Nashville Gas Company, which at the time served 61,000 customers, and, between 1986 and 1995, signed on 20,000 new customers each year. In 1984, Piedmont opened a Houston office and formed a joint venture with natural gas marketers in Texas that allowed it to market wholesale gas to other utilities and large-volume customers beyond its three-state area. By 1990, Piedmont was serving 415,000 customers, and its continued success was attracting notice. Duke Power, provider of electrical service in the Piedmont region and longtime Piedmont competitor, began to seek ways to counteract the company's aggressive marketing and growth in the residential and small commercial markets.

Piedmont continued to grow at a remarkable rate throughout the early 1990s. In August 1991 John Birch, an analyst at

Equitable Securities in Nashville, Tennessee, called Piedmont "one of the best utility stories in the United States." The company continued to add customers—a record 28,100 customers in 1993—and common stock dividends grew at a rate above the industry average between 1991 and 1996. In 1995, Piedmont recorded a net income of $38 million and was honored by the Newcomen Society of the United States, an organization founded in 1923 to promote and recognize important contributions to free enterprise. John Maxheim was selected by *Financial World Magazine* as CEO of the year that same year in the gas utility category.

New Challenges and Joint Ventures

The gas business continued to change, and Piedmont had to diversify to adapt to new circumstances. As deregulation progressed during the middle and late 1990s, the company formed an increasing number of joint ventures with other utilities and natural gas suppliers. In 1994, Piedmont's subsidiary, Piedmont Energy Company, became a 51 percent partner in Resource Energy Services Company, L.L.C., which focused on providing gas acquisition, transportation, and storage services to industrial and large commercial customers in the Southeast. In 1995, Piedmont Intrastate Pipeline Company, a division of one of the Piedmont subsidiaries, Piedmont Energy, joined with several other utilities to extend the Cardinal Pipeline of North Carolina 65 miles to a point in the vicinity of Raleigh. That same year, Intrastate announced plans with Transco and two other North Carolina utilities to build a liquefied natural gas terminal near Transco's main line in North Carolina under a joint venture called Pine Needle LNG Company.

Among Piedmont's most important joint ventures was the formation of SouthStar Energy Services, LLC, with AGL Resources of Atlanta and Dynergy, Inc. of Houston, the holding company for Atlanta Gaslight, the southeast's largest natural gas distributor. In addition to selling natural gas to industry and large commercial customers in the eight-state southeast region, SouthStar was formed to provide electricity and natural gas to residential and small business customers. In the fall of 1998, when Georgia became the first state in the region to open its utility market to competition, SouthStar, doing business as Georgia Natural Gas Services, began marketing unregulated natural gas services to its customers.

Competition also increased with deregulation. In 1995, the NCUC awarded natural gas service in four North Carolina counties to newcomer Frontier Utilities over Piedmont's competing bid. Two years later, Piedmont protested plans by BASF, a chemical company and manufacturer of plastics, pharmaceuticals, and crop protection products, to buy its natural gas directly from Transco, Piedmont's supplier. In order to meet the challenges of future deregulated competition, Piedmont began a process of cost cutting. In 1994, the company sold properties acquired during the early 1970s on which it had sought natural gas deposits; the production from its finds no longer justified administrative costs. Piedmont also ended its natural gas appliance sales and installation business in 1996 after 45 years of involvement when revenues no longer justified expenses. In 1997, the company eliminated 126 positions from its work force to help ensure that Piedmont would remain competitive.

Throughout the late 1990s, Piedmont continued to prepare to meet the challenges of the increasingly competitive gas market. Natural gas doubled its share of the home heating market between 1992 and 1998, during which time Piedmont expanded both its customer base and earnings. In 1997, the company enjoyed a net income of $54.1 million, an 11.4 percent increase over the previous year. The mild winter of 1997–98 made a dent in sales, but Piedmont continued to add new customers at a much faster rate than most utilities across the nation. In 1998, the NCUC granted Piedmont permission to use $26.2 million from specially designated and regulated expansion funds to expand its service into three more North Carolina counties. Piedmont was providing services to 673,000 customers in that year and had grown into the second largest gas utility in the southeastern United States.

Principal Subsidiaries

Piedmont Energy Company, Inc.; Piedmont Intrastate Pipeline Company, Inc.; Piedmont Interstate Pipeline Company, Inc.; PNG Energy Company; Piedmont Energy Partners, Inc.; Tennessee Gas Company.

Further Reading

"Analyst Says Duke Needs 'To Fight' Competitive Threat from Piedmont," *Electric Utility Week,* December 10, 1990, p. 9.

"Buyout Could Put Other Gas Companies on the Market," *Asheville Citizen Times,* November 17, 1998, p. B8.

"Distributors Seek Nationwide Conference on Issues Confronting FERC as Gas Industry Moves Toward Deregulation," *Foster Natural Gas Report,* April 15, 1982, p. 12.

Johnson, Leslie Williams, "Piedmont Natural Gas Enters New Territory as Georgia, Others Deregulate," *Charlotte Observer,* July 16, 1998, p. B5.

"N.C. Residential Gas Market Booming, But Consumption Lowest in Region," *Gas Utility Report,* June 19, 1998, p. 2.

"Piedmont Joins Two Texas Marketers to Provide Wide Range of Services," *Gas Utility Report,* January 21, 1994, p. 2.

"Piedmont, Nonutility Company Battle over Right to Serve Rural N.C. Area," *Gas Utility Report,* July 21, 1995, p. 1.

"Utility Players; Speculation Regarding Publicly Owned Stocks," *Business North Carolina,* August 1991, p. 49.

—Carrie Rothburd

PlayCORE

PlayCore, Inc.

1212 Barbary Drive
Janesville, Wisconsin 53545
U.S.A.
(608) 755-4768
Fax: (608) 755-4763
Web site: http://www.playcore.com

Public Company
Incorporated: 1985 as Swing-N-Slide Corporation
Employees: 516
Sales: $89 million (1997)
Stock Exchanges: American
Symbol: PCO
SICs: 3949 Sporting & Athletic Goods, Not Elsewhere
    Classified

PlayCore, Inc. is one of the fastest growing and most innovative commercial and consumer playground equipment firms in the United States. The company has three core divisions, including: Swing-N-Slide, the consumer products division; GameTime, the commercial products division; and Pentes Play, the soft-contained equipment division. Swing-N-Slide, whose do-it-yourself wooden playground equipment is the leader of the market in the United States, is located in Janesville, Wisconsin, and promotes and sells its products through hardware and home service centers; GameTime, whose manufacturing facilities are situated in Fort Payne, Alabama, designs and markets playground systems to municipalities, amusement parks, school districts, and park districts across America and is recognized as one of the largest makers of modular and custom commercial outdoor playground equipment; and Pentes Play is one of America's leading designers and manufacturers of indoor soft-contained play equipment. GameTime, Inc., purchased in 1997, and Pentes Play, Inc., acquired in 1998, are the first two steps management has taken at PlayCore to implement its strategy to become the world's leading supplier of playground and children's recreation products. By the middle of 1998, both through the acquisition of GameTime and a new global marketing strat-

egy, PlayCore was able to report that international sales accounted for six percent of the company's total sales volume.

Early History

During the mid-1980s Thomas and Michelle Baer, residents of Janesville, Wisconsin, thought that a do-it-yourself hardware kit using standardized lumber to build swing sets would be a low-cost alternative to the then predominant wooden swing sets everyone bought for their children. Thomas Baer had been looking quite some time for a high-quality swing set for his children, but was unwilling to pay $750 for the pre-cut swing sets that he could find. Baer finally decided to design a wood swing set that included everything such as rings, chain, swing hangers, brackets, and plans, but without the wood. The wood was to be purchased at a local lumberyard. When Baer finished building the swing set design of his own, he realized that he had completed the entire wood swing set for less than $200.

Even though the Baers put their own money into starting a venture to manufacture these hardware kits, however, they found that more capital was required to make the enterprise a sustainable success. They approached the DRS Investment Group, also located in Janesville, and suggested a partnership to underwrite the costs of starting a company. An agreement having been signed among all parties, Swing-N-Slide, Inc. was formed to manufacture and market do-it-yourself wooden home playground equipment. Thomas Baer became the company's first president and CEO.

Within a few years the company was growing at a torrid rate. Swing sets, which included an assembly plan, swing hangers, chains and seats, brackets, and a complete breakdown of the lumber, number of nails, and tools required to finish the kit, were selling better than anticipated. By the early 1990s the company had introduced a total of six basic designs for swing set kits. Equally successful were the company's climbing units. Five basic designs were manufactured, each complete with an assembly plan, climbing rope, climbing ladder, tarp, fasteners, assembly hardware and, similar to the swing set kits, a list of the required lumber, number of nails, and tools to complete the kit.

In addition to swing set kits and climbing units, the company manufactured plastic slides for use on all of the kits. Although the firm initially made metal slides, management quickly decided that plastic slides were of a higher quality since they are longer, can be manufactured in a wide variety of colors, are not susceptible to rust, and do not become as hot in the sun as metal slides commonly do. To augment its product line, the company also designed, manufactured, and marketed numerous accessories that complemented its swing set kits and climbing units, such as climbing ropes, metal and wood swing hangers, nets, merry-go-rounds, tarps, ladders, and swing set seats. In 1988 the company's accessories product line included only eleven items. By the early 1990s, however, more than 30 items were sold as accessories to swing set kits and climbing units.

Growth and Development in the Early 1990s

The early 1990s were boom years for the company. Once only available through lumber yards, by 1992 the company's products could be purchased through a number of different home center stores—a total of more than 6,000 retail outlets—including 19 of the 20 largest home center chains with operations throughout the United States. Swing-N-Slide's product mix also was a telling sign of good times: swing sets accounted for 17 percent of sales, climbing units for 23 percent of sales, slides for 34 percent of sales, and accessories for 26 percent of sales. From 1989 to 1992 the company's total sales volume increased from $7.8 million to $46 million, adding up to an astounding near 500 percent increase. Gross profit and operating income also skyrocketed during the same period. In fact, the company's gross profit margin hovered around 50 percent, twice the figure of other swing set manufacturers.

Perhaps the best news for those individuals, especially the Baers, who were instrumental in establishing the company, came when Swing-N-Slide became a public company in 1992. With an initial public offering at $11 per share on the Nasdaq stock exchange, the company sold 2.6 million shares. The Baers became millionaires overnight. Although the following summer of 1993, with floods throughout the Midwest and an increase of lumber prices by 15 percent, saw the stock lose 46 percent of its value, within another six months the company's stock price jumped back and stabilized at $12.50 per share.

During the mid-1990s, however, Swing-N-Slide fell into a design and marketing routine. Sales had peaked in 1993, with

profitability leveling off, and gross profit margins stagnating. The year 1994 was the same for the company. In 1995 net sales amounted to a disappointing $45 million. But this was not the end of it. Even more disappointing was the net sales total for 1996—$41 million. Unfortunately, it seemed as if the company had a brief success and was destined to head for bankruptcy courts. In a move that was designed to shake up management and return the company to respectable profitability, the board of directors decided to release Thomas Baer as head of the company and hire a new president and chief executive officer by the name of Frederick L. Contino, a manager with extensive experience in the playground and play systems industry.

Without hesitating, Contino streamlined management and services, expanding the company's presence in the retail home center and outlet market, and focused on designing new and better playground systems. Most important of all, however, was Contino's strategy to grow the company through a comprehensive acquisitions plan. The first step in his plan was to purchase GameTime, Inc., located in Fort Payne, Alabama. A leading supplier of commercial outdoor playground equipment for public parks, public schools, municipalities, day care centers, campgrounds, churches, hotels, and amusement parks, GameTime was a perfect complement to Swing-N-Slide's product line. With a well-known reputation for innovative designs, product longevity, and customer satisfaction, GameTime, Inc. brought with it three primary brands, PrimeTime, PowerScape, and TotTime. The company's PrimeTime brand is a play system that can be used anywhere, featuring an easy-to-build bolt-through fastening system. GameTime's PowerScape brand is one of the premier play systems used in the United States, with patented, factory-installed locks, galvanized steel or aluminum support posts, and modular roofs on certain systems. The Tot-Time brand is an innovative play system designed especially for two- to five-year-olds, using PrimeTime construction techniques and featuring lower and higher deck heights. GameTime also manufactures StreetScape, a highly innovative product line including commercial outdoor furniture for use in shopping malls, parks, and a variety of urban environments.

When acquired by Swing-N-Slide, the GameTime product line was sold by 21 independent representatives throughout the United States and by 25 independent international distributors around the world. With an industry certification granted by the International Organization of Standardization, GameTime products were in growing demand from countries outside the United States. The acquisition of GameTime not only doubled the net sales of Swing-N-Slide almost immediately, but provided it with an international distribution network that management was keen to develop.

There were other advantages to the acquisition as well. Swing-N-Slide's consumer sales were seasonal, with most of its business conducted during the first two quarters of the year. GameTime, on the other hand, sold about 65 percent of its product line during the second and third quarters of the year. The two companies also complemented each other with regard to their manufacturing capacities. GameTime previously had outsourced its thermoform production of bubble windows and panels, but was able to take advantage of Swing-N-Slide's manufacturing plant in Janesville, Wisconsin. Simultaneously, Swing-N-Slide was able to take advantage of GameTime's efficiency in metal fabrication and commercial production, to hasten and improve Swing-N-Slide's Tuff Kids product line, a rock-bottom-priced line of commercial playground equipment and systems.

By the end of 1997 Swing-N-Slide's net sales had jumped to $89 million, an increase of 114 percent over 1996. The number of employees also had increased from 241 to 516 workers. Keeping this many employees was an indication that Contino was strongly committed to expanding the company's product line and marketing capacity.

By mid-1998 the company reported net sales of $62 million, an increase of 36 percent over the same time in 1997. Operating income and profitability also increased substantially during the first six months of 1998.

With such favorable financial indicators, Contino continued to move the company forward. In 1998 the company changed its name from Swing-N-Slide, Inc. to PlayCore, Inc., to emphasize the company's focus on playgrounds and play systems. In May of 1998 Contino convinced the board of directors to approve the purchase of Pentes Play, Inc., one of America's leading designers and marketers of indoor soft-contained play equipment. Based in Charlotte, North Carolina, Pentes Play, Inc. previously had outsourced almost all of its manufacturing needs. The acquisition, however, enabled the company to use the production facilities at PlayCore's plant in Janesville, Wisconsin.

The Late 1990s and Beyond

The acquisitions made by PlayCore transformed the company from a seasonal consumer playground and play systems manufacturer into a highly integrated company with the ability to produce and market its product line not only in the United States, but in many foreign countries. Adding more than $70 million in revenues, management's strategy has been enormously successful. In addition, the company's distribution strength has been enhanced significantly through GameTime's market leadership in supplying play equipment to schools, churches, and park districts, as well as in other applications. Along with PlayCore's growing retail distribution network through its Swing-N-Slide division, customers such as Home Depot, Lowe's, Builders Square, 84 Lumber, and Ace Hardware are part of the company's growing success.

With the number of children in the five- to 12-year age range estimated to increase through the early years of the 21st century, new schools will be opening throughout the United States. The expanding economy has led management at PlayCore to believe that numerous city governments will have the funds to remodel old parks and playgrounds and construct new ones. PlayCore has every intention of taking advantage of this opportunity.

Principal Divisions

GameTime; Pentes Play; Swing-N-Slide.

Further Reading

"Outdoors '95," *Sporting Goods Business,* August 1995, p. 72.
Savitz, Eric J., "Big Swing," *Barrons,* August 17, 1992, pp. 16–17.
Teitelbaum, Richard S., "Children a Mixed Blessing: Not To These Stocks," *Fortune,* November 29, 1993, p. 27.
——, "Swing-N-Slide," *Fortune,* December 28, 1992, p. 55.
Yohalem, Kathy C., "A Word for It, Or Maybe Two," *Sporting Goods Business,* August 1995, p. 94.
Young, Kevin, "Standard Operations," *Sporting Goods Business,* August 1995, p. 48.

—Thomas Derdak

Pleasant Company

8400 Fairway Place
Middleton, Wisconsin 53562
U.S.A.
(608) 836-4848
(800) 845-0005
Fax: (608) 836-1999
Web site: http://www.pleasantco.com

Wholly Owned Subsidiary of Mattel Inc.
Incorporated: 1986
Employees: 850
Sales: $300 million (1998 est.)
SICs: 5961 Catalog & Mail-Order Houses; 2721
    Periodicals, Publishing, or Publishing & Printing

Pleasant Company is one of the United States' premiere manufacturers of children's dolls. Its American Girls collection embodies girls from different periods in American history, such as Kirsten, a Swedish immigrant pioneer girl of the 1850s, and Josefina, a Mexican-American girl living in northern New Mexico in the 1820s. The high-quality dolls, which retail for close to $100, are accompanied by a wealth of historically accurate accessories. Pleasant Company also sells books about each of its doll characters and publishes *American Girl Magazine,* with more than 700,000 subscribers. Pleasant Company is one of the top ten publishers of children's magazines in the United States and is in the top 20 of children's book publishers. The company also finds itself in the top 20 among direct mail enterprises, as the dolls are sold almost exclusively by mail. The company operates doll-related tours or shows at six living history museums around the country and opened its first retail space, a combination theater-restaurant-store, in Chicago in 1998. Pleasant Company manufactures girls' clothing as well as doll outfits and sells a line of baby dolls and accessories in addition to its main American Girl line. The company operates out of a warehouse and distribution facility in Middleton, Wisconsin, with additional sites in nearby southeastern Wisconsin. The company was privately held until 1998, when it was bought by Mattel Inc.

Early History

Pleasant Company was the brainchild of Pleasant Rowland, an entrepreneur with a background in education and a fervent dream. Rowland was raised on Chicago's North Shore and educated at Wells College. After graduating from Wells, she taught elementary school for six years during the 1960s. In 1968 Rowland became a television news anchor in San Francisco. While on assignment as a reporter, she met a representative of an educational publishing company, Boston Educational Research. Impressed with her skills and interest in children's materials, Boston Educational Research hired Rowland away from the television station, and she became director of product development there from 1971 to 1978. At that company she developed several children's reading textbooks, which were used widely by school systems across the country. Royalties from her textbooks gave Rowland enough money to buy the *Children's Magazine Guide* in 1981, a library resource aimed at elementary school children. Rowland tripled the circulation of the publication in the 1980s and then sold it in 1989.

Although she had worked with children's educational materials for most of her career, the idea for her American Girls doll collection did not gel until Rowland visited the historical site at Williamsburg, Virginia sometime in the early 1980s. Rowland was impressed with the exhibits at Colonial Williamsburg, but dismayed that there were no books in the gift shop that she deemed suitable for children. So Rowland decided to write a children's guide to Williamsburg. She sold the idea to the Colonial Williamsburg Foundation and eventually produced an illustrated family guidebook for them. She grew excited about teaching history to children and searched for other ways to reach kids. Her resolve to make historical dolls was strengthened when she examined the mass market dolls that were currently available. The choices for girls between the ages of seven and 11 ranged from glitzy, buxom Barbie to bland, babyish Cabbage Patch dolls, with little in between. Rowland decided to develop something completely different: a finely made, historically accurate doll that would teach children about history and inspire their imaginations.

Rowland eschewed outside consultants and put together her enterprise her own way. She found one nicely made doll in a back room at Marshall Fields in Chicago and, from a tag on its underwear, located its German manufacturer. Intensive research at the Smithsonian Institution in Washington and at New York's Fashion Institute of Technology led to prototype designs for three dolls. Kirsten, a Swedish pioneer girl, Samantha, a wealthy Victorian orphan, and Molly, a bespectacled nine-year-old in the waning years of World War II, were the first three products in the American Girl line. Each doll was accompanied by a book, an audiocassette, and a painstakingly detailed collection of optional accessories. Rowland rented a warehouse in Madison, Wisconsin, where she had been living since the early 1980s, for her first manufacturing and distribution center. By Christmas season 1986 the American Girl collection was ready to go. Rowland and a small staff put together a lavish catalog and mailed it to upscale consumers on lists Rowland purchased. She also placed advertisements in a few select magazines such as the *New Yorker* and *Smithsonian*.

The dolls were high-priced, but that did not seem to deter discriminating consumers, and the American Girl line found a niche. By 1989 annual sales had grown to $30 million. Staff had grown from an initial three to 140 full-time workers. The company added hundreds to its payroll in its busy Christmas season. To accommodate its growth, the company moved from its Madison headquarters to nearby Middleton, Wisconsin and filled a 150,000-square-foot office and processing space. Pleasant's mailing list, which had started with 500,000 names, grew to eight million over the first three years.

Managing Growth in the Early 1990s

With the company clearly thriving, Pleasant began to diversify its product line. In 1990 the company brought out a different set of dolls, its New Baby Collection. These baby dolls did not have the historical theme of the American Girls collection, yet they were intended as educational tools as well as playthings. The dolls were meant to help prepare toddlers for the actual arrival of a new baby in the family. The dolls had lifelike faces and could be bought with a barrage of useful accessories such as diaper bags, clothes, baby powder, bibs, and bassinets. A series of novels now accompanied the American Girls collection, a set of six books about each character. Similarly, the New Baby dolls came with a pop-up book and a collection of toddler clothes to match the dolls' clothes.

As the company grew, it needed more professional staff. Rowland hired an executive away from Land's End, another successful Wisconsin mail-order firm, and lured a marketing specialist from Miller Brewing. Rowland also hired manufacturing directors who were skilled at dealing with firms in Asia, where most of the accessories were made. Yet Rowland herself kept a firm grip on the creative aspect of the business. She hired

authors to produce the novels about the American Girl characters, yet they apparently wrote them in close accordance with Rowland's ideas. Her vision was central to the corporation, and she was uncompromising regarding quality. The American Girl novels, she explained in an interview with *Milwaukee* magazine in July 1991, were to celebrate "family, hard work, honesty, courage, reliability and responsibility." In other words, a strong ethical message accompanied the dolls, and this carried through to every aspect of their production. They were packaged in an eco-friendly, water-soluble packaging, and Rowland herself had been known to take employees into her home for extended hand-sewing sessions when accessories were behind schedule. The doll accessories were exceedingly detailed and always thoroughly researched. For example, each of the dolls had a lunch box and miniature lunch, with different foods exemplifying what would have been typical for the doll's putative time period and social station. As an accessory to an accessory, one doll's picnic lunch could be accompanied by six plastic ants.

By 1991, after only five years in business, Pleasant Company's sales were nearly $50 million. The American Girl line added a new doll, Felicity, a girl living just before the American Revolution. She debuted at Colonial Williamsburg, the site that first inspired Rowland to manufacture historical dolls. Felicity's unveiling was attended by more than 10,000 people, despite pricey tickets of $30 for children, $50 for adults. Two years later the company launched Addy, its first African-American doll. Addy was a slave who escaped to freedom in Philadelphia in 1864. She had been in development for more than three years, and the company was aided by a panel of seven African-American scholars. Giving Pleasant perhaps its first bout of negative publicity, two of the illustrators for the Addy books resigned in anger before the product was finished, claiming that the company wanted to change their pictures to make the slaves look happier and better-fed. Despite this unpleasantness, Addy debuted to crowds even greater than those for Felicity, drawing 15,000 girls across the country to bookstores and libraries where special events heralded the new doll.

Pleasant's product was a hit, seemingly secure in the niche it had created. Now managing future growth was the problem. The greatest pitfall of the toy industry is that big hits often become passé after a few years, and successful companies end up bankrupt. Pleasant Company decided to expand by extending its publishing business. In 1992 the company began putting out *American Girl* magazine. This was geared to girls aged 7 to 12 and featured fiction and nonfiction about girls in different historical periods, as well as feature articles on current topics, and craft ideas and paper dolls. The magazine was not as closely tied to the doll line as the novels about Kirsten and her cohorts and was meant to be a "celebration of girlhood," according to Rowland. Within two years the magazine had 350,000 subscribers.

In 1994 Pleasant Company launched another publishing venture, a grade-school curriculum unit called America at School based on five American Girls books. The curriculum package included books based on the school experiences of the American Girls dolls, a teacher's guide and activity cards, historical maps, and the option to rent or buy the American Girls dolls and their school-related accessories such as miniature desks and books. The unit was intended to boost language arts and social studies skills for third-to-fifth graders and show that girls had a significant place in history. This was the first time that American Girls products were aimed at boys, who would be naturally part of a class using the curriculum. Pleasant also brought out a new line of activity books for sale in bookstores and museums. This American Girls Pastimes collection featured a cookbook, a craft book, a paper doll book, and theater kit for each of five American Girl characters.

The next year the company brought out two new products. The American Girl of Today collection featured contemporary dolls, and Bitty Baby was a new collection of realistic baby dolls. A set of books also accompanied the American Girl of Today collection, similar to the historical novels but about girls in the United States in the 1990s.

After Ten Years

By its tenth anniversary Pleasant Company was among the top ten children's magazine publishers in the country, with 660,000 paid subscribers to *American Girl.* The company sought to bring history to life through its doll characters in a new way that year, beginning museum tours led by the fictional girls. Felicity led a tour of Colonial Williamsburg, and the pioneer girl Kirsten led a tour of Gammelgården in Scandia, Minnesota.

From the museum tours it was just a short step to envision a retail store/entertainment center that would bring Pleasant's products to life. The company designed an ambitious space on Chicago's fashionable downtown Miracle Mile, combining a restaurant, a theater, and a store for dolls, clothes, books, and accessories. When American Girl Place opened in November, 1998, it proved to be as meticulously detailed as the dolls themselves. The fine china in the café matched the wallpaper, and the café chairs held doll-sized booster seats so girls could lunch comfortably with their mute companions. The theater was sized for girls and meant to be unintimidating. Exhibits of the historical dolls with all of their paraphernalia were sealed museumlike behind glass. It was the only place in the country where the entire historical collection was displayed, and the only place the dolls could be bought retail. Boutiques in the three-story building also offered American Girl Gear, the clothing line for girls that matched the dolls' outfits, and a bookstore for all of the various Pleasant Company publications.

Acquisition in 1998

Founder Pleasant Rowland claimed to have had the idea for American Girl Place for 13 years, that is, since she began the company. But shortly before the lavish retail space opened, she did something no one had foreseen. On June 15, 1998 Rowland announced the sale of her company to Mattel Inc. for $700 million. Mattel, the world's largest toy company, with revenues of close to $5 billion at the time of the acquisition, was the maker of Barbie, the antithesis of the American Girl line. In part it was Rowland's horror at Barbie that led her to develop her dolls in the first place. Barbie was a cheap mass market product available in toy stores across the globe, an icon of femininity, whose fantasy accessories had little in common with the detailed and realistic historical frills that accompanied the American Girls dolls. Pleasant Company's products had been surrounded from the beginning by the halo of education and ethics, especially pronounced in the family values promoted by the American Girl books. Barbie and Mattel shared little of that. Mattel believed that it had a lot to learn from Pleasant Company's success, however, and wanted to embark on direct marketing and in publishing books about its brand-name toys. So although the fit of Pleasant with Mattel seemed unlikely from the smaller company's perspective, it made good sense to Mattel. Pleasant Rowland was to become a vice-chairman of Mattel, and the company would remain in Middleton, with no announced changes in its marketing strategy or goals.

Further Reading

Alexander, Suzanne, "Doll Line Is History—and a Pleasant Hit," *Wall Street Journal,* August 22, 1991, p. B1.
Allen, Hayward, "Pleasant Rowland," *Wisconsin Trails,* January/February 1990, p. 46.
"The American Girls Put the Past in Pastime," *Publisher's Weekly,* August 8, 1994, p. 35.
Bannon, Lisa, " 'Hi, Barbie! I'm Samantha. Can I Boost Your Sales?,' " *Wall Street Journal,* June 16, 1998, p. B1.
Conroy, Mary, "Doll Firm Comes Long Way After Starting with 3 Workers," *Capital Times* (Madison, Wis.), May 19, 1990.
Ivey, Mike, "Mattel Buys Pleasant Co. for $700 Million," *Capital Times* (Madison, Wis.), June 15, 1998, p. 1A.
Moore, Todd, "Unpleasantries at Pleasant Co.," *Capital Times* (Madison, Wis.), September 16, 1993, p. 1A.
"Pleasant Dreams," *Milwaukee,* July 1991, p. 29.
Weintraub, Joanne, "Dolls Provide a Creative Alternative," *Milwaukee Journal,* November 23, 1986, p. 1G.

—A. Woodward

Pluma, Inc.

801 Fieldcrest Road
Eden, North Carolina 27288
U.S.A.
(336) 635-4000
Fax: (336) 635-3488
Web site: http://www.plumainc.com

Public Company
Incorporated: 1986
Employees: 2,400
Sales: $134.6 million (1997)
Stock Exchanges: New York
Ticker Symbol: PLU
SICs: 2253 Knit Outerwear Mills; 2329 Men's & Boys'
    Clothing, Not Elsewhere Classified; 2339 Women's
    Misses & Juniors' Outerwear, Not Elsewhere
    Classified; 5136 Men's and Boys' Clothing &
    Furnishings; 5137 Women's, Children's & Infants'
    Clothing & Accessories; 5699 Miscellaneous Apparel
    & Accessory Stores

Pluma, Inc. is a vertically integrated manufacturer and distributor of high-quality fleece and jersey activewear, selling its products under its own brand names to both retailers and wholesalers. In addition, it sells to screen printers and embroiderers who sell the company's products to a wide variety of retailers. The company name is derived from the Latin word for fleece.

Mid-1980s Founding

Pluma was founded in Eden, North Carolina, in 1986 by R. Duke Ferrell, Jr., George Wade, G. Walker Box, C. Monroe Light, and two other executives at Bassett Walker, Inc., a fleece manufacturer based in Martinsville, Virginia, that was acquired by VF Corp. in 1984. Pluma's beginnings were reportedly so modest that Wade—the company's first president and chief executive officer—and two others shared an office and a telephone dropped from the second-floor window each morning

and pulled up each evening. The company's original product was fleece sweatsuits made with heavier fabrics in order to tap a high-end market that most large manufacturers had ignored.

Pluma posted annual profits from its inception and had sales of about $60 million in 1989. The company added heavyweight cotton jersey products suitable for outerwear in 1990 in order to diversify its product mix and use its manufacturing base more efficiently. By 1992, Pluma had revenues of $83.6 million, net income of $4.8 million, was employing 1,500 people, and had six plants to do its knitting, dyeing, cutting, and sewing. Most of its customers during this time were screen printers who put college and athletic-team logos on its clothing and sold the goods to university bookstores and department stores. Ferrell succeeded Wade as president of the company in 1992 and as chief executive officer in 1993.

Pluma's annual revenues increased each year, passing the $100 million mark in 1995. Net income was more variable, falling to $3.8 million in 1993, rising to $4.3 million in 1994, but then dropping to $1.1 million in 1995. The latter figure excluded a $2 million charge to bring the company's sales and marketing in-house and a $3.3 million writeoff for doubtful accounts. At the close of the year Pluma purchased Box & Co., which had been its first exclusive sales agent. G. Walker Box then became chairman of Pluma's board. In 1996 revenues surged to $127.8 million and net income to a record $5.8 million. Fleece accounted for 63 percent of sales and jersey for 37 percent.

Public Offering in the Mid-1990s

Pluma went public in February 1997, marketing 2.5 million shares of common stock (about 32 percent of the total) at $12 a share. In addition, existing shareholders sold another 600,000 shares. The nearly $30 million raised by the company from the sale was applied to reduce its outstanding debt, which had reached $43.6 million at the end of 1996 under a revolving credit facility.

In its preliminary prospectus, Pluma revealed that it was selling its activewear to such major branded sports companies as Adidas, Nike, and Starter, and also to such entertainment firms as Walt Disney, Busch Gardens, and Hard Rock Cafe. It was also marketing its products under its own Pluma, Santee, and Snowbank labels to such retailers as Sam's Club, a division of Wal-Mart Stores. Other customers included wholesale distributors, screen printers, and embroiderers.

During this time Pluma introduced an all-cotton fleece pique and a five-way stretch fleece in a cotton and Spandex blend. The company stated that it had made significant investments for the sake of efficiency, including upgrading knitting equipment, adding computerized monitoring and control systems for its dyeing processes, and installing new machines to improve cutting and sewing. Among its innovations was a patented tandem sewing table.

According to Pluma's prospectus, the company was competing in an activewear industry that grew to about $40 billion at retail in 1996. Major competitors were said to include diversified companies such as Fruit of the Loom, Inc., VF Corp., and Sara Lee Corp., and fleecewear specialties such as Oneita Industries, Russell Corp., and Tultex Corp. Pluma attributed the growth of activewear to increased fitness and the "casualization of America," which had led to an increased acceptance of fleece and jersey products.

The company listed as another asset what it described as "The versatility of fleece and jersey fabric," which "coupled with technological advances in product development and manufacturing, has significantly improved product design and quality, resulting in increased consumer demand." It observed that the basic styles of fleece and jersey activewear are not "primarily driven by fashion trends or fads, contributing to the stability of product demand."

Just before the end of 1997, Pluma announced it had completed the acquisition of substantially all of the assets of Frank L. Robinson Co., a Los Angeles-based wholesale distributor. Founded in 1936, this company was operating two facilities in California and in 1996 posted revenues of about $48 million while serving more than 3,000 customers. At this time Pluma also acquired Stardust Corp., a wholesale distributor founded in 1988 and based in Verona, Wisconsin. Stardust was serving more than 6,000 customers in the apparel industry and had revenues of about $64 million in 1996. This purchase of two former customers, at a cost of $68 million, enabled Pluma to make strides toward a national distribution network and thereby bring the company closer to the ultimate consumer—the retail customer.

Also in 1997, Pluma became a partner with a Mexican corporation in a joint venture located in Aguascalientes, Mex-

ico, which began sewing a small portion of its products. During the year Pluma also contracted with four independent Mexican contractors to sew some of its goods.

Pluma reported revenues of $134.6 million for 1997 but net income of only $2 million, partly because switching to the new computer system had caused production interruptions. Management also relocated some operations, delaying shipments as much as six weeks. The company lost money during the first half of 1998, shipping fewer goods than usual to its acquired distributors in order to reduce inventory and taking a $1.6 million charge. It also lost money in the third quarter, increasing its loss during the first nine months of the year to $5.3 million, even though sales had increased by 46 percent to $144.9 million. After reaching a high of $16.50 a share at mid-year 1997, Pluma's stock skidded to about $7 a share in early 1998 and dropped below $1 a share at times later in the year.

The company expected to save on labor costs by establishing another joint venture in Mexico with a company that would sew some of its goods in Mexico's state of Chihuahua. Pluma anticipated that it might have up to 30 percent of its products sewn in Mexico in 1998. It was also pursuing the possibility of having another 20 percent of its goods sewn in Honduras. In October 1998 Pluma said it had initiated several cost-cutting measures, including eliminating more than 11 percent of its approximately 850 non-manufacturing employees, or about four percent of its total employees. The staff reductions, as well as planned salary cuts for senior company executives, were expected to reduce annual expenses by about $2.4 million.

Securities analysts generally agreed with the company that many of Pluma's problems were only temporary. One industry observer expressed her confidence in the company's long-term outlook once the computer system was fully installed. However, she also noted, "It's difficult to totally maintain your profit and margins when you have someone like Fruit of the Loom consistently cutting prices."

Products and Facilities in the Late 1990s

Pluma's fleece products in 1997 included various styles, colors, and weights of tops and bottoms in all-cotton and varying blends of cotton and polyester. The company also was manufacturing all-cotton jersey tops and bottoms designed for outerwear in two different weights. Fleece products accounted for 61 percent of Pluma's sales in 1997 and jersey products for the remaining 39 percent. Jersey products generally were cheaper and generated lower profit margins than fleece. The company was selling products under its own Pluma, Santee, and Snowbank brand names to retail and wholesale customers.

Pluma's fleece products in 1997 included a variety of styles and colors of tops and bottoms on 7½-, 9-, 10-, and 11-ounce weights in cotton/polyester blends starting at half-cotton/half-polyester and progressing to all-cotton. Pluma also manufactured 5½- and 7-ounce all-jersey tops and bottoms designed for outerwear. The company cited these advantages, relative to the products of most of its competitors: fleece and jersey tops fuller cut and heavier weight; higher-stitch-count fabrics to reduce shrinkage, provide a better printing surface, and increase softness; air-jet spun yarn for its half-cotton, half-polyester fleece fabric, in order to prevent pilling; Spandex to retain shape for all the company's ribbed fabrics; greater detail in its sewing processes to enhance durability and appearance; and advanced finishing techniques, including the application of softeners and napping (brushing), to give its fleece fabrics more bulk and softer texture.

Branded accounts constituted 23 percent of Pluma's net sales in 1997. These accounts consisted of customers such as Adidas and Starter and required the company to meet exact specifications of manufacturing, such as styling, color, screen printing, and embroidery. Retail customers were responsible for 41 percent of net sales. Pluma's main customer in 1997 was Sam's Club, which marketed and sold Pluma-labeled products and accounted for 31 percent of the company's net sales. Other retail customers included Miller's Outpost, which sold its own private-label products manufactured by Pluma or products with Pluma's Santee label. Pluma also granted a license to Kayser Roth Corp., allowing it to manufacture and distribute socks to Sam's Club under the Pluma brand name.

Branded and retail customers generated higher gross margins for the company than its other customers, screen printers and embroiderers (11 percent in 1997), wholesale distributors (17 percent), and entertainment (eight percent). Screen printers and embroiderers such as Endless Design and Embroidery Services were typically purchasing basic products from Pluma to which they added design and logos and then resold these products to a wide variety of retailers, ranging from small souvenir and resort stores to large nationwide department stores.

Wholesale distributors such as Skyline and Alpha, in addition to Pluma-acquired Robinson and Stardust, generally purchased the company's goods in large volume for further distribution to companies such as Guess? as well as to small companies typically more difficult for Pluma to service. All products sold to wholesale customers contained Pluma's Santee label. Entertainment accounts included customers such as Walt Disney, Busch Gardens, and Hard Rock Cafe. These clients demanded a basic product on which designs were printed or embroidered for souvenir sales.

Pluma's main factory was in Eden, where it had machinery for circular knitting, pressured dyeing, finishing, and cutting. Sewing of preassembled parts was being performed in Eden and also in company facilities in Altavista, Chatham, Martinsville, Rocky Mount, and Vesta, Virginia. In addition, some 15 percent of Pluma's products were being sewn by independent contractors in 1997. Packaging and distribution were being performed in Martinsville.

G. Walker Box was Pluma's largest stockholder in early 1998, with nearly ten percent of the shares. Other stockholders with more than five percent of the shares included Ferrell, Wade, and a Goldman, Sachs & Co. partnership. Pluma's long-term debt was $40 million at the end of 1997.

Further Reading

Brady, Jennifer L., "Pluma: Going for an IPO," *WWD/Women's Wear Daily,* February 24, 1997, p. 34.

Eldridge, Lisa, "At the Top of Their Form," *Business North Carolina,* July 1990, p. 17.

Gibson, Dale, "Will Pluma Get Fleeced in a Tough Market?" *Business North Carolina,* September 1998, p. 22+.

Nelson, Luann, "Leading by Taking Orders," *Business North Carolina,* June 1992, p. 26+.

"Pluma Reports Loss of $2.7 Million in Third Quarter as Sales Rose 40.1%," *WWD/Women's Wear Daily,* November 3, 1998, p. 23.

Truitt, Forrest H. II, "Pluma Acquires Frank L. Robinson Co.," *Business Wire,* December 30, 1997.

—Robert Halasz

Powerhouse Technologies, Inc.

2311 South 7th Avenue
Bozeman, Montana 59715
U.S.A.
(406) 585-6617
Fax: (406) 585-6609
Web site: http://www.pwrh.com

Public Company
Incorporated: 1991 as Video Lottery Technologies, Inc.
Employees: 830
Sales: $201.2 million (1998)
Stock Exchanges: NASDAQ
Ticker Symbol: PWRH
SICs: 3999 Manufacturing Industries; 7372 Prepackaged
    Software; 6719 Holding Companies

Powerhouse Technologies, Inc. is a leader in the development, manufacture, marketing and operation of gaming and wagering systems in the on-line lottery, video lottery, casino gaming, and pari-mutuel wagering markets. Video lottery operations include video terminals on which games such as poker, blackjack, bingo and keno can be played. The company designs and produces on-line computer systems for state lotteries, and places their gaming machines in casinos, riverboat gambling operations, and Native American gaming locations. The company also owns and operates a racetrack in Sunland Park, New Mexico. Powerhouse operates its business through four wholly owned subsidiaries, Automated Wagering International, Inc. (AWI), Video Lottery Consultants, Inc. (VLC), United Wagering Systems (UWS)—more commonly known by the trade name of its principal subsidiary, United Tote—and Sunland Park.

The Early Years

The roots of Powerhouse Technologies, Inc. can be traced to an earlier company called Video Lottery Technologies, Inc. This company was incorporated in 1991 as a holding company for six corporations that had previously been under the control of numerous individuals, including Larry Lippon. VLC, the principal operating subsidiary of the new entity, was a producer and marketer of video lottery terminals and the central control system software. VLC had been incorporated in 1985, but did not achieve profitability until 1988. The other operating subsidiaries that were combined to form Video Lottery Technologies were Raven's D & R Music, Inc., Automatic Music Service of Billings, Inc., Automation First, Inc., Lucky Lady, Inc., and Piper Lance, Inc. Automation First, Inc., operated three coin-operated machine routes in Montana; Lucky Lady, Inc. operated two video-lottery-licensed food and beverage establishments in Montana; and Piper Lance, Inc. owned and operated an airplane that was used by the other subsidiaries on a rental basis.

The new holding company was reorganized just prior to the initial public offering, as it acquired certain assets and all of the outstanding common stock of the subsidiaries, which until that time had been held by 15 different individuals. After the offering, the new entity's chief executive officer, Larry Lippon, owned 39.1 percent of the company. The company's president, Richard Barber, owned 9.7 percent, and another 10.9 percent was owned by other company executives who had joined together in a resolve to discourage future takeovers by outsiders. Proceeds of the offering were used to repay the debt incurred when acquiring the subsidiaries, to repay indebtedness to banks and certain other individuals, and to finance expansion of their principal facility.

The Background of Lotteries Prior to the 1990s

Historically, most lottery systems have been operated by state, local, and foreign governmental authorities. In the United States, lottery revenues are often designated by each individual state for particular purposes: education, aid to the elderly, economic development, conservation, and so on. While only two states were authorizing traditional lotteries in 1970, that number had grown to 32 states and the District of Columbia by 1990—and the growth of lottery operations continued to accelerate. Accounting for the rise in overall gross consumer spending in the gaming industry (including all forms of legal gaming, such as horse races, casinos, bingo, lotteries, etc.) were increases in the number of gaming jurisdictions, as well as increases in

Company Perspectives:

These guiding principles reflect the quality and integrity of Powerhouse's products, services and people, and are critical to the realization of the Company's business vision: Our customers are our priority; Our purpose is to produce above average returns for our shareholders through long-term earnings growth; We provide innovative technology, quality products, and responsive service to our customers; We produce value for our customers and receive fair compensation for that value; We help our people by providing growth opportunities, a team environment, and fair compensation; We take pride in honoring our commitments and 'doing what we say we will do'; We are professional and maintain the highest level of ethics; We plan carefully and do it right the first time; We are positive, yet direct and candid in all our communications; We bring power and energy to everything we do.

spending on existing gaming, which rose to $247 billion by 1989. By 1991, governments in 88 countries had authorized traditional lotteries, including lotto, numbers, and keno—all of which typically create nontax revenues.

The relatively new idea of video lottery came into being in Montana, South Dakota, and three Canadian provinces as a means of generating new sources of gaming revenues. Video lottery used video terminals to provide low-stakes entertainment gaming without increasing general taxation. Video lottery terminals have been used as part of a government-run central control system, as well as on a stand-alone basis. One of the subsidiaries of Video Lottery Technologies—VLC—designed terminals connected to a jurisdiction-wide control system in South Dakota, Newfoundland, Nova Scotia, and New Brunswick. The system was monitored by a central computer using telephonic communications; for example, in Montana, terminals internally recorded net revenues, and owners at each location were required to report amounts to authorities for taxation.

Innovations in the Early 1990s

The success of the terminals that VLC had designed to connect to a central control system within one jurisdiction prompted its new parent company to design and install a multi-jurisdictional control system for video lottery. Within the industry, Video Lottery Technologies had begun as the only company focused primarily on government-authorized video lottery operations, as opposed to traditional lottery systems, casino gaming, or other forms of video gaming. The company's ability to expand and generate greater revenues and earnings was dependent upon government approval of jurisdiction-wide video lottery operations. Through its direct sales force the company began marketing terminals and software that had been manufactured in its principal facility in Bozeman, Montana. The products were sold to independent operators of coin-operated amusement machines in Montana, South Dakota and New Brunswick, and to the government-operated Atlantic Lottery Commission in Newfoundland and Nova Scotia. The control

system software was designed to run on any model or multi-module configuration of the IBM System/88 family of mainframe computers.

In addition to obtaining revenues from the granting of their software licenses, use of software, maintenance, and installation services, as well as the sale of video terminals, three of the company's subsidiaries sold amusement machines such as pinball machines, pool tables, CD players, and jukeboxes. Certain subsidiaries also operated licensed food and beverage establishments in Billings, Montana—in locations that also operated their video lottery terminals. These locations served as testing grounds for new equipment and software concepts.

Changes within the industry in the early to mid-1990s prompted Video Lottery Technologies to create a strategic planning committee for the purpose of considering alternative opportunities and to formulate a long-term strategic plan. Mark Spagnolo, who had served on the company's board of directors and as the designee for Electronic Data Systems Corp., was appointed as the new CEO.

Soon thereafter, the company introduced its new release of the MasterLink advanced on-line lottery central control system to the Delaware Lottery. The company also released the new Ovation terminals for lotteries in Delaware and Minnesota.

Challenges in the Mid-1990s

Beginning in 1994, profits at Video Lottery began to slide. Total revenues had increased from $174.6 million in 1993 to $188.8 million in 1994, bolstered by the acquisition of the UWS subsidiary and an increase in video lottery gaming revenues. However, the company's ensuing revenue declines were attributed to a "poor reputation for customer service, high management turnover and quarter-after-quarter losses," according to a March 6, 1998 *Investor's Business Daily*.

In response, the company began to pursue new state contracts. In 1995, Video Lottery Technologies reported that it was awarded a contract to lease 600 additional lottery terminals to the Oregon Lottery; a preliminary award of a five-year on-line lottery services contract with the Arizona lottery to the AWI subsidiary; and a recommendation from the Nevada State Gaming Control Board to the Nevada Gaming Commission for the approval of a license for the manufacture and distribution of gaming devices and operation of a gaming route.

However, AWI's contract with the state of Arizona was canceled in 1996 due to problems related to the implementation of the on-line system. Thus, the company continued to reorganize. The addition of new subsidiaries since the company had been incorporated in 1991, and the continual shift in focus brought on by the changing demands of gaming consumers, prompted Video Lottery Technologies to change its name in 1997 to Powerhouse Technologies, Inc. The company promoted Richard Haddrill to the CEO position in June 1997, with the hope that he would lead the company out of the tough times.

One of the things Haddrill blamed for the company's three years of heavy losses was what he called "A bad marriage to Electronic Data Systems (EDS), which had been our technology partner for three years," according to *Investor's Business Daily*.

The partnership and the revolving door of top executives, he explained, "resulted in an active board of directors that tried to run the company, and it's difficult to run a company by committee." Another complaint with EDS, according to Haddrill, was that customer service deteriorated greatly while they ran Powerhouse's systems.

In 1994, Video Lottery Technologies had outsourced its on-line lottery business to EDS, who had purchased 545,454 shares of Video Lottery Technologies' common stock and almost two million shares of its preferred stock. The companies had signed a ten year agreement in which EDS became responsible for providing numerous services that were primarily related to the company's AWI subsidiary. When the deterioration of services became apparent, Powerhouse moved to end the partnership, resulting in EDS's claim that Powerhouse would have to pay them a $39 million settlement. Instead, Haddrill worked out a deal that allowed Powerhouse to pay EDS back $27 million in a note payable over seven years. Part of the deal stipulated that EDS would have to give back all of the computer equipment it was using to service Powerhouse customers, plus the company stock that it owned. After the split, Powerhouse began bringing more of its operations in-house, having transferred lottery personnel and services back to AWI.

The End of the Century and Beyond

After its reorganization, the Powerhouse strategy included the further funding of its Video Lottery Consultants unit, which invented multiple casino games for the casino marketplace. Haddrill's other priorities involved growing Powerhouse's AWI unit by winning back customers that had signed on with competitors, and by pursuing new state contracts. The company focused on introducing new on-line lottery technology, beginning with the 1996 software contract for the Maryland lottery. The company positioned itself against GTECH Holdings, Inc., which held a 50 percent share of the worldwide market for lottery systems, and which competed aggressively with AWI for several contracts. AWI only held a seven percent share of the market.

Even after Powerhouse introduced four additional systems, it lost the contract to run the Texas lottery, which company officials predicted would have saved that state $80 million dollars over four years. Instead, the contract was awarded to rival GTECH Holdings. Offsetting that disappointment, however, were contracts awarded to Powerhouse by the state of Florida—one of the largest lotteries in the world—and in New Mexico, where the company was contracted to install up to 300 casino gaming machines at its Sunland Park racetrack.

Sunland Park had become another development target for Haddrill's new strategy. Although the racetrack itself had not been a very profitable venture up to that point—it had been classified as a discontinued operation in late 1995—management decided to reconsider. They reopened the venture with the expectation that gaming machine revenues would offset the racing segment.

Moreover, the company projected that its United Tote Division was capable of providing the expertise in the racing arena, which would influence the sales of gaming machines to other racetracks, as well as providing the skills to expand through initiating more gaming legislation. United Tote returned to profitability one year later, following a vote by the New Mexico legislature that allowed casino gaming at pari-mutuel racetracks including the Company's racetrack in Sunland Park. The bill allowed the operation of up to 300 video gaming machines per pari-mutuel racetrack facility for up to 12 hours per day.

Internationally, in 1997 AWI was awarded a $12 million contract for supplying a lottery system and equipment for an established Latin American lottery. Furthermore, the VLC subsidiary received a 500 machine order from the Canadian Province of Quebec, and completed installation of a control system and terminals in Norway for the Norwegian Red Cross. The VLC subsidiary was licensed in parts of South Africa, giving direct access to one of the world's largest new video lottery markets. Company reports estimated the market's potential at 45,000-70,000 machines. Permanent licenses were also granted to VLC in Nevada and New Jersey, two of the largest gaming machine markets in the United States, and the California State Lottery ordered in excess of 2,000 instant ticket validation terminals.

Meanwhile, the gaming machine segment had successfully gained approval and licenses to sell video gaming machines in numerous jurisdictions in 1996 including New Jersey, Minnesota, Wisconsin, Connecticut and Arizona. This raised the number of jurisdictions in which the company could sell gaming machines to 43. The VLC subsidiary introduced the newest version of video machines: the Winning Touch Power Series with state-of-the-art enhanced graphics, sound, and color capabilities.

In 1997, Powerhouse received the ISO-9002 certification, which is an international standard of quality covering all facets of the manufacturing process. Powerhouse began exploring the future possibility of penetration into new markets including New South Wales, Australia, and new parts of Canada and South Africa.

It remains to be seen whether AWI, Powerhouse's principal source of revenues, can remain competitive with on-line lottery giant, GTECH, which in 1997 supplied systems to 29 of the 38 U.S. on-line lottery jurisdictions and had a strong presence internationally. Subsidiary AWI's success is largely related to innovative game design and its technological advancements. In the meantime, revenues in Powerhouse's other segments have continued to rise and offer testament to the effectiveness of the most recent management team's efforts.

Principal Subsidiaries

Automated Wagering International, Inc.; Video Lottery Consultants, Inc.; United Wagering Systems, Inc.; Sunland Park.

Further Reading

Parets, Robyn Taylor, "High Stakes, New Powerhouse CEO Polishes Company's Image, Operations," *Investor's Business Daily,* March 6, 1998.

—Terri Mozzone

Premier Parks, Inc.

11501 Northeast Expressway
Oklahoma City, Oklahoma 73131
U.S.A.
(405) 475-2500
Fax: (405) 475-2555
Web site: http://www.sixflags.com

Public Company
Incorporated: 1994
Employees: 11,142
Sales: $193.9 million (1997)
Stock Exchanges: New York
Ticker Symbol: PKS
SICs: 7796 Amusement Parks

With its 1998 acquisition of Six Flags, Premier Parks, Inc. became the world's largest regional theme park and the second leading amusement park operation in the United States, Walt Disney being the first. The Oklahoma City-based company runs 31 family-oriented theme parks in the United States and Europe. Premier estimates that up to 90 percent of the country's population lives within a day's drive of one of its 17 Six Flags parks. Premier is renowned for buying struggling parks and turning them around with expansion and aggressive marketing strategies that target families. Premier's parks feature thrill rides, such as the 70 mph Mr. Freeze roller coaster, animal attractions, upscale restaurants, shows, merchandise outlets, elaborate picnic areas and kiddie attractions, and water slides. Premier amusement parks host about 40 million guests a year, and the average Six Flags visitor spends $30 to $35 at a park, including admission.

Humble Beginnings

Premier Parks originally operated as the Tierco Group, Inc., an Oklahoma-based real estate company. The company purchased the sleepy Frontier City theme park in Oklahoma City in 1982 for $1.2 million. Tierco had no intention of entering into the amusement park business, however. Company officials described Frontier City as "beat up" and "run down"; they planned to demolish the park, subdivide the land, and build a shopping center. However, given the economic downturns prompted by an oil bust in Oklahoma, developers lost interest in the idea of converting the park into a shopping center. So in 1984 Tierco hired Gary Story as general manager of Frontier City and sunk about $39 million into improving the park.

Story began his career in the amusement park business when he was 16, when he was employed to sweep park streets at St. Louis Six Flags. After ten years of service in various capacities there, including that of manager of attractions, Story worked for amusement parks in Mexico and in Australia. As the new manager of Frontier City, he would quadruple that park's attendance and revenues. Under his leadership, two new rides and a petting zoo were added to the park along with a new ticket booth, sales office, and improved food service.

In 1988, Tierco shifted its strategic direction from real estate to amusement parks. It sold much of its property during this time, which generated capital to reinvest in Frontier City. Once this reinvestment paid off in terms of increased business and profits, more capital became available, which meant further growth. Tierco purchased Oklahoma City's White Water waterpark in 1991 (the name later being changed to White Water Bay). The company realized the key to boosting a park's attendance was to add new and exciting rides and make it more attractive to families. It converted White Water's old gang slide into a dual racing slide where two two-passenger boats raced against each other and the clock. New picnic areas were added, one with a beachcomber theme, and the activity pool was converted into a pirate's cove. Eventually, Tierco added the Blue Marlin Grill, an upscale sit-down restaurant.

Tierco acquired the financially troubled Wild World in Largo, Maryland, in 1992 and later changed that park's name to Adventure World. With a $500,000 investment, Tierco expanded Wild World's kiddie section and remodeled its buildings to give the park a tropical look and feel. Story was promoted to executive vice-president after the purchase of Wild World. In 1994, he was promoted again to president and chief operating officer (COO).

Since Tierco was on its way to becoming a "premier" regional theme park operator, in 1994 it changed its name to

Premier Parks, Inc. Kieran E. Burke, chairman and chief executive officer (CEO), noted that the new name signified the beginning of a new era for the company. "We hope to acquire several more parks in the next few years and perhaps expand into other areas of the entertainment business," Burke said in a December 12, 1994 article in *Amusement Business*.

A Decade of Growth

During the next few years, Premier picked up speed. The company acquired the following three parks in 1995 from Funtime Parks, Inc.: Geauga Lake in Cleveland, Ohio; Wyandot Lake in Columbus, Ohio; and Darien Lake, near Buffalo, New York. In 1996 Premier added the following parks to its portfolio: Elitch Gardens in Denver, Colorado; Waterworld USA waterparks in Sacramento and Concord, California; and Great Escape and Splashwater Kingdom at Lake George, New York.

Premier went public in 1996 and raised nearly $70 million through an initial offering at $18 a share. The company planned to use the money to expand its ten parks and acquire new ones. In 1997, Premier purchased Riverside Park, near Boston; Kentucky Kingdom, in Louisville, Kentucky; and Marine World, near San Francisco. A second public offering at $29 a share raised an additional two million dollars. Nearly 8.8 million people visited Premier's parks in 1996, making it the second largest chain in the world by attendance.

Burke explained the company's success in the February 24, 1997 issue of *Amusement Business*: "We built a strong base with Frontier City in the 1980s, and based on that, we were able to raise $50 million in private equity to acquire our first three parks." Burke said that the success of Premier's first three parks propelled it into its public offering, which raised the capital the company needed to purchase the additional parks.

In December 1997, Premier entered a definitive agreement to purchase Walibi Family Parks in Europe. Walibi owned three parks in France, two in Belgium, and one in the Netherlands. The transaction was valued at $140 million for all six parks. After the acquisition of the Walibi parks, Premier controlled 20 parks with a combined 1997 attendance of approximately 14.5 million and became the third largest regional theme park in the world.

The 1998 Purchase of Six Flags

In 1998 Premier purchased the 12-park Six Flags chain from Times Warner and Boston Ventures. The $1.9 billion purchase was the largest acquisition in amusement park history. Forty-nine percent of Six Flags was owned by Times Warner and 51 percent by Boston Ventures, a private investment firm. Premier agreed to assume a daunting $890 million in debt to purchase the parks. Amusement park officials were stunned by the purchase and referred to Premier's move as "bold" and "gutsy." Some worried Premier had grown too large too fast and wondered whether the company could generate enough profits to cover its debt.

With the Six Flags parks in its possession, Premier was the largest regional theme park chain in the world and the second largest amusement park operator in the United States. The acquisition was considered second in industry importance only to the opening of Disneyland in 1955, an event that redefined the future of the amusement park industry. Premier's attendance base was nearly 40 million in 1997—Disney's was 86 million.

As part of the Six Flags transaction, Premier received a long-term licensing agreement giving it exclusive theme park rights in the United States and Canada for all Warner Brothers and DC comics animated cartoons and comic book characters, including Bugs Bunny, Batman, Superman, Daffy Duck, and the Looney Toons characters. The company also owned the worldwide rights to the Six Flags moniker—the most recognized theme park brand name in the world next to Disney. Premier officials felt the Six Flags name was the common thread that would unite all of its parks together. Premier converted Kentucky Kingdom to a Six Flags park in June 1998, as well as four more parks in 1999: Six Flags Marine World, Six Flags Elitch Gardens, Six Flags Darien Lake, and Six Flags America, formerly Adventure World. Any park without Six Flags as part of its name was designated "Six Flags Properties." The company hoped to covert more parks to Six Flags in the future. "It has been proven that the addition of the Six Flags name helps grow business," Story told *Amusement Business* in November 1998. Management decided to keep Premier Parks as the company's legal name, however, and to trade the company's stocks under Premier Parks (PKS) on the New York Stock Exchange.

Although Premier's value was rocketing skyward, its journey was not without a few twists and turns. A few months after the purchase of Six Flags, rumors spread that the company's cash flow for the parks was below expectations, and Premier's stock tumbled 35 percent. Premier executives referred to the stock drop as a "huge overreaction" and pointed out that the original 13 Premier Parks were exceeding expectations. They claimed that the problems with the Six Flags Parks were a result of missteps made by previous management. Prior to its acquisition by Premier, Six Flags had started to languish as part of a conglomerate. According to the 1997 year-end issue of *Amusement Business*, only two of the nine Six Flags amusement parks had an attendance increase from 1996. Premier believed that a lack of capital growth had stagnated Six Flags and the company had mistakenly targeted most of its advertising toward teens when it should have focused on families. "We know in this business, mothers tend to be the gatekeepers for seven out of ten of our visitors," Story said in an article in the *Fort Worth Star-Telegram*. In response, Premier redesigned the Six Flags marketing strategy so that its ads also targeted women aged 18 to 49.

To remedy the troubles at Six Flags, Premier planned to cut costs and expand and improve its new parks. The company shut down Six Flags' Parsippany, New Jersey, headquarters, eliminating 450 full-time positions. Premier has only 35 employees at the corporate level, most of them at its headquarters in Oklahoma City. Known as a lean corporation with a risk-taking mentality, Premier's small but efficient corporate staff believed that the company's trim managerial structure, with only a few levels of management, helped streamline communication between upper management and consumers. Premier also cut staff at the park level. Since amusement parks are seasonal, management did not see the need for a large, year-round staff.

In 1999, Premier announced that it was going to invest $200 million in improvements for its 25 domestic parks. Some of the beneficiaries included Six Flags Great Adventure in Jackson, New Jersey; Six Flags Fiesta Texas in San Antonio, Texas; Six Flags St. Louis; and Six Flags Over Texas in Dallas. The largest expansions took place at Six Flags Great Adventure. Its $42 million in renovations there represented the largest single-year investment ever made at the park. The addition of 25 new rides increased the number of rides at the park by 50 percent. "We declare war on lines. Our guests will have more rides to ride and, with the increased capacity, they will be able to more fully enjoy the Park's extensive entertainment presentation. The scope of the overall expansion is nothing short of spectacular," Burke commented in a 1999 press release. Premier unveiled "Medusa, the world's first "floorless" roller coaster, at Six Flags Great Adventure in 1999. The high-intensity thrill attraction was a giant "supercoaster" that plunged through twists, turns, and sudden drops at over 60 mph. Unlike traditional roller coasters in which passengers ride above or below the track, riders on Medusa were suspended between tracks with nothing above or below them. With the addition of Medusa, Six Flags Great Adventure had 13 roller coasters, more than any other park on the East Coast.

Hurricane Harbor, in Fort Worth, Texas, also underwent substantial renovations to create a haven for families at the park. Premier spent $3 million on a massive interactive play area and a Caribbean-themed area in the largest capital investment ever at the park. The main addition for 1999 was Hook's Lagoon. The 40,000 square-foot attraction included a pirate shop, three pools, and a five-story "treehouse."

As the century drew to a close, executives at Premier were confident that the company was back on track. Premier stock ended 1998 with a 49 percent gain. Premier officials claimed that, even if the company never acquired another park, its internal growth would completely satisfy its stockholders. While Premier has grown into a world-class corporation, Story insisted the company had no intention of relocating its Oklahoma headquarters: "It's where we started. We have a great team of people from Oklahoma. It's a great community with a high quality of life. . . . There's no reason to contemplate going

anywhere else," he said, adding "I call Oklahoma the best kept secret in America."

Principal Divisions

Six Flags America; Six Flags AstroWorld and Waterworld; Six Flags Darien Lake; Six Flags Elitch Gardens; Six Flags Fiesta Texas; Six Flags Great Adventure; Six Flags Great America; Six Flags Kentucky Kingdom; Six Flags Magic Mountain and Hurricane Harbor; Six Flags Marine World; Six Flags Over Georgia; Six Flags Over Texas and Hurricane Harbor; Six Flags St. Louis; Frontier City Theme Park and White Water Bay; Geauga Lake Amusement Park; The Great Escape and Splashwater Kingdom; Riverside Theme Park; Waterworld USA; Wyandot Lake Adventure Park; Walibi Group (Belgium; France; The Netherlands).

Further Reading

Bunyan, Clytie, "Theme Park Crossing New Frontiers," *The Sunday Oklahoman,* April 26, 1998.
O'Brien, Tim, "Industry Stunned, Excited About Premier Move," *Amusement Business,* February 16, 1998, p. 2.
——, "Premier Converts More to Six Flags," *Amusement Business,* November 2, 1998, p. 1.
——, "Premier Planning Growth Through Park Acquisitions," *Amusement Business,* December 12, 1994, p. 1.
——, "Rapid Growth of Premier Spurred by Successful Public Stock Offerings," *Amusement Business,* February 24, 1997, p. 22.
——, "Restructuring, Renaming, Renovations: Tierco Group Prepares Parks for '92," *Amusement Business,* March 23, 1002, p. 17.
——, "Six Flags Acquisition a 'Premier' Purchase," *Amusement Business,* February 16, 1998, p. 1.
——, "Six Months Later, Six Flags Parks a Sign of Merging Corporate Cultures," *Amusement Business,* November 2, 1998, p. 44.
Potts, Gregory, "Premier Parks Expands Six Flags Brand Name," *The Journal Record,* October 29, 1998.
"Premier Parks Announces Acquisition Agreement; Premier Parks to Become Majority Owner of Walibi," *Business Wire,* December 16, 1997.
"Six Flags Over Texas Announces Blockbuster 1999 Expansion Plans," *PR Newswire,* November 4, 1998, p. 6148.
West, Sandy, "Premier Parks Taking Ground from Walt Disney," *The Boulder News,* January 2, 1999.
Wood, Sean, "Hurricane Harbor Moves to Broaden Family Appeal," *The Fort Worth Star-Telegram,* December 2, 1998.
——, "Ready to Ride Premier Parks Overhauls Six Flags Parks, Management," *The Fort Worth Star-Telegram,* November 17, 1998.
——, "Six Flags to Build New Attractions at Arlington, Texas, Theme Park." *Knight-Ridder/Tribune Business News,* December 3, 1998.
"Six Flags Great Adventure Announces Historic $42 Million Expansion for '99 Season," *Business Wire,* January 20, 1999.

—Tracey Vasil Biscontini

Response Oncology, Inc.

1775 Moriah Woods Boulevard
Memphis, Tennessee 38117
U.S.A.
(901) 761-7000
Fax: (901) 763-7045

Public Company
Incorporated: 1994
Employees: 53
Sales: $101.9 million
Stock Exchanges: NASDAQ
Ticker Symbol: ROIX
SICs: 8093 Specialty Outpatient Facilities

Response Oncology, Inc. is one of the fastest growing cancer management companies in the United States. The firm has three core businesses, including the provision of highly sophisticated, state-of-the-art treatment services through a network of outpatient facilities supervised by practicing oncologists; the organization and implementation of extensive clinical research in association with leading pharmaceutical companies throughout the United States; and ownership and management of nonmedical operations of oncology practices directed by physicians. With more than 400 medical oncologists associated with Response Oncology through these various activities, the company has grown rapidly since the mid-1990s. By the summer of 1998 the company reported that its network amounted to 28 wholly owned outpatient facilities called IMPACT Centers, 15 managed programs, and nine IMPACT Centers operating as joint ventures with hospitals across the nation. With its headquarters located in Memphis, Tennessee, the company has wholly owned centers in Florida, Georgia, Indiana, Louisiana, Michigan, Minnesota, North Carolina, Missouri, New Mexico, Pennsylvania, South Carolina, Tennessee, Texas, and Virginia.

Early History

The founder and driving force behind Response Oncology, Inc. is William H. West, a practicing oncologist who devoted his life to providing more accessible advanced cancer treatments to patients throughout the United States. As the medical profession and academic research facilities made significant discoveries in the field of cancer treatment during the 1970s and 1980s, West became worried that these discoveries might be delayed in reaching both rural areas across America and practice settings that were not ready to administer such advanced cancer treatments. Moreover, West wanted to provide the same quality and level of advanced treatment to all cancer patients, not just those who were fortunate enough to be treated at urban and regional academic medical centers. The cornerstone of West's belief was that all cancer institutions, academic research facilities, medical centers, and practicing oncologists must collaborate through the sharing of research, experimental data, patient treatment results, and professional knowledge and experience. According to West, this type of close cooperation was the only way that major strides could be achieved in the clinical management and treatment of cancer.

West's vision led him to establish Response Technologies, Inc., initially operating as a wholly owned subsidiary of Seafield Capital Corporation, an investment firm that provided capital for his dream to come true. In addition to his idealism, West was a savvy entrepreneur whose desire was to provide an effective advanced cancer treatment delivery system while also reducing the ever-burgeoning costs for the treatment. After his agreement with Seafield was finalized, therefore, the ambitious doctor formed partnerships with leading cancer specialists across America to provide standardized clinical techniques that would not only increase survival rates among cancer patients but also reduce costs.

In 1989, through his partnerships West established a nationwide network of centers that provided high-dose chemotherapy to cancer patients. Along with the clinical treatment, West also developed a sophisticated cancer management infrastructure that included well-defined treatment strategies and that accurately monitored patient results. Yet West's focus on high-dose chemotherapy treatment was extremely controversial, since a large segment of both the nation's practicing oncologists and insurance companies were reluctant to embrace a treatment known for its high risk to patients and its booming costs. In addition, high-dose chemotherapy treatment was available only at the more prestigious academic medical centers and, most important, more than one out of ten patients died of complications related to the treatment during the early years of its development and implementation.

Under the direction of West, Response Technologies forged ahead in developing safer methods for high-dose chemotherapy treatment, while also paying close attention to reducing costs. Building on previous research and clinical trials conducted by numerous academic medical centers in the United States and Europe, Response Technologies implemented a method of stem cell harvest that facilitated and lessened the time of a patient's recovery from the treatment.

The newly developed treatment eschewed the extraction of bone marrow from the patient involved in the traditional method and replaced it with a chemotherapy schedule and mild drug regime that facilitated the stem cells into the patient's blood for harvesting. The next step was to extract the stem cells from the blood and then freeze them at one of the company's treatment centers. After receiving a high dose of chemotherapy, the patient's immune system then was bolstered by the infusion of his own stem cells, which immediately replaced the cells depleted by the high-dose chemotherapy treatment. This new method of treatment soon was used by the company and its practicing oncologists for patients with breast cancer, recurrent lymphoma, and a wide variety of other types of cancer.

At the same time it implemented this method of stem cell harvesting, rather than treating patients at hospital locations, Response Technologies re-engineered the delivery of high-dose chemotherapy services by providing treatment at one of the company's growing network of what were called IMPACT Centers (Implementing Advanced Cancer Treatment), which not only created a more relaxing environment for patients, since it was likely that one of the treatment facilities was located near the patient's residence, but significantly reduced costs. As his company grew, Dr. West was able to fulfill one of his dreams by assuring patients who required treatment that they would have access to the most advanced methods of treatment to date.

Growth and Development in the Early 1990s

During the early 1990s Response Technologies grew at a steady but not rapid rate, primarily due to the reluctance of many oncologists to accept wholeheartedly high-dose chemotherapy treatment as a regular option for cancer patients. That situation changed dramatically in 1995 with the publication of randomized data that justified the company's strategy of promoting high-dose chemotherapy treatment. A randomized trial for high-dose chemotherapy treatment for recurrent lymphoma was published by the *New England Journal of Medicine,* and it corroborated the company's position that its method of treatment should be the standard type of care for patients with the disease. In an unrelated randomized study on patients with multiple myeloma, originating from France and presented at a session of the American Society for Hematology, more than 50 percent of the patients in the trial survived five years when treated with high-dose chemotherapy, in contrast with 12 percent of the patients who received a standard-dose treatment.

The randomized studies and their data were interpreted by the company as a vindication of the hypothesis that high-dose chemotherapy would gain widespread acceptance both with the general public and oncology specialists across the United States. Although low-dose chemotherapy was considered standard treatment for patients with multiple myeloma, denial of high-dosage treatment by insurance companies and other payors who argued that such treatment was experimental became less common. In fact, immediately after the publication of the aforementioned randomized studies of high-dose chemotherapy, referrals of patients for this type of treatment rose dramatically during 1996. The number of women who had breast cancer and underwent high-dose chemotherapy treatment immediately after surgery increased to an all-time high.

At the beginning of 1996, having changed its name from Response Technologies, Inc. to Response Oncology, Inc., company management made a strategic decision to diversify and implement a physician practice management. This long-term management services agreement extended to all nonmedical aspects of the operations of oncology practices affiliated with the company. Under the agreement, Response Oncology was responsible for arranging facilities, providing equipment and supplies, hiring personnel, and conducting all management and financial consulting services. Starting with a nine-member oncology practice in Miami, Florida, within a short period of time the company had entered into a complete practice management services agreement with nine more oncological practices in other areas of Florida and in Knoxville, Tennessee. By the end of 1996 the company operated wholly owned centers in 13 states, managed centers in nine states, and jointly owned centers in eight states. This activity and expansion of the company's services contributed to a skyrocketing increase of revenues totaling more than $67 million at the end of fiscal 1996.

The year 1997 was the most successful yet for the company. One of the important developments was the growing attention given by pharmaceutical firms and biotechnology companies to Response Oncology's clinical research and site management program. Having already established an efficient network of physicians, research nurses, and willing patients, the company designed a system to implement clinical trials with the utmost speed and precision. During 1997 alone, more than 32 major clinical trials were conducted by the company on the behalf of pharmaceutical firms around the world, one of the most significant including the phase three trial of Leucotropin, an innovative drug used to fight cancer. An added benefit, of course, and one that enhanced the reputation of the company among its growing number of patients, was that the trials provided affiliated physicians with the ability to provide their patients earlier access to revolutionary drugs and new treatment techniques.

The expansion of the company's network of high-dose chemotherapy centers across the United States, with the added demand from oncologists and patients alike, gave further credibility to its treatment strategy. Referrals of patients for high-dose chemotherapy treatment was gaining wider and wider acceptance throughout the country. Growing rapidly, Response Oncology added a total of seven new IMPACT Centers to its burgeoning network in the year 1997, with a total of 49 centers across 25 states either owned or managed by the end of the fiscal year.

In July of 1997 most of the company's stock was made available to the general public for purchasing. The board of directors at Seafield Capital Corporation, Response Oncology's former parent company, announced its plan to distribute the firm's stock to its shareholders, which resulted in the company becoming a public entity for the first time in its short but successful life span. Response Oncology's treatment strategy and financial performance had firmly convinced Seafield's board of directors that a greater number of investors would be interested in the company.

Looking Toward the Future

Response Oncology's net revenue for the first six months of 1998 amounted to a little more than $62 million, in comparison with $50 million during the same period in 1997, an increase of 24 percent. In fact, the company experienced impressive financial success during this time, including an increase of pharmaceutical sales to physicians, an increase in practice management fees, and an increase in revenue from the IMPACT Centers.

With an innovative approach to delivering new technologies for the treatment of cancer patients in a cost-effective manner, Response Oncology is at the forefront of what might become a revolution in medical practice. Astute management and sound fiscal strategies should enable the company to remain ahead of its competition for years to come.

Further Reading

Connelly, Mary, "More Dealers Join Ford's Drive To Boost Breast Cancer Research," *Automotive News,* November 9, 1998, p. 44.

"Four Costliest Outpatient Procedures," *Hospitals & Health Networks,* September 20, 1998, p. 32.

Hudson, Teresa, "Short Stays or Short Cuts?," *Hospitals & Health Networks,* March 5, 1998, p. 36.

Lutz, Sandy, "Suit Signals Cancer Services Fight," *Modern Healthcare,* April 15, 1996, p. 24.

Snow, Charlotte, "Post-acute Progress: Outpatient, Rehab Services Experience Most Growth," *Modern Healthcare,* May 26, 1997, p. 74.

Weissenstein, Eric, "Hospitals, Congress Fight Over Outpatient PPS," *Modern Healthcare,* September 7, 1998, p. 6.

—Thomas Derdak

Riviana Foods Inc.

2777 Allan Parkway
P.O. Box 2636
Houston, Texas 77252-2141
U.S.A.
(713) 529-3251
Fax: (713) 529-1661
Web sites: http://www.carolinarice.com;
    http://www.mahatmarice.com;
    http://www.successrice.com

Public Company
Incorporated: 1986
Employees: 2,656
Sales: $450 million (1998)
Stock Exchanges: NASDAQ
Ticker Symbol: RVFD
SICs: 0112 Rice; 2044 Rice Milling; 5149 Groceries and
    Related Products; 5431 Fresh Fruits and Vegetables

Riviana Foods Inc. is the largest processor and marketer of rice products in the United States. The company buys rough or green rice from independent growers and processes it at plants located in Louisiana, Texas, Arkansas, and Tennessee. Although none of its brands of packaged rice outsells Uncle Ben's Converted brand of rice, Riviana leads the industry in total sales of rice produced for domestic consumption. Riviana's familiar brands include Mahatma, Success, Carolina, River, and WaterMaid. Under these names, Riviana sells an array of processed rice in different grains and types, including dried, instant, prepared, and brown rice. The company also provides various supermarket and grocery chains with rice under private labels and food manufacturers with bulk rice for an array of processed foods, including breakfast cereals. In addition, its foreign subsidiaries in Belgium and the United Kingdom sell rice and processed foods in Europe, while those in Central America process and sell fruits, vegetables, cookies, and fruit drinks.

Origin and Early Development: 1910–30

By 1910, American rice growers and millers faced a serious problem—a market glut created by overproduction and a price that had bottomed out. The industry was plagued by its haphazard, inefficient system of small, independent mills, which were driving milling costs up and quality down. In 1911, looking for a solution for Louisiana rice producers, a consortium of millers merged to become Louisiana State Rice Company.

The move was spearheaded by Frank A. Godchaux, Sr., the general manager of two mills in rural Louisiana. The consortium soon chartered Louisiana State Rice Milling Company of New Orleans (LSRMC), created to improve both the efficiency of the mills and the quality of their rice. It combined the assets of more than 30 of the state's 70 rice mills.

LSRMC had tough going in its early years. It was unable to eliminate depressed prices resulting from excessive production, cheap foreign competition, and a frustrating lack of domestic interest in rice as a food staple. In 1916, it reorganized as the Louisiana State Rice Milling Company, Inc. (LSRMCI), still hoping to solve the problems nagging the industry. LSRMCI combined 12 Louisiana mills, but it quickly added two mills in both Arkansas and Texas. It could not shake off the industry's doldrums, however, and struggled for several years. Its one bright point was the 1919–20 season, when it recorded a promising surplus of about $320,000. But it would not prove as successful again until the mid-1930s, despite its valiant efforts to promote its product domestically. By 1924, the company had divested several marginal and idle properties, leaving a cluster of six mills in south-central Louisiana, one in Arkansas, and a California subsidiary.

In 1925, LSRMCI also began standardizing its rice merchandising, marketing its best quality short-grain Blue Rose rice in 100 pound pockets, soon to be sold under the Water-Maid brand name. In that same year, Godchaux and some associated investors acquired a controlling interest in the company, and Godchaux's son, Frank A. Godchaux, Jr., entered the business. Over the next four years, the Godchauxs sold the California

Company Perspectives:

We are focusing on achieving meaningful improvements in profitability by: utilizing technology to improve the efficiency of our operations; exploring new ways to provide the products that today's consumers want and need; seeking joint venture partners that offer unique expertise or market position; evaluating acquisition opportunities that are a good strategic fit with our existing operations; and controlling expenses and administrative costs.

subsidiary and got their finances in good enough shape to survive the economic debacle that started in 1929.

The Depression and War Years: 1930–45

The Great Depression hit the rice industry hard. It devastated export sales, forcing American farmers and mills to hold surpluses that in turn caused prices to plummet, leaving the industry in total disarray. Under the Administration of Franklin D. Roosevelt, there were efforts to bail farmers and millers out through price supports, but many of the New Deal initiatives were delayed by legal entanglements. By 1935, the industry faced the unhappy prospect of having the largest unsold surplus in its history. The government responded by imposing a processing tax designed to curtail milling enough to stabilize the industry, but, delayed by the Supreme Court, it went into effect too late to help the industry.

Through careful management, LSRMCI fared better than many of its competitors. It survived and even prospered some during the 1930s. It managed by redoubling its marketing efforts. It also introduced the popular Mahatma brand, its name for its finest long-grain rice. But there was luck, too; unlike many other banks, LSRMCI's banks remained solvent through the bad years.

In the 1936–37 season, Frank A. Godchaux, Jr., replaced his father as president of LSRMCI and took charge of managing the company's operations. He ran into immediate difficulties the following year, when farmers held their crops with the futile hope that economic conditions at both home and abroad would improve, forcing prices up. But LSRMCI weathered this and other problems to become, by the early 1940s, the best managed operation in the industry.

World War II brought its own special problems. Both the Lend-Lease and Selective Service Acts had a negative impact on the rice industry, as did the closing of foreign markets. Unable to make solid market projections, LSRMCI had to pass up an opportunity to purchase its chief competitor, the Standard Rice Milling Company, after that company's president and principal stockholder, W.R. Morrow, died. The war convinced the Godchauxs that greater attention should be given to marketing packaged rice for household table use. It also brought a major account with Kellogg, which used LSRMCI's Water Maid rice for its famous Rice Krispies cereal.

Recovery and Merger: 1946–65

LSRMCI had serious postwar problems, including government allegations of price control and mandatory set aside violations. Competition was also picking up. In 1946, the Champion Rice Milling Company emerged, soon becoming the River Brand Rice Mills, Inc. It purchased the Southern Rice Sales Co. and several other enterprises. Southern, founded in 1911 by Julius R. Ross, had proved a troublesome marketing rival of LSRMCI since its had begun packaging and selling rice under the ''Carolina'' and ''River Brand'' names in the late 1920s. Combining that marketing ability and the milling capacity of four mills, River quickly became a major headache for LSRMCI, demanding as much attention as commodity-market fluctuations, consumer tastes, and federal regulations.

The competition spurred greater marketing efforts by LSRMCI. To promote its sales, the company put more funds into advertising, which, in the 1950s, included television spots and the publication of free recipe books that garnered national attention. In 1950, Frank A. Godchaux III joined the company and was soon named vice-president, charged with sales. He faced toughening competition, especially from Uncle Ben's Converted rice, which, thanks to its ads on the Gary Moore television show, was quickly growing in popularity. In spite of the increasing success of converted and ''minute'' rices, and America's emerging fast-food life style, LSRMCI doggedly pursued the principle that rice was an economy food and delayed marketing value-added lines.

The 1950s proved a troublesome decade for LSRMCI. It faced decreasing profit margins and stagnant sales. However, these factors did stimulate company efforts to improve its efficiency, largely through modernizing and centralizing billing and accounting operations. Some relief came in the late 1950s, when new government programs permitted commercial rice stocks to qualify for subsidies, even when exported. It was a timely measure, for in 1961, after the Castro regime came to power in Cuba, the punitive trade embargo closed one of LSRMCI's more lucrative markets.

By the early 1960s, Frank A. Godchaux III was pressing for innovations geared to America's new love affair with quick and easy foods. The company introduced Mahatma Yellow Rice, using real saffron, and sped up its research on a freeze-dried method of producing a quick-cooking rice. It was also trying to find a more effective milling method of removing rice hulls, research in which River Brand Rice Mills was also engaged. In 1964, the two companies pooled their efforts, forming Food Engineering International (FEI), a jointly-owned and financed research and development company.

By that year, almost total control of the company's day-to-day operations had passed to Frank A. Godchaux III and his brother, Charles R. Godchaux. Frank became president after his grandfather's death in 1965. Surrounded by an older management team mostly recruited by their grandfather, the younger Godchauxs grew concerned about the company's future prospects and began merger negotiations with River Brand, their FEI partner. They felt that, in tandem, the two companies could compete successfully in the domestic table-rice market then dominated by Uncle

Ben's and Minute rice brands. On September 2, 1965, through a stock-exchange arrangement, the two companies merged under the River name—later changed to Riviana Foods Inc.—with Frank A. Godchaux III as chairman of its board. Riviana soon began aggressive marketing in the convenience food market through both expansion and diversification.

Diversifying and the Colgate Merger: 1966–76

Riviana first started streamlining its operations by centering its milling and packaging facilities in Houston, Memphis, and Abbeville, Louisiana. It also looked for new export markets, especially in South Africa, where it owned Quix-Riviana Foods (Pty) Ltd. But most importantly, Riviana started acquiring other food-product companies. These included the Pangburn Company, a candy maker and marketer; the Austex Foods Division of Frito-Lay, Inc., which processed convenience-food items like tamales and chili; the Hill's Packing Company, a processor and seller of pet foods; Hebrew National Kosher Foods, a processor of meat products; the Romanoff Caviar Company, which marketed imported and domestic caviar and manufactured dehydrated, granulated instant beef and vegetable and chicken flavored products under the MBT brand name; and several small restaurant chains and delicatessens, including Trini's, a chain of Mexican food restaurants in Texas.

Riviana's expansion also necessitated organizational changes. The company soon established four operating divisions: the Grocery Products, Specialty Foods, International, and Retail Divisions. Each of these operated as a profit center with full authority over the policies of the subsidiaries under its control. All divisions prospered and grew, especially those milling and marketing rice products, the demand for which greatly escalated during the Vietnam War. The company also pursued new foreign markets. In 1970, it purchased Central American food processing and distribution properties from W.R. Grace & Co., including Pozuelo S.A. in Costa Rica and Alimentos Kern de Guatemala, S.A., producers and marketers of a wide variety of foods.

In the domestic market, diversification produced promising results, but Riviana's staple remained rice, which accounted for about 50 percent of its sales. Overall, sales between 1965 and 1970 climbed from about $30 million to almost $145 million. By 1968, Riviana's success had gained it a listing on the New York Stock Exchange. It also attracted the attention of Colgate-Palmolive Company's CEO, David R. Foster, who had begun his own campaign of aggressive diversification. In June 1976, Colgate bought Riviana by trading 1.1 shares of Colgate for each share of Riviana common, a sale amounting to about $180 million. Theoretically, Riviana was to continue as a quasi-independent division under its own management, thus Riviana viewed the merger as an opportunity for even faster growth. Reality would soon dampen those expectations.

Divestments and an End to Colgate's Ownership: 1976–86

Larger sales gains from the merger with Colgate simply failed to materialize. Both domestic and international economic problems slowed the sale of rice products, though Riviana's subsidiaries did well, particularly Hill's Pet Food, Hebrew National, and the Central American operations. In 1977, Riviana reorganized, hoping to reverse steadily declining rice sales. It created Riviana Rice USA, a new division in control of domestic rice sales and marketing, with Charles R. Godchaux as president. Frank A. Godchaux III also reorganized his division, Riviana International Inc. However, stiff competition from nonprofit farmer-owned cooperatives continued to erode the company's market share and force prices down. In 1978, Riviana attempted to gain back its lost ground by more aggressive pricing and by building a new parboil plant, strategies that worked to a very limited degree and still left Riviana struggling to maintain its financial equilibrium.

In 1979, Foster, in ill health, resigned as Colgate's CEO and chairman. Colgate then began selling off what Foster himself had called "rundown acquisitions." Over the next two years, it sold off all of Riviana's domestic subsidiaries except Hill, leaving only Hill's Pet Nutrition, Riviana Rice USA, and Riviana International intact. Then, in 1980, Riviana struck a new nadir. In ill health, the company's president and CEO resigned. While Hill's remained quite profitable, Riviana, with just a seven percent market share, was losing out to the rice cooperatives. Other problems followed. The company lost a major mill in Memphis to fire in 1983 and took a temporary market beating when national publicity argued that a long-used crop fumigant was contaminating its rice products. Facing the possibility of Colgate's selling off what remained of Riviana's holdings, the Godchauxs began organizing an investment group to purchase the company back.

In 1986, operating as Lastarmco, Inc., controlled by the Godchauxs, the investors bought all of Riviana's holdings except the Hill's subsidiary. The basic price Lastarmco paid in a complex agreement was $23.9 million. The new company was incorporated as a private company—Louisiana State Rice Milling Company, Inc. (LSRM)—and merged with Lastarmco. In 1987, its name changed to Riviana Foods Inc. The Godchaux family held about 62 percent of new company's stock, and Frank A. Godchaux III and Charles R. Godchaux served, respectively, as chairman and vice-chairman of the board of directors.

Promise and Growth: 1987–99

With net sales of $244 million and a $9.3 million profit in 1987, Riviana quickly demonstrated renewed promise. It benefitted from supportive farm legislation and the rising per capita consumption of rice in the United States, which, in 1991, at 20.5 pounds a year, was almost three times what it had been in 1961. Determined to reduce its dependency on the volatile bulk-rice commodities market, the company continued to pursue an increased share of the convenient instant rice market then dominated by General Foods. In 1988, it built a new research and development facility in Houston, and the next year opened its new Food Service Kitchen at the Houston Technical Center, where it tested food service equipment with consumer rice products. Riviana also entered a 1989 agreement with Riceland Foods, Inc., the nation's leading rice processor. Named Rivland Partnership, the joint enterprise set out to make and market rice flour from a new facility in Jonesboro and within a year was dominating that market.

There were still problems in Riviana's re-emergence as an industry leader. After four years of growth, in 1994 Riviana's net income dropped, despite an increase in sales. The company then decided to go public once again, and in December 1995 requested the SEC's permission to offer 21.6 percent of its privately-owned common stock. At the same time, Riviana's operational leadership passed to Joseph Hafner, the company's president and CEO, but the Godchauxs continued to hold a controlling interest in the company.

In 1995, Riviana's sales reached $427 million, returning the company to its projected levels of sales and profits. In fact, its net income, at $19.13 million, rocketed to 71 percent over the previous year's net. Since then, the company has had a slow but steady increase in both figures. It has also undertaken some new steps towards broadening its markets. For example, in 1997, Riviana began working with Tiger Oats Ltd. in South Africa, with plans to market value-added rice products there. Increasingly dependent on its lines of packaged rice for its profits, Riviana would continue its aggressive search for additional convenience-food markets.

Since domestic rice consumption was continuing to rise, Riviana was expected to fare well into the next century. In the United States, it sold its branded and private-label rice products to all but one of the top 20 supermarket chains in 1999. Only its Central American subsidiaries were going through an unstable period, plagued by destructive weather, economic problems, and political unrest. Hafner remained optimistic, however, confident that the region would stabilize and that Riviana would be able to use its branded-market position as a base for the introduction of new lines and upgraded packaging. Further expansion and product development should enhance Riviana's presence, both at home and abroad.

Principal Subsidiaries

Riviana International Inc., consisting of Pozuelo, S.A. (Costa Rica); Alimentos Kern de Guatemala, S.A.; Boost Distribution C.V. (Belgium); Steven & Brothers Ltd. (U.K.)

Further Reading

"Board Approves Buyback of 1 Million Shares," *The Wall Street Journal*, August 31, 1998, pp. B3, B2.

Buss, Dale, "Spilling the Beans: Better Dehydration Technologies Pave the Way for New Legions of Legumes," *Food Processing*, December 1996, p. 65.

Elder, Laura Elizabeth, "The Riceman Cometh," *Houston Business Journal*, March 8, 1996, p. 16A.

Moore, John Robert, *Grist for the Mill: An Entrepreneurial History of Louisiana State Rice Milling Company, 1911–1965, River Brand Rice Milling Company, 1946–1965, and Riviana Foods, 1965–1991*, Lafayette, La.: Center for Louisiana Studies, 1999.

Pybus, Kenneth R., "Riviana Foods Returns to Wall Street With New IPO," *Houston Business Journal*, January 6, 1995, p. 1.

—John W. Fiero

Saga Communications, Inc.

73 Kercheval Avenue
Grosse Pointe Farms, Michigan 48236
U.S.A.
(313) 886-7070
Fax: (313) 886-7150

Public Company
Incorporated: 1986
Employees: 747
Sales: $66.3 million (1997)
Stock Exchanges: American
Ticker Symbol: SGA
SICs: 4832 Radio Broadcasting Stations; 4833 Television
  Broadcasting Stations

In the Nordic language, "saga" means an ongoing adventure. According to Ed Christian, Saga Communications, Inc.'s founder, chairman, president, and CEO, "This is how I view my company and my life. Our company is really an ongoing adventure." Starting with three AM and five FM radio stations that he acquired in 1986 from Josephson International, Christian built Saga into a company that owned and operated 24 FM and 13 AM radio stations, two state radio networks, and one television station. It also had a 50 percent interest in seven FM stations in Reykjavik, Iceland, the country's capital. Saga's strategy was to acquire top-billing radio and television stations in mid-sized markets. It achieved top rankings in those markets through programming and marketing, attracting a disproportionate share of advertising dollars and becoming a dominant force in the markets in which it operated.

Founding by Ed Christian in 1986

Saga Communications was incorporated in May 1986. The company was founded by Ed Christian, who was born in 1944 in Grosse Pointe, Michigan. As a child he dreamed of becoming a radio disk jockey. In 1986 he raised $38.5 million to buy out Josephson International's radio division, which he had been running for ten years, and renamed it Saga Communications. It owned three AM and five FM radio stations.

Christian was from the small Michigan town of St. Helen's. Throughout college he worked at local radio stations in Roger City, Lansing, and Flint, both as a weekend anchor and as a salesperson. After graduating from Wayne State University in 1966 with a bachelor's degree in mass communications, he became an account executive for WCAR-AM-FM in Detroit.

After a couple of job changes and a master's degree in management from Central Michigan University, Christian decided at the age of 26 to buy a radio station in a small market. He purchased WCER-AM-FM in Charlotte, Michigan, in 1970. After three years, he sold out and made a deal with State Mutual Life Insurance Co. to run a Detroit radio station, WNIC-AM-FM, that it had repossessed. WNIC was in dire financial straits, and State Farm wanted to get it back on its feet so it could be sold. After changing the format to adult contemporary, the station started to come back. After three years it was sold to Josephson International for $4 million. Christian remained with WNIC as the station's general manager.

Marvin Josephson, head of Josephson International, wanted to build a radio division, and Christian was selected to help build the group. In 1986 Josephson decided to stop acquiring stations and sell the division. He wanted Christian to buy it, and he did. Christian, who realized he knew how to run radio stations but did not know a lot about financing them, had prepared himself by studying finance, so he was ready when Josephson wanted to sell.

Christian initially owned all of the voting stock in Saga Communications, but he made equity shares of the company available to individual station managers and key personnel in the company. He told *Broadcasting,* "The company is more of a confederacy than anything else." His philosophy was to let local managers have control of their own destiny.

Initial Public Offering: 1992

When Saga Communications announced it planned to file for an initial public offering (IPO) of stock in 1992, it owned 15 radio stations in medium-sized markets. In its filing with the Securities and Exchange Commission (SEC), it reported 1991 revenues of $25.9 million, operating income of $9.4 million, and an operating profit of $3.4 million. However, interest payments on $39.5 million of debt resulted in a pre-tax loss of $2.1 million.

The company planned to sell 2.3 million share of Class A common stock to raise $27.6 million, with net proceeds to the company of $19.8 million. CEO and chairman Ed Christian would retain control of the company through his ownership of the company's Class B stock, which had 10 times the voting rights of the Class A stock being offered. The company planned to continue to operate in medium-sized markets, or those ranked from 20th to 130th in size.

Saga made two acquisitions in the fall of 1992. It acquired WIXY-FM in Champaign, Illinois, for $250,000 in September, and WVEM-FM in Springfield, Illinois, for $1.5 million in October, bringing the total number of stations owned to 17. The acquisitions resulted in Saga owning two stations in each market.

Later in the year the company amended its SEC filing, and in December 1992 the company went public. All existing shareholders and partners in the firm exchanged their shares for either Class A or Class B common stock. On August 12, 1993, 685,000 shares of Class A stock were sold at $17.75 per share through underwriter First Boston Corporation. First Boston was a principal stockholder in the company through its Boston Ventures Limited Partnership, which also held much of Saga's debt.

New Rules on Station Ownership: 1993

Starting in 1993, the Federal Communications Commission (FCC) relaxed its rules on radio station ownership, permitting companies to own up to two AM and two FM stations in a single market as long as the collective market share controlled by the stations at the time of purchase did not exceed 25 percent. Previously, companies were limited to owning a single AM and single FM station in each market.

In May 1993 Saga Communications acquired its third radio station in Portland, Maine, with the acquisition of WYNZ-AM-FM for between $800,000 and $900,000. It already owned WGAN-AM and WMGX-FM in Portland. In November the company entered into an agreement to acquire a second station in Milwaukee, WLZR-AM-FM, for $7 million. It already owned WKLH-FM in Milwaukee. The acquisition of WLZR was completed in 1994.

For fiscal 1993 (ending December 31) Saga reported net income of $757,000 on net operating revenue of $34.6 million. Those figures reflected the 1993 acquisitions of KIOA-FM (Des

Moines, Iowa), KXTK-AM (Des Moines), WYNZ (Portland, Maine), WZAN-AM (Portland), and WQQL (Springfield, Illinois), as well as the results of a local marketing agreement for WAFX-FM of Norfolk, Virginia.

Continued Strategy of Acquisitions: 1994

In June 1994 Saga Communications entered the television market by purchasing KOAM-TV from Scarecrow Holdings for $8.55 million. The station served the Joplin, Missouri, and Pittsburg, Kansas, market. For 1994, net operating revenue increased to $44.4 million, and net income jumped to $2.3 million. Those figures reflected the 1994 acquisitions of WLZR (Milwaukee), WJYI (Milwaukee), WAFX (Norfolk), and KOAM-TV. In 1995, net operating revenue rose to $49.7 million, and net income was $2.7 million. No acquisitions were made during 1995.

Telecom Act of 1996 Affects Station Ownership

With the passage of the Telecommunications Act of 1996, companies could own as many as eight radio stations in a single market. The Telecommunications Act also lifted the limitations on the number of radio stations one organization could own in total. As a result, there was a frenzy of buying in the radio industry, as several companies sought to acquire as many stations as possible. In the process, many of them also acquired a substantial amount of debt.

Saga chose to adhere to its program of acquisitions, but it did not wish to assume a lot of debt. It proceeded cautiously, continuing to acquire top-billing stations in medium-sized markets. In February 1996 Saga entered into an agreement with Roy H. Park Broadcasting of the Midwest, Inc. to purchase WNAX-AM and WNAX-FM of Yankton, South Dakota, for $7 million. WNAX-AM was an agricultural station, and WNAX-FM was an oldies station. Both served the Sioux City, Iowa, market from their base in Yankton.

In July 1996 Saga began operating two AM and two FM radio stations serving the Springfield, Illinois, market under a local market agreement. The four stations—WTAX-AM, WDBR-FM, WVAX-AM, and WYXY-FM—were acquired by Saga on May 5, 1997, for $6 million.

Saga began operating radio station KAZR-FM serving Des Moines, Iowa, on August 1, under a local marketing agreement. Saga closed the acquisition of the station on March 14, 1997, for a purchase price of $2.7 million. During 1996 the company also acquired an additional AM and an FM station in Portland, Maine.

Net operating revenue for 1996 rose to $56.2 million, and net income increased to $3.9 million. Those figures reflected the 1996 acquisitions of WNAX-AM-FM (Yankton, South Dakota) and WPOR-AM-FM (Portland, Maine), as well as local market agreements for WDBR (Springfield, Illinois), WYXY (Springfield, Illinois), WTAX (Springfield, Illinois), WVAX (Springfield, Illinois), and KAZR (Des Moines).

Acquiring Nine More Radio Stations: 1997

Saga acquired another FM radio station in Des Moines, KLTI-FM, in April 1997 after operating the station under a local market agreement since January. The acquisition price was $3.2 million.

In March 1997 Saga acquired two more radio stations in Milwaukee, WFMR-FM and WFMI-FM, for $5 million, bringing its total to five stations in that market. WFMR-FM, which historically served the fine arts community of Milwaukee, was bought from Harris Classical Broadcasting Co. WFMI-FM was purchased from Harbish Co. Saga changed WFMI's call letters to WPNT-FM, "The Point," and changed its format. Following the acquisitions, Saga Communications owned a total of 36 radio stations.

In November 1997 Saga acquired WQLL-FM, serving Manchester, New Hampshire, for $3.4 million, after operating the station under a local market agreement since July. Saga also acquired its first statewide radio network in November when it purchased The Illinois Radio Network for $1.75 million. This regional and state news and sports information network served more than 45 stations throughout Illinois. The company planned to increase the number of affiliates to around 65 or 70 by the end of 1998.

Net revenues for 1997 increased nearly 18 percent to $66.3 million, and net income rose 15.4 percent to $4.5 million. The increase in revenues was attributed to the company's aggressive acquisitions program, which resulted in Saga buying nine radio stations in four markets during 1997.

Focusing on Medium-Sized Markets

According to 1997 rankings, Saga was operating 37 radio stations in markets ranked from 28th (Columbus, Ohio) to 232nd (Sioux City, Iowa) at the end of the year. It owned multiple stations in the following markets: four FM stations and one AM station in Milwaukee, Wisconsin, ranked 31st; two FM stations and one AM station in Norfolk, Virginia, ranked 39th; four FM stations and two AM stations in Des Moines, Iowa, ranked 67th; three FM stations and three AM stations in Portland, Maine, ranked 82nd; one FM station and one AM station in Springfield, Massachusetts, ranked 85th; four FM stations and two AM stations in Springfield, Illinois, ranked 139th; two FM stations and one AM station in Manchester, New Hampshire, ranked 140th; and two FM stations in Champaign, Illinois, ranked 165th.

The company's single television station, KOAM-TV, served the Joplin, Missouri, and Pittsburg, Kansas, market, which was ranked 146th by number of television households. It was the top-ranked station of four in the market and was a CBS affiliate.

Acquisitions Continue in 1998

Saga closed on its second network acquisition, The Michigan Radio Network, in March 1998 for a price of not more than $1.5 million subject to certain adjustments. Like The Illinois Radio Network, The Michigan Radio Network was a regional and state news and sports information network. At the time of the acquisition, it had more than 55 affiliated radio stations. Saga planned to add ten additional affiliates in 1998. Saga believed that it could acquire state radio networks at a lower multiple of cash flow than it could acquire individual radio stations. The company planned to acquire several more state radio networks in the future.

In June 1998 Saga acquired a 50 percent interest in an Icelandic Corporation, Finn Midill, ehf., that owned six FM radio stations serving Iceland's capital, Reykjavik, for $1.1 million. Saga became aware of radio opportunities in Iceland in 1997, when a group of station managers were rewarded with an Icelandic fishing trip for exceeding their budget targets. Christian himself is of Icelandic heritage, and he served as the Honorary Consul of Iceland for Michigan, Ohio, and Indiana.

Saga expanded its television station holdings in July 1998 when it entered into an agreement to purchase KAVU-TV, an ABC affiliate, and a low power Univision affiliate serving the Victoria, Texas, market for $11.9 million in cash and stock. Saga also assumed an existing local market agreement to operate KVCT-TV, a Fox affiliate in Victoria.

Saga entered a new market, Bellingham, Washington, in July 1998, when it agreed to acquire KGMI-AM and KISM-FM for $8 million. In August 1998 Saga's board of directors authorized a stock repurchase program. The company felt its stock was undervalued. On June 24 it had hit a 52-week low of $14 per share. Under the program the company intended to repurchase up to $2 million of its Class A common stock. At this point, the company owned 24 FM and 13 AM radio stations, two state radio networks, one TV station, and a 50 percent interest in seven FM stations in Reykjavik, Iceland.

Outlook Calls for More Acquisitions

At the end of 1998, Saga appeared committed to its strategy of acquiring radio and television stations in medium-sized markets. Through its ownership of multiple stations, it could achieve dominance in those markets through programming and marketing initiatives. At the same time, the company was committed to keeping its total debt at manageable levels, and it was not likely to take on substantial debt simply for the sake of acquiring more stations.

Further Reading

"Detroit Free Press Michigan Memo Column," *Knight-Ridder/Tribune Business News,* February 27, 1996.
"Detroit Free Press Michigan Memo Column," *Knight-Ridder/Tribune Business News,* August 11, 1998.
Farber, Erica, "Publisher's Profile: Ed Christian," *R & R,* August 21, 1998, p. 112.
Lilly, Stephen, "Merger Mania Grips Radio Industry," *Business First-Columbus,* November 1, 1993, p. 1.
"Saga Communications Inc., Saying Its Stock Is Undervalued, Plans to Buy Back Its Shares through Open-Market Purchase," *Broadcasting and Cable,* August 24, 1998, p. 73.
"Saga Expands in Milwaukee," *Mediaweek,* March 10, 1997, p. 26.
"The Saga of Ed Christian," *Broadcasting,* December 28, 1987, p. 87.
"Saga's Game," *Broadcasting and Cable,* March 2, 1998, p. 30.
"Transactions," *Television Digest,* June 13, 1994, p. 8.
Viles, Peter, "Saga to Make Public Offering," *Broadcasting,* May 4, 1992, p. 57.
"WLZR-AM-FM," *Billboard,* November 20, 1993, p. 78.
"WVEM(FM) Springfield, Ill., Was Sold by Daniel Menghini to Saga Communications for $1.5 Million," *Broadcasting,* October 5, 1992, p. 69.
"WYNZ-AM-FM Portland, Me., Has Been Sold," *Broadcasting and Cable,* May 10, 1993, p. 65.

—David Bianco

SAUDI ARABIAN AIRLINES
الخطوط الجوية العربية السعودية

Saudi Arabian Airlines

P.O. Box 620
Jeddah, 21231
Kingdom of Saudi Arabia
(966-2) 686-0000
Fax: (966-2) 686-4552
Web site: http://www.saudiairlines.com

State-Owned Company
Incorporated: 1945
Employees: 24,842
Sales: $4.66 billion (1997)
SICs: 4516 Air Transportation, Scheduled

Saudi Arabian Airlines (Saudia) is the national airline of the Kingdom of Saudi Arabia and the largest airline in the Middle East. It flies 12 billion passengers per year. The airline carries many observers as they make an annual pilgrimage, the hajj, to the holiest of destinations in the Muslim world. Saudia Arabian religious practice prevents the carrier from serving alcoholic beverages to passengers and also informs certain personnel policies.

1940s Origins

The origin of Saudi Arabian Airlines goes back to April 1945, when U.S. President Franklin D. Roosevelt presented a single Douglas DC-3 to King Abdul Aziz ibn Saud. This aircraft was quickly put into service to transport passengers and mail between the country's three main cities: Jeddah, Riyadh, and Dhahran. By the end of 1945 an additional four DC-3 aircraft had been purchased by the Saudi Arabian government. Under the aegis of the Saudi Ministry of Defense and utilizing the existing government equipment and personnel, Saudi Arabian Airlines was formed in September 1946. In October of the same year the first international flight took off for Jerusalem, returning via Beirut carrying pilgrims bound for Mecca. By the end of the year the first overseas office was taking bookings in Cairo.

The first of the scheduled operations using these aircraft began in 1947 with a service between Riyadh, Hofuf, Dhahran, and the summer capital, Jeddah. There also were regular international flights to Cairo, Damascus, and Beirut. By 1949 the fleet had expanded to 13 aircraft with more DC-3s and the airline's first Bristol 170 nose-loading freight aircraft.

The close relationship between Saudi Arabia and the growing American interests in the region continued in the 1950s when management and technical services for the fledgling airline were provided by Trans World Airlines (TWA) of the United States. The fleet of DC-3s was expanded in the early 1950s with the addition of ten Convair 340s, two Douglas DC-4s from the United States, and another Bristol 170 freighter from England. The fleet expansion was undertaken in response, in part, to the great demand from Islamic pilgrims wishing to travel to the two holy mosques in the Kingdom of Saudi Arabia. The early international expansion of the airline's network was dictated in large part by this demand and by the end of 1953 services operating to Amman, Jordan; Asmara, Ethiopia; Bahrain; Basra, Iraq; Istanbul, Turkey; Karachi, Pakistan; and Kuwait.

On the domestic front, the airline's role in the kingdom's economic development was significant. In a state more than five times the size of California with a population of less than ten million in the 1950s, air travel proved to be the only fast and efficient method of connecting many of the scattered and remote towns and cities. In the mid-1950s airports at the domestic centers of Madinah, Buraydah, Najran, Jizan, and Khamis Mushayt were modernized and upgraded and joined the expanding domestic network.

Saudia moved into the jet age in 1962 with the acquisition of two Boeing 720s with long-range capabilities and seating capacities of 119 passengers each. The new aircraft were put into service on the Cairo, Amman, and Beirut routes. In February 1963 a royal decree was issued by King Faisal making Saudi Arabian Airlines a legally independent, commercial entity with its own board of directors. The decree also stipulated a pattern for future growth through modernization and expansion of the airline business and through the provision of training facilities and backup services.

Going International in the 1960s

The mid-1960s saw a steady integration of the airline into the international airline community. In 1965 it joined the Arab

Company Perspectives:

Since the airline's humble beginning in 1945 with a single DC-3, finally becoming one of the world's great modern carriers, Saudi Arabian Airlines has been contributing to the country's training and development of manpower and skills and continuing development and repeated successes that can be traced to corporate dedication to the highest level of passenger service and to efficient use of state-of-the-art civil aviation technology.

Air Carriers Organization (AACO) and inaugurated a new service to Bombay the following year. In 1967 Saudi Arabian Airlines became a member of the International Air Transport Association (IATA) and inaugurated its first European service to Geneva, Frankfurt, and London. A new livery also was introduced on the fleet of airliners in 1972, and the name "Saudia" was adopted as a shorter alternative to the longer official name.

By the early 1970s Saudi Arabia was benefiting from significant economic expansion as a result of the activities of foreign oil companies in the kingdom. With the exception of the ruling sheiks, the kingdom itself was not receiving an adequate share of the profits of the massive international oil business. Following the 1973 to 1974 oil price hikes that were promoted vigorously by Saudi Arabian representation at the Organization of Petroleum Exporting Countries (OPEC), revenues from the oil business increased dramatically. Much of the new wealth was invested outside the kingdom, but a sizable proportion was invested in the domestic economy and infrastructure. This gave a further boost to Saudia's activities as demand for internal and external freight flights increased, as did the number of foreign workers entering the kingdom for short- or long-term contracts.

In 1973 Saudia carried a little more than one million passengers for the first time. By 1975 the annual number of passengers carried had risen to three million. This unprecedented increase in demand was given a further impetus in 1975 when a fare cut of 25 percent was announced by the airline for all domestic routes. To meet the new demand, the fleet expansion program was accelerated. Between the beginning of 1975 and the end of 1976, the fleet had grown through the purchase of two Fokker F-27s, five more Boeing 707s, nine Boeing 737s, and seven long-haul Lockheed Tristars.

The cargo division of Saudia was the next area to see a major expansion. In 1977 three DC-8 freighter aircraft were leased together with three more Tristars, two Boeing 707s, and two 737s, and for the first time the airline leased two Boeing 747s. The first of the kingdom's chain of new international airports in Jeddah neared completion and the contract was signed to build "Saudia City"—at 1.5 million square meters, the largest housing complex ever built by any airline for its staff.

In 1978 the high level of re-equipment and expansion continued. In that year three more Boeing 737s were purchased and an additional 747 was leased to meet demand on the long-haul

routes. The following year the airline opened the $40 million Flight Training Center in Jeddah equipped with the latest flight training equipment. This was designed to ensure that the airline's requirements for qualified crews would be met up to and beyond the year 2000.

The rapid expansion of the middle to late 1970s was not sustainable in the long term, and in 1980 a five-year development plan was announced that placed emphasis on upgrading service and ensuring a controlled expansion of about 30 percent more passengers carried each year. The plan made provision for ordering new wide-bodied aircraft: eight Boeing 747-100s, two 747-SPs, and 11 Airbus A300-600s. By the end of the five-year plan in 1985, an additional provision had been made for the purchase of ten Boeing 747-300s, five of which entered service that year.

By the end of the five-year plan, the fleet had grown to 104 mostly modern jet liners, and the total number of passengers carried had increased by more than threefold to a stable 10.8 million in 1985. Of these, about seven million were carried on domestic routes, a number significantly lower than that of the record-breaking previous year when the total stood at 11.34 million passengers.

The year 1985 was also Saudia's 40th anniversary year. Looking back over the history of his company, Captain Ahmed Mattar, Saudia's Director General, said at the time, "Throughout its history, Saudia has been committed to growth and progress, incorporating at every opportunity the latest technical developments in the highly competitive field of international air transport. There has been no time in the last 40 years when Saudia has been content to stand still."

In recognition of his contribution to Saudia and to the international airline business, the following year Captain Mattar was appointed to the executive committees of AACO and IATA. By the 40th anniversary year, Saudia had seen a great expansion in demand for its cargo services from companies in the oil, petrochemical, and associated industrial sectors for the rapid transportation of high-value industrial equipment and tools. That year saw the total weight of cargo handled increase to 165 million kilograms, an increase of more than 20 percent from the previous year.

Continuing Expansion in the 1980s

In the mid-1980s Saudia also started the implementation of cargo handling for other airlines operating flights into the kingdom. Saudia's growing cargo handling activities were boosted in 1983 with the opening of the new Saudi Air Cargo Building (SACB) at the new King Khaled International Airport in Riyadh. With equipment to handle more than 140,000 metric tons a year, the facility became the largest of its kind in the Middle East and one of the most sophisticated in the world in terms of information and cargo-handling technology. The SACB included a special docking facility that allowed up to three 747 aircraft to unload directly into the freight handling terminal.

Also during the mid-1980s, Saudia's expansion was still progressing, with Africa and Europe seeing a large portion of the expansion. In April 1986 twice weekly flights were started to Kano, Nigeria. In May flights were introduced to Cameroon and Senegal, and in June flights to Amsterdam and Brussels commenced. Saudia's cargo business continued to expand during 1988 with the first flight from the kingdom to the new Saudia cargo freight handling hub in Taiwan. The following year Saudia took delivery of its first custom-built Boeing 747-F freighter with a capacity of 100 tons. The aircraft was put to work immediately on the Far East freight route.

The year 1990 was perhaps Saudia's most traumatic to date. The Iraqi invasion and occupation of Kuwait, followed by the eventual military action to force the Iraqis out of Kuwait, caused great disruption to the world economy and especially to the airline business for many months after the fighting had stopped. For Saudia the immediate effect of the Iraqi invasion was the disruption of scheduled services within the region. Services to Baghdad and Kuwait were suspended and all other regional and long-haul flights suffered some form of disruption. With the airline's main business centers in Jeddah, Riyhad, and Dhahran acting as important logistical bases for the massive military buildup in the region, airspace for military use became a priority.

One year after the end of the Gulf War, only 75 percent of the air services within the region that were halted during the conflict had been resumed. Furthermore, intraregional air traffic had fallen by almost 30 percent compared with the 1989 level.

For Saudia, the financial impact of the Gulf War in terms of reduced revenue and higher insurance premiums forced the airline to freeze its plan for a fleet modernization program involving the replacement of all of the company's Boeing 737s, some of which were more than 20 years old. The *Middle East Economic Digest* quoted Saudia's executive vice-president for operations, Adnan Dabbagh, as saying: "We did have a plan anticipating some fleet replacements but, with the crisis, everything is being postponed until things get back to normal." Dabbagh confirmed plans to dispose of the fleet of 737s, but noted that they could not be replaced until financing became available for new aircraft.

Over the course of its development, Saudia has tended to follow a policy of business expansion in response to growing demand. The airline has benefited greatly from its domestic market, which has expanded rapidly and steadily. This approach has resulted in a stabilization of passenger volumes in recent years. According to *Jane's Airline Directory,* Saudia's prudent approach "has protected the airline from the worst of the economic and traffic downturn in the Middle East generally, following the rapid decline in the oil price."

Although the airline's rapid expansion has been remarkable, its operating losses of $163.5 million in 1990, along with the prospect of increasing competition between the other regional and national carriers, created some uncertainty for Saudia over the next few years. This was compounded by Saudi Arabia's poor relations with a number of its geographically close neighbors, including Iraq, Iran, and Israel. To date, however, the airline also had proved that good relations with close neighbors was not a prerequisite for successful business.

Beyond the 1990s

As Saudia depended on other countries for labor, in the 1990s it intensified its training program to ensure a supply of Saudi workers and pilots. At the time, all of the female flight attendants were foreigners; the other half of the cabin crew were all Saudi, as were three-quarters of the technical staff.

In 1994, in the wake of the Persian Gulf War, President Clinton announced a $6 billion order was forthcoming from Saudia Arabia, and all of it would be for U.S. aircraft at the expense of Airbus Industrie. The next year, Saudia ordered 23 Boeing 777s and five Boeing 747 jumbo jets, as well as four MD-11 aircraft and 29 MD-90 built by McDonnel Douglas. The latter aircraft featured the Honeywell Pegasus advanced flight management system, making Saudia the launch customer for these avionics. The massive order came to be worth $7.5 billion. The first Boeings, scheduled to arrive in 1997, were delivered late amid rumors of financing problems on the part of the Saudis. Although oil forecasts were better than expected, the country carried a nearly $5 billion budget deficit and Gulf War debt.

To provide extra capacity without further taxing its capital resources, in early 1997 the company leased four Boeing 747 aircraft from an Icelandic firm. Later that year it was reported that J.P. Morgan would be issuing a seven-year, $4.33 billion syndicated loan to facilitate its first payments on the 61-aircraft order it made in 1995.

Many national airlines in the Middle East struggled in the 1990s, prompting a call for an "open skies" policy among regional carriers. Jordan's Prince Faisal Bin Al Hussein challenged the efficacy of major carriers serving such short routes with half-full jumbo jets. Prince Faisal implored that developing a regional network in the area would actually create more business for the large state airlines in the long run. Arab-Israeli tension remained a volatile barrier to the type of regional cooperation Prince Faisal was seeking.

In the spring of 1998 the airline's Khalid bin Bakr announced a shift in the culture of the airline intended to smooth the way towards privatization. New company colors were part of the scheme. Saudia was expanding its cargo operations at the same time.

Principal Subsidiaries

Saudi Cargo; Saudia Catering.

Further Reading

Chronology of Saudia, Jeddah, Saudi Arabia: Saudi Arabian Airlines, 1992.
Holden and Johns, *The House of Saud,* New York: Holt, 1981.
Lenorovitz, Jeffrey M., "US Claims Victory in Saudia Aircraft Buy," *Aviation Week and Space Technology,* February 21, 1994, pp. 32–33.
Mann, Mimi, "Executive Briefing," *Middle East Executive Reports,* April 1998, pp. 4–7.
Morrocco, John D., "Regionals Slow to Start, While Majors Struggle," *Aviation Week and Space Technology,* November 10, 1997, pp. 69–70.

Nelms, Douglas W., "Searching for the Future," *Air Transport World,* April 1992, p. 107.

Proctor, Paul, "US Manufacturers to Build 61 Transports for Saudia," *Aviation Week and Space Technology,* June 26, 1995.

"Saudi Arabia Resorts to Jumbo Aircraft Loan as Finances Tighten Again," *International Trade Finance,* November 21, 1997, pp. 1–2.

"Saudia Facilities Maintain 34 Aircraft in Three Years," *Arab News,* Jeddah, April 6, 1986.

"Saudia Takes Its Place Amongst Top International Airlines," *Wall Street Journal,* May 9, 1986.

Vandyk, Anthony, "Arabian Night into Day," *Air Transport World,* June 1995.

——, "A Goal of 'Saudization'," *Air Transport World,* September 1993.

—Stephen Kremer
—updated by Frederick C. Ingram

Simon Property Group, Inc.

115 W. Washington Street
Indianapolis, Indiana 46204
U.S.A.
(317) 636-1600
Fax: (317) 263-2318
Web site: http://www.simon.com

Public Company
Incorporated: 1960 as Melvin Simon & Associates
Employees: 6,300
Sales: $1.41 billion (1998)
Stock Exchanges: New York
Ticker Symbol: SPG
SICs: 6798 Real Estate Investment Trusts; 6552 Real
Estate Developers; 1542 Building Contractors

Simon Property Group, Inc. is a self-administered, self-managed real estate investment trust (REIT). With ownership or interest in more than 240 properties and a total market capitalization of $17 billion, the Indianapolis, Indiana-based company is the largest REIT in the world. Through subsidiary partnerships, Simon owns, develops, manages, leases, and expands retail properties in 35 states, totaling approximately 180 million square feet of gross leasable area. Simon's properties—primarily shopping malls, community shopping centers, and specialty and mixed-use properties—attract more than 1.6 billion shopping visits yearly. Since its initial public offering in December 1993, the company has more than tripled in size.

Starting Small in the 1960s

The shopping mall empire that is Simon Property Group began in 1960, when Melvin Simon, a leasing agent for an Indiana real estate firm, asked his brothers Herbert and Fred to leave New York and join him in Indiana. With a degree in accounting from the City College of New York, Simon had enlisted in the Army and been stationed at Fort Benjamin Harrison's Army Finance Center near Indianapolis, Indiana.

After his military discharge, he remained in the Indianapolis area, took a job as a leasing agent, and set about learning the real estate business. Soon, he realized that there was a promising future in developing retail shopping centers. Petitioning his brothers for assistance, Simon founded Melvin Simon & Associates (MSA) and began his career as a developer.

The Simon brothers' first developments were small, open-air plazas, usually including a grocery store or drug store as an anchor. The company's first wholly-owned shopping plaza opened in Bloomington, Indiana, in August 1960 and was followed rapidly by four similar centers in the Indianapolis area. Within a short period of time, the Simons' reputation as good managers attracted larger retail tenants, such as Sears and Woolworth's. Signing leases with major retailers made the company more attractive to the bank, and the brothers were able to borrow enough capital to cover construction costs for ongoing projects, and still have enough to finance new projects. The company's first developments outside of Indiana came when the S.S. Kresge Company signed deals with MSA to develop four of the first Kmart department stores in the Midwest—in Indiana, Illinois, and Michigan. On the heels of these developments came a deal for developing three properties in Colorado, including the company's first fully-enclosed shopping mall, University Mall in Fort Collins. Opened in 1964, this first enclosed mall was built around an existing Montgomery Ward store. Working with the Montgomery Ward representatives allowed MSA to develop a pivotal relationship with a major retailer—the first of many.

The Simons brought their enclosed mall concept back to Indiana later in 1964, opening the first two enclosed malls in Indiana, in Anderson and Bloomington. The company continued to expand in the coming few years, adding an average of 1,000,000 square feet of retail space each year. By 1967, MSA owned and operated more than 3,000,000 square feet. The size of Simon's individual properties was also becoming more ambitious as the company grew. In 1975, MSA opened Towne East Square in Wichita, Kansas, the first enclosed mall with more than 1,000,000 square feet. The company made an improvement in its corporate structure around the same time. In the mid-1970s, MSA formed a separate management division charged

Company Perspectives:

Simon Property Group is about building shareholder value in the retail real estate business. It's about providing retailers with world class venues in which they can build lasting and mutually beneficial relationships with their customers. And it's about providing our shareholders with consistent and reliable performance. As a real estate investment trust (REIT), we provide an opportunity for investors to participate in the ownership of commercial real estate. As the world's largest retail real estate investment trust, we are committed to use our vast resources and marketing expertise to serve our constituents—shoppers, retailers, investors and other strategic partners. Our vision is to be the industry's unquestioned leader. We accomplish this by developing new retail properties, enhancing the performance of our existing portfolio, growing our company through acquisitions, and creating new revenue opportunities from the millions of customers that pass through our doors every year.

with tending to its existing properties. The newly formed division provided marketing and technical services, quality control, and landscaping and design assistance to ensure a degree of consistent managerial and operational quality throughout the Simon portfolio.

A New Direction in the 1980s: Moving Back Downtown

Much of MSA's early success was premised on a changing demographic. As suburban areas grew in popularity, more and more urban dwellers left the cities and moved into outlying areas. Retail, in the form of community plazas and enclosed malls, followed these suburbanites into their new neighborhoods, making it easier and more convenient for them to shop near their homes than to travel to downtown retailers. A lack of parking in many cities' downtown areas and the resulting hassle for shoppers contributed to the trend toward mall shopping.

By the late 1970s, hundreds of downtowns across America were in decline, as both residents and businesses moved into outlying areas, leaving city interiors all but empty. In the early 1980s, Simon, which was by that time opening three or more enclosed malls each year, turned its attentions to urban redevelopment. The company was asked to become involved in three redevelopment projects in midwestern cities with declining downtowns. One of the cities was Simon's home base, Indianapolis. After more than ten years in the planning stage and almost three years in construction phases, Simon's downtown Indianapolis project, Circle Centre, opened. This 800,000-square foot shopping and entertainment complex, which included a 3,000-car parking garage, gave downtown Indianapolis a much-needed boost and reaffirmed Simon's commitment to urban redevelopment.

MSA's success with urban redevelopment in Indianapolis and other cities led the Simons to consider a slightly different project: mixed-use properties. Based on the theory that sites located right next to large metropolitan areas could be used for retail, business, *and* residential construction, MSA began its first mixed-use project in Arlington, Virginia. Joining forces with a New York development firm, MSA developed an 800,000 square foot retail complex, coupled with a Ritz-Carlton hotel and a 160,000 square foot office building. The company also began planning a similar site in Jersey City, New Jersey, which would include not only retail and office space, but hotels, apartments, condos, a marina, and other recreational facilities.

Something for Everyone in the 1990s

In the early 1990s, MSA broke new ground in retail real estate development again when they began to rethink the concept of the traditional enclosed shopping mall. The Simons reasoned that by marrying the shopping experience with a range of entertainment options, they could attract more visitors who would stay for longer periods of time. In addition to retail shops—the malls' bread and butter—MSA began to include amusement arcades and interesting architectural and design features. "We try to make malls for everybody," explained Herb Simon in a 1998 interview for *Northwest Airlines World Traveler.* "If the older population, teenagers and families can feel very comfortable there, then the more successful the mall is going to be. It becomes a destination, rather than just a place to go buy a pair of pants and leave," he reasoned.

One of the first examples of Simon's entertainment-shopping hybrid was The Forum Shops at Caesars in Las Vegas, developed in partnership with The Gordon Company of Los Angeles. Built between Caesars Palace and The Mirage hotels, this development was designed to recreate a Roman street, complete with robotic animated statues, fountains, and simulated Mediterranean sky. It opened in May of 1992. In August 1992, MSA followed its Las Vegas development with perhaps its best-known project, the Mall of America. This vast, 4.2 million square foot entertainment and retail complex, developed in partnership with the Triple Five Corporation, was located near the Minneapolis/St. Paul airport. The Mall of America included the four anchor stores of Bloomingdale's, Macy's, Nordstrom, and Sears; more than 500 specialty shops; a seven-acre family theme park; an 18-hole miniature golf course; and an entertainment section complete with a 14-screen cinema, eight nightclubs, and a walk-through aquarium.

The beginning of the 1990s also saw the addition of Melvin Simon's oldest son David to the family business. With an M.B.A. from Columbia University and a background as a Wall Street investment banker, David entered MSA as its executive vice-president and chief financial officer, becoming president and chief executive officer in 1994. Under David Simon's guidance, the company began an aggressive renovation program designed to upgrade several of the older properties in the Simon portfolio. Beginning in 1992, the company began enhancing several properties each year, by expansion of existing space and/or remodeling entrances and common areas. In addition to its renovation program, Simon implemented three discrete management programs designed to, respectively, target emerging retail concepts; collaborate with onsite mall management onsite to increase operational efficiency; and audit individual mall security programs.

IPO and Subsequent Consolidation

Melvin Simon & Associates took the majority of its assets to Wall Street at the close of 1993 through the formation of Simon Property Group (SPG). SPG's $840 million initial public offering was at that time the largest in U.S. history, and the company began trading on the New York Stock Exchange under the ticker symbol SPG.

The remainder of the 1990s was characterized by mergers, acquisitions, and strategic partnerships for SPG, following the national industry trend toward consolidation. In 1996, Simon announced its merger with DeBartolo Realty Corp. The newly combined Simon DeBartolo Group owned seven percent of all regional malls in the United States and managed or owned almost 200 properties in 33 states, making it the largest public retail real estate company in North America. The following year, Simon expanded its portfolio yet again with the acquisition of The Retail Property Trust, a private Massachusetts business trust that owned ten enclosed malls and one community center. 1998 brought another merger, this time with Corporate Property Investors (CPI), a privately held New York-City-based REIT. The CPI merger added 23 malls and four office buildings to the Simon portfolio, making the company larger than its next four competitors combined. These two acquisitions also gave Simon an even stronger presence in several major metropolitan markets, including New York, Chicago, Los Angeles, Boston, Atlanta, and Pittsburgh.

At the same time Simon was building its portfolio through mergers and acquisitions, the company was also exploring growth options via strategic alliances. By developing partnerships with other REITs, Simon was able to pursue joint-venture projects, tapping other companies' areas of expertise, sharing project costs, and expanding smoothly into new markets. The first such partnership began in 1997 with the New Jersey-based Chelsea GCA Realty, Inc., known for developing outlet malls. In 1998, the Simon/Chelsea partnership announced plans to develop two outlet sites, in Houston and Orlando. Simon also partnered with the Virginia-based Mills Corporation to develop four specialty retail projects in Texas, California, Arizona, and North Carolina; and with New York-based DLJ Real Estate Capital Partners and Ohio-based Madison Marquette to acquire and develop entertainment-oriented projects. At the close of 1998, Simon announced a new 50-50 partnership with The Macerich Company of Santa Monica, California, formed to acquire a portfolio of 12 existing malls in eight states. In 1998, the company also dropped the ''DeBartolo,'' from its name, reverting back to its previous Simon Property Group, when Edward DeBartolo resigned from the company's board.

In 1997, Simon created an innovative marketing initiative, Simon Brand Ventures (SBV), which was designed to capitalize on economies of scale. By leveraging the combined buying power of the company's customers and retailers, SBV's ultimate goal was to provide Simon both shoppers and retail tenants with products, benefits, and discounts that no other mall could provide. Toward this end, the Merchant Services arm of Simon Brand Ventures set about establishing ''preferred customer'' relationships with vendors, enabling Simon's retailers to purchase services, supplies, and products and below-market rates. By the end of 1998, the company had established more than 20 such relationships with vendors supplying a wide range of services—from waste removal to customer traffic analysis.

At the same time, SBV implemented new ways to reward Simon shoppers, and thereby inspire brand loyalty. One of the first initiatives was the MALLPeRKS program, which rewarded shoppers with one point for every dollar spent in a Simon mall tenant shop. Shoppers were able to use their accumulated points to purchase retail items at reduced prices. MALLPeRKS, the shopping center industry's only national customer loyalty plan, met with promising response in its first year. By the end of 1998, more than 2,000,000 shoppers were enrolled in the program. In a similar initiative, Simon Brand Ventures partnered with VISA to create a MALL V.I.P. credit card that offered users a two percent rebate on purchases in over 400 malls across the nation and a one percent rebate on purchases made elsewhere.

Other strategic alliances followed. At the beginning of 1998, the company announced that it would partner with PepsiCo, Inc. to develop a nationwide ''Teen Affinity Program.'' The program, designed to drive teen brand loyalty, positioned Simon to benefit from the Pepsi ''GeneratioNext'' campaign and gave Pepsi exclusive vending rights in all Simon mall common space. A subsequent deal with Microsoft and the AIM Smart Corporation provided shoppers with free Internet access, email, and in-mall interactive shopping services. Another 1997 alliance, with AmeriCash, SMARTALK, and Diebold, served to develop an inaugural Electronic Concierge ATM Network, which offers shoppers access to cash, prepaid phone cards, and gift certificates.

Looking Ahead: International and Domestic Expansion

In the six years following its IPO, Simon Property Group more than tripled in size, growing revenues from $406 million to $1.4 billion. Further expansion was underway by the end of 1998, with 5,000,000 square feet of new development projects under construction in Atlanta, Orlando, Charlotte, North Carolina, and Hurst, Texas. Grand openings for the new projects were planned for 1999 and 2000. Renovations and expansions of seven existing properties in the Simon portfolio were also scheduled for completion during the same time frame.

In addition to continued domestic growth, the early years of the 21st century should see the Simon empire expand into new geographic markets. In 1998, the company made its entry into the European retail real estate market when it joined with two other investment firms—Argo II and Harvard Private Capital Group, Inc.—to acquire 44 percent ownership in the Paris-based real estate developer, lessor, and manager, Groupe BEG, S.A. The agreement was structured to allow Simon, Argo, and Harvard to gain controlling interest in BEG over a period of time. Meanwhile, it's association with BEG should allow Simon to take advantage of already-formed relationships with major European retailers, and provide opportunities for future growth in the market. ''Simon's investment in Groupe BEG enables our company to seek growth and consolidation opportunities in the European market which is fundamentally strong,'' said David Simon in a June 4, 1998 press release, adding ''Our expansion into the European marketplace represents an opportunity to generate revenue and additional FFO and potentially enhances our position as solution providers to retailers expanding into international markets.''

The company's marketing arm, Simon Brand Ventures, was also poised to move in new directions as the century drew to a close. In early 1999, the company announced a partnership with Time Inc. Custom Publishing, a division of Time Inc. The partnership was formed to produce a national lifestyle magazine targeted to mall shoppers, the first publication of its kind. The planned magazine, named *S,* would be published monthly and would contain national and local lifestyle features, announcements and coverage of mall-specific events, promotions, and special offerings. Circulation was expected to run approximately 2.2 million copies per month.

Further Reading

''Merger Makes Simon DeBartolo No. 1,'' *Chain Store Age,* May 1997, p. 80.

Newman, Jeff, and Greg Andrews, ''Swelled Simon to ''Wreak Havoc,'' *Indiana Business Journal,* April 7, 1996, p. 1.

Pollock, Will, ''Simon DeBartolo Surges Forward,'' *Shopping Center World,* May 1998.

Riha, John, ''Mall Magicians,'' *Northwest Airlines World Traveler,* March 1998, p. 48.

''Simon DeBartolo Group Goes Shopping,'' *Buildings,* April 1998, p. 18.

''Simon DeBartolo Group,'' *National Real Estate Investor,* September 1997, p. 17.

''Simon Says Name Change,'' *Long Island Business News,* August 3, 1998, p. 7A.

—Shawna Brynildssen

Simon Transportation Services Inc.

5175 West 2100 South
West Valley City, Utah 84120-1252
U.S.A.
(801) 924-7000
(800) 777-9100
Fax: (800) 688-1152
Web site: http://www.simn.com

Public Company
Incorporated: 1972 as Dick Simon Trucking, Inc.
Employees: 2,135
Sales: $193.5 million (1998)
Stock Exchanges: NASDAQ
Ticker Symbol: SIMN
SICs: 4213 Trucking Except Local; 6719 Holding
    Companies, Not Elsewhere Classified; 5078
    Refrigeration Equipment & Supplies

Simon Transportation Services Inc. serves customers throughout the lower 48 states and also Canada and Mexico. From its headquarters in the Salt Lake City suburb of West Valley City and five other terminals in the Los Angeles, Houston, Phoenix, Portland, and Atlanta areas, Simon ships mainly food products for firms such as North American Logistic Services (M&M Mars), Albertson's, Nestlé Frozen Food Company, and ConAgra Frozen Foods. Its fleet of 53-foot refrigerated trailers is the largest of its kind in the United States. Simon uses modern computers and telecommunications to manage its growing fleet and provide better customer relations. The company in 1999 remains a family firm (though publicly owned) under the leadership of founder Dick Simon and three sons.

Getting Started

Richard D. "Dick" Simon loved trucks from his early childhood. "All I ever wanted to be was a truck driver," said Simon. Born in Provo, Utah, in 1937, Simon grew up on a ranch near Meridian, Idaho, where his grandfather and two uncles had trucks to haul timber from the mountains and then eventually to Provo and Springville, Utah, for house construction. On the return trip, the trucks hauled coke from Geneva Steel back to Idaho.

In 1955 Dick Simon traded his new car for a 2-ton tractor and 32-foot trailer. He made his first trip hauling feed from Provo to southern California ranchers and then returning with a load of fish meal from Long Beach. Other jobs followed, but his truck wore out, so he drove trucks owned by others.

Simon purchased his first diesel tractor with a refrigerated trailer in 1963 when he was 26 years old. He drove a route from Utah to Arizona and Los Angeles and then back home. "In those days I never slept. I was driving all the time," said Simon in a typescript record. His wife Valene provided crucial support in those early years by doing the bookkeeping and occasionally driving for him, so he could get some sleep.

With his first driver, Simon established what he called the "Round Robin." They picked up produce in Idaho, added vegetables and fruit in the border town of Nogales, Arizona, then hauled the refrigerated contents to Los Angeles and returned to Utah with California produce.

Early Expansion

Simon admitted that eventually his nonstop driving days had to end. "By the time I was 35 I couldn't do it anymore," said Simon. "However, I was in a position where I could bring on more drivers and equipment." Thus Simon in 1972 ended his sole proprietorship and incorporated as Dick Simon Trucking, Inc.

To provide for his growing family, Simon decided to expand his fleet. He took his young children on the road with him, and they accepted various odd jobs around the company offices and gradually the second generation of the family business assumed more responsibility. By the time daughter Sherry was in high school and son Dick Simon, Jr. ("King"), was in junior high, son Lyn worked in the office, and son Kelle drove for the growing company. Kelle had begun working for the firm in the late 1970s when it had about 25 trucks.

About that time, Simon Trucking adopted its familiar "Sweet Simon" skunk logo. Since the firm hauled perfume and cosmetics in some trucks, they had a sweet smell. According to Dick Simon, one day he took his fragrant rig to a Salt Lake City detailer who was so good that Simon let him have his artistic way. At first he was angry with the skunks holding "Sweet Simon" flags painted on his truck. However, many people, including his wife, loved the skunk image, so Simon adopted it as the official company logo.

By the early 1980s, Simon Trucking operated 26 tractors. Then the grocery chain Smith's Food King signed a contract that required Simon to quickly double the size of his fleet. For some time the company remained at about 65 trailers, but by 1988 Simon's contract with Smith's helped it grow to 97 tractors and 225 trailers.

One of the biggest challenges for all trucking firms was deregulation based on the Motor Carriers Act of 1980. Previously, the federal government strictly controlled interstate trucking, with the Interstate Commerce Commission giving permits to companies for designated routes. Under those circumstances, firms more or less were guaranteed a profit. With deregulation, more trucks were on the road but cargo amounts did not increase at the same rate, thus intensifying competition and reducing freight rates by about half.

Manufacturers and consumers loved trucking deregulation, but the trucking industry did not. For example, there was a threefold increase in the number of bankruptcies in trucking and related industries by 1987, according to Otis Winn of the Utah Motor Transport Association in the September 20, 1987 *Deseret News*. By 1987, 33 of the nation's 45 public trucking firms operating before deregulation had gone out of business. Furthermore, because many truckers made little if any money, maintenance was sometimes reduced, leading to serious safety concerns.

The 1990s

By the early 1990s Simon Trucking had survived deregulation and was growing rapidly. Gross revenues increased from $31 million in 1991 to almost $41 million in 1992, almost $58 million in 1993, and about $72 million in 1994. Since the company was paying huge amounts of interest to borrow money for its expansion, it reduced its growth rate in 1995 to just 4.9 percent.

Meanwhile, Dick Simon Trucking faced competitors, such as Frozen Food Express Industries, Inc., a Dallas-based public firm founded in 1945. With 1996 sales of $311.4 million, Frozen Food Express was in the mid-1990s North America's largest temperature-controlled trucking firm. Other firms competing against Simon included KLLM Transport Services, Aasche Transportation, US 1 Industries, and Marten Transport.

Confronted by tough competition and internal financial difficulties, Kelle Simon, then vice-president of maintenance and fleet purchasing, and Lyn Simon, vice-president of sales and marketing, pushed their father to consider taking the firm public, but Dick Simon refused to budge. Finally he saw the necessity of such a major move, especially with the firm's debt-to-capital ratio at 57 percent. Thus on November 17, 1995, Simon Transportation Services Inc. was launched with its stock offered on the NASDAQ. Dick Simon Trucking remained a subsidiary. "Going public was the best thing we ever did," said Dick Simon in his typescript manuscript. "Instead of paying $20,000 a month in interest on a line of credit, we now collect the money."

In 1996 the new public corporation used some of the $19.7 million raised in its IPO to trade in 350 older tractors and buy over 650 new ones. According to Renee Weaver, a Wheat First Butcher Singer analyst in the August 1996 *Investor's Business Daily*, "Any diesel engine since 1993 had a big advancement in their fuel efficiency, so it had fewer expenses for upkeep."

Simon's updated fleet helped attract new customers in 1996: Kellogg Company; M&M Mars, a division of Mars Inc.; Tootsie Roll Industries Inc.; and the baking division of CPC International Inc. In the summer of 1996 it shipped its first load to Mexico.

That purchase and others in the late 1990s resulted in Simon Transportation having a very young fleet. In 1998 the firm owned a total of 1,644 tractors made by Freightliner, Peterbilt, Volvo, and International. Every tractor was purchased in 1996, 1997, or 1998, and its average trailer age was just two years. Almost all of Simon's over 2,500 trailers were refrigerated vans. In May 1998 the company announced that it had phased out its 48-foot refrigerated trailers, so all trailers were the 53-foot models. In 1998 the company also planned to purchase an additional 400 tractors and 800 trailers.

In July 1997 Simon Trucking moved to its new 60,000-square-foot headquarters and 70,000-square-foot maintenance facility in West Valley City, a suburb of Salt Lake City. Located on 55.2 acres, the new facilities included the latest technology in the trucking industry for repair, service, and communications. Simon sold its original property, including eight acres and some buildings, to the Murray City government for use as a public works complex.

CEO Dick Simon celebrated the opening by commissioning Dan Christensen, company artist and marketing representative, to paint a portrait of Shadrach Roundy, one of Utah's original pioneers and Simon's ancestor. Simon grew up hearing stories about Roundy, one of his heroes. Simon felt inspired to continue that pioneering spirit by using the latest technology in his business.

For example, each Simon truck included the QUALCOMM satellite communication system. In 1992 Simon Trucking became the 13th company in the world to completely install this global positioning system (GPS), which provided exact location of each truck and miles remaining for delivery. The QUALCOMM satellite transmitted positions to its headquarters in San

Diego and then that data was transmitted via modem to Simon's mainframe computer. If a truck was late, all parties would be notified electronically and sometimes alternative routes would be planned.

At Simon's new headquarters, huge computer screens displayed the positions of its trucks, national weather data, load data, and other information. No wonder this central dispatch room was called the "War Room." This high-tech approach to trucking earned Simon coverage on the popular television series "20/20" in early 1998. It also was a key component in maintaining the firm's status as a core carrier for some large customers, resulting in fixed routes, higher profit margins, and first bids on upcoming projects.

By 1997 each Simon truck also carried its individual "radio frequency identification (RFID) tag." The SmartPass RFID System was developed by Amtech Systems Corporation. Using RFID readers, which cost about $2,500 each, terminal managers could tell when a truck entered the terminal. The RFID also provided automated fueling that improved record-keeping and kept fuel costs to a minimum.

In addition, inhouse software linked to the RFID system provided even more data. "With our vehicle maintenance software, when this vehicle enters the yard, it (the system) says, 'It needs this type of service, it needs an oil change, the tires need to be checked,' " said Bob Slaughter, Simon Trucking's director of management information systems in the May 25, 1997 *Deseret News.* "Every single person here, even our mechanics, are on the computer. All the information is shared. It's hard to measure those things in terms of dollars, but I don't know what price tag you put on things when information is available to everybody."

Terminal operations in West Valley City demonstrated the efficiency of Simon Trucking's high-tech approach. Every day an average of 225 trucks received oil changes, which took only 15 minutes, during which other routine maintenance checks and lubrication were completed. Simon also recapped its own tires, completing between 60 and 80 daily.

In the unregulated trucking industry, firms like Simon that could afford the latest technology naturally gained the upper hand competing against the nation's 25,000 small trucking companies. Manufacturers wanted to save transportation expenses, which ranged from three to six percent of their total costs.

Simon's largest customers from January to July 1998 included the following: North American Logistic Services, Albertson's, Inc., Nestlé Frozen Food Company, ConAgra Frozen Foods, Hunt Wesson, Inc., Kraft Foods, Inc., Coors Brewing Company, Foster Farms, Lamb-Weston, Inc., Proctor & Gamble, The Pillsbury Company, Fred Meyer, Kellogg Company, Tropicana Products, Pilgrim's Pride, The Kroger Company, Costco, and Hershey. Other Salt Lake City trucking firms besides Simon expanded in the late 1990s, including C.R. England, which built a 65,000-square-foot facility that included a theater, library, gym, and sleeping quarters for 200. According to the Utah Department of Transportation, the state's commercial trucking industry increased by 11 percent in 1995 and 1996. Most expansions occurred along 2100 South, a main east-west route close to interstate highways. This growth, part of the

state's booming economy, helped Salt Lake City continue its tradition as the "Crossroads of the West."

In June 1998 the company started the Simon Driver School to train its own drivers, including those with no experience, to reduce the number of tractors sitting idly without drivers. Like more and more companies, applicants could apply online.

Simon also raised its driver wages in 1998. "The wage increases cut our operating margin substantially, but we believe it was necessary to remain competitive in a very tight market for drivers," said Dick Simon in his firm's November 1998 online newsletter *Simon Says.*

Simon Transportation experienced a mixed fiscal year 1998, ending September 30. Revenue increased 25 percent from fiscal 1997 to almost $194 million. In its November 1998 newsletter, the company emphasized its positive finances, such as having $60 million in net worth and reduced long-term debt and no liens on any of its properties. CFO Alban Lang concluded that "the company is financially very strong, probably stronger than over 95% of the trucking companies across the country."

The bad news was that Simon Transportation's stock price per share declined significantly. By early December 1998 it had fallen to about $6, far below its recent high of about $25 per share in early October 1997. The company blamed its stock decline on an unusually high number of accidents, a delayed order for new Freightliner tractors, and its new Atlanta terminal costing more than expected.

Simon Transportation's poor stock performance in 1998 influenced some company shareholders and their Los Angeles attorney Lionel Z. Glancy in December 1998 to file a lawsuit in Utah federal court against Dick Simon, Kelle Simon, and Alban Lang. The three were accused in this proposed class-action lawsuit of insider trading when they sold almost $3 million worth of company stock between January 15 and February 12, 1998, just before the stock value started to plummet. CFO Lang said those stock sales had been planned months earlier, long before any knowledge of financial problems.

In 1998 Simon Transportation continued as a family business. Founder Dick Simon owned about 22 percent of Simon Transportation's stock, and he remained at the helm as its board chairman, president, and CEO. Kelle Simon, age 36, served as vice-president of maintenance and fleet purchasing, while Lyn Simon, age 33, was the firm's vice-president of sales and marketing, and Richard D. Simon, Jr., age 26, served as vice-president of operations.

Principal Subsidiaries

Dick Simon Trucking, Inc.

Further Reading

Berry, Kate, "Cool Course," *Investor's Business Daily,* August 1996.
Collins, Lois, "Trucking: Few in Business Singing Praises of Deregulation," *Deseret News,* September 20, 1987, pp. M1–M2.
Macklin, Gary, "Dick Simon Trucking Builds Nation's Largest Fleet of 53-Ft. Reefer Vans," *Refrigerated Transporter,* November 1996.

Mitchell, Lesley, "Trucking Firms Bring Life to Salt Lake City," *Press Dispatch* (Victorville and Barstow, California), November 23, 1997, p. B6.

Much, Marilyn, "Trucker Pulling Ahead with Superior Service," *Investor's Business Daily,* June 5, 1997.

Oberbeck, Steven, "Lawsuit Accuses Top Simon Transportation Executives of Insider Trading," *Salt Lake Tribune,* December 8, 1998, p. B10.

"QUALCOMM and Dick Simon Trucking Featured on ABC's '20/20,'" *Transportation Times,* spring/summer 1998.

"Sweet Smell of Success," *Panorama* (Equillon Lubricants' periodical), July 1998, pp. 14–18.

Thomson, Linda, "Truckin' Toward 2000: Firms Like England, Simon Use Up-to-Date Technology to Keep Ahead in Competitive Industry," *Deseret News,* May 25, 1997.

—David M. Walden

A great way to fly
SINGAPORE AIRLINES

Singapore Airlines Ltd.

P.O. Box 501
Airmail Transit Centre
Singapore, 918101
Republic of Singapore
(65)5423333
Fax: (65)5456083

State-Owned Company
Incorporated: 1972 as Singapore Airlines
Employees: 13,500
Sales: S $7,72 billion (US $4.96 billion) (1998)
SICs: 4512 Air Transportation, Scheduled

Singapore Airlines Ltd. (SIA), the national airline of Singapore and a major carrier in the Pacific region with routes to Europe and North America, is known for its unparalleled customer service as well as for its continuing efforts to upgrade its aircraft and technology. SIA is 54 percent owned by the Singapore government with minor shareholdings by Delta Airlines and Swissair. A long-established strategic seaport, Singapore is an important transit point for travel to other areas of the Far East. Even during times of severe recession in the airline industry, SIA has been the world's most consistently profitable airline and, unlike most, a virtual stranger to debt. The "Singapore Girl" flies to 90 cities in 40 countries.

Imperial Origins

SIA was incorporated in 1972, and its origins date back to the formation of Malayan Airways Limited (MAL). In 1936 the British government and Imperial Airways localized air transport in Singapore and Malaya (now Malaysia) by forming MAL. This new airline was owned and operated by Imperial Airways and the Ocean Steam Ship Company and was formally incorporated in Singapore in October 1937. During this time, however, an Australian company, Wearne Brothers, began scheduled airline services between what was to be MAL's prime route, Malaya to Singapore. The first chairman of MAL, Frank Lane, concluded that the market could not accommodate two carriers

operating this route. Consequently, MAL remained inactive for the next ten years. World War II and the Japanese occupation of the region ruled out commercial air transport, and during this period Wearne Brothers went bankrupt and ceased operations. In 1946 Singapore's airport reopened, and Britain's renamed national carrier, British Overseas Airways Corporation (BOAC), agreed to relinquish its control of MAL to a local concern, the Singapore Straits Steamship Company. In May 1947 MAL began scheduled services with two Airspeed Consul airplanes, six pilots, six radio operators, a dozen administrative personnel, and a few ground crew members. One month later a third aircraft was added.

The new airline was successful; commercial air transport increased dramatically after World War II, and initial services between Singapore and the Malaysian city of Kuala Lumpur were fully booked at M $35 each way. By the end of 1947 MAL had introduced three DC-3s into its fleet, and within a year of its first flight the airline was carrying 5,000 passengers every month. Over the next two years Bangkok, Rangoon, and Borneo were added to the destination list, and three more DC-3s were purchased; during this time MAL gained membership to the International Air Transport Association (IATA). Rapidly growing as a major air transport center, Singapore began to attract such established carriers as Air India. In 1955 the new Paya Lebar Airport, capable of accommodating jets and large planes, was completed.

In August 1957 Malaya received its independence from Great Britain, signaling dramatic changes for MAL. The government of Malaya took a holding in the company, and the Singapore Straits Steamship Company sold its shareholding to BOAC and the Australian airline Qantas. As a result of this restructuring, the Malayan government, BOAC, and Qantas each held a 33 percent stake in MAL. The airline added two Viscounts to its fleet in 1959 and began offering service to Hong Kong in 1958. Furthermore, MAL entered the jet age with the loan of a Comet from BOAC to service its international routes. Profitable every year since 1948, the company was proving to be a sound investment for its partners.

In 1963 the Federation of Malaysia was formed, comprising the former British colonies of Singapore, Sarawak, and Sabah.

The airline was renamed Malaysian Airways Ltd. Under the leadership of Keith Hamilton, who joined MAL in 1960 after 12 years with Qantas, the company opened an office in New York to promote travel to Malaysia. In 1965 Singapore achieved its independence from Malaysia and the governments of Malaysia and Singapore acquired joint majority control of the airline in 1966, renaming it Malaysia-Singapore Airlines (MSA). The year 1968 marked the opening of a new 16-story headquarters building in Singapore, the commencement of service to Tokyo, and the purchase of three Boeing 707s and five 737s, making MSA competitive with other large jet operators. By 1971 service to Rome, London, Frankfurt, and Sydney was available.

Birth of Singapore Airlines

In April 1970 Malaysia announced that it would establish its own national carrier for domestic and international flights. This resulted in the dissolution of MSA and equal distribution of assets between Malaysia and Singapore. Singapore received all the Boeing aircraft, the facilities in Singapore, and overseas offices in 18 countries. Malaysia received the remaining aircraft, facilities within Malaysia, and a cash payment from Singapore to make up the difference. In June of 1972 Singapore Airlines Limited was formed; its first chairperson was the former joint chief of MSA, J.Y. Pillay. In July of 1972 Singapore Airlines (or SIA as it came to be known) purchased its first Boeing 747s, which would become the mainstay of its fleet. The purchase of these aircraft coincided with an increase in frequency of flights to such destinations as Zurich, Athens, Frankfurt, Osaka, London, and Kuala Lumpur, which it now serviced 11 times daily. An immediate concern of SIA was to become known as a leader in international air travel. To this end, the company conceived a marketing strategy that stressed its commitment to passenger comfort and service and established the airline's distinctive group of air hostesses. Nicknamed the ''Singapore Girls,'' the stewardesses, wearing custom-designed oriental sarongs, became recognized for their friendly and efficient service.

In addition to its marketing campaign, SIA launched a successful behind-the-scenes lobbying effort to convince various countries to grant the airline access to their airports. To cope with its growing number of flights and planes, SIA established a subsidiary called Singapore Airport Terminal Services Ltd.

(SATS) in 1973. The company also embarked on a large-scale training program for all of its staff that included a S $20 million training center and several state-of-the-art flight simulators. By 1975 SIA's lobbying, marketing, and staff training efforts began to pay off with a 54 percent increase in passenger traffic that year alone. The fleet now consisted of seven Boeing 747s, 14 707s, and five 737s.

In addition to facing a large increase in passenger traffic, SIA had to accommodate a surge in operating costs, brought about not only by increased expenditures but also by huge increases in the price of oil in 1973 and 1977. SIA survived this crisis by adopting a companywide cost-cutting program and relying on its loyal customer base. In 1976 SIA's annual passenger volume passed the two million mark—doubling the 1973 volume—and SIA ranked third among airlines in the Far East Asia region, behind Japan Air Lines and All Japan Airlines. In 1977 SIA's lobbying of the United States government to grant access rights paid off, and it began service to San Francisco, Guam, and Honolulu. Also during this year SIA and the Singapore government announced plans for a vast new airport in the city of Changi, featuring a new headquarters building for SIA, a freight terminal for SATS, and an in-flight catering center. The government provided a five-year plan for the construction of the airport, which was scheduled for completion in 1981.

In July 1977 SIA announced a joint operation with British Airways to provide Concorde jet service between Singapore and London, an arrangement intended to bring prestige to SIA and help British Airways fully exploit the potential of its new supersonic aircraft. Featuring the SIA yellow-and-black logo on one side and the British Airways logo on the other, the aircraft had its maiden flight on December 9, 1977, but service was halted after three flights because of protests from the Malaysian government over environmental damage the Concorde caused while in Malaysian airspace. Full service resumed 13 months later on a thrice weekly basis via an alternate route and with a stop at Bahrain in the Persian Gulf. The service was terminated, however, in November 1980. Nevertheless, the project was deemed a marketing victory, and SIA became known as one of only four airlines to operate the supersonic aircraft.

1980s Expansion

In the early 1980s SIA continued to expand its services in the United States. Weekly flights to Los Angeles via Tokyo began at the end of 1980. The following year marked the opening of Singapore's new airport at Changi, offering improved service to visitors in Singapore and giving SIA the opportunity to expand its fleet. During this time, the comforts of the new airport, along with SIA's renowned customer service, resulted in SIA being named the top airline in the Asia Pacific region by customer preference. In response to a growing demand, six Boeing 747-300s (known as ''Big Tops'') were acquired, as well as seven Airbus A310s, to help SIA in its large-capacity routes. The purchases were part of a plan conceived in 1978 to replace the airline's entire fleet to decrease maintenance costs and increase punctuality. The workhorse of SIA's fleet has been the Boeing 747, which accounted for 90 percent of the airline's flight revenues; the company had purchased more than 50 of the aircraft, including a single order for 20 in February 1986, worth US $3.3 billion to Boeing.

By 1987 SIA's destination network spanned 54 cities in 37 countries, and the airline had installed one of the world's most modern computer centers, with a staff of 350, to coordinate and control its flights and other operations. In recognition of the airline's 40th anniversary that year, SIA engineers restored the airline's first plane, the Airspeed Consul. Furthermore, the Singapore government, which held 73 percent of SIA, floated part of its holding on the Singapore Stock Exchange, giving foreigners the opportunity to own up to 20 percent of the airline. Employee holdings remained significant at 17 percent.

Still Climbing in the 1990s

In 1989 SIA teamed with Delta and Swiss Air to create a formidable global alliance. By 1998 the carrier was also inking agreements with Lufthansa and Air Canada. It aggressively promoted similar arrangements with Ansett and Air New Zealand, which greatly increased SIA's presence in the South Pacific.

Although the carrier continued to grow in the 1990s, controlling costs remained a necessary priority. SIA used its younger, lower-cost SilkAir subsidiary to cover gaps in its route network. The company continued to expand its network, which included 68 cities in 40 countries in 1994. In response to rising labor expenses, SIA began shopping overseas for personnel, establishing a software developer in Bombay and investing in a Chinese maintenance facility and a Cambodian start-up airline. It continued to seek opportunities to invest in other Asian carriers, such as China Airlines and Thai Airways International.

In 1992 SIA spun off its maintenance unit, SIA Engineering, which also continued to grow, building a new hangar at the Changi Airport. In 1998 SIA Engineering entered into joint ventures with Hamilton Standard and Pratt and Whitney. In 1995 the ground-handling subsidiary, SATS Airport Services, opened a $150 million multi-tier airfreight terminal.

SIA lobbied worldwide for freer markets in the 1990s, which it said held the key to industry profits. The traditional system of regulation, bilateral agreements between individual nations, could only hinder the world's airlines with inefficiency, according to company officials. In 1992–93 SIA earned an operating profit of $548 million. This figure reached $657 million in just two years.

Still, the pressures of competition induced SIA to install a "cabin management interactive system" in every seat. The CMIS gave passengers a six-inch screen with a choice of six movies, as well as video games, telephones, etc. The consoles cost $4 million per plane to install. Other liabilities accrued when the carrier had problems selling jets as they reached an age of five years. It finally resorted to leasing the aircraft in slow resale markets.

The Asian financial crisis severely cut into SIA's earnings in the late 1990s, prompting it to examine its global route network for poorly performing routes. Service to Berlin was canceled in early 1999. Still, SIA used its ample cash reserves to further upgrade passenger amenities, spending $300 million to renovate the cabins of its aircraft. The first two 747s to receive the upgrade were painted in an exotic livery reminiscent of a tropical sunset. SIA prefixed its traditional slogan "A great way to fly" with "Now more than ever."

Principal Subsidiaries

Singapore Airport Terminal Services Ltd.; SATS Apron Services Pte. Ltd.; SATS Airport Services Pte. Ltd.; SATS Catering Pte. Ltd.; SATS Security Services Private Limited; SilkAir (Singapore) Private Limited; Tradewinds Tours & Travel Private Limited; Singapore Aviation and General Insurance Company (Pte.) Limited; SIA Engineering Company Private Limited; Singapore Flying College Pte. Ltd.; Aero Laundry & Lines Services Private Limited; Abacus Travel Systems Pte. Ltd. (61%); Singapore Jamco Private Limited (51%); Cargo Community Network Pte. Ltd. (51%); Star Kingdom Investment Limited (Hong Kong); SH tours Ltd. (United Kingdom); Auspice Limited (Channel Islands); Singapore Airlines (Mauritius) Ltd. (Mauritius); Airline Software Development Consultancy India (Pvt) Limited (51%); Eagle Services Asia (49%).

Further Reading

Allen, Roy, *SIA: Take-Off to Success,* Singapore: SIA, 1990.
Bociurkiw, Michael, "Time for Champagne," *Forbes,* December 14, 1998.
Donoghue, J.A., "Superior, Innovative and Adept," *Air Transport World,* June 1994, pp. 30–39.
"Flying Beauty," *Economist,* December 14, 1991.
Leung, James, "Winging Their Way to Global Might," *Asian Business,* December 1996, pp. 24–34.
Tanzer, Andrew, "The Prime Minister Is a Demanding Shareholder," *Forbes,* April 2, 1990, pp. 152–53.
Westlake, Michael, "Success in the Air," *Far Eastern Economic Review,* October 15, 1987, pp. 78–81.

—Dylan Tanner
—updated by Frederick C. Ingram

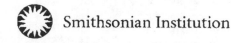 Smithsonian Institution

Smithsonian Institution

1000 Jefferson Drive S.W.
Washington, DC 20560
U.S.A.
(202) 357-1300
Fax: (202) 786-2377
Web site: http://www.si.edu

Public Institution
Founded: 1846
Employees: 6,300
Revenues: $552 million (1998)

The Smithsonian Institution is the largest museum, education, and research system in the world, with 16 museums and galleries, the National Zoological Park, and ten research centers, all with free admittance. It is the home of the Hope Diamond, the Wright brothers' airplane, the original Star Spangled Banner, and some 140 million other items, and it attracts more than 28 million visitors a year. The Smithsonian also produces records and tapes through Smithsonian Folkways Recordings; publishes books and magazines; produces television documentaries, home videos, and radio shows; operates 16 museum stores and mail order and on-line catalogs; conducts numerous educational activities through its membership programs; and annually sponsors a juried craft show and the Festival of American Folklife. In fiscal 1998, 72 percent of the Smithsonian's revenues came from its annual federal appropriation. The remainder came from gifts and grants, contracts, investments, membership programs, and sales.

A Provision in a Will: 1829

The man who endowed the Smithsonian Institution was born in France in 1765, the illegitimate son of Hugh Smithson, the first Duke of Northumberland, and Elizabeth Keate Hungerford Macie, a widow connected to the royal family. Named James Lewis Macie, he took his father's name after his mother's death in 1800.

A graduate of Oxford and an avid scientist, James Smithson traveled throughout Europe studying chemistry, mineralogy,

and geology. He wrote 27 articles for scientific journals dealing with topics ranging from a better way to make coffee to the chemical makeup of a woman's teardrop. His personal library contained 213 volumes, and a type of zinc carbonate was renamed *smithsonite* in his honor.

When Smithson died in 1829, he left the bulk of his estate to his nephew, Henry Hungerford. A clause in his will, however, stated that should Hungerford die without heirs (legitimate or illegitimate), the estate would go to "the United States of America to found at Washington, under the name of Smithsonian Institution, an Establishment for the increase and diffusion of knowledge . . ."

Smithson's provision was newsworthy in both Europe and the United States when it first became known, and newspapers tried to figure out why this man, who had never visited the United States, might leave the nation his estate. Although he may have had other reasons, one purpose was revenge: "My name," Smithson wrote, "shall live in the memory of man when the titles of the Northumberlands and Percys are extinct and forgotten."

What Now?: 1835–46

When Henry Hungerford died childless in 1835, the country, or at least those governing it, had to decide whether to accept the estate. President Andrew Jackson thought it was a good idea, but was not sure it was constitutional to accept the bequest. When he asked Congress to pass legislation making that possible, he ran into opposition from those who believed, as the Smithsonian accounted, that "acceptance of the Smithson bequest . . . on behalf of the entire nation would abridge states' rights." The two senators from South Carolina were among the strongest opponents. Senator John C. Calhoun believed Congress had no authority to accept the gift, and Senator William Campbell Preston, while also questioning the constitutionality, complained that "[E]very whippersnapper vagabond . . . might think it proper to have his name distinguished in the same way."

Despite such concerns, Congress authorized the acceptance of the bequest on July 1, 1836 and established a select committee to decide what to do with the estate, then worth $515,169. The nation spent the next ten years debating what this new institution should be. The first proposals were for a national university—to train teachers, to teach natural history, to teach the classics, to improve social conditions through applied sciences. Over the years, the debate broadened to create a national museum, an institute to promote science, a national library, an institute to support basic scientific research, or a national observatory.

Finally, on August 10, 1846, legislation containing many of these ideas, but eliminating the national university, was signed by President James K. Polk. The "Act To Establish the Smithsonian Institution" created a charitable trust, with its administration, independent of the government, the responsibility of the Institution's Secretary and Board of Regents, consisting of three members of the House of Representatives, three Senators, and nine private citizens appointed by a joint resolution of Congress. The vice-president of the United States and the chief justice of the Supreme Court served as ex officio members.

Creating the Institution: 1846–78

The Board of Regents selected Joseph Henry, a prominent physicist, as the first Secretary, or chief executive. Henry envisioned the Smithsonian as a scientific research institute and undertook such activities as organizing volunteer weather observers who telegraphed weather information from around the country to the Smithsonian where scientists collected and recorded the data. Henry also initiated the research report series *Smithsonian Contributions to Knowledge* to overcome the high cost of scientific publication. In 1850 he created the International Exchange Service, a low-cost system whereby American scientists could gain access to scholarly publications from Europe and elsewhere.

The legislation that created the Institution required that the public have access to the Institution. Henry himself conducted public lectures, along with "a number of distinguished gentlemen . . . whose character will tend to give due importance to the communications."

In 1855 Henry moved his family into the second floor of the newly completed Smithsonian Building. Designed by James Renwick, Jr., it resembled a 12th century Italian Romanesque castle and housed offices, laboratories, art gallery, science museum, and lecture hall, with living space for resident scientists in the tower. The red brick building quickly became known as "The Castle," and when Henry's meteorologists received word of impending storms, they signaled nearby ports from the tower. Henry worked hard to keep his Institution separate from politics

so as not to endanger support in Congress. He took no position on Darwin's theory of evolution and made sure no flag of any sort flew over the Smithsonian Building during the Civil War.

In 1879 Congress established the Smithsonian's Bureau of Ethnology, and its head, Civil War veteran and scientist John Wesley Powell, initiated wide-ranging research in archeology, linguistics, and physical anthropology. Powell was also a director of the U.S. Geological Survey, and according to Ken Ringle in a *Washington Post* article, "The linkage would become something of a model in future years for the Smithsonian. It put science to work for the U.S. government while the quasi-independence of the institution and its strong-willed leaders served to insulate scholars and scientists from the political pressures of the day."

Developing a National Museum: 1850–87

When Henry died in 1878, he was succeeded by his assistant of 28 years, Spencer Fullerton Baird. An avid naturalist and collector, Baird had received the first grant from the Institution for scientific exploration and field research in 1848. Two years later he arrived at the Smithsonian with two railroad cars full of natural specimens, considerably augmenting the Institution's few boxes of minerals and plants.

As Assistant Secretary, he was in charge of the Department of Exploration, and his efforts included teaching a generation of naturalists how to prepare specimens for museum collections. He instructed and supplied naturalists attached to just about any expedition heading west, making the Smithsonian a center for information about the natural history of North America. In 1858 the Congress designated the Smithsonian The National Museum of the United States.

In 1876 the United States celebrated its Centennial with an exposition in Philadelphia. When the exposition closed, 42 boxcars of artifacts were donated to the Smithsonian, ranging from an 1876 locomotive from California to Samuel F.B. Morse's original telegraph to military uniforms to 19th century household items. Needing more space for all of these artifacts, the Smithsonian erected the U.S. National Museum (now the Arts and Industries Building), which opened in 1881.

In 1883 the Smithsonian accepted from the National Institute museum at the Patent Office a collection that included George Washington memorabilia. By the end of Baird's tenure as Secretary in 1887, the Smithsonian was far more than an institute for scientific research. The National Museum had more than 2.5 million artifacts and specimens, organized into collections that concentrated on the natural history and people of North America and on the country's national identity.

Animals, Art, and War Machines: 1887–1963

Samuel Langley, a physician, astronomer, and aircraft inventor, succeeded Baird and served until 1906. One of his first actions was to create the Children's Room at the Castle, claiming "Knowledge begins in wonder." During his tenure, the Institution established the Smithsonian Astrophysical Observatory (1890) and the National Zoological Park (1891), the first zoo created with a mission of breeding native wildlife.

Langley left one legacy that was less enriching. For nearly 40 years, the Smithsonian claimed that Langley built the "first man carrying plane capable of sustained flight," beating the Wright brothers. Not until 1942, when the Institution corrected its records, did Orville Wright agree to place the original Flyer in the Smithsonian.

In 1910 the third Smithsonian building opened, the National Museum of Natural History, with nearly 11 acres of floor space that also housed offices and art works and was the first Smithsonian museum to be open on Sunday. Charles Freer's donation of his priceless collection of American and Oriental art greatly enhanced the Smithsonian's reputation and added significantly to its art holdings. The Freer Gallery, built especially for the collection, opened in 1923. The construction was paid for with an additional $1 million Freer contributed for that purpose.

After World War I, tanks, uniforms, and gas masks were placed on exhibit, an indication of the continuing relationship between Smithsonian scientists and the government, with an increasing emphasis on research useful to the military. The scientists' investigations over the years ranged from recoilless gun design to rocketry and shark repellent, and their research on tropical islands provided information for the military during the war in the Pacific.

In 1946 Barro Colorado Island in Panama, the first biological reserve in the Americas, became part of the Smithsonian. The reserve had been established in 1923, on an island created when the Panama Canal was built. Scientists conducted long-term studies in tropical biology on the Isthmus and established a marine science program.

Reshaping an Institution: 1964–69

The 20 years in which Sidney Dillon Ripley was Secretary was a period of tremendous growth for the Smithsonian. An ornithologist, Ripley believed that museums should be "points of contact" with all people, not just some place to visit on a Sunday afternoon or a high school field trip. He also wanted the Smithsonian to be a center of ideas and a "company of scholars."

The National Museum of History and Technology (now the Museum of American History) opened in 1964, and Ripley set out to make the Mall between the Smithsonian's buildings more inviting to people. At his urging, roads were closed to traffic and replaced with broad paths lined with benches. Ripley also installed a carousel in front of the Castle and, in 1965, held the first Festival of American Folklife, filling the Mall for 12 weeks with exhibits, dancers, food, and music from all over the United States and 35 other countries.

Ripley also pushed the Smithsonian's museum offerings beyond the Mall, and outside Washington, DC. In 1967–68 four new Smithsonian museums opened. The Anacostia Museum brought a museum to the people of the southeastern section of the city and examined the African American experience in Washington, DC. The Old Patent Office, a few blocks north of the Mall and once the site of the National Institute museum, became the home of the National Museum of American Art and the National Portrait Gallery. In New York City, Ripley leased the Fifth Avenue Carnegie mansion to house the Cooper-Hewitt, National Design Museum, which became part of the Smithsonian.

Ripley also enhanced the Institution's research activities. He established the Smithsonian Environmental Research Center on Chesapeake Bay in 1965 and, in 1996, renamed Barro Colorado Institute the Smithsonian Tropical Research Institute (STRI).

Ripley's Building Boom: 1970–84

The decade of the 1970s saw the fruition of several of Ripley's dreams and efforts. He had worked hard to convince Joseph Hirshhorn to donate his massive collection of modern art to the Smithsonian and to gain support and money to build a museum for the works. At the same time he persuaded President Lyndon Johnson to save the abandoned Renwick Gallery from being torn down and make it once again a public museum. In 1972 the Smithsonian opened the Hirshhorn Museum and Sculpture Garden on the Mall and the Renwick Gallery a block from the White House. Many people laughed at the Hirshhorn's bagel-like shape or questioned whether crafts (the focus of the Renwick) were art, but both additions proved to be popular.

Broadening the reach of (and the support for) the Smithsonian, Ripley began publishing the monthly *Smithsonian* magazine and instituted Smithsonian Institution Traveling Exhibition Service (SITES), sending wide varieties of exhibits to communities around the country. He also added the Archives of American Art to the Smithsonian and made appropriations for the National Zoo part of the overall Smithsonian requests to Congress. This latter step increased and stabilized funds for the zoo and made it possible to renovate and add facilities there.

Even as he broadened the scope of the Smithsonian, Ripley did not forget its scientific purposes. In the early 1970s STRI began expanding its work to conduct tropical research throughout Latin America, Asia, and Africa. He also increased research at the National Zoo and, in conjunction with Harvard University, established an astrophysical observatory in Arizona.

One of Ripley's major contributions, and the most visited museum in the world, the National Air and Space Museum, opened in 1976. Two years later the Smithsonian took over an existing collection, establishing the National Museum of African Art. Ripley also began the Smithsonian's first inventory, an undertaking that would take five years and cost $8 million. The result: fully indexed and cross-referenced computer files identifying some 100 million items, including 114,429 bird's eggs, 20 pipe organs, and 14 million postage stamps.

Ripley made a significant impact on the Smithsonian, on Washington, DC, and on the field of museums. During his two decades as Secretary, eight new museums and seven new research or conservation and storage facilities opened, outreach efforts proved successful, the number of visitors more than doubled, and the annual budget grew to more than $300 million, with half coming from Congress.

Changing Financial Picture: 1984–94

Robert McCormick Adams, an archeologist, served as Secretary from 1984 to 1994 and continued to make the Smithsonian an open, inviting place. In 1987 the Arthur M. Sackler

Gallery of Asian Art opened, and the Anacostia Museum, which had expanded to include the Center for African American History and Culture, moved to a new building. In 1989 Congress established the National Museum of the American Indian and a year later the National Postal Museum. In 1993 the Postal Museum's collection of postal history and philatelic items moved to its new home in the historic City Post Office, a Beaux Arts building a few blocks north of the Mall. In 1994 the George Gustav Heye Center of the National Museum of the American Indian opened in lower Manhattan, in the historic Alexander Hamilton U.S. Custom House.

During the 1990s museums across the country faced service cuts and staff reductions as federal money for the arts decreased. Although its federal appropriation actually increased, the money did not keep up with inflation, and the Smithsonian was forced to eliminate extended summer hours, offer buyouts to staff, leave some vacancies unfilled, and change exhibitions less often. Many museums, including the Smithsonian, turned to corporate sponsors for projects and exhibits.

The ability to raise money and extensive management skills were critical considerations in the selection of Ira Michael Heyman as the tenth Secretary of the Smithsonian in 1994. The retired chancellor of the University of California at Berkeley and a lawyer, Heyman's selection broke the tradition of the Secretary being a scientist.

1994 to the Present

Heyman spent five years as Secretary, successfully steering the institution through financial difficulties, unifying its management structure, and improving relationships with Congress. He generated several very large gifts and initiated a capital campaign. He also promoted the Smithsonian through extensive exchange programs and an exceedingly popular web site. But it was a less than tranquil period, as controversies erupted over various exhibitions ranging from the Enola Gay, the airplane that dropped the atomic bomb on Hiroshima, to a forum at the 50th anniversary of Israel.

The issues of what and how things were displayed at a museum was not new, nor was it limited to the Smithsonian Institution. At its core were differences about the role of public museums: to present one or different viewpoints, to display revered objects or explain (interpret) history. Pressure for the Smithsonian and other public institutions to present noncontroversial exhibits was seen by some as appropriate and others as censorship. The growing dependence on corporate funding only served to expand the voices influencing such decisions. Finances and politics had been intertwined in the Smithsonian's role since the institution was established. Heyman's successors each would make their mark on that relationship and on "The Nation's Attic" itself.

Principal Museums

Anacostia Museum and Center for African American History and Culture; Arts and Industries Building; Cooper-Hewitt, National Design Museum; Freer Gallery of Art; Hirshhorn Museum and Sculpture Garden; National Air and Space Museum; National Museum of American Art; National Museum of American History; National Museum of the American Indian; National Museum of Natural History; National Portrait Gallery; National Postal Museum; National Zoological Park; Renwick Gallery; Arthur M. Sackler Gallery; Smithsonian Institution Building. [principal_research_facilities] Archives of American Art; Center for Folklife Programs and Cultural Studies; Smithsonian Center for Materials Research and Education; Conservation and Research Center; Marine Station at Link Port; Smithsonian Astrophysical Observatory; Smithsonian Environmental Research Center; Smithsonian Tropical Research Institute; Center for Latino Initiatives.

Further Reading

Arnett, Elsa C., "150 Years at the Smithsonian," *News & Record* (Greensboro, N.C.), August 10, 1996, p. D1.
Bonner, Alice, "Smithsonian Finds Its Attic Full of Treasure," *Washington Post,* August 27, 1981, p. A1.
Davis, Lou, "Who Was on First, First?," *Air Transport World,* January 1993, p. 85.
Forgey, Benjamin, "Ripley's Believe It and Build," *Washington Post,* September 15, 1984, p. C1.
"From Smithson to Smithsonian: The Birth of an Institution," http://www.sil.si.edu/exhibits/smithson, 1998.
Goldberger, Paul, "Historical Shows on Trial: Who Judges?," *New York Times,* February 11, 1996, p. B1.
Goode, George Brown, "Biographical Sketch of Spencer Fullerton Baird," *Marine Fisheries Review* (U.S. Department of Commerce, Washington, DC), January 1, 1996, p. 40.
Mulligan, Kate, "Nation's Venerable Institution," *Washington Times,* April 25, 1996, p. M4.
Page, Jake, "From Back-Lot Menagerie to Nascent BioPark in Only a Hundred Years," *Smithsonian,* July 1989, p. 26.
Parks, Edward, "Secretary S. Dillon Ripley Retires After Twenty Years of Innovation," *Smithsonian,* September 1984, p. 76.
Ringle, Ken, "Smithsonian: The Greatest of the Mall," *Washington Post,* August 10, 1996, p. A1.
"The Smithsonian Institution Fact Sheet," Washington, DC: Smithsonian Institution, March 1998.
Trescott, Jacqueline, "Heyman To Leave Smithsonian," *Washington Post,* January 23, 1999, p. A1.
Van Dyne, Larry, "Storming the Castle," *Washingtonian,* August 1994.
Wellborn, Stanley N., "New Guard for Treasures at Smithsonian," *U.S. News & World Report,* September 24, 1984, p. 68.
Wiencek, Henry, "Smithsonian Institution," in *The Smithsonian Guide to Historic America: Virginia and the Capital Region,* New York: Stewart, Tabori & Chang, 1989, p. 47.

—Ellen D. Wernick

Snap-On, Incorporated

10801 Corporate Drive
Kenosha, Wisconsin 53141-1430
U.S.A.
(414) 656-5200
Fax: (414) 656-5577
Web site: http://www.snapon.com

Public Company
Incorporated: 1920 as Snap-On Wrench Company
Employees: 11,700
Sales: $1.77 billion (1998)
Stock Exchanges: New York
Ticker Symbol: SNA
SICs: 3423 Hand & Edge Tools, Not Elsewhere
   Classified; 3546 Power-Driven Handtools; 3825
   Instruments for Electrical Signal Measurement; 3559
   Special Industry Machinery, Not Elsewhere Classified

Snap-On, Incorporated is one of the largest and most successful manufacturers and marketers of hand tools, power tools, shop equipment, diagnostic equipment, collision repair equipment, and emissions/safety equipment in the United States. The company makes hand tools such as wrenches, sockets, pliers, ratchets, screwdrivers; power tools such as pneumatic (air) and corded (electric) drills, sanders, and polishers; and a host of other items like wheel balancing and alignment equipment for cars, tool chests and cabinets for industrial, automotive, and aerospace storage applications, and engine and emission analyzing equipment. Snap-On markets its entire range of products through an extensive international network of subsidiaries, dealers, and representatives. The company considers itself the originator of the mobile van method of marketing hand tools.

Early History

Snap-On was founded in 1920 by Joe Johnson and William A. Seidemann. Prior to Johnson's idea for "interchangeable sockets," the socket wrenches used by mechanics were one-piece units. Professional auto mechanics quickly recognized the efficiency and flexibility that resulted from pairing many sockets with few handles. From the beginning, sales were generated by demonstrating the benefits of the novel tool sets directly to the customers. New tools were added to the line, and a catalog was published in 1923. By 1925, 165 salesmen were demonstrating and distributing Snap-On tools.

Stanton Palmer, a former factory sales representative, served as president of the corporation from 1921 until his death ten years later. At that time, Snap-On sought financial help from one of its principal creditors, Forged Steel Products Company, whose owner, William E. Myers, became Snap-On's new president. When Myers died in 1939, Joe Johnson, the corporation's conceptual founder, became the president of both Snap-On and Forged Steel.

Under Johnson's leadership the sales force continued to grow. During World War II, when supplying the military's needs caused tool shortages in the civilian market, Snap-On began releasing available stock to its sales force, in an attempt to maintain goodwill with the civilian customer base. By 1945 all salesmen were carrying stock and making immediate deliveries to their customers. Shortly thereafter, Snap-On made each seller an independent businessperson in an assigned territory.

The Postwar Era of Growth and Prosperity

Subsidiaries in Canada and Mexico aided growth in the 1950s. The Snap-On product line also was expanded. Corporate acquisitions of specialized companies brought products that addressed the mechanic's need for increasingly complex diagnostic tune-up and maintenance equipment. During this period, Snap-On also acquired its system of branches (which had operated previously as independent outlets). Branch acquisitions permitted Snap-On greater control over the marketing and distribution systems.

Victor M. Cain became president upon Johnson's retirement in 1959. In 1965 a Snap-On branch was opened in the United Kingdom. An important patent on the "flank drive" design of wrenches was also awarded in 1965, after years of legal debate. The "flank drive" design produced wrenches with a superior grip, less likely to round the corners of 12-point fasteners under high torque conditions.

Growth and Expansion in the 1970s and 1980s

Snap-On's growth was dramatic in the period that followed. Sales increased from $66.2 million in 1969 to $373.6 million in 1979, while profits increased from $6 million to $42.6 million. Norman E. Lutz became president in 1974, overseeing growth in the worldwide sales force to more than 3,000. In 1978 Lutz became chair and chief executive officer (CEO), and Edwin C. Schindler became president. That year Snap-On stock was first listed on the New York Stock Exchange.

The early 1980s saw rapid changes in the company's management. In 1982 Lutz retired and was replaced by Schindler as chairperson, while William B. Rayburn became president; the following year Schindler died, and Rayburn became the company's chairperson and CEO. A slight decrease in both revenue and earnings in 1982 was attributed to that year's recession. Snap-On examined operations and took measures to improve profitability through reducing expenses as well as marketing more aggressively. Even in this disappointing year, however, net earnings were significant at $37.3 million on $430.5 million in net sales, or 8.7 percent of sales.

Snap-On continued to cultivate its image as the foremost supplier of well-crafted products and customer-oriented service. During the 1980s, Snap-On became the sole supplier of tools to NASA for the space shuttles. In 1984 Snap-On acquired an equity stake of approximately 34 percent in Balco, Inc., a developer of engine diagnostic and wheel service equipment. The frequency of visits to customers had increased to weekly in some cases, and the vans carried $50,000 to $200,000 of hand tools and equipment inventory. Additional services provided by dealers, such as cleaning previously purchased Snap-On tools every six months, allowed dealers to identify and recommend replacement of worn-out tools. Although Snap-on was beginning to face competition from a variety of sources, including Sears, Roebuck & Co., the Mac Tools subsidiary of Stanley Works, the Matco Tools subsidiary of Chicago Pneumatic, and various Japanese companies, Snap-On was able to maintain its premium prices because of the services it offered and the customer relationships in place.

Snap-On has stated that its market share cannot be determined, but in October 1986, *Forbes* estimated that "with its long head start and 49 percent of the market, Snap-On has as many dealers tooling about as all of its competitors combined." At this time, Snap-On was distributing two million catalogs each year. The 350-page catalogs were considered Snap-On's "most valuable single marketing tool" by Rayburn, who told *Forbes* that "our industrial people leave them with buyers, purchasing agents and requisition people. Our dealers leave them with shop owners and mechanics. When there is a mechanical problem, they look in the catalog for a tool that can solve it."

In 1988 new Chairperson Marion Gregory faced a new challenge for Snap-On. An increasing number of lawsuits were filed by former and current dealers in state courts around the United States. The claims included allegations of misrepresentation, contract violations, and causing emotional distress. In an early case, George Owens, a former dealer, claimed that he was pressured to divide his territory with another dealer. A California jury awarded $6.9 million in damages, an amount later reduced in settlement. Other lawsuits claimed misrepresentation of potential profits to dealers, automatic billing of dealers by Snap-On for certain tools provided to the dealers for promotional purposes, and pressure to extend credit.

Snap-On's general policy was to consider settlement as preferable to litigation; the company accrued or paid a total of $7.9 million, $16.6 million, and $16.2 million for litigation-related costs in 1989, 1990, and 1991, respectively, before "determining to pursue more cases to final determination and apply a more stringent policy toward settlement," per Snap-On's 1991 Annual Report. Snap-On also asserted claims of its own against its insurance carriers with respect to coverage on certain dealer claims.

The 1990s and Beyond

In 1991 Robert A. Cornog, formerly the president of Macwhyte Company, became chairperson, president, and CEO of Snap-On, ending a long tradition of filling these positions from within the company. Also that year, Snap-On began to enroll all new U.S. dealers as franchisees and offered the option of applying for a franchise to existing dealers. Snap-On viewed the conversion to a franchise program as an opportunity to establish greater control over the marketing and business activities of its dealers. The program was not designed to increase revenues, and costs in new group insurance programs, stock purchase programs, and special volume-purchase discounts were expected to offset franchise fees. As an inducement to convert, Snap-On waived initial and some recurring franchise fees for existing dealers. Nonetheless, most existing dealers did not elect to apply for franchises.

Snap-On issued common stock valued at approximately $21.2 million to acquire the remaining interest in Balco, Inc. in 1991. The corporation also announced its intention to consolidate product inventories from 51 branch warehouses to four regional distribution centers. By this time, operations were conducted in subsidiaries located in Canada, the United Kingdom, Mexico, Germany, Australia, Japan, and The Netherlands. Sales in other countries accounted for 17 percent of total revenue, though only five percent of operating income.

Net earnings, which had been down from earlier levels for three years in a row, were still $34.3 million on net revenue of

$881.7 million or 8.3 percent of net revenue in 1991, despite the recession in the United States and Canada. This translated to an after-tax return on average shareholders' equity of 11.4 percent, considerably below the 18 to 23 percent level that Snap-On had enjoyed in the years 1983–89. In response, Snap-On reorganized its management structure to allow separate accountability for its three business areas: Finance, Manufacturing and Technology, and Marketing and Distribution.

As Snap-On management looked to the end of the 20th century, management recognized that the corporation would have to adjust to fundamental changes in its business to achieve the high levels of return it sought. Believing that improved automotive quality and warranty programs had caused slower repair volume growth and had shifted work to the auto dealers, Snap-On determined to develop new products and services for existing customers while reaching out to the new markets as well.

Snap-On management began to consider whether other services, such as a credit card for general use, might profitably be offered to its credit-proven customers, who were in weekly contact with Snap-On dealers. Outside sourcing of products, which already accounted for 35 percent of Snap-On's manufacturing, was considered an opportunity for cost savings. International and industrial markets were seen as offering a possible means toward the growth to which Snap-On had always been accustomed.

In maintaining its strategy in searching for new markets, during the late 1990s management at Snap-On decided to enter into a licensing agreement with Stylus Writing Instruments to manufacture and market office products under its own brand name. Snap-On office tools, such as staples, staple removers, and tape dispensers, were marketed with the designation, "Made in the USA." In reaching the agreement, management at Stylus promised that all Snap-On office tools would be "ergonomic and durable, with unique styling and colors." At the same time, Snap-On made an about-face and ventured into direct consumer retail sales by reaching a private label pact with Lowe's Home Improvement Warehouse. Inaugurating a private label tool line known as Kobalt, the two companies were positioning themselves to compete against Sears' Craftsman brand, Wal-Mart's Popular Mechanics, and Home Depot's Husky brand name tool line. The expansion into retail sales was expected to increase the company's 1997 revenues of $1.7 billion by at least five percent, perhaps more. Since sales of Snap-On hand tools was estimated to increase at 1.5 percent, management considered the entry into retail sales well worth the effort and risk.

Snap-On announced a comprehensive plan to restructure its entire operation during the summer of 1998, including the elimination of more than 1,000 jobs to increase profitability. The plan was designed to close five manufacturing facilities and five warehouses, discontinue a number of product lines, consolidate some business units, and close more than 40 small sales offices throughout North America and Europe.

With more than 200 patents and numerous pending patent applications, Snap-On continues to encourage its research and development team to challenge the ordinary way of doing things. The company has been at the forefront of designing new tools for many industrial, medical diagnostic, automotive, and aerospace applications and also will remain one of the most innovative marketers within the tool manufacturing industry for years to come.

Principal Subsidiaries

Snap-On Tools of Canada Ltd.; Snap-On Tools Limited; Snap-On Tools International, Ltd. (F.S.C.); Herramientas Snap-On de Mexico, S.A.; Snap-On Tools GmbH (Germany); Snap-On Tools Import and Wholesale Pty. Ltd.; Snap-On Tools Netherlands B.V.; Snap-On Tools Japan, K.K.; Snap-On Tools (Europe) Limited; Snap-On AG (Germany); ATI Industries, Inc.; Balco, Inc.; Sun Electric Corp; Sioux Tools, Inc.; Wheeltronic, Ltd.; Edge Diagnostic Systems; Consolidated Devices, Inc.; John Bean Company; Credit Corp SPC LLC; Hoffman Werkstatt-Technik GmbH (Germany); Nu-Tech Industries, Inc.

Further Reading

"Coming Soon to an Office Desk Near You: Snap-On Tools," *Brandweek,* September 28, 1998, p. 5.

Fanning, Deirdre, "Monkey Wrench at Snap-On Tools," *Forbes,* June 27, 1988.

Kerwin, Kathleen, "GM: Modular Plants Won't Be a Snap," *Business Week,* November 9, 1998, pp. 168–72.

——, "Lowe's to Compete in PL Tool Race," *Discount Store News,* November 23, 1998, p. 1.

Smith, Geoffrey N., "Snap-On's Proprietary Ingredient," *Forbes,* October 6, 1986.

——, "Snap-On Plans Restructuring," *American Metal Market,* July 6, 1998.

—Marcia McDermott
—updated by Thomas Derdak

Société Air France

45, rue de Paris
95747
Roissy CDG Cedex
France
33-1-41-56-78-00
Fax: 33-1-41-56-70-29
Web site: http://www.airfrance.fr

State-Owned Company (94.3%)
Incorporated: 1933 as Société Air France
Employees: 50,000
Sales: FFr 60.72 billion ($9.81 billion) (1998)
SICs: 4516 Air Transportation, Scheduled; 4522 Air
    Transportation, Nonscheduled

One of the world's largest airlines, Société Air France is trying to shake a somewhat troubled reputation and a socialist work ethic to become known as Europe's finest carrier. Its fleet of approximately 205 aircraft includes several of the unique, supersonic Concordes and numerous Airbus and Boeing planes. More than 33 million passengers a year fly Air France which is also a key deliverer of air freight.

In the Beginning

Air France emerged in the early 1930s, when the possibilities for large-scale commercial air transport were swiftly expanding. Recognizing the benefits likely to arise from coordination and an end to competition, four private French air transport companies—Air Union, SGTA, CIDNA, and Air Orient—merged in August of 1933 and took over another enterprise, Aéropostale, to create Société Air France.

The new company soon became France's most prominent airline and expanded steadily during the 1930s, as the demand for air transport grew. The company created extensive networks for carrying passengers, cargo, and mail in various parts of the world until, by the start of World War II in 1939, Air France was recognized as one of the world's leading air carriers.

The outbreak of the war and the German occupation of much of France ended this period of expansion for Société Air France and crippled the company's chances of maintaining its services. Most of the airline's activities were suspended until the war ended in 1945.

Postwar Nationalization

The end of World War II sparked a wave of support within the French government for nationalization of key industries as the best method of harnessing the country's resources to rebuild what had been destroyed during the war and strengthen the French economy. Considered one of the country's main connections with the rest of the world, Air France was a prime target, and in 1948 Société Air France became the Compagnie Nationale Air France, with the French government holding the bulk of the company's stock.

Nationalization allowed Air France access to much greater financial resources than had previously been the case, both through the government's injection of capital and the benefits of government backing in securing loans. Thus, aided by a period of global economic growth, rising demand for air transport, and dramatic improvements in aircraft technology, the company was able to sustain a long period of expansion.

During the 1950s and 1960s Air France developed an extensive network of tourist paths, increasing both the number of routes it served and the frequency of flights. The company improved its operations by using the fastest and newest propeller aircraft, including the Super Constellation, a plane capable of flying up to 500 kilometers per hour. These changes enabled Air France to expand its network from a total of 250,000 km in 1953 to 325,000 km in 1960.

The development of commercial jet aircraft, which afforded larger capacity and shorter journey times, during the 1960s enabled Air France to undertake another important improvement in its operations. The company began using Caravelle and Boeing 707 jets and in 1962 became involved in a joint venture with British Airways to develop a supersonic jet aircraft, the Concorde, at an estimated cost to each partner of between £75 million and £85 million.

Company Perspectives:

Being the best European airline . . . involves improving our customer's satisfaction on a daily basis and providing the most attractive products and services at the best value. Air France must be a global brand meeting the needs of customers from all over the world. We will increase the range of our destinations both directly and through an alliance network. We will be a customer-driven organization. We will be reliable. We will improve our commercial efficiency by developing closer relationships with our distributors and customers. This is our commitment.

By 1970 Air France's network had grown to 500,000 km, and its acquisition of new jet aircraft, including the Boeing 727 and 747 and the Airbus 300, ensured its position as one of the world's leading international carriers. In the mid-1970s the company began using the newly developed Concorde for commercial flights. The Concorde project, however, proved far more expensive than originally expected: by 1982 it had cost the French and British governments a total of nearly £1.8 billion, more than ten times the original estimates.

1980s: Deregulation Era

Throughout the 1980s the world airline industry, which had remained relatively stable for decades, showed signs of change. Deregulation of the U.S. industry in the early part of the decade radically altered conditions in one of the key airline markets, while the prospect of a single European market emerging in the 1990s compelled European airlines to examine their operations, build alliances with other carriers, and diversify their business bases.

Like other airlines, Air France was affected by the changing conditions. In 1987, amid widespread rumors that he would be responsible for preparing the company for privatization, Jacques Friedmann, former head of the Compagnie Générale Maritime et Financière, was appointed chair of Société Air France by the conservative French government of Jacques Chirac. A plan to sell 15 percent of Air France's stock on the Paris stock exchange, though, was postponed indefinitely in October.

The government deregulated the domestic French airline market by allowing charter companies to compete against Société Air France and a private carrier, Air Inter, for domestic routes. Air France responded to this change by fighting for control of Air Inter against Union des Transports Aériens (UTA), Air France's main private rival. Both companies increased their stakes in Air Inter, but the dispute ended in a stalemate with Air France and UTA each holding 35 percent of the company.

Meanwhile, Air France was building alliances with other European airlines to branch out into other industries. Among such collaborations was its investment of 25 percent of the capital to develop a joint computer reservations system called Amadeus with the German airline Lufthansa, the Spanish carrier Iberia, and Scandinavian Airlines. The consortium estimated the cost of developing the system at $300 million.

In September 1988 the newly elected Socialist government chose Bernard Attali, a prominent Socialist, to take over for Jacques Friedmann as chair of Air France. Widely regarded as a political move, the replacement was officially linked with the crash three months before of a new Air France A320 Airbus at the Mulhouse air show, in which three people were killed.

The change in leadership removed the immediate possibility of privatization for Air France, but the company continued to seek acquisitions and new alliances. In July 1989 Air France paid FFr 240 million for a 35 percent stake in TAT, a regional passenger carrier and parcels and express delivery company based in Tours. TAT was the fourth-largest air carrier in France. In September 1989 Air France signed a cooperation agreement with Lufthansa in response to the changing conditions and to moves by British Airways, then the largest Western European airline, to build new alliances in Europe and America. The accordance entailed cooperation in all aspects of management and operations, including joint negotiations with aircraft manufacturers, harmonized aircraft acquisition programs, joint development of new long-distance routes, and the establishment of permanent management structures between the two companies.

The Perilous 1990s

Air France made another crucial strategic move in January 1990, when it bought 70 percent of UTA from Chargeurs S.A., giving it authority over UTA's extensive network in tropical Africa and the South Pacific as well as control of Air Inter, which dominated the French domestic airline industry. The takeover made Air France the largest airline in Western Europe. The European Commission's competition commissioner, Sir Leon Brittan, tried to block the takeover on the grounds that it would restrict competition. After ten months of negotiations, though, he approved the deal on the condition that the French government allow independent carriers to compete on several routes and that Air France sell its 35 percent holding in TAT.

In late 1990, however, the expansion that Air France and other airlines were planning was put to a halt. The Iraqi invasion of Kuwait pushed oil prices sharply higher and ultimately caused a huge dent in passenger demand. Citing soaring fuel costs and higher insurance premiums, Air France launched an economy drive and spending freeze in September, stopping all ground investments that had been planned for 1990, canceling all nonessential building and computer investments, and suspending recruitment.

Air France continued to look for international alliances, and in September 1990 signed a commercial agreement with USAir, a leading domestic airline in the United States, to cooperate on transatlantic routes. A worsening economic and financial climate, however, was limiting the possibilities for expansion. In November, a few days after the EC approved the UTA takeover, UTA and Air Inter announced that they were no longer making a profit. After years of growing profits, Air France recorded a loss of FFr 668 million for 1990. The group estimated that the crisis in the Persian Gulf had cost it FFr 1.7 billion in 1990 alone.

In early 1991 the EC responded to the worsening position of the airlines by suspending its restrictive competition rules, allowing them limited state support and more flexibility in pricing and assessing costs. Bernard Attali illustrated the extent of the problem in the April 12, 1992, issue of the *Guardian*: "We are in a period of very great crisis. It is the greatest crisis ever in air transport."

In May 1991 the French government announced that it would inject FFr 2 billion in fresh capital into Air France and in August gave the company approval to raise up to FFr 5 billion more from other sources. In November, after the EC had approved the government grant, the airline announced that the state-owned Banque Nationale de Paris would pay FFr 1.25 billion for an 8.8 percent stake in the company.

The worsening of the Persian Gulf crisis in early 1991 and the ensuing war was detrimental to airlines. Air France incurred a loss of FFr 1.16 billion in the first six months of 1991. The company responded to the predicament by appointing a management consultancy firm, Andersen Consulting, to undertake a nine-month study of how the company could cut costs in the face of increased competition from American and Asian airlines.

As a result of the study, Air France announced in September 1991 that it would merge its routes with those of UTA, cutting 3,000 jobs, or nearly eight percent of its work force, by the end of 1993, saving £150 million a year, and phasing out the UTA brand name. Air France also announced that it would sell its headquarters in central Paris for FFr 1.6 billion and move its offices to Charles de Gaulle airport by 1995. The company reported another loss of FFr 685 million for 1991. Despite a slight increase in turnover, a restructuring, and a slight upturn in traffic, it did not expect to make a profit until 1993 at the earliest.

In January 1992 Air France became the first Western airline to acquire shares in an existing Eastern European carrier. The company led a consortium, along with the European Bank for Reconstruction and Development and Caisse des Dépôts et Consignations, that paid a total of $60 million for a 40 percent stake in the Czechoslovakian airline Ceskeslovenske Aerolinie. The two carriers began combining their activities, using Paris and Prague as shared bases.

Also in early 1992, the pressures of the tight market were displayed in a series of disputes between Air France and U.S. carriers over transatlantic routes. Each side slashed prices to undercut the other, and a dispute over the amount of extra capacity the American airlines could add to their European routes during summer months resulted in France renouncing a bilateral air traffic agreement it had signed with the United States in 1946.

Air France signed another partnership agreement in April 1992, this time with the state-owned Belgian airline Sabena. Air France agreed to acquire as much as BFr 6 billion of a BFr 15 billion issue of Sabena shares by 1994, giving it a 37 percent stake in the carrier. The companies consented to integrate their activities at Brussels, Charles de Gaulle, and Orly airports.

Also during this time Air France announced an in-principle accordance with Lufthansa to merge its Meridien hotel chain with Lufthansa's Kempinski chain, creating an 80-hotel group with annual sales of nearly £565 million. By June 1992, however, the only firm result was a marketing agreement between the two, and no timetable for a merger had been set.

Edouard Balladur became prime minister of France in March 1993. He proposed privatizing 21 large companies, including Air France. In the face of a paralyzing but popular strike in the fall of 1993, the government canceled plans to cut wages and eliminate 4,000 jobs. It feared similar strikes in other troubled industries. France floundered in a recession characterized by severe unemployment, afflicting nearly 12 percent of the work force. Meanwhile Air France hemorrhaged money, losing $650 million in the first six months of 1993.

In April, Chairman Christian Blanc finally announced that the previously-rejected restructuring had been approved by Air France unions. However, it was contingent upon the European Commission's approval of yet another government bail-out, this time in the amount of FFr 20 billion ($3.4 billion). *The Economist* noted this spurred resentment among unsubsidized European carriers such as British Airways, which owned a fifty percent share of French domestic carrier TAT.

French resources were severely taxed when Flight 8969 was hijacked in Algeria by Muslim terrorists. Although three passengers were executed before the plane was allowed to leave the country, a French commando unit rescued the remainder after it refueled in Marseilles.

In 1995 Air France announced plans to enter the commercial data communications business, in direct competition with France Telecom. The company's extensive computerized reservations system provided the rationale behind the venture. It already had 50 air transportation clients, and expected revenues of $40 million per year from the venture.

After losing $3.5 billion in seven years, Air France posted a profit in 1996, when earnings were FFr 394 million. Blanc cut 5,000 jobs through attrition and trimmed costs by one-fifth. Blanc also resisted Jacques Chirac's urging to buy only Airbus aircraft. Thanks to these practical, but politically unpopular efforts, Air France posted even larger profits in 1997.

Chairman and CEO Christian Blanc, frustrated at government intervention of the airline's majority privatization scheme, resigned in September 1997. He had guided the airline to profitability, but the concessions he gained from workers rested on the promise of eventual compensation in company stock. If only a minority stake were sold, too few shares (less than ten percent) would land on the market to make the employees' share of thirty percent very valuable. Jean-Cyril Spinetta became the company's next chairman.

French tourism was booming in 1997, again making it the most popular tourist destination in the world. During this time Air France merged with domestic carrier Air Inter. An ouster of conservatives in June 1997, however, threatened Air France's plans to go public. In February 1998 a partial privatization plan was announced that would reduce the government's share from 95 percent to 53 percent. In March this plan was postponed until autumn.

Air France pilots went on strike in June 1998. They objected to plans to cut their salaries in exchange for equity. *The Economist* reported the strike cost FFr 100 million ($17 million) per day.

In the summer of 1998, the planned privatization was rescheduled for early 1999. This plan called for the sale of only 20 percent of the company, expected to raise between FFr 15 billion and FFr 20 billion.

By November 1998, the main pilots' union had agreed to a three-year contract that would reduce costs by $90 million per year. With an initial public offering planned for 1999, most of the union's pilots opted to reduce their wages in exchange for company stock.

Principal Subsidiaries

Air Intel, Air France Industries, Air France Cargo.

Further Reading

Egan, Jack, "Equality, Fraternity, and Inefficiency," *U.S. News and World Report,* June 23, 1997.
"European 100: Air France," *Information Week,* December 11, 1995.
"Deja Vu," *Economist,* October 30, 1993.
"Flying Low with Air France," *Economist,* October 30, 1993.
"Flying Tackle," *Economist,* June 6, 1998.
Sancton, Thomas, "Anatomy of a Hijack," *Time,* January 9, 1995.
"Whitewash," *Economist,* April 16, 1994.

—Richard Brass
—updated by Frederick C. Ingram

Société du Louvre

58, Boulevard Gouvion-Saint-Cyr
75017 Paris
France
(33) 1.40.68.53.50
Fax: 1.40.68.53.45
Web sites: http://www.concorde-hotels.com; http://www.campanile.fr; http://www.clarine.com

Public Subsidiary of Taittinger S.A.
Incorporated: 1855 as Fabre-Cauchard-Henriot et Cie
Employees: 5,956
Sales: FFr 3.72 billion (US$600 million) (1997)
Stock Exchanges: Paris
Ticker Symbol: Louvre
SICs: Holding Companies

Société du Louvre does not run that Paris museum, but its properties are almost as distinguished. Société du Louvre is a holding company that oversees active and investment control of subsidiary companies in three primary categories: hotels, luxury goods, and light industry. Governed by the Taittinger family since the 1950s, Société du Louvre is also a subsidiary of the Taittinger champagne company. Directly or indirectly, the Taittinger family controls more than 40 percent of Société du Louvre's stock and more than 60 percent of the company's voting rights. Anne-Claire Taittinger Bonnemaison was named company president in 1997, taking over from her father, Jean Taittinger. If the Taittinger name has become inextricably linked with Société du Louvre, that is also because of the family's active participation in the company's day to day operations: many of the company's top positions are held by Taittinger family members and close associates. In the 1990s the company, under pressure from minority shareholders, has taken steps to limit this family involvement, however.

Hotels represent Société du Louvre's principal activity, with nearly 70 percent of the company's total revenues in 1997. The company's hotel holdings are operated under two separate subsidiaries. The first and flagship subsidiary is the Concorde Hotels group. Representing some of the world's most distinguished hotels, including the famed Hotel Crillon in Paris, the Martinez in Cannes, Concorde Hotels represents more than 70 hotels worldwide and specializes in the luxury hotel category.

While luxury hotels have long formed a centerpiece of the Société du Louvre portfolio, the company has built a strong European position in the mid-class and budget accommodations categories through subsidiary Envergure. This subsidiary represents Europe's second largest hotel group (behind leader Accor), with more than 625 hotels and restaurants representing more than 38,000 rooms. Envergure hotels and restaurants are grouped under five different brands: Campanile, with more than 360 two-star hotel-restaurants; the three-star chain of Blue Marine hotels and restaurants; the single-star Premier Classe chain; Clarine, consisting of more than 35 hotels, primarily located in city centers; and the Côte à Côte chain of restaurants, founded in 1996.

In addition to its hotel holdings, Société du Louvre has claimed a strong position in the world's luxury goods markets through its Annick Goutal perfume subsidiary and especially through its majority control of famed crystal maker Baccarat, founded in 1764. Contrasting these holdings is Société du Louvre's light industry subsidiaries, particularly Deville, founded in 1846, a leading maker of heating and cooking products, which had formed part of the group since 1979.

In the late 1990s, Société du Louvre has been under attack by various investors, including François Pinault and Asher Edelman, who have made no secret of their separate ambitions to seize control of the company. An attempt by Edelman, who built a shareholding position of more than 10 percent by August 1998 once again placed the reserved Taittingers in the spotlight. The willingness of some family members to convert their stock to cash has led some observers to believe that one day such attempts might succeed. For the moment, however, the Taittinger family's control—spread across more than 100 family members—remains firm.

Luxuriating Since the 1850s

With roots extending to the mid-19th century, Société du Louvre's name would epitomize luxury in the 20th century.

Founded in 1855 as the limited partnership Fabre-Cauchard-Henriot et Cie, the group's initial vocation was in the retail sphere. The partnership operated its own stores for more than 100 years, before abandoning its distribution activities in the 1970s. By then, the company had built up an impressive portfolio of hotels. Its name would change to Société du Louvre by 1898, reflecting at once the company's ownership of the Hotel du Louvre and its base in Paris.

During the 20th century, Société du Louvre continued to build its portfolio of properties, located not only in Paris but throughout France, gaining the company an impressive list of Parisian properties, as well as a number of the world's most prestigious names in luxury accommodations. Its presence in the real estate industry led Société du Louvre to extend its financial activities into the investment community, with the creation of the Banque du Louvre, specializing in brokering and other investment and investment management activities.

By the mid-1950s, the Taittinger family—already proprietors of one of the world's leading champagne labels—had built a leading shareholding position in Société du Louvre, to the extent that the group quickly became synonymous with the Taittinger name and subsidiary of the Taittinger family business. The first of the Taittinger clan to arrive at the helm of Société du Louvre was Pierre Taittinger, who took over the company's management in 1955. The elder Taittinger—the first of three generations of the Taittinger family to lead the group in the 20th century—soon placed the group more firmly within the family's ownership, buying up shares in Société du Louvre and succeeding in placing the group's important real estate holding, including hotels and a number of France's largest and most prominent department stores, under direct control of the Taittinger champagne empire.

Hotel Expansion in the 1970s

Pierre Taittinger ceded Société du Louvre's leadership to son Guy Taittinger by the 1960s. The first generation of Taittingers had consolidated the group's position as a holder of prime Parisian and French department store, hotel, and other real estate properties, including such landmarks as the Hotel Crillon, widely considered among the world's most beautiful hotels, the Hotel Lutetia, the company's namesake hotel, and Hotel du Louvre, overlooking the museum and other grand hotels. The second generation of Taittingers led the way to establishing Société du Louvre as a European leader in hotel accommodations.

Guy Taittinger began building the company by dismantling a number of its investments, shedding significant parts of the company's real-estate holdings, including many of its department stores. In turn, the company began expanding its hotel purchases, as well as building the hotel extension to the Palais des Congrès, one of Europe's largest convention centers. The Hotel Concorde-Lafayette, a towering structure located on the Parisian rim and featuring 1,000 rooms, crowned Guy Taittinger's achievements in 1974. By then, Société du Louvre had moved more firmly in the direction of hotel ownership and management: in 1970, the group created the Concorde hotel insignia to group its growing list of luxury hotels, whether company-owned or managed under contract. With its attention

fixed on the hotel trade, Société du Louvre jettisoned its department store activities in 1973.

While Société du Louvre's initial focus had been on the luxury hotel category, it soon saw the chance to expand into new accommodation categories. In 1974, the group purchased a position in a small chain of budget hotels operated by the Société Française de Promotion et Développement Hôtelier. The chain, renamed Campanile in 1976, became the spearhead to the development of Société du Louvre as one of Europe's leading hotel groups. The period also marked a transition in the group's leadership, as Jean Taittinger became president at his brother Guy Taittinger's death.

Jean Taittinger not only diversified the company's hotel holdings, he also diversified its activities. In 1979, Société du Louvre moved beyond the accommodation categories with the acquisition of Compagnie Financière Deville. Created as a foundry in 1846, Deville took on its specialty by the 1880s, that of heating equipment, especially coal- and wood-burning furnaces. In the 1950s, Deville extended its product range to the production of oil-burning stoves and ovens, quickly becoming the French leader in this category. Deville's high-end kitchen equipment was supplemented in the 1970s with a line of coal-burning stoves, as well as a range of electric appliances targeted at the high-end kitchen.

While the Deville acquisition brought the company into light industry, Société du Louvre was also extending its hotel holdings, particularly with the gradual acquisition of the Hotel Martinez, long a Cannes landmark, by 1982, and the purchase of the Hotel Ambassador in 1989.

Hotel and Luxury Leader in the 1990s

Société du Louvre had also begun to seek further diversification, with a focus on the luxury goods category. In 1985, the group formed a partnership with perfumer Annick Goutal. Launched in 1981 by the designer, Annick Goutal perfumes quickly found success among consumers in the high-end perfume segment, especially in the United States. As Annick Goutal moved into retail operations, opening its first Paris boutique, the perfumer caught the interest of Jean Taittinger. In 1985, Société du Louvre entered Annick Goutal as a 50 percent partnership; in 1988 the group took full control of Annick Goutal—leading to its founder's departure—and the perfumer's four Paris boutiques.

Société du Louvre's next move confirmed its taste for luxury: in 1988 the company acquired 12 percent of the famed Cristalleries Baccarat. Founded in 1764, Baccarat had established itself as one of the world's great designers of crystal ware by the mid-19th century. Baccarat designs graced the palaces of much of European royalty, before becoming a favorite among the rising numbers of wealthy Americans. By the 20th century, the company's name had reached legendary status. Baccarat went public in 1978; the company's fortunes soared during the economic boom of the 1980s. Eager to expand its name into new markets, particularly the rapidly developing economies in the Asia Pacific region, Baccarat received expansion capital with the Société du Louvre into its shareholding structure. Société du Louvre continued to advance its position, building its share of Baccarat's stock to 25 percent in 1990, then 47 percent in 1992, before reaching majority control of 51.7 percent in the late 1990s—even as Baccarat's growth was slowed by the extended economic recession of the early 1990s, and the later collapse of much of the Asian economies in the late 1990s.

Annick Goutal's fortunes also slumped in the early 1990s. Caught by the gloomy economic climate, and seemingly lost without the guidance of its founder, Annick Goutal began losing money in the 1990s. However, an agreement reached between Société du Louvre and Annick Goutal returned the designer to the perfumer's creative lead. The perfume design and retail company returned to profitability by the late 1990s.

The hotel world also underwent a crisis in the early 1990s. The combination of overbuilding and the collapse of the worldwide economy at the start of the decade, coupled with travelers' fears arising from the Persian Gulf War, saw occupancy rates plunge. Yet Société du Louvre, which by then had created the subsidiary Envergure Group to guide its non-luxury hotel activities, chose this period to accelerate its growth in the hotel accommodations market.

Between 1992 and 1998, Société du Louvre more than tripled the number of hotel beds under its control. This was accomplished not only by the rapid expansion of its Campanile chain—which had opened to franchising after a long period of reluctance by the Société du Louvre—but also by the strong growth seen in several newly created Envergure labels. Designed to span the range of price categories, Envergure's insignias grew to include the three-star hotel chain Blue Marine, the budget accommodation chain Première Classe, and the chain of two-star Clarine hotels, launched in 1995. Société du Louvre also reinforced its restaurant holdings, launching the Côte à Côte concept of grill restaurants. The company's commitment to hotels and restaurants as its primary source of growth could be seen as well in its sale of its position in the Bank du Louvre to CCP in 1997.

By the middle of the decade, Société du Louvre had grown to become Europe's second largest hotel group, after the giant Accor. The company remained far behind such world leaders as Choice Hotels, however. In addition, the 1990s saw the company's independence threatened. With the difficult economic climate, the company struggled to maintain the all-important occupancy rates. The company's stock price, too, softened— and Société du Louvre quickly became attractive to a number of outside investors eager to add the company's collection of prestigious names to their own portfolios. Perhaps the most tenacious suitor was the American Asher Edelman, who succeeded in building up a position of 11 percent in the company's stock by the end of 1997, and who formally announced his interest in acquiring majority control of Société du Louvre's shares.

These shares, however, remained under the Taittinger family's control, bound by a family pact not to sell shares to outsiders. Yet, with the company paying reduced share benefits, many of the Taittinger family's more than 100 shareholding heirs were finding themselves hard-pressed to pay the hefty estate taxes demanded by the French government. While principal decision-making remained among the majority shareholders in the Taittinger family, represented especially by the Jean Taittinger branch, the company was still forced to tread lightly, particularly as the group's non-family shareholders (including members of the Peugeot group) had begun to demand a clearing out of Taittinger family members from the leadership of many of the group's subsidiaries and operations. Nonetheless, the company was able to rebuff Edelman's several attempts to buy control through 1998.

In 1997, Jean Taittinger retired from the lead of Société du Louvre. His daughter, Anne-Claire Taittinger Bonnemaison was named in his stead as company president. The member of the new Taittinger generation at Société du Louvre's helm had spent nearly 20 years in the company's management, including taking leadership of Baccarat in 1994 and returning that company to revenue growth and profitability for the second half of the decade. Despite continued concerns about the safety of the Taittinger's shareholding position, Anne-Claire Taittinger inherited control of a company set for still greater expansion, particularly through the growth and franchising of the units of its Envergure subsidiary. The return to economic growth—and the upswing in the hotel industry—spelled an optimistic future for the Société du Louvre.

Principal Subsidiaries

International Concorde Hotel Company; Groupe Envergure; Groupe Baccarat; Groupe Deville; Annick Goutal; Louvre Corporation.

Further Reading

Besses-Boumard, Pascale, "La Société du Louvre veut doubler son parc hôtelier économique," *Les Echos,* October 6, 1998, p. 20.
de la Rocque, Jean-Pierre, "La tribu Taittinger sous pression," *L'Express,* December 18, 1997.
Epinay, Bénédicte, "Annick Goutal commence à équilibré ses comptes," *Les Echos,* November 21, 1997, p. 12.
Herzlich, Guy, "Les hôtels Concorde se font agressifs," *Le Monde,* October 18, 1991, p. 33.
Ramadier, Sylvie, "Après de forts investissements, le groupe du Louvre enregistre les premiers signes de reprise," *Les Echos,* June 8, 1994, p. 3.
Renault, Enguérand, "La famille Taittinger tente de résister au siège de sa fortresse," *Le Monde,* August 16, 1998, p. 10.

—M. L. Cohen

Southern Union Company

504 Lavaca Street, Suite 800
Austin, Texas 78701
U.S.A.
(512) 477-5852
Fax: (512) 477-3879
Web site: http://www.southernunionco.com

Public Company
Incorporated: 1932 as Southern Union Utilities Company
Employees: 1,595
Sales: $669.3 million (1998)
Stock Exchanges: New York
Ticker Symbol: SUG
SICs: 4924 Natural Gas Distribution; 6552 Subdividers and Developers Not Elsewhere Classified

Southern Union Company is a publicly owned international holding company for public utilities and other energy-related businesses; the company's principal line of business is the distribution of natural gas. As the 16th largest natural gas distributor in the United States, the company serves over one million customers through its three divisions: Southern Union Gas in Texas, Missouri Gas Energy, and Atlantic Utilities in Florida. The Southern Union Gas division distributes natural gas to approximately 511,000 agricultural, commercial, industrial, and residential customers in Texas, including the cities of Austin, Brownsville, El Paso, Galveston, and Port Arthur. The Missouri Gas Energy division distributes natural gas to approximately 482,000 customers in western Missouri, including the cities of Kansas City and St. Joseph. Atlantic Utilities in Florida is a natural gas and propane distribution firm that serves several communities in Florida. Southern Union's focus is to provide safe, reliable, and low-cost energy. The company believes that the diversity of its geographic operations reduce weather-related risk and risk affiliated with local economic conditions, and it strives for selected growth, mainly in the natural gas industry, while providing various customers "one-stop shopping" for their energy needs.

Early 20th Century Origins and Growth

The company reportedly traces its origins to the 1929 founding of Wink Gas Co. in the West Texas town of Wink. Despite the onset of the Great Depression, Texas was at that time experiencing a boom in the oil business, and the company's business was steady. By 1932, the company had reorganized as a holding company, known as Southern Union Utilities Co. and overseeing the operations of subsidiaries Southern Union Gas Co., New Mexico Gas Co., New Mexico Eastern Gas Co., and Texas Southwestern Gas Co. To better reflect its focus on gas over utilities in general, the company merged all of its assets into the Southern Union Gas Co. in 1942.

The period that followed was characterized by expansion through acquisition. For instance, on January 26, 1944, the company purchased for $2.7 million from Lone Star Gas Company a gas distribution system serving approximately 17,000 customers in the El Paso vicinity. During this time, the company also purchased leases for lands in Louisiana, and by 1949 had acquired for $350,000 the gas facilities of Durango Natural Gas Company in Durango, Colorado. Southern Union cemented its presence in Austin, Texas, when it merged with the Texas Public Service Company in 1949. The company also acquired a gas distribution system with 24,000 customers in Albuquerque, New Mexico.

Throughout the 1950s and 1960s, Southern Union formed wholly owned subsidiaries to oversee the operations of its increasingly far-reaching holdings. The Southern Union Gathering Company was formed to assume operation of the company's gas gathering pipeline system across 50,000 acres of Blanco gas field in San Juan Basin. In 1967, Southern Union Realty Company was formed as a wholly owned subsidiary.

The energy crisis effected by the OPEC oil embargo in the 1970s prompted the company to search further afield for natural resources, and the Southern Union Exploration Co. was formed as a subsidiary in 1974. Also that year, another wholly owned subsidiary, Southern Union Oil Products Company, was formed primarily to sell and distribute refined oil products it had purchased from a refinery owned by Famariss Oil and Refining Company, itself a subsidiary of Famariss Oil Corporation.

Southern Union Oil Products Co. acquired Famariss Oil Corp. in September 1975. Company development over the next 15 years included efforts to consolidate Southern Union's wide array of interests, which by that time included the Southern Union Financial Corporation, Southern Union Processing Co., Southern Union Refining Co., and others.

New Leadership in the 1990s

Perhaps because of its series of acquisitions and mergers in the 1970s and 1980s, many of which had proved unprofitable, Southern Union began the next decade nearly bankrupt. On February 6, 1990, Metro Mobile CTS, a company specializing in cellular telephone licenses, acquired Southern Union for $175 million. The cash transaction was structured in such a way that Southern Union survived the merger as an independent corporate entity with a new group of shareholders (Metro Mobile's), a new board of directors, and three new senior officers, including the new CEO, chairman, and controlling shareholder, George L. Lindemann.

Lindemann was an entrepreneur from New York who had graduated from Wharton and gone on to make millions establishing highly successful businesses whose focuses ranged from contact lenses to cable companies to cellular telephone licenses. When his Metro Mobile CTS company acquired Southern Union, Lindemann admitted knowing nothing about the natural gas business. However, in a 1993 article in *Forbes,* he maintained that contact lenses, cable television, and cellular phones, and, even natural gas distribution "look a lot more different than they are. They're all service oriented; they're all very similar as far as the back office is concerned."

Lindemann brought in Peter H. Kelley to serve as the company's president, and together they set about reorganizing and consolidating Southern Union's customer service operations and bolstering the company's customer base with the acquisition of several new distribution systems in Texas.

Distinguishing itself as an innovator while at the same time making use of excess natural gas supplies in the off-season, Southern Union became involved in converting cars and trucks to run on natural gas. Although this business segment represented a small percentage of the company's sales volume, it was regarded as potentially very profitable given stipulations of the Clean Air Act of 1990 that the country's more polluted urban areas work to reduce pollution by using alternative fuels.

1993 was a year of major acquisitions for the company. In July of that year, Southern Union purchased Eagle Pass Natural Gas Company for $2 million, which added more than 3,800 customers to the company's central Texas region. Also during this time, plans were announced for the acquisition of certain Missouri natural gas distribution operations of Western Resources, Inc., based in Kansas City, Missouri. In September 1993, Southern Union acquired the Rio Grande Valley Gas Company from Valero Energy Corporation for about $30.5 million. The purchase comprised 1,552 miles of distribution lines serving almost 76,000 customers in south Texas.

Under Lindemann and Kelley, expansion also involved moving further north into states where colder weather could provide more stable annual revenues to offset the cyclical nature of gas distribution. In January 1994, the Western Resources, Inc. $400.3 million acquisition was finalized. The Missouri Acquisition gave Southern Union a Kansas office from which to grow its natural gas vehicle market and added 460,00 customers to its operations, nearly doubling the size of its service base. By having the Missouri Gas Energy (MGE) division under its operating belt, Southern Union became one of the 15 major gas utilities in the United States. The company soon was able to declare a three-for-two stock split, and by year-end 1994, the company's sales of $374.5 million had almost doubled 1992 sales figures.

The Missouri Acquisition helped establish Southern Union as a sales and market-driven company, with management committed to reaching profitable growth in an increasingly competitive business arena. Management had three strategies for achieving their objectives, including: promoting new sales opportunities and markets for natural gas; improving financial and operating performance; and growing the company through development of existing systems and specific acquisitions of new systems.

1996 was also a year of innovation and new markets for Southern Union. The company created Energy WorX, Inc. as a subsidiary to fill a void in the natural gas training industry. Energy WorX developed computer-based training courses on natural gas industry topics, and saved the company training costs. Southern Union also entered the propane market when subsidiary SUPro acquired propane distribution facilities in El Paso, Texas, which served 1,100 customers. SUPro installed centralized distribution systems in regions that were geographically beyond the natural gas mains and were financially incapable of expanding the gas lines. The long-term goal of the company was to first secure the customers' loyalty with economical propane distribution. Then, when development permitted the expansion of the natural gas lines, Southern Union would convert these same customers to natural gas consumption.

By year-end 1996, Southern Union had reached $620.4 million in sales and recorded its sixth consecutive year of earnings and revenues growth. A triumph for Southern Union occurred when *Fortune* magazine named the company among its October 1996 list of America's 100 fastest-growing companies, the only utility to make the list.

In 1997, Southern Union implemented an Automated Meter Reading (AMR) system throughout the MGE division's facilities. This advanced technology cost the company about $28 million; however, the investment provided greater quality customer service and decreased overall operating expenses by allowing the company to collect gas consumption data via a remote computer transmission device, reducing a traditionally labor-intensive process.

Transition to Deregulation and Beyond

In 1998, impending deregulation of the energy industry and the increasingly competitive environment for consumers loomed large for Southern Union. In response, in January of that year Southern Union acquired for $22 million the Atlantic Utilities Corporation in Miami, Florida, a natural gas and propane distribution firm that served several communities in Florida. The Florida market was targeted for nontraditional applications of natural gas for annual use, such as desiccant technology, gas-fired peak shaving equipment, natural gas-powered air conditioning, and natural gas-fired cogeneration.

As it neared the close of the century, Southern Union was providing natural gas services in Florida, Missouri, Texas, and Mexico. Even with pending deregulation of the energy industry, and competition heating up, Southern Union appeared to have the equipment, organization, and personnel in place to guarantee reliable service to consumers well on into the next millennium.

Principal Subsidiaries

Mercado Gas Services Inc.; Energy WorX Inc.; SUPro, Lavaca Realty Company; Southern Transmission Company; Southern Union Energy International Inc. (SUEI); Norteño Pipeline Company; ConTigo Inc.; Southern Union Total Energy Systems, Inc.; Energia Estrella del Sur, S.A. de C.V. (Mexico; 42%).

Principal Divisions

Southern Union Gas; Missouri Gas Energy; Atlantic Utilities.

Further Reading

Atlas, Riva, "The Golden Touch," *Forbes,* October 18, 1995, pp. 52–56.

"Southern Union Acquires Florida Company," *Business Wire,* January 12, 1998, p. 1.

"Southern Union Buys Firm," *Oil Daily,* October 5, 1993, p. 5.

"Southern Union Completes Acquisition," *Fortnightly,* March 15, 1994, p. 8.

"Southern Union to Buy Some Properties Of Western Resources for $360 Million," *Wall Street Journal,* July 12, 1993, p. B4.

"Suit Filed as Part of Effort To Stop 2 Utilities' Merger," *Wall Street Journal,* August 21, 1996, p. B3.

"Western, Oneok End Talks; Sale to Southern Union Proceeds, *Oil Daily,* July 19, 1993, p. 3.

—Kim L. Messeri

Spiegel, Inc.

3500 Lacey Road
Downers Grove, Illinois 60515-5432
U.S.A.
(630) 986-8800
(800) 732-7772
Fax: (630) 769-2012
Web site: http://www.spiegel.com

Public Company
Incorporated: 1893 as Spiegel House Furnishings
   Company
Employees: 12,400
Sales: $2.94 billion (1998)
Stock Exchanges: NASDAQ
Ticker Symbol: SPGLA
SICs: 5961 Mail Order Houses; 5621 Women's Clothing
   Stores; 5651 Family Clothing Stores; 5399
   Miscellaneous General Merchandise Stores; 6141
   Personal Credit Institutions; 5611 Men's & Boys
   Clothing Stores; 5941 Sporting Goods Stores

Spiegel, Inc. is a leading U.S. retailer of apparel, accessories, and home furnishings. Perhaps best known for its namesake *Spiegel* catalog, the company distributes numerous other catalogs under such names as *Newport News* and *Eddie Bauer.* The company also operates several specialty retail stores, including Spiegel outlet stores and Eddie Bauer, Inc. The latter sells men's and women's casual and sports apparel. The main target market for the apparel and home furnishings featured in Spiegel's catalogs and stores consists primarily of middle-class working women, ranging in age from 21 to 59. Spiegel, Inc. is 90 percent owned by members of Germany's Otto family, whose Otto-Versand GmbH is one of the largest catalog retailers in the world.

The Early Years

For the first 100 years of its history, Spiegel was primarily a family business. The company was founded in 1865 by Joseph Spiegel, the son of a German rabbi. After spending the final few months of the Civil War in a Confederate prison camp, Spiegel settled in Chicago, where his brother-in-law, Henry Liebenstein, ran a successful furniture business. With Liebenstein's assistance, Spiegel opened J. Spiegel and Company, a small home furnishings retail operation located on Wabash Avenue in Chicago's loop.

The business was quite successful in its early years. In 1871, however, the Great Chicago Fire destroyed most of the area's business district, including the Spiegel store. After the fire, Spiegel and a partner named Jacob Cahn rebuilt the business, and by 1874 the company was prospering again under the leadership of the two men. Cahn retired from the business in 1879, at which time the company was growing impressively. In 1885 Spiegel began running regular advertisements in several Chicago newspapers, and the following year the company moved to a larger building on State Street. Spiegel's two oldest sons, Modie and Sidney, were brought into the business during this time.

Spiegel issued its first catalogs in 1888. The catalogs were made available to potential customers who lived outside the city. Because a mail order system did not yet exist, the catalogs served instead to lure people into the downtown store. By 1892, however, business had taken a turn for the worse, as many customers were slow to pay for their purchases. With debts mounting, the company went bankrupt. At Modie Spiegel's urging, the company reinvented itself as Spiegel House Furnishings Company of Chicago in 1893. The principal difference was that the new company, like many others in the furniture business, sold on credit. The decision to offer installment plans, and the timing of the decision, made possible Spiegel's remarkable expansion over the next several decades.

Expansion in the Early 1900s

The new Spiegel was an instant hit, and the first branch store was opened on Chicago's South Side in 1898. Another South Side branch went into operation three years later. The company's slogan—"We Trust the People!"—reflected its emphasis on credit merchandising. In 1903 Joseph Spiegel's third son, Arthur, entered the business with a plan to develop mail order operations for Spiegel. After a couple years of lobbying, Arthur convinced the company hierarchy to open a mail order department, and in 1905 Spiegel became the first company to offer credit through the mail. The new service was reflected by the addition of a word to the company motto, which began to read: "We Trust the People—Everywhere!" The response was phenomenal, and soon a huge, previously untapped base of customers was ordering from Spiegel's mail order catalog.

In 1906 Spiegel's mail order sales were nearly $1 million, far exceeding anyone's expectations. To handle the overwhelming success of the mail order operation, a new company—Spiegel, May, Stern and Company—was formed, allowing the Spiegel House Furnishings Company to devote its limited resources to conventional retailing, rather than assume the debts associated with building up the mail order segment. Arthur was named president of the new company.

Spiegel then began to diversify its line of products, offering apparel for the first time in 1912. After a couple of unsuccessful partnerships with independent clothing manufacturers, Spiegel, May, Stern and Company began offering its own line of women's apparel. The "Martha Lane Adams" line—named after its fictional designer—was so successful that it quickly became a wholly owned subsidiary of Spiegel, May, Stern, and Company and earned its own catalog. Martha Lane Adams' sales grew to nearly $2 million by 1916. That same year, Arthur Spiegel died of pneumonia at the young age of 32.

Spiegel's next marketing breakthrough came in 1926, when company executive Ed Swikard introduced a promotional idea involving Congoleum floor covering. Swikard engineered a mailing to more than nine million residences, offering a pre-cut Congoleum package at a low cost. The response was again overwhelming, and company sales reached a record $16 million for the year, with a net profit of $4 million. In 1928 Spiegel, May, Stern and Company went public, although the Spiegel family retained a controlling interest. The following year, just as the Great Depression was setting in, the Spiegels began gradually liquidating their retail furniture business. By 1932 the last Spiegel furniture store in Chicago closed its doors.

Post-Depression Ups and Downs

After experiencing considerable economic losses in the early years of the Depression, Spiegel entered a period of terrific growth and profits beginning in 1933. During this time, M.J. Spiegel, son of Modie, took over the leadership of the company. Spurred by a remarkably liberal credit policy ("No Charge for Credit"), the company's sales rose from $7.1 million in 1932 to more than $56 million by 1937. Furthermore, a $300,000 net

loss was transformed into $2.5 million in profits. The strategy behind this growth involved the aggressive marketing of easy credit as the company's most important commodity. When sales began to level off in 1938, Spiegel reacted by shifting its attention to consumers in a higher income bracket. The company began adding dozens of brand names with national reputations to its catalog. The new approach was referred to as the "quality concept," and it brought success.

The onset of World War II, however, was disastrous for Spiegel. Because so much manufacturing had been shifted to wartime production, many of the products that were popular catalog items were no longer available in large quantities. Moreover, a shortage of labor affected the company's operations, and when buying on credit was officially discouraged by the U.S. government, Spiegel management had to discard its "No Charge for Credit" policy. In 1942 and 1943 combined, the company lost $3.8 million. To reverse this trend, Spiegel began to open retail outlets once again in 1944, hoping to mimic the success of its larger competitors, Sears, Roebuck & Co. and Montgomery Ward. That year, Spiegel acquired 46 Sally dress shops in Illinois. Several other chains were purchased over the next few years, and by 1948 Spiegel was operating 168 retail stores featuring a wide range of merchandise, including clothing, furniture, and auto supplies.

After an initial success in retail, the costs of retail operations began to outweigh the benefits. By the mid-1950s, Spiegel was again concentrating on its former mainstay, mail order sales on credit. Although nearly all of the company's retail outlets were sold off by 1954, several catalog shopping centers were retained so that customers could ask questions and place orders with company representatives. The following year, Spiegel unveiled its Budget Power Plan, a liberal policy under which customers were offered a line of credit sometimes as high as $1,000, with very low monthly payments. The idea was to add as many names as possible to the Spiegel customer list. The company also began to include a widening range of products in its catalogs; by 1960 Spiegel was even shipping pets. By that time, sales were considerably more than $200 million and nearly two million people had Spiegel credit accounts.

The 1960s and 1970s

In 1965, after a century of operation as a family business, Spiegel was purchased by Beneficial Finance Company. Spiegel stockholders received shares of Beneficial stock, and Spiegel became a wholly owned subsidiary. During the early 1970s, several charges were leveled against Spiegel by the Federal Trade Commission (FTC) regarding some of the company's marketing tactics. In 1971, for example, the FTC accused Spiegel of failing to adequately disclose credit terms in some of its statements and catalog ads. The company also was cited for its handling of credit life insurance policies, as well as for offering free home trials without informing customers that credit approval was required before a product would be shipped. Moreover, in 1974, the FTC charged that Spiegel's debt collection policies treated customers unfairly. Most of the complaints brought by FTC during this period were settled by minor changes in company practices, and serious action by the government was avoided for the most part.

Rising interest rates in the mid-1970s made financing credit accounts costly. Also during that time, Spiegel began to feel the pressure of competition from discount stores such as Kmart, which were rapidly establishing a national presence. In 1976, to help turn the company around, Beneficial hired Henry "Hank" Johnson, a veteran of the mail order operations of Montgomery Ward and Avon. One of Johnson's first moves was to streamline company management. Dozens of executives were let go, and overall employment was cut in half over the next five years, from 7,000 in 1976 to 3,500 in 1981. Johnson also closed Spiegel's remaining catalog stores.

Perhaps more important, Johnson sought to change Spiegel's image to that of a "fine department store in print." Accordingly, the Spiegel catalog was completely revamped; low-budget items were replaced by upscale apparel and accessories for career women. Merchandise bearing designer labels began appearing in 1980, when the company introduced a line of Gloria Vanderbilt products.

A New Focus in the 1980s

Spiegel soon became a trendsetter in the catalog business, which was booming as a whole during the early 1980s. The company's sales grew at an impressive pace of 25 to 30 percent a year. Although Spiegel still ranked fourth in catalog sales during this time—trailing Sears, J.C. Penney, and Montgomery Ward—the company's moves were being followed closely by its larger competitors.

In 1982 Beneficial sold Spiegel to Otto-Versand GmbH, a huge, private West German company prominent in catalog sales. Between 1982 and 1983, Spiegel's revenue shot from $394 million to $513 million, and the company's pre-tax profits more than doubled, reaching $22.5 million in 1983. The following year, control of Spiegel was transferred from Otto-Versand itself to members of its controlling family, the Ottos. Under its new ownership, Spiegel's transformation into an outlet for higher-end products continued.

In 1984 Spiegel began distributing specialty catalogs in addition to its four primary catalogs; 25 of these specialty catalogs were in circulation by 1986, featuring Italian imports, plus-sized clothing, and other specialty items. That year, Spiegel mailed a total of 130 million catalogs, at a cost of $100 million, and company sales surpassed the $1 billion mark for the first time. Also during this time, a new president and CEO, John Shea, was named.

In 1987 six million shares of nonvoting stock was sold to the public, marking the first time since 1965 that Spiegel was not completely privately held. The following year, Spiegel acquired Eddie Bauer, Inc., a retail chain specializing in sportswear and outdoor equipment. Eddie Bauer, which also maintained a catalog operation, had annual sales of $260 million. In the first year following the acquisition, the chain was expanded from 60 to 99 stores.

By 1989 Spiegel had become the number three catalog retailer in the United States, with a total circulation of about 200 million catalogs, including 60 different specialty catalogs, and an active customer base of five million.

New Additions in the Early 1990s

In 1990 Spiegel acquired First Consumers National Bank, which began issuing credit cards and statements to Spiegel and Eddie Bauer customers. That year, the company enhanced its image as the premier catalog for career women through an advertising campaign that featured actress Candice Bergen, who portrayed a career woman on the situation comedy "Murphy Brown." The campaign also featured a specialty catalog promoted by Bergen, emphasizing the inconvenience of department store shopping and the relative ease of shopping by catalog.

The company also began to expand its retail outlet operations based on lines from its catalogs. Spiegel stores included For You From Spiegel, which offered large-sized women's apparel, and Crayola Kids, providing a line of children's apparel first launched in 1991. In spite of these innovations, the company's growth stagnated because of national economic recession, and earnings declined sharply in 1991. Slight gains were realized the following year as Spiegel's revenue topped $2 billion. Eddie Bauer performed particularly well, having grown to 265 stores.

In August 1993 Spiegel announced its purchase of New Hampton, Inc., a catalog company specializing in moderately priced women's clothing. Later that year, Spiegel unveiled a new specialty catalog, E Style, featuring a clothing line aimed at African-American women. E Style represented a partnership between Spiegel and Ebony magazine that was formed as a means of targeting an untapped market of Spiegel consumers while also offering African-American women a clothing line more suited to their tastes. That same year, Sears discontinued its Big Book catalog sales operation and Spiegel and other specialty catalog retailers scurried to pick up the leftovers and increase their own share of the market.

Spiegel reported total revenues of $2.6 billion in 1993. Sales at Eddie Bauer stores reached $1 billion that year, bolstered by 30 new outlets that had opened. Between Spiegel and Eddie Bauer, 81 different catalogs, with a total circulation of more than 313 million, were distributed in 1993. The company's specialty retail stores also performed well in 1993, generating $840 million in sales.

Innovations in the Mid-1990s

In 1994 Spiegel formed a joint venture with Time Warner Entertainment to create two home shopping services for cable television. One of the services was named "Catalog 1," and was planned as a one-channel showcase for a roster of numerous upscale catalog retailers, each of which would sell its goods using innovative entertainment-style shows. Participants in Catalog 1 in 1994 were The Bombay Company, Crate & Barrel, Eddie Bauer, The Nature Company, Neiman Marcus, The Sharper Image, Spiegel, Viewer's Edge, and Williams Sonoma. The channel was tested in five markets that year: Rochester, New York; Milwaukee, Wisconsin; Nashua, New Hampshire; Columbus, Ohio; and Pittsburgh, Pennsylvania.

Spiegel also teamed up with Lillian Vernon, Lands' End, and other catalogers in 1994 to create a computerized CD-ROM catalog. The company also formed a partnership with MCI

Communications Corporation that was aimed at increasing both companies' customer bases. MCI began offering a $35 Spiegel gift certificate to any customer who changed his or her long distance telephone service to MCI. MCI also offered an additional $20 certificate to any customer who remained an MCI user for at least six months. Around this time, Spiegel also seriously began considering an entrance into the electronic shopping market through an online service such as America Online (AOL).

In 1995 Spiegel did just that—but at the expense of its year-old Catalog 1 venture. By this time, Catalog 1 had begun airing in three more test markets, raising its total presence to eight cities. Time Warner and Spiegel were beginning to decide, however, that there was greater potential gain in launching a web site for Catalog 1 and capitalizing on the increasing popularity of the Internet. Therefore, they scaled back their cable television operation and began working on a home page through Time Warner's popular Pathfinder site.

Spiegel also initiated an entrance into the Canadian market in 1995 and planned to distribute its catalog there by the spring of 1996. Previous strong Eddie Bauer business in Canada aided the company's decision to move in on a larger scale, as did the company's good distribution agreements in Canada. Meanwhile, Eddie Bauer was doing extremely well in Japan, where the company had placed numerous retail stores throughout the previous few years.

The year 1996 marked the most profitable year in Eddie Bauer's history up to that point, and Spiegel's revenues benefited. Eddie Bauer's merchandise was so popular that year, in fact, that the company suffered through many delays in shipping and out-of-stock merchandise occurrences that were direct results of increased consumer demand. Eddie Bauer also made headlines in 1996 when it introduced ''Balance Day'' to its employees, which was an extra day off per year to do anything they wanted. The addition demonstrated the company's commitment to providing innovative benefits to its workers, and employees began referring to it as ''call in well day.'' The company also made an effort to find ways to offer its single workers benefits that were equal to those offered to its workers with families.

The End of the Century and Beyond

Spiegel achieved $3.06 billion in 1997 revenue, with approximately $1.8 billion of that stemming from its Eddie Bauer operations. Regardless of Eddie Bauer's huge contribution to its parent company, however, the subsidiary had a very rough year. Following the immense demand for its products in 1996, the company mistakenly overproduced and overstocked in 1997. In addition, the new Eddie Bauer merchandise offerings did not hit home with consumers; thus the company was left with too much stock and no means of selling it all. In the August 17, 1998 issue of the *Puget Sound Business Journal,* Eddie Bauer's president and CEO, Rick Fersch, commented on the company's problems: ''We were overplanned, overstocked, overstyled, overcolored—and it was overwarm (last winter) and that meant trouble.'' The company began formulating plans to turn things around in 1998.

The year 1998, however, brought with it additional challenges for the Eddie Bauer enterprise and, subsequently, for Bauer's parent company. Warmer than usual winter weather, brought about by a highly publicized weather phenomenon known as ''El Nino,'' once again hurt Bauer's sales figures. Spiegel's overall revenues for the year dropped to $2.94 billion as a result.

Spiegel set out to halt its downward spiral and achieve profitability again. The company redesigned its *Spiegel* catalog, which had become something of an amalgam of differing—and often conflicting—items and images. The company created a catalog solely to target the working woman and organized its main catalog so as not to place $1,000 designer outfits adjacent to $20 casual shirts, for example. Eddie Bauer also launched efforts to get itself back on track.

By the end of the year, Spiegel announced that its efforts had been fruitful and that the company had achieved earnings once again. Although its revenue dipped during 1998, the company inked a profit and achieved positive cash flow, according to a fiscal year-end document released by Spiegel in early 1999. Eddie Bauer's performance was again disappointing during the year, but Spiegel's other lesser-known subsidiary catalog, *Newport News,* posted solid results. Late in the year, rumors surfaced that the company's positive results had led to numerous unsolicited purchase offers, including one from Arizona-based IG Holdings.

As the new millennium approached, Spiegel had many obstacles to overcome but was headed in the right direction. Having spent many decades in the shadow of companies such as Sears, Roebuck & Co. and Montgomery Ward, Spiegel had come to be regarded as a leader in the catalog shopping industry by the 1990s. Relying on its past proven ability to adapt to changes in customer tastes and trends in competition, the company was attempting to maintain this status.

Principal Subsidiaries

Eddie Bauer, Inc.; New Hampton, Inc.; First Consumer's National Bank; Spiegel Acceptance Corporation; Cara Corporation.

Further Reading

''Aggressive Approach To Credit Sales Pays Off in Bigger Net for Spiegel,'' *Barron's,* January 2, 1961, p. 20.

''Bauer Propels Spiegel,'' *Chain Store Age Executive with Shopping Center Age,* November 1994, p. 26.

''Beneficial Finance and Spiegel, Inc., Propose Merger,'' *Wall Street Journal,* June 1, 1965, p. 30.

''Beneficial Sets Spiegel Merger,'' *New York Times,* August 6, 1965, p. 33.

''Beneficial's Spiegel To Close Remaining 131 Catalog Stores,'' *Wall Street Journal,* February 10, 1978, p. 16.

''Besieged Spiegel,'' *Business Week,* June 15, 1946, p. 92.

Byrne, Harlan, ''Spiegel Inc.,'' *Barron's,* August 14, 1989, p. 102.

''Canada,'' *Direct Marketing,* October 1995, p. 44.

Chandler, Susan, ''Retail Executive Seeks To Redesign Spiegel Catalog,'' *Chicago Tribune,* April 22, 1998.

Collins, Lisa, ''Spiegel's Big Order: Salvage Lousy Year,'' *Crain's Chicago Business,* October 21, 1991, p. 1.

Cooper, Colleen, ''Good Connection,'' *Incentive,* August 1994, p. 101.

Cornell, James, Jr., *The People Get the Credit,* Chicago: Spiegel, Inc., 1964.

Csatari, Jeffrey, "Hard Driving a Bargain," *Men's Health,* May 1995, p. 27.

"Cyber shopping," *Information Week,* February 13, 1995, p. 20.

"Fashions with Pizzazz," *Ebony,* September 1993, p. 132.

Fitzgerald, Kate, "Spiegel Expands Retail Holdings," *Advertising Age,* July 15, 1991, p. 12.

——, "Spiegel Pans Department Stores," *Advertising Age,* April 2, 1990, p. 41.

George, Melissa, "Why Eddie Bauer Is Lost in the Woods," *Crain's Chicago Business,* August 10, 1998, p. 1.

Gerosa, Melina, "That's Entertainment?," *Entertainment Weekly,* April 22, 1994, p. 8.

Johnson, Henry, "Spiegel's New, Winning Spirit Based on Target Marketing," *Direct Marketing,* August 1982, pp. 58–63.

Kim, Nancy J., "Bauer Hits the Recovery Trail," *Puget Sound Business Journal,* August 17, 1998.

Kleiman, Carol, "A Fair Shake for Single Workers," *Chicago Tribune,* December 20, 1998.

"Markets Announced for Catalog 1," *Direct Marketing,* April 1994, p. 9.

Miller, Cyndee, "Catalogs Alive, Thriving," *Marketing News,* February 28, 1994, p. 1.

——, "Major Catalogers, Niche Players Carve Up Mail Order Market," *Marketing News,* September 27, 1993, p. 1.

"Montgomery Ward, Spiegel Cited by FTC on Credit Charge," *Wall Street Journal,* February 11, 1971, p. 30.

Neal, Mollie, Gattuso, Greg, Santoro, Elaine, and Incremona, Amy, "Catalogers Brace for Holiday Rush," *Direct Marketing,* January 1995, p. 7.

"New Catalog Channel Unveiled," *Direct Marketing,* March 1994, p. 8.

Oneal, Michael, "Wall Street Isn't Buying Spiegel's High-Gloss Look," *Business Week,* October 19, 1987, p. 62.

Palmeri, Christopher, "Indoor Outdoorsman," *Forbes,* March 29, 1993, p. 43.

"Resurgent Spiegel," *Business Week,* May 18, 1946, p. 86.

Santoro, Elaine, "Spiegel Debuts E Style," *Direct Marketing,* November 1993, p. 8.

Smalley, Orange, and Sturdivant, Frederick, *The Credit Merchants,* Carbondale: Southern Illinois University Press, 1973.

"Spiegel, Inc. Reports Fourth-Quarter and Full-Year 1998 Results," *PRNewswire,* February 16, 1999.

"Spiegel Launches Catalog for Working Women," *Direct Marketing,* November 1998, p. 11.

Strom, Stephanie, "Home Shopping Plans for Spiegel-Time Warner," *New York Times,* September 28, 1993, p. D5.

Veverka, Mark, "Spiegel Broadens with Catalog Buy," *Crain's Chicago Business,* September 6, 1993, p. 9.

Williams, Winston, "The Metamorphosis of Spiegel," *New York Times,* July 15, 1984, p. F8.

—Robert R. Jacobson
—updated by Laura E. Whiteley

Steelcase®

Steelcase, Inc.

901 44th Street
Grand Rapids, Michigan 49508
U.S.A.
(616) 247-2710
(800) 333-9939
Fax: (616) 246-4041
Web site: http://www.steelcase.com

Public Company
Incorporated: 1912 as Metal Office Furniture Company
Employees: 16,400
Sales: $3.26 billion (1998)
Stock Exchanges: New York
Ticker Symbol: SCS
SICs: 2521 Wood Office Furniture; 2522 Office
    Furniture, Except Wood; 3429 Hardware, Not
    Elsewhere Classified

Known since 1984 as "The Office Environment Company," Steelcase, Inc. is the world's leading designer and manufacturer of office furniture. The company, launched in 1912 with a single product and 15 employees, supplies thousands of products worldwide produced in over 20 million square feet of manufacturing, shipping, and administrative facilities. A network of more than 650 independent dealers sells Steelcase metal and wood office furniture, systems furniture, seating, computer support furniture, desks, tables, credenzas, filing cabinets, and office lighting. The company also offers computer-assisted programs for those who plan, provide, and manage offices; office-worker public opinion surveys; and leasing programs.

According to *Everybody's Business: A Field Guide to the Leading 400 Companies,* "This company, more than any other, is responsible for the look of the modern office. Since 1968, they've been the industry leader, earning a reputation as the General Motors of the office furniture industry." Steelcase's sales figures confirm its leadership. At $3.26 billion in worldwide sales, of which some $2.76 billion is domestic, the company has more than twice the sales volume of its nearest competitor.

Origins in 1912

Steelcase was incorporated as the Metal Office Furniture Company on March 16, 1912, in Grand Rapids, Michigan. Although the new company had a novel idea—fabricating furniture from sheet metal—it received little notice in "The Furniture City," which already had nearly 60 furniture manufacturers.

Peter M. Wege proposed the Metal Office Furniture Company to a group of investors. Wege had been a designer and executive at the Safe Cabinet Company and the General Fireproofing Company, both in Ohio, and had received several patents for all or portions of sheet-metal structures he had designed. He was aware of the benefits of steel furniture. At the turn of the 20th century, mergers were leading to larger companies, larger office and administrative staffs, larger buildings, and an increased office furniture market. However, while new brick and steel construction techniques were making building exteriors less flammable and skyscrapers a reality, office interiors, cluttered with wooden furniture and other combustibles, were still being heated and lighted by open flame appliances. An added fire risk was the use of smoking materials; ashes dumped into the popular wicker wastebaskets caused many office fires. A fire in one of the higher structures was an inferno firefighters could not effectively battle.

Wege persuaded the investors, some of whom were with the Macey Furniture Company, that steel office furniture's strength, durability, and fireproof qualities made sense. The Macey Company agreed to purchase and market all of the shelving, tables, files, and fireproof safes manufactured by the new company. Metal Office Furniture Company's first officers were A.W. Hompe, president (also president of Macey Company); Peter M. Wege, vice-president and general manager; and Walter D. Idema, secretary-treasurer. Two years later, when the agreement with Macey was severed, Hompe stepped down, Wege became president and general manager, Fred W. Tobey became vice-president, and Idema remained secretary-treasurer. David

432

D. Hunting joined Metal Office in 1914 to establish a marketing network. He became secretary in 1920, and the Wege-Idema-Hunting management team was set for the next three decades.

On August 7, 1912, the first filing cases and safes made by Metal Office were delivered to Macey sales outlets. By the end of the year, Metal Office had $13,000 in sales, and by the end of the first full year of operation, it had $76,000 in sales, an amount equal to the initial capitalization.

In 1914 Metal Office hit on an idea that solved the problem of carelessly flicked cigar and cigarette ashes: The Victor, a fireproof steel wastebasket. Touted for its strength and durability, the wastebasket could also be color coordinated with other furniture. Victor became an official trademark in 1918 and eventually became an expanded line of products. Metal Office had two other unusual products that enjoyed short-term popularity. The Liberty Bond Box was used for storing war bonds, while the Servidor was a double-doored product into which hotel guests put room service orders or clothes to be cared for. Service personnel tended to the guests' needs from the hall side without disturbing them.

The concern over fire safety led to Metal Office's first government contract and to its becoming a desk manufacturer. While businesses were slow to replace wooden furniture with the more expensive metal furniture, government architects specified it, citing the fire threat. David Hunting heard that metal furniture was to be used in the renovation of the 50-year-old Boston Customs House. Although Metal Office did not make desks, Hunting conferred with Wege and Idema and they agreed Metal Office should submit a bid. The bid was for 192 desks at $44 each. After the lowest bidder's product was deemed unacceptable, Metal Office, as the next lowest bidder, was asked to send a sample of a desk for examination. Wege and Chris Sonne designed a desk, and a prototype was built to send to Washington the next week. Unlike the low bidder's desk, which was held together by loose bolts, theirs had welds and crimped metal and did not come apart during shipping. Metal Office got the order and filled it in 90 days.

A Focus on Design in the 1920s

In 1921 Metal Office hired media consultant Jim Turner to convince the public that wooden office furniture was a thing of the past. Turner coined the name Steelcase to describe the indestructible quality of the furniture. Steelcase was officially registered as a trademark in August 1921. Because office furnishers never entirely gave up their perception that offices, and especially executive offices, should have wooden furniture, the company pursued ways to make metal furniture more attractive. It implemented spray-painting in 1924 to give furniture a smoother, more even coat and in 1928 developed a wood-graining process. Metal Office manufactured fashionable roll-top desks in oak and mahogany wood-grain on metal.

During the 1930s Metal Office produced some attention-getting furniture, including a futuristic, island-based desk displayed at the World's Fair in Chicago. In 1937 the company collaborated with world-famous architect Frank Lloyd Wright to produce furniture for the "great workroom" for the offices of S.C. Johnson & Sons in Racine, Wisconsin.

Over the years, Metal Office/Steelcase won several more government contracts. During World War II, the brunt of the forced cutback in the use of steel by metal furniture manufacturers was tempered by the U.S. Navy's order for "Shipboard Furniture." The company had to recruit plant personnel to meet increased production and the loss of workers to the military. Many of the new employees were the mothers, wives, and sweethearts of soldiers.

A piece of Steelcase naval furniture was used for the historic signing of the surrender documents ending World War II. A mahogany table had been prepared on September 2, 1945, for the signing by Japanese Foreign Minister Mamoru Shigemitsu and the Supreme Commander of the Allied Forces, General Douglas MacArthur, but the table was too small for the documents. The ceremony was completed on a Steelcase rectangular folding table from the crew's mess, spread with a green tablecloth.

Metal Office utilized what it had learned in building furniture with interchangeable parts for ships when it introduced the first standard sizing of desks based on a 15-inch multiple in 1949. The Multiple 15 concept became an industry standard; it also served as the basis for other modular furniture developed by Steelcase.

A Name Change in 1954

In 1954 the Metal Office Furniture Company officially changed its name to Steelcase, Inc. Walter Idema thought the name change would eliminate confusion with the products of other metal furniture manufacturers. That same year, Steelcase became the first in the industry to offer office furniture in colors, announcing Sunshine Styling colors inspired by the twilight haze over the Arizona mountains: Desert Sage, Autumn Haze, and Blond Tan. The innovation was made possible by acrylic paints that made it easier for workers to change colors. In 1959 the company introduced Convertibles, auxiliary pieces with rigid steel frames and suspended cabinets and pedestals that permitted working arrangements to be individually designed to suit each worker, and Convertiwalls, steel and glass panels attached at slotted posts, which could be wired for telephone or electrical connections.

In the 1960s Steelcase product engineers developed Chromattecs, a method devised to soften the mirror-like finish of traditional chrome. The resulting new line featured "matte-textured acrylics and classic personal fabrics." In 1965 Steelcase established itself as the industry leader, achieving record sales volume for the United States and Canada. Mobiles, introduced in 1968, was the first product incorporating the concept of systems furniture. The line combined the features of Multiple 15, Sunshine Styling, and Convertibles to create more private workstations, completely furnished with desks, shelving, walls, and broadside dividers.

In 1971 Steelcase offered its first comprehensive systems furniture line, Movable Walls, and, in 1973, introduced the Series 9000 Systems Furniture line. The Designs in Wood line, introduced in 1972, addressed the negative perception of metal furniture. The furniture featured exterior hardwood paneling with drawer and pedestal interiors of steel. In 1975 Steelcase brought out the Sensor chair, the first office chair to sense and support the body's movements according to the occupant's height, weight, and preference.

In 1992, looking to a future relying increasingly on teamwork and wireless technology, Steelcase demonstrated Harbor, a prototype product of the office of the future, and Commons, a concept that used open space to quickly reconfigure into an ad hoc meeting area. The company also announced a partnership with Motorola, Inc. to develop wireless technology in office furniture.

Steelcase products, not surprisingly, have won numerous design awards, including the Distinguished Engineering Award from the Consulting Engineers Council of Michigan for an innovative steam-generating, waste-disposal system, and a national award from the President's Council on Environmental Quality for a process that curbed pollutants in its painting process.

Direct descendants of Metal Office Furniture Company founders held many key executive positions in the successor firm, Steelcase, Inc. They included Robert Pew (who married the daughter of investor Henry Idema), chairman; his son, Robert Pew III, president of Steelcase North American operations; Peter Wege, vice-chairman; and William Crawford, president of a design subsidiary. Prior to 1994, only two Steelcase chief executives, Frank Merlotti and Jerry Myers, had not been descendants of the founders.

Frank Merlotti, who came up through the manufacturing ranks, was credited with changing how the company approached the process of product development and production. The World Class Manufacturing (WCM) plan implemented during his tenure had five principles: quality, faster throughput, elimination of waste, product group focus, and employee involvement or empowerment. The plan was put into practice at the $111 million Corporate Development Center opened in 1989. The pyramid-shaped facility had ten laboratories, giving it the most comprehensive research capability in the office furniture industry. It also provided an interdisciplinary creative environment where designers, engineers, marketers, and others worked in neighborhoods focused on the development of a particular product.

A Bumpy Ride in the Early 1990s

Steelcase's status as a privately held company was threatened in 1992, when an estimated one million shares of the rarely traded stock passed to the brokerage firm of Robert W. Baird & Co. from the estate of an heiress of one of the founding families. Baird sold the shares to outsiders, including one buyer who accumulated 30,000 shares and distributed them to allies in an attempt to force Steelcase to go public. The descendants of the founders joined ranks and used a reverse stock split to force the outsiders to sell their Steelcase stock back to the company.

Following a 20-year boom in office furniture sales propelled by an increasing number of office jobs, Steelcase was experiencing flat sales in the early 1990s because of a recession and widespread corporate downsizing. Although Steelcase had to make cutbacks and short-term layoffs, it was determined to avoid the fate of the automakers. The company embarked on aggressive product development, broadened its overseas base, and continued to keep the needs of its employees and dealers a priority, while striving to cut administrative and manufacturing costs.

These changes were largely due to the efforts of President and CEO Jerry Myers, who had been running Steelcase since 1990. Myers, an outsider to the family-held company, had no furniture industry experience prior to joining Steelcase. As Myers attempted to implement his vision of a leaner, more internationally competitive company, he began to encounter resistance in both the manufacturing shop and the boardroom. Steelcase, like most western Michigan furniture companies, was not unionized, but treated its employees much like family, rewarding them with profit sharing and a strong benefits package. The Grand Rapids furniture manufacturing community was shocked when in 1993 many Steelcase employees began meeting with organizers from unions such as the Teamsters and the United Auto Workers. Employees cited changing work rules, reduced benefits, and several years of low profit sharing checks as motivating factors. Members of the company's founding families were also becoming increasingly frustrated with the direction Myers was taking Steelcase, as well as the company's lackluster earnings figures. Steelcase announced its first annual loss in history for the fiscal year ending in February 1994, and in July Myers was asked to resign by the board of directors.

His replacement was James Hackett, who had been with the company in several executive capacities, notably as president of the Turnstone subsidiary, a successful lower-priced furniture line that had been introduced in September 1993. Hackett's approach was to take Steelcase "back to basics," though a number of Myers's cost-cutting and international expansion initiatives were left in place. Earnings were back on track by the end of the next fiscal year, with 1996's totals the strongest since 1991. U.S. sales were $2.16 billion, with total worldwide sales standing at $2.6 billion.

A major setback for Steelcase occurred at the end of 1996, when the company was ordered to pay archrival Haworth $211.5 million to settle an 11-year-old patent infringement lawsuit. While many companies would be crippled or wiped out by such a ruling, Steelcase was doing so well that it was still able to record a small profit for the year.

After 86 years of private ownership, the company finally went public in 1998. In February over 12 million shares were offered on the New York Stock Exchange, sold by John Hunting and Peter Wege, descendants of the company's founders. Both planned to use their proceeds to fund charitable trusts. The stock offering only represented ten percent of the total shares, the rest remaining in family hands.

The stock entered the market at $28 per share, but its value had dropped by more than $10 by year-end; the large number of shares still in family control was cited as one reason for the disappointing showing. Another was the fact that Steelcase was having a slow year, with its estimate of a three percent annual sales increase less than half the eight percent industry average. Analysts attributed this to purchasing cutbacks at *Fortune* 500 companies, the global economic downturn, and a relatively stagnant product mix. Steelcase's major product introduction for 1998 had been the Pathways integrated office architecture package. Pathways was eight years and $150 million in development, and the company stood firmly behind it as the office design standard of the future. However, it was not catching on as rapidly as had been hoped.

As Steelcase neared the millennium, it remained the number one manufacturer of office furniture in the world. Although it had gone public, the company was still firmly under the control of the heirs of its founding fathers. Following several turbulent years in the early 1990s, the company had gotten back on track for future growth with the introduction of its Pathways system and an ongoing program of international expansion.

Principal Subsidiaries

Steelcase Canada, Ltd.; Metropolitan Furniture Corp.; Brayton International, Inc.; DesignTex Fabrics Inc.; Office Details, Inc.; Wigand Corporation; Steelcase Strafor S.A. (50%; France); Attwood Corporation; Steelcase Financial Services, Inc.; Revest Inc.

Principal Divisions

Steelcase U.S.; Steelcase Design Partnership; Steelcase International; Steelcase Furniture Management Coalition; Steelcase Wood Furniture; Turnstone.

Further Reading

"The Best of 1989," *Business Week,* January 8, 1990.

Blake, Laura, "Steelcase's Changes Cap Tumultuous Year," *Grand Rapids Business Journal,* December 26, 1994, p. 5.

"The Eternal Coffee Break," *Economist,* March 7, 1992.

"4 of Top 100 in State," *Flint Journal,* January 23, 1993.

Ghering, Mike, "Patent Dispute Spotlights Busy Field," *Grand Rapids Business Journal,* January 6, 1997, p. 1.

"A Glimpse of the 'Flex' Future, at Steelcase, Offering Variable Hours, Pay and Perks Benefits the Firm and Its Workers," *Newsweek,* August 1, 1988.

Harger, Jim, "Union Effort Is a Wake-up Call, Steelcase Chief Says," *Grand Rapids Press,* November 7, 1993, p. A1.

Howes, Daniel, "What Went Wrong at Steelcase," *Gannett News Service,* August 11, 1994.

Leith, Scott, "Steelcase Chief Remains Optimistic About Future," *Grand Rapids Press,* September 29, 1998, p. B6.

Lyne, Jack, "Steelcase CEO Jerry Myers: Creating the Office of the Future—Now," *Site Selection and Industrial Development,* October 1992.

Molinari, Deanne, "Steelcase Filing Unlocks Secrets," *Grand Rapids Business Journal,* December 15, 1997, p. 1.

Morgan, Hal, and Kerry Tucker, *Companies That Care: The Most Family-Friendly Companies in America—What They Offer and How They Got That Way,* New York: Simon and Schuster, 1991.

Moskowitz, Milton, et. al., editors, *Everybody's Business: A Field Guide to the 400 Leading Companies in America,* New York: Doubleday, 1990.

Nelson-Horchler, Joani, "Take-Home Dinners (From the Company Cafeteria)," *Industry Week,* December 3, 1990.

"Office Furniture Firms in Michigan Design to Ensure Business Future," *Flint Journal,* November 11, 1990.

Radigan, Mary, and Amber Veverka, "Steelcase Optimistic Despite $70 Million Loss," *Grand Rapids Press,* May 5, 1994, p. A1.

Servaas, Lois, *Steelcase: The First 75 Years,* Grand Rapids, Mich.: Steelcase, Inc., 1987.

Shellum, Bernie, "The Steelcase Way; Its Stock Battle Over, the Office Furniture Maker Forges Ahead," *Detroit Free Press,* June 8, 1992.

Sheridan, John N., "Frank Merlotti: A Master of Empowerment," *Industry Week,* January 7, 1991.

Simison, Robert L., "Steelcase Goes Public and Shares Jump 22% Over Offer Price in Intraday Trade," *Wall Street Journal,* February 19, 1998, p. A8.

"Steelcase Lays Off 460 More Workers," *Flint Journal,* January 21, 1993.

"Steelcase Uses Leaves of Absence of 60 Days to Avert Big Layoffs," *Detroit Free Press,* April 5, 1991.

Verespej, Michael A., "America's Best Plants: IW's Second Annual Survey. Steelcase: Grand Rapids," *Industry Week,* October 21, 1991.

Veverka, Amber, "Steelcase Celebrates Return to Good Times," *Grand Rapids Press,* May 18, 1995, p. A1.

Wells, Garrison, "Steelcase Sales Down $14.4 Million in Third Quarter," *Grand Rapids Press,* December 19, 1998, p. D4.

—Doris Morris Maxfield
—updated by Frank Uhle

SÜDZUCKER

Südzucker AG

Maximilianstrasse 10
D-68165 Mannheim
Germany
(49) (621) 421-0
Fax: (49) (621) 421-393
Web site: http://www.suedzucker.de

Public Company
Incorporated: 1926 as Süddeutsche Zucker AG
Employees: 20,394
Sales: DM 8.18 billion (1998)
Stock Exchanges: Frankfurt Berlin Münich Stuttgart
    Hanover Hamburg Düsseldorf
Ticker Symbol: SZUG
SICs: 0133 Sugarcane & Sugar Beets; 2024 Ice Cream &
    Frozen Desserts; 2037 Frozen Fruits, Fruit Juices &
    Vegetables; 2038 Frozen Specialties, Not Elsewhere
    Classified; 2048 Prepared Feeds & Feed Ingredients
    for Animals & Fowls, Except Dogs & Cats; 2051
    Bread & Other Bakery Products, Except Cookies &
    Crackers; 2053 Frozen Bakery Products, Except
    Bread; 2063 Beet Sugar; 2064 Candy & Other
    Confectionery Products; 2066 Chocolate & Cocoa
    Products; 2869 Industrial Organic Chemicals, Not
    Elsewhere Classified; 5191 Farm Supplies

Südzucker AG is the largest sugar producer in the European Union (EU) with an annual production of three million metric tons and an EU market share of 16.4 percent in 1998. The German company is also one of the European leaders in other food markets including ice cream, frozen food, and industrial baked goods, which constitute about 40 percent of its business. Südzucker expanded its traditional sugar business—which was derived from 33 sugar production facilities and contributed about 60 percent of the company's sales in 1998—into eastern Europe in the 1990s. In 1998, the company's market share in sugar production reached 15 percent in the Czech Republic, 37 percent in Hungary, and 20 percent in Romania. Südzucker is

also active in the areas of sugar substitute products, starch, and confectionery. The Süddeutsche Zuckerrüben-Verwertungs-genossenschaft (SVZG), the holding organization of southern German beet farmers, is the majority owner of Südzucker. The Deutsche Bank holds a ten percent share in the company's capital. Südzucker's major subsidiaries include the German Schöller group, the AGRANA group in Austria, and Raffinerie Tirlemontoise in Belgium.

A Sugar Giant Founded in 1926

In 1747 Andreas Sigismund Markgraf, a German physicist, discovered that the "Runkelrübe," a type of beet, contained sugar. After Markgraf's student Franz Carl Archard displayed samples of the "Sweet Salt of Beets" to the Prussian King Friedrich Wilhelm III, the king provided a loan in 1802 to build the first German sugar factory. Between 1836 and 1856 about a dozen sugar production enterprises were founded in states in southwestern Germany, and by the end of the 19th century many more had been started.

On March 15, 1926, the member companies of the Interessengemeinschaft Süddeutscher Zuckerfabriken, an organization that represented most sugar producers of southern Germany, merged to form Süddeutsche Zucker AG. The company had its headquarters in Mannheim and share capital of 30 million German Reichsmarks (RM). The member companies included the Badische Gesellschaft für Zuckerfabrikation AG with factories in Waghäusel, Züttlingen, and Rheingau; the Zuckerfabrik Frankenthal AG with production facilities in Frankenthal, Regensburg, Friedensau, and Gernsheim; the Zuckerfabrik Heilbronn AG; the Zuckerfabrik Stuttgart AG with facilities in Stuttgart-Bad Cannstadt and Gross-Umstadt; and the Zuckerfabrik Offstein AG with factories in Offstein and Gross-Gerau. At the first meeting the new management team decided not to manage the factories as subsidiaries, but to divide them into two bigger firms, one in Frankenthal and one in Stuttgart, which would then manage all facilities in the surrounding areas.

In fiscal 1928–29, the new sugar giant employed 6,200 people, processed nine million metric tons of sugar beets and produced 1.3 million metric tons of sugar. After the merger, all

Company Perspectives:

Nature is our partner. Südzucker views itself as a dynamic corporation which understands its responsibility towards nature. In the agriculture and production divisions, solutions must be developed which are ecologically and economically sound. Südzucker stands for competence and experience when it comes to secure the steady high quality standard of a natural food product. Flexibility in planning and innovation are the basis for our company's future. As part of its growth strategy, Südzucker is also involved in other areas of the food industry outside the traditional sugar business and it has developed into a food company.

facilities were modernized and equipped with state-of-the-art technology. At the beginning of the 1930s, Süddeutsche Zucker AG ran the most modern sugar production facilities in Germany. In 1929–30, production peaked at 2.25 million metric tons of raw sugar. To better utilize refinery capacity, Südzucker bought additional amounts of raw sugar from northern German producers that year and afterwards.

However, the sugar industry at that time was confronted with difficult market conditions. German sugar producers were suffering in particular from competition by government-subsidized Polish and Czech sugar factories. As a result, in 1929 the German government raised import tariffs on sugar and established a maximum retail price to protect German customers. Sugar prices on the world market were low because of an oversupply from sugar-producing nations around the world such as Cuba, Java, England, Poland, Czechoslovakia, and Hungary. After those countries failed to reach a compromise at various conferences, and the export of sugar began to produce losses for German sugar producers who also refused to cut back production, the German government in 1931 began regulating German sugar production. The so-called "Zuckerwirtschaftsgesetz" (Sugar Industry Law) established fixed prices for sugar beets over a long period of time, enabling farmers to better plan crops. Delivery contracts with sugar factories also guaranteed that farmers would be able to sell their harvest and that they could expect a certain income at a certain time.

While shares were divided between many shareholders when the Süddeutsche Zucker-AG was founded, it was concentrated in the hands of only three corporate shareholders seven years later. In 1931, a group of upper managers examined the company's financial situation, which at the time had RM 33 million in bank debts. Heavy investment in new technologies had pushed up capacity, while government restrictions limited output and prices. Consequently, production facilities were running at only 60 percent of capacity. The subsequent measures to improve this situation included closing down the facilities in Züttlingen, Gernsheim, and Friedensau; centralization of the buying departments; reorganization of the factory in Frankenthal; and the acquisition of various shares in other companies. Südzucker sales rose by about 20 percent from RM 150 million in 1929–30 to RM 177 in 1937–38. At the same time, the number of employees dropped by 15 percent to 5100 in 1936–37. In 1937, the company operated a variety of facilities:

three factories for the production of white sugar; three factories which produced white as well as raw sugar; and one refinery. It also owned six sugar beet farms and operated some 50 others under a lease contract. Südzucker also held between 61 and 100 percent of shares of various sugar producers mostly in southwestern and southeastern parts of Germany, as well as shares in various other companies such as mill operations, a maker of conserved food, a brewery, and a Swiss chocolate maker. During World War II, sugar production as well as the supply of raw materials and workers was administrated by the German government. In 1943 the sugar refinery Frankenthal was bombed heavily, and the central office building in Mannheim was completely destroyed.

New Beginnings After World War II

After World War II, the almost completely destroyed sugar factory in Frankenthal was closed down. In all, the German sugar industry lost 128 out of 201 sugar factories and six out of 13 sugar refineries which were located in the zone occupied by the Russian army. Only 29 percent of all land used for sugar beet farming before the war was located in the territory of what later became the Federal Republic of Germany (FRG). Accordingly, 62 percent of the sugar consumed in that area in 1946–47 had to be imported. Sugar supply became a crucial issue for the German food industry. Most of the imported sugar came from Cuba. In order to save coal, the military government required it to be distributed in its unrefined form as it was imported. However, in 1948 German sugar producers who wanted to utilize unused capacities convinced the military government to allow them to refine Cuban raw sugar into white sugar.

In 1949, the newly erected Südzucker headquarters in Mannheim were reopened. Südzucker undertook every effort to make the technology in its factories suitable for processing the Cuban raw sugar as quickly as possible. In the following years, more sugar producers competed to purchase the imported raw sugar. At the same time, domestic sugar beet production rose by 29 percent in 1950 alone, and Südzucker was not able to process the entire amount of sugar beets harvested within its territory. With the foundation of the FRG, new regulations were worked out for the German economy, including the food sector, based on a more liberal model. In 1950, the "Gesetz über den Verkehr mit Zucker"—the so-called "sugar law"—was issued by the new West German government. It included guidelines on buying and processing sugar beets as well as on the production and storage of sugar, and allowed the parties involved to set their own prices. At the same time, holding organizations of the sugar farmers and manufacturers were reorganized.

Beet Farmers Become Shareholders in the 1950s

One of the most influential decisions for Südzucker was made by farmers in September 1950. Under the leadership of Dr. Hans Hege, a plant cultivation specialist who at the time headed the holding organization of southern German beet farmers, they founded the Süddeutscher Zuckerrüben-Verwertungsgenossenschaft (SVZG). The main goal of the new organization was to raise funds to build new sugar factories. This was not the first attempt of sugar beet farmers to participate in the profits from further refining of their harvest. However, it was the first successful one. Shortly after the war, farmers again embraced a plan for building their own factory. Due to a shortage in production capacity in 1950, the Bavarian Ministry of Agriculture learned of the idea, and invited both parties to a meeting. Because the Ministry offered favorable grants and loans to farmers who participated in the project, Südzucker's attitude was essentially positive. However, the farmers were only willing to cooperate if they could be majority holders of the new factory. In addition, if the new company were later merged with Südzucker, they wanted 26 percent of all Südzucker shares. Hege preferred a partnership between the farmers and the industry, but Südzucker felt their demands were unacceptable.

While the farmers started looking for other land—it was very unlikely that Südzucker would allow them to build their own factory on the company's property—the Bavarian Ministry of Agriculture made it clear that the laws allowed them to forbid Südzucker to build a factory without the farmer's participation. They also informed Südzucker that they would help the farmers raise finances to build a factory independently. Finally, after year-long negotiations and encouraged by additional funding from the American Marshall Fund which also wanted farmers to have 51 percent ownership of the new company, Südzucker signed the deal. In July 1951, the Zuckerfabrik Franken GmbH headquartered in Ochsenfurt was founded as a limited liability company with capital of DM 6 million. Dr. Hans Hege became the first chairman of the board. From 1951 until 1968, Südzucker's board of directors was headed by Hermann J. Abs, a man who always tried to find compromises that matched the interests of Südzucker as well as the farmers. The Süddeutsche Zucker AG brought the new company the complete equipment of the desiccation plant Ochsenfurt, an asset worth DM 2.5 million. Due to enormously rising prices, it cost about DM 33.5 million, 40 percent more than originally planned, to build the new facility. Equipped with the latest machinery, it started production in November 1952. Only two years later, the factory was running at maximum capacity.

Expanding Capacities in Europe in the Next Three Decades

As a result of a new law, two representatives of Südzucker employees joined the company's board of directors in fiscal 1953–54. The sugar yield in that year reached prewar levels for the first time. In 1956–57, Südzucker built a new factory in Rain am Lech, which was financed primarily by selling off shares of companies not involved in sugar production. It applied a new technological concept which included continuous extraction in an extraction tower and sugar storage in silos instead of sacks. Later, it became the only Südzucker facility to produce sugar cubes and sugar in fluid form. In 1957, 17 percent of the beet harvest in the Ochsenfurt area could not be processed in Südzucker's facilities. Therefore, in the fall of 1958, the management committees of the Zuckerfabrik Franken GmbH decided to build a new factory in Zell am Main which was finished in 1960. Another new facility was built in Plattling in 1961–62. It was the only Südzucker facility able to produce a thick sugar concentrate which could be stored and further processed in the "slow time" between sugar "campaigns," which began at the beet harvest in September and usually concluded by the end of a year when all the beets had been processed. Later it employed a new recycling technology which transformed the lime which

was used to eliminate non-sugar elements out of the raw juice into fertilizer. In 1965, the Süddeutsche Zuckervertrieb GmbH, of which Südzucker held 52 percent of the capital, was founded in Frankfurt/Main by four southern German sugar manufacturers. From July 1968 on, this venture marketed a major part of the participating company's products.

After the European Common Market was founded in 1957, German regulation of the sugar market was replaced by broader European laws. The new "EWG-Zuckermarktordnung" became effective in July 1968. Among other things, it determined production quotas for the Union's sugar-producing countries and a minimum price to the farmers for quantities produced within the quotas. For all quantities over quotas which were exported by the producers, the European regulations subsidized price differences between the world and the domestic market. The subsidies were financed by a production fee paid by the beet farmers. In the new European market, cheaper products such as fondant, sweets, and sweet baked goods from other European countries competed with German sugar producers by lowering domestic demand from food companies. Since the EU regulations for the sugar market were introduced, production quotas and price regulations were updated regularly.

Restructuring and Diversification in the 1970s and 1980s

In the 1970s, the German economy was shaken by currency turbulence, the oil crisis in 1973, and the subsequent worldwide recession. Those circumstances, along with the rising influence of the new European regulations on the sugar market, led to an era of restructuring and diversification within the German sugar industry. As a result, 20 percent of the sugar factories still in existence in 1970 had disappeared by 1986. Südzucker reacted by making production more efficient and by diversifying into new markets.

First, production facilities were restructured around the three main areas of influence in Hessen-Pfalz, Baden-Würtemberg, and Bavaria. After old sites in Heilbronn, Stuttgart, and Züttlingen were closed down, a new production facility was built in Offenau in 1971, which processed sugar beets harvested from the Bodensee area up to the river Main. The remaining older Südzucker facilities in Gross-Gerau, Offstein/Pfalz, Waghäusel/Baden, Regensburg, and Worms were modernized and capacity optimized during the 1970s and 1980s. Südzucker's central research and development department located in Offstein, "Palatinit," developed a sugar substitute and introduced it to the German market. Another strategy Südzucker pursued was to optimize sugar beet quality. Studies in the 1960s showed that intensive fertilizing did not automatically yield better results. On the contrary, over-fertilized beets were of lower quality and caused processing problems. Therefore, Südzucker started a campaign to optimize nitrogen fertilization. Between 1979 and 1981, they tested the so-called "EUF-method" (Electro-Ultra-Filtration) and opened a laboratory that tested soil probes from beet farmers. Based on the results, farmers received fertilizing recommendations.

After an earlier attempt to diversify by purchasing a high-quality food producer had failed in the 1970s, Südzucker adopted a new approach in the 1980s. In 1983, together with two major banks, Südzucker participated in a newly founded holding company, the Agrar-Industrie-Holding GmbH, which was set up in Mannheim with the goal of purchasing and administering shares in various companies involved in agriculture and the food industry. One of the most important acquisitions of that time was made in 1984–85 by acquiring a 15 percent share in Milchhof-Eiskrem GmbH & Co. KG (MEK) in Mettmann, a producer of milk and ice cream with above-average growth potential. In 1986, negotiations began regarding the possibility of a merger of Süddeutsche Zucker AG with Zuckerfabrik Franken GmbH. In 1988, Zuckerfabrik Franken GmbH and Süddeutsche Zucker-AG merged. The new corporation, headquartered in Mannheim, was named Südzucker AG Mannheim/Ochsenfurt. With 16 production facilities in Germany, the firm became the largest sugar manufacturer in the country. Zuckerfabrik Franken brought a 49 percent share in the German Schöller group—the second largest German ice cream maker at the time after Unilever's Nestlé group—into the marriage which later became one of the most important strategic growth markets for the new group.

Striving for Leadership in New Markets in the 1990s

After Germany was reunited in 1990, Südzucker began to do business in the new German Länder in former East Germany. Sugar sales grew in the two-digit range when the opening of the new east German market led to increased demand for sugar from producers—primarily West German—of beverages, baked goods, ice cream, candy, and milk products. In February 1991, Südzucker GmbH in Zeitz was officially registered as a fully-owned subsidiary responsible for all East German facilities. The 13 companies taken over by Südzucker were restructured between 1990 and 1994 with an investment of DM 800 million. Eight were closed as inefficient while the five remaining were equipped with state-of-the-art technology. In Zeitz, a new factory was built with a beet processing capacity of 10,000 metric tons a day which opened in 1993. After almost 20 years, Südzucker introduced a new package design for food retail sugar products in 1992.

With the acquisition of new shares in foreign sugar manufacturers, Südzucker became the largest sugar producer in the European Union, and extended its market borders further. In 1990, Südzucker took over the Belgian Raffinerie Tirlemontoise S.A. in Brussels. Through a participation in the DM 800 million Austrian AGRANA group, Südzucker not only gained control over the Austrian sugar market, but also a market share of over 30 percent in the Hungarian sugar market and an important share in the starch markets of those two countries. In return, the AGRANA group acquired a minority share in Südzucker which fluctuated between 1.4 and 6.4 percent in the following years.

Another growth market was Isomalt, Südzucker's easy-to-process sugar substitute product first introduced to the German market in 1990. Isomalt, marketed by Südzucker's subsidiary Palatinit Süßungsmittel GmbH, is made out of beet sugar, but contains only half the calories and is therefore suitable for diabetics. It is produced in a new facility in Offstein, Germany, and sold worldwide, primarily to the confectionery industry. In 1996, sales reached about DM 100 million, about 90 percent coming from exports.

Sales of the Schöller group grew by 28 percent in 1991 to DM 1.56 billion after two new ice cream factories were opened in East Germany and in Hungary. Beginning in 1994, Südzucker's ice cream, frozen food, and baked goods sectors outgrew its traditional sugar division which at that time still generated about 80 percent of group sales. That same year, in order to centralize all subsidiaries and minority shares in those markets under the umbrella of the Schöller group, the Schöller Holding GmbH & Co. KG headquartered in Nürnberg was founded with 65 percent of the shares held by Südzucker. In 1995, Theo Spettmann became Südzucker's new speaker of the executive board, after his predecessor Klaus Fleck suffered a fatal accident. Spettmann emphasized a strategic orientation as an international food company. In 1996, Südzucker purchased a majority in Freiberger, the leading European producer of frozen pizza, pasta, and baguettes which in 1998 was integrated as a 100 percent subsidiary. In 1997, the Schöller group acquired two companies, the Danish Hjem-Is-Group, the most important Scandinavian direct marketer of ice cream, and an ice cream producer in Turkey.

As a result of these activities, net profits grew by over 28 percent and reached DM 286 million in fiscal 1996–97. With over 20,000 employees in 1998, Südzucker headed towards DM 10 billion in sales, to be achieved mainly by cost reductions in its West German facilities; entering new sugar markets in Belarus, Lithuania and the Ukraine; and making the ice cream and frozen foods division as strong as the sugar business.

Principal Subsidiaries

Südzucker International GmbH; Südzucker GmbH; Raffinerie Tirlemontoise S.A. (Belgium; 74.7%); AGRANA Beteiligungs-AG (Austria; 42.6%); Palatinit Süssungsmittel GmbH; Schöller Holding GmbH & Co. KG (65%); Freiberger Lebensmittel GmbH & Co. Produktions-und Vertriebs KG.

Further Reading

"Bei Südzucker dauert die Wachstumsphase weiter an," *Frankfurter Allgemeine Zeitung*, July 17, 1997.
"Der Einfluß von Südzucker reicht von Belgien bis Österreich," *Frankfurter Allgemeine Zeitung*, July 13, 1994.
Die Natur ist unser Partner, Mannheim, Germany: Südzucker AG Mannheim Ochsenfurt, 1993, 55 p.
Pohl, Manfred, Südzucker 1837–1897, Mainz, Germany: v. Hase & Koehler, 1987, 210 p.
"Die Südzucker-Gruppe hat Osteuropa fest im Blick," *Frankfurter Allgemeine Zeitung*, November 15, 1993, p. 20.
"Südzucker drängt weiter nach Ost-und Südsteuropa," *Frankfurter Allgemeine Zeitung*, July 15, 1998.
"Südzucker erwartet Wachstum im zuckerfreien Bereich," *Frankfurter Allgemeine Zeitung*, July 17, 1996.
"Südzucker sieht das größere Wachstumspotential im Osten," *Frankfurter Allgemeine Zeitung*, June 28, 1995, p. 19.
"Südzucker übernimmt den Eiskremhersteller Schöller," *Frankfurter Allgemeine Zeitung*, August 26, 1994, p. 22.
"Südzucker verstärkt den Einfluß in Österreich und Osteuropa," *Frankfurter Allgemeine Zeitung*, July 16, 1993.
"Das starke Wachstum soll die Rendite von Südzucker nicht schmälern," *Frankfurter Allgemeine Zeitung*, July 19, 1995.

—Evelyn Hauser

Suprema Specialties, Inc.

P.O. Box 280
Paterson, New Jersey 07543-0280
U.S.A.
(201) 684-2900
(888) 882-3966
Fax: (201) 684-8680
Web site: http://www.supremachez.com

Public Company
Incorporated: 1983
Employees: 140
Sales: $108.1 (1998)
Stock Exchanges: NASDAQ
Ticker Symbol: CHEZ
SICs: 2022 Natural Processed & Imitation Cheese; 5143 Dairy Products, Except Dried or Canned

Suprema Specialties, Inc. manufactures, processes, and markets a variety of premium, gourmet, natural cheese products, using both imported and domestic cheeses. It principally markets its product line under the Suprema Di Avellino brand name. The company's cheese products contain no preservatives, additives, sweeteners, dehydrated fillers, or artificial flavorings. Retail customers include supermarkets, grocery stores, delicatessens, and gourmet shops. The company also sells its products to food manufacturers and to distributors who market the products to restaurants, hotels, and caterers.

Private Company: 1983–91

Suprema Specialties was founded in 1983 by Mark Cocchiola and his brother-in-law, Paul Lauriero. It began as a small family business distributing imported gourmet Italian cheeses—specifically, pecorino romano and parmesan—in the New York City metropolitan area, grating and shredding them, and selling them in cups under a proprietary name. Prior to founding Suprema, Cocchiola and Lauriero had been co-owners of Long Island Diary Distributors, Inc. since 1975, even though Cocchiola was only 19 at the time and Lauriero only five years older.

By fiscal 1988 (the year ended July 31, 1988), Suprema Specialties had annual net sales of $9.25 million. The company lost $46,000 that year. In fiscal 1989 (the year ended June 30, 1989), net sales rose to $10.4 million, and the company had net earnings of $72,000. These figures rose to $12.5 million and $296,000, respectively, in fiscal 1990. For the following year they were $15.4 million for net sales and $143,000 for net earnings. Suprema made its initial public offering in April 1991, selling one million shares of common stock at $3.50 a share. Following this sale, Cocchiola retained 37 percent of the common stock and Lauriero kept 17 percent.

Suprema Specialties was, in mid-1991, processing and marketing the same cheeses, but from Argentina as well as Italy, and it had introduced additional lines of mozzarella and ricotta cheese products, including ''lite'' versions of these products containing less fat and fewer calories. Provolone was added the following year. The company had relocated in late 1989 to Paterson, New Jersey, which was now the site for its grating, shredding, and packaging operations. A significant portion of its products was now being packaged in bags and shakers as well as cups. Certain products were packaged in shrink-wrapped plastic and plastic pillow packs, ranging in size from one to ten pounds, or in customized sizes, for food service distributors and food manufacturers.

During the 1980s Suprema Specialties expanded its customer base from the New York metropolitan area to New England and Pennsylvania. By mid-1991 it had expanded its marketing efforts to include the Chicago and Baltimore/Washington metropolitan areas, as well as Florida and California. Retail customers, including several regional supermarket chains, accounted for 71 percent of the company's sales in fiscal 1991. Food service industry distributors, who, in large part, bought in bulk, accounted for most of the remainder. About half of Suprema's bulk cheese requirements were manufactured by foreign producers in fiscal 1991.

Adding Manufacturing Operations: 1991–97

The proceeds from Suprema Specialties' initial public sale of stock allowed it to begin manufacturing cheese from raw milk at a leased plant in Manteca, California, the assets of which were purchased from A&J Foods Inc. in November 1991 for $480,000. The company chose California because milk prices were about ten percent lower there and it was one of two states that did not follow industry pricing and standards. Suprema began production with ricotta and mozzarella for the food service industry and parmesan and romano shipped to Paterson for processing and sale. The plant began producing provolone for shipment to Paterson the following fiscal year.

In 1992 Suprema Specialties became the first cheese company to pursue national distribution of Lite Parmesan and Lite Romano cheeses to the delicatessen departments of grocery stores. These freshly grated products, which came in resealable cups, contained 50 percent less fat, one third fewer calories, and at least 25 percent less cholesterol than regular parmesan and romano cheese. (A "lite" version of provolone was added in fiscal 1995.)

Suprema Specialties, by mid-1993, was marketing its product line principally under the Suprema Di Avellino brand name. The company had stepped up its sales to food service distributors and food manufacturers, so that retail customers accounted for only 47 percent of net sales in fiscal 1993. This proportion was to fall further, to 31 percent in fiscal 1994 and 19 percent in fiscal 1995. By contrast, sales to food service companies accounted for about 69 percent of total sales in fiscal 1995 and sales to food manufacturers accounted for another 12 percent. Net sales rose from $23.5 million in fiscal 1992 to $27.4 million in 1993, $32 million in 1994, and $52.1 million in 1995. Net earnings were $335,000, $621,000, $429,000, and $912,000, respectively.

Suprema Specialties' customers in 1994 included supermarket chains such as Pathmark, Foodtown, and Stop & Shop. Its customers also included pizzamakers. The company's Paterson headquarters was a processing center where workers trimmed wheels of cheese to remove mold, then placed the wheels into machines that grated, packaged, and labeled them. The Manteca plant was expanded in size during 1994–95.

Suprema Specialties leased a 72,000-square-foot plant in 1996 in Ogdensburg, New York, to process whey and produce mozzarella and provolone cheeses. "Acquiring this East Coast plant," said Cocchiola, "will now complement our West Coast operations and should strengthen our competitive position." Also in 1996, Suprema purchased its leased facility in Paterson, which had been expanded to include a refrigerated/freezer storage facility in addition to the company's executive offices and its production and shipping facilities.

These acquisitions were financed by a secondary public offering in June 1996 of one million shares of common stock issued by the company, in addition to 500,000 shares offered by selling stockholders, at a purchase price of $5.50 per share. The net proceeds to the company came to about $4.5 million. When the underwriter exercised his option shortly after to purchase 225,000 shares at the same price, it brought the company additional net proceeds of about $1 million. Cocchiola held 16.3 percent of the common stock and Lauriero held 9.6 percent in October 1997.

Suprema Specialties, in October 1997, took an extraordinary charge of about $1 million for prepayment penalties and associated fees pertaining to the prepayment of subordinated debt. It also repurchased warrants to purchase 354,990 shares of common stock. Company debt was retired by means of a $10 million bridge loan replaced in March 1998 by a $10.5 million subordinate loan from Albion Alliance Mezzanine Fund, L.P. and the Equitable Life Assurance Society of the United States. At the same time, the senior lender, Fleet Bank, N.A., increased its revolving credit line to the company to $25 million.

Suprema Specialties in 1998

Suprema Specialties' net sales rose from $65.1 million in fiscal 1996 to $88.3 million in fiscal 1997 and $108.1 million in fiscal 1998. Net income, $1.4 million in 1996, fell to $120,781 in 1997, which the company attributed primarily to a $944,000 write-off of its marketing service agreements, but increased to $2.4 million in 1998, despite an extraordinary charge of $1,011,000 for prepayment penalties related to the early extinguishment of the subordinated debt and related fees. The long-term debt at the end of fiscal 1998 was $35.5 million.

At the end of fiscal 1998 Suprema Specialties was manufacturing bulk cheeses at its Manteca and Ogdensburg facilities and purchasing bulk cheeses from foreign sources—primarily from Europe and, to a lesser extent, South America—and from domestic sources. Bulk cheese was being repackaged and sold to food service distributors and food manufacturers under the Suprema Di Avellino name or on a private-label basis, or it was being grated or shredded and packaged by Suprema and sold to retail customers under the Suprema Di Avellino name in clear plastic cups, bags, and shakers. The company also was selling certain of its products in shrink-wrapped plastic packaging and plastic pillow packs ranging in size from one to ten pounds or in customized sizes for food service distributors and food manufacturers.

Suprema's product line, which it marketed, for the most part, under the Suprema Di Avellino brand name, primarily consisted of grated and shredded imported and domestic parmesan and romano cheeses, imported pecorino (sheep's milk) romano cheese (including "lite" versions of these products with less fat and fewer calories), bulk mozzarella, ricotta, and provolone cheese. Sales of mozzarella, ricotta, and provolone cheese products manufactured at Suprema's Manteca and Ogdensburg facilities accounted for 71.8 percent of the company's revenues in fiscal 1998. The Manteca plant was manufacturing mozzarella, parmesan, provolone, ricotta, romano, lite parmesan, and lite romano. The Ogdensburg plant was manufacturing mozzarella and provolone. Both facilities also were converting whey into WPC, a sweet, high-protein food substance.

Suprema Specialties received gold, silver, and bronze medals at several prestigious cheese contests in 1998 for outstanding quality and taste of its mozzarella and provolone cheeses. The company also announced that it was installing a whey-drying operation to allow it to process whey from the concentrated state into a powdered form, thereby increasing its value when sold. Whey by-products were a vital and growing segment of the cheese industry and were being distributed both nationally and internationally to industries such as pharmaceutical, confectionery, dairy foods, and bakeries.

Sales of bulk cheese products to food service industry distributors and food manufacturers under the Suprema Di Avellino name or on a private-label basis accounted for 41 percent of the company's revenues in fiscal 1998. Supermarket customers included King Kullen, Shop-Rite, BJ's, Foodtown, Stop'N Shop, D'Agostino's, Super Valu, and Giant. Sales to food service companies accounted for about 88 percent of the company's revenues in fiscal 1998, food manufacturers accounted for about six percent, and retailers accounted for about six percent. A&J Cheese Co. was the leading single customer in fiscal 1998, accounting for 18 percent of the company's revenues. A milk cooperative was Suprema's leading provider in the fiscal year, accounting for almost 25 percent of its supplies.

Principal Subsidiaries

Suprema Northeast, Inc.; Suprema Specialties West, Inc.

Further Reading

Coleman-Lochner, Lauren, "The Big Cheeses: Companies Carving Paths to Success," *Bergen (New Jersey) Record,* October 21, 1994, p. D7.
Flower, Michael A., and Douglas Jones, "Suprema Specialties Acquires Assets of California Cheese-Making Facilities of A&J Foods," *Business Wire,* November 8, 1991.
——, "Suprema Specialties Announces New Lite Grated Cheeses," *Business Wire,* March 18, 1992.
"Suprema Specialties' New Plant Opens," *Dairy Foods,* October 1996, p. 12.

—Robert Halasz

Supreme International Corporation

3000 NW 107th Avenue
Miami, Florida 33172
U.S.A.
(305) 592-2830
Fax: (305) 594-2307
Web site: http://www.supreme.com

Public Company
Founded: 1966
Employees: 335
Sales: $190.6 million (1998)
Stock Exchanges: NASDAQ
Ticker Symbol: SUPI
SICs: 5136 Men's & Boys' Clothing

Supreme International Corporation is one of the top suppliers of men's and boys' casual clothing in the country and the leading men's sportswear company in the southern United States. The company represents over 30 brands, and designs, imports, and markets sportswear and casual clothing under a broad array of labels, including Natural Issue, Munsingwear, and Grand Slam. Its apparel is sold to department, chain, and specialty stores, mass merchants, and golf pro shops in the United States, Canada, and Puerto Rico. Headquartered in Miami, Florida, the company has offices in seven locations around the globe and produces its clothing in Asia, Latin America, and Mexico. The Feldenkreis family owns about 43 percent of the company.

Starting with Car Parts: 1961–65

George Feldenkreis started his first import business in 1956 while a law student in his native Cuba. George and his brother imported Japanese products such as Formica and car parts and sold them on the island. But in 1961, after Fidel Castro came to power, George immigrated to the United States along with his pregnant wife and year-old son. He had $700, a law degree not recognized in his newly adopted country, and some business contacts in Japan.

To support his family he decided to start another import business, because, as he told the *South Florida Business Journal* in 1986, "Cubans were more experienced with import techniques than American because so much of the Cuban economy depended on imports."

After improving his English and studying trade statistics from the U.S. Department of Commerce, Feldenkreis founded Carfel Inc. and began importing automobile and motorcycle parts from Japan.

John Kennedy was president and few Americans drove Japanese cars. But Feldenkreis believed that would change. His first big sale occurred when a New York firm ordered $4,000 worth of clutch plates. With a loan from his father, Feldenkreis went to Japan, renewed his contacts there and made new ones. Carfel was on its way.

Expanding into Apparel: 1966–88

In 1966, Carfel had annual sales of about $3 million. That year, Feldenkreis and his brother began importing children's school uniforms to Puerto Rico. The following year he formed a new company, Supreme International Corporation, and added guayaberas, the open-neck, pleated shirt popular with Hispanic men, to his offerings. The shirts were made by a Japanese firm, with Feldenkreis importing and wholesaling them in Florida and Puerto Rico.

Feldenkreis gradually expanded his companies to the point that he was selling his imports throughout North America as well as in England. Carfel represented the biggest part of the sales, importing auto and motorcycle parts from several Asian countries. Supreme International was growing, however. The company began importing men's pants and knit shirts as well as the guayaberas from Asia and sold the clothing to major merchandisers such as Sears, Kmart, and J.C. Penney. Supreme's shirts ranged in price from $9.50 to $60.

By 1981, the Feldenkreis importing group was a $30 million business, although Supreme International represented only $5 million of that total. In addition to Carfel and Supreme, the

---

Company Perspectives:

For 30 years, we've scouted international markets for the highest quality and lowest cost manufacturers of apparel. Because of these sourcing capabilities, we've become one of the few companies to profitably service the full spectrum of apparel retail distribution channels.

---

group included Master International Inc., United Trading Co., and Diamond Electronics Inc.

George's son Oscar joined the business full-time early in the 1980s, after dropping out of the University of Miami. More alert to fashion trends than his father, Oscar made Supreme International's products more upscale and expanded product lines. As he told Larry Briger of the *Miami Herald,* "We were positioned as an importer of parochial, children's back-to-school uniforms, and guayaberas. I felt we could be more successful by finding niches . . . that could be filled and be recognized by name brands."

His early attempts at creating Supreme's own brands were not big hits. He first introduced the Feldini brand of Italian-style dress pants, well-made and half the price of Italian pants, but slow to sell. He then brought out the Gianni Abozzi and Simultaneous lines of sport shirts, but had to discontinue the Gianni Abozzi line. "We didn't have a theme or direction," Oscar explained in a 1995 *Forbes* article. "You have to develop a brand or a name that is easy for the customer to say."

Focusing on Name Brands: 1989–94

Oscar found that brand in 1989, with the introduction of Natural Issue. "We were kicking around some ideas on a brand that would be part of what was happening at the time—recycling, natural fibers, the environment," Oscar told *Forbes.* The new line started with printed silk and rayon sports shirts and quickly added 100 percent cotton printed shirts. The shirts retailed at $26 and were an immediate hit, putting Supreme in direct competition with well-known brands such as Dockers and Izod. The line boosted Supreme's sales by over $2.5 million in the first year, to $18 million.

By 1991, Oscar was heading Supreme International as executive vice-president for marketing and sales. Due to his efforts (and Natural Issue), in fiscal 1990 Supreme International accounted for 39 percent of the overall sales of the Feldenkreis family holdings.

Going Public and Acquiring More Brand Names: 1993–94

For fiscal 1993, ended January 31, 1993, Supreme International had revenues of $33.5 million, an increase of more than 24 percent over fiscal 1992, with growth in all its product lines. Net income tripled in the same period, to $1.8 million. In May, Feldenkreis took the company public, raising some $13.8 million. George was chairman and chief executive officer and Oscar was president and chief operating officer.

With that financial cushion, the company went on a buying spree, scooping up brand labels. With a cash bid of $360,000, Supreme International won a bankruptcy court auction for Publix Group LP in August. This brought Supreme the designer licenses for the Adolfo and Albert Nipon brands of shirts as well as for private labels for dress and sport shirts including Career Club, Cotton Mill, and CC Sport.

The following month the company acquired Miami-based Alexander Martin Corp. which made sports shirts, casual pants, and swimwear for the Big & Tall segment of men's clothing. The purchase gave Supreme International a manufacturing base in the United States and doubled the company's volume in that portion of the industry, with the Alexander Martin, Al Mar Sports, and Active Sport U.S.A. labels. At the same time, the company acquired the Gianfranco Ruffini license for dress shirts and casual pants.

Revenues for fiscal 1994 more than doubled, reaching $75 million in sales with earnings of over $4 million. Both *Forbes* and *Business Week* named Supreme International one of the year's best small companies. All this occurred while rivals such as Izod, USA Classic, and Munsingwear were in financial trouble. George Feldenkreis credited the company's success to its sourcing capabilities and distribution channels. "A lot of men's wear companies really don't have the sourcing capabilities that we have," Feldenkreis told the *Daily News Record* in 1993. "We have been close to that sourcing group for 25 years, and I think that's been a big part of our success."

Responding to the Casual Trend: 1994–95

Another factor in Supreme's growth was its ability to quickly respond to fashion trends with attractive products. The company's process was fairly simple. Its art department at headquarters sent computer-designed prints (more than 2,000 in 1993) to company offices in Asia and Guatemala which contracted with over 40 production companies to make the clothes. The shirts, pants, and other apparel were shipped to two warehouses in Miami and distributed to stores in North America, Puerto Rico, and Latin America. As Leslie McCall, an analyst with Oppenheimer & Co. Inc. explained in a 1995 *Investor's Business Daily* article, "Supreme is way ahead of the game for a company of its size. The CAD [computer assisted design] system gives Supreme a jump on fashion trends and allows them to beat the market at value-for-price. When a particular trend hits the streets . . . Supreme can get more . . . shirt styles out in a shorter amount of time for less money than the competition."

In the United States, which received more than 80 percent of the products, retail outlets ranged from Macy's and Federated Department Stores to Sears and Kmart. Department stores and chains represented 80 percent of Supreme's customers and the remainder were specialty stores. "Supreme has a tremendous niche in quality men's apparel," an industry analyst explained in a 1994 *USA Today* article.

Sales continued to increase, reaching $90 million for fiscal 1995. While adding new brands, Supreme kept its Natural Issue brand fresh and out front. J.C. Penney, for example, established Natural Issue Focus Shops in 250 stores, with exclusive displays of Supreme's products. In the spring of 1995, the company introduced Textures by Natural Issue, a collection of high-end men's clothing. It also licensed the production of Natural Issue underwear and sleepwear, and began designing and producing cold weather clothing such as jackets and sweaters for men and boys. That move positioned Supreme as a year-round supplier.

That fall, Supreme International raised $17 million through a second public offering and used the proceeds to repay debt. The company ended the year with sales of $121.1 million, although 1995 had been a tough one for most manufacturers and retailers of men's wear.

Going for the Golfer: 1996–97

The company started 1996 by repurchasing shares of its common stock, considering the price undervalued. Then, in March, Supreme International announced it would acquire Miami-based Jolem Imports for around $3 million. Jolem was a ten-year old private company that made casual clothes aimed at younger Hispanic men. Its brands included Tippos and Sun Splash. This niche complemented Supreme's other lines, attracting a different customer base.

But the big men's wear news in the mid-1990s was the growing popularity of golf and golf apparel. That market had long been dominated by lines such as Greg Norman and Jack Nicklaus, made by Reebok and Hartmarx, respectively, and licensed by individual golfers, or brands dedicated solely to golf wear, including Munsingwear, with its Penguin logo.

The appearance of Tiger Woods, the aging of baby boomers, and the continuing move to casual clothing, made golf and the sport's pants, sweaters, and knit shirts more popular. Citing figures released by the PGA early in 1996, *Bobbin* reported "the largest group of golfers, 23.9 percent, are affluent, career-oriented male baby boomers." Moreover, with the National Golf Foundation finding that the number of male golfers had increased more than 27 percent since the mid-1980s, men's clothing manufacturers could not ignore that market. Long consigned to pro shops at country clubs, golf wear began appearing in department stores, mass market venues, and specialty shops. Polo Ralph Lauren, which started its golf line in 1989, was soon joined by Tommy Hilfiger, Georgio Armani, and Haggar, and department stores began introducing private label collections, such as Federated's Arnold Palmer, Dayton Hudson/Marshall Field's Payne Stewart, and Nordstrom's Callaway.

Supreme International moved into the golf market, spending $18 million in cash to acquire the domestic and certain international trademarks of Munsingwear Inc. More than 100 years old, Munsingwear produced the first golf shirt, in 1954, and introduced the first designer logo, its penguin. For its money, Supreme received the Munsingwear brand, a golf label sold to mass merchandisers including Bradlees and Montgomery Ward; Penguin Sport, another golf line sold through Sears and Kohl's; and the Grand Slam line, distributed through Federated Department Stores, May Department Stores, and Dayton Hudson. With the acquisition of Munsingwear's Grand Slam Tour brand, Supreme also gained access to the "green grass" golf pro shop distribution channel.

As George Feldenkreis told *Daily News Record* in a September 10, 1996 interview, "We're going to have multiple labels to sell all channels of distribution . . . . We have more brands to offer to mass merchandisers and regional chains. They want brands because established names don't want to go down to that level of distribution." Supreme International also gained the royalties from Munsingwear's licenses, including sales of the Penguin and other logoed shirts, golf balls, umbrellas, and shoes, as well as its $50 million men's underwear business licensed to Fruit of the Loom.

However, the company was not depending solely on acquisitions to keep growing. During the year, Supreme International introduced Corporate Gear, a new private brand developed for Sears especially for Casual Friday wear. Supreme International's two purchases, combined with increased sales of its own labels, resulted in sales for fiscal 1997 of $155.7 million.

1997 to the Present

Supreme International continued to grow, following a business strategy based on increasing brand name recognition, diversifying product lines, seeking private label opportunities, and pursuing acquisition and licensing opportunities. It purchased Crossings sweaters, opened a new, $18 million headquarters, warehouse, and distribution center, and signed top designer Andrew Fezza. It also arranged more licensing deals, introducing a Ping line of golf clothes and signing an agreement with PNB Nation Clothing, thus expanding its presence in the growing young men's market segment. Under that license, PNB Nation designed and marketed the clothing and Supreme was responsible for sourcing and sales. Revenue for fiscal 1998 reached $190.7 million.

The "Asian flu," which hurt U.S. exporters during 1998, enabled Supreme International to reduce its costs, as imports became less expensive. The company concentrated on its Munsingwear brands during the year, introducing an advertising campaign and creating the Munsingwear.com web site. Supreme used the web site to steer Internet users to nearby stores which sold the products seen on the site. Following a successful test launch in 1997, Supreme added its new Munsingwear Lifestyle label to products sold to regional mass merchants. Lifestyle targeted the dress casual sportswear market, but was positioned beside the popular Slammer brand golf wear. As a Supreme official told *Daily News Record*, "What we did was to expand a very familiar golf and sportswear label into a new area. We traded on the authenticity and the recognition value of the brand to extend it into new lifestyle areas."

At the end of 1998, Supreme announced the purchase of the John Henry shirt line, which it had previously licensed, and the Manhattan shirt brands, including Lady Manhattan, from Salant Corporation for $35 million. The purchase helped Supreme further broaden its brand portfolio and gave it a much stronger position in the men's dress shirt segment. It also increased the company's international business, since Manhattan was the number two brand of dress shirts in China. Supreme indicated it would likely introduce a brand of Manhattan sportswear. "Manhattan has been boxed in as a dress shirt brand, which it shouldn't be," Feldenkreis told the *Miami Herald*. "We plan to broaden its appeal." Supreme also announced it would license its Munsingwear, Penguin Sport, and Natural Issue labels to Fishman & Tobin, Inc. to produce and market boys' sportswear.

The company that began as an importer of school uniforms and guayaberas had become a major manufacturer of men's and boys' clothing. Its labels could be found in just about every segment of retail, from Saks Fifth Avenue to Kmart to regional chains. While almost half its revenues came from the sale of knit shirts, it also produced dress, flannel, linen, and cotton shirts, slacks, shorts, sweaters, and jackets, and licensed underwear and boys' clothes. In addition, it was the leading distributor in the country of guayabera shirts. As the consolidation in wholesale continued, the company felt well positioned to meet its customers needs for a wide variety of design apparel.

Further Reading

Abend, Jules, "New Entrants Crowding Golf Category," *Bobbin,* November 1996, p. 90.

Altaner, David, "Shirts for All," *Sun-Sentinel* (Fort Lauderdale), March 12, 1998, p. 1D.

Auerbach, Jonathan, "Supreme Gets All Publix Shirt Labels," *Daily News Record,* August 27, 1993, p. 17.

Benko, Laura B., "The New America: Supreme International Corp." *Investor's Business Daily,* October 9, 1995, p. A6.

D'Innocenzio, Anne, "Supreme International Plans to Go Public," *Daily News Record,* April 30, 1993, p. 10.

"Dream Wasn't Farfetched, After All," *Miami Herald,* June 6, 1994, p. 9BM.

"Feldenkreis Got Big Jump on Imports from Orient," *South Florida Business Journal,* April 7, 1986, p. 37.

Geller, Stan, "Munsingwear a Supreme Buy," *Daily News Record,* May 24, 1996, p. 1.

——, "The Supreme Choice: Munsingwear Gets a Dressy Edge," *Daily News Record,* September 28, 1998, p. 2.

Gwynne, S.C., "The Coming Storm," *Time,* November 9, 1998, p. 122A.

Lloyd, Brenda, "Supreme International Reaping Rewards of 3 Decades of Hard Work," *Daily News Record,* July 13, 1994, p. 7.

"Making the Internet Work for Supreme International," *Business Wire,* June 8, 1998.

Randall, Eric D., "Menswear Maker a 'Supreme' Deal," *USA Today,* August 18, 1994, p. 3B.

Reveron, Derek, "The Importer Who Spotted Japan Before Japan Was Hot," *Miami Herald,* March 12, 1990, p. 9BM.

Ryan, Thomas J. "Most Men's Wear Stocks Hobble in '95," *Daily News Record,* January 3, 1996.

——, "Supreme International Sees Big Growth in Brands," *Daily News Record,* December 30, 1993, p. 3.

Spevack, Rachel, "Supreme International Sees Green with Munsingwear Labels in Hand," *Daily News Record,* September 10, 1996, p. 3.

"Supreme in Deal to Acquire Jolem," *Daily News Record,* May 9, 1996, p. 10.

"Supreme International, Inc.; Initial Public Offering Generated $13.8 Million," *Daily News Record,* May 27, 1993, p. 8.

"Supreme International Inks Deal to Acquire Alexander Martin," *Daily News Record,* August 5, 1993, p. 12.

"Urban Apparel Firm PNB Nation Joining Supreme International," *Business Wire,* May 27, 1998.

Youngblood, Dick, "Smaller Is Better," *Star Tribune* (Minneapolis), January 26, 1998, p. 1D.

Walker, Elaine, "Supreme International Grows Out of Its Old Florida Home," *Miami Herald,* March 12, 1998.

Walsh, Matt, "Winning Team," *Forbes,* March 27, 1995, p. 66.

Whitefield, Mimi, "Miami-Based Supreme Will Buy Salant Dress Shirt Brands," *Miami Herald,* December 31, 1998.

—Ellen D. Wernick

Sybase, Inc.

6475 Christie Avenue
Emeryville, California 94608
U.S.A.
(510) 922-3500
Fax: (510) 922-3210
Web site: http://www.sybase.com

Public Company
Incorporated: 1984
Employees: 5,200
Sales: $903.9 million (1997)
Stock Exchanges: NASDAQ
Ticker Symbol: SYBS
SICs: 7372 Prepackaged Software

Sybase, Inc. is one of the ten largest independent software companies in the world. The company's main area of emphasis is in developing relational database management systems for network computer environments. Approximately half of Sybase's revenues come from the sale of its products, but the company also offers other services such as consulting and technical support. Founded in the mid-1980s in Silicon Valley, the company has grown steadily, establishing a strong market share and a worldwide network of customers.

Sybase's Beginnings

Sybase was founded in 1984 by Mark Hoffman and Robert Epstein. Hoffman had previously worked as an executive at a company called Britton Lee, which pioneered the field of database computing. He joined Epstein, who had helped to create an early relational program called Ingres while working toward his Ph.D. at the University of California at Berkeley. Together, the two set out to market a cutting-edge relational database management system (RDBMS), which would organize information and make it available to many computers in a network.

After gathering a corps of experienced programmers, the company spent more than two years working on its debut product.

During that time, Sybase's activities were funded by a consortium of venture capital firms, including Hambrecht & Quist and Kleiner Perkins Caufield & Byers. In late 1986, Sybase shipped its first test programs, entering a market that others had pioneered five years earlier. In May 1987, Sybase formally released the SYBASE system, the first high-performance RDBMS for online applications. Rather than having a vast central bank of data stored in a large mainframe computer, the SYBASE System provided for a client/server computer architecture.

Client/server computer systems logically broke up monolithic applications into separate components that interrelated over a network for faster processing. The system linked hardware and software into a complex web in which information resources were distributed over multiple computer systems. Clients (individual desktop computers) and servers (databases) moved information and tools back and forth between themselves in order to most efficiently fulfill a company's needs. With the SYBASE system, companies could maintain the integrity of and control over information that a mainframe gave them, but could also make use of that information in a much more widespread and efficient manner.

The SYBASE system was based on Structured Query Language (SQL), a standard IBM computer programming language, and consisted of two parts—the DataServer and the DataToolset. The first component allowed an entire network of computers to gain access to a database at the same time. The second provided the building blocks for programs that developed applications, wrote reports, and performed queries. In its use of SQL, the company provided an advance in computer software that no other company had made.

In order to give its program the greatest possible capabilities, Sybase made the decision to limit its use to a small number of strategic hardware platforms. The company chose to market SYBASE for use only on DEC, IBM, and UNIX-based computers. Sybase invested heavily in training for its technical support staff to reassure its potential customers that they could rely on the company for help in using its products. Eschewing middlemen or software dealers, the company relied on direct sales to distribute SYBASE, establishing a network of sales offices across the United States and an office in London.

Company Perspectives:

Sybase's products, combined with its world-class professional services and partner technologies, provide a comprehensive platform for delivering the integrated solutions businesses need to be successful.

Success in the Late 1980s

In the first year after its release, Sybase's software formed some important alliances. In September 1987, the Pyramid Technology Corporation began selling its own hardware and Sybase software as a package deal. In October 1987, Sun Microsystems, Inc., another computer maker, bought 40 copies of the Sybase program for its own internal use. After seven months of sales, Sybase was able to report revenues of $6 million, as its product notched quarterly sales of $3 million. The company moved from losses to a profit in the third quarter of the year. At that time, Sybase also received an infusion of $3.3 million in capital from Apple Computer.

In January 1988, software giant Microsoft revealed that it had made an agreement with Sybase in 1986 that would allow Microsoft to license the company's technology. As a result of this agreement, Microsoft SQL Server for the company's OS/2 computer operating system was released. SQL Server retrieved information faster than similar programs, and was the first to update all outlying databases in a network instantaneously if the central databank was revised.

With this partnership, Microsoft helped to establish Sybase in the industry by codeveloping and selling versions of the company's products for use on its operating systems. The first arrangement of this kind came shortly after Microsoft's announcement, when the Ashton-Tate software company moved to release SQL Server for use on machines that ran on DOS, the IBM-standard operating system. This program was known as Ashton-Tate/Microsoft SQL Server, and was marketed both individually and in conjunction with the company's dBase product.

Within a year of SYBASE's release, the program had established a strong following in the corporate and government world. Due to its power, Sybase targeted its sales in part to customers who required online transaction processing—or real-time computer operations—such as banks.

At the end of 1988, Sybase formed Sybase Canada, and three months later the company also set up a French subsidiary. In March 1989, Sybase toyed with the idea of selling stock to the public in order to generate some working capital, but finally announced that it would postpone this step to a later date. Six months later, the company announced that it had, instead, received additional funding from the Lotus Development Corporation, a software company that acquired 15 percent of Sybase's stock.

In October 1989, Sybase released additional products, introducing the SYBASE Open Client/Server Interfaces—new software programs that provided generic client/server communication, allowing for greater connectivity within computer networks. With these new offerings, and its earlier system, Sybase notched sales of $56 million in 1989.

The Early 1990s

In January 1990, Sybase paid $3.5 million for D&N Systems, Inc., an integrated database consulting firm which it renamed SQL Solutions, Inc. Sybase increased its penetration of the government market in early 1990, when the company successfully marketed its products to NASA, the Army, and the Air Force's Military Airlift Command. These clients made particular use of the Sybase program's capacity to keep data secure and confidential. The company also expanded internationally, when in June 1990 Sybase formed a joint venture with HCL America, called HCL Sybase, to sell its programs in Singapore.

Despite this growth, Sybase's earnings had slowed in the late 1980s, and the company reported several quarters of losses. In August 1990, Sybase cut its staff by five percent, laying off 50 members of its 800-member workforce in an effort to cut costs. To shore up its returns, the company also began to seek out clients in the financial services field. Offering customers the ability to process transactions in real time, Sybase had lined up 20 of Wall Street's 22 largest brokers within the next few years.

Sybase also introduced new products that were designed to help IBM mainframe computers become part of a client/server system. These programs were the first to join local area network (LAN) technology to mainframe technology. In addition, Sybase introduced joint marketing ventures with its investor, Lotus, creating interface software for Lotus 1-2-3 and packaging the company's spreadsheet with its own SQL Server. At the end of the year, Lotus increased its ownership of Sybase from 15 to 25 percent by buying Ashton-Tate's shares in the company.

In March 1991, Sybase made its second acquisition, purchasing Deft Software, Inc. Five months later, the company made its initial public offering of stock. This move brought about a new accountability to Wall Street investors, and Sybase saw its European sales fall short of expectations. In an effort to redress this failing, the company set out to unify and upgrade its European operations, eliminating country managers and instituting other changes.

With its new infusion of capital, Sybase merged with SQ Software, Inc., in June 1992, and purchased Gain Technology, Inc.—a vendor of object-based, multimedia application development tools—in September of that year. Gain's principal product was GainMomentum, a software program that allowed different forms of data to be included in the company's client/server computer architecture. Two months after this purchase, Sybase announced its latest generation of software. Dubbed the System 10 product family, these programs were designed to provide a framework for companies to switch over their computer operations from older mainframe models to client/server systems. By the end of 1992, Sybase posted revenues of $265 million.

In April 1993, Sybase introduced the first component of System 10, called OmniSQL Gateway. This program connected the various parts of a computer network, enabling users at any point to gain access to changes being made anywhere on the system. This quality was known as "transparent interoperability." Building on the program of its acquisition, Gain Technology, the company introduced a family of products called "Momentum." These included Build Momentum and Enterprise Momentum, both of which were environments for building applications. With these tools, programmers could create visually appealing programs for corporate employees to use when negotiating their company's computer system.

In the summer of 1993, Sybase also completed a reorganization of its operations. With more than 2,000 employees, the company had grown rapidly, and it needed to better define its corporate goals. In order to do this, Sybase divided its activities into two groups, the Tools Technology Group and the Server & Connectivity Group.

Later that year, Sybase completed its rollout of the System 10 components, which included SQL Server 10 and Back-up Server; Open Client/Server APIs; and SQL Monitor and SA Companion, which were used to manage computer systems. In the next month, Sybase also released its Replication Server, which allowed computer users to build reliable systems to keep computer operations running for online transaction processing.

By the end of 1993, Sybase's revenue had reached $427 million, and earnings were $44 million. The company's growth rate was 61 percent, which made Sybase the world's second largest supplier of enterprise client/server RDBS software. With this gain, the company moved ahead of its competitor Informix, and came up on the heels of industry leader Oracle.

Sybase had achieved this growth not only through the consistent introduction of solid products, but also by emphasizing customer service and prompt delivery of new software. During the course of 1993, the company dramatically increased the size of its customer service and support divisions. Sybase also opened three new technical support service centers in Burlington, Massachusetts; Tokyo; and Mexico City. Including the employees hired to staff these outposts, Sybase increased its staff by 1,400 people throughout the course of the year.

Sybase's strong growth had also been driven by the company's rapid international expansion. After its successful revamp of foreign operations, overseas sales had doubled in 1993, boosted by 82 percent growth in Europe and an extremely strong 182 percent gain in Asia and Latin America. These operations accounted for more than a quarter of the company's revenues. Throughout the course of 1993, Sybase added new subsidiaries in Belgium, Italy, Spain, Switzerland, and Mexico. Overall, it had ten foreign subsidiaries and 39 international distributors.

On the first day of 1994, Sybase purchased Oasis Group plc, a British firm that helped companies choose and build computer systems. With this alliance, Sybase positioned itself as a provider of a complete range of services for customers upgrading their computer operations. Later in January, Sybase also announced that it would purchase MicroDecisionWare, Inc., a producer of networking software. With this merger, Sybase hoped to become the market leader in this field.

One month later, Sybase enhanced its software offerings to government agencies when it released Secure SQL Server 10, which offered secure and practical RDBMS applications. In April 1994, Sybase announced a new generation of software that would expand a company's computer network over telephone lines to take in other businesses and clients. Sybase embarked upon this project with its partner Tele-Communications, Inc., to produce programs to control the traffic over such large-scale extended enterprise systems. In addition, the company rushed to release its Navigation Server, a program that implemented the newest parallel-processing technology. Also in 1994, the company announced Enterprise CONNECT, an interoperability framework, and purchased Expressway Technologies, whose technology later served as the foundation for the Sybase IQ product and the Warehouse WORKS framework.

The Mid-1990s and Beyond

In early 1995, Sybase merged with Powersoft, the leading client/server tools vendor at the time. The merger created the world's sixth largest independent software company. Sybase then added to its scope in May 1995 by acquiring SDP, a French company whose focus laid in developing tools for data modeling. SDP's technology allowed users to design and reverse-engineer multiple databases. Soon thereafter, Sybase introduced a new family of database products called System 11. This was the biggest launch in Sybase's history.

In 1996 the company formed an agreement to merge again, this time with Visual Components, Inc. The merger led to the creation of a new Powersoft components division, with the express purpose of delivering reusable software such as spreadsheets, spell-checking modules, and charting tools. Around that same time, Sybase introduced web.works, which was a program that allowed business applications to be delivered on the Internet. The company broke the $1 billion mark in annual sales in 1996, achieving revenue of $1.01 billion.

Annual revenue decreased the following year, as a result of a surprising turn of events in Sybase's Japanese subsidiary. While completing its financial audit at the end of the year, Sybase found that its operation in Japan had committed serious violations of the company's rules for recognizing revenue. Thus, although the company had thought that it had achieved profits throughout the first three quarters of the fiscal year, in truth it ended up posting losses. The company's overall revenue in 1997 dropped to a somewhat disappointing $903.9 million.

Nevertheless, the company was pleased with what it had accomplished throughout the year. According to CEO Mitchell Kertzman in his letter to shareholders, "We dramatically improved our technology across all our product lines, we maintained a strong balance sheet . . . . Today, Sybase is the only enterprise software solutions company whose technology fully embraces the open standards of the software industry."

Sybase needed a turnaround, however, and thus hired John Chen to take over as president and CEO. For three years prior to his arrival, Sybase had achieved around a billion dollars in revenue, only to fail to make a profit. Chen set about the task of solving this problem. He decided that one of his favorite pastimes—golf—could provide an answer. As stated by Jamie

Beckett in the October 20, 1998 edition of the *San Francisco Chronicle,* "Sybase was like a player on a difficult course who used the same club no matter what hole or hazard he faced."

Chen initiated some changes within the company that eventually led to some positive changes. For example, one of his first orders of business as CEO was to create a portable computer database software division, in order to capitalize on the ever increasing popularity of laptop computing in the late 1990s. Sybase also added web-based customer service in 1998. By mid-1998, the company had halted its continuous string of money-losing quarters with a break-even second quarter. Then, in the third quarter the company finally posted a profit—$2.2 million for the three months ending September 30, 1998.

With a loyal customer base despite its mid-decade slump, Sybase was firmly established in a field laden with opportunity as the 1990s drew to a close. The company's strong record of past performance indicated that it had potential to succeed in the competitive software programming market of the coming century. Its ability to continue generating profits and further its turnaround efforts, however, would determine its true future success.

Principal Subsidiaries

SQL Solutions, Inc.; Deft Software, Inc.; Oasis Group P.L.C.

Further Reading

Beckett, Jamie, "Turning Around Sybase: CEO Found Strategy Through Golf," *San Francisco Chronicle,* October 20, 1998, p. B1.

Brandt, Richard, "Sybase Steps Out of the Shadows," *Business Week,* April 18, 1994.

Davey, Tom, "Three Bay Area Companies Lead Pack in Database Race," *San Francisco Business Times,* June 17–23, 1994.

Eisenhart, Mary, "Connectivity Solutions in Data Base Management," *Microtimes,* March 1988.

Garner, Rochelle, and Houston, Patrick, "Inside People," *PC Week,* September 20, 1993.

Houston, Patrick, "Learning from a Rival's Reorg," *PC Week,* June 13, 1994.

Knowles, Anne, "A Software Start-up with Hardware Back-Up," *Electronic Business,* January 15, 1988.

Siegmann, Ken, "Data Management Takes Off," *San Francisco Chronicle,* May 9, 1994.

—Elizabeth Rourke
—updated by Laura E. Whiteley

Target Stores

33 S. Sixth Street
P.O. Box 1392
Minneapolis, Minnesota 55440-1392
U.S.A.
(612) 304-6073
Fax: (612) 304-0730
Web site: http://www.targetstores.com

Division of Dayton Hudson Corporation
Incorporated: 1961
Employees: 166,000
Sales: $20.37 billion (1997)
SICs: 5331 Variety Stores

Target Stores, Inc. is a division of Dayton Hudson Corporation, and is the third of the "Big 3" in U.S. discount retailing, behind Wal-Mart and Kmart. Curiously enough, Target opened its first store the very same year as did Wal-Mart and Kmart, in 1962. Since that time, Target's growth has been nothing short of meteoric. The company operates over 850 stores in 41 states, including 75 Target Greatlands, 14 SuperTargets, and 298 Targets with pharmacies. Part of the company's success lies in its ability to combine bargain prices with fashionable, branded merchandise and excellent customer service. The company's commitment to this is reflected in its motto: "Expect More. Pay Less."

The Early Years

Dayton's department stores began planning a Target discount chain in 1961 when it foresaw a rising public demand for lower-priced, mass merchandise available in a convenient, friendly environment. According to company literature, the Target name and red and white bull's-eye logo were selected for their visual impact and the underlying message that the stores would be aimed at offering customers the best prices. When Target was incorporated in September 1961, there were a handful of high-volume, low-margin discount retailers doing business around the country; nonetheless, Target claimed to be the first to offer quality national brands in a comfortable, attractive

setting. As Target expanded during the 1960s, consumer attitudes toward discount retailers changed dramatically, from mild disdain to enthusiastic acceptance.

The first Target store actually opened in 1962 in Roseville, Minnesota, a northern tier suburb of Minneapolis and St. Paul. The test store conformed to the specifications of later Target stores, which were generally sized between 80,000 and 135,000 square feet and emphasized wide aisles, well-marked displays, ample checkout lines, and a clean, inviting atmosphere. Plans for Target were still in an embryonic stage when the first store was opened; therefore, the management of Dayton's consulted with the management of a fashionable, upscale department store chain in Georgia named Rich's, which was planning a similar new discount retailing entry in its home market—Richway stores. According to a 1989 Target advertisement/retrospective, "the two teams shared ideas and strategies" and "did not see themselves as competitors, but as collaborators." Central to the strategy of each parent company was locating its discount offspring in major markets near major thoroughfares. The Minnesota-Georgia planning sessions obviously rewarded Target during the short-term, but also in the long-term: later in 1989, when Target was prepared to enter the Southeast, the Richway chain proved an ideal acquisition candidate that facilitated a strong Target entry into the region.

By the end of Target's introductory year, four stores had been opened. By 1966 the subsidiary had made its first foray outside of Minnesota with the opening of two stores in Denver, Colorado. Within the next four years, Target had 17 stores in four states. The company closed the decade with 40 percent average annual growth over four years and annual sales of $100 million.

Expansion in the 1970s

During the 1970s, Target matured not only in terms of size (80 stores in 11 states by 1979, with $1.12 billion in sales) but also in terms of technology (electronic cash registers for improved inventory control) and corporate identity (toy safety campaigns, shopping events for seniors and the disabled, and various outreach programs). The tone for Target's aggressive expansion was set in 1971 when the subsidiary acquired a 16-store retail chain serving the markets of Colorado, Oklahoma, and Iowa. It was through such opportunistic purchases—as well as through the regular addition of new stores—that Target was able to become Dayton Hudson's top revenue producer by 1975.

Unlike other discount and mass merchandisers, Target had a department store heritage instead of dimestore roots. This proved to be valuable in terms of its growth potential, allowing the store chain to negotiate deals with manufacturers that might have been difficult otherwise. For example, premier brand-name manufacturers were formerly accustomed to establishing exclusive relationships with department stores, and often avoided the distribution of their goods in mass merchandising channels. Target's connection to Dayton's, however—in addition to changing attitudes about discount retailing—helped fuel Target's success.

Nevertheless, Target's ascendancy was not without problems. In 1973 the chain had 46 stores and was facing two consecutive years of decreased earnings. New management, in the form of replacement President Stephen Pistner and Merchandising Executive Kenneth Macke (who eventually became president of Target and then chairman and CEO of Dayton Hudson, retiring in 1993), arrived and took stock. In a 1986 *Star Tribune* article, Macke commented, "Target had grown very fast and they'd forgotten a little about the most important person: the customer."

In 1974, Target initiated a rapid turnaround that began with a one-year halt to new store additions. Other steps included the creation of a management team to review Target's objectives; the creation of a quality assurance committee to review the manufacture and pricing of private-label products; the addition of new brand-name selections; the renovation of store interiors and displays; and the advent of color promotional inserts in Sunday newspapers. These steps were designed to demonstrate Target's high reputation to its customers, as well as its commitment to good products at low prices.

The discount chain also implemented policies and events that demonstrated its commitment to the surrounding communities. For example, midway through the decade, Target began hosting special shopping events for senior citizens and people with disabilities. The store also initiated a toy safety campaign, and its employees began the practice of donating money to such causes as United Way (within a decade, Target team members reached a milestone by donating over $1 million in this fashion).

Revitalized, Target continued its transition from an expanding subsidiary to the central growth division of Dayton Hudson, a transformation that became especially overt between 1977 and 1982. At the beginning of this five-year period, Target's operating profits represented just 26 percent of overall corporate profits; by 1982, department store profits had plunged from 58 percent to 25 percent, while Target earnings had risen to a solid 33 percent, approximately the same as the Mervyn's chain (acquired by Dayton's in 1978).

Acquisitions in the 1980s

Target launched into the 1980s with the acquisition of Ayr-Way Stores, a 40-outlet chain operating in Illinois, Ohio, Indiana, and Kentucky. Prior to the purchase, Target had operated stores in Illinois; the other three states were new territories for the company. Three years later the company acquired 33 FedMart sites in southern California and Arizona.

According to Neal St. Anthony in the April 7, 1986 edition of the *Minneapolis Star Tribune,* analysts were particularly worried about Target's acquisition of 28 closed FedMart stores in the highly competitive region of southern California. Some believed that to compete there, Target would have to follow other mass merchants and begin offering liquor and groceries as well as clothing and household items. In addition, FedMart employed union workers, Target did not. However, these and other obstacles were overcome, and California soon became the state in which Target had by far the most stores, the most retail square feet, and generated the most revenue.

In addition to catapulting Target firmly into the "Big Three," the successful California expansion won the approval of Wall Street and kudos from a number of other sources. In 1984 the University of California's School of Business Administration named Dayton Hudson Corporation, of which Target formed no small part, the "best managed company in the U.S.A." Target closed the decade with several highlights, including a large expansion into the Southeast, recognition as the Discounter of the Year, and sponsorship of the International Trans-Antarctica Expedition. By 1989 the company operated 399 stores in 31 states and boasted annual sales of $7.52 billion.

New Growth in the 1990s

In 1990 Target opened a new prototype store in Apple Valley, Minnesota. Called Target Greatland, it was a megastore featuring wider aisles, color-coded signs and graphics, broader product offerings, and "Food Avenue" and "Guest Services" areas. The Greatland concept proved to be quite successful, and continued to be implemented throughout the 1990s, serving also as a guide for the approximately twice-per-decade remodeling of existing stores. During 1990 Target also unveiled a market strategy to introduce Target stores into smaller cities (exactly the opposite strategy of giant rival Wal-Mart), as well as total quality and micromarketing programs. This last was designed to capitalize on the unique needs and interests of different communities and regions, through merchandise reflecting, for example, the local climate or local sports teams.

In 1991 Bill Saporito, writing for *Fortune,* posed the question "Is Wal-Mart Unstoppable?" According to him, the stage for a three-way showdown in discount retailing was set: "In the next five years the three biggest outfits—the Marts, K and Wal, as well as the less well known Target stores . . . will be on one collision course after another. . . . By 1995 the three, which now control 70 percent of the discount department store business, will overlap in about 40 percent of their territories, up from 15 percent today." The outcome was by no means any clearer by mid-decade, though Kmart appeared to be experiencing the greatest difficulty in maintaining profits. Kmart's situation actually led to a shareholder revolt and divestiture request in mid-1994, initiated by certain large institutional investors.

However, a glimpse of the mounting battle in the form of price wars was offered in 1993 by articles in the *Star Tribune* and *U.S. News & World Report*. Both reported on a skirmish between Wal-Mart and Target, in which certain Wal-Mart stores apparently used flawed price comparison advertising. Target retaliated with ads headed "This Never Would Have Happened If Sam Walton Were Alive," charging that Wal-Mart was posting inflated or misleading prices on Target items. Wal-Mart responded in kind, and Target requested an investigation by the Better Business Bureau. The whole price brouhaha was underscored in May 1993 when Wal-Mart began phasing out its slogan "Always the low price. Always" to "Always low prices. Always," perhaps confirming the belief that price wars in discount retailing are ultimately unsustainable. Experts admitted that not even the largest companies in the industry could conceivably hope to offer the best prices on all products all of the time.

Meanwhile, a primary focus for Target was a reinvestment in its employees. Beginning in 1989, Target staff had been trained through an intensive course called "Target U." to treat customers as guests and to generate a "fast, fun, friendly" shopping environment. According to Ronald Henkoff in *Fortune*, "The new training has had a dramatic impact on employee turnover, which peaked at 89 percent among hourly workers in 1989—the year Target U. was born—and dropped to 59 percent in 1992. Customer service, as measured by the stores' semiannual surveys, has been on a steady upward trend." The 1993 Target annual report announced the company's commitment to institute this "Guest Culture"—"modeled on the practices of premier customer services companies such as Disney"—nationwide.

Target's most prominent goal in the mid-1990s was to seek out opportunities for new growth. During 1993, the company entered the Chicago market with 18 stores. Another 32 stores were added to existing markets in the Midwest, Southeast, and Southwest. By the close of 1995, the company operated 670 stores throughout the United States, including two new prototype SuperTarget stores, which offered grocery items in addition to Target's regular merchandise.

The first SuperTarget store was opened in Omaha, Nebraska, in 1995, and the second store soon followed in Lawrence, Kansas. Target had studied the best grocery stores in the country prior to developing SuperTarget, and had then integrated those ideas into the already successful Target Greatland concept. The company hoped that the concept would result in a one-stop, no-hassle shopping experience for its customers. Success

came quickly, and Target soon opened six more SuperTargets in Nebraska, Iowa, and Utah the following year.

Target also expanded its offerings chainwide in 1995, introducing three new services on a national level: a bridal gift registry, a baby shower gift registry, and the Target Guest Card—the company's own credit card. Club Wedd, the bridal registry, had been in existence for a few years already, but the company took the concept nationwide in 1995 by linking all Target stores through a computer system that would allow people to access and use a couple's gift registry at any Target throughout the United States. The Lullaby Club—a registry for baby gifts—soon followed. As for the Target Guest Card, the company issued its card to customers and then allowed them to use the card at any of the parent company's retail stores. Conversely, customers could also use a Hudson's card to make purchases at Target.

The End of the Century and Beyond

In 1996, Target continued its expansion efforts, adding 71 new stores throughout the United States, including an entrance into the metro market of Washington, D.C. By the end of the year, the company was operating 736 stores throughout the country, and had achieved annual revenues of $17.85 billion.

The company also continued its efforts to give something back to the communities that it served. In 1996, Dayton Hudson and its many retail divisions made grants of approximately $25 million. The following year, that figure rose to $39 million, including $2.8 million in scholarships that were given to high school seniors who had been involved in their communities. At the local level, Target stores contributed to the arts, education, and family violence prevention efforts. On a national scale, the company made contributions to the Washington Memorial Restoration project, the St. Jude Children's Research Program, United Way, Habitat for Humanity, and its own National Wildlife Federation club for kids—EarthSavers.

By far one of the most popular community support efforts, though, was Target's Take Charge of Education program. Initiated in 1997, the program allowed Target Guest Card holders to sign up the school of their choice to receive one percent of their Guest Card purchase amounts. Within two years, over 300,000 schools were registered, and over $800,000 had been given to these schools. Furthermore, in 1999 the company pledged to give back more than $1 million a week to the communities in which it did business. Examples of this generosity were seen immediately in January 1999, when tornados tore apart two cities in the state of Tennessee, and Target offered relief to the victims.

Target's strategy, one of the most imitated among mass merchandisers in the country, had always been a model of simplicity: provide customers with quality products at low prices. In 1986, Target's first president, Douglas Dayton, had remarked that Dayton Hudson "would have been a fading retail entity" without Target. This was even more evident 15 years later, as the company and the communities it served approached the end of the 20th century, and Target Stores continued to achieve success.

Further Reading

Apgar, Sally, "Target Accuses Wal-Mart of Not Playing Fair When Posting Comparative Prices," *Minneapolis Star Tribune,* March 25, 1993, p. 1D.

"Big Three Discounters Top Big Builders List," *Chain Store Age Executive,* December 1993, p. 114.

Fitzgerald, Kate, "Bob Thacker: Target," *Advertising Age,* July 5, 1993, p. S18.

Grant, Linda, and Warren Cohen, "Shopping's Big Chill," *U.S. News & World Report,* July 12, 1993, p. 44.

Hendrix, Kimberly D., "Discount Stores Fared Well During Recession," *Chain Store Age Executive,* August 1992, p. 19A.

Henkoff, Ronald, "Companies That Train Best," *Fortune,* March 22, 1993, p. 73.

"In Retailing, Price Stranglehold Lessens," *Advertising Age,* November 1, 1993, pp. S6, S18.

Ortega, Bob, "Wal-Mart Bows to Pricing Reality by Changing 4 Letters," *Wall Street Journal,* May 21, 1993, p. B1.

Papa, Mary Bader, "William Andres: Executive of the Year," *Corporate Report Minnesota,* January 1984, pp. 57–63.

St. Anthony, Neal, "Target Stores Have Made Their Mark: Discount Offspring Now Powers Parent Firm," *Minneapolis Star Tribune,* April 7, 1986, p. 1M.

Saporito, Bill, "Is Wal-Mart Unstoppable?" *Fortune,* May 6, 1991, pp. 50–59.

Schafer, Lee, "The Best Defense," *Corporate Report Minnesota,* June 1989, pp. 31–35.

Stavig, Vicki, "A Sight to Be Sold," *Corporate Report Minnesota,* April 1986, p. 37.

—Jay P. Pederson
—updated by Laura E. Whiteley

Teck Corporation

200 Burrard Street
Vancouver, British Columbia
V6C 3L9
Canada
(604) 687-1117
Fax: (604) 687-6100
Web site: http://www.teckcorp.ca

Public Company
Incorporated: 1913 as Teck-Hughes Gold Mines, Ltd.
Employees: 3,154
Sales: $503.9 million (1998)
Stock Exchanges: Toronto Vancouver Montreal
Ticker Symbol: D.TIH
SICs: 1041 Gold Ores; 1021 Copper Ores; 1031 Lead &
   Zinc Ores

Teck Corporation is one of the world's fastest growing diversified mine development and operating companies, producing gold, silver, copper, zinc, niobium and metallurgical coal. Teck is the largest shareholder in Cominco Ltd., a world leader in zinc and lead as well as a producer of copper. The company has working interests in 11 mines located across Canada and a copper mine in Chile. Teck projects usually involve partnerships or joint ventures with other companies, with Teck operating as the builder and project manager. Teck partners include Adrian Resources, AMAX Inc., Soquem Ltee, Cambior Inc., Inmet Mining Corporation, Kuwait Investment Office, TVX, Rio Algom, Nissho Iwai, Homestake Mining Co., Aur Resources Inc., Cominco Ltd., ENAMI and Sociedad Minera Pudahuel Ltda. (SMP). Their projects include explorations in Australia, Argentina, Bolivia, Brazil, Canada, Central Asia, Chile, Indonesia, Mexico, Panama, Peru, the United States, Venezuela, and West Africa.

The Early Years: Yukon Gold Discovered in 1896

In 1896, gold was discovered in the Yukon Territory at Bonanza Creek by prospector George Washington Carmack.

The following July, two steamers carried Yukon prospectors and gold valued at over $1.2 million into the ports of Seattle and San Francisco—a ground-breaking event that opened the famous Klondike Gold Rush of the 1890s. Within two years thousands of men and women trekked north, inspired by dreams of mining their fortunes. Some were more fortunate than the majority, forming businesses that grew and prospered. Such was the case with the Yukon Consolidated Gold Corporation (YCGC), which would eventually grow to become the largest operator in the area. Between 1932 and 1966, YCGC produced 1.7 million ounces of gold, all from the rich river gravels. In later years, YCGC became part of Teck Corporation through a 1978 amalgamation actuated by Norman Keevil.

Norman Keevil—father of the 1990s Teck Corporation President and CEO Norman B. Keevil—began operating as a copper miner when he started the Temagami Mining Company, Ltd., following the discovery of high-grade copper deposits in Ontario's Lake Temagami region. After purchasing several other mining operations and merging with others, Keevil would eventually form Teck Corporation. Teck was derived from the Teck-Hughes Gold Mining Company at Kirkland Lake, Ontario—an operation that had been created in 1913. At that time, Teck-Hughes was a relatively small company with a few small gold mines.

The 1960s–1980s: Growth as a Mining Development Company

Norman Keevil's son, Norman B. Keevil, began working for Toronto-based Teck-Hughes Gold Mines Ltd. in 1962. The younger Keevil shared his father's interest in geology, according to David Berman of *Canadian Business,* but planned "to pursue a career in academia and actually accepted a job in the geology and geophysics department of a U.S. university." After half a dozen or so refusals to his father's request that he join Teck, the younger Keevil finally relented. Under his youthful and ambitious direction, the company moved it's base to Vancouver, British Columbia, where it grew into a substantial mining development company and began a new phase of rapid expansion. Norman B. Keevil was appointed President and CEO in 1981.

Jewelry fabrication was the largest commercial use for gold—one of Teck's principal products—and usually ac-

Company Perspectives:

Teck's mission is to be the leader in new mine development and operations, by providing the best in engineering talent and systems, having a strong financing capacity and by dealing with our partners on a fair and open basis. Teck projects come in on time and on budget. We welcome new opportunities for successful mine development and the opportunity to establish relationships with new partners.

counted for about 25 percent of the company's revenues. In 1980, Teck developed a placer gold operation around the area of the Klondike Gold Rush near Dawson City, Yukon Territory. Digging and scraping was conducted adjacent to an area which was mined by dredging between the years of 1914 to 1921. Due to its location in the permafrost-zone, the harsh climate dictated that the operation was seasonal. During the mining season, the surface operation used large CAT tractors and scrapers to mine 800,000 cubic yards per year, resulting in 210,000 cubic yards of paygravel that was washed through a sluicebox. On average, 23 people were employed to produce approximately 7,000 ounces of gold per season, making the Klondike Placer Gold Mine one of the largest and most successful alluvial mining operations in the Yukon.

During this time, the David Bell Mine was discovered by David Bell in 1981. Teck managed the development and construction of the mine in the Hemlo Gold camp of Northern Ontario. According to company reports, the mine was developed through a 1,160 meter production shaft, and mining was done by process of longhold stoping (working a steplike part of a mine where ore, etc. is being extracted) with delayed cemented hydraulic backfill. The mill utilized a two-stage grinding circuit, employing semi-autogenous grinding and ball milling. Gold was recovered from solution using carbon in pulp. The gold was recovered from carbon by pressure stripping and was then electrowon from strip solution. Cathodes were smelted to produce dore bullion. Homestake Mining Company shared a 50 percent joint venture interest in the Bell Mine project.

By the end of the decade, the Williams Gold Mine was the largest gold mine in Canada, producing 450,000 ounces of gold per year. In 1989, the Supreme Court of Canada upheld a 1986 Supreme Court of Ontario judgment awarding the Williams Gold Mine to Teck and its 50 percent joint venture partner Corona Corporation, which would later become the Homestake Mining Company. Teck's experienced management resulted in reductions in operating costs of 20 percent per ton, while increasing throughput by 1,000 tons per day. The facility operated the largest gold milling plant in Canada, using semi-autogenous grinding and a gold recovery circuit which was later expanded to produce 6,000 tons per day.

Expansion and Joint Ventures in the Early 1990s

As a means of balancing the volatile gold market and supply fluctuations, Teck began expanding into the major production of base metal products in the 1990s. In 1991, the Metall Mining Corporation—a Toronto-based subsidiary of Metallgesellschaft AG of Frankfurt, Germany—traded most of its holdings in Cominco Ltd. to MIM Holdings Ltd. (an Australian metals and coal producer) and Teck Corporation, in a stock transfer worth about $170 million. At the same time, Metall strengthened its holdings in MIM and Teck with the intention of pursuing joint-venture base metal projects that were being considered by those companies. Metall acquired 3.7 million shares of Teck's Class A and Class B stock, increasing its Teck holdings to 14.1 percent.

Metall's strategy was to streamline its investments by having one strategic investment in North America and one in the Pacific Rim area, because those areas were considered to be the main mining areas in the world. It also valued Teck and MIM as successful and reliable joint-venture partners. Cominco was the world's largest zinc concentrate producer with its Red Dog, Sullivan, and Polaris mines and would later become the third largest refined zinc producer with its Trail zinc and lead operation and its Cajamarquilla zinc refinery in Peru. After the 1995 acquisition of the Cajamarquilla refinery, Cominco worked to steadily increase its production of zinc.

Cominco was also a significant producer of copper, a substance which was used primarily in electrical wires. Cominco's copper holdings mainly included its 50 percent interest in Highland Valley Copper and its 47.25 percent interest in the Quebrada Blanca copper mine in Chile. Norman B. Keevil explained to Edward Worden of *American Metal Market* that the Quebrada Blanca Mine's extraction and electrowinning operation would be "bypassing the smelting and refining charges which have been escalating considerably in recent years." Worden reported that the state-owned Empresa Nacional de Mineria retained a ten percent interest in the project, while Sociedad Minera Pudahuel Ltda y Cia held a five percent carried interest in exchange for the use of its patented leaching technology.

Teck reported that 1991 profits declined 59 percent compared with 1990 figures, which was an occurrence attributed to lower metal prices and lower gold production. In the following year, Teck bought over 15 percent of Arauco Resources Corp., a two-year-old junior exploration company that had recently gone public. The company also had numerous gold mining prospects in Chile, plus five copper prospects in Argentina. Teck also increased its share in Pacific Sentinel Gold Corp., a Vancouver exploration company.

Teck and Cominco jointly ran an extensive exploration project in Chile. The joint venture built up a very large property inventory in the high Andes and the coastal copper belts of northern Chile. During this period, Cominco was reporting substantial losses—partly attributed to the company's nickel smelting operations, which were shut down for several months. Thus, Teck also reported losses related to its 22 percent equity interest in Cominco.

In addition to diversification, a continual search for resource development locations remained critical to Teck's future profitability. The company managed an exploration team and a business development team in order to discover, identify, and acquire the reserves which would potentially become operating mines. Teck's early explorations traditionally concentrated on Canadian sites, but became increasingly active internationally as the company began exhausting Canadian options. New exploration opportunities were discovered outside of North America, and offices were established in Singapore, Mexico, Peru, Panama and Chile. The company began planning for further expansion into nearly every country in South America.

Voisey Bay Discovery: 1993

One of the most important mineral discoveries of the century in Canada was the Voisey Bay nickel deposit in Labrador. Vancouver-based Diamond Fields Resources Inc. had discovered the huge deposit almost by accident, and later maintained the majority interest in the mining project. The deposit was found by two prospectors who stumbled across it in 1993. They were looking for diamonds on behalf of their company, and had almost given up at the end of their three-month search. After surveying a 15,000-square-mile area, they were heading home by helicopter when they spotted a gossan, and took samples that were found to be filled with copper sulfide. In addition to nickel, the site also contained substantial amounts of copper and cobalt, with high-grade ore reserve estimates of approximately 25 million metric tons. Annual production of 100 million pounds of nickel and 60 million pounds of copper were estimated. The site was especially attractive due to its high grades of ore and its proximity to the surface, which was expected to cut normal production costs in half.

More than 20 major mining companies expressed interest in participating in the Voisey Bay enterprise. Teck paid $108 million for a 10.4 percent stake in Diamond Fields. Then, due to Teck's experience with open-pit mines, Diamond Fields Resources awarded Teck the approximately $1.5 million contract to conduct a feasibility study "to address mining and concentrate production, power and water supplies, repair facilities and roads, among other things," according to Craig Schiffer in an August 31, 1995 *American Metal Market* article. It was estimated that total annual revenues of $288 million and a cash flow of $216 million could be expected from the site. Production was scheduled to begin in approximately late 1999, pending successful negotiations with both governmental entities and the Innuit and Innu Tribes, whose traditional hunting grounds and fisheries were located in the coastal waters off Voisey Bay.

The End of the Century and Beyond: Focusing on the Environment

One of the great challenges facing the mining industry has always been to minimize environmental risks. Teck reported that it had adopted a philosophy of prevention, rather than reaction: environmental concerns were addressed throughout the entire process, so as to avoid problems that would need solving later. The company claimed that it tries to emphasize "local concerns and values, environmental conditions, the mining and milling methods used, and techniques for pollution prevention and reclamation technologies." Teck reported that its overall environmental performance at its operations sites continued to be excellent in 1997, with greater than 98.5 percent compliance for effluent water quality. At their Williams/David Bell tailings basin, a water transfer system was established to pump water from the basin into a polishing pond so as to

eliminate the need for cyanide treatment. This also allowed the mines to control ammonia levels, and reduced the concentrations of contaminates. Environmental management teams were established to investigate opportunities for recycling at all operations—including the recycling of oil, batteries, scrap metal, paper, and hazardous waste.

Even with all of the company's prevention efforts, two spills occurred in 1997. One took place at the company's Quyintette operation, due to the failure of a decant pipe on a newly-constructed sediment pond. The result was the spill of approximately 800,000 cubic meters of non-toxic sediment-laden pond water into the Murray River. The other occurred at the Tarmoola operation in Australia, when a feed line to the tailings pond burst, releasing 150 tons of tailings. Cleanup was implemented and corrective steps undertaken to prevent future occurrences.

Near the end of the 1990s, approximately 44 percent of Teck's total revenues came from the production of coal, which accounted for $50 million of the company's total mine operating profit in 1997. Its coal operations included the Elkview Mine (located in southeastern British Columbia), the Bullmoose Mine (located in northeastern British Columbia), and the Quintette Mine (also located in northeastern British Columbia). A Coal Task Force was established in 1997 to seek coal development opportunities in Canada as well as in other locations around the globe. The Task Force began by targeting government representatives, mine operators, investment bankers and coal property owners for discussion about operating within their various countries. The Task Force also began investigating methods of working with other coal producers in Canada for the purpose of improving the structure of transportation, port and sales operations.

Also in 1997, the discovery of a massive sulphide deposit in Zacatecas State, Mexico, indicated reserves of copper, zinc, gold, and silver that could be of potential value to Teck following further drilling and metallurgical testing. The company's net interest in the discovery was 52.5 percent. Teck was also involved in a Colorado-based chemical pilot plant for the purpose of converting titanium concentrate to commercial grade pigment. A 1998 feasibility study was conducted to determine its viability. The site contains the largest titanium resource known to be located in North America.

Teck implemented other promising base metal explorations in 1998 in Argentina, Chile, and Mexico, as well as in the Bathurst district of New Brunswick. The company's other investments included a 25 percent share interest in Golden Knight Resources, which holds an interest in the Tarkwa gold mine which is under construction in Ghana, West Africa; a 42 percent interest in Camelot Resources NL, an Australian company which shares a joint-venture with Teck in the Tarmoola gold mine in Western Australia and the Northern Territories; along with other recent investments valued at approximately $89 million.

Prices for most metals were volatile near the end of the 1990s, with gold suffering the largest decline when its price dropped from $369 to $288 per ounce in 1997 alone. Teck reports indicated that the gold decline was influenced less by consumption than by the policies of central banks. Gold prices were expected to recover although it was thought that the practice of forward selling (promising a product to customers and accepting payment before the product was actually available) could moderate the amount of recovery.

Following the weak metal prices, Teck reviewed its expenditure levels, including the cost of exploration and capital spending at the mines. It was decided that the development of the Lobo-Marte, Nuteck, and Petaquilla projects would be deferred. Furthermore, the Klondike placer operation was permanently shut down after the 1997 season, as was the Afton copper mine. Regardless of these decisions—and actually, due to them—the company remained in strong financial condition as it neared the 21st century, and was optimistic about its potential to increase production at its other facilities.

Principal Subsidiaries

Camelot Resources NL (Australia); Central Asian Gold Corp.; Minera Teck Chile, S.A.; Mineral Teck dos Brasil Ltda. (Brazil); Minera Teck Panama, S.A.; Minera Teck Peru, S.A.; Minera Teck S.A. de C.V., Mexico; Nunachiaq Corporation; Teck Australia Pty Ltd.; Teck-Bullmoose Coal Inc.; Teck Exploration Ltd.; Teck Financial Corporation Ltd. (Bermuda); Teck Gold Ltd. (Bermuda); Teck-Hemlo Inc.; Teck Mining Group Ltd.; Teck Resources Inc.; Teck Resources International Ltd. (Bermuda).

Further Reading

Berman, David, "Mission: Excellence," *Canadian Business,* December 1996, p. 71.

"Canadians Stalled in Kazakhstan," *American Metal Market,* January 14, 1997, p. 1.

Caney, Derek, J., "Cominco Resources Incurs C$5.1 M 3rd-qtr. Loss," *American Metal Market,* November 5, 1993, p. 7.

Dunn, Brian, "Voisey Bay Discovery Looms Larger by the Minute; Among Biggest Nickel, Copper, and Cobalt Finds," *American Metal Market,* May 2, 1995, p. 2.

"Inmet to Sell Stake in Teck," *American Metal Market,* April 15, 1996, p. 2.

"Lobo-Marte Gold Project Planned," *American Metal Market,* December 9, 1996, p. 5.

"Metall Acquires Teck Corp. Shares," *American Metal Market,* July 5, 1993, p. 8.

Mumford, Christopher, "Metall Boosting MIM, Teck Stake Via Stock Swap," *American Metal Market,* October 18, 1991, p. 1.

Schiffer, Craig, "Teck Chosen for Voisey Bay Study," *American Metal Market,* August 31, 1995, p. 2.

"Teck Boosts Stake in Arauco," *American Metal Market,* April 30, 1993, p. 5.

"Teck, Camelot Team for Mt. Edon Buyout," *American Metal Market,* February 5, 1997, p. 4.

"Teck Corp. Earnings Register a Dip," *American Metal Market,* November 17, 1993, p. 6.

"Teck's Profits Plummet 59 Percent," *American Metal Market,* February 24, 1992, p. 5.

Worden, Edward, "Teck Links Up With Cominco to Develop Quebrada Blanca," *American Metal Market,* December 9, 1991, p. 2.

—Terri Mozzone

Tengelmann Group

Wissollstrasse 5-43
45478 Mülheim an der Ruhr
Germany
(49) 208 5806 0
Fax: (49) 208 5806 6401
Web site: http://www.tengelmann.de

Private Company
Founded: 1867
Employees: 200,000
Sales: DM 53 billion (US $34 billion) (1997)
SICs: 5411 Grocery Stores

Privately held Tengelmann Group is among the world's largest retail supermarket and distribution groups, ranking number four behind Wal-Mart of the United States and Germany's Rewe and Metro AG. With some 7,700 supermarkets, hypermarkets, discount markets, drugstores, and other specialty retail stores, Tengelmann is present in much of Europe, but especially in Germany, The Netherlands, Hungary, Austria, Poland, Italy, Spain, France, and the Czech Republic. In the United States and Canada, Tengelmann is represented through its majority control of the Great Atlantic and Pacific Tea Company, better known to North America's shoppers as A&P, but also including the Kohls, Waldbaums, Super Fresh, and Food Emporium banners in the United States, and the Dominion and Miracle Food Mart names in Canada.

On the European continent, Tengelmann is present in nearly every food retail segment. In Germany, in addition to the flagship Tengelmann chain of supermarkets, the company also operates the Grosso and Magnet hypermarket formats, Kaiser's supermarkets, the Ledi deep discount formula, the Plus convenience store chain, and the Obi do-it-yourself chain of building and hardware supplies. Beyond Germany, Tengelmann is represented by such names as Skala Co-Op (Hungary); Italy's Superal, operated in partnership with the grocery chain of that country's PAM Group; and Hermans Groep (The Netherlands).

Beyond retail distribution, Tengelmann long has been a major producer and distributor of such products as coffee and tea as well as candy and other confectionery goods, notably of the Gummi Bear brand. Tengelmann also has expanded into meat distribution and features an extensive line of private label products, under various labels, including the A&P label. In addition, Tengelmann operates as a wholesaler to third party distributors.

Tengelmann remains the property of the founding Scholl/Haub family. Erivan Haub, great-grandson of the company's founder, and responsible for much of the company's expansion and diversification, has been at the company's helm since the late 1960s. In the 1990s, the elder Haub has been joined by his sons, Christian, who became A&P CEO in 1998, and Karl-Erivan, who has been in charge of the company's European division since 1997.

From Coffee to Retail in the 19th Century

In the early 1800s the Scholl family provided ferry services on the Rhine River from their Mülheim home, near the border with The Netherlands. Joining the family business in midcentury was Louise Scholl. By then, the building of a bridge had ended the need for the family's ferry service. The family now oriented its business toward river cargo, serving the growing industrial presence of the Ruhr valley region. Among the cargo the family carried were products from the German and other European colonies, including spices, tea, cacao, and coffee, which arrived in the Dutch ports to be transported throughout Europe.

Louise Scholl married Wilhelm Schmitz in 1867. Schmitz had operated a wholesale business, under the name of Schmitz & Lindgens, with a focus on colonial products. Upon their marriage, Schmitz and Scholl joined their business interests, forming the trading firm Wilh. Schmitz-Scholl. Louise Scholl would continue to play an active leadership role in the new Schmitz-Scholl family business.

The growing popularity of coffee led Schmitz-Scholl to explore a new market. For most of the century, coffee reached the end consumer as unroasted green beans. Customers were required to roast their own coffee, for better or worse. Wilhelm Schmitz saw an opportunity to provide an expanded service to his customers, and he determined to roast his own coffee for sale. His efforts would remain on a small scale, until the 1880s, when the company purchased an industrial-sized roasting oven. In that year the company opened a new coffee roasting plant, across the street from the company's office headquarters.

By the mid-1880s the Schmitz-Schollschen Rösterei was producing more than 1,000 pounds of coffee each day. After adding a second roaster, the company moved its coffee roasting operations to a new, larger production plant.

The death of Wilhelm Schmitz in 1887 brought the next generation of the family's leadership: sons Karl and Wilhelm Schmitz-Scholl took over the company's operations and began orienting the company toward further expansion. The brothers began advertising their products, and the Scholl coffees soon reached new popularity under the Plantagen (plantation) Koffie and Storch (stork) Koffie brand names.

The popularity of the company's products would again lead the Scholls to expand their operations. The Scholls were dissatisfied with their distribution arrangements—the company used third party distributors or sold directly to retailers, methods that could not provide a certain inflow of orders. In addition, the Scholls took pride in the quality of their products, in particular their coffee, a pride that was not always reflected in the care with which retailers stored and displayed their products. In the 1890s, therefore, the company determined to take their products' distribution under the company's wing.

The first Scholl family retail store opened in 1893 and was called Tengelmann's, after long-time employee Emil Tengelmann, so that the Scholl family name would avoid being associated with the then socially unacceptable retail trade. A retail subsidiary, Firma Hamburger Kaffee-Import-Geschäft Emil Tengelmann, was set up under the Schmitz-Scholl operation. The Tengelmann store featured the company's coffees, cacao, and teas, as well as other grocery items.

20th Century Distribution Giant

The new distribution format was a huge success. The Scholls quickly expanded the Tengelmann concept from a single store to a true retail organization with branches spreading throughout Germany. Driving this growth was the company's coffee, which had become a popular brand name. The Scholl-Tengelmann operation would quickly become one of Germany's—and Europe's—leading coffee importers. The success of its wholesale and retail distribution activities encouraged the company to increase its production capacity. At the turn of the century the company opened three new grocery branches, which featured their own coffee roasting plants. The Tengelmann stores also were beginning to feature a wider assortment of goods, expanding to become full-fledged grocery stores.

Among the company's import products were such items as vanilla, anise, cinnamon, cane sugar, and other spices, which, coupled with the firm's cacao imports, would lead the Scholl-Tengelmann concern to expand in a new direction. At the turn of the century the company began producing its own sweets and confectionery products, establishing a second production line.

This would take the form of the Rheinische Zuckerwarenfabrik GmbH, established in Dusseldorf in 1906 under the direction of Wilhelm Schmitz-Scholl. Among the candies that would later bring international success to the company were its Gummi Bears.

The launch into candies was followed quickly by the construction of the company's own chocolate and cacao factory, in Mülheim, which opened in 1912. The company's chocolate and cacao products would be sold under the Wissoll brand name, formed by the contraction of the Wilh. Schmitz-Scholl company name. Wissoll would later become the umbrella name for all of the group's candy and confectionery products, which included brand names Lohmann, Galasana, Nipi, and Risco, in addition to the Gummi Bear and other candy items. In the 1920s the company began selling its candy products on the international market.

By the outbreak of the First World War, the Schmitz-Scholl company boasted more than 560 Tengelmann groceries. The hostilities—and the blockade of Germany by the Allies—would force the company to adapt its product assortment, limiting its offers. With the German defeat and the reparations toll, which included the loss of parts of German territory, including the Ruhr valley region, Tengelmann itself lost some 160 of its grocery stores. The postwar period would bring a depression and rampant inflation—to the extent that the mark became virtually worthless. To continue operations, Tengelmann—as the company now began to call itself—adapted its product assortment, adding inexpensive items such as ersatz coffee and pudding powders.

The institution of the Weimar Republic in the 1920s helped stabilize the Germany economy. Tengelmann, too, would profit from the return to growth by engaging on an expansion drive, dividing its operations now into regional divisions. The Tengelmann store design underwent a thorough modernization, and the leaner, more efficiently organized group looked forward to further expansion. The Weimar Republic was short-lived. By the beginning of the 1930s, however, a new economic depression, exacerbating the volatility of the German political scene, enabled the Nazi power grab. The Tengelmann group, too, had come under new leadership. With the death of Karl Schmitz-Scholl in 1993, son Karl Jr. became the company's chief.

The Nazis' power base among the fading small merchant class, among others, led to official measures against nationally operating grocery and department store chains. Among these measures was a stiff revenue tax. Tengelmann, associating with other firms, was able to gain an exemption from the revenue tax, at least for non-Jewish companies. But Tengelmann's expansion efforts were nonetheless thwarted by protectionist policies that barred the opening of new branches or factories. The outbreak of the Second World War placed Tengelmann's operations under the ultimate control of the Nazi government.

The end of the war had left not only the Reich in ruins, but much of Tengelmann as well. Its urban-based stores and factories had not been spared the bombing of the country by the Allied forces, while many of its undestroyed factories now were located in Soviet-controlled East Germany. Moreover, the shortage of goods following the war would make it difficult for the company to resume its operations; on top of this, company chief Karl Schmitz-Scholl had been placed in jail. Nonetheless, Tengelmann was able to resume operations in 1945, under direction of Schmitz-Scholl's sister Elisabeth Haub. The company reopened shop using mobile trailers. Product assortment was limited, but the company developed several powdered products meant as protein supplements.

Postwar Expansion

Tengelmann was once again back on its feet in the 1950s. The company participated fully in the German economic reconstruction that would spark an economic boom that would last into the 1980s. Perhaps the most significant move that would enable Tengelmann to become one of the country's top grocery concerns was the institution of an innovative shopping concept in 1953. That concept had been brought back from the United States by Karl Schmitz-Scholl Jr.'s nephew, Erivan Haub. Then 20 years old, Haub had been sent to the United States to spend time working for American supermarkets. There, Haub discovered the relatively new self-service concept that was quickly becoming a mainstay of the U.S. grocery market. Haub suggested that Tengelmann, too, adopt the self-service concept.

The first self-service Tengelmann opened its doors in 1953. The success of the new concept was immediate. By the end of the 1950s Tengelmann had restructured all of its stores to the self-service format. The company proved quick to adopt new technologies as well, including electric cash registers and computerized data processing. During the 1960s the company also began to seek expanding its retail operations into newly developing segments. The first was a new department store concept, which would become known as the hypermarket, which combined traditional supermarket operations with an expanded range of products, from hardware to small appliances to books and records, and more. In 1967 Tengelmann inaugurated its first hypermarket, under the Grosso-Markt name. The Grosso-Markt followed upon the launch of another concept store: the Tenga markets. These smaller stores took an opposite approach: vastly reduced product assortment at discount prices. Launched in 1966, the Tenga would eventually give way to other Tengelmann store names, including the Ledi and Plus discount formats.

By 1968 Tengelmann had grown into a nationwide chain of more than 400 branch operations, including more than 350 Tengelmann supermarkets, a growing number of Tenga discount stores and Grosso-Markt hypermarkets, and the company's chocolate production operations. That year the company topped the DM 1 billion mark for the first time.

The death of Karl Schmitz-Scholl in 1969 brought nephew Erivan Haub to the company's leadership. Haub, who had already introduced the self-service concept to the company, would be the chief architect of Tengelmann's greatest expansion. Whereas Tengelmann's previous expansion had been primarily internal, under Haub the company would begin a string of important acquisitions that would not only strengthen the company's domestic position, but also transform it into an international major player while continuing its internal expansion, including the launch of a new Tengelmann Markt category, positioned between the discount and grocery format and the larger supermarket format, in 1970.

Tengelmann's first acquisition came in 1971, when the company bought up its struggling arch-rival, Kaiser's Kaffee Geschäft AG. Founded in 1880, Kaiser's had grown into a chain of more than 500 supermarkets with revenues of DM 875 million. The company had run into difficulties, however, in the late 1960s. The acquisition by Tengelmann brought a restructuring of the Kaiser chain, including the conversion of a number of its smaller stores to the Tengelmann Plus format. Those stores, launched in 1972, took over the company's Tenga discount operations, expanding the small store format to include fresh fruits and vegetables as well. Through the 1970s the company made a number of other domestic acquisitions, including firms such as C.F. Beck, Wedi, Carisch, Hillko, Bronner, Schwörer, and Schade & Füllgrabe.

At the same time the company was expanding domestically, it was looking toward international expansion. A first step was taken with the acquisition of the Austrian supermarket chain, Löwa, in 1972. This acquisition was followed at the end of the 1970s by the acquisition of a 24 percent controlling share of the Great Atlantic and Pacific Tea Company and its A&P chain of supermarkets. Once the world's largest supermarket chain, with more than 12,000 branches, A&P had fallen into disarray by the 1970s. Under Tengelmann's control, however, A&P was able to restructure rapidly and revitalize its operations, returning to profitability in the early 1980s. Tengelmann would continue to acquire shares in A&P, reaching more than 55 percent by the late 1990s.

During the 1980s Tengelmann would expand into The Netherlands, purchasing that country's number four supermarket group, the Hermans Groep. By the end of the decade Tengelmann had moved into two more European countries: Italy, with the acquisition of the Superal chain, and Hungary, with the acquisition of the Skala-Coop chain of supermarkets. If Tengelmann's international acquisition drive had come in part in response to the increasingly limited growth opportunities in Germany, due to market saturation and tightening restrictions on the opening of new supermarkets, the company nevertheless sought means to continue its growth in Germany.

For this growth, Tengelmann began to diversify beyond its traditional food-oriented distribution. In 1985 the company bought a share in the holding company Obi, and its chain of Obi do-it-yourself (DIY) hardware and building supply stores. By the end of the 1990s Obi could claim the crown as the German market's number one DIY chain. Tengelmann next moved into clothing and accessories, with the launch of the discount center Rudis Reste Rampe and the takeover of the Modea clothing store chain.

The 1990s and Beyond

In the 1990s Tengelmann's international expansion continued, with the extension of its Plus and other store formats into new markets, including Hungary and Poland. The end of the Cold War, which opened these markets, also brought down the Berlin Wall—and restored many of Tengelmann's properties and factories that had been under Soviet control for nearly 50 years. The German reunification, however, would put extreme pressure on the Germany economy—at a time when the world was entering a global recession. Tengelmann would come to feel the brunt of the difficult economic period, especially the heightened competition that raged among supermarketers. In particular, a new category—that of the deep discount market— forced Tengelmann to respond, by opening its own chain of Ledi deep discount stores.

Tengelmann also would face a public relations crisis, brought on by the company's announcement of plans to build a supermarket on the site of the Ravensbrück concentration camp. International protests forced the company to back down from the plan. With profits under increasing pressure into the mid-1990s, Tengelmann was forced to restructure its operations. After taking the decision to expand the Ledi deep discount formula, which reached more than 250 stores in 1998, Tengelmann announced its intention to convert its Plus stores from the discount format to a new convenience store format. In 1998 the company also reached an agreement to merge its Italian supermarket operations with Italy's PAM supermarket group. At the same time Erivan Haub moved to confirm the family's intention to maintain control of its supermarket empire. After appointing eldest son Karl-Erivan Haub the company's European director in 1997, the elder Haub named youngest son Christian Haub leader of Tengelmann's A&P group.

Principal Operating Units

Tengelmann; Grosso/Magnet; Hermans Groep; Kaiser's; Modea; Obi; Plus; Skala Co-Op; Superal; Cheers; A&P (55%).

Further Reading

''A&P's Haub Is Calling for Private-Label Growth,'' *Supermarket News,* November 23, 1998.

Baumeister, Rosemarie, ed., *Ein Jahrhundert Tengelmann,* Mülheim an der Ruhr: Unternehmensgruppe Tengelman, 1993.

''Changes at Tengelmann Boost Store Brands,'' *Private Label,* November 1998.

''Haub Zeichnet Ein Trübes Bild für den Lebensmittelhandel,'' *Frankfurter Allgemeine Zeitung,* December 18, 1998.

''Lebensmittelkette Kaiser's Strafft Filialnetz und Geht Neue Wege,'' *Die Welt,* December 16, 1998.

—M.L. Cohen

Thai Airways International Public Company Limited

89 Vibhavadi Rangsit Road
Bangkok 10900
Thailand
(66) 2 513-0121
Fax: (66) 2 513-3398
Web site: http//www.thaiair.com

Public Company
Incorporated: 1947 as Thai Airways Company
Employees: 21,500
Sales: B 105,493 million (US$ 3.12 billion) (1997)
Stock Exchanges: Bangkok
SICs: 4512 Air Transportation, Scheduled

Thai Airways International Public Company Limited is one of the most influential companies in that emerging Asian country. It is an example of the growing success and significance of Asian national carriers, which have carved a niche in ferrying industrial goods from the Far East to Western markets and in serving Western business and leisure travelers. Thailand's location ensures the carrier a considerable piece of the growing Asian air travel market.

Origins

Airplanes were seen over the Thai capital of Bangkok as early as 1911, but it was not until 1947 that the government of Thailand established a national airline of its own, Thai Airways Company. The country had recognized a need for such an airline network during post-World War II reconstruction. Until then, rivers and canals had been the traditional mode of transportation. The postwar years saw these replaced by highways and roads as main transport arteries, and the aviation industry developing worldwide at the time not surprisingly also had an impact on Thailand.

The original Thai Airways Company was a modest affair— three DC-6 prop-jets; each had 70 seats. Thai Airways' first head office in Bangkok was situated on New Road, directly across from the main post office. From these headquarters passengers could purchase tickets to nine domestic destinations, including the jungle resorts of Chiang Mai in the North, Lampang in the center of the country, and the pristine beaches of Hat Yai to the south.

In 1954 the Thai government identified 130 airfields throughout the country, 104 of which were functional. Thailand's main airport was Don Maung, outside Bangkok. Thai Airways expanded abroad in 1959 with the help of Scandinavian airline SAS, which assumed a 30 percent shareholding in a new subsidiary, Thai Airways International Ltd. SAS brought technical and managerial expertise and its old propeller planes to the fledgling national carrier; in return, SAS was awarded landing rights in Hong Kong.

Approximately 83,000 passengers were carried to nine Asian destinations in 1960, the first year of Thai's service. Routes included those from Bangkok to Calcutta, India, via Rangoon, Burma; Bangkok to Tokyo via Hong Kong and Taipei, Taiwan; and flights to Phnom Penh, Cambodia; Saigon, Vietnam; Kuala Lumpur, Malaysia; and Singapore. The airline's staff numbered 477. That year its pilots flew a total of 8,147 hours.

Thai owed much then, as now, to its unique location. At the crossroads between East and West, North and South, Thailand is a sought-after stopover on numerous flights by airlines from around the world, a situation that has afforded the airline considerable leverage in securing reciprocal landing rights in European and North American airports. Even in the 1990s, Thai remained in a strong bargaining position: long-range jumbo jets flying from Europe to Asia may skip India or the Middle East on their way to Australia, but they need to refuel in either Bangkok or its rival Singapore.

In 1964 Thai added a Caravelle SE-210 jet aircraft to its fleet, which allowed the first scheduled service to Osaka, Japan; Kathmandu, Nepal; and Bali, Indonesia. The aircraft was able to fly between Bangkok and Hong Kong without refueling. It carried 72 passengers and had a takeoff weight of 48 tons. This meant it could carry a payload of ten tons and would burn off three tons of fuel each hour in the air.

Company Perspectives:

Thai's distinctive livery incorporates the colours associated with Thailand: the shining gold found in its temples, the magenta of its shimmering silks and the rich purples of its orchids. Our logo has been likened to an orchid but is simply a symbol meant to convey the essence of Thailand; its soft, curving lines combined with a speed line to suggest effortless flight. Similarly, our slogan "Smooth as Silk" derives from the texture and luxurious look of Thailand's most famous creation: silk. It suggests both the way we fly our aircraft and the way we hope passengers feel when they fly with us, wrapped in comfort and pleasure.

Catching Tourists with Silk in the 1960s and 1970s

By the mid-1960s Thailand had become a tourist destination for Westerners traveling in Asia. The lure of the Orient was clear to Thai's founders; they recognized that the development of the company's regional route network would depend on access to tourist destinations both in Thailand and throughout Asia. The airline did its best to promote these locales, investing in advertising and public relations. Colorful pamphlets encouraged tour operators and travel writers to visit Asian resorts, and word of mouth in turn inspired other wayfarers to make the trip.

In 1969 the company entered the packaged holiday market with Royal Orchid Holidays, offering the flexibility of individually planned tour itineraries combined with the cost savings usually found only in large group tours. Thai did not, however, want to replace the travel agent, who traditionally sold tours to travelers; nor did it wish to replace tour operators in the field, who looked after travelers once they arrived at each of their tour destinations. Instead, Thai operated as the middleman, bringing travelers and tour operators together, thus putting more people on its planes. By 1972 Thai was ranked 44th among the world's international airlines, one place behind rival Philippine Airlines.

To emphasize the romance of the Orient, Thai's air hostesses began wearing traditional Thai silk costumes. Western airlines had been known to criticize their Asian counterparts for exploitation of their hostesses, who, it was charged, were required to maintain a submissive role—traditional in some Asian cultures—in order to offer what the airline perceived as first-rate cabin service. Although space limitations in cabins prohibited traditional costumes by the 1990s, by which time hostesses had switched to more comfortable two-piece silk uniforms, the philosophy persisted. In October 1991 airline president Kaset Rojananil announced a change in hiring policy at the airline: an applicant's physical beauty would be weighed before her educational qualifications. "Intelligent women tend not to be good-looking," he noted, according to *AsiaWeek*. Kaset, also a military general and member of the junta then ruling Thailand, maintained that applicants should be screened "the way beauty pageant judging panels select contestants."

Beginning in the late 1960s, Thai also benefited greatly from Asians increasingly traveling to the West. Despite the twin oil shocks of the 1970s, the number of Asians traveling to the West grew by an average of 17 percent a year during the decade—the airline carried 1.31 million passengers to 26 destinations in 1976 alone. By the mid-1970s, Thai's staff had grown to 4,631, making the airline one of the nation's largest employers. Vacancies for cabin hostesses and stewards routinely elicited thousands of inquiries. The 1981–82 world recession, however, had a dampening effect, bringing growth in passenger numbers down to 10 percent during those years. Passenger traffic to Asia was encouraged, though, by the success of James Clavell's popular novel *Shogun* and the completion of the Tokyo Disneyland, which attracted six million visitors in its first six months of business, in 1981.

As a state-owned airline, Thai was also charged with flying the national flag and acting as an overseas ambassador for Thailand. This included sponsoring leading Thai artists appearing overseas, including musicians and classical dance troupes. Beginning in the 1970s, the growing airline also began supporting community efforts in the region. In 1979, for example, the airline initiated the Asian SAE Write Awards to promote Asian literature.

Aside from establishing international goodwill, these efforts sent a message to Thai competitors that the airline would pursue every avenue to establish dominance in the region. American airlines, like Northwest Orient, Pan American, and United, also expanded into Asia in the 1970s. Regional rivals Singapore Airlines, Philippine Airlines, and Japan Air Lines Co., which were government-owned, were also competing ferociously for market share in the key corridor between London and Sydney and on the Bangkok-Tokyo route.

Modernizing for the 1980s

In 1975 the national carrier made a bid toward modernization when it changed its quaint logo—a dancer in classical dress silhouetted behind lettering that spelled out the word "Thai"—to a distinctive purple and gold symbol approximating the graceful curves of an orchid.

Part of Thai's success has always been attributed to the quality of its in-flight meals. By the early 1990s Thai's flight kitchen at Don Maung Airport catered to 44 international airlines stopping over in Bangkok. In 1980 the airline established Air Lanka Catering Services Ltd., a 50–50 joint venture with Air Lanka to develop and operate a modern flight kitchen in Colombo, Sri Lanka. A decade later, Thai established Phuket Air Catering Co. Ltd., in which it held a 25 percent stake in partnership with the Phuket Pearl Hotel. The facility served 2,500 meals daily to flights moving through Phuket, in southern Thailand.

Another extension of the airline was its supply of aviation fuel. In 1983 Thai established Bangkok Aviation Fuel Services Ltd. (BAFS) at Don Maung Airport. The carrier took a 32 percent stake of BAFS, which operated from a depot near the airport housing storage tanks containing 51 million liters of jet fuel. Underground pipes from the depot to aircraft parking bays carried the fuel to customers. As an offshoot of BAFS, Thai in 1990 launched Fuel Pipeline Transportation Ltd. in partnership with Thailand's state-owned oil enterprises and various multinational oil companies. The aim of the new company was to improve fuel distribution by constructing a 68-kilometer pipe-line from the oil refinery and depot at Bangchak and Chong-nonsee, in Bangkok's dock area, to Don Maung Airport.

Thai also made inroads into the hotel business. In 1983 it obtained a 24 percent stake in the 775-room Royal Orchid K Hotel in central Bangkok. It also maintained a 40 percent stake in the 440-room Bangkok Airport Hotel, adjacent to Don Maung Airport.

Cargo was also another key element of the airline's business. In 1985 the carrier built a 14-acre "Cargo Village," in which goods scheduled for shipment to Europe, North America, and other parts of Asia were stored. Thai could carry up to 700 tons of cargo on flights to any of its 13 European destinations. The airline boasted that fresh orchids and popular tropical fruits like rambutan and pineapple could be delivered to Don Maung Airport late in the afternoon and appear on store shelves in London or Paris the following afternoon. Cargo growth signifi-cantly fueled revenue for Thai. The airline recorded revenues of B 12.6 million in 1980–81 and B 23.8 million in 1985–86 before posting a record revenue base of B 51.9 million in 1990–91.

Products for export, including textiles, VCRs, fashion prod-ucts, and high-tech manufacturing tools—were also being in-creasingly shipped to global destinations, and promoted, by Thai Airway. The importance of such flights grew as companies worldwide adopted just-in-time inventory control.

Military Influence on the 1990s

In 1988 Chatichai Choonhavan's new administration in-stalled air force generals at the top posts of the airline. This ushered in a period of corruption and diminished international stature that would be widely criticized in Western media. In April, Thai International merged with Thai Airways, its one-time corporate parent.

By 1990 Thai was carrying just over 8.1 million passengers yearly and counted a staff of 18,272. The carrier's pilots flew 143,032 hours that year on 60 jet aircraft. The fleet included four 747-400 jets and six 747-200 jets. Thai Airways posted a profit of $139 million in fiscal 1990; however, the *Far Eastern Economic Review* reported that creative accounting disguised what was in fact the company's first loss in 20 years.

With an eye toward future growth, Bangkok planned to build a new airport at Don Maung scheduled to open in 2000, when more than 20 million travelers were expected. This venture called for massive investment, including purchasing 27 new jet aircraft between 1992 and 1996. Thai's staff in this period was expected to increase from roughly 18,000 to 30,000 employees. To fund this expansion, the airline announced in January 1992 that it would list 20 percent ownership of the company on the Bangkok Stock Exchange. By turning to the private sector, Thai Airways International signaled a move away from full state control—a direction mirrored in the early 1990s across the airline industry as alliances and mergers between competing airlines proliferated.

In testament to its growing importance in Thai society, the airline began hosting a number of national events. In 1991 these included Bangkok's bicentennial celebrations, Visit Thailand Year, and Arts & Crafts Year. The following year saw Thai host Thailand's National Heritage Year. Among the sports events the company began sponsoring annually were the Pro-fessional Golf Association's Thai Open and Ladies' Open. The airline also continued to host a number of international tennis competitions.

In 1991, a military coup overthrew Chatichai Choonhavan. Military-sponsored candidates won their elections, and students were shot at subsequent pro-democracy protests in Bangkok in May. After five years of Thai Air Force control, a mostly civilian board was appointed in September 1992. Finance Min-istry official Pandit Bunyapana replaced Gun Pimarnthip as chairman, while Chatrachai Bunyananta replaced as president another air force general, Air Chief Marshal Veera Kitchathorn, who had been implicated in the May killings. Chatrachai was a 20-year company veteran who had worked his way up the ranks and was credited with much of the airline's success in the mid-1980s. The new leadership effected a modest turnaround nearly immediately.

Chatrachai's work involved a complete restructuring in or-der to compete with the megacarriers venturing into Thai airspace. The airline needed to standardize its fleet; 18 different types were too many to fly efficiently. Dispatch reliability proved a persistent problem due to the lack of cash for buying suitable equipment. The company's planes were typically only operated four or five hours per day, less than half the rates achieved by other airlines.

Some lackluster international routes, such as Seattle and Toronto, were dropped. The domestic market proved most un-profitable, thanks to impossibly low government-mandated fares. Years of nepotism had also helped swell the company's roster to 20,000, providing another target for cutbacks.

A Future As a Public Company

The company launched a successful initial public offering in early 1993. Approximately ten percent of the company's owner-ship became private. Plans to offer another tenth of the shares were soon put into place, but they were quashed by profits that did not meet expectations. In fact, in July 1996, the government canceled the airline's refleeting program. Still, management persisted in lobbying for ways to reduce government ownership of the carrier. Nevertheless, upon the resignation of Amaret Sila-on in 1995, Air Chief Marshal Siripong Thongyai assumed command of the airline, which seemed to reverse the company's progression into professional management.

Thai International was again accepting aircraft deliveries in late 1997, necessitating more capital investments. The company finally became 100 percent publicly traded. In order to escape the crowded and expensive Bangkok International Airport, the company built a $120 maintenance facility, the Thai Aircraft Engineering Service Co. Ltd., in the Gulf of Thailand.

After weathering coups, government meddling, and the other, less exotic factors that make managing airlines a chal-lenge, Thai International managed to regain a measure of inter-national prestige. An agreement between Thai International and Lufthansa developed into the powerful Star Alliance, which also included Air Canada, United Airlines, and SAS. In November 1998 the company was named one of the world's top ten airlines by *Condé Nast.* It was not immune to tragedy, however, as one of the carrier's Airbus 310s crashed one month later. (One of these same models had crashed in Thailand in July 1992.) Singapore Airlines and Lufthansa planned to buy shares of Thai Airways in 1999, in order to counter the overtures of British Airways and Quantas into the Asian market.

Principal Subsidiaries

Bangkok Aviation Fuel Services Ltd. (30.7%); Phuket Air Catering Co. Ltd. (30%); Royal Orchid Hotel (Thailand) Ltd. (24%); Amadeus Marketing SA (8%); Aeronautical Radio of Thailand Ltd. (4%); Air Lanka Catering Services Ltd. (Sri Lanka; 40%).

Further Reading

Handley, Paul, "Change of Pilot," *Far Eastern Economic Review,* September 1992, p. 17.

"Have a Pleasant Flight," *AsiaWeek,* October 11, 1991.

Hill, Leonard, "Thai'd in Knots," *Air Transport World,* October 1996, pp. 48–56.

Mhatre, Kamlakar, "Burdens Bared in Bangkok," *Air Transport World,* February 1993, pp. 80–83.

Proctor, Paul, "New Chief Acts to End Woes at Thai Airways," *Aviation Week and Space Technology,* November 30, 1992, p. 41.

Thai Airways International—32nd Anniversary, Bangkok: Thai Airways Public Relations, 1992.

"Thais Approve New 777 Trent Order," *Flight International,* February 11, 1992.

Thomas, Geoffrey, "Asians Become Darlings of Alliance Investors," *Aviation Week and Space Technology,* May 4, 1998, pp. 24–25.

—Etan Vlessing
—updated by Frederick C. Ingram

Thomaston Mills, Inc.

P.O. Box 311
115 E. Main Street
Thomaston, Georgia 30286
U.S.A.
(706) 647-7131
Fax: (706) 646-5082
Web site: http://www.thomastonmills.com

Public Company
Incorporated: 1899
Employees: 2,246
Sales: $280.7 million (1998)
Stock Exchanges: NASDAQ
Ticker Symbol: TMSTA
SICs: 2200 Textile Mill Products; 2211 Brandwoven
   Fabric Mills, Cotton; 2261 Finishing Plants, Cotton;
   2390 Miscellaneous Fabricated Textile Products

Based in Thomaston, Georgia, Thomaston Mills, Inc. produces textiles for industrial and consumer use. The company, founded in 1899, faced challenges from foreign competition in the 1980s, and suffered during the economic recession of the early 1990s. In 1998, it had sales of $280.7 million, and though losses were up, so were sales per employee. "The year just ended was disappointing," admitted President and CEO Neil H. Hightower in the company's 1998 annual report; however, he proposed a number of measures to increase profits in the coming year. Hightower's promise seemed to reflect an eternal truth about the textile industry in general, and the company in particular, formulated by his uncle George Hightower in a speech 15 years before and excerpted as the epigraph to *Hard Times, Good Times,* a centennial history of the company: "Thomaston's textile industry has grown. It has grown all the time, all through the years, hard times, good times, bad times, all times. The textile industry has always been that way; it's always been the best of times and the worst of times. That never changes. It's a fight all the time and a joy and a pleasure to be involved in it. It's a wonderful business." The company's long and varied

history gave observers plenty of reason to predict more good times ahead for Thomaston Mills.

Upson County Gets a Cotton Mill

Thomaston Mills is located in the west central Georgia county of Upson, whose principal town is Thomaston. By the latter part of the 20th century, Thomaston Mills was the county's primary employer by a wide margin, but in the 1890s Upson County was without a major industrial presence. Editorials in the local paper, the *Thomaston Times,* called for the founding of a cotton mill, and in the last month of the 19th century, Robert E. Hightower and R.A. Matthews established Thomaston Cotton Mills.

In the depressed economy of the rural South, still reeling from the Civil War a generation after the conclusion of hostilities, the foundation of a new industrial concern was a cause for excitement. The mill soon became a major employer, and within a short time it had greatly affected the local economy. Yet the early years were also ones of struggle. Ill health forced Matthews to retire, and while on a trip to New York City in 1901, Hightower secured a new investor in James E. Reynolds. With Reynolds's help, Hightower rescued the company from a brush with bankruptcy, and in the years that followed, would steer it into its first great period of growth.

Hightower had built a diversified resume as an apparel merchant, railroad executive, and banker. A devoted Methodist, he based his business principles on the New Testament parable of the talents, in which a merchant rewards or punishes employees on the basis of how wisely they use money he has entrusted to them. Thus he continually reinvested profits in the company. Between 1901 and 1926, the mill grew from a 5,000-spindle operation to a plant of some 75,000 spindles; and after expanding the original mill in the years between 1906 and 1910, Hightower added a second plant, containing 25,000 spindles, in 1915. Two years later, in 1917, Thomaston Mills opened yet another 25,000-spindle facility, this one dedicated to manufacturing a fabric used in making automobile tires. Directing its efforts increasingly toward the tire-cord market—Thomaston Mills counted both B.F. Goodrich and Firestone among its clients—the company replaced the equipment in Mill Number Two, and put the mill's old machines to use in Peerless Mill, chartered in 1919. The company built a mill village to house 600 employees who would work in the new facility, and set up the Thomaston Bleachery, an operation for finishing textiles, in 1924.

Sticking Together Through the Depression

In 1926, Thomaston Mills signed a $100 million contract with B.F. Goodrich and the Fisk Rubber Company to provide them with 50,000 tons of tire fabrics over the next decade. As a result, the company experienced unprecedented expansion, adding among other facilities a new mill (dubbed Martha Mill in honor of Hightower's wife), along with another village to house its workers. Thomaston also purchased new plants, including one in Griffin, Georgia; and modernized existing facilities.

Hightower's eldest son, Harrison, became CEO of Thomaston Mills in 1925, while the father—known as "Mr. Bobby"—moved into the position of chairman. The Wall Street crash four years later hit the company hard, and after years of continued growth and expansion, Thomaston Mills faced a series of setbacks. The senior management took pay cuts, the company sold off facilities, and the company's stock value dropped. Mr. Bobby even lost title to his own home.

An already bad situation became desperate when the Fisk Rubber Company went bankrupt. As Charles Josey wrote in *Hard Times, Good Times,* "Making matters even worse, the mills had already purchased the cotton necessary to deliver its 1930 commitment to its enormous contract with Fisk. When a 100-boxcar train was loaded with cotton and headed north to be sold for whatever it would bring, there seemed little hope for the company. Debts piled up, and the company found itself being placed into receivership by The First National City Bank of New York." Yet the Hightower family, and the larger "family" of Thomaston Mills and the town, stuck together through these lean years. Often the company provided food for employees, and distributed gifts to their children at Christmastime.

The company's leadership had learned a lesson in the Fisk debacle, and thenceforth Thomaston Mills never put itself in the position of devoting more than five percent of its production to a single client. During the 1930s, the company developed strategic relationships with two distributors: F.F. Myers in Akron, Ohio, which acted in a distribution capacity for Thomaston Mills' tire-related production; and J.P. Stevens, which similarly distributed its non-industrial products. By 1935, two years before the death of Mr. Bobby, Thomaston Mills was out of receivership and on the road to new growth.

Heightened Focus on Employee Needs in the Postwar Years

Under the leadership of Harrison Hightower, the company underwent consolidation of its operations, along with improvement of its facilities. During the 1930s, union agitators had attempted to organize the employees of Thomaston Mills, but they had little success due to the strong sense of family that blurred the lines between management and labor. Exemplary of the company's commitment to its employees was a renovation of the mill villages that it underwent as soon as it came out of receivership. Ronnie VanHouten, who later became corporate secretary, recalled life growing up in the village: "We certainly didn't think of ourselves as being 'owned' by the company; we were part of it. . . . If something happened to one person, everyone knew . . . and grieved for them in times of trouble."

During World War II, Thomaston Mills redirected its production for wartime, producing tire cord, industrial fabrics, and material for uniforms. It also maintained a much-reduced line of goods for consumer use; but with the end of the war in 1945, the consumer market reemerged as a priority along with plans for expansion and modernization of the company. The latter changes included formation of a personnel department—an innovative concept in late 1940s rural Georgia—along with a company newspaper, the *Spinning Wheel,* which ran folksy news items by, for, and about mill workers. Typical was this item: "Cecil thinks he's something since he has a 1935 Ford. Better watch out folks!"

This was just one of the employee-oriented creations developed under the leadership of Harrison, who was also heavily involved in community work such as the establishment of a school for millworkers' children, opened in 1946. He led efforts to improve education in textile engineering at Georgia Tech, where the textile industry building is named in his honor. In addition, he established Community Enterprises, Inc., a charitable organization which undertook a number of projects to improve community life in Thomaston.

With the death of Harrison in 1947, leadership of Thomaston Mills, Inc.—it had changed its name in 1945—went to his younger brother Rob. Like his brother before him, Rob put an emphasis on employees, in particular by encouraging participation in the popular company baseball and basketball teams. Rob Hightower died in 1952, and the last of Mr. Bobby's sons, Julian, became CEO. He would remain at the helm for almost 20 years, until 1971, during a period of great change for America—and for Thomaston Mills.

Computers, Direct Sales, and Other Changes

A symbol of the new world of the 1950s was the two-story school building Thomaston Mills built for the children of the community: among its many state-of-the-art amenities was a brand-new 1955 computerized communication system. This was just one of several local building projects fostered by Julian, who Josey in his company history characterized as a leader motivated as much by aesthetic as by humanitarian concerns. Like his brothers, he took especial care of the employees, and introduced a number of innovations. Under his leadership, the company in 1966 added a new data-processing system to facilitate management of operations. Although its early computers were ungainly and limited in function, from this start Thomaston Mills developed an information-management framework upon which it would build in the coming decades.

Julian, who died in 1987, turned over the reins of leadership to William Harrison Hightower, Jr., his brother Harrison's oldest son, who became CEO in 1972. Billy, as he was called, set about changing the terms of the company's relationship with J.P. Stevens, which had become increasingly rocky—a fact exacerbated by a decline in the tire-cord market. Under Billy's watch, the company disengaged from Stevens and began directly marketing its own goods. Billy also began developing brand names for the company, which previously had maintained a relatively low profile with regard to the public. Taking his cue from Stuckey's, which marketed candies through company-owned stores along interstate highways in the South, Billy opened six Thomaston Mills stores. Through these, the company sold varieties of apparel and other consumer products, including bed linens.

Thomaston Mills, which had formerly maintained a focus in tire cord and other industrial products, showed its new consumer-oriented approach with the introduction of patterned sheets under the brand name "Thomaston American Mood Prints" in 1970. Over the decade that followed, it would add numerous patterns to the collection, and this led to new distribution relationships with companies such as Ely and Walker of Memphis, Tennessee. Ultimately it would form even more lucrative alliances, including one with retail giant Kmart in the mid-1970s. In the 1980s, it expanded its retail lines with Rattlers Brand hunting gear, made of snakeproof Cordura nylon. But Thomaston Mills certainly did not confine itself to retail: along with other areas, it developed a strong line in institutional linens such that travelers at New York's tony Plaza Hotel—as well as those staying at Motel 6—were likely to sleep on Thomaston Mills sheets.

Among Billy Hightower's other important moves was the establishment of an export department, and when he retired in the early 1980s, the company's board noted that sales under his leadership had risen from $46.6 million in the 1969 fiscal year to $137.7 million in 1981. At the end of his tenure as leader, the company opened a 64,700-square-foot weaving plant in Zebulon, Georgia.

Staying Competitive in the 1980s and 1990s

In 1982, George Hightower, Billy's younger brother, became CEO. George faced the vicissitudes of a changing market, and it fell to him not only to close the company stores in 1984, but to sell off the mill villages. The company also stopped producing broadcloth and shirts.

Driving the latter move were factors which would increasingly come to haunt Thomaston Mills in the years that followed: government interference and foreign competition. A company executive recalled in *Hard Times, Good Times:* "Because of the [U.S.] Department of Agriculture's rules on cotton, the Japanese mills could buy United States cotton, delivered in Japan, cheaper than we could buy the same cotton here in America. They could buy cotton ten-to-twelve cents a pound cheaper than we could. Also, the Japanese had retooled their industry with the very finest combed goods and weaving facilities; so, they literally drove us out of the business. We had to shift to heavy goods, such as denim twills, drills, et cetera. And this involved a major retooling."

With the retirement of George Hightower in 1986, Neil Hightower—son of Billy and grandson of Harrison—assumed leadership of Thomaston Mills. Like his uncle George before him, Neil had to confront situations new to the company's leadership. Seeking to cut costs, U.S. businesses had drastically reduced inventories, and therefore expected suppliers to provide goods quickly and efficiently as needed. This required the creation of a company transportation fleet and a department to run it. By 1997, the year when Thomaston Mills began outsourcing its transportation, the company's fleet included some 17 tractors and 62 trailers. Another change was the creation of two classes of stock, one voting and the other nonvoting, to encourage greater liquidity without diluting the influence of the Hightower family.

On the retail front, the company moved increasingly into the department store market, and this required expansion of the bedding design staff. The "snake-bite-proof" Rattlers brand proved enormously successful, with annual sales of some seven million units, and in January 1998 the company sold the line to Rutter Rex of New Orleans. Another important development came in the fall of 1998, when the company reorganized the sales structure that had existed more or less unchanged since the split with J.P. Stevens. This led to the creation of divisions such as Apparel Fabrics and Apparel Sales.

A Century-Old Company in a Global Marketplace

A number of changes had been spurred by the increasing influence of the global marketplace, heightened through trade agreements such as NAFTA (North American Free Trade Agreement), signed in 1993. Despite the fact that many jobs go to Third World countries, the efficiency of U.S. facilities ensures their continued importance in part because of the capital-intensive nature of the business: moving factories is simply not a viable option. Nonetheless, Thomaston Mills has had to adjust to a changing landscape in order to remain as competitive as possible.

When it comes to maintaining an edge in a changing marketplace, computers are an important tool; but perhaps most important, in the case of Thomaston Mills at least, are its people. "The folks who run Thomaston Mills have a gallant, self-effacing demeanor that's quintessentially Southern," wrote Susan Harte in the *Atlanta Journal and Constitution.* "Don't be fooled. They also ooze grit from every pore, and have no intention of allowing their family-controlled textile company to become a casualty of its beleaguered industry."

With their strong sense of community, the company's personnel are vitally aware of their long history, and of the other storms they have weathered in the preceding century. Thus as the company faced losses in 1998 due in part to the Asian financial crisis, Neil Hightower was able to take a long view. Explaining to stockholders a plan whereby the company would introduce new lines, close some facilities, and reinstate strategic relationships with old customers, he said, "We are not looking for a quick turn. We are going to be smaller before we are profitable, but we are all committed to meeting the challenge."

Principal Divisions

Apparel Products; Industrial Products; Consumer Products; Retail Store.

Further Reading

Adler, Sam, "A Mill's Heading Upstairs: Thomaston Opens with J.G. Hook," *HFN: The Weekly Newspaper for the Home Furnishing Network,* February 19, 1996, p. 29.

Allgood, Lyn, "Thomaston Mills Paring Operations," *Atlanta Business Chronicle,* September 9, 1985, p. 1A.

Glover, Charles, "A Look at Thomaston Mills," *Atlanta Journal and Constitution,* December 29, 1991, p. H1.

Harte, Susan, "Bright Spot in Textile Production: Thomaston Mills Adjusts to Remain Dominant Player," *Atlanta Journal and Constitution,* December 29, 1991, p. H1.

Isaacs, McCallister, III, "Distribution for All Seas: Thomaston Mills Revamps Distribution Center," *Textile World,* August 1998, p. 37.

Josey, Charles, *Hard Times, Good Times: 1899–1999, The First 100 Years of Thomaston Mills,* Thomaston, Ga.: Thomaston Mills, 1999.

Lloyd, Brenda, "Hightower Sets Thomaston's Turnaround Plans," *Daily News Record,* October 5, 1998, p. 2.

——, "Thomaston Execs See Return to Profitability in '98," *Daily News Record,* October 6, 1997, p. 1.

"Thomaston's Team Spirit Scores Big with Buyers," *Textile World,* June 1992, p. 30.

—Judson Knight

TNT Post Group N.V.

Post Office Box 1300
1100 KG Amsterdam
Netherlands
(20) 500 60 00
Fax: (20) 500 70 00
Web site: http://www.tntpost-group.com

Public Company
Incorporated: 1998
Employees: 100,666
Sales: NLG 15.2 billion (US $7.53 billion) (1997)
Stock Exchanges: Amsterdam New York London
    Frankfurt
Ticker Symbol: TP
SICs: 4212 Local Trucking Without Storage; 4215
    Courier Services, Except by Air; 4225 General Ware-
    housing & Storage; 4513 Air Courier Services; 4731
    Arrangement of Transportation of Freight & Cargo

TNT Post Group N.V. (TPG) provides domestic and international mail services, express distribution, and logistic services. It includes the Dutch postal service, which is the first such service to be part of a publicly traded company, and is considered one of the most efficient postal operators in the world, delivering 22 million mail items every day. The company's mail division also offers domestic services such as direct marketing, direct mail, and unaddressed advertising, and the company provides international bulk mailing services. Under the TNT brand, the company's express services distribute documents, parcels, and freight internationally, constituting one of the four main players in the market (along with United Parcel Service, FedEx, and DHL). Logistics includes the management of a customer's entire supply chain, encompassing transport, stock management, order picking, and information systems management. TPG's logistics sector specializes in specific industry segments, most notably medical supplies and automotive parts. TNT Post Group has branches in 55 countries and operates in more than 200 countries.

TNT Post Group is essentially a combination of the Dutch post office and Australia-based TNT Limited. Prior to the 1980s European post offices were typically included within state-owned post and telephone companies, known as PTTs. In the 1980s these companies began to be privatized, with the Netherlands PTT gaining its independence in 1989 and then emerging as a public company, Koninklijke PTT Nederland N.V. (KPN), in 1994. Two years later KPN acquired TNT. In June 1998 TNT Post Group was demerged from KPN, creating a new entity focused on mail, express, and logistics and leaving KPN purely a telecommunications firm.

Dutch Postal Service's Early History

In the early 18th century cities were the main purveyors of postal services in The Netherlands, known at the time as the Dutch Republic of the United Provinces. Over time the cities acceded their roles as postmasters to the provinces, leading to the 1752 creation of the Statenpost, which held monopolies on domestic service and had improved relations with foreign postal services. The United Provinces were taken over by France in 1795 and transformed into the Batavian Republic, which was modeled on the revolutionary French republic. Thus in 1799 the Statenpost was reorganized into a single national service based on the French model.

Napoleon changed the Batavian Republic into the kingdom of Holland in 1806. The following year the Dutch postal service became part of the Ministry of Finance, with the first Postal Act setting up regulations on the collection, transport, and delivery of letters. Rates were made uniform across the entire nation, based on weights and distances. Required to make significant contributions to the Treasury, the postal service seemed to many Dutch citizens to be a tax-raising organization rather than a public service body. Meantime, after the fall of Napoleon, the kingdom of The Netherlands gained its independence in 1815 at the Congress of Vienna.

In the second half of the 19th century the Dutch postal service evolved into a more modern entity. The Postal Act of 1850 mandated that the postal service existed to serve the public interest. Postal tariffs were simplified, and the postage stamp made its debut in 1852. That same year, every municipality in The Netherlands acquired what were essentially "post offices," places where letters were posted for delivery and collected. The Netherlands could boast of a well-run postal service by 1870. New services, including the postcard and parcel post, were soon added.

Automation and Restructuring in the 20th Century

The Great Depression had a profound effect on the postal service. Rates were reduced and efforts were made to cut costs. The first steps toward mechanization were taken, including the 1931 debut of the Marchand Transforma, which was the first sorting machine, capable of sorting mail into 400 destinations with the help of an operator feeding in the mail by hand. In another cost-cutting move, the number of daily deliveries was reduced from three to two. Despite this, increased efficiency enabled mail to be delivered faster, with items posted by 6:00 in the evening being delivered the following morning. A more commercially savvy postal service also launched a major—for the era—advertising campaign.

The postal service operated in the red following World War II. Once again, rates were raised and cost-cutting measures were undertaken, particularly attempts to control labor costs. In 1949 a national analysis of processing and delivery statistics led to the closure of some smaller post offices. Needing to become even more efficient, the postal service restructured operations in the 1960s and 1970s so that certain tasks were concentrated within larger units. Mail began to be processed at 18 (later reduced to 12) "mail interchange centers," where highly efficient sorting and canceling machines were installed. In 1977 the postcode made its debut, allowing further automation, with mail now being sorted down to a postman's route rather than a city. Deliveries were reduced to one round per day during the 1970s. By the mid-1980s the postal service was profitable.

Privatized in 1989, Floated in 1994

The Netherlands PTT, which included both the Dutch postal service and the state-run telephone monopoly, gained its independence from government control in 1989 although it remained state owned. Netherlands PTT became a private company called PTT Nederland N.V., with PTT Post and PTT Telecom subsidiaries. PTT Post—headed by President Ad J. Scheepbouwer—now had much greater latitude to seek out opportunities for growth at a time when traditional postal services were being rocked by the increasing popularity of telex, fax, and e-mail, in addition to the rapid ascendance of international express delivery services.

Privatization opened the door to PTT Post gaining in a short period a commanding portion of the "remailing" sector. Remailing involved taking in bulk consignments from foreign corporate clients and then wrapping, addressing, labeling, and shipping the mail to a specified list of customers in another country. Such services often provided cost savings to the clients, as well as delivery faster than that of the clients' domestic postal service. In 1992 PTT Post launched an ambitious automation program, eventually dubbed Briefpost 2000, which aimed to increase the percentage of machine-sorted post from the 25 percent of 1990 to about 90 percent by 2000. The result would be not only reduced costs but also improved service quality.

Another key—and particularly bold—post-privatization move came in 1992 when PTT Post joined with the postal services of Sweden, France, Germany, and Canada to acquire 50 percent of GD Express Worldwide (GDEW). The other half-interest in GDEW remained with TNT Limited, which had created it. Operating under the trade name TNT Express Worldwide, GDEW combined the express mail and parcel activities of TNT and the five postal services. This marked the beginning of the increasingly close relationship between PTT Post and TNT.

In June 1994 The Netherlands state sold to the public 30 percent of its shares in PTT Nederland, which was renamed Koninklijke PTT Nederland N.V. (KPN). The NLG 6.8 billion (US $3.9 billion) raised marked the largest initial public offering in Dutch history. KPN obtained a listing on the Amsterdam Stock Exchange. The flotation was unusual in that most European PTTs were split into separate postal and telecom companies before being taken public. The decision not to do so indicated the strong position that PTT Post held, strong enough to stand alongside PTT Telecom in a publicly traded company. In late 1995 The Netherlands sold another 25 percent of KPN through a secondary offering, leaving the state without a controlling interest in the company. Shares began trading on the New York Stock Exchange for the first time, and then in 1996 listings were added in Frankfurt and London. It was also in 1996 that KPN acquired full control of both TNT and GDEW.

TNT's Early History

TNT Limited began in 1946 when Ken W. Thomas started operating a one-man trucking business in Sydney, Australia. After several years of steady growth, he incorporated the business as a private company in 1951. Continuing growth over the next decade, with the expansion of the company's fleet and extension of its routes across Australia, led to its incorporation as a public company in 1962, under the name Thomas Nationwide Transport Limited (TNT), and listing on the Sydney Stock Exchange the following year. Access to public funds allowed the company to continue expanding until, as the end of the decade approached, the limits of the Australian trucking market became apparent and TNT began to look for opportunities to extend its business beyond Australia. The chance came in 1967, a key year in TNT's history, when the company merged with another growing Australian transport enterprise, the Alltrans Group. Like TNT, Alltrans was another company that began in a small way in the optimistic environment of postwar Australia. One of Alltrans's two principal shareholders, Peter Abeles, was a refugee from war-torn Hungary. Abeles stepped off a ship in

Sydney in the late 1940s with £4,000. With a partner, George Rockey, he bought two trucks on time payment, named them *Samson* and *Delilah,* and, like Thomas, set about building up his business. Abeles would spend weeks driving his car through the Australian bush, drumming up contracts for the fledgling business. Although the merger with TNT involved discarding the Alltrans name and Thomas remaining head of the merged group, Abeles soon emerged as the driving force in the company, its key strategist, and its public face.

The merger gave TNT its first international operations via Alltrans's activities in New Zealand, which had begun in 1964. The size of the new group gave it the base required to begin expanding internationally. TNT began an ambitious international acquisition program, starting with its entry into the tough U.S. trucking industry through the purchase of a California truck line, Walkup's Merchant Express Inc., in 1969. In 1970 TNT bought Gill Interprovincial Lines in Canada and acquired one-third of a shipping company, Bulkships. Over the next two years, the expansion continued with the purchase of another Canadian operator, Scott Transport, one-sixth of the Union Steamship Co. of New Zealand Ltd., and TNT's entry into the U.S. air transport business through a joint venture with Shulman Transport Enterprises Inc. In 1972 the company also opened a small office in the United Kingdom, its first European presence. These swift moves were not without problems, however. The U.S. trucking industry was a difficult market for a newcomer. TNT's efforts to move into this market were accompanied by a series of wildcat strikes, mysterious bombings, and arson attacks. The damage caused by this interference was the first in a number of problems that would affect TNT's U.S. operations for years.

The company continued with its acquisition plans, aimed at attaining Abeles's vision of an integrated global transport operation. In 1973 TNT went into partnership with two West German companies to form an international ship brokering company, Montan TNT Pty Ltd. It also formed Kwikasair Ltd., an express delivery service between the United Kingdom and continental Europe. TNT's U.S. base also was expanded, through the purchase in the same year of Overland Western Ltd., a trucking company operating in Ontario and New York and Michigan, and of Acme Fast Freight Inc. The company also began developing a strong South American presence in 1973 when it bought 70 percent of the Brazilian transport group Pampa OTT and established Kwikasair Brazil.

Failed Takeover of Ansett in 1972

It was TNT's activities within Australia, however, that suddenly brought the company to international attention in 1972. TNT had continued to grow steadily since the 1967 merger, and it was well on its way to becoming the country's dominant transport group. In 1972 the company tried to accelerate the process by launching a hostile takeover bid for Ansett Transport Industries Limited (Ansett), the operator of one of Australia's two major domestic airlines. Protected from free competition by a government-endorsed airline duopoly, Ansett was a highly profitable company that would have secured TNT's position as Australia's leading carrier. Ansett's chairman and founder, Sir Reginald Ansett, was a tough adversary. At the height of the battle he called on the Victorian state government, headed by

his personal friend Sir Henry Bolte, for assistance. The government ruled that it was unacceptable for a company based in Victoria to be taken over by a company from New South Wales, and it stopped the takeover. TNT withdrew with 23 percent of Ansett's shares, but kept a close eye on Ansett.

The failed bid for Ansett did not stop TNT's international growth program, which continued through the mid-1970s with a series of acquisitions, particularly in the United Kingdom and Canada, that the company was using as launch pads for later growth in Europe and the United States, respectively. In 1975 Abeles foreshadowed the company's next international step when he launched an attack on international shipping conferences and the effect these cartels had on the global transport industry and trade prospects. The following year TNT directly challenged one of the most powerful of these cartels, the North Atlantic Freight Conference, comprising some of the world's largest shipping companies, by operating a nonconference container shipping service, Trans Freight Lines, on the Atlantic run.

Ten years after the merger between TNT and Alltrans, TNT had become Australia's major transport group, despite its failure to take over Ansett, and was a growing presence internationally. The group's annual revenue had increased tenfold from A $46 million in 1967 to A $462.7 million by 1977, while its after-tax profits had risen over the same period from A $956,000 to A $15.3 million. Such a swift expansion, however, had left the group exposed to a wide range of fluctuating markets and economies. TNT had bought heavily, was a relative newcomer in many of its markets, and was losing money from some of its operations in the difficult U.S. market. In 1977 to 1978, for the first time since its public incorporation in 1961, TNT's profits fell.

Gained 50 Percent of Ansett in 1979

The company responded with a recovery strategy aimed at rationalizing its international activities to cut out the weaker activities and build up other operations to the point where they were more prominent than the Australian operations. The program began in 1979 with the sale of the U.S. trucking company Acme Fast Freight, which had lost money every year since being acquired in 1973. The group also cut a loss-making stake in Nigerian Shipping Operations from 100 percent to 25 percent. By 1980, the company projected, more than half of its profits would for the first time be earned outside Australia. These projections were overshadowed later in 1979, when a new takeover battle for Ansett Transport Industries Limited began. With Sir Henry Bolte gone and a more liberalized corporate climate in Australia, two groups, Ampol Petroleum and Bell Resources, began buying Ansett shares heavily. TNT entered the battle, which also involved Rupert Murdoch's The News Corporation Limited. Just as the latter emerged as the likely victor, it suddenly became clear that TNT's stake was large enough to prevent Murdoch's company from taking control. The two companies agreed to share control of Ansett, with 50 percent each. Ansett's operations included a major Australian domestic airline, Ansett Australia, as well as freight services and tourist resort operations.

The cash flow provided by its share of Ansett gave TNT renewed strength to pursue its international expansion plans. The company changed its international focus to concentrate on the United Kingdom and Europe as its most important growth area. This focus became clear in October 1980 when, sponsored by the British merchant bank Hambros, TNT was listed on the London Stock Exchange, after removing itself from the Toronto and Vancouver exchanges earlier in the year. TNT was now well placed to expand into Europe, although it continued to look for openings in the United States, buying another trucking and warehousing company, Pilot Freight Carriers, while Trans Freight Lines doubled its size by buying another container line, Seatrain International.

The impact TNT's services were having in its new markets was indicated in 1982 in a confidential U.K. Post Office report that stated that a new TNT private parcel delivery service, Homefast, would pose a serious threat to the Royal Mail parcels network. TNT took a significant step toward building a European freight network in 1983 when it bought Skypak, IPEC Holdings Ltd.'s international courier operations, which operated in 26 countries. Combined with TNT's existing courier networks, this gave the group bases in 49 countries and provided access to Middle and Far East markets. Four months after the Skypak acquisition, TNT bought IPEC Europe, the leader in the European international express freight market, complete with more than 60 purpose-built terminals and 600 radio-equipped vehicles.

With its Ansett stake and its growing international business, TNT itself became a prime candidate for takeover in the early 1980s. One of Australia's most skilled takeover operators, Robert Holmes à Court, stalked TNT through 1981 and 1982 but was held off, although at one stage Ansett and another of TNT's associates, McIlwraith McEachern Limited, were called upon to pay more than A $60 million for a strategic stake in TNT to protect it from predators.

The vulnerability of a widespread transport group to the cyclical movements of economies became clear again when the company's profits plunged by half in 1982 to 1983. A recession in Australia had severely cut freight volumes, while in other markets competition had forced TNT to reduce its rates and thus its profit margin. TNT continued to pour money into expansion, however, opening a steady stream of operations and services in the United Kingdom, where it was a pioneer in the area of overnight delivery service, as it had been in Australia, and constantly looking out for new acquisition or expansion opportunities in Europe. In view of its international emphasis, the company changed its name in 1985 from Thomas Nationwide Transport Limited to simply TNT Limited (TNT).

A key event for TNT's European operation occurred in 1986 and came in large part by virtue of the close relationship that had developed between Abeles and Rupert Murdoch since the Ansett takeover. When Murdoch planned to move his British national newspapers in London from Fleet Street to a new plant in Wapping, in the face of fierce resistance from the printing unions, he also anticipated problems from the unions at British Rail, which distributed all of his publications nationwide. Murdoch, therefore, worked closely with TNT, whose U.K. manager, Alan Jones, built up a fleet of trucks in the weeks leading up to the transfer to Wapping. The weekend before the move, Jones hired 550 drivers, and when Wapping began operating, TNT's trucks rolled through the gates and the picket lines.

For TNT the effort paid off, as the company was awarded the contract to distribute all of Murdoch's British papers, providing a massive boost to the company's U.K. operation. The plan also marked the end of British Rail's dominance of the newspaper distribution market, as more publishers followed Murdoch's lead and switched to road distribution.

Emerged as Leading Diversified Transport Group by 1987

In the late 1980s TNT emerged from a period that could have damaged a company with a different approach. Faced with a recession and exposed in a number of geographical areas, TNT under Abeles spent heavily on expansion and outlasted the problems. The company was particularly well positioned in the £500 million-a-year European express delivery market, which was growing at 50 percent a year. The emphasis on Europe was shown by the fact that the company's European turnover grew by an average of almost 50 percent a year from when the U.K. office was opened in 1972 to 1987. By 1987 TNT had become the world's largest diversified transportation group, with operations in 105 countries. Abeles indicated that the company was moving into a new phase when he said in the *Sunday Times,* June 28, 1987, ''The growing pains of setting up and consolidating into a truly worldwide transportation group are coming to an end.''

From its wider base, TNT began a new series of developments aimed at furthering its reach in its existing markets, particularly in Europe. In 1987 the company sold its last shares in the U.S. shipping company Trans Freight Lines, which had been unsuccessful in its attempt to penetrate the tight North Atlantic shipping business and had lost a net A $80 million since 1976. TNT also unloaded another big loss-making U.S. operation, the trucking business TNT Pilot, which had lost more than A $60 million since 1980. In 1987 TNT made one of its biggest investments when it negotiated a right of first refusal of five years' production of British Aerospace's new BAe 146 Quiet Trader freight aircraft, worth an estimated total of about £1 billion, and used the first 18 planes to establish a trans-European air express freight network servicing 17 countries.

TNT also pushed toward the goal of running a new freight airline in Europe. In 1988 it merged its European express freight division with that of its biggest competitor, Scandinavian Airline System's Air de Cologne, and bought a 75 percent stake in the leading Spanish domestic freight carrier, Unitransa. It also bought KLM Airlines' parcel express business, XP, and linked its air freight business in Europe with its road operations, creating a formidable new network, TNT Express Europe. By mid-1989 the European operations accounted for 35 percent of TNT's total worldwide assets, double the proportion of just two years before. Abeles's eyes were clearly fixed on the coming of the single European market in 1992, and his strategy of dominating the highly segmented European freight industry by offering a comprehensive range of services between and within all European countries appeared to be working.

The late 1980s also marked TNT's extension into Eastern Europe, just in time for the collapse of the Eastern Bloc in 1989 and 1990. The company formed a joint venture with the Hungarian airline Malev in 1988, created TNT Aeroflot—a joint venture with Russia's Aeroflot—in 1989, and started a joint venture with Yugoslavia's airline JAT in 1990. As other countries in the region became liberalized, TNT moved toward similar operations throughout Eastern Europe. It also expanded in Southeast Asia, investing in joint ventures with the Philippine Aerospace Development Corporation to develop the Philippines as a regional hub.

Troubled Period Began in 1989

From late 1989, however, TNT encountered a series of serious problems. The problems began in August 1989 when Australia's domestic airline pilots resigned en masse as part of a campaign to secure a 29.7 percent salary increase that was outside the government's six percent wages accord and centralized system. Accordingly, the pilots' union's industrial awards were cancelled by the Industrial Relations Commission. The four airlines, namely Ansett Airlines, East-West Airlines, government-owned Australian Airlines, and IPEC Aviation, slowly rebuilt their airlines by employing pilots on individual contracts. This took several months and was completed by March 1990. The number of pilots reemployed was significantly lower than prior to the dispute. The dispute, which lasted for months, ended in favor of the airlines, but caused serious damage to the airlines' revenue. At the height of the dispute, Ansett was estimated to be losing A $10 million a week. TNT's profits for the September quarter of 1989 were 70 percent lower than for the same period a year before.

The damage subsided after the dispute, but hopes for a return to profit growth disappeared in 1990, when Australia, the United Kingdom, and North America fell into recession. As usual, the economic downturn hit the transport industry hard, and TNT's broad exposure in these regions left it open to a severe drop in revenue. This problem was compounded in Australia in November 1990, when the federal government deregulated the domestic airline industry and ended the two-airline agreement that had protected Ansett's share of the air market for so long. Compass Airlines, a new company headed by a former Ansett employee, entered the market and began offering big fare reductions, forcing Ansett Australia, East-West Airlines, and Australian Airlines to introduce fare discounts of up to 61 percent, further slashing revenue.

These problems—along with debt totaling A $2.2 billion—caused a surge of concern in financial markets about TNT's capacity to generate liquidity in tough times. In January 1991 the company's share price on the Australian Stock Exchange fell to a record low of A 75¢. Because of the unfavorable market conditions, the company decided not to issue A $200 million of preference shares, issuing later, in April 1991, 50 million new ordinary shares of A 50¢ at a premium of A $1.00 to ease its liquidity problems. The hardest blow came when TNT revealed that it had lost nearly A $197 million for the fiscal year ending in June 1991.

TNT Focused on Core Areas in the 1990s

TNT's board responded to this crisis with a reassessment of the company's growth strategy. The company simplified its structure by focusing on three core areas: international express delivery, domestic express delivery, and TNT's contract business with major manufacturers for the delivery of goods in certain sectors, such as automotive parts. Assets not fitting into these core areas became candidates for divestment. One of the first such selloffs came in March 1992 when TNT spun off its U.S. regional motor carriers into TNT Freightways (renamed USFreightways in February 1996). The initial public offering of 75 percent of the new company's stock raised US $280.3 million and left TNT with a 25 percent stake. Also in March 1992 TNT completed the acquisition of Chronoservice, a leading French express carrier, which filled a gap in the company's network of domestic express businesses in Europe. TNT reached an agreement with rival Federal Express whereby it would subcontract the delivery of inbound FedEx packages to ten European countries, a deal consummated that same month. Later in 1992 came the establishment of GD Express Worldwide (GDEW)—which allowed TNT to remove A $600 million in long-term debt from its balance sheet—and the start of the TNT-PTT Post relationship. An era also came to an end in 1992 when the colorful and autocratic Abeles stepped aside as managing director, replaced by the lower-key David Mortimer.

Abeles remained on the TNT board but only until September 1993 when he and four other directors resigned following a boardroom disagreement over how to handle the company's troubled balance sheet. Debt had been reduced to A $1.12 billion, but TNT posted losses of A $195.4 million for fiscal 1992 and A $256.7 million (US $171.1 million) for fiscal 1993. With A $400 million in debt due for repayment in both fiscal 1994 and 1995, the company was forced to step up its divestment program. In 1994 TNT sold the bulk of its shipping and development division for about A $125 million (US $89 million). Also divested was a car auctioning service in Australia. For fiscal 1994 TNT posted a profit of A $105.1 million (US $78 million), in large part because of a turnaround in Ansett Airlines and reduced losses at GDEW, which had been suffering the effects of aggressive competition.

KPN Acquired TNT in December 1996

In September 1996 TNT continued to narrow its interests when it sold its 50 percent interest in Ansett to Air New Zealand for A $475 million. Three months later Koninklijke PTT Nederland (KPN) completed a friendly A $2 billion (US $1.58 billion) takeover of TNT, in one of the largest mergers in Dutch history. KPN also gained full control of GDEW as the other postal service partners in the venture sold out. The combination of PTT Post and TNT created the most extensive express mail network in Europe and one of the world's four largest time-sensitive distribution and logistics groups (along with United Parcel Service, FedEx, and DHL). TNT activities related to mail, express, and logistics were integrated into PTT Post. Other TNT assets—including freight, shipping, and aircraft leasing—were soon sold off.

The combined PTT Post/TNT operations now generated about half of KPN's total revenue, compared with one-third before the acquisition of TNT. But on June 29, 1998, TNT Post Group N.V. (TPG)—the mail, express, and logistics operations of KPN—were demerged from KPN and listed independently on the stock exchanges of Amsterdam, New York, London, and Frankfurt. KPN shareholders received one share of TPG stock for each KPN share they held. The Dutch government held a 44 percent stake in TPG at the outset. Given that the company included the national postal service of the country—an entity of vital importance—the government retained the special right to approve resolutions that would fundamentally alter the group structure of TPG and could increase its stake to a controlling 51 percent in certain circumstances ''only to safeguard the general interest.'' The government confirmed its intention not to reduce its stake below one-third before 2004. In addition, the government had the right to appoint three of the nine members of the TPG supervisory board. Ad J. Scheepbouwer was named chairman of the board of management.

The culmination of PTT Post's Briefpost 2000 initiative came in November 1998 with the opening of six new sorting centers, which replaced the 12 mail interchange centers that had been used to sort mail. The state-of-the-art sorting machines not only greatly increased the percentage of automatically sorted mail, but also led to cost savings from the elimination of 4,500 jobs. Most of the people who lost their jobs were transferred to other positions within TPG. In any event, the completion of Briefpost 2000 provided a solid beginning for the newly independent company, which appeared—based on its long history of innovation, daring, and forward-thinking—to be well positioned to thrive in the increasingly competitive environment of the early 21st century, when European postal services' monopoly on letter delivery was expected to be removed.

Principal Operating Units

PTT Post (including Letters, Parcel Service, International & Consumer, Media Service, Document Handling, and Post Offices [50%]); TNT (including International Mail, TNT International Express, TNT South Europe [Italy/France/Spain], TNT Benelux, TNT United Kingdom, TNT Germany, TNT North America, and TNT Australia/Asia).

Further Reading

Brady, Diane, ''Delivery Giants Race to Provide Overnight Service to Asian Cities,'' *Wall Street Journal,* August 7, 1995, p. B6A.

Brown, Kevin, ''Takeover Drive Puts TNT on Road to Profit,'' *Financial Times,* March 25, 1992, p. 26.

Cramb, Gordon, ''Offer Values TPG at Fl 22bn,'' *Financial Times,* June 29, 1998, p. 28.

——, ''TNT Post Group Tops Forecast at Halfway,'' *Financial Times,* September 1, 1998, p. 17.

Cramb, Gordon, and Nikki Tait, ''Wrapping Up the Old with the New,'' *Financial Times,* October 3, 1996, p. 28.

du Bois, Martin, ''KPN Grows To Challenge Delivery Giants,'' *Wall Street Journal,* December 17, 1996, p. A6.

''Dutch Government Set To Divest Control of KPN,'' *Privatisation International,* October 1995, pp. 1+.

Milbank, Dana, ''Dutch Service Hopes To Deliver World's Mail,'' *Wall Street Journal,* July 28, 1994, pp. B1, B6.

Murdoch, Adrian, ''Postman Pat He Ain't,'' *CA Magazine* (Scotland), August 1998, pp. 34+.

Salomon, Alan, ''Delivering a Market Battle: Courier Wars Darken Skies Over Europe, Asia as FedEx, TNT, DHL Battle for Domination,'' *Advertising Age,* July 17, 1995, p. I-18.

Tait, Nikki, ''TNT Losses Mount as Directors Quit,'' *Financial Times,* September 9, 1993, p. 34.

——, ''TNT Sells Shipping Businesses,'' *Financial Times,* February 23, 1994, p. 31.

''TNT Sale May Signal Industry Trend,'' *Logistics Management,* January 1997, p. 26.

van de Krol, Ronald, ''KPN Floats into Land of the Giants,'' *Financial Times,* July 21, 1993, p. 23.

Witcher, S. Karene, ''Sir Peter's Reign Dismays TNT Critics,'' *Wall Street Journal,* August 28, 1991, p. A4.

Witcher, S. Karene, and Martin du Bois, ''Dutch Telecommunications Firm KPN Offers $1.58 Billion for Australia's TNT,'' *Wall Street Journal,* October 3, 1996, p. A9.

—Richard Brass
—updated by David E. Salamie

Todhunter International, Inc.

222 Lakeview Avenue
Suite 1500
West Palm Beach, Florida 33401
U.S.A.
(561) 655-8977
Fax: (561) 655-9718
Web site: http://www.todhunter.com

Public Company
Incorporated: 1964
Employees: 335
Sales: $75.1 million (1998)
Stock Exchanges: American
Ticker Symbol: THT
SICs: 2084 Wines, Brandy & Brandy Spirits
    (Manufacturers); 2082 Malt Beverages
    (Manufacturers); 2085 Distillers; 2086 Bottlers; 5099
    Importers & Exporters; 5181 Beer & Ale—
    Wholesale; 5182 Wines—Wholesale

Todhunter International, Inc. produces alcoholic and nonalcoholic products, as well as by-products and related products. Its primary business is in rum, brandies, wines, and various other spirits, some of which it bottles itself—most notably under the Cruzan Rum and Porfidio Tequila labels—and some of which it sells to other beverage companies, who bottle it. In addition, it bottles various light alcoholic drinks, including wine coolers and cocktails, for other liquor companies. Alcohol-related products and by-products include vinegar, cooking wines, industrial alcohol, and residuum, a by-product sold as animal feed. Todhunter had more than $75 million in annual revenues in 1998.

1960s Beginnings in the Bahamas

Todhunter was founded in 1964 by A. Kenneth Pincourt, Jr., who into the 1990s remained the company's chairman. As for its unusual name, there is undoubtedly a story behind it, but it is not one the company relates in its promotional literature. Established in the Bahamas, where it was able to operate tax-free, the company continued its ties with the island nation long after it moved to its U.S. mainland location in West Palm Beach, Florida.

During the 1970s Todhunter began to experience explosive growth, and in 1987 it signed a wine cooler production agreement with a giant in the spirits industry, Joseph E. Seagram & Sons, Inc. In 1989 it bought up all of the production facilities in Florida belonging to its biggest competitor and on October 13, 1992 made an initial public offering (IPO) of its stock. At that time the stock was traded on NASDAQ; five years later, in October 1997, the company would switch to the American Stock Exchange (AMEX).

Thus the early history of Todhunter, with the exception of its offshore founding, is not unlike that of most American companies. The production of rum, in which Todhunter participates, has an exotic reputation, however, due to its association with the West Indies and the rich history of that region. When Todhunter acquired the Cruzan Rum label in the mid-1990s, the company also acquired an intriguing history. Todhunter makes much of the latter in its promotional literature.

The Rich History of Cruzan

A list of "Significant Dates of St. Croix and Cruzan Distillery History" published by Todhunter begins all the way back in 1493, when the "First 'Cruise Ship' docks in St. Croix: Christopher Columbus, on second voyage, with 17 ships and 1,500 men, sails into Salt River Bay of the island he names Santa Cruz. Calls it a 'lush garden.' Claims island for Spain. Encounters the indigenous population called Ay-Ay. Brings sugar cane to the West Indies, a prelude to the Piña Colada." The history then proceeds to the 17th and 18th centuries, when European powers—England, The Netherlands, Spain, France, and the Knights of Malta—"play 'capture the flag.'" Again, there is more than a touch of romance to this history: "Pirates and buccaneers based in the islands disrupt trade; bury treasure."

The history continues with a number of interesting facts—including the information that Denmark, not a major New

World colonist, owned St. Croix from the 1700s until 1917—to the point when the Nelthropp family became established on the island. They eventually controlled the Diamond Estate distillery, later renamed Cruzan Distillery. The latter was shut down for nearly 15 years beginning in 1919, while the United States (by then the owners of the Virgin Islands) underwent Prohibition. In the 1930s Donald Carr (''Hardy'') Nelthropp—future president of Cruzan when it became a subsidiary of Todhunter—was born, and in 1961 Schenley Distilleries bought Cruzan, though the latter continued to run its own operation.

''Over the years,'' according to Todhunter, ''Hardy Nelthropp has seen many changes in the rum industry, including the closing of other distilleries in St. Croix, until only his own remains; change in ownership of the Cruzan Distillery; and changes in consumer consumption trends. However, Hardy has persevered, making, as he proudly asserts, 'Only one product: rum—good, clean rum of the highest quality.' Today, the business is owned by Todhunter International . . . but it is still operated by Hardy in recognition of his many talents, skills, and dedication.''

Growth and Growing Pains in the Early 1990s

Cruzan was the most notable of Todhunter's several acquisitions during the early to mid-1990s. The label came to it as part of its purchase of Virgin Islands Rum Industries, announced by Todhunter executives in January 1994. In addition to Cruzan, through which Virgin Islands Rum sold its product throughout the United States, the company also supplied bulk rum to bottlers and distillers throughout the country. At the same time it purchased Virgin Islands Rum, Todhunter announced the acquisition of Yellowstone Distillery in Louisville, Kentucky, where it would begin producing fortified wine late in 1994.

During those years of growth the company also experienced a few growing pains. In January 1993 it announced the resignation of one of its leading officers, Peter D. Kuc, who was leaving to pursue other interests. Along with this transition, there was a shuffle of executives as Chief Operating Officer (COO) Arnold R. Beinstein became vice-chairman of the board; Vice-President of Sales Dennis C. Mitchell replaced Beinstein as COO; and Treasurer Troy Edwards became chief financial officer (CFO).

Todhunter also was hit with a fine of more than $780,000 by the Environmental Protection Agency (EPA) in July 1993. The federal agency charged that by burning small quantities of alcohol by-products on five occasions in 1991 and 1992, the company was attempting to destroy waste illegally. Todhunter responded that it was simply using the alcohol, according to Pincourt in the *South Florida Business Journal,* to ''reduce water pollution and our use of imported fuel oil. We believe that the by-products are clean-burning and present no potential for harm to human health or the environment.''

Another challenge came in the form of a fire at Todhunter's Lake Alfred, Florida distillery in September 1993. Damage was estimated at $3 million, including inventory. The fire was contained within a tank storage facility area and a barrel warehouse where the company aged its rum.

But along with the growing pains was noticeable growth, and Wall Street certainly paid attention. Thus *Fortune* profiled Todhunter in November 1993 as one of its ''Companies to Watch.'' Richard S. Teitelbaum of that magazine identified several factors influencing Todhunter's increasing success: ''The company,'' he wrote, ''makes high-octane ingredients that liquor producers blend with everything from whiskey to blueberry brandy. Because alcohol consumption is declining, [leading alcohol companies such as] Heublein, Seagram, Brown-Forman, and others are trying hard to cut costs, and Todhunter's sauces are among the least expensive around.'' Teitelbaum in turn attributed the low prices to the quantity of ''cheap, abundant oranges'' at its Florida location: specifically, the company had a ''pipeline'' from a Minute Maid orange juice factory nearby, which sent pulp and other citrus residue to Todhunter's Auburndale, Florida distillery. There Todhunter turned this into citrus brandy, which tastes relatively benign but packs a staggering 189-proof punch.

The Blair Debacle in the 1990s

Along with its acquisitions in 1994, Todhunter sold off its assets in Todhunter-Mitchell & Co., a firm based in Freeport, Bahamas, to Butler & Sands of Nassau. In addition, the company had acquired Blair Importers along with Virgin Islands Rum, but this second purchase did not prove as successful as its predecessor. Blair, importer of Yago Sangria, a Spanish wine, turned into an $11 million loss on Todhunter's books in 1995, and by September the parent company was announcing the sale of its troubled subsidiary. ''We shut it down . . . because it wasn't making any money,'' Pincourt told the *Palm Beach Post,* adding ''We had high hopes for it, but it didn't work out.''

Blair held distribution rights for Cruzan, which Todhunter retained; the remainder of the company went to David Sherman Corp. of St. Louis, Missouri for $6 million. Later Pincourt and other company officials would hold that Blair's management deliberately overvalued their company, and in November 1995 they filed an $11 million arbitration claim. The former owners of Blair filed a counterclaim, charging that Todhunter still owed them $2.8 million for assumed debts, along with as much as $8 million in stock. In January 1998 Todhunter settled with Blair, agreeing to pay the $2.8 million. As for the remainder, this would be settled through nonbinding mediation, but ''If it doesn't settle through mediation within 60 days,'' Pincourt told the *Palm Beach Post,* ''then we go back to fighting.''

Despite what the *Palm Beach Daily Business Review* described in a headline as a ''Sour Deal's Aftertaste,'' Todhunter remained an attractive stock. According to Mike Vogel of the Palm Beach publication, ''Its best margins are in making bulk alcohol products—fortified citrus wine, brandy and spirits, cane spirits and rum—for other manufacturers to use in their products. It also has made good money in recent years bottling other alcohol and non-alcohol beverages, and by making vinegar.'' After starting at $6 a share in 1992, the company's stock had risen to $16 in 1994, before the Blair debacle. As of October 1997, when it made the switch to the American Stock Exchange, the company's stock had hit a 52-week high of $10.38.

Todhunter, which had previously tangled with the EPA, in March 1998 had to take on another government agency: the

Internal Revenue Service (IRS). Again, the ill-fated Blair Importers adventure had come back to haunt the company. Because it had purchased Blair for $8 million and sold it for $6 million a year later, Todhunter attempted to take a deduction of $2.1 million, most of which it claimed was for "sales promotion." The IRS refused to allow the deduction, but Todhunter filed a petition to appeal.

Moving into the Limelight in the Late 1990s

In a September 1998 profile of Todhunter subsidiary Florida Distillers, Paul Power, Jr., of *The Ledger* in Lakeland, Florida wrote that "since most of its production traditionally has been used for manufacturing other companies' spirits, the group is little known. It threw itself into the spotlight about five years ago when its vats at the Lake Alfred distillery ignited. . . . Now it's trying to catapult itself in a different but equally dramatic fashion, shifting from a somewhat anonymous company that sells tankers of ingredients, to a concern that wants to steal alcohol sales from Bacardi and other marketing giants."

Not only the subsidiary, but the parent company, increasingly bid for recognition in its own right—rather than merely as a bottler of others' products—as the 1990s drew to a close. With its creation of the Todhunter Imports Ltd. division, along with the introduction of 14 new proprietary labels, Todhunter had made "a grand entrance into the rum and super-premium tequila markets," wrote Kavita Varma in the *South Florida Business Journal.* "So grand," she went on to say, "that in an upcoming episode of the CBS drama 'Dellaventura,' a Todhunter brand will make its television debut. In a scene where actor Danny Aiello is looking for someone in a bar, the bartender says, 'You can't miss him. He drinks Porfidio'."

"We were too dependent on others succeeding with their brands," Thomas Valdes, a former Bacardi executive and later head of Todhunter Imports, told Varma. "Once in a while they would make a mistake, and we could feel it. So we had to take control of that," he noted. Take control they had, launching the 14 new labels and adding 21 distributors who would help the company sell to an affluent market. Overall demand for alcohol was down, but demand for a higher premium in rum and tequila was up. "Those rums are doing a lot of volume now," said Jay Maltby, another former Bacardi executive hired by Pincourt. "People want flavor."

Principal Subsidiaries

Florida Distillers Company; Todhunter Bahamas Limited (Bahamas); Todhunter Imports; Cruzan Rum Distillery, Ltd. (Virgin Islands); Todhunter Foods.

Further Reading

Berzof, Ken, "Analyst Has His Favorite Liquid Stocks," *Courier-Journal* (Louisville, Kentucky), July 24, 1994, p. 1E.
Egerton, Judith, "Company Wants To Set Up Winery at Distillery Site," *Courier-Journal* (Louisville, Kentucky), September 17, 1993, p. D1.
Hartman, Lauren R., "Goldwasser Glitters with No-Label Look," *Packaging Digest,* December 1997, p. 42.
Herubin, Danielle, "Liquor Firm Shuts Down Subsidiary," *Palm Beach Post,* September 23, 1995, p. 5B.
Hosford, Christopher, "Todhunter Hit with EPA Charge Alleging Illegal Fuel Burning," *South Florida Business Journal,* July 23, 1993, p. 8.
Power, Paul, Jr., "Into the Limelight: Local Distillery Moving from Supplier to Brand-Name Retailer," *The Ledger* (Lakeland, Florida), September 6, 1998, p. E1.
Ringle, Bill, "Todhunter Wants Break in $1.4 Million Dispute with IRS," *Palm Beach Post,* March 18, 1998, p. 8B.
Teitelbaum, Richard S., "Todhunter," *Fortune,* January 11, 1993, p. 81.
Utley, Michael, "Firm Settles Claim for $2.8 Million," *Palm Beach Post,* January 9, 1998, p. 7D.
Varma, Kavita, "A New Shot for Todhunter," *South Florida Business Journal,* January 30, 1998, p. 1A.
Vogel, Mike, "Sour Deal's Aftertaste Burning," *Palm Beach Daily Business Review,* October 8, 1997, p. A1.

—Judson Knight

Unique Casual Restaurants, Inc.

One Corporate Place
55 Ferncroft Road
Danvers, Massachusetts 01923
U.S.A.
(978) 774-6606
Fax: (978) 750-1414

Public Company
Incorporated: 1973 as Daka, Inc.
Employees: 8,000
Sales: $215.3 million (1998)
Stock Exchanges: NASDAQ
Ticker Symbol: UNIQ
SICs: 5812 Eating Places

A restaurant operator undergoing extensive change, Unique Casual Restaurants, Inc. owns, operates, and franchises a chain of restaurants under the Champps Americana banner, but prior to late 1998 the company's holdings were far more plentiful and diverse. At its peak, when Unique Casual operated as Daka International, the company's assets included a quarter-billion-dollar contract feeding business, a more than 200-unit restaurant chain named Fuddruckers, and a specialty concepts division that operated multi-unit restaurants such as Great Bagel and Coffee Co. and French Quarter Coffee Co. Financial problems in 1996 precipitated major divestitures in 1997 and 1998 that stripped the company of roughly 75 percent of its annual revenue volume and left it dependent on Champps Americana for its existence. In 1999 the Champps Americana chain comprised approximately 30 restaurants that offered a casual menu of pizza, burgers, chicken, and fish in a combination sports bar and entertainment dining environment.

Origins and 1988 Fuddruckers Merger

Unique Casual's predecessor, a company named Daka, Inc., was founded by Terry Vince, a British citizen who arrived in the United States in the late 1950s. Upon his arrival in the United States, Vince began working as a chef-manager at the foodser-

vice division of transportation giant Greyhound, eventually working his way up to research and development director during his ten-year tenure. When he left in 1968, Vince joined Servomation Wilbur (later Service America Inc.), a contract feeding company that managed and operated dining facilities for corporate and institutional clients. Vince spent five years at Service America's predecessor, then left in 1973 to start his own contract feeding company, an enterprise he named Daka, Inc. From the beginning, Vince strove to provide what he called "low-profile, highly personalized, state-of-the-art" service. He avoided displaying the Daka name in the dining facilities he operated, convinced that the name of a contract foodservice provider "means nothing to the diner anyway." Instead, Vince chose modern and unique names under which to operate his facilities, thereby decreasing the institutional "feel" of the dining rooms and, as he perceived it, increasing the longevity of the contract with the client. Although in large part unknown because of Vince's reluctance to use the Daka name for promotion, the company prospered and grew, acquiring a sufficient volume of clients to enable diversification into hotel ownership. Vince's acquisition of several hotel properties was followed by the acquisition of Fuddruckers, a gourmet hamburger chain. Although the addition of Fuddruckers, like the acquisition of the hotels, pointed to Vince's growing prominence as a businessman, the combination of the two diversifications ultimately led to his departure from the company he had started in 1973.

The 1988 acquisition of Fuddruckers brought with it the talents and services of William H. Baumhauer, Fuddruckers president and chairman. Baumhauer was graduated with a degree in accounting from Florida Atlantic University, although accounting was not his first choice. "I wanted a professional degree—to be a doctor or lawyer," Baumhauer once remarked, "but I didn't have the money. I went into accounting for all the wrong reasons." Despite his disinclination, Baumhauer proved to be a particularly adept accountant, earning enough respect during his 11 years as a public accountant to be presented with a number of enticing professional opportunities. In one month in 1982, Baumhauer was offered three executive positions: president of a freight airline company in Miami, president of a real estate subsidiary owned by a large insurance company, and chief financial officer of Fuddruckers, which at the time operated five restaurants and was looking to convert to public ownership. Lured by the risk and the financial rewards of joining the ambitious yet modestly sized hamburger chain, Baumhauer chose the position at Fuddruckers and helped the company through its 1983 initial public offering. For the next two years, Baumhauer had little time to reflect on his choice, as he assisted in the company's prolific expansion from a five-restaurant enterprise into a 100-unit chain. In January 1985 Fuddruckers' founder, Phil Romano, retired, paving the way for Baumhauer's promotion to president. Two months later Baumhauer took over as chairman as well, building on his influence over the fast-growing chain. Unfortunately for Baumhauer, Romano's departure was a timely one and Baumhauer's ascension to the top of Fuddruckers' executive ranks was not. The company was strapped for cash, its resources exhausted by the rapid expansion, and Baumhauer was faced with mustering a revival. He restructured the company, and for the next two years he closed unprofitable restaurants, reevaluated Fuddruckers' franchisees, and implemented wholesale changes within the company's executive ranks. "We were fortunate to survive," he later remarked. "We had no money, no good operations, and we started every Monday looking at how to make payroll Friday."

By 1987 Fuddruckers was once again profitable, its number of restaurants pared to 80. Buoyed by Fuddruckers' resurgence, Baumhauer was skeptical when a broker suggested a merger with another company involved in another area of the foodservice industry—Vince's Daka. After meeting with Vince, however, Baumhauer reconsidered, and their talks led to the November 1988 formation of Daka International, parent company of Daka, Inc., Fuddruckers, and the hotel properties acquired by Vince. The union of the two companies created an enviable enterprise: annual sales exceeded $360 million, foodservice accounts numbered 500, hotel properties comprised six Ramada units, and the restaurant segment of the business constituted 120 Fuddruckers units, 47 of which were operated under franchise agreements. Within months, however, differences between Baumhauer and Vince began to surface. Their disagreement centered on the hotel properties, whose value had plummeted amid an anemic real estate market during the late 1980s and the first hints of the early 1990s national economic recession. The differences evidently were irreconcilable because in November 1990 Vince left the company. One year later the hotel properties were divested, sold to Vince for $5 million worth of Daka International stock. For the second time in his career as a corporate executive, Baumhauer had ascended to the position of sole command.

Strategy Set for the 1990s

In the aftermath of Vince's 1990 exit, Baumhauer fine-tuned Daka International's operations. Unprofitable Fuddruckers were closed, restructuring efforts took place, and he implemented a strategy of acquiring franchised Fuddruckers units in selected markets. For the first time since 1984, Fuddruckers was advertised on television. Baumhauer also raised capital by selling stock to investors on two occasions, leading up to his 1993 proclamation that he would double the size of Daka International during the ensuing three years. The 1993–96 period saw Daka International expand mightily, and not just in the number of Fuddruckers restaurants. The contract feeding operations housed within Daka, Inc. generated the majority of Daka International's revenues, a

reality not lost on Baumhauer despite his allegiance to the Fuddruckers chain. Building on a base of more than 500 foodservice operations in the eastern half of the United States, Baumhauer pressed ahead, acquiring 102 educational foodservice accounts from Service America Inc. in August 1993. Including accounts primarily in Florida, Georgia, New Jersey, and Pennsylvania, the deal with Service America added $80 million in new business and was followed by the acquisition of the education and corporate accounts belonging to Service Master, worth another $81 million. Baumhauer made equally bold moves in other segments of Daka International's business, particularly within the company's restaurant division. In early 1996 a $69 million stock swap added another restaurant chain, the 15-unit Champps Americana chain, featuring multitiered dining rooms, open kitchens, video screens, and disc jockeys. Baumhauer was "thrilled to get the concept," referring to the combination entertainment and sports bar restaurants scattered in Minnesota, Texas, and New Jersey, and welcomed the addition of the chain's $80 million a year in sales. A short time later, in April 1996, Baumhauer acquired another chain, the 18-unit Great Bagel and Coffee Co., described as a combination specialty coffee retailer, bagel bakery, and grab-and-go deli.

While the acquisition campaign that added foodservice contracts and the two restaurant chains was being conducted, Baumhauer also directed his energies toward developing expansion internally. Between 1993 and 1996 he oversaw the development of Daka International's specialty concepts division, which created concepts to be used as in-house vehicles in the company's institutional foodservice accounts and in locations not managed by the company. French Quarter Coffee Co. and Good Natural Café were two examples of the concepts created by Daka International's specialty concepts division, appearing in company-managed dining rooms and at Home Depot, General Cinema, Macy's, and Texaco. It was through this segment of Daka International's ever-expanding business that news of Baumhauer's biggest deal emerged, one that would have a profound effect on the entire operations of the company.

In July 1996 discount store chain Kmart Corp. and Daka International announced a joint venture of mammoth proportions. Under the terms of the proposed venture, Baumhauer's company would take over operation of 1,850 Kmart in-store restaurants, including 550 Little Caesar pizza franchise stores and any other restaurants opened during the 15-year agreement between Daka International and Kmart. By committing to invest $51 million in the restaurants over a three-year period, Daka International would gain a majority 51 percent stake in the restaurants and control foodservice operations capable of doubling Daka International's revenue volume. By all measures, it was an enticing deal, but negotiations stalled between the two parties as the summer progressed. Frustration over the delay was compounded severely when the financial figures for the previous year were announced. Net income for the year had plunged from $9.2 million to $905,000, and sales had dropped five percent, causing investors to eye the company negatively. Amid concerns that Daka International's portfolio of businesses was too diverse, the company's stock price slumped, dropping from a high of $34 per share in 1995 to $10 per share after the depressed financial figures were released. The situation was exacerbated by the yet-to-materialize agreement with Kmart and was aggravated further when the joint venture was abandoned entirely before the end of 1996. In the aftermath of these pernicious events, sweeping changes were made, pervasive alterations that stripped away much of Daka International to create Unique Casual Restaurants, Inc.

Late 1990s Divestitures

To solve Daka International's pressing financial problems, a two-step process was arranged for execution in May 1997. The first step in the plan entailed the sale of the company's foodservice division, the $285 million in sales generated by the corporate, educational, and other contract feeding clients that represented the origins of the Daka name. Compass Group USA Inc., a subsidiary of London, England-based Compass Group PLC, paid $195 million in cash and assumed the debt of the former Daka, Inc. The divestiture left Baumhauer in charge of the commercial restaurant businesses, comprising Fuddruckers, Champps Americana, and Great American Bagel and Coffee Co.—250 commercial units in all, with annual sales eclipsing $325 million. The second step of the plan involved spinning off the commercial holdings formerly owned by Daka International to shareholders and creating a new corporate entity, a company named Unique Casual Restaurants, Inc.

The two-step transaction was completed in July 1997, with Baumhauer assuming control of Unique Casual as chairman and chief executive officer. Thanks to the spin-off and the divestiture of the contract feeding operations, the new company began its corporate life virtually debt-free and better able to focus on solving some of the problems that had surfaced in 1996 and led to crippling losses. Chief among these problems was the ailing Fuddruckers chain, whose low profitability had precipitated the need to restructure and start anew. Many of the newer Fuddruckers units—those opened during the 1993 to 1996 period—had performed poorly, while the older units had suffered from declining sales. In response, Baumhauer announced plans in July 1997 to close between ten and 12 underperforming Fuddruckers, to halt expansion of company-owned Fuddruckers in 1998, and to invigorate sales at the older Fuddruckers units. To increase sales, the company began experimenting with several product introductions such as $8 to $9 steak and grilled chicken breast platters to increase the average bill recorded during dinner hours. Concurrently, the company turned its attention to its other major chain, the Champps Americana restaurants. While operating under the auspices of Daka International, Champps Americana had suffered from a lack of sufficient capital, unable to expand amid the financial crisis that existed from the first day of its acquisition. Baumhauer, with Unique Casual's nearly debt-free balance sheet to work from, was able to expand the chain for the first time and build upon the 12-restaurant base in existence in mid-1997. As part of his plans for the future success of his three commercial holdings, Baumhauer projected the establishment of five or six Champps Americana restaurants by the end of 1998.

Nine months after focus was centered on the progress of Fuddruckers, Champps Americana, and the specialty concepts division's contender, Great Bagel and Coffee Co., there were small yet encouraging signs of improvement. By mid-1998 same-store sales had increased at Fuddruckers, four new Champps Americana restaurants had opened, with three more units slated for openings by the end of 1998, and the company-owned portfolio of Great Bagel and Coffee Co. units had been increased by the acquisition of eight restaurants from a Phoenix franchisee. Financially, the company was on the mend, but there was still much to be done. The first nine months of Unique Casual's existence resulted in a net loss of $374,000, but the total represented a significant increase from the $8.55 million loss reported for the nine-month period of the previous year. Perhaps because an immediate turnaround had not been effected, the company again turned to divestitures for help in improving its financial health. Before the end of 1998 the company sold its 204-unit Fuddruckers chain, stripping itself of more than 60 percent of its revenue. Another portion of the company's financial might was removed in late 1998 when the Great Bagel and Coffee Co. chain was closed, leaving Unique Casual as a single-concept restaurant company dependent on its roughly 30 Champps Americana chain. As the company prepared for the future, having undergone a complete transformation from the Daka International of the early 1990s, all attention was focused on the success and expansion of the Champps Americana chain. Entering 1999, Unique Casual anticipated opening at least six new restaurants in the coming year.

Principal Subsidiaries

Champps Americana; Restaurant Consulting Service, Inc. (50%).

Further Reading

Allen, Robin Lee, "Unique Begins To Fine-Tune Concepts; Daka Creation Has Debt-Free Focus on Restaurant Biz," *Nation's Restaurant News,* July 28, 1997, p. 3.
——, "William H. Baumhauer: Known for His Financial Savvy and Cunning Strategizing, Daka's Chairman Always Plays To Win," *Nation's Restaurant News,* October 14, 1996, p. 152.
——, "Cost-Cutting Measures Cited To Boost at Daka," *Nation's Restaurant News,* September 14, 1992, p. 14.
Carlino, Bill, "Daka Buys Stake in La Salsa Chain; Plans To Pair Quick-Service Taqueria Concept with Fuddruckers Brand," *Nation's Restaurant News,* February 5, 1996, p. 1.
——, "Daka's Overhaul Rewarded with 21% Jump in Earnings," *Nation's Restaurant News,* October 11, 1993, p. 14.
——, "Fuddruckers and Earnings Problems Block Fast Track for Daka," *Nation's Restaurant News,* September 23, 1996, p. 11.
Coeyman, Marjorie, "Going Gringo," *Restaurant Business,* June 10, 1996, p. 44.
"Daka International Buys 50% Interest in 11-Unit Champps," *Nation's Restaurant News,* May 2, 1994, p. 2.
"Daka To Sell Hotels to Vince," *Nation's Restaurant News,* September 23, 1991, p. 2.
Keegan, Peter O., "Terry Vince," *Nation's Restaurant News,* May 21, 1990, p. 92.
King, Paul, " 'Unique' Deal: Compass Buys Daka International," *Nation's Restaurant News,* June 9, 1997, p. 1.
"Kmart Cooks Up Plan To Turn Around Restaurants," *Discount Store News,* August 5, 1996, p. 1.
Labate, John, "Daka International," *Fortune,* November 14, 1994, p. 258.
Postman, Lore, "Compass Group USA of Charlotte, N.C. Buys Daka's Food Service Unit," *Knight-Ridder/Tribune Business News,* May 29, 1997, p. 52.

—Jeffrey L. Covell

Utah Power and Light Company

700 N.E. Multnomah Street
Suite 1600
Portland, Oregon 97232-4116
U.S.A.
(503) 731-2000
(888) 221-7070
Fax: (503) 731-2136

Wholly Owned Division of PacifiCorp
Incorporated: 1912
Employees: 10,087 (PacifiCorp)
Sales: $3.7 billion (PacifiCorp 1997 U.S. sales)
SICs: 4911 Electric Services

Utah Power and Light Company (UP&L) is the major provider of electrical power in Utah and the Intermountain West. Since its creation in 1912, it has acquired more than 100 small power producers and supplied power for the area's homes, companies, and cities. UP&L has encouraged the use of electrical consumption by promoting appliances and the benefits of modern electrified life. It has endured many challenges from the Great Depression to the energy crisis of the 1970s, when it began emphasizing energy conservation and finding new sources of energy. In 1989 UP&L became a subsidiary of Portland-based PacifiCorp, which operates in seven states: Oregon, Utah, Washington, Montana, Idaho, California, and Wyoming. In late 1998 Scotland-based ScottishPower began the acquisition of PacifiCorp, but government approval was pending. Heavily regulated historically by state laws and policies, UP&L and most electric utility firms face a major change from probable energy deregulation and increased competition as the century ends.

Preliminary Power Developments in Utah

Strange as it may seem, Utah played a key role in the history of electrical power. While Utah was still a federal territory, in 1880 the Salt Lake Power, Light, and Heating Company was formed. Following London, New York, San Francisco, and Cleveland, in 1881 Salt Lake City became the world's fifth city to electrify with a central station source of electricity. Dr. John

McCormick in his history of UP&L described this dramatic moment: "At 8 p.m. the lights came on. Even a blind man would have known it because a loud shout went up from the assembled spectators, and those who had remained inside until the last moment rushed out into the already crowded streets. At first there was only a faint, pale glow, but it gradually grew brighter and brighter until each lamp 'glowed like a sun, being fully as dazzling to the eye and lighting up every nook and corner within their reach with the brightness of noonday'."

One of the first main uses of electricity was to run streetcars. The Salt Lake City Street Railway Company in 1872 had started the city's first streetcars pulled by horses and mules. In 1889 electricity replaced the animals in Salt Lake City's trolleys, allowing some families to live further from downtown. Ogden, Provo, and Logan, Utah also had electric streetcars.

Electric streetcars within cities led to electric trains between cities. Five such interurban trains were built in Utah, starting in 1891 with the Bamberger line between Salt Lake City and Ogden, originally a steam-powered line. Other interurban electric lines were built across the nation, reaching a peak of 15,580 miles in 1916.

Although people marveled at the changes from the electrical revolution, for a generation rival power companies wasted resources fighting each other. For example, different firms erected their own power lines, resulting in a maze of electric, telephone, and trolley lines in Salt Lake City. Plants remained small and inefficient, and rural consumers seldom received power. McCormick called it a "nightmare."

Well into the 20th century, consumers could get electricity only part-time. When the moon was bright, the lights went out in Salt Lake City. Plus, power was unreliable because of frequent equipment failure and vandalism. At the turn of the century, only about 20 Utah communities in nine of the state's 27 counties had electricity.

Early 20th-Century Incorporation

On September 6, 1912, Utah Power & Light Company was incorporated in Maine as a subsidiary of Electric Bond and Share Corporation (EBASCO). General Electric (GE) had started EBASCO in 1905 as a New York City holding company to consolidate small power companies in Utah, Idaho, and Colorado into stable entities that could purchase GE-manufactured equipment. EBASCO's 200-plus operating companies in 30 states supplied 14 percent of the nation's power in the mid-1920s.

Such consolidation was a major trend in the electrical industry in the early 20th century. By 1929, 16 holding companies provided more than 80 percent of the nation's electricity. Smaller firms simply did not have the capital and could not attract enough investors for the increasingly complex technology and huge service areas that needed access to electricity.

UP&L on November 22, 1912 acquired Telluride Power Company with its five power plants that served southeastern Idaho, western Colorado, and northern Utah. Telluride had started and UP&L finished a major hydroelectric and irrigation project on Bear Lake that McCormick said was "one of the first multipurpose reclamation developments in the nation." On February 7, 1913 Utah Power purchased another major firm, Knight Consolidated Power, started by Provo's Jesse Knight to provide electricity to his mines mainly in the Tintic Mining District south of Provo. Two months later, in April 1913, UP&L purchased Idaho Power and Transportation Company, Ltd. with its three plants serving customers in southeastern Idaho. And then in 1915 Utah Power made its fourth major early acquisition, that of Utah Light and Traction, which operated five power plants for Salt Lake City customers.

Utah Power eventually acquired some 130 companies. In addition to the four major acquisitions, it purchased shortly after its founding the Park City Light, Heat, and Power Company; Preston, Idaho's Idaho-Utah Electric Company; Shelley, Idaho's Gem State Light and Power Company; Provo's The Electric Company; the Camp Floyd Electric Company in Mercur, Utah; and several other small firms in Utah and Idaho. By 1922 UP&L operated 40 generating plants and had nearly doubled its miles of power lines to integrate its system. About half of its total capacity came from its Bear River hydroelectric plants.

The company also emphasized stimulating demand for power in its early years. Its Sales Department told consumers electricity was necessary for modern life, not just a luxury for the rich. It advertised the benefits of electric fans, blankets, irons, and toasters produced initially after the turn of the century. Since few dealers were available, the company sold and serviced electric stoves and refrigerators. To appeal to the new generation, it placed appliances such as stoves in public schools for cooking classes. Utah Power demonstrated the new labor-saving devices in schools and churches and even on sidewalks. In 1917 UP&L produced two movies promoting the advantages of electricity, not only for lighting, but for electric sewing machines, vacuum cleaners, and other new equipment.

Meanwhile, most industries, from mines to cement factories, had been electrified by 1922. That included agriculture, which increasingly used electric pumps for irrigation. UP&L pushed city lights to prevent crime.

World War I stressed the company due to labor and material shortages. Women helped make up for the men who left for the military after the Congress declared war in 1917.

The Twenties and the Great Depression

Utah Power enjoyed prosperity in the Roaring Twenties, when many American corporations increased their production and stock prices rose for many years. UP&L built three new plants in the 1920s, including its first steam plant, which marked the start of the declining role for hydroelectricity. It acquired 17 small power firms in Utah, Idaho, and Wyoming between 1922 and 1929.

The only negative aspect of that era, from the power company's perspective, was the increasing use of cars and trucks, which slowly replaced the electric trolley cars and interurban trains. According to McCormick, trolley use in Utah peaked in 1914 when only 6,216 cars were registered in the state. By 1929 Utah residents registered 112,000 cars, and the number of trolley passengers had declined rapidly. The power company tried a hybrid vehicle. In 1928 it pioneered the use of a rubber-tired trolley bus powered by overhead electrical lines. To gain further flexibility, internal combustion engines replaced the electrical lines, resulting in the modern bus that could go anywhere.

In 1929 the Great Depression began, and Utah Power suffered along with the rest of the nation. Utah's unemployment rate in 1932 reached 35.8 percent, the fourth highest in the United States. UP&L's customers, revenues, and kilowatt hours all began to decline in 1929. Plus, the company from 1932 to 1940 doubled its taxes to all levels of government and was forced in the 1930s to reduce its power rates by Utah's Public Service Commission. In 1935 Utah Power admitted that "it had been fighting for its very existence" for the previous five years. Provo and also Delta, Colorado rejected UP&L during the Depression in favor of their own municipal power agencies; the power company succeeded in defeating similar proposals in Salt Lake City, Ogden, and Montrose, Colorado.

UP&L survived the depression by drastically cutting its work force and the wages of its remaining workers. The company also eliminated salaries for board members, reduced dividends, and ended its free services on electrical appliances.

Increasing Demand from World War II

The Great Depression finally ended as the United States prepared to fight World War II. UP&L geared up to meet the electrical needs of the state's new military bases and defense-related companies. In the company's history book, UP&L's former President E.M. Naughton said, "The nineteen-forties were a busy time for the people of Utah Power & Light. In many ways it was like a three-ring circus."

New military installations needing power included Fort Douglas, Camp Kearns, Wendover Air Force Base, Ogden Arsenal, Hill Field's General Depot, Clearfield Naval Supply Depot, Tooele Army Depot, Dugway Proving Ground, and the Deseret Chemical Depot. The federal government built the huge Geneva Steel plant in Utah County, which was sold after World War II to U.S. Steel. Other defense plants that helped increase power demands included Salt Lake City's Remington Small Arms Plant with peak employment of 10,000, the Eitel McCullough Radio Tube Plant, and the Standard Parachute Company in Manti.

Such plants had to work around the clock, so Utah Power had to scramble to keep its systems working. That proved rather difficult because of war shortages of copper, steel, and rubber. The company sometimes was forced to use substitutes, for example, iron for copper. Meter readers used bicycles instead of cars. Overtime was common for Utah Power workers, not surprising in light of the 27 percent increase in output between 1940 and 1943.

Postwar Developments as an Independent Firm

As required by the 1935 Public Utility Holding Company Act, Utah Power on January 1, 1946 changed from an EBASCO subsidiary to an independent company with a new board of local directors. They led a company that for the next 20 years or so kept prices low and enjoyed steady expansion and prosperity. By 1967 its customers numbered 275,000, about double from the 140,000 in 1945.

Using mainly new coal-fired plants, Utah Power had doubled its 1945 output by 1954 and then again doubled that capacity by 1963, when it could produce 1,064,275 kilowatts. The company spent $313 million from the end of the war to 1967 on new construction. For example, it spent $6 million to build at the mouth of Provo Canyon the second unit of the Hale Plant, with generating capacity of 44,000 kilowatts. Coal for the Hale Plant and other facilities came mostly from Utah's Carbon County, a major coal source since the late 1800s.

After not advertising during World War II, Utah Power renewed that effort in the postwar years. It promoted "Better Living Electrically" by emphasizing the benefits of television in the late 1940s and the 1950s, air conditioning starting in the late 1950s, and the all-electric home in the 1960s. The company in 1953 started a national advertising program to attract new businesses to Utah, citing the area's abundant natural resources, open spaces, good transportation, and numerous recreation opportunities.

The 1960s brought some major changes to Utah Power. The firm began using mainframe computers in 1961 to automate its accounting. Half of the firm's 31 hydroelectric plants by 1964 were unattended because of computerization. Centralized computers in 1966 controlled the company's electrical production and transmission to gain the best balance of fuel prices and efficiency, system security, and power purchases from outside companies. In addition, a microwave radio system improved communication between power plants, substations, and company headquarters.

In 1958 Utah Power began participating in the development of atomic energy. Along with 51 other utilities, it formed High Temperature Reactor Development Associates, Inc. (HTRDA) to fund research and development of a new plant. HTRDA, General Atomic, Bechtel Corporation, and the Philadelphia Electric Company built and operated the nation's first gas-cooled nuclear plant built by private enterprise. Nuclear energy did not, however, fulfill the high hopes of UP&L President G.M. Gadsby, who in the firm's corporate history said, "With the availability of a great new energy source—atomic power . . . the millennium of physical comfort is almost at hand."

The Difficult 1970s and 1980s

Starting around 1970, UP&L faced some major challenges fueled by rapid population growth. Its customer base expanded from 282,000 in 1968 to almost 500,000 in 1984. To meet the demand, Utah Power built some huge and very expensive plants: the third Naughton Plant unit near Kemmerer, Wyoming and five 400,000-kilowatt units at the Huntington and Hunter plants in Emery County, Utah. To save money on these and other coal-fired plants, Utah Power in the early 1970s began purchasing its own coal mines with several hundred million tons of reserves. By the early 1980s only about five percent of its power came from hydroelectric dams, compared with 90 percent in 1946.

This expansion cost consumers a pretty penny. Starting in 1971, the Utah Public Service Commission allowed UP&L to raise its rates every year due to increasing inflation. For example, between 1975 and 1980 the cost of coal increased 150 percent. Its new plants cost the firm $1,000 per kilowatt, far more than the $129 per kilowatt to build the oldest of the 13 steam-generating plants it owned in 1980.

Not surprisingly, many complained about rising power rates. That kept Utah Power's public relations staff busy trying to explain why the increases were necessary. For example, the company told how increasing environmental regulations impacted power rates. Utah Power also started programs to help those struggling to pay their utility bill. It started in 1983 the Project Share program that was administered by the Red Cross to help the needy. And it began working with social workers to help families contact state and local government agencies that provided help not only for electrical bills, but also for medical care and other assistance.

After the Arab oil embargo in 1973, Utah Power implemented an energy conservation policy that was just the opposite of what was done in the early 20th century. It published booklets and gave demonstrations on how to save energy. It worked with architects and contractors to help them design and build more energy-efficient structures. Houses became more air-tight and thus saved energy, but that also resulted in increased indoor air pollution as an unintended side effect.

Like other energy companies around the world, Utah Power in the 1970s began exploring alternative energy sources, including solar power and the possibility of using garbage to create energy. It built one of the nation's first geothermal plants in 1984. Located at the Roosevelt Hot Springs near Milford, Utah, this geothermal plant had a capacity of 20,000 kilowatts. The company in 1984 also formed a wholly owned subsidiary called Energy National, Inc. to explore alternative energy sources.

In 1975 Utah Power sold its subsidiary Western Colorado Power Company for $20.7 million to a group of four rural cooperatives called the Western Colorado Power Agency. The sale had little impact on UP&L, however, because the subsidiary accounted for only two percent of its income.

Aquisition, Deregulation, and Diversification: Late 1980s–90s

In 1987 UP&L and PacifiCorp announced they had agreed to merge in a $1.85 billion stock swap. Utah Power had considered merging with other utilities, including Public Service Company of New Mexico. Headquartered in Portland, PacifiCorp originated in 1910, about the same time as UP&L. The agreement allowed Utah Power to retain its name and Salt Lake City offices, but it would operate as a PacifiCorp subsidiary. Verl Topham, UP&L's president/CEO, became a board member of PacifiCorp.

This deal was not finalized until 1989 because of regulatory requirements. The Federal Energy Regulatory Commission required PacifiCorp to open its power lines to independent producers under certain situations. In spite of criticism from other power companies, PacifiCorp agreed in order to gain the advantages of merging with UP&L. PacifiCorp gained access through UP&L lines to distribute its power to California and the Southwest. PacifiCorp, whose demand peaked in winter, and UP&L, with peak demands in the summer, both benefited from the merger. In 1989 PacifiCorp received 37.2 percent of its electricity revenues from Utah customers and 29.6 percent from Oregon.

In December 1995 Utah Power announced it would close 13 customer service offices in Utah and five in Idaho to cut costs and expand modern payment options. Company representatives said that 85 percent of the firm's customers already used the mail system or phones to make payments and that UP&L would expand the use of electronic transfers and 24-hour telephone services.

In 1996 California started a new trend by passing legislation deregulating the energy industry. According to the power industry in December 1998, 12 states had passed laws allowing what it called retail choice in power. Utah was not on the list, but its lawmakers had looked into energy deregulation. Utah Power supported deregulation, since power from any producer would be transmitted over its lines. At the end of the century, it was a major issue faced by Utah Power and its parent company PacifiCorp.

To prepare for deregulation, PacifiCorp and Utah Power in 1997 diversified their services and products, with advice from the law firm Stoel Rives LLP. Offered to all PacifiCorp customers in its seven-state market, this new "Simple Choice" program included new payment options, extended appliance warranties, surge suppressors, DISH Network Satellite TV, carbon monoxide detectors, and payment protection in case of customers' death, disability, or unemployment. Other new items included cell phones, paging, wireless modems, Internet services, home security services, a parts hotline, and on-call repair assistance for the do-it-yourself consumer.

In 1998 Utah Power began building 12 substations to power the Utah Transit Authority's light rail system from downtown Salt Lake City to the suburb of Sandy. Thus the company came full circle by again supplying power to electric trains that were so crucial in its early history around the turn of the century.

In December 1998 company representatives announced that Scotland-based ScottishPower plc had agreed to purchase PacifiCorp, pending approval by the Securities and Exchange Commission, the Nuclear Regulatory Commission, the Federal Energy Regulatory Commission, and state regulatory bodies. If accepted, the deal was reported to be the first time a foreign company purchased an entire American electric firm. Utah Power spokesmen stated, however, that the firm's 580,000 Utah customers would not see many changes and that UP&L would continue as a PacifiCorp subsidiary.

Further Reading

Lewis, Scott M., "PacifiCorp," in *International Directory of Company Histories,* Detroit: St. James Press, 1992, pp. 688–90.

McCormick, John S., *The Power to Make Good Things Happen: Past, Present, Future: The History of Utah Power and Light Company,* Salt Lake City: UP&L, 1990.

Oberbeck, Steven, "Sale of PacifiCorp Is Far from a Done Deal," *Salt Lake Tribune,* December 8, 1998, pp. B10, B14.

"Pacificorp Receives Utah Rate Reduction Order," *PR Newswire,* March 5, 1999.

"Revolution in the Power Industry," *Forbes* (special advertising section), December 14, 1998.

Thomson, Linda, "Deregulation Is a Highly Charged Issue," *Deseret News* (Web Edition), May 29, 1997.

——, "Utah Power Gives Push to 'Simple Choice,' " *Deseret News* (Web Edition), May 30, 1997.

—David M. Walden

Vendôme Luxury Group plc

27 Nightsbridge
London SW1X 7WB
England
(44) 171 838 8500
Fax: (44) 171 838 8555
Web site: http://www.richemont.ch/Vendôme

Wholly Owned Subsidiary of Compagnie Financière Richemont
Incorporated: 1993
Employees: 8,000
Sales: SFr 3.43 billion (US $2.38 billion) (1997)
SICs: 6719 Holding Companies, Not Elsewhere Classified

Vendôme Luxury Group plc is nearly synonymous with luxury. Since its formation in 1993, the Vendôme Luxury Group has operated one of the world's most distinguished collections of luxury goods businesses, include its chief revenue generator Cartier, and names including Mont Blanc, Lancel, Baume & Mercier, Vacheron Constantin, Chloé, Piaget, and Alfred Dunhill. The 13 member companies of the Vendôme group combined to create more than SFr 3.4 billion in sales in 1997. These sales are generated through the company's several store brands, including the famed Cartier house and the company's latest venture, the Art of Leather store concept, launched in Singapore in 1998 and offering leather products from many of the group's labels. Vendôme operates nearly 600 company-owned stores in some 140 countries; an additional 10,000 locations are authorized to sell group products.

From its incorporation, Vendôme's chief shareholder has been the Compagnie Financière Richemont, the Switzerland-based holding set up by South Africa's Rupert family to group its tobacco, luxury products, and other interests. Already holding 70 percent of Vendôme, in December 1997 Richemont bought up the remaining 30 percent of the luxury groups, consolidating Vendôme under Richemont's operations. When, in January 1999, Richemont announced its intention to sell its tobacco operations, which included worldwide brand Rothmans

and others, to rival British American Tobacco (BAT), creating the world's fourth largest tobacco company, Vendôme took on a central role in the Richemont holding, which also includes media and other interests in the United States and Europe.

After a difficult decade in the 1990s and despite the economic collapse in many of Vendôme's important Asian markets, Vendôme has shown irresistible appeal to the world's wealthy, with sales marking new growth in 1998. Vendôme continues to be led by Joseph Kanoui, the French banker who has long been the chief architect of the Rupert family luxury goods holdings. Kanoui's wife, Micheline, has achieved international fame in her own right as Cartier's lead jewelry designer.

Family Beginnings in the 1940s

When Vendôme was formed in October 1993, the luxury goods group already boasted nearly two centuries of history. The Vendôme Luxury Goods Group was created in that year after the Rupert family of South Africa broke up its holdings into two separate entities, both grouped under the family's Switzerland-based Compagnie Financière Richemont. Tobacco holdings were placed under the Rothmans name, and the family's luxury goods holdings, especially its Alfred Dunhill and Cartier firms, were placed under the Vendôme banner. Richemont sold 30 percent of the new, London-based Vendôme group to the public, retaining 70 percent. Vendôme nonetheless would operate independently for more than five years, before being brought back fully under Richemont's—and the Rupert family's—control.

The Rupert family of South Africa was an unlikely candidate to become one of the world's foremost luxury goods manufacturers. The family empire was started in 1941 by Anton Rupert, who then operated a dry cleaning business. In the late 1940s, however, Rupert decided to enter the tobacco industry, taking out a loan to launch his own tobacco company. The company's first cigarette brand was named Rembrandt, and it became popular among South African smokers. By the 1950s Rupert found himself at the head of one of the continent's leading tobacco firms.

Rupert soon entered the world tobacco market. In 1955 he expanded his business beyond the African continent by buying up the popular European brand Rothmans. Soon after, the company acquired the Peter Stuyvesant brand name as well. By the 1970s, Rupert, who would shortly be joined by son Johann Rupert, had built up one of the top five tobacco companies in the world. Rupert also had begun an interest into other activities, building up a wide-ranging holdings portfolio. Among these holdings was a growing interest in luxury products, including control of the Alfred Dunhill brand of smoking and other accessories and the world-renowned Cartier name. The Chloé label, founded in the 1950s, joined the group's holdings in the early 1980s.

Cartier would take the first steps to joining the growing Rupert empire in the mid-1970s when a group of investors, lead by Joseph Kanoui, bought up the flagging New York branch of the famed jeweler. Three years later, in 1979, the rest of the Cartier operations was acquired. At the same time, Johann Rupert was adding to the family's empire. After pursuing a merchant banking career in the 1970s, with stints at Chase Manhattan Bank and Lazard Frères in New York, the younger Rupert returned to South Africa to found the Rand Merchant Bank. As Anton Rupert looked toward retirement, Johann Rupert took an active role in the family's Rembrandt company, which had grown to become a vast holding vehicle for both tobacco and luxury goods assets. In 1988 the younger Rupert organized a company breakup, splitting the family's holdings into two companies, the Switzerland-based Richemont, which grouped the family's Rothmans and Dunhill tobacco operations, and the South African-based Rembrandt, which controlled the family's other holdings.

By the time Johann Rupert took over the family's business in 1993, the Rembrandt-Rothman group had taken control of more than 85 percent of South Africa's tobacco industry and had taken the number four position among world-leading tobacco companies, behind Philip Morris, British American Tobacco, and RJR Nabisco. The continuing strong tobacco sales and profits would provide fuel for Rupert's further expansion of the family empire, as he transformed Vendôme from a holding organization for the family's luxury goods businesses to one of the world's leading collections of exclusive luxury goods brands.

By the late 1990s the Vendôme name seemed synonymous with luxury. Strong growth, despite a sustained European economic recession, had enabled the company to top SFr 1.7 billion in annual sales. The booming economies of the Asian region were chiefly responsible for the company's continued profits, as some of the Vendôme stable found as much as 60 percent or more of sales in that part of the world. The collapse of the Asian economic miracle in 1997 would seem to end Vendôme's own growth. If nothing else, Vendôme's share price was battered by an increasingly nervous market, dropping by more than 40 percent in 1997.

Buoyed by Richemont's strong tobacco performance, Johann Rupert launched a bid to regain control of the remaining 30 percent of the Vendôme empire. Reasoning that the group's luxury brands were not well understood by the stock market, Rupert would pay approximately US $2 billion to bring Vendôme fully under Richemont control. Full control of Vendôme seemed to have inspired the Ruperts to begin a transformation away from tobacco. In January 1999 Richemont announced its agreement to merge its Rothmans tobacco group with British American Tobacco, creating the world's third largest tobacco company. The Rupert family had not fully divested of the product that had helped found their empire, however; the Rothmans sale gave the Richemont holding company a 35 percent stake in BAT.

Grouping Luxury in the 1990s

By the start of the 1990s, with the family's luxury goods holdings pressured by the poor worldwide economic climate and the family's tobacco holdings under pressure from a growing antitobacco sentiment, the family's holdings were once again reorganized, creating publicly held Vendôme Luxury Goods PLC, with Richemont holding 70 percent of the new company's shares, and the Rothmans International group, directly controlled by Richemont and including the Rupert family's vast tobacco interests.

Foremost among the new Vendôme company's subsidiaries were its Cartier and Alfred Dunhill operations. Both enjoyed long-held reputations among the world's most exclusive brand names. Cartier was founded by apprentice jeweler Louis François Cartier, who purchased the jewelry shop of his Parisian mentor in 1847. Cartier's simplified lines contrasted with the era's more flamboyant designs, bringing the young Cartier to the attention of the Parisian nobility. A series of private commissions, notably from Princess Mathilde, cousin to Napoleon, who would become an early Cartier patron, helped establish Cartier as a leading name in Parisian jewelry design. Cartier's son Louis François Alfred would help solidify the Cartier reputation, but it was Alfred's three sons who took Cartier worldwide. Louis-Joseph Cartier took the lead of the original Paris branch, Jacques-Théodule Cartier brought the company to London, and Pierre-Camille Cartier opened Cartier's New York branch. Among the company's successes would be Cartier New York's sale of the Hope diamond, the launch of the famed Panther icon, and the introduction of the invisible setting.

If the Cartier name had maintained its luster through the first half of the 20th century, the deaths of the third generation of Cartiers would bring on a slow decline of the company's fortunes. In the 1970s the Cartier house was taken over by Robert Hocq and Joseph Kanoui, who, with managing director Alain Dominique Perrin, would revitalize the Cartier name and extend its products to include a vast array of accessories, ranging from handbags to pens, lighters, and perfumes. At the end of the 1970s Cartier was bought up by the Rupert family, joining another family holding, Alfred Dunhill.

Alfred Dunhill already had undergone a similar expansion from its original leather goods focus to include a broad range of exclusive products, including watches, cigarette lighters, pipes, and other smoking accessories, as well as its own line of men's clothing. Beginning with his family's harness-making business in 1893, Alfred Dunhill began producing related products such as saddles and clothing suitable for equestrian sports. A commitment to high quality would serve Dunhill in his next venture, that of the introduction in 1896 of a range of motorist clothing and accessories, becoming one of the first to cater to the newly emerging automotive market. The success of Dunhill Motorities, as the line was called, extended to products such as watches, goggles, headlamps, horns, and luggage. The company's move into pipe tobaccos and smoking accessories followed at the turn of the century, including the introduction of the famed Unique lighter, which would remain a company hallmark through the end of the century. Dunhill would capitalize on its brand name, expanding throughout Europe and opening a string of retail shops around the world, moving into North America and Hong Kong in the 1950s, and extending to Australia and Japan in the 1960s. After introducing its men's clothing line in the 1970s, Dunhill joined the growing Rupert empire, which also included famed fountain pen maker Mont Blanc.

The launch of the Vendôme group brought together not only Cartier and Alfred Dunhill, but noted Paris designer group Chloé—which would receive worldwide attention when it appointed Stella McCartney, daughter of Paul McCartney, as its lead designer—and other world renowned names, including Piaget and Karl Lagerfeld. In the 1990s Vendôme continued to expand its holdings, acquiring famed fountain pen maker Mont Blanc and Geneva-based watchmakers Baume & Mercier and Vacheron Constantin, which, together with Piaget, produced much of the world's most exclusive timepieces. Italian watchmaker Panerai joined the Vendôme group in the late 1990s, bringing that company's exclusive watches—previously limited to the Italian navy—to the general public for the first time.

Watches took on even greater importance to Vendôme's sales in the 1990s. After acquiring famed watchmaker Baume & Mercier, Vendôme reached an agreement with Sheik Ahmed Zaki Yamani to buy the former Saudi Arabian Oil Minister's stake in another Geneva-based watchmaker, Vacheron Constantin. For a purchase price estimated as high as SFr 110 million, Vendôme added one of the world's most exclusive ranges of watches. With prices of Vacheron Constantin watches beginning at US $6,000 and reaching US $3 million and beyond, the Vacheron Constantin name added yet more luster to the Vendôme roster of exclusive worldwide brands.

In 1997 Vendôme added the Lancel brand name and that company's exclusive line of handbags and other leather goods and accessories. The purchase, for SFr 342 million, brought in Lancel's 85 boutiques. Primarily located in France, the Lancel stores included the company's landmark Place d'Opera boutique, which had opened in 1929. Under the purchase agreement, Vendôme acquired 90 percent of Lancel, with an option on the remaining shares over a five-year period. The addition of Lancel boosted the leather goods category to the second place of Vendôme's top revenue generators.

The Lancel brand brought a younger image appeal to complement Vendôme's existing lineup of leather goods brands. Lancel expanded a product category already represented by the Seeger label, one of the world's most exclusive producers of suitcases, briefcases, purses, and other travel, business, and handbags. In the 1990s Seeger, too, launched itself into the retail arena, opening its first boutiques in Hong Kong, Singapore, and Frankfurt, Germany in 1995. Over the next three years the Seeger chain would expand to include locations in Bangkok, Berlin, Costa Mesa, Jakarta, Kuala Lumpur, Madrid, New York, Osaka, San Francisco, and Sydney.

The appointment of Stella McCartney as Chloé's lead designer in 1997 received international attention; widely considered at the outset as an excellent publicity stunt, the move would take on more legitimacy with the highly successful reception of McCartney's first collections. Whereas Chloé represented the luxury ready-to-wear category, Vendôme's other garment interests reached into separate niches. For one, the company continued to work on rebuilding the Sulka name. Acquired by Richemont in 1989, Sulka had enjoyed a period of unrivaled popularity among the world's elite during the first half of the 20th century. But the famed Sulka men's suit faded into near-oblivion in the second half of the century after the death of the company's founders, surviving more as an exhibit in the Metropolitan Museum of Art than as a retail item. In the 1990s, however, Richemont and, later, Vendôme would work to revive the Sulka name, targeting once again an exclusive clientele. The company launched a new Sulka shop concept in Chicago and Beverly Hills, which, in addition to the complete line of Sulka products (the company aims to dress the "Sulka Man" completely) also offered laundry and dry cleaning services for Sulka products. The successful launch of the new concept was to be extended to Sulka's New York and London branches; expansion to ten boutiques worldwide was expected to be achieved by the end of the first decade of the 21st century.

Vendôme would take on even greater importance for the Rupert family as the 20th century drew to an end. After selling off its control of its tobacco interests to BAT, Richemont would become even more focused on its luxury goods holdings. The move seemed well-timed: the tobacco industry could only look forward to increasingly embattled positions, while the luxury goods market, after years of pressure from a slow worldwide economy, appeared to have once again returned to a growth cycle. Vendôme's collection of exclusive names promised to keep the company at the top of the luxury industry.

Principal Divisions

Cartier; Alfred Dunhill; Lancel; Mont Blanc; Piaget; Vacheron Constantin; Hackett; Chloé; Sulka; Panerai; Purdy.

Further Reading

Cope, Nigel, "Luxury Goods Dynasty with Humble Origins," *Independent,* January 12, 1999, p. 13.
——, "Vendome Ahead in Jewelry Boom," *Independent,* November 27, 1997, p. 27.
Helgadottir, Birna, "Fashion Victim," *The European,* December 4, 1997, p. 26.
Kroll, Luisa, "Smoke This," *Forbes,* July 6, 1998, p. 272.
Okun, Stacey, "The Legend and the Legacy: The House of Cartier Celebrates 150 Years of History and Romance," *Town & Country Monthly,* March 1, 1997, p. 122.
Pratley, Nils, "Vendome Gives Go-Ahead to Pounds 1bn Purchase," *Daily Telegraph,* December 23, 1997.
Rawsthorn, Alice, and Victor Mallet, "Taking the Long View," *Financial Times,* January 12, 1999.

—M. L. Cohen

Viasoft Inc.

3033 North 44th Street
Phoenix, Arizona 85018-7296
U.S.A.
(602) 952-0050
(888) VIASOFT (842-7638)
Fax: (602) 840-4068
Web site: http://www.viasoft.com

Public Company
Founded: 1983 as Software Renovation Technology
Employees: 561
Sales: $113.7 million (1998)
Stock Exchanges: NASDAQ
Ticker Symbol: VIAS
SICs: 7371 Computer Programming Services; 7372
   Prepackaged Software; 7379 Computer Related
   Service, Not Elsewhere Classified

Viasoft Inc. is best known as a leading provider of highly-integrated information technology (IT) solutions for businesses. Its product line consists of integrated technology, software products, and related specialized, professional consulting services, which are typically designed to manage and automate the evolution of large-scale existing COBOL applications software systems. For example, the company's line consists of programs to extract and build comprehensive information on programs and applications; systems designed to automate the process of analyzing and understanding complex COBOL logic; systems designed to implement desired program changes without introducing undesirable side effects; programs to isolate and extract specific business functions from a program; tools designed to promote speed and accuracy in code testing and debugging; and systems to synthesize comprehensive program information directly from the source code and organize it. Viasoft's products also assist in the evolution of other information technology (IT) assets, showcasing the technology and services to capture, consolidate, reuse, and evolve critical IT assets. The company also offers professional services designed to help customers address the Year 2000 (Y2K) century date conversion requirements for existing applications and technical support and maintenance for products.

The Early Years

The company which eventually became Viasoft was founded in 1983 in Sunnyvale, California, as Software Renovation Technology. In January 1985, the company moved its corporate headquarters from California's Silicon Valley to Phoenix, Arizona, with the backing of a group of venture capitalists. This move was made under the direction of entrepreneur LeRoy Ellison, who had previously been the founding president of Kapex Corp., which also developed software to aid programmers and was later acquired by Computer Associates International. After the move, Ellison named Kent Petzold—formerly Director of Western Operations for Pansophic—to the position of President and Chief Executive Officer. The company arrived in the Valley of the Sun with a handful of employees and a product that had yet to be introduced into the market.

In 1986, the company changed its name to Viasoft, combining the Latin phrase for ''by way of'' with the word ''soft,'' which was short for ''software.'' During that year, the company released *VIA/Insight*—a program understanding tool—as its first generally available product. The next product that was developed and marketed was *SmartTest* (renamed *VIA/SmartTest*), which was a tool used for testing and debugging. *SmartTest* was followed by *SmartEdit* (renamed *VIA/SmartEdit*), a COBOL-intelligent editor.

Viasoft's business took on a new dimension when the company began to emphasize software solutions rather than individual tools. The first solution introduced was Viasoft's *Insourcing,* which combined the company's *Existing Systems Workbench (ESW)* toolset with services for enhanced systems maintenance. The *ESW* products provided the advanced technology necessary to gain in-depth understanding of computer applications, and to automate time-consuming programming tasks—both of which are vital to the effective management of a company's business. Viasoft's unique core technology unraveled the intricacies of these complex applications, providing a thorough understanding of how the applications work. *ESW* provided integrated functionality to manage every aspect of system maintenance and enhancement, while also providing the technological foundation for a range of company-wide initiatives, including Y2K conversion, portfolio assessment, application re-engineering, maintenance productivity improvement, and a transition to new computer architectures.

In 1988, the company established its Annual International Users Conference, to assist companies in application development and systems engineering. Within a decade, the conference would boast more than 700 attendees, representing some 400 companies from 23 countries.

In December 1989, the company joined forces with PC tools developer Micro Focus Inc. to create COBOL tools, allowing cooperative applications in which processing is shared between PCs and mainframes. The tools conformed to the Common User Access (CUA) rules of IBM's Systems Application Architecture (SAA). Prior to this alliance, Viasoft had been solely a mainframe supplier, and saw the venture with Micro Focus as a chance to build compatible user interfaces between PCs and mainframes. The alliance also produced a new line of complementary COBOL code-editing, testing, and debugging tools from both companies for designing cooperative-processing applications.

An Expanding Focus in The Early 1990s

By 1990, the company was marketing four computer-aided software engineering (CASE) products throughout the world (priced at nearly $40,000 each) and boasted some 150 employees. Sales for the previous fiscal year had topped $12.5 million, and Viasoft had posted profits for two years in a row. The company continued to develop and enhance its *ESW* products and add solutions.

In June of 1990, the company released *VIA/SmartDoc,* an intelligent tool for programmers which automatically generated full documentation for COBOL programs. It was the first documentation tool to understand the internal logic of COBOL programs and how they handle data. It collected information directly from the program source code, then analyzed and organized that information into detailed documentation.

Later that year, in September 1990, the company's board of directors returned Chairman of the Board Ellison to the company's top executive slot, replacing Petzold at Viasoft's helm. That year, Ellison was also named an Entrepreneur of the Year in Arizona. Steven D. Whiteman, formerly senior vice-president of sales and international operations for Systems Center Inc., a developer and marketer of network and systems management software, joined the company as vice-president of sales

and marketing in December 1990. He would go on to become Viasoft's president in May 1993, chief executive officer in January 1994, and chairman in April 1997.

By 1992, a growing number of information systems managers were moving their programming tools from the mainframe to the PC, because developers could no longer afford the delays that went along with building software in a mainframe time-sharing environment. At that time, Viasoft sped up its move away from work in mainframe environments and toward the personal computer market.

That year, the company created a Client Services Division to support its customers' efforts in code renovation and engineering using the company's products. The new division provided consulting partnerships with customer staffs to provide technology transfer, which was designed to speed up customer adoption and success with Viasoft tools. The division also began to offer product training courses.

It was around that same time that the company introduced *Via/Insight-OS/2,* a version of its COBOL analysis package for mainframes that was designed as part of its existing *ESW* tools for rebuilding and maintenance of mainframe COBOL systems. The program, however, was designed to run on *OS/2 Presentation Manager* as part of the company's transition to PCs. The program's introduction was a major step in Viasoft's quest to transform itself into a PC CASE company over the next two years. That same year, the Viasoft also released OS/2 versions of its other development tools: its COBOL re-engineering tool *Via/Renaissance* (a COBOL re-engineering tool that broke applications into smaller, more manageable part); an *OS/2 Presentation Manager* version of the company's mainframe COBOL analysis package (which displayed the code, structure charts, and documentation in different windows, giving developers rapid access to the information they need to make decisions); and *Via/Recap* (designed to measure the quality of complex COBOL programs).

By mid-1992, Viasoft's client list included telecommunications giant Pacific Bell, who used the company's software to isolate, extract, and reuse code from existing COBOL systems in new systems without harming original programs. Viasoft had also formed a partnership with Atlanta-based KnowledgeWare Inc., to provide redevelopment tools to expand IBM's Application Development/Cycle (AD/Cycle) CASE software. This was done to meet the needs of users for software maintenance products, as IBM added Viasoft to its International Alliance for AD/Cycle. AD/Cycle products emphasized designing and building new applications, but customers demanded more CASE tools for enhancing their many aging COBOL applications. So the addition of Viasoft to the alliance was indicative of Big Blue's support for the art of re-engineering existing code, which was the process of analyzing and cleaning up applications code through housekeeping tasks; the elimination of dataname redundancies; making code ready for change; and preparing code to add or move to another hardware platform. IBM and most of its AD/Cycle business partners had previously focused on new application development instead of working with existing applications. KnowledgeWare, already a member of the alliance, developed the Application Development Workbench (ADW)/Maintenance Workstation, an OS/2 front end to

IBM's *Inspector, Pinpoint,* and *Recoder* mainframe redevelopment tools. IBM soon began selling five Viasoft mainframe-based re-engineering products.

Also in 1992, the company enhanced its *ESW* product line with a Common User Access (CUA) interface, Structured Query Language (SQL) database support in all *ESW* components, and an interface to Computer Associates International, Inc.'s CA-IDMS mainframe databases, which provided access to program functions through action bars, pop-up windows, and pull-down menus.

New Problems and New Solutions in the Mid-1990s

In 1993, the "Year 2000 Problem" (Y2K) was brought to the world's attention by Canadian consultant Peter de Jager, who wrote an article called "Doomsday" in the September 1993 issue of *Computerworld.* The problem, involving misinterpretation of "00" in two-digit date fields in computer systems as 1900 instead of 2000, loomed over the entire information technology industry as it moved toward the 21st Century. Analysts and computer experts throughout the world predicted two main scenarios: either computer systems would revert to dates in the year 1900, or they would crash completely. Faced with the realization that most companies and organizations lacked the staff, tools, processes, and systems knowledge to effectively handle this challenge, Viasoft and other similar companies turned their attention toward the growing market of correcting the problem. The move proved to be wise; Viasoft's total revenue for 1993 (prior to Y2K being a significant part of the company's work) had reached $20.6 million, but with a net loss of $3.3 million. The following year, however, total revenues climbed to $26.0 million, and the company achieved a net income of $3.7 million.

By February 1994, the company had more than 700 clients in 24 countries, and net export earnings had reached almost $6 million. By March of that year, the company was a recognized name in the Mexican software market, with a client list that included Bancomer—one of Mexico's largest banking chains. By August, Viasoft had introduced the $45,000 *VIA/Alliance* program as a part of its *ESW* line. Complete with a set of cross-reference supports for creating detailed reports on existing applications, and able to format information into a DB/2 database, *VIA/Alliance* was designed to allow developers to perform impact analysis, inventory source code and job control language so that firms could view the reusable code available to them.

By late 1994, railroad pioneer Union Pacific Railroad Co. had joined the Who's Who list of Viasoft clients. Union Pacific had a history of consistently deploying technology to keep ahead of its competition, and utilized Viasoft's *ESW* product line to enhance its software maintenance operations. Use of Viasoft's products made the job of operating some 750 trains—180,000 freight cars daily—over more than 17,000 miles of track more feasible for the Omaha-based railroad company. In April 1996, the Union Pacific addressed its Y2K compliance problem by again bringing in Viasoft to perform an impact assessment of its old codes.

Having achieved a great deal of success and having landed a number of big-name clients, Viasoft launched a successful ini-

tial public offering (IPO) in March 1995. By mid-year, the company started what is now known as the "Providers" program, which generated wider market penetration.

In 1995, Kevin Schick of Gartner Group, Inc., a highly-respected, publicly-traded computer consulting firm, estimated that fixing the Year 2000 problem (which he called "the biggest single information project the world has ever faced") could cost as much as $600 billion, "a suitably terrifying number that grabbed the world by the throat," as described in the August 1996 issue of *Fortune.* It launched a flurry of articles on the problem. In April 1995, Viasoft released *Enterprise 2000,* a Y2K software and consulting package aimed at helping companies convert legacy systems to handle dates after 1999. The program comprised an impact-analysis component, development of a project plan, and implementation of that plan—all of which were marketed separately, with the first piece being offered for $30,000. Viasoft's total revenue for 1995 rose to $31.0 million, with a net income of $5.2 million.

In October 1996, the company joined forces with IBS Conversions Inc. to expand the platforms available for Viasoft's Y2K solution. Together, they incorporated Chicago-based IBS' Y2K date analysis and scanning services for companies with AS/400 systems into Viasoft's *Enterprise 2000* product, enabling programmers to identify faulty date codes and estimate costs necessary for conversion projects. Later that year, Viasoft also entered a joint agreement with KPMG Peat Marwick LLP to market the latter's year 2000 consulting services with Viasoft's millennium programming software.

The company ended 1996 with the acquisition of R&O Software-Technik GmbH, which added the "*Rochade*" repository to Viasoft's product line. The *Rochade* repository is a specialized IT database that allows an organization to capture, reuse, and evolve information assets. Its architecture, power, and stability also provide a solid environment for the integration of all IT assets in a company, while managing complexity, facilitating communication, and providing a company-wide view of business processes. To do this, *Rochade* leverages the latest information technology, including client/server architecture, Internet and Intranets, object orientation, and graphical user interfaces (GUIs). This enables the reuse of IT information for initiatives such as data warehousing, modernization of systems, tool integration, the Y2K conversion process, and European implementation. Total year-end revenues for fiscal 1996 jumped to $43.6 million, with a net income of $6.2 million.

The End of the Century and Beyond

In 1998, Viasoft assembled the technologies for *OnMark 2000,* its distributed Y2K solution, and unveiled a suite of tools for European implementation. In January of that year, the company acquired EraSoft Technologies, a Calgary, Alberta, Canada-based provider of Y2K assessment and analysis software for desktop environments, for $7.75 million in cash.

In February 1998, The Mutual Life Insurance Company of New York (MONY) selected the company's *ESW* integrated suite of software development tools to complete its Y2K code conversion compliance project. The 155 year-old mutual life insurance company, which sold the nation's first mutual life insurance policy, installed the technology at its Syracuse, New York site, which provides customer-related services to more than a million MONY policyholders and clients throughout the world. Also in February, the company gained Caldor Inc. as one of its Y2K clients. The fourth-largest discount department store chain in the United States, with 157 stores in ten states and annual sales of approximately $2.6 billion, Caldor acquired the technology in order to have its mainframe systems maintained at the highest possible levels in order to expand its business functions and keep its information technology costs low.

In June 1998, the company further bolstered its growing client list by signing a licensing agreement with the fifth-largest chemical company in the world—Dow Chemical Co.—for the use of Viasoft's *ESW2000*. Although the company's stock fluctuated from 1997–98, the Year 2000 Problem continued to plague Global 5000 companies, and Viasoft's Y2K programs offered solutions. Thus, the company could count on steady business growth as the millennium grew near.

As the end of the century approached, Viasoft was serving customers throughout the world, including many "Global 5000" corporations and similarly sized organizations, through a worldwide network of independent distributors. Viasoft had domestic sales offices located in the following U.S. cities: Roswell, Georgia; Chicago, Illinois; Dallas, Texas; Herndon, Virginia; and Westford, Massachusetts. The company also possessed international sales offices located in the following countries: Australia, Belgium, France, Germany, Japan, The Netherlands, and The United Kingdom. Competitors have included Alydaar; BindView Development Corp.; Data Dimensions; McCabe and Associates Inc.; Micro Focus/Burl Software Laboratories; NetSuite; SEEC Inc.; Sterling Software, Inc.; and KnowledgeWare Inc.

Further Reading

Ambrosio, Johanna, "IBM Picks Viasoft as AD/Cycle Member," *Computerworld,* July 13, 1992, p. 8.
Ballou, Melinda-Carol, "Viasoft's VIA/Alliance Helps Decipher Legacy Code," *Computerworld,* August 15, 1994, p. 16.
Burden, Kevin, "Firing Line: Viasoft's VIA/Alliance Provides a Road Map to Legacy COBOL Code, but Requires Its Sister Products to Perform Redevelopment," *Computerworld,* September 26, 1994, p. 115.
"Dow Signs with Viasoft," *PC Week,* June 8, 1998, p. 76.
Evans, David, "Don't Shoot the Messenger," *Computer Weekly,* June 6, 1996, p. 36.
Fehr-Snyder, Kerry, "Earnings Up at Phoenix's Viasoft; Firm Prevents Year-2000 Computer Errors," *Knight-Ridder/Tribune Business News,* April 24, 1996.
——, "Phoenix's Viasoft Sues Fired Executive," *Knight-Ridder/Tribune Business News,* April 11, 1996.
——, "Wall Street Clobbers Phoenix-Based Viasoft," *Knight-Ridder/Tribune Business News,* October 22, 1997.
Jensen, Tom, and Mary Ellen Yates, "LeRoy Ellison: Energetic Entrepreneur Works Tirelessly to Aid Small Business Growth in Arizona," *Business Journal—Serving Phoenix & the Valley of the Sun,* July 2, 1990, p. 12.
"Kent Petzold," *Business Journal—Serving Phoenix & the Valley of the Sun,* September 10, 1990, p. 12B.
"KPMG, Viasoft in Pact," *Computerworld,* December 2, 1996, p. 81.
Luebke, Cathy, "Viasoft Inc. Continues Record Growth," *Business Journal—Serving Phoenix & the Valley of the Sun,* February 7, 1992, p. 3.
——, "Viasoft Names New President, Charts Course for Fast Growth," *Business Journal—Serving Phoenix & the Valley of the Sun,* October 29, 1990, p. 8.
Nocera, Joseph, "The Story of '00," *Fortune,* August 19, 1996, p. 50.
Pallatto, John, "KnowledgeWare and Viasoft to Bolster IBM AD/Cycle Line," *PC Week,* July 20, 1992, p. 61.
——, "Micro Focus, Viasoft Forge Links Between PC, Host COBOL Tools," *PC Week,* December 18, 1989, p. 63.
——, "Viasoft Adds OS/2 Interface to VIA/Insight COBOL Tool," *PC Week,* February 24, 1992, p. 59.
Schine, Eric, "From Hero to Zero in Nine Weeks: Al Holland Seemed Like a Godsend to Viasoft. What Happened?," *Business Week,* June 24, 1996, p. 146.
"Viasoft Buys in to Y2K," *Computerworld,* January 19, 1998, p. 41.
"Viasoft Helps Organizations Plan for Revisions in Year 2000," *PC Week,* April 17, 1995, p. 23.
"Viasoft Inc.," *Business Journal—Serving Phoenix & the Valley of the Sun,* June 28, 1996, p. 101B.
"Viasoft Inc.," *New York Times,* September 15, 1997, p. C10.
"Viasoft Inc.," *Wall Street Journal,* September 18, 1997, p. C23.
"Viasoft Inc.," *Wall Street Journal,* April 10, 1998, p. B10.
Waxler, Caroline, "After the Millennium," *Forbes,* March 9, 1998, p. 230.
Wolf, Kenneth, "Viasoft Inc.," *Journal of Commerce and Commercial,* February 4, 1994, p. 5A.

—Daryl F. Mallett

Vickers plc

Vickers House
2 Bessborough Gardens
London SW1V 2JE
England
(44) 171 828-7777
Fax: (44) 171 331-3964
Web site: http://www.vickers.plc.uk

Public Company
Incorporated: 1829 as Naylor, Hutchinson, Vickers &
    Company
Employees: 10,381
Sales: UK £1.19 billion (US $1.96 billion) (1997)
Stock Exchanges: London OTC
Ticker Symbols: VKRSY
SICs: 3511 Turbines & Turbine Generator Sets; 3795
    Tanks & Tank Components

One of the central figures in British industrial history, Vickers plc of England was reorganized in 1998 to produce an engineering and manufacturing complex capturing leading market shares in three core divisions: Vickers Defense Systems, which produces armaments systems, tanks, and other armored vehicles, including the Challenger 2 tank introduced in 1997; the Sweden-based Kamewa group, which designs and manufactures marine propulsion systems; and Ross Catherall, the brand name under which Vickers operates its turbine components division. Notably absent among this list is the former Vickers Medical Equipment Division, sold in 1997, and the Rolls Royce and Cosworth automotive divisions, sold to Volkswagen to great fanfare in 1998. The company also jettisoned its luxury yacht business, Cantieri Riva.

Vickers's reorganization is proving more than a simple reduction of its activities. In December 1998 the company announced its intention to purchase Norway's Ulstein Holding ASA, a leading marine propulsion systems producer. At the same time, Vickers has made moves to remain at the forefront of the rapidly consolidating European defense industry. In January 1999 Vickers and France's Giat announced plans to enter into a joint venture to produce tanks and other armored vehicles. The joint venture follows upon the closing of one of the two Vickers tank production plants in 1998.

Vickers is led by Chairman Colin Chandler and Chief Executive Officer Paul Buysse. Although the company's revenues of nearly £1.2 billion produced after-tax losses of £2.2 million in 1997, its reorganization is expected to improve its position as early as year-end 1998.

18th-Century Industrial Origins

Edward Vickers was the driving force behind the formation of a new steel production business in Sheffield, the center of early 18th-century British steel production. The Vickers family was already well established in the region at the beginning of the century. While Edward Vickers operated the Vickers family's milling business, his father-in-law, George Naylor, was chief of the Naylor & Sanderson steel and iron production firm, and his brother William entered the steel trade with the operation of a rolling mill. When the Naylor & Sanderson partnership was dissolved in 1829, Edward Vickers stepped in to take over the Naylor side of the business, combining his brother's rolling mill with the company's existing operations, which was now renamed Naylor, Hutchinson, Vickers & Company.

Soon after its formation, the new company bought up a neighboring steel mill. The company's early years were marked by steady growth; by the end of the 1830s the company was already one of the region's leading steel works and the Vickers family was among its leading citizens. The company's expansion would take on greater steam from the 1840s, however, with its introduction into the booming U.S. market. For this, the company enlisted the aid of Ernst Benzon; unlike the founding families, Benzon's background was in sales, and he would become responsible for bringing the company's steel and iron products to the United States and other foreign markets. Benzon would quickly become a partner in the company, which changed its name to Vickers Sons & Company in 1867.

A new generation of Vickers already had taken over the company's operation by then. Most significant among the Vickers Sons was Tom Vickers. With a strong engineering background, Tom Vickers, who joined the company at the age of 22, would be responsible for developing the steel company's engineering side—to the extent that the company would soon become known more for its products, which included steel tires, propellers, shafts, and other components but also would extend into shipbuilding and armaments before the end of the century, than for its steel production. An important Vickers product of the era was its armor plating, necessary for protecting the British fleet from the increasing hitting power of the modern gun.

Vickers's decision to enter fully into the armaments industry was taken in 1888, when the company accepted a government commission to manufacture entire gun assemblies, not merely their components. From armaments, the company quickly expanded into shipbuilding, becoming the first private British firm to produce complete marine defense solutions. By the turn of the century Vickers had established itself as one of the British Empire's—and the world's—leading military suppliers. The company had made two important purchases to achieve this rapid growth. The first came with the purchase, in 1888, of the Naval Construction & Armaments Company Limited. Barrow, the shipbuilder's location, would soon become synonymous with Vickers, and function as the site of many Vickers engineering triumphs. Vickers quickly built out the Barrow yards. From an initial employee count of less than 900, the Barrow yards reached more than 5,000 by 1897, producing the Royal Navy's destroyers, cruisers, and other battleships on nearly 300 acres of dockyards.

A second important acquisition followed at the end of the 1890s, with the purchase of Maxim Nordenfelts, maker of the Maxim machine gun, which had played an important role in the Boer War and would remain a key component of the British armed forces entering World War I. The addition of Maxim gave the company a new name for the start of the new century: Vickers Sons and Maxim Ltd.

Weathering the World Wars

Vickers's importance to the British armed forces effort extended beyond its manufacturing and into its engineering endeavors. The company would continue to develop stronger armor plating and ''big guns'' for its battleships, while on the offense the company's products would extend to include submarines, torpedos, the invention of the first battle-ready tanks, and moves into the new heavier-than-aircraft industry, with both tanks and aircraft often powered by Rolls Royce engines. At the outbreak of the First World War, Vickers would prove its strategic importance to the English cause, drastically increasing production and enabling the country to hold the line until the late American arrival to win the war.

On the civilian side, Vickers also had entered the automobile business, forming the Wolseley Tool and Motor Car Company Limited in 1901. Although much of the company's expansion in the first decades of the century would be directed toward its armaments businesses, including acquisitions that brought the company fire control systems production capacity, among others, the period following the ''War to End All Wars'' would see the company attempt the difficult adjustment to a civilian market.

Vickers turned to an obvious market, that of converting its warship production to merchant shipbuilding production. But the company quickly sought opportunities in a vast number of new products and industries, including optical instruments; bicycles; machines; tools; engine manufacturing; production for the railroad industry, including the manufacture of locomotives; sporting guns; sewing machines; furniture; and many others. The company also would attempt to rival the Ford motor cars with its own inexpensive, mass-produced automobile. Its most significant move of the time, however, was the acquisition of the Metropolitan Company, a leading railroad cars manufacturer and electrical power supplier; the purchase, for the price of nearly 13 million pounds, created the Metropolitan-Vickers Electrical Company in 1919.

The British economy soon would enter into a grand slump that would last through much of the decade and see an important transformation of Vickers. While Vickers struggled through the economic recession, its long-time rival, Armstrong Whitworth, the nation's leading defense industry manufacturer, was heading toward collapse. The situation reached a head in 1926, when the Vickers and Armstrong operations were merged into a new company. Former subsidiary operations, which by then included the Metropolitan-Vickers Electrical Company and the International Paper Company, among other diverse interests, were shed. Vickers regrouped around a core defense industries focus; for its steel-making interests, it created a new company, the English Steel Corporation.

The buildup to the Second World War would give the newly expanded Vickers a boost. While the company's shipbuilding division geared up to an important series of orders, not only for its battleships and cruisers, but as well for its submarines, another Vickers product family was finding strong demand. Vickers aircraft had already played a strong role in World War I. At the end of that war, the company introduced its Vimy, which made international headlines by being the first plane to cross the Atlantic in a single direct flight. The Vimy, originally designed as a bomber, was quickly adapted to civilian needs, becoming among the first passenger-oriented airliners. The company continued to lead the British aircraft industry into the 1930s, when production began on the landmark Spitfire. Over the next decade, Vickers would produce nearly 22,000 Spitfires. The Spitfire, joined by the Wellington bomber, of which more than 11,000 were built, was credited with helping England resist—and then turn the tide—of the Nazi war effort.

Indeed, Vickers production was devoted entirely to armaments during the years of the Second World War, producing not only tanks and other armored vehicles, battleships, and aircraft, but guns and munitions as well. By the end of the war, Vickers had produced some 225 ships, including eight aircraft carriers and 123 submarines. Its tank production numbered in the tens of thousands, and the company alone provided for some two-thirds of the country's light artillery needs.

Postwar Adjustments

While the rest of the United Kingdom was celebrating the Allied victory, Vickers was forced to look hard at its postwar prospects. Despite government reassurance of a gradual slowdown in armaments orders (contrasted with the sharp breakoff of orders at the end of the First World War), Vickers would still be required to develop new markets for the peacetime economy. The new conditions forced Vickers to redefine itself.

In the immediate postwar period, Vickers identified four main areas for its business: aircraft; shipbuilding, including submarines; steel production; and engineering. The company's aircraft production would make a number of important advances, including the 1950s introduction of the Viscount turbo-prop jet plane. In shipbuilding, Vickers would become the first builder of a British nuclear-powered submarine. The company's engineering efforts would once again take it into the diversified manufacturing field, as the Vickers name became associated with products ranging from sewing machines and copiers, none of which provided the hoped-for success. A particularly flagrant failure was Vickers's attempt to move into the production of tractors. With the postwar economy booming, the company saw a vast market for its tractors, both in the United Kingdom and throughout the world. But the company's tank building experience did not translate well to the tractor market, which required far simpler systems than the company was accustomed to building. The tractor project would remain a stone of the company's books for more than a decade, before being ended finally in the 1960s.

Different difficulties were in store for Vickers's steel production arm. The rise of the Labor Party to government control in the 1950s meant the fulfillment of Labor's promise to nationalize a number of strategic industries, including the coal and gas industries, but also the steel industry. The government took control of Vickers's steel division at the beginning of the 1950s; the return of the Conservatives to the government leadership in 1954 would put the former Vickers steel works on the auction block. Vickers hastened to buy back its former division, paying a handsome price for the privilege. Control of steel production would only last as long as the next Labor Party nationalization effort, conducted in the 1960s, which saw the definitive end of Vickers's steel production activity in mid-decade.

After ending its tractor production in the early 1960s, Vickers had moved to step up its production of copy machines, acquiring a number of British-based businesses. Yet the company found it difficult to compete against industry leaders such as Xerox. A more successful diversification came from the company's move into medical instruments, which would remain a Vickers division until the late 1990s.

As Vickers struggled to redefine itself during the 1970s, the company was hit once again by British government policies. In 1977 both the company's aerospace (which by then included a partnership role in the Concorde project) and shipbuilding divisions were taken over by the government. The losses of these two core divisions cut out more than one-half of Vickers's revenues and more than two-thirds of its annual profits. The amputated operation was forced to look elsewhere for boosting its business.

Redefining for the 1990s

A partial answer came in 1980, when Vickers agreed to acquire Rolls Royce Motors. Long a supplier of engines for Vickers's tanks and aircraft, Rolls Royce had reached the verge of financial collapse at the end of the 1970s. As part of the acquisition, former Rolls Royce CEO David Plastow was placed in the Vickers lead. Plastow would take Vickers on an extensive restructuring through the 1980s, drastically streamlining the company's operations. After eliminating nearly half of the company's more than 50 subsidiaries, including many of its noncore activities, the company began to refocus on building several strategic markets, including boosting its medical instruments division and purchasing Kamewa, the Sweden-based world leader in propeller and other naval propulsion systems. The 1986 Kamewa purchase was followed in 1987 by the purchase of the Leeds tank production plant of the Royal Ordnance department; added to Vickers's existing tank production facilities, the purchase established Vickers as the country's leading producer of tanks and armored vehicles.

Colin Chandler replaced Plastow as director and then CEO of Vickers in the early 1990s. By then the company was struggling through a new global recession that had hit most of its divisions. The company's tank production would be bolstered by the British army's order of 130 Challenger 2 tanks—that order would eventually be increased to nearly 400 of this latest Vickers design, a contract worth more than £1.3 billion. The first of the Challenger 2 tanks were turned over to the British army in 1998. Yet the company was still searching for future orders from other governments, casting the profitability of the venture in doubt. With few orders on its books, Vickers decided to close its Leeds tanks factory in 1998. By then, Vickers had lost its title of largest British armored vehicle maker—which went to the merged operations of Alvis PLC and GKN PLC in 1998. In response to this merger, and to the increasing consolidation of the European defense industry, Vickers reached a joint venture agreement to product tanks and other armored vehicles with France's Giat, maker of the Leclerc tank.

In 1998 Vickers, now under the leadership of CEO Paul Buysse, made international headlines with the sale of its Rolls Royce division. Rolls Royce had been struggling throughout the 1990s, with the worldwide recession and Persian Gulf War cutting deeply into demand for the division's luxury vehicles; the Asian economic collapse of the late 1990s would further increase the division's difficulties. Added to this, Rolls Royce, which had not introduced a new model in nearly 20 years, was hard pressed to find these development resources. In the mid-1990s the division slashed its work force and reorganized its production methods. The company also began work on the latest Rolls Royce model, the Silver Seraph, introduced in 1998. Nonetheless, Vickers began looking to shed the luxury division. Initial suitors for the prestigious luxury name had included BMW and Mercedes Benz, but the Rolls Royce Motors division finally would go to Volkswagen, which also added Vickers Cosworth racing engines subsidiary under its Audi subsidiary.

The Rolls Royce sale had followed on the sale of another long-time Vickers division, its medical equipment arm. Another division to go was the company's Cantieri Riva luxury yacht and powerboat operations. Meanwhile, Vickers regrouped around three core divisions: Vickers Defense Systems, including tank production; turbine engine components, produced especially by the company's Ross Catherall subsidiary; and propulsion technologies, which included its Kamewa subsidiaries and the 1998 acquisition of the complementary activities of Ulstein Holding. The new Vickers, while maintaining a foothold in the company's tradition, seemed to have successfully bridged the transition to the next 150 years of Vickers history.

Principal Subsidiaries

Brown Brothers & Company Ltd; Michell Bearings; Turbine Components Division; Specialist Engines; Ross Catherall Ceramics Ltd; Ross & Catherall Ltd; Trucast Ltd; Vickers Aerospace Components; Vickers Airmotive; Vickers Bridging; Vickers Defence Systems; Vickers Precision Machining; Vickers Pressings; Vickers Properties Ltd; Aquamaster-Rauma Ltd; Kamewa Benelux Bv; Kamewa Hägglunds; Kamewa Italia S.R.L.; Kamewa Sarl; Mst Marine Schiffstechnik Gmbh; Mst Marine Schiffstechnik Gmbh; Ff-Jet Ltd; Kamewa Ab; Kamewa Denmark A/S; Kamewa Finland Oy; Certified Alloy Products Inc.; Kamewa Canada Inc.; Kamewa USA Inc.; Trucast Inc. Kamewa Australia Pty Ltd; Kamewa Hong Kong; Kamewa Korea Co. Ltd; Kamewa Singapore Pte Ltd; Kamewa Japan Kk.

Further Reading

Evans, Harold, *Vickers: Against the Odds,* London: Hodder and Stoughton, 1978.
Scott, J.D., *Vickers: A History,* London: Weidenfeld and Nicolson, 1962.

—M.L. Cohen

VNU N.V.

Ceylonpoort 5-25
P.O. Box 4028
2027 AA Haarlem
The Netherlands
(31) 23 546 3463
Fax: (31) 23 546 3912
Web site: http://www.vnu.com

Public Company
Incorporated: 1964 as Verenigde Nederlandse
    Uitgeverijsbedrijven NV
Employees: 10,808
Sales: NLG 3.92 billion (US $1.93 billion) (1997)
Stock Exchanges: Amsterdam Brussels Luxembourg OTC
    (ADR)
Ticker Symbol: VNUVY
SICs: 2721 Periodicals; 2711 Newspapers; 2741
    Miscellaneous Publishing

The Netherlands' publishing group VNU N.V. has built an international position in consumer and business publications, marketing resources, telephone directories, and regional newspapers. VNU publishes more than 150 consumer magazine titles in The Netherlands, where the company leads this market with a 60 percent share; and in Belgium, the United Kingdom, France, Hungary, and the Czech Republic. The company's titles include *Panorama, Magriet, Humo, Vlata, Yes, Meglepetés, Feeling,* and *Libelle,* giving VNU a total yearly circulation of more than 300 million. The company's regional newspaper holdings are limited to The Netherlands, with a focus on the southern provinces. Titles include *Dagblad De Limburger, De Gelderlander, Brabants Dagblad, BN/DeStem,* and *Eindhovens Dagblad.* These titles, with total circulation of 850,000, give VNU 18 percent of the Dutch regional newspaper market. The company also has begun to offer regionally oriented electronic newspapers, accessible through the cable television system.

VNU's international presence is focused more particularly on the business world. VNU has built a strong presence in the business and trade publication and information market, with more than 90 publications in Europe and more than 30 publications in the United States. VNU's Business Information Europe division has a strong presence in the computer magazine and periodical segment, where the company's titles—in The Netherlands, Belgium, France, Italy, Spain, Hungary, and the United Kingdom—place VNU as a leader in this category. The company's U.S. publications include *Billboard, Adweek,* and the *Hollywood Reporter.* The company's U.S. presence is focused strongly on the media, music, marketing, entertainment and related markets, as well as on the restaurant and food industries and healthcare markets.

A rising position in the VNU organization is held by the company's telephone directory division. Boosted by the 1998 acquisition of ITT World Directories, the newly renamed VNU World Directories division publishes telephone directories and offers related products and services in The Netherlands, Belgium, Ireland, Portugal, Puerto Rico, and South Africa, under such well-known brand names as the Gouden Gids, the Golden Pages, and Pages d'Or. The company's directories are focused particularly on the business-to-business market. The acquisition of ITT World Directories cost VNU more than US $2 billion.

VNU also publishes and produces for the educational market, including Dutch- and French-language textbooks, magazines, classroom aids, software, and other products. Until the summer of 1998, VNU also had held a presence in the Dutch and Belgium television markets. The company has since all but exited these markets. VNU continues to seek acquisitions to bolster its target markets: after purchasing an Atlanta, Georgia-based trade publisher in October 1998, the company increased its position in the telephone and electronic information service, Scoot Nederland, operated in cooperation with Freepages, of the United Kingdom.

Uniting Publishers in the 1960s

The Verenigde Nederlandse Uitgeverijen, or United Dutch Publishers, was formed in 1964 by the merger of two important

Catholic publishing groups, Cebema and De Spaarnestad. Both companies originated around the turn of the century. Cebema was the successor to the Teulings publishing and printing concern operated by the Teulings family. Founded by Coenraad Nicolaas Teulings in 1884, the company's original activity was as a small printing concern. From printing, the company, located in 's-Hertogenbosch, quickly expanded to include binding activities, which in turn led the company toward full-fledged publishing and distribution operations. By the start of the First World War, the Teulings house, which would be led by successive generations of the Teulings family, had become a nationally operating publishing company.

The second half of the later VNU was founded in Haarlem in 1906 as De Spaarnestad, a printing house with the particular mission of rescuing the troubled operations of the *Nieuwe Haarlemsche Courant* newpaper. The De Spaarnestad concern also took a Catholic orientation—its acquisition of newspaper *De Tijd* in 1931 would give it one of The Netherlands' most influential Catholic newspapers. By this time, the Teulings house, which would soon take on the Cebema name, also had been growing rapidly. In 1919 Cebema acquired the book publisher L.C.G. Malmberg, enabling the company to expand strongly into this market. In the 1930s Cebema boosted its magazine and newspaper publishing operations with the launch of the Amsterdam-based De Geïllustreerde Pers in 1936 and the acquisition of the Nederlandse Diepdruk Inrichting in 1937.

By the mid-1960s, both companies counted a number of important Dutch publications among their operations, with Cebema publishing the popular magazines *Margriet* and *Revu,* as well as three prominent Brabant province daily newspapers; De Spaarnestad for its part published the equally popular magazines *Panorama* and *Libelle,* and included among its subsidiaries the publishing firms Internationale Uitgeversmaatschappij and De Tijd/Maasbode. Direct competitors for the most part, both Cebema and De Spaarnestad were numbered among The Netherlands' largest publishing houses.

When the two companies fused, Cebema's 1,700 employees were joined by De Spaarnestad's 2,600 employees to create what the Dutch publishing industry saw as a new publishing giant, with operations in the most prominent publishing segments of newspapers, consumer magazines, and book publishing, while continuing its printing operations. VNU quickly asserted itself, beginning a string of acquisitions to consolidate its position as an industry leader. In 1967 VNU added Het Nieuwsblad van het Zuiden, a publisher of important regional newspapers with a focus on the southern (and more Catholic-oriented) Dutch provinces. That same year brought book publisher Het Spectrum, a publisher of Catholic market books. The Het Spectrum acquisition marked the secularization of VNU, however; after being merged into VNU, Het Spectrum exited the religious book market to focus on fiction and translations.

VNU closed out the 1960s with the purchases of two more important Dutch industry companies. In 1968 VNU added the Offsetdrukkerij Smeets, then a leading European offset printing firm. At the same time VNU further strengthened its printing capacity with the addition of the publishing and printing operations of the Nederlandse Rotogravure Maatschappij (NRM), based in Leiden.

Reorienting Toward the Turn of the Century

The 1970s would see continued growth for VNU, but also a shift in its direction. The acquisitions of publisher Intermediair and its trade journal titles in 1973, the industrial bookbinding operations of Belgium's Reliure Industrielle de Barchon in 1974, followed by the 1975 acquisition of Diligentia, another publisher of trade journals, had made clear VNU's new orientation toward the business publication market in particular and the magazine and periodicals market in general. This new direction was the result, in part, of the company's restructuring moves made during the decade. After finding it difficult to digest its many acquisitions in the early part of the 1970s, VNU hired management consultants to help reorganize and refocus the company.

The results of this restructuring brought VNU to exit the book publishing market altogether by the end of the 1970s. After selling off its book publishing operations, VNU concentrated on building its business information segment, particularly on the international front, with a strong interest in the U.S. market. VNU also began extending its consumer magazine titles, not only within The Netherlands and Dutch-speaking Belgium, but into other European countries as well. Two U.S. acquisitions were made at the end of the 1970s: those of Computing Publications and Business and Career and Business Publications.

VNU continued to expand its European trade and consumer magazine base during the 1980s, while continuing to build on its position as a dominant Dutch and Belgian regional newspaper and magazine publisher. Meanwhile, its attention turned to boosting its U.S. presence. In 1985 VNU acquired database and business information provider Disclosure. While this company would be resold in 1994, fetching a price of US $200 million, VNU used Disclosure as a springboard for building a wider U.S. position in business information services.

VNU's early moves into the U.S. trade magazine market offered less than satisfactory results. In 1986 VNU purchased Hayden Publications and its computer industry titles such as *Personal Computing* and *Computer Decisions.* A bottoming of the computer market at the end of the decade, however, led to severe losses. After less than three years with VNU, Hayden's titles were put up for sale.

Back home in The Netherlands, VNU continued to strengthen its position. The acquisition of Audet in 1988 gave it the top position in the Dutch regional newspaper market, expanding VNU's titles to include such important regional papers as *Dagblad De Limburger, De Gelderlander, Brabants Dag-blad, BN/DeStem,* and *Eindhovens Dagblad.* At the same time, VNU began developing an interest in another market entirely: television. On the European scale, VNU would enter the British, Spanish, French, and Italian markets, while continuing to strengthen its Belgian presence.

The decision by the Dutch government in the late 1980s to allow advertising in the country's television system—which had been entirely commercial-free until then—sent a shock through VNU. With much of its revenues generated by advertising, VNU reasoned that the opening of television to advertising would cause a deep cut in its own revenues. To protect itself, then, VNU began acquiring interests in a number of burgeoning television stations. These included an 11 percent share of the Belgian VTM, a position which VNU would raise to 44 percent by the mid-1990s, and a 19 percent share—later doubled—in RTL4, the first commercial television station to begin broad-casting specifically to the Dutch market.

Unlike other countries, almost all of The Netherlands' homes were linked to cable television systems, which provided the primary source of television and radio broadcast reception. VNU's television holdings would lead it to explore using the cable system's teletext service to provide electronic newspaper services.

In the 1990s VNU began looking for new markets to conquer. Specific targets included the Eastern European countries, emerging from Soviet domination to develop free market systems in the 1990s. At the start of the decade, newsstands in these countries featured a new title, *Moscow Magazine,* published by VNU. After establishing positions in the Hungarian and Polish markets, VNU made a strong move into the Czech Republic, acquiring Kwety Ceske, that country's largest publisher of consumer-oriented magazines.

VNU also made the decision to focus more strongly on its publishing operations. In the early 1990s the company sold off its graphics division. In 1993 VNU sold its printing operations to Koninglijke De Boer Boekhoven. The company next sold Disclosure, in 1995, to the United States' Primark for $200 million. VNU followed that sale with the purchase of the U.S.-based SRDS, strengthening its share of the North American business information market. This acquisition followed upon VNU's 1993 purchase of BPI Communications, which added famed industry titles including *Billboard* and the *Hollywood Reporter* to VNU's growing list of U.S. trade periodical titles.

In the late 1990s VNU would continue its penchant for redefining its operations. In March 1997 the company announced its plan to reorganize its consumer magazine holdings into a single operating division; the company's many magazine titles would be grouped into nine subdivisions according to target market (women's, men's, youth, living, etc.), with a tenth division providing business and other backup services.

At the end of 1997 VNU announced its intention to perform one of its largest acquisitions to date. This acquisition, of the directories publishing arm of ITT Sheraton, was finalized in February 1998. For the price of US $2.1 billion, VNU acquired ITT World Directories' leading position in six markets, includ-ing The Netherlands and Belgian, and its brand ownership of the Gouden Gids (the Dutch Yellow Pages). The newly acquired division, renamed as VNU World Directories, not only added a new market to VNU, but a new core product focus. The company's interest in the directories market—with its extenda-bility into the booming Internet directories market—was explained in part as well by the relatively steady advertising revenues generated by the division's primarily business-to-business directory publications.

Meanwhile, VNU had lost interest in the television market. The threatened collapse of print advertising that was to follow in the wake of commercial television never materialized. In August 1998 VNU sold off nearly all of its television holdings, retaining only a minority share in a local television network. At the end of 1998 VNU would continue to build around its new redefined core markets, acquiring U.S.-based trade publisher Shore-Varrone and its *Display & Design Ideas* and *Sport Trend* titles, among others, in October; acquiring 49 percent—with the option of 100 percent ownership in 2003—of retail and food industry software developer RMS, based in Connecticut; acquiring in May 1998 *Drama-Logue,* an actors' trade magazine, 65 percent of Sunshine Group Worldwide, and three Young/Conway Publications periodicals; and closing the year with an increase of its position in telephone and online information service Scoot Nederland, operated in partnership with Britain's Freepages. As the publishing industry underwent a transition toward a reduced number of globally operating megapublishers, including Wolters Kluwer and Reed Elsevier, also of The Netherlands, and Germany's Bertelsmann Group, VNU clearly had staked out its own growth targets for the future.

Principal Subsidiaries

VNU Tijdschriften BV (Netherlands); Accres Uitgevers BV (Netherlands); Admedia NV/SA (Netherlands); De Geïllustreerde Pers/MC VOF (Netherlands; 50%); Uitgeverij Woudestein BV (Netherlands); Mediaxis (Belgium); VNU Magazine Group International BV (Netherlands); British European Associated Publishers Ltd. (UK); Erasmus Press Kiadói (Hungary); Figyelö Publishing Ltd. (Hungary); Mona Praha VOS (Czech Republic); VNU Dagbladengroep BV (Netherlands); VNU World Directories Inc. (Belgium); VNU Business Information Europe BV (Netherlands); Benelux Periodieken BV (Netherlands); Array Publications (Netherlands; 85%); Learned Information (Europe; UK); Gruppo Editoriale Jackson Srl (Italy); VNU Publications France SA; Diligentia Business Press NV (Belgium); Business Publications España (25%); Claritas (USA; UK; France; Italy; Spain; Germany; Switzerland; Sweden; Austria); VNU USA Inc.; Spectra Marketing Systems Inc. (USA); Trade Dimensions/National Research Bureau (USA); Competitive Media Reporting (USA); National Research Group Inc. (USA); Interactive Market Systems (UK; Canada; USA); Broadcast Data Systems (USA; 89%); BPI Communications Inc. (USA); Bill Communications Inc. (USA).

Further Reading

"Dutch Publisher Acquires U.S. Trade Publications," *New York Times,* May 21, 1998.

"Louter goed nieuws bij uitgeversconcern VNU," *De Telegraaf-i,* March 20, 1998.

"VNU nu bijna geheel uit tv-activiteiten," *De Telegraaf-i,* July 18, 1998.

"VNU sluit miljardenlening voor overname," *Het Financieele Dagblad,* June 2, 1998.

"VNU To Sell Broadcasting Interests," *Screen Digest,* May 1, 1998.

"VNU ziet enorme voordelen in koop World Directories," *De Telegraaf-i,* December 20, 1997.

—M.L. Cohen

Vorwerk & Co.

Mühlenweg 17-37
D-42270 Wuppertal
Germany
(49) 202 564 0
Fax: (49) 202 564 1301
Web site: http://www.vorwerk.de

Private Company
Incorporated: 1883 as Teppichfabrik Vorwerk & Co.
Employees: 14,827
Sales: DM 2.44 billion (1997)
SICs: 5722 Household Appliance Stores; 5023
   Homefurnishings; 5719 Miscellaneous Home
   Furnishing Stores; 6341 Insurance & Diversified
   Financial Companies; 3635 Household Vacuum
   Cleaners; 3631 Household Cooking Equipment; 2273
   Carpets & Rugs

For more than 100 years, Vorwerk & Co. has been a fixture in German and international homes. Vorwerk & Co. designs, manufacturers, and sells household appliances, and fitted kitchens, chiefly through a direct sales network. Vorwerk also distributes its own and third-party kitchen and bathroom equipment through its Brugman subsidiary. The company also designs, produces, and sells carpeting to commercial and industrial customers, as well as under contract to third-party carpet suppliers. In addition to its interiors businesses, Vorwerk operates an Industrial Services branch, grouping its banking and insurance wing and other financial services, security and other business premises services, and data processing services, including software sales and design.

Direct sales remains Vorwerk's primary revenue source. The company's direct sales organization, which dates back to the 1930s, has made Vorwerk the German market leader in certain home appliance segments, and especially in the vacuum cleaner segment. In some categories, such as carpet cleaners, Vorwerk has captured more than 90 percent of the German

market. Where many companies have abandoned the door-to-door approach, Vorwerk continues to step up its commitment to this sales channel, not only in its native Germany, but on the international front as well. The company has been able to adopt the sales technique to fit the specifics of different cultures. Vorwerk's direct sales force, known as "advisors" within the company and numbering more than 20,000 worldwide in 1998, have shown especially promising results in the Far East and Pacific Rim regions. In all, Vorwerk claims a success rate of more than one sale per three home visits. Vorwerk advisors, while not directly employed by the company, nonetheless are given the opportunity to advance into management positions.

While vacuum cleaners have become synonymous with Vorwerk's German clients since the 1930s, Vorwerk has developed two more direct sales products, adapting its distribution concept to meet each category. Since 1985, the company has vaunted the performance of its Thermomix cooking system, an all-in-one unit meant to replace many if not most kitchen appliances. Sales of the Thermomix appliance are accomplished through the so-called Sales Party, in which the Vorwerk advisor consults with the party's host or hostess on the menu for the evening, then prepares the meal in front of the guests. Vorwerk claims an 85 percent sales success rate using the Party Sales approach.

Vorwerk also provides a line of fitted kitchens, a modular concept which can be adapted to meet the space requirements of its customers. Vorwerk's fitted kitchens are also distributed via the door-to-door approach. The kitchens, which are self-standing units with their own rear wall, can be re-designed to meet a customer's changing needs, and, should the customer move, the fitted kitchen can be taken along and adapted to the customer's new kitchen space. In the late 1990s, Vorwerk's fitted kitchen sales remained limited to Germany. With its Netherlands-based Brugman subsidiary, acquired in 1991, Vorwerk has expanded its kitchen sales, under the Brugman brand name, into the Netherlands as well.

Vorwerk's carpeting subsidiary, representing the company's founding product, concentrates sales on the commercial and industrial markets, placing its products in such facilities as hotels and office buildings. Vorwerk also designs and produces carpeting under contract to third-party distributors. Carpeting remains a relatively small percentage of Vorwerk's sales, at less than 10 percent of total sales in 1997. On the rise is the company's Industrial services, which groups Vorwerk's banking and insurance subsidiary, akf bank GmbH & Co., and other services, including software development and distribution, and security and other business premises services.

Vorwerk remains a privately owned, family-controlled company. The Scheid family has provided company leadership since 1904. However, in the late 1990s, Vorwerk appears to be edging towards a more open financial structure. Vorwerk is also making moves to increase its international presence, building up markets throughout Europe, with an emphasis on the Eastern European countries, as well as its Far Eastern sales. Germany remains the company's primary revenue source, with more than 58 percent of corporate sales.

19th-Century Carpeting Specialist

Vorwerk & Co. was founded by brothers Carl and Adolf Vorwerk in 1883 as Teppichfabrik Vorwerk & Co. The company's focus, as its name implied, was the production of carpeting for the domestic German market. While Vorwerk & Co. would soon expand its product line, carpeting remained a key company product throughout the 20th century.

Vorwerk's 20th-century growth began with the Scheid family's participation in the company, which was structured as a limited partnership. In 1904, August Mittelsten Scheid took over Vorwerk & Co.'s leadership, the first of four generations of Scheid family leadership in the new century. Under Scheid, Vorwerk & Co. began to expand its operations. In 1908, the company-run machine shop used for supplying its carpet production activities was converted to a full-fledged production facility for the manufacturing of machinery.

Vorwerk's focus on carpeting, coupled with its increasing production capacity, combined to launch the company into a new direction, one that came to define the company for much of its domestic clientele for more than 70 years. In 1929, the company invented its Kobold vacuum cleaning system. In German folklore, a kobold was an imp—often mischievous—said to inhabit people's homes. The Kobold vacuum cleaner quickly found acceptance in the German home, as Vorwerk & Co. now provided not only carpeting, but a means to clean carpets as well.

In order to sell its vacuum cleaners, Vorwerk & Co. adopted the then popular direct sales approach. Sending its sales force door-to-door, the company reasoned, enabled the customer to witness Vorwerk's products' qualities in their own homes.

Seeing the results on their own floors and carpets gave customers confidence in Vorwerk products. Indeed, Vorwerk's sales approach inspired its domestic customers to make Vorwerk the country's top supplier of vacuum cleaners—a position the company continued to hold through the end of the 20th century. Where others abandoned the direct sales approach, Vorwerk & Co. continued to maintain and reinforce its sales formula to a German market highly receptive to this type of sales method.

By the 1930s, Vorwerk & Co. had begun to diversify its domestic appliance line, adding production of refrigerators in 1937. The following year, Vorwerk & Co. went international, opening its first foreign subsidiary in Italy. That country, supplied by Vorwerk Folletto, as the subsidiary was called, remained Vorwerk & Co.'s largest foreign market throughout the rest of the century.

Postwar Growth

If Vorwerk & Co. had been able to continue its home appliance and carpeting production during the Nazi rise to power in Germany, the German invasion of Poland and the subsequent start of World War II forced Vorwerk & Co. to convert its production to supply the Nazi war effort. By 1943, as the Allies turned the tide of the war, and as raw materials and manpower became increasingly rare in a Germany heading toward defeat, Vorwerk & Co. was forced to cut its own operations, shutting down its direct sales force and ending production of its vacuum cleaners. In the same year, August Scheid retired, replaced by sons Erich and Werner Mittelsten Scheid.

The German defeat enabled Vorwerk & Co. to resume production of its Kobold vacuum cleaners in 1945. With the younger Scheid generation at the company's lead, Vorwerk & Co's direct sales force once again took to the country's doorsteps. The postwar reconstruction and the German ''economic miracle'' provided Vorwerk with a receptive market for its vacuum cleaners and other appliances. In 1959, the company launched a new line of electric-powered carpet brushes, dubbed the Europas.

Where Vorwerk's sales had remained largely domestic, the company now expanded into new directions as the concept of the European market began to take on reality in the late 1950s and 1960s. In 1961, Vorwerk & Co. set up a new subsidiary for its foreign operations, under the name Auslandsholding Vorwerk & Co. This subsidiary was renamed as Vorwerk International in 1971. The following year, the company expanded its carpeting production, moving to new quarters in Gehrden.

The sustained economic boom that marked the 1960s not only in Germany but throughout Europe and the United States helped encourage a trend towards building massive corporate conglomerates. Vorwerk & Co. too was inspired by this trend, as the company began to seek markets beyond its traditional manufacturing base. After launching a financial services unit in 1968, Vorwerk & Co. reorganized the company, separating its manufacturing operations into three distinct subsidiaries: Elektrowerke (electric), Teppichwerke (carpeting), and Möbelstoffwerke (upholstery materials).

The arrival of a new generation of the Scheid family, in the person of Jôrg Mittelsten Scheid, who led the company through the end of the century, marked the start of a more vigorous diversification period. To financial services, Vorwerk & Co. added a new data processing arm, the subsidiary ZEDA Informationsverarbeitung. While both its banking service and data processing brought the company beyond its traditional appliance and carpet orientation, Vorwerk's next expansion seemed more organic. In 1974, the company created its Hygienic Service Gebâudereiniging und Umweltplfege GmbH subsidiary, renamed as Hectas in 1997. As the name implied, the new subsidiary complemented the company's industrial carpeting installations with building cleaning and maintenance services.

On the appliance side, Vorwerk & Co. marked the 1970s with the launch of two new product categories: a new line of vacuum cleaners and carpet cleaners, and the company's fitted kitchen concept. Sold through the direct sales channel, the fitted kitchen provided a complete, modular kitchen unit that could be adapted to customers' homes. The Vorwerk direct sales ''advisor'' helped the customer plan the kitchen, which was then manufactured in a new Vorwerk production facility established for this product line. A more or less independent structure, with its own back wall, the fitted kitchen could be refitted according to clients' changing needs, and even follow the customer, should the client move to a new home.

Vorwerk's fitted kitchen concept caught on in the domestic German market. By the 1990s, the company would sell more than 8,500 fitted kitchens per year, while continuing to limit these sales to the domestic market. Rather than export the fitted kitchen, however, Vorwerk began looking for another channel for entering the foreign market for kitchens. In 1991, the company purchased Brugman Keukens, a Netherlands-based kitchens manufacturer with a chain of retail kitchen specialist stores. Vorwerk & Co. adapted the Brugman concept and imported it to the German market.

The 1980s also saw the introduction of a major new product for Vorwerk & Co. In 1985, the company founded its Vorwerk & Co. Thermomix GmbH for the manufacturing and distribution of the Thermomix home cooking appliance. A multipurpose, all-in-one appliance, the Thermomix was designed to replace many of the common tools and appliances used in the modern kitchen. For the new product, Vorwerk & Co. also introduced a new sales method. While continuing its direct sales approach, marketing and distribution of the Thermomix took on the ''party sales'' approach that had proven effective for Mary Kay Cosmetics and others. The party sales method was effective for Vorwerk as well: the company was able to claim a sales per demonstration success rate of 85 percent.

In the 1990s, Vorwerk & Co. in response began preparing to step up its international activity to the long economic crisis in Europe, and especially the recessionary period provoked by the difficulties of the German reunification. The company's sales expanded into Germany's Eastern European neighbors, as well as through other Western European markets. Vorwerk & Co. also targeted the Far East for product growth, bringing its door-to-door sales approach to the countries of that region. In keeping with its international growth objectives, Vorwerk & Co. restructured its operations in 1997, regrouping its subsidiaries into four distinct divisions: Direct Sales; Specialist Retail; Carpeting; and Industrial Services.

Perhaps the most important transformation Vorwerk planned to implement, however, was the change in its corporate management and ownership structure. In 1998, the company moved closer towards its announced goal of replacing its traditional family-owned structure with a more modern family-run business group.

Principal Subsidiaries

Vorwerk & Co. Interholding GmbH; Vorwerk Asia Pte Ltd. (Singapore); Vorwerk Austria Ges.m.b.H.; Vorwerk Folletto (Italy); Vorwerk Contempora S.r.l. (Italy); Vorwerk CS (Czech); Vorwerk Elektrowerke GmbH & Co.; Vorwerk Deutschland Stiftung & Co.; Vorwerk & Co. Thermomix GmbH; Vorwerk España (Spain); Vorwerk France; VISOFI S.A. (France); Vorwerk Semco S.A. (France); Vorwerk Nippon K.K. (Japan); Vorwerk Polska sp.z.o.o. (Poland); Vorwerk Portugal Electrodomesticos Lda.; Vorwerk Shanghai Home Care Systems Co., Ltd. (China); Vorwerk Tornado AG; Vorwerk U.K. Ltd.; Vorwerk USA Company, L.P.; akf bank GmbH & Co.; akf leasing Gmbh & Co.; Hectas Gebäudedienste Stiftung & Co. (95%); Hectas Gebäudereinigung Stiftung & Co.; Hectas Sicherheitsdienste GmbH; Hectas Gebäudemanagement GmbH & Co.; Vorwerk & Co. Teppichwerke GmbH & Co.; Brugman C.V.; Brugman GmbH & Co.

Principal Divisions

Direct Sales; Specialist Retail; Carpeting; and Industrial Services.

Further Reading

''Vorwerk & Co.—Datum zur Unternehmensgeschichte,'' Wuppertal, Germany: Vorwerk & Co.: 1991.

—M. L. Cohen

BURPEE®

W. Atlee Burpee & Co.

300 Park Avenue
Warminster, Pennsylvania 18974
U.S.A.
(215) 674-4900
Fax: (215) 441-0647
Web site: http://www.burpee.com

Private Company
Founded: 1876
Employees: 250 (est.)
Sales: $100 million (1998 est.)
SICs: 0181 Ornamental Nursery Products; 5191 Farm Supplies; 5961 Catalog & Mail-Order Houses

W. Atlee Burpee & Co., a private family-owned company founded in Philadelphia in 1876 by 18-year-old W. Atlee Burpee, has been the leading U.S. seed supplier for over 120 years. Although purchased by General Foods during their acquisition spree in the early 1970s, Burpee once again came into family hands in 1988. The company has bred more flowers and vegetables for American gardeners than all other seed companies combined. Before Burpee, U.S. seed companies were founded and run by large agricultural landowners who grew extra amounts of their main crops for seed; few new products entered the market in those days. Burpee was the first ''modern'' seed company based entirely on plant breeding and product innovation. David Burpee, Atlee's son, was the first commercial horticulturist to recognize the potential of hybridization; with his colleagues David revolutionized the growing of flowers and of vegetables. In 1991, George J. Ball, Inc. (Ball)—another successful horticultural company that was one of Burpee's major breeding partners—merged with Burpee. George Jacob Ball was a breeder of sweet peas, asters, and calendulas. His grandson, George Ball, Jr., now serves as Burpee's president and CEO. Currently, Burpee has the largest private seed-testing laboratory in the United States and continues to maintain experimental/developmental stations in Pennsylvania, California, Illinois, and Florida. Burpee sells seeds of over 500 vegetable and herb varieties and 600 kinds of flowers.

Many heirloom vegetables and flowers are available as transplants. The company also offers a rich assortment of perennial plants, bulbs for spring and for summer, fruits, shrubs, vines, and trees. Flowers account for approximately half of the company's sales. Additionally, Burpee sells seed-starting supplies, gardening tools, accessories, even greenhouses. Since 1876 Burpee has guaranteed all its products to the full amount of the purchase price. Within a year of purchase, unsatisfied customers may ask for a replacement or a refund.

Early Farming and Gardening: 1876–87

When the great Philadelphia Centennial Exposition opened on May 10, 1876, ''the United States was still recovering from the cataclysmic upheaval of the Civil War, the agonies of Reconstruction, and a severe economic depression,'' wrote Robert Elman in a short biography titled ''The Legacy of W. Atlee Burpee.'' However, Elman went on to say, for many Americans, the industrial revolution and westward expansion generated ''an almost unrestrained optimism—faith in scientific, social, and cultural progress resulting from self-reliant, individual achievement.'' When 18-year-old W. Atlee Burpee (*Burpee* was the Americanized form of the French Canadian Huguenot *Beaupé*) went to the Exposition, like many others he marveled at electric arc lights and many other mechanical and industrial exhibits but was especially fascinated by displays of agricultural advances. The young man's hobby already had expanded from his early breeding of poultry to the breeding of livestock, dogs, and plants.

By the mid-19th century, the crucial genetic experiments of Gregor Johann Mendel (the Father of Modern Genetics) and Charles Darwin's comments on selective breeding were beginning to appear in scientific publications and were available in major libraries in Philadelphia and elsewhere. Elman commented that young Atlee was an avid researcher and in all probability ''was familiar with Mendel's famous 1866 report entitled *Experiments with Plant Hybrids* as well as with reports by the very active British breeders of livestock, poultry, grains, and vegetables.'' As early as during his mid-teens, Atlee corresponded with English breeders and quickly received recognition when reports on his experiments were published in England.

Atlee's father was a surgeon and hoped his son would choose the same professional career but Atlee disliked his studies at the University of Pennsylvania Medical School and braved Dr. Burpee's anger by dropping out. His sympathetic mother, however, loaned Atlee $1,000 to start his own business for breeding poultry. For about two years the W. Atlee Burpee Company was quite successful; then, the need for repeat business and for a product that could be shipped more easily resulted in Atlee's beginning to breed dogs (especially an excellent strain of border collies), hogs, sheep, goats, and even calves. It was not long before the young entrepreneur realized that shipping feed and seed would not only be less expensive than shipping animals but would also be marketable to immigrant farmers who yearned for vegetables like those of "the old country."

Atlee had always been preoccupied with improvement and innovation. His belief that European growers had the key to quality led him to tour Europe every year to take notes and to obtain seed stock from German, Dutch, and Scandinavian vegetable breeders (recognized as the best in that field) and from state-of-the-art English breeders of flowers. He corresponded with foreign breeders who came to visit him and exchanged mail-order catalogues with them. By the 1880s, the Burpee Company was the world's fastest-growing mail-order company; it supplied the Northeast and the Midwest with seed and livestock.

Developing Seeds for America: 1888–1915

In 1888, Atlee bought the Fordhook farm, near Doylestown, Pennsylvania; here he used selective breeding to create what became internationally known as a plant development facility for improving and adapting the best European vegetables and flowers to growing conditions in the United States. By the 1890s, the Burpee Company was the largest seed company in the world; it also had introduced a new cabbage variety, called Surehead; an improved carrot, called Long Orange; better varieties of celery, peppers, and radishes; Iceberg lettuce; and the Stringless Green Pod Bean. A simple, forthright slogan, which the company kept as its motto, expressed the reliability of the seeds: "Burpee's Seeds Grow."

Occasionally, it was during his travels in the United States that Atlee found seeds to produce superior vegetables and flowers. For instance, he bought seeds for the first Bush Lima Beans from Asa Palmer—a Chester, Pennsylvania farmer who had obtained three seeds from an unusual plant in his lima bean garden: it had three little pods each of which contained one bean. Asa planted the three beans the following season: two of them grew into low bushes bearing a generous yield of lima beans. Until then lima beans had been grown only on poles. Asa sold the seeds to Atlee, and by 1907 the bush lima bean, named "The Fordhook," was the home gardener's favorite. "Lima bean aficionados," said biographer Elman, spoke of "being 'Fordhooked.'"

A similar case was that of Golden Bantam Corn. Originally, yellow corn was used only as feed for livestock and poultry; civilized people ate white corn. But William Chambers of Greenfield, Massachusetts, developed a yellow mutant sweet corn that became locally famous. At Chambers's death, one of his friends sold a handful of the mutant's yellow kernels to Atlee. The result was that Golden Bantam, the first yellow sweet corn, was listed in the *Burpee Catalogue* in 1902. During the Burpee Company's early years, most of its customers were farmers rather than gardeners; in fact, the first Burpee catalogs were called *Burpee's Farm Annual*. In 1890 vegetables were featured on the first 87 pages, flowers in the next 41 pages, and a 32-page supplement covered the availability of collie dogs, poultry, hogs, sheep, farm and garden tools, and a few late-entry flowers and vegetables. Flowers, nevertheless, accounted for a large part of the mail-order market.

Eager to provide better service to the western part of the country, Atlee in 1909 established Floradale Farms at Lompoc, in Santa Barbara County, California. This site, in a valley protected by a mountain range, had an ideally cool temperature exempt from great fluctuations; it was constantly humid and not subject to heavy sporadic rains. Lompoc—like Erfurt in Germany, East Anglia in the United Kingdom, and certain valleys in Kaskmir, India—endured as one of the world's best places for the production of outdoor flower seeds. Atlee also wanted to produce hardy seeds for cool weather agricultural and floral crops, especially sweet peas—one of the early 20th century's favorite annual garden flowers. During the following decades the company added other breeding and growing facilities, mainly in Florida, Illinois, Pennsylvania, northern California, and Costa Rica.

While in California Atlee visited his cousin, Luther Burbank—already famous for his multiple crossbreedings, graftings, and production of outstanding potatoes, plums, berries, and many ornamental plants. The cousins knew of each other's work and established a close relationship. When Atlee died in 1915, his company was mailing a million catalogs a year. His 22-year-old son, David, became head of the company and maintained close ties with Luther Burbank, who had started a small seed company. When Burbank died in 1926, David bought his company and acquired the rights to the seeds as well as to his cousin's experimental work—including the breeding records, or "stud book"—and added Burbank's splendid flowers and vegetables to the Burpee line.

World Wars and the Seed Industry: 1915–45

David (known as D.B.) managed the company only a short time before World War I almost completely shut down availability of the European seeds used for selective breeding at Burpee's experimental facilities. At that time Germany was a major producer of seeds—as well as a world center of plant research. Burpee also relied on seeds from France, Holland, and especially from England. Fortunately, Atlee's foresight of trade disruptions caused by wars had led him to establish Floradale Farms in California to develop seeds suited to the U.S. climate. Following in his father's footsteps, David opened six other regional breeding sites and sales offices in the United States and Mexico during World War I. In "The Legacy," Elman quoted from David Burpee's notes to illustrate how the young man dedicated his professional skill to meeting his country's needs: " 'Food will win the war,' we were told by Washington and I decided the best way I could help our country's war effort was by showing people how to grow a good share of their food right in their own back yards. To dramatize this, I set up what we called 'War Gardens' in a number of cities." Burpee continued, "The biggest attention-getter was the one in New York. It was in Union Square, directly opposite an imitation battleship bristling with wooden guns aimed at the tomatoes and cabbages . . . . It was a huge success. I would guess that that garden alone must have started thousands of people gardening."

Thus, the "War Gardens" of World War I planted the idea of the "Victory Gardens" that became so popular during World War II. In the intervening years D.B. gradually departed from the selective breeding in vogue with horticulturists until the late 1930s in order to practice hybridization (crossbreeding). He found that crossing two strains of the same species or of different species created an entirely new product that was stronger-growing and more disease-resistant than either of its parents. According to "The Legacy," D.B. became "a leading expert in hybridization, his greatest contribution to American plant development, and was the first commercial horticulturist to recognize the potential of hybrids. His firm was to gardening what Macintosh was to the development of personal computers." Working with his colleagues, D.B. developed the first successful hybrid flower, the Double Hybrid Nasturtium (1934). Then came the 1937 introduction of the Burpee Red and Gold Hybrid Marigold.

In fact, marigolds were D.B.'s favorite flowers and remained Burpee's most popular flower seeds. In a search for an odorless marigold (some people did not like the terpene odor emitted by marigold foliage), D.B. bought seeds from Europe, Africa, Asia, Australia, and South America. But not until he received seeds from Reverend Carter D. Holton, who had discovered an odorless marigold in China, did Burpee succeed in producing an odorless plant bursting with shimmering golden blossoms, which yielded the seeds that brought about production of the Crown of Gold Marigold.

A significant horticultural innovation occurred in the 1940s when Burpee's experimental breeders began to "shock" the chromosome structures of flowers with tiny amounts of colchicine, a poisonous alkaloid obtained from the autumn crocus, and thereby empowered the plants to emerge in dramatic new forms. Snapdragons—plants especially inclined to benefit from colchicine—burst forth in dazzling colors, as in the Bright Scarlet and the Rosabel versions of the Super Terra Snapdragons. Researchers also used colchicine to transform the wildflower known as the Black-Eyed Susan into the garden flower called the Gloriosa Daisy, and to produce the seven-inch-diameter blossoms of the Ruffled Jumbo Scarlet Zinnia.

Postwar Years and the Hybrid Revolution: 1945–89

World War II brought about many changes in everyday life, including farming and gardening. While adult males served in the armed forces, labor shortages drew more women than ever into the workforce but, motivated by patriotism, food shortages, and the tight economy, these women and their children tended Victory Gardens. During the years of the Great Depression, many farmers had moved to cities in search of better-paying jobs; they, too, tilled Victory Gardens. The Burpee breeders turned their attention to producing vegetables ideally suited to home gardening. Two outstanding results in 1945 were the Burpee Hybrid Cucumber and the Fordhook Hybrid Tomato. In 1949 came Burpee's legendary Big Boy Tomato, which remained a popular favorite and was the ancestor of all the best tomato varieties that followed.

With the coming of peaceful times, a strong economy, and the end of food shortages, city and suburban gardeners turned their Victory Gardens into pleasure gardens where, as hobbyists, they cultivated flowers as well as vegetables. As the quest for floral hybrids intensified, Burpee breeders brought forth beautiful new strains of marigolds, zinnias, nasturtiums, and snapdragons—to name but a few hybrids. As a matter of fact, Burpee breeders had basically invented marigolds and zinnias from seeds of Central American wildflowers. The Burpee company diversified and pioneered the bedding-plant industry and saw sales of its "color packet" retail business soar to new heights.

During the next 20 years, Burpee worked closely with another horticultural company, George J. Ball, Inc. (Ball). This firm, founded in 1902 outside of Chicago by George Jacob Ball, initially supplied cut and pot flowers to florists, and later expanded its sales to greenhouses and the food-processing industry; for instance, Ball supplied varieties of tomatoes that best suited the manufacturing of tomato paste and ketchup. By mid-century, Ball was an important producer of seeds for both flowers and vegetables. In the 1970s, Ball and its subsidiary—PanAmerican Seeds—also were major suppliers of many of Burpee's new varieties, especially the impatiens, which Burpee thought a major breakthrough for gardeners. Ball pioneered ever better varieties of dwarf impatiens and produced colorful modern varieties, such as the Super Elfin, the bold orange Tango, winner of the All-America Award, and the African Queen—the world's first yellow impatiens for the garden. Impatiens, virtually unknown in the mid-19th century, became the nation's most popular bedding plant: American gardeners needed color for shade, and the impatiens was an instantaneous hit. By the 1980s, Burpee and Ball had become interdependent. Ball supplied an ever increasing number of new products while Burpee won over an ever growing number of eager home gardeners.

Toward the 21st Century: 1990 and Beyond

The companies merged in 1991. George Ball, Jr., who was ardently involved in flower development, came from his firm's research-and-production department to become president and CEO of W. Atlee Burpee & Co. and be the driving force behind the development of new colors and larger, more graceful plants better suited to naturalistic garden design. By the end of the

1990s, the company stocked seed for more than 500 different vegetable and herb varieties and over 600 kinds of flowers, including the largest selection of heirloom vegetables and flowers available anywhere. Many of the most popular flowers and vegetables also were available as custom-grown transplants (known as Sure Start Plants). These were shipped by express mail to arrive on Thursday or Friday for weekend planting at the right planting date for a customer's climate zone. To assure compatibility of climate and to eliminate risk, these Sure Starts were grown in four locations across the country. In 1998 Burpee introduced Ruby Queen, a hybrid sweet corn with deep red kernels. It took five years for plant geneticists to bring pink-kerneled corn through ten generations to achieve Ruby Queen's deep red. By 1999 Burpee offered 175 new and bestselling flowers and vegetables as plants, including 61 old-fashioned vegetable and flower varieties.

Burpee's seeds and seed kits could be found in most good hardware stores and garden centers across the country. The company's retail racks offered a select line that varied according to region and from store to store, sometimes presenting up to 500 different varieties of flowers, vegetables, and herbs. These seed packets included such unique selections as a sunflower garden, a wide range of perennials, and the first-ever bilingual Spanish/English assortment featuring varieties of Latin American heritage. Burpee's full product line—including seed starting supplies, greenhouses, and gardening tools and accessories—was available through its catalogs, of which six very different versions were published between November and July of every year—and from its Online Catalog at the Burpee web site. By this time, Burpee was mailing a total of approximately six million catalogs a year.

The company's authoritative reference guides (some of which are listed below) offered gardeners comprehensive and in-depth information from gardening experts on essential and timely gardening topics. In addition, a "3D Virtual Garden Tour" was available to visitors of Burpee's web site. As the 21st century drew near, W. Atlee Burpee & Co. continued its quest for the highest possible quality of seeds, remained dedicated to conscientious service, and strove for steady improvement of an always expanding selection of flowers and vegetables that "made gardening easier and more rewarding" for its customers.

Further Reading

Bales, Suzanne Frutig, *The Burpee American Gardening Series,* New York: Macmillan Publishing Company, 1993.

Burpee Basics, New York: Macmillan Publishing Company, 1998–99.

Burpee 3d Garden Designer & Encyclopedia (CD-ROM), New York: Macmillan Digital Publishing Company, 1998.

Cutler, Karan D., et al, *Burpee Complete Vegetable & Herb Gardener: A Guide to Growing Your Garden Organically*, New York: Macmillan Publishing Company, 1997, 416 p.

Elman, Robert, "The Legacy of W. Atlee Burpee," *Burpee Home Gardener Magazine,* Winter/Spring 1996; reprinted as a separate booklet, Warminster, Penn.: W. Atlee Burpee & Co., 15 p.

Hefferman, Maureen, *Burpee Seed Starter: A Guide to Growing Flower, Vegetable, and Herb Seeds Indoors and Outdoors,* New York: Macmillan Publishing Company, 1997, 224 p.

Hefferman, Maureen, et al, *Burpee Complete Gardener: A Comprehensive, Up-to-Date, Fully Illustrated Reference for Gardeners at All Levels,* New York: Macmillan Publishing Company, 1995, 432 p.

—Gloria A. Lemieux

Winnebago Industries, Inc.

605 W. Crystal Lake Road
Forest City, Iowa 50436
U.S.A.
(515) 582-3535
Fax: (515) 582-6966
Web site: http://www.winnebagoind.com

Public Company
Incorporated: 1958 as Modernistic Industries of Iowa
Employees: 2,800
Sales: $438 million (1997)
Stock Exchanges: New York Midwest Pacific
Ticker Symbol: WGO
SICs: 3716 Motor Homes

Winnebago Industries, Inc. is one of the largest manufacturers of mobile homes within the United States. Sold under the Winnebago, Rialta, Ultimate, Vectra, and Itasca brand names, these self-contained vehicles are aimed at the recreational and leisure markets through an extensive dealer network throughout the United States and Canada. Built with state-of-the-art computer-aided design and manufacturing systems, on highly efficient assembly lines similar to the automotive industry, the company has grown into one of the leaders in the industry. Winnebago Industries celebrated its 40th anniversary in fiscal 1998 by introducing new designs for over 75 percent of its motor homes.

Early History

Winnebago Industries was formed in Forest City, Iowa, as a community project. In the early 1950s local businesspeople were eager to establish factory jobs for those leaving farms to seek work in Minneapolis or beyond. The town—with a population of 2,500 in 1955—formed a trust, the Forest City Industrial Development, to attract industrial ventures to their area.

In these postwar years, Forest City businessman John K. Hanson had noticed the growing popularity of recreational trailers among travelers on holiday. Hanson bought two trailer models to learn more about the burgeoning industry before approaching the Industrial Development trustees with a possible venture. In October 1957 the trustees voted to investigate making travel trailers, and Hanson became chairman of the search committee.

During a three-day drive, $20,000 came in from the Forest City community to begin the business venture. Forest City Industries was born, its board of directors including Paul Carse, president, Bob Smith, secretary, and John K. Hanson, treasurer. Smith and Hanson eventually struck a deal with Modernistic Industries Inc., a trailer factory based in California, for Modernistic Industries of Iowa to become a subsidiary. They would build Modernistic's "Aljo" brand trailers for the Midwest market under supervision from California.

Work began at Modernistic Industries of Iowa on January 29, 1958. The first trailer rolled off the assembly line in mid-March. The trailer could sleep five people, had kitchen and lounging facilities, and cost $895. Because of the great demand for these trailers, a host of Forest City natives broke away to form Forest City Industries Inc., a rival to the Modernistic Industries operation. This development unsettled Modernistic management, which was led by C.T. McCreary.

The Aljo plant was shut down for Labor Day weekend and did not reopen as planned for the new 1959 model production in September. After negotiations failed to reopen the Forest City plant by February 1959, five local businessmen purchased the trailer company, and John K. Hanson offered to manage it for the coming year. Modernistic Industries of Iowa survived the year and by 1959 it had 17 employees. On February 28, 1961, the company's name was changed to Winnebago Industries, Inc.

Growth, Diversification, and the Challenge of Success

In 1973 Winnebago Industries, by now the continent's largest recreational vehicle maker, had amassed more than 400 acres of land holdings in Forest City, including 46.5 acres of factory floor space, or two million square feet in all. Winnebago has since increased its land holdings to 860 acres.

To encourage superior after-sales service, the company had invited more than 1,000 dealer personnel to the Forest City head

Company Perspectives:

More people are choosing the RV lifestyle than ever before. These are exciting times. Enormous opportunities lie ahead for us. To meet the challenges of the next 40 years and beyond, we will continue to work not only harder, but smarter, to be able to continue to further increase our production capacity, market share, financial results, and ultimately our value for every Winnebago Industries Shareholder.

office for service school classes. Also in 1973, Winnebago established two subsidiaries: Winnebago Realty Corporation and Winnebago International Corporation. The realty arm was formed to help dealers establish or enlarge outlets at selected sites, while the international arm was meant to forge overseas markets for the company's products.

In 1974 the company began to feel the full brunt of 1973's oil shortage, which discouraged sales of gas-guzzling motor homes. Compounding financial difficulties, the United States suffered a mild recession that year, further denting consumer spending. To compensate, Winnebago diversified its holdings. The Maroff Division was formed to market a new Eze-Hauler fifth-wheel trailer for use on farms. In addition, the company moved into the mass-transportation market during a time of mounting energy conservation. Winnebago buses were unveiled to encourage companies to bring employees from outlying areas to work, thus saving on gas consumption.

At the end of 1974 Winnebago's payroll stood at 1,600 people. In order to revive sales of recreational vehicles amid the OPEC oil embargo, a Grand Giveaway program was established. Under the plan, motor home buyers were offered merchandise premiums. In 1976 John Hanson removed himself from day-to-day management of the company, stepping in as vice-chairman. Gerald Boman was elected chairman of the board and John V. Hanson, son of the founder, became president and chief executive officer.

A year later, the company began constructing a 126,000-square-foot factory in Riverside, California, to build motor homes. In addition, a 66,000-square-foot plant was leased in Asheville, North Carolina, to build van conversions. Also in 1977, Winnebago celebrated the manufacture of its 100,000th motor home. Journalists from across the United States turned out for the event.

In October of that year, another boardroom shuffle saw J. Harold Bragg become chairman and chief executive officer of the company. John V. Hanson retained his position as president, but Gerald Boman became senior vice-president of the company. The change was attributed to growing demands on the company, on top of continuing shocks from the domestic energy shortage. The response required more senior managerial experience in the boardroom.

But the boardroom renewal did not succeed. In March 1979 company founder John K. Hanson stepped in to end what he termed, according to *The Winnebago Story, 1958–1988,* "a

difference in management philosophy." J. Harold Bragg and John V. Hanson were replaced by John K. Hanson, who ended his semi-retirement to become chairman and chief executive officer of the company. This boardroom crisis was a precursor of a general business downturn. In May 1979 motor home production at Winnebago was halted for six weeks to reduce excess inventory owing to reduced consumer demand. A continuing drop in revenues led to the sale of the newly built Riverside, California, plant.

Restructuring in the 1980s

The 1980 lines of motor homes were smaller and more fuel efficient. Winnebago's new LLT trailer, for example, came in 16- and 18-foot models and had a road-to-roof height of just 86 inches. A more easily towed trailer was seen to be more fuel efficient for car owners on the highway. High interest rates and undercutting attempts at financing new vehicle purchases by consumers made 1980 a difficult trading year for Winnebago. That year, inventory, debt load, and overhead expenses were reduced. The company's workforce was substantially reduced—from 4,000 employees in January 1979 to 1,000 by August 1980.

Remaining employees began working in quality circles in 1981 to improve productivity. That year, Winnebago had a net positive cash position of $23.7 million at its fiscal year-end. This allowed the company to invest its own funds where only a few years earlier it had to borrow amid high interest rates.

With a more assured business future, Winnebago saw yet another boardroom shuffle in 1981. John K. Hanson remained as chairman of the board, but Ronald E. Haugen assumed presidency of the company. John K. Hanson was feeling more confident about Winnebago's comeback. He was quoted as saying in *The Winnebago Story*: "We've done our homework and . . . are about to enter a period of rapid growth." An increase in sales allowed more investment in the development of fuel-efficient vehicles, and the company's workforce was expanded to 1,350 people in 1982.

In the spring of 1983, the company enlisted a number of companies to manufacture a line of Winnebago brand products—from outdoor apparel to backpacks, rubberized air mattresses, picnic jugs, and coolers. Winnebago received royalties for the use of its company logo under the licensing arrangements in more than 2,000 retail outlets across the United States. Sales that year reached $239.26 million, up sharply from $146.6 million a year earlier. Earnings in 1984 were even better: profits totalled $27.8 million, or $1.10 a share (an increase of 77 percent on 1983 earnings). Rising sales were in part attributed to increased demand for the company's LeSharo and Itasca Phasar brand vehicle lines.

In order to further improve productivity, Winnebago moved part of its sewing operation from Forest City, Iowa, to Juarez, Mexico, in 1984. This was part of a long-range plan to move labor-intensive manufacturing from Forest City to cheaper labor markets.

Capital expenditure at Winnebago reached $24 million in 1985, as the company continued modernizing its manufacturing operations. Winnebago followed the suit of the big three automakers in Detroit, who were developing modernized operations—including computer-aided design and manufacturing facilities. Winnebago installed a "System 85" telephone system encompassing its entire workforce and dealer network. Yet another innovation was the Education Center, where Winnebago employees were instructed in the latest electronic and computer techniques being introduced on the shop floor.

Changes to the Winnebago boardroom in 1985 included John V. Hanson rejoining the company management as deputy chairman. In 1986 Gerald Gilbert became president and chief executive officer of the company, while Richard Berreth was appointed executive vice-president of operations. Also that year, Winnebago entered the *Fortune* 500 list of major U.S. companies, ranking number 500 in sales and 340 in net income.

In October 1986 Winnebago diversified its portfolio by acquiring majority control of Cycle Video, Inc., a satellite courier business specializing in transmitting television commercials from advertising agencies to broadcast affiliates. Also that month, Winnebago celebrated the manufacture of its 200,000th motor home. Sales for 1987 were posted at $406.4 million, leading to earnings of $19.97 million, or 78 cents per share. Changes made that year to promote increased productivity included strengthening the marketing department and expanding its training program for dealers.

More management changes occurred in 1989, following poor earnings performance a year earlier. Sales in 1988 had reached $430 million, but earnings slipped to $2.7 million, or 11 cents per share. In September, Gerald Gilbert was replaced as president and CEO of the company by a seven-person management council appointed to manage day-to-day operations. John K. Hanson said of the company's performance that year, according to a 1988 annual report: "The company failed to fully participate in the growth of the motor home industry during the second half of the year."

On the international sales front, Winnebago signed a 1988 agreement with Winnebago Trading GmbH, based in Hamburg, Germany, to sell its motor vehicles in 14 European markets. The company also reached an agreement that same year with the Tokyo-based Mitsubishi Corporation to sell Winnebago products in Japan.

But the company's fortunes did not improve in 1989. Winnebago posted a loss of $4.67 million on sales of $437.5 million in 1989. The beginning of the recession that year had dented consumer confidence and demand for motor homes decreased. Still, John K. Hanson saw grounds for optimism about his company's future. The United States was seeing an increase in the population of elderly people able to afford recreational vehicles. In addition, international markets for motor homes continued to mature, especially in Europe and Japan.

The 1990s and Prospects for a New Millennium

That optimism was short-lived, however. Revenues for the company plunged to $332.8 million in 1990 from $437.5 million a year earlier. Earnings continued to be in the red; this time the posted loss was $17.8 million. The effects of the Persian Gulf War—which drove up the price of oil and raised fears of an oil shortage at the gas pumps—undercut sales in the motor home division. In addition, the Cycle-Sat subsidiary continued to post operating losses. To stem losses, Winnebago began an austerity program in 1990 and increased the marketing of its Warrior and Spirit micro-mini motor home models, which offered superior fuel efficiency.

Fred Dohrmann, appointed chief operating officer of Winnebago in 1990, added the position of president to his nameplate in 1991 as the company continued to struggle amid the gathering recession. Company sales, dented by the impact of the Gulf War, continued a slide of 34 percent to $222.6 million for fiscal 1991. An earnings loss in 1991 was posted at $29.3 million, or $1.18 per share.

John K. Hanson termed the year a difficult one for the company. The manufacture of commercial vehicles was discontinued to direct more investment toward the recreational motor home division, the company's core business. Sales of motor homes in 1991, at $180.8 million, represented 81.2 percent of total company sales. In 1992 sales for the company increased to $294.9 million. The company, however, continued to lose money and posted a net loss of $10.5 million. Nonetheless, the recession had eased in 1992, and the Gulf War and its harmful trading effects had ended.

During the mid- and late 1990s, Winnebago Industries continued to struggle. Yet, by 1997, the company's management had implemented a comprehensive revitalization strategy that brought life back to the company. Most of Winnebago's non-RV holdings were sold off, and the company returned to what it did best, namely, manufacture recreational vehicles. All new 33- and 36-foot designs for the Winnebago Chieftain and Itasca Sunflyer, loaded with innovative and functional amenities such as a galley/coach slideout, a dinette/couch slideout, and a bed/wardrobe slideout where a queen-sized bed and mirrored wardrobe are moved out to reveal nearly 132 cubic feet of added living space, soon became the envy of the industry and two of the most popular RVs on the market. The company also made the commitment to install the latest technological advancements in RV manufacturing, thus resulting in the increase of its original equipment manufacturing program that brought in over $30 million in new sales during 1998. All of these measures contributed to a cash reserve of over $50 million by the end of fiscal 1998, and growing confidence within management that the company was ready to embark on a growth through acquisitions strategy, with the intention of enhancing its ability to build and market top-quality motor homes.

Although Winnebago Industries will need to work hard in order to maintain profitability, recent demographic studies indicate that the company should be confident about its future. Moreover, as long as there are people who want to travel in the comfortable and relaxing surroundings of their own motor home, Winnebago Industries will provide them with the most luxurious recreational vehicle on the market.

Principal Subsidiaries

Winnebago Acceptance Corporation; Winnebago R.V., Inc.; Winnebago Realty Corporation; Winnebago Products, Inc.

Further Reading

Goldenberg, Sherman, "Winnebago Sharper Focus: Hanson Family Says Company Not for Sale," *RV Business,* October 1997, pp. 13–32.

Kisiel, Ralph, "Winnebago Introduces Revamped Rialta," *Automotive News,* January 13, 1997.

Miller, Joe, "Winnebago Climbs Back into Conversion Vans," *Automotive News,* May 11, 1998.

"Winnebago Adopts Cross-Functional Product Approach," *RV Business,* October 1997, p. 13, 37.

The Winnebago Story: 1958–1988, Forest City, Iowa: Winnebago Industries Public Relations, 1988.

—Etan Vlessing
—updated by Thomas Derdak

Worms et Cie

55, rue de la Boetie
75008 Paris
France
(33) 1.44.13.38.00
Fax: (33) 1.44.13.38.83

Public Subsidiary of Someal
Incorporated: 1848
Employees: 33
Sales: FFr 1 billion (US$ 207.7 million) (1996)
Stock Exchanges: Paris
Ticker Symbol: Worms
SICs: 6719 Holding Companies, Not Elsewhere
Classified

One of the most illustrious names in French financial history, Worms et Cie has functioned since the 1980s primarily as a holding company for various investments along two primary lines: insurance and industrial agrochemical, with an emphasis on paper and sugar production. In the late 1990s, however, Worms et Cie has undergone an important transition. After being attacked in a hostile takeover attempt by François Pinault, of the Artémis Group and Pinault-Printemps-Redoute, the formerly independent, family-controlled investment firm agreed to sell its Athena insurance subsidiary to Assurances Generales de France (AGF), a longtime investor and ally. At the same time, Worms et Cie agreed to be acquired—together with its remaining holdings, including its controlling shares of the Saint Louis industrial group and the Arjo Wiggins Appleton paper group—by Someal, an investment partnership controlled by another longtime Worms et Cie ally, the Agnelli family of Italy, via its Ifil investment vehicle. Someal is comprised of Ifil and members of the former shareholding group of Worms et Cie.

With an estimated worth of more than FFr 30 billion in 1998, Worms et Cie retains control of Saint Louis, the second largest sugar producer in France, as well as a controlling share of the Arjo Wiggins Appleton paper manufacturing group. Worms et Cie has not entirely abandoned its financial investment wing,

retaining its control of the Permal Group, a New York-based investment fund management firm. The change in the structure of the company, which had been operated as a limited partnership—chiefly among Worms and related founding family shareholders—throughout the company's 150-year history, marks a new era for the holding group. The company will also enter the year 2000 without a Worms family member at the helm; the last of the founding family directors, Nicholas Clive Worms, relinquished his active participation in Worms et Cie's daily operations at the time of its acquisition by Someal. Longtime Worms et Cie director Dominique Auburtin remains the company's chief executive.

The new Worms et Cie enters the liberty of the free market with an absence of debt, a war chest of some FFr 4 billion, and a strengthened management. With its focus no longer split between insurance and industry, Worms et Cie is expected to continue building its industrial portfolio.

Coal Beginning in the 19th Century

The acquisition of Worms et Cie by Someal marked the end of more than 150 years of active Worms family leadership in the company that bears its name. Although the family would come to represent the new French financial ''nobility'' in the 20th century, Worms et Cie had decidedly common origins. Born in 1801, Hypolite Worms, a wholesaler and shipping agent, opened an office in Paris in 1841. The end of the French monarchy, reestablished on the heels of the French revolution, was once again in the air, falling before the brief civil war of 1848. In that same year, Worms, together with a number of associates, the families of whom would remain shareholders in the company until the end of the 20th century, began importing English coal to France.

Worms and his associates reorganized the company, forming Worms et Cie, a limited partnership that remained in place until the mid-1990s. Among the features of this partnership was a pyramid-like structure of a small number of directors. For much of the company's history, these directors were also among the company's capitalists. As Worms et Cie diversified over the decades, individual directors typically became responsible for a particular branch of the company's development. For much of the company's history, however, a member of the Worms family provided the company's leadership.

The end of the 1848 civil war led to the creation—and brief existence—of the Second Republic. One of the preoccupations of the new civil government was the rising rate of unemployment, particularly in the Parisian region, as the provincial population began a shift to the city center. The government created "national workshops" (*ateliers nationaux*) with the goal of providing work for the country's unemployed. While this policy had the effect of attracting still more of the population to the capital city—and further exacerbating the unemployment problem—the availability of a cheap and abundant labor force and the rise in industrial activity came at the right time for Worms et Cie and its coal import business.

Worms et Cie prospered, and continued to see its fortunes—and financial influence—rise, even after the foundering of the Second Republic and the rise to power of Emperor Napoleon III in the formation of the Second Empire in 1852. Under Napoleon, the industrialization of France took on a new pace, fueling the demand for coal—and the growth of Worms et Cie. France's increasingly international interests, in parallel with Napoleon III's belligerence, led Worms et Cie to develop a new direction: that of shipping operations. Launched in 1856, the shipping wing of Worms et Cie soon became its principal activity and led the company to expand its operations on an international level.

The company's first foreign office was opened in Port Saïd, Egypt, in 1869. The company's operations soon spread throughout northern Africa, especially among France's zone of colonial influence. By then Hypolite Worms was preparing to pass on the company's leadership to the next generation, his nephew Henri Goudchaux. Under Goudchaux, Worms et Cie's shipping empire took on an even greater influence, even as Napoleon III's empire collapsed, replaced by the more durable Third Republic.

While coal-burning steam engines had provided the backbone of the Industrial Revolution, the end of the 19th century saw the emergence of a new type of engine requiring a new type of fuel source: petroleum. Worms et Cie adapted to the new market, expanding its trade activities to include the sale of petroleum, at first for Marcus Samuel & Co., beginning in 1892, and, starting in 1986, Shell of the Netherlands, with principal ports at Egypt, Marseilles, and the Sudan.

20th-Century Industrial-Financiers

In the early years of the 20th century, a new Worms name joined the company's group of directors: Hypolite Worms, born in 1889 and named for his grandfather, who had died in 1877. While Henri Goudchaux's interest had focused on expanding Worms et Cie's shipping activities, the younger Hypolite Worms was interested in bringing Worms et Cie beyond merchant activities and into the industrial and financial realms. A first step toward becoming one of France's leading industrial concerns was the company's move into shipbuilding. Encouraged by the French government, preoccupied with fighting World War I, Worms et Cie opened its shipyard near Le Havre

in 1916, supplying merchant and other ships. Worms et Cie itself made use of its shipyards, building up a fleet of ocean-going vessels that led the company to create the Nouvelle Compagnie Havraise Pénninsulaire (NCHP), in 1934, launching the company in long-haul shipping.

Meanwhile, Hypolite Worms had brought the company's growing influence to bear on the financial market in the postwar era. In 1928, Worms formed its Services Bancaires (banking services), which evolved into the Banque Worms in the 1960s. In the 1930s, Worms et Cie quickly became a prominent source of investment capital in France's industrial landscape, including financing the creation of the national airline, Air France. On the industrial front, Worms et Cie opened a new subsidiary, Société Française de Transports Pétroliers, dedicated to oceangoing petroleum transportation.

Worms et Cie, which maintained close ties with England, continued operations through World War II, angering the Vichy French authorities; yet the refusal to interrupt its activities also brought the company into difficulties with the French justice system, eager to purge the country of its collaborationist taint, in the postwar years. The company was not, however, convicted of collaborationist activities, and the charges against it were dropped.

In the meantime, Hypolite Worms extended the company's financial activities into the insurance industry, taking shares in companies La Préservatrice and La Foncière in 1949. Both companies were nearly as old as Worms et Cie. La Préservatrice had been founded in 1861 in Brussels, before becoming a French corporation in 1877, building up a network of 450 branch offices by the turn of the century. La Foncière was founded in 1877, developing fire, transport, and life insurance activities, and worldwide operations by the turn of the century. Under Worms et Cie's control, the two companies established the basis for the later formation of Athena Assurances, formed in 1989.

Evolving in the Postwar Era

Worms et Cie's financial activities took on a greater importance for the company in the postwar years, as France's economy boomed with the postwar reconstruction effort. In the 1950s, Worms et Cie began offering complete financing for the construction of factories located outside of France. Worms et Cie's banking wing took on a new dimension with the establishment of the Banque Worms in the mid-1960s, which led to the company's move into real estate leasing with the creation of a new subsidiary, Unibail, in 1968. While the company built its financial activities, it began to slow its industrial operations, closing its shipyard in 1966, and ending its Worms shipping line in 1968. The rest of the company's maritime activities were brought under the umbrella group Compagnie Navale Worms in the early 1970s.

At the start of the 1970s, Worms et Cie took over Pechelbronn, a holding company which took on the role of an important investment vehicle for the firm, and was renamed as Worms et Cie during a company reorganization in 1991. The 1970s proved a quiet time for the company; while continuing its maritime activity, the company's banking arm, and in particular

Banque Worms, had become its central activity. The company's industrial activity consisted chiefly of a series of investments, gaining shares in Saint Louis and Arjomari Prioux, but also in such names as Lancel and Dior, and in General Biscuit and Presses de la Cité. But Worms et Cie's leadership was aging, and the company, which had grown to be identified with establishment France, was seen as slipping toward decline.

The nationalization of the Banque Worms by the French government provided something of a wake-up call for the company. Deprived of its central business, Worms et Cie recognized a need for a new generation of management—and the reappearance of a Worms at the company's helm. Nicholas Clive Worms, born in 1942 and the sole male heir to the family fortune, had joined the family firm in 1970, but was not elevated to a director's position until the early 1980s. Worms quickly surrounded himself with an able group of directors, notably Jean-Phillipe Thierry, leading the insurance wing, while turning his personal attention to the company's industrial investments.

Under Nicholas Worms, the company moved towards a dual focus on insurance and industrial investments. After the loss of Banque Worms—which had its main branch in the company's traditional headquarters—Worms et Cie quickly regrouped its financial activities into Banque Demachy, which became Demachy Worms et Cie at the end of the decade. Worms et Cie also maintained parts of its maritime operations through the 1990s—in 1986, Worms et Cie took over the former Elf subsidiary Compagnie Nationale de Navigation, which became the new name for the company's ship-fittings operations. In the same period, Worms et Cie interrupted its shipping operations, selling off the Nouvelle Compagnie Havraise Péninsulaire. The company did not rebuild its shipping activity until the mid-1990s, taking over the management of Total's petroleum transport fleet. This became something of a Worms et Cie specialty, especially with the partnership agreement reached with Compagnie Maritime Belge in 1995.

By the 1990s, however, the company's insurance arm, Athena, had taken on the central role. Formed in 1989 with the merger of Worms et Cie's Préservatrice Foncière Assurances, with GPA Assurances (former Groupe des Populaires d'Assurances, and including Proxima, CGS, and Athena Banque), Athena reached FFr 18 billion in revenues by the mid-1990s. At the same time, Worms et Cie focused its industrial investments on two vehicles: the group Saint Louis, one of the France's leading sugar producers and distributors, and the Arjo Wiggins Appleton paper manufacturing group. In each of these, Worms et Cie built controlling shareholder positions.

After nearly 150 years as a limited partnership, Worms et Cie, which by the 1990s counted nearly 100 partners among the heirs of the founding families, as well as investors among Italy's Agnelli family, and others, reorganized as a public shareholding company in 1996. The change exposed the company to a hostile takeover threat by François Pinault. One of France's most successful entrepreneurs, Pinault had already built the distribution empire Pinault-Printemps-Redoute, grouping the famed department stores with the country's leading

catalog sales firm, as well as other retail activities, including the FNAC chain of book, music, computer, and stereo stores. However, Pinault was also president of Artemis, a fast-growing name in the country's financial-insurance circles. Pinault saw an opening to add Athena to the Artemis portfolio, and rapidly built up a shareholding position in Worms et Cie.

Pinault struck in September 1997 with an offer of FFr 410 per share in cash, valuing Worms et Cie at some FFr 28 billion. Worms et Cie scrambled to shield itself from the hostile takeover attempt. By the beginning of October 1997, the company had found its white knights. Two of the Worms et Cie's major shareholders and longtime investment allies—the insurance group AGF and the Agnelli family holding vehicle Ifil—responded to Pinault's cash offer with a stock and cash offer worth FFr 465 per share. This offer, which raised Worms et Cie's valuation to FFr 32 billion, took a two-pronged approach. The Athena insurance subsidiary was acquired by AGF, as part of its bid to strengthen its share of the French insurance market. Worms et Cie instead regrouped around its industrial investments, principally its control of Saint Louis and Arjo Wiggins, with a new owner: Someal, a holding company composed of the Worms family (28.2 percent), Ifil (56.5 percent), and AGF (15.3 percent).

The deal was accepted in December 1997, placing Worms et Cie out of reach of Pinault. But the deal also meant the end of active Worms family management in the firm, as Nicholas Clive Worms stepped aside to a board position, with leadership taken by Dominique Auburtin. In addition to the firm's former industrial and maritime holdings, the new ownership also took on certain Ifil holdings, including its positions in the hotel and travel group Accor and the Agnelli family's shares in Danone. With its focus on industrial investments, the ''new'' Worms et Cie was poised to continue its legacy as a pillar of French economic history.

Principal Subsidiaries

Générale Sucrière; Permal Group; Compagnie Nationale de Navigation (52%); Lancel (20%); Arjo Wiggins Appleton (40%).

Further Reading

Abescat, Bruno, ''Le retour des Worms,'' *Nouvel Observateur,* May 29, 1987, p. 45.

Almi, Jannick, ''Worms et Cie: la contre-attaque des AGF,'' *La Vie Française,* October 11, 1997, p. 14.

Bertier, Etienne, ''Les Volte-Face de MM. Worms,'' *L'Expansion,* April 1, 1988, p. 201.

Chaperon, Isabelle, ''Worms & Cie: une mutation conduite à pas comptés,'' *Les Echos,* September 22, 1997, p. 27.

Chevrillon, Hedwige, and Yannick Le Bourdonnec, ''Worms, le retour aux valeurs familiales,'' *L'Expansion,* July 17, 1993, p. 118.

Denis, Anne, and Pascalle Santi, ''Worms et Cie: l'avenir d'Athena au centre de la strategie,'' *Les Echos,* February 25, 1997, p. 17.

''Le nouveau Worms & Cie affiche une stratégie centrée sur l'industrie,'' *Les Echos,* September 5, 1998, p. 22.

—M. L. Cohen

Yahoo! Inc.

3420 Central Expressway
Santa Clara, California 95051
U.S.A.
(408) 731-3300
Fax: (408) 731-3301
Web site: http://www.yahoo.com

Public Company
Incorporated: 1995
Employees: 475
Sales: $203.3 million (1998)
Stock Exchanges: NASDAQ
Ticker Symbol: YHOO
SICs: 7375 Information Retrieval Services; 7374 Data Processing & Preparation; 7372 Prepackaged Software; 7379 Computer Services, Not Elsewhere Classified

Yahoo! Inc. is one of the world's leading Internet media companies. Using its seemingly never-ending compilation of links to other web sites, as well as its extensive searchable database, the company helps Internet users throughout the world navigate the World Wide Web. Anyone can access the Yahoo! web site for free, because it is funded not by subscriptions, but by the advertisers who pay to promote their products there. The company leads its competitors in the amount of user traffic at its site, with over 95 million pages of information viewed through Yahoo! each day. The company also offers Internet users other peripheral services, such as free e-mail accounts (Yahoo! Mail), online chat areas (Yahoo! Chat), and news tailored to each user's demographic or geographic area (Yahoo! News). About 30 percent of Yahoo! is owned by Japan's Softbank Corp., while company founders Jerry Yang and David Filo each own approximately 13 percent.

Humble Beginnings

Yahoo! Inc. got its start in 1994 as the hobby of two Stanford University Ph.D. students who were procrastinating the writing of their doctoral dissertations. Jerry Yang and David Filo—both of whom were candidates in Stanford's electrical engineering doctoral program—spent much of their free time surfing the World Wide Web and cataloging their favorite web sites. In doing so, they created a web site of their own, which linked Internet users to Yang's and Filo's favorite places in cyberspace. At that time, their site was called "Jerry's Guide to the World Wide Web."

As their web site grew—both in size and in the number of links from which it was composed—the number of people who used the site also increased dramatically. Thus, Yang and Filo began spending more and more time on their new hobby, gradually converting the homemade list into a customized database that users could search through to locate web sites related to specific interests. The database itself was originally located on Yang's Stanford student computer workstation, named "akebono," while the search engine was located on Filo's computer, "konishiki" (the two computers were named after legendary Hawaiian sumo wrestlers).

As for the transformation of the database's name from "Jerry's Guide to the World Wide Web" to "Yahoo!," the two men became bored with the original tag and set about to change it late one night while bumming around in their trailer on the Stanford campus. Looking to mimic the phrase/acronym "Yet Another Compiler Compiler" (YACC)—a favorite among Unix aficionados—Yang and Filo came up with "Yet Another Hierarchical Officious Oracle" (YAHOO). Browsing through Webster's online edition around midnight, they decided that the general definition of a yahoo—rude and uncouth—was fitting. Yang was known for his foul language, and Filo was described as being blunt. The two considered themselves to be a couple of major yahoos, and thus the name which would soon become a household brand was born.

It was not long before the Yahoo! database became too large to remain on the Stanford University computer system. In early 1995, Marc Andreessen—cofounder of Netscape Communications—invited Yang and Filo to move Yahoo! to the larger computer system housed at Netscape. Stanford benefited greatly from this move, in that its computer system finally returned to normal after having been inundated by Yahoo!'s activity and the computing resources that it required for a year.

Expansion in 1995

Commercialization soon followed. Yang and Filo began selling advertisement space on their site in order to fund further growth. The duo soon realized that it was going to be too difficult to manage both the creative and the administrative aspects of the Yahoo! enterprise. They recruited Tim Koogle, also a former Stanford student, to come aboard as CEO. Prior to his arrival at Yahoo!, Koogle had put himself through engineering school by rebuilding engines and restoring cars, and had then gone on to work at Motorola and InterMec Corp.

One of Koogle's first moves as Yahoo! CEO was to bring in Jeff Mallett as COO. Mallett was a former member of the Canadian men's national soccer team, who at age 22 began running the sales, marketing, and business development aspects of his parents' telecommunications company—Island Pacific Telephone in Vancouver. Prior to joining the Yahoo! gang, he also gained experience in marketing at Reference Software and WordPerfect, and acted as vice-president and general manager of Novell Inc.'s consumer division. Together, Koogle and Mallett began transforming Yahoo! from a homegrown list of interesting web sites into the most popular stop along the information highway.

Koogle and Mallett soon became known as "the parents" at Yahoo!'s corporate headquarters. While Yang and Filo would arrive at work wearing T-shirts and sneakers, Koogle and Mallett preferred Italian silk ties. Many viewed the foursome's working relationship as that of kids with ideas and the adults that they found to transform the ideas into reality. In the August 6, 1998 edition of the *San Francisco Chronicle,* analyst Andrea Williams of Volpe Brown Whelan & Co. referred to Koogle and Mallett as "Yahoo's equivalent of the Wizard of Oz, pulling the strings from behind the scenes . . . . Americans are captivated by the idea of two college kids like Yang and Filo starting an incredible service. But [Mallett] and [Koogle] have turned it into a business that advertisers and investors understand and respect."

The majority of Yahoo!'s revenue came through banner advertising deals. In basic terms, Yahoo! sold space on its web pages to companies wishing to promote their products to the demographic that frequented the Yahoo! site. The purchased space not only acted as a visual advertisement (such as in a magazine), but was also often an actual link to the advertiser's own web site. Thus, a simple click on a banner ad by an Internet user could immediately transport that user to the advertiser's web site. In this sense, banner ads were somewhat superior to other forms of advertisement in that no other method of advertising (television, print media, etc.) had ever led consumers to a company quite so immediately.

As another means of generating revenue, Yahoo! also struck up distribution deals with web sites that were looking to increase their own traffic. For example, Yahoo! itself was not an online retailer, but boasted a lot of user traffic at its site. An online retailer, however, might have goods to sell but a need to first increase traffic at its own site in order to sell those goods. A distribution deal would pair the two sites, with Yahoo! leading its customer traffic to the retailer's site in exchange for a cut of the transaction revenues whenever customers made purchases. In this sense, Yahoo! (along with competitors such as Excite, Infoseek, and Lycos) came to be known as a "portal"—a gateway to the rest of the Internet.

Through banner advertising and distribution deals, Yahoo! was able to continue offering its services to web surfers for free, as opposed to online services such as America Online (AOL), Prodigy, and Microsoft Network. The latter three charged monthly fees for the use of their offerings. Although these online service companies' offerings were often more graphically intricate and visually pleasing than the Yahoo! site, they were essentially offering the same thing as Yahoo!—and for a lot more money. According to Jonathan Littman in the July 20, 1998 edition of *Upside Today,* "Yahoo, much like Amazon.com, built a natural Internet brand through its simple desire to satisfy customers." It was not long before Yahoo!'s user base was comparable to that of industry giant AOL, even though its 1995 revenues topped off at only around $1 million.

1996: The Birth of a Brand Name

In 1996, Yahoo! went public, offering shares of its stock for $13. In the first day of trading alone, the company's stock price sailed to $43, and its estimated valuation was quoted at upwards of $300 million—more than 15 times its eventual 1996 revenues of approximately $20 million. Around that time, Yahoo! decided to start promoting itself in the public advertising arena. Another former Stanford graduate—Karen Edwards—was brought aboard as the Yahoo! "brand marketer," and immediately lined up ad agency Black Rocket of San Francisco to handle Yahoo!'s account. Black Rocket was composed of four independent advertising executives who, ironically, owned no computers.

That spring, Yahoo! used almost its entire advertising budget for 1996 to run its first national-scale ad campaign on television. Luckily, the ad was an immediate hit. In the television spot, a fisherman used Yahoo! to obtain some baiting tips, and then proceeded to land multiple gigantic fish. According to Jonathan Littman in a July 20, 1998 edition of *Upside Today,* "The faux testimonial captured the Net's spirit without being the least bit techie." From this campaign arose the company tagline "Do you Yahoo!?" Yahoo! executives hoped that the efforts would help their company blossom into a full-fledged media company.

The quest to turn the Yahoo! name into a major brand took a few wacky turns along the way. For example, Edwards decided that the Yahoo! name simply needed to be out in the public eye as much as possible, regardless of the manner in which it appeared. Yahoo! posters began appearing at many outdoor locations, such as sporting events, concerts, and even construction sites. The Yahoo! logo was placed everywhere, with one of the most notable places being a tattoo on the rear-end of a Yahoo!'s financial pages' senior producer, when he made good on a lost bet. It was also plastered on the side of the San Jose Sharks' Zamboni ice machine, and printed onto items such as Ben & Jerry's ice cream containers and Visa cards. The yellow and purple Yahoo! logo even appeared shrink-wrapped onto five Yahoo! employees' cars, and one spring Edwards planted her flower garden at home in yellow gladioli and purple petunias.

1997–98: Acquisitions and Further Expansion

As Yahoo! became a certifiable household brand name, the company began striving to further satisfy the needs of its users. Following the trend set by online service companies such as

AOL, Yahoo! added services and features such as chat areas, Yellow Pages, online shopping, and news. The company also added a feature called ''My Yahoo!,'' which was a personalized front page for regular users that displayed information tailored to each user's interests. The company also teamed up with Visa to create an Internet shopping mall (an idea that was later aborted); with publisher Ziff-Davis to create ''Yahoo! Internet Life'' (an online and print magazine which never came to fruition); and with Netscape to develop a topic-based Internet navigation service to be used with the Netscape Communicator browser software.

By 1997, Internet surfers were using Yahoo! to view approximately 65 million pages of electronic data each day. That year, Yahoo! acquired online white-pages provider Four11 for $95 million. The purchase gave Yahoo! access to Four11's e-mail capabilities, which when integrated into Yahoo!'s offerings allowed the company to provide its users with free e-mail (Yahoo! Mail) as well. By mid-1998, over 40 million people were logging on to Yahoo! each month—12 million of whom had become registered Yahoo! e-mail users. To put those numbers into perspective, one can consider the following: at that time, only 30 million people were tuning in to network-leader NBC's top-rated show (''ER'') each week, and the number of Yahoo! e-mail users was comparable to that of online service giant AOL.

In July 1998, Yahoo! received a $250 million investment from Japan's Softbank Corp., increasing Softbank's share of the company to approximately 31 percent. Yahoo!'s market valuation at that time was $6.9 billion—much higher than that of most other media companies. As an emerging media company, Yahoo! began to move into the Internet access market that year through the launch of Yahoo! Online. To do so, the company initially formed a partnership with MCI WorldCom, but the arrangement deteriorated later that year. Thus, Yahoo! struck up a deal with communications giant AT&T, to provide Internet access through AT&T's WorldNet service.

Also in 1998, Yahoo! replaced Digital Equipment's Alta Vista with California-based search engine specialist Inktomi, as the supplier of Yahoo!'s search engine. Yahoo! then purchased Viaweb, a producer of Internet software programs. The acquisition resulted in the posting of a one-time $44 million charge in 1998. Yahoo! planned to use Viaweb's software to start a new service, which would allow its users to set up their own web sites for the purpose of buying and selling goods online.

In October 1998, Yahoo! purchased Yoyodyne Entertainment for 280,664 shares of Yahoo! common stock. Yoyodyne added its permission-based direct marketing capabilities to Yahoo!, which also obtained the company's database of consumers, valuable demographic information, and other Yoyodyne assets. Prior to the acquisition, much of Yoyodyne's direct marketing was done through online games and sweepstakes at Internet sites such as EZSpree.com, GetRichClick.com, EZVenture.com, and EZWheels.com. Yahoo! announced that while those four sites would remain intact after the integration of Yoyodyne into Yahoo!, the former company's overall brand would be phased out.

By the end of the year, Yahoo!'s user traffic had increased considerably since 1997, with web surfers viewing approximately 95 million pages of information through Yahoo! each day—a huge increase from the previous year's average.

The End of the Century and Beyond

By the end of the 20th century, the computer industry—and the Internet industry in particular—was becoming increasingly inundated with new players. In July 1998, NBC had purchased a 19 percent interest in Snap!—another portal operated by CNET Inc. Disney followed suit by grabbing a 43 percent stake in Infoseek Corporation; At Home Corporation purchased Excite, Inc.; and Microsoft Corporation increased promotion of its MSN portal. Even America Online made moves to increase its scope through the acquisition of Netscape and its Netcenter portal. Nobody wanted to be left out of the Internet game, since many analysts predicted that it would be the next true media industry.

By the end of the 1990s, it was approximated that 90 million people throughout the world had Internet access and were surfing the web on a somewhat regular basis. According to International Data Corp. in the September 7, 1998 edition of *Business Week,* it was predicted that figure would balloon to 328 million people by 2002. As stated by *Business Week*'s Himelstein, Green, Siklos, and Yang, ''What's emerging faster than many imagined is a Net generation that rises not to its newspapers and TV news shows but to its coffee and glowing computer screens. Some 64 percent of cybersurfers watch less TV now than they did before their Web-cruising days, while 48 percent are not reading as much, according to market researchers Strategis Group.''

Yahoo! tried to maintain its large share of the market by continuing to focus on its users and their satisfaction. Recognizing that it would only take one click of a computer mouse for a Yahoo! user to defect to one of its competitors, the company made moves to provide its users with even more. In January 1999, Yahoo! announced the purchase of GeoCities, the third most-visited web site in December 1998—directly behind top-rated AOL.com, and second-rated Yahoo.com. The GeoCities site was a creator of electronic communities for people. Based on people's interests, GeoCities allowed its users to set up their own personal home pages. Yahoo! hoped that the acquisition of GeoCities would bring many of that site's users to Yahoo!, and vice versa.

As the 21st century approached, many people felt that the Internet industry was nearing a shakeout, through which only a handful of companies would survive. Yahoo! was poised to weather the storm, however, and possessed the resources to do so. As the first Internet company to go public and the first to turn a profit, as well as the first to advertise itself on national television, Yahoo!'s brand was well known and its site was rated at the top of the heap. According to analyst Paul Noglows of Hambrecht & Quist Inc. in the September 7, 1998 edition of *Business Week,* ''Yahoo has the potential to emerge as the first pure Internet giant.'' Its ability to do so in the computer-dependent environment of the 21st century seemed certain.

Further Reading
Alden, Christopher J., ''Kingmaker,'' *Red Herring,* August 1998.

Hansell, Saul, ''Yahoo to Acquire GeoCities,'' *The New York Times,* January 28, 1999.

Himelstein, Linda, Heather Green, Richard Siklos, and Catherine Yang, ''Yahoo!: The Company, the Strategy, the Stock,'' *Business Week,* September 7, 1998.

Mittner, Greta, ''Yahoo Plays Yoyodyne's Game,'' *Red Herring Online,* October 13, 1998.

Napoli, Lisa, ''Yoyodyne Deal Signals Next Stage of Marketing,'' *New York Times,* October 14, 1998.

Swartz, Jon, ''Yahoo's Other Dynamic Duo,'' *San Francisco Chronicle,* August 6, 1998, p. D3.

—Laura E. Whiteley

INDEX TO COMPANIES

Index to Companies

Listings in this index are arranged in alphabetical order under the company name. Company names beginning with a letter or proper name such as Eli Lilly & Co. will be found under the first letter of the company name. Definite articles (The, Le, La) are ignored for alphabetical purposes as are forms of incorporation that precede the company name (AB, NV). Company names printed in bold type have full, historical essays on the page numbers appearing in bold. Updates to entries that appeared in earlier volumes are signified by the notation (**upd.**). Company names in light type are references within an essay to that company, not full historical essays. This index is cumulative with volume numbers printed in bold type.

523

INDEX TO INDUSTRIES

Index to Industries

ENGINEERING & MANAGEMENT SERVICES

ENTERTAINMENT & LEISURE

FINANCIAL SERVICES: BANKS

FINANCIAL SERVICES: NON-BANKS

FOOD PRODUCTS

FOOD SERVICES & RETAILERS

HEALTH & PERSONAL CARE PRODUCTS

HEALTH CARE SERVICES

INSURANCE

Washington National Corporation, 12
Willis Corroon Group plc, 25
"Winterthur" Schweizerische
    Versicherungs-Gesellschaft, III
The Yasuda Fire and Marine Insurance
    Company, Limited, III
The Yasuda Mutual Life Insurance
    Company, Limited, III
"Zürich" Versicherungs-Gesellschaft, III

LEGAL SERVICES

Baker & McKenzie, 10
King & Spalding, 23
Milbank, Tweed, Hadley & McCloy, 27
Paul, Hastings, Janofsky & Walker LLP,
    27
Pre-Paid Legal Services, Inc., 20
Skadden, Arps, Slate, Meagher & Flom, 18
Sullivan & Cromwell, 26

MANUFACTURING

A.O. Smith Corporation, 11
A.T. Cross Company, 17
AAF-McQuay Incorporated, 26
AAON, Inc., 22
ABC Rail Products Corporation, 18
ACCO World Corporation, 7
Acme-Cleveland Corp., 13
Ag-Chem Equipment Company, Inc., 17
AGCO Corp., 13
Aisin Seiki Co., Ltd., III
Aktiebolaget Electrolux, 22 (upd.)
Aktiebolaget SKF, III
Alfa-Laval AB, III
Alliant Techsystems, Inc., 8
Allied Healthcare Products, Inc., 24
Allied Products Corporation, 21
Allied Signal Engines, 9
AlliedSignal Inc., 22 (upd.)
Allison Gas Turbine Division, 9
American Business Products, Inc., 20
American Homestar Corporation, 18
American Tourister, Inc., 16
Ameriwood Industries International Corp.,
    17
AMETEK, Inc., 9
Ampex Corporation, 17
Analogic Corporation, 23
Anchor Hocking Glassware, 13
Andersen Corporation, 10
Andreas Stihl, 16
Anthem Electronics, Inc., 13
Applied Materials, Inc., 10
Applied Power, Inc., 9
ARBED S.A., 22 (upd.)
Arctco, Inc., 16
Armor All Products Corp., 16
Armstrong World Industries, Inc., III; 22
    (upd.)
Atlas Copco AB, III
Avery Dennison Corporation, 17 (upd.)
Avondale Industries, Inc., 7
Badger Meter, Inc., 22
Baker Hughes Incorporated, III
Baldor Electric Company, 21
Baldwin Piano & Organ Company, 18
Baldwin Technology Company, Inc., 25
Ballantyne of Omaha, Inc., 27
Ballard Medical Products, 21
Bally Manufacturing Corporation, III
Barnes Group Inc., 13
Bassett Furniture Industries, Inc., 18
Bath Iron Works Corporation, 12
Beckman Coulter, Inc., 22
Beckman Instruments, Inc., 14
Belden Inc., 19
Bell Sports Corporation, 16

Beloit Corporation, 14
Benjamin Moore and Co., 13
Berry Plastics Corporation, 21
BIC Corporation, 8; 23 (upd.)
BICC PLC, III
Binks Sames Corporation, 21
Binney & Smith Inc., 25
Biomet, Inc., 10
BISSELL, Inc., 9
The Black & Decker Corporation, III; 20
    (upd.)
Blount, Inc., 12
Blyth Industries, Inc., 18
BMC Industries, Inc., 17
Borden, Inc., 22 (upd.)
Borg-Warner Automotive, Inc., 14
Borg-Warner Corporation, III
Bridgeport Machines, Inc., 17
Briggs & Stratton Corporation, 8; 27 (upd.)
BRIO AB, 24
Brother Industries, Ltd., 14
Brown & Sharpe Manufacturing Co., 23
Broyhill Furniture Industries, Inc., 10
Brunswick Corporation, III; 22 (upd.)
BTR Siebe plc, 27
Bucyrus International, Inc., 17
Bugle Boy Industries, Inc., 18
Bulgari S.p.A., 20
Bulova Corporation, 13
Bundy Corporation, 17
Burelle S.A., 23
Burton Snowboards Inc., 22
Bush Industries, Inc., 20
Butler Manufacturing Co., 12
Callaway Golf Company, 15
Cannondale Corporation, 21
Caradon plc, 20 (upd.)
Carl-Zeiss-Stiftung, III
Carrier Corporation, 7
Casio Computer Co., Ltd., III
Caterpillar Inc., III; 15 (upd.)
Cessna Aircraft Company, 27 (upd.)
Champion Enterprises, Inc., 17
Chanel, 12
Chart Industries, Inc., 21
Chromcraft Revington, Inc., 15
Cincinnati Milacron Inc., 12
Circon Corporation, 21
Citizen Watch Co., Ltd., III
Clarcor Inc., 17
Clark Equipment Company, 8
Clayton Homes Incorporated, 13
The Clorox Company, 22 (upd.)
Cobra Golf Inc., 16
Cockerill Sambre Group, 26 (upd.)
Colt's Manufacturing Company, Inc., 12
Columbia Sportswear Company, 19
Congoleum Corp., 18
Converse Inc., 9
Corrpro Companies, Inc., 20
Crane Co., 8
Crown Equipment Corporation, 15
Cuisinart Corporation, 24
Culligan International Company, 12
Curtiss-Wright Corporation, 10
Cutter & Buck Inc., 27
Daewoo Group, III
Daikin Industries, Ltd., III
Danaher Corporation, 7
Daniel Industries, Inc., 16
Deere & Company, III
Defiance, Inc., 22
Department 56, Inc., 14
Detroit Diesel Corporation, 10
Deutsche Babcock A.G., III
Diebold, Incorporated, 7; 22 (upd.)
Dixon Industries, Inc., 26
Dixon Ticonderoga Company, 12

Donnelly Corporation, 12
Douglas & Lomason Company, 16
Dover Corporation, III
Dresser Industries, Inc., III
Drexel Heritage Furnishings Inc., 12
Drypers Corporation, 18
Duracell International Inc., 9
Durametallic, 21
Duriron Company Inc., 17
Eagle-Picher Industries, Inc., 8; 23 (upd.)
Eastman Kodak Company, III; 7 (upd.)
Eddie Bauer Inc., 9
Ekco Group, Inc., 16
Elano Corporation, 14
Electrolux Group, III
Eljer Industries, Inc., 24
Elscint Ltd., 20
Enesco Corporation, 11
Escalade, Incorporated, 19
Essilor International, 21
Esterline Technologies Corp., 15
Ethan Allen Interiors, Inc., 12
The Eureka Company, 12
Fanuc Ltd., III; 17 (upd.)
Farah Incorporated, 24
Fedders Corp., 18
Federal Signal Corp., 10
Fender Musical Instruments Company, 16
Figgie International Inc., 7
Firearms Training Systems, Inc., 27
First Brands Corporation, 8
Fisher Controls International, Inc., 13
Fisher Scientific International Inc., 24
Fisher-Price Inc., 12
Fisons plc, 9
Fleetwood Enterprises, Inc., III; 22 (upd.)
Flexsteel Industries Inc., 15
Florsheim Shoe Company, 9
Fort James Corporation, 22 (upd.)
Foxboro Company, 13
Framatome SA, 19
Frigidaire Home Products, 22
Frymaster Corporation, 27
FSI International, Inc., 17
Fuji Photo Film Co., Ltd., III; 18 (upd.)
Fuqua Enterprises, Inc., 17
The Furukawa Electric Co., Ltd., III
G.S. Blodgett Corporation, 15
The Gates Corporation, 9
GE Aircraft Engines, 9
GEA AG, 27
Gehl Company, 19
GenCorp Inc., 8; 9
General Housewares Corporation, 16
Gerber Scientific, Inc., 12
Giddings & Lewis, Inc., 10
The Gillette Company, 20 (upd.)
GKN plc, III
Gleason Corporation, 24
The Glidden Company, 8
Goody Products, Inc., 12
The Gorman-Rupp Company, 18
Goulds Pumps Inc., 24
Graco Inc., 19
Grinnell Corp., 13
Groupe André, 17
Groupe Legis Industries, 23
Grow Group Inc., 12
The Gunlocke Company, 23
H.B. Fuller Company, 8
Hach Co., 18
Haemonetics Corporation, 20
Halliburton Company, III
Hardinge Inc., 25
Harland and Wolff Holdings plc, 19
Harmon Industries, Inc., 25
Harnischfeger Industries, Inc., 8
Harsco Corporation, 8

MATERIALS

MINING & METALS

PAPER & FORESTRY

PERSONAL SERVICES

PETROLEUM

PUBLISHING & PRINTING

RUBBER & TIRE

TELECOMMUNICATIONS

UTILITIES

WASTE SERVICES

NOTES ON CONTRIBUTORS

Notes on Contributors

AZZATA, Gerry. Freelance writer, researcher, and editor based in Medford, Massachusetts.

BIANCO, David. Freelance writer, editor, and publishing consultant.

BISCONTINI, Tracey Vasil. Pennsylvania-based freelance writer, editor, and columnist.

BROWN, Susan Windisch. Freelance writer and editor.

BRYNILDSSEN, Shawna. Freelance writer and editor based in Bloomington, Indiana.

COHEN, M. L. Novelist and freelance writer living in Paris.

COVELL, Jeffrey L. Freelance writer and corporate history contractor.

DERDAK, Thomas. Freelance writer and adjunct professor of philosophy at Loyola University of Chicago.

FIERO, John W. Freelance writer, researcher, and consultant.

HALASZ, Robert. Former editor in chief of *World Progress* and *Funk & Wagnalls New Encyclopedia Yearbook*; author, *The U.S. Marines* (Millbrook Press, 1993).

HAUSER, Evelyn. Freelance writer and marketing specialist based in Northern California.

INGRAM, Frederick C. South Carolina-based business writer who has contributed to *GSA Business, Appalachian Trailway News,* the *Encyclopedia of Business,* the *Encyclopedia of Global Industries,* the *Encyclopedia of Consumer Brands,* and other regional and trade publications.

KEPOS, Paula. Product Manager for a major online information service.

KNIGHT, Judson. Freelance writer based in Atlanta.

LEMIEUX, Gloria A. Freelance writer and editor living in Nashua, New Hampshire.

MALLETT, Daryl F. Freelance writer and editor; actor; contributing editor and series editor at The Borgo Press; series editor of SFRA Press's *Studies in Science Fiction, Fantasy and Horror*; associate editor of Gryphon Publications and for *Other Worlds Magazine*; founder and owner of Angel Enterprises, Jacob's Ladder Books, and Dustbunny Productions.

MARTIN, Rachel. Denver-based freelance writer.

MESSERI, Kim L. Austin-based freelance editor, researcher, and writer specializing in the high-tech and hospitality industries.

MOZZONE, Terri. Iowa-based freelance writer.

ROTHBURD, Carrie. Freelance technical writer and editor, specializing in corporate profiles, academic texts, and academic journal articles.

SALAMIE, David E. Co-owner of InfoWorks Development Group, a reference publication development and editorial services company; contributor to such reference works as *Encyclopedia of American Industries,* and *Encyclopedia of Global Industries.*

TRADII, Mary. Freelance writer based in Denver, Colorado.

UHLE, Frank. Ann Arbor-based freelance writer; movie projectionist, disc jockey, and staff member of *Psychotronic Video* magazine.

WALDEN, David M. Freelance writer and historian in Salt Lake City; adjunct history instructor at Salt Lake City Community College.

WERNICK, Ellen. Freelance writer and editor.

WHITELEY, Laura. Memphis-based freelance writer and editor.

WOODWARD, A. Freelance writer and editor.